Collins
English
Thesaurus

HarperCollins Publishers
Westerhill Road
Bishopbriggs
Glasgow
G64 2QT

This Edition 2012

Reprint 10 9 8 7 6 5 4 3 2 1

ISBN 978-0-00-748743-1

Collins® is a registered trademark of
HarperCollins Publishers Limited

www.collinslanguage.com

A catalogue record for this book is
available from the British Library.

Typeset by Wordcraft

Printed in Great Britain by
Clays Ltd, St Ives plc

Acknowledgements
We would like to thank those authors and
publishers who kindly gave permission for
copyright material to be used in the Collins
Corpus. We would also like to thank Times
Newspapers Ltd for providing valuable data.

Contents

EDITORIAL STAFF

EDITORS
Lorna Gilmour

FOR THE PUBLISHERS
Morven Dooner
Elaine Higgleton
Lorna Knight

Main entry words	Main entry words are printed in bold type: **altogether**
Parts of speech	Parts of speech are shown (in small capitals) when the entry has more than one part of speech. Where a word has several senses for one part of speech, the senses are numbered: **abandon** *verb* **1**
Alternatives	Alternatives are introduced by an equals sign: = The key synonym for each sense is underlined, with other alternatives given in roman: **absorb 1** = <u>soak up</u>, suck up, receive, digest, imbibe **2** = <u>engross</u>, involve, engage, fascinate, rivet, captivate
Opposites	Opposites are introduced by an equals sign with a line through it ≠ partially

ABBREVIATIONS USED IN THIS THESAURUS

AD	anno Domini
adj	adjective
adv	adverb
anat	anatomy
archit	architecture
astrol	astrology
Aust	Australia(n)
BC	before Christ
biol	biology
Brit	British
Canad	Canadian
chem	chemistry
C of E	Church of England
conj	conjunction
E	East
eg	for example
esp	especially
etc	et cetera
fem	feminine
foll	followed
geom	geometry
hist	history
interj	interjection
lit	literary
masc	masculine
med	medicine
NZ	New Zealand

a

abandon VERB 1 = <u>leave</u>, strand, ditch, forsake, run out on, desert, dump 2 = <u>stop</u>, give up, halt, pack in (*Brit. informal*), discontinue, leave off ≠ continue 3 = <u>give up</u>, yield, surrender, relinquish ≠ keep
● NOUN = <u>recklessness</u>, wildness ≠ restraint

abandonment = <u>desertion</u>, leaving, forsaking

abbey = <u>monastery</u>, convent, priory, nunnery, friary

abduct = <u>kidnap</u>, seize, carry off, snatch (*slang*)

abide VERB = <u>tolerate</u>, suffer, accept, bear, endure, put up with, take, stand
● PHRASES **abide by something** = <u>obey</u>, follow, agree to, carry out, observe, fulfil, act on, comply with

abiding = <u>enduring</u>, lasting, continuing, permanent, persistent, everlasting ≠ brief

ability 1 = <u>capability</u>, potential, competence, proficiency ≠ inability 2 = <u>skill</u>, talent, expertise, competence, aptitude, proficiency, cleverness

able = <u>capable</u>, qualified, efficient, accomplished, competent, skilful, proficient ≠ incapable

abnormal = <u>unusual</u>, different, odd, strange, extraordinary, remarkable, exceptional, peculiar ≠ normal

abnormality 1 = <u>strangeness</u>, peculiarity, irregularity, singularity 2 = <u>anomaly</u>, oddity, exception, peculiarity, deformity, irregularity

abolish = <u>do away with</u>, end, destroy, eliminate, cancel, get rid of, ditch (*slang*), throw out ≠ establish

abolition = <u>eradication</u>, ending, end, destruction, wiping out, elimination, cancellation, termination

abort 1 = <u>terminate</u> (*a pregnancy*), miscarry 2 = <u>stop</u>, end, finish, check, arrest, halt, cease, axe (*informal*)

abortion = <u>termination</u>, miscarriage, deliberate miscarriage

abound = <u>be plentiful</u>, thrive, flourish, be numerous, proliferate, be abundant, be thick on the ground

about PREPOSITION 1 = <u>regarding</u>, on, concerning, dealing with, referring to, relating to, as regards 2 = <u>near</u>, around, close to, nearby, beside, adjacent to, in the neighbourhood of
● ADVERB = <u>approximately</u>, around, almost, nearly, approaching, close to, roughly, just about

above 1 = <u>over</u>, upon, beyond, on top of, exceeding, higher than ≠ under 2 = <u>senior to</u>, over, ahead of, in charge of, higher than, superior to, more powerful than

abroad = <u>overseas</u>, out of the country, in foreign lands

abrupt 1 = <u>sudden</u>, unexpected, rapid, surprising, quick, rash, precipitate ≠ slow 2 = <u>curt</u>, brief, short, rude, impatient, terse, gruff, succinct ≠ polite

absence 1 = <u>time off</u>, leave, break, vacation, recess, truancy, absenteeism, nonattendance 2 = <u>lack</u>, deficiency, omission, scarcity, want, need, shortage, dearth

absent ADJECTIVE 1 = <u>away</u>, missing, gone, elsewhere, unavailable, nonexistent ≠ present 2 = <u>absent-minded</u>, blank, vague, distracted, vacant, preoccupied, oblivious, inattentive ≠ alert
● PHRASES **absent yourself** = <u>stay away</u>, withdraw, keep away, play truant

absolute 1 = <u>complete</u>, total, perfect, pure, sheer, utter, outright, thorough 2 = <u>supreme</u>, sovereign, unlimited, ultimate, full, unconditional, unrestricted, pre-eminent 3 = <u>autocratic</u>, supreme, all-powerful, imperious, domineering, tyrannical

absolutely = <u>completely</u>, totally, perfectly, fully, entirely, altogether, wholly, utterly ≠ somewhat

absorb 1 = <u>soak up</u>, suck up, receive, digest, imbibe 2 = <u>engross</u>, involve, engage, fascinate, rivet, captivate

absorbed = <u>engrossed</u>, lost, involved, gripped, fascinated, caught up, wrapped up, preoccupied

absorbing = <u>fascinating</u>, interesting, engaging, gripping, compelling, intriguing, enticing, riveting ≠ boring

absorption 1 = <u>soaking up</u>, consumption, digestion, sucking up 2 = <u>immersion</u>, involvement, concentration, fascination, preoccupation, intentness

abstract ADJECTIVE = <u>theoretical</u>, general, academic, speculative, indefinite, hypothetical, notional, abstruse ≠ actual

● NOUN = <u>summary</u>, résumé, outline, digest, epitome, rundown, synopsis, précis ≠ expansion

● VERB = <u>extract</u>, draw, pull, remove, separate, withdraw, isolate, pull out ≠ add

absurd = <u>ridiculous</u>, crazy (*informal*), silly, foolish, ludicrous, unreasonable, irrational, senseless ≠ sensible

abundance = <u>plenty</u>, bounty, exuberance, profusion, plethora, affluence, fullness, fruitfulness ≠ shortage

abundant = <u>plentiful</u>, full, rich, liberal, generous, ample, exuberant, teeming ≠ scarce

abuse NOUN 1 = <u>maltreatment</u>, damage, injury, hurt, harm, exploitation, manhandling, ill-treatment 2 = <u>insults</u>, blame, slights, put-downs, censure, reproach, scolding, defamation 3 = <u>misuse</u>, misapplication

● VERB 1 = <u>ill-treat</u>, damage, hurt, injure, harm, molest, maltreat, knock about *or* around ≠ care for 2 = <u>insult</u>, offend, curse, put down, malign, scold, disparage, castigate ≠ praise

abusive 1 = <u>violent</u>, rough, cruel, savage, brutal, vicious, destructive, harmful ≠ kind 2 = <u>insulting</u>, offensive, rude, degrading, scathing, contemptuous, disparaging, scurrilous ≠ complimentary

academic ADJECTIVE 1 = <u>scholastic</u>, educational 2 = <u>scholarly</u>, learned, intellectual, literary, erudite, highbrow, studious 3 = <u>theoretical</u>, abstract, speculative, hypothetical, impractical, notional, conjectural

● NOUN = <u>scholar</u>, intellectual, don, master, professor, fellow, lecturer, tutor, acca (*Austral. slang*)

accelerate 1 = <u>increase</u>, grow, advance, extend, expand, raise, swell, enlarge ≠ fall 2 = <u>expedite</u>, further, speed up, hasten ≠ delay 3 = <u>speed up</u>, advance, quicken, gather momentum ≠ slow down

acceleration = <u>hastening</u>, hurrying, stepping up (*informal*), speeding up, quickening

accent NOUN = <u>pronunciation</u>, tone, articulation, inflection, brogue, intonation, diction, modulation

● VERB = <u>emphasize</u>, stress, highlight, underline, underscore, accentuate

accept 1 = <u>receive</u>, take, gain, pick up, secure, collect, get, obtain 2 = <u>acknowledge</u>, believe, allow, admit, approve, recognize, yield, concede

acceptable = <u>satisfactory</u>, fair, all right, suitable, sufficient, good enough, adequate, tolerable ≠ unsatisfactory

acceptance 1 = <u>accepting</u>, taking, receiving, obtaining, acquiring, reception, receipt 2 = <u>acknowledgement</u>, agreement, approval, recognition, admission, consent, adoption, assent

accepted = <u>agreed</u>, common, established, traditional, approved, acknowledged, recognized, customary ≠ unconventional

access 1 = <u>admission</u>, entry, passage 2 = <u>entrance</u>, road, approach, entry, path, gate, opening, passage

accessible = <u>handy</u>, near, nearby, at hand, within reach, at your fingertips, reachable, achievable ≠ inaccessible

accessory 1 = <u>extra</u>, addition, supplement, attachment, adjunct, appendage 2 = <u>accomplice</u>, partner, ally, associate (*in crime*), assistant, helper, colleague, collaborator

accident 1 = <u>crash</u>, smash, wreck, collision 2 = <u>misfortune</u>, disaster, tragedy, setback, calamity, mishap, misadventure 3 = <u>chance</u>, fortune, luck, fate, hazard, coincidence, fluke, fortuity

accidental 1 = <u>unintentional</u>, unexpected, incidental, unforeseen, unplanned ≠ deliberate 2 = <u>chance</u>, random, casual, unplanned, fortuitous, inadvertent

accidentally = <u>unintentionally</u>, incidentally, by accident, by chance, inadvertently, unwittingly, randomly, haphazardly ≠ deliberately

acclaim VERB = <u>praise</u>, celebrate, honour, cheer, admire, hail, applaud, compliment

● NOUN = <u>praise</u>, honour, celebration, approval, tribute, applause, kudos, commendation ≠ criticism

accommodate 1 = <u>house</u>, put up, take in, lodge, shelter, entertain, cater for 2 = <u>help</u>, support, aid, assist, cooperate with, abet, lend a hand to 3 = <u>adapt</u>, fit, settle, alter, adjust, modify, comply, reconcile

accommodating = <u>obliging</u>, willing,

kind, friendly, helpful, polite, cooperative, agreeable ≠ unhelpful

accommodation = <u>housing</u>, homes, houses, board, quarters, digs (*Brit. informal*), shelter, lodging(s)

accompaniment 1 = <u>backing music</u>, backing, support, obbligato 2 = <u>supplement</u>, extra, addition, companion, accessory, complement, decoration, adjunct

accompany 1 = <u>go with</u>, lead, partner, guide, attend, conduct, escort, shepherd 2 = <u>occur with</u>, belong to, come with, supplement, go together with, follow

accompanying = <u>additional</u>, extra, related, associated, attached, attendant, complementary, supplementary

accomplish = <u>realize</u>, produce, effect, finish, complete, manage, achieve, perform ≠ fail

accomplished = <u>skilled</u>, able, professional, expert, masterly, talented, gifted, polished ≠ unskilled

accomplishment 1 = <u>achievement</u>, feat, act, stroke, triumph, coup, exploit, deed 2 = <u>accomplishing</u>, finishing, carrying out, conclusion, bringing about, execution, completion, fulfilment

accord NOUN 1 = <u>treaty</u>, contract, agreement, arrangement, settlement, pact, deal (*informal*) 2 = <u>sympathy</u>, agreement, harmony, unison, rapport, conformity ≠ conflict

● PHRASES **accord with something** = <u>agree with</u>, match, coincide with, fit with, correspond with, conform with, tally with, harmonize with

accordingly 1 = <u>consequently</u>, so, thus, therefore, hence, subsequently, in consequence, ergo 2 = <u>appropriately</u>, correspondingly, properly, suitably, fitly

account NOUN 1 = <u>description</u>, report, story, statement, version, tale, explanation, narrative 2 = <u>importance</u>, standing, concern, value, note, worth, weight, honour

● PLURAL NOUN (*Commerce*) = <u>ledgers</u>, books, charges, bills, statements, balances, tallies, invoices

● VERB = <u>consider</u>, rate, value, judge, estimate, think, count, reckon

accountability = <u>responsibility</u>, liability, culpability, answerability, chargeability

accountable = <u>answerable</u>, subject, responsible, obliged, liable, amenable, obligated, chargeable

accountant = <u>auditor</u>, book-keeper, bean counter (*informal*)

accumulate = <u>build up</u>, increase, be stored, collect, gather, pile up, amass, hoard ≠ disperse

accumulation 1 = <u>collection</u>, increase, stock, store, mass, build-up, pile, stack 2 = <u>growth</u>, collection, gathering, build-up

accuracy = <u>exactness</u>, precision, fidelity, authenticity, correctness, closeness, veracity, truthfulness ≠ inaccuracy

accurate 1 = <u>precise</u>, close, correct, careful, strict, exact, faithful, explicit ≠ inaccurate 2 = <u>correct</u>, true, exact, spot-on (*Brit. informal*)

accurately 1 = <u>precisely</u>, correctly, closely, truly, strictly, exactly, faithfully, to the letter 2 = <u>exactly</u>, closely, correctly, precisely, strictly, faithfully, explicitly, scrupulously

accusation = <u>charge</u>, complaint, allegation, indictment, recrimination, denunciation, incrimination

accuse 1 = <u>point a or the finger at</u>, blame for, denounce, hold responsible for, impute blame to ≠ exonerate 2 = <u>charge with</u>, indict for, impeach for, censure with, incriminate for ≠ absolve

accustom = <u>familiarize</u>, train, discipline, adapt, instruct, school, acquaint, acclimatize

accustomed 1 = <u>used</u>, trained, familiar, given to, adapted, acquainted, in the habit of, familiarized ≠ unaccustomed 2 = <u>usual</u>, established, expected, common, standard, traditional, normal, regular ≠ unusual

ace NOUN 1 (*Cards, dice*) = <u>one</u>, single point 2 (*Informal*) = <u>expert</u>, star, champion, authority, professional, master, specialist, guru

● ADJECTIVE (*Informal*) = <u>great</u>, brilliant, fine, wonderful, excellent, outstanding, superb, fantastic (*informal*), booshit (*Austral. slang*), exo (*Austral. slang*), sik (*Austral. slang*), ka pai (*N.Z.*)

ache VERB = <u>hurt</u>, suffer, burn, pain, smart, sting, pound, throb

● NOUN = <u>pain</u>, discomfort, suffering, hurt, throbbing, irritation, tenderness, pounding

achieve = <u>accomplish</u>, fulfil, complete, gain, perform, do, get, carry out

achievement = <u>accomplishment</u>, effort,

feat, deed, stroke, triumph, coup, exploit

acid 1 = <u>sour</u>, tart, pungent, acerbic, acrid, vinegary ≠ sweet **2** = <u>sharp</u>, cutting, biting, bitter, harsh, barbed, caustic, vitriolic ≠ kindly

acknowledge 1 = <u>admit</u>, own up, allow, accept, reveal, grant, declare, recognize ≠ deny **2** = <u>greet</u>, address, notice, recognize, salute, accost ≠ snub **3** = <u>reply to</u>, answer, notice, recognize, respond to, react to, retort to ≠ ignore

acquaintance 1 = <u>associate</u>, contact, ally, colleague, comrade ≠ intimate **2** = <u>relationship</u>, connection, fellowship, familiarity ≠ unfamiliarity

acquire = <u>get</u>, win, buy, receive, gain, earn, secure, collect ≠ lose

acquisition 1 = <u>acquiring</u>, gaining, procurement, attainment **2** = <u>purchase</u>, buy, investment, property, gain, prize, asset, possession

acquit VERB = <u>clear</u>, free, release, excuse, discharge, liberate, vindicate ≠ find guilty
● PHRASES **acquit yourself** = <u>behave</u>, bear yourself, conduct yourself, comport yourself

act VERB **1** = <u>do something</u>, perform, function **2** = <u>perform</u>, mimic
● NOUN **1** = <u>deed</u>, action, performance, achievement, undertaking, exploit, feat, accomplishment **2** = <u>pretence</u>, show, front, performance, display, attitude, pose, posture **3** = <u>law</u>, bill, measure, resolution, decree, statute, ordinance, enactment **4** = <u>performance</u>, show, turn, production, routine, presentation, gig (*informal*), sketch

acting NOUN = <u>performance</u>, playing, performing, theatre, portrayal, impersonation, characterization, stagecraft
● ADJECTIVE = <u>temporary</u>, substitute, interim, provisional, surrogate, stopgap, pro tem

action 1 = <u>deed</u>, act, performance, achievement, exploit, feat, accomplishment **2** = <u>measure</u>, act, manoeuvre **3** = <u>lawsuit</u>, case, trial, suit, proceeding, dispute, prosecution, litigation **4** = <u>energy</u>, activity, spirit, force, vitality, vigour, liveliness, vim **5** = <u>effect</u>, working, process, operation, activity, movement, functioning, motion **6** = <u>battle</u>, fight, conflict, clash, contest, encounter, combat, engagement

activate = <u>start</u>, move, initiate, rouse, mobilize, set in motion, galvanize ≠ stop

active 1 = <u>busy</u>, involved, occupied, lively, energetic, bustling, on the move, strenuous ≠ sluggish **2** = <u>energetic</u>, quick, alert, dynamic, lively, vigorous, animated, forceful ≠ inactive **3** = <u>in operation</u>, working, acting, at work, in action, operative, in force, effectual

activist = <u>militant</u>, partisan

activity 1 = <u>action</u>, labour, movement, energy, exercise, spirit, motion, bustle ≠ inaction **2** = <u>pursuit</u>, project, scheme, pleasure, interest, hobby, pastime

actor *or* **actress** = <u>performer</u>, player, Thespian, luvvie (*informal*)

actual = <u>real</u>, substantial, concrete, definite, tangible

actually = <u>really</u>, in fact, indeed, truly, literally, genuinely, in reality, in truth

acute 1 = <u>serious</u>, important, dangerous, critical, crucial, severe, grave, urgent **2** = <u>sharp</u>, shooting, powerful, violent, severe, intense, fierce, piercing **3** = <u>perceptive</u>, sharp, keen, smart, sensitive, clever, astute, insightful ≠ slow

adamant = <u>determined</u>, firm, fixed, stubborn, uncompromising, resolute, unbending, obdurate ≠ flexible

adapt 1 = <u>adjust</u>, change, alter, modify, accommodate, conform, acclimatize **2** = <u>convert</u>, change, transform, alter, modify, tailor, remodel

adaptation 1 = <u>acclimatization</u>, naturalization, familiarization **2** = <u>conversion</u>, change, variation, adjustment, transformation, modification, alteration

add 1 = <u>count up</u>, total, reckon, compute, add up, tot up ≠ take away **2** = <u>include</u>, attach, supplement, adjoin, augment, affix, append

addict 1 = <u>junkie</u> (*informal*), freak (*informal*), fiend (*informal*) **2** = <u>fan</u>, lover, nut (*slang*), follower, enthusiast, admirer, buff (*informal*), junkie (*informal*)

addicted
● PHRASES **addicted to** = <u>hooked on</u>, dependent on, accustomed to (*slang*), habituated to

addiction = <u>dependence</u>, habit, obsession, craving, enslavement *with to* = <u>love of</u>, passion for, attachment to

addition NOUN 1 = <u>extra</u>, supplement, increase, gain, bonus, extension, accessory, additive 2 = <u>inclusion</u>, adding, increasing, extension, attachment, insertion, incorporation, augmentation ≠ removal 3 = <u>counting up</u>, totalling, adding up, computation, totting up ≠ subtraction
● PHRASES **in addition to** = <u>as well as</u>, along with, on top of, besides, to boot, additionally, over and above, to say nothing of

additional = <u>extra</u>, new, other, added, further, fresh, spare, supplementary

address NOUN 1 = <u>location</u>, home, place, house, point, position, situation, site 2 = <u>speech</u>, talk, lecture, discourse, sermon, dissertation, homily, oration
● VERB = <u>speak to</u>, talk to, greet, hail, approach, converse with, korero (N.Z.)

adept ADJECTIVE = <u>skilful</u>, able, skilled, expert, practised, accomplished, versed, proficient ≠ unskilled
● NOUN = <u>expert</u>, master, genius, hotshot (informal), dab hand (Brit. informal)

adequate 1 = <u>passable</u>, acceptable, average, fair, satisfactory, competent, mediocre, so-so (informal) ≠ inadequate 2 = <u>sufficient</u>, enough ≠ insufficient

adhere to = <u>stick to</u>, attach to, cling to, glue to, fix to, fasten to, hold fast to, paste to

adjacent ADJECTIVE = <u>adjoining</u>, neighbouring, nearby ≠ far away
● PREPOSITION **with to** = <u>next to</u>, touching, close to, neighbouring, beside, near to, adjoining, bordering on

adjoin = <u>connect with</u> or to, join, link with, touch on, border on

adjoining = <u>connecting</u>, touching, bordering, neighbouring, next door, adjacent, abutting

adjourn = <u>postpone</u>, delay, suspend, interrupt, put off, defer, discontinue ≠ continue

adjust 1 = <u>adapt</u>, change, alter, accustom, conform 2 = <u>change</u>, reform, alter, adapt, revise, modify, amend, make conform 3 = <u>modify</u>, alter, adapt

adjustable = <u>alterable</u>, flexible, adaptable, malleable, movable, modifiable

adjustment 1 = <u>alteration</u>, change, tuning, repair, conversion, modifying, adaptation, modification 2 = <u>acclimatization</u>, orientation, change,

regulation, amendment, adaptation, revision, modification

administer 1 = <u>manage</u>, run, control, direct, handle, conduct, command, govern 2 = <u>dispense</u>, give, share, provide, apply, assign, allocate, allot 3 = <u>execute</u>, give, provide, apply, perform, carry out, impose, implement

administration 1 = <u>management</u>, government, running, control, handling, direction, conduct, application 2 = <u>directors</u>, board, executive(s), employers 3 = <u>government</u>, leadership, regime

administrative = <u>managerial</u>, executive, directing, regulatory, governmental, organizational, supervisory, directorial

administrator = <u>manager</u>, head, official, director, executive, boss (informal), governor, supervisor, baas (S. African)

admirable = <u>praiseworthy</u>, good, great, fine, wonderful, excellent, brilliant, outstanding, booshit (Austral. slang), exo (Austral. slang), sik (Austral. slang), ka pai (N.Z.) ≠ deplorable

admiration = <u>regard</u>, wonder, respect, praise, approval, recognition, esteem, appreciation

admire 1 = <u>respect</u>, value, prize, honour, praise, appreciate, esteem, approve of ≠ despise 2 = <u>adore</u>, like, love, take to, fancy (Brit. informal), treasure, cherish, glorify 3 = <u>marvel at</u>, look at, appreciate, delight in, wonder at, be amazed by, take pleasure in, gape at

admirer 1 = <u>fan</u>, supporter, follower, enthusiast, partisan, disciple, devotee 2 = <u>suitor</u>, lover, boyfriend, sweetheart, beau, wooer

admission 1 = <u>admittance</u>, access, entry, introduction, entrance, acceptance, initiation, entrée 2 = <u>confession</u>, declaration, revelation, allowance, disclosure, acknowledgement, unburdening, divulgence

admit 1 = <u>confess</u>, confide, own up, come clean (informal) 2 = <u>allow</u>, agree, accept, reveal, grant, declare, acknowledge, recognize ≠ deny 3 = <u>let in</u>, allow, receive, accept, introduce, take in, initiate, give access to ≠ keep out

adolescence = <u>teens</u>, youth, minority, boyhood, girlhood

adolescent ADJECTIVE 1 = <u>young</u>, junior,

teenage, juvenile, youthful, childish, immature, boyish **2** = <u>teenage</u>, young, teen (*informal*)

● **NOUN** = <u>teenager</u>, girl, boy, kid (*informal*), youth, lad, minor, young man

adopt 1 = <u>take on</u>, follow, choose, maintain, assume, take up, engage in, become involved in **2** = <u>take in</u>, raise, nurse, mother, rear, foster, bring up, take care of ≠ abandon

adoption 1 = <u>fostering</u>, adopting, taking in **2** = <u>embracing</u>, choice, taking up, selection, assumption, endorsement, appropriation, espousal

adore = <u>love</u>, honour, admire, worship, esteem, cherish, revere, dote on ≠ hate

adoring = <u>admiring</u>, loving, devoted, fond, affectionate, doting ≠ hating

adorn = <u>decorate</u>, array, embellish, festoon

adrift **ADJECTIVE 1** = <u>drifting</u>, afloat, unmoored, unanchored **2** = <u>aimless</u>, goalless, directionless, purposeless

● **ADVERB** = <u>wrong</u>, astray, off course, amiss, off target, wide of the mark

adult **NOUN** = <u>grown-up</u>, mature person, person of mature age, grown or grown-up person, man or woman

● **ADJECTIVE 1** = <u>fully grown</u>, mature, grown-up, of age, ripe, fully fledged, fully developed, full grown **2** = <u>pornographic</u>, blue, dirty, obscene, filthy, indecent, lewd, salacious

advance **VERB 1** = <u>progress</u>, proceed, come forward, make inroads, make headway ≠ retreat **2** = <u>accelerate</u>, speed, promote, hasten, bring forward **3** = <u>improve</u>, rise, develop, pick up, progress, upgrade, prosper, make strides **4** = <u>suggest</u>, offer, present, propose, advocate, submit, prescribe, put forward ≠ withhold **5** = <u>lend</u>, loan, supply on credit ≠ withhold payment

● **NOUN 1** = <u>down payment</u>, credit, loan, fee, deposit, retainer, prepayment **2** = <u>attack</u>, charge, strike, assault, raid, invasion, offensive, onslaught **3** = <u>improvement</u>, development, gain, growth, breakthrough, step, headway, inroads

● **ADJECTIVE** = <u>prior</u>, early, beforehand

● **PHRASES** **in advance** = <u>beforehand</u>, earlier, ahead, previously

advanced = <u>sophisticated</u>, foremost, modern, revolutionary, up-to-date, higher, leading, recent ≠ backward

advancement = <u>promotion</u>, rise, gain, progress, improvement, betterment, preferment

advantage 1 = <u>benefit</u>, help, profit, favour ≠ disadvantage **2** = <u>lead</u>, sway, dominance, precedence **3** = <u>superiority</u>, good

adventure 1 = <u>venture</u>, experience, incident, enterprise, undertaking, exploit, occurrence, caper **2** = <u>excitement</u>, action, passion, thrill, animation, commotion

adventurous = <u>daring</u>, enterprising, bold, reckless, intrepid, daredevil ≠ cautious

adversary = <u>opponent</u>, rival, enemy, competitor, foe, contestant, antagonist ≠ ally

adverse 1 = <u>harmful</u>, damaging, negative, destructive, detrimental, hurtful, injurious, inopportune ≠ beneficial **2** = <u>unfavourable</u>, hostile, unlucky **3** = <u>negative</u>, opposing, hostile, contrary, dissenting, unsympathetic, ill-disposed

advert (*Brit. informal*) = <u>advertisement</u>, notice, commercial, ad (*informal*), announcement, poster, plug (*informal*), blurb

advertise = <u>publicize</u>, promote, plug (*informal*), announce, inform, hype, notify, tout

advertisement = <u>advert</u> (*Brit. informal*), notice, commercial, ad (*informal*), announcement, poster, plug (*informal*), blurb

advice = <u>guidance</u>, help, opinion, direction, suggestion, instruction, counsel, counselling

advise 1 = <u>recommend</u>, suggest, urge, counsel, advocate, caution, prescribe, commend **2** = <u>notify</u>, tell, report, announce, warn, declare, inform, acquaint

adviser = <u>counsellor</u>, guide, consultant, aide, guru, mentor, helper, confidant

advisory = <u>advising</u>, helping, recommending, counselling, consultative

advocate **VERB** = <u>recommend</u>, support, champion, encourage, propose, promote, advise, endorse ≠ oppose

● **NOUN 1** = <u>supporter</u>, spokesman, champion, defender, campaigner, promoter, counsellor, proponent **2** (*Law*) = <u>lawyer</u>, attorney, solicitor, counsel, barrister

affair 1 = <u>matter</u>, business, happening, event, activity, incident, episode, topic

2 = relationship, romance, intrigue, fling, liaison, flirtation, amour, dalliance

affect¹ 1 = influence, concern, alter, change, manipulate, act on, bear upon, impinge upon **2** = emotionally move, touch, upset, overcome, stir, disturb, perturb

**affect² ** = put on, assume, adopt, pretend, imitate, simulate, contrive, aspire to

affected = pretended, artificial, contrived, put-on, mannered, unnatural, feigned, insincere ≠ genuine

affection = fondness, liking, feeling, love, care, warmth, attachment, goodwill, aroha (N.Z.)

affectionate = fond, loving, kind, caring, friendly, attached, devoted, tender ≠ cool

affiliate = associate, unite, join, link, ally, combine, incorporate, amalgamate

affinity 1 = attraction, liking, leaning, sympathy, inclination, rapport, fondness, partiality, aroha (N.Z.) ≠ hostility **2** = similarity, relationship, connection, correspondence, analogy, resemblance, closeness, likeness ≠ difference

affirm 1 = declare, state, maintain, swear, assert, testify, pronounce, certify ≠ deny **2** = confirm, prove, endorse, ratify, verify, validate, bear out, substantiate ≠ refute

affirmative = agreeing, confirming, positive, approving, consenting, favourable, concurring, assenting ≠ negative

afflict = torment, trouble, pain, hurt, distress, plague, grieve, harass

affluent = wealthy, rich, prosperous, loaded (slang), well-off, opulent, well-heeled (informal), well-to-do ≠ poor

afford 1 = have the money for, manage, bear, pay for, spare, stand, stretch to **2** = bear, stand, sustain, allow yourself **3** = give, offer, provide, produce, supply, yield, render

affordable = inexpensive, cheap, reasonable, moderate, modest, low-cost, economical ≠ expensive

afraid 1 = scared, frightened, nervous, terrified, shaken, startled, fearful, cowardly ≠ unafraid **2** = reluctant, frightened, scared, unwilling, hesitant, loath, disinclined, unenthusiastic **3** = sorry, apologetic, regretful, sad, distressed, unhappy ≠ pleased

after PREPOSITION = at the end of, following, subsequent to ≠ before

● ADVERB = following, later, next, succeeding, afterwards, subsequently, thereafter

RELATED WORD

prefix: post-

aftermath = effects, results, wake, consequences, outcome, sequel, end result, upshot

again 1 = once more, another time, anew, afresh **2** = also, in addition, moreover, besides, furthermore

against 1 = beside, on, up against, in contact with, abutting **2** = opposed to, anti (informal), hostile to, in opposition to, averse to, opposite to **3** = in opposition to, resisting, versus, counter to, in the opposite direction of **4** = in preparation for, in case of, in anticipation of, in expectation of, in provision for

RELATED WORDS

prefixes: anti-, counter-

age NOUN **1** = years, days, generation, lifetime, length of existence **2** = old age, experience, maturity, seniority, majority, senility, decline (of life), advancing years ≠ youth **3** = time, day(s), period, generation, era, epoch

● VERB **1** = grow old, decline, weather, fade, deteriorate, wither **2** = mature, season, condition, soften, mellow, ripen

aged = old, getting on, grey, ancient, antique, elderly, antiquated ≠ young

agency 1 = business, company, office, firm, department, organization, enterprise, establishment **2** (Old-fashioned) = medium, means, activity, vehicle, instrument, mechanism

agenda = programme, list, plan, schedule, diary, calendar, timetable

agent 1 = representative, rep (informal), negotiator, envoy, surrogate, go-between **2** = author, worker, vehicle, instrument, operator, performer, catalyst, doer **3** = force, means, power, cause, instrument

aggravate 1 = make worse, exaggerate, intensify, worsen, exacerbate, magnify, inflame, increase ≠ improve **2** (Informal) = annoy, bother, provoke, irritate, nettle, get on your nerves (informal) ≠ please

aggregate NOUN = total, body, whole, amount, collection, mass, sum, combination

● ADJECTIVE = collective, mixed, combined,

collected, accumulated, composite, cumulative

● VERB = **combine**, mix, collect, assemble, heap, accumulate, pile, amass

aggression 1 = **hostility**, malice, antagonism, antipathy, ill will, belligerence, destructiveness, pugnacity 2 = **attack**, campaign, injury, assault, raid, invasion, offensive, onslaught

aggressive 1 = **hostile**, offensive, destructive, belligerent, unfriendly, contrary, antagonistic, pugnacious, aggers (*Austral. slang*), biffo (*Austral. slang*) ≠ friendly 2 = **forceful**, powerful, convincing, effective, enterprising, dynamic, bold, militant ≠ submissive

agitate 1 = **stir**, beat, shake, disturb, toss, rouse 2 = **upset**, worry, trouble, excite, distract, unnerve, disconcert, fluster ≠ calm

agony = **suffering**, pain, distress, misery, torture, discomfort, torment, hardship

agree 1 = **concur**, be as one, sympathize, assent, see eye to eye, be of the same opinion ≠ disagree 2 = **correspond**, match, coincide, tally, conform 3 = **suit**, get on, befit

agreement 1 = **treaty**, contract, arrangement, alliance, deal (*informal*), understanding, settlement, bargain 2 = **concurrence**, harmony, compliance, union, agreeing, consent, unison, assent ≠ disagreement 3 = **correspondence**, similarity, consistency, correlation, conformity, compatibility, congruity ≠ difference

agricultural = **farming**, country, rural, rustic, agrarian

agriculture = **farming**, culture, cultivation, husbandry, tillage

ahead 1 = **in front**, in advance, towards the front, frontwards 2 = **at an advantage**, in advance, in the lead 3 = **in the lead**, winning, leading, at the head, to the fore, at an advantage 4 = **in front**, before, in advance, in the lead

aid NOUN = **help**, backing, support, benefit, favour, relief, promotion, assistance ≠ hindrance

● VERB 1 = **help**, support, serve, sustain, assist, avail, subsidize, be of service to ≠ hinder 2 = **promote**, help, further, forward, encourage, favour, facilitate, pave the way for

aide = **assistant**, supporter, attendant, helper, right-hand man, second

ailing 1 = **weak**, failing, poor, flawed, unstable, unsatisfactory, deficient 2 = **ill**, poorly, sick, weak, crook (*Austral. & N.Z. informal*), unwell, infirm, under the weather (*informal*), indisposed

ailment = **illness**, disease, complaint, disorder, sickness, affliction, malady, infirmity

aim VERB 1 = **try for**, seek, work for, plan for, strive, set your sights on 2 = **point**

● NOUN = **intention**, point, plan, goal, design, target, purpose, desire

air NOUN 1 = **wind**, breeze, draught, gust, zephyr 2 = **atmosphere**, sky, heavens, aerosphere 3 = **tune**, song, theme, melody, strain, lay, aria 4 = **manner**, appearance, look, aspect, atmosphere, mood, impression, aura

● PLURAL NOUN = **affectation**, arrogance, pretensions, pomposity, swank (*informal*), hauteur, haughtiness, superciliousness

● VERB 1 = **publicize**, reveal, exhibit, voice, express, display, circulate, make public 2 = **ventilate**, expose, freshen, aerate

▓▓ RELATED WORD

adjective: aerial

airborne = **flying**, floating, in the air, hovering, gliding, in flight, on the wing

airing 1 = **ventilation**, drying, freshening, aeration 2 = **exposure**, display, expression, publicity, vent, utterance, dissemination

airplane (*U.S. & Canad.*) = **plane**, aircraft, jet, aeroplane, airliner

aisle = **passageway**, path, lane, passage, corridor, alley, gangway

alarm NOUN 1 = **fear**, panic, anxiety, fright, apprehension, nervousness, consternation, trepidation ≠ calmness 2 = **danger signal**, warning, bell, alert, siren, alarm bell, hooter, distress signal

● VERB = **frighten**, scare, panic, distress, startle, dismay, daunt, unnerve ≠ calm

alarming = **frightening**, shocking, scaring, disturbing, distressing, startling, horrifying, menacing

alcoholic NOUN = **drunkard**, drinker, drunk, toper, lush (*slang*), tippler, wino (*informal*), inebriate, alko *or* alco (*Austral. slang*)

● ADJECTIVE = **intoxicating**, hard, strong, stiff, brewed, fermented, distilled

alert ADJECTIVE 1 = **attentive**, awake,

vigilant, watchful, on the lookout, circumspect, observant, on guard ≠ careless **2** = quick-witted, bright, sharp
● NOUN = warning, signal, alarm, siren ≠ all clear
● VERB = warn, signal, inform, alarm, notify, tip off, forewarn ≠ lull

alien ADJECTIVE **1** = foreign, strange, imported, unknown, exotic, unfamiliar **2** = strange, new, foreign, novel, unknown, exotic, unfamiliar, untried ≠ similar
● NOUN = foreigner, incomer, immigrant, stranger, outsider, newcomer, asylum seeker ≠ citizen

alienate = antagonize, anger, annoy, offend, irritate, hassle (*informal*), estrange

alienation = estrangement, setting against, separation, turning away, disaffection, remoteness

alight¹ 1 = get off, descend, get down, disembark, dismount **2** = land, light, settle, come down, descend, perch, touch down, come to rest ≠ take off

alight² = lit up, bright, brilliant, shining, illuminated, fiery

align 1 = ally, side, join, associate, affiliate, cooperate, sympathize **2** = line up, order, range, regulate, straighten, even up

alike ADJECTIVE = similar, close, the same, parallel, resembling, identical, corresponding, akin ≠ different
● ADVERB = similarly, identically, equally, uniformly, correspondingly, analogously ≠ differently

alive 1 = living, breathing, animate, subsisting, existing, functioning, in the land of the living (*informal*) ≠ dead **2** = in existence, existing, functioning, active, operative, in force, on-going, prevalent ≠ inoperative **3** = lively, active, vital, alert, energetic, animated, agile, perky ≠ dull

all PRONOUN **1** = the whole amount, everything, the total, the aggregate, the totality, the sum total, the entirety, the entire amount **2** = every, each, every single, every one of, each and every
● ADJECTIVE = complete, greatest, full, total, perfect, entire, utter
● ADVERB = completely, totally, fully, entirely, absolutely, altogether, wholly, utterly

allegation = claim, charge, statement, declaration, accusation, assertion, affirmation

allege = claim, charge, challenge, state, maintain, declare, assert, uphold ≠ deny

alleged = claimed, supposed, declared, assumed, so-called, apparent, stated, described

allegiance = loyalty, devotion, fidelity, obedience, constancy, faithfulness ≠ disloyalty

allergic = sensitive, affected by, susceptible, hypersensitive

allergy = sensitivity, reaction, susceptibility, antipathy, hypersensitivity, sensitiveness

alleviate = ease, reduce, relieve, moderate, soothe, lessen, lighten, allay

alley = passage, walk, lane, pathway, alleyway, passageway, backstreet

alliance = union, league, association, agreement, marriage, connection, combination, coalition ≠ division

allied 1 = united, linked, related, combined, integrated, affiliated, cooperating, in league **2** = connected, linked, associated

allocate = assign, grant, distribute, designate, set aside, earmark, give out, consign

allocation 1 = allowance, share, portion, quota, lot, ration **2** = assignment, allowance, allotment

allow VERB **1** = permit, approve, enable, sanction, endure, license, tolerate, authorize ≠ prohibit **2** = let, permit, sanction, authorize, license, tolerate, consent to, assent to ≠ forbid **3** = give, provide, grant, spare, devote, assign, allocate, set aside **4** = acknowledge, accept, admit, grant, recognize, yield, concede, confess
● PHRASES **allow for something** = take something into account, consider, plan for, accommodate, provide for, make provision for, make allowances for, make concessions for

allowance 1 = portion, lot, share, amount, grant, quota, allocation, stint **2** = pocket money, grant, fee, payment, ration, handout, remittance **3** = concession, discount, reduction, repayment, deduction, rebate

all right 1 = satisfactory, O.K. *or* okay (*informal*), average, fair, sufficient, standard, acceptable, good enough ≠ unsatisfactory **2** = well, O.K. *or* okay (*informal*), whole, sound, fit, safe, healthy, unharmed ≠ ill

ally NOUN = partner, friend, colleague, associate, mate, comrade, helper, collaborator, cobber (*Austral. & N.Z. old-fashioned informal*), E hoa (*N.Z.*) ≠ opponent

● PHRASES **ally yourself with something** *or* **someone** = unite with, associate with, unify, collaborate with, join forces with, band together with

almost = nearly, about, close to, virtually, practically, roughly, just about, not quite

alone ADJECTIVE 1 = solitary, isolated, separate, apart, by yourself, unaccompanied, on your tod (*slang*) ≠ accompanied 2 = lonely, abandoned, isolated, solitary, forsaken, forlorn, destitute

● ADVERB 1 = solely, only, individually, singly, exclusively, uniquely 2 = by yourself, independently, unaccompanied, without help, on your own, without assistance ≠ with help

aloud = out loud, clearly, plainly, distinctly, audibly, intelligibly

already = before now, before, previously, at present, by now, by then, even now, just now

also = and, too, further, in addition, as well, moreover, besides, furthermore

alter 1 = modify, change, reform, vary, transform, adjust, adapt, revise 2 = change, turn, vary, transform, adjust, adapt

alternate VERB 1 = interchange, change, fluctuate, take turns, oscillate, chop and change 2 = intersperse, interchange, exchange, swap, stagger, rotate

● ADJECTIVE = alternating, interchanging, every other, rotating, every second, sequential

alternative NOUN = substitute, choice, other (*of two*), option, preference, recourse

● ADJECTIVE = different, other, substitute, alternate

alternatively = or, instead, otherwise, on the other hand, if not, then again, as an alternative, as another option

although = though, while, even if, even though, whilst, albeit, despite the fact that, notwithstanding

altogether 1 = absolutely, quite, completely, totally, perfectly, fully, thoroughly, wholly 2 = completely, fully, entirely, thoroughly, wholly, in every respect ≠ partially 3 = on the whole, generally, mostly, in general, collectively, all things considered, on average, for the most part 4 = in total, in all, all told, taken together, in sum, everything included

always 1 = habitually, regularly, every time, consistently, invariably, perpetually, without exception, customarily ≠ seldom 2 = forever, for keeps, eternally, for all time, evermore, till the cows come home (*informal*), till Doomsday 3 = continually, constantly, all the time, forever, repeatedly, persistently, perpetually, incessantly

amass = collect, gather, assemble, compile, accumulate, pile up, hoard

amateur = nonprofessional, outsider, layman, dilettante, layperson, non-specialist, dabbler

amaze = astonish, surprise, shock, stun, alarm, stagger, startle, bewilder

amazement = astonishment, surprise, wonder, shock, confusion, admiration, awe, bewilderment

amazing = astonishing, surprising, brilliant, stunning, overwhelming, staggering, sensational (*informal*), bewildering

ambassador = representative, minister, agent, deputy, diplomat, envoy, consul, attaché

ambiguity = vagueness, doubt, uncertainty, obscurity, equivocation, dubiousness

ambiguous = unclear, obscure, vague, dubious, enigmatic, indefinite, inconclusive, indeterminate ≠ clear

ambition 1 = goal, hope, dream, target, aim, wish, purpose, desire 2 = enterprise, longing, drive, spirit, desire, passion, enthusiasm, striving

ambitious = enterprising, spirited, daring, eager, intent, enthusiastic, hopeful, striving ≠ unambitious

ambush VERB = trap, attack, surprise, deceive, dupe, ensnare, waylay, bushwhack (*U.S.*)

● NOUN = trap, snare, lure, waylaying

amend VERB = change, improve, reform, fix, correct, repair, edit, alter

● PLURAL NOUN (*usually in* make amends) = compensation, redress, reparation, restitution, atonement, recompense

amendment 1 = <u>addition</u>, change, adjustment, attachment, adaptation, revision, modification, alteration **2** = <u>change</u>, improvement, repair, edit, remedy, correction, revision, modification

amenity = <u>facility</u>, service, advantage, comfort, convenience

amid or **amidst 1** = <u>during</u>, among, at a time of, in an atmosphere of **2** = <u>in the middle of</u>, among, surrounded by, amongst, in the midst of, in the thick of

ammunition = <u>munitions</u>, rounds, shot, shells, powder, explosives, armaments

amnesty = <u>general pardon</u>, mercy, pardoning, immunity, forgiveness, reprieve, remission (*of penalty*), clemency

among or **amongst 1** = <u>in the midst of</u>, with, together with, in the middle of, amid, surrounded by, amidst, in the thick of **2** = <u>in the group of</u>, one of, part of, included in, in the company of, in the class of, in the number of **3** = <u>between</u>, to

amount NOUN = <u>quantity</u>, measure, size, supply, mass, volume, capacity, extent
● PHRASES **amount to something 1** = <u>add up to</u>, mean, total, equal, constitute, comprise, be equivalent to **2** = <u>come to</u>, become, develop into, advance to, progress to, mature into

ample 1 = <u>plenty of</u>, generous, lavish, abundant, plentiful, expansive, copious, profuse ≠ insufficient **2** = <u>large</u>, full, extensive, generous, abundant, bountiful

amply = <u>fully</u>, completely, richly, generously, abundantly, profusely, copiously ≠ insufficiently

amuse 1 = <u>entertain</u>, please, delight, charm, cheer, tickle ≠ bore **2** = <u>occupy</u>, interest, involve, engage, entertain, absorb, engross

amusement 1 = <u>enjoyment</u>, entertainment, cheer, mirth, merriment ≠ boredom **2** = <u>diversion</u>, fun, pleasure, entertainment **3** = <u>pastime</u>, game, sport, joke, entertainment, hobby, recreation, diversion

amusing = <u>funny</u>, humorous, comical, droll, interesting, entertaining, comic, enjoyable ≠ boring

anaesthetic NOUN = <u>painkiller</u>, narcotic, sedative, opiate, anodyne, analgesic, soporific
● ADJECTIVE = <u>pain-killing</u>, dulling, numbing, sedative, deadening, anodyne, analgesic, soporific

analogy = <u>similarity</u>, relation, comparison, parallel, correspondence, resemblance, correlation, likeness

analyse 1 = <u>examine</u>, test, study, research, survey, investigate, evaluate, inspect **2** = <u>break down</u>, separate, divide, resolve, dissect, think through

analysis = <u>examination</u>, test, inquiry, investigation, interpretation, breakdown, scanning, evaluation

analytical or **analytic** = <u>rational</u>, organized, exact, precise, logical, systematic, inquiring, investigative

anarchy = <u>lawlessness</u>, revolution, riot, disorder, confusion, chaos, disorganization ≠ order

anatomy 1 = <u>structure</u>, build, make-up, frame, framework, composition **2** = <u>examination</u>, study, division, inquiry, investigation, analysis, dissection

ancestor 1 = <u>forefather</u>, predecessor, precursor, forerunner, forebear, antecedent, tupuna or tipuna (*N.Z.*) ≠ descendant

ancient 1 = <u>classical</u>, old, former, past, bygone, primordial, primeval, olden **2** = <u>very old</u>, aged, antique, archaic, timeworn **3** = <u>old-fashioned</u>, dated, outdated, obsolete, out of date, unfashionable, outmoded, passé ≠ up-to-date

and 1 = <u>also</u>, including, along with, together with, in addition to, as well as **2** = <u>moreover</u>, plus, furthermore

anecdote = <u>story</u>, tale, sketch, short story, yarn, reminiscence, urban myth, urban legend

angel 1 = <u>divine messenger</u>, cherub, archangel, seraph **2** (*Informal*) = <u>dear</u>, beauty, saint, treasure, darling, jewel, gem, paragon

anger NOUN = <u>rage</u>, outrage, temper, fury, resentment, wrath, annoyance, ire ≠ calmness
● VERB = <u>enrage</u>, outrage, annoy, infuriate, incense, gall, madden, exasperate ≠ soothe

angle 1 = <u>gradient</u>, bank, slope, incline, inclination **2** = <u>intersection</u>, point, edge, corner, bend, elbow, crook, nook **3** = <u>point of view</u>, position, approach, direction, aspect, perspective, outlook, viewpoint

angry = <u>furious</u>, cross, mad (*informal*),

outraged, annoyed, infuriated, incensed, enraged, tooshie (*Austral. slang*), off the air (*Austral. slang*) ≠ calm

angst = anxiety, worry, unease, apprehension ≠ peace of mind

anguish = suffering, pain, distress, grief, misery, agony, torment, sorrow

animal NOUN 1 = creature, beast, brute 2 = brute, devil, monster, savage, beast, bastard (*informal, offensive*), villain, barbarian
• ADJECTIVE = physical, gross, bodily, sensual, carnal, brutish, bestial

animate ADJECTIVE = living, live, moving, alive, breathing, alive and kicking
• VERB = enliven, excite, inspire, move, fire, stimulate, energize, kindle ≠ inhibit

animated = lively, spirited, excited, enthusiastic, passionate, energetic, ebullient, vivacious ≠ listless

animation = liveliness, energy, spirit, passion, enthusiasm, excitement, verve, zest

announce = make known, tell, report, reveal, declare, advertise, broadcast, disclose ≠ keep secret

announcement 1 = statement, communication, broadcast, declaration, advertisement, bulletin, communiqué, proclamation 2 = declaration, report, reporting, revelation, proclamation

annoy = irritate, trouble, anger, bother, disturb, plague, hassle (*informal*), madden ≠ soothe

annoying = irritating, disturbing, troublesome, maddening, exasperating ≠ delightful

annual 1 = once a year, yearly 2 = yearlong, yearly

annually 1 = once a year, yearly, every year, per year, by the year, every twelve months, per annum 2 = per year, yearly, every year, by the year, per annum

anomaly = irregularity, exception, abnormality, inconsistency, eccentricity, oddity, peculiarity, incongruity

anonymous 1 = unnamed, unknown, unidentified, nameless, unacknowledged, incognito ≠ identified 2 = unsigned, uncredited, unattributed ≠ signed

answer VERB = reply, explain, respond, resolve, react, return, retort ≠ ask
• NOUN 1 = reply, response, reaction, explanation, comeback, retort, return,

defence ≠ question 2 = solution, resolution, explanation 3 = remedy, solution

anthem = song of praise, carol, chant, hymn, psalm, paean, chorale, canticle

anthology = collection, selection, treasury, compilation, compendium, miscellany

anticipate 1 = expect, predict, prepare for, hope for, envisage, foresee, bank on, foretell 2 = await, look forward to, count the hours until

anticipation = expectancy, expectation, foresight, premonition, prescience, forethought

antics = clowning, tricks, mischief, pranks, escapades, playfulness, horseplay, tomfoolery

antique NOUN = period piece, relic, bygone, heirloom, collector's item, museum piece
• ADJECTIVE = vintage, classic, antiquarian, olden

anxiety = uneasiness, concern, worry, doubt, tension, angst, apprehension, misgiving ≠ confidence

anxious 1 = eager, keen, intent, yearning, impatient, itching, desirous ≠ reluctant 2 = uneasy, concerned, worried, troubled, nervous, uncomfortable, tense, fearful ≠ confident

apart 1 = to pieces, to bits, asunder 2 = away from each other, distant from each other 3 = aside, away, alone, isolated, to one side, by yourself 4 *with from* = except for, excepting, other than, excluding, besides, not including, aside from, but

apartment 1 (*U.S.*) = flat, room, suite, penthouse, crib 2 = rooms, quarters, accommodation, living quarters

apathy = lack of interest, indifference, inertia, coolness, passivity, nonchalance, torpor, unconcern ≠ interest

apiece = each, individually, separately, for each, to each, respectively, from each ≠ all together

apologize = say sorry, express regret, ask forgiveness, make an apology, beg pardon

apology NOUN = regret, explanation, excuse, confession
• PHRASES **apology for something** *or* **someone** = mockery of, excuse for, imitation of, caricature of, travesty of, poor

substitute for

appal = <u>horrify</u>, shock, alarm, frighten, outrage, disgust, dishearten, revolt

appalling 1 = <u>horrifying</u>, shocking, alarming, awful, terrifying, horrible, dreadful, fearful ≠ reassuring 2 = <u>awful</u>, dreadful, horrendous

apparatus 1 = <u>organization</u>, system, network, structure, bureaucracy, hierarchy, setup (*informal*), chain of command 2 = <u>equipment</u>, tackle, gear, device, tools, mechanism, machinery, appliance

apparent 1 = <u>seeming</u>, outward, superficial, ostensible ≠ actual 2 = <u>obvious</u>, marked, visible, evident, distinct, manifest, noticeable, unmistakable ≠ unclear

apparently = <u>seemingly</u>, outwardly, ostensibly

appeal VERB 1 = <u>plead</u>, ask, request, pray, beg, entreat ≠ refuse
● NOUN 1 = <u>plea</u>, call, application, request, prayer, petition, overture, entreaty ≠ refusal 2 = <u>attraction</u>, charm, fascination, beauty, allure ≠ repulsiveness
● PHRASES **appeal to someone** = <u>attract</u>, interest, draw, please, charm, fascinate, tempt, lure

appealing = <u>attractive</u>, engaging, charming, desirable, alluring, winsome ≠ repellent

appear 1 = <u>look (like or as if)</u>, seem, occur, look to be, come across as, strike you as 2 = <u>come into view</u>, emerge, occur, surface, come out, turn up, be present, show up (*informal*) ≠ disappear

appearance 1 = <u>look</u>, form, figure, looks, manner, expression, demeanour, mien (*literary*) 2 = <u>arrival</u>, presence, introduction, emergence 3 = <u>impression</u>, air, front, image, illusion, guise, façade, pretence

appease 1 = <u>pacify</u>, satisfy, calm, soothe, quiet, placate, mollify, conciliate ≠ anger 2 = <u>ease</u>, calm, relieve, soothe, alleviate, allay

appendix = <u>supplement</u>, postscript, adjunct, appendage, addendum, addition

appetite 1 = <u>hunger</u> 2 = <u>desire</u>, liking, longing, demand, taste, passion, stomach, hunger ≠ distaste

applaud 1 = <u>clap</u>, encourage, praise, cheer, acclaim ≠ boo 2 = <u>praise</u>, celebrate, approve, acclaim, compliment, salute, commend, extol ≠ criticize

applause = <u>ovation</u>, praise, cheers, approval, clapping, accolade, big hand

appliance = <u>device</u>, machine, tool, instrument, implement, mechanism, apparatus, gadget

applicable = <u>appropriate</u>, fitting, useful, suitable, relevant, apt, pertinent ≠ inappropriate

applicant = <u>candidate</u>, claimant, inquirer

application 1 = <u>request</u>, claim, appeal, inquiry, petition, requisition 2 = <u>effort</u>, work, industry, trouble, struggle, pains, commitment, hard work

apply VERB 1 = <u>request</u>, appeal, put in, petition, inquire, claim, requisition 2 = <u>be relevant</u>, relate, refer, be fitting, be appropriate, fit, pertain, be applicable 3 = <u>use</u>, exercise, carry out, employ, implement, practise, exert, enact 4 = <u>put on</u>, work in, cover with, lay on, paint on, spread on, rub in, smear on
● PHRASES **apply yourself to something** = <u>work hard at</u>, concentrate on, try at, commit yourself to, buckle down to (*informal*), devote yourself to, be diligent in, dedicate yourself to

appoint 1 = <u>assign</u>, name, choose, commission, select, elect, delegate, nominate ≠ fire 2 = <u>decide</u>, set, choose, establish, fix, arrange, assign, designate ≠ cancel

appointed 1 = <u>decided</u>, set, chosen, established, fixed, arranged, assigned, designated 2 = <u>assigned</u>, named, chosen, selected, elected, delegated, nominated 3 = <u>equipped</u>, provided, supplied, furnished, fitted out

appointment 1 = <u>selection</u>, naming, election, choice, nomination, assignment 2 = <u>job</u>, office, position, post, situation, place, employment, assignment 3 = <u>meeting</u>, interview, date, arrangement, engagement, fixture, rendezvous, assignation

appraisal = <u>assessment</u>, opinion, estimate, judgment, evaluation, estimation

appreciate 1 = <u>enjoy</u>, like, value, respect, prize, admire, treasure, rate highly ≠ scorn 2 = <u>be aware of</u>, understand, realize, recognize, perceive, take account of, be sensitive to, sympathize with ≠ be unaware of 3 = <u>be grateful</u>, be obliged, be thankful, give thanks, be indebted, be in debt, be appreciative ≠ be ungrateful for **4** = increase, rise, grow, gain, improve, enhance, soar ≠ fall

appreciation 1 = admiration, enjoyment **2** = gratitude, thanks, recognition, obligation, acknowledgment, indebtedness, thankfulness, gratefulness ≠ ingratitude **3** = awareness, understanding, recognition, perception, sympathy, consciousness, sensitivity, realization ≠ ignorance **4** = increase, rise, gain, growth, improvement, escalation, enhancement ≠ fall

apprehension 1 = anxiety, concern, fear, worry, alarm, suspicion, dread, trepidation ≠ confidence **2** = arrest, catching, capture, taking, seizure ≠ release **3** = awareness, understanding, perception, grasp, comprehension ≠ incomprehension

apprentice = trainee, student, pupil, novice, beginner, learner, probationer ≠ master

approach VERB **1** = move towards, reach, near, come close, come near, draw near **2** = make a proposal to, speak to, apply to, appeal to, proposition, solicit, sound out, make overtures to **3** = set about, tackle, undertake, embark on, get down to, launch into, begin work on, commence on ● NOUN **1** = advance, coming, nearing, appearance, arrival, drawing near **2** = access, way, drive, road, passage, entrance, avenue, passageway **3** *often plural* = proposal, offer, appeal, advance, application, invitation, proposition, overture **4** = way, means, style, method, technique, manner

appropriate ADJECTIVE = suitable, fitting, relevant, to the point, apt, pertinent, befitting, well-suited ≠ unsuitable ● VERB **1** = seize, claim, acquire, confiscate, usurp, impound, commandeer, take possession of ≠ relinquish **2** = allocate, allow, budget, devote, assign, designate, set aside, earmark ≠ withhold **3** = steal, take, nick (*slang, chiefly Brit.*), pocket, pinch (*informal*), lift (*informal*), embezzle, pilfer

approval 1 = consent, agreement, sanction, blessing, permission, recommendation, endorsement, assent **2** = favour, respect, praise, esteem, acclaim, appreciation, admiration, applause

≠ disapproval

approve VERB = agree to, allow, pass, recommend, permit, sanction, endorse, authorize ≠ veto ● PHRASES **approve of something** *or* **someone** = favour, like, respect, praise, admire, commend, have a good opinion of, regard highly

apt 1 = appropriate, fitting, suitable, relevant, to the point, pertinent ≠ inappropriate **2** = inclined, likely, ready, disposed, prone, liable, given, predisposed **3** = gifted, skilled, quick, talented, sharp, capable, smart, clever ≠ slow

arbitrary = random, chance, subjective, inconsistent, erratic, personal, whimsical, capricious ≠ logical

arbitration = decision, settlement, judgment, determination, adjudication

arc = curve, bend, bow, arch, crescent, half-moon

arcade = gallery, cloister, portico, colonnade

arch[1] NOUN **1** = archway, curve, dome, span, vault **2** = curve, bend, bow, crook, arc, hunch, sweep, hump ● VERB = curve, bridge, bend, bow, span, arc

arch[2] = playful, sly, mischievous, saucy, pert, roguish, frolicsome, waggish

archetypal = typical, standard, model, original, classic, ideal, prototypic *or* prototypical

architect = designer, planner, draughtsman, master builder

architecture 1 = design, planning, building, construction **2** = construction, design, style **3** = structure, design, shape, make-up, construction, framework, layout, anatomy

archive NOUN = record office, museum, registry, repository ● PLURAL NOUN = records, papers, accounts, rolls, documents, files, deeds, chronicles

arctic (*Informal*) = freezing, cold, frozen, icy, chilly, glacial, frigid

Arctic = polar, far-northern, hyperborean

ardent 1 = enthusiastic, keen, eager, avid, zealous ≠ indifferent **2** = passionate, intense, impassioned, lusty, amorous, hot-blooded ≠ cold

area 1 = region, quarter, district, zone, neighbourhood, locality **2** = part, section, sector, portion **3** = realm, part, department, field, province, sphere, domain

arena 1 = ring, ground, field, theatre, bowl, pitch, stadium, enclosure 2 = scene, world, area, stage, field, sector, territory, province

argue 1 = quarrel, fight, row, clash, dispute, disagree, squabble, bicker 2 = discuss, debate, dispute 3 = claim, reason, challenge, insist, maintain, allege, assert, uphold

argument 1 = reason, case, reasoning, ground(s), defence, logic, polemic, dialectic 2 = debate, questioning, claim, discussion, dispute, controversy, plea, assertion 3 = quarrel, fight, row, clash, dispute, controversy, disagreement, feud ≠ agreement

arise 1 = happen, start, begin, follow, result, develop, emerge, occur 2 (*Old-fashioned*) = get to your feet, get up, rise, stand up, spring up, leap up 3 = get up, wake up, awaken, get out of bed

aristocrat = noble, lord, lady, peer, patrician, grandee, aristo (*informal*), peeress

aristocratic = upper-class, lordly, titled, elite, gentlemanly, noble, patrician, blue-blooded ≠ common

arm¹ = upper limb, limb, appendage

arm² VERB = equip, provide, supply, array, furnish, issue with, deck out, accoutre
● PLURAL NOUN = weapons, guns, firearms, weaponry, armaments, ordnance, munitions, instruments of war

armed = carrying weapons, protected, equipped, primed, fitted out

armour = protection, covering, shield, sheathing, armour plate, chain mail, protective covering

armoured = protected, mailed, reinforced, toughened, bulletproof, armour-plated, steel-plated, ironclad

army 1 = soldiers, military, troops, armed force, legions, infantry, military force, land force 2 = vast number, host, gang, mob, flock, array, legion, swarm

aroma = scent, smell, perfume, fragrance, bouquet, savour, odour, redolence

around PREPOSITION 1 = surrounding, about, enclosing, encompassing, framing, encircling, on all sides of, on every side of 2 = approximately, about, nearly, close to, roughly, just about, in the region of, circa (*used with dates*)

● ADVERB 1 = everywhere, about, throughout, all over, here and there, on all sides, in all directions, to and fro 2 = near, close, nearby, at hand, close at hand

arouse 1 = stimulate, encourage, inspire, prompt, spur, provoke, rouse, stir up ≠ quell 2 = inflame, move, excite, spur, provoke, stir up, agitate 3 = awaken, wake up, rouse, waken

arrange 1 = plan, agree, prepare, determine, organize, construct, devise, contrive, jack up (*N.Z. informal*) 2 = put in order, group, order, sort, position, line up, organize, classify, jack up (*N.Z. informal*) ≠ disorganize 3 = adapt, score, orchestrate, harmonize, instrument

arrangement 1 *often plural* = plan, planning, provision, preparation 2 = agreement, contract, settlement, appointment, compromise, deal (*informal*), pact, compact 3 = display, system, structure, organization, exhibition, presentation, classification, alignment 4 = adaptation, score, version, interpretation, instrumentation, orchestration, harmonization

array NOUN 1 = arrangement, show, supply, display, collection, exhibition, line-up, mixture 2 (*Poetic*) = clothing, dress, clothes, garments, apparel, attire, finery, regalia
● VERB 1 = arrange, show, group, present, range, display, parade, exhibit 2 = dress, clothe, deck, decorate, adorn, festoon, attire

arrest VERB 1 = capture, catch, nick (*slang, chiefly Brit.*), seize, detain, apprehend, take prisoner ≠ release 2 = stop, end, limit, block, slow, delay, interrupt, suppress ≠ speed up 3 = fascinate, hold, occupy, engage, grip, absorb, entrance, intrigue
● NOUN 1 = capture, bust (*informal*), detention, seizure ≠ release 2 = stoppage, suppression, obstruction, blockage, hindrance ≠ acceleration

arresting = striking, surprising, engaging, stunning, impressive, outstanding, remarkable, noticeable ≠ unremarkable

arrival 1 = appearance, coming, arriving, entrance, advent, materialization 2 = coming, happening, taking place, emergence, occurrence, materialization 3 = newcomer, incomer, visitor, caller, entrant

arrive 1 = come, appear, turn up, show up (*informal*), draw near ≠ depart 2 = occur, happen, take place 3 (*Informal*) = succeed, make it (*informal*), triumph, do well, thrive, flourish, be successful, make good

arrogance = conceit, pride, swagger, insolence, high-handedness, haughtiness, superciliousness, disdainfulness ≠ modesty

arrogant = conceited, proud, cocky, overbearing, haughty, scornful, egotistical, disdainful ≠ modest

arrow 1 = dart, flight, bolt, shaft (*archaic*), quarrel 2 = pointer, indicator, marker

arsenal = armoury, supply, store, stockpile, storehouse, ammunition dump, arms depot, ordnance depot

art 1 = artwork, style of art, fine art, creativity 2 = skill, craft, expertise, competence, mastery, ingenuity, virtuosity, cleverness

article 1 = feature, story, paper, piece, item, creation, essay, composition 2 = thing, piece, unit, item, object, device, tool, implement 3 = clause, point, part, section, item, passage, portion, paragraph

articulate ADJECTIVE = expressive, clear, coherent, fluent, eloquent, lucid ≠ incoherent
● VERB 1 = express, say, state, word, declare, phrase, communicate, utter 2 = pronounce, say, talk, speak, voice, utter, enunciate

artificial 1 = synthetic, manufactured, plastic, man-made, non-natural 2 = insincere, forced, affected, phoney *or* phony (*informal*), false, contrived, unnatural, feigned ≠ genuine 3 = fake, mock, imitation, bogus, simulated, sham, counterfeit ≠ authentic

artillery = big guns, battery, cannon, ordnance, gunnery

artistic 1 = creative, cultured, original, sophisticated, refined, aesthetic, discerning, eloquent ≠ untalented 2 = beautiful, creative, elegant, stylish, aesthetic, tasteful ≠ unattractive

as CONJUNCTION = when, while, just as, at the time that
● PREPOSITION 1 = in the role of, being, under the name of, in the character of 2 = in the way that, like, in the manner that 3 = since, because, seeing that, considering that, on account of the fact that

ashamed 1 = embarrassed, sorry, guilty, distressed, humiliated, self-conscious, red-faced, mortified ≠ proud 2 = reluctant, embarrassed

ashore = on land, on the beach, on the shore, aground, to the shore, on dry land, shorewards, landwards

aside ADVERB = to one side, separately, apart, beside, out of the way, on one side, to the side
● NOUN = interpolation, parenthesis

ask 1 = inquire, question, quiz, query, interrogate ≠ answer 2 = request, appeal to, plead with, demand, beg 3 = invite, bid, summon

asleep = sleeping, napping, dormant, dozing, slumbering, snoozing (*informal*), fast asleep, sound asleep

aspect 1 = feature, side, factor, angle, characteristic, facet 2 = position, view, situation, scene, prospect, point of view, outlook 3 = appearance, look, air, condition, quality, bearing, attitude, cast

aspiration = aim, plan, hope, goal, dream, wish, desire, objective

aspire to = aim for, desire, hope for, long for, seek out, wish for, dream about, set your heart on

ass 1 = donkey, moke (*slang*) 2 = fool, idiot, twit (*informal*, *chiefly Brit.*), oaf, jackass, blockhead, halfwit, numbskull *or* numskull, dorba *or* dorb (*Austral. slang*), bogan (*Austral. slang*)

assassin = murderer, killer, slayer, liquidator, executioner, hit man (*slang*), hatchet man (*slang*)

assassinate = murder, kill, eliminate (*slang*), take out (*slang*), terminate, hit (*slang*), slay, liquidate

assault NOUN = attack, raid, invasion, charge, offensive, onslaught, foray ≠ defence
● VERB = strike, attack, beat, knock, bang, slap, smack, thump

assemble 1 = gather, meet, collect, rally, come together, muster, congregate ≠ scatter 2 = bring together, collect, gather, rally, come together, muster, amass, congregate 3 = put together, join, set up, build up, connect, construct, piece together, fabricate ≠ take apart

assembly 1 = gathering, group, meeting, council, conference, crowd, congress, collection, hui (*N.Z.*), runanga (*N.Z.*) **2** = <u>putting together</u>, setting up, construction, building up, connecting, piecing together

assert VERB **1** = <u>state</u>, argue, maintain, declare, swear, pronounce, affirm, profess ≠ deny **2** = <u>insist upon</u>, stress, defend, uphold, put forward, press, stand up for ≠ retract

● PHRASES **assert yourself** = <u>be forceful</u>, put your foot down (*informal*), put yourself forward, make your presence felt, exert your influence

assertion 1 = <u>statement</u>, claim, declaration, pronouncement **2** = <u>insistence</u>, stressing, maintenance

assertive = <u>confident</u>, positive, aggressive, forceful, emphatic, insistent, feisty (*informal, chiefly U.S. & Canad.*), pushy (*informal*) ≠ meek

assess 1 = <u>judge</u>, estimate, analyse, evaluate, rate, value, check out, weigh up **2** = <u>evaluate</u>, rate, tax, value, estimate, fix, impose, levy

assessment 1 = <u>judgment</u>, analysis, evaluation, valuation, appraisal, rating, opinion, estimate **2** = <u>evaluation</u>, rating, charge, fee, toll, levy, valuation

asset NOUN = <u>benefit</u>, help, service, aid, advantage, strength, resource, attraction ≠ disadvantage

● PLURAL NOUN = <u>property</u>, goods, money, funds, effects, capital, riches, finance

assign 1 = <u>give</u>, set, grant, allocate, give out, consign, allot, apportion **2** = <u>select for</u>, post, commission, elect, appoint, delegate, nominate, name **3** = <u>attribute</u>, credit, put down, set down, ascribe, accredit

assignment = <u>task</u>, job, position, post, commission, exercise, responsibility, duty

assist 1 = <u>help</u>, support, aid, cooperate with, abet, lend a helping hand to **2** = <u>facilitate</u>, help, further, serve, aid, forward, promote, speed up ≠ hinder

assistance = <u>help</u>, backing, support, aid, cooperation, helping hand ≠ hindrance

assistant = <u>helper</u>, ally, colleague, supporter, aide, second, attendant, accomplice

associate VERB **1** = <u>connect</u>, link, ally, identify, join, combine, attach, fasten ≠ separate **2** = <u>socialize</u>, mix, accompany, mingle, consort, hobnob ≠ avoid

● NOUN = <u>partner</u>, friend, ally, colleague,

mate (*informal*), companion, comrade, affiliate, cobber (*Austral. & N.Z. old-fashioned informal*), E hoa (*N.Z.*)

association 1 = <u>group</u>, club, society, league, band, set, pack, collection **2** = <u>connection</u>, union, joining, pairing, combination, mixture, blend, juxtaposition

assorted = <u>various</u>, different, mixed, varied, diverse, miscellaneous, sundry, motley ≠ similar

assume 1 = <u>presume</u>, think, believe, expect, suppose, imagine, fancy, take for granted ≠ know **2** = <u>take on</u>, accept, shoulder, take over, put on, enter upon **3** = <u>simulate</u>, affect, adopt, put on, imitate, mimic, feign, impersonate **4** = <u>take over</u>, take, appropriate, seize, commandeer ≠ give up

assumed = <u>false</u>, made-up, fake, bogus, counterfeit, fictitious, make-believe ≠ real

assumption 1 = <u>presumption</u>, belief, guess, hypothesis, inference, conjecture, surmise, supposition **2** = <u>taking on</u>, managing, handling, shouldering, putting on, taking up, takeover, acquisition **3** = <u>seizure</u>, taking, takeover, acquisition, appropriation, wresting, confiscation, commandeering

assurance 1 = <u>promise</u>, statement, guarantee, commitment, pledge, vow, declaration, assertion ≠ lie **2** = <u>confidence</u>, conviction, certainty, self-confidence, poise, faith, nerve, aplomb ≠ self-doubt

assure 1 = <u>convince</u>, encourage, persuade, satisfy, comfort, reassure, hearten, embolden **2** = <u>make certain</u>, ensure, confirm, guarantee, secure, make sure, complete, seal **3** = <u>promise to</u>, pledge to, vow to, guarantee to, swear to, confirm to, certify to, give your word to

assured 1 = <u>confident</u>, certain, positive, poised, fearless, self-confident, self-assured, dauntless ≠ self-conscious **2** = <u>certain</u>, sure, ensured, confirmed, settled, guaranteed, fixed, secure ≠ doubtful

astonish = <u>amaze</u>, surprise, stun, stagger, bewilder, astound, daze, confound

astounding = <u>amazing</u>, surprising, brilliant, impressive, astonishing, staggering, sensational (*informal*), bewildering

astute = <u>intelligent</u>, sharp, clever, subtle, shrewd, cunning, canny, perceptive

≠ stupid

asylum 1 (*Old-fashioned*) = <u>mental hospital</u>, hospital, institution, psychiatric hospital, madhouse (*informal*) 2 = <u>refuge</u>, haven, safety, protection, preserve, shelter, retreat, harbour

athlete = <u>sportsperson</u>, player, runner, competitor, sportsman, contestant, gymnast, sportswoman

athletic ADJECTIVE = <u>fit</u>, strong, powerful, healthy, active, trim, strapping, energetic ≠ feeble
● PLURAL NOUN = <u>sports</u>, games, races, exercises, contests, sporting events, gymnastics, track and field events

atmosphere 1 = <u>air</u>, sky, heavens, aerosphere 2 = <u>feeling</u>, character, environment, spirit, surroundings, tone, mood, climate

atom = <u>particle</u>, bit, spot, trace, molecule, dot, speck

atrocity 1 = <u>act of cruelty</u>, crime, horror, evil, outrage, abomination 2 = <u>cruelty</u>, horror, brutality, savagery, wickedness, barbarity, viciousness, fiendishness

attach 1 = <u>affix</u>, stick, secure, add, join, couple, link, tie ≠ detach 2 = <u>ascribe</u>, connect, attribute, assign, associate

attached ADJECTIVE = <u>spoken for</u>, married, partnered, engaged, accompanied
● PHRASES **attached to** = <u>fond of</u>, devoted to, affectionate towards, full of regard for

attachment 1 = <u>fondness</u>, liking, feeling, relationship, regard, attraction, affection, affinity, aroha (*N.Z.*) ≠ aversion 2 = <u>accessory</u>, fitting, extra, component, extension, supplement, fixture, accoutrement

attack VERB 1 = <u>assault</u>, strike (at), mug, ambush, tear into, set upon, lay into (*informal*) ≠ defend 2 = <u>invade</u>, occupy, raid, infringe, storm, encroach 3 = <u>criticize</u>, blame, abuse, condemn, knock (*informal*), put down, slate (*informal*), have a go (at) (*informal*)
● NOUN 1 = <u>assault</u>, charge, campaign, strike, raid, invasion, offensive, blitz ≠ defence 2 = <u>criticism</u>, censure, disapproval, abuse, bad press, vilification, denigration, disparagement 3 = <u>bout</u>, fit, stroke, seizure, spasm, convulsion, paroxysm

attacker = <u>assailant</u>, assaulter, raider, intruder, invader, aggressor, mugger

attain 1 = <u>obtain</u>, get, reach, complete, gain, achieve, acquire, fulfil 2 = <u>reach</u>, achieve, acquire, accomplish

attempt VERB = <u>try</u>, seek, aim, struggle, venture, undertake, strive, endeavour
● NOUN 1 = <u>try</u>, go (*informal*), shot (*informal*), effort, trial, bid, crack (*informal*), stab (*informal*) 2 = <u>attack</u>

attend VERB 1 = <u>be present</u>, go to, visit, frequent, haunt, appear at, turn up at, patronize ≠ be absent 2 = <u>pay attention</u>, listen, hear, mark, note, observe, heed, pay heed ≠ ignore
● PHRASES **attend to something** = <u>apply yourself to</u>, concentrate on, look after, take care of, see to, get to work on, devote yourself to, occupy yourself with

attendance 1 = <u>presence</u>, being there, attending, appearance 2 = <u>turnout</u>, audience, gate, congregation, house, crowd, throng, number present

attendant NOUN = <u>assistant</u>, guard, servant, companion, aide, escort, follower, helper
● ADJECTIVE = <u>accompanying</u>, related, associated, accessory, consequent, resultant, concomitant

attention 1 = <u>thinking</u>, thought, mind, consideration, scrutiny, heed, deliberation, intentness 2 = <u>care</u>, support, concern, treatment, looking after, succour, ministration 3 = <u>awareness</u>, regard, notice, recognition, consideration, observation, consciousness ≠ inattention

attic = <u>loft</u>, garret, roof space

attitude 1 = <u>opinion</u>, view, position, approach, mood, perspective, point of view, stance 2 = <u>position</u>, bearing, pose, stance, carriage, posture

attract 1 = <u>allure</u>, draw, persuade, charm, appeal to, win over, tempt, lure (*informal*) ≠ repel 2 = <u>pull</u>, draw, magnetize

attraction 1 = <u>appeal</u>, pull (*informal*), charm, lure, temptation, fascination, allure, magnetism 2 = <u>pull</u>, magnetism

attractive 1 = <u>seductive</u>, charming, tempting, pretty, fair, inviting, lovely, pleasant ≠ unattractive 2 = <u>appealing</u>, pleasing, inviting, tempting, irresistable ≠ unappealing

attribute VERB = <u>ascribe</u>, credit, refer, trace, assign, charge, allocate, put down
● NOUN = <u>quality</u>, feature, property,

character, element, aspect, characteristic, distinction

audience 1 = spectators, company, crowd, gathering, gallery, assembly, viewers, listeners 2 = interview, meeting, hearing, exchange, reception, consultation

aura = air, feeling, quality, atmosphere, tone, mood, ambience

austerity 1 = plainness, simplicity, starkness 2 = asceticism, self-discipline, sobriety, puritanism, self-denial

authentic 1 = real, pure, genuine, valid, undisputed, lawful, bona fide, dinkum (*Austral. & N.Z. informal*), true-to-life ≠ fake 2 = accurate, legitimate, authoritative

authenticity 1 = genuineness, purity 2 = accuracy, certainty, validity, legitimacy, faithfulness, truthfulness

author 1 = writer, composer, novelist, hack, creator, scribbler, scribe, wordsmith 2 = creator, father, producer, designer, founder, architect, inventor, originator

authoritarian ADJECTIVE = strict, severe, autocratic, dictatorial, dogmatic, tyrannical, doctrinaire ≠ lenient
● NOUN = disciplinarian, dictator, tyrant, despot, autocrat, absolutist

authoritative 1 = commanding, masterly, imposing, assertive, imperious, self-assured ≠ timid 2 = reliable, accurate, valid, authentic, definitive, dependable, trustworthy ≠ unreliable

authority 1 *usually plural* = powers that be, government, police, officials, the state, management, administration, the system 2 = prerogative, influence, power, control, weight, direction, command, licence, mana (*N.Z.*) 3 = expert, specialist, professional, master, guru, virtuoso, connoisseur, fundi (*S. African*) 4 = command, power, control, rule, management, direction, mastery

authorize 1 = empower, commission, enable, entitle, mandate, accredit, give authority to 2 = permit, allow, grant, approve, sanction, license, warrant, consent to ≠ forbid

automatic 1 = mechanical, automated, mechanized, push-button, self-propelling ≠ done by hand 2 = involuntary, natural, unconscious, mechanical, spontaneous, reflex, instinctive, unwilled ≠ conscious

autonomous = self-ruling, free, independent, sovereign, self-sufficient, self-governing, self-determining

autonomy = independence, freedom, sovereignty, self-determination, self-government, self-rule, self-sufficiency, home rule, rangatiratanga (*N.Z.*) ≠ dependency

availability = accessibility, readiness, handiness, attainability

available = accessible, ready, to hand, handy, at hand, free, to be had, achievable ≠ in use

avalanche 1 = snow-slide, landslide, landslip 2 = large amount, barrage, torrent, deluge, inundation

avant-garde = progressive, pioneering, experimental, innovative, unconventional, ground-breaking ≠ conservative

avenue = street, way, course, drive, road, approach, route, path

average NOUN = standard, normal, usual, par, mode, mean, medium, norm
● ADJECTIVE 1 = usual, standard, general, normal, regular, ordinary, typical, commonplace ≠ unusual 2 = mean, middle, medium, intermediate, median ≠ minimum
● VERB = make on average, be on average, even out to, do on average, balance out to
● PHRASES **on average** = usually, generally, normally, typically, for the most part, as a rule

avert 1 = ward off, avoid, prevent, frustrate, fend off, preclude, stave off, forestall 2 = turn away, turn aside

avoid 1 = prevent, stop, frustrate, hamper, foil, inhibit, avert, thwart 2 = refrain from, bypass, dodge, eschew, escape, duck (out of) (*informal*), fight shy of, shirk from 3 = keep away from, dodge, shun, evade, steer clear of, bypass

await 1 = wait for, expect, look for, look forward to, anticipate, stay for 2 = be in store for, wait for, be ready for, lie in wait for, be in readiness for

awake ADJECTIVE = not sleeping, sleepless, wide-awake, aware, conscious, aroused, awakened, restless ≠ asleep
● VERB 1 = wake up, come to, wake, stir, awaken, rouse 2 = alert, stimulate, provoke, revive, arouse, stir up, kindle

awaken 1 = stimulate, provoke, alert, stir up, kindle 2 = awake, wake, revive, arouse, rouse

award NOUN = prize, gift, trophy, decoration, grant, bonsela (*S. African*), koha (*N.Z.*)

● VERB 1 = present with, give, grant, hand out, confer, endow, bestow 2 = grant, give, confer

aware = informed, enlightened, knowledgeable, learned, expert, versed, up to date, in the picture ≠ ignorant

awareness

● PHRASES **awareness of** = knowledge of, understanding of, recognition of, perception of, consciousness of, realization of, familiarity with

away ADJECTIVE = absent, out, gone, elsewhere, abroad, not here, not present, on vacation

● ADVERB 1 = off, elsewhere, abroad, hence, from here 2 = aside, out of the way, to one side 3 = at a distance, far, apart, remote, isolated 4 = continuously, repeatedly, relentlessly, incessantly, interminably, unremittingly, uninterruptedly

awe NOUN = wonder, fear, respect, reverence, horror, terror, dread, admiration ≠ contempt

● VERB = impress, amaze, stun, frighten, terrify, astonish, horrify, intimidate

awesome = awe-inspiring, amazing, stunning, impressive, astonishing, formidable, intimidating, breathtaking

awful 1 = disgusting, offensive, gross, foul, dreadful, revolting, sickening, frightful, festy (*Austral. slang*) yucko (*Austral. slang*) 2 = bad, poor, terrible, appalling, foul, rubbish (*slang*), dreadful, horrendous ≠ wonderful, ka pai (*N.Z.*) 3 = shocking, dreadful 4 = unwell, poorly (*informal*), ill, terrible, sick, crook (*Austral. & N.Z. informal*), off-colour, under the weather (*informal*)

awfully 1 (*Informal*) = very, extremely, terribly, exceptionally, greatly, immensely, exceedingly, dreadfully 2 = badly, woefully, dreadfully, disgracefully, wretchedly, unforgivably, reprehensibly

awkward 1 = embarrassing, difficult, sensitive, delicate, uncomfortable, humiliating, disconcerting, inconvenient, barro (*Austral. slang*) ≠ comfortable 2 = inconvenient, difficult, troublesome, cumbersome, unwieldy, unmanageable, clunky (*informal*) ≠ convenient 3 = clumsy, lumbering, bumbling, unwieldy,

ponderous, ungainly, gauche, gawky, unco (*Austral. slang*) ≠ graceful

axe NOUN = hatchet, chopper, tomahawk, cleaver, adze

● VERB 1 (*Informal*) = abandon, end, eliminate, cancel, scrap, cut back, terminate, dispense with 2 (*Informal*) = dismiss, fire (*informal*), sack (*informal*), remove, get rid of

● PHRASES **the axe** (*Informal*) = the sack (*informal*), dismissal, the boot (*slang*), termination, the chop (*slang*)

axis = pivot, shaft, axle, spindle, centre line

b

baas (*S. African*) = master, bo (*informal*), chief, ruler, commander, head, overlord, overseer

baby NOUN = child, infant, babe, bairn (*Scot.*), newborn child, babe in arms, ankle-biter (*Austral. slang*), tacker (*Austral. slang*)

● ADJECTIVE = small, little, minute, tiny, mini, wee, miniature, petite

back NOUN 1 = spine, backbone, vertebrae, spinal column, vertebral column 2 = rear ≠ front 3 = reverse, rear, other side, wrong side, underside, flip side

● ADJECTIVE 1 = rear ≠ front 2 = rearmost, hind, hindmost 3 = previous, earlier, former, past, elapsed ≠ future 4 = tail, end, rear, posterior

● VERB 1 = support, help, aid, champion, defend, promote, assist, advocate ≠ oppose 2 = subsidize, help, support, sponsor, assist

backbone 1 = spinal column, spine, vertebrae, vertebral column 2 = strength of character, character, resolution, nerve, daring, courage, determination, pluck

backer 1 = supporter, second, angel (*informal*), patron, promoter, subscriber, helper, benefactor 2 = advocate, supporter, patron, sponsor, promoter

backfire = fail, founder, flop (*informal*), rebound, boomerang, miscarry, misfire

background 1 = upbringing, history, culture, environment, tradition, circumstances **2** = experience, grounding, education **3** = circumstances, history, conditions, situation, atmosphere, environment, framework, ambience

backing 1 = support, encouragement, endorsement, moral support **2** = assistance, support, help, aid, sponsorship, patronage

backlash = reaction, response, resistance, retaliation, repercussion, counterblast, counteraction

backward 1 = underdeveloped, undeveloped **2** = slow, behind, retarded, underdeveloped, subnormal, half-witted, slow-witted

backwards *or* **backward** = towards the rear, behind you, in reverse, rearwards

bacteria = microorganisms, viruses, bugs (*slang*), germs, microbes, pathogens, bacilli

bad 1 = harmful, damaging, dangerous, destructive, unhealthy, detrimental, hurtful, ruinous ≠ beneficial **2** = poor **3** = unfavourable, distressing, unfortunate, grim, unpleasant, gloomy, adverse **4** = inferior, poor, inadequate, faulty, unsatisfactory, defective, imperfect, substandard, bush-league (*Austral. & N.Z. informal*), half-pie (*N.Z. informal*), bodger *or* bodgie (*Austral. slang*) ≠ satisfactory **5** = incompetent, poor, useless, incapable, unfit, inexpert **6** = grim, severe, hard, tough **7** = wicked, criminal, evil, corrupt, immoral, sinful, depraved ≠ virtuous **8** = naughty, defiant, wayward, mischievous, wicked, unruly, impish, undisciplined ≠ well-behaved **9** = rotten, off, rank, sour, rancid, mouldy, putrid, festy (*Austral. slang*)

badge 1 = image, brand, stamp, identification, crest, emblem, insignia **2** = mark, sign, token

badger = pester, harry, bother, bug (*informal*), bully, plague, hound, harass

badly 1 = poorly, incorrectly, carelessly, inadequately, imperfectly, ineptly ≠ well **2** = severely, greatly, deeply, seriously, desperately, intensely, exceedingly **3** = unfavourably, unsuccessfully

baffle = puzzle, confuse, stump, bewilder, confound, perplex, mystify, flummox ≠ explain

bag NOUN = sack, container, sac, receptacle
- **VERB 1** = get, land, score (*slang*), capture, acquire, procure **2** = catch, kill, shoot, capture, acquire, trap

baggage = luggage, things, cases, bags, equipment, gear, suitcases, belongings

baggy = loose, slack, bulging, sagging, sloppy, floppy, roomy, ill-fitting ≠ tight

bail NOUN (*Law*) = security, bond, guarantee, pledge, warranty, surety
- **PHRASES bail out** = escape, withdraw, get away, retreat, make your getaway, break free *or* out ♦ **bail something** *or* **someone out** (*Informal*) = save, help, release, aid, deliver, recover, rescue, get out

bait NOUN = lure, attraction, incentive, carrot (*informal*), temptation, snare, inducement, decoy
- **VERB** = tease, annoy, irritate, bother, mock, wind up (*Brit. slang*), hound, torment

baked = dry, desert, seared, scorched, barren, sterile, arid, torrid

bakkie (*S. African*) = truck, pick-up, van, lorry, pick-up truck

balance VERB 1 = stabilize, level, steady ≠ overbalance **2** = weigh, consider, compare, estimate, contrast, assess, evaluate, set against **3** (*Accounting*) = calculate, total, determine, estimate, settle, count, square, reckon
- **NOUN 1** = equilibrium, stability, steadiness, evenness ≠ instability **2** = stability, equanimity, steadiness **3** = parity, equity, fairness, impartiality, equality, correspondence, equivalence **4** = remainder, rest, difference, surplus, residue **5** = composure, stability, restraint, self-control, poise, self-discipline, equanimity, self-restraint

balcony 1 = terrace, veranda **2** = upper circle, gods, gallery

bald 1 = hairless, depilated, baldheaded **2** = plain, direct, frank, straightforward, blunt, rude, forthright, unadorned

ball = sphere, drop, globe, pellet, orb, globule, spheroid

balloon = expand, rise, increase, swell, blow up, inflate, bulge, billow

ballot = vote, election, voting, poll, polling, referendum, show of hands

ban VERB 1 = prohibit, bar, block, veto, forbid, boycott, outlaw, banish ≠ permit 2 = bar, prohibit, exclude, forbid, disqualify, preclude, debar, declare ineligible
● NOUN = prohibition, restriction, veto, boycott, embargo, injunction, taboo, disqualification, rahui (*N.Z.*) ≠ permission

band¹ 1 = ensemble, group, orchestra, combo 2 = gang, company, group, party, team, body, crowd, pack

band² = headband, strip, ribbon

bandage NOUN = dressing, plaster, compress, gauze
● VERB = dress, cover, bind, swathe

bandit = robber, outlaw, raider, plunderer, mugger (*informal*), looter, highwayman, desperado

bang NOUN 1 = explosion, pop, clash, crack, blast, slam, discharge, thump 2 = blow, knock, stroke, punch, bump, sock (*slang*), smack, thump
● VERB 1 = resound, boom, explode, thunder, thump, clang 2 = bump, knock, elbow, jostle 3 *often with* **on** = hit, strike, knock, belt (*informal*), slam, thump, clatter
● ADVERB = exactly, straight, square, squarely, precisely, slap, smack, plumb (*informal*)

banish 1 = exclude, ban, dismiss, expel, throw out, eject, evict 2 = expel, exile, outlaw, deport ≠ admit 3 = get rid of, remove

bank¹ NOUN 1 = financial institution, repository, depository 2 = store, fund, stock, source, supply, reserve, pool, reservoir
● VERB = deposit, keep, save

bank² NOUN 1 = side, edge, margin, shore, brink 2 = mound, banking, rise, hill, mass, pile, heap, ridge, kopje *or* koppie (*S. African*) 3 = mass
● VERB = tilt, tip, pitch, heel, slope, incline, slant, cant

bank³ = row, group, line, range, series, file, rank, sequence

bankrupt = insolvent, broke (*informal*), ruined, wiped out (*informal*), impoverished, in the red, destitute, gone bust (*informal*) ≠ solvent

bankruptcy = insolvency, failure, disaster, ruin, liquidation

banner = flag, standard, colours, placard, pennant, ensign, streamer

banquet = feast, spread (*informal*), dinner, meal, revel, repast, hakari (*N.Z.*)

bar NOUN 1 = public house, pub (*informal, chiefly Brit.*), counter, inn, saloon, tavern, canteen, watering hole (*facetious slang*) 2 = rod, staff, stick, stake, rail, pole, paling, shaft 3 = obstacle, block, barrier, hurdle, hitch, barricade, snag, deterrent ≠ aid
● VERB 1 = lock, block, secure, attach, bolt, blockade, barricade, fortify 2 = block, restrict, restrain, hamper, thwart, hinder, obstruct, impede 3 = exclude, ban, forbid, prohibit, keep out of, disallow, shut out of, blackball ≠ admit

barbarian 1 = savage, monster, beast, brute, yahoo, swine, sadist 2 = lout, yahoo, bigot, philistine, hoon (*Austral. & N.Z.*), cougan (*Austral. slang*), scozza (*Austral. slang*), bogan (*Austral. slang*), boor, vulgarian

bare 1 = naked, nude, stripped, uncovered, undressed, unclothed, unclad, without a stitch on (*informal*) ≠ dressed 2 = simple, spare, stark, austere, spartan, unadorned, unembellished, unornamented ≠ adorned 3 = plain, simple, basic, obvious, sheer, patent, evident, stark

barely = only just, just, hardly, scarcely, at a push ≠ completely

bargain NOUN 1 = good buy, discount purchase, good deal, steal (*informal*), snip (*informal*), giveaway, cheap purchase 2 = agreement, deal (*informal*), promise, contract, arrangement, settlement, pledge, pact
● VERB = negotiate, deal, contract, mediate, covenant, stipulate, transact, cut a deal

barge = canal boat, lighter, narrow boat, flatboat

bark¹ VERB = yap, bay, howl, snarl, growl, yelp, woof
● NOUN = yap, bay, howl, snarl, growl, yelp, woof

bark² = covering, casing, cover, skin, layer, crust, cortex (*Anatomy, botany*), rind

barracks = camp, quarters, garrison, encampment, billet

barrage 1 = bombardment, attack, bombing, assault, shelling, battery, volley, blitz 2 = torrent, mass, burst, stream, hail, spate, onslaught, deluge

barren 1 = desolate, empty, desert, waste ≠ fertile 2 (*Old-fashioned*) = infertile, sterile, childless, unproductive

barricade NOUN = barrier, wall, fence,

blockade, obstruction, rampart, bulwark, palisade

● VERB = <u>bar</u>, block, defend, secure, lock, bolt, blockade, fortify

barrier = <u>barricade</u>, wall, bar, fence, boundary, obstacle, blockade, obstruction

base¹ NOUN 1 = <u>bottom</u>, floor, lowest part ≠ top 2 = <u>support</u>, stand, foot, rest, bed, bottom, foundation, pedestal 3 = <u>foundation</u>, institution, organization, establishment 4 = <u>centre</u>, post, station, camp, settlement, headquarters, starting point 5 = <u>home</u>, house, pad (slang), residence 6 = <u>essence</u>, source, basis, root, core

● VERB 1 = <u>ground</u>, found, build, establish, depend, construct, derive, hinge 2 = <u>place</u>, set, post, station, establish, locate, install

base² = <u>dishonourable</u>, evil, disgraceful, shameful, immoral, wicked, sordid, despicable, scungy (Austral. & N.Z.) ≠ honourable

bash NOUN (Informal) = <u>attempt</u>, go (informal), try, shot (informal), bid, crack (informal), stab (informal)

● VERB (Informal) = <u>hit</u>, beat, strike, knock, smash, belt (informal), slap, sock (slang)

basic ADJECTIVE 1 = <u>fundamental</u>, main, essential, primary, vital, principal, cardinal, elementary 2 = <u>vital</u>, needed, important, key, necessary, essential, primary, crucial 3 = <u>essential</u>, key, vital, fundamental ≠ secondary 4 = <u>main</u>, key, essential, primary 5 = <u>plain</u>, simple, classic, unfussy, unembellished

● PLURAL NOUN = <u>essentials</u>, principles, fundamentals, nuts and bolts (informal), nitty-gritty (informal), rudiments, brass tacks (informal)

basically = <u>essentially</u>, mainly, mostly, principally, fundamentally, primarily, at heart, inherently

basis 1 = <u>arrangement</u>, way, system, footing, agreement 2 = <u>foundation</u>, support, base, ground, footing, bottom, groundwork

bask = <u>lie</u>, relax, lounge, sprawl, loaf, lie about, swim in, sunbathe, outspan (S. African)

bass = <u>deep</u>, low, resonant, sonorous, low-pitched, deep-toned

batch = <u>group</u>, set, lot, crowd, pack, collection, quantity, bunch

bath NOUN = <u>wash</u>, cleaning, shower, soak, cleansing, scrub, scrubbing, douche

● VERB = <u>clean</u>, wash, shower, soak, cleanse, scrub, bathe, rinse

bathe 1 = <u>swim</u> 2 = <u>wash</u>, clean, bath, shower, soak, cleanse, scrub, rinse 3 = <u>cleanse</u>, clean, wash, soak, rinse 4 = <u>cover</u>, flood, steep, engulf, immerse, overrun, suffuse, wash over

baton = <u>stick</u>, club, staff, pole, rod, crook, cane, mace, mere (N.Z.), patu (N.Z.)

batter = <u>beat</u>, hit, strike, knock, bang, thrash, pound, buffet

battery = <u>artillery</u>, ordnance, gunnery, gun emplacement, cannonry

battle NOUN 1 = <u>fight</u>, attack, action, struggle, conflict, clash, encounter, combat, biffo (Austral. slang) ≠ peace 2 = <u>conflict</u>, campaign, struggle, dispute, contest, crusade 3 = <u>campaign</u>, drive, movement, push, struggle

● VERB 1 = <u>wrestle</u>, war, fight, argue, dispute, grapple, clamour, lock horns 2 = <u>struggle</u>, work, labour, strain, strive, toil, go all out (informal), give it your best shot (informal)

battlefield = <u>battleground</u>, front, field, combat zone, field of battle

batty = <u>crazy</u>, odd, mad, eccentric, peculiar, daft (informal), touched, potty (Brit. informal), off the air (Austral. slang), porangi (N.Z.)

bay¹ = <u>inlet</u>, sound, gulf, creek, cove, fjord, bight, natural harbour

bay² = <u>recess</u>, opening, corner, niche, compartment, nook, alcove

bay³ VERB = <u>howl</u>, cry, roar (used of hounds), bark, wail, growl, bellow, clamour

● NOUN = <u>cry</u>, roar (used of hounds), bark, howl, wail, growl, bellow, clamour

bazaar 1 = <u>market</u>, exchange, fair, marketplace 2 = <u>fair</u>, fête, gala, bring-and-buy

be = <u>be alive</u>, live, exist, survive, breathe, be present, endure

beach = <u>shore</u>, coast, sands, seaside, water's edge, seashore

beached = <u>stranded</u>, grounded, abandoned, deserted, wrecked, ashore, marooned, aground

beacon = <u>signal</u>, sign, beam, flare, lighthouse, bonfire, watchtower

bead = <u>drop</u>, tear, bubble, pearl, dot, drip, blob, droplet

beam VERB 1 = <u>smile</u>, grin 2 = <u>transmit</u>,

show, air, broadcast, cable, send out, relay, televise **3** = <u>radiate</u>, flash, shine, glow, glitter, glare, gleam
● NOUN **1** = <u>ray</u>, flash, stream, glow, streak, shaft, gleam, glint **2** = <u>rafter</u>, support, timber, spar, plank, girder, joist **3** = <u>smile</u>, grin

bear VERB **1** = <u>carry</u>, take, move, bring, transfer, conduct, transport, haul ≠ put down **2** = <u>support</u>, shoulder, sustain, endure, uphold, withstand ≠ give up **3** = <u>display</u>, have, show, hold, carry, possess **4** = <u>suffer</u>, experience, go through, sustain, stomach, endure, brook, abide **5** = <u>bring yourself to</u>, allow, accept, permit, endure, tolerate **6** = <u>produce</u>, generate, yield, bring forth **7** = <u>give birth to</u>, produce, deliver, breed, bring forth, beget **8** = <u>exhibit</u>, hold, maintain **9** = <u>conduct</u>, carry, move, deport
● PHRASES **bear something out** = <u>support</u>, prove, confirm, justify, endorse, uphold, substantiate, corroborate

bearer 1 = <u>agent</u>, carrier, courier, herald, envoy, messenger, conveyor, emissary **2** = <u>carrier</u>, runner, servant, porter

bearing NOUN **1** usually with **on** or **upon** = <u>relevance</u>, relation, application, connection, import, reference, significance, pertinence ≠ irrelevance **2** = <u>manner</u>, attitude, conduct, aspect, behaviour, posture, demeanour, deportment
● PLURAL NOUN = <u>way</u>, course, position, situation, track, aim, direction, location

beast 1 = <u>animal</u>, creature, brute **2** = <u>brute</u>, monster, savage, barbarian, fiend, swine, ogre, sadist

beastly = <u>unpleasant</u>, mean, awful, nasty, rotten, horrid, disagreeable ≠ pleasant

beat VERB **1** = <u>batter</u>, hit, strike, knock, pound, smack, thrash, thump **2** = <u>pound</u>, strike, hammer, batter, thrash **3** = <u>throb</u>, thump, pound, quake, vibrate, pulsate, palpitate **4** = <u>hit</u>, strike, bang **5** = <u>flap</u>, thrash, flutter, wag **6** = <u>defeat</u>, outdo, trounce, overcome, crush, overwhelm, conquer, surpass
● NOUN **1** = <u>throb</u>, pounding, pulse, thumping, vibration, pulsating, palpitation, pulsation **2** = <u>route</u>, way, course, rounds, path, circuit
●PHRASES **beat someone up** (Informal) = <u>assault</u>, attack, batter, thrash, set about, set upon, lay into (informal), beat the living daylights out of (informal)

beaten 1 = <u>stirred</u>, mixed, whipped, blended, whisked, frothy, foamy **2** = <u>defeated</u>, overcome, overwhelmed, cowed, thwarted, vanquished

beautiful = <u>attractive</u>, pretty, lovely, charming, tempting, pleasant, handsome, fetching ≠ ugly

beauty 1 = <u>attractiveness</u>, charm, grace, glamour, elegance, loveliness, handsomeness, comeliness ≠ ugliness **2** = <u>good-looker</u>, lovely (slang), belle, stunner (informal)

because CONJUNCTION = <u>since</u>, as, in that
● PHRASES **because of** = <u>as a result of</u>, on account of, by reason of, thanks to, owing to

beckon = <u>gesture</u>, sign, wave, indicate, signal, nod, motion, summon

become 1 = <u>come to be</u>, develop into, be transformed into, grow into, change into, alter to, mature into, ripen into **2** = <u>suit</u>, fit, enhance, flatter, embellish, set off

becoming 1 = <u>flattering</u>, pretty, attractive, enhancing, neat, graceful, tasteful, well-chosen ≠ unflattering **2** = <u>appropriate</u>, seemly, fitting, suitable, proper, worthy, in keeping, compatible ≠ inappropriate

bed 1 = <u>bedstead</u>, couch, berth, cot, bunk, divan **2** = <u>plot</u>, area, row, strip, patch, ground, land, garden **3** = <u>bottom</u>, ground, floor **4** = <u>base</u>, footing, basis, bottom, foundation, underpinning, groundwork, bedrock

before PREPOSITION **1** = <u>earlier than</u>, ahead of, prior to, in advance of ≠ after **2** = <u>in front of</u>, ahead of, in advance of **3** = <u>in the presence of</u>, in front of **4** = <u>ahead of</u>, in front of, in advance of
● ADVERB **1** = <u>previously</u>, earlier, sooner, in advance, formerly ≠ after **2** = <u>in the past</u>, earlier, once, previously, formerly, hitherto, beforehand
▰▰ RELATED WORDS
prefixes: ante-, fore-, pre-

beforehand = <u>in advance</u>, before, earlier, already, sooner, ahead, previously, in anticipation

beg 1 = <u>implore</u>, plead with, beseech, request, petition, solicit, entreat **2** = <u>scrounge</u>, bum (informal), touch (someone) for (slang), cadge, sponge on (someone) for, freeload (slang), seek charity, solicit charity ≠ give

beggar = tramp, bum (*informal*), derelict, drifter, down-and-out, pauper, vagrant, bag lady (*chiefly U.S.*), derro (*Austral. slang*)

begin 1 = start, commence, proceed ≠ stop 2 = commence, start, initiate, embark on, set about, instigate, institute, make a beginning 3 = start talking, start, initiate, commence 4 = come into existence, start, appear, emerge, arise, originate, come into being 5 = emerge, start, spring, stem, derive, originate ≠ end

beginner = novice, pupil, amateur, newcomer, starter, trainee, apprentice, learner ≠ expert

beginning 1 = start, opening, birth, origin, outset, onset, initiation, inauguration ≠ end 2 = outset, start, opening, birth, onset, commencement 3 = origins

behave 1 = act 2 *often reflexive* = be well-behaved, mind your manners, keep your nose clean, act correctly, conduct yourself properly ≠ misbehave

behaviour 1 = conduct, ways, actions, bearing, attitude, manner, manners, demeanour 2 = action, performance, operation, functioning

behind PREPOSITION 1 = at the rear of, at the back of, at the heels of 2 = after, following 3 = supporting, for, backing, on the side of, in agreement with 4 = causing, responsible for, initiating, at the bottom of, instigating 5 = later than, after
● ADVERB 1 = after, next, following, afterwards, subsequently, in the wake (of) ≠ in advance of 2 = behind schedule, delayed, running late, behind time ≠ ahead 3 = overdue, in debt, in arrears, behindhand
● NOUN (*Informal*) = bottom, butt (*U.S. & Canad. informal*), buttocks, posterior

being 1 = individual, creature, human being, living thing 2 = life, reality ≠ nonexistence 3 = soul, spirit, substance, creature, essence, organism, entity

beleaguered 1 = harassed, troubled, plagued, hassled (*informal*), badgered, persecuted, pestered, vexed 2 = besieged, surrounded, blockaded, beset, encircled, assailed, hemmed in

belief 1 = trust, confidence, conviction ≠ disbelief 2 = faith, principles, doctrine, ideology, creed, dogma, tenet, credo 3 = opinion, feeling, idea, impression, assessment, notion, judgment, point of view

believe 1 = think, judge, suppose, estimate, imagine, assume, gather, reckon 2 = accept, trust, credit, depend on, rely on, have faith in, swear by, be certain of ≠ disbelieve

believer = follower, supporter, convert, disciple, devotee, apostle, adherent, zealot ≠ sceptic

bellow VERB = shout, cry (out), scream, roar, yell, howl, shriek, bawl
● NOUN = shout, cry, scream, roar, yell, howl, shriek, bawl

belly = stomach, insides (*informal*), gut, abdomen, tummy, paunch, potbelly, corporation (*informal*), puku (*N.Z.*)

belong = go with, fit into, be part of, relate to, be connected with, pertain to

belonging = fellowship, relationship, association, loyalty, acceptance, attachment, inclusion, affinity

belongings = possessions, goods, things, effects, property, stuff, gear, paraphernalia

beloved = dear, loved, valued, prized, admired, treasured, precious, darling

below PREPOSITION 1 = under, underneath, lower than 2 = less than, lower than 3 = subordinate to, subject to, inferior to, lesser than
● ADVERB 1 = lower, down, under, beneath, underneath 2 = beneath, following, at the end, underneath, at the bottom, further on

belt 1 = waistband, band, sash, girdle, girth, cummerbund 2 = conveyor belt, band, loop, fan belt, drive belt 3 (*Geography*) = zone, area, region, section, district, stretch, strip, layer

bemused = puzzled, confused, baffled, at sea, bewildered, muddled, perplexed, mystified

bench NOUN 1 = seat, stall, pew 2 = worktable, stand, table, counter, trestle table, workbench
● PHRASES **the bench** = court, judges, magistrates, tribunal, judiciary, courtroom

benchmark = reference point, gauge, yardstick, measure, level, standard, model, par

bend VERB = twist, turn, wind, lean, hook, bow, curve, arch
● NOUN = curve, turn, corner, twist, angle, bow, loop, arc

beneath PREPOSITION 1 = <u>under</u>, below, underneath, lower than ≠ over 2 = <u>inferior to</u>, below 3 = <u>unworthy of</u>, unfitting for, unsuitable for, inappropriate for, unbefitting

● ADVERB = <u>underneath</u>, below, in a lower place

RELATED WORD
prefix: sub-

beneficial = <u>favourable</u>, useful, valuable, helpful, profitable, benign, wholesome, advantageous ≠ harmful

beneficiary 1 = <u>recipient</u>, receiver, payee 2 = <u>heir</u>, inheritor

benefit NOUN 1 = <u>good</u>, help, profit, favour ≠ harm 2 = <u>advantage</u>, aid, favour, assistance

● VERB 1 = <u>profit from</u>, make the most of, gain from, do well out of, reap benefits from, turn to your advantage 2 = <u>help</u>, aid, profit, improve, enhance, assist, avail ≠ harm

benign 1 = <u>benevolent</u>, kind, kindly, warm, friendly, obliging, sympathetic, compassionate ≠ unkind 2 (*Medical*) = <u>harmless</u>, innocent, innocuous, curable, inoffensive, remediable ≠ malignant

bent ADJECTIVE 1 = <u>misshapen</u>, twisted, angled, bowed, curved, arched, crooked, distorted ≠ straight 2 = <u>stooped</u>, bowed, arched, hunched

● NOUN = <u>inclination</u>, ability, leaning, tendency, preference, penchant, propensity, aptitude

● PHRASES **bent on** = <u>intent on</u>, set on, fixed on, predisposed to, resolved on, insistent on

bequeath 1 = <u>leave</u>, will, give, grant, hand down, endow, bestow, entrust 2 = <u>give</u>, accord, grant, afford, yield, lend, pass on, confer

berth NOUN 1 = <u>bunk</u>, bed, hammock, billet 2 (*Nautical*) = <u>anchorage</u>, haven, port, harbour, dock, pier, wharf, quay

● VERB (*Nautical*) = <u>anchor</u>, land, dock, moor, tie up, drop anchor

beside PREPOSITION = <u>next to</u>, near, close to, neighbouring, alongside, adjacent to, at the side of, abreast of

● PHRASES **beside yourself** = <u>distraught</u>, desperate, distressed, frantic, frenzied, demented, unhinged, overwrought

besides PREPOSITION = <u>apart from</u>, barring, excepting, other than, excluding, as well (as), in addition to, over and above

● ADVERB = <u>also</u>, too, further, otherwise, in addition, as well, moreover, furthermore

besiege 1 = <u>harass</u>, harry, plague, hound, hassle (*informal*), badger, pester 2 = <u>surround</u>, enclose, blockade, encircle, hem in, shut in, lay siege to

best ADJECTIVE = <u>finest</u>, leading, supreme, principal, foremost, pre-eminent, unsurpassed, most accomplished

● NOUN = <u>finest</u>, top, prime, pick, flower, cream, elite, crème de la crème (*French*)

● ADVERB = <u>most highly</u>, most fully, most deeply

bestow = <u>present</u>, give, award, grant, commit, hand out, lavish, impart ≠ obtain

bet VERB = <u>gamble</u>, chance, stake, venture, hazard, speculate, wager, risk money

● NOUN = <u>gamble</u>, risk, stake, venture, speculation, flutter (*informal*), punt, wager

betray 1 = <u>be disloyal to</u>, dob in (*Austral. slang*), double-cross (*informal*), stab in the back, be unfaithful to, inform on *or* against 2 = <u>give away</u>, reveal, expose, disclose, uncover, divulge, unmask, let slip

betrayal = <u>disloyalty</u>, sell-out (*informal*), deception, treason, treachery, trickery, double-cross (*informal*), breach of trust ≠ loyalty

better ADVERB 1 = <u>to a greater degree</u>, more completely, more thoroughly 2 = <u>in a more excellent manner</u>, more effectively, more attractively, more advantageously, more competently, in a superior way ≠ worse

● ADJECTIVE 1 = <u>well</u>, stronger, recovering, cured, fully recovered, on the mend (*informal*) ≠ worse 2 = <u>superior</u>, finer, higher-quality, surpassing, preferable, more desirable ≠ inferior

between = <u>amidst</u>, among, mid, in the middle of, betwixt

RELATED WORD
prefix: inter-

beverage = <u>drink</u>, liquid, liquor, refreshment

beware 1 = <u>be careful</u>, look out, watch out, be wary, be cautious, take heed, guard against something 2 = <u>avoid</u>, mind

bewilder = <u>confound</u>, confuse, puzzle, baffle, perplex, mystify, flummox, bemuse

bewildered = <u>confused</u>, puzzled, baffled, at sea, muddled, perplexed, at a loss, mystified

beyond 1 = <u>on the other side of</u>
2 = <u>after</u>, over, past, above 3 = <u>past</u>
4 = <u>except for</u>, but, save, apart from, other than, excluding, besides, aside from
5 = <u>exceeding</u>, surpassing, superior to, out of reach of 6 = <u>outside</u>, over, above

bias NOUN = <u>prejudice</u>, leaning, tendency, inclination, favouritism, partiality
≠ impartiality
● VERB = <u>influence</u>, colour, weight, prejudice, distort, sway, warp, slant

biased = <u>prejudiced</u>, weighted, one-sided, partial, distorted, slanted

bid NOUN 1 = <u>attempt</u>, try, effort, go (*informal*), shot (*informal*), stab (*informal*), crack (*informal*) 2 = <u>offer</u>, price, amount, advance, proposal, sum, tender
● VERB 1 = <u>make an offer</u>, offer, propose, submit, tender, proffer 2 = <u>wish</u>, say, call, tell, greet 3 = <u>tell</u>, ask, order, require, direct, command, instruct

bidding = <u>order</u>, request, command, instruction, summons, beck and call

big 1 = <u>large</u>, great, huge, massive, vast, enormous, substantial, extensive ≠ small
2 = <u>important</u>, significant, urgent, far-reaching ≠ unimportant 3 = <u>powerful</u>, important, prominent, dominant, influential, eminent 4 = <u>grown-up</u>, adult, grown, mature, elder, full-grown
≠ young 5 = <u>generous</u>, good, noble, gracious, benevolent, altruistic, unselfish, magnanimous

bill¹ NOUN 1 = <u>charges</u>, rate, costs, score, account, statement, reckoning, expense 2 = <u>act of parliament</u>, measure, proposal, piece of legislation, projected law 3 = <u>list</u>, listing, programme, card, schedule, agenda, catalogue, inventory
4 = <u>advertisement</u>, notice, poster, leaflet, bulletin, circular, handout, placard
● VERB 1 = <u>charge</u>, debit, invoice, send a statement to, send an invoice to
2 = <u>advertise</u>, post, announce, promote, plug (*informal*), tout, publicize, give advance notice of

bill² = <u>beak</u>, nib, neb (*archaic*, *dialect*), mandible

bind VERB 1 = <u>oblige</u>, make, force, require, engage, compel, constrain, necessitate
2 = <u>tie</u>, join, stick, secure, wrap, knot, strap, lash ≠ untie
● NOUN (*Informal*) = <u>nuisance</u>, inconvenience, hassle (*informal*), drag

(*informal*), spot (*informal*), difficulty, bore, dilemma, uphill (*S. African*)

binding = <u>compulsory</u>, necessary, mandatory, obligatory, irrevocable, unalterable, indissoluble ≠ optional

binge (*Informal*) = <u>bout</u>, spell, fling, feast, stint, spree, orgy, bender (*informal*)

biography = <u>life story</u>, life, record, account, profile, memoir, CV, curriculum vitae

bird = <u>feathered friend</u>, fowl, songbird
▨ RELATED WORDS
adjective: avian
male: cock
female: hen
young: chick, fledg(e)ling, nestling
collective nouns: flock, flight
habitation: nest

birth 1 = <u>childbirth</u>, delivery, nativity, parturition ≠ death 2 = <u>ancestry</u>, stock, blood, background, breeding, pedigree, lineage, parentage
▨ RELATED WORD
adjective: natal

bit¹ 1 = <u>slice</u>, fragment, crumb, morsel
2 = <u>piece</u>, scrap 3 = <u>jot</u>, iota 4 = <u>part</u>

bit² = <u>curb</u>, check, brake, restraint, snaffle

bite VERB = <u>nip</u>, cut, tear, wound, snap, pierce, pinch, chew
● NOUN 1 = <u>snack</u>, food, piece, taste, refreshment, mouthful, morsel, titbit
2 = <u>wound</u>, sting, pinch, nip, prick

biting 1 = <u>piercing</u>, cutting, sharp, frozen, harsh, penetrating, arctic, icy 2 = <u>sarcastic</u>, cutting, stinging, scathing, acrimonious, incisive, virulent, caustic

bitter 1 = <u>resentful</u>, angry, offended, sour, sore, acrimonious, sullen, miffed (*informal*)
≠ happy 2 = <u>freezing</u>, biting, severe, intense, raw, fierce, chill, stinging ≠ mild
3 = <u>sour</u>, sharp, acid, harsh, tart, astringent, acrid, unsweetened ≠ sweet

bitterness 1 = <u>resentment</u>, hostility, indignation, animosity, acrimony, rancour, ill feeling, bad blood 2 = <u>sourness</u>, acidity, sharpness, tartness, acerbity

bizarre = <u>strange</u>, unusual, extraordinary, fantastic, weird, peculiar, eccentric, ludicrous ≠ normal

black 1 = <u>dark</u>, raven, ebony, sable, jet, dusky, pitch-black, swarthy ≠ light
2 = <u>gloomy</u>, sad, depressing, grim, bleak, hopeless, dismal, ominous ≠ happy
3 = <u>terrible</u>, bad, devastating, tragic,

fatal, catastrophic, ruinous, calamitous **4** = <u>wicked</u>, bad, evil, corrupt, vicious, immoral, depraved, villainous ≠ good **5** = <u>angry</u>, cross, furious, hostile, sour, menacing, moody, resentful ≠ happy

blackmail NOUN = <u>threat</u>, intimidation, ransom, extortion, hush money (*slang*)
● VERB = <u>threaten</u>, squeeze, compel, intimidate, coerce, dragoon, extort, hold to ransom

blame VERB **1** = <u>hold responsible</u>, accuse, denounce, indict, impeach, incriminate, impute ≠ absolve **2** = <u>attribute to</u>, credit to, assign to, put down to, impute to **3** (used in negative constructions) = <u>criticize</u>, condemn, censure, reproach, chide, find fault with ≠ praise
● NOUN = <u>responsibility</u>, liability, accountability, onus, culpability, answerability ≠ praise

bland 1 = <u>dull</u>, boring, plain, flat, dreary, run-of-the-mill, uninspiring, humdrum ≠ exciting **2** = <u>tasteless</u>, insipid, flavourless, thin

blank ADJECTIVE **1** = <u>unmarked</u>, white, clear, clean, empty, plain, bare, void ≠ marked **2** = <u>expressionless</u>, empty, vague, vacant, deadpan, impassive, poker-faced (*informal*) ≠ expressive
● NOUN **1** = <u>empty space</u>, space, gap **2** = <u>void</u>, vacuum, vacancy, emptiness, nothingness

blanket NOUN **1** = <u>cover</u>, rug, coverlet **2** = <u>covering</u>, sheet, coat, layer, carpet, cloak, mantle, thickness
● VERB = <u>coat</u>, cover, hide, mask, conceal, obscure, cloak

blast NOUN **1** = <u>explosion</u>, crash, burst, discharge, eruption, detonation **2** = <u>gust</u>, rush, storm, breeze, puff, gale, tempest, squall **3** = <u>blare</u>, blow, scream, trumpet, wail, resound, clamour, toot
● VERB = <u>blow up</u>, bomb, destroy, burst, ruin, break up, explode, shatter

blatant = <u>obvious</u>, clear, plain, evident, glaring, manifest, noticeable, conspicuous ≠ subtle

blaze VERB **1** = <u>burn</u>, glow, flare, be on fire, go up in flames, be ablaze, fire, flame **2** = <u>shine</u>, flash, beam, glow, flare, glare, gleam, radiate
● NOUN **1** = <u>inferno</u>, fire, flames, bonfire, combustion, conflagration **2** = <u>flash</u>, glow, glitter, flare, glare, gleam, brilliance,

radiance

bleach = <u>lighten</u>, wash out, blanch, whiten

bleak 1 = <u>dismal</u>, dark, depressing, grim, discouraging, gloomy, hopeless, dreary ≠ cheerful **2** = <u>exposed</u>, empty, bare, barren, desolate, windswept, weather-beaten, unsheltered ≠ sheltered **3** = <u>stormy</u>, severe, rough, harsh, tempestuous, intemperate

bleed 1 = <u>lose blood</u>, flow, gush, spurt, shed blood **2** = <u>blend</u>, run, meet, unite, mix, combine, flow, fuse **3** (*Informal*) = <u>extort</u>, milk, squeeze, drain, exhaust, fleece

blend VERB **1** = <u>mix</u>, join, combine, compound, merge, unite, mingle, amalgamate **2** = <u>go well</u>, match, fit, suit, go with, correspond, complement, coordinate **3** = <u>combine</u>, mix, link, integrate, merge, unite, amalgamate
● NOUN = <u>mixture</u>, mix, combination, compound, brew, union, synthesis, alloy

bless 1 = <u>sanctify</u>, dedicate, ordain, exalt, anoint, consecrate, hallow ≠ curse **2** = <u>endow</u>, give to, provide for, grant for, favour, grace, bestow to ≠ afflict

blessed = <u>holy</u>, sacred, divine, adored, revered, hallowed, sanctified, beatified

blessing 1 = <u>benefit</u>, help, service, favour, gift, windfall, kindness, good fortune ≠ disadvantage **2** = <u>approval</u>, backing, support, agreement, favour, sanction, permission, leave ≠ disapproval **3** = <u>benediction</u>, grace, dedication, thanksgiving, invocation, commendation, consecration, benison ≠ curse

blight NOUN **1** = <u>curse</u>, suffering, evil, corruption, pollution, plague, hardship, woe ≠ blessing **2** = <u>disease</u>, pest, fungus, mildew, infestation, pestilence, canker
● VERB = <u>frustrate</u>, destroy, ruin, crush, mar, dash, wreck, spoil, crool or cruel (*Austral. slang*)

blind 1 = <u>sightless</u>, unsighted, unseeing, eyeless, visionless ≠ sighted **2** *often with* **to** = <u>unaware of</u>, unconscious of, ignorant of, indifferent to, insensitive to, oblivious of, unconcerned about, inconsiderate of ≠ aware **3** = <u>unquestioning</u>, prejudiced, wholesale, indiscriminate, uncritical, unreasoning, undiscriminating

blindly 1 = <u>thoughtlessly</u>, carelessly, recklessly, indiscriminately, senselessly, heedlessly 2 = <u>wildly</u>, aimlessly

blink VERB 1 = <u>flutter</u>, wink, bat 2 = <u>flash</u>, flicker, wink, shimmer, twinkle, glimmer
● PHRASES **on the blink** (*Slang*) = <u>not working (properly)</u>, faulty, defective, playing up, out of action, malfunctioning, out of order

bliss 1 = <u>joy</u>, ecstasy, euphoria, rapture, nirvana, felicity, gladness, blissfulness ≠ misery 2 = <u>beatitude</u>, blessedness

blister = <u>sore</u>, boil, swelling, cyst, pimple, carbuncle, pustule

blitz = <u>attack</u>, strike, assault, raid, offensive, onslaught, bombardment, bombing campaign

bloc = <u>group</u>, union, league, alliance, coalition, axis

block NOUN 1 = <u>piece</u>, bar, mass, brick, lump, chunk, hunk, ingot 2 = <u>obstruction</u>, bar, barrier, obstacle, impediment, hindrance
● VERB 1 = <u>obstruct</u>, close, stop, plug, choke, clog, stop up, bung up (*informal*) ≠ clear 2 = <u>obscure</u>, bar, obstruct 3 = <u>shut off</u>, stop, bar, hamper, obstruct

blockade = <u>stoppage</u>, block, barrier, restriction, obstacle, barricade, obstruction, impediment

bloke (*Informal*) = <u>man</u>, person, individual, character (*informal*), guy (*informal*), fellow, chap

blonde or **blond** 1 = <u>fair</u>, light, flaxen 2 = <u>fair-haired</u>, golden-haired, tow-headed

blood 1 = <u>lifeblood</u>, gore, vital fluid 2 = <u>family</u>, relations, birth, descent, extraction, ancestry, lineage, kinship

bloodshed = <u>killing</u>, murder, massacre, slaughter, slaying, carnage, butchery, blood-letting

bloody 1 = <u>cruel</u>, fierce, savage, brutal, vicious, ferocious, cut-throat, warlike 2 = <u>bloodstained</u>, raw, bleeding, blood-soaked, blood-spattered

bloom NOUN 1 = <u>flower</u>, bud, blossom 2 = <u>prime</u>, flower, beauty, height, peak, flourishing, heyday, zenith 3 = <u>glow</u>, freshness, lustre, radiance ≠ pallor
● VERB 1 = <u>flower</u>, blossom, open, bud ≠ wither 2 = <u>grow</u>, develop, wax 3 = <u>succeed</u>, flourish, thrive, prosper, fare well ≠ fail

blossom NOUN = <u>flower</u>, bloom, bud, efflorescence, floret
● VERB 1 = <u>bloom</u>, grow, develop, mature

2 = <u>succeed</u>, progress, thrive, flourish, prosper 3 = <u>flower</u>, bloom, bud

blow¹ VERB 1 = <u>move</u>, carry, drive, sweep, fling, buffet, waft 2 = <u>be carried</u>, flutter 3 = <u>exhale</u>, breathe, pant, puff 4 = <u>play</u>, sound, pipe, trumpet, blare, toot
● PHRASES **blow something up** 1 = <u>explode</u>, bomb, blast, detonate, blow sky-high 2 = <u>inflate</u>, pump up, fill, expand, swell, enlarge, puff up, distend 3 = <u>magnify</u>, increase, extend, expand, widen, broaden, amplify ◆ **blow up** 1 = <u>explode</u>, burst, shatter, erupt, detonate 2 (*Informal*) = <u>lose your temper</u>, rage, erupt, see red (*informal*), become angry, hit the roof (*informal*), fly off the handle (*informal*), go crook (*Austral. & N.Z. slang*), blow your top

blow² 1 = <u>knock</u>, stroke, punch, bang, sock (*slang*), smack, thump, clout (*informal*) 2 = <u>setback</u>, shock, disaster, reverse, disappointment, catastrophe, misfortune, bombshell

bludge (*Austral. & N.Z. informal*) = <u>slack</u>, skive (*Brit. informal*), idle, shirk

blue ADJECTIVE 1 = <u>depressed</u>, low, sad, unhappy, melancholy, dejected, despondent, downcast ≠ happy 2 = <u>smutty</u>, obscene, indecent, lewd, risqué, X-rated (*informal*) ≠ respectable
● PLURAL NOUN = <u>depression</u>, gloom, melancholy, unhappiness, low spirits, the dumps (*informal*), doldrums

blueprint 1 = <u>scheme</u>, plan, design, system, programme, proposal, strategy, pattern 2 = <u>plan</u>, scheme, pattern, draft, outline, sketch

bluff¹ NOUN = <u>deception</u>, fraud, sham, pretence, deceit, bravado, bluster, humbug
● VERB = <u>deceive</u>, trick, fool, pretend, cheat, con, fake, mislead

bluff² NOUN = <u>precipice</u>, bank, peak, cliff, ridge, crag, escarpment, promontory
● ADJECTIVE = <u>hearty</u>, open, blunt, outspoken, genial, ebullient, jovial, plain-spoken ≠ tactful

blunder NOUN = <u>mistake</u>, slip, fault, error, oversight, gaffe, slip-up (*informal*), indiscretion ≠ correctness
● VERB 1 = <u>make a mistake</u>, blow it (*slang*), err, slip up (*informal*), foul up, put your foot in it (*informal*) ≠ be correct 2 = <u>stumble</u>, fall, reel, stagger, lurch

blunt ADJECTIVE 1 = frank, forthright, straightforward, rude, outspoken, bluff, brusque, plain-spoken ≠ tactful 2 = dull, rounded, dulled, edgeless, unsharpened ≠ sharp

• VERB = dull, weaken, soften, numb, dampen, water down, deaden, take the edge off ≠ stimulate

blur NOUN = haze, confusion, fog, obscurity, indistinctness

• VERB 1 = become indistinct, become vague, become hazy, become fuzzy 2 = obscure, make indistinct, mask, obfuscate, make vague, make hazy

blush VERB = turn red, colour, glow, flush, redden, go red (as a beetroot), turn scarlet ≠ turn pale

• NOUN = reddening, colour, glow, flush, pink tinge, rosiness, ruddiness, rosy tint

board NOUN 1 = plank, panel, timber, slat, piece of timber 2 = council, directors, committee, congress, advisers, panel, assembly, trustees 3 = meals, provisions, victuals, daily meals

• VERB = get on, enter, mount, embark ≠ get off

boast VERB 1 = brag, crow, vaunt, talk big (slang), blow your own trumpet, show off, be proud of, congratulate yourself on, skite (Austral. & N.Z. informal) ≠ cover up 2 = possess, exhibit

• NOUN = bragging ≠ disclaimer

bob = bounce, duck, hop, oscillate

bodily = physical, material, actual, substantial, tangible, corporal, carnal, corporeal

body 1 = physique, build, form, figure, shape, frame, constitution 2 = torso, trunk 3 = corpse, dead body, remains, stiff (slang), carcass, cadaver 4 = organization, company, group, society, association, band, congress, institution 5 = main part, matter, material, mass, substance, bulk, essence 6 = expanse, mass, sweep

▓▓ RELATED WORDS
adjectives: corporal, physical

bog = marsh, swamp, slough, wetlands, fen, mire, quagmire, morass, pakihi (N.Z.)

bogey = bugbear, bête noire, horror, nightmare, bugaboo

bogus = fake, false, artificial, forged, imitation, sham, fraudulent, counterfeit ≠ genuine

Bohemian ADJECTIVE often not cap. = unconventional, alternative, artistic, unorthodox, arty (informal), offbeat, left bank, nonconformist ≠ conventional

• NOUN often not cap. = nonconformist, rebel, radical, eccentric, maverick, hippy, dropout, individualist

boil[1] = simmer, bubble, foam, seethe, fizz, froth, effervesce

boil[2] = pustule, gathering, swelling, blister, carbuncle

bold 1 = fearless, enterprising, brave, daring, heroic, adventurous, courageous, audacious ≠ timid 2 = impudent, forward, confident, rude, cheeky, brazen, shameless, insolent ≠ shy

bolster = support, help, boost, strengthen, reinforce, shore up, augment

bolt NOUN 1 = pin, rod, peg, rivet 2 = bar, catch, lock, latch, fastener, sliding bar

• VERB 1 = lock, close, bar, secure, fasten, latch 2 = dash, fly 3 = gobble, stuff, wolf, cram, gorge, devour, gulp, guzzle

bomb NOUN = explosive, mine, shell, missile, device, rocket, grenade, torpedo

• VERB = blow up, attack, destroy, assault, shell, blitz, bombard, torpedo

bombard 1 = attack, assault, besiege, beset, assail 2 = bomb, shell, blitz, open fire, strafe, fire upon

bombardment = bombing, attack, assault, shelling, blitz, barrage, fusillade

bond NOUN 1 = tie, union, coupling, link, association, relation, connection, alliance 2 = fastening, tie, chain, cord, shackle, fetter, manacle 3 = agreement, word, promise, contract, guarantee, pledge, obligation, covenant

• VERB 1 = form friendships, connect 2 = fix, hold, bind, connect, glue, stick, paste, fasten

bonus 1 = extra, prize, gift, reward, premium, dividend 2 = advantage, benefit, gain, extra, plus, asset, icing on the cake

book NOUN 1 = work, title, volume, publication, tract, tome 2 = notebook, album, journal, diary, pad, notepad, exercise book, jotter

• VERB = reserve, schedule, engage, organize, charter, arrange for, make reservations

●PHRASES **book in** = register, enter

booklet = brochure, leaflet, hand-out, pamphlet, folder, mailshot, handbill

boom NOUN 1 = expansion, increase,

development, growth, jump, boost, improvement, upsurge ≠ decline **2** = <u>bang</u>, crash, clash, blast, burst, explosion, roar, thunder

● **VERB 1** = <u>increase</u>, flourish, grow, develop, expand, strengthen, swell, thrive ≠ fall **2** = <u>bang</u>, roll, crash, blast, explode, roar, thunder, rumble

boon 1 = <u>benefit</u>, blessing, godsend, gift **2** = <u>gift</u>, favour

boost VERB = <u>increase</u>, develop, raise, expand, add to, heighten, enlarge, amplify ≠ decrease

● **NOUN 1** = <u>rise</u>, increase, jump, addition, improvement, expansion, upsurge, upturn ≠ fall **2** = <u>encouragement</u>, help

boot = <u>kick</u>, punt, put the boot in(to) (*slang*), drop-kick

border NOUN 1 = <u>frontier</u>, line, limit, bounds, boundary, perimeter, borderline **2** = <u>edge</u>, margin, verge, rim

● **VERB** = <u>edge</u>, bound, decorate, trim, fringe, rim, hem

bore¹ = <u>drill</u>, mine, sink, tunnel, pierce, penetrate, burrow, puncture

bore² VERB = <u>tire</u>, fatigue, weary, wear out, jade, be tedious, pall on, send to sleep ≠ excite

● **NOUN** = <u>nuisance</u>, pain (*informal*), yawn (*informal*), anorak (*informal*)

bored = <u>fed up</u>, tired, wearied, uninterested, sick and tired (*informal*), listless, brassed off (*Brit. slang*), hoha (*N.Z.*)

boredom = <u>tedium</u>, apathy, weariness, monotony, sameness, ennui, flatness, world-weariness ≠ excitement

boring = <u>uninteresting</u>, dull, tedious, tiresome, monotonous, flat, humdrum, mind-numbing

borrow 1 = <u>take on loan</u>, touch (someone) for (*slang*), scrounge (*informal*), cadge, use temporarily ≠ lend **2** = <u>steal</u>, take, copy, adopt, pinch (*informal*)

boss NOUN = <u>manager</u>, head, leader, director, chief, master, employer, supervisor, baas (*S. African*)

●**PHRASES boss someone around** (*Informal*) = <u>order around</u>, dominate, bully, oppress, push around (*slang*)

bother VERB 1 = <u>trouble</u>, concern, worry, alarm, disturb, disconcert, perturb **2** = <u>pester</u>, plague, harass, hassle (*informal*), inconvenience ≠ help

● **NOUN** = <u>trouble</u>, problem, worry,

difficulty, fuss, irritation, hassle (*informal*), nuisance, uphill (*S. African*) ≠ help

bottle shop (*Austral. & N.Z.*) = <u>off-licence</u> (*Brit.*), liquor store (*U.S. & Canad.*), bottle store (*S. African*), package store (*U.S. & Canad.*), offie or offy (*Brit. informal*)

bottle store (*S. African*) = <u>off-licence</u> (*Brit.*), liquor store (*U.S. & Canad.*), bottle shop (*Austral. & N.Z.*), package store (*U.S. & Canad.*), offie or offy (*Brit. informal*)

bottom NOUN 1 = <u>lowest part</u>, base, foot, bed, floor, foundation, depths ≠ top **2** = <u>underside</u>, sole, underneath, lower side **3** = <u>buttocks</u>, behind (*informal*), rear, backside, rump, seat, posterior

● **ADJECTIVE** = <u>lowest</u>, last ≠ higher

bounce VERB 1 = <u>rebound</u>, recoil, ricochet **2** = <u>bound</u>, spring, jump, leap, skip, gambol

● **NOUN 1** = <u>springiness</u>, give, spring, resilience, elasticity, recoil **2** (*Informal*) = <u>life</u>, go (*informal*), energy, zip (*informal*), vigour, exuberance, dynamism, vivacity

bound¹ 1 = <u>compelled</u>, obliged, forced, committed, pledged, constrained, beholden, duty-bound **2** = <u>tied</u>, fixed, secured, attached, tied up, fastened, pinioned **3** = <u>certain</u>, sure, fated, doomed, destined

bound² 1 = <u>surround</u>, confine, enclose, encircle, hem in, demarcate **2** = <u>limit</u>, restrict, confine, restrain, circumscribe

bound³ VERB 1 = <u>leap</u>, bob, spring, jump, bounce, skip, vault

● **NOUN** = <u>leap</u>, bob, spring, jump, bounce, hurdle, skip, vault

boundary 1 = <u>frontier</u>, edge, border, barrier, margin, brink **2** = <u>edges</u>, limits, fringes, extremities **3** = <u>dividing line</u>, borderline

bounds = <u>boundary</u>, limit, edge, border, confine, verge, rim, perimeter

bouquet 1 = <u>bunch of flowers</u>, spray, garland, wreath, posy, buttonhole, corsage, nosegay **2** = <u>aroma</u>, smell, scent, perfume, fragrance, savour, odour, redolence

bourgeois = <u>middle-class</u>, traditional, conventional, materialistic, hidebound

bout 1 = <u>period</u>, term, fit, spell, turn, interval **2** = <u>round</u>, series, session, cycle, sequence, stint **3** = <u>fight</u>, match, competition, struggle, contest, set-to, encounter, engagement

bow¹ VERB = <u>bend</u>, bob, nod, stoop, droop, genuflect
● NOUN = <u>bending</u>, bob, nod, obeisance, kowtow, genuflection
bow² (*Nautical*) = <u>prow</u>, head, stem, fore, beak
bowels 1 = <u>guts</u>, insides (*informal*), intestines, innards (*informal*), entrails, viscera, vitals 2 = <u>depths</u>, hold, inside, deep, interior, core, belly
bowl¹ = <u>basin</u>, plate, dish, vessel
bowl² = <u>throw</u>, hurl, launch, cast, pitch, toss, fling, chuck (*informal*)
box¹ NOUN = <u>container</u>, case, chest, trunk, pack, package, carton, casket
● VERB = <u>pack</u>, package, wrap, encase, bundle up
box² = <u>fight</u>, spar, exchange blows
boxer = <u>fighter</u>, pugilist, prizefighter
boy = <u>lad</u>, kid (*informal*), youth, fellow, youngster, schoolboy, junior, stripling
boycott = <u>embargo</u>, reject, snub, black ≠ support
boyfriend = <u>sweetheart</u>, man, lover, beloved, admirer, suitor, beau, date
brace VERB 1 = <u>steady</u>, support, secure, stabilize 2 = <u>support</u>, strengthen, steady, reinforce, bolster, fortify, buttress
● NOUN = <u>support</u>, stay, prop, bolster, bracket, reinforcement, strut, truss
bracing = <u>refreshing</u>, fresh, stimulating, crisp, brisk, exhilarating, invigorating ≠ tiring
brain = <u>intelligence</u>, understanding, sense, intellect
brake NOUN = <u>control</u>, check, curb, restraint, constraint, rein
● VERB = <u>slow</u>, decelerate, reduce speed
branch 1 = <u>bough</u>, shoot, arm, spray, limb, sprig, offshoot 2 = <u>office</u>, department, unit, wing, chapter, bureau 3 = <u>division</u>, part, section, subdivision, subsection 4 = <u>discipline</u>, section, subdivision
brand NOUN 1 = <u>trademark</u> 2 = <u>label</u>, mark, sign, stamp, symbol, logo, trademark, marker
● VERB 1 = <u>stigmatize</u>, mark, expose, denounce, disgrace, discredit, censure 2 = <u>mark</u>, burn, label, stamp, scar
brash = <u>bold</u>, rude, cocky, pushy (*informal*), brazen, impertinent, insolent, impudent ≠ timid
brave ADJECTIVE = <u>courageous</u>, daring, bold, heroic, adventurous, fearless, resolute, audacious ≠ timid
● VERB = <u>confront</u>, face, suffer, tackle, endure, defy, withstand, stand up to ≠ give in to
bravery = <u>courage</u>, nerve, daring, pluck, spirit, fortitude, heroism, mettle ≠ cowardice
brawl NOUN = <u>fight</u>, clash, fray, skirmish, scuffle, punch-up (*Brit. informal*), fracas, altercation, biffo (*Austral. slang*)
● VERB = <u>fight</u>, scrap (*informal*), wrestle, tussle, scuffle
breach 1 = <u>nonobservance</u>, abuse, violation, infringement, trespass, transgression, contravention, infraction ≠ compliance 2 = <u>opening</u>, crack, split, gap, rift, rupture, cleft, fissure
bread 1 = <u>food</u>, fare, kai (*N.Z. informal*), nourishment, sustenance 2 (*Slang*) = <u>money</u>, cash, dough (*slang*)
breadth 1 = <u>width</u>, spread, span, latitude, broadness, wideness 2 = <u>extent</u>, range, scale, scope, compass, expanse
break VERB 1 = <u>shatter</u>, separate, destroy, crack, snap, smash, crush, fragment ≠ repair 2 = <u>fracture</u>, crack, smash 3 = <u>burst</u>, tear, split 4 = <u>disobey</u>, breach, defy, violate, disregard, flout, infringe, contravene ≠ obey 5 = <u>stop</u>, cut, suspend, interrupt, cut short, discontinue 6 = <u>disturb</u>, interrupt 7 = <u>end</u>, stop, cut, drop, give up, abandon, suspend, interrupt 8 = <u>weaken</u>, undermine, tame, subdue, demoralize, dispirit 9 = <u>be revealed</u>, be published, be announced, be made public, be proclaimed, be let out 10 = <u>reveal</u>, tell, announce, declare, disclose, proclaim, make known 11 = <u>beat</u>, top, better, exceed, go beyond, excel, surpass, outstrip
● NOUN 1 = <u>fracture</u>, opening, tear, hole, split, crack, gap, fissure 2 = <u>interval</u>, pause, interlude, intermission 3 = <u>holiday</u>, leave, vacation, time off, recess, awayday 4 (*Informal*) = <u>stroke of luck</u>, chance, opportunity, advantage, fortune, opening
● PHRASES **break off** = <u>stop talking</u>, pause ◆ **break out** = <u>begin</u>, start, happen, occur, arise, set in, commence, spring up ◆ **break something off** = <u>detach</u>, separate, divide, cut off, pull off, sever, part, remove ◆ **break something up** = <u>stop</u>, end, suspend, dismantle, terminate, disband, diffuse ◆ **break up** 1 = <u>finish</u>, be

suspended, adjourn **2** = <u>split up</u>, separate, part, divorce

breakdown = <u>collapse</u>

break-in = <u>burglary</u>, robbery, breaking and entering

breakthrough = <u>development</u>, advance, progress, discovery, find, invention, step forward, leap forwards

breast = <u>bosom(s)</u>, front, chest, bust

breath = <u>inhalation</u>, breathing, pant, gasp, gulp, wheeze, exhalation, respiration

breathe 1 = <u>inhale and exhale</u>, pant, gasp, puff, gulp, wheeze, respire, draw in breath **2** = <u>whisper</u>, sigh, murmur

breathless 1 = <u>out of breath</u>, panting, gasping, gulping, wheezing, short-winded **2** = <u>excited</u>, curious, eager, enthusiastic, impatient, on tenterhooks, in suspense

breathtaking = <u>amazing</u>, exciting, stunning (*informal*), impressive, thrilling, magnificent, astonishing, sensational

breed NOUN **1** = <u>variety</u>, race, stock, type, species, strain, pedigree **2** = <u>kind</u>, sort, type, variety, brand, stamp

● VERB **1** = <u>rear</u>, tend, keep, raise, maintain, farm, look after, care for **2** = <u>reproduce</u>, multiply, propagate, procreate, produce offspring, bear young, bring forth young **3** = <u>produce</u>, cause, create, generate, bring about, arouse, give rise to, stir up

breeding = <u>refinement</u>, culture, taste, manners, polish, courtesy, sophistication, cultivation

breeze NOUN = <u>light wind</u>, air, draught, gust, waft, zephyr, breath of wind, current of air

● VERB = <u>sweep</u>, move briskly, pass, sail, hurry, glide, flit

brew VERB **1** = <u>boil</u>, make, soak, steep, stew, infuse (*tea*) **2** = <u>make</u>, ferment **3** = <u>start</u>, develop, gather, foment **4** = <u>develop</u>, form, gather, foment

● NOUN = <u>drink</u>, preparation, mixture, blend, liquor, beverage, infusion, concoction

bribe NOUN = <u>inducement</u>, pay-off (*informal*), sweetener (*slang*), kickback (*U.S.*), backhander (*slang*), enticement, allurement

● VERB = <u>buy off</u>, reward, pay off (*informal*), corrupt, suborn, grease the palm *or* hand of (*slang*)

bribery = <u>corruption</u>, inducement, buying off, payola (*informal*), palm-greasing

(*slang*)

bridge NOUN = <u>arch</u>, span, viaduct, flyover, overpass

● VERB **1** = <u>span</u>, cross **2** = <u>reconcile</u>, resolve

brief ADJECTIVE = <u>short</u>, quick, fleeting, swift, short-lived, momentary, ephemeral, transitory ≠ long

● VERB **1** = <u>inform</u>, prime, prepare, advise, fill in (*informal*), instruct, put in the picture (*informal*), keep (someone) posted

● NOUN = <u>summary</u>, résumé, outline, sketch, abstract, digest, epitome, rundown

briefing 1 = <u>conference</u>, priming **2** = <u>instructions</u>, information, priming, directions, preparation, guidance, rundown

briefly 1 = <u>quickly</u>, shortly, hastily, momentarily, hurriedly **2** = <u>in outline</u>, in brief, in a nutshell, concisely

brigade 1 = <u>corps</u>, company, force, unit, division, troop, squad, team **2** = <u>group</u>, band, squad, organization

bright 1 = <u>vivid</u>, rich, brilliant, glowing, colourful **2** = <u>shining</u>, glowing, dazzling, gleaming, shimmering, radiant, luminous, lustrous **3** = <u>intelligent</u>, smart, clever, aware, sharp, enlightened, astute, wide-awake ≠ stupid **4** = <u>clever</u>, smart, ingenious **5** = <u>sunny</u>, clear, fair, pleasant, lucid, cloudless, unclouded ≠ cloudy

brighten 1 = <u>light up</u>, shine, glow, gleam, lighten ≠ dim **2** = <u>enliven</u>, animate, make brighter, vitalize **3** = <u>become brighter</u>, light up, glow, gleam

brilliance *or* **brilliancy 1** = <u>cleverness</u>, talent, wisdom, distinction, genius, excellence, greatness, inventiveness ≠ stupidity **2** = <u>brightness</u>, intensity, sparkle, dazzle, lustre, radiance, luminosity, vividness ≠ darkness **3** = <u>splendour</u>, glamour, grandeur, magnificence, éclat, illustriousness

brilliant 1 = <u>intelligent</u>, sharp, intellectual, clever, profound, penetrating, inventive, perspicacious ≠ stupid **2** = <u>expert</u>, masterly, talented, gifted, accomplished ≠ untalented **3** = <u>splendid</u>, famous, celebrated, outstanding, superb, magnificent, glorious, notable **4** = <u>bright</u>, shining, intense, sparkling, glittering, dazzling, vivid, radiant ≠ dark

brim NOUN = <u>rim</u>, edge, border, lip, margin, verge, brink

● VERB **1** = <u>be full</u>, spill, well over, run over

2 = <u>fill</u>, well over, fill up, overflow

bring VERB 1 = <u>fetch</u>, take, carry, bear, transfer, support, deliver, transport, convey

2 = <u>take</u>, guide, conduct, escort 3 = <u>cause</u>, produce, create, effect, occasion, result in, contribute to, inflict

● PHRASES **bring someone up** = <u>rear</u>, raise, support, train, develop, teach, breed, foster ◆ **bring something about** = <u>cause</u>, produce, create, effect, achieve, generate, accomplish, give rise to ◆ **bring something off** = <u>accomplish</u>, achieve, perform, succeed, execute, pull off, carry off ◆ **bring something up** = <u>mention</u>, raise, introduce, point out, refer to, allude to, broach

brink = <u>edge</u>, limit, border, lip, margin, boundary, skirt, frontier

brisk 1 = <u>quick</u>, lively, energetic, active, vigorous, bustling, sprightly, spry ≠ slow

2 = <u>short</u>, brief, blunt, abrupt, terse, gruff, brusque, monosyllabic

briskly = <u>quickly</u>, smartly, promptly, rapidly, readily, actively, efficiently, energetically

bristle NOUN = <u>hair</u>, spine, thorn, whisker, barb, stubble, prickle

● VERB 1 = <u>stand up</u>, rise, stand on end

2 = <u>be angry</u>, rage, seethe, flare up, bridle, see red

brittle = <u>fragile</u>, delicate, crisp, crumbling, frail, crumbly, breakable, friable ≠ tough

broad 1 = <u>wide</u>, large, ample, generous, expansive 2 = <u>large</u>, huge, vast, extensive, ample, spacious, expansive, roomy ≠ narrow 3 = <u>full</u>, general, comprehensive, complete, wide, sweeping, wide-ranging, thorough 4 = <u>universal</u>, general, common, wide, sweeping, worldwide, widespread, wide-ranging 5 = <u>general</u>, loose, vague, approximate, indefinite, ill-defined, inexact, unspecific

broadcast NOUN = <u>transmission</u>, show, programme, telecast

● VERB 1 = <u>transmit</u>, show, air, radio, cable, beam, send out, relay 2 = <u>make public</u>, report, announce, publish, spread, advertise, proclaim, circulate

broaden = <u>expand</u>, increase, develop, spread, extend, stretch, swell, supplement ≠ restrict

brochure = <u>booklet</u>, advertisement, leaflet, hand-out, circular, pamphlet, folder, mailshot

broekies (S. African informal) = <u>underpants</u>, pants, briefs, drawers, knickers, panties, boxer shorts, Y-fronts®, underdaks (Austral. slang)

broke (Informal) = <u>penniless</u>, short, ruined, bust (informal), bankrupt, impoverished, in the red, insolvent ≠ rich

broken 1 = <u>interrupted</u>, incomplete, erratic, intermittent, fragmentary, spasmodic, discontinuous 2 = <u>imperfect</u>, halting, hesitating, stammering, disjointed 3 = <u>smashed</u>, burst, shattered, fragmented, fractured, severed, ruptured, separated 4 = <u>defective</u>, not working, imperfect, out of order, on the blink (slang), kaput (informal)

broker = <u>dealer</u>, agent, trader, supplier, merchant, negotiator, mediator, intermediary

bronze = <u>reddish-brown</u>, copper, tan, rust, chestnut, brownish

brood NOUN 1 = <u>offspring</u>, issue, clutch, litter, progeny 2 = <u>children</u>, family, nearest and dearest, flesh and blood, ainga (N.Z.)

● VERB = <u>think</u>, obsess, muse, ponder, agonize, mull over, mope, ruminate

brook = <u>stream</u>, burn (Scot. & Northern English), rivulet, beck, watercourse, rill

brother 1 = <u>male sibling</u> 2 = <u>monk</u>, cleric, friar, religious

▇ RELATED WORD
adjective: fraternal

brotherly = <u>fraternal</u>, friendly, neighbourly, sympathetic, affectionate, benevolent, kind, amicable

brown ADJECTIVE 1 = <u>brunette</u>, bay, coffee, chocolate, chestnut, hazel, dun, auburn

2 = <u>tanned</u>, bronze, tan, sunburnt

● VERB = <u>fry</u>, cook, grill, sear, sauté

browse 1 = <u>skim</u>, scan, glance at, survey, look through, look round, dip into, leaf through 2 = <u>graze</u>, eat, feed, nibble

bruise NOUN = <u>discoloration</u>, mark, injury, blemish, contusion

● VERB 1 = <u>hurt</u>, injure, mark 2 = <u>damage</u>, mark, mar, discolour

brush¹ NOUN 1 = <u>broom</u>, sweeper, besom 2 = <u>conflict</u>, clash, confrontation, skirmish, tussle 3 = <u>encounter</u>, meeting, confrontation, rendezvous

● VERB 1 = <u>clean</u>, wash, polish, buff

2 = <u>touch</u>, sweep, kiss, stroke, glance, flick, scrape, graze

● PHRASES **brush someone off**

(*Slang*) = ignore, reject, dismiss, snub, disregard, scorn, disdain, spurn ♦ **brush something up** or **brush up on something** = revise, study, go over, cram, polish up, read up on, relearn, bone up on (*informal*)

brush² = shrubs, bushes, scrub, undergrowth, thicket, copse, brushwood

brutal 1 = cruel, savage, vicious, ruthless, callous, sadistic, heartless, inhuman ≠ kind 2 = harsh, tough, severe, rough, rude, indifferent, insensitive, callous ≠ sensitive

brutality = cruelty, atrocity, ferocity, savagery, ruthlessness, barbarism, inhumanity, viciousness

bubble NOUN = air ball, drop, bead, blister, blob, droplet, globule

• VERB 1 = boil, seethe 2 = foam, fizz, froth, percolate, effervesce 3 = gurgle, splash, murmur, trickle, ripple, babble, burble, lap

bubbly 1 = lively, happy, excited, animated, merry, bouncy, elated, sparky 2 = frothy, sparkling, fizzy, effervescent, carbonated, foamy

buckle NOUN = fastener, catch, clip, clasp, hasp

• VERB 1 = fasten, close, secure, hook, clasp 2 = distort, bend, warp, crumple, contort 3 = collapse, bend, twist, fold, give way, subside, cave in, crumple

bud NOUN = shoot, branch, sprout, sprig, offshoot

• VERB = develop, grow, shoot, sprout, burgeon, burst forth

budding = developing, beginning, growing, promising, potential, burgeoning, fledgling, embryonic

budge 1 = move, stir 2 = dislodge, move, push, transfer, shift, stir

budget NOUN = allowance, means, funds, income, finances, resources, allocation

• VERB = plan, estimate, allocate, cost, ration, apportion

buff¹ ADJECTIVE = fawn, tan, beige, yellowish, straw-coloured, sand-coloured, yellowish-brown

• VERB = polish, smooth, brush, shine, rub, wax, brighten, burnish

buff² (*Informal*) = expert, fan, addict, enthusiast, admirer, devotee, connoisseur, aficionado, fundi (*S. African*)

buffer = safeguard, screen, shield, cushion, intermediary, bulwark

buffet 1 = smorgasbord 2 = snack bar, café, cafeteria, brasserie, refreshment counter

bug NOUN 1 (*Informal*) = illness, disease, virus, infection, disorder, sickness, ailment, affliction 2 = fault, error, defect, flaw, glitch, gremlin

• VERB 1 = tap, eavesdrop, listen in on 2 (*Informal*) = annoy, bother, disturb, irritate, hassle (*informal*), pester, vex, get on your nerves (*informal*)

build VERB = construct, make, raise, put up, assemble, erect, fabricate, form ≠ demolish

• NOUN = physique, form, body, figure, shape, structure, frame

building = structure, house, construction, dwelling, erection, edifice, domicile

build-up = increase, development, growth, expansion, accumulation, enlargement, escalation

bulge VERB 1 = swell out, project, expand, stick out, protrude, puff out, distend 2 = stick out, stand out, protrude

• NOUN 1 = lump, swelling, bump, projection, hump, protuberance, protrusion ≠ hollow 2 = increase, rise, boost, surge, intensification

bulk 1 = size, volume, dimensions, magnitude, substance, immensity, largeness 2 = weight, size, mass, heaviness, poundage 3 = majority, mass, most, body, best part, lion's share, better part, preponderance

bullet = projectile, ball, shot, missile, slug, pellet

bulletin = report, account, statement, message, communication, announcement, dispatch, communiqué

bully NOUN = persecutor, tough, oppressor, tormentor, bully boy, browbeater, coercer, ruffian

• VERB 1 = persecute, intimidate, torment, oppress, pick on, victimize, terrorize, push around (*slang*) 2 = force, coerce, browbeat, hector, domineer

bump VERB 1 = knock, hit, strike, crash, smash, slam, bang 2 = jerk, shake, bounce, rattle, jog, lurch, jolt

• NOUN 1 = knock, blow, impact, collision, thump 2 = thud, crash, knock, bang, smack, thump 3 = lump, swelling, bulge, hump, nodule, protuberance, contusion

bumper = exceptional, excellent, exo (*Austral. slang*), massive, jumbo (*informal*), abundant, whopping (*informal*), bountiful

bunch NOUN 1 = group, band, crowd, party, team, gathering, gang, flock 2 = bouquet, sheaf 3 = cluster, clump

●PHRASES **bunch together** *or* **up** = group, mass, collect, assemble, cluster, huddle

bundle NOUN = bunch, group, collection, mass, pile, stack, heap, batch

● VERB = push, thrust, shove, throw, rush, hurry, jostle, hustle

●PHRASES **bundle someone up** = wrap up, swathe

bungle = mess up, blow (*slang*), ruin, spoil, blunder, botch, make a mess of, muff, crool *or* cruel (*Austral. slang*) ≠ accomplish

bungling = incompetent, blundering, clumsy, inept, cack-handed (*informal*), maladroit, ham-fisted (*informal*), unco (*Austral. slang*)

bunk *or* **bunkum** (*Informal*) = nonsense, rubbish, garbage (*informal*), hot air (*informal*), twaddle, moonshine, baloney (*informal*), hogwash, bizzo (*Austral. slang*), bull's wool (*Austral. & N.Z. slang*), kak (*S. African taboo slang*)

buoy = float, guide, signal, marker, beacon

buoyant ADJECTIVE = cheerful, happy, upbeat (*informal*), carefree, jaunty, chirpy (*informal*), light-hearted ≠ gloomy

● ADJECTIVE = floating, light

burden NOUN 1 = trouble, worry, weight, responsibility, strain, affliction, onus, millstone 2 = load, weight, cargo, freight, consignment, encumbrance

● VERB = weigh down, worry, load, tax, bother, handicap, oppress, inconvenience

bureau 1 = agency 2 = office, department, section, branch, station, unit, division, subdivision 3 = desk, writing desk

bureaucracy 1 = government, officials, authorities, administration, the system, civil service, corridors of power 2 = red tape, regulations, officialdom

bureaucrat = official, officer, administrator, civil servant, public servant, functionary, mandarin

burglar = housebreaker, thief, robber, pilferer, filcher, cat burglar, sneak thief

burglary = breaking and entering, housebreaking, break-in

burial = funeral, interment, obsequies, entombment, exequies

burn 1 = be on fire, blaze, be ablaze,

smoke, flame, glow, flare, go up in flames 2 = set on fire, light, ignite, kindle, incinerate 3 = scorch, toast, sear, char, singe 4 = be passionate, be aroused, be inflamed 5 = seethe, fume, be angry, simmer, smoulder

burning 1 = intense, passionate, eager, ardent, fervent, impassioned, vehement ≠ mild 2 = blazing, fiery, smouldering, glowing 3 = flashing, blazing, flaming, gleaming, fiery 4 = crucial, important, pressing, significant, essential, vital, critical, acute

burrow NOUN = hole, shelter, tunnel, den, lair, retreat

● VERB 1 = dig, tunnel, excavate 2 = delve, search, probe, ferret, rummage, forage, fossick (*Austral. & N.Z.*)

burst VERB 1 = explode, blow up, break, split, crack, shatter, puncture, rupture 2 = rush, run, break, break out, erupt, spout, gush forth 3 = barge, charge, rush, shove

● NOUN 1 = rush, surge, outbreak, outburst, spate, gush, torrent, spurt 2 = explosion, crack, blast, bang, discharge

● ADJECTIVE = ruptured, flat, punctured, split, rent

bury 1 = inter, lay to rest, entomb, consign to the grave, inhume ≠ dig up 2 = hide, cover, conceal, stash (*informal*), secrete, stow away ≠ uncover 3 = sink, embed, immerse, enfold 4 = forget

bush NOUN = shrub, plant, hedge, thicket, shrubbery

● PHRASES **the bush** = the wilds, brush, scrub, woodland, backwoods, scrubland

business 1 = trade, selling, industry, manufacturing, commerce, dealings 2 = establishment, company, firm, concern, organization, corporation, venture, enterprise 3 = profession, work, job, line, trade, career, function, employment 4 = matter, issue, subject, point, problem, responsibility, task, duty 5 = concern, affair

businessman = executive, director, manager, merchant, capitalist, administrator, entrepreneur, tycoon

bust[1] = bosom, breasts, chest, front

bust[2] (*Informal*) VERB 1 = break, smash, split, burst, shatter, fracture, rupture 2 = arrest, catch, raid

● PHRASES **go bust** = go bankrupt, fail, be

ruined, become insolvent

bustle VERB = hurry, rush, fuss, hasten, scuttle, scurry, scamper ≠ idle
● NOUN = activity, to-do, stir, excitement, fuss, flurry, commotion, ado ≠ inactivity

bustling = busy, full, crowded, active, lively, buzzing, humming, swarming

busy ADJECTIVE 1 = active, industrious, rushed off your feet ≠ idle 2 = occupied with, working, engaged in, on duty, employed in, hard at work ≠ unoccupied 3 = hectic, full, exacting, energetic
●PHRASES **busy yourself** = occupy yourself, be engrossed, immerse yourself, involve yourself, absorb yourself, employ yourself, engage yourself

but CONJUNCTION = however, still, yet, nevertheless
● PREPOSITION = except (for), save, bar, barring, excepting, excluding, with the exception of
● ADVERB = only, just, simply, merely

butcher NOUN = murderer, killer, slaughterer, slayer, destroyer, executioner, cut-throat, exterminator
● VERB 1 = slaughter, prepare, carve, cut up, dress, cut, clean, joint 2 = kill, slaughter, massacre, destroy, cut down, assassinate, slay, liquidate

butt¹ 1 = end, handle, shaft, stock, shank, hilt, haft 2 = stub, tip, leftover, fag end (*informal*)

butt² = target, victim, dupe, laughing stock, Aunt Sally

butt³ VERB = knock, push, bump, thrust, ram, shove, poke, prod
●PHRASES **butt in** 1 = interfere, meddle, intrude, heckle, barge in (*informal*), stick your nose in, put your oar in 2 = interrupt, cut in, break in, chip in (*informal*)

butt⁴ = cask, barrel

butterfly

▋ RELATED WORDS
young: caterpillar, chrysalis *or* chrysalid
enthusiast: lepidopterist

buy VERB = purchase, get, pay for, obtain, acquire, invest in, shop for, procure ≠ sell
● NOUN = purchase, deal, bargain, acquisition, steal (*informal*), snip (*informal*), giveaway

by PREPOSITION 1 = through, through the agency of 2 = via, over, by way of 3 = near, past, along, close to, closest to, neighbouring, next to, beside
● ADVERB = nearby, close, handy, at hand, within reach

bypass 1 = get round, avoid 2 = go round, circumvent, depart from, deviate from, pass round, detour round ≠ cross

cab = taxi, minicab, taxicab, hackney carriage

cabin 1 = room, berth, quarters, compartment 2 = hut, shed, cottage, lodge, shack, chalet, shanty, whare (*N.Z.*)

cabinet 1 = cupboard, case, locker, dresser, closet, press, chiffonier 2 *often cap.* = council, committee, administration, ministry, assembly, board

cad (*Old-fashioned, informal*) = scoundrel (*slang*), rat (*informal*), bounder (*Brit. old-fashioned slang*), rotter (*slang, chiefly Brit.*), heel

café = snack bar, restaurant, cafeteria, coffee shop, brasserie, coffee bar, tearoom, lunchroom

cage = enclosure, pen, coop, hutch, pound

cake = block, bar, slab, lump, cube, loaf, mass

calculated = deliberate, planned, considered, intended, intentional, designed, aimed, purposeful ≠ unplanned

calculating = scheming, sharp, shrewd, cunning, sly, devious, manipulative, crafty ≠ direct

calculation 1 = computation, working out, reckoning, estimate, forecast, judgment, result, answer 2 = planning, intention, deliberation, foresight, contrivance, forethought, premeditation

calibre *or* (*U.S.*) **caliber** 1 = worth, quality, ability, talent, capacity, merit, distinction, stature 2 = standard, level, quality, grade 3 = diameter, bore, gauge, measure

call VERB 1 = name, entitle, dub, designate, term, style, label, describe as 2 = cry, shout, scream, yell, whoop ≠ whisper **3** = <u>phone</u>, telephone, ring (up) (*informal*, *chiefly Brit.*) **4** = <u>hail</u>, summon **5** = <u>summon</u>, gather, rally, assemble, muster, convene ≠ dismiss **6** = <u>waken</u>, arouse, rouse

● NOUN **1** = <u>visit</u> **2** = <u>request</u>, order, demand, appeal, notice, command, invitation, plea **3** (*usually used in a negative construction*) = <u>need</u>, cause, reason, grounds, occasion, excuse, justification **4** = <u>attraction</u>, pull (*informal*), appeal, lure, allure, magnetism **5** = <u>cry</u>, shout, scream, yell, whoop ≠ whisper

● PHRASES **call for someone** = <u>fetch</u>, pick up, collect ◆ **call for something 1** = <u>demand</u>, order, request, insist on, cry out for **2** = <u>require</u>, need, involve, demand, occasion, entail, necessitate

calling = <u>profession</u>, trade, career, mission, vocation, life's work

calm ADJECTIVE **1** = <u>cool</u>, relaxed, composed, sedate, collected, dispassionate, unemotional, self-possessed ≠ excited **2** = <u>still</u>, quiet, smooth, mild, serene, tranquil, balmy, windless ≠ rough

● NOUN **1** = <u>peacefulness</u>, peace, serenity **2** = <u>stillness</u>, peace, quiet, hush, serenity, tranquillity, repose, peacefulness **3** = <u>peace</u>, calmness ≠ disturbance

● VERB **1** = <u>soothe</u>, quiet, relax, appease, still, allay, assuage, quieten ≠ excite **2** = <u>placate</u>, hush, pacify, mollify ≠ aggravate

camouflage NOUN **1** = <u>protective colouring</u> **2** = <u>disguise</u>, cover, screen, blind, mask, cloak, masquerade, subterfuge

● VERB = <u>disguise</u>, cover, screen, hide, mask, conceal, obscure, veil ≠ reveal

camp[1] = <u>camp site</u>, tents, encampment, bivouac, camping ground

camp[2] (*Informal*) = <u>affected</u>, mannered, artificial, posturing, ostentatious, effeminate

campaign 1 = <u>drive</u>, appeal, movement, push (*informal*), offensive, crusade **2** = <u>operation</u>, drive, attack, movement, push, offensive, expedition, crusade

canal = <u>waterway</u>, channel, passage, conduit, duct, watercourse

cancel VERB **1** = <u>call off</u>, drop, forget about **2** = <u>annul</u>, abolish, repeal, abort, do away with, revoke, eliminate

● PHRASES **cancel something out** = <u>counterbalance</u>, offset, make up for, compensate for, neutralize, nullify, balance out

cancellation 1 = <u>abandonment</u> **2** = <u>annulment</u>, abolition, repeal, elimination, revocation

cancer 1 = <u>growth</u>, tumour, malignancy **2** = <u>evil</u>, corruption, sickness, pestilence

candidate = <u>contender</u>, competitor, applicant, nominee, entrant, claimant, contestant, runner

cannabis = <u>marijuana</u>, pot (*slang*), dope (*slang*), grass (*slang*), hemp, dagga (*S. African*)

cannon = <u>gun</u>, big gun, field gun, mortar

canon 1 = <u>rule</u>, standard, principle, regulation, formula, criterion, dictate, statute **2** = <u>list</u>, index, catalogue, roll

canopy = <u>awning</u>, covering, shade, sunshade

cap 1 (*Informal*) = <u>beat</u>, top, better, exceed, eclipse, surpass, transcend, outstrip **2** = <u>top</u>, crown **3** = <u>complete</u>, crown

capability = <u>ability</u>, means, power, potential, capacity, qualification(s), competence, proficiency ≠ inability

capable 1 = <u>able</u> ≠ incapable **2** = <u>accomplished</u>, qualified, talented, gifted, efficient, competent, proficient ≠ incompetent

capacity 1 = <u>ability</u>, facility, gift, genius, capability, aptitude, aptness, competence *or* competency **2** = <u>size</u>, room, range, space, volume, extent, dimensions, scope **3** = <u>function</u>, position, role, post, office

cape = <u>headland</u>, point, head, peninsula, promontory

capital NOUN = <u>money</u>, funds, investment(s), cash, finances, resources, assets, wealth

● ADJECTIVE (*Old-fashioned*) = <u>first-rate</u>, fine, excellent, superb

capitalism = <u>private enterprise</u>, free enterprise, private ownership, laissez faire *or* laisser faire

capsule 1 = <u>pill</u>, tablet, lozenge **2** (*Botany*) = <u>pod</u>, case, shell, vessel, sheath, receptacle, seed case

captain 1 = <u>leader</u>, boss, master, skipper, head, chief **2** = <u>commander</u>, skipper

captivate = <u>charm</u>, attract, fascinate, entrance, enchant, enthral, beguile, allure ≠ repel

captive ADJECTIVE = <u>confined</u>, caged,

imprisoned, locked up, enslaved, incarcerated, ensnared, subjugated
● NOUN = **prisoner**, hostage, convict, prisoner of war, detainee, internee

captivity = **confinement**, custody, detention, imprisonment, incarceration, internment

capture VERB = **catch**, arrest, take, bag, secure, seize, collar (*informal*), apprehend ≠ release
● NOUN = **arrest**, catching, trapping, imprisonment, seizure, apprehension, taking, taking captive

car 1 = **vehicle**, motor, wheels (*informal*), auto (*U.S.*), automobile, jalopy (*informal*), motorcar, machine 2 (*U.S. & Canad.*) = **(railway) carriage**, coach, cable car, dining car, sleeping car, buffet car, van

cardinal = **principal**, first, leading, chief, main, central, key, essential ≠ secondary

care VERB = **be concerned**, mind, bother, be interested, be bothered, give a damn, concern yourself
● NOUN 1 = **custody**, keeping, control, charge, management, protection, supervision, guardianship 2 = **caution**, attention, pains, consideration, heed, prudence, vigilance, forethought ≠ carelessness 3 = **worry**, concern, pressure, trouble, responsibility, stress, anxiety, disquiet ≠ pleasure
● PHRASES **care for someone** 1 = **look after**, mind, tend, attend, nurse, minister to, watch over 2 = **love**, desire, be fond of, want, prize ◆ **care for something or someone** = **like**, enjoy, take to, relish, be fond of, be keen on, be partial to ◆ **take care of** 1 = **look after**, mind, watch, protect, tend, nurse, care for, provide for 2 = **deal with**, manage, cope with, see to, handle

career NOUN = **occupation**, calling, employment, pursuit, vocation, livelihood, life's work
● VERB = **rush**, race, speed, tear, dash, barrel (along) (*informal*, (*chiefly U.S. & Canad.*), bolt, hurtle

careful 1 = **cautious**, scrupulous, circumspect, chary, thoughtful, discreet ≠ careless 2 = **thorough**, full, particular, precise, intensive, in-depth, meticulous, conscientious ≠ casual 3 = **prudent**, sparing, economical, canny, provident, frugal, thrifty

careless 1 = **slapdash**, irresponsible, sloppy (*informal*), cavalier, offhand, neglectful, slipshod, lackadaisical ≠ careful 2 = **negligent**, hasty, thoughtless, unthinking, forgetful, absent-minded, remiss ≠ careful 3 = **nonchalant**, casual, offhand, artless, unstudied ≠ careful

caretaker = **warden**, keeper, porter, superintendent, curator, custodian, watchman, janitor

cargo = **load**, goods, contents, shipment, freight, merchandise, baggage, consignment

caricature NOUN = **parody**, cartoon, distortion, satire, send-up (*Brit. informal*), travesty, takeoff (*informal*), lampoon
● VERB = **parody**, take off (*informal*), mock, distort, ridicule, mimic, send up (*Brit. informal*), lampoon

carnage = **slaughter**, murder, massacre, holocaust, havoc, bloodshed, shambles, mass murder

carnival = **festival**, fair, fête, celebration, gala, jubilee, jamboree, revelry

carol = **song**, hymn, Christmas song

carp = **find fault**, complain, criticize, reproach, quibble, cavil, pick holes ≠ praise

carpenter = **joiner**, cabinet-maker, woodworker

carriage 1 = **vehicle**, coach, trap, gig, cab, wagon, hackney, conveyance 2 = **bearing**, posture, gait, deportment, air

carry VERB 1 = **convey**, take, move, bring, bear, transfer, conduct, transport 2 = **transport**, take, transfer 3 = **transmit**, transfer, spread, pass on 4 = **win**, gain, secure, capture, accomplish
● PHRASES **carry on** 1 = **continue**, last, endure, persist, keep going, persevere 2 (*Informal*) = **make a fuss**, misbehave, create (*slang*), raise Cain ◆ **carry something on** = **engage in**, conduct, carry out, undertake, embark on, enter into ◆ **carry something out** = **perform**, effect, achieve, realize, implement, fulfil, accomplish, execute

carry-on (*Informal*, *chiefly Brit.*) = **fuss**, disturbance, racket, commotion

carton = **box**, case, pack, package, container

cartoon 1 = **drawing**, parody, satire, caricature, comic strip, takeoff (*informal*), lampoon, sketch 2 = **animation**, animated film, animated cartoon

carve 1 = <u>sculpt</u>, cut, chip, whittle, chisel, hew, fashion 2 = <u>etch</u>, engrave

cascade NOUN = <u>waterfall</u>, falls, torrent, flood, shower, fountain, avalanche, deluge
● VERB = <u>flow</u>, fall, flood, pour, plunge, surge, spill, tumble

case[1] 1 = <u>situation</u>, event, circumstance(s), state, position, condition, context, contingency 2 = <u>instance</u>, example, occasion, specimen, occurrence 3 (*Law*) = <u>lawsuit</u>, trial, suit, proceedings, dispute, action

case[2] 1 = <u>cabinet</u>, box, chest, holder 2 = <u>container</u>, carton, canister, casket, receptacle 3 = <u>suitcase</u>, bag, grip, holdall, portmanteau, valise 4 = <u>crate</u>, box 5 = <u>covering</u>, casing, shell, jacket, envelope, capsule, sheath, wrapper

cash = <u>money</u>, funds, notes, currency, silver, brass (*Northern English dialect*), dough (*slang*), coinage

cast NOUN 1 = <u>actors</u>, company, players, characters, troupe, dramatis personae 2 = <u>type</u>, sort, kind, style, stamp
● VERB 1 = <u>choose</u>, name, pick, select, appoint, assign, allot 2 = <u>bestow</u>, give, level, direct 3 = <u>give out</u>, spread, deposit, shed, distribute, scatter, emit, radiate 4 = <u>throw</u>, launch, pitch, toss, thrust, hurl, fling, sling 5 = <u>mould</u>, set, found, form, model, shape

caste = <u>class</u>, order, rank, status, stratum, social order

castle = <u>fortress</u>, keep, palace, tower, chateau, stronghold, citadel

casual 1 = <u>careless</u>, relaxed, unconcerned, blasé, offhand, nonchalant, lackadaisical ≠ serious 2 = <u>chance</u>, unexpected, random, accidental, incidental ≠ planned 3 = <u>informal</u>, leisure, sporty, non-dressy ≠ formal

casualty 1 = <u>fatality</u>, death, loss, wounded 2 = <u>victim</u>, sufferer

cat = <u>feline</u>, pussy (*informal*), moggy (*slang*), puss (*informal*), ballarat (*Austral. informal*), tabby

▨▨▨ RELATED WORDS
adjective: feline
male: tom
female: tabby
young: kitten

catalogue or (*U.S.*) **catalog** NOUN = <u>list</u>, record, schedule, index, register, directory, inventory, gazetteer
● VERB = <u>list</u>, file, index, register, classify, inventory, tabulate, alphabetize

catastrophe = <u>disaster</u>, tragedy, calamity, cataclysm, trouble, adversity, fiasco

catch VERB 1 = <u>capture</u>, arrest, trap, seize, snare, apprehend, ensnare, entrap ≠ free 2 = <u>trap</u>, capture, snare, ensnare, entrap 3 = <u>seize</u>, get, grab, snatch 4 = <u>grab</u>, take, grip, seize, grasp, clutch, lay hold of ≠ release 5 = <u>discover</u>, surprise, find out, expose, detect, catch in the act, take unawares 6 = <u>contract</u>, get, develop, suffer from, incur, succumb to, go down with ≠ escape
● NOUN 1 = <u>fastener</u>, clip, bolt, latch, clasp 2 (*Informal*) = <u>drawback</u>, trick, trap, disadvantage, hitch, snag, stumbling block, fly in the ointment ≠ advantage
● PHRASES **catch on** 1 (*Informal*) = <u>understand</u>, see, find out, grasp, see through, comprehend, twig (*Brit. informal*), get the picture 2 = <u>become popular</u>, take off, become trendy, come into fashion

catching = <u>infectious</u>, contagious, transferable, communicable, transmittable ≠ non-infectious

category = <u>class</u>, grouping, heading, sort, department, type, division, section

cater
● PHRASES **cater for something** or **someone** 1 = <u>provide for</u>, supply, purvey 2 = <u>take into account</u>, consider, bear in mind, make allowance for, have regard for

cattle = <u>cows</u>, stock, beasts, livestock, bovines

▨▨▨ RELATED WORDS
adjective: bovine
collective nouns: drove, herd

cause NOUN 1 = <u>origin</u>, source, spring, agent, maker, producer, root, beginning ≠ result 2 = <u>reason</u>, call, need, grounds, basis, incentive, motive, motivation 3 = <u>aim</u>, movement, principle, ideal, enterprise
● VERB = <u>produce</u>, create, lead to, result in, generate, induce, bring about, give rise to ≠ prevent

caution NOUN 1 = <u>care</u>, discretion, heed, prudence, vigilance, alertness, forethought, circumspection ≠ carelessness 2 = <u>reprimand</u>, warning, injunction, admonition

● **VERB 1** = <u>warn</u>, urge, advise, alert, tip off, forewarn **2** = <u>reprimand</u>, warn, admonish, give an injunction to

cautious = <u>careful</u>, guarded, wary, tentative, prudent, judicious, circumspect, cagey (*informal*) ≠ careless

cavalry = <u>horsemen</u>, horse, mounted troops ≠ infantrymen

cave = <u>hollow</u>, cavern, grotto, den, cavity

cavity = <u>hollow</u>, hole, gap, pit, dent, crater

cease 1 = <u>stop</u>, end, finish, come to an end ≠ start **2** = <u>discontinue</u>, end, stop, finish, conclude, halt, terminate, break off ≠ begin

celebrate 1 = <u>rejoice</u>, party, enjoy yourself, carouse, live it up (*informal*), make merry, put the flags out, kill the fatted calf **2** = <u>commemorate</u>, honour, observe, toast, drink to, keep **3** = <u>perform</u>, observe, preside over, officiate at, solemnize

celebrated = <u>renowned</u>, popular, famous, distinguished, well-known, prominent, acclaimed, notable ≠ unknown

celebration 1 = <u>party</u>, festival, gala, jubilee, festivity, revelry, red-letter day, merrymaking **2** = <u>commemoration</u>, honouring, remembrance **3** = <u>performance</u>, observance, solemnization

celebrity 1 = <u>personality</u>, star, superstar, big name, dignitary, luminary, big shot (*informal*), V.I.P. ≠ nobody **2** = <u>fame</u>, reputation, distinction, prestige, prominence, stardom, renown, repute ≠ obscurity

cell 1 = <u>room</u>, chamber, lock-up, compartment, cavity, cubicle, dungeon, stall **2** = <u>unit</u>, group, section, core, nucleus, caucus, coterie

cement NOUN 1 = <u>mortar</u>, plaster, paste **2** = <u>sealant</u>, glue, gum, adhesive

● **VERB** = <u>stick</u>, join, bond, attach, seal, glue, plaster, weld

cemetery = <u>graveyard</u>, churchyard, burial ground, necropolis, God's acre

censor = <u>expurgate</u>, cut, blue-pencil, bowdlerize

censure VERB = <u>criticize</u>, blame, condemn, denounce, rebuke, reprimand, reproach, scold ≠ applaud

● **NOUN** = <u>disapproval</u>, criticism, blame, condemnation, rebuke, reprimand,

reproach, stick (*slang*) ≠ approval

central 1 = <u>inner</u>, middle, mid, interior ≠ outer **2** = <u>main</u>, chief, key, essential, primary, principal, fundamental, focal ≠ minor

centre NOUN = <u>middle</u>, heart, focus, core, nucleus, hub, pivot, kernel ≠ edge

● **VERB** = <u>focus</u>, concentrate, cluster, revolve, converge

ceremonial ADJECTIVE = <u>formal</u>, public, official, ritual, stately, solemn, liturgical, courtly ≠ informal

● **NOUN** = <u>ritual</u>, ceremony, rite, formality, solemnity

ceremony 1 = <u>ritual</u>, service, rite, observance, commemoration, solemnities **2** = <u>formality</u>, ceremonial, propriety, decorum

certain 1 = <u>sure</u>, convinced, positive, confident, satisfied, assured ≠ unsure **2** = <u>bound</u>, sure, fated, destined ≠ unlikely **3** = <u>inevitable</u>, unavoidable, inescapable **4** = <u>known</u>, true, positive, conclusive, unequivocal, undeniable, irrefutable, unquestionable ≠ doubtful **5** = <u>fixed</u>, decided, established, settled, definite ≠ indefinite

certainly = <u>definitely</u>, surely, truly, undoubtedly, without doubt, undeniably, indisputably, assuredly

certainty 1 = <u>confidence</u>, trust, faith, conviction, assurance, sureness, positiveness ≠ doubt **2** = <u>inevitability</u> ≠ uncertainty **3** = <u>fact</u>, truth, reality, sure thing (*informal*), banker

certificate = <u>document</u>, licence, warrant, voucher, diploma, testimonial, authorization, credential(s)

certify = <u>confirm</u>, declare, guarantee, assure, testify, verify, validate, attest

chain NOUN 1 = <u>tether</u>, coupling, link, bond, shackle, fetter, manacle **2** = <u>series</u>, set, train, string, sequence, succession, progression

● **VERB** = <u>bind</u>, confine, restrain, handcuff, shackle, tether, fetter, manacle

chairman *or* **chairwoman 1** = <u>director</u>, president, chief, executive, chairperson **2** = <u>master of ceremonies</u>, spokesman, chair, speaker, MC, chairperson

challenge NOUN 1 = <u>dare</u>, provocation, wero (*N.Z.*) **2** = <u>test</u>, trial, opposition, confrontation, ultimatum

● **VERB 1** = <u>dispute</u>, question, tackle,

confront, defy, object to, disagree with, take issue with **2** = **dare**, invite, defy, throw down the gauntlet **3** = **test 4** = **question**, interrogate

chamber 1 = **hall**, room **2** = **council**, assembly, legislature, legislative body **3** = **room**, bedroom, apartment, enclosure, cubicle **4** = **compartment**

champion NOUN 1 = **winner**, hero, victor, conqueror, title holder **2** = **defender**, guardian, patron, backer, protector, upholder

● **VERB** = **support**, back, defend, promote, advocate, fight for, uphold, espouse

chance NOUN 1 = **probability**, odds, possibility, prospect, likelihood ≠ certainty **2** = **opportunity**, opening, occasion, time **3** = **accident**, fortune, luck, fate, destiny, coincidence, providence ≠ design **4** = **risk**, speculation, gamble, hazard

● **VERB** = **risk**, try, stake, venture, gamble, hazard, wager

change NOUN 1 = **alteration**, innovation, transformation, modification, mutation, metamorphosis, difference, revolution **2** = **variety**, break (informal), departure, variation, novelty, diversion ≠ monotony **3** = **exchange**, trade, conversion, swap, substitution, interchange

● **VERB 1** = **alter**, reform, transform, adjust, revise, modify, reorganize, restyle ≠ keep **2** = **shift**, vary, transform, alter, modify, mutate ≠ stay **3** = **exchange**, trade, replace, substitute, swap, interchange

channel NOUN 1 = **means**, way, course, approach, medium, route, path, avenue **2** = **strait**, sound, route, passage, canal, waterway **3** = **duct**, artery, groove, gutter, furrow, conduit

● **VERB** = **direct**, guide, conduct, transmit, convey

chant NOUN = **song**, carol, chorus, melody, psalm

● **VERB** = **sing**, chorus, recite, intone, carol

chaos = **disorder**, confusion, mayhem, anarchy, lawlessness, pandemonium, bedlam, tumult ≠ orderliness

chaotic = **disordered**, confused, uncontrolled, anarchic, tumultuous, lawless, riotous, topsy-turvy

chap (Informal) = **fellow**, man, person, individual, character, guy (informal), bloke (Brit. informal)

chapter 1 = **section**, part, stage, division,

episode, topic, segment, instalment **2** = **period**, time, stage, phase

character 1 = **personality**, nature, attributes, temperament, complexion, disposition **2** = **nature**, kind, quality, calibre **3** = **reputation**, honour, integrity, good name, rectitude **4** = **role**, part, persona **5** = **eccentric**, card (informal), original, oddball (informal) **6** = **symbol**, mark, sign, letter, figure, device, rune, hieroglyph

characteristic NOUN = **feature**, mark, quality, property, attribute, faculty, trait, quirk

● **ADJECTIVE** = **typical**, special, individual, representative, distinguishing, distinctive, peculiar, singular ≠ rare

characterize = **distinguish**, mark, identify, brand, stamp, typify

charge VERB 1 = **accuse**, indict, impeach, incriminate, arraign ≠ acquit **2** = **attack**, assault, assail ≠ retreat **3** = **rush**, storm, stampede **4** = **fill**, load

● **NOUN 1** = **price**, rate, cost, amount, payment, expense, toll, expenditure **2** = **accusation**, allegation, indictment, imputation ≠ acquittal **3** = **care**, trust, responsibility, custody, safekeeping **4** = **duty**, office, responsibility, remit **5** = **ward**, pupil, protégé, dependant **6** = **attack**, rush, assault, onset, onslaught, stampede, sortie ≠ retreat

charisma = **charm**, appeal, personality, attraction, lure, allure, magnetism, force of personality

charismatic = **charming**, appealing, attractive, influential, magnetic, enticing, alluring

charitable 1 = **benevolent**, liberal, generous, lavish, philanthropic, bountiful, beneficent ≠ mean **2** = **kind**, understanding, forgiving, sympathetic, favourable, tolerant, indulgent, lenient ≠ unkind

charity 1 = **charitable organization**, fund, movement, trust, endowment **2** = **donations**, help, relief, gift, contributions, assistance, hand-out, philanthropy, koha (N.Z.) ≠ meanness **3** = **kindness**, humanity, goodwill, compassion, generosity, indulgence, altruism, benevolence, aroha (N.Z.) ≠ ill will

charm NOUN 1 = **attraction**, appeal,

fascination, allure, magnetism
≠ repulsiveness 2 = <u>talisman</u>, trinket, amulet, fetish 3 = <u>spell</u>, magic, enchantment, sorcery, makutu (*N.Z.*)
● VERB 1 = <u>attract</u>, delight, fascinate, entrance, win over, enchant, captivate, beguile ≠ repel 2 = <u>persuade</u>, seduce, coax, beguile, sweet-talk (*informal*)

charming = <u>attractive</u>, pleasing, appealing, fetching, delightful, cute, seductive, captivating ≠ unpleasant

chart NOUN = <u>table</u>, diagram, blueprint, graph, plan, map
● VERB 1 = <u>plot</u>, map out, delineate, sketch, draft, tabulate 2 = <u>monitor</u>, follow, record, note, document, register, trace, outline

charter NOUN 1 = <u>document</u>, contract, permit, licence, deed, prerogative 2 = <u>constitution</u>, laws, rules, code
● VERB 1 = <u>hire</u>, commission, employ, rent, lease 2 = <u>authorize</u>, permit, sanction, entitle, license, empower, give authority

chase VERB 1 = <u>pursue</u>, follow, track, hunt, run after, course 2 = <u>drive away</u>, drive, expel, hound, send away, send packing, put to flight 3 = <u>rush</u>, run, race, shoot, fly, speed, dash, bolt
● NOUN = <u>pursuit</u>, race, hunt, hunting

chat VERB = <u>talk</u>, gossip, jaw (*slang*), natter, blather, blether (*Scot.*)
● NOUN = <u>talk</u>, tête-à-tête, conversation, gossip, heart-to-heart, natter, blather, blether (*Scot.*), korero (*N.Z.*)

chatter VERB = <u>prattle</u>, chat, rabbit on (*Brit. informal*), babble, gab (*informal*), natter, blather, schmooze (*slang*)
● NOUN = <u>prattle</u>, chat, gossip, babble, gab (*informal*), natter, blather, blether (*Scot.*)

cheap 1 = <u>inexpensive</u>, reduced, keen, reasonable, bargain, low-priced, low-cost, cut-price ≠ expensive 2 = <u>inferior</u>, poor, worthless, second-rate, shoddy, tawdry, tatty, trashy, bodger *or* bodgie (*Austral. slang*) ≠ good 3 (*Informal*) = <u>despicable</u>, mean, contemptible, scungy (*Austral. & N.Z.*) ≠ decent

cheat VERB = <u>deceive</u>, trick, fool, con (*informal*), mislead, rip off (*slang*), fleece, defraud
● NOUN = <u>deceiver</u>, sharper, shark, charlatan, trickster, con man (*informal*), double-crosser (*informal*), swindler, rorter (*Austral. slang*)

check VERB 1 *often with* **out** = <u>examine</u>, test, study, look at, research, investigate, monitor, vet ≠ overlook 2 = <u>stop</u>, limit, delay, halt, restrain, inhibit, hinder, obstruct ≠ further
● NOUN 1 = <u>examination</u>, test, research, investigation, inspection, scrutiny, once-over (*informal*) 2 = <u>control</u>, limitation, restraint, constraint, obstacle, curb, obstruction, stoppage

cheek (*Informal*) = <u>impudence</u>, nerve, disrespect, audacity, lip (*slang*), temerity, chutzpah (*U.S. & Canad. informal*), insolence

cheeky = <u>impudent</u>, rude, forward, insulting, saucy, audacious, pert, disrespectful ≠ respectful

cheer VERB 1 = <u>applaud</u>, hail, acclaim, clap ≠ boo 2 = <u>hearten</u>, encourage, comfort, uplift, brighten, cheer up, buoy up, gladden ≠ dishearten
● NOUN = <u>applause</u>, ovation, plaudits, acclamation
● PHRASES **cheer someone up** = <u>comfort</u>, encourage, hearten, enliven, gladden, gee up, jolly along (*informal*)
◆ **cheer up** = <u>take heart</u>, rally, perk up, buck up (*informal*)

cheerful 1 = <u>happy</u>, optimistic, enthusiastic, jolly, merry, upbeat (*informal*), buoyant, cheery ≠ sad 2 = <u>pleasant</u> ≠ gloomy

chemical = <u>compound</u>, drug, substance, synthetic substance, potion

chemist = <u>pharmacist</u>, apothecary (*obsolete*), dispenser

cherish 1 = <u>cling to</u>, prize, treasure, hold dear, cleave to ≠ despise 2 = <u>care for</u>, love, support, comfort, look after, shelter, nurture, hold dear ≠ neglect 3 = <u>harbour</u>, nurse, sustain, foster, entertain

chest 1 = <u>breast</u>, front 2 = <u>box</u>, case, trunk, crate, coffer, casket, strongbox
▬ RELATED WORD
adjective: pectoral

chew = <u>munch</u>, bite, grind, champ, crunch, gnaw, chomp, masticate

chic = <u>stylish</u>, smart, elegant, fashionable, trendy (*Brit. informal*) ≠ unfashionable

chief NOUN = <u>head</u>, leader, director, manager, boss (*informal*), captain, master, governor, baas (*S. African*), ariki (*N.Z.*) ≠ subordinate
● ADJECTIVE = <u>primary</u>, highest, leading, main, prime, key, premier, supreme

≠ minor

chiefly 1 = <u>especially</u>, essentially, principally, primarily, above all 2 = <u>mainly</u>, largely, usually, mostly, in general, on the whole, predominantly, in the main

child 1 = <u>youngster</u>, baby, kid (*informal*), infant, babe, juvenile, toddler, tot, littlie (*Austral. informal*), ankle-biter (*Austral. slang*), tacker (*Austral. slang*) 2 = <u>offspring</u>

▨▨ RELATED WORDS
adjective: filial
prefix: paedo-

childbirth = <u>child-bearing</u>, labour, delivery, lying-in, confinement, parturition

childhood = <u>youth</u>, minority, infancy, schooldays, immaturity, boyhood *or* girlhood

childish 1 = <u>youthful</u>, young, boyish *or* girlish 2 = <u>immature</u>, juvenile, foolish, infantile, puerile ≠ mature

chill VERB 1 = <u>cool</u>, refrigerate, freeze 2 = <u>dishearten</u>, depress, discourage, dismay, dampen, deject
● NOUN 1 = <u>coldness</u>, bite, nip, sharpness, coolness, rawness, crispness, frigidity 2 = <u>shiver</u>, frisson
● ADJECTIVE = <u>chilly</u>, biting, sharp, freezing, raw, bleak, chilly, wintry

chilly 1 = <u>cool</u>, fresh, sharp, crisp, penetrating, brisk, draughty, nippy ≠ warm 2 = <u>unfriendly</u>, hostile, unsympathetic, frigid, unresponsive, unwelcoming ≠ friendly

china¹ = <u>pottery</u>, ceramics, ware, porcelain, crockery, tableware, service

china² (*Brit. & S. African informal*) = <u>friend</u>, pal, mate (*informal*), buddy (*informal*), companion, best friend, intimate, comrade, cobber (*Austral. & N.Z. old-fashioned informal*), E hoa (*N.Z.*)

chip NOUN 1 = <u>fragment</u>, shaving, wafer, sliver, shard 2 = <u>scratch</u>, nick, notch 3 = <u>counter</u>, disc, token
● VERB 1 = <u>nick</u>, damage, gash 2 = <u>chisel</u>, whittle

choice NOUN 1 = <u>range</u>, variety, selection, assortment 2 = <u>selection</u>, preference, pick 3 = <u>option</u>, say, alternative
● ADJECTIVE = <u>best</u>, prime, select, excellent, exclusive, elite, booshit (*Austral. slang*), exo (*Austral. slang*), sik (*Austral. slang*)

choke 1 = <u>suffocate</u>, stifle, smother, overpower, asphyxiate 2 = <u>strangle</u>, throttle, asphyxiate 3 = <u>block</u>, clog,

obstruct, bung, constrict, congest, stop, bar

choose 1 = <u>pick</u>, prefer, select, elect, adopt, opt for, designate, settle upon ≠ reject 2 = <u>wish</u>, want

chop = <u>cut</u>, fell, hack, sever, cleave, hew, lop

chore = <u>task</u>, job, duty, burden, hassle (*informal*), errand

chorus NOUN 1 = <u>refrain</u>, response, strain, burden 2 = <u>choir</u>, singers, ensemble, vocalists, choristers
● PHRASES **in chorus** = <u>in unison</u>, as one, all together, in concert, in harmony, in accord, with one voice

christen 1 = <u>baptize</u>, name 2 = <u>name</u>, call, term, style, title, dub, designate

Christmas = <u>festive season</u>, Noël, Xmas (*informal*), Yule (*archaic*), Yuletide (*archaic*)

chronicle VERB = <u>record</u>, tell, report, enter, relate, register, recount, set down
● NOUN = <u>record</u>, story, history, account, register, journal, diary, narrative

chuck (*Informal*) 1 = <u>throw</u>, cast, pitch, toss, hurl, fling, sling, heave 2 often with *away* or *out* = <u>throw out</u>, dump (*informal*), scrap, get rid of, ditch (*slang*), dispose of, dispense with, jettison 3 = <u>give up</u> *or* <u>over</u>, leave, abandon, cease, resign from, pack in 4 (*Austral. & N.Z. informal*) = <u>vomit</u>, throw up (*informal*), spew, heave (*slang*), puke (*slang*), barf (*U.S. slang*), chunder (*slang, chiefly Austral.*)

chuckle = <u>laugh</u>, giggle, snigger, chortle, titter

chum (*Informal*) = <u>friend</u>, mate (*informal*), pal (*informal*), companion, comrade, crony, cobber (*Austral. & N.Z. old-fashioned informal*), E hoa (*N.Z.*)

chunk = <u>piece</u>, block, mass, portion, lump, slab, hunk, nugget

churn 1 = <u>stir up</u>, beat, disturb, swirl, agitate 2 = <u>swirl</u>, toss

cinema 1 = <u>pictures</u>, movies, picture-house, flicks (*slang*) 2 = <u>films</u>, pictures, movies, big screen (*informal*), motion pictures, silver screen

circle NOUN 1 = <u>ring</u>, disc, hoop, halo 2 = <u>group</u>, company, set, club, society, clique, coterie
● VERB 1 = <u>go round</u>, ring, surround, enclose, envelop, encircle, circumscribe, circumnavigate 2 = <u>wheel</u>, spiral

circuit 1 = <u>course</u>, tour, track, route,

journey 2 = racetrack, course, track, racecourse 3 = lap, tour, revolution, orbit

circular ADJECTIVE 1 = round, ring-shaped 2 = circuitous, cyclical, orbital

● NOUN = advertisement, notice, ad (*informal*), announcement, advert (*Brit. informal*), press release

circulate 1 = spread, issue, publish, broadcast, distribute, publicize, disseminate, promulgate 2 = flow, revolve, rotate, radiate

circulation 1 = distribution, currency, readership 2 = bloodstream, blood flow 3 = flow, circling, motion, rotation 4 = spread, distribution, transmission, dissemination

circumstance 1 *usually plural* = situation, condition, contingency, state of affairs, lie of the land 2 *usually plural* = detail, event, particular, respect 3 *usually plural* = situation, state, means, position, station, status 4 = chance, the times, accident, fortune, luck, fate, destiny, providence

cite = quote, name, advance, mention, extract, specify, allude to, enumerate

citizen = inhabitant, resident, dweller, denizen, subject, townsman

▋ RELATED WORD
adjective: civil

city = town, metropolis, municipality, conurbation

▋ RELATED WORD
adjective: civic

civic = public, municipal, communal, local

civil 1 = civic, political, domestic, municipal ≠ state 2 = polite, obliging, courteous, considerate, affable, well-mannered ≠ rude

civilization 1 = society, people, community, nation, polity 2 = culture, development, education, progress, enlightenment, sophistication, advancement, cultivation

civilize = cultivate, educate, refine, tame, enlighten, sophisticate

civilized 1 = cultured, educated, sophisticated, enlightened, humane ≠ primitive 2 = polite, mannerly, tolerant, gracious, courteous, well-behaved, well-mannered

claim VERB 1 = assert, insist, maintain, allege, uphold, profess 2 = demand, call for, ask for, insist on

● NOUN 1 = assertion, statement, allegation, declaration, pretension, affirmation, protestation 2 = demand, application, request, petition, call 3 = right, title, entitlement

clamour = noise, shouting, racket, outcry, din, uproar, commotion, hubbub

clamp NOUN = vice, press, grip, bracket, fastener

● VERB = fasten, fix, secure, brace, make fast

clan 1 = family, group, society, tribe, fraternity, brotherhood, ainga (*N.Z.*), ngai (*N.Z.*) 2 = group, set, circle, gang, faction, coterie, cabal

clap = applaud, cheer, acclaim ≠ boo

clarify = explain, interpret, illuminate, clear up, simplify, make plain, elucidate, throw *or* shed light on

clarity 1 = clearness, precision, simplicity, transparency, lucidity, straightforwardness ≠ obscurity 2 = transparency, clearness ≠ cloudiness

clash VERB 1 = conflict, grapple, wrangle, lock horns, cross swords, war, feud, quarrel 2 = disagree, conflict, vary, counter, differ, contradict, diverge, run counter to 3 = not go, jar, not match 4 = crash, bang, rattle, jar, clatter, jangle, clang, clank

● NOUN 1 = conflict, fight, brush, confrontation, collision, showdown (*informal*) 2 = disagreement, difference, argument, dispute, dissent, difference of opinion

clasp VERB = grasp, hold, press, grip, seize, squeeze, embrace, clutch

● NOUN 1 = grasp, hold, grip, embrace, hug 2 = fastening, catch, grip, hook, pin, clip, buckle, brooch

class NOUN 1 = group, set, division, rank 2 = type, set, sort, kind, category, genre

● VERB = classify, group, rate, rank, brand, label, grade, designate

classic ADJECTIVE 1 = typical, standard, model, regular, usual, ideal, characteristic, definitive, dinki-di (*Austral. informal*) 2 = masterly, best, finest, world-class, consummate, first-rate ≠ second-rate 3 = lasting, enduring, abiding, immortal, undying, ageless, deathless

● NOUN = standard, masterpiece, prototype, paradigm, exemplar, model

classification = categorization, grading, taxonomy, sorting, analysis, arrangement

classify = categorize, sort, rank, arrange,

grade, catalogue, pigeonhole, tabulate

classy (*Informal*) = high-class, exclusive, superior, elegant, stylish, posh (*informal, chiefly Brit.*), up-market, top-drawer

clause = section, condition, article, chapter, passage, part, paragraph

claw NOUN 1 = nail, talon 2 = pincer

● VERB = scratch, tear, dig, rip, scrape, maul, mangulate (*Austral. slang*), lacerate

clean ADJECTIVE 1 = hygienic, fresh, sterile, pure, purified, antiseptic, sterilized, uncontaminated ≠ contaminated 2 = spotless, fresh, immaculate, impeccable, flawless, unblemished, unsullied ≠ dirty 3 = moral, good, pure, decent, innocent, respectable, upright, honourable ≠ immoral 4 = complete, final, whole, total, perfect, entire, decisive, thorough

● VERB = cleanse, wash, scrub, rinse, launder, scour, purify, disinfect ≠ dirty

cleanse = purify, clear, purge 1 = absolve, clear, purge, purify 2 = clean, wash, scrub, rinse, scour

clear ADJECTIVE 1 = comprehensible, explicit, understandable ≠ confused 2 = distinct ≠ indistinct 3 = obvious, plain, apparent, evident, distinct, pronounced, manifest, blatant ≠ ambiguous 4 = certain, sure, convinced, positive, satisfied, resolved, definite, decided ≠ confused 5 = transparent, see-through, translucent, crystalline, glassy, limpid, pellucid ≠ opaque 6 = unobstructed, open, free, empty, unhindered, unimpeded ≠ blocked 7 = bright, fine, fair, shining, sunny, luminous, cloudless, light ≠ cloudy 8 = untroubled, clean, pure, innocent, immaculate, unblemished, untarnished

● VERB 1 = unblock, free, loosen, extricate, open, disentangle 2 = remove, clean, wipe, cleanse, tidy (up), sweep away 3 = brighten, break up, lighten 4 = pass over, jump, leap, vault, miss 5 = absolve, acquit, vindicate, exonerate ≠ blame

clear-cut = straightforward, specific, plain, precise, black-and-white, explicit, definite, unequivocal

clearly 1 = obviously, undoubtedly, evidently, distinctly, markedly, overtly, undeniably, beyond doubt 2 = legibly, distinctly 3 = audibly, distinctly, intelligibly, comprehensibly

clergy = priesthood, ministry, clerics, clergymen, churchmen, the cloth, holy orders

clever 1 = intelligent, bright, talented, gifted, smart, knowledgeable, quick-witted ≠ stupid 2 = shrewd, bright, ingenious, resourceful, canny ≠ unimaginative 3 = skilful, talented, gifted ≠ inept

cliché = platitude, stereotype, commonplace, banality, truism, hackneyed phrase

client = customer, consumer, buyer, patron, shopper, patient

cliff = rock face, overhang, crag, precipice, escarpment, scar, bluff

climate = weather, temperature

climax = culmination, top, summit, height, highlight, peak, high point, zenith

climb VERB 1 = ascend, scale, mount, go up, clamber, shin up 2 = clamber, descend, scramble, dismount 3 = rise, go up, soar, ascend, fly up

● PHRASES **climb down** = back down, withdraw, yield, concede, retreat, surrender, give in, cave in (*informal*)

clinch 1 = secure, close, confirm, conclude, seal, sew up (*informal*), set the seal on 2 = settle, decide, determine

cling 1 = clutch, grip, embrace, grasp, hug, hold on to, clasp 2 = stick to, adhere to

clinical = unemotional, cold, scientific, objective, detached, analytic, impersonal, dispassionate

clip¹ VERB 1 = trim, cut, crop, prune, shorten, shear, snip, pare 2 (*Informal*) = smack, strike, knock, punch, thump, clout (*informal*), cuff, whack

● NOUN (*Informal*) = smack, strike, knock, punch, thump, clout (*informal*), cuff, whack

clip² = attach, fix, secure, connect, pin, staple, fasten, hold

cloak NOUN 1 = cape, coat, wrap, mantle 2 = covering, layer, blanket, shroud

● VERB 1 = cover, coat, wrap, blanket, shroud, envelop 2 = hide, cover, screen, mask, disguise, conceal, obscure, veil

clog = obstruct, block, jam, hinder, impede, congest

close¹ VERB 1 = shut, lock, fasten, secure ≠ open 2 = shut down, finish, cease 3 = wind up, finish, shut down, terminate 4 = block up, bar, seal ≠ open 5 = end, finish, complete, conclude, wind up, terminate ≠ begin **6** = <u>clinch</u>, confirm, secure, conclude, seal, sew up (*informal*), set the seal on **7** = <u>come together</u>, join, connect ≠ separate

● NOUN = <u>end</u>, ending, finish, conclusion, completion, finale, culmination, denouement

close² **1** = <u>near</u>, neighbouring, nearby, handy, adjacent, adjoining, cheek by jowl ≠ far **2** = <u>intimate</u>, loving, familiar, thick (*informal*), attached, devoted, confidential, inseparable ≠ distant **3** = <u>noticeable</u>, marked, strong, distinct, pronounced **4** = <u>careful</u>, detailed, intense, minute, thorough, rigorous, painstaking **5** = <u>even</u>, level, neck and neck, fifty-fifty (*informal*), evenly matched **6** = <u>imminent</u>, near, impending, at hand, nigh ≠ far away **7** = <u>stifling</u>, oppressive, suffocating, stuffy, humid, sweltering, airless, muggy ≠ airy

closed **1** = <u>shut</u>, locked, sealed, fastened ≠ open **2** = <u>shut down</u>, out of service **3** = <u>exclusive</u>, select, restricted **4** = <u>finished</u>, over, ended, decided, settled, concluded, resolved, terminated

cloth = <u>fabric</u>, material, textiles

clothe = <u>dress</u>, array, robe, drape, swathe, attire, fit out, garb ≠ undress

clothes = <u>clothing</u>, wear, dress, gear (*informal*), outfit, costume, wardrobe, garments

clothing = <u>clothes</u>, wear, dress, gear (*informal*), outfit, costume, wardrobe, garments

cloud NOUN = <u>mist</u>, haze, vapour, murk, gloom

● VERB **1** = <u>confuse</u>, distort, impair, muddle, disorient **2** = <u>darken</u>, dim, be overshadowed

clout (*Informal*) VERB = <u>hit</u>, strike, punch, slap, sock (*slang*), smack, thump, clobber (*slang*)

● NOUN **1** = <u>thump</u>, blow, punch, slap, sock (*slang*), wallop (*informal*) **2** = <u>influence</u>, power, authority, pull, weight, prestige, mana (*N.Z.*)

clown NOUN **1** = <u>comedian</u>, fool, comic, harlequin, joker, jester, prankster, buffoon **2** = <u>fool</u>, idiot, twit (*informal*, *chiefly Brit.*), imbecile (*informal*), ignoramus, dolt, blockhead, dorba *or* dorb (*Austral. slang*), bogan (*Austral. slang*)

● VERB *usually with* **around** = <u>play the fool</u>, mess about, jest, act the fool

club NOUN **1** = <u>association</u>, company, group, union, society, lodge, guild, fraternity **2** = <u>stick</u>, bat, bludgeon, truncheon, cosh (*Brit.*), cudgel

● VERB = <u>beat</u>, strike, hammer, batter, bash, bludgeon, pummel, cosh (*Brit.*)

clue = <u>indication</u>, lead, sign, evidence, suggestion, trace, hint, suspicion

clump NOUN = <u>cluster</u>, group, bunch, bundle

● VERB = <u>stomp</u>, thump, lumber, tramp, plod, thud

clumsy = <u>awkward</u>, lumbering, bumbling, ponderous, ungainly, gauche, gawky, uncoordinated, unco (*Austral. slang*) ≠ skilful

cluster NOUN = <u>gathering</u>, group, collection, bunch, knot, clump, assemblage

● VERB = <u>gather</u>, group, collect, bunch, assemble, flock, huddle

clutch VERB **1** = <u>hold</u>, grip, embrace, grasp, cling to, clasp **2** = <u>seize</u>, catch, grab, grasp, snatch

● PLURAL NOUN = <u>power</u>, hands, control, grip, possession, grasp, custody, sway

clutter NOUN = <u>untidiness</u>, mess, disorder, confusion, litter, muddle, disarray, jumble ≠ order

● VERB = <u>litter</u>, scatter, strew, mess up ≠ tidy

coach NOUN **1** = <u>instructor</u>, teacher, trainer, tutor, handler **2** = <u>bus</u>, charabanc

● VERB = <u>instruct</u>, train, prepare, exercise, drill, tutor

coalition = <u>alliance</u>, union, association, combination, merger, conjunction, bloc, confederation

coarse **1** = <u>rough</u>, crude, unfinished, homespun, impure, unrefined, unprocessed, unpolished ≠ smooth **2** = <u>vulgar</u>, rude, indecent, improper, earthy, smutty, ribald, indelicate

coast NOUN = <u>shore</u>, border, beach, seaside, coastline, seaboard

● VERB = <u>cruise</u>, sail, drift, taxi, glide, freewheel

coat NOUN **1** = <u>fur</u>, hair, skin, hide, wool, fleece, pelt **2** = <u>layer</u>, covering, coating, overlay

● VERB = <u>cover</u>, spread, plaster, smear

coax = <u>persuade</u>, cajole, talk into, wheedle, sweet-talk (*informal*), prevail upon, entice, allure ≠ bully

cobber (*Austral. & N.Z. old-fashioned informal*) = friend, pal, mate (*informal*), buddy (*informal*), china (*Brit. & S. African informal*), best friend, intimate, comrade, E hoa (*N.Z.*)

cocktail = mixture, combination, compound, blend, mix

cocky or **cockie** (*Austral. & N.Z. informal*) = farmer, smallholder, crofter (*Scot.*), grazier, agriculturalist, rancher

code 1 = principles, rules, manners, custom, convention, ethics, maxim, etiquette, kawa (*N.Z.*), tikanga (*N.Z.*) 2 = cipher, cryptograph

coherent 1 = consistent, reasoned, organized, rational, logical, meaningful, systematic, orderly ≠ inconsistent 2 = articulate, lucid, comprehensible, intelligible ≠ unintelligible

coil 1 = wind, twist, curl, loop, spiral, twine 2 = curl, wind, twist, snake, loop, twine, wreathe

coin NOUN = money, change, cash, silver, copper, specie
● VERB = invent, create, make up, forge, originate, fabricate

coincide 1 = occur simultaneously, coexist, synchronize, be concurrent 2 = agree, match, accord, square, correspond, tally, concur, harmonize ≠ disagree

coincidence = chance, accident, luck, fluke, stroke of luck, happy accident

cold ADJECTIVE 1 = chilly, freezing, bleak, arctic, icy, frosty, wintry, frigid ≠ hot 2 = distant, reserved, indifferent, aloof, frigid, undemonstrative, standoffish ≠ emotional 3 = unfriendly, indifferent, frigid ≠ friendly
● NOUN = coldness, chill, frigidity, frostiness, iciness

collaborate 1 = work together, team up, join forces, cooperate, play ball (*informal*), participate 2 = conspire, cooperate, collude, fraternize

collaboration 1 = teamwork, partnership, cooperation, association, alliance 2 = conspiring, cooperation, collusion, fraternization

collaborator 1 = co-worker, partner, colleague, associate, team-mate, confederate 2 = traitor, turncoat, quisling, fraternizer

collapse VERB 1 = fall down, fall, give way, subside, cave in, crumple, fall apart at the seams 2 = fail, fold, founder, break down, fall through, come to nothing, go belly-up (*informal*)
● NOUN 1 = falling down, ruin, falling apart, cave-in, disintegration, subsidence 2 = failure, slump, breakdown, flop, downfall 3 = faint, breakdown, blackout, prostration

collar (*Informal*) = seize, catch, arrest, grab, capture, nail (*informal*), nab (*informal*), apprehend

colleague = fellow worker, partner, ally, associate, assistant, team-mate, comrade, helper

collect 1 = gather, save, assemble, heap, accumulate, amass, stockpile, hoard ≠ scatter 2 = assemble, meet, rally, cluster, come together, convene, converge, congregate ≠ disperse

collected = calm, cool, composed, poised, serene, unperturbed, unruffled, self-possessed ≠ nervous

collection 1 = accumulation, set, store, mass, pile, heap, stockpile, hoard 2 = compilation, accumulation, anthology 3 = group, company, crowd, assembly, cluster, assortment 4 = gathering 5 = contribution, donation, alms 6 = offering, offertory

collective 1 = joint, united, shared, combined, corporate, unified ≠ individual 2 = combined, aggregate, composite, cumulative ≠ separate

collide 1 = crash, clash, meet head-on, come into collision 2 = conflict, clash, be incompatible, be at variance

collision 1 = crash, impact, accident, smash, bump, pile-up (*informal*), prang (*informal*) 2 = conflict, opposition, clash, encounter, disagreement, incompatibility

colony = settlement, territory, province, possession, dependency, outpost, dominion, satellite state

colour or (*U.S.*) **color** NOUN 1 = hue, tone, shade, tint, colourway 2 = paint, stain, dye, tint, pigment, colorant
● VERB = blush, flush, redden

colourful 1 = bright, brilliant, psychedelic, variegated, multicoloured ≠ drab 2 = interesting, rich, graphic, lively, distinctive, vivid, picturesque ≠ boring

column 1 = <u>pillar</u>, support, post, shaft, upright, obelisk 2 = <u>line</u>, row, file, rank, procession, cavalcade

coma = <u>unconsciousness</u>, trance, oblivion, stupor

comb 1 = <u>untangle</u>, arrange, groom, dress 2 = <u>search</u>, hunt through, rake, sift, scour, rummage, ransack, forage, fossick (*Austral. & N.Z.*)

combat NOUN = <u>fight</u>, war, action, battle, conflict, engagement, warfare, skirmish ≠ peace
● VERB = <u>fight</u>, oppose, resist, defy, withstand, do battle with ≠ support

combination 1 = <u>mixture</u>, mix, blend, composite, amalgamation, coalescence 2 = <u>association</u>, union, alliance, coalition, federation, consortium, syndicate, confederation

combine 1 = <u>amalgamate</u>, mix, blend, integrate, merge ≠ <u>join together</u>, link, connect, integrate, merge, amalgamate 3 = <u>unite</u>, associate, team up, get together, collaborate, join forces, join together, pool resources ≠ split up

come VERB 1 = <u>approach</u>, near, advance, move towards, draw near 2 = <u>arrive</u>, turn up (*informal*), show up (*informal*) 3 = <u>reach</u>, extend, come up to, come as far as 4 = <u>happen</u>, fall, occur, take place, come about, come to pass 5 = <u>be available</u>, be made, be offered, be produced, be on offer
● PHRASES **come across as something** *or* **someone** = <u>seem</u>, look, seem to be, appear to be, give the impression of being ♦ **come across someone** = <u>meet</u>, encounter, run into, bump into (*informal*) ♦ **come across something** = <u>find</u>, discover, notice, unearth, stumble upon, chance upon = <u>be obtained</u>, be from, issue, emerge, flow, arise, originate, emanate

comeback 1 (*Informal*) = <u>return</u>, revival, rebound, resurgence, rally, recovery, triumph 2 = <u>response</u>, reply, retort, retaliation, riposte, rejoinder

comedian = <u>comic</u>, wit, clown, funny man, humorist, wag, joker, jester, dag (*N.Z. informal*)

comedy 1 = <u>light entertainment</u> ≠ tragedy, soapie (*Austral. slang*) 2 = <u>humour</u>, fun, joking, farce, jesting, hilarity ≠ seriousness

comfort NOUN 1 = <u>ease</u>, luxury, wellbeing, opulence 2 = <u>consolation</u>, succour, help, support, relief, compensation ≠ annoyance
● VERB = <u>console</u>, reassure, soothe, hearten, commiserate with ≠ distress

comfortable 1 = <u>pleasant</u>, homely, relaxing, cosy, agreeable, restful ≠ unpleasant 2 = <u>at ease</u>, happy, at home, contented, relaxed, serene ≠ uncomfortable 3 (*Informal*) = <u>well-off</u>, prosperous, affluent, well-to-do, comfortably-off, in clover (*informal*)

comforting = <u>consoling</u>, encouraging, cheering, reassuring, soothing, heart-warming ≠ upsetting

comic ADJECTIVE = <u>funny</u>, amusing, witty, humorous, farcical, comical, droll, jocular ≠ sad
● NOUN = <u>comedian</u>, funny man, humorist, wit, clown, wag, jester, dag (*N.Z. informal*), buffoon

coming ADJECTIVE = <u>approaching</u>, near, forthcoming, imminent, in store, impending, at hand, nigh
● NOUN = <u>arrival</u>, approach, advent

command VERB 1 = <u>order</u>, tell, charge, demand, require, direct, bid, compel ≠ beg 2 = <u>have authority over</u>, lead, head, control, rule, manage, handle, dominate ≠ be subordinate to
● NOUN 1 = <u>order</u>, demand, instruction, requirement, decree, directive, ultimatum, commandment 2 = <u>domination</u>, control, rule, mastery, power, government 3 = <u>management</u>, power, control, charge, authority, supervision

commander = <u>leader</u>, chief, officer, boss, head, captain, bass (*S. African*), ruler

commanding = <u>dominant</u>, controlling, dominating, superior, decisive, advantageous

commemorate = <u>celebrate</u>, remember, honour, recognize, salute, pay tribute to, immortalize ≠ ignore

commence 1 = <u>embark on</u>, start, open, begin, initiate, originate, instigate, enter upon ≠ stop 2 = <u>start</u>, open, begin, go ahead ≠ end

commend 1 = <u>praise</u>, acclaim, applaud, compliment, extol, approve, speak highly of ≠ criticize 2 = <u>recommend</u>, suggest, approve, advocate, endorse

comment VERB 1 = <u>remark</u>, say, note,

mention, point out, observe, utter
2 *usually with* **on** = <u>remark on</u>, explain,
talk about, discuss, speak about, say
something about, allude to, elucidate
● NOUN 1 = <u>remark</u>, statement, observation
2 = <u>note</u>, explanation, illustration,
commentary, exposition, annotation,
elucidation

commentary 1 = <u>narration</u>, report,
review, explanation, description, voice-
over 2 = <u>analysis</u>, notes, review, critique,
treatise

commentator 1 = <u>reporter</u>, special
correspondent, sportscaster 2 = <u>critic</u>,
interpreter, annotator

commercial 1 = <u>mercantile</u>, trading
2 = <u>materialistic</u>, mercenary, profit-making

commission VERB = <u>appoint</u>, order,
contract, select, engage, delegate,
nominate, authorize
● NOUN 1 = <u>duty</u>, task, mission, mandate,
errand 2 = <u>fee</u>, cut, percentage, royalties,
rake-off (*slang*) 3 = <u>committee</u>, board,
representatives, commissioners,
delegation, deputation

commit 1 = <u>do</u>, perform, carry out,
execute, enact, perpetrate 2 = <u>put in</u>
<u>custody</u>, confine, imprison ≠ release

commitment 1 = <u>dedication</u>, loyalty,
devotion
≠ indecisiveness 2 = <u>responsibility</u>, tie,
duty, obligation, liability, engagement

common 1 = <u>usual</u>, standard, regular,
ordinary, familiar, conventional, routine,
frequent ≠ rare 2 = <u>popular</u>, general,
accepted, standard, routine, widespread,
universal, prevailing 3 = <u>shared</u>, collective
4 = <u>ordinary</u>, average, typical, dinki-di
(*Austral. informal*) ≠ important 5 = <u>vulgar</u>,
inferior, coarse, plebeian ≠ refined
6 = <u>collective</u>, public,
community, social, communal ≠ personal

commonplace ADJECTIVE = <u>everyday</u>,
common, ordinary, widespread, mundane,
banal, run-of-the-mill, humdrum ≠ rare
● NOUN = <u>cliché</u>, platitude, banality, truism

common sense = <u>good sense</u>, sound
judgment, level-headedness, prudence,
gumption (*Brit. informal*), horse sense,
native intelligence, wit

communal = <u>public</u>, shared, general,
joint, collective
≠ private

commune = <u>community</u>, collective,

cooperative, kibbutz

communicate 1 = <u>contact</u>, talk, speak,
make contact, get in contact 2 = <u>make</u>
<u>known</u>, declare, disclose, pass on,
proclaim, transmit, convey, impart ≠ keep
secret 3 = <u>pass on</u>, transfer, spread,
transmit

communication 1 = <u>contact</u>,
conversation, correspondence, link,
relations 2 = <u>passing on</u>, circulation,
transmission, disclosure, imparting,
dissemination, conveyance 3 = <u>message</u>,
news, report, word, information,
statement, announcement, disclosure

communism *usually cap.* = <u>socialism</u>,
Marxism, collectivism, Bolshevism, state
socialism

communist *often cap.* = <u>socialist</u>, Red
(*informal*), Marxist, Bolshevik, collectivist

community = <u>society</u>, people, public,
residents,
commonwealth, general public, populace,
state

commuter = <u>daily traveller</u>, passenger,
suburbanite

compact[1] ADJECTIVE 1 = <u>closely packed</u>,
solid, thick, dense, compressed,
condensed, pressed together ≠ loose
2 = <u>concise</u>, brief, to the point, succinct,
terse ≠ lengthy
● VERB = <u>pack closely</u>, stuff, cram,
compress, condense, tamp ≠ loosen

compact[2] = <u>agreement</u>, deal,
understanding, contract,
bond, arrangement, treaty, bargain

companion 1 = <u>friend</u>, partner, ally,
colleague, associate, mate (*informal*),
comrade, accomplice, cobber (*Austral. &
N.Z. old-fashioned informal*) 2 = <u>assistant</u>,
aide, escort, attendant

company 1 = <u>business</u>, firm, association,
corporation, partnership, establishment,
syndicate, house 2 = <u>group</u>, set,
community, band, crowd, collection,
gathering, assembly 3 = <u>troop</u>, unit,
squad, team 4 = <u>companionship</u>, society,
presence, fellowship 5 = <u>guests</u>, party,
visitors, callers

comparable 1 = <u>equal</u>, equivalent,
on a par, tantamount, a match for,
proportionate, commensurate, as good as
≠ unequal 2 = <u>similar</u>,
related, alike, corresponding,
akin, analogous, of a piece, cognate

comparative = relative, qualified, by comparison

compare VERB = contrast, balance, weigh, set against, juxtapose
- PHRASES **compare to something** = liken to, parallel, identify with, equate to, correlate to, mention in the same breath as ♦ **compare with something** = be as good as, match, approach, equal, compete with, be on a par with, be the equal of, hold a candle to

comparison 1 = contrast, distinction, differentiation, juxtaposition 2 = similarity, analogy, resemblance, correlation, likeness, comparability

compartment 1 = section, carriage, berth 2 = bay, booth, locker, niche, cubicle, alcove, pigeonhole, cubbyhole

compass = range, field, area, reach, scope, limit, extent, boundary

compassion = sympathy, understanding, pity, humanity, mercy, sorrow, kindness, tenderness, aroha (*N.Z.*) ≠ indifference

compassionate = sympathetic, understanding, pitying, humanitarian, charitable, humane, benevolent, merciful ≠ uncaring

compatible 1 = consistent, in keeping, congruous ≠ inappropriate 2 = like-minded, harmonious, in harmony ≠ incompatible

compel = force, make, railroad (*informal*), oblige, constrain, coerce, impel, dragoon

compelling 1 = convincing, telling, powerful, forceful, conclusive, weighty, cogent, irrefutable 2 = pressing, binding, urgent, overriding, imperative, unavoidable, coercive, peremptory 3 = fascinating, gripping, irresistible, enchanting, enthralling, hypnotic, spellbinding, mesmeric ≠ boring

compensate 1 = recompense, repay, refund, reimburse, remunerate, make good 2 = make amends, make up for, atone, make it up to someone, pay for, do penance, cancel out, make reparation 3 = balance, cancel (out), offset, make up for, redress, counteract, counterbalance

compensation 1 = reparation, damages, recompense, remuneration, restitution, reimbursement 2 = recompense, amends, reparation, restitution, atonement

compete 1 = contend, fight, vie, challenge, struggle, contest, strive 2 = take part, participate, be in the running, be a competitor, be a contestant, play

competence 1 = ability, skill, talent, capacity, expertise, proficiency, capability ≠ incompetence 2 = fitness, suitability, adequacy, appropriateness ≠ inadequacy

competent 1 = able, skilled, capable, proficient ≠ incompetent 2 = fit, qualified, suitable, adequate ≠ unqualified

competition 1 = rivalry, opposition, struggle, strife 2 = opposition, field, rivals, challengers 3 = contest, event, championship, tournament, head-to-head

competitive 1 = cut-throat, aggressive, fierce, ruthless, relentless, antagonistic, dog-eat-dog 2 = ambitious, pushing, opposing, aggressive, vying, contentious, combative

competitor 1 = rival, adversary, antagonist 2 = contestant, participant, contender, challenger, entrant, player, opponent

compilation = collection, treasury, accumulation, anthology, assortment, assemblage

compile = put together, collect, gather, organize, accumulate, marshal, garner, amass

complacency = smugness, satisfaction, contentment, self-congratulation, self-satisfaction

complacent = smug, self-satisfied, pleased with yourself, resting on your laurels, contented, satisfied, serene, unconcerned ≠ insecure

complain = find fault, moan, grumble, whinge (*informal*), carp, groan, lament, whine

complaint 1 = protest, objection, grievance, charge 2 = grumble, criticism, moan, lament, grievance, grouse, gripe (*informal*) 3 = disorder, problem, disease, upset, illness, sickness, ailment, affliction

complement VERB = enhance, complete, improve, boost, crown, add to, set off, heighten
- NOUN 1 = accompaniment, companion, accessory, completion, finishing touch, rounding-off, adjunct, supplement 2 = total, capacity, quota, aggregate, contingent, entirety

complementary = matching,

companion, corresponding, compatible, reciprocal, interrelating, interdependent, harmonizing ≠ incompatible

complete ADJECTIVE 1 = <u>total</u>, perfect, absolute, utter, outright, thorough, consummate, out-and-out 2 = <u>whole</u>, full, entire ≠ partial 3 = <u>entire</u>, full, whole, intact, unbroken, faultless ≠ incomplete 4 = <u>unabridged</u>, full, entire 5 = <u>finished</u>, done, ended, achieved, concluded, fulfilled, accomplished ≠ unfinished 6 = <u>perfect</u>, finish off, round off, crown ≠ spoil
● VERB 1 = <u>finish</u>, conclude, end, close, settle, wrap up (*informal*), finalize ≠ start 2 = <u>fill in</u>, fill out

completely = <u>totally</u>, entirely, wholly, utterly, perfectly, fully, absolutely, altogether

completion = <u>finishing</u>, end, close, conclusion, fulfilment, culmination, fruition

complex ADJECTIVE 1 = <u>compound</u>, multiple, composite, manifold, heterogeneous, multifarious 2 = <u>complicated</u>, difficult, involved, elaborate, tangled, intricate, tortuous, convoluted ≠ simple
● NOUN 1 = <u>structure</u>, system, scheme, network, organization, aggregate, composite 2 (*Informal*) = <u>obsession</u>, preoccupation, phobia, fixation, fixed idea, idée fixe (*French*)

complexion 1 = <u>skin</u>, colour, colouring, hue, skin tone, pigmentation 2 = <u>nature</u>, character, make-up 3 = <u>perspective</u>, look, light, appearance, aspect, angle, slant

complexity = <u>complication</u>, involvement, intricacy, entanglement

complicate = <u>make difficult</u>, confuse, muddle, entangle, involve ≠ simplify

complicated 1 = <u>involved</u>, difficult, puzzling, troublesome, problematic, perplexing ≠ simple 2 = <u>complex</u>, involved, elaborate, intricate, convoluted, labyrinthine ≠ understandable

complication 1 = <u>problem</u>, difficulty, obstacle, drawback, snag, uphill (*S. African*) 2 = <u>complexity</u>, web, confusion, intricacy, entanglement

compliment NOUN = <u>praise</u>, honour, tribute, bouquet, flattery, eulogy

≠ criticism
● PLURAL NOUN 1 = <u>greetings</u>, regards, respects, good wishes, salutation ≠ insult 2 = <u>congratulations</u>, praise, commendation
● VERB = <u>praise</u>, flatter, salute, congratulate, pay tribute to, commend, extol, wax lyrical about ≠ criticize

complimentary 1 = <u>flattering</u>, approving, appreciative, congratulatory, commendatory ≠ critical 2 = <u>free</u>, donated, courtesy, honorary, on the house, gratuitous, gratis

comply = <u>obey</u>, follow, observe, submit to, conform to, adhere to, abide by, acquiesce with ≠ defy

component NOUN = <u>part</u>, piece, unit, item, element, ingredient, constituent
● ADJECTIVE = <u>constituent</u>, inherent, intrinsic

compose VERB 1 = <u>put together</u>, make up, constitute, comprise, make, build, form, fashion ≠ destroy 2 = <u>create</u>, write, produce, invent, devise, contrive 3 = <u>arrange</u>, make up, construct, put together, order, organize
● PHRASES **compose yourself** = <u>calm</u>, control, collect, quiet, soothe, pull yourself together

composed = <u>calm</u>, cool, collected, relaxed, poised, at ease, serene, sedate ≠ agitated

composition 1 = <u>design</u>, structure, make-up, organization, arrangement, formation, layout, configuration 2 = <u>creation</u>, work, piece, production, opus, masterpiece 3 = <u>essay</u>, exercise, treatise, literary work 4 = <u>production</u>, creation, making, fashioning, formation, putting together, compilation, formulation

compound NOUN = <u>combination</u>, mixture, blend, composite, fusion, synthesis, alloy, medley ≠ element
● ADJECTIVE = <u>complex</u>, multiple, composite, intricate ≠ simple
● VERB 1 = <u>intensify</u>, add to, complicate, worsen, heighten, exacerbate, aggravate, magnify ≠ lessen 2 = <u>combine</u>, unite, mix, blend, synthesize, amalgamate, intermingle ≠ divide

comprehend = <u>understand</u>, see, take in, perceive, grasp, conceive, make out, fathom ≠ misunderstand

comprehension = <u>understanding</u>,

grasp, conception, realization, intelligence, perception, discernment ≠ incomprehension

comprehensive = broad, full, complete, blanket, thorough, inclusive, exhaustive, all-inclusive ≠ limited

compress 1 = squeeze, crush, squash, press **2** = condense, contract, concentrate, shorten, abbreviate

comprise 1 = be composed of, include, contain, consist of, take in, embrace, encompass **2** = make up, form, constitute, compose

compromise NOUN = give-and-take, agreement, settlement, accommodation, concession, adjustment, trade-off ≠ disagreement

• VERB **1** = meet halfway, concede, make concessions, give and take, strike a balance, strike a happy medium, go fifty-fifty (*informal*) ≠ disagree **2** = undermine, expose, embarrass, weaken, prejudice, discredit, jeopardize, dishonour ≠ support

compulsive 1 = obsessive, confirmed, chronic, persistent, addictive, uncontrollable, incurable, inveterate **2** = fascinating, gripping, absorbing, compelling, captivating, enthralling, hypnotic, engrossing **3** = irresistible, overwhelming, compelling, urgent, neurotic, uncontrollable, driving

compulsory = obligatory, forced, required, binding, mandatory, imperative, requisite, de rigueur (*French*) ≠ voluntary

compute = calculate, total, count, reckon, figure out, add up, tally, enumerate

comrade = companion, friend, partner, ally, colleague, associate, fellow, co-worker, cobber (*Austral. & N.Z. old-fashioned informal*)

con (*Informal*) VERB = swindle, trick, cheat, rip off (*slang*), deceive, defraud, dupe, hoodwink

• NOUN = swindle, trick, fraud, deception, scam (*slang*), sting (*informal*)

conceal 1 = hide, bury, cover, screen, disguise, obscure, camouflage ≠ reveal **2** = keep secret, hide, disguise, mask, suppress, veil ≠ show

concede 1 = admit, allow, accept, acknowledge, own, grant, confess ≠ deny **2** = give up, yield, hand over, surrender, relinquish, cede ≠ conquer

conceive 1 = imagine, envisage,

comprehend, visualize, think, believe, suppose, fancy **2** = think up, create, design, devise, formulate, contrive **3** = become pregnant, get pregnant, become impregnated

concentrate 1 = focus your attention on, focus on, pay attention to, be engrossed in, put your mind to, keep your mind on, apply yourself to, give your mind to ≠ pay no attention to **2** = focus, centre, converge, bring to bear **3** = gather, collect, cluster, accumulate, congregate ≠ scatter

concentrated 1 = condensed, rich, undiluted, reduced, evaporated, thickened, boiled down **2** = intense, hard, deep, intensive, all-out (*informal*)

concentration 1 = attention, application, absorption, single-mindedness, intentness ≠ inattention **2** = focusing, centring, consolidation, convergence, bringing to bear, intensification, centralization **3** = convergence, collection, mass, cluster, accumulation, aggregation ≠ scattering

concept = idea, view, image, theory, notion, conception, hypothesis, abstraction

conception 1 = idea, plan, design, image, concept, notion **2** = impregnation, insemination, fertilization, germination

concern NOUN **1** = anxiety, fear, worry, distress, unease, apprehension, misgiving, disquiet **2** = worry, care, anxiety **3** = affair, issue, matter, consideration **4** = care, interest, attentiveness **5** = business, job, affair, responsibility, task **6** = company, business, firm, organization, corporation, enterprise, establishment **7** = importance, interest, bearing, relevance

• VERB **1** = worry, trouble, bother, disturb, distress, disquiet, perturb, make anxious **2** = be about, cover, deal with, go into, relate to, have to do with **3** = be relevant to, involve, affect, regard, apply to, bear on, have something to do with, pertain to

concerned 1 = worried, troubled, upset, bothered, disturbed, anxious, distressed, uneasy ≠ indifferent **2** = involved, interested, active, mixed up, implicated, privy to

concerning = regarding, about, re, touching, respecting, relating to, on the subject of, with reference to

concession 1 = compromise, agreement, settlement, accommodation, adjustment, trade-off, give-and-take 2 = privilege, right, permit, licence, entitlement, indulgence, prerogative 3 = reduction, saving, grant, discount, allowance 4 = surrender, yielding, conceding, renunciation, relinquishment

conclude 1 = decide, judge, assume, gather, work out, infer, deduce, surmise 2 = come to an end, end, close, finish, wind up ≠ begin 3 = bring to an end, end, close, finish, complete, wind up, terminate, round off ≠ begin 4 = accomplish, effect, bring about, carry out, pull off

conclusion 1 = decision, opinion, conviction, verdict, judgment, deduction, inference 2 = end, ending, close, finish, completion, finale, termination, bitter end 3 = outcome, result, upshot, consequence, culmination, end result

concrete 1 = specific, precise, explicit, definite, clear-cut, unequivocal ≠ vague 2 = real, material, actual, substantial, sensible, tangible, factual ≠ abstract

condemn 1 = denounce, damn, criticize, disapprove, censure, reprove, upbraid, blame ≠ approve 2 = sentence, convict, damn, doom, pass sentence on ≠ acquit

condemnation = denunciation, blame, censure, disapproval, reproach, stricture, reproof

condition NOUN 1 = state, order, shape, nick (*Brit. informal*), trim 2 = situation, state, position, status, circumstances 3 = requirement, terms, rider, restriction, qualification, limitation, prerequisite, proviso 4 = health, shape, fitness, trim, form, kilter, state of health, fettle 5 = ailment, problem, complaint, weakness, malady, infirmity
● PLURAL NOUN = circumstances, situation, environment, surroundings, way of life, milieu
● VERB = train, teach, adapt, accustom

conditional = dependent, limited, qualified, subject to, contingent, provisional, with reservations ≠ unconditional

condone = overlook, excuse, forgive, pardon, turn a blind eye to, look the other way, make allowance for, let pass ≠ condemn

conduct VERB 1 = carry out, run, control, manage, direct, handle, organize, administer 2 = accompany, lead, escort, guide, steer, convey, usher
● NOUN 1 = management, running, control, handling, administration, direction, organization, guidance 2 = behaviour, ways, bearing, attitude, manners, demeanour, deportment
● PHRASES **conduct yourself** = behave yourself, act, carry yourself, acquit yourself, deport yourself, comport yourself

confer 1 = discuss, talk, consult, deliberate, discourse, converse 2 = grant, give, present, accord, award, hand out, bestow

conference = meeting, congress, discussion, convention, forum, consultation, seminar, symposium, hui (*N.Z.*)

confess 1 = admit, acknowledge, disclose, confide, own up, come clean (*informal*), divulge ≠ cover up 2 = declare, allow, reveal, confirm, concede, assert, affirm, profess

confession = admission, revelation, disclosure, acknowledgment, exposure, unbosoming

confidant or **confidante** = close friend, familiar, intimate, crony, alter ego, bosom friend

confide = tell, admit, reveal, confess, whisper, disclose, impart, divulge

confidence NOUN 1 = trust, belief, faith, dependence, reliance, credence ≠ distrust 2 = self-assurance, courage, assurance, aplomb, boldness, self-possession, nerve ≠ shyness ≠ secret
● PHRASES **in confidence** = in secrecy, privately, confidentially, between you and me (and the gatepost), (just) between ourselves

confident 1 = certain, sure, convinced, positive, secure, satisfied, counting on ≠ unsure 2 = self-assured, positive, assured, bold, self-confident, self-reliant, sure of yourself ≠ insecure

confidential 1 = secret, private, intimate, classified, privy, off the record, hush-hush (*informal*) 2 = secretive, low, soft, hushed

confine VERB 1 = imprison, enclose, shut up, intern, incarcerate, hem in, keep, cage 2 = restrict, limit
● PLURAL NOUN = limits, bounds, boundaries, compass, precincts, circumference, edge

confirm 1 = prove, support, establish,

back up, verify, validate, bear out, substantiate **2** = <u>ratify</u>, establish, sanction, endorse, authorize **3** = <u>strengthen</u>, establish, fix, secure, reinforce, fortify

confirmation 1 = <u>proof</u>, evidence, testimony, verification, ratification, validation, corroboration, authentication ≠ repudiation **2** = <u>affirmation</u>, approval, acceptance, endorsement, ratification, assent, agreement ≠ disapproval

confirmed = <u>long-established</u>, seasoned, chronic, hardened, habitual, ingrained, inveterate, dyed-in-the-wool

confiscate = <u>seize</u>, appropriate, impound, commandeer, sequester ≠ give back

conflict NOUN 1 = <u>dispute</u>, difference, opposition, hostility, disagreement, friction, strife, fighting ≠ agreement **2** = <u>struggle</u>, battle, clash, strife **3** = <u>battle</u>, war, fight, clash, contest, encounter, combat, strife ≠ peace
● VERB = <u>be incompatible</u>, clash, differ, disagree, collide, be at variance ≠ agree

conflicting = <u>incompatible</u>, opposing, clashing, contrary, contradictory, inconsistent, paradoxical, discordant ≠ agreeing

conform 1 = <u>fit in</u>, follow, adjust, adapt, comply, obey, fall in with, toe the line **2** = <u>fulfil</u>, meet, match, suit, satisfy, agree with, obey, abide by

confound = <u>bewilder</u>, baffle, confuse, astound, perplex, mystify, flummox, dumbfound

confront 1 = <u>tackle</u>, deal with, cope with, meet head-on **2** = <u>trouble</u>, face, perturb, bedevil **3** = <u>challenge</u>, face, oppose, tackle, encounter, defy, stand up to, accost ≠ evade

confrontation = <u>conflict</u>, fight, contest, set-to (*informal*), encounter, showdown (*informal*), head-to-head

confuse 1 = <u>mix up with</u>, take for, muddle with **2** = <u>bewilder</u>, puzzle, baffle, perplex, mystify, fluster, faze, flummox **3** = <u>obscure</u>, cloud, make more difficult

confused 1 = <u>bewildered</u>, puzzled, baffled, at sea, muddled, perplexed, taken aback, disorientated ≠ enlightened **2** = <u>disorderly</u>, disordered, chaotic, mixed up, jumbled, untidy, in disarray, topsy-turvy ≠ tidy

confusing = <u>bewildering</u>, puzzling, misleading, unclear, baffling, contradictory, perplexing ≠ clear

confusion 1 = <u>bewilderment</u>, doubt, uncertainty ≠ enlightenment **2** = <u>disorder</u>, chaos, turmoil, upheaval, muddle, shambles, commotion ≠ order

congestion = <u>overcrowding</u>, crowding, jam, clogging, bottleneck

congratulate = <u>compliment</u>, pat on the back, wish joy to

congratulations PLURAL NOUN = <u>good wishes</u>, greetings, compliments, best wishes, felicitations
● INTERJECTION = <u>good wishes</u>, greetings, compliments, best wishes, felicitations

congregation = <u>parishioners</u>, brethren, crowd, assembly, flock, fellowship, multitude, throng

congress 1 = <u>meeting</u>, council, conference, assembly, convention, conclave, hui (*N.Z.*), runanga (*N.Z.*) **2** = <u>legislature</u>, council, parliament, House of Representatives (*N.Z.*)

conjure VERB = <u>produce</u>, generate, bring about, give rise to, make, create, effect, produce as if by magic
● PHRASES **conjure something up** = <u>bring to mind</u>, recall, evoke, recreate, recollect, produce as if by magic

connect 1 = <u>link</u>, join, couple, attach, fasten, affix, unite ≠ separate **2** = <u>associate</u>, join, link, identify, lump together

connected = <u>linked</u>, united, joined, coupled, related, allied, associated, combined

connection 1 = <u>association</u>, relationship, link, bond, relevance, tie-in **2** = <u>communication</u>, alliance, attachment, liaison, affinity, union **3** = <u>link</u>, coupling, junction, fastening, tie **4** = <u>contact</u>, friend, ally, associate, acquaintance

conquer 1 = <u>seize</u>, obtain, acquire, occupy, overrun, annex, win **2** = <u>defeat</u>, overcome, overthrow, beat, master, crush, overpower, quell ≠ lose to **3** = <u>overcome</u>, beat, defeat, master, overpower

conquest 1 = <u>takeover</u>, coup, invasion, occupation, annexation, subjugation **2** = <u>defeat</u>, victory, triumph, overthrow, rout, mastery

conscience 1 = <u>principles</u>, scruples, moral sense, sense of right and wrong, still small voice **2** = <u>guilt</u>, shame, regret, remorse, contrition, self-reproach

conscious 1 *often with of* = aware of, alert to, responsive to, sensible of ≠ unaware **2** = deliberate, knowing, studied, calculated, self-conscious, intentional, wilful, premeditated ≠ unintentional **3** = awake, wide-awake, sentient, alive ≠ asleep

consciousness = awareness, understanding, knowledge, recognition, sensibility, realization, apprehension

consecutive = successive, running, succeeding, in turn, uninterrupted, sequential, in sequence

consensus = agreement, general agreement, unanimity, common consent, unity, harmony, assent, concord, kotahitanga (*N.Z.*)

consent NOUN = agreement, sanction, approval, go-ahead (*informal*), permission, compliance, assent, acquiescence ≠ refusal
● VERB = agree, approve, permit, concur, assent, acquiesce ≠ refuse

consequence 1 = result, effect, outcome, repercussion, issue, sequel, end result, upshot **2** = importance, concern, moment, value, account, weight, import, significance

consequently = as a result, thus, therefore, hence, subsequently, accordingly, for that reason, thence

conservation 1 = preservation, saving, protection, maintenance, safeguarding, upkeep, guardianship, safekeeping **2** = economy, saving, thrift, husbandry

conservative ADJECTIVE = traditional, conventional, cautious, sober, reactionary, die-hard, hidebound ≠ radical
● NOUN = traditionalist, reactionary, die-hard, stick-in-the-mud (*informal*) ≠ radical

Conservative ADJECTIVE = Tory, Republican (*U.S.*), right-wing
● NOUN = Tory, Republican (*U.S.*), right-winger

conserve 1 = save, husband, take care of, hoard, store up, use sparingly ≠ waste **2** = protect, keep, save, preserve

consider 1 = think, see, believe, rate, judge, suppose, deem, view as **2** = think about, reflect on, weigh, contemplate, deliberate, ponder, meditate, ruminate **3** = bear in mind, remember, respect, think about, take into account, reckon with, take into consideration, make allowance for

considerable = large, goodly, great, marked, substantial, noticeable, plentiful, appreciable ≠ small

considerably = greatly, very much, significantly, remarkably, substantially, markedly, noticeably, appreciably

consideration 1 = thought, review, analysis, examination, reflection, scrutiny, deliberation **2** = thoughtfulness, concern, respect, kindness, tact, considerateness **3** = factor, point, issue, concern, element, aspect **4** = payment, fee, reward, remuneration, recompense, tip

considering = taking into account, in the light of, bearing in mind, in view of, keeping in mind, taking into consideration

consist VERB
● PHRASES **consist in something** = lie in, involve, reside in, be expressed by, subsist in, be found *or* contained in
♦ **consist of something** = be made up of, include, contain, incorporate, amount to, comprise, be composed of

consistency 1 = agreement, regularity, uniformity, constancy, steadiness, steadfastness, evenness **2** = texture, density, thickness, firmness, viscosity, compactness

consistent 1 = steady, even, regular, stable, constant, persistent, dependable, unchanging ≠ erratic **2** = compatible, agreeing, in keeping, harmonious, in harmony, consonant, in accord, congruous ≠ incompatible **3** = coherent, logical, compatible, harmonious, consonant ≠ contradictory

consolation = comfort, help, support, relief, cheer, encouragement, solace, succour

console = comfort, cheer, soothe, support, encourage, calm, succour, express sympathy for ≠ distress

consolidate 1 = strengthen, secure, reinforce, fortify, stabilize **2** = combine, unite, join, merge, unify, amalgamate, federate

conspicuous = obvious, clear, patent, evident, noticeable, blatant, salient ≠ inconspicuous

conspiracy = plot, scheme, intrigue, collusion, machination

conspire 1 = plot, scheme, intrigue,

manoeuvre, contrive, machinate, plan
2 = <u>work together</u>, combine, contribute,
cooperate, concur, tend

constant 1 = <u>continuous</u>, sustained,
perpetual, interminable, unrelenting,
incessant, ceaseless, nonstop ≠ occasional
2 = <u>unchanging</u>, even, fixed, permanent,
stable, steady, uniform, invariable
≠ changing **3** = <u>faithful</u>, true, devoted,
loyal, stalwart, staunch, trustworthy, trusty
≠ undependable

constantly = <u>continuously</u>, always, all
the time, invariably, continually, endlessly,
perpetually, incessantly ≠ occasionally

constituent NOUN **1** = <u>voter</u>, elector,
member of the electorate **2** = <u>component</u>,
element, ingredient, part, unit, factor
● ADJECTIVE = <u>component</u>, basic, essential,
integral, elemental

constitute 1 = <u>represent</u>, be, consist
of, embody, exemplify, be equivalent to
2 = <u>make up</u>, form, compose, comprise

constitution 1 = <u>state of health</u>, build,
body, frame, physique, physical condition
2 = <u>structure</u>, form, nature, make-up,
composition, character, disposition

constitutional = <u>legitimate</u>, official, legal,
chartered, statutory, vested

constrain 1 = <u>restrict</u>, confine, curb,
restrain, constrict, straiten, check **2** = <u>force</u>,
bind, compel, oblige, necessitate, coerce,
impel, pressurize

constraint 1 = <u>restriction</u>, limitation, curb,
rein, deterrent, hindrance, check **2** = <u>force</u>,
pressure, necessity, restraint, compulsion,
coercion

construct 1 = <u>build</u>, make, form, create,
fashion, shape, manufacture, assemble
≠ demolish **2** = <u>create</u>, make, form,
compose, put together

construction 1 = <u>building</u>, creation,
composition **2** (*Formal*) = <u>interpretation</u>,
reading, explanation, rendering, inference

constructive = <u>helpful</u>, positive,
useful, practical, valuable, productive
≠ unproductive

consult 1 = <u>ask</u>, refer to, turn to, take
counsel, pick (someone's) brains, question
2 = <u>confer</u>, talk, compare notes **3** = <u>refer to</u>,
check in, look in

consultant = <u>specialist</u>, adviser,
counsellor, authority

consultation 1 = <u>discussion</u>, talk, council,
conference, dialogue **2** = <u>meeting</u>,
interview, session, appointment,
examination, deliberation, hearing

consume 1 = <u>eat</u>, swallow, devour, put
away, gobble (up), eat up **2** = <u>use up</u>,
spend, waste, absorb, exhaust, squander,
dissipate, expend **3** = <u>destroy</u>, devastate,
demolish, ravage, annihilate, lay waste
4 *often passive* = <u>obsess</u>, dominate, absorb,
preoccupy, eat up, monopolize, engross

consumer = <u>buyer</u>, customer, user,
shopper, purchaser

consumption 1 = <u>using up</u>, use,
loss, waste, expenditure, exhaustion,
depletion, dissipation **2** (*Old-fashioned*)
= <u>tuberculosis</u>, T.B.

contact NOUN **1** = <u>communication</u>, link,
association, connection, correspondence
2 = <u>touch</u>, contiguity **3** = <u>connection</u>,
colleague, associate, liaison, acquaintance,
confederate
● VERB = <u>get</u> *or* be in touch with, call,
reach, approach, write to, speak to,
communicate with

contain 1 = <u>hold</u>, incorporate,
accommodate, enclose, have capacity for
2 = <u>include</u>, consist of, embrace, comprise,
embody, comprehend **3** = <u>restrain</u>,
control, hold in, curb, suppress, hold back,
stifle, repress

container = <u>holder</u>, vessel, repository,
receptacle

contaminate = <u>pollute</u>, infect, stain,
corrupt, taint, defile, adulterate, befoul
≠ purify

contamination = <u>pollution</u>, infection,
corruption, poisoning, taint, impurity,
contagion, defilement

contemplate 1 = <u>consider</u>, plan, think of,
intend, envisage, foresee **2** = <u>think about</u>,
consider, ponder, reflect upon, ruminate
(upon), muse over, deliberate over
3 = <u>look at</u>, examine, inspect, gaze at, eye
up, view, study, regard

contemporary ADJECTIVE **1** = <u>modern</u>,
recent, current, up-to-date, present-day,
à la mode, newfangled, present ≠ old-
fashioned **2** = <u>coexisting</u>, concurrent,
contemporaneous
● NOUN = <u>peer</u>, fellow, equal

contempt = <u>scorn</u>, disdain, mockery,
derision, disrespect, disregard ≠ respect

contend 1 = <u>argue</u>, hold, maintain, allege,
assert, affirm **2** = <u>compete</u>, fight, struggle,
clash, contest, strive, vie, jostle

content¹ NOUN 1 = <u>subject matter</u>, material, theme, substance, essence, gist 2 = <u>amount</u>, measure, size, load, volume, capacity
● PLURAL NOUN = <u>constituents</u>, elements, load, ingredients

content² ADJECTIVE = <u>satisfied</u>, happy, pleased, contented, comfortable, fulfilled, at ease, gratified
● NOUN = <u>satisfaction</u>, ease, pleasure, comfort, peace of mind, gratification, contentment
● PHRASES **content yourself with something** = <u>satisfy yourself with</u>, be happy with, be satisfied with, be content with

contented = <u>satisfied</u>, happy, pleased, content, comfortable, glad, thankful, gratified ≠ discontented

contentious = <u>argumentative</u>, wrangling, bickering, quarrelsome, querulous, cavilling, disputatious, captious

contest NOUN 1 = <u>competition</u>, game, match, trial, tournament 2 = <u>struggle</u>, fight, battle, conflict, dispute, controversy, combat
● VERB 1 = <u>compete in</u>, take part in, fight in, go in for, contend for, vie in 2 = <u>oppose</u>, question, challenge, argue, debate, dispute, object to, call in or into question

contestant = <u>competitor</u>, candidate, participant, contender, entrant, player

context 1 = <u>circumstances</u>, conditions, situation, ambience 2 = <u>frame of reference</u>, background, framework, relation, connection

contingency = <u>possibility</u>, happening, chance, event, incident, accident, emergency, eventuality

continual 1 = <u>constant</u>, interminable, incessant, unremitting ≠ erratic 2 = <u>frequent</u>, regular, repeated, recurrent ≠ occasional

continually 1 = <u>constantly</u>, always, all the time, forever, incessantly, nonstop, interminably 2 = <u>repeatedly</u>, often, frequently, many times, over and over, persistently

continuation 1 = <u>continuing</u>, lasting, carrying on, keeping up, endurance, perpetuation, prolongation 2 = <u>addition</u>, extension, supplement, sequel, resumption, postscript

continue 1 = <u>keep on</u>, go on, maintain, sustain, carry on, persist in, persevere, stick at ≠ stop 2 = <u>go on</u>, progress, proceed, carry on, keep going 3 = <u>resume</u>, return to, take up again, proceed, carry on, recommence, pick up where you left off ≠ stop 4 = <u>remain</u>, last, stay, survive, carry on, live on, endure, persist ≠ quit

continuing = <u>lasting</u>, sustained, enduring, ongoing, in progress

continuity = <u>cohesion</u>, flow, connection, sequence, succession, progression

continuous = <u>constant</u>, extended, prolonged, unbroken, uninterrupted, unceasing ≠ occasional

contract NOUN = <u>agreement</u>, commitment, arrangement, settlement, bargain, pact, covenant
● VERB 1 = <u>agree</u>, negotiate, pledge, bargain, undertake, come to terms, covenant, make a deal ≠ refuse 2 = <u>constrict</u>, confine, tighten, shorten, compress, condense, shrivel 3 = <u>tighten</u>, narrow, shorten ≠ stretch 4 = <u>lessen</u>, reduce, shrink, diminish, decrease, dwindle ≠ increase 5 = <u>catch</u>, get, develop, acquire, incur, be infected with, go down with, be afflicted with ≠ avoid

contraction 1 = <u>tightening</u>, narrowing, shortening, constricting, shrinkage 2 = <u>abbreviation</u>, reduction, shortening, compression

contradict 1 = <u>dispute</u>, deny, challenge, belie, fly in the face of, be at variance with 2 = <u>negate</u>, deny, rebut, controvert ≠ confirm

contradiction 1 = <u>conflict</u>, inconsistency, contravention, incongruity 2 = <u>negation</u>, opposite, denial

contradictory = <u>inconsistent</u>, conflicting, opposed, opposite, contrary, incompatible, paradoxical

contrary ADJECTIVE 1 = <u>opposite</u>, different, opposed, clashing, counter, reverse, adverse, contradictory ≠ in agreement 2 = <u>perverse</u>, difficult, awkward, intractable, obstinate, stroppy (*Brit. slang*), cantankerous, disobliging ≠ cooperative
● NOUN = <u>opposite</u>, reverse, converse, antithesis

contrast NOUN = <u>difference</u>, opposition, comparison, distinction, foil, disparity, divergence, dissimilarity
● VERB 1 = <u>differentiate</u>, compare, oppose, distinguish, set in opposition 2 = <u>differ</u>, be

contrary, be at variance, be dissimilar

contribute VERB = give, provide, supply, donate, subscribe, chip in (*informal*), bestow

● PHRASES **contribute to something** = be partly responsible for, lead to, be instrumental in, be conducive to, help

contribution = gift, offering, grant, donation, input, subscription, koha (*N.Z.*)

contributor = donor, supporter, patron, subscriber, giver

contrive 1 = devise, plan, fabricate, create, design, scheme, manufacture, plot 2 = manage, succeed, arrange, manoeuvre

contrived = forced, planned, laboured, strained, artificial, elaborate, unnatural, overdone ≠ natural

control NOUN 1 = power, authority, management, command, guidance, supervision, supremacy, charge 2 = restraint, check, regulation, brake, limitation, curb 3 = self-discipline, self-restraint, restraint, self-command 4 = switch, instrument, button, dial, lever, knob

● PLURAL NOUN = instruments, dash, dials, console, dashboard, control panel

● VERB 1 = have power over, manage, direct, handle, command, govern, administer, supervise 2 = limit, restrict, curb 3 = restrain, limit, check, contain, curb, hold back, subdue, repress

controversial = disputed, contentious, at issue, debatable, under discussion, open to question, disputable

controversy = argument, debate, row, dispute, quarrel, squabble, wrangling, altercation

convene 1 = call, gather, assemble, summon, bring together, convoke 2 = meet, gather, assemble, come together, congregate

convenience 1 = benefit, good, advantage 2 = suitability, fitness, appropriateness 3 = usefulness, utility ≠ uselessness 4 = accessibility, availability, nearness 5 = appliance, facility, comfort, amenity, labour-saving device, help

convenient 1 = suitable, fit, handy, satisfactory 2 = useful, practical, handy, serviceable, labour-saving ≠ useless 3 = nearby, available, accessible, handy, at hand, within reach, close at hand, just round the corner ≠ inaccessible

4 = appropriate, timely, suitable, helpful

convention 1 = custom, practice, tradition, code, usage, protocol, etiquette, propriety, kawa (*N.Z.*), tikanga (*N.Z.*) 2 = agreement, contract, treaty, bargain, pact, protocol 3 = assembly, meeting, council, conference, congress, convocation, hui (*N.Z.*), runanga (*N.Z.*)

conventional 1 = proper, conservative, respectable, genteel, conformist 2 = ordinary, standard, normal, regular, usual 3 = traditional, accepted, orthodox, customary 4 = unoriginal, routine, stereotyped, banal, prosaic, run-of-the-mill, hackneyed ≠ unconventional

converge VERB = come together, meet, join, combine, gather, merge, coincide, intersect

● PHRASES **converge on something** = close in on, arrive at, move towards, home in on, come together at

conversation = talk, discussion, dialogue, tête-à-tête, conference, chat, gossip, discourse, korero (*N.Z.*)

■ **RELATED WORD**
adjective: colloquial

conversion 1 = change, transformation, metamorphosis 2 = adaptation, reconstruction, modification, alteration, remodelling, reorganization

convert VERB 1 = change, turn, transform, alter, transpose 2 = adapt, modify, remodel, reorganize, customize, restyle 3 = reform, convince, proselytize

● NOUN = neophyte, disciple, proselyte

convey 1 = communicate, impart, reveal, relate, disclose, make known, tell 2 = carry, transport, move, bring, bear, conduct, fetch

convict VERB = find guilty, sentence, condemn, imprison, pronounce guilty

● NOUN = prisoner, criminal, lag (*slang*), felon, jailbird

conviction 1 = belief, view, opinion, principle, faith, persuasion, creed, tenet, kaupapa (*N.Z.*) 2 = certainty, confidence, assurance, firmness, certitude

convince 1 = assure, persuade, satisfy, reassure 2 = persuade, induce, coax, talk into, prevail upon, bring round to the idea of

convincing = persuasive, credible, conclusive, telling, powerful, impressive, plausible, cogent ≠ unconvincing

cool ADJECTIVE 1 = <u>cold</u>, chilled, refreshing, chilly, nippy ≠ warm 2 = <u>calm</u>, collected, relaxed, composed, sedate, self-controlled, unruffled, unemotional ≠ agitated 3 = <u>unfriendly</u>, distant, indifferent, aloof, lukewarm, offhand, unenthusiastic, unwelcoming ≠ friendly 4 = <u>unenthusiastic</u>, indifferent, lukewarm, unwelcoming
● VERB 1 = <u>lose heat</u>, cool off ≠ warm (up) 2 = <u>make cool</u>, freeze, chill, refrigerate, cool off ≠ warm (up)
● NOUN 1 = <u>coldness</u>, chill, coolness 2 (*Slang*) = <u>calmness</u>, control, temper, composure, self-control, poise, self-discipline, self-possession
cooperate = <u>work together</u>, collaborate, coordinate, join forces, conspire, pull together, pool resources, combine your efforts ≠ conflict
cooperation = <u>teamwork</u>, unity, collaboration, give-and-take, combined effort, esprit de corps, kotahitanga (*N.Z.*) ≠ opposition
cooperative 1 = <u>shared</u>, joint, combined, collective, collaborative 2 = <u>helpful</u>, obliging, accommodating, supportive, responsive, onside (*informal*)
cope VERB = <u>manage</u>, get by (*informal*), struggle through, survive, carry on, make the grade, hold your own
● PHRASES **cope with something** = <u>deal with</u>, handle, struggle with, grapple with, wrestle with, contend with, weather
copy NOUN = <u>reproduction</u>, duplicate, replica, imitation, forgery, counterfeit, likeness, facsimile ≠ original
● VERB 1 = <u>reproduce</u>, replicate, duplicate, transcribe, counterfeit ≠ create 2 = <u>imitate</u>, act like, emulate, behave like, follow, repeat, mirror, ape
cord = <u>rope</u>, line, string, twine
cordon NOUN = <u>chain</u>, line, ring, barrier, picket line
● PHRASES **cordon something off** = <u>surround</u>, isolate, close off, fence off, separate, enclose, picket, encircle
core 1 = <u>centre</u> 2 = <u>heart</u>, essence, nucleus, kernel, crux, gist, nub, pith
corner NOUN 1 = <u>angle</u>, joint, crook 2 = <u>bend</u>, curve 3 = <u>space</u>, hideaway, nook, hide-out
● VERB 1 = <u>trap</u>, catch, run to earth 2 (usually with *market* as object)

= <u>monopolize</u>, take over, dominate, control, hog (*slang*), engross
corporation 1 = <u>business</u>, company, concern, firm, society, association, organization, enterprise 2 = <u>town council</u>, council, municipal authorities, civic authorities
corps = <u>team</u>, unit, regiment, detachment, company, band, division, troop
corpse = <u>body</u>, remains, carcass, cadaver, stiff (*slang*)
correct ADJECTIVE 1 = <u>accurate</u>, right, true, exact, precise, flawless, faultless, O.K. or okay (*informal*) ≠ inaccurate 2 = <u>right</u>, standard, appropriate, acceptable, proper, precise 3 = <u>proper</u>, seemly, standard, fitting, kosher (*informal*) ≠ inappropriate
● VERB 1 = <u>rectify</u>, remedy, redress, right, reform, cure, adjust, amend ≠ spoil 2 = <u>rebuke</u>, discipline, reprimand, chide, admonish, chastise, chasten, reprove ≠ praise
correction 1 = <u>rectification</u>, improvement, amendment, adjustment, modification, alteration, emendation 2 = <u>punishment</u>, discipline, reformation, admonition, chastisement, reproof, castigation
correctly = <u>rightly</u>, right, perfectly, properly, precisely, accurately
correctness 1 = <u>truth</u>, accuracy, precision, exactitude, exactness, faultlessness 2 = <u>decorum</u>, propriety, good manners, civility, good breeding
correspond 1 = <u>be consistent</u>, match, agree, accord, fit, square, tally, conform ≠ differ 2 = <u>communicate</u>, write, keep in touch, exchange letters
correspondence 1 = <u>communication</u>, writing, contact 2 = <u>letters</u>, post, mail 3 = <u>relation</u>, match, agreement, comparison, harmony, coincidence, similarity, correlation
correspondent 1 = <u>reporter</u>, journalist, contributor, hack 2 = <u>letter writer</u>, pen friend *or* pen pal
corresponding = <u>equivalent</u>, matching, similar, related, complementary, reciprocal, analogous
corridor = <u>passage</u>, alley, aisle, hallway, passageway
corrupt ADJECTIVE 1 = <u>dishonest</u>, bent (*slang*), crooked (*informal*), fraudulent, unscrupulous, venal, unprincipled

≠ honest **2** = <u>depraved</u>, vicious, degenerate, debased, profligate, dissolute **3** = <u>distorted</u>, doctored, altered, falsified
● VERB **1** = <u>bribe</u>, fix (*informal*), buy off, suborn, grease (someone's) palm (*slang*) **2** = <u>deprave</u>, pervert, subvert, debauch ≠ reform **3** = <u>distort</u>, doctor, tamper with

corruption 1 = <u>dishonesty</u>, fraud, bribery, extortion, venality, shady dealings (*informal*) **2** = <u>depravity</u>, vice, evil, perversion, decadence, wickedness, immorality **3** = <u>distortion</u>, doctoring, falsification

cosmetic = <u>superficial</u>, surface, nonessential

cosmic 1 = <u>extraterrestrial</u>, stellar **2** = <u>universal</u>, general, overarching

cosmopolitan = <u>sophisticated</u>, cultured, refined, cultivated, urbane, well-travelled, worldly-wise ≠ unsophisticated

cost NOUN **1** = <u>price</u>, worth, expense, charge, damage (*informal*), amount, payment, outlay **2** = <u>loss</u>, suffering, damage, injury, penalty, hurt, expense, harm
● PLURAL NOUN = <u>expenses</u>, spending, expenditure, overheads, outgoings, outlay, budget
● VERB **1** = <u>sell at</u>, come to, set (someone) back (*informal*), be priced at, command a price of **2** = <u>lose</u>, deprive of, cheat of

costly 1 = <u>expensive</u>, dear, stiff, steep (*informal*), highly-priced, exorbitant, extortionate ≠ inexpensive **2** = <u>damaging</u>, disastrous, harmful, catastrophic, loss-making, ruinous, deleterious

costume = <u>outfit</u>, dress, clothing, uniform, ensemble, livery, apparel, attire

cosy 1 = <u>comfortable</u>, homely, warm, intimate, snug, comfy (*informal*), sheltered **2** = <u>snug</u>, warm, comfortable, sheltered, comfy (*informal*), tucked up **3** = <u>intimate</u>, friendly, informal

cottage = <u>cabin</u>, lodge, hut, shack, chalet, whare (*N.Z.*)

cough VERB = <u>clear your throat</u>, bark, hack
● NOUN = <u>frog</u> *or* tickle in your throat, bark, hack

council 1 = <u>committee</u>, governing body, board **2** = <u>governing body</u>, parliament, congress, cabinet, panel, assembly, convention, conference, runanga (*N.Z.*)

counsel NOUN **1** = <u>advice</u>, information, warning, direction, suggestion,

recommendation, guidance **2** = <u>legal adviser</u>, lawyer, attorney, solicitor, advocate, barrister
● VERB = <u>advise</u>, recommend, advocate, warn, urge, instruct, exhort

count VERB **1** *often with* **up** = <u>add (up)</u>, total, reckon (up), tot up, calculate, compute, tally, number **2** = <u>matter</u>, be important, carry weight, tell, rate, weigh, signify **3** = <u>consider</u>, judge, regard, deem, think of, rate, look upon **4** = <u>include</u>, number among, take into account *or* consideration
● NOUN = <u>calculation</u>, poll, reckoning, sum, tally, numbering, computation, enumeration
● PHRASES **count on** *or* **upon something** *or* **someone** = <u>depend on</u>, trust, rely on, bank on, take for granted, lean on, reckon on, take on trust

counter VERB **1** = <u>oppose</u>, meet, block, resist, parry, deflect, repel, rebuff **2** = <u>retaliate</u>, answer, reply, respond, retort, hit back, rejoin, strike back ≠ yield
● ADVERB = <u>opposite to</u>, against, versus, conversely, in defiance of, at variance with, contrariwise ≠ in accordance with

counterpart = <u>opposite number</u>, equal, twin, equivalent, match, fellow, mate

countless = <u>innumerable</u>, legion, infinite, myriad, untold, limitless, incalculable, immeasurable ≠ limited

country 1 = <u>nation</u>, state, land, commonwealth, kingdom, realm, people **2** = <u>people</u>, community, nation, society, citizens, inhabitants, populace, public **3** = <u>countryside</u>, provinces, sticks (*informal*), farmland, outback (*Austral. & N.Z.*), green belt, backwoods, bush (*N.Z. & S. African*) ≠ town **4** = <u>territory</u>, land, region, terrain

countryside = <u>country</u>, rural areas, outback (*Austral. & N.Z.*), green belt, sticks (*informal*)

county = <u>province</u>, district, shire

coup = <u>masterstroke</u>, feat, stunt, action, exploit, manoeuvre, deed, accomplishment

couple NOUN = <u>pair</u>, two, brace, duo, twosome
● PHRASES **couple something to something** = <u>link to</u>, connect to, pair with, unite with, join to, hitch to, yoke to

coupon = <u>slip</u>, ticket, certificate, token,

voucher, card

courage = bravery, nerve, resolution, daring, pluck, heroism, mettle, gallantry ≠ cowardice

courageous = brave, daring, bold, gritty, fearless, gallant, intrepid, valiant ≠ cowardly

courier 1 = messenger, runner, carrier, bearer, envoy 2 = guide, representative, escort, conductor

course NOUN 1 = route, way, line, road, track, direction, path, passage 2 = procedure, plan, policy, programme, method, conduct, behaviour, manner 3 = progression, order, unfolding, development, movement, progress, flow, sequence 4 = classes, programme, schedule, lectures, curriculum 5 = racecourse, circuit 6 = period, time, duration, term, passing
- VERB 1 = run, flow, stream, gush, race, speed, surge 2 = hunt, follow, chase, pursue
- PHRASES of course = naturally, certainly, obviously, definitely, undoubtedly, needless to say, without a doubt, indubitably

court NOUN 1 = law court, bar, bench, tribunal 2 = palace, hall, castle, manor 3 = royal household, train, suite, attendants, entourage, retinue, cortege
- VERB 1 = cultivate, seek, flatter, solicit, pander to, curry favour with, fawn upon 2 = invite, seek, attract, prompt, provoke, bring about, incite 3 = woo, go (out) with, date, take out, run after, walk out with, set your cap at

courtesy 1 = politeness, good manners, civility, gallantry, graciousness, affability, urbanity 2 = favour, kindness, indulgence

courtyard = yard, square, piazza, quadrangle, plaza, enclosure, cloister, quad (informal)

cove = bay, sound, inlet, anchorage

covenant = promise, contract, agreement, commitment, arrangement, pledge, pact

cover VERB 1 = conceal, hide, mask, disguise, obscure, veil, cloak, shroud ≠ reveal 2 = clothe, dress, wrap, envelop ≠ uncover 3 = overlay, blanket 4 = coat, cake, plaster, smear, envelop, spread, encase, daub 5 = submerge, flood, engulf, overrun, wash over 6 = travel over, cross,

traverse, pass through or over 7 = protect, guard, defend, shield 8 = consider, deal with, investigate, describe, tell of 9 = report on, write about, commentate on, relate, tell of, narrate, write up 10 = pay for, fund, provide for, offset, be enough for
- NOUN 1 = protection, shelter, shield, defence, guard, camouflage, concealment 2 = insurance, protection, compensation, indemnity, reimbursement 3 = covering, case, top, coating, envelope, lid, canopy, wrapper 4 = bedclothes, bedding, sheets, blankets, quilt, duvet, eiderdown 5 = jacket, case, wrapper 6 = disguise, front, screen, mask, veil, façade, pretext, smoke screen

covering NOUN = cover, coating, casing, wrapping, layer, blanket
- ADJECTIVE = explanatory, accompanying, introductory, descriptive

covet = long for, desire, envy, crave, aspire to, yearn for, lust after, set your heart on

coward = wimp, chicken (slang), scaredy-cat (informal), yellow-belly (slang)

cowardly = faint-hearted, scared, spineless, soft, yellow (informal), weak, chicken (slang), fearful, sookie (N.Z.) ≠ brave

cowboy = cowhand, drover, rancher, stockman, cattleman, herdsman, gaucho (S. American)

crack VERB 1 = break, split, burst, snap, fracture, splinter 2 = snap, ring, crash, burst, explode, pop, detonate 3 (Informal) = hit, clip (informal), slap, smack, clout (informal), cuff, whack 4 = break, cleave 5 = solve, work out, resolve, clear up, fathom, decipher, suss (out) (slang), get to the bottom of 6 = break down, collapse, yield, give in, give way, succumb, lose control, be overcome
- NOUN 1 = break, chink, gap, fracture, rift, cleft, crevice, fissure 2 = split, break, fracture 3 = snap, pop, crash, burst, explosion, clap, report 4 (Informal) = blow, slap, smack, clout (informal), cuff, whack, clip (informal) 5 (Informal) = joke, dig, gag (informal), quip, jibe, wisecrack, witticism, funny remark
- ADJECTIVE (Slang) = first-class, choice, excellent, ace, elite, superior, world-class, first-rate

crackdown = clampdown, crushing, repression, suppression

cracked = broken, damaged, split, chipped, flawed, faulty, defective, imperfect

cradle NOUN 1 = crib, cot, Moses basket, bassinet 2 = birthplace, beginning, source, spring, origin, fount, fountainhead, wellspring

● VERB = hold, support, rock, nurse, nestle

craft 1 = vessel, boat, ship, plane, aircraft, spacecraft 2 = occupation, work, business, trade, employment, pursuit, vocation, handicraft 3 = skill, art, ability, technique, know-how (*informal*), expertise, aptitude, artistry

craftsman = skilled worker, artisan, master, maker, wright, technician, smith

cram 1 = stuff, force, jam, shove, compress 2 = pack, fill, stuff 3 = squeeze, press, pack in 4 = study, revise, swot, bone up (*informal*), mug up (*slang*)

cramp[1] = spasm, pain, ache, contraction, pang, stitch, convulsion, twinge

cramp[2] = restrict, hamper, inhibit, hinder, handicap, constrain, obstruct, impede

cramped = restricted, confined, overcrowded, crowded, packed, uncomfortable, closed in, congested ≠ spacious

crash NOUN 1 = collision, accident, smash, wreck, prang (*informal*), bump, pile-up (*informal*) 2 = smash, clash, boom, bang, thunder, racket, din, clatter 3 = collapse, failure, depression, ruin, downfall

● VERB 1 = fall, plunge, topple, lurch, hurtle, overbalance, fall headlong 2 = plunge, hurtle 3 = collapse, fail, go under, be ruined, go bust (*informal*), fold up, go to the wall, go belly up (*informal*)

● PHRASES **crash into** = collide with, hit, bump into, drive into, plough into

crate = container, case, box, packing case, tea chest

crater = hollow, hole, depression, dip, cavity

crave 1 = long for, yearn for, hanker after, want, desire, hope for, lust after 2 (*Informal*) = beg, ask for, seek, petition, pray for, plead for, solicit, implore

craving = longing, hope, desire, yen (*informal*), hunger, appetite, yearning, thirst

crawl VERB = creep, slither, inch, wriggle, writhe, worm your way, advance slowly ≠ run

● PHRASES **crawl to someone** = grovel, creep, fawn, toady, humble yourself

craze = fad, fashion, trend, rage, enthusiasm, vogue, mania, infatuation

crazed = mad, crazy, raving, insane, lunatic, berko (*Austral. slang*), off the air (*Austral. slang*), porangi (*N.Z.*)

crazy 1 (*Informal*) = ridiculous, absurd, foolish, ludicrous, senseless, preposterous, idiotic, nonsensical, porangi (*N.Z.*) ≠ sensible 2 = insane, mad, unbalanced, deranged, nuts (*slang*), crazed, demented, off the air (*Austral. slang*), out of your mind, porangi (*N.Z.*) ≠ sane 3 = fanatical, wild (*informal*), mad, devoted, enthusiastic, passionate, infatuated ≠ uninterested

cream NOUN 1 = lotion, ointment, oil, essence, cosmetic, paste, emulsion, salve 2 = best, elite, prime, pick, flower, crème de la crème (*French*)

● NOUN *or* ADJECTIVE = off-white, ivory, yellowish-white

creamy 1 = milky, buttery 2 = smooth, soft, velvety, rich

crease NOUN 1 = fold, line, ridge, groove, corrugation 2 = wrinkle, line, crow's-foot

● VERB 1 = crumple, rumple, fold, double up, corrugate 2 = wrinkle, crumple, screw up

create 1 = cause, lead to, occasion, bring about 2 = make, produce, invent, compose, devise, originate, formulate, spawn ≠ destroy 3 = appoint, make, establish, set up, invest, install, constitute

creation 1 = universe, world, nature, cosmos 2 = invention, production, achievement, brainchild (*informal*), concoction, handiwork, pièce de résistance (*French*), magnum opus 3 = making, generation, formation, conception, genesis 4 = setting up, development, production, institution, foundation, establishment, formation, inception

creative = imaginative, gifted, artistic, inventive, original, inspired, clever, ingenious

creativity = imagination, inspiration, ingenuity, originality, inventiveness, cleverness

creator 1 = maker, father, author, designer, architect, inventor, originator 2 *usually with cap.* = God, Maker

creature 1 = living thing, being, animal, beast, brute **2** = person, man, woman, individual, soul, human being, mortal

credentials 1 = qualifications, ability, skill, fitness, attribute, capability, eligibility, aptitude **2** = certification, document, reference(s), papers, licence, passport, testimonial, authorization

credibility = believability, reliability, plausibility, trustworthiness

credible 1 = believable, possible, likely, reasonable, probable, plausible, conceivable, imaginable ≠ unbelievable **2** = reliable, honest, dependable, trustworthy, sincere, trusty ≠ unreliable

credit NOUN **1** = praise, honour, recognition, approval, tribute, acclaim, acknowledgment, kudos **2** = source of satisfaction or pride, asset, honour, feather in your cap **3** = prestige, reputation, standing, position, influence, regard, status, esteem **4** = belief, trust, confidence, faith, reliance, credence
● VERB = believe, rely on, have faith in, trust, accept
● PHRASES **credit someone with something** = attribute to, assign to, ascribe to, impute to

creed = belief, principles, doctrine, dogma, credo, catechism, articles of faith

creek 1 = inlet, bay, cove, bight, firth or frith (Scot.) **2** (U.S., Canad., Austral., & N.Z.) = stream, brook, tributary, bayou, rivulet, watercourse, runnel

creep VERB = sneak, steal, tiptoe, slink, skulk, approach unnoticed
● NOUN (Slang) = bootlicker (informal), sneak, sycophant, crawler (slang), toady
● PHRASES **give someone the creeps** (Informal) = disgust, frighten, scare, repel, repulse, make your hair stand on end, make you squirm

crescent = meniscus, sickle, new moon

crest 1 = top, summit, peak, ridge, highest point, pinnacle, apex, crown **2** = tuft, crown, comb, plume, mane **3** = emblem, badge, symbol, insignia, device

crew 1 = (ship's) company, hands, (ship's) complement **2** = team, squad, gang, corps, posse **3** (Informal) = crowd, set, bunch (informal), band, pack, gang, mob, horde

crime 1 = offence, violation, trespass, felony, misdemeanour, misdeed, transgression, unlawful act **2** = lawbreaking, corruption, illegality, vice, misconduct, wrongdoing

criminal NOUN = lawbreaker, convict, offender, crook (informal), villain, culprit, sinner, felon, rorter (Austral. slang), skelm (S. African)
● ADJECTIVE **1** = unlawful, illicit, lawless, wrong, illegal, corrupt, crooked (informal), immoral ≠ lawful **2** (Informal) = disgraceful, ridiculous, foolish, senseless, scandalous, preposterous, deplorable

cripple 1 = disable, paralyse, lame, maim, incapacitate, weaken, hamstring **2** = damage, destroy, ruin, spoil, impair, put paid to, put out of action ≠ help

crippled = disabled, handicapped, paralysed, lame, incapacitated

crisis 1 = emergency, plight, predicament, trouble, deep water, meltdown (informal), dire straits **2** = critical point, climax, height, crunch (informal), turning point, culmination, crux, moment of truth

crisp 1 = firm, crunchy, crispy, crumbly, fresh, brittle, unwilted ≠ soft **2** = bracing, fresh, refreshing, brisk, invigorating ≠ warm **3** = clean, smart, trim, neat, tidy, spruce, well-groomed, well-pressed

criterion = standard, test, rule, measure, principle, gauge, yardstick, touchstone

critic 1 = judge, authority, expert, analyst, commentator, pundit, reviewer, connoisseur **2** = fault-finder, attacker, detractor, knocker (informal)

critical 1 = crucial, decisive, pressing, serious, vital, urgent, all-important, pivotal ≠ unimportant **2** = grave, serious, acute, precarious ≠ safe **3** = disparaging, disapproving, scathing, derogatory, nit-picking (informal), censorious, fault-finding, captious ≠ complimentary **4** = analytical, penetrating, discriminating, discerning, perceptive, judicious ≠ undiscriminating

criticism 1 = fault-finding, censure, disapproval, disparagement, stick (slang), flak (informal), bad press, character assassination **2** = analysis, assessment, judgment, commentary, evaluation, appreciation, appraisal, critique

criticize = find fault with, censure, disapprove of, knock (informal), condemn, carp, put down, slate (informal) ≠ praise

crook NOUN (Informal) = criminal, rogue, cheat, thief, shark, villain, robber, racketeer, skelm (*S. African*)

● **ADJECTIVE** (*Austral. & N.Z. informal*) = ill, sick, poorly (*informal*), unhealthy, seedy (*informal*), unwell, queasy, out of sorts (*informal*)

● **PHRASES go (off) crook** (*Austral. & N.Z. informal*) = lose your temper, be furious, rage, go mad, lose it (*informal*), crack up (*informal*), see red (*informal*), blow your top

crooked 1 = bent, twisted, curved, irregular, warped, out of shape, misshapen ≠ straight **2** = deformed, distorted **3** = zigzag, winding, twisting **4** = at an angle, uneven, slanting, squint, awry, lopsided, askew, off-centre **5** (*Informal*) = dishonest, criminal, illegal, corrupt, unlawful, shady (*informal*), fraudulent, bent (*slang*) ≠ honest

crop NOUN 1 = yield, produce, gathering, fruits, harvest, vintage, reaping

● **VERB 1** = graze, eat, browse, feed on, nibble **2** = cut, trim, clip, prune, shear, snip, pare, lop

● **PHRASES crop up** (*Informal*) = happen, appear, emerge, occur, arise, turn up, spring up

cross VERB 1 = go across, pass over, traverse, cut across, move across, travel across **2** = span, bridge, go across, extend over **3** = intersect, intertwine, crisscross **4** = oppose, interfere with, obstruct, block, resist, impede **5** = interbreed, mix, blend, cross-pollinate, crossbreed, hybridize, cross-fertilize, intercross

● **NOUN 1** = crucifix **2** = trouble, worry, trial, load, burden, grief, woe, misfortune **3** = mixture, combination, blend, amalgam, amalgamation **4** = crossroads, crossing, junction, intersection

● **ADJECTIVE** = angry, annoyed, put out, grumpy, short, ill-tempered, irascible, tooshie (*Austral. slang*), in a bad mood, hoha (*N.Z.*) ≠ good-humoured

● **PHRASES cross something out** *or* **off** = strike off *or* out, eliminate, cancel, delete, blue-pencil, score off *or* out

crouch = bend down, kneel, squat, stoop, bow, duck, hunch

crow = gloat, triumph, boast, swagger, brag, exult, blow your own trumpet

crowd NOUN 1 = multitude, mass, throng, army, host, pack, mob, swarm **2** = group, set, lot, circle, gang, bunch (*informal*),

clique **3** = audience, spectators, house, gate, attendance

● **VERB 1** = flock, mass, collect, gather, stream, surge, swarm, throng **2** = squeeze, pack, pile, bundle, cram **3** = congest, pack, cram

crowded = packed, full, busy, cramped, swarming, teeming, congested, jam-packed

crown NOUN 1 = coronet, tiara, diadem, circlet **2** = laurel wreath, trophy, prize, honour, garland, laurels, wreath **3** = high point, top, tip, summit, crest, pinnacle, apex

● **VERB 1** = install, honour, dignify, ordain, inaugurate **2** = top, cap, be on top of, surmount **3** = cap, finish, complete, perfect, round off, put the finishing touch to, be the climax *or* culmination of **4** (*Slang*) = strike, belt (*informal*), bash, hit over the head, box, punch, cuff, biff (*slang*)

● **PHRASES the Crown 1** = monarch, ruler, sovereign, emperor *or* empress, king *or* queen **2** = monarchy, sovereignty, royalty

crucial 1 (*Informal*) = vital, important, pressing, essential, urgent, momentous, high-priority **2** = critical, central, key, psychological, decisive, pivotal

crude 1 = rough, basic, makeshift **2** = simple, rudimentary, basic, primitive, coarse, clumsy, rough-and-ready **3** = vulgar, dirty, rude, obscene, coarse, indecent, tasteless, smutty ≠ tasteful **4** = unrefined, natural, raw, unprocessed ≠ processed

crudely 1 = roughly, basically **2** = simply, roughly, basically, coarsely **3** = vulgarly, rudely, coarsely, crassly, obscenely, lewdly, impolitely, tastelessly

cruel 1 = brutal, ruthless, callous, sadistic, inhumane, vicious, monstrous, unkind ≠ kind **2** = bitter, ruthless, traumatic, grievous, unrelenting, merciless, pitiless

cruelly 1 = brutally, severely, mercilessly, in cold blood, callously, monstrously, sadistically, pitilessly **2** = bitterly, deeply, severely, ruthlessly, mercilessly, grievously, pitilessly, traumatically

cruelty = brutality, ruthlessness, depravity, inhumanity, barbarity, callousness, spitefulness, mercilessness

cruise NOUN 1 = sail, voyage, boat trip, sea trip

● **VERB 1** = sail, coast, voyage **2** = travel

along, coast, drift, keep a steady pace

crumb 1 = <u>bit</u>, grain, fragment, shred, morsel 2 = <u>morsel</u>, scrap, shred, snippet, soupçon (*French*)

crumble 1 = <u>disintegrate</u>, collapse, deteriorate, decay, fall apart, degenerate, tumble down, go to pieces 2 = <u>crush</u>, fragment, pulverize, pound, grind, powder, granulate 3 = <u>collapse</u>, deteriorate, decay, fall apart, degenerate, go to pieces, go to wrack and ruin

crumple 1 = <u>crush</u>, squash, screw up, scrumple 2 = <u>crease</u>, wrinkle, rumple, ruffle, pucker 3 = <u>collapse</u>, sink, go down, fall 4 = <u>break down</u>, fall, collapse, give way, cave in, go to pieces 5 = <u>screw up</u>

crunch VERB = <u>chomp</u>, champ, munch, chew noisily, grind
● NOUN (*Informal*) = <u>critical point</u>, test, crisis, emergency, crux, moment of truth

crusade NOUN 1 = <u>campaign</u>, drive, movement, cause, push 2 = <u>holy war</u>
● VERB = <u>campaign</u>, fight, push, struggle, lobby, agitate, work

crush VERB 1 = <u>squash</u>, break, squeeze, compress, press, pulverize 2 = <u>crease</u>, wrinkle, crumple 3 = <u>overcome</u>, overwhelm, put down, subdue, overpower, quash, quell, stamp out 4 = <u>demoralize</u>, depress, devastate, discourage, humble, put down (*slang*), humiliate, squash
● NOUN = <u>crowd</u>, mob, horde, throng, pack, mass, jam, huddle

crust = <u>layer</u>, covering, coating, skin, surface, shell

cry VERB 1 = <u>weep</u>, sob, shed tears, blubber, snivel ≠ laugh 2 = <u>shout</u>, scream, roar, yell, howl, call out, exclaim, shriek ≠ whisper
● NOUN 1 = <u>weep</u>, sob, bawl, blubber 2 = <u>shout</u>, call, scream, roar, yell, howl, shriek, bellow 3 = <u>appeal</u>, plea
● PLURAL NOUN = <u>weeping</u>, sobbing, blubbering, snivelling
● PHRASES **cry off** (*Informal*) = <u>back out</u>, withdraw, quit, excuse yourself

cuddle VERB 1 = <u>hug</u>, embrace, fondle, cosset 2 = <u>pet</u>, hug, bill and coo
● PHRASES **cuddle up** = <u>snuggle</u>

cue = <u>signal</u>, sign, hint, prompt, reminder, suggestion

culminate = <u>end up</u>, close, finish, conclude, wind up, climax, come to a head, come to a climax

culprit = <u>offender</u>, criminal, felon, guilty party, wrongdoer, miscreant, evildoer, transgressor

cult 1 = <u>sect</u>, faction, school, religion, clique, hauhau (*N.Z.*) 2 = <u>craze</u>, fashion, trend, fad 3 = <u>obsession</u>, worship, devotion, idolization

cultivate 1 = <u>farm</u>, work, plant, tend, till, plough 2 = <u>develop</u>, establish, foster 3 = <u>court</u>, seek out, run after, dance attendance upon 4 = <u>improve</u>, refine

cultural 1 = <u>ethnic</u>, national, native, folk, racial 2 = <u>artistic</u>, educational, aesthetic, enriching, enlightening, civilizing, edifying

culture 1 = <u>the arts</u> 2 = <u>civilization</u>, society, customs, way of life 3 = <u>lifestyle</u>, habit, way of life, mores 4 = <u>refinement</u>, education, enlightenment, sophistication, good taste, urbanity

cultured = <u>refined</u>, intellectual, educated, sophisticated, enlightened, well-informed, urbane, highbrow ≠ uneducated

cunning ADJECTIVE 1 = <u>crafty</u>, sly, devious, artful, sharp, wily, Machiavellian, shifty ≠ frank 2 = <u>ingenious</u>, imaginative, sly, devious, artful, Machiavellian 3 = <u>skilful</u>, clever ≠ clumsy
● NOUN 1 = <u>craftiness</u>, guile, trickery, deviousness, artfulness, slyness ≠ candour 2 = <u>skill</u>, subtlety, ingenuity, artifice, cleverness ≠ clumsiness

cup 1 = <u>mug</u>, goblet, chalice, teacup, beaker, bowl 2 = <u>trophy</u>

cupboard = <u>cabinet</u>, press

curb VERB = <u>restrain</u>, control, check, restrict, suppress, inhibit, hinder, retard
● NOUN = <u>restraint</u>, control, check, brake, limitation, rein, deterrent, bridle

cure VERB 1 = <u>make better</u>, correct, heal, relieve, remedy, mend, ease 2 = <u>restore to health</u>, restore, heal 3 = <u>preserve</u>, smoke, dry, salt, pickle
● NOUN = <u>remedy</u>, treatment, antidote, panacea, nostrum

curiosity 1 = <u>inquisitiveness</u>, interest, prying, snooping (*informal*), nosiness (*informal*) 2 = <u>oddity</u>, wonder, sight, phenomenon, spectacle, freak, novelty, rarity

curious ADJECTIVE 1 = <u>inquisitive</u>, interested, questioning, searching, inquiring, meddling, prying, nosy (*informal*) ≠ uninterested 2 = <u>strange</u>, unusual, bizarre, odd, novel, rare,

extraordinary, unexpected
● **ADJECTIVE** ≠ ordinary

curl NOUN 1 = ringlet, lock 2 = twist, spiral, coil, kink, whorl 3 = crimp, wave, perm
● **VERB** 1 = twirl, turn, bend, twist, curve, loop, spiral, coil 2 = wind

curly = wavy, curled, curling, fuzzy, frizzy

currency 1 = money, coinage, legal tender, notes, coins 2 = acceptance, popularity, circulation, vogue, prevalence

current NOUN 1 = flow, course, undertow, jet, stream, tide, progression, river 2 = draught, flow, breeze, puff 3 = mood, feeling, spirit, atmosphere, trend, tendency, undercurrent
● **ADJECTIVE** 1 = present, fashionable, up-to-date, contemporary, trendy (*Brit. informal*), topical, present-day, in fashion ≠ out-of-date 2 = prevalent, common, accepted, popular, widespread, customary, in circulation

curse VERB 1 = swear, cuss (*informal*), blaspheme, take the Lord's name in vain 2 = abuse, damn, scold, vilify
● **NOUN** 1 = oath, obscenity, blasphemy, expletive, profanity, imprecation, swearword 2 = malediction, jinx, anathema, hoodoo (*informal*), excommunication 3 = affliction, plague, scourge, trouble, torment, hardship, bane

cursed = under a curse, damned, doomed, jinxed, bedevilled, accursed, ill-fated

curtail = reduce, diminish, decrease, dock, cut back, shorten, lessen, cut short

curtain = hanging, drape (*chiefly U.S.*), portière

curve NOUN = bend, turn, loop, arc, curvature
● **VERB** = bend, turn, wind, twist, arch, snake, arc, coil

curved = bent, rounded, twisted, bowed, arched, serpentine, sinuous

cushion NOUN = pillow, pad, bolster, headrest, beanbag, hassock
● **VERB** 1 = protect 2 = soften, dampen, muffle, mitigate, deaden, suppress, stifle

custody 1 = care, charge, protection, supervision, safekeeping, keeping 2 = imprisonment, detention, confinement, incarceration

custom 1 = tradition, practice, convention, ritual, policy, rule, usage, kaupapa (*N.Z.*) 2 = habit, way, practice,

procedure, routine, wont 3 = customers, business, trade, patronage

customary 1 = usual, common, accepted, established, traditional, normal, ordinary, conventional ≠ unusual 2 = accustomed, regular, usual

customer = client, consumer, regular (*informal*), buyer, patron, shopper, purchaser

customs = import charges, tax, duty, toll, tariff

cut VERB 1 = slit, score, slice, slash, pierce, penetrate 2 = chop, split, slice, dissect 3 = carve, slice 4 = sever, cut in two 5 = shape, carve, engrave, chisel, form, score, fashion, whittle 6 = slash, wound 7 = clip, mow, trim, prune, snip, pare, lop 8 = trim, shave, snip 9 = reduce, lower, slim (down), diminish, slash, decrease, cut back ≠ increase 10 = abridge, edit, shorten, curtail, condense, abbreviate ≠ extend 11 = delete, take out, expurgate 12 = hurt, wound, upset, sting, hurt someone's feelings 13 (*Informal*) = ignore, avoid, slight, blank (*slang*), snub, spurn, cold-shoulder, turn your back on ≠ greet 14 = cross, bisect
● **NOUN** 1 = incision, nick, stroke, slash, slit 2 = gash, nick, wound, slash, laceration 3 = reduction, fall, lowering, slash, decrease, cutback 4 (*Informal*) = share, piece, slice, percentage, portion 5 = style, look, fashion, shape

cutback = reduction, cut, retrenchment, economy, decrease, lessening

cute = appealing, sweet, attractive, engaging, charming, delightful, lovable, winsome

cutting = hurtful, wounding, bitter, malicious, scathing, acrimonious, barbed, sarcastic ≠ kind

cycle = series of events, circle, revolution, rotation

cynic = sceptic, doubter, pessimist, misanthrope, misanthropist, scoffer

cynical 1 = sceptical, mocking, pessimistic, scoffing, contemptuous, scornful, distrustful, derisive ≠ trusting 2 = unbelieving, sceptical, disillusioned, pessimistic, disbelieving, mistrustful ≠ optimistic

cynicism 1 = scepticism, pessimism, misanthropy 2 = disbelief, doubt, scepticism, mistrust

d

dab VERB 1 = <u>pat</u>, touch, tap 2 = <u>apply</u>, daub, stipple

● NOUN 1 = <u>spot</u>, bit, drop, pat, smudge, speck 2 = <u>touch</u>, stroke, flick

daft (*Informal, chiefly Brit.*) 1 = <u>stupid</u>, crazy, silly, absurd, foolish, idiotic, witless, crackpot (*informal*), off the air (*Austral. slang*) 2 = <u>crazy</u>, mad, touched, nuts (*slang*), crackers (*Brit. slang*), insane, demented, deranged, off the air (*Austral. slang*), porangi (*N.Z.*)

dag NOUN (*N.Z. informal*) = <u>joker</u>, comic, wag, wit, comedian, clown, humorist, prankster

● PHRASES **rattle your dags** (*N.Z. informal*) = <u>hurry up</u>, get a move on, step on it (*informal*), get your skates on (*informal*), make haste

dagga (*S. African*) = <u>cannabis</u>, marijuana, pot (*slang*), dope (*slang*), hash (*slang*), grass (*slang*), weed (*slang*), hemp

daily ADVERB = <u>every day</u>, day by day, once a day

● ADJECTIVE = <u>everyday</u>, diurnal, quotidian

dam NOUN = <u>barrier</u>, wall, barrage, obstruction, embankment

● VERB = <u>block up</u>, restrict, hold back, barricade, obstruct

damage VERB = <u>spoil</u>, hurt, injure, harm, ruin, crush, devastate, wreck ≠ fix

● NOUN 1 = <u>destruction</u>, harm, loss, injury, suffering, hurt, ruin, devastation ≠ improvement 2 (*Informal*) = <u>cost</u>, price, charge, bill, amount, payment, expense, outlay

● PLURAL NOUN (*Law*) = <u>compensation</u>, fine, satisfaction, amends, reparation, restitution, reimbursement, atonement

damaging = <u>harmful</u>, detrimental, hurtful, ruinous, deleterious, injurious, disadvantageous ≠ helpful

dame = <u>lady</u>, baroness, dowager, grande dame (*French*), noblewoman, peeress

damn = <u>criticize</u>, condemn, blast, denounce, put down, censure ≠ praise

damned (*Slang*) = <u>infernal</u>, detestable, confounded, hateful, loathsome

damp ADJECTIVE = <u>moist</u>, wet, soggy, humid, dank, sopping, clammy, dewy ≠ dry

● NOUN = <u>moisture</u>, liquid, drizzle, dampness, wetness, dankness ≠ dryness

● VERB = <u>moisten</u>, wet, soak, dampen, moisturize

● PHRASES **damp something down** = <u>curb</u>, reduce, check, diminish, inhibit, stifle, allay, pour cold water on

dampen 1 = <u>reduce</u>, check, moderate, dull, restrain, stifle, lessen 2 = <u>moisten</u>, wet, spray, make damp

dance VERB 1 = <u>prance</u>, trip, hop, skip, sway, whirl, caper, jig 2 = <u>caper</u>, trip, spring, jump, bound, skip, frolic, cavort

● NOUN = <u>ball</u>, social, hop (*informal*), disco, knees-up (*Brit. informal*), discotheque, B and S (*Austral. informal*)

dancer = <u>ballerina</u>, Terpsichorean

danger 1 = <u>jeopardy</u>, vulnerability 2 = <u>hazard</u>, risk, threat, menace, peril, pitfall

dangerous = <u>perilous</u>, risky, hazardous, vulnerable, insecure, unsafe, precarious, breakneck ≠ safe

dangerously = <u>perilously</u>, alarmingly, precariously, recklessly, riskily, hazardously, unsafely

dangle 1 = <u>hang</u>, swing, trail, sway, flap, hang down 2 = <u>wave</u> 3 = <u>offer</u>, flourish, brandish, flaunt

dare 1 = <u>risk doing</u>, venture, presume, make bold (*archaic*), hazard doing 2 = <u>challenge</u>, provoke, defy, taunt, goad, throw down the gauntlet

daring ADJECTIVE = <u>brave</u>, bold, adventurous, reckless, fearless, audacious, intrepid, daredevil ≠ timid

● NOUN = <u>bravery</u>, nerve (*informal*), courage, spirit, bottle (*Brit. slang*), pluck, audacity, boldness ≠ timidity

dark ADJECTIVE 1 = <u>dim</u>, murky, shady, shadowy, grey, dingy, unlit, poorly lit 2 = <u>black</u>, brunette, ebony, dark-skinned, sable, dusky, swarthy ≠ fair 3 = <u>evil</u>, sinister, vile, wicked, infernal 4 = <u>secret</u>, hidden, mysterious, concealed 5 = <u>gloomy</u>, sad, grim, miserable, bleak, dismal, pessimistic, melancholy ≠ cheerful

● NOUN 1 = <u>darkness</u>, shadows, gloom, dusk, obscurity, murk, dimness, semi-darkness 2 = <u>night</u>, twilight, evening, evo (*Austral. slang*), dusk, night-time, nightfall

darken 1 = <u>cloud</u>, obscure, dim, overshadow, blacken ≠ brighten 2 = <u>make dark</u>, blacken

darkness = <u>dark</u>, shadows, shade, gloom, blackness, murk, duskiness

darling NOUN = <u>beloved</u>, love, dear, dearest, angel, treasure, precious, sweetheart

● ADJECTIVE = <u>beloved</u>, dear, treasured, precious, adored, cherished

dart = <u>dash</u>, run, race, shoot, fly, speed, spring, tear

dash VERB 1 = <u>rush</u>, run, race, shoot, fly, career, speed, tear ≠ dawdle 2 = <u>throw</u>, cast, pitch, slam, toss, hurl, fling, chuck (*informal*) 3 = <u>crash</u>, break, smash, shatter, splinter

● NOUN 1 = <u>rush</u>, run, race, sprint, dart, spurt, sortie 2 = <u>drop</u>, little, bit, shot (*informal*), touch, spot, trace, hint ≠ lot 3 (*Old-fashioned*) = <u>style</u>, spirit, flair, flourish, verve, panache, élan, brio

dashing 1 (*Old-fashioned*) = <u>stylish</u>, smart, elegant, flamboyant, sporty, jaunty, showy 2 = <u>bold</u>, spirited, gallant, swashbuckling, debonair ≠ dull

data = <u>information</u>, facts, figures, details, intelligence, statistics

date NOUN 1 = <u>time</u>, stage, period 2 = <u>appointment</u>, meeting, arrangement, commitment, engagement, rendezvous, tryst, assignation 3 = <u>partner</u>, escort, friend

● VERB 1 = <u>put a date on</u>, assign a date to, fix the period of 2 = <u>become dated</u>, become old-fashioned

● PHRASES **date from** or **date back to** (with a *time* or *date* as object) = <u>come from</u>, belong to, originate in, exist from, bear a date of

dated = <u>old-fashioned</u>, outdated, out of date, obsolete, unfashionable, outmoded, passé, old hat ≠ modern

daunting = <u>intimidating</u>, alarming, frightening, discouraging, unnerving, disconcerting, demoralizing, off-putting (*Brit. informal*) ≠ reassuring

dawn NOUN 1 = <u>daybreak</u>, morning, sunrise, daylight, aurora (*poetic*), crack of dawn, sunup, cockcrow 2 (*Literary*) = <u>beginning</u>, start, birth, rise, origin, emergence, advent, genesis

● VERB 1 = <u>begin</u>, start, rise, develop, emerge, unfold, originate 2 = <u>grow light</u>, break, brighten, lighten

● PHRASES **dawn on** or **upon someone** = <u>hit</u>, strike, occur to, register (*informal*), become apparent, come to mind, come into your head

day 1 = <u>twenty-four hours</u> 2 = <u>daytime</u>, daylight 3 = <u>date</u> 4 = <u>time</u>, age, era, period, epoch

daylight = <u>sunlight</u>, sunshine, light of day

daze VERB = <u>stun</u>, shock, paralyse, numb, stupefy, benumb

● NOUN (usually used in the phrase *in a daze*) = <u>shock</u>, confusion, distraction, trance, bewilderment, stupor, trancelike state

dazzle VERB 1 = <u>impress</u>, amaze, overwhelm, astonish, overpower, bowl over (*informal*), take your breath away 2 = <u>blind</u>, confuse, daze, bedazzle

● NOUN = <u>splendour</u>, sparkle, glitter, brilliance, magnificence, razzmatazz (*slang*)

dazzling = <u>splendid</u>, brilliant, stunning, glorious, sparkling, glittering, sensational (*informal*), virtuoso ≠ ordinary

dead ADJECTIVE 1 = <u>deceased</u>, departed, late, perished, extinct, defunct, passed away ≠ alive 2 = <u>boring</u>, dull, dreary, flat, plain, humdrum, uninteresting 3 = <u>not working</u>, useless, inactive, inoperative ≠ working 4 = <u>numb</u>, frozen, paralysed, insensitive, inert, deadened, immobilized, unfeeling 5 (usually used of *centre, silence,* or *stop*) = <u>total</u>, complete, absolute, utter, outright, thorough, unqualified 6 (*Informal*) = <u>exhausted</u>, tired, worn out, spent, done in (*informal*), all in (*slang*), drained, knackered (*slang*)

● NOUN = <u>middle</u>, heart, depth, midst

● ADVERB (*Informal*) = <u>exactly</u>, completely, totally, directly, fully, entirely, absolutely, thoroughly

deadline = <u>time limit</u>, cutoff point, target date or time, limit

deadlock 1 = <u>impasse</u>, stalemate, standstill, gridlock, standoff 2 = <u>tie</u>, draw, stalemate, impasse, standstill, gridlock, standoff, dead heat

deadly 1 = <u>lethal</u>, fatal, deathly, dangerous, devastating, mortal, murderous, malignant 2 (*Informal*) = <u>boring</u>, dull, tedious, flat, monotonous, uninteresting, mind-numbing, wearisome

deaf 1 = hard of hearing, without hearing, stone deaf **2** = oblivious, indifferent, unmoved, unconcerned, unsympathetic, impervious, unhearing

deal NOUN **1** (*Informal*) = agreement, understanding, contract, arrangement, bargain, transaction, pact **2** = amount, quantity, measure, degree, mass, volume, share, portion

● PHRASES **deal in something** = sell, trade in, stock, traffic in, buy and sell

◆ **deal something out** = distribute, give, share, assign, allocate, dispense, allot, mete out ◆ **deal with something** = be concerned with, involve, concern, touch, regard, apply to, bear on, pertain to

◆ **deal with something** or **someone** = handle, manage, treat, cope with, take care of, see to, attend to, get to grips with

dealer = trader, merchant, supplier, wholesaler, purveyor, tradesman

dear ADJECTIVE **1** = beloved, close, valued, favourite, prized, treasured, precious, intimate ≠ hated **2** (*Brit. informal*) = expensive, costly, high-priced, pricey (*informal*), at a premium, overpriced, exorbitant ≠ cheap

● NOUN = darling, love, dearest, angel, treasure, precious, beloved, loved one

dearly (*Formal*) **1** = very much, greatly, extremely, profoundly **2** = at great cost, at a high price

death 1 = dying, demise, end, passing, departure ≠ birth **2** = destruction, finish, ruin, undoing, extinction, downfall ≠ beginning

▌▌▌ RELATED WORDS
adjectives: fatal, lethal, mortal

deathly = deathlike, white, pale, ghastly, wan, pallid, ashen

debacle or **débâcle** = disaster, catastrophe, fiasco

debate NOUN = discussion, talk, argument, dispute, analysis, conversation, controversy, dialogue

● VERB **1** = discuss, question, talk about, argue about, dispute, examine, deliberate **2** = consider, reflect, think about, weigh, contemplate, deliberate, ponder, ruminate

debris = remains, bits, waste, ruins, fragments, rubble, wreckage, detritus

debt NOUN = debit, commitment, obligation, liability

● PHRASES **in debt** = owing, liable, in the red (*informal*), in arrears

debtor = borrower, mortgagor

debut = entrance, beginning, launch, coming out, introduction, presentation, first appearance, initiation

decay VERB **1** = rot, spoil, crumble, deteriorate, perish, decompose, moulder, go bad **2** = decline, diminish, crumble, deteriorate, fall off, dwindle, lessen, wane ≠ grow

● NOUN **1** = rot, corruption, mould, blight, decomposition, gangrene, canker, caries **2** = decline, collapse, deterioration, failing, fading, degeneration ≠ growth

deceased = dead, late, departed, expired, defunct, lifeless

deceive = take in, trick, fool (*informal*), cheat, con (*informal*), mislead, dupe, swindle

decency 1 = propriety, correctness, decorum, respectability, etiquette **2** = courtesy, politeness, civility, graciousness, urbanity, courteousness

decent 1 = satisfactory, fair, all right, reasonable, sufficient, good enough, adequate, ample ≠ unsatisfactory **2** = proper, becoming, seemly, fitting, appropriate, suitable, respectable, befitting ≠ improper **3** (*Informal*) = good, kind, friendly, neighbourly, generous, helpful, obliging, accommodating **4** = respectable, pure, proper, modest, chaste, decorous

deception 1 = trickery, fraud, deceit, cunning, treachery, guile, legerdemain ≠ honesty **2** = trick, lie, bluff, hoax, decoy, ruse, subterfuge

decide 1 = make a decision, make up your mind, reach or come to a decision, choose, determine, conclude ≠ hesitate **2** = resolve, answer, determine, conclude, clear up, ordain, adjudicate, adjudge **3** = settle, determine, resolve

decidedly = definitely, clearly, positively, distinctly, downright, unequivocally, unmistakably

decision 1 = judgment, finding, ruling, sentence, resolution, conclusion, verdict, decree **2** = decisiveness, purpose, resolution, resolve, determination, firmness, forcefulness, strength of mind or will

decisive 1 = crucial, significant, critical,

influential, momentous, conclusive, fateful ≠ uncertain **2** = <u>resolute</u>, decided, firm, determined, forceful, incisive, trenchant, strong-minded ≠ indecisive

deck = <u>decorate</u>, dress, clothe, array, adorn, embellish, festoon, beautify

declaration 1 = <u>announcement</u>, proclamation, decree, notice, notification, edict, pronouncement **2** = <u>affirmation</u>, profession, assertion, revelation, disclosure, acknowledgment, protestation, avowal **3** = <u>statement</u>, testimony

declare 1 = <u>state</u>, claim, announce, voice, express, maintain, assert, proclaim **2** = <u>testify</u>, state, swear, assert, affirm, bear witness, vouch **3** = <u>make known</u>, reveal, show, broadcast, confess, communicate, disclose

decline VERB **1** = <u>fall</u>, drop, lower, sink, fade, shrink, diminish, decrease ≠ rise **2** = <u>deteriorate</u>, weaken, pine, decay, worsen, languish, degenerate, droop ≠ improve **3** = <u>refuse</u>, reject, turn down, avoid, spurn, abstain, say 'no' ≠ accept ● NOUN **1** = <u>depression</u>, recession, slump, falling off, downturn, dwindling, lessening ≠ rise **2** = <u>deterioration</u>, failing, weakening, decay, worsening, degeneration ≠ improvement

décor or **decor** = <u>decoration</u>, colour scheme, ornamentation, furnishing style

decorate 1 = <u>adorn</u>, trim, embroider, ornament, embellish, festoon, beautify, grace **2** = <u>do up</u>, paper, paint, wallpaper, renovate (*informal*), furbish **3** = <u>pin a medal on</u>, cite, confer an honour on or upon

decoration 1 = <u>adornment</u>, trimming, enhancement, elaboration, embellishment, ornamentation, beautification **2** = <u>ornament</u>, trimmings, garnish, frill, bauble **3** = <u>medal</u>, award, star, ribbon, badge

decorative = <u>ornamental</u>, fancy, pretty, attractive, for show, embellishing, showy, beautifying

decrease VERB **1** = <u>drop</u>, decline, lessen, lower, shrink, diminish, dwindle, subside **2** = <u>reduce</u>, cut, lower, moderate, weaken, diminish, cut down, shorten ≠ increase ● NOUN = <u>lessening</u>, decline, reduction, loss, falling off, dwindling, contraction, cutback ≠ growth

decree NOUN **1** = <u>law</u>, order, ruling, act,

command, statute, proclamation, edict **2** = <u>judgment</u>, finding, ruling, decision, verdict, arbitration ● VERB = <u>order</u>, rule, command, demand, proclaim, prescribe, pronounce, ordain

dedicate 1 = <u>devote</u>, give, apply, commit, pledge, surrender, give over to **2** = <u>offer</u>, address, inscribe

dedicated = <u>committed</u>, devoted, enthusiastic, single-minded, zealous, purposeful, wholehearted ≠ indifferent

dedication 1 = <u>commitment</u>, loyalty, devotion, allegiance, adherence, single-mindedness, faithfulness, wholeheartedness ≠ indifference **2** = <u>inscription</u>, message, address

deduct = <u>subtract</u>, remove, take off, take away, reduce by, knock off (*informal*), decrease by ≠ add

deduction 1 = <u>conclusion</u>, finding, verdict, judgment, assumption, inference **2** = <u>reasoning</u>, thinking, thought, analysis, logic **3** = <u>discount</u>, reduction, cut, concession, decrease, rebate, diminution **4** = <u>subtraction</u>, reduction, concession

deed 1 = <u>action</u>, act, performance, achievement, exploit, feat **2** (*Law*) = <u>document</u>, title, contract

deep ADJECTIVE **1** = <u>big</u>, wide, broad, profound, yawning, bottomless, unfathomable ≠ shallow **2** = <u>intense</u>, great, serious (*informal*), acute, extreme, grave, profound, heartfelt ≠ superficial **3** = <u>sound</u>, profound, unbroken, undisturbed, untroubled **4** = <u>absorbed</u>, lost, gripped, preoccupied, immersed, engrossed, rapt **5** = <u>dark</u>, strong, rich, intense, vivid ≠ light **6** = <u>low</u>, booming, bass, resonant, sonorous, low-pitched ≠ high **7** = <u>secret</u>, hidden, mysterious, obscure, abstract, esoteric, mystifying, arcane **8** = <u>far</u>, a long way, a good way, miles, a great distance ● NOUN = <u>middle</u>, heart, midst, dead ● PHRASES **the deep** (*Poetic*) = <u>the ocean</u>, the sea, the waves, the main, the high seas, the briny (*informal*)

deepen 1 = <u>intensify</u>, increase, grow, strengthen, reinforce, escalate, magnify **2** = <u>dig out</u>, excavate, scoop out, hollow out

deeply = <u>thoroughly</u>, completely, seriously, sadly, severely, gravely, profoundly, intensely

de facto ADJECTIVE = actual, real, existing
● ADVERB = in fact, really, actually, in effect, in reality

default VERB = fail to pay, dodge, evade, neglect
● NOUN 1 (usually in phrase by default or in default of) = failure, neglect, deficiency, lapse, omission, dereliction 2 = nonpayment, evasion

defeat VERB 1 = beat, crush, overwhelm, conquer, master, rout, trounce, vanquish ≠ surrender 2 = frustrate, foil, thwart, ruin, baffle, confound, balk, get the better of
● NOUN 1 = conquest, beating, overthrow, rout ≠ victory 2 = frustration, failure, reverse, setback, thwarting

defect NOUN = deficiency, failing, fault, error, flaw, imperfection
● VERB = desert, rebel, quit, revolt, change sides

defence or (U.S.) **defense** NOUN
1 = protection, cover, security, guard, shelter, safeguard, immunity 2 = armaments, weapons 3 = argument, explanation, excuse, plea, justification, vindication, rationalization 4 = plea (Law), testimony, denial, alibi, rebuttal
● PLURAL NOUN = shield, barricade, fortification, buttress, rampart, bulwark, fortified pa (N.Z.)

defend 1 = protect, cover, guard, screen, preserve, look after, shelter, shield 2 = support, champion, justify, endorse, uphold, vindicate, stand up for, speak up for

defendant = the accused, respondent, prisoner at the bar

defender 1 = supporter, champion, advocate, sponsor, follower 2 = protector, guard, guardian, escort, bodyguard

defensive 1 = protective, watchful, on the defensive, on guard 2 = oversensitive, uptight (informal)

defer = postpone, delay, put off, suspend, shelve, hold over, procrastinate, put on ice (informal)

defiance = resistance, opposition, confrontation, contempt, disregard, disobedience, insolence, insubordination ≠ obedience

defiant = resisting, rebellious, daring, bold, provocative, audacious, antagonistic, insolent ≠ obedient

deficiency 1 = lack, want, deficit, absence, shortage, scarcity, dearth ≠ sufficiency 2 = failing, fault, weakness, defect, flaw, drawback, shortcoming, imperfection

deficit = shortfall, shortage, deficiency, loss, arrears

define 1 = mark out, outline, limit, bound, delineate, circumscribe, demarcate 2 = describe, interpret, characterize, explain, spell out, expound 3 = establish, specify, designate

definite 1 = specific, exact, precise, clear, particular, fixed, black-and-white, cut-and-dried (informal) ≠ vague 2 = clear, black-and-white, unequivocal, unambiguous, guaranteed, cut-and-dried (informal) 3 = noticeable, marked, clear, decided, striking, particular, distinct, conspicuous 4 = certain, decided, sure, settled, convinced, positive, confident, assured ≠ uncertain

definitely = certainly, clearly, surely, absolutely, positively, without doubt, unquestionably, undeniably

definition 1 = description, interpretation, explanation, clarification, exposition, elucidation, statement of meaning 2 = sharpness, focus, clarity, contrast, precision, distinctness

definitive 1 = final, convincing, absolute, clinching, decisive, definite, conclusive, irrefutable 2 = authoritative, greatest, ultimate, reliable, exhaustive, superlative

deflect = turn aside, bend

defy = resist, oppose, confront, brave, disregard, stand up to, spurn, flout

degenerate VERB = decline, slip, sink, decrease, deteriorate, worsen, decay, lapse
● ADJECTIVE = depraved, corrupt, low, perverted, immoral, decadent, debauched, dissolute

degrade = demean, disgrace, humiliate, shame, humble, discredit, debase, dishonour ≠ ennoble

degree = amount, stage, grade

delay VERB 1 = put off, suspend, postpone, shelve, defer, hold over 2 = hold up, detain, hold back, hinder, obstruct, impede, bog down, set back ≠ speed (up)
● NOUN = hold-up, wait, setback, interruption, stoppage, impediment, hindrance

delegate NOUN = representative, agent, deputy, ambassador, commissioner, envoy, proxy, legate

● VERB 1 = entrust, transfer, hand over, give, pass on, assign, consign, devolve 2 = appoint, commission, select, contract, engage, nominate, designate, mandate

delegation 1 = deputation, envoys, contingent, commission, embassy, legation 2 = commissioning, assignment, devolution, committal

delete = remove, cancel, erase, strike out, obliterate, efface, cross out, expunge

deliberate ADJECTIVE 1 = intentional, meant, planned, intended, conscious, calculated, wilful, purposeful ≠ accidental 2 = careful, measured, slow, cautious, thoughtful, circumspect, methodical, unhurried ≠ hurried

● VERB = consider, think, ponder, discuss, debate, reflect, consult, weigh

deliberately = intentionally, on purpose, consciously, knowingly, wilfully, by design, in cold blood, wittingly

deliberation 1 = consideration, thought, reflection, calculation, meditation, forethought, circumspection 2 = discussion, talk, conference, debate, analysis, conversation, dialogue, consultation

delicacy 1 = fragility, flimsiness 2 = daintiness, charm, grace, elegance, neatness, prettiness, slenderness, exquisiteness 3 = difficulty 4 = sensitivity, understanding, consideration, diplomacy, discretion, tact, thoughtfulness, sensitiveness 5 = treat, luxury, savoury, dainty, morsel, titbit 6 = lightness, accuracy, precision, elegance, sensibility, purity, subtlety, refinement

delicate 1 = fine, elegant, exquisite, graceful 2 = subtle, fine, delicious, faint, refined, understated, dainty ≠ bright 3 = fragile, weak, frail, brittle, tender, flimsy, dainty, breakable 4 = skilled, precise, deft 5 = diplomatic, sensitive, thoughtful, discreet, considerate, tactful ≠ insensitive

delicious = delectable, tasty, choice, savoury, dainty, mouthwatering, scrumptious (*informal*), appetizing, lekker (*S. African slang*), yummo (*Austral. slang*) ≠ unpleasant

delight NOUN = pleasure, joy, satisfaction, happiness, ecstasy, enjoyment, bliss, glee ≠ displeasure

● VERB = please, satisfy, thrill, charm, cheer, amuse, enchant, gratify ≠ displease

● PHRASES **delight in** *or* **take (a) delight in something** *or* **someone** = like, love, enjoy, appreciate, relish, savour, revel in, take pleasure in

delightful = pleasant, charming, thrilling, enjoyable, enchanting, agreeable, pleasurable, rapturous ≠ unpleasant

deliver 1 = bring, carry, bear, transport, distribute, convey, cart 2 *sometimes with up* = hand over, commit, give up, yield, surrender, turn over, relinquish, make over 3 = give, read, present, announce, declare, utter 4 = strike, give, deal, launch, direct, aim, administer, inflict 5 (*Dated*) = release, free, save, rescue, loose, liberate, ransom, emancipate

delivery 1 = handing over, transfer, distribution, transmission, dispatch, consignment, conveyance 2 = consignment, goods, shipment, batch 3 = speech, utterance, articulation, intonation, elocution, enunciation 4 = childbirth, labour, confinement, parturition

delusion = misconception, mistaken idea, misapprehension, fancy, illusion, hallucination, fallacy, false impression

demand VERB 1 = request, ask (for), order, expect, claim, seek, insist on, exact 2 = challenge, ask, question, inquire 3 = require, want, need, involve, call for, entail, necessitate, cry out for ≠ provide

● NOUN 1 = request, order 2 = need, want, call, market, claim, requirement

demanding = difficult, trying, hard, taxing, wearing, challenging, tough, exacting ≠ easy

demise 1 = failure, end, fall, defeat, collapse, ruin, breakdown, overthrow 2 (*Euphemistic*) = death, end, dying, passing, departure, decease

democracy = self-government, republic, commonwealth

Democrat ADJECTIVE = left-wing, Labour
● NOUN = left-winger

democratic = self-governing, popular, representative, autonomous, populist, egalitarian

demolish 1 = knock down, level, destroy, dismantle, flatten, tear down, bulldoze, raze ≠ build 2 = destroy, wreck, overturn, overthrow, undo

demolition = knocking down, levelling, destruction, explosion, wrecking, tearing down, bulldozing, razing

demon 1 = evil spirit, devil, fiend, goblin, ghoul, malignant spirit, atua (*N.Z.*), wairua (*N.Z.*) **2** = wizard, master, ace (*informal*), fiend

demonstrate 1 = prove, show, indicate, make clear, manifest, testify to **2** = show, express, display, indicate, exhibit, manifest **3** = march, protest, rally, object, parade, picket, remonstrate, express disapproval, hikoi (*N.Z.*) **4** = describe, show, explain, teach, illustrate

demonstration 1 = march, protest, rally, sit-in, parade, picket, mass lobby, hikoi (*N.Z.*) **2** = display, show, performance, explanation, description, presentation, exposition **3** = indication, proof, testimony, confirmation, substantiation **4** = exhibition, display, expression, illustration

den 1 = lair, hole, shelter, cave, haunt, cavern, hide-out **2** (*Chiefly U.S.*) = study, retreat, sanctuary, hideaway, sanctum, cubbyhole

denial 1 = negation, contradiction, dissent, retraction, repudiation ≠ admission **2** = refusal, veto, rejection, prohibition, rebuff, repulse **3** = renunciation, giving up, rejection, abdication, repudiation, forswearing, disavowal, relinquishment

denomination 1 = religious group, belief, sect, persuasion, creed, school, hauhau (*N.Z.*) **2** = unit, value, size, grade

denounce 1 = condemn, attack, censure, revile, vilify, stigmatize **2** = report, dob in (*Austral. slang*)

dense 1 = thick, heavy, solid, compact, condensed, impenetrable, close-knit ≠ thin **2** = heavy, thick, opaque, impenetrable **3** = stupid (*Informal*), thick, dull, dumb (*informal*), dozy (*Brit. informal*), stolid, dopey (*informal*), moronic ≠ bright

density 1 = tightness, thickness, compactness, impenetrability, denseness **2** = mass, bulk, consistency, solidity

dent VERB = make a dent in, press in, gouge, hollow, push in
● NOUN = hollow, chip, indentation, depression, impression, pit, dip, crater, ding (*Austral. & N.Z. dated informal*)

deny 1 = contradict, disagree with, rebuff, negate, rebut, refute ≠ admit **2** = renounce, reject, retract, repudiate,

disown, recant, disclaim **3** = refuse, forbid, reject, rule out, turn down, prohibit, withhold, preclude ≠ permit

depart 1 = leave, go, withdraw, retire, disappear, quit, retreat, exit ≠ arrive **2** = deviate, vary, differ, stray, veer, swerve, diverge, digress

department = section, office, unit, station, division, branch, bureau, subdivision

departure 1 = leaving, going, retirement, withdrawal, exit, going away, removal, exodus ≠ arrival **2** = retirement, going, withdrawal, exit, going away, removal **3** = shift, change, difference, variation, innovation, novelty, deviation, divergence

depend 1 = be determined by, be based on, be subject to, hang on, rest on, revolve around, hinge on, be subordinate to **2** = count on, turn to, trust in, bank on, lean on, rely upon, reckon on

dependent *or* (*U.S. sometimes*) **dependant** ADJECTIVE = reliant, vulnerable, helpless, powerless, weak, defenceless ≠ independent
● PHRASES **dependent on** *or* **upon 1** = reliant on, relying on **2** = determined by, depending on, subject to, influenced by, conditional on, contingent on

depict 1 = illustrate, portray, picture, paint, outline, draw, sketch, delineate **2** = describe, present, represent, outline, characterize

deplete = use up, reduce, drain, exhaust, consume, empty, lessen, impoverish ≠ increase

deplore = disapprove of, condemn, object to, denounce, censure, abhor, take a dim view of

deploy (used of troops or military resources) = use, station, position, arrange, set out, utilize

deployment (used of troops or military resources) = use, stationing, spread, organization, arrangement, positioning, utilization

deport = expel, exile, throw out, oust, banish, expatriate, extradite, evict

depose = oust, dismiss, displace, demote, dethrone, remove from office

deposit NOUN **1** = down payment, security, stake, pledge, instalment, retainer, part payment **2** = accumulation, mass, build-up, layer **3** = sediment, grounds, residue, lees, precipitate, silt, dregs

● VERB 1 = <u>put</u>, place, lay, drop 2 = <u>store</u>, keep, put, bank, lodge, entrust, consign

depot 1 = <u>arsenal</u>, warehouse, storehouse, repository, depository 2 (*Chiefly U.S. & Canad.*) = <u>bus station</u>, station, garage, terminus

depreciation = <u>devaluation</u>, fall, drop, depression, slump, deflation

depress 1 = <u>sadden</u>, upset, distress, discourage, grieve, oppress, weigh down, make sad ≠ cheer 2 = <u>lower</u>, cut, reduce, diminish, decrease, lessen ≠ raise 3 = <u>devalue</u>, depreciate, cheapen 4 = <u>press down</u>, push, squeeze, lower, flatten, compress, push down

depressed 1 = <u>sad</u>, blue, unhappy, discouraged, fed up, mournful, dejected, despondent 2 = <u>poverty-stricken</u>, poor, deprived, disadvantaged, run-down, impoverished, needy 3 = <u>lowered</u>, devalued, weakened, depreciated, cheapened 4 = <u>sunken</u>, hollow, recessed, indented, concave

depressing = <u>bleak</u>, sad, discouraging, gloomy, dismal, harrowing, saddening, dispiriting

depression 1 = <u>despair</u>, misery, sadness, dumps (*informal*), the blues, melancholy, unhappiness, despondency 2 = <u>recession</u>, slump, economic decline, stagnation, inactivity, hard *or* bad times 3 = <u>hollow</u>, pit, dip, bowl, valley, dent, cavity, indentation

deprivation 1 = <u>lack</u>, denial, withdrawal, removal, expropriation, dispossession 2 = <u>want</u>, need, hardship, suffering, distress, privation, destitution

deprive = <u>dispossess</u>, rob, strip, despoil, bereave

deprived = <u>poor</u>, disadvantaged, needy, in need, lacking, bereft, destitute, down at heel ≠ prosperous

depth 1 = <u>deepness</u>, drop, measure, extent 2 = <u>insight</u>, wisdom, penetration, profundity, discernment, sagacity, astuteness, profoundness ≠ superficiality 3 = <u>breadth</u>

deputy = <u>substitute</u>, representative, delegate, lieutenant, proxy, surrogate, second-in-command, legate

derelict ADJECTIVE = <u>abandoned</u>, deserted, ruined, neglected, discarded, forsaken, dilapidated

● NOUN = <u>tramp</u>, outcast, drifter, down-and-out, vagrant, bag lady, derro (*Austral. slang*)

descend VERB 1 = <u>fall</u>, drop, sink, go down, plunge, dive, tumble, plummet ≠ rise 2 = <u>get off</u> 3 = <u>go down</u>, come down, walk down, move down, climb down 4 = <u>slope</u>, dip, incline, slant

● PHRASES **be descended from** = <u>originate from</u>, derive from, spring from, proceed from, issue from

descent 1 = <u>fall</u>, drop, plunge, coming down, swoop 2 = <u>slope</u>, drop, dip, incline, slant, declivity 3 = <u>decline</u>, deterioration, degeneration 4 = <u>origin</u>, extraction, ancestry, lineage, family tree, parentage, genealogy, derivation

describe 1 = <u>relate</u>, tell, report, explain, express, recount, recite, narrate 2 = <u>portray</u>, depict 3 = <u>trace</u>, draw, outline, mark out, delineate

description 1 = <u>account</u>, report, explanation, representation, sketch, narrative, portrayal, depiction 2 = <u>calling</u>, naming, branding, labelling, dubbing, designation 3 = <u>kind</u>, sort, type, order, class, variety, brand, category

desert¹ = <u>wilderness</u>, waste, wilds, wasteland

desert² 1 = <u>abandon</u>, leave, quit (*informal*), forsake 2 = <u>leave</u>, abandon, strand, maroon, walk out on (*informal*), forsake, jilt, leave stranded ≠ take care of 3 = <u>abscond</u>

deserted 1 = <u>empty</u>, abandoned, desolate, neglected, vacant, derelict, unoccupied 2 = <u>abandoned</u>, neglected, forsaken

deserve = <u>merit</u>, warrant, be entitled to, have a right to, rate, earn, justify, be worthy of

deserved = <u>well-earned</u>, fitting, due, earned, justified, merited, proper, warranted

deserving = <u>worthy</u>, righteous, commendable, laudable, praiseworthy, meritorious, estimable ≠ undeserving

design VERB 1 = <u>plan</u>, draw, draft, trace, outline, devise, sketch, formulate 2 = <u>create</u>, plan, fashion, propose, invent, conceive, originate, fabricate 3 = <u>intend</u>, mean, plan, aim, purpose

● NOUN 1 = <u>pattern</u>, form, style, shape, organization, arrangement, construction

2 = <u>plan</u>, drawing, model, scheme, draft, outline, sketch, blueprint **3** = <u>intention</u>, end, aim, goal, target, purpose, object, objective

designate 1 = <u>name</u>, call, term, style, label, entitle, dub **2** = <u>choose</u>, reserve, select, label, flag, assign, allocate, set aside **3** = <u>appoint</u>, name, choose, commission, select, elect, delegate, nominate

designer 1 = <u>couturier</u> **2** = <u>producer</u>, architect, deviser, creator, planner, inventor, originator

desirable 1 = <u>advantageous</u>, useful, valuable, helpful, profitable, of service, convenient, worthwhile ≠ disadvantageous **2** = <u>popular</u> ≠ unpopular **3** = <u>attractive</u>, appealing, pretty, fair, inviting, lovely, charming, sexy (*informal*) ≠ unattractive

desire NOUN **1** = <u>wish</u>, want, longing, hope, urge, aspiration, craving, thirst **2** = <u>lust</u>, passion, libido, appetite, lasciviousness

● VERB = <u>want</u>, long for, crave, hope for, ache for, wish for, yearn for, thirst for

despair NOUN = <u>despondency</u>, depression, misery, gloom, desperation, anguish, hopelessness, dejection

● VERB = <u>lose hope</u>, give up, lose heart

desperate 1 = <u>grave</u>, pressing, serious, severe, extreme, urgent, drastic **2** = <u>last-ditch</u>, daring, furious, risky, frantic, audacious

desperately = <u>gravely</u>, badly, seriously, severely, dangerously, perilously

desperation 1 = <u>misery</u>, worry, trouble, despair, agony, anguish, unhappiness, hopelessness **2** = <u>recklessness</u>, madness, frenzy, impetuosity, rashness, foolhardiness

despise = <u>look down on</u>, loathe, scorn, detest, revile, abhor ≠ admire

despite = <u>in spite of</u>, in the face of, regardless of, even with, notwithstanding, in the teeth of, undeterred by

destination = <u>stop</u>, station, haven, resting-place, terminus, journey's end

destined = <u>fated</u>, meant, intended, certain, bound, doomed, predestined

destiny 1 = <u>fate</u>, fortune, lot, portion, doom, nemesis **2** *usually cap.* = <u>fortune</u>, chance, karma, providence, kismet, predestination, divine will

destroy 1 = <u>ruin</u>, crush, devastate, wreck, shatter, wipe out, demolish, eradicate

2 = <u>slaughter</u>, kill

destruction 1 = <u>ruin</u>, havoc, wreckage, demolition, devastation, annihilation **2** slaughter, extermination, eradication **3** = <u>slaughter</u>

destructive = <u>devastating</u>, fatal, deadly, lethal, harmful, damaging, catastrophic, ruinous

detach 1 = <u>separate</u>, remove, divide, cut off, sever, disconnect, tear off, disengage ≠ attach **2** = <u>free</u>, remove, separate, isolate, cut off, disengage

detached 1 = <u>objective</u>, neutral, impartial, reserved, impersonal, disinterested, unbiased, dispassionate ≠ subjective **2** = <u>separate</u>, disconnected, discrete, unconnected, undivided

detachment 1 = <u>indifference</u>, fairness, neutrality, objectivity, impartiality, coolness, remoteness, nonchalance **2** (*Military*) = <u>unit</u>, party, force, body, squad, patrol, task force

detail NOUN **1** = <u>point</u>, fact, feature, particular, respect, factor, element, aspect **2** = <u>fine point</u>, particular, nicety, triviality **3** (*Military*) = <u>party</u>, force, body, duty, squad, assignment, fatigue, detachment

● VERB = <u>list</u>, relate, catalogue, recount, rehearse, recite, enumerate, itemize

detailed = <u>comprehensive</u>, full, complete, minute, particular, thorough, exhaustive, all-embracing ≠ brief

detain 1 = <u>hold</u>, arrest, confine, restrain, imprison, intern, take prisoner, hold in custody **2** = <u>delay</u>, hold up, hamper, hinder, retard, impede, keep back, slow up *or* down

detect 1 = <u>discover</u>, find, uncover, track down, unmask **2** = <u>notice</u>, see, spot, note, identify, observe, recognize, perceive

detective = <u>investigator</u>, cop (*slang*), private eye, sleuth (*informal*), private investigator, gumshoe (*U.S. slang*)

detention = <u>imprisonment</u>, custody, quarantine, confinement, incarceration ≠ release

deter 1 = <u>discourage</u>, inhibit, put off, frighten, intimidate, dissuade, talk out of **2** = <u>prevent</u>, stop

deteriorate = <u>decline</u>, worsen, degenerate, slump, go downhill ≠ improve

determination = <u>resolution</u>, purpose, resolve, dedication, fortitude, persistence, tenacity, perseverance ≠ indecision

determine 1 = <u>affect</u>, decide, regulate, ordain 2 = <u>settle</u>, learn, establish, discover, find out, work out, detect, verify 3 = <u>decide on</u>, choose, elect, resolve 4 = <u>decide</u>, conclude, resolve, make up your mind

determined = <u>resolute</u>, firm, dogged, intent, persistent, persevering, single-minded, tenacious

deterrent = <u>discouragement</u>, obstacle, curb, restraint, impediment, check, hindrance, disincentive ≠ incentive

devastate = <u>destroy</u>, ruin, sack, wreck, demolish, level, ravage, raze

devastation = <u>destruction</u>, ruin, havoc, demolition, desolation

develop 1 = <u>grow</u>, advance, progress, mature, evolve, flourish, ripen 2 = <u>establish</u>, set up, promote, generate, undertake, initiate, embark on, cultivate 3 = <u>form</u>, establish, breed, generate, originate 4 = <u>expand</u>, extend, work out, elaborate, unfold, enlarge, broaden, amplify

development 1 = <u>growth</u>, increase, advance, progress, spread, expansion, evolution, enlargement 2 = <u>establishment</u>, forming, generation, institution, invention, initiation, inauguration, instigation 3 = <u>event</u>, happening, result, incident, improvement, evolution, unfolding, occurrence

deviant ADJECTIVE = <u>perverted</u>, sick (*informal*), twisted, warped, kinky (*slang*) ≠ normal
● NOUN = <u>pervert</u>, freak, misfit

device 1 = <u>gadget</u>, machine, tool, instrument, implement, appliance, apparatus, contraption 2 = <u>ploy</u>, scheme, plan, trick, manoeuvre, gambit, stratagem, wile

devil NOUN 1 = <u>evil spirit</u>, demon, fiend, atua (*N.Z.*), wairua (*N.Z.*) 2 = <u>brute</u>, monster, beast, barbarian, fiend, terror, swine, ogre 3 = <u>person</u>, individual, soul, creature, thing, beggar 4 = <u>scamp</u>, rogue, rascal, scoundrel, scallywag (*informal*), nointer (*Austral. slang*)
● PHRASES **the Devil** = <u>Satan</u>, Lucifer, Prince of Darkness, Mephistopheles, Evil One, Beelzebub, Old Nick (*informal*)

devise = <u>work out</u>, design, construct, invent, conceive, formulate, contrive,

dream up

devoid *with of* = <u>lacking in</u>, without, free from, wanting in, bereft of, empty of, deficient in

devote = <u>dedicate</u>, give, commit, apply, reserve, pledge, surrender, assign

devoted = <u>dedicated</u>, committed, true, constant, loyal, faithful, ardent, staunch ≠ disloyal

devotee = <u>enthusiast</u>, fan, supporter, follower, admirer, buff (*informal*), fanatic, adherent

devotion NOUN 1 = <u>love</u>, passion, affection, attachment, fondness 2 = <u>dedication</u>, commitment, loyalty, allegiance, fidelity, adherence, constancy, faithfulness ≠ indifference 3 = <u>worship</u>, reverence, spirituality, holiness, piety, godliness, devoutness ≠ irreverence
● PLURAL NOUN = <u>prayers</u>, religious observance, church service, divine office

devour 1 = <u>eat</u>, consume, swallow, wolf, gulp, gobble, guzzle, polish off (*informal*) 2 = <u>enjoy</u>, take in, read compulsively *or* voraciously

devout = <u>religious</u>, godly, pious, pure, holy, orthodox, saintly, reverent ≠ irreverent

diagnose = <u>identify</u>, determine, recognize, distinguish, interpret, pronounce, pinpoint

diagnosis = <u>identification</u>, discovery, recognition, detection

diagram = <u>plan</u>, figure, drawing, chart, representation, sketch, graph

dialogue 1 = <u>discussion</u>, conference, exchange, debate 2 = <u>conversation</u>, discussion, communication, discourse

diary 1 = <u>journal</u>, chronicle 2 = <u>engagement book</u>, Filofax®, appointment book

dictate VERB = <u>speak</u>, say, utter, read out
● NOUN 1 = <u>command</u>, order, decree, demand, direction, injunction, fiat, edict 2 = <u>principle</u>, law, rule, standard, code, criterion, maxim
● PHRASES **dictate to someone** = <u>order (about)</u>, direct, lay down the law, pronounce to

dictator = <u>absolute ruler</u>, tyrant, despot, oppressor, autocrat, absolutist, martinet

dictatorship = <u>absolute rule</u>, tyranny, totalitarianism, authoritarianism, despotism, autocracy, absolutism

dictionary = <u>wordbook</u>, vocabulary,

glossary, lexicon

die VERB 1 = <u>pass away</u>, expire, perish, croak (*slang*), give up the ghost, snuff it (*slang*), peg out (*informal*), kick the bucket (*slang*), cark it (*Austral. & N.Z. slang*) ≠ live 2 = <u>stop</u>, fail, halt, break down, run down, stop working, peter out, fizzle out 3 = <u>dwindle</u>, decline, sink, fade, diminish, decrease, decay, wither ≠ increase
● PHRASES **be dying for something** = <u>long for</u>, want, desire, crave, yearn for, hunger for, pine for, hanker after

diet¹ NOUN 1 = <u>food</u>, provisions, fare, rations, kai (*N.Z. informal*), nourishment, sustenance, victuals 2 = <u>fast</u>, regime, abstinence, regimen
● VERB = <u>slim</u>, fast, lose weight, abstain, eat sparingly ≠ overindulge

diet² *often cap.* = <u>council</u>, meeting, parliament, congress, chamber, convention, legislature

differ 1 = <u>be dissimilar</u>, contradict, contrast with, vary, belie, depart from, diverge, negate ≠ accord 2 = <u>disagree</u>, clash, dispute, dissent ≠ agree

difference 1 = <u>dissimilarity</u>, contrast, variation, change, variety, diversity, alteration, discrepancy ≠ similarity 2 = <u>remainder</u>, rest, balance, remains, excess 3 = <u>disagreement</u>, conflict, argument, clash, dispute, quarrel, contretemps ≠ agreement

different 1 = <u>dissimilar</u>, opposed, contrasting, changed, unlike, altered, inconsistent, disparate 2 = <u>various</u>, varied, diverse, assorted, miscellaneous, sundry 3 = <u>unusual</u>, special, strange, extraordinary, distinctive, peculiar, uncommon, singular

differentiate 1 = <u>distinguish</u>, separate, discriminate, contrast, mark off, make a distinction, tell apart, set off *or* apart 2 = <u>make different</u>, separate, distinguish, characterize, single out, segregate, individualize, mark off 3 = <u>become different</u>, change, convert, transform, alter, adapt, modify

difficult 1 = <u>hard</u>, tough, taxing, demanding, challenging, exacting, formidable, uphill ≠ easy 2 = <u>problematical</u>, involved, complex, complicated, obscure, baffling, intricate, knotty ≠ simple 3 = <u>troublesome</u>, demanding, perverse, fussy, fastidious, hard to please, refractory, unaccommodating ≠ cooperative

difficulty 1 = <u>problem</u>, trouble, obstacle, hurdle, dilemma, complication, snag, uphill (*S. African*) 2 = <u>hardship</u>, strain, awkwardness, strenuousness, arduousness, laboriousness

dig VERB 1 = <u>hollow out</u>, mine, quarry, excavate, scoop out 2 = <u>delve</u>, tunnel, burrow 3 = <u>turn over</u> 4 = <u>search</u>, hunt, root, delve, forage, dig down, fossick (*Austral. & N.Z.*) 5 = <u>poke</u>, drive, push, stick, punch, stab, thrust, shove
● NOUN 1 = <u>cutting remark</u>, crack (*slang*), insult, taunt, sneer, jeer, barb, wisecrack (*informal*) 2 = <u>poke</u>, thrust, nudge, prod, jab, punch

digest VERB 1 = <u>ingest</u>, absorb, incorporate, dissolve, assimilate 2 = <u>take in</u>, absorb, grasp, soak up
● NOUN = <u>summary</u>, résumé, abstract, epitome, synopsis, précis, abridgment

dignity 1 = <u>decorum</u>, gravity, majesty, grandeur, respectability, nobility, solemnity, courtliness 2 = <u>self-importance</u>, pride, self-esteem, self-respect

dilemma = <u>predicament</u>, problem, difficulty, spot (*informal*), mess, puzzle, plight, quandary

dilute 1 = <u>water down</u>, thin (out), weaken, adulterate, make thinner, cut (*informal*) ≠ condense 2 = <u>reduce</u>, weaken, diminish, temper, decrease, lessen, diffuse, mitigate ≠ intensify

dim ADJECTIVE 1 = <u>poorly lit</u>, dark, gloomy, murky, shady, shadowy, dusky, tenebrous 2 = <u>cloudy</u>, grey, gloomy, dismal, overcast, leaden ≠ bright 3 = <u>unclear</u>, obscured, faint, blurred, fuzzy, shadowy, hazy, bleary ≠ distinct 4 = <u>stupid</u> (*Informal*), thick, dull, dense, dumb (*informal*), daft (*informal*), dozy (*Brit. informal*), obtuse ≠ bright
● VERB 1 = <u>turn down</u>, fade, dull 2 = <u>grow or become faint</u>, fade, dull, grow or become dim 3 = <u>darken</u>, dull, cloud over

dimension 1 = <u>aspect</u>, side, feature, angle, facet 2 = <u>extent</u>, size

diminish 1 = <u>decrease</u>, decline, lessen, shrink, dwindle, wane, recede, subside ≠ grow 2 = <u>reduce</u>, cut, decrease, lessen, lower, curtail ≠ increase

din = <u>noise</u>, row, racket, crash, clamour, clatter, uproar, commotion ≠ silence

dine = <u>eat</u>, lunch, feast, sup

dinkum (*Austral. & N.Z. informal*) = <u>genuine</u>, honest, natural, frank, sincere, candid, upfront (*informal*), artless

dinner 1 = <u>meal</u>, main meal, spread (*informal*), repast **2** = <u>banquet</u>, feast, repast, hakari (*N.Z.*)

dip VERB **1** = <u>plunge</u>, immerse, bathe, duck, douse, dunk **2** = <u>drop (down)</u>, fall, lower, sink, descend, subside **3** = <u>slope</u>, drop (down), descend, fall, decline, sink, incline, drop away

● NOUN **1** = <u>plunge</u>, ducking, soaking, drenching, immersion, douche **2** = <u>nod</u>, drop, lowering, slump, sag **3** = <u>hollow</u>, hole, depression, pit, basin, trough, concavity

● PHRASES **dip into something** = <u>sample</u>, skim, glance at, browse, peruse

diplomacy 1 = <u>statesmanship</u>, statecraft, international negotiation **2** = <u>tact</u>, skill, sensitivity, craft, discretion, subtlety, delicacy, finesse ≠ tactlessness

diplomat = <u>official</u>, ambassador, envoy, statesman, consul, attaché, emissary, chargé d'affaires

diplomatic 1 = <u>consular</u>, official, foreign-office, ambassadorial, foreign-politic **2** = <u>tactful</u>, politic, sensitive, subtle, delicate, polite, discreet, prudent ≠ tactless

dire = <u>desperate</u>, pressing, critical, terrible, crucial, extreme, awful, urgent

direct ADJECTIVE = <u>quickest</u>, shortest

● ADVERB **1** = <u>straight</u>, through ≠ circuitous **2** = <u>first-hand</u>, personal, immediate ≠ indirect **3** = <u>clear</u>, specific, plain, absolute, definite, explicit, downright, point-blank ≠ ambiguous **4** = <u>straightforward</u>, open, straight, frank, blunt, honest, candid, forthright ≠ indirect **5** = <u>verbatim</u>, exact, word-for-word, strict, accurate, faithful, letter-for-letter **6** = <u>non-stop</u>, straight

● VERB **1** = <u>aim</u>, point, level, train, focus **2** = <u>guide</u>, show, lead, point the way, point in the direction of **3** = <u>control</u>, run, manage, lead, guide, handle, conduct, oversee **4** = <u>order</u>, command, instruct, charge, demand, require, bid **5** = <u>address</u>, send, mail, route, label

direction NOUN **1** = <u>way</u>, course, line, road, track, bearing, route, path **2** = <u>management</u>, control, charge, administration, leadership, command, guidance, supervision

● PLURAL NOUN = <u>instructions</u>, rules, information, plan, briefing, regulations, recommendations, guidelines

directive = <u>order</u>, ruling, regulation, command, instruction, decree, mandate, injunction

directly 1 = <u>straight</u>, unswervingly, without deviation, by the shortest route, in a beeline **2** = <u>immediately</u>, promptly, right away, straightaway **3** (*Old-fashioned*) = <u>at once</u>, as soon as possible, straightaway, forthwith **4** = <u>honestly</u>, openly, frankly, plainly, point-blank, unequivocally, truthfully, unreservedly

director = <u>controller</u>, head, leader, manager, chief, executive, governor, administrator, baas (*S. African*)

dirt 1 = <u>filth</u>, muck, grime, dust, mud, impurity, kak (*S. African taboo slang*) **2** = <u>soil</u>, ground, earth, clay, turf, loam

dirty ADJECTIVE **1** = <u>filthy</u>, soiled, grubby, foul, muddy, polluted, messy, grimy, festy (*Austral. slang*) ≠ clean **2** = <u>dishonest</u>, illegal, unfair, cheating, crooked, fraudulent, treacherous, unscrupulous ≠ honest **3** = <u>obscene</u>, indecent, blue, offensive, filthy, pornographic, sleazy, lewd ≠ decent

● VERB = <u>soil</u>, foul, stain, spoil, muddy, pollute, blacken, defile ≠ clean

disability = <u>handicap</u>, affliction, disorder, defect, impairment, infirmity

disable = <u>handicap</u>, cripple, damage, paralyse, impair, incapacitate, immobilize, enfeeble

disabled = <u>differently abled</u>, physically challenged, handicapped, weakened, crippled, paralysed, lame, incapacitated ≠ able-bodied

disadvantage 1 = <u>drawback</u>, trouble, handicap, nuisance, snag, inconvenience, downside ≠ advantage **2** = <u>harm</u>, loss, damage, injury, hurt, prejudice, detriment, disservice ≠ benefit

disagree 1 = <u>differ (in opinion)</u>, argue, clash, dispute, dissent, quarrel, take issue with, cross swords ≠ agree **2** = <u>make ill</u>, upset, sicken, trouble, hurt, bother, distress, discomfort

disagreement = <u>argument</u>, row, conflict, clash, dispute, dissent, quarrel, squabble ≠ agreement

disappear 1 = <u>vanish</u>, recede, evanesce

≠ appear **2** = <u>pass</u>, fade away **3** = <u>cease</u>, dissolve, evaporate, perish, die out, pass away, melt away, leave no trace

disappearance 1 = <u>vanishing</u>, going, passing, melting, eclipse, evaporation, evanescence **2** = <u>flight</u>, departure **3** = <u>loss</u>, losing, mislaying

disappoint = <u>let down</u>, dismay, fail, disillusion, dishearten, disenchant, dissatisfy, disgruntle

disappointment 1 = <u>regret</u>, discontent, dissatisfaction, disillusionment, chagrin, disenchantment, dejection, despondency **2** = <u>letdown</u>, blow, setback, misfortune, calamity, choker (*informal*) **3** = <u>frustration</u>

disapproval = <u>displeasure</u>, criticism, objection, condemnation, dissatisfaction, censure, reproach, denunciation

disapprove = <u>condemn</u>, object to, dislike, deplore, frown on, take exception to, take a dim view of, find unacceptable ≠ approve

disarm 1 = <u>demilitarize</u>, disband, demobilize, deactivate **2** = <u>win over</u>, persuade

disarmament = <u>arms reduction</u>, demobilization, arms limitation, demilitarization, de-escalation

disarming = <u>charming</u>, winning, irresistible, persuasive, likable *or* likeable

disarray 1 = <u>confusion</u>, disorder, indiscipline, disunity, disorganization, unruliness ≠ order **2** = <u>untidiness</u>, mess, chaos, muddle, clutter, shambles, jumble, hotchpotch ≠ tidiness

disaster 1 = <u>catastrophe</u>, trouble, tragedy, ruin, misfortune, adversity, calamity, cataclysm **2** = <u>failure</u>, mess, flop (*informal*), catastrophe, debacle, cock-up (*Brit. slang*), washout (*informal*)

disastrous 1 = <u>terrible</u>, devastating, tragic, fatal, catastrophic, ruinous, calamitous, cataclysmic **2** = <u>unsuccessful</u>

disbelief = <u>scepticism</u>, doubt, distrust, mistrust, incredulity, unbelief, dubiety ≠ belief

discard = <u>get rid of</u>, drop, throw away *or* out, reject, abandon, dump (*informal*), dispose of, dispense with ≠ keep

discharge VERB **1** = <u>release</u>, free, clear, liberate, pardon, allow to go, set free **2** = <u>dismiss</u>, sack (*informal*), fire (*informal*), remove, expel, discard, oust, cashier **3** = <u>carry out</u>, perform, fulfil, accomplish,

do, effect, realize, observe **4** = <u>pay</u>, meet, clear, settle, square (up), honour, satisfy, relieve **5** = <u>pour forth</u>, release, leak, emit, dispense, ooze, exude, give off **6** = <u>fire</u>, shoot, set off, explode, let off, detonate, let loose (*informal*)

● NOUN **1** = <u>release</u>, liberation, clearance, pardon, acquittal **2** = <u>dismissal</u>, notice, removal, the boot (*slang*), expulsion, the push (*slang*), marching orders (*informal*), ejection **3** = <u>emission</u>, ooze, secretion, excretion, pus, seepage, suppuration **4** = <u>firing</u>, report, shot, blast, burst, explosion, volley, salvo

disciple 1 = <u>apostle</u> **2** = <u>follower</u>, student, supporter, pupil, devotee, apostle, adherent ≠ teacher

discipline NOUN **1** = <u>control</u>, authority, regulation, supervision, orderliness, strictness **2** = <u>punishment</u>, penalty, correction, chastening, chastisement, castigation **3** = <u>self-control</u>, control, restraint, self-discipline, willpower, self-restraint, orderliness **4** = <u>training</u>, practice, exercise, method, regulation, drill, regimen **5** = <u>field of study</u>, area, subject, theme, topic, course, curriculum, speciality

● VERB **1** = <u>punish</u>, correct, reprimand, castigate, chastise, chasten, penalize, bring to book **2** = <u>train</u>, educate

disclose 1 = <u>make known</u>, reveal, publish, relate, broadcast, confess, communicate, divulge ≠ keep secret **2** = <u>show</u>, reveal, expose, unveil, uncover, lay bare, bring to light ≠ hide

disclosure 1 = <u>revelation</u>, announcement, publication, leak, admission, declaration, confession, acknowledgment **2** = <u>uncovering</u>, publication, revelation, divulgence

discomfort 1 = <u>pain</u>, hurt, ache, throbbing, irritation, tenderness, pang, malaise ≠ comfort **2** = <u>uneasiness</u>, worry, anxiety, doubt, distress, misgiving, qualms, trepidation ≠ reassurance **3** = <u>inconvenience</u>, trouble, difficulty, bother, hardship, irritation, nuisance, uphill (*S. African*)

discontent = <u>dissatisfaction</u>, unhappiness, displeasure, regret, envy, restlessness, uneasiness

discontented = <u>dissatisfied</u>, unhappy, fed up, disgruntled, disaffected, vexed, displeased ≠ satisfied

discount NOUN = <u>deduction</u>, cut, reduction, concession, rebate
● VERB 1 = <u>mark down</u>, reduce, lower 2 = <u>disregard</u>, reject, ignore, overlook, discard, set aside, dispel, pass over
discourage 1 = <u>dishearten</u>, depress, intimidate, overawe, demoralize, put a damper on, dispirit, deject ≠ hearten 2 = <u>put off</u>, deter, prevent, dissuade, talk out of ≠ encourage
discourse 1 = <u>conversation</u>, talk, discussion, speech, communication, chat, dialogue 2 = <u>speech</u>, essay, lecture, sermon, treatise, dissertation, homily, oration, whaikorero (*N.Z.*)
discover 1 = <u>find out</u>, learn, notice, realize, recognize, perceive, detect, uncover 2 = <u>find</u>, come across, uncover, unearth, turn up, dig up, come upon
discovery 1 = <u>finding out</u>, news, revelation, disclosure, realization 2 = <u>invention</u>, launch, institution, pioneering, innovation, inauguration 3 = <u>breakthrough</u>, find, development, advance, leap, invention, step forward, quantum leap 4 = <u>finding</u>, revelation, uncovering, disclosure, detection
discredit VERB 1 = <u>disgrace</u>, shame, smear, humiliate, taint, disparage, vilify, slander ≠ honour 2 = <u>dispute</u>, question, challenge, deny, reject, discount, distrust, mistrust
● NOUN = <u>disgrace</u>, scandal, shame, disrepute, stigma, ignominy, dishonour, ill-repute ≠ honour
discreet = <u>tactful</u>, diplomatic, guarded, careful, cautious, wary, prudent, considerate ≠ tactless
discrepancy = <u>disagreement</u>, difference, variation, conflict, contradiction, inconsistency, disparity, divergence
discretion 1 = <u>tact</u>, consideration, caution, diplomacy, prudence, wariness, carefulness, judiciousness ≠ tactlessness 2 = <u>choice</u>, will, pleasure, preference, inclination, volition
discriminate VERB = <u>differentiate</u>, distinguish, separate, tell the difference, draw a distinction
● PHRASES **discriminate against someone** = <u>treat differently</u>, single out, victimize, treat as inferior, show bias against, show prejudice against
discriminating = <u>discerning</u>, particular, refined, cultivated, selective, tasteful,

fastidious ≠ undiscriminating
discrimination 1 = <u>prejudice</u>, bias, injustice, intolerance, bigotry, favouritism, unfairness 2 = <u>discernment</u>, taste, judgment, perception, subtlety, refinement
discuss = <u>talk about</u>, consider, debate, examine, argue about, deliberate about, converse about, confer about
discussion 1 = <u>talk</u>, debate, argument, conference, conversation, dialogue, consultation, discourse, korero (*N.Z.*) 2 = <u>examination</u>, investigation, analysis, scrutiny, dissection
disdain NOUN = <u>contempt</u>, scorn, arrogance, derision, haughtiness, superciliousness
● VERB = <u>scorn</u>, reject, slight, disregard, spurn, deride, look down on, sneer at
disease = <u>illness</u>, condition, complaint, infection, disorder, sickness, ailment, affliction
diseased = <u>unhealthy</u>, sick, infected, rotten, ailing, sickly, unwell, crook (*Austral. & N.Z. informal*), unsound
disgrace NOUN 1 = <u>shame</u>, degradation, disrepute, ignominy, dishonour, infamy, opprobrium, odium ≠ honour 2 = <u>scandal</u>, stain, stigma, blot, blemish
● VERB = <u>shame</u>, humiliate, discredit, degrade, taint, sully, dishonour, bring shame upon ≠ honour
disgraceful = <u>shameful</u>, shocking, scandalous, unworthy, ignominious, disreputable, contemptible, dishonourable
disgruntled = <u>discontented</u>, dissatisfied, annoyed, irritated, put out, grumpy, vexed, displeased, hoha (*N.Z.*)
disguise NOUN = <u>costume</u>, mask, camouflage
● VERB = <u>hide</u>, cover, conceal, screen, mask, suppress, withhold, veil
disguised 1 = <u>in disguise</u>, masked, camouflaged, undercover, incognito 2 = <u>false</u>, artificial, forged, fake, mock, imitation, sham, counterfeit
disgust NOUN 1 = <u>loathing</u>, revulsion, hatred, dislike, nausea, distaste, aversion, repulsion ≠ liking 2 = <u>outrage</u>, shock, anger, hurt, fury, resentment, wrath, indignation
● VERB = <u>sicken</u>, offend, revolt, put off, repel, nauseate ≠ delight

disgusting 1 = <u>sickening</u>, foul, revolting, gross, repellent, nauseating, repugnant, loathsome, festy (*Austral. slang*), yucko (*Austral. slang*) **2** = <u>appalling</u>, shocking, awful, offensive, dreadful, horrifying

dish 1 = <u>bowl</u>, plate, platter, salver **2** = <u>food</u>, fare, recipe

dishonest 1 = <u>deceitful</u>, corrupt, crooked (*informal*), lying, bent (*slang*), false, cheating, treacherous ≠ honest

disintegrate = <u>break up</u>, crumble, fall apart, separate, shatter, splinter, break apart, go to pieces

dislike VERB = <u>hate</u>, object to, loathe, despise, disapprove of, detest, recoil from, take a dim view of ≠ like
● NOUN = <u>hatred</u>, hostility, disapproval, distaste, animosity, aversion, displeasure, antipathy ≠ liking

dismal 1 = <u>bad</u>, awful, dreadful, rotten (*informal*), terrible, poor, dire, abysmal **2** = <u>sad</u>, gloomy, dark, depressing, discouraging, bleak, dreary, sombre ≠ happy **3** = <u>gloomy</u>, depressing, dull, dreary ≠ cheerful

dismantle = <u>take apart</u>, strip, demolish, disassemble, take to pieces *or* bits

dismay NOUN **1** = <u>alarm</u>, fear, horror, anxiety, dread, apprehension, nervousness, consternation **2** = <u>disappointment</u>, frustration, dissatisfaction, disillusionment, chagrin, disenchantment, discouragement
● VERB **1** = <u>alarm</u>, frighten, scare, panic, distress, terrify, appal, startle **2** = <u>disappoint</u>, upset, discourage, daunt, disillusion, let down, dishearten, dispirit

dismiss 1 = <u>reject</u>, disregard **2** = <u>banish</u>, dispel, discard, set aside, cast out, lay aside, put out of your mind **3** = <u>sack</u>, fire (*informal*), remove (*informal*), axe (*informal*), discharge, lay off, cashier, give notice to **4** = <u>let go</u>, free, release, discharge, dissolve, liberate, disperse, send away

dismissal = <u>the sack</u>, removal, notice, the boot (*slang*), expulsion (*informal*), the push (*slang*), marching orders (*informal*)

disobey 1 = <u>defy</u>, ignore, rebel, disregard, refuse to obey **2** = <u>infringe</u>, defy, refuse to obey, flout, violate, contravene, overstep, transgress

disorder 1 = <u>illness</u>, disease, complaint, condition, sickness, ailment, affliction, malady **2** = <u>untidiness</u>, mess, confusion, chaos, muddle, clutter, shambles, disarray **3** = <u>disturbance</u>, riot, turmoil, unrest, uproar, commotion, unruliness, biffo (*Austral. slang*)

disorderly 1 = <u>untidy</u>, confused, chaotic, messy, jumbled, shambolic (*informal*), disorganized, higgledy-piggledy (*informal*) ≠ tidy **2** = <u>unruly</u>, disruptive, rowdy, turbulent, tumultuous, lawless, riotous, ungovernable

dispatch *or* **despatch** VERB **1** = <u>send</u>, consign **2** = <u>kill</u>, murder, destroy, execute, slaughter, assassinate, slay, liquidate **3** = <u>carry out</u>, perform, fulfil, effect, finish, achieve, settle, dismiss
● NOUN = <u>message</u>, news, report, story, account, communication, bulletin, communiqué

dispel = <u>drive away</u>, dismiss, eliminate, expel, disperse, banish, chase away

dispense VERB **1** = <u>distribute</u>, assign, allocate, allot, dole out, share out, apportion, deal out **2** = <u>prepare</u>, measure, supply, mix **3** = <u>administer</u>, operate, carry out, implement, enforce, execute, apply, discharge
● PHRASES **dispense with something** *or* **someone 1** = <u>do away with</u>, give up, cancel, abolish, brush aside, forgo **2** = <u>do without</u>, get rid of, dispose of, relinquish

disperse 1 = <u>scatter</u>, spread, distribute, strew, diffuse, disseminate, throw about **2** = <u>break up</u>, separate, scatter, dissolve, disband ≠ gather **3** = <u>dissolve</u>, break up

displace 1 = <u>replace</u>, succeed, supersede, oust, usurp, supplant, take the place of **2** = <u>move</u>, shift, disturb, budge, misplace

display VERB **1** = <u>show</u>, present, exhibit, put on view ≠ conceal **2** = <u>expose</u>, show, reveal, exhibit, uncover **3** = <u>demonstrate</u>, show, reveal, register, expose, disclose, manifest **4** = <u>show off</u>, parade, exhibit, sport (*informal*), flash (*informal*), flourish, brandish, flaunt
● NOUN **1** = <u>proof</u>, exhibition, demonstration, evidence, expression, illustration, revelation, testimony **2** = <u>exhibition</u>, show, demonstration, presentation, array **3** = <u>ostentation</u>, show, flourish, fanfare, pomp **4** = <u>show</u>, exhibition, parade, spectacle, pageant

disposable 1 = <u>throwaway</u>, nonreturnable **2** = <u>available</u>, expendable, consumable

disposal NOUN = <u>throwing away</u>, dumping (*informal*), scrapping, removal, discarding, jettisoning, ejection, riddance

● PHRASES **at your disposal** = <u>available</u>, ready, to hand, accessible, handy, at hand, on tap, expendable

dispose VERB = <u>arrange</u>, put, place, group, order, distribute, array

● PHRASES **dispose of someone** = <u>kill</u>, murder, destroy, execute, slaughter, assassinate, slay, liquidate ◆ **dispose of something** 1 = <u>get rid of</u>, destroy, dump (*informal*), scrap, discard, unload, jettison, throw out *or* away 2 = <u>deal with</u>, manage, treat, handle, settle, cope with, take care of, see to

disposition 1 = <u>character</u>, nature, spirit, make-up, constitution, temper, temperament 2 = <u>tendency</u>, inclination, propensity, habit, leaning, bent, bias, proclivity 3 = <u>arrangement</u>, grouping, ordering, organization, distribution, placement

dispute NOUN 1 = <u>disagreement</u>, conflict, argument, dissent, altercation 2 = <u>argument</u>, row, clash, controversy, contention, feud, quarrel, squabble

● VERB 1 = <u>contest</u>, question, challenge, deny, doubt, oppose, object to, contradict 2 = <u>argue</u>, fight, clash, disagree, fall out (*informal*), quarrel, squabble, bicker

disqualify = <u>ban</u>, rule out, prohibit, preclude, debar, declare ineligible

disregard VERB = <u>ignore</u>, discount, overlook, neglect, pass over, turn a blind eye to, make light of, pay no heed to ≠ pay attention to

● NOUN = <u>ignoring</u>, neglect, contempt, indifference, negligence, disdain, disrespect

disrupt 1 = <u>interrupt</u>, stop, upset, hold up, interfere with, unsettle, obstruct, cut short 2 = <u>disturb</u>, upset, confuse, disorder, spoil, disorganize, disarrange

disruption = <u>disturbance</u>, interference, interruption, stoppage

disruptive = <u>disturbing</u>, upsetting, disorderly, unsettling, troublesome, unruly ≠ well-behaved

dissatisfaction = <u>discontent</u>, frustration, resentment, disappointment, irritation, unhappiness, annoyance, displeasure

dissatisfied = <u>discontented</u>, frustrated,

unhappy, disappointed, fed up, disgruntled, displeased, unsatisfied ≠ satisfied

dissent = <u>disagreement</u>, opposition, protest, resistance, refusal, objection, discord, demur ≠ assent

dissident NOUN = <u>protester</u>, rebel, dissenter, demonstrator, agitator

● ADJECTIVE = <u>dissenting</u>, disagreeing, nonconformist, heterodox

dissolve 1 = <u>melt</u>, soften, thaw, liquefy, deliquesce 2 = <u>end</u>, suspend, break up, wind up, terminate, discontinue, dismantle, disband

distance 1 = <u>space</u>, length, extent, range, stretch, gap, interval, span 2 = <u>aloofness</u>, reserve, detachment, restraint, stiffness, coolness, coldness, standoffishness

distant 1 = <u>far-off</u>, far, remote, abroad, out-of-the-way, far-flung, faraway, outlying ≠ close 2 = <u>remote</u> 3 = <u>reserved</u>, withdrawn, cool, remote, detached, aloof, unfriendly, reticent ≠ friendly 4 = <u>faraway</u>, blank, vague, distracted, vacant, preoccupied, oblivious, absent-minded

distinct 1 = <u>different</u>, individual, separate, discrete, unconnected ≠ similar 2 = <u>striking</u>, dramatic, outstanding, noticeable, well-defined 3 = <u>definite</u>, marked, clear, decided, obvious, evident, noticeable, conspicuous ≠ vague

distinction 1 = <u>difference</u>, contrast, variation, differential, discrepancy, disparity, dissimilarity 2 = <u>excellence</u>, importance, fame, merit, prominence, greatness, eminence, repute 3 = <u>feature</u>, quality, characteristic, mark, individuality, peculiarity, distinctiveness, particularity 4 = <u>merit</u>, honour, integrity, excellence, rectitude

distinctive = <u>characteristic</u>, special, individual, unique, typical, peculiar, singular, idiosyncratic ≠ ordinary

distinctly 1 = <u>definitely</u>, clearly, obviously, plainly, patently, decidedly, markedly, noticeably 2 = <u>clearly</u>, plainly

distinguish 1 = <u>differentiate</u>, determine, separate, discriminate, decide, judge, ascertain, tell the difference 2 = <u>characterize</u>, mark, separate, single out, set apart 3 = <u>make out</u>, recognize, perceive, know, see, tell, pick out, discern

distinguished = <u>eminent</u>, noted, famous, celebrated, well-known, prominent, esteemed, acclaimed ≠ unknown

distort 1 = misrepresent, twist, bias, disguise, pervert, slant, colour, misinterpret **2** = deform, bend, twist, warp, buckle, mangle, mangulate (*Austral. slang*), disfigure, contort

distortion 1 = misrepresentation, bias, slant, perversion, falsification **2** = deformity, bend, twist, warp, buckle, contortion, malformation, crookedness

distract 1 = divert, sidetrack, draw away, turn aside, lead astray, draw *or* lead away from **2** = amuse, occupy, entertain, beguile, engross

distracted = agitated, troubled, puzzled, at sea, perplexed, flustered, in a flap (*informal*)

distraction 1 = disturbance, interference, diversion, interruption **2** = entertainment, recreation, amusement, diversion, pastime

distraught = frantic, desperate, distressed, distracted, worked-up, agitated, overwrought, out of your mind

distress NOUN 1 = suffering, pain, worry, grief, misery, torment, sorrow, heartache **2** = need, trouble, difficulties, poverty, hard times, hardship, misfortune, adversity

• **VERB** = upset, worry, trouble, disturb, grieve, torment, harass, agitate

distressed 1 = upset, worried, troubled, distracted, tormented, distraught, agitated, wretched **2** = poverty-stricken, poor, impoverished, needy, destitute, indigent, down at heel, straitened

distressing = upsetting, worrying, disturbing, painful, sad, harrowing, heart-breaking

distribute 1 = hand out, pass round **2** = circulate, deliver, convey **3** = share, deal, allocate, dispense, allot, dole out, apportion

distribution 1 = delivery, mailing, transportation, handling **2** = sharing, division, assignment, rationing, allocation, allotment, apportionment **3** = spread, organization, arrangement, placement

district = area, region, sector, quarter, parish, neighbourhood, vicinity, locality

distrust VERB = suspect, doubt, be wary of, mistrust, disbelieve, be suspicious of ≠ trust

• **NOUN** = suspicion, question, doubt, disbelief, scepticism, mistrust, misgiving, wariness ≠ trust

disturb 1 = interrupt, trouble, bother, plague, disrupt, interfere with, hassle, inconvenience **2** = upset, concern, worry, trouble, alarm, distress, unsettle, unnerve ≠ calm **3** = muddle, disorder, mix up, mess up, jumble up, disarrange

disturbance 1 = disorder, fray, brawl, fracas, commotion, rumpus **2** = upset, bother, distraction, intrusion, interruption, annoyance

disturbed 1 (*Psychiatry*) = unbalanced, troubled, disordered, unstable, neurotic, upset, deranged, maladjusted ≠ balanced **2** = worried, concerned, troubled, upset, bothered, nervous, anxious, uneasy ≠ calm

disturbing = worrying, upsetting, alarming, frightening, distressing, startling, unsettling, harrowing

ditch NOUN = channel, drain, trench, dyke, furrow, gully, moat, watercourse

• **VERB 1** (*Slang*) = get rid of, dump (*informal*), scrap, discard, dispose of, dispense with, jettison, throw out *or* overboard **2** (*Slang*) = leave, drop, abandon, dump (*informal*), get rid of, forsake

dive VERB 1 = plunge, drop, duck, dip, descend, plummet **2** = go underwater **3** = nose-dive, plunge, crash, swoop, plummet

• **NOUN** = plunge, spring, jump, leap, lunge, nose dive

diverse 1 = various, mixed, varied, assorted, miscellaneous, several, sundry, motley **2** = different, unlike, varying, separate, distinct, disparate, discrete, dissimilar

diversify = vary, change, expand, spread out, branch out

diversion 1 = distraction, deviation, digression **2** = pastime, game, sport, entertainment, hobby, relaxation, recreation, distraction **3** (*Chiefly Brit.*) = detour, roundabout way, indirect course **4** (*Chiefly Brit.*) = deviation, departure, straying, divergence, digression

diversity 1 = difference, multiplicity, heterogeneity, diverseness **2** = range, variety, scope, sphere

divert 1 = redirect, switch, avert, deflect, deviate, turn aside **2** = distract, sidetrack, lead astray, draw *or* lead away from **3** = entertain, delight, amuse, please, charm, gratify, beguile, regale

divide 1 = <u>separate</u>, split, segregate, bisect ≠ join 2 *sometimes with* **up** = <u>share</u>, distribute, allocate, dispense, allot, mete, deal out 3 = <u>split</u>, break up, come between, estrange, cause to disagree

dividend = <u>bonus</u>, share, cut (*informal*), gain, extra, plus, portion, divvy (*informal*)

divine ADJECTIVE 1 = <u>heavenly</u>, spiritual, holy, immortal, supernatural, celestial, angelic, superhuman 2 = <u>sacred</u>, religious, holy, spiritual, blessed, revered, hallowed, consecrated 3 (*Informal*) = <u>wonderful</u>, perfect, beautiful, excellent, lovely, glorious, marvellous, splendid
● VERB = <u>guess</u>, suppose, perceive, discern, infer, deduce, apprehend, surmise

division 1 = <u>separation</u>, dividing, splitting up, partition, cutting up 2 = <u>sharing</u>, sharing, distribution, assignment, rationing, allocation, allotment, apportionment 3 = <u>disagreement</u>, split, rift, rupture, abyss, chasm, variance, discord ≠ unity 4 = <u>department</u>, group, branch 5 = <u>part</u>, bit, piece, section, class, category, fraction

divorce NOUN = <u>separation</u>, split, break-up, parting, split-up, rift, dissolution, annulment
● VERB = <u>separate</u>, split up, part company, dissolve your marriage

dizzy 1 = <u>giddy</u>, faint, light-headed, swimming, reeling, shaky, wobbly, off balance 2 = <u>confused</u>, dazzled, at sea, bewildered, muddled, bemused, dazed, disorientated

do VERB 1 = <u>perform</u>, achieve, carry out, complete, accomplish, execute, pull off 2 = <u>make</u>, prepare, fix, arrange, look after, see to, get ready 3 = <u>solve</u>, work out, resolve, figure out, decode, decipher, puzzle out 4 = <u>be adequate</u>, be sufficient, satisfy, suffice, pass muster, cut the mustard, meet requirements 5 = <u>produce</u>, make, create, develop, manufacture, construct, invent, fabricate
● NOUN (*Informal*, *chiefly Brit. & N.Z.*) = <u>party</u>, gathering, function, event, affair, occasion, celebration, reception
● PHRASES **do away with something** = <u>get rid of</u>, remove, eliminate, abolish, discard, put an end to, dispense with, discontinue ◆ **do without something** *or* **someone** = <u>manage without</u>, give up, dispense with, forgo, kick (*informal*), abstain from, get along without

dock¹ NOUN = <u>port</u>, haven, harbour, pier, wharf, quay, waterfront, anchorage
● VERB 1 = <u>moor</u>, land, anchor, put in, tie up, berth, drop anchor 2 (*of spacecraft*) = <u>link up</u>, unite, join, couple, rendezvous, hook up

dock² 1 = <u>cut</u>, reduce, decrease, diminish, lessen ≠ increase 2 = <u>deduct</u>, subtract 3 = <u>cut off</u>, crop, clip, shorten, curtail, cut short

doctor NOUN = <u>physician</u>, medic (*informal*), general practitioner, medical practitioner, G.P.
● VERB 1 = <u>change</u>, alter, interfere with, disguise, pervert, tamper with, tinker with, misrepresent 2 = <u>add to</u>, spike, cut, mix something with something, dilute, water down, adulterate

doctrine = <u>teaching</u>, principle, belief, opinion, conviction, creed, dogma, tenet, kaupapa (*N.Z.*)

document NOUN = <u>paper</u>, form, certificate, report, record, testimonial, authorization
● VERB = <u>support</u>, certify, verify, detail, validate, substantiate, corroborate, authenticate

dodge VERB 1 = <u>duck</u>, dart, swerve, sidestep, shoot, turn aside 2 = <u>evade</u>, avoid, escape, get away from, elude 3 = <u>avoid</u>, evade, shirk
● NOUN = <u>trick</u>, scheme, ploy, trap, device, fraud, manoeuvre, deception

dodgy 1 (*Brit., Austral., & N.Z*) = <u>nasty</u>, offensive, unpleasant, revolting, distasteful, repellent, obnoxious, repulsive 2 (*Brit., Austral., & N.Z*) = <u>risky</u>, difficult, tricky, dangerous, delicate, uncertain, dicey (*informal, chiefly Brit.*), chancy (*informal*) 3 = <u>second rate</u>, poor, inferior, mediocre, shoddy, bush-league (*Austral. & N.Z. informal*), half-pie (*N.Z. informal*), bodger *or* bodgie (*Austral. slang*)

dog NOUN = <u>hound</u>, canine, pooch (*slang*), cur, man's best friend, kuri *or* goorie (*N.Z.*), brak (*S. African*)
● VERB 1 = <u>plague</u>, follow, trouble, haunt, hound, torment 2 = <u>pursue</u>, follow, track, chase, trail, hound, stalk
● PHRASES **go to the dogs** (*Informal*) = <u>deteriorate</u>, degenerate, be in decline, go downhill (*informal*), go down the drain, go to pot, go to ruin
■■■ RELATED WORDS

adjective: canine
female: bitch
young: pup, puppy
dogged = determined, persistent, stubborn, resolute, tenacious, steadfast, obstinate, indefatigable ≠ irresolute
dole NOUN = share, grant, gift, allowance, handout, koha (*N.Z.*)
● PHRASES **dole something out** = give out, distribute, assign, allocate, hand out, dispense, allot, apportion
dolphin
  RELATED WORD
collective noun: school
domestic ADJECTIVE 1 = home, internal, native, indigenous 2 = household, home, family, private 3 = home-loving, homely, housewifely, stay-at-home, domesticated 4 = domesticated, trained, tame, pet, house-trained
● NOUN = servant, help, maid, daily, char (*informal*), charwoman
dominant 1 = main, chief, primary, principal, prominent, predominant, pre-eminent ≠ minor 2 = controlling, ruling, commanding, supreme, governing, superior, authoritative
dominate 1 = control, rule, direct, govern, monopolize, tyrannize, have the whip hand over 2 = tower above, overlook, survey, stand over, loom over, stand head and shoulders above
domination = control, power, rule, authority, influence, command, supremacy, ascendancy
don = put on, get into, dress in, pull on, change into, get dressed in, clothe yourself in, slip on or into
donate = give, present, contribute, grant, subscribe, endow, entrust, impart
donation = contribution, gift, subscription, offering, present, grant, hand-out, koha (*N.Z.*)
donor = giver, contributor, benefactor, philanthropist, donator ≠ recipient
doom NOUN 1 = destruction, ruin, catastrophe, downfall 2 = fate, fortune
● VERB = condemn, sentence, consign, destine
doomed = hopeless, condemned, ill-fated, fated, unhappy, unfortunate, cursed, unlucky
door = opening, entry, entrance, exit, doorway

dope NOUN 1 (*Slang*) = drugs, narcotics, opiates, dadah (*Austral. slang*) 2 (*Informal*) = idiot, fool, twit (*informal, chiefly Brit.*), dunce, simpleton, dimwit (*informal*), nitwit (*informal*), dumb-ass (*slang*), dorba or dorb (*Austral. slang*), bogan (*Austral. slang*)
● VERB = drug, knock out, sedate, stupefy, anaesthetize, narcotize
dorp (*S. African*) = town, village, settlement, municipality, kainga or kaika (*N.Z.*)
dose 1 = measure, amount, allowance, portion, prescription, ration, draught, dosage 2 = quantity, measure, supply, portion
dot NOUN = spot, point, mark, fleck, jot, speck, speckle
● VERB = spot, stud, fleck, speckle
● PHRASES **on the dot** = on time, promptly, precisely, exactly (*informal*), to the minute, on the button (*informal*), punctually
double ADJECTIVE 1 = matching, coupled, paired, twin, duplicate, in pairs 2 = dual, enigmatic, twofold
● VERB 1 = multiply by two, duplicate, increase twofold, enlarge, magnify 2 = fold up or over
● NOUN = twin, lookalike, spitting image, clone, replica, dead ringer (*slang*), Doppelgänger, duplicate
● PHRASES **at** or **on the double** = at once, now, immediately, directly, quickly, promptly, straight away, right away
♦ **double as something** or **someone** = function as, serve as
doubt NOUN 1 = uncertainty, confusion, hesitation, suspense, indecision, hesitancy, lack of conviction, irresolution ≠ certainty 2 = suspicion, scepticism, distrust, apprehension, mistrust, misgivings, qualms ≠ belief
● VERB 1 = be uncertain, be sceptical, be dubious 2 = waver, hesitate, vacillate, fluctuate 3 = disbelieve, question, suspect, query, distrust, mistrust, lack confidence in ≠ believe
doubtful 1 = unlikely, unclear, dubious, questionable, improbable, debatable, equivocal ≠ certain 2 = unsure, uncertain, hesitant, suspicious, hesitating, sceptical, tentative, wavering ≠ certain
doubtless = probably, presumably, most

likely

down ADJECTIVE = <u>depressed</u>, low, sad, unhappy, discouraged, miserable, fed up, dejected

● VERB (*Informal*) = <u>swallow</u>, drink (down), drain, gulp (down), put away (*informal*), toss off

downfall = <u>ruin</u>, fall, destruction, collapse, disgrace, overthrow, undoing, comeuppance (*slang*)

downgrade = <u>demote</u>, degrade, take down a peg (*informal*), lower *or* reduce in rank ≠ promote

downright = <u>complete</u>, absolute, utter, total, plain, outright, unqualified, out-and-out

down-to-earth = <u>sensible</u>, practical, realistic, matter-of-fact, sane, no-nonsense, unsentimental, plain-spoken

downward = <u>descending</u>, declining, heading down, earthward

draft NOUN 1 = <u>outline</u>, plan, sketch, version, rough, abstract 2 = <u>money order</u>, bill (of exchange), cheque, postal order

● VERB = <u>outline</u>, write, plan, produce, create, design, draw, compose

drag VERB = <u>pull</u>, draw, haul, trail, tow, tug, jerk, lug

● NOUN (*Slang*) = <u>nuisance</u>, bore, bother, pest, hassle (*informal*), inconvenience, annoyance

drain VERB 1 = <u>remove</u>, draw, empty, withdraw, tap, pump, bleed 2 = <u>empty</u> 3 = <u>flow out</u>, leak, trickle, ooze, seep, exude, well out, effuse 4 = <u>drink up</u>, swallow, finish, put away (*informal*), quaff, gulp down 5 = <u>exhaust</u>, wear out, strain, weaken, fatigue, debilitate, tire out, enfeeble 6 = <u>consume</u>, exhaust, empty, use up, sap, dissipate

● NOUN 1 = <u>sewer</u>, channel, pipe, sink, ditch, trench, conduit, duct 2 = <u>reduction</u>, strain, drag, exhaustion, sapping, depletion

drama 1 = <u>play</u>, show, stage show, dramatization 2 = <u>theatre</u>, acting, stagecraft, dramaturgy 3 = <u>excitement</u>, crisis, spectacle, turmoil, histrionics

dramatic 1 = <u>exciting</u>, thrilling, tense, sensational, breathtaking, electrifying, melodramatic, climactic 2 = <u>theatrical</u>, Thespian, dramaturgical 3 = <u>expressive</u> 4 = <u>powerful</u>, striking, impressive, vivid, jaw-dropping ≠ ordinary

drape = <u>cover</u>, wrap, fold, swathe

drastic = <u>extreme</u>, strong, radical, desperate, severe, harsh

draught 1 = <u>breeze</u>, current, movement, flow, puff, gust, current of air 2 = <u>drink</u>

draw VERB 1 = <u>sketch</u>, design, outline, trace, portray, paint, depict, mark out 2 = <u>pull</u>, drag, haul, tow, tug 3 = <u>extract</u>, take, remove 4 = <u>deduce</u>, make, take, derive, infer 5 = <u>attract</u> 6 = <u>entice</u>

● NOUN 1 = <u>tie</u>, deadlock, stalemate, impasse, dead heat 2 (*Informal*) = <u>appeal</u>, pull (*informal*), charm, attraction, lure, temptation, fascination, allure

● PHRASES **draw on** or **upon something** = <u>make use of</u>, use, employ, rely on, exploit, extract, take from, fall back on

drawback = <u>disadvantage</u>, difficulty, handicap, deficiency, flaw, hitch, snag, downside ≠ advantage

drawing = <u>picture</u>, illustration, representation, cartoon, sketch, portrayal, depiction, study

drawn = <u>tense</u>, worn, stressed, tired, pinched, haggard

dread VERB = <u>fear</u>, shrink from, cringe at the thought of, quail from, shudder to think about, have cold feet about (*informal*), tremble to think about

● NOUN = <u>fear</u>, alarm, horror, terror, dismay, fright, apprehension, trepidation

dreadful 1 = <u>terrible</u>, shocking, awful, appalling, horrible, fearful, hideous, atrocious 2 = <u>serious</u>, terrible, awful, horrendous, monstrous, abysmal 3 = <u>awful</u>, terrible, horrendous, frightful

dream NOUN 1 = <u>vision</u>, illusion, delusion, hallucination 2 = <u>ambition</u>, wish, fantasy, desire, pipe dream 3 = <u>daydream</u> 4 = <u>delight</u>, pleasure, joy, beauty, treasure, gem, marvel, pearler (*Austral. slang*)

● VERB 1 = <u>have dreams</u>, hallucinate 2 = <u>daydream</u>, stargaze, build castles in the air *or* in Spain

● PHRASES **dream of something** or **someone** = <u>daydream about</u>, fantasize about

dreamer = <u>idealist</u>, visionary, daydreamer, utopian, escapist, Walter Mitty, fantasist

dreary = <u>dull</u>, boring, tedious, drab, tiresome, monotonous, humdrum, uneventful ≠ exciting

drench = <u>soak</u>, flood, wet, drown, steep, swamp, saturate, inundate

dress NOUN 1 = <u>frock</u>, gown, robe

2 = <u>clothing</u>, clothes, costume, garments, apparel, attire, garb, togs
• VERB **1** = <u>put on clothes</u>, don clothes, slip on *or* into something ≠ undress **2** = <u>clothe</u> **3** = <u>bandage</u>, treat, plaster, bind up **4** = <u>arrange</u>, prepare, get ready

dribble VERB **1** = <u>run</u>, drip, trickle, drop, leak, ooze, seep, fall in drops **2** = <u>drool</u>, drivel, slaver, slobber

drift VERB **1** = <u>float</u>, go (aimlessly), bob, coast, slip, sail, slide, glide **2** = <u>wander</u>, stroll, stray, roam, meander, rove, range **3** = <u>stray</u>, wander, digress, get off the point **4** = <u>pile up</u>, gather, accumulate, amass, bank up
• NOUN **1** = <u>pile</u>, bank, mass, heap, mound, accumulation **2** = <u>meaning</u>, point, gist, direction, import, intention, tendency, significance

drill NOUN **1** = <u>bit</u>, borer, gimlet, boring tool **2** = <u>training</u>, exercise, discipline, instruction, preparation, repetition **3** = <u>practice</u>
• VERB **1** = <u>bore</u>, pierce, penetrate, sink in, puncture, perforate **2** = <u>train</u>, coach, teach, exercise, discipline, practise, rehearse

drink VERB **1** = <u>swallow</u>, sip, suck, gulp, sup, guzzle, imbibe, quaff **2** = <u>booze</u> (*informal*), tipple, tope, hit the bottle (*informal*)
• NOUN **1** = <u>glass</u>, cup, draught **2** = <u>beverage</u>, refreshment, potion, liquid **3** = <u>alcohol</u>, booze (*informal*), liquor, spirits, the bottle (*informal*), hooch *or* hootch (*informal, chiefly U.S. & Canad.*)

drip VERB = <u>drop</u>, splash, sprinkle, trickle, dribble, exude, plop
• NOUN **1** = <u>drop</u>, bead, trickle, dribble, droplet, globule, pearl **2** (*Informal*) = <u>weakling</u>, wet (*Brit. informal*), weed (*informal*), softie (*informal*), mummy's boy (*informal*), namby-pamby

drive VERB **1** = <u>go (by car)</u>, ride (by car), motor, travel by car **2** = <u>operate</u>, manage, direct, guide, handle, steer **3** = <u>push</u>, propel **4** = <u>thrust</u>, push, hammer, ram **5** = <u>herd</u>, urge, impel **6** = <u>force</u>, press, prompt, spur, prod, constrain, coerce, goad
• NOUN **1** = <u>run</u>, ride, trip, journey, spin (*informal*), outing, excursion, jaunt **2** = <u>initiative</u>, energy, enterprise, ambition, motivation, zip (*informal*), vigour, get-up-and-go **3** = <u>campaign</u>, push, crusade, action, effort, appeal

drop VERB **1** = <u>fall</u>, decline, diminish **2** *often with away* = <u>decline</u>, fall, sink **3** = <u>plunge</u>, fall, tumble, descend, plummet **4** = <u>drip</u>, trickle, dribble, fall in drops **5** = <u>sink</u>, fall, descend **6** = <u>quit</u>, give up, axe (*informal*), kick (*informal*), relinquish, discontinue
• NOUN **1** = <u>decrease</u>, fall, cut, lowering, decline, reduction, slump, fall-off **2** = <u>droplet</u>, bead, globule, bubble, pearl, drip **3** = <u>dash</u>, shot (*informal*), spot, trace, sip, tot, trickle, mouthful **4** = <u>fall</u>, plunge, descent
• PHRASES **drop off 1** = <u>fall asleep</u>, nod (off), doze (off), snooze (*informal*), have forty winks (*informal*) **2** = <u>decrease</u>, lower, decline, shrink, diminish, dwindle, lessen, subside ◆ **drop out** = <u>leave</u>, stop, give up, withdraw, quit, pull out, fall by the wayside ◆ **drop out of something** = <u>discontinue</u>, give up, quit

drought = <u>water shortage</u>, dryness, dry spell, aridity ≠ flood

drove *often plural* = <u>herd</u>, company, crowds, collection, mob, flocks, swarm, horde

drown 1 = <u>go down</u>, go under **2** = <u>drench</u>, flood, soak, steep, swamp, saturate, engulf, submerge **3** = <u>overwhelm</u>, overcome, wipe out, overpower, obliterate, swallow up

drug NOUN **1** = <u>medication</u>, medicine, remedy, physic, medicament **2** = <u>dope</u> (*slang*), narcotic (*slang*), stimulant, opiate, dadah (*Austral. slang*)
• VERB = <u>knock out</u>, dope (*slang*), numb, deaden, stupefy, anaesthetize

drum VERB = <u>pound</u>, beat, tap, rap, thrash, tattoo, throb, pulsate
• PHRASES **drum something into someone** = <u>drive into</u>, hammer into, instil into, din into, harp on about to

drunk ADJECTIVE **1** = <u>intoxicated</u>, plastered (*slang*), drunken, merry (*Brit. informal*), under the influence (*informal*), tipsy, legless (*informal*), inebriated, out to it (*Austral. & N.Z. slang*), babalas (*S. African*)
• NOUN = <u>drunkard</u>, alcoholic, lush (*slang*), boozer (*informal*), wino (*informal*), inebriate, alko *or* alco (*Austral. slang*)

dry ADJECTIVE **1** = <u>dehydrated</u>, dried-up, arid, parched, desiccated ≠ wet **2** = <u>thirsty</u>, parched **3** = <u>sarcastic</u>, cynical, low-key, sly, sardonic, deadpan, droll, ironical **4** = <u>dull</u>, boring, tedious, dreary, tiresome, monotonous, run-of-the-mill, humdrum ≠ interesting **5** = plain, simple, bare, basic, stark, unembellished

● VERB **1** = drain, make dry **2** often with **out** = dehydrate, make dry, desiccate, sear, parch, dehumidify ≠ wet

● PHRASES **dry up** or **out** = become dry, harden, wither, shrivel up, wizen

dual = twofold, double, twin, matched, paired, duplicate, binary, duplex

dubious 1 = suspect, suspicious, crooked, dodgy (*Brit., Austral., & N.Z. informal*), questionable, unreliable, fishy (*informal*), disreputable ≠ trustworthy **2** = unsure, uncertain, suspicious, hesitating, doubtful, sceptical, tentative, wavering ≠ sure

duck 1 = bob, drop, lower, bend, bow, dodge, crouch, stoop **2** (*Informal*) = dodge, avoid, escape, evade, elude, sidestep, shirk **3** = dunk, wet, plunge, dip, submerge, immerse, douse, souse

due ADJECTIVE **1** = expected, scheduled **2** = fitting, deserved, appropriate, justified, suitable, merited, proper, rightful **3** = payable, outstanding, owed, owing, unpaid, in arrears

● ADVERB = directly, dead, straight, exactly, undeviatingly

● NOUN = right(s), privilege, deserts, merits, comeuppance (*informal*)

● PLURAL NOUN = membership fee, charges, fee, contribution, levy

duel NOUN **1** = single combat, affair of honour **2** = contest, fight, competition, clash, encounter, engagement, rivalry

● VERB = fight, struggle, clash, compete, contest, contend, vie with, lock horns

duff (*Brit., Austral., & N.Z. informal*) = bad, poor, useless, inferior, unsatisfactory, defective, imperfect, substandard, bodger or bodgie (*Austral. slang*)

dull ADJECTIVE **1** = boring, tedious, dreary, flat, plain, monotonous, run-of-the-mill, humdrum ≠ exciting **2** = lifeless, indifferent, apathetic, listless, unresponsive, passionless ≠ lively **3** = cloudy, dim, gloomy, dismal, overcast, leaden ≠ bright **4** = blunt, blunted, unsharpened ≠ sharp

● VERB = relieve, blunt, lessen, moderate, soften, alleviate, allay, take the edge off

duly 1 = properly, fittingly, correctly, appropriately, accordingly, suitably, deservedly, rightfully **2** = on time,

promptly, punctually, at the proper time

dumb 1 = unable to speak, mute ≠ articulate **2** = silent, mute, speechless, tongue-tied, wordless, voiceless, soundless, mum **3** (*Informal*) = stupid, thick, dull, foolish, dense, unintelligent, asinine, dim-witted (*informal*) ≠ clever

dummy NOUN **1** = model, figure, mannequin, form, manikin **2** = imitation, copy, duplicate, sham, counterfeit, replica **3** (*Slang*) = fool, idiot, dunce, oaf, simpleton, nitwit (*informal*), blockhead, dumb-ass (*slang*), dorba or dorb (*Austral. slang*), bogan (*Austral. slang*)

● ADJECTIVE = imitation, false, fake, artificial, mock, bogus, simulated, sham

dump VERB **1** = drop, deposit, throw down, let fall, fling down **2** = get rid of, tip, dispose of, unload, jettison, empty out, throw away or out **3** = scrap, get rid of, abolish, put an end to, discontinue, jettison, put paid to

● NOUN **1** = rubbish tip, tip, junkyard, rubbish heap, refuse heap **2** (*Informal*) = pigsty, hole (*informal*), slum, hovel

dunny (*Austral. & N.Z. old-fashioned informal*) = toilet, lavatory, bathroom, loo (*Brit. informal*), W.C., bog (*slang*), Gents or Ladies, can (*U.S. & Canad. slang*), bogger (*Austral. slang*), brasco (*Austral. slang*)

duplicate VERB **1** = repeat, reproduce, copy, clone, replicate **2** = copy

● ADJECTIVE = identical, matched, matching, twin, corresponding, twofold

● NOUN **1** = copy, facsimile **2** = photocopy, copy, reproduction, replica, carbon copy

durable 1 = hard-wearing, strong, tough, reliable, resistant, sturdy, long-lasting ≠ fragile **2** = enduring, continuing, dependable, unwavering, unfaltering

duration = length, time, period, term, stretch, extent, spell, span

dusk = twilight, evening, evo (*Austral. slang*), nightfall, sunset, dark, sundown, eventide, gloaming (*Scot. poetic*) ≠ dawn

dust NOUN **1** = grime, grit, powder **2** = particles

● VERB = sprinkle, cover, powder, spread, spray, scatter, sift, dredge

dusty = dirty, grubby, unclean, unswept

duty NOUN **1** = responsibility, job, task, work, role, function, obligation, assignment **2** = tax, toll, levy, tariff, excise

● PHRASES **on duty** = at work, busy,

engaged, on active service

dwarf VERB 1 = <u>tower above</u> or <u>over</u>, dominate, overlook, stand over, loom over, stand head and shoulders above 2 = <u>eclipse</u>, tower above or over, put in the shade, diminish

● ADJECTIVE = <u>miniature</u>, small, baby, tiny, diminutive, bonsai, undersized

● NOUN = <u>gnome</u>, midget, Lilliputian, Tom Thumb, pygmy or pigmy

dwell (*Formal or literary*) = <u>live</u>, reside, lodge, abide

dwelling (*Formal or literary*) = <u>home</u>, house, residence, abode, quarters, lodging, habitation, domicile, whare (*N.Z.*)

dwindle = <u>lessen</u>, decline, fade, shrink, diminish, decrease, wane, subside ≠ increase

dye VERB = <u>colour</u>, stain, tint, tinge, pigment

● NOUN = <u>colouring</u>, colour, pigment, stain, tint, tinge, colorant

dying 1 = <u>near death</u>, moribund, in extremis (*Latin*), at death's door, not long for this world 2 = <u>final</u>, last, parting, departing 3 = <u>failing</u>, declining, foundering, diminishing, decreasing, dwindling, subsiding

dynamic = <u>energetic</u>, powerful, vital, go-ahead, lively, animated, high-powered, forceful ≠ apathetic

dynasty = <u>empire</u>, house, rule, regime, sovereignty

e

each DETERMINER = <u>every</u>, every single

● PRONOUN = <u>every one</u>, all, each one, each and every one, one and all

● ADVERB = <u>apiece</u>, individually, for each, to each, respectively, per person, per head, per capita

eager 1 = <u>anxious</u>, keen, hungry, impatient, itching, thirsty ≠ unenthusiastic 2 = <u>keen</u>, interested, intense, enthusiastic,

passionate, avid (*informal*), fervent ≠ uninterested

ear = <u>sensitivity</u>, taste, discrimination, appreciation

RELATED WORD
adjective: aural

early ADVERB 1 = <u>in good time</u>, beforehand, ahead of schedule, in advance, with time to spare ≠ late 2 = <u>too soon</u>, before the usual time, prematurely, ahead of time ≠ late

● ADJECTIVE 1 = <u>first</u>, opening, initial, introductory 2 = <u>premature</u>, forward, advanced, untimely, unseasonable ≠ belated 3 = <u>primitive</u>, first, earliest, young, original, undeveloped, primordial, primeval ≠ developed

earmark 1 = <u>set aside</u>, reserve, label, flag, allocate, designate, mark out 2 = <u>mark out</u>, identify, designate

earn 1 = <u>be paid</u>, make, get, receive, gain, net, collect, bring in 2 = <u>deserve</u>, win, gain, attain, justify, merit, warrant, be entitled to

earnest 1 = <u>serious</u>, grave, intense, dedicated, sincere, thoughtful, solemn, ardent ≠ frivolous 2 = <u>determined</u>, dogged, intent, persistent, persevering, resolute, wholehearted ≠ half-hearted

earnings = <u>income</u>, pay, wages, revenue, proceeds, salary, receipts, remuneration

earth 1 = <u>world</u>, planet, globe, sphere, orb, earthly sphere 2 = <u>ground</u>, land, dry land, terra firma 3 = <u>soil</u>, ground, land, dust, clay, dirt, turf, silt

earthly 1 = <u>worldly</u>, material, secular, mortal, temporal, human ≠ spiritual 2 = <u>sensual</u>, worldly, physical, fleshly, bodily, carnal 3 (*Informal*) = <u>possible</u>, likely, practical, feasible, conceivable, imaginable

ease NOUN 1 = <u>straightforwardness</u>, simplicity, readiness 2 = <u>comfort</u>, luxury, leisure, relaxation, prosperity, affluence, rest, repose ≠ hardship 3 = <u>peace of mind</u>, peace, content, quiet, comfort, happiness, serenity, tranquillity ≠ agitation

● VERB 1 = <u>relieve</u>, calm, soothe, lessen, alleviate, lighten, lower, relax ≠ aggravate 2 = <u>reduce</u>, diminish, lessen, slacken 3 = <u>move carefully</u>, edge, slip, inch, slide, creep, manoeuvre

easily = <u>without difficulty</u>, smoothly, readily, comfortably, effortlessly, with ease, straightforwardly

easy 1 = <u>simple</u>, straightforward, no trouble, not difficult, effortless, painless, uncomplicated, child's play (*informal*) ≠ hard **2** = <u>untroubled</u>, relaxed, peaceful, serene, tranquil, quiet **3** = <u>carefree</u>, comfortable, leisurely, trouble-free, untroubled, cushy (*informal*) ≠ difficult **4** = <u>tolerant</u>, soft, mild, laid-back (*informal*), indulgent, easy-going, lenient, permissive ≠ strict

eat 1 = <u>consume</u>, swallow, chew, scoff (*slang*), devour, munch, tuck into (*informal*), put away **2** = <u>have a meal</u>, lunch, breakfast, dine, snack, feed, graze (*informal*), have lunch

ebb VERB 1 = <u>flow back</u>, go out, withdraw, retreat, wane, recede **2** = <u>decline</u>, flag, diminish, decrease, dwindle, lessen, subside, fall away
● **NOUN** = <u>flowing back</u>, going out, withdrawal, retreat, wane, low water, low tide, outgoing tide

eccentric ADJECTIVE = <u>odd</u>, strange, peculiar, irregular, quirky, unconventional, idiosyncratic, outlandish ≠ normal
● **NOUN** = <u>crank</u> (*informal*), character (*informal*), oddball (*informal*), nonconformist, weirdo *or* weirdie (*informal*)

echo NOUN 1 = <u>reverberation</u>, ringing, repetition, answer, resonance, resounding **2** = <u>copy</u>, reflection, clone, reproduction, imitation, duplicate, double, reiteration
● **VERB 1** = <u>reverberate</u>, repeat, resound, ring, resonate **2** = <u>recall</u>, reflect, copy, mirror, resemble, imitate, ape

eclipse NOUN = <u>obscuring</u>, covering, blocking, shading, dimming, extinction, darkening, blotting out
● **VERB** = <u>surpass</u>, exceed, overshadow, excel, transcend, outdo, outclass, outshine

economic 1 = <u>financial</u>, industrial, commercial **2** = <u>profitable</u>, successful, commercial, rewarding, productive, lucrative, worthwhile, viable **3** (*Informal*) = <u>economical</u>, cheap, reasonable, modest, low-priced, inexpensive

economical 1 = <u>thrifty</u>, sparing, careful, prudent, provident, frugal, parsimonious, scrimping ≠ extravagant **2** = <u>efficient</u>, sparing, cost-effective, money-saving, time-saving ≠ wasteful

economy 1 = <u>financial system</u>, financial state **2** = <u>thrift</u>, restraint, prudence, husbandry, frugality, parsimony

ecstasy = <u>rapture</u>, delight, joy, bliss, euphoria, fringe, verge, elation ≠ agony

ecstatic = <u>rapturous</u>, entranced, joyous, elated, overjoyed, blissful, euphoric, enraptured

edge NOUN 1 = <u>border</u>, side, limit, outline, boundary, fringe, verge, brink **2** = <u>verge</u>, point, brink, threshold **3** = <u>advantage</u>, lead, dominance, superiority, upper hand, head start, ascendancy, whip hand **4** = <u>power</u>, force, bite, effectiveness, incisiveness, powerful quality **5** = <u>sharpness</u>, point, bitterness, keenness
● **VERB 1** = <u>inch</u>, ease, creep, slink, steal, sidle, move slowly **2** = <u>border</u>, fringe, hem, pipe
● **PHRASES on edge** = <u>tense</u>, nervous, impatient, irritable, apprehensive, edgy, ill at ease, on tenterhooks

edit = <u>revise</u>, improve, correct, polish, adapt, rewrite, condense, redraft

edition = <u>version</u>, copy, issue, programme (*TV*, *Radio*), printing, volume, impression, publication

educate = <u>teach</u>, school, train, develop, improve, inform, discipline, tutor

educated 1 = <u>cultured</u>, intellectual, learned, sophisticated, refined, cultivated, enlightened, knowledgeable ≠ uncultured **2** = <u>taught</u>, schooled, coached, informed, tutored, instructed, nurtured, well-informed ≠ uneducated

education 1 = <u>teaching</u>, schooling, training, development, discipline, instruction, nurture, tuition **2** = <u>learning</u>, schooling, cultivation, refinement

educational 1 = <u>academic</u>, school, learning, teaching, scholastic, pedagogical, pedagogic **2** = <u>instructive</u>, useful, cultural, illuminating, enlightening, informative, instructional, edifying

eerie = <u>uncanny</u>, strange, frightening, ghostly, weird, mysterious, scary (*informal*), sinister

effect NOUN 1 = <u>result</u>, consequence, conclusion, outcome, event, end result, upshot **2** = <u>impression</u>, feeling, impact, influence **3** = <u>purpose</u>, impression, sense, intent, essence, thread, tenor
● **PLURAL NOUN** = <u>belongings</u>, goods, things, property, stuff, gear, possessions, paraphernalia
● **VERB** = <u>bring about</u>, produce, complete,

achieve, perform, fulfil, accomplish, execute

effective 1 = <u>efficient</u>, successful, useful, active, capable, valuable, helpful, adequate ≠ ineffective 2 = <u>powerful</u>, strong, convincing, persuasive, telling, impressive, compelling, forceful ≠ weak 3 = <u>virtual</u>, essential, practical, implied, implicit, tacit, unacknowledged 4 = <u>in operation</u>, official, current, legal, active, in effect, valid, operative ≠ inoperative

efficiency 1 = <u>effectiveness</u>, power, economy, productivity, organization, cost-effectiveness, orderliness 2 = <u>competence</u>, expertise, capability, professionalism, proficiency, adeptness

efficient 1 = <u>effective</u>, successful, structured, productive, systematic, streamlined, cost-effective, methodical ≠ inefficient 2 = <u>competent</u>, professional, capable, organized, productive, proficient, businesslike, well-organized ≠ incompetent

effort 1 = <u>attempt</u>, try, endeavour, shot (*informal*), bid, essay, go (*informal*), stab (*informal*) 2 = <u>exertion</u>, work, trouble, energy, struggle, application, graft, toil

egg NOUN = <u>ovum</u>, gamete, germ cell
● PHRASES **egg someone on** = <u>incite</u>, push, encourage, urge, prompt, spur, provoke, prod

eject 1 = <u>throw out</u>, remove, turn out, expel (*slang*), oust, banish, drive out, evict 2 = <u>bail out</u>, escape, get out

elaborate ADJECTIVE 1 = <u>complicated</u>, detailed, studied, complex, precise, thorough, intricate, painstaking 2 = <u>ornate</u>, involved, complex, fancy, complicated, intricate, baroque, ornamented ≠ plain
● VERB 1 = <u>develop</u>, flesh out 2 = <u>expand (upon)</u>, extend, enlarge (on), amplify, embellish, flesh out, add detail (to) ≠ simplify

elastic 1 = <u>flexible</u>, supple, rubbery, pliable, plastic, springy, pliant, tensile ≠ rigid 2 = <u>adaptable</u>, yielding, variable, flexible, accommodating, tolerant, adjustable, supple ≠ inflexible

elbow = <u>joint</u>, angle, curve

elder ADJECTIVE = <u>older</u>, first, senior, first-born
● NOUN = <u>older person</u>, senior

elect 1 = <u>vote for</u>, choose, pick, determine, select, appoint, opt for, settle on 2 = <u>choose</u>, decide, prefer, select, opt

election 1 = <u>vote</u>, poll, ballot, referendum, franchise, plebiscite, show of hands 2 = <u>appointment</u>, picking, choice, selection

electric 1 = <u>electric-powered</u>, powered, cordless, battery-operated, electrically-charged, mains-operated 2 = <u>charged</u>, exciting, stirring, thrilling, stimulating, dynamic, tense, rousing

elegance = <u>style</u>, taste, grace, dignity, sophistication, grandeur, refinement, gracefulness

elegant = <u>stylish</u>, fine, sophisticated, delicate, handsome, refined, chic, exquisite ≠ inelegant

element NOUN 1 = <u>component</u>, part, unit, section, factor, principle, aspect, foundation 2 = <u>group</u>, faction, clique, set, party, circle 3 = <u>trace</u>, suggestion, hint, dash, suspicion, tinge, smattering, soupçon
● PLURAL NOUN = <u>weather conditions</u>, climate, the weather, wind and rain, atmospheric conditions, powers of nature
● PHRASES **be in your element** = <u>be in a situation you enjoy</u>, be in your natural environment, be in familiar surroundings

elementary = <u>simple</u>, clear, easy, plain, straightforward, rudimentary, uncomplicated, undemanding ≠ complicated

elevate 1 = <u>promote</u>, raise, advance, upgrade, exalt, kick upstairs (*informal*), aggrandize, give advancement to 2 = <u>increase</u>, lift, raise, step up, intensify, move up, hoist, raise high 3 = <u>raise</u>, lift, heighten, uplift, hoist, lift up, raise up, hike up

elevated 1 = <u>exalted</u>, important, august, grand, superior, noble, dignified, high-ranking 2 = <u>high-minded</u>, fine, grand, noble, inflated, dignified, sublime, lofty ≠ humble 3 = <u>raised</u>, high, lifted up, upraised

elicit 1 = <u>bring about</u>, cause, derive, bring out, evoke, give rise to, draw out, bring forth 2 = <u>obtain</u>, extract, exact, evoke, wrest, draw out, extort

eligible 1 = <u>entitled</u>, fit, qualified, suitable ≠ ineligible 2 = <u>available</u>, free, single, unmarried, unattached

eliminate = <u>remove</u>, end, stop, withdraw,

get rid of, abolish, cut out, dispose of

elite = aristocracy, best, pick, cream, upper class, nobility, crème de la crème (*French*), flower ≠ rabble

eloquent 1 = silver-tongued, moving, powerful, effective, stirring, articulate, persuasive, forceful ≠ inarticulate **2** = expressive, telling, pointed, significant, vivid, meaningful, indicative, suggestive

elsewhere = in *or* to another place, away, abroad, hence (*archaic*), somewhere else, not here, in other places, in *or* to a different place

elude 1 = evade, escape, lose, avoid, flee, duck (*informal*), dodge, get away from **2** = escape, baffle, frustrate, puzzle, stump, foil, be beyond (someone), thwart

elusive 1 = difficult to catch, tricky, slippery, difficult to find, evasive, shifty **2** = indefinable, fleeting, subtle, indefinite, transient, intangible, indescribable, transitory

emanate = flow, emerge, spring, proceed, arise, stem, derive, originate

embargo NOUN = ban, bar, restriction, boycott, restraint, prohibition, moratorium, stoppage, rahui (*N.Z.*)
● VERB = block, stop, bar, ban, restrict, boycott, prohibit, blacklist

embark VERB = go aboard, climb aboard, board ship, step aboard, go on board, take ship ≠ get off
● PHRASES **embark on something** = begin, start, launch, enter, take up, set out, set about, plunge into

embarrass = shame, distress, show up (*informal*), humiliate, disconcert, fluster, mortify, discomfit

embarrassed = ashamed, shamed, uncomfortable, awkward, abashed, humiliated, uneasy, unsettled

embarrassing = humiliating, upsetting, compromising, delicate, uncomfortable, awkward, sensitive, troublesome, barro (*Austral. slang*)

embarrassment 1 = shame, distress, showing up (*informal*), humiliation, discomfort, unease, self-consciousness, awkwardness **2** = problem, difficulty, nuisance, source of trouble, thorn in your flesh **3** = predicament, problem, difficulty (*informal*), mess, jam (*informal*), plight, scrape (*informal*), pickle (*informal*)

embody 1 = personify, represent, stand

for, manifest, exemplify, symbolize, typify, actualize **2** = incorporate, include, contain, combine, collect, take in, encompass

embrace VERB **1** = hug, hold, cuddle, seize, squeeze, clasp, envelop, canoodle (*slang*) **2** = accept, support, welcome, adopt, take up, seize, espouse, take on board **3** = include, involve, cover, contain, take in, incorporate, comprise, encompass
● NOUN = hug, hold, cuddle, squeeze, clinch (*slang*), clasp

embroil = involve, mix up, implicate, entangle, mire, ensnare, enmesh

embryo 1 = foetus, unborn child, fertilized egg **2** = germ, beginning, source, root, seed, nucleus, rudiment

emerge 1 = come out, appear, surface, rise, arise, turn up, spring up, emanate ≠ withdraw **2** = become apparent, come out, become known, come to light, crop up, transpire, become evident, come out in the wash

emergence 1 = coming, development, arrival, surfacing, rise, appearance, arising, turning up **2** = disclosure, publishing, broadcasting, broadcast, publication, declaration, revelation, becoming known

emergency NOUN = crisis, danger, difficulty, accident, disaster, necessity, plight, scrape (*informal*)
● ADJECTIVE **1** = urgent, crisis, immediate **2** = alternative, extra, additional, substitute, replacement, temporary, makeshift, stopgap

emigrate = move abroad, move, relocate, migrate, resettle, leave your country

eminent = prominent, noted, respected, famous, celebrated, distinguished, well-known, esteemed ≠ unknown

emission = giving off *or* out, release, shedding, leak, radiation, discharge, transmission, ejaculation

emit 1 = give off, release, leak, transmit, discharge, send out, radiate, eject ≠ absorb **2** = utter, produce, voice, give out, let out

emotion 1 = feeling, spirit, soul, passion, excitement, sensation, sentiment, fervour **2** = instinct, sentiment, sensibility, intuition, tenderness, gut feeling, soft-heartedness

emotional 1 = psychological, private, personal, hidden, spiritual, inner **2** = moving, touching, affecting, stirring, sentimental, poignant, emotive, heart-rending **3** = <u>passionate</u>, sentimental, temperamental, excitable, demonstrative, hot-blooded **4** = <u>emotive</u>, sensitive, controversial, delicate, contentious, heated, inflammatory, touchy

emphasis 1 = <u>importance</u>, attention, weight, significance, stress, priority, prominence **2** = <u>stress</u>, accent, force, weight

emphasize 1 = <u>highlight</u>, stress, underline, draw attention to, dwell on, play up, make a point of, give priority to ≠ minimize **2** = <u>stress</u>, accentuate, lay stress on

emphatic 1 = <u>forceful</u>, positive, definite, vigorous, unmistakable, insistent, unequivocal, vehement ≠ hesitant **2** = <u>significant</u>, pronounced, decisive, resounding, conclusive

empire 1 = <u>kingdom</u>, territory, province, federation, commonwealth, realm, domain **2** = <u>organization</u>, company, business, firm, concern, corporation, consortium, syndicate

▪ RELATED WORD
adjective: imperial

empirical *or* **empiric** = <u>first-hand</u>, direct, observed, practical, actual, experimental, pragmatic, factual ≠ hypothetical

employ 1 = <u>hire</u>, commission, appoint, take on, retain, engage, recruit, sign up **2** = <u>use</u>, apply, exercise, exert, make use of, utilize, ply, bring to bear **3** = <u>spend</u>, fill, occupy, involve, engage, take up, make use of, use up

employed 1 = <u>working</u>, in work, having a job, in employment, in a job, earning your living ≠ out of work **2** = <u>busy</u>, active, occupied, engaged, hard at work, in harness, rushed off your feet ≠ idle

employee = <u>worker</u>, labourer, workman, staff member, member of staff, hand, wage-earner, white-collar worker

employer 1 = <u>boss</u> (*informal*), manager, head, leader, director, chief, owner, master, baas (*S. African*) **2** = <u>company</u>, business, firm, organization, establishment, outfit (*informal*)

employment 1 = <u>job</u>, work, position, trade, post, situation, profession, occupation **2** = <u>taking on</u>, commissioning, appointing, hire, hiring, retaining, engaging, appointment **3** = <u>use</u>,

application, exertion, exercise, utilization

empower 1 = <u>authorize</u>, allow, commission, qualify, permit, sanction, entitle, delegate **2** = <u>enable</u>, equip, emancipate, give means to, enfranchise

empty ADJECTIVE **1** = <u>bare</u>, clear, abandoned, deserted, vacant, free, void, desolate ≠ full **2** = <u>meaningless</u>, cheap, hollow, vain, idle, futile, insincere **3** = <u>worthless</u>, meaningless, hollow, pointless, futile, senseless, fruitless, inane ≠ meaningful

● VERB **1** = <u>clear</u>, drain, void, unload, pour out, unpack, remove the contents of ≠ fill **2** = <u>exhaust</u>, consume the contents of, void, deplete, use up ≠ replenish **3** = <u>evacuate</u>, clear, vacate

emulate = <u>imitate</u>, follow, copy, mirror, echo, mimic, model yourself on

enable 1 = <u>allow</u>, permit, empower, give someone the opportunity, give someone the means ≠ prevent **2** = <u>authorize</u>, allow, permit, qualify, sanction, entitle, license, warrant ≠ stop

enact 1 = <u>establish</u>, order, command, approve, sanction, proclaim, decree, authorize **2** = <u>perform</u>, play, present, stage, represent, put on, portray, depict

enchant = <u>fascinate</u>, delight, charm, entrance, dazzle, captivate, enthral, beguile

enclose *or* **inclose 1** = <u>surround</u>, circle, bound, fence, confine, close in, wall in, encircle **2** = <u>send with</u>, include, put in, insert

encompass 1 = <u>include</u>, hold, cover, admit, deal with, contain, take in, embrace **2** = <u>surround</u>, circle, enclose, close in, envelop, encircle, fence in, ring

encounter VERB **1** = <u>experience</u>, meet, face, suffer, have, go through, sustain, endure **2** = <u>meet</u>, confront, come across, bump into (*informal*), run across, come upon, chance upon, meet by chance

● NOUN **1** = <u>meeting</u>, brush, confrontation, rendezvous, chance meeting **2** = <u>battle</u>, conflict, clash, contest, run-in (*informal*), confrontation, head-to-head

encourage 1 = <u>inspire</u>, comfort, cheer, reassure, console, hearten, cheer up, embolden ≠ discourage **2** = <u>urge</u>, persuade, prompt, spur, coax, egg on ≠ dissuade **3** = <u>promote</u>, back, support, increase, foster, advocate, stimulate, endorse ≠ prevent

encouragement 1 = <u>inspiration</u>, support, comfort, comforting, cheer, cheering, reassurance, morale boosting 2 = <u>urging</u>, prompting, stimulus, persuasion, coaxing, egging on, incitement 3 = <u>promotion</u>, backing, support, endorsement, stimulation, furtherance

end NOUN 1 = <u>close</u>, ending, finish, expiry, expiration ≠ beginning 2 = <u>conclusion</u>, ending, climax, completion, finale, culmination, denouement, consummation ≠ start 3 = <u>finish</u>, close, stop, resolution, conclusion, closure, completion, termination 4 = <u>extremity</u>, limit, edge, border, extent, extreme, margin, boundary 5 = <u>tip</u>, point, head, peak, extremity 6 = <u>purpose</u>, point, reason, goal, target, aim, object, mission 7 = <u>outcome</u>, resolution, conclusion 8 = <u>death</u>, dying, ruin, destruction, passing on, doom, demise, extinction 9 = <u>remnant</u>, butt, stub, scrap, fragment, stump, remainder, leftover

● VERB 1 = <u>stop</u>, finish, halt, cease, wind up, terminate, call off, discontinue ≠ start 2 = <u>finish</u>, close, conclude, wind up, culminate, terminate, come to an end, draw to a close ≠ begin

▬ RELATED WORDS
adjectives: final, terminal, ultimate

endanger = <u>put at risk</u>, risk, threaten, compromise, jeopardize, imperil, put in danger, expose to danger ≠ save

endearing = <u>attractive</u>, winning, pleasing, appealing, sweet, engaging, charming, pleasant

endeavour (*Formal*) VERB = <u>try</u>, labour, attempt, aim, struggle, venture, strive, aspire

● NOUN = <u>attempt</u>, try, effort, trial, bid, venture, enterprise, undertaking

ending = <u>finish</u>, end, close, conclusion, summing up, completion, finale, culmination ≠ start

endless = <u>eternal</u>, infinite, continual, unlimited, interminable, incessant, boundless, everlasting ≠ temporary

endorse 1 = <u>approve</u>, back, support, champion, promote, recommend, advocate, uphold 2 = <u>sign</u>, initial, countersign, sign on the back of

endorsement = <u>approval</u>, backing, support, favour, recommendation,

acceptance, agreement, upholding

endow 1 = <u>provide</u>, favour, grace, bless, supply, furnish, endue 2 = <u>finance</u>, fund, pay for, award, confer, bestow, bequeath, donate money to 3 = <u>imbue</u>

endowment = <u>provision</u>, funding, award, grant, gift, contribution, subsidy, donation, koha (*N.Z.*)

endurance 1 = <u>staying power</u>, strength, resolution, determination, patience, stamina, fortitude, persistence 2 = <u>permanence</u>, stability, continuity, duration, longevity, durability, continuance

endure 1 = <u>experience</u>, suffer, bear, meet, encounter, cope with, sustain, undergo 2 = <u>last</u>, continue, remain, stay, stand, go on, survive, live on

enemy = <u>foe</u>, rival, opponent, the opposition, competitor, the other side, adversary, antagonist ≠ friend

energetic 1 = <u>forceful</u>, determined, active, aggressive, dynamic, vigorous, hard-hitting, strenuous 2 = <u>lively</u>, active, dynamic, vigorous, animated, tireless, bouncy, indefatigable ≠ lethargic 3 = <u>strenuous</u>, hard, taxing, demanding, tough, exhausting, vigorous, arduous

energy 1 = <u>strength</u>, might, stamina, forcefulness 2 = <u>liveliness</u>, drive, determination, pep, vitality, vigour, verve, resilience 3 = <u>power</u>

enforce 1 = <u>carry out</u>, apply, implement, fulfil, execute, administer, put into effect, put into action 2 = <u>impose</u>, force, insist on

engage 1 *with* **in** = <u>participate in</u>, join in, take part in, undertake, embark on, enter into, become involved in, set about 2 = <u>captivate</u>, catch, arrest, fix, capture 3 = <u>occupy</u>, involve, draw, grip, absorb, preoccupy, immerse, engross 4 = <u>employ</u>, appoint, take on, hire, retain, recruit, enlist, enrol ≠ dismiss 5 = <u>set going</u>, apply, trigger, activate, switch on, energize, bring into operation 6 (*Military*) = <u>begin battle with</u>, attack, take on, encounter, fall on, battle with, meet, assail

engaged 1 = <u>occupied</u>, working, employed, busy, tied up 2 = <u>betrothed</u>, promised, pledged, affianced, promised in marriage ≠ unattached 3 = <u>in use</u>, busy, tied up, unavailable ≠ free

engagement 1 = <u>appointment</u>, meeting, interview, date, commitment, arrangement, rendezvous **2** = betrothal, marriage contract, troth (*archaic*), agreement to marry **3** = battle, fight, conflict, action, struggle, clash, encounter, combat **4** = participation, joining, taking part, involvement

engaging = charming, interesting, pleasing, attractive, lovely, entertaining, winning, fetching (*informal*) ≠ unpleasant

engine = machine, motor, mechanism, generator, dynamo

engineer NOUN **1** = designer, producer, architect, developer, deviser, creator, planner, inventor **2** = worker, specialist, operator, practitioner, operative, driver, conductor, technician

● VERB **1** = design, plan, create, construct, devise **2** = bring about, plan, effect, set up (*informal*), scheme, arrange, plot, mastermind

engraving = print, carving, etching, inscription, plate, woodcut, dry point

engulf 1 = immerse, swamp, submerge, overrun, inundate, envelop, swallow up **2** = overwhelm, overcome, crush, swamp

enhance = improve, better, increase, lift, boost, add to, strengthen, reinforce ≠ reduce

enjoy 1 = take pleasure in or from, like, love, appreciate, relish, delight in, be pleased with, be fond of ≠ hate **2** = have, use, own, experience, possess, have the benefit of, reap the benefits of, be blessed or favoured with

enjoyable = pleasurable, good, great, fine, nice, satisfying, lovely, entertaining ≠ unpleasant

enjoyment 1 = pleasure, liking, fun, delight, entertainment, joy, happiness, relish **2** = benefit, use, advantage, favour, possession, blessing

enlarge VERB **1** = expand, increase, extend, add to, build up, widen, intensify, broaden ≠ reduce **2** = grow, increase, extend, expand, swell, become bigger, puff up, grow larger

● PHRASES **enlarge on something** = expand on, develop, add to, fill out, elaborate on, flesh out, expatiate on, give further details about

enlighten = inform, tell, teach, advise, counsel, educate, instruct, illuminate

enlightened = informed, aware, reasonable, educated, sophisticated, cultivated, open-minded, knowledgeable ≠ ignorant

enlightenment = understanding, learning, education, knowledge, instruction, awareness, wisdom, insight

enlist 1 = join up, join, enter (into), register, volunteer, sign up, enrol **2** = recruit, take on, hire, sign up, call up, muster, mobilize, conscript **3** = obtain, get, gain, secure, engage, procure

enormous = huge, massive, vast, extensive, tremendous, gross, immense, gigantic ≠ tiny

enough DETERMINER = sufficient, adequate, ample, abundant, as much as you need, as much as is necessary

● PRONOUN = sufficiency, plenty, sufficient, abundance, adequacy, right amount, ample supply

● ADVERB = sufficiently, amply, reasonably, adequately, satisfactorily, abundantly, tolerably

enrage = anger, infuriate, incense, madden, inflame, exasperate, antagonize, make you angry ≠ calm

enrich 1 = enhance, develop, improve, boost, supplement, refine, heighten, augment **2** = make rich, make wealthy, make affluent, make prosperous, make well-off

enrol 1 = enlist, register, be accepted, be admitted, join up, put your name down for, sign up or on **2** = recruit, take on, enlist

en route = on or along the way, travelling, on the road, in transit, on the journey

ensemble 1 = group, company, band, troupe, cast, orchestra, chorus **2** = collection, set, body, whole, total, sum, combination, entity **3** = outfit, suit, get-up (*informal*), costume

ensue = follow, result, develop, proceed, arise, stem, derive, issue ≠ come first

ensure 1 = make certain, guarantee, secure, make sure, confirm, warrant, certify **2** = protect, defend, secure, safeguard, guard, make safe

entail = involve, require, produce, demand, call for, occasion, need, bring about

enter 1 = come or go in or into, arrive, set foot in somewhere, cross the threshold of somewhere, make an entrance ≠ exit **2** = penetrate, get in, pierce, pass into, perforate **3** = join, start work at, begin work at, enrol in, enlist in ≠ leave **4** = participate in, join (in), be involved in, get involved in, play a part in, partake in, associate yourself with, start to be in **5** = begin, start, take up, move into, commence, set out on, embark upon **6** = compete in, contest, join in, fight, sign up for, go in for **7** = record, note, register, log, list, write down, take down, inscribe

enterprise 1 = firm, company, business, concern, operation, organization, establishment, commercial undertaking **2** = venture, operation, project, adventure, undertaking, programme, pursuit, endeavour **3** = initiative, energy, daring, enthusiasm, imagination, drive, ingenuity, originality

enterprising = resourceful, original, spirited, charm, daring, bold, enthusiastic, imaginative, energetic

entertain 1 = amuse, interest, please, delight, charm, enthral, cheer, regale **2** = show hospitality to, receive, accommodate, treat, put up, lodge, be host to, have company of **3** = consider, imagine, think about, contemplate, conceive of, bear in mind, keep in mind, give thought to

entertainment 1 = enjoyable, fun, pleasure, leisure, relaxation, recreation, enjoyment, amusement **2** = pastime, show, sport, performance, treat, presentation, leisure activity

enthusiasm = keenness, interest, passion, motivation, relish, zeal, zest, fervour

enthusiast = fan, supporter, lover, follower, addict, buff (*informal*), fanatic, devotee

enthusiastic = keen, committed, eager, passionate, vigorous, avid, fervent, zealous ≠ apathetic

entice = lure, attract, invite, persuade, tempt, induce, seduce, lead on

entire = whole, full, complete, total, gross

entirely = completely, totally, absolutely, fully, altogether, thoroughly, wholly, utterly ≠ partly

entitle 1 = give the right to, allow, enable, permit, sanction, license, authorize, empower **2** = call, name, title, term, label, dub, christen, give the title of

entity = thing, being, individual, object, substance, creature, organism

entrance¹ 1 = way in, opening, door, approach, access, entry, gate, passage ≠ exit **2** = appearance, coming in, entry, arrival, introduction ≠ exit **3** = admission, access, entry, entrée, admittance, permission to enter, right of entry

entrance² 1 = enchant, delight, charm, fascinate, dazzle, captivate, enthral, beguile ≠ bore **2** = mesmerize, bewitch, hypnotize, put a spell on, cast a spell on, put in a trance

entrant = competitor, player, candidate, entry, participant, applicant, contender, contestant

entrenched *or* **intrenched** = fixed, set, rooted, well-established, ingrained, deep-seated, deep-rooted, unshakeable *or* unshakable

entrepreneur = businessman *or* businesswoman, tycoon, executive, industrialist, speculator, magnate, impresario, business executive

entrust *or* **intrust 1** = give custody of, deliver, commit, delegate, hand over, turn over, confide **2** = assign

entry 1 = admission, access, entrance, admittance, entrée, permission to enter, right of entry **2** = coming in, entering, appearance, arrival, entrance ≠ exit **3** = introduction, presentation, initiation, inauguration, induction, debut, investiture **4** = record, listing, account, note, statement, item **5** = way in, opening, door, approach, access, gate, passage, entrance

envelope = wrapping, casing, case, covering, cover, jacket, sleeve, wrapper

environment 1 = surroundings, setting, conditions, situation, medium, circumstances, background, atmosphere **2** = habitat, home, surroundings, territory, terrain, locality, natural home

environmental = ecological, green

environmentalist = conservationist, ecologist, green

envisage 1 = imagine, contemplate, conceive (of), visualize, picture, fancy, think up, conceptualize **2** = foresee, see, expect, predict, anticipate, envision

envoy 1 = ambassador, diplomat, emissary **2** = messenger, agent, representative, delegate, courier, intermediary, emissary

envy NOUN = covetousness, resentment, jealousy, bitterness, resentfulness, enviousness (*informal*)

● **VERB 1** = be jealous (of), resent, begrudge, be envious (of) **2** = covet, desire, crave, aspire to, yearn for, hanker after

epidemic 1 = outbreak, plague, growth, spread, scourge, contagion **2** = spate, plague, outbreak, wave, rash, eruption, upsurge

episode 1 = event, experience, happening, matter, affair, incident, adventure, occurrence **2** = instalment, part, act, scene, section, chapter, passage **3** = period, attack, spell, phase, bout

equal ADJECTIVE 1 = identical, the same, matching, equivalent, uniform, alike, corresponding ≠ unequal **2** = fair, just, impartial, egalitarian, unbiased, even-handed ≠ unfair **3** = even, balanced, fifty-fifty (*informal*), evenly matched ≠ uneven
● **NOUN** = match, equivalent, twin, counterpart
● **VERB 1** = amount to, make, come to, total, level, parallel, tie with, equate ≠ be unequal to **2** = be equal to, match, reach **3** = be as good as, match, compare with, equate with, measure up to, be as great as

equality 1 = fairness, equal opportunity, equal treatment, egalitarianism, fair treatment, justness ≠ inequality **2** = sameness, balance, identity, similarity, correspondence, parity, likeness, uniformity ≠ disparity

equate 1 = identify, associate, connect, compare, relate, mention in the same breath, think of in connection with **2** = make equal, match, even up **3** = be equal to, parallel, compare with, liken, be commensurate with, correspond with or to

equation = equating, comparison, parallel, correspondence

equilibrium = stability, balance, symmetry, steadiness, evenness, equipoise

equip 1 = supply, provide for, stock, arm, array, furnish, fit out, kit out **2** = prepare, qualify, educate, get ready

equipment = apparatus, stock, supplies, stuff, tackle, gear, tools, provisions

equitable = even-handed, just, fair, reasonable, proper, honest, impartial, unbiased

equivalent NOUN = equal, counterpart, twin, parallel, match, opposite number
● **ADJECTIVE** = equal, same, comparable,

parallel, identical, alike, corresponding, tantamount ≠ different

era = age, time, period, date, generation, epoch, day or days

eradicate = wipe out, eliminate, remove, destroy, get rid of, erase, extinguish, obliterate

erase 1 = delete, cancel out, wipe out, remove, eradicate, obliterate, blot out, expunge **2** = rub out, remove, wipe out, delete

erect VERB 1 = build, raise, set up, construct, put up, assemble, put together ≠ demolish **2** = found, establish, form, create, set up, institute, organize, put up
● **ADJECTIVE** = upright, straight, stiff, vertical, elevated, perpendicular, pricked-up ≠ bent

erode 1 = disintegrate, crumble, deteriorate, corrode, break up, grind down, waste away, wear down or away **2** = destroy, consume, crumble, eat away, corrode, break up, grind down, abrade **3** = weaken, destroy, undermine, diminish, impair, lessen, wear away

erosion 1 = disintegration, deterioration, wearing down or away, grinding down **2** = deterioration, undermining, destruction, weakening, attrition, eating away, abrasion, grinding down

erotic = sexual, sexy (*informal*), crude, explicit, sensual, seductive, vulgar, voluptuous

erratic = unpredictable, variable, unstable, irregular, inconsistent, uneven, unreliable, wayward ≠ regular

error = mistake, slip, blunder, oversight, howler (*informal*), bloomer (*Brit. informal*), miscalculation, solecism

erupt 1 = explode, blow up, emit lava **2** = discharge, expel, emit, eject, spout, throw off, pour forth, spew forth or out **3** = gush, burst out, pour forth, belch forth, spew forth or out **4** = start, break out, began, explode, flare up, burst out, boil over **5** (*Medical*) = break out, appear, flare up

escalate 1 = grow, increase, extend, intensify, expand, surge, mount, heighten ≠ decrease **2** = increase, develop, extend, intensify, expand, build up, heighten ≠ lessen

escape VERB 1 = get away, flee, take off, fly, bolt, slip away, abscond, make a break for it **2** = <u>avoid</u>, miss, evade, dodge, shun, elude, duck, steer clear of **3** = <u>leak out</u>, flow out, gush out, emanate, seep out, exude, spill out, pour forth

● NOUN **1** = <u>getaway</u>, break, flight, breakout **2** = <u>avoidance</u>, evasion, circumvention **3** = <u>relaxation</u>, recreation, distraction, diversion, pastime **4** = <u>leak</u>, emission, outpouring, seepage, issue, emanation

escort NOUN **1** = <u>guard</u>, bodyguard, train, convoy, entourage, retinue, cortege **2** = <u>companion</u>, partner, attendant, guide, beau, chaperon

● VERB = <u>accompany</u>, lead, partner, conduct, guide, shepherd, usher, chaperon

especially 1 = <u>notably</u>, mostly, strikingly, conspicuously, outstandingly **2** = <u>very</u>, specially, extremely, remarkably, unusually, exceptionally, markedly, uncommonly

espionage = <u>spying</u>, intelligence, surveillance, counter-intelligence, undercover work

essay NOUN = <u>composition</u>, study, paper, article, piece, assignment, discourse, tract

● VERB (*Formal*) = <u>attempt</u>, try, undertake, endeavour

essence 1 = <u>fundamental nature</u>, nature, being, heart, spirit, soul, core, substance **2** = <u>concentrate</u>, spirits, extract, tincture, distillate

essential ADJECTIVE **1** = <u>vital</u>, important, needed, necessary, critical, crucial, key, indispensable ≠ unimportant **2** = <u>fundamental</u>, main, basic, principal, cardinal, elementary, innate, intrinsic ≠ secondary

● NOUN = <u>prerequisite</u>, fundamental, necessity, must, basic, sine qua non (*Latin*), rudiment

establish 1 = <u>set up</u>, found, create, institute, constitute, inaugurate **2** = <u>prove</u>, confirm, demonstrate, certify, verify, substantiate, corroborate, authenticate **3** = <u>secure</u>, form, ground, settle

establishment NOUN **1** = <u>creation</u>, founding, setting up, foundation, institution, organization, formation, installation **2** = <u>organization</u>, company, business, firm, concern, operation, institution, corporation

● PHRASES **the Establishment** = <u>the</u> <u>authorities</u>, the system, the powers that be, the ruling class

estate 1 = <u>lands</u>, property, area, grounds,

domain, manor, holdings **2** = <u>area</u>, centre, park, development, site, zone, plot **3** (*Law*) = <u>property</u>, capital, assets, fortune, goods, effects, wealth, possessions

esteem NOUN = <u>respect</u>, regard, honour, admiration, reverence, estimation, veneration

● VERB = <u>respect</u>, admire, think highly of, love, value, prize, treasure, revere

estimate VERB **1** = <u>calculate roughly</u>, value, guess, judge, reckon, assess, evaluate, gauge **2** = <u>think</u>, believe, consider, rate, judge, hold, rank, reckon

● NOUN **1** = <u>approximate calculation</u>, guess, assessment, judgment, valuation, guesstimate (*informal*), rough calculation, ballpark figure (*informal*) **2** = <u>assessment</u>, opinion, belief, appraisal, evaluation, judgment, estimation

estuary = <u>inlet</u>, mouth, creek, firth, fjord

etch 1 = <u>engrave</u>, cut, impress, stamp, carve, imprint, inscribe **2** = <u>corrode</u>, eat into, burn into

etching = <u>print</u>, impression, carving, engraving, imprint, inscription

eternal 1 = <u>everlasting</u>, lasting, permanent, enduring, endless, perpetual, timeless, unending ≠ transitory **2** = <u>interminable</u>, endless, infinite, continual, immortal, never-ending, everlasting ≠ occasional

eternity 1 (*Theology*) = <u>the afterlife</u>, heaven, paradise, the next world, the hereafter **2** = <u>perpetuity</u>, immortality, infinity, timelessness, endlessness **3** = <u>ages</u>

ethical 1 = <u>moral</u>, behavioural **2** = <u>right</u>, morally acceptable, good, just, fair, responsible, principled ≠ unethical

ethics = <u>moral code</u>, standards, principles, morals, conscience, morality, moral values, moral principles, tikanga (*N.Z.*)

ethnic or **ethnical** = <u>cultural</u>, national, traditional, native, folk, racial, genetic, indigenous

euphoria = <u>elation</u>, joy, ecstasy, rapture, exhilaration, jubilation ≠ despondency

evacuate 1 = <u>remove</u>, clear, withdraw, expel, move out, send to a safe place **2** = <u>abandon</u>, leave, clear, desert, quit, withdraw from, pull out of, move out of

evade 1 = <u>avoid</u>, escape, dodge, get away from, elude, steer clear of, sidestep, duck ≠ face **2** = <u>avoid answering</u>, parry, fend off, fudge, hedge, equivocate

evaluate = assess, rate, judge, estimate, reckon, weigh, calculate, gauge

evaporate 1 = disappear, vaporize, dematerialize, vanish, dissolve, dry up, fade away, melt away 2 = dry up, dry, dehydrate, vaporize, desiccate 3 = fade away, disappear, vanish, dissolve, melt away

eve 1 = night before, day before, vigil 2 = brink, point, edge, verge, threshold

even 1 = regular, stable, constant, steady, smooth, uniform, unbroken, uninterrupted ≠ variable 2 = level, straight, flat, smooth, true, steady, uniform, parallel ≠ uneven 3 = equal, like, matching, similar, identical, comparable ≠ unequal 4 = equally matched, level, tied, on a par, neck and neck, fifty-fifty (*informal*), all square ≠ ill-matched 5 = square, quits, on the same level, on an equal footing 6 = calm, composed, cool, well-balanced, placid, unruffled, imperturbable, even-tempered ≠ excitable

evening = dusk (*archaic*), night, sunset, twilight, sundown, gloaming (*Scot. poetic*), close of day, evo (*Austral. slang*)

event 1 = incident, happening, experience, affair, occasion, proceeding, business, circumstance 2 = competition, game, tournament, contest, bout

eventual = final, overall, concluding, ultimate

eventually = in the end, finally, one day, after all, some time, ultimately, at the end of the day, when all is said and done

ever 1 = at any time, at all, in any case, at any point, by any chance, on any occasion, at any period 2 = always, for ever, at all times, evermore 3 = constantly, continually, perpetually

every = each, each and every, every single

everybody = everyone, each one, the whole world, each person, every person, all and sundry, one and all

everyday = ordinary, common, usual, routine, stock, customary, mundane, run-of-the-mill ≠ unusual

everyone = everybody, each one, the whole world, each person, every person, all and sundry, one and all

everything = all, the lot, the whole lot, each thing

everywhere 1 = all over, all around, the world over, high and low, in every nook and cranny, far and wide *or* near, to *or* in every place 2 = all around, all over, in every nook and cranny, ubiquitously, far and wide *or* near, to *or* in every place

evidence NOUN 1 = proof, grounds, demonstration, confirmation, verification, corroboration, authentication, substantiation 2 = sign(s), suggestion, trace, indication 3 = testimony, statement, submission, avowal
● VERB = show, prove, reveal, display, indicate, witness, demonstrate, exhibit

evident = obvious, clear, plain, apparent, visible, manifest, noticeable, unmistakable ≠ hidden

evidently 1 = obviously, clearly, plainly, undoubtedly, manifestly, without question, unmistakably 2 = apparently, seemingly, outwardly, ostensibly, so it seems, to all appearances

evil NOUN 1 = wickedness, bad, vice, sin, wrongdoing, depravity, badness, villainy 2 = harm, suffering, hurt, woe 3 = act of cruelty, crime, ill, horror, outrage, misfortune, mischief, affliction
● ADJECTIVE 1 = wicked, bad, malicious, immoral, sinful, malevolent, depraved, villainous 2 = harmful, disastrous, destructive, dire, catastrophic, pernicious, ruinous 3 = demonic, satanic, diabolical, hellish, devilish, infernal, fiendish 4 = offensive, nasty, foul, unpleasant, vile, noxious, disagreeable, pestilential 5 = unfortunate, unfavourable, ruinous, calamitous

evoke = arouse, cause, induce, awaken, give rise to, stir up, rekindle, summon up ≠ suppress

evolution 1 = rise, development, adaptation, natural selection, Darwinism, survival of the fittest 2 = development, growth, advance, progress, working out, expansion, extension, unfolding

evolve 1 = develop, metamorphose, adapt yourself 2 = grow, develop, advance, progress, mature 3 = work out, develop, progress, expand, unfold

exact ADJECTIVE = accurate, correct, true, right, specific, precise, definite, faultless ≠ approximate
● VERB 1 = demand, claim, force, command, extract, compel, extort 2 = inflict, apply, administer, mete out, deal out

exacting 1 = demanding, hard, taxing,

difficult, tough ≠ easy 2 = strict, severe, harsh, rigorous, stringent

exactly 1 = accurately, correctly, precisely, faithfully, explicitly, scrupulously, truthfully, unerringly 2 = precisely, specifically, bang on (*informal*), to the letter

exaggerate = overstate, enlarge, embroider, amplify, embellish, overestimate, overemphasize, pile it on about (*informal*)

examination 1 = checkup, analysis, going-over (*informal*), exploration, health check, check 2 = exam, test, research, paper, investigation, practical, assessment, quiz

examine 1 = inspect, study, survey, investigate, explore, analyse, scrutinize, peruse 2 = check, analyse, check over 3 = test, question, assess, quiz, evaluate, appraise 4 = question, quiz, interrogate, cross-examine, grill (*informal*), give the third degree to (*informal*)

example 1 = instance, specimen, case, sample, illustration, particular case, particular instance, typical case 2 = illustration, model, ideal, standard, prototype, paradigm, archetype, paragon 3 = warning, lesson, caution, deterrent

exceed 1 = surpass, better, pass, eclipse, beat, cap (*informal*), top, be over 2 = go over the limit of, go beyond, overstep

excel VERB = be superior, eclipse, beat, surpass, transcend, outdo, outshine
● PHRASES **excel in** or **at something** = be good at, shine at, be proficient in, show talent in, be skilful at, be talented at

excellence = high quality, merit, distinction, goodness, superiority, greatness, supremacy, eminence

excellent = outstanding, good, great, fine, cool (*informal*), brilliant, very good, superb, booshit (*Austral. slang*), exo (*Austral. slang*), sik (*Austral. slang*) ≠ terrible

except or **except for** PREPOSITION = apart from, but for, saving, barring, excepting, other than, excluding, omitting
● VERB = exclude, leave out, omit, disregard, pass over

exception = special case, freak, anomaly, inconsistency, deviation, oddity, peculiarity, irregularity

exceptional 1 = remarkable, special, excellent, extraordinary, outstanding,

superior, first-class, marvellous ≠ average 2 = unusual, special, odd, strange, extraordinary, unprecedented, peculiar, abnormal ≠ ordinary

excerpt = extract, part, piece, section, selection, passage, fragment, quotation

excess 1 = surfeit, surplus, overload, glut, superabundance, superfluity ≠ shortage 2 = overindulgence, extravagance, profligacy, debauchery, dissipation, intemperance, indulgence, prodigality ≠ moderation

excessive 1 = immoderate, too much, extreme, exaggerated, unreasonable, disproportionate, undue, uncontrolled 2 = inordinate, unfair, unreasonable, disproportionate, undue, unwarranted, exorbitant, extortionate

exchange VERB = interchange, change, trade, switch, swap, barter, give to each other, give to one another
● NOUN 1 = conversation, talk, word, discussion, chat, dialogue, natter, powwow 2 = interchange, trade, switch, swap, trafficking, swapping, substitution, barter

excite 1 = thrill, inspire, stir, provoke, animate, rouse, exhilarate, inflame 2 = arouse, provoke, rouse, stir up 3 = titillate, thrill, stimulate, turn on (*slang*), arouse, get going (*informal*), electrify

excitement = exhilaration, action, activity, passion, thrill, animation, furore, agitation

exciting 1 = stimulating, dramatic, gripping, stirring, thrilling, sensational, rousing, exhilarating ≠ boring 2 = titillating, stimulating, arousing, erotic

exclaim = cry out, declare, shout, proclaim, yell, utter, call out

exclude 1 = keep out, bar, ban, refuse, forbid, boycott, prohibit, disallow ≠ let in 2 = omit, reject, eliminate, rule out, miss out, leave out ≠ include 3 = eliminate, reject, ignore, rule out, leave out, set aside, omit, pass over

exclusion 1 = ban, bar, veto, boycott, embargo, prohibition, disqualification 2 = elimination, missing out, rejection, leaving out, omission

exclusive 1 = select, fashionable, stylish, restricted, posh (*informal, chiefly Brit.*), chic, high-class, up-market ≠ unrestricted 2 = sole, full, whole, complete, total, entire, absolute, undivided ≠ shared **3** = <u>entire</u>, full, whole, complete, total, absolute, undivided **4** = <u>limited</u>, unique, restricted, confined, peculiar

excursion **1** = <u>trip</u>, tour, journey, outing, expedition, ramble, day trip, jaunt

excuse NOUN = <u>justification</u>, reason, explanation, defence, grounds, plea, apology, vindication ≠ accusation
● VERB **1** = <u>justify</u>, explain, defend, vindicate, mitigate, apologize for, make excuses for ≠ blame **2** = <u>forgive</u>, pardon, overlook, tolerate, acquit, turn a blind eye to, exonerate, make allowances for **3** = <u>free</u>, relieve, exempt, release, spare, discharge, let off, absolve ≠ convict

execute **1** = <u>put to death</u>, kill, shoot, hang, behead, decapitate, guillotine, electrocute **2** = <u>carry out</u>, effect, implement, accomplish, discharge, administer, prosecute, enact **3** = <u>perform</u>, carry out, accomplish

execution **1** = <u>killing</u>, hanging, the death penalty, the rope, capital punishment, beheading, the electric chair, the guillotine **2** = <u>carrying out</u>, performance, operation, administration, prosecution, enforcement, implementation, accomplishment

executive NOUN **1** = <u>administrator</u>, official, director, manager, chairman, managing director, controller, chief executive officer **2** = <u>administration</u>, government, directors, management, leadership, hierarchy, directorate
● ADJECTIVE = <u>administrative</u>, controlling, directing, governing, regulating, decision-making, managerial

exemplify = <u>show</u>, represent, display, demonstrate, illustrate, exhibit, embody, serve as an example of

exempt ADJECTIVE = <u>immune</u>, free, excepted, excused, released, spared, not liable to ≠ liable
● VERB = <u>grant immunity</u>, free, excuse, release, spare, relieve, discharge, let off

exemption = <u>immunity</u>, freedom, relief, exception, discharge, release, dispensation, absolution

exercise VERB **1** = <u>put to use</u>, use, apply, employ, exert, utilize, bring to bear, avail yourself of **2** = <u>train</u>, work out, practise, keep fit, do exercises
● NOUN **1** = <u>use</u>, practice, application,

operation, discharge, implementation, fulfilment, utilization **2** = <u>exertion</u>, training, activity, work, labour, effort, movement, toil **3** = <u>manoeuvre</u>, campaign, operation, movement, deployment **4** = <u>task</u>, problem, lesson, assignment, practice

exert VERB = <u>apply</u>, use, exercise, employ, wield, make use of, utilize, bring to bear
● PHRASES **exert yourself** = <u>make an effort</u>, work, labour, struggle, strain, strive, endeavour, toil

exhaust **1** = <u>tire out</u>, fatigue, drain, weaken, weary, sap, wear out, debilitate **2** = <u>use up</u>, spend, consume, waste, go through, run through, deplete, squander

exhausted **1** = <u>worn out</u>, tired out, drained, spent, bushed (*informal*), done in (*informal*), all in (*slang*), fatigued ≠ invigorated **2** = <u>used up</u>, consumed, spent, finished, depleted, dissipated, expended ≠ replenished

exhaustion **1** = <u>tiredness</u>, fatigue, weariness, debilitation **2** = <u>depletion</u>, emptying, consumption, using up

exhibit **1** = <u>show</u>, reveal, display, demonstrate, express, indicate, manifest **2** = <u>display</u>, show, set out, parade, unveil, put on view

exhibition **1** = <u>show</u>, display, representation, presentation, spectacle, showcase, exposition **2** = <u>display</u>, show, performance, demonstration, revelation

exile NOUN **1** = <u>banishment</u>, expulsion, deportation, eviction, expatriation **2** = <u>expatriate</u>, refugee, outcast, émigré, deportee
● VERB = <u>banish</u>, expel, throw out, deport, drive out, eject, expatriate, cast out

exist **1** = <u>live</u>, be present, survive, endure, be in existence, be, have breath **2** = <u>occur</u>, be present **3** = <u>survive</u>, stay alive, make ends meet, subsist, eke out a living, scrape by, scrimp and save, support yourself

existence **1** = <u>reality</u>, being, life, subsistence, actuality **2** = <u>life</u>, situation, way of life, life style

existent = <u>in existence</u>, living, existing, surviving, standing, present, alive, extant

exit NOUN **1** = <u>way out</u>, door, gate, outlet, doorway, gateway, escape route ≠ entry **2** = <u>departure</u>, withdrawal, retreat, farewell, going, goodbye, exodus, decamping
● VERB = <u>depart</u>, leave, go out, withdraw,

retire, quit, retreat, go away ≠ enter

exodus = <u>departure</u>, withdrawal, retreat, leaving, flight, exit, migration, evacuation

exotic 1 = <u>unusual</u>, striking, strange, fascinating, mysterious, colourful, glamorous, unfamiliar ≠ ordinary 2 = <u>foreign</u>, alien, tropical, external, naturalized

expand VERB 1 = <u>get bigger</u>, increase, grow, extend, swell, widen, enlarge, become bigger ≠ contract 2 = <u>make bigger</u>, increase, develop, extend, widen, enlarge, broaden, magnify ≠ reduce 3 = <u>spread (out)</u>, stretch (out), unfold, unravel, diffuse, unfurl, unroll

● PHRASES **expand on something** = <u>go into detail about</u>, embellish, elaborate on, develop, flesh out, expound on, enlarge on, expatiate on

expansion 1 = <u>increase</u>, development, growth, spread, magnification, amplification 2 = <u>enlargement</u>, increase, growth, opening out

expatriate NOUN = <u>exile</u>, refugee, emigrant, émigré

● ADJECTIVE = <u>exiled</u>, refugee, banished, emigrant, émigré, expat

expect 1 = <u>think</u>, believe, suppose, assume, trust, imagine, reckon, presume 2 = <u>anticipate</u>, look forward to, predict, envisage, await, hope for, contemplate 3 = <u>require</u>, demand, want, call for, ask for, hope for, insist on

expectation 1 = <u>projection</u>, supposition, assumption, belief, forecast, likelihood, probability, presumption 2 = <u>anticipation</u>, hope, promise, excitement, expectancy, apprehension, suspense

expedition = <u>journey</u>, mission, voyage, tour, quest, trek

expel 1 = <u>throw out</u>, exclude, ban, dismiss, kick out (*informal*), ask to leave, turf out (*informal*), debar ≠ let in 2 = <u>banish</u>, exile, deport, evict, force to leave ≠ take in 3 = <u>drive out</u>, discharge, force out, let out, eject, issue, spew, belch

expenditure 1 = <u>spending</u>, payment, expense, outgoings, cost, outlay 2 = <u>consumption</u>, using, output

expense = <u>cost</u>, charge, expenditure, payment, spending, outlay

expensive = <u>costly</u>, high-priced, lavish, extravagant, dear, stiff, steep (*informal*), pricey ≠ cheap

experience NOUN 1 = <u>knowledge</u>, practice, skill, contact, expertise, involvement, exposure, participation 2 = <u>event</u>, affair, incident, happening, encounter, episode, adventure, occurrence

● VERB = <u>undergo</u>, feel, face, taste, go through, sample, encounter, endure

experienced = <u>knowledgeable</u>, skilled, tried, tested, seasoned, expert, veteran, practised ≠ inexperienced

experiment NOUN 1 = <u>test</u>, trial, investigation, examination, procedure, demonstration, observation, try-out 2 = <u>research</u>, investigation, analysis, observation, research and development, experimentation

● VERB = <u>test</u>, investigate, trial, research, try, examine, pilot, sample

experimental 1 = <u>test</u>, trial, pilot, preliminary, provisional, tentative, speculative, exploratory 2 = <u>innovative</u>, new, original, radical, creative, ingenious, avant-garde, inventive

expert NOUN = <u>specialist</u>, authority, professional, master, genius, guru, pundit, maestro, fundi (*S. African*) ≠ amateur

● ADJECTIVE = <u>skilful</u>, experienced, professional, masterly, qualified, talented, outstanding, practised ≠ unskilled

expertise = <u>skill</u>, knowledge, know-how (*informal*), facility, judgment, mastery, proficiency, adroitness

expire 1 = <u>become invalid</u>, end, finish, conclude, close, stop, run out, cease 2 = <u>die</u>, depart, perish, kick the bucket (*informal*), depart this life, meet your maker, cark it (*Austral. & N.Z. slang*), pass away *or* on

explain 1 = <u>make clear *or* plain</u>, describe, teach, define, resolve, clarify, clear up, simplify 2 = <u>account for</u>, excuse, justify, give a reason for

explanation 1 = <u>reason</u>, answer, account, excuse, motive, justification, vindication 2 = <u>description</u>, report, definition, teaching, interpretation, illustration, clarification, simplification

explicit 1 = <u>clear</u>, obvious, specific, direct, precise, straightforward, definite, overt ≠ vague 2 = <u>frank</u>, specific, graphic, unambiguous, unrestricted, unrestrained, uncensored ≠ indirect

explode 1 = <u>blow up</u>, erupt, burst, go off, shatter 2 = <u>detonate</u>, set off, discharge,

let off 3 = lose your temper, rage, erupt, become angry, hit the roof (*informal*), go crook (*Austral. & N.Z. slang*) **4** = increase, grow, develop, extend, advance, shoot up, soar, boost **5** = disprove, discredit, refute, demolish, repudiate, put paid to, invalidate, debunk

exploit VERB **1** = take advantage of, abuse, use, manipulate, milk, misuse, ill-treat, play on *or* upon **2** = make the best use of, use, make use of, utilize, cash in on (*informal*), capitalize on, use to good advantage, profit by *or* from
● NOUN = feat, act, achievement, enterprise, adventure, stunt, deed, accomplishment

exploitation = misuse, abuse, manipulation, using, ill-treatment

exploration 1 = expedition, tour, trip, survey, travel, journey, reconnaissance **2** = investigation, research, survey, search, inquiry, analysis, examination, inspection

explore 1 = travel around, tour, survey, scout, reconnoitre **2** = investigate, consider, research, survey, search, examine, probe, look into

explosion 1 = blast, crack, burst, bang, discharge, report, blowing up, clap **2** = increase, rise, development, growth, boost, expansion, enlargement, escalation **3** = outburst, fit, storm, attack, surge, flare-up, eruption **3** = outbreak, flare-up, eruption, upsurge

explosive NOUN = bomb, mine, shell, missile, rocket, grenade, charge, torpedo
● ADJECTIVE **1** = unstable, dangerous, volatile, hazardous, unsafe, perilous, combustible, inflammable **2** = sudden, rapid, marked, unexpected, startling, swift, abrupt **3** = fiery, violent, volatile, stormy, touchy, vehement

expose 1 = uncover, show, reveal, display, exhibit, present, unveil, lay bare ≠ hide **2** = make vulnerable, subject, endanger, leave open, jeopardize, put at risk, imperil, lay open

exposure 1 = hypothermia, frostbite, extreme cold, intense cold **2** = uncovering, showing, display, exhibition, revelation, presentation, unveiling

express VERB **1** = state, communicate, convey, articulate, say, word, voice, declare **2** = show, indicate, exhibit, demonstrate, reveal, intimate, convey, signify
● ADJECTIVE **1** = explicit, clear, plain, distinct,

definite, unambiguous, categorical **2** = specific, exclusive, particular, sole, special, singular, clear-cut, especial **3** = fast, direct, rapid, priority, prompt, swift, high-speed, speedy

expression 1 = statement, declaration, announcement, communication, utterance, articulation **2** = indication, demonstration, exhibition, display, showing, show, sign, symbol **3** = look, countenance, face, air, appearance, aspect **4** = phrase, saying, word, term, remark, maxim, idiom, adage

expressive = vivid, striking, telling, moving, poignant, eloquent ≠ impassive

expulsion 1 = ejection, exclusion, dismissal, removal, eviction, banishment **2** = discharge, emission, spewing, secretion, excretion, ejection, seepage, suppuration

exquisite 1 = beautiful, elegant, graceful, pleasing, attractive, lovely, charming, comely ≠ unattractive **2** = fine, beautiful, lovely, elegant, precious, delicate, dainty **3** = intense, acute, severe, sharp, keen, extreme

extend 1 = spread out, reach, stretch **2** = stretch, stretch out, spread out, straighten out **3** = last, continue, go on, stretch, carry on **4** = protrude, project, stand out, bulge, stick out, hang, overhang, jut out **5** = widen, increase, expand, add to, enhance, supplement, enlarge, broaden ≠ reduce **6** = make longer, prolong, lengthen, draw out, spin out, drag out ≠ shorten **7** = offer, present, confer, stick out, impart, proffer ≠ withdraw

extension 1 = annexe, addition, supplement, appendix, appendage **2** = lengthening, extra time, continuation, additional period of time **3** = development, expansion, widening, increase, broadening, enlargement, diversification

extensive ADJECTIVE = large, considerable, substantial, spacious, wide, broad, expansive
● ADJECTIVE ≠ confined **2** = comprehensive, complete, wide, pervasive ≠ restricted **3** = great, vast, widespread, large-scale, far-reaching, far-flung, voluminous ≠ limited

extent 1 = magnitude, amount, scale, level, stretch, expanse **2** = size, area, length, width, breadth

exterior NOUN = <u>outside</u>, face, surface, covering, skin, shell, coating, façade
● ADJECTIVE = <u>outer</u>, outside, external, surface, outward, outermost ≠ inner

external 1 = <u>outer</u>, outside, surface, outward, exterior, outermost ≠ internal 2 = <u>foreign</u>, international, alien, extrinsic ≠ domestic 3 = <u>outside</u>, visiting ≠ inside

extinct = <u>dead</u>, lost, gone, vanished, defunct ≠ living

extinction = <u>dying out</u>, destruction, abolition, oblivion, extermination, annihilation, eradication, obliteration

extra ADJECTIVE 1 = <u>additional</u>, more, added, further, supplementary, auxiliary, ancillary ≠ vital 2 = <u>surplus</u>, excess, spare, redundant, unused, leftover, superfluous
● NOUN = <u>addition</u>, bonus, supplement, accessory ≠ necessity
● ADVERB 1 = <u>in addition</u>, additionally, over and above 2 = <u>exceptionally</u>, very, specially, especially, particularly, extremely, remarkably, unusually

extract VERB 1 = <u>take out</u>, draw, pull, remove, withdraw, pull out, bring out 2 = <u>pull out</u>, remove, take out, draw, uproot, pluck out 3 = <u>elicit</u>, obtain, force, draw, derive, glean, coerce
● NOUN 1 = <u>passage</u>, selection, excerpt, cutting, clipping, quotation, citation 2 = <u>essence</u>, solution, concentrate, juice, distillation

extraordinary 1 = <u>remarkable</u>, outstanding, amazing, fantastic, astonishing, exceptional, phenomenal, extremely good ≠ unremarkable 2 = <u>unusual</u>, strange, remarkable, uncommon ≠ ordinary

extravagant 1 = <u>wasteful</u>, lavish, prodigal, profligate, spendthrift ≠ economical 2 = <u>excessive</u>, outrageous, over the top (*slang*), unreasonable, preposterous ≠ moderate

extreme ADJECTIVE 1 = <u>great</u>, highest, supreme, acute, severe, maximum, intense, ultimate ≠ mild 2 = <u>severe</u>, radical, strict, harsh, rigid, drastic, uncompromising 3 = <u>radical</u>, excessive, fanatical, immoderate ≠ moderate 4 = <u>farthest</u>, furthest, far, remotest, far-off, outermost, most distant ≠ nearest
● NOUN = <u>limit</u>, end, edge, opposite, pole, boundary, antithesis, extremity

extremely = <u>very</u>, particularly, severely, terribly, unusually, exceptionally, extraordinarily, tremendously

extremist NOUN = <u>radical</u>, activist, militant, fanatic, die-hard, bigot, zealot
● ADJECTIVE = <u>extreme</u>, wild, passionate, frenzied, obsessive, fanatical, fervent, zealous

eye NOUN 1 = <u>eyeball</u>, optic (*informal*), organ of vision, organ of sight 2 *often plural* = <u>eyesight</u>, sight, vision, perception, ability to see, power of seeing 3 = <u>appreciation</u>, taste, recognition, judgment, discrimination, perception, discernment 4 = <u>observance</u>, observation, surveillance, vigil, watch, lookout 5 = <u>centre</u>, heart, middle, mid, core, nucleus
● VERB = <u>look at</u>, view, study, watch, survey, observe, contemplate, check out (*informal*)

▓▓▓ RELATED WORDS
adjectives: ocular, ophthalmic, optic

f

fable 1 = <u>legend</u>, myth, parable, allegory, story, tale 2 = <u>fiction</u>, fantasy, myth, invention, yarn (*informal*), fabrication, urban myth, tall story (*informal*) ≠ fact

fabric 1 = <u>cloth</u>, material, stuff, textile, web 2 = <u>framework</u>, structure, make-up, organization, frame, foundations, construction, constitution 3 = <u>structure</u>, foundations, construction, framework

fabulous 1 = (*Informal*) = <u>wonderful</u>, excellent, brilliant, superb, spectacular, fantastic (*informal*), marvellous, sensational (*informal*) ≠ ordinary 2 = <u>astounding</u>, amazing, extraordinary, remarkable, incredible, astonishing, unbelievable, breathtaking 3 = <u>legendary</u>, imaginary, mythical, fictitious, made-up, fantastic, invented, unreal

façade 1 = <u>front</u>, face, exterior 2 = <u>show</u>, front, appearance, mask, exterior, guise, pretence, semblance

face NOUN 1 = <u>countenance</u>, features, profile, mug (*slang*), visage 2 = <u>expression</u>, look, air, appearance, aspect, countenance 3 = <u>side</u>, front, outside, surface, exterior, elevation, vertical surface

• VERB 1 = <u>look onto</u>, overlook, be opposite, look out on, front onto 2 = <u>confront</u>, meet, encounter, deal with, oppose, tackle, experience, brave 3 *often with up to* = <u>accept</u>, deal with, tackle, acknowledge, cope with, confront, come to terms with, meet head-on

facilitate = <u>further</u>, help, forward, promote, speed up, pave the way for, make easy, expedite ≠ hinder

facility 1 *often plural* = <u>amenity</u>, means, aid, opportunity, advantage, resource, equipment, provision 2 = <u>opportunity</u>, possibility, convenience 3 = <u>ability</u>, skill, efficiency, fluency, proficiency, dexterity, adroitness 4 = <u>ease</u>, fluency, effortlessness ≠ difficulty

fact 1 = <u>truth</u>, reality, certainty, verity ≠ fiction 2 = <u>event</u>, happening, act, performance, incident, deed, occurrence, fait accompli (*French*)

faction 1 = <u>group</u>, set, party, gang, bloc, contingent, clique, coterie 2 = <u>dissension</u>, division, conflict, rebellion, disagreement, variance, discord, infighting ≠ agreement

factor = <u>element</u>, part, cause, influence, item, aspect, characteristic, consideration

factory = <u>works</u>, plant, mill, workshop, assembly line, shop floor

factual = <u>true</u>, authentic, real, correct, genuine, exact, precise, dinkum (*Austral. & N.Z. informal*), true-to-life ≠ fictitious

faculty NOUN 1 = <u>ability</u>, power, skill, facility, capacity, propensity, aptitude ≠ failing 2 = <u>department</u>, school 3 = <u>teaching staff</u>, staff, teachers, professors, lecturers (*chiefly U.S.*)

• PLURAL NOUN = <u>powers</u>, reason, senses, intelligence, wits, capabilities, mental abilities, physical abilities

fad = <u>craze</u>, fashion, trend, rage, vogue, whim, mania

fade 1 = <u>become pale</u>, bleach, wash out, discolour, lose colour, decolour 2 = <u>make pale</u>, dim, bleach, wash out, blanch, discolour, decolour 3 = <u>grow dim</u>, fade away, become less loud 4 = <u>dwindle</u>,

disappear, vanish, melt away, decline, dissolve, wane, die away

fail VERB 1 = <u>be unsuccessful</u>, founder, fall, break down, flop (*informal*), fizzle out (*informal*), come unstuck, miscarry ≠ succeed 2 = <u>disappoint</u>, abandon, desert, neglect, omit, let down, forsake, be disloyal to 3 = <u>stop working</u>, stop, die, break down, stall, cut out, malfunction, conk out (*informal*) 4 = <u>wither</u>, perish, sag, waste away, shrivel up 5 = <u>go bankrupt</u>, collapse, fold (*informal*), close down, go under, go bust (*informal*), go out of business, be wound up 6 = <u>decline</u>, deteriorate, degenerate 7 = <u>give out</u>, dim, peter out, die away, grow dim

• PHRASES **without fail** = <u>without exception</u>, regularly, constantly, invariably, religiously, unfailingly, conscientiously, like clockwork

failing NOUN = <u>shortcoming</u>, fault, weakness, defect, deficiency, flaw, drawback, blemish ≠ strength

• PREPOSITION = <u>in the absence of</u>, lacking, in default of

failure 1 = <u>lack of success</u>, defeat, collapse, breakdown, overthrow, miscarriage, fiasco, downfall ≠ success 2 = <u>loser</u>, disappointment, flop (*informal*), write-off, no-hoper (*chiefly Austral.*), dud (*informal*), black sheep, washout (*informal*), dead duck (*slang*) 3 = <u>bankruptcy</u>, crash, collapse, ruin, closure, winding up, downfall, going under ≠ prosperity

faint ADJECTIVE 1 = <u>dim</u>, low, soft, faded, distant, vague, unclear, muted ≠ clear 2 = <u>slight</u>, weak, feeble, unenthusiastic, remote, slim, vague, slender 3 = <u>dizzy</u>, giddy, light-headed, weak, exhausted, wobbly, muzzy, woozy (*informal*) ≠ energetic

• VERB = <u>pass out</u>, black out, lose consciousness, keel over (*informal*), go out, collapse, swoon (*literary*), flake out (*informal*)

• NOUN = <u>blackout</u>, collapse, coma, swoon (*literary*), unconsciousness

faintly 1 = <u>slightly</u>, rather, a little, somewhat, dimly 2 = <u>softly</u>, weakly, feebly, in a whisper, indistinctly, unclearly

fair¹ 1 = <u>unbiased</u>, impartial, even-handed, unprejudiced, just, reasonable, proper, legitimate ≠ unfair 2 = <u>respectable</u>, average, reasonable, decent, acceptable, moderate, adequate, satisfactory **3** = <u>light</u>, golden, blonde, blond, yellowish, fair-haired, light-coloured, flaxen-haired **4** = <u>fine</u>, clear, dry, bright, pleasant, sunny, cloudless, unclouded **5** = <u>beautiful</u>, pretty, attractive, lovely, handsome, good-looking, bonny, comely ≠ ugly

fair² = <u>carnival</u>, show, fête, festival, exhibition, mart, bazaar, gala

fairly 1 = <u>equitably</u>, objectively, legitimately, honestly, justly, lawfully, without prejudice, dispassionately **2** = <u>moderately</u>, rather, quite, somewhat, reasonably, adequately, pretty well, tolerably **3** = <u>positively</u>, really, simply, absolutely **4** = <u>deservedly</u>, objectively, honestly, justifiably, justly, impartially, equitably, without fear or favour

fairness = <u>impartiality</u>, justice, equity, legitimacy, decency, disinterestedness, rightfulness, equitableness

fairy = <u>sprite</u>, elf, brownie, pixie, puck, imp, leprechaun, peri

fairy tale or **fairy story 1** = <u>folk tale</u>, romance, traditional story **2** = <u>lie</u>, fiction, invention, fabrication, untruth, urban myth, tall story, urban legend

faith 1 = <u>confidence</u>, trust, credit, conviction, assurance, dependence, reliance, credence ≠ distrust **2** = <u>religion</u>, church, belief, persuasion, creed, communion, denomination, dogma ≠ agnosticism

faithful 1 = <u>loyal</u>, true, committed, constant, devoted, dedicated, reliable, staunch ≠ disloyal **2** = <u>accurate</u>, close, true, strict, exact, precise

fake ADJECTIVE = <u>artificial</u>, false, forged, counterfeit, put-on, pretend (*informal*), mock, imitation ≠ genuine
● NOUN **1** = <u>forgery</u>, copy, fraud, reproduction, dummy, imitation, hoax, counterfeit **2** = <u>charlatan</u>, deceiver, sham, quack
● VERB **1** = <u>forge</u>, copy, reproduce, fabricate, counterfeit, falsify **2** = <u>sham</u>, put on, pretend, simulate, feign, go through the motions of

fall VERB **1** = <u>drop</u>, plunge, tumble, plummet, collapse, sink, go down, come down ≠ rise **2** = <u>decrease</u>, drop, decline, go down, slump, diminish, dwindle, lessen ≠ increase **3** = <u>be overthrown</u>, surrender, succumb, submit, capitulate, be conquered, pass into enemy hands ≠ triumph **4** = <u>be killed</u>, die, perish, meet your end ≠ survive **5** = <u>occur</u>, happen, come about, chance, take place, befall, come to pass
● NOUN **1** = <u>drop</u>, slip, plunge, dive, tumble, descent, plummet, nose dive **2** = <u>decrease</u>, drop, lowering, decline, reduction, slump, dip, lessening **3** = <u>collapse</u>, defeat, downfall, ruin, destruction, overthrow, submission, capitulation

false 1 = <u>incorrect</u>, wrong, mistaken, misleading, faulty, inaccurate, invalid, erroneous ≠ correct **2** = <u>untrue</u>, fraudulent, trumped up, fallacious, untruthful ≠ true **3** = <u>artificial</u>, forged, fake, reproduction, replica, imitation, bogus, simulated ≠ real

falter 1 = <u>hesitate</u>, delay, waver, vacillate ≠ persevere **2** = <u>tumble</u>, totter **3** = <u>stutter</u>, pause, stumble, hesitate, stammer

fame = <u>prominence</u>, glory, celebrity, stardom, reputation, honour, prestige, stature ≠ obscurity

familiar 1 = <u>well-known</u>, recognized, common, ordinary, routine, frequent, accustomed, customary ≠ unfamiliar **2** = <u>friendly</u>, close, dear, intimate, amicable ≠ formal **3** = <u>relaxed</u>, easy, friendly, comfortable, intimate, casual, amicable **4** = <u>disrespectful</u>, forward, bold, intrusive, presumptuous, impudent, overfamiliar

familiarity 1 = <u>acquaintance</u>, experience, understanding, knowledge, awareness, grasp ≠ unfamiliarity **2** = <u>friendliness</u>, intimacy, ease, openness, informality, sociability ≠ formality **3** = <u>disrespect</u>, forwardness, overfamiliarity, cheek, presumption, boldness ≠ respect

family 1 = <u>relations</u>, relatives, household, folk (*informal*), kin, nuclear family, next of kin, kith and kin, ainga (*N.Z.*) **2** = <u>children</u>, kids (*informal*), offspring, little ones, littlies (*Austral. informal*) **3** = <u>ancestors</u>, house, race, tribe, clan, dynasty, line of descent **4** = <u>species</u>, group, class, system, order, network, genre, subdivision

famine = <u>hunger</u>, want, starvation, deprivation, scarcity, dearth

famous = <u>well-known</u>, celebrated, acclaimed, noted, distinguished, prominent, legendary, renowned ≠ unknown

fan¹ NOUN = <u>blower</u>, ventilator, air

conditioner
● **VERB** = <u>blow</u>, cool, refresh, air-condition, ventilate

fan² = <u>supporter</u>, lover, follower, enthusiast, admirer, buff (*informal*), devotee, aficionado

fanatic = <u>extremist</u>, activist, militant, bigot, zealot

fancy **ADJECTIVE** = <u>elaborate</u>, decorative, extravagant, intricate, baroque, ornamental, ornate, embellished ≠ plain
● **NOUN 1** = <u>whim</u>, thought, idea, desire, urge, notion, humour, impulse **2** = <u>delusion</u>, dream, vision, fantasy, daydream, chimera
● **VERB 1** = <u>wish for</u>, want, desire, hope for, long for, crave, yearn for, thirst for **2** (*Informal*) = <u>be attracted to</u>, find attractive, lust after, like, take to, be captivated by, have a thing about (*informal*), have eyes for **3** = <u>suppose</u>, think, believe, imagine, reckon, conjecture, think likely

fantastic 1 (*Informal*) = <u>wonderful</u>, great, excellent, very good, smashing (*informal*), superb, tremendous (*informal*), magnificent, booshit (*Austral. slang*), exo (*Austral. slang*), sik (*Austral. slang*) ≠ ordinary **2** = <u>strange</u>, bizarre, grotesque, fanciful, outlandish **3** = <u>implausible</u>, unlikely, incredible, absurd, preposterous, cock-and-bull (*informal*)

fantasy or (*Archaic*) **phantasy**
1 = <u>daydream</u>, dream, wish, reverie, flight of fancy, pipe dream **2** = <u>imagination</u>, fancy, invention, creativity, originality

far **ADVERB 1** = <u>a long way</u>, miles, deep, a good way, afar, a great distance **2** = <u>much</u>, greatly, very much, extremely, significantly, considerably, decidedly, markedly
● **ADJECTIVE** *often with* **off** = <u>remote</u>, distant, far-flung, faraway, out-of-the-way, far-off, outlying, off the beaten track ≠ near

farce 1 = <u>comedy</u>, satire, slapstick, burlesque, buffoonery **2** = <u>mockery</u>, joke, nonsense, parody, shambles, sham, travesty

fare **NOUN 1** = <u>charge</u>, price, ticket price, ticket money **2** = <u>food</u>, provisions, board, rations, kai (*N.Z. informal*), nourishment, sustenance, victuals, nutriment
● **VERB** = <u>get on</u>, do, manage, make out, prosper, get along

farewell **INTERJECTION** = <u>goodbye</u>, bye (*informal*), so long, see you, take care, good morning, bye-bye (*informal*), good day, haere ra (*N.Z.*)
● **NOUN** = <u>goodbye</u>, parting, departure, leave-taking, adieu, valediction, sendoff (*informal*)

farm **NOUN** = <u>smallholding</u>, ranch (*chiefly U.S. & Canad.*), farmstead, station (*Austral. & N.Z.*), vineyard, plantation, croft (*Scot.*), grange, homestead
● **VERB** = <u>cultivate</u>, work, plant, grow crops on, keep animals on

fascinate = <u>entrance</u>, absorb, intrigue, rivet, captivate, enthral, beguile, transfix ≠ bore

fascinating = <u>captivating</u>, engaging, gripping, compelling, intriguing, very interesting, irresistible, enticing ≠ boring

fascination = <u>attraction</u>, pull, magic, charm, lure, allure, magnetism, enchantment

fashion **NOUN 1** = <u>style</u>, look, trend, rage, custom, mode, vogue, craze **2** = <u>method</u>, way, style, manner, mode
● **VERB** = <u>make</u>, shape, cast, construct, form, create, manufacture, forge

fashionable = <u>popular</u>, in fashion, trendy (*Brit. informal*), in (*informal*), modern, with it (*informal*), stylish, chic ≠ unfashionable

fast¹ **ADJECTIVE 1** = <u>quick</u>, flying, rapid, fleet, swift, speedy, brisk, hasty ≠ slow **2** = <u>fixed</u>, firm, sound, stuck, secure, tight, jammed, fastened ≠ unstable **3** = <u>dissipated</u>, wild, exciting, loose, extravagant, reckless, self-indulgent, wanton **4** = <u>close</u>, firm, devoted, faithful, steadfast
● **ADVERB 1** = <u>quickly</u>, rapidly, swiftly, hastily, hurriedly, speedily, in haste, at full speed ≠ slowly **2** = <u>securely</u>, firmly, tightly, fixedly **3** = <u>fixedly</u>, firmly, soundly, deeply, securely, tightly

fast² **VERB** = <u>go hungry</u>, abstain, go without food, deny yourself
● **NOUN** = <u>fasting</u>, diet, abstinence

fasten 1 = <u>secure</u>, close, do up **2** = <u>tie</u>, bind, tie up **3** = <u>fix</u>, join, link, connect, attach, affix

fat **ADJECTIVE 1** = <u>overweight</u>, large, heavy, plump, stout, obese, tubby, portly ≠ thin **2** = <u>fatty</u>, greasy, adipose, oleaginous, oily ≠ lean
● **NOUN** = <u>fatness</u>, flesh, bulk, obesity, flab, blubber, paunch, fatty tissue

fatal 1 = <u>disastrous</u>, devastating, crippling, catastrophic, ruinous, calamitous, baleful, baneful ≠ minor 2 = <u>lethal</u>, deadly, mortal, causing death, final, killing, terminal, malignant ≠ harmless

fate 1 = <u>destiny</u>, chance, fortune, luck, the stars, providence, nemesis, kismet 2 = <u>fortune</u>, destiny, lot, portion, cup, horoscope

fated = <u>destined</u>, doomed, predestined, preordained, foreordained

father NOUN 1 = <u>daddy</u> (*informal*), dad (*informal*), male parent, pop (*U.S. informal*), old man (*Brit. informal*), pa (*informal*), papa (*old-fashioned informal*), pater 2 = <u>founder</u>, author, maker, architect, creator, inventor, originator, prime mover 3 *usually cap.* = <u>priest</u>, minister, vicar, parson, pastor, cleric, churchman, padre (*informal*) 4 *usually plural* = <u>forefather</u>, predecessor, ancestor, forebear, progenitor, tupuna *or* tipuna (*N.Z.*)

● VERB = <u>sire</u>, parent, conceive, bring to life, beget, procreate, bring into being, give life to

▓▓▓ RELATED WORD
adjective: paternal

fatherly = <u>paternal</u>, kindly, protective, supportive, benign, affectionate, patriarchal, benevolent

fatigue NOUN = <u>tiredness</u>, lethargy, weariness, heaviness, languor, listlessness ≠ freshness

● VERB = <u>tire</u>, exhaust, weaken, weary, drain, wear out, take it out of (*informal*), tire out ≠ refresh

fatty = <u>greasy</u>, fat, creamy, oily, adipose, oleaginous, suety, rich

fault NOUN 1 = <u>responsibility</u>, liability, guilt, accountability, culpability 2 = <u>mistake</u>, slip, error, blunder, lapse, oversight, indiscretion, howler (*informal*) 3 = <u>failing</u>, weakness, defect, deficiency, flaw, shortcoming, blemish, imperfection ≠ strength

● VERB = <u>criticize</u>, blame, complain, condemn, moan about, censure, hold (someone) responsible, find fault with

● PHRASES **find fault with something** *or* **someone** = <u>criticize</u>, complain about, whinge about (*informal*), whine about (*informal*), quibble, carp at, take to task, pick holes in ◆ **to a fault** = <u>excessively</u>, unduly, in the extreme, overmuch, immoderately

faulty 1 = <u>defective</u>, damaged, malfunctioning, broken, flawed, impaired, imperfect, out of order 2 = <u>incorrect</u>, flawed, unsound

favour NOUN 1 = <u>approval</u>, goodwill, commendation, approbation ≠ disapproval 2 = <u>favouritism</u>, preferential treatment 3 = <u>support</u>, backing, aid, assistance, patronage, good opinion 4 = <u>good turn</u>, service, benefit, courtesy, kindness, indulgence, boon, good deed ≠ wrong

● VERB 1 = <u>prefer</u>, opt for, like better, incline towards, choose, pick, desire, go for ≠ object to 2 = <u>indulge</u>, reward, side with, smile upon 3 = <u>support</u>, champion, encourage, approve, advocate, subscribe to, commend, stand up for ≠ oppose 4 = <u>help</u>, benefit

favourable 1 = <u>positive</u>, encouraging, approving, praising, reassuring, enthusiastic, sympathetic, commending ≠ disapproving 2 = <u>affirmative</u>, agreeing, confirming, positive, assenting, corroborative 3 = <u>advantageous</u>, promising, encouraging, suitable, helpful, beneficial, auspicious, opportune ≠ disadvantageous

favourite ADJECTIVE = <u>preferred</u>, favoured, best-loved, most-liked, special, choice, dearest, pet

● NOUN = <u>darling</u>, pet, blue-eyed boy (*informal*), beloved, idol, fave (*informal*), teacher's pet, the apple of your eye

fear NOUN 1 = <u>dread</u>, horror, panic, terror, fright, alarm, trepidation, fearfulness 2 = <u>bugbear</u>, bête noire, horror, nightmare, anxiety, terror, dread, spectre

● VERB 1 = <u>be afraid of</u>, dread, shudder at, be fearful of, tremble at, be terrified by, take fright at, shake in your shoes about 2 = <u>regret</u>, feel, suspect, have a feeling, have a hunch, have a sneaking suspicion, have a funny feeling

● PHRASES **fear for something** *or* **someone** = <u>worry about</u>, be anxious about, feel concern for

fearful 1 = <u>scared</u>, afraid, alarmed, frightened, nervous, terrified, petrified ≠ unafraid 2 = <u>timid</u>, afraid, frightened, scared, alarmed, nervous, uneasy, jumpy ≠ brave 3 = <u>frightful</u>, terrible, awful, dreadful, horrific, dire, horrendous, gruesome

feasible = practicable, possible, reasonable, viable, workable, achievable, attainable, likely ≠ impracticable

feast NOUN 1 = banquet, repast, spread (*informal*), dinner, treat, hakari (*N.Z.*) 2 = festival, holiday, fête, celebration, holy day, red-letter day, religious festival, saint's day
● VERB = eat your fill, wine and dine, overindulge, consume, indulge, gorge, devour, pig out (*slang*)

feat = accomplishment, act, performance, achievement, enterprise, undertaking, exploit, deed

feather NOUN = plume
● PLURAL NOUN = plumage, plumes, down

feature NOUN 1 = aspect, quality, characteristic, property, factor, trait, hallmark, facet 2 = article, report, story, piece, item, column 3 = highlight, attraction, speciality, main item
● PLURAL NOUN = face, countenance, physiognomy, lineaments
● VERB 1 = spotlight, present, emphasize, play up, foreground, give prominence to 2 = star, appear, participate, play a part

federation = union, league, association, alliance, combination, coalition, partnership, consortium

fed up = cheesed off, depressed, bored, tired, discontented, dissatisfied, glum, sick and tired (*informal*), hoha (*N.Z.*)

fee = charge, price, cost, bill, payment, wage, salary, toll

feeble 1 = weak, frail, debilitated, sickly, puny, weedy (*informal*), infirm, effete ≠ strong 2 = inadequate, pathetic, insufficient, lame 3 = unconvincing, poor, thin, tame, pathetic, lame, flimsy, paltry ≠ effective

feed VERB 1 = cater for, provide for, nourish, provide with food, supply, sustain, cook for, wine and dine 2 = graze, eat, browse, pasture 3 = eat, drink milk
● NOUN 1 = food, fodder, provender, pasturage 2 (*Informal*) = meal, spread (*informal*), dinner, lunch, tea, breakfast, feast, supper

feel VERB 1 = experience, bear 2 = touch, handle, manipulate, finger, stroke, paw, caress, fondle 3 = be aware of 4 = perceive, detect, discern, experience, notice, observe 5 = sense, be aware,

be convinced, have a feeling, intuit 6 = believe, consider, judge, deem, think, hold
● NOUN 1 = texture, finish, touch, surface, surface quality 2 = impression, feeling, air, sense, quality, atmosphere, mood, aura

feeling 1 = emotion, sentiment 2 = opinion, view, attitude, belief, point of view, instinct, inclination 3 = passion, emotion, intensity, warmth 4 = ardour, love, care, warmth, tenderness, fervour 5 = sympathy, understanding, concern, pity, sensitivity, compassion, sorrow, sensibility 6 = sensation, sense, impression, awareness 7 = sense of touch, perception, sensation 8 = impression, idea, sense, notion, suspicion, hunch, inkling, presentiment 9 = atmosphere, mood, aura, ambience, feel, air, quality

fell 1 = cut down, cut, level, demolish, knock down, hew 2 = knock down

fellow 1 (*Old-fashioned*) = man, person, individual, character, guy (*informal*), bloke (*Brit. informal*), chap (*informal*) 2 = associate, colleague, peer, partner, companion, comrade, crony

fellowship 1 = society, club, league, association, organization, guild, fraternity, brotherhood 2 = camaraderie, brotherhood, companionship, sociability

feminine = womanly, pretty, soft, gentle, tender, delicate, ladylike ≠ masculine

fence NOUN = barrier, wall, defence, railings, hedge, barricade, hedgerow, rampart
● VERB *often with in or off* = enclose, surround, bound, protect, pen, confine, encircle

ferocious 1 = fierce, violent, savage, ravening, predatory, rapacious, wild ≠ gentle 2 = cruel, bitter, brutal, vicious, ruthless, bloodthirsty

ferry NOUN = ferry boat, boat, ship, passenger boat, packet boat, packet
● VERB = transport, bring, carry, ship, take, run, shuttle, convey

fertile = productive, rich, lush, prolific, abundant, plentiful, fruitful, teeming ≠ barren

fertility = fruitfulness, abundance, richness, fecundity, luxuriance, productiveness

fertilizer = compost, muck, manure, dung, bone meal, dressing

festival 1 = celebration, fair, carnival, gala, fête, entertainment, jubilee, fiesta 2 = holy day, holiday, feast, commemoration, feast day, red-letter day, saint's day, fiesta

festive = celebratory, happy, merry, jubilant, cheery, joyous, joyful, jovial ≠ mournful

fetch 1 = bring, pick up, collect, go and get, get, carry, deliver, transport 2 = sell for, make, raise, earn, realize, go for, yield, bring in

fetching = attractive, charming, cute, enticing, captivating, alluring, winsome

feud NOUN = hostility, row, conflict, argument, disagreement, rivalry, quarrel, vendetta
● VERB = quarrel, row, clash, dispute, fall out, contend, war, squabble

fever = excitement, frenzy, ferment, agitation, fervour, restlessness, delirium

few = not many, one or two, scarcely any, rare, meagre, negligible, sporadic, sparse

fiasco = flop, failure, disaster, mess (*informal*), catastrophe, debacle, cock-up (*Brit. slang*), washout (*informal*)

fibre = thread, strand, filament, tendril, pile, texture, wisp

fiction 1 = tale, story, novel, legend, myth, romance, narration, creative writing 2 = lie, invention, fabrication, falsehood, untruth, urban myth, tall story, urban legend

fictional = imaginary, made-up, invented, legendary, unreal, nonexistent

fiddle VERB 1 *usually with* **with** = fidget, play, finger, tamper, mess about *or* around 2 *usually with* **with** = tinker, adjust, interfere, mess about *or* around 3 (*Informal*) = cheat, cook (*informal*), fix, diddle (*informal*), wangle (*informal*)
● NOUN 1 (*Brit. informal*) = fraud, racket, scam (*slang*), fix, swindle 2 = violin

fiddling = trivial, small, petty, trifling, insignificant, unimportant, pettifogging, futile

fidelity 1 = loyalty, devotion, allegiance, constancy, faithfulness, dependability, trustworthiness, staunchness ≠ disloyalty 2 = accuracy, precision, correspondence, closeness, faithfulness, exactness, scrupulousness ≠ inaccuracy

field NOUN 1 = meadow, land, green, lea (*poetic*), pasture 2 = speciality, line, area, department, territory, discipline, province, sphere 3 = line, reach, sweep 4 = competitors, competition, candidates, runners, applicants, entrants, contestants
● VERB 1 (*Informal*) = deal with, answer, handle, respond to, reply to, deflect, turn aside 2 (*Sport*) = retrieve, return, stop, catch, pick up

fierce 1 = ferocious, wild, dangerous, cruel, savage, brutal, aggressive, menacing, aggers (*Austral. slang*), biffo (*Austral. slang*) ≠ gentle 2 = intense, strong, keen, relentless, cut-throat 3 = stormy, strong, powerful, violent, intense, raging, furious, howling ≠ tranquil

fiercely = ferociously, savagely, passionately, furiously, viciously, tooth and nail, tigerishly, with no holds barred

fiery 1 = burning, flaming, blazing, on fire, ablaze, aflame, afire 2 = excitable, fierce, passionate, irritable, impetuous, irascible, hot-headed

fight VERB 1 = oppose, campaign against, dispute, contest, resist, defy, contend, withstand 2 = battle, combat, do battle 3 = engage in, conduct, wage, pursue, carry on
● NOUN 1 = battle, campaign, movement, struggle 2 = conflict, clash, contest, encounter 3 = brawl, scrap (*informal*), confrontation, rumble (*U.S. & N.Z. slang*), duel, skirmish, tussle, biffo (*Austral. slang*) 4 = row, argument, dispute, quarrel, squabble 5 = resistance, spirit, pluck, militancy, belligerence, pluckiness

fighter 1 = boxer, wrestler, pugilist, prize fighter 2 = soldier, warrior, fighting man, man-at-arms

figure NOUN 1 = digit, character, symbol, number, numeral 2 = shape, build, body, frame, proportions, physique 3 = personage, person, individual, character, personality, celebrity, big name, dignitary 4 = diagram, drawing, picture, illustration, representation, sketch 5 = design, shape, pattern 6 = price, cost, value, amount, total, sum
● VERB 1 *usually with* **in** = feature, act, appear, contribute to, play a part, be featured 2 = calculate, work out, compute, tot up, total, count, reckon, tally
● PHRASES **figure something** *or* **someone out** = understand, make out, fathom, see, solve, comprehend, make sense of, decipher

figurehead = nominal head, titular head, front man, puppet, mouthpiece

file¹ NOUN 1 = folder, case, portfolio, binder 2 = dossier, record, information, data, documents, case history, report, case 3 = line, row, chain, column, queue, procession

● VERB 1 = arrange, order, classify, put in place, categorize, pigeonhole, put in order 2 = register, record, enter, log, put on record 3 = march, troop, parade, walk in line, walk behind one another

file² = smooth, shape, polish, rub, scrape, rasp, abrade

fill 1 = top up, fill up, make full, become full, brim over 2 = swell, expand, become bloated, extend, balloon, fatten 3 = pack, crowd, squeeze, cram, throng 4 = stock, supply, pack, load 5 = plug, close, stop, seal, cork, bung, block up, stop up 6 = saturate, charge, pervade, permeate, imbue, impregnate, suffuse 7 = fulfil, hold, perform, carry out, occupy, execute, discharge 8 *often with* **up** = satisfy, stuff, glut

filling NOUN = stuffing, padding, filler, wadding, inside, insides, contents

● ADJECTIVE = satisfying, heavy, square, substantial, ample

film NOUN 1 = movie, picture, flick (*slang*), motion picture 2 = cinema, the movies 3 = layer, covering, cover, skin, coating, dusting, tissue, membrane

● VERB 1 = photograph, record, shoot, video, videotape, take 2 = adapt for the screen, make into a film

filter VERB 1 = purify, treat, strain, refine, riddle, sift, sieve, winnow 2 = trickle, seep, percolate, escape, leak, penetrate, ooze, dribble

● NOUN = sieve, mesh, gauze, strainer, membrane, riddle, sifter

filthy 1 = dirty, foul, polluted, squalid, slimy, unclean, putrid, festy (*Austral. slang*) 2 = grimy, muddy, blackened, grubby, begrimed, festy (*Austral. slang*) 3 = obscene, corrupt, indecent, pornographic, lewd, depraved, impure, smutty

final 1 = last, latest, closing, finishing, concluding, ultimate, terminal ≠ first 2 = irrevocable, absolute, definitive, decided, settled, definite, conclusive, irrefutable

finale = climax, ending, close, conclusion, culmination, denouement, last part, epilogue ≠ opening

finally 1 = eventually, at last, in the end, ultimately, at length, at long last, after a long time 2 = lastly, in the end, ultimately 3 = in conclusion, lastly, in closing, to conclude, to sum up, in summary

finance VERB = fund, back, support, pay for, guarantee, invest in, underwrite, endow

● NOUN = economics, business, money, banking, accounts, investment, commerce

● PLURAL NOUN = resources, money, funds, capital, cash, affairs, budgeting, assets

financial = economic, business, commercial, monetary, fiscal, pecuniary

find VERB 1 = discover, uncover, spot, locate, detect, come across, hit upon, put your finger on ≠ lose 2 = encounter, meet, recognize 3 = observe, learn, note, discover, notice, realize, come up with, perceive

● NOUN = discovery, catch, asset, bargain, acquisition, good buy

● PHRASES **find something out** = learn, discover, realize, observe, perceive, detect, become aware, come to know

fine¹ 1 = excellent, good, striking, masterly, very good, impressive, outstanding, magnificent ≠ poor 2 = satisfactory, good, all right, suitable, acceptable, convenient, fair, O.K. *or* okay (*informal*) 3 = thin, light, narrow, wispy 4 = delicate, light, thin, sheer, flimsy, wispy, gossamer, diaphanous ≠ coarse 5 = stylish, expensive, elegant, refined, tasteful, quality 6 = exquisite, delicate, fragile, dainty 7 = minute, exact, precise, nice 8 = keen, minute, nice, sharp, acute, subtle, precise, hairsplitting 9 = brilliant, quick, keen, alert, clever, penetrating, astute 10 = sunny, clear, fair, dry, bright, pleasant, clement, balmy ≠ cloudy

fine² NOUN = penalty, damages, punishment, forfeit, financial penalty

● VERB = penalize, charge, punish

finger = touch, feel, handle, play with, manipulate, paw (*informal*), maul, toy with

finish VERB 1 = stop, close, complete, conclude, cease, wrap up (*informal*), terminate, round off ≠ start 2 = get done, complete, conclude 3 = end, stop, conclude, wind up, terminate

4 = <u>consume</u>, dispose of, devour, polish off, eat, get through **5** = <u>use up</u>, empty, exhaust **6** = <u>coat</u>, polish, stain, texture, wax, varnish, gild, veneer **7** *usually with off* = <u>destroy</u>, defeat, overcome, bring down, ruin, dispose of, rout, put an end to **8** *usually with off* = <u>kill</u>, murder, destroy, massacre, butcher, slaughter, slay, exterminate

● NOUN **1** = <u>end</u>, close, conclusion, run-in, completion, finale, culmination, cessation ≠ beginning **2** = <u>surface</u>, polish, shine, texture, glaze, veneer, lacquer, lustre

finished 1 = <u>over</u>, done, through, ended, closed, complete, executed, finalized ≠ begun **2** = <u>ruined</u>, done for (*informal*), doomed, through, lost, defeated, wiped out, undone

fire NOUN **1** = <u>flames</u>, blaze, combustion, inferno, conflagration, holocaust **2** = <u>passion</u>, energy, spirit, enthusiasm, excitement, intensity, sparkle, vitality **3** = <u>bombardment</u>, shooting, firing, shelling, hail, volley, barrage, gunfire

● VERB **1** = <u>let off</u>, shoot, shell, set off, discharge, detonate **2** = <u>shoot</u>, explode, discharge, detonate, pull the trigger **3** (*Informal*) = <u>dismiss</u>, sack (*informal*), get rid of, discharge, lay off, make redundant, cashier, give notice **4** *sometimes with* **up** = <u>inspire</u>, excite, stir, stimulate, motivate, awaken, animate, rouse

fireworks 1 = <u>pyrotechnics</u>, illuminations, feux d'artifice **2** (*Informal*) = <u>trouble</u>, row, storm, rage, uproar, hysterics

firm¹ 1 = <u>hard</u>, solid, dense, set, stiff, compacted, rigid, inflexible ≠ soft **2** = <u>secure</u>, fixed, rooted, stable, steady, fast, embedded, immovable ≠ unstable **3** = <u>strong</u>, close, tight, steady **4** = <u>strict</u>, unshakeable, resolute, inflexible, unyielding, unbending **5** = <u>determined</u>, resolved, definite, set on, adamant, resolute, inflexible, unyielding ≠ wavering **6** = <u>definite</u>, hard, clear, confirmed, settled, fixed, hard-and-fast, cut-and-dried (*informal*)

firm² = <u>company</u>, business, concern, association, organization, corporation, venture, enterprise

firmly 1 = <u>securely</u>, safely, tightly **2** = <u>immovably</u>, securely, steadily, like a rock, unflinchingly, unshakeably **3** = <u>steadily</u>, securely, tightly, unflinchingly

4 = <u>resolutely</u>, staunchly, steadfastly, definitely, unwaveringly, unchangeably

first ADJECTIVE **1** = <u>earliest</u>, original, primordial **2** = <u>initial</u>, opening, earliest, maiden, introductory **3** = <u>top</u>, best, winning, premier **4** = <u>elementary</u>, key, basic, primary, fundamental, cardinal, rudimentary, elemental **5** = <u>foremost</u>, highest, greatest, leading, head, ruling, chief, prime

● ADVERB = <u>to begin with</u>, firstly, initially, at the beginning, in the first place, beforehand, to start with, at the outset

● NOUN = <u>novelty</u>, innovation, originality, new experience

● PHRASES **from the first** = <u>from the start</u>, from the beginning, from the outset, from the very beginning, from the introduction, from the starting point, from the inception, from the commencement

fish = <u>angle</u>, net, cast, trawl

fit¹ VERB **1** = <u>adapt</u>, shape, arrange, alter, adjust, modify, tweak (*informal*), customize **2** = <u>place</u>, insert **3** = <u>suit</u>, meet, match, belong to, conform to, correspond to, accord with, be appropriate to **4** = <u>equip</u>, provide, arm, prepare, fit out, kit out

● ADJECTIVE **1** = <u>appropriate</u>, suitable, right, becoming, seemly, fitting, skilled, correct ≠ inappropriate **2** = <u>healthy</u>, strong, robust, sturdy, well, trim, strapping, hale ≠ unfit

fit² **1** = <u>seizure</u>, attack, bout, spasm, convulsion, paroxysm **2** = <u>bout</u>, burst, outbreak, outburst, spell

fitness 1 = <u>appropriateness</u>, competence, readiness, eligibility, suitability, propriety, aptness **2** = <u>health</u>, strength, good health, vigour, good condition, wellness, robustness

fitting NOUN = <u>accessory</u>, part, piece, unit, component, attachment

● ADJECTIVE = <u>appropriate</u>, suitable, proper, apt, right, becoming, seemly, correct ≠ unsuitable

fix VERB **1** = <u>place</u>, join, stick, attach, set, position, plant, link **2** = <u>decide</u>, set, choose, establish, determine, settle, arrange, arrive at **3** = <u>arrange</u>, organize, sort out, see to, fix up, make arrangements for **4** = <u>repair</u>, mend, service, correct, restore, see to, overhaul, patch up **5** = <u>focus</u>, direct at, fasten on **6** (*Informal*) = <u>rig</u>, set up (*informal*), influence, manipulate, fiddle (*informal*)

● NOUN (*Informal*) = <u>mess</u>, corner, difficulty, dilemma, embarrassment, plight, pickle (*informal*), uphill (*S. African*)

● PHRASES **fix someone up** = <u>provide</u>, supply, bring about, lay on, arrange for

◆ **fix something up** = <u>arrange</u>, plan, settle, fix, organize, sort out, agree on, make arrangements for

fixed 1 = <u>inflexible</u>, set, steady, resolute, unwavering ≠ wavering 2 = <u>immovable</u>, set, established, secure, rooted, permanent, rigid ≠ mobile 3 = <u>agreed</u>, set, planned, decided, established, settled, arranged, resolved

fizz 1 = <u>bubble</u>, froth, fizzle, effervesce, produce bubbles 2 = <u>sputter</u>, buzz, sparkle, hiss, crackle

flag¹ NOUN = <u>banner</u>, standard, colours, pennant, ensign, streamer, pennon

● VERB = <u>mark</u>, identify, indicate, label, pick out, note

● PHRASES **flag something** or **someone down** = <u>hail</u>, stop, signal, wave down

flag² = <u>weaken</u>, fade, weary, falter, wilt, wane, sag, languish

flagging = <u>weakening</u>, declining, waning, fading, deteriorating, wearying, faltering, wilting

flair 1 = <u>ability</u>, feel, talent, gift, genius, faculty, mastery, knack 2 = <u>style</u>, taste, dash, chic, elegance, panache, discernment, stylishness

flake NOUN = <u>chip</u>, scale, layer, peeling, shaving, wafer, sliver

● VERB = <u>chip</u>, peel (off), blister

flamboyant 1 = <u>camp</u> (*informal*), dashing, theatrical, swashbuckling 2 = <u>showy</u>, elaborate, extravagant, ornate, ostentatious 3 = <u>colourful</u>, striking, brilliant, glamorous, stylish, dazzling, glitzy (*slang*), showy

flame NOUN 1 = <u>fire</u>, light, spark, glow, blaze, brightness, inferno 2 (*Informal*) = <u>sweetheart</u>, partner, lover, girlfriend, boyfriend, heart-throb (*Brit.*), beau

● VERB = <u>burn</u>, flash, shine, glow, blaze, flare, glare

flank 1 = <u>side</u>, hip, thigh, loin 2 = <u>wing</u>, side, sector, aspect

flap VERB 1 = <u>flutter</u>, wave, flail 2 = <u>beat</u>, wave, thrash, flutter, wag, vibrate, shake

● NOUN 1 = <u>flutter</u>, beating, waving,

shaking, swinging, swish 2 (*Informal*) = <u>panic</u>, state (*informal*), agitation, commotion, sweat (*informal*), dither (*chiefly Brit.*), fluster, tizzy (*informal*)

flare NOUN = <u>flame</u>, burst, flash, blaze, glare, flicker

● VERB 1 = <u>blaze</u>, flame, glare, flicker, burn up 2 = <u>widen</u>, spread, broaden, spread out, dilate, splay

flash NOUN = <u>blaze</u>, burst, spark, beam, streak, flare, dazzle, glare

● VERB 1 = <u>blaze</u>, shine, beam, sparkle, flare, glare, gleam, light up 2 = <u>speed</u>, race, shoot, fly, tear, dash, whistle, streak 3 (*Informal*) = <u>show quickly</u>, display, expose, exhibit, flourish, show off, flaunt

● ADJECTIVE (*Informal*) = <u>ostentatious</u>, smart, trendy, showy

flat¹ ADJECTIVE 1 = <u>even</u>, level, levelled, smooth, horizontal ≠ uneven 2 = <u>punctured</u>, collapsed, burst, blown out, deflated, empty 3 = <u>used up</u>, finished, empty, drained, expired 4 = <u>absolute</u>, firm, positive, explicit, definite, outright, downright, unequivocal 5 = <u>dull</u>, dead, empty, boring, depressing, tedious, lacklustre, tiresome ≠ exciting 6 = <u>without energy</u>, empty, weak, tired, depressed, drained, weary, worn out 7 = <u>monotonous</u>, boring, dull, tedious, tiresome, unchanging

● ADVERB = <u>completely</u>, directly, absolutely, categorically, precisely, exactly, utterly, outright

● PHRASES **flat out** (*Informal*) = <u>at full speed</u>, all out, to the full, hell for leather (*informal*), as hard as possible, at full tilt, for all you are worth

flat² = <u>apartment</u>, rooms, quarters, digs, suite, penthouse, living quarters

flatly = <u>absolutely</u>, completely, positively, categorically, unequivocally, unhesitatingly

flatten 1 = <u>level</u>, squash, compress, trample, iron out, even out, smooth off 2 = <u>destroy</u>, level, ruin, demolish, knock down, pull down, raze

flatter 1 = <u>praise</u>, compliment, pander to, sweet-talk (*informal*), wheedle, soft-soap (*informal*), butter up 2 = <u>suit</u>, become, enhance, set off, embellish, do something for, show to advantage

flattering 1 = <u>becoming</u>, kind, effective, enhancing, well-chosen ≠ unflattering

2 = <u>ingratiating</u>, complimentary, fawning, fulsome, laudatory, adulatory ≠ uncomplimentary

flavour NOUN **1** = <u>taste</u>, seasoning, flavouring, savour, relish, smack, aroma, zest ≠ blandness **2** = <u>quality</u>, feeling, feel, style, character, tone, essence, tinge

● VERB = <u>season</u>, spice, add flavour to, enrich, infuse, imbue, pep up, leaven

flaw = <u>weakness</u>, failing, defect, weak spot, fault, blemish, imperfection, chink in your armour

flawed 1 = <u>damaged</u>, defective, imperfect, blemished, faulty **2** = <u>erroneous</u>, incorrect, invalid, wrong, mistaken, false, faulty, unsound

flee = <u>run away</u>, escape, bolt, fly, take off (informal), depart, run off, take flight

fleet = <u>navy</u>, task force, flotilla, armada

fleeting = <u>momentary</u>, passing, brief, temporary, short-lived, transient, ephemeral, transitory ≠ lasting

flesh NOUN **1** = <u>fat</u>, muscle, tissue, brawn **2** = <u>fatness</u>, fat, adipose tissue, corpulence, weight **3** = <u>meat</u> **4** = <u>physical nature</u>, carnality, human nature, flesh and blood, sinful nature

● PHRASES **your own flesh and blood** = <u>family</u>, blood, relations, relatives, kin, kith and kin, blood relations, kinsfolk, ainga (N.Z.)

flexibility 1 = <u>elasticity</u>, pliability, springiness, pliancy, give (informal) **2** = <u>adaptability</u>, openness, versatility, adjustability **3** = <u>complaisance</u>, accommodation, give and take, amenability

flexible 1 = <u>pliable</u>, plastic, elastic, supple, lithe, springy, pliant, stretchy ≠ rigid **2** = <u>adaptable</u>, open, variable, adjustable, discretionary ≠ inflexible

flick VERB **1** = <u>jerk</u>, pull, tug, lurch, jolt **2** = <u>strike</u>, tap, remove quickly, hit, touch, stroke, flip, whisk

● PHRASES **flick through something** = <u>browse</u>, glance at, skim, leaf through, flip through, thumb through, skip through

flicker VERB **1** = <u>twinkle</u>, flash, sparkle, flare, shimmer, gutter, glimmer **2** = <u>flutter</u>, waver, quiver, vibrate

● NOUN **1** = <u>glimmer</u>, flash, spark, flare, gleam **2** = <u>trace</u>, breath, spark, glimmer, iota

flight¹ 1 = <u>journey</u>, trip, voyage

2 = <u>aviation</u>, flying, aeronautics **3** = <u>flock</u>, group, unit, cloud, formation, squadron, swarm, flying group

**flight² **= <u>escape</u>, fleeing, departure, retreat, exit, running away, exodus, getaway

fling VERB = <u>throw</u>, toss, hurl, launch, cast, propel, sling, catapult

● NOUN = <u>binge</u>, good time, bash, party, spree, night on the town, rave-up (Brit. slang)

flip VERB **1** = <u>flick</u>, switch, snap, slick **2** = <u>spin</u>, turn, overturn, turn over, roll over **3** = <u>toss</u>, throw, flick, fling, sling

● NOUN = <u>toss</u>, throw, spin, snap, flick

flirt VERB **1** = <u>chat up</u>, lead on (informal), make advances at, make eyes at, philander, make sheep's eyes at **2** usually with **with** = <u>toy with</u>, consider, entertain, play with, dabble in, trifle with, give a thought to, expose yourself to

● NOUN = <u>tease</u>, philanderer, coquette, heart-breaker

float 1 = <u>glide</u>, sail, drift, move gently, bob, coast, slide, be carried **2** = <u>be buoyant</u>, hang, hover ≠ sink **3** = <u>launch</u>, offer, sell, set up, promote, get going ≠ dissolve

floating 1 = <u>uncommitted</u>, wavering, undecided, indecisive, vacillating, sitting on the fence (informal), unaffiliated, independent **2** = <u>free</u>, wandering, variable, fluctuating, unattached, movable

flock NOUN **1** = <u>herd</u>, group, flight, drove, colony, gaggle, skein **2** = <u>crowd</u>, company, group, host, collection, mass, gathering, herd

● VERB **1** = <u>stream</u>, crowd, mass, swarm, throng **2** = <u>gather</u>, crowd, mass, collect, assemble, herd, huddle, converge

flog = <u>beat</u>, whip, lash, thrash, whack, scourge, hit hard, trounce

flood NOUN **1** = <u>deluge</u>, downpour, inundation, tide, overflow, torrent, spate **2** = <u>torrent</u>, flow, rush, stream, tide, abundance, glut, profusion **3** = <u>series</u>, stream, avalanche, barrage, spate, torrent **4** = <u>outpouring</u>, rush, stream, surge, torrent

● VERB **1** = <u>immerse</u>, swamp, submerge, inundate, drown, cover with water **2** = <u>pour over</u>, swamp, run over, overflow, inundate **3** = <u>engulf</u>, sweep into, overwhelm, surge into, swarm into, pour into **4** = <u>saturate</u>, fill, choke, swamp, glut, oversupply, overfill **5** = <u>stream</u>, flow, rush, pour, surge

floor NOUN 1 = <u>ground</u> 2 = <u>storey</u>, level, stage, tier

● VERB 1 (*Informal*) = <u>disconcert</u>, stump, baffle, confound, throw (*informal*), defeat, puzzle, bewilder 2 = <u>knock down</u>, fell, knock over, prostrate, deck (*slang*)

flop VERB 1 = <u>slump</u>, fall, drop, collapse, sink 2 = <u>hang down</u>, hang, dangle, sag, droop 3 (*Informal*) = <u>fail</u>, fold (*informal*), founder, fall flat, come unstuck, misfire, go belly-up (*slang*) ≠ succeed

● NOUN (*Informal*) = <u>failure</u>, disaster, fiasco, debacle, washout (*informal*), nonstarter ≠ success

floppy = <u>droopy</u>, soft, loose, limp, sagging, baggy, flaccid, pendulous

floral = <u>flowery</u>, flower-patterned

flounder 1 = <u>falter</u>, struggle, stall, slow down, run into trouble, come unstuck (*informal*), be in difficulties, hit a bad patch 2 = <u>dither</u>, struggle, blunder, be confused, falter, be in the dark, be out of your depth 3 = <u>struggle</u>, struggle, toss, thrash, stumble, fumble, grope

flourish VERB 1 = <u>thrive</u>, increase, advance, progress, boom, bloom, blossom, prosper ≠ fail 2 = <u>succeed</u>, move ahead, go places (*informal*) 3 = <u>grow</u>, thrive, flower, succeed, bloom, blossom, prosper 4 = <u>wave</u>, brandish, display, shake, wield, flaunt

● NOUN 1 = <u>wave</u>, sweep, brandish, swish, swing, twirl 2 = <u>show</u>, display, parade, fanfare 3 = <u>curlicue</u>, sweep, decoration, swirl, plume, embellishment, ornamentation

flourishing = <u>thriving</u>, successful, blooming, prospering, rampant, going places, in the pink

flow VERB 1 = <u>run</u>, course, rush, sweep, move, pass, roll, flood 2 = <u>pour</u>, move, sweep, flood, stream 3 = <u>issue</u>, follow, result, emerge, spring, proceed, arise, derive

● NOUN = <u>stream</u>, current, movement, motion, course, flood, drift, tide

flower NOUN 1 = <u>bloom</u>, blossom, efflorescence 2 = <u>elite</u>, best, prime, finest, pick, choice, cream, crème de la crème (*French*) 3 = <u>height</u>, prime, peak

● VERB 1 = <u>bloom</u>, open, mature, flourish, unfold, blossom 2 = <u>blossom</u>, grow, develop, progress, mature, thrive, flourish, bloom

RELATED WORD
adjective: floral

fluctuate 1 = <u>change</u>, swing, vary, alternate, waver, veer, seesaw 2 = <u>shift</u>, oscillate

fluent = <u>effortless</u>, natural, articulate, well-versed, voluble

fluid NOUN = <u>liquid</u>, solution, juice, liquor, sap

● ADJECTIVE = <u>liquid</u>, flowing, watery, molten, melted, runny, liquefied ≠ solid

flurry 1 = <u>commotion</u>, stir, bustle, flutter, excitement, fuss, disturbance, ado 2 = <u>gust</u>, shower, gale, swirl, squall, storm

flush¹ VERB 1 = <u>blush</u>, colour, glow, redden, turn red, go red 2 *often with* **out** = <u>cleanse</u>, wash out, rinse out, flood, swill, hose down 3 = <u>expel</u>, drive, dislodge

● NOUN = <u>blush</u>, colour, glow, reddening, redness, rosiness

flush² 1 = <u>level</u>, even, true, flat, square 2 (*Informal*) = <u>wealthy</u>, rich, well-off, in the money (*informal*), well-heeled (*informal*), replete, moneyed

flutter VERB 1 = <u>beat</u>, flap, tremble, ripple, waver, quiver, vibrate, palpitate 2 = <u>flit</u>

● NOUN 1 = <u>tremor</u>, tremble, shiver, shudder, palpitation 2 = <u>vibration</u>, twitching, quiver 3 = <u>agitation</u>, state (*informal*), confusion, excitement, flap (*informal*), dither (*chiefly Brit.*), commotion, fluster

fly 1 = <u>take wing</u>, soar, glide, wing, sail, hover, flutter, flit 2 = <u>pilot</u>, control, operate, steer, manoeuvre, navigate 3 = <u>airlift</u>, send by plane, take by plane, take in an aircraft 4 = <u>flutter</u>, wave, float, flap 5 = <u>display</u>, show, flourish, brandish 6 = <u>rush</u>, race, shoot, career, speed, tear, dash, hurry 7 = <u>pass swiftly</u>, pass, glide, slip away, roll on, flit, elapse, run its course 8 = <u>leave</u>, get away, escape, flee, run for it, skedaddle (*informal*), take to your heels

flying = <u>hurried</u>, brief, rushed, fleeting, short-lived, hasty, transitory

foam NOUN = <u>froth</u>, spray, bubbles, lather, suds, spume, head

● VERB = <u>bubble</u>, boil, fizz, froth, lather, effervesce

focus VERB 1 = <u>concentrate</u>, centre, spotlight, direct, aim, pinpoint, zoom in 2 = <u>fix</u>, train, direct, aim

• NOUN 1 = <u>centre</u>, focal point, central point 2 = <u>focal point</u>, heart, target, hub

foe VERB 1 = <u>enemy</u>, rival, opponent, adversary, antagonist ≠ friend

fog = <u>mist</u>, gloom, haze, smog, murk, miasma, peasouper (*informal*)

foil[1] = <u>thwart</u>, stop, defeat, disappoint, counter, frustrate, hamper, balk

foil[2] = <u>complement</u>, relief, contrast, antithesis

fold VERB 1 = <u>bend</u>, crease, double over 2 (*Informal*) = <u>go bankrupt</u>, fail, crash, collapse, founder, shut down, go under, go bust (*informal*)

• NOUN = <u>crease</u>, gather, bend, overlap, wrinkle, pleat, ruffle, furrow

folk 1 = <u>people</u>, persons, individuals, men and women, humanity, inhabitants, mankind, mortals 2 *usually plural* = <u>family</u>, parents, relations, relatives, tribe, clan, kin, kindred, ainga (*N.Z.*)

follow 1 = <u>accompany</u>, attend, escort, go behind, tag along behind, come behind 2 = <u>pursue</u>, track, dog, hunt, chase, shadow, trail, hound ≠ avoid 3 = <u>come after</u>, go after, come next ≠ precede 4 = <u>result</u>, issue, develop, spring, flow, proceed, arise, ensue 5 = <u>obey</u>, observe, adhere to, stick to, heed, conform to, keep to, pay attention to ≠ ignore 6 = <u>succeed</u>, replace, come after, take over from, come next, supersede, supplant, take the place of 7 = <u>understand</u>, realize, appreciate, take in, grasp, catch on (*informal*), comprehend, fathom 8 = <u>keep up with</u>, support, be interested in, cultivate, be a fan of, keep abreast of

follower = <u>supporter</u>, fan, disciple, devotee, apostle, pupil, adherent, groupie (*slang*) ≠ leader

following ADJECTIVE 1 = <u>next</u>, subsequent, successive, ensuing, later, succeeding, consequent 2 = <u>coming</u>, about to be mentioned

• NOUN = <u>supporters</u>, backing, train, fans, suite, clientele, entourage, coterie

folly = <u>foolishness</u>, nonsense, madness, stupidity, indiscretion, lunacy, imprudence, rashness ≠ wisdom

fond ADJECTIVE 1 = <u>loving</u>, caring, warm, devoted, tender, adoring, affectionate, indulgent ≠ indifferent 2 = <u>unrealistic</u>, empty, naive, vain, foolish, deluded, overoptimistic, delusive ≠ sensible

• PHRASES **fond of** 1 = <u>attached to</u>, in love with, keen on, attracted to, having a soft spot for, enamoured of 2 = <u>keen on</u>, into (*informal*), hooked on, partial to, having a soft spot for, addicted to

fondly 1 = <u>lovingly</u>, tenderly, affectionately, amorously, dearly, possessively, with affection, indulgently 2 = <u>unrealistically</u>, stupidly, vainly, foolishly, naively, credulously

food = <u>nourishment</u>, fare, diet, tucker (*Austral. & N.Z. informal*), rations, nutrition, cuisine, refreshment, nibbles, kai (*N.Z. informal*)

fool NOUN 1 = <u>simpleton</u>, idiot, mug (*Brit. slang*), dummy (*slang*), git (*Brit. slang*), twit (*informal, chiefly Brit.*), dunce, imbecile (*informal*), dorba or dorb (*Austral. slang*), bogan (*Austral. slang*) ≠ genius 2 = <u>dupe</u>, mug (*Brit. slang*), sucker (*slang*), stooge (*slang*), laughing stock, pushover (*informal*), fall guy (*informal*) 3 = <u>jester</u>, clown, harlequin, buffoon, court jester

• VERB = <u>deceive</u>, mislead, delude, trick, take in, con (*informal*), dupe, beguile

foolish = <u>unwise</u>, silly, absurd, rash, senseless, foolhardy, ill-judged, imprudent ≠ sensible

footing 1 = <u>basis</u>, foundation, base position, groundwork 2 = <u>relationship</u>, position, basis, standing, rank, status, grade

footpath (*Austral. & N.Z.*) = <u>pavement</u>, sidewalk (*U.S. & Canad.*)

footstep = <u>step</u>, tread, footfall

foray = <u>raid</u>, sally, incursion, inroad, attack, assault, invasion, swoop

forbid = <u>prohibit</u>, ban, disallow, exclude, rule out, veto, outlaw, preclude ≠ permit

forbidden = <u>prohibited</u>, banned, vetoed, outlawed, taboo, out of bounds, proscribed

forbidding = <u>threatening</u>, severe, frightening, hostile, menacing, sinister, daunting, ominous ≠ inviting

force VERB 1 = <u>compel</u>, make, drive, press, oblige, constrain, coerce, impel 2 = <u>push</u>, thrust, propel 3 = <u>break open</u>, blast, wrench, prise, wrest

• NOUN 1 = <u>compulsion</u>, pressure, violence, constraint, oppression, coercion, duress, arm-twisting (*informal*) 2 = <u>power</u>, might, pressure, energy, strength, momentum, impulse, vigour ≠ weakness **3** = <u>intensity</u>, vigour, vehemence, fierceness, emphasis **4** = <u>army</u>, unit, company, host, troop, squad, patrol, regiment

● PHRASES **in force 1** = <u>valid</u>, working, current, effective, binding, operative, operational, in operation **2** = <u>in great numbers</u>, all together, in full strength

forced 1 = <u>compulsory</u>, enforced, mandatory, obligatory, involuntary, conscripted ≠ voluntary **2** = <u>false</u>, affected, strained, wooden, stiff, artificial, contrived, unnatural ≠ natural

forceful 1 = <u>dynamic</u>, powerful, assertive ≠ weak **2** = <u>powerful</u>, strong, convincing, effective, compelling, persuasive, cogent

forecast NOUN = <u>prediction</u>, prognosis, guess, prophecy, conjecture, forewarning
● VERB = <u>predict</u>, anticipate, foresee, foretell, divine, prophesy, augur, forewarn

forefront = <u>lead</u>, centre, front, fore, spearhead, prominence, vanguard, foreground

foreign = <u>alien</u>, exotic, unknown, strange, imported, remote, external, unfamiliar ≠ native

foreigner = <u>alien</u>, incomer, immigrant, non-native, stranger, settler

foremost = <u>leading</u>, best, highest, chief, prime, primary, supreme, most important

foresee = <u>predict</u>, forecast, anticipate, envisage, prophesy, foretell

forever 1 = <u>evermore</u>, always, ever, for good, for keeps, for all time, in perpetuity, till the cows come home (*informal*) **2** = <u>constantly</u>, always, all the time, continually, endlessly, persistently, eternally, perpetually

forfeit VERB = <u>relinquish</u>, lose, give up, surrender, renounce, be deprived of, say goodbye to, be stripped of
● NOUN = <u>penalty</u>, fine, damages, forfeiture, loss, mulct

forge 1 = <u>form</u>, build, create, establish, set up, fashion, shape, frame **2** = <u>fake</u>, copy, reproduce, imitate, counterfeit, feign, falsify **3** = <u>create</u>, make, work, found, form, model, fashion, shape

forget 1 = <u>neglect</u>, overlook, omit, not remember, be remiss, fail to remember **2** = <u>leave behind</u>, lose, lose sight of, mislay

forgive = <u>excuse</u>, pardon, not hold something against, understand, acquit, condone, let off (*informal*), turn a blind eye to ≠ blame

forgiveness = <u>pardon</u>, mercy, absolution, exoneration, amnesty, acquittal, remission

forgotten = <u>unremembered</u>, lost, past, left behind, omitted, bygone, past recall

fork = <u>branch</u>, part, separate, split, divide, diverge, subdivide, bifurcate

forked = <u>branching</u>, split, branched, divided, angled, pronged, zigzag, Y-shaped

form NOUN **1** = <u>type</u>, sort, kind, variety, class, style **2** = <u>shape</u>, formation, configuration, structure, pattern, appearance **3** = <u>condition</u>, health, shape, nick (*informal*), fitness, trim, fettle **4** = <u>document</u>, paper, sheet, questionnaire, application **5** = <u>procedure</u>, etiquette, use, custom, convention, usage, protocol, wont, kawa (*N.Z.*), tikanga (*N.Z.*) **6** = <u>class</u>, year, set, rank, grade, stream
● VERB **1** = <u>arrange</u>, combine, line up, organize, assemble, draw up **2** = <u>make</u>, produce, fashion, build, create, shape, construct, forge **3** = <u>constitute</u>, make up, compose, comprise **4** = <u>establish</u>, start, launch **5** = <u>take shape</u>, grow, develop, materialize, rise, appear, come into being, crystallize **6** = <u>draw up</u>, devise, formulate, organize **7** = <u>develop</u>, pick up, acquire, cultivate, contract

formal 1 = <u>serious</u>, stiff, detached, official, correct, conventional, remote, precise ≠ informal **2** = <u>official</u>, authorized, endorsed, certified, solemn **3** = <u>ceremonial</u>, traditional, solemn, ritualistic, dressy **4** = <u>conventional</u>, established, traditional

formality 1 = <u>correctness</u>, seriousness, decorum, protocol, etiquette **2** = <u>convention</u>, procedure, custom, ritual, rite

format = <u>arrangement</u>, form, style, make-up, look, plan, design, type

formation 1 = <u>establishment</u>, founding, forming, setting up, starting, production, generation, manufacture **2** = <u>development</u>, shaping, constitution, moulding, genesis **3** = <u>arrangement</u>, grouping, design, structure, pattern, organization, array, configuration

former = <u>previous</u>, one-time, erstwhile, earlier, prior, sometime, foregoing ≠ current

formerly = <u>previously</u>, earlier, in the past, at one time, before, lately, once

formidable 1 = <u>impressive</u>, great, powerful, tremendous, mighty, terrific, awesome, invincible 2 = <u>intimidating</u>, threatening, terrifying, menacing, dismaying, fearful, daunting, frightful ≠ encouraging

formula = <u>method</u>, plan, policy, rule, principle, procedure, recipe, blueprint

formulate 1 = <u>devise</u>, plan, develop, prepare, work out, invent, forge, draw up 2 = <u>express</u>, detail, frame, define, specify, articulate, set down, put into words

fort NOUN = <u>fortress</u>, keep, camp, tower, castle, garrison, stronghold, citadel, fortified pa (N.Z.)

● PHRASES **hold the fort** (*Informal*) = <u>take responsibility</u>, cover, stand in, carry on, take over the reins, deputize, keep things on an even keel

forte = <u>speciality</u>, strength, talent, strong point, métier, long suit (*informal*), gift ≠ weak point

forth 1 (*Formal or old-fashioned*) = <u>forward</u>, out, away, ahead, onward, outward 2 = <u>out</u>

forthcoming 1 = <u>approaching</u>, coming, expected, future, imminent, prospective, impending, upcoming 2 = <u>available</u>, ready, accessible, at hand, in evidence, obtainable, on tap (*informal*) 3 = <u>communicative</u>, open, free, informative, expansive, sociable, chatty, talkative

fortify 1 = <u>protect</u>, defend, strengthen, reinforce, support, shore up, augment, buttress 2 = <u>strengthen</u>, add alcohol to ≠ dishearten

fortitude = <u>courage</u>, strength, resolution, grit, bravery, backbone, perseverance, valour

fortress = <u>castle</u>, fort, stronghold, citadel, redoubt, fastness, fortified pa (N.Z.)

fortunate 1 = <u>lucky</u>, favoured, jammy (*Brit. slang*), in luck ≠ unfortunate 2 = <u>well-off</u>, rich, successful, wealthy, prosperous, affluent, opulent, well-heeled (*informal*) 3 = <u>providential</u>, fortuitous, felicitous, timely, helpful, convenient, favourable, advantageous

fortunately = <u>luckily</u>, happily, as luck would have it, providentially, by good luck, by a happy chance

fortune NOUN 1 = <u>wealth</u>, means, property, riches, resources, assets, possessions, treasure ≠ poverty 2 = <u>luck</u>, fluke (*informal*), stroke of luck, serendipity, twist of fate, run of luck 3 = <u>chance</u>, fate, destiny, providence, the stars, Lady Luck, kismet

● PLURAL NOUN = <u>destiny</u>, lot, experiences, history, condition, success, means, adventures

forward ADVERB 1 = <u>forth</u>, on, ahead, onwards ≠ backward(s) 2 = <u>on</u>, onward, onwards

● ADJECTIVE 1 = <u>leading</u>, first, head, front, advance, foremost 2 = <u>future</u>, advanced, premature, prospective 3 = <u>presumptuous</u>, familiar, bold, cheeky, brash, pushy (*informal*), brazen, shameless ≠ shy

● VERB 1 = <u>further</u>, advance, promote, assist, hurry, hasten, expedite 2 = <u>send on</u>, send, post, pass on, dispatch, redirect

fossick (*Austral. & N.Z.*) = <u>search</u>, hunt, explore, ferret, check, forage, rummage

foster 1 = <u>bring up</u>, mother, raise, nurse, look after, rear, care for, take care of 2 = <u>develop</u>, support, further, encourage, feed, promote, stimulate, uphold ≠ suppress

foul ADJECTIVE 1 = <u>dirty</u>, unpleasant, stinking, filthy, grubby, repellent, squalid, repulsive, festy (*Austral. slang*), yucko (*Austral. slang*) ≠ clean 2 = <u>obscene</u>, crude, indecent, blue, abusive, coarse, vulgar, lewd 3 = <u>unfair</u>, illegal, crooked, shady (*informal*), fraudulent, dishonest, unscrupulous, underhand 4 = <u>offensive</u>, bad, wrong, evil, corrupt, disgraceful, shameful, immoral ≠ admirable

● VERB = <u>dirty</u>, stain, contaminate, pollute, taint, sully, defile, besmirch ≠ clean

found = <u>establish</u>, start, set up, begin, create, institute, organize, constitute

foundation 1 = <u>basis</u> *often plural* = <u>substructure</u>, underpinning, groundwork, bedrock, base, footing, bottom 3 = <u>setting up</u>, institution, instituting, organization, settlement, establishment, initiating, originating

founder[1] = <u>initiator</u>, father, author, architect, creator, beginner, inventor, originator

founder[2] 1 = <u>fail</u>, collapse, break down, fall through, be unsuccessful, come unstuck, miscarry, misfire **2** = <u>sink</u>, go down, be lost, submerge, capsize, go to the bottom

fountain 1 = <u>font</u>, spring, reservoir, spout, fount, water feature, well **2** = <u>jet</u>, stream, spray, gush **3** = <u>source</u>, fount, wellspring, cause, origin, derivation, fountainhead

fowl = <u>poultry</u>

foyer = <u>entrance hall</u>, lobby, reception area, vestibule, anteroom, antechamber

fraction = <u>percentage</u>, share, section, slice, portion

fracture NOUN **1** = <u>break</u>, split, crack **2** = <u>cleft</u>, opening, split, crack, rift, rupture, crevice, fissure

● VERB **1** = <u>break</u>, crack **2** = <u>split</u>, separate, divide, rend, fragment, splinter, rupture

fragile 1 = <u>unstable</u>, weak, vulnerable, delicate, uncertain, insecure, precarious, flimsy **2** = <u>fine</u>, weak, delicate, frail, brittle, flimsy, dainty, easily broken ≠ durable **3** = <u>delicate</u>, fine, charming, elegant, neat, exquisite, graceful, petite **4** = <u>unwell</u>, poorly, weak, delicate, crook (*Austral. & N.Z. informal*), shaky, frail, feeble, sickly

fragment NOUN = <u>piece</u>, bit, scrap, particle, portion, shred, speck, sliver

● VERB **1** = <u>break</u>, shatter, crumble, disintegrate, splinter, come apart, break into pieces, come to pieces ≠ fuse **2** = <u>break up</u>, split up

fragrance 1 = <u>scent</u>, smell, perfume, bouquet, aroma, sweet smell, sweet odour, redolence ≠ stink **2** = <u>perfume</u>, scent, cologne, eau de toilette, eau de Cologne, toilet water, Cologne water

fragrant = <u>aromatic</u>, perfumed, balmy, redolent, sweet-smelling, sweet-scented, odorous ≠ stinking

frail 1 = <u>feeble</u>, weak, puny, infirm ≠ strong **2** = <u>flimsy</u>, weak, vulnerable, delicate, fragile, insubstantial

frame NOUN **1** = <u>casing</u>, framework, structure, shell, construction, skeleton, chassis **2** = <u>physique</u>, build, form, body, figure, anatomy, carcass

● VERB **1** = <u>mount</u>, case, enclose **2** = <u>surround</u>, ring, enclose, encompass, envelop, encircle, hem in **3** = <u>devise</u>, draft, compose, sketch, put together, draw up, formulate, map out

● PHRASES **frame of mind** = <u>mood</u>, state, attitude, humour, temper, outlook, disposition, mind-set

framework 1 = <u>system</u>, plan, order,

scheme, arrangement, the bare bones **2** = <u>structure</u>, body, frame, foundation, shell, skeleton

frank = <u>candid</u>, open, direct, straightforward, blunt, sincere, outspoken, honest ≠ secretive

frankly 1 = <u>honestly</u>, sincerely, in truth, candidly, to tell you the truth, to be frank, to be frank with someone, to be honest **2** = <u>openly</u>, freely, directly, plainly, bluntly, candidly, without reserve

frantic 1 = <u>frenzied</u>, wild, furious, distracted, distraught, berserk, at the end of your tether, beside yourself, berko (*Austral. slang*) ≠ calm **2** = <u>hectic</u>, desperate, frenzied, fraught (*informal*), frenetic

fraternity 1 = <u>companionship</u>, fellowship, brotherhood, kinship, camaraderie **2** = <u>circle</u>, company, guild **3** = <u>brotherhood</u>, club, union, society, league, association

fraud 1 = <u>deception</u>, deceit, treachery, swindling, trickery, duplicity, double-dealing, chicanery ≠ honesty **2** = <u>scam</u>, deception (*slang*) **3** = <u>hoax</u>, trick, con (*informal*), deception, sham, spoof (*informal*), prank, swindle **4** (*Informal*) = <u>impostor</u>, fake, hoaxer, pretender, charlatan, fraudster, swindler, phoney *or* phony (*informal*)

fraudulent = <u>deceitful</u>, crooked (*informal*), untrue, sham, treacherous, dishonest, swindling, double-dealing ≠ genuine

fray = <u>wear thin</u>, wear, rub, wear out, chafe

freak ADJECTIVE = <u>abnormal</u>, chance, unusual, exceptional, unparalleled

● NOUN **1** (*Informal*) = <u>enthusiast</u>, fan, nut (*slang*), addict, buff (*informal*), fanatic, devotee, fiend (*informal*) **2** = <u>aberration</u>, eccentric, anomaly, oddity, monstrosity, malformation **3** = <u>weirdo or weirdie</u> (*informal*), eccentric, character (*informal*), oddball (*informal*), nonconformist

free ADJECTIVE **1** = <u>complimentary</u>, for free (*informal*), for nothing, unpaid, for love, free of charge, on the house, without charge **2** = <u>allowed</u>, permitted, unrestricted, unimpeded, clear, able **3** = <u>at liberty</u>, loose, liberated, at large, on the loose ≠ confined **4** = <u>independent</u>, unfettered, footloose **5** = <u>available</u>, empty, spare, vacant, unused, unoccupied, untaken **6** = <u>generous</u>, liberal, lavish, unstinting, unsparing ≠ mean

● VERB **1** = <u>clear</u>, disengage, cut loose, release, rescue, extricate **2** = <u>release</u>, liberate, let out, set free, deliver, loose, untie, unchain ≠ confine **3** = <u>disentangle</u>, extricate, disengage, loose, unravel, disconnect, untangle

freedom 1 = <u>independence</u>, democracy, sovereignty, self-determination, emancipation, autarchy, rangatiratanga (*N.Z.*) **2** = <u>liberty</u>, release, discharge, emancipation, deliverance ≠ captivity **3** = <u>licence</u>, latitude, free rein, opportunity, discretion, carte blanche, blank cheque ≠ restriction

freely 1 = <u>abundantly</u>, liberally, lavishly, extravagantly, copiously, unstintingly, amply **2** = <u>openly</u>, frankly, plainly, candidly, unreservedly, straightforwardly, without reserve **3** = <u>willingly</u>, readily, voluntarily, spontaneously, without prompting, of your own free will, of your own accord

freeway (*U.S. & Austral.*) = <u>motorway</u> (*Brit.*), autobahn (*German*), autoroute (*French*), autostrada (*Italian*)

freeze 1 = <u>ice over</u> or up, harden, stiffen, solidify, become solid **2** = <u>chill</u> **3** = <u>fix</u>, hold, limit, hold up **4** = <u>suspend</u>, stop, shelve, curb, cut short, discontinue

freezing 1 = <u>icy</u>, biting, bitter, raw, chill, arctic, frosty, glacial **2** = <u>frozen</u>, very cold

freight 1 = <u>transportation</u>, traffic, delivery, carriage, shipment, haulage, conveyance, transport **2** = <u>cargo</u>, goods, load, delivery, burden, shipment, merchandise, consignment

French = <u>Gallic</u>

frenzied 1 = <u>uncontrolled</u>, wild, crazy, furious, frantic, frenetic, feverish, rabid

frenzy 1 = <u>fury</u>, passion, rage, seizure, hysteria, paroxysm, derangement ≠ calm

frequent ADJECTIVE = <u>common</u>, repeated, usual, familiar, everyday, persistent, customary, recurrent ≠ infrequent

● VERB = <u>visit</u>, attend, haunt, be found at, patronize, hang out at (*informal*), visit often, go to regularly ≠ keep away

frequently 1 = <u>often</u>, commonly, repeatedly, many times, habitually, not infrequently, much ≠ infrequently

fresh 1 = <u>additional</u>, more, new, other, added, further, extra, supplementary **2** = <u>natural</u>, unprocessed, unpreserved

≠ preserved **3** = <u>new</u>, original, novel, different, recent, modern, up-to-date, unorthodox ≠ old **4** = <u>invigorating</u>, clean, pure, crisp, bracing, refreshing, brisk, unpolluted ≠ stale **5** = <u>cool</u>, cold, refreshing, brisk, chilly, nippy **6** = <u>lively</u>, keen, alert, refreshed, vigorous, energetic, sprightly, spry ≠ weary **7** = <u>cheeky</u> (*Informal*), impertinent, forward, familiar, audacious, disrespectful, presumptuous, insolent ≠ well-mannered

fret = <u>worry</u>, brood, agonize, obsess, lose sleep, upset yourself, distress yourself

friction 1 = <u>conflict</u>, hostility, resentment, disagreement, animosity, discord, bad blood, dissension **2** = <u>resistance</u>, rubbing, scraping, grating, rasping, chafing, abrasion **3** = <u>rubbing</u>, scraping, grating, rasping, chafing, abrasion

friend 1 = <u>companion</u>, pal, mate (*informal*), buddy (*informal*), best friend, close friend, comrade, chum (*informal*), cobber (*Austral. & N.Z.*), E hoa (*N.Z. old-fashioned informal*) ≠ foe **2** = <u>supporter</u>, ally, associate, sponsor, patron, well-wisher

friendly 1 = <u>amiable</u>, welcoming, warm, neighbourly, pally (*informal*), helpful, sympathetic, affectionate = <u>amicable</u>, warm, familiar, pleasant, intimate, informal, cordial, congenial ≠ unfriendly

friendship 1 = <u>attachment</u>, relationship, bond, link, association, tie **2** = <u>friendliness</u>, affection, harmony, goodwill, intimacy, familiarity, rapport, companionship ≠ unfriendliness

fright 1 = <u>fear</u>, shock, alarm, horror, panic, dread, consternation, trepidation ≠ courage **2** = <u>scare</u>, start, turn, surprise, shock, jolt, the creeps (*informal*), the willies (*slang*)

frighten = <u>scare</u>, shock, alarm, terrify, startle, intimidate, unnerve, petrify ≠ reassure

frightened = <u>afraid</u>, alarmed, scared, terrified, shocked, startled, petrified, flustered

frightening = <u>terrifying</u>, shocking, alarming, startling, horrifying, menacing, scary (*informal*), fearful

fringe NOUN **1** = <u>border</u>, edging, edge, trimming, hem, frill, flounce **2** = <u>edge</u>, limits, border, margin, outskirts, perimeter, periphery, borderline

● ADJECTIVE = <u>unofficial</u>, alternative, radical,

innovative, avant-garde, unconventional, unorthodox

front NOUN 1 = <u>head</u>, start, lead, forefront 2 = <u>exterior</u>, face, façade, frontage 3 = <u>foreground</u>, fore, forefront, nearest part 4 = <u>front line</u>, trenches, vanguard, firing line 5 (*Informal*) = <u>disguise</u>, cover, blind, mask, cover-up, cloak, façade, pretext

• ADJECTIVE 1 = <u>foremost</u>, at the front ≠ back 2 = <u>leading</u>, first, lead, head, foremost, topmost

• VERB = <u>face onto</u>, overlook, look out on, have a view of, look over *or* onto

frontier = <u>border</u>, limit, edge, boundary, verge, perimeter, borderline, dividing line

frost = <u>hoarfrost</u>, freeze, rime

frown VERB = <u>glare</u>, scowl, glower, make a face, look daggers, knit your brows, lour *or* lower

• NOUN = <u>scowl</u>, glare, glower, dirty look

frozen 1 = <u>icy</u>, hard, solid, frosted, arctic, ice-covered, icebound 2 = <u>chilled</u>, cold, iced, refrigerated, ice-cold 3 = <u>ice-cold</u>, freezing, numb, very cold, frigid, frozen stiff

fruit 1 = <u>produce</u>, crop, yield, harvest 2 *often plural* = <u>result</u>, reward, outcome, end result, return, effect, benefit, profit

frustrate = <u>thwart</u>, stop, check, block, defeat, disappoint, counter, spoil, crool *or* cruel (*Austral. slang*) ≠ further

frustrated = <u>disappointed</u>, discouraged, infuriated, exasperated, resentful, embittered, disheartened

frustration 1 = <u>annoyance</u>, disappointment, resentment, irritation, grievance, dissatisfaction, exasperation, vexation 2 = <u>obstruction</u>, blocking, foiling, spoiling, thwarting, circumvention

fudge = <u>misrepresent</u>, hedge, stall, flannel (*Brit. informal*), equivocate

fuel = <u>incitement</u>, ammunition, provocation, incentive

fugitive = <u>runaway</u>, refugee, deserter, escapee

fulfil 1 = <u>carry out</u>, perform, complete, achieve, accomplish ≠ neglect 2 = <u>achieve</u>, realize, satisfy, attain, consummate, bring to fruition 3 = <u>satisfy</u>, please, content, cheer, refresh, gratify, make happy 4 = <u>comply with</u>, meet, fill, satisfy, observe, obey, conform to, answer

fulfilment = <u>achievement</u>, implementation, completion, accomplishment, realization, attainment, consummation

full 1 = <u>filled</u>, stocked, brimming, replete, complete, loaded, saturated ≠ empty 2 = <u>satiated</u>, having had enough, replete 3 = <u>extensive</u>, complete, generous, adequate, ample, abundant, plentiful ≠ incomplete 4 = <u>comprehensive</u>, complete, exhaustive, all-embracing 5 = <u>rounded</u>, strong, rich, powerful, intense, pungent 6 = <u>plump</u>, rounded, voluptuous, shapely, well-rounded, buxom, curvaceous 7 = <u>voluminous</u>, large, loose, baggy, billowing, puffy, capacious, loose-fitting ≠ tight 8 = <u>rich</u>, strong, deep, loud, distinct, resonant, sonorous, clear ≠ thin

full-scale = <u>major</u>, wide-ranging, all-out, sweeping, comprehensive, thorough, in-depth, exhaustive

fully 1 = <u>completely</u>, totally, perfectly, entirely, altogether, thoroughly, wholly, utterly 2 = <u>in all respects</u>, completely, totally, entirely, altogether, thoroughly, wholly

fumble = <u>grope</u>, flounder, scrabble, feel around

fume VERB = <u>rage</u>, seethe, see red (*informal*), storm, rant, smoulder, get hot under the collar (*informal*)

• PLURAL NOUN = <u>smoke</u>, gas, exhaust, pollution, vapour, smog

fun NOUN 1 = <u>amusement</u>, sport, pleasure, entertainment, recreation, enjoyment, merriment, jollity 2 = <u>enjoyment</u>, pleasure, mirth ≠ gloom

• ADJECTIVE = <u>enjoyable</u>, entertaining, pleasant, amusing, lively, diverting, witty, convivial

• PHRASES **make fun of something or someone** = <u>mock</u>, tease, ridicule, poke fun at, laugh at, mimic, parody, send up (*Brit. informal*)

function NOUN 1 = <u>purpose</u>, business, job, use, role, responsibility, task, duty 2 = <u>reception</u>, party, affair, gathering, bash (*informal*), social occasion, soiree, do (*informal*)

• VERB 1 = <u>work</u>, run, operate, perform, go 2 = <u>act</u>, operate, perform, behave, do duty, have the role of

functional 1 = <u>practical</u>, utilitarian, serviceable, hard-wearing, useful

2 = <u>working</u>, operative, operational, going, prepared, ready, viable, up and running

fund NOUN = <u>reserve</u>, stock, supply, store, collection, pool

● PLURAL NOUN = <u>money</u>, capital, cash, finance, means, savings, resources, assets

● VERB = <u>finance</u>, back, support, pay for, subsidize, provide money for, put up the money for

fundamental 1 = <u>central</u>, key, basic, essential, primary, principal, cardinal ≠ incidental **2** = <u>basic</u>, essential, underlying, profound, elementary, rudimentary

fundamentally 1 = <u>basically</u>, at heart, at bottom **2** = <u>essentially</u>, radically, basically, primarily, profoundly, intrinsically

fundi (*S. African*) = <u>expert</u>

funeral = <u>burial</u>, committal, laying to rest, cremation, interment, obsequies, entombment

funny 1 = <u>humorous</u>, amusing, comical, entertaining, comic, witty, hilarious, riotous ≠ unfunny **2** = <u>comic</u>, comical **3** = <u>peculiar</u>, odd, strange, unusual, bizarre, curious, weird, mysterious **4** = <u>ill</u>, poorly (*informal*), sick, odd, crook (*Austral. & N.Z. informal*), ailing, unhealthy, unwell, off-colour (*informal*)

furious 1 = <u>angry</u>, raging, fuming, infuriated, incensed, enraged, inflamed, very angry, tooshie (*Austral. slang*) ≠ pleased **2** = <u>violent</u>, intense, fierce, savage, turbulent, vehement, unrestrained

furnish 1 = <u>decorate</u>, fit out, stock, equip **2** = <u>supply</u>, give, offer, provide, present, grant, hand out

furniture = <u>household goods</u>, furnishings, fittings, house fittings, goods, things (*informal*), possessions, appliances

furore = <u>commotion</u>, to-do, stir, disturbance, outcry, uproar, hullabaloo

further *or* **farther** ADVERB = <u>in addition</u>, moreover, besides, furthermore, also, to boot, additionally, into the bargain

● ADJECTIVE = <u>additional</u>, more, new, other, extra, fresh, supplementary

● VERB = <u>promote</u>, help, develop, forward, encourage, advance, work for, assist ≠ hinder

furthermore = <u>moreover</u>, further, in addition, besides, too, as well, to boot, additionally

furthest *or* **farthest** = <u>most distant</u>, extreme, ultimate, remotest, furthermost, outmost

fury 1 = <u>anger</u>, passion, rage, madness, frenzy, wrath, impetuosity ≠ calmness **2** = <u>violence</u>, force, intensity, severity, ferocity, savagery, vehemence, fierceness ≠ peace

fuss NOUN **1** = <u>commotion</u>, to-do, bother, stir, excitement, ado, hue and cry, palaver **2** = <u>bother</u>, trouble, struggle, hassle (*informal*), nuisance, inconvenience, hindrance **3** = <u>complaint</u>, row, protest, objection, trouble, argument, squabble, furore

● VERB = <u>worry</u>, flap (*informal*), fret, fidget, take pains, be agitated, get worked up

futile = <u>useless</u>, vain, unsuccessful, pointless, worthless, fruitless, ineffectual, unprofitable ≠ useful

future NOUN **1** = <u>time to come</u>, hereafter, what lies ahead **2** = <u>prospect</u>, expectation, outlook

● ADJECTIVE = <u>forthcoming</u>, coming, later, approaching, to come, succeeding, fated, subsequent ≠ past

fuzzy 1 = <u>frizzy</u>, fluffy, woolly, downy **2** = <u>indistinct</u>, blurred, vague, distorted, unclear, bleary, out of focus, ill-defined ≠ distinct

gadget = <u>device</u>, thing, appliance, machine, tool, implement, invention, instrument

gag¹ NOUN = <u>muzzle</u>, tie, restraint

● VERB **1** = <u>suppress</u>, silence, muffle, curb, stifle, muzzle, quieten **2** = <u>retch</u>, heave

gag² (*Informal*) = <u>joke</u>, crack (*slang*), funny (*informal*), quip, pun, jest, wisecrack (*informal*), witticism

gain VERB **1** = <u>acquire</u>, get, receive, pick up, secure, collect, gather, obtain **2** = <u>profit</u>, get, land, secure, collect, gather, capture, acquire ≠ lose **3** = <u>put on</u>, increase in,

gather, build up **4** = <u>attain</u>, get, reach, get to, secure, obtain, acquire, arrive at
- NOUN **1** = <u>rise</u>, increase, growth, advance, improvement, upsurge, upturn, upswing **2** = <u>profit</u>, return, benefit, advantage, yield, dividend ≠ loss
- PLURAL NOUN = <u>profits</u>, earnings, revenue, proceeds, winnings, takings
- PHRASES **gain on something** or **someone** = <u>get nearer to</u>, close in on, approach, catch up with, narrow the gap on

gala = <u>festival</u>, fête, celebration, carnival, festivity, pageant, jamboree

gale 1 = <u>storm</u>, hurricane, tornado, cyclone, blast, typhoon, tempest, squall **2** (*Informal*) = <u>outburst</u>, scream, roar, fit, storm, shout, burst, explosion

gall = <u>annoy</u>, provoke, irritate, trouble, disturb, madden, exasperate, vex

gallop 1 = <u>run</u>, race, career, speed, bolt **2** = <u>dash</u>, run, race, career, speed, rush, sprint

gamble NOUN **1** = <u>risk</u>, chance, venture, lottery, speculation, uncertainty, leap in the dark ≠ certainty **2** = <u>bet</u>, flutter (*informal*), punt (*chiefly Brit.*), wager
- VERB **1** = <u>take a chance</u>, speculate, stick your neck out (*informal*) **2** = <u>risk</u>, chance, hazard, wager **3** = <u>bet</u>, play, game, speculate, punt, wager, have a flutter (*informal*)

game NOUN **1** = <u>pastime</u>, sport, activity, entertainment, recreation, distraction, amusement, diversion ≠ job **2** = <u>match</u>, meeting, event, competition, tournament, clash, contest, head-to-head **3** = <u>amusement</u>, joke, entertainment, diversion **4** = <u>wild animals</u> or birds, prey, quarry **5** = <u>scheme</u>, plan, design, trick, plot, tactic, manoeuvre, ploy
- ADJECTIVE **1** = <u>willing</u>, prepared, ready, keen, eager, interested, desirous **2** = <u>brave</u>, courageous, spirited, daring, persistent, gritty, intrepid, plucky ≠ cowardly

gang = <u>group</u>, crowd, pack, company, band, bunch, mob

gangster = <u>hoodlum</u> (*chiefly U.S.*), crook (*informal*), bandit, hood (*U.S. slang*), robber, mobster (*U.S. slang*), racketeer, ruffian, tsotsi (*S. African*)

gap 1 = <u>opening</u>, space, hole, break, crack, slot, aperture, cleft **2** = <u>interval</u>, pause, interruption, respite, lull, interlude,

breathing space, hiatus **3** = <u>difference</u>, gulf, contrast, disagreement, discrepancy, inconsistency, disparity, divergence

gape 1 = <u>stare</u>, wonder, goggle, gawp (*Brit. slang*), gawk **2** = <u>open</u>, split, crack, yawn

gaping = <u>wide</u>, great, open, broad, vast, yawning, wide open, cavernous

garland NOUN = <u>wreath</u>, band, bays, crown, honours, laurels, festoon, chaplet
- VERB = <u>adorn</u>, crown, deck, festoon, wreathe

garment often plural = <u>clothes</u>, dress, clothing, gear (*slang*), uniform, outfit, costume, apparel

garnish NOUN = <u>decoration</u>, embellishment, adornment, ornamentation, trimming
- VERB = <u>decorate</u>, adorn, ornament, embellish, trim ≠ strip

garrison NOUN **1** = <u>troops</u>, group, unit, section, command, armed force, detachment **2** = <u>fort</u>, fortress, camp, base, post, station, stronghold, fortification, fortified pa (*N.Z.*)
- VERB = <u>station</u>, position, post, install, assign, put on duty

gas 1 = <u>fumes</u>, vapour **2** (*U.S., Canad., & N.Z.*) = <u>petrol</u>, gasoline

gasp VERB = <u>pant</u>, blow, puff, choke, gulp, catch your breath
- NOUN = <u>pant</u>, puff, gulp, sharp intake of breath

gate = <u>barrier</u>, opening, door, entrance, exit, gateway, portal

gather 1 = <u>congregate</u>, assemble, collect, meet, mass, come together, muster, converge ≠ scatter **2** = <u>assemble</u>, collect, bring together, muster, call together ≠ disperse **3** = <u>collect</u>, assemble, accumulate, mass, muster, garner, amass, stockpile **4** = <u>pick</u>, harvest, pluck, reap, garner, glean **5** = <u>build up</u>, rise, increase, grow, expand, swell, intensify, heighten **6** = <u>understand</u>, believe, hear, learn, assume, conclude, presume, infer **7** = <u>fold</u>, tuck, pleat

gathering 1 = <u>assembly</u>, group, crowd, meeting, conference, company, congress, mass, hui (*N.Z.*), runanga (*N.Z.*) **2** = <u>collecting</u>, obtaining, attainment

gauge VERB **1** = <u>measure</u>, calculate, evaluate, value, determine, count, weigh, compute **2** = <u>judge</u>, estimate, guess, assess, evaluate, rate, appraise, reckon

- NOUN = <u>meter</u>, dial, measuring instrument

gay ADJECTIVE 1 = <u>homosexual</u>, lesbian, queer (*informal or derogatory*), moffie (*S. African slang*) 2 = <u>cheerful</u>, lively, sparkling, merry, upbeat (*informal*), buoyant, cheery, carefree ≠ sad 3 = <u>colourful</u>, rich, bright, brilliant, vivid, flamboyant, flashy, showy ≠ drab

- NOUN = <u>homosexual</u>, lesbian, auntie or aunty (*Austral. slang*), lily (*Austral. slang*) ≠ heterosexual

gaze VERB = <u>stare</u>, look, view, watch, regard, gape

- NOUN = <u>stare</u>, look, fixed look

gazette = <u>newspaper</u>, paper, journal, periodical, news-sheet

gear NOUN 1 = <u>mechanism</u>, works, machinery, cogs, cogwheels, gearwheels 2 = <u>equipment</u>, supplies, tackle, tools, instruments, apparatus, paraphernalia, accoutrements 3 = <u>clothing</u>, wear, dress, clothes, outfit, costume, garments, togs

- VERB *with* **to** *or* **towards** = <u>equip</u>, fit, adjust, adapt

gem 1 = <u>precious stone</u>, jewel, stone 2 = <u>treasure</u>, prize, jewel, pearl, masterpiece, humdinger (*slang*), taonga (*N.Z.*)

general 1 = <u>widespread</u>, accepted, popular, public, common, broad, extensive, universal ≠ individual 2 = <u>overall</u>, complete, total, global, comprehensive, blanket, inclusive, all-embracing ≠ restricted 3 = <u>universal</u>, overall, widespread, collective, across-the-board ≠ exceptional 4 = <u>vague</u>, loose, blanket, sweeping, unclear, approximate, woolly, indefinite ≠ specific

generally 1 = <u>usually</u>, commonly, typically, normally, on the whole, by and large, ordinarily, as a rule ≠ occasionally 2 = <u>commonly</u>, widely, publicly, universally, extensively, popularly, conventionally, customarily ≠ individually

generate = <u>produce</u>, create, make, cause, give rise to, engender ≠ end

generation 1 = <u>age group</u>, peer group 2 = <u>age</u>, period, era, time, lifetime, span, epoch

generic = <u>collective</u>, general, common, wide, comprehensive, universal, blanket, inclusive ≠ specific

generosity 1 = <u>liberality</u>, charity, bounty, munificence, beneficence, largesse *or* largess 2 = <u>magnanimity</u>, goodness, kindness, selflessness, charity, unselfishness, high-mindedness, nobleness

generous 1 = <u>liberal</u>, lavish, charitable, hospitable, bountiful, open-handed, unstinting, beneficent ≠ mean 2 = <u>magnanimous</u>, kind, noble, good, high-minded, unselfish, big-hearted 3 = <u>plentiful</u>, lavish, ample, abundant, full, rich, liberal, copious ≠ meagre

genesis = <u>beginning</u>, origin, start, birth, creation, formation, inception ≠ end

genius 1 = <u>brilliance</u>, ability, talent, capacity, gift, bent, excellence, flair 2 = <u>master</u>, expert, mastermind, maestro, virtuoso, whiz (*informal*), hotshot (*informal*), brainbox, fundi (*S. African*) ≠ dunce

genre = <u>type</u>, group, order, sort, kind, class, style, species

gentle 1 = <u>kind</u>, kindly, tender, mild, humane, compassionate, meek, placid ≠ unkind 2 = <u>slow</u>, easy, slight, moderate, gradual, imperceptible 3 = <u>moderate</u>, light, soft, slight, mild, soothing ≠ violent

gentlemanly = <u>chivalrous</u>, refined, polite, civil, courteous, gallant, genteel, well-mannered

genuine 1 = <u>authentic</u>, real, actual, true, valid, legitimate, veritable, bona fide, dinkum (*Austral. & N.Z. informal*) ≠ counterfeit 2 = <u>heartfelt</u>, sincere, honest, earnest, real, true, frank, unaffected ≠ affected 3 = <u>sincere</u>, honest, frank, candid, dinkum (*Austral. & N.Z. informal*), guileless ≠ hypocritical

germ 1 = <u>microbe</u>, virus, bug (*informal*), bacterium, bacillus, microorganism 2 = <u>beginning</u>, root, seed, origin, spark, embryo, rudiment

gesture NOUN = <u>sign</u>, action, signal, motion, indication, gesticulation

- VERB = <u>signal</u>, sign, wave, indicate, motion, beckon, gesticulate

get VERB 1 = <u>become</u>, grow, turn, come to be 2 = <u>persuade</u>, convince, induce, influence, entice, incite, impel, prevail upon 3 (*Informal*) = <u>annoy</u>, upset, anger, disturb, trouble, bug (*informal*), irritate, gall 4 = <u>obtain</u>, receive, gain, acquire, win, land, net, pick up 5 = <u>fetch</u>, bring, collect 6 = <u>understand</u>, follow, catch, see, realize, take in, perceive, grasp **7** = <u>catch</u>, develop, contract, succumb to, fall victim to, go down with, come down with **8** = <u>arrest</u>, catch, grab, capture, seize, take, nab (*informal*), apprehend

● PHRASES **get at someone** = <u>criticize</u>, attack, blame, put down, knock (*informal*), nag, pick on, disparage ◆ **get at something 1** = <u>reach</u>, touch, grasp, get (a) hold of, stretch to **2** = <u>find out</u>, learn, reach, reveal, discover, acquire, detect, uncover **3** = <u>imply</u>, mean, suggest, hint, intimate, lead up to, insinuate ◆ **get by** = <u>manage</u>, survive, cope, fare, exist, get along, make do, muddle through ◆ **get something across** = <u>communicate</u>, pass on, transmit, convey, impart, bring home, make known, put over

ghastly = <u>horrible</u>, shocking, terrible, awful, dreadful, horrendous, hideous, frightful ≠ lovely

ghost 1 = <u>spirit</u>, soul, phantom, spectre, spook (*informal*), apparition, wraith, atua (*N.Z.*), kehua (*N.Z.*), wairua (*N.Z.*) **2** = <u>trace</u>, shadow, suggestion, hint, suspicion, glimmer, semblance

▦ RELATED WORD
adjective: spectral

ghostly = <u>unearthly</u>, phantom, eerie, supernatural, spooky (*informal*), spectral

giant ADJECTIVE = <u>huge</u>, vast, enormous, tremendous, immense, titanic, gigantic, monumental ≠ tiny

● NOUN = <u>ogre</u>, monster, titan, colossus

gidday *or* **g'day** (*Austral. & N.Z.*) = <u>hello</u>, hi (*informal*), greetings, how do you do?, good morning, good evening, good afternoon, welcome, kia ora (*N.Z.*)

gift 1 = <u>donation</u>, offering, present, contribution, grant, legacy, hand-out, endowment, bonsela (*S. African*), koha (*N.Z.*) **2** = <u>talent</u>, ability, capacity, genius, power, capability, flair, knack

gifted = <u>talented</u>, able, skilled, expert, masterly, brilliant, capable, clever ≠ talentless

gigantic = <u>huge</u>, large, giant, massive, enormous, tremendous, immense, titanic ≠ tiny

giggle VERB = <u>laugh</u>, chuckle, snigger, chortle, titter, twitter

● NOUN = <u>laugh</u>, chuckle, snigger, chortle, titter, twitter

girl = <u>female child</u>, lass, lassie (*informal*),

miss, maiden (*archaic*), maid (*archaic*)

give VERB **1** = <u>perform</u>, do, carry out, execute **2** = <u>communicate</u>, announce, transmit, pronounce, utter, issue **3** = <u>produce</u>, make, cause, occasion, engender **4** = <u>present</u>, contribute, donate, provide, supply, award, grant, deliver ≠ take **5** = <u>concede</u>, allow, grant **6** = <u>surrender</u>, yield, devote, hand over, relinquish, part with

● PHRASES **give in** = <u>admit defeat</u>, yield, concede, collapse, quit, submit, surrender, succumb ◆ **give something away** = <u>reveal</u>, expose, leak, disclose, betray, uncover, let out, divulge ◆ **give something off** *or* **out** = <u>emit</u>, produce, release, discharge, send out, throw out, exude ◆ **give something up** = <u>abandon</u>, stop, quit, cease, renounce, leave off, desist

glad 1 = <u>happy</u>, pleased, delighted, contented, gratified, joyful, overjoyed ≠ unhappy **2** (*Archaic*) = <u>pleasing</u>, happy, cheering, pleasant, cheerful, gratifying

gladly 1 = <u>happily</u>, cheerfully, gleefully **2** = <u>willingly</u>, freely, happily, readily, cheerfully, with pleasure ≠ reluctantly

glamorous 1 = <u>attractive</u>, elegant, dazzling ≠ unglamorous **2** = <u>exciting</u>, glittering, prestigious, glossy ≠ unglamorous

glamour 1 = <u>charm</u>, appeal, beauty, attraction, fascination, allure, enchantment **2** = <u>excitement</u>, magic, thrill, romance, prestige, glitz (*slang*)

glance VERB = <u>peek</u>, look, view, glimpse, peep ≠ scrutinize

● NOUN = <u>peek</u>, look, glimpse, peep, dekko (*slang*) ≠ good look

glare VERB **1** = <u>scowl</u>, frown, glower, look daggers, lour *or* lower **2** = <u>dazzle</u>, blaze, flare, flame

● NOUN **1** = <u>scowl</u>, frown, glower, dirty look, black look, lour *or* lower **2** = <u>dazzle</u>, glow, blaze, flame, brilliance

glaring 1 = <u>obvious</u>, gross, outrageous, manifest, blatant, conspicuous, flagrant, unconcealed ≠ inconspicuous **2** = <u>dazzling</u>, strong, bright, glowing, blazing ≠ subdued

glaze NOUN = <u>coat</u>, finish, polish, shine, gloss, varnish, enamel, lacquer

● VERB = <u>coat</u>, polish, gloss, varnish, enamel, lacquer

gleam VERB = <u>shine</u>, flash, glow, sparkle, glitter, shimmer, glint, glimmer
• NOUN 1 = <u>glimmer</u>, flash, beam, glow, sparkle 2 = <u>trace</u>, suggestion, hint, flicker, glimmer, inkling

glide = <u>slip</u>, sail, slide

glimpse NOUN = <u>look</u>, sighting, sight, glance, peep, peek
• VERB = <u>catch sight of</u>, spot, sight, view, spy, espy

glitter VERB = <u>shine</u>, flash, sparkle, glare, gleam, shimmer, twinkle, glint
• NOUN 1 = <u>glamour</u>, show, display, splendour, tinsel, pageantry, gaudiness, showiness 2 = <u>sparkle</u>, flash, shine, glare, gleam, sheen, shimmer, brightness

global 1 = <u>worldwide</u>, world, international, universal 2 = <u>comprehensive</u>, general, total, unlimited, exhaustive, all-inclusive ≠ limited

globe 1 = <u>planet</u>, world, earth, sphere, orb

gloom 1 = <u>darkness</u>, dark, shadow, shade, twilight, dusk, obscurity, blackness ≠ light 2 = <u>depression</u>, sorrow, woe, melancholy, unhappiness, despondency, dejection, low spirits ≠ happiness

gloomy 1 = <u>dark</u>, dull, dim, dismal, black, grey, murky, dreary ≠ light 2 = <u>miserable</u>, sad, pessimistic, melancholy, glum, dejected, dispirited, downcast ≠ happy 3 = <u>depressing</u>, bad, dreary, sombre, dispiriting, disheartening, cheerless

glorious 1 = <u>splendid</u>, beautiful, brilliant, shining, superb, gorgeous, dazzling ≠ dull 2 = <u>delightful</u>, fine, wonderful, excellent, marvellous, gorgeous 3 = <u>illustrious</u>, famous, celebrated, distinguished, honoured, magnificent, renowned, eminent ≠ ordinary

glory NOUN 1 = <u>honour</u>, praise, fame, distinction, acclaim, prestige, eminence, renown ≠ shame 2 = <u>splendour</u>, majesty, greatness, grandeur, nobility, pomp, magnificence, pageantry
• VERB = <u>triumph</u>, boast, relish, revel, exult, take delight, pride yourself

gloss¹ = <u>shine</u>, gleam, sheen, polish, brightness, veneer, lustre, patina

gloss² NOUN = <u>interpretation</u>, comment, note, explanation, commentary, translation, footnote, elucidation
• VERB = <u>interpret</u>, explain, comment, translate, annotate, elucidate

glossy = <u>shiny</u>, polished, shining, glazed,

bright, silky, glassy, lustrous ≠ dull

glow NOUN = <u>light</u>, gleam, splendour, glimmer, brilliance, brightness, radiance, luminosity ≠ dullness
• VERB 1 = <u>shine</u>, burn, gleam, brighten, glimmer, smoulder 2 = <u>be pink</u>

glowing 1 = <u>complimentary</u>, enthusiastic, rave (*informal*), ecstatic, rhapsodic, laudatory, adulatory ≠ scathing 2 = <u>aglow</u>, bright, radiant ≠ pale

glue NOUN = <u>adhesive</u>, cement, gum, paste
• VERB = <u>stick</u>, fix, seal, cement, gum, paste, affix

go VERB 1 = <u>move</u>, travel, advance, journey, proceed, pass, set off ≠ stay 2 = <u>leave</u>, withdraw, depart, move out, slope off, make tracks 3 = <u>elapse</u>, pass, flow, fly by, expire, lapse, slip away 4 = <u>be given</u>, be spent, be awarded, be allotted 5 = <u>function</u>, work, run, move, operate, perform ≠ fail 6 = <u>match</u>, correspond, fit, suit, chime, harmonize 7 = <u>serve</u>, help, tend
• NOUN 1 = <u>attempt</u>, try, effort, bid, shot (*informal*), crack (*informal*) 2 = <u>turn</u>, shot (*informal*), stint 3 (*Informal*) = <u>energy</u>, life, drive, spirit, vitality, vigour, verve, force
• PHRASES **go off** 1 = <u>depart</u>, leave, quit, go away, move out, decamp, slope off 2 = <u>explode</u>, fire, blow up, detonate, come about 3 (*Informal*) = <u>go bad</u>, turn, spoil, rot, go stale ♦ **go out** 1 = <u>see someone</u>, court, date (*informal, chiefly U.S.*), woo, go steady (*informal*), be romantically involved with 2 = <u>be extinguished</u>, die out, fade out ♦ **go through something** 1 = <u>suffer</u>, experience, bear, endure, brave, undergo, tolerate, withstand 2 = <u>search</u>, look through, rummage through, rifle through, hunt through, fossick through (*Austral. & N.Z.*), ferret about in 3 = <u>examine</u>, check, search, explore, look through

goal = <u>aim</u>, end, target, purpose, object, intention, objective, ambition

god = <u>deity</u>, immortal, divinity, divine being, supreme being, atua (*N.Z.*)

godly = <u>devout</u>, religious, holy, righteous, pious, good, saintly, god-fearing

gogga (*S. African*) = <u>insect</u>, bug, creepy-crawly (*Brit. informal*)

golden 1 = <u>yellow</u>, blonde, blond, flaxen ≠ dark 2 = <u>successful</u>, glorious, prosperous, rich, flourishing, halcyon ≠ worst

3 = promising, excellent, favourable, opportune ≠ unfavourable

gone 1 = missing, lost, away, vanished, absent, astray **2** = past, over, ended, finished, elapsed

good ADJECTIVE **1** = excellent, great, fine, pleasing, acceptable, first-class, splendid, satisfactory, booshit (*Austral. slang*), exo (*Austral. slang*), sik (*Austral. slang*) ≠ bad **2** = proficient, able, skilled, expert, talented, clever, accomplished, first-class ≠ bad **3** = beneficial, useful, helpful, favourable, wholesome, advantageous ≠ harmful **4** = honourable, moral, worthy, ethical, upright, admirable, honest, righteous ≠ bad **5** = well-behaved, polite, orderly, obedient, dutiful, well-mannered ≠ naughty **6** = kind, kindly, friendly, obliging, charitable, humane, benevolent, merciful ≠ unkind **7** = true, real, genuine, proper, dinkum (*Austral. & N.Z. informal*) **8** = full, complete, extensive ≠ scant **9** = considerable, large, substantial, sufficient, adequate, ample **10** = valid, convincing, compelling, legitimate, authentic, persuasive, bona fide ≠ invalid **11** = convenient, timely, fitting, appropriate, suitable ≠ inconvenient

● NOUN **1** = benefit, interest, gain, advantage, use, profit, welfare, usefulness ≠ disadvantage **2** = virtue, goodness, righteousness, worth, merit, excellence, morality, rectitude ≠ evil

● PHRASES **for good** = permanently, finally, for ever, once and for all, irrevocably

goodbye NOUN = farewell, parting, leave-taking

● INTERJECTION = farewell, see you, see you later, ciao (*Italian*), cheerio, adieu, ta-ta, au revoir (*French*), haere ra (*N.Z.*)

goodness 1 = virtue, honour, merit, integrity, morality, honesty, righteousness, probity ≠ badness **2** = excellence, value, quality, worth, merit, superiority **3** = nutrition, benefit, advantage, wholesomeness, salubriousness **4** = kindness, charity, humanity, goodwill, mercy, compassion, generosity, friendliness

goods 1 = merchandise, stock, products, stuff, commodities, wares **2** = property, things, effects, gear, possessions, belongings, trappings, paraphernalia

goodwill = friendliness, friendship, benevolence, amity, kindliness

gore[1] = blood, slaughter, bloodshed, carnage, butchery

gore[2] = pierce, wound, transfix, impale

gorge NOUN = ravine, canyon, pass, chasm, cleft, fissure, defile, gulch

● VERB **1** = overeat, devour, gobble, wolf, gulp, guzzle **2** *usually reflexive* = stuff, feed, cram, glut

gorgeous 1 = magnificent, beautiful, superb, spectacular, splendid, dazzling, sumptuous ≠ shabby **2** = delightful, good, great, wonderful, excellent, lovely, fantastic, pleasant ≠ awful **3** (*Informal*) = beautiful, lovely, stunning (*informal*), elegant, handsome, exquisite, ravishing ≠ ugly

gospel 1 = doctrine, news, teachings, message, revelation, creed, credo, tidings **2** = truth, fact, certainty, the last word

gossip NOUN **1** = idle talk, scandal, hearsay, tittle-tattle, small talk, chitchat, blether, chinwag (*Brit. informal*) **2** = busybody, chatterbox (*informal*), chatterer, scandalmonger, gossipmonger

● VERB = chat, chatter, jaw (*slang*), blether

gourmet = connoisseur, foodie (*informal*), bon vivant (*French*), epicure, gastronome

govern 1 = rule, lead, control, command, manage, direct, guide, handle **2** = restrain, control, check, master, discipline, regulate, curb, tame

government 1 = administration, executive, ministry, regime, powers-that-be **2** = rule, authority, administration, sovereignty, governance, statecraft

governor = leader, administrator, ruler, head, director, manager, chief, executive, baas (*S. African*)

gown = dress, costume, garment, robe, frock, garb, habit

grab = snatch, catch, seize, capture, grip, grasp, clutch, snap up

grace NOUN **1** = elegance, poise, ease, polish, refinement, fluency, suppleness, gracefulness ≠ ungainliness **2** = manners, decency, etiquette, consideration, propriety, tact, decorum ≠ bad manners **3** = indulgence, mercy, pardon, reprieve **4** = benevolence, favour, goodness, goodwill, generosity, kindness, kindliness ≠ ill will **5** = prayer, thanks, blessing, thanksgiving, benediction **6** = favour, regard, respect, approval, approbation, good opinion ≠ disfavour

● VERB 1 = adorn, enhance, decorate, enrich, set off, ornament, embellish 2 = honour, favour, dignify ≠ insult

graceful 1 = elegant, easy, pleasing, beautiful ≠ inelegant 2 = polite, mannerly, charming, gracious, civil, courteous, well-mannered

gracious = courteous, polite, civil, accommodating, kind, friendly, cordial, well-mannered ≠ ungracious

grade VERB = classify, rate, order, class, group, sort, range, rank

● NOUN 1 = class 2 degree 3 = level, rank, group, class, stage, category, echelon

gradual = steady, slow, regular, gentle, progressive, piecemeal, unhurried ≠ sudden

gradually = steadily, slowly, progressively, gently, step by step, little by little, by degrees, unhurriedly

graduate 1 = mark off, grade, proportion, regulate, gauge, calibrate, measure out 2 = classify, rank, grade, group, order, sort, arrange

graft NOUN 1 = shoot, bud, implant, sprout, splice, scion 2 (*Informal*) = labour, work, effort, struggle, sweat, toil, slog, exertion

● VERB 1 = join, insert, transplant, implant, splice, affix 2 = work, labour, struggle, sweat (*informal*), slave, strive, toil

grain 1 = seed, kernel, grist 2 = cereal, corn 3 = bit, piece, trace, scrap, particle, fragment, speck, morsel 4 = texture, pattern, surface, fibre, weave, nap

grand 1 = impressive, great, large, magnificent, imposing, splendid, regal, stately ≠ unimposing 2 = ambitious, great, grandiose 3 = superior, great, dignified, stately 4 = excellent, great (*informal*), fine, wonderful, outstanding, smashing (*informal*), first-class, splendid ≠ bad

grandeur = splendour, glory, majesty, nobility, pomp, magnificence, sumptuousness, sublimity

grant NOUN = award, allowance, donation, endowment, gift, subsidy, hand-out

● VERB 1 = give, allow, present, award, permit, assign, allocate, hand out 2 = accept, allow, admit, acknowledge, concede

graphic 1 = vivid, clear, detailed, striking, explicit, expressive ≠ vague 2 = pictorial, visual, diagrammatic ≠ impressionistic

grapple 1 = deal, tackle, struggle, take on, confront, get to grips, address yourself to 2 = struggle, fight, combat, wrestle, battle, clash, tussle, scuffle

grasp VERB 1 = grip, hold, catch, grab, seize, snatch, clutch, clinch 2 = understand, realize, take in, get, see, catch on, comprehend, catch *or* get the drift of

● NOUN 1 = grip, hold, possession, embrace, clutches, clasp 2 = understanding, knowledge, grip, awareness, mastery, comprehension 3 = reach, power, control, scope

grasping = greedy, acquisitive, rapacious, avaricious, covetous, snoep (*S. African informal*) ≠ generous

grate 1 = shred, mince, pulverize 2 = scrape, grind, rub, scratch, creak, rasp

grateful = thankful, obliged, in (someone's) debt, indebted, appreciative, beholden

grating[1] = grille, grid, grate, lattice, trellis, gridiron

grating[2] = irritating, harsh, annoying, jarring, unpleasant, raucous, strident, discordant ≠ pleasing

gratitude = thankfulness, thanks, recognition, obligation, appreciation, indebtedness, gratefulness ≠ ingratitude

grave[1] = tomb, vault, crypt, mausoleum, sepulchre, pit, burying place

grave[2] 1 = serious, important, critical, pressing, threatening, dangerous, acute, severe ≠ trifling 2 = solemn, sober, sombre, dour, unsmiling ≠ carefree

graveyard = cemetery, churchyard, burial ground, charnel house, necropolis

gravity 1 = seriousness, importance, significance, urgency, severity, acuteness, weightiness, momentousness ≠ triviality 2 = solemnity, seriousness, gravitas ≠ frivolity

graze[1] = feed, crop, browse, pasture

graze[2] VERB 1 = scratch, skin, scrape, chafe, abrade 2 = touch, brush, rub, scrape, shave, skim, glance off

● NOUN = scratch, scrape, abrasion

greasy = fatty, slippery, oily, slimy, oleaginous

great 1 = large, big, huge, vast, enormous, immense, gigantic, prodigious ≠ small 2 = important, serious, significant, critical, crucial, momentous ≠ unimportant

3 = <u>famous</u>, outstanding, remarkable, prominent, renowned, eminent, illustrious, noteworthy **4** (*Informal*) = <u>excellent</u>, fine, wonderful, superb, fantastic (*informal*), tremendous (*informal*), marvellous (*informal*), terrific (*informal*), booshit (*Austral. slang*), exo (*Austral. slang*), sik (*Austral. slang*) ≠ poor **5** = <u>very</u>, really, extremely, exceedingly

greatly = <u>very much</u>, hugely, vastly, considerably, remarkably, enormously, immensely, tremendously

greatness 1 = <u>grandeur</u>, glory, majesty, splendour, pomp, magnificence **2** = <u>fame</u>, glory, celebrity, distinction, eminence, note, renown, illustriousness

greed *or* **greediness 1** = <u>gluttony</u>, voracity **2** = <u>avarice</u>, longing, desire, hunger, craving, selfishness, acquisitiveness, covetousness ≠ generosity

greedy 1 = <u>gluttonous</u>, insatiable, voracious, ravenous, piggish **2** = <u>avaricious</u>, grasping, selfish, insatiable, acquisitive, rapacious, materialistic, desirous ≠ generous

green ADJECTIVE **1** = <u>verdant</u>, leafy, grassy **2** = <u>ecological</u>, conservationist, environment-friendly, ozone-friendly, non-polluting **3** = <u>inexperienced</u>, new, raw, naive, immature, gullible, untrained, wet behind the ears (*informal*) **4** = <u>jealous</u>, grudging, resentful, envious, covetous
● NOUN = <u>lawn</u>, common, turf, sward

greet 1 = <u>salute</u>, hail, say hello to, address, accost **2** = <u>welcome</u>, meet, receive, karanga (*N.Z.*), mihi (*N.Z.*) **3** = <u>receive</u>, take, respond to, react to

greeting = <u>welcome</u>, reception, salute, address, salutation, hongi (*N.Z.*), kia ora (*N.Z.*)

grey 1 = <u>dull</u>, dark, dim, gloomy, drab **2** = <u>boring</u>, dull, anonymous, faceless, colourless, nondescript, characterless **3** = <u>pale</u>, wan, pallid, ashen **4** = <u>ambiguous</u>, uncertain, neutral, unclear, debatable

grief = <u>sadness</u>, suffering, regret, distress, misery, sorrow, woe, anguish ≠ joy

grievance = <u>complaint</u>, gripe (*informal*), axe to grind

grieve 1 = <u>mourn</u>, suffer, weep, lament **2** = <u>sadden</u>, hurt, injure, distress, wound, pain, afflict, upset ≠ gladden

grim = <u>terrible</u>, severe, harsh, forbidding, formidable, sinister

grind VERB **1** = <u>crush</u>, mill, powder, grate, pulverize, pound, abrade, granulate **2** = <u>press</u>, push, crush, jam, mash, force down **3** = <u>grate</u>, scrape, gnash **4** = <u>sharpen</u>, polish, sand, smooth, whet
● NOUN = <u>hard work</u> (*Informal*), labour, sweat (*informal*), chore, toil, drudgery

grip VERB **1** = <u>grasp</u>, hold, catch, seize, clutch, clasp, take hold of **2** = <u>engross</u>, fascinate, absorb, entrance, hold, compel, rivet, enthral
● NOUN **1** = <u>clasp</u>, hold, grasp **2** = <u>control</u>, rule, influence, command, power, possession, domination, mastery **3** = <u>hold</u>, purchase, friction, traction **4** = <u>understanding</u>, sense, command, awareness, grasp, appreciation, mastery, comprehension

gripping = <u>fascinating</u>, exciting, thrilling, entrancing, compelling, riveting, enthralling, engrossing

grit NOUN **1** = <u>gravel</u>, sand, dust, pebbles **2** = <u>courage</u>, spirit, resolution, determination, guts (*informal*), backbone, fortitude, tenacity
● VERB = <u>clench</u>, grind, grate, gnash

gritty 1 = <u>rough</u>, sandy, dusty, rasping, gravelly, granular **2** = <u>courageous</u>, dogged, determined, spirited, brave, resolute, tenacious, plucky

groan VERB **1** = <u>moan</u>, cry, sigh **2** (*Informal*) = <u>complain</u>, object, moan, grumble, gripe (*informal*), carp, lament, whine
● NOUN **1** = <u>moan</u>, cry, sigh, whine **2** (*Informal*) = <u>complaint</u>, protest, objection, grumble, grouse, gripe (*informal*)

groom NOUN **1** = <u>stableman</u>, stableboy, hostler *or* ostler (*archaic*) **2** = <u>newly-wed</u>, husband, bridegroom, marriage partner
● VERB **1** = <u>brush</u>, clean, tend, rub down, curry **2** = <u>smarten up</u>, clean, tidy, preen, spruce up, primp **3** = <u>train</u>, prime, prepare, coach, ready, educate, drill, nurture

groove = <u>indentation</u>, cut, hollow, channel, trench, flute, trough, furrow

grope = <u>feel</u>, search, fumble, flounder, fish, scrabble, cast about, fossick (*Austral. & N.Z.*)

gross ADJECTIVE **1** = <u>flagrant</u>, blatant, rank, sheer, utter, grievous, heinous, unmitigated ≠ qualified **2** = <u>vulgar</u>, offensive, crude, obscene, coarse,

indelicate ≠ decent **3** = fat, obese, overweight, hulking, corpulent ≠ slim **4** = total, whole, entire, aggregate, before tax, before deductions ≠ net
● VERB = earn, make, take, bring in, rake in (*informal*)

grotesque 1 = unnatural, bizarre, strange, fantastic, distorted, deformed, outlandish, freakish ≠ natural **2** = absurd, preposterous ≠ natural

ground NOUN **1** = earth, land, dry land, terra firma **2** = arena, pitch, stadium, park (*informal*), field, enclosure
● PLURAL NOUN **1** = estate, land, fields, gardens, territory **2** = reason, cause, basis, occasion, foundation, excuse, motive, justification **3** = dregs, lees, deposit, sediment
● VERB **1** = base, found, establish, set, settle, fix **2** = instruct, train, teach, initiate, tutor, acquaint with, familiarize with

group NOUN = crowd, party, band, pack, gang, bunch
● VERB = arrange, order, sort, class, classify, marshal, bracket

grove = wood, plantation, covert, thicket, copse, coppice, spinney

grow 1 = develop, get bigger ≠ shrink **2** = get bigger, spread, swell, stretch, expand, enlarge, multiply **3** = cultivate, produce, raise, farm, breed, nurture, propagate **4** = become, get, turn, come to be **5** = originate, spring, arise, stem, issue **6** = improve, advance, progress, succeed, thrive, flourish, prosper

grown-up NOUN = adult, man, woman
● ADJECTIVE = mature, adult, of age, fully-grown

growth 1 = increase, development, expansion, proliferation, enlargement, multiplication ≠ decline **2** = progress, success, improvement, expansion, advance, prosperity ≠ failure **3** (*Medical*) = tumour, cancer, swelling, lump, carcinoma (*Pathology*), sarcoma (*Medical*)

grudge NOUN = resentment, bitterness, grievance, dislike, animosity, antipathy, enmity, rancour ≠ goodwill
● VERB = resent, mind, envy, covet, begrudge ≠ welcome

gruelling = exhausting, demanding, tiring, taxing, severe, punishing, strenuous, arduous ≠ easy

gruesome = horrific, shocking, terrible, horrible, grim, ghastly, grisly, macabre ≠ pleasant

grumble VERB **1** = complain, moan, gripe (*informal*), whinge (*informal*), carp, whine, grouse, bleat **2** = rumble, growl, gurgle
● NOUN **1** = complaint, protest, objection, moan, grievance, grouse, gripe (*informal*), grouch (*informal*) **2** = rumble, growl, gurgle

guarantee VERB **1** = ensure, secure, assure, warrant, make certain **2** = promise, pledge, undertake
● NOUN **1** = promise, pledge, assurance, certainty, word of honour **2** = warranty, contract, bond

guard VERB = protect, defend, secure, mind, preserve, shield, safeguard, watch over
● NOUN **1** = sentry, warder, warden, custodian, watch, lookout, watchman, sentinel **2** = shield, security, defence, screen, protection, safeguard, buffer

guarded = cautious, reserved, careful, suspicious, wary, prudent, reticent, circumspect

guardian = keeper, champion, defender, guard, warden, curator, protector, custodian

guerrilla = freedom fighter, partisan, underground fighter

guess VERB **1** = estimate, predict, work out, speculate, conjecture, postulate, hypothesize ≠ know **2** = suppose, think, believe, suspect, judge, imagine, reckon, fancy
● NOUN **1** = estimate, speculation, judgment, hypothesis, conjecture, shot in the dark ≠ certainty **2** = supposition, idea, theory, hypothesis

guest = visitor, company, caller, manu(w)hiri (*N.Z.*)

guidance = advice, direction, leadership, instruction, help, management, teaching, counselling

guide NOUN **1** = handbook, manual, guidebook, instructions, catalogue **2** = directory, street map **3** = escort, leader, usher **4** = pointer, sign, landmark, marker, beacon, signpost, guiding light, lodestar **5** = model, example, standard, ideal, inspiration, paradigm
● VERB **1** = lead, direct, escort, conduct, accompany, shepherd, usher, show the way **2** = steer, control, manage,

direct, handle, command, manoeuvre
3 = <u>supervise</u>, train, teach, influence,
advise, counsel, instruct, oversee

guild = <u>society</u>, union, league, association,
company, club, order, organization

guilt 1 = <u>shame</u>, regret, remorse,
contrition, guilty conscience, self-
reproach ≠ pride **2** = <u>culpability</u>, blame,
responsibility, misconduct, wickedness,
sinfulness, guiltiness ≠ innocence

guilty 1 = <u>ashamed</u>, sorry, rueful, sheepish,
contrite, remorseful, regretful, shamefaced
≠ proud **2** = <u>culpable</u>, responsible,
to blame, offending, erring, at fault,
reprehensible, blameworthy ≠ innocent

guise 1 = <u>form</u>, appearance, shape, aspect,
mode, semblance **2** = <u>pretence</u>, disguise,
aspect, semblance

gulf 1 = <u>bay</u>, bight, sea inlet **2** = <u>chasm</u>,
opening, split, gap, separation, void, rift, abyss

gum NOUN = <u>glue</u>, adhesive, resin, cement,
paste
● **VERB** = <u>stick</u>, glue, affix, cement, paste

gun = <u>firearm</u>, shooter (*slang*), piece
(*slang*), handgun

gunman = <u>armed man</u>, gunslinger (*U.S.
slang*)

guru 1 = <u>authority</u>, expert, leader, master,
pundit, Svengali, fundi (*S. African*)
2 = <u>teacher</u>, mentor, sage, master, tutor

gush VERB 1 = <u>flow</u>, run, rush, flood, pour,
stream, cascade, spurt **2** = <u>enthuse</u>, rave,
spout, overstate, effuse
● **NOUN** = <u>stream</u>, flow, rush, flood, jet,
cascade, torrent, spurt

gut NOUN = <u>paunch</u> (*Informal*), belly, spare
tyre (*Brit. slang*), potbelly, puku (*N.Z.*)
● **PLURAL NOUN 1** = <u>intestines</u>, insides
(*informal*), stomach, belly, bowels, innards
(*informal*), entrails **2** (*Informal*) = <u>courage</u>,
spirit, nerve, daring, pluck, backbone,
bottle (*slang*), audacity
● **VERB 1** = <u>disembowel</u>, clean **2** = <u>ravage</u>,
empty, clean out, despoil
● **ADJECTIVE** = <u>instinctive</u>, natural, basic,
spontaneous, intuitive, involuntary,
heartfelt, unthinking

gutter = <u>drain</u>, channel, ditch, trench,
trough, conduit, sluice

guy (*Informal*) = <u>man</u>, person, fellow, lad,
bloke (*Brit. informal*), chap

Gypsy or **Gipsy** = <u>traveller</u>, roamer,
wanderer, Bohemian, rover, rambler,
nomad, Romany

compulsion

h

habit 1 = <u>mannerism</u>, custom, way,
practice, characteristic, tendency, quirk,
propensity **2** = <u>addiction</u>, dependence,
compulsion

hack¹ = <u>cut</u>, chop, slash, mutilate, mangle,
mangulate (*Austral. slang*), hew, lacerate

hack² = <u>reporter</u>, writer, correspondent,
journalist, scribbler, contributor, literary
hack

hail¹ VERB 1 = <u>acclaim</u>, honour,
acknowledge, cheer, applaud ≠ condemn
2 = <u>salute</u>, greet, address, welcome, say
hello to, halloo ≠ snub **3** = <u>flag down</u>,
summon, signal to, wave down
● **PHRASES hail from somewhere**
= <u>come from</u>, be born in, originate in, be a
native of, have your roots in

hail² NOUN 1 = <u>hailstones</u>, sleet, hailstorm,
frozen rain **2** = <u>shower</u>, rain, storm, battery,
volley, barrage, bombardment, downpour
● **VERB 1** = <u>rain</u>, shower, pelt **2** = <u>batter</u>, rain,
bombard, pelt, rain down on, beat down
upon

hair = <u>locks</u>, mane, tresses, shock, mop,
head of hair

hairdresser = <u>stylist</u>, barber, coiffeur *or*
coiffeuse

hairy 1 = <u>shaggy</u>, woolly, furry, stubbly,
bushy, unshaven, hirsute **2** (*Slang*)
= <u>dangerous</u>, risky, unpredictable,
hazardous, perilous

hale (*Old-fashioned*) = <u>healthy</u>, well,
strong, sound, fit, flourishing, robust,
vigorous

half NOUN = <u>fifty per cent</u>, equal part
● **ADJECTIVE** = <u>partial</u>, limited, moderate,
halved
● **ADVERB** = <u>partially</u>, partly, in part
▩ **RELATED WORDS**
prefixes: bi-, demi-, hemi-, semi-

halfway ADVERB = <u>midway</u>, to *or* in the
middle
● **ADJECTIVE** = <u>midway</u>, middle, mid, central,
intermediate, equidistant

hall 1 = <u>passage</u>, lobby, corridor, hallway,

foyer, entry, passageway, entrance hall
2 = meeting place, chamber, auditorium, concert hall, assembly room

hallmark 1 = trademark, sure sign, telltale sign **2** (*Brit.*) = mark, sign, device, stamp, seal, symbol

halt VERB **1** = stop, break off, stand still, wait, rest ≠ continue **2** = come to an end, stop, cease **3** = hold back, end, check, block, curb, terminate, cut short, bring to an end ≠ aid
● NOUN = stop, end, close, pause, standstill, stoppage ≠ continuation

halting 1 = faltering, stumbling, awkward, hesitant, laboured, stammering, stuttering

halve 1 = cut in half, reduce by fifty per cent, decrease by fifty per cent, lessen by fifty per cent **2** = split in two, cut in half, bisect, divide in two, share equally, divide equally

hammer 1 = hit, drive, knock, beat, strike, tap, bang **2** (*Informal*) = defeat, beat, thrash, trounce, run rings around (*informal*), wipe the floor with (*informal*), drub

hamper = hinder, handicap, prevent, restrict, frustrate, hamstring, interfere with, obstruct ≠ help

hand NOUN **1** = palm, fist, paw (*informal*), mitt (*slang*) **2** = worker, employee, labourer, workman, operative, craftsman, artisan, hired man **3** = round of applause, clap, ovation, big hand **4** = writing, script, handwriting, calligraphy
● VERB = give, pass, hand over, present to, deliver

handbook = guidebook, guide, manual, instruction book

handcuff VERB = shackle, secure, restrain, fetter, manacle
● PLURAL NOUN = shackles, cuffs (*informal*), fetters, manacles

handful 1 = few, sprinkling, small amount, smattering, small number ≠ a lot

handicap NOUN **1** = disability, defect, impairment, physical abnormality **2** = disadvantage, barrier, restriction, obstacle, limitation, drawback, stumbling block, impediment ≠ advantage **3** = advantage, head start
● VERB = hinder, limit, restrict, burden, hamstring, hamper, hold back, impede ≠ help

handle NOUN = grip, hilt, haft, stock

● VERB **1** = manage, deal with, tackle, cope with **2** = deal with, manage **3** = control, manage, direct, guide, manipulate, manoeuvre **4** = hold, feel, touch, pick up, finger, grasp

handsome 1 = good-looking, attractive, gorgeous, elegant, personable, dishy (*informal, chiefly Brit.*), comely ≠ ugly **2** = generous, large, princely, liberal, considerable, lavish, ample, abundant ≠ mean

handy 1 = useful, practical, helpful, neat, convenient, easy to use, manageable, user-friendly ≠ useless **2** = convenient, close, available, nearby, accessible, on hand, at hand, within reach ≠ inconvenient **3** = skilful, skilled, expert, adept, deft, proficient, adroit, dexterous ≠ unskilled

hang VERB **1** = dangle, swing, suspend **2** = lower, suspend, dangle **3** = lean **4** = execute, lynch, string up (*informal*)
● PHRASES **get the hang of something** = grasp, understand, learn, master, comprehend, catch on to, acquire the technique of ◆ **hang back** = be reluctant, hesitate, hold back, recoil, demur

hangover = aftereffects, morning after (*informal*)

hang-up (*Informal*) = preoccupation, thing (*informal*), problem, block, difficulty, obsession, mania, inhibition

hank = coil, roll, length, bunch, piece, loop, clump, skein

happen 1 = occur, take place, come about, result, develop, transpire (*informal*), come to pass **2** = chance, turn out (*informal*)

happening = event, incident, experience, affair, proceeding, episode, occurrence

happily 1 = luckily, fortunately, providentially, opportunely **2** = joyfully, cheerfully, gleefully, blithely, merrily, gaily, joyously **3** = willingly, freely, gladly, with pleasure

happiness = pleasure, delight, joy, satisfaction, ecstasy, bliss, contentment, elation ≠ unhappiness

happy 1 = pleased, delighted, content, thrilled, glad, cheerful, merry, ecstatic **2** = contented, joyful, blissful ≠ sad **3** = fortunate, lucky, timely, favourable, auspicious, propitious, advantageous ≠ unfortunate

harass = annoy, trouble, bother, harry, plague, hound, hassle (*informal*), persecute

harassed = hassled, worried, troubled, strained, under pressure, tormented, distraught (*informal*), vexed

harassment = hassle, trouble, bother, irritation, persecution (*informal*), nuisance, annoyance, pestering

harbour NOUN = port, haven, dock, mooring, marina, pier, wharf, anchorage
● VERB = hold, bear, maintain, nurse, retain, foster, entertain, nurture **2** = shelter, protect, hide, shield, provide refuge, give asylum to

hard ADJECTIVE **1** = tough, strong, firm, solid, stiff, rigid, resistant, compressed ≠ soft **2** = difficult, involved, complicated, puzzling, intricate, perplexing, impenetrable, thorny ≠ easy **3** = exhausting, tough, exacting, rigorous, gruelling, strenuous, arduous, laborious ≠ easy **4** = harsh, cold, cruel, stern, callous, unkind, unsympathetic, pitiless ≠ kind **5** = grim, painful, distressing, harsh, unpleasant, intolerable, grievous, disagreeable
● ADVERB **1** = strenuously, steadily, persistently, doggedly, diligently, energetically, industriously, untiringly **2** = intently, closely, carefully, sharply, keenly **3** = forcefully, strongly, heavily, sharply, severely, fiercely, vigorously, intensely ≠ softly

harden 1 = solidify, set, freeze, cake, bake, clot, thicken, stiffen **2** = accustom, season, toughen, train, inure, habituate

hardened 1 = habitual, chronic, shameless, inveterate, incorrigible ≠ occasional **2** = seasoned, experienced, accustomed, toughened, inured, habituated ≠ naive

hardly 1 = barely, only just, scarcely, just, with difficulty, with effort ≠ completely **2** = only just, just, barely, scarcely

hardship = suffering, need, difficulty, misfortune, adversity, tribulation, privation ≠ ease

hardy = strong, tough, robust, sound, rugged, sturdy, stout ≠ frail

harm VERB **1** = injure, hurt, wound, abuse, ill-treat, maltreat ≠ heal **2** = damage, hurt, ruin, spoil
● NOUN **1** = injury, suffering, damage, ill, hurt, distress **2** = damage, loss, ill, hurt, misfortune, mischief ≠ good

harmful = damaging, dangerous, negative, destructive, hazardous, unhealthy, detrimental, hurtful ≠ harmless

harmless 1 = safe, benign, wholesome, innocuous, nontoxic ≠ dangerous **2** = inoffensive, innocent, innocuous, gentle, tame, unobjectionable

harmony 1 = accord, peace, agreement, friendship, sympathy, cooperation, rapport, compatibility ≠ conflict **2** = tune, melody, unison, tunefulness, euphony ≠ discord

harness VERB = exploit, control, channel, employ, utilize, mobilize
● NOUN = equipment, tackle, gear, tack

harrowing = distressing, disturbing, painful, terrifying, traumatic, tormenting, agonizing, nerve-racking

harry = pester, bother, plague, harass, hassle (*informal*), badger, chivvy

harsh 1 = severe, hard, tough, stark, austere, inhospitable **2** = bleak, freezing, severe, icy **3** = cruel, savage, ruthless, barbarous, pitiless **4** = hard, severe, cruel, stern, pitiless ≠ kind **5** = drastic, punitive, Draconian **6** = raucous, rough, grating, strident, rasping, discordant, guttural, dissonant ≠ soft

harshly = severely, roughly, cruelly, strictly, sternly, brutally

harvest NOUN **1** = harvesting, picking, gathering, collecting, reaping, harvest-time **2** = crop, yield, year's growth, produce
● VERB = gather, pick, collect, bring in, pluck, reap

hassle (*Informal*) NOUN = trouble, problem, difficulty, bother, grief (*informal*), uphill (*S. African*), inconvenience
● VERB = bother, bug (*informal*), annoy, hound, harass, badger, pester

hasten = rush, race, fly, speed, dash, hurry (up), scurry, make haste ≠ dawdle

hastily 1 = quickly, rapidly, promptly, speedily **2** = hurriedly, rashly, precipitately, impetuously

hatch 1 = incubate, breed, sit on, brood, bring forth **2** = devise, design, invent, put together, conceive, brew, formulate, contrive

hate VERB **1** = detest, loathe, despise, dislike, abhor, recoil from, not be able to

bear ≠ love **2** = dislike, detest, shrink from, recoil from, not be able to bear ≠ like **3** = be unwilling, regret, be reluctant, hesitate, be sorry, be loath, feel disinclined
● NOUN = dislike, hostility, hatred, loathing, animosity, aversion, antipathy, enmity ≠ love

hatred = hate, dislike, animosity, aversion, revulsion, antipathy, enmity, repugnance ≠ love

haul VERB = drag, draw, pull, heave
● NOUN = yield, gain, spoils, catch, harvest, loot, takings, booty

haunt VERB = plague, trouble, obsess, torment, possess, stay with, recur, prey on
● NOUN = meeting place, hangout (*informal*), rendezvous, stamping ground

haunted 1 = possessed, ghostly, cursed, eerie, spooky (*informal*), jinxed **2** = preoccupied, worried, troubled, plagued, obsessed, tormented

haunting = evocative, poignant, unforgettable

have VERB **1** = own, keep, possess, hold, retain, boast, be the owner of **2** = get, obtain, take, receive, accept, gain, secure, acquire **3** = suffer, experience, undergo, sustain, endure, be suffering from **4** = give birth to, bear, deliver, bring forth, beget **5** = experience, go through, undergo, meet with, come across, run into, be faced with
● PHRASES **have someone on** = tease, kid (*informal*), wind up (*Brit. slang*), trick, deceive, take the mickey, pull someone's leg ◆ **have something on** = wear, be wearing, be dressed in, be clothed in, be attired in ◆ **have to** to **1** = must, should, be forced, ought, be obliged, be bound, have got to, be compelled **2** = have got to, must

haven = sanctuary, shelter, retreat, asylum, refuge, oasis, sanctum

havoc 1 = devastation, damage, destruction, ruin **2** (*Informal*) = disorder, confusion, chaos, disruption, mayhem, shambles

hazard NOUN = danger, risk, threat, problem, menace, peril, jeopardy, pitfall
● VERB = jeopardize, risk, endanger, threaten, expose, imperil, put in jeopardy
● PHRASES **hazard a guess** = guess, conjecture, presume, take a guess

hazardous = dangerous, risky, difficult, insecure, unsafe, precarious, perilous, dicey (*informal*, chiefly *Brit.*) ≠ safe

haze = mist, cloud, fog, obscurity, vapour

head NOUN **1** = skull, crown, pate, nut (*slang*), loaf (*slang*) **2** = mind, reasoning, understanding, thought, sense, brain, brains (*informal*), intelligence **3** = top, crown, summit, peak, crest, pinnacle **4** (*Informal*) = head teacher, principal **5** = leader, president, director, manager, chief, boss (*informal*), captain, master
● ADJECTIVE = chief, main, leading, first, prime, premier, supreme, principal
● VERB **1** = lead, precede, be the leader of, be *or* go first, be *or* go at the front of, lead the way **2** = top, lead, crown, cap **3** = be in charge of, run, manage, lead, control, direct, guide, command
● PHRASES **go to your head 1** = intoxicate **2** = make someone conceited, puff someone up, make someone full of themselves ◆ **head over heels** = completely, thoroughly, utterly, intensely, wholeheartedly, uncontrollably

headache 1 = migraine, head (*informal*), neuralgia **2** = problem (*Informal*), worry, trouble, bother, nuisance, inconvenience, bane, vexation

heading = title, name, caption, headline, rubric

heady 1 = exciting, thrilling, stimulating, exhilarating, intoxicating **2** = intoxicating, strong, potent, inebriating

heal 1 *sometimes with* **up** = mend, get better, get well, cure, regenerate, show improvement **2** = cure, restore, mend, make better, remedy, make good, make well ≠ injure

health 1 = condition, state, shape, constitution, fettle **2** = wellbeing, strength, fitness, vigour, good condition, soundness, robustness, healthiness ≠ illness **3** = state, condition, shape

healthy 1 = well, fit, strong, active, robust, in good shape (*informal*), in the pink, in fine fettle ≠ ill **2** = wholesome, beneficial, nourishing, nutritious, salutary, hygienic, salubrious ≠ unwholesome **3** = invigorating, beneficial, salutary, salubrious

heap NOUN **1** = pile, lot, collection, mass, stack, mound, accumulation, hoard **2** *often plural* (*Informal*) = a lot, lots (*informal*), plenty, masses, load(s) (*informal*), great

deal, tons, stack(s)
● VERB *sometimes with* **up** = pile, collect,
gather, stack, accumulate, amass, hoard
● PHRASES **heap something on
someone** = load with, confer on, assign
to, bestow on, shower upon

hear 1 = overhear, catch, detect **2** = listen
to **3** (*Law*) = try, judge, examine,
investigate **4** = learn, discover, find out,
pick up, gather, ascertain, get wind of
(*informal*)

hearing = inquiry, trial, investigation,
industrial tribunal

heart NOUN **1** = emotions, feelings, love,
affection **2** = nature, character, soul,
constitution, essence, temperament,
disposition **3** = root, core, centre, nucleus,
hub, gist, nitty-gritty (*informal*), nub
4 = courage, will, spirit, purpose, bottle
(*Brit. informal*), resolution, resolve,
stomach
● PHRASES **by heart** = from *or* by memory,
verbatim, word for word, pat, word-
perfect, by rote, off by heart, off pat
▨▨▨▨ RELATED WORD
adjective: cardiac

heat VERB *sometimes with* **up** = warm (up),
cook, boil, roast, reheat, make hot ≠ chill
● NOUN **1** = warmth, hotness, temperature
≠ cold **2** = hot weather, warmth,
closeness, high temperature, heatwave,
warm weather, hot climate, mugginess
3 = passion, excitement, intensity, fury,
fervour, vehemence ≠ calmness
▨▨▨▨ RELATED WORD
adjective: thermal

heated 1 = impassioned, intense, spirited,
excited, angry, furious, fierce, lively ≠ calm
2 = wound up, worked up, keyed up, het
up (*informal*)

heaven NOUN **1** = paradise, next world,
hereafter, nirvana (*Buddhism, Hinduism*),
bliss, Zion (*Christianity*), life everlasting,
Elysium *or* Elysian fields (*Greek myth*)
2 (*Informal*) = happiness, paradise, ecstasy,
bliss, utopia, rapture, seventh heaven
● PHRASES **the heavens** (*Old-fashioned*)
= sky, ether, firmament

heavenly 1 = celestial, holy, divine,
blessed, immortal, angelic ≠ earthly
2 (*Informal*) = wonderful, lovely, delightful,
beautiful, divine (*informal*), exquisite,
sublime, blissful ≠ awful

heavily 1 = excessively, to excess,

very much, a great deal, considerably,
copiously, without restraint, immoderately
2 = densely, closely, thickly, compactly
3 = hard, clumsily, awkwardly, weightily

heavy 1 = weighty, large, massive, hefty,
bulky, ponderous ≠ light **2** = intensive,
severe, serious, concentrated, fierce,
excessive, relentless **3** = considerable,
large, huge, substantial, abundant,
copious, profuse ≠ slight

hectic = frantic, chaotic, heated, animated,
turbulent, frenetic, feverish ≠ peaceful

hedge VERB = prevaricate, evade, sidestep,
duck, dodge, flannel (*Brit. informal*),
equivocate, temporize
● PHRASES **hedge against something**
= protect against, insure against, guard
against, safeguard against, shield against,
cover against

heed (*Formal*) VERB = pay attention to,
listen to, take notice of, follow, consider,
note, observe, obey ≠ ignore
● NOUN = thought, care, mind, attention,
regard, respect, notice ≠ disregard

heel (*Slang*) = swine, cad (*Brit. informal*),
bounder (*Brit. old-fashioned slang*), rotter
(*slang, chiefly Brit.*)

hefty (*Informal*) = big, strong, massive,
strapping, robust, muscular, burly, hulking
≠ small

height 1 = tallness, stature, highness,
loftiness ≠ shortness **2** = altitude,
measurement, highness, elevation,
tallness ≠ depth **3** = peak, top, crown,
summit, crest, pinnacle, apex ≠ valley
4 = culmination, climax, zenith, limit,
maximum, ultimate ≠ low point

heighten = intensify, increase, add to,
improve, strengthen, enhance, sharpen,
magnify

heir = successor, beneficiary, inheritor,
heiress (*fem.*), next in line

hell 1 = the underworld, the abyss, Hades
(*Greek myth*), hellfire, the inferno, fire and
brimstone, the nether world, the bad
fire (*informal*) **2** (*Informal*) = torment,
suffering, agony, nightmare, misery,
ordeal, anguish, wretchedness

hello 1 = hi (*informal*), greetings, how do
you do?, good morning, good evening,
good afternoon, welcome, kia ora (*N.Z.*),
gidday *or* g'day (*Austral. & N.Z.*)

helm (*Nautical*) = tiller, wheel, rudder

help VERB **1** *sometimes with* **out** = aid,

support, assist, cooperate with, abet, lend a hand, succour ≠ hinder **2** = improve, ease, relieve, facilitate, alleviate, mitigate, ameliorate ≠ make worse **3** = assist, aid, support **4** = resist, refrain from, avoid, prevent, keep from

● NOUN = assistance, aid, support, advice, guidance, cooperation, helping hand ≠ hindrance

helper = assistant, ally, supporter, mate, second, aide, attendant, collaborator

helpful 1 = cooperative, accommodating, kind, friendly, neighbourly, sympathetic, supportive, considerate **2** = useful, practical, profitable, constructive **3** = beneficial, advantageous

helping = portion, serving, ration, piece, dollop (*informal*), plateful

helpless = powerless, weak, disabled, incapable, paralysed, impotent, infirm ≠ powerful

hem NOUN = edge, border, margin, trimming, fringe

● PHRASES **hem something** or **someone in 1** = surround, confine, enclose, shut in **2** = restrict, confine, beset, circumscribe

hence = therefore, thus, consequently, for this reason, in consequence, ergo, on that account

herald VERB = indicate, promise, usher in, presage, portend, foretoken

● NOUN **1** (*Often literary*) = forerunner, sign, signal, indication, token, omen, precursor, harbinger **2** = messenger, courier, proclaimer, announcer, crier, town crier

herd = flock, crowd, collection, mass, drove, mob, swarm, horde

hereditary 1 = genetic, inborn, inbred, transmissible, inheritable **2** (*Law*) = inherited, passed down, traditional, ancestral

heritage = inheritance, legacy, birthright, tradition, endowment, bequest

hero 1 = protagonist, leading man **2** = star, champion, victor, superstar, conqueror **3** = idol, favourite, pin-up (*slang*), fave (*informal*)

heroic = courageous, brave, daring, fearless, gallant, intrepid, valiant, lion-hearted ≠ cowardly

heroine 1 = protagonist, leading lady, diva, prima donna **2** = idol, favourite, pin-up (*slang*), fave (*informal*)

hesitate 1 = waver, delay, pause, wait, doubt, falter, dither (*chiefly Brit.*), vacillate ≠ be decisive **2** = be reluctant, be unwilling, shrink from, think twice, scruple, demur, hang back, be disinclined ≠ be determined

hesitation = reluctance, reservation(s), misgiving(s), ambivalence, qualm(s), unwillingness, scruple(s), compunction

hidden 1 = secret, veiled, latent **2** = concealed, secret, covert, unseen, clandestine, secreted, under wraps

hide¹ 1 = conceal, stash (*informal*), secrete, put out of sight ≠ display **2** = go into hiding, take cover, keep out of sight, hole up, lie low, go underground, go to ground, go to earth **3** = keep secret, suppress, withhold, keep quiet about, hush up, draw a veil over, keep dark, keep under your hat ≠ disclose **4** = obscure, cover, mask, disguise, conceal, veil, cloak, shroud ≠ reveal

hide² = skin, leather, pelt

hideous = ugly, revolting, ghastly, monstrous, grotesque, gruesome, grisly, unsightly ≠ beautiful

hiding (*Informal*) = beating, whipping, thrashing, licking (*informal*), spanking, walloping (*informal*), drubbing

hierarchy = grading, ranking, social order, pecking order, class system, social stratum

high ADJECTIVE **1** = tall, towering, soaring, steep, elevated, lofty ≠ short **2** = extreme, great, acute, severe, extraordinary, excessive ≠ low **3** = strong, violent, extreme, blustery, squally, sharp **4** = important, chief, powerful, superior, eminent, exalted ≠ lowly **5** = high-pitched, piercing, shrill, penetrating, strident, sharp, acute, piping ≠ deep **6** (*Informal*) = intoxicated, stoned (*slang*), tripping (*informal*)

● ADVERB = way up, aloft, far up, to a great height

high-flown = extravagant, elaborate, pretentious, exaggerated, inflated, lofty, grandiose, overblown ≠ straightforward

highlight VERB = emphasize, stress, accent, show up, underline, spotlight, accentuate, call attention to ≠ play down

● NOUN = high point, peak, climax, feature, focus, focal point, high spot ≠ low point

highly = extremely, very, greatly, vastly, exceptionally, immensely, tremendously

hijack = <u>seize</u>, take over, commandeer, expropriate

hike NOUN = <u>walk</u>, march, trek, ramble, tramp, traipse

● VERB = <u>walk</u>, march, trek, ramble, tramp, back-pack

hilarious 1 = <u>funny</u>, entertaining, amusing, hysterical, humorous, comical, side-splitting 2 = <u>merry</u>, uproarious, rollicking ≠ serious

hill = <u>mount</u>, fell, height, mound, hilltop, tor, knoll, hillock, kopje or koppie (S. African)

hinder = <u>obstruct</u>, stop, check, block, delay, frustrate, handicap, interrupt ≠ help

hint NOUN 1 = <u>clue</u>, suggestion, implication, indication, pointer, allusion, innuendo, intimation 2 often plural = <u>advice</u>, help, tip(s), suggestion(s), pointer(s) 3 = <u>trace</u>, touch, suggestion, dash, suspicion, tinge, undertone

● VERB sometimes with at = <u>suggest</u>, indicate, imply, intimate, insinuate

hire VERB 1 = <u>employ</u>, commission, take on, engage, appoint, sign up, enlist 2 = <u>rent</u>, charter, lease, let, engage

● NOUN 1 = <u>rental</u>, hiring, rent, lease 2 = <u>charge</u>, rental, price, cost, fee

hiss VERB 1 = <u>whistle</u>, wheeze, whiz, whirr, sibilate 2 = <u>jeer</u>, mock, deride

● NOUN = <u>fizz</u>, buzz, hissing, fizzing, sibilation

historic = <u>significant</u>, notable, momentous, famous, extraordinary, outstanding, remarkable, ground-breaking ≠ unimportant

historical = <u>factual</u>, real, documented, actual, authentic, attested ≠ contemporary

history 1 = <u>the past</u>, antiquity, yesterday, yesteryear, olden days 2 = <u>chronicle</u>, record, story, account, narrative, recital, annals

hit VERB 1 = <u>strike</u>, beat, knock, bang, slap, smack, thump, clout (informal) 2 = <u>collide with</u>, run into, bump into, clash with, smash into, crash against, bang into 3 = <u>affect</u>, damage, harm, ruin, devastate, overwhelm, touch, impact on 4 = <u>reach</u>, gain, achieve, arrive at, accomplish, attain

● NOUN 1 = <u>shot</u>, blow 2 = <u>blow</u>, knock, stroke, belt (informal), rap, slap, smack, clout (informal) 3 = <u>success</u>, winner, triumph, smash (informal), sensation

● PHRASES **hit it off** (Informal) = <u>get on</u> (well) with, click (slang), be on good terms, get on like a house on fire (informal)

◆ **hit on** or **upon something** = <u>think up</u>, discover, arrive at, invent, stumble on, light upon, strike upon

hitch NOUN = <u>problem</u>, catch, difficulty, hold-up, obstacle, drawback, snag, uphill (S. African), impediment

● VERB 1 (Informal) = <u>hitchhike</u>, thumb a lift 2 = <u>fasten</u>, join, attach, couple, tie, connect, harness, tether

● PHRASES **hitch something up** = <u>pull up</u>, tug, jerk, yank

hitherto (Formal) = <u>previously</u>, so far, until now, thus far, heretofore

hobby = <u>pastime</u>, relaxation, leisure pursuit, diversion, avocation, (leisure) activity

hoist VERB = <u>raise</u>, lift, erect, elevate, heave

● NOUN = <u>lift</u>, crane, elevator, winch

hold VERB 1 = <u>embrace</u>, grasp, clutch, hug, squeeze, cradle, clasp, enfold 2 = <u>restrain</u> ≠ release 3 = <u>accommodate</u>, take, contain, seat, have a capacity for 4 = <u>consider</u>, think, believe, judge, regard, assume, reckon, deem ≠ deny 5 = <u>occupy</u>, have, fill, maintain, retain, possess, hold down (informal) 6 = <u>conduct</u>, convene, call, run, preside over ≠ cancel 7 = <u>detain</u>, confine, imprison, impound ≠ release

● NOUN 1 = <u>grip</u>, grasp, clasp 2 = <u>foothold</u>, footing 3 = <u>control</u>, influence, mastery, mana (N.Z.)

holder 1 = <u>owner</u>, bearer, possessor, keeper, proprietor 2 = <u>case</u>, cover, container

hold-up 1 = <u>robbery</u>, theft, mugging (informal), stick-up (slang, chiefly U.S.) 2 = <u>delay</u>, wait, hitch, setback, snag, traffic jam, stoppage, bottleneck

hole 1 = <u>cavity</u>, pit, hollow, chamber, cave, cavern 2 = <u>opening</u>, crack, tear, gap, breach, vent, puncture, aperture 3 = <u>burrow</u>, den, earth, shelter, lair 4 (Informal) = <u>hovel</u>, dump (informal), dive (slang), slum 5 (Informal) = <u>predicament</u>, spot (informal), fix (informal), mess, jam (informal), dilemma, scrape (informal), hot water (informal)

holiday 1 = <u>vacation</u>, leave, break, time off, recess 2 = <u>festival</u>, fête, celebration, feast, gala

hollow ADJECTIVE 1 = <u>empty</u>, vacant, void,

unfilled ≠ solid **2** = worthless, useless, vain, meaningless, pointless, futile, fruitless ≠ meaningful **3** = dull, low, deep, muted, toneless, reverberant ≠ vibrant

● NOUN **1** = cavity, hole, bowl, depression, pit, basin, crater, trough ≠ mound **2** = valley, dale, glen, dell, dingle ≠ hill

● VERB *often followed by* **out** = scoop out, dig out, excavate, gouge out

holocaust 1 = devastation, destruction, genocide, annihilation, conflagration **2** = genocide, massacre, annihilation

holy 1 = sacred, blessed, hallowed, venerable, consecrated, sacrosanct, sanctified ≠ unsanctified **2** = devout, godly, religious, pure, righteous, pious, virtuous, saintly ≠ sinful

homage = respect, honour, worship, devotion, reverence, deference, adulation, adoration ≠ contempt

home NOUN **1** = dwelling, house, residence, abode, habitation, pad (*slang*), domicile **2** = birthplace, homeland, home town, native land

● ADJECTIVE **1** = domestic, local, internal, native

● PHRASES **at home 1** = in, present, available **2** = at ease, relaxed, comfortable, content, at peace ◆ **bring something home to someone** = make clear, emphasize, drive home, press home, impress upon

homeland = native land, birthplace, motherland, fatherland, country of origin, mother country

homeless = destitute, displaced, dispossessed, down-and-out

homely 1 = comfortable, welcoming, friendly, cosy, homespun **2** = plain, simple, ordinary, modest ≠ elaborate

homicide = murder, killing, manslaughter, slaying, bloodshed

hone 1 = improve, better, enhance, upgrade, refine, sharpen, help **2** = sharpen, point, grind, edge, file, polish, whet

honest 1 = trustworthy, upright, ethical, honourable, reputable, truthful, virtuous, law-abiding ≠ dishonest **2** = open, direct, frank, plain, sincere, candid, forthright, upfront (*informal*) ≠ secretive

honestly 1 = ethically, legally, lawfully, honourably, by fair means **2** = frankly, plainly, candidly, straight (out), truthfully, to your face, in all sincerity

honesty 1 = integrity, honour, virtue, morality, probity, rectitude, truthfulness, trustworthiness **2** = frankness, openness, sincerity, candour, bluntness, outspokenness, straightforwardness

honorary = nominal, unofficial, titular, in name *or* title only

honour NOUN **1** = integrity, morality, honesty, goodness, fairness, decency, probity, rectitude ≠ dishonour **2** = prestige, credit, reputation, glory, fame, distinction, dignity, renown ≠ disgrace **3** = reputation, standing, prestige, image, status, stature, good name, cachet **4** = acclaim, praise, recognition, compliments, homage, accolades, commendation ≠ contempt **5** = privilege, credit, pleasure, compliment

● VERB **1** = acclaim, praise, decorate, commemorate, commend **2** = respect, value, esteem, prize, appreciate, adore ≠ scorn **3** = fulfil, keep, carry out, observe, discharge, live up to, be true to **4** = pay, take, accept, pass, acknowledge ≠ refuse

honourable 1 = principled, moral, ethical, fair, upright, honest, virtuous, trustworthy **2** = proper, respectable, virtuous, creditable

hook NOUN **1** = fastener, catch, link, peg, clasp

● VERB **1** = fasten, fix, secure, clasp **2** = catch, land, trap, entrap

hooked 1 = bent, curved, aquiline, hook-shaped **2** (*Informal*) = obsessed, addicted, taken, devoted, turned on (*slang*), enamoured **3** (*Informal*) = addicted, dependent, using (*informal*), having a habit

hooligan = delinquent, vandal, hoon (*Austral. & N.Z.*), ruffian, lager lout, yob *or* yobbo (*Brit. slang*), cougan (*Austral. slang*), scozza (*Austral. slang*), bogan (*Austral. slang*)

hoop = ring, band, loop, wheel, round, girdle, circlet

hop VERB = jump, spring, bound, leap, skip, vault, caper

● NOUN = jump, step, spring, bound, leap, bounce, skip, vault

hope VERB = believe, look forward to, cross your fingers

● NOUN = belief, confidence, expectation, longing, dream, desire, ambition, assumption ≠ despair

hopeful 1 = optimistic, confident, looking forward to, buoyant, sanguine, expectant ≠ despairing 2 = promising, encouraging, bright, reassuring, rosy, heartening, auspicious ≠ unpromising

hopefully = optimistically, confidently, expectantly, with anticipation

hopeless = impossible, pointless, futile, useless, vain, no-win, unattainable

horde = crowd, mob, swarm, host, band, pack, drove, gang

horizon = skyline, view, vista

horizontal = level, flat, parallel

horrible 1 (*Informal*) = dreadful, terrible, awful, nasty, cruel, mean, unpleasant, horrid ≠ wonderful 2 = terrible, appalling, terrifying, shocking, grim, dreadful, revolting, ghastly

horrific = horrifying, shocking, appalling, awful, terrifying, dreadful, horrendous, ghastly

horrify 1 = terrify, alarm, frighten, scare, intimidate, petrify, make your hair stand on end ≠ comfort 2 = shock, appal, dismay, sicken, outrage ≠ delight

horror 1 = terror, fear, alarm, panic, dread, fright, consternation, trepidation 2 = hatred, disgust, loathing, aversion, revulsion, repugnance, odium, detestation ≠ love

horse = nag, mount, mare, colt, filly, stallion, steed (*archaic or literary*), moke (*Austral. slang*), yarraman *or* yarramin (*Austral.*), gee-gee (*slang*)

▓ RELATED WORDS
adjectives: equestrian, equine
male: stallion
female: mare
young: foal, colt, filly

hospitality = welcome, warmth, kindness, friendliness, sociability, conviviality, neighbourliness, cordiality

host¹ *or* **hostess** NOUN 1 = master of ceremonies, proprietor, innkeeper, landlord *or* landlady 2 = presenter, compere (*Brit.*), anchorman *or* anchorwoman
● VERB = present, introduce, compere (*Brit.*), front (*informal*)

host² 1 = multitude, lot, load (*informal*), wealth, array, myriad, great quantity, large number 2 = crowd, army, pack, drove, mob, herd, legion, swarm

hostage = captive, prisoner, pawn

hostile 1 = antagonistic, opposed, contrary, ill-disposed 2 = unfriendly, belligerent, antagonistic, rancorous, ill-disposed ≠ friendly 3 = inhospitable, adverse, uncongenial, unsympathetic, unwelcoming ≠ hospitable

hostility NOUN 1 = unfriendliness, hatred, animosity, spite, bitterness, malice, venom, enmity ≠ friendliness 2 = opposition, resentment, antipathy, aversion, antagonism, ill feeling, ill-will, animus ≠ approval
● PLURAL NOUN = warfare, war, fighting, conflict, combat, armed conflict ≠ peace

hot 1 = heated, boiling, steaming, roasting, searing, scorching, scalding 2 = warm, close, stifling, humid, torrid, sultry, sweltering, balmy ≠ cold 3 = spicy, pungent, peppery, piquant, biting, sharp ≠ mild 4 = intense, passionate, heated, spirited, fierce, lively, animated, ardent 5 = new, latest, fresh, recent, up to date, just out, up to the minute, bang up to date (*informal*) ≠ old 6 = popular, hip, fashionable, cool, in demand, sought-after, must-see, in vogue ≠ unpopular 7 = fierce, intense, strong, keen, competitive, cut-throat 8 = fiery, violent, raging, passionate, stormy ≠ calm

hound = underline{harass}, harry, bother, provoke, annoy, torment, hassle (*informal*), badger
▓ RELATED WORD
collective noun: pack

house NOUN 1 = home, residence, dwelling, pad (*slang*), homestead, abode, habitation, domicile, whare (*N.Z.*) 2 = household, family 3 = firm, company, business, organization, outfit (*informal*) 4 = assembly, parliament, Commons, legislative body 5 = dynasty, tribe, clan
● VERB 1 = accommodate, quarter, take in, put up, lodge, harbour, billet 2 = contain, keep, hold, cover, store, protect, shelter 3 = take, accommodate, sleep, provide shelter for, give a bed to
● PHRASES on the house = free, for free (*informal*), for nothing, free of charge, gratis

household = family, home, house, family circle, ainga (*N.Z.*)

housing 1 = accommodation, homes, houses, dwellings, domiciles 2 = case, casing, covering, cover, shell, jacket, holder, container

hover 1 = <u>float</u>, fly, hang, drift, flutter 2 = <u>linger</u>, loiter, hang about or around (*informal*) 3 = <u>waver</u>, fluctuate, dither (*chiefly Brit.*), oscillate, vacillate

however = <u>but</u>, nevertheless, still, though, yet, nonetheless, notwithstanding, anyhow

howl VERB 1 = <u>bay</u>, cry 2 = <u>cry</u>, scream, roar, weep, yell, wail, shriek, bellow
● NOUN 1 = <u>baying</u>, cry, bay, bark, barking, yelping 2 = <u>cry</u>, scream, roar, bay, wail, shriek, clamour, bawl

hub = <u>centre</u>, heart, focus, core, middle, focal point, nerve centre

huddle VERB 1 = <u>curl up</u>, crouch, hunch up 2 = <u>crowd</u>, press, gather, collect, squeeze, cluster, flock, herd
● NOUN (*Informal*) = <u>discussion</u>, conference, meeting, hui (*N.Z.*), powwow, confab (*informal*), korero (*N.Z.*)

hue = <u>colour</u>, tone, shade, dye, tint, tinge

hug VERB = <u>embrace</u>, cuddle, squeeze, clasp, enfold, hold close, take in your arms
● NOUN = <u>embrace</u>, squeeze, bear hug, clinch (*slang*), clasp

huge = <u>enormous</u>, large, massive, vast, tremendous, immense, gigantic, monumental ≠ tiny

hui (*N.Z.*) = <u>meeting</u>, gathering, assembly, conference, congress, rally, convention, get-together (*informal*)

hull = <u>framework</u>, casing, body, covering, frame

hum 1 = <u>drone</u>, buzz, murmur, throb, vibrate, purr, thrum, whir 2 (*Informal*) = <u>be busy</u>, buzz, bustle, stir, pulse, pulsate

human ADJECTIVE = <u>mortal</u>, manlike ≠ nonhuman
● NOUN = <u>human being</u>, person, individual, creature, mortal, man or woman ≠ nonhuman

humane = <u>kind</u>, compassionate, understanding, forgiving, tender, sympathetic, benign, merciful ≠ cruel

humanitarian ADJECTIVE
1 = <u>compassionate</u>, charitable, humane, benevolent, altruistic 2 = <u>charitable</u>, philanthropic, public-spirited
● NOUN = <u>philanthropist</u>, benefactor, Good Samaritan, altruist

humanity 1 = <u>the human race</u>, man, mankind, people, mortals, humankind, Homo sapiens 2 = <u>human nature</u>, mortality 3 = <u>kindness</u>, charity, compassion, sympathy, mercy, philanthropy, fellow feeling, kind-heartedness

humble ADJECTIVE 1 = <u>modest</u>, meek, unassuming, unpretentious, self-effacing, unostentatious ≠ proud 2 = <u>lowly</u>, poor, mean, simple, ordinary, modest, obscure, undistinguished ≠ distinguished
● VERB = <u>humiliate</u>, disgrace, crush, subdue, chasten, put (someone) in their place, take down a peg (*informal*) ≠ exalt

humidity = <u>damp</u>, moisture, dampness, wetness, moistness, dankness, clamminess, mugginess

humiliate = <u>embarrass</u>, shame, humble, crush, put down, degrade, chasten, mortify ≠ honour

humiliating = <u>embarrassing</u>, shaming, humbling, mortifying, crushing, degrading, ignominious, barro (*Austral. slang*)

humiliation = <u>embarrassment</u>, shame, disgrace, humbling, put-down, degradation, indignity, ignominy

humorous = <u>funny</u>, comic, amusing, entertaining, witty, comical, droll, jocular ≠ serious

humour NOUN 1 = <u>comedy</u>, funniness, fun, amusement, funny side, jocularity, facetiousness, ludicrousness ≠ seriousness 2 = <u>mood</u>, spirits, temper, disposition, frame of mind 3 = <u>joking</u>, comedy, wit, farce, jesting, wisecracks (*informal*), witticisms
● VERB = <u>indulge</u>, accommodate, go along with, flatter, gratify, pander to, mollify ≠ oppose

hunch NOUN = <u>feeling</u>, idea, impression, suspicion, intuition, premonition, inkling, presentiment
● VERB = <u>crouch</u>, bend, curve, arch, draw in

hunger NOUN 1 = <u>appetite</u>, emptiness, hungriness, ravenousness 2 = <u>starvation</u>, famine, malnutrition, undernourishment 3 = <u>desire</u>, appetite, craving, ache, lust, yearning, itch, thirst
● PHRASES **hunger for** or **after something** = <u>want</u>, desire, crave, long for, wish for, yearn for, hanker after, ache for

hungry 1 = <u>starving</u>, ravenous, famished, starved, empty, voracious, peckish (*informal*, *chiefly Brit.*) 2 = <u>eager</u>, keen, craving, yearning, greedy, avid, desirous, covetous

hunk = <u>lump</u>, piece, chunk, block, mass, wedge, slab, nugget

hunt VERB = <u>stalk</u>, track, chase, pursue, trail, hound

● NOUN = <u>search</u>, hunting, investigation, chase, pursuit, quest

● PHRASES **hunt for something** or **someone** = <u>search for</u>, look for, seek for, forage for, scour for, fossick for (*Austral. & N.Z.*), ferret about for

hurdle 1 = <u>obstacle</u>, difficulty, barrier, handicap, hazard, uphill (*S. African*), obstruction, stumbling block 2 = <u>fence</u>, barrier, barricade

hurl = <u>throw</u>, fling, launch, cast, pitch, toss, propel, sling

hurricane = <u>storm</u>, gale, tornado, cyclone, typhoon, tempest, twister (*U.S. informal*), willy-willy (*Austral.*)

hurried 1 = <u>hasty</u>, quick, brief, rushed, short, swift, speedy 2 = <u>rushed</u>, perfunctory, speedy, hasty, cursory

hurry VERB 1 = <u>rush</u>, fly, dash, scurry, scoot ≠ dawdle 2 = <u>make haste</u>, rush, get a move on (*informal*), step on it (*informal*)

● NOUN = <u>rush</u>, haste, speed, urgency, flurry, quickness ≠ slowness

hurt VERB 1 = <u>injure</u>, damage, wound, cut, disable, bruise, scrape, impair ≠ heal 2 = <u>ache</u>, be sore, be painful, burn, smart, sting, throb, be tender 3 = <u>harm</u>, injure, ill-treat, maltreat 4 = <u>upset</u>, distress, pain, wound, annoy, grieve, sadden

● NOUN = <u>distress</u>, suffering, pain, grief, misery, sorrow, heartache, wretchedness ≠ happiness

● ADJECTIVE 1 = <u>injured</u>, wounded, damaged, harmed, cut, bruised, scarred ≠ healed 2 = <u>upset</u>, wounded, crushed, offended, aggrieved, tooshie (*Austral. slang*) ≠ calmed

hurtle = <u>rush</u>, charge, race, shoot, fly, speed, tear, crash

husband NOUN = <u>partner</u>, spouse, mate, better half (*humorous*)

● VERB = <u>conserve</u>, budget, save, store, hoard, economize on, use economically ≠ squander

hush VERB = <u>quieten</u>, silence, mute, muzzle, shush

● NOUN = <u>quiet</u>, silence, calm, peace, tranquillity, stillness

hut 1 = <u>cabin</u>, shack, shanty, hovel, whare (*N.Z.*) 2 = <u>shed</u>, outhouse, lean-to, lockup

hybrid 1 = <u>crossbreed</u>, cross, mixture, compound, composite, amalgam, mongrel, half-breed 2 = <u>mixture</u>, compound, composite, amalgam

hygiene = <u>cleanliness</u>, sanitation, disinfection, sterility

hymn 1 = <u>religious song</u>, song of praise, carol, chant, anthem, psalm, paean 2 = <u>song of praise</u>, anthem, paean

hype (*Slang*) = <u>publicity</u>, promotion, plugging (*informal*), razzmatazz (*slang*), brouhaha, ballyhoo (*informal*)

hypocrisy = <u>insincerity</u>, pretence, deception, cant, duplicity, deceitfulness ≠ sincerity

hypothesis = <u>theory</u>, premise, proposition, assumption, thesis, postulate, supposition

hysteria = <u>frenzy</u>, panic, madness, agitation, delirium, hysterics

hysterical 1 = <u>frenzied</u>, frantic, raving, distracted, distraught, crazed, overwrought, berko (*Austral. slang*) ≠ calm 2 (*Informal*) = <u>hilarious</u>, uproarious, side-splitting, comical ≠ serious

icy 1 = <u>cold</u>, freezing, bitter, biting, raw, chill, chilly, frosty ≠ hot 2 = <u>slippery</u>, glassy, slippy (*informal* or *dialect*), like a sheet of glass 3 = <u>unfriendly</u>, cold, distant, aloof, frosty, frigid, unwelcoming ≠ friendly

idea 1 = <u>notion</u>, thought, view, teaching, opinion, belief, conclusion, hypothesis 2 = <u>understanding</u>, thought, view, opinion, concept, impression, perception 3 = <u>intention</u>, aim, purpose, object, plan, objective

ideal NOUN 1 = <u>epitome</u>, standard, dream, pattern, perfection, last word, paragon 2 = <u>model</u>, prototype, paradigm

● ADJECTIVE = <u>perfect</u>, best, model, classic, supreme, ultimate, archetypal, exemplary

≠ imperfect

ideally = <u>in a perfect world</u>, all things being equal, if you had your way

identical = <u>alike</u>, matching, twin, duplicate, indistinguishable, interchangeable ≠ different

identification 1 = <u>discovery</u>, recognition, determining, establishment, diagnosis, confirmation, divination 2 = <u>recognition</u>, naming, distinguishing, confirmation, pinpointing 3 = <u>connection</u>, relationship, association 4 = <u>understanding</u>, relationship, involvement, unity, sympathy, empathy, rapport, fellow feeling

identify VERB 1 = <u>recognize</u>, place, name, remember, spot, diagnose, make out, pinpoint 2 = <u>establish</u>, spot, confirm, demonstrate, pick out, certify, verify, mark out

● PHRASES **identify something** or **someone with something** or **someone** = <u>equate with</u>, associate with ◆ **identify with someone** = <u>relate to</u>, respond to, feel for, empathize with

identity = <u>individuality</u>, self, character, personality, existence, originality, separateness

idiot = <u>fool</u>, moron, twit (*informal*, *chiefly Brit.*), chump, imbecile, cretin, simpleton, halfwit, galah (*Austral. & N.Z. informal*), dorba or dorb (*Austral. slang*), bogan (*Austral. slang*)

idle ADJECTIVE 1 = <u>unoccupied</u>, unemployed, redundant, inactive ≠ occupied 2 = <u>unused</u>, inactive, out of order, out of service 3 = <u>lazy</u>, slow, slack, sluggish, lax, negligent, inactive, inert ≠ busy 4 = <u>useless</u>, vain, pointless, unsuccessful, ineffective, worthless, futile, fruitless ≠ useful

● VERB often with **away** = <u>fritter</u>, lounge, potter, loaf, dally, loiter, dawdle, laze

idol 1 = <u>hero</u>, pin-up, favourite, pet, darling, beloved (*slang*), fave (*informal*) 2 = <u>graven image</u>, god, deity

if 1 = <u>provided</u>, assuming, given that, providing, supposing, presuming, on condition that, as long as 2 = <u>when</u>, whenever, every time, any time

ignite 1 = <u>catch fire</u>, burn, burst into flames, inflame, flare up, take fire 2 = <u>set fire to</u>, light, set alight, torch, kindle

ignorance 1 = <u>lack of education</u>, stupidity, foolishness ≠ knowledge

2 with **of** = <u>unawareness of</u>, inexperience of, unfamiliarity with, innocence of, unconsciousness of

ignorant 1 = <u>uneducated</u>, illiterate ≠ educated 2 = <u>insensitive</u>, rude, crass 3 with **of** = <u>uninformed of</u>, unaware of, oblivious to, innocent of, unconscious of, inexperienced of, uninitiated about, unenlightened about ≠ informed

ignore 1 = <u>pay no attention to</u>, neglect, disregard, slight, overlook, scorn, spurn, rebuff ≠ pay attention to 2 = <u>overlook</u>, discount, disregard, reject, neglect, shrug off, pass over, brush aside 3 = <u>snub</u>, slight, rebuff

ill ADJECTIVE 1 = <u>unwell</u>, sick, poorly (*informal*), diseased, weak, crook (*Austral. & N.Z. slang*), ailing, frail ≠ healthy 2 = <u>harmful</u>, bad, damaging, evil, foul, unfortunate, destructive, detrimental ≠ favourable

● NOUN = <u>problem</u>, trouble, suffering, worry, injury, hurt, strain, harm ≠ good

● ADVERB 1 = <u>badly</u>, unfortunately, unfavourably, inauspiciously 2 = <u>hardly</u>, barely, scarcely, just, only just, by no means, at a push ≠ well

illegal = <u>unlawful</u>, banned, forbidden, prohibited, criminal, outlawed, illicit, unlicensed ≠ legal

illicit 1 = <u>illegal</u>, criminal, prohibited, unlawful, illegitimate, unlicensed, unauthorized, felonious ≠ legal 2 = <u>forbidden</u>, improper, immoral, guilty, clandestine, furtive

illness = <u>sickness</u>, disease, infection, disorder, bug (*informal*), ailment, affliction, malady

illuminate 1 = <u>light up</u>, brighten ≠ darken 2 = <u>explain</u>, interpret, make clear, clarify, clear up, enlighten, shed light on, elucidate ≠ obscure

illuminating = <u>informative</u>, revealing, enlightening, helpful, explanatory, instructive ≠ confusing

illusion 1 = <u>delusion</u>, misconception, misapprehension, fancy, fallacy, false impression, false belief 2 = <u>false impression</u>, appearance, impression, deception, fallacy ≠ reality 3 = <u>fantasy</u>, vision, hallucination, trick, spectre, mirage, daydream, apparition

illustrate 1 = <u>demonstrate</u>, emphasize 2 = <u>explain</u>, sum up, summarize, bring

home, point up, elucidate
illustrated = pictured, decorated,
pictorial
illustration 1 = example, case, instance,
sample, specimen, exemplar 2 = picture,
drawing, painting, image, print, plate,
figure, portrait
image 1 = thought, idea, vision, concept,
impression, perception, mental picture,
conceptualization 2 = figure of speech
3 = reflection, likeness, mirror image
4 = figure, idol, icon, fetish, talisman
5 = replica, copy, reproduction,
counterpart, clone, facsimile, spitting
image (*informal*), Doppelgänger
6 = picture, photo, photograph,
representation, reproduction, snapshot
imaginary = fictional, made-up, invented,
imagined, unreal, hypothetical, fictitious,
illusory ≠ real
imagination 1 = creativity, vision,
invention, ingenuity, enterprise, originality,
inventiveness, resourcefulness 2 = mind's
eye, fancy
imaginative = creative, original, inspired,
enterprising, clever, ingenious, inventive
≠ unimaginative
imagine 1 = envisage, see, picture, plan,
think of, conjure up, envision, visualize
2 = believe, think, suppose, assume,
suspect, guess (*informal, chiefly U.S. &
Canad.*), take it, reckon
imitate 1 = copy, follow, repeat, echo,
emulate, ape, simulate, mirror 2 = do an
impression of, mimic, copy
imitation NOUN 1 = replica, fake,
reproduction, sham, forgery,
counterfeiting, likeness, duplication
2 = copying, resemblance, mimicry
3 = impression, impersonation
● ADJECTIVE = artificial, mock, reproduction,
dummy, synthetic, man-made, simulated,
sham ≠ real
immaculate 1 = clean, spotless, neat,
spruce, squeaky-clean, spick-and-span
≠ dirty 2 = pure, perfect, impeccable,
flawless, faultless, above reproach
≠ corrupt 3 = perfect, flawless, impeccable,
faultless, unblemished, untarnished,
unexceptionable ≠ tainted
immediate 1 = instant, prompt,
instantaneous, quick, on-the-spot, split-
second ≠ later 2 = nearest, next, direct,
close, near ≠ far

immediately = at once, now, instantly,
straight away, directly, promptly, right
away, without delay
immense = huge, great, massive, vast,
enormous, extensive, tremendous, very
big ≠ tiny
immerse 1 = engross, involve, absorb,
busy, occupy, engage 2 = plunge, dip,
submerge, sink, duck, bathe, douse, dunk
immigrant = settler, incomer, alien,
stranger, outsider, newcomer, migrant,
emigrant
imminent = near, coming, close,
approaching, gathering, forthcoming,
looming, impending ≠ remote
immoral = wicked, bad, wrong, corrupt,
indecent, sinful, unethical, depraved
≠ moral
immortal ADJECTIVE 1 = timeless, eternal,
everlasting, lasting, traditional, classic,
enduring, perennial ≠ ephemeral
2 = undying, eternal, imperishable,
deathless ≠ mortal
● NOUN 1 = hero, genius, great 2 = god,
goddess, deity, divine being, immortal
being, atua (*N.Z.*)
immune
● PHRASES immune from = exempt from,
free from ◆ immune to 1 = resistant
to, free from, protected from, safe from,
not open to, spared from, secure against,
invulnerable to 2 = unaffected by,
invulnerable to
immunity 1 = exemption, amnesty,
indemnity, release, freedom,
invulnerability 2 with to = resistance
to, protection from, resilience to,
inoculation against, immunization from
≠ susceptibility to
impact NOUN 1 = effect, influence,
consequences, impression, repercussions,
ramifications 2 = collision, contact, crash,
knock, stroke, smash, bump, thump
● VERB = hit, strike, crash, clash, crush, ram,
smack, collide
impair = worsen, reduce, damage, injure,
harm, undermine, weaken, diminish
≠ improve
impaired = damaged, flawed, faulty,
defective, imperfect, unsound
impasse = deadlock, stalemate, standstill,
dead end, standoff
impatient 1 = cross, annoyed, irritated,
prickly, touchy, bad-tempered, intolerant,

ill-tempered ≠ easy-going **2** = eager, longing, keen, anxious, hungry, enthusiastic, restless, avid ≠ calm

impeccable = faultless, perfect, immaculate, flawless, squeaky-clean, unblemished, unimpeachable, irreproachable ≠ flawed

impending = looming, coming, approaching, near, forthcoming, imminent, upcoming, in the pipeline

imperative = urgent, essential, pressing, vital, crucial ≠ unnecessary

imperial = royal, regal, kingly, queenly, princely, sovereign, majestic, monarchial

impetus 1 = incentive, push, spur, motivation, impulse, stimulus, catalyst, goad **2** = force, power, energy, momentum

implant 1 = insert, fix, graft **2** = instil, infuse, inculcate

implement VERB = carry out, effect, carry through, complete, apply, perform, realize, fulfil ≠ hinder

● NOUN = tool, machine, device, instrument, appliance, apparatus, gadget, utensil

implicate VERB = incriminate, involve, embroil, entangle, inculpate ≠ dissociate

● PHRASES **implicate something or someone in something** = involve in, associate with

implication NOUN = suggestion, hint, inference, meaning, significance, presumption, overtone, innuendo

● PLURAL NOUN = consequences, result, developments, upshot

implicit 1 = implied, understood, suggested, hinted at, taken for granted, unspoken, inferred, tacit ≠ explicit **2** = inherent, underlying, intrinsic, latent, ingrained, inbuilt **3** = absolute, full, complete, firm, fixed, constant, utter, outright

implied = suggested, indirect, hinted at, implicit, unspoken, tacit, undeclared, unstated

imply 1 = suggest, hint, insinuate, indicate, intimate, signify **2** = involve, mean, entail, require, indicate, point to, signify, presuppose

import VERB = bring in, buy in, ship in, introduce

● NOUN **1** (*Formal*) = significance, concern, value, weight, consequence, substance, moment, magnitude **2** = meaning,

implication, significance, sense, intention, substance, drift, thrust

importance 1 = significance, interest, concern, moment, value, weight, import, consequence **2** = prestige, standing, status, rule, authority, influence, distinction, esteem, mana (*N.Z.*)

important 1 = significant, critical, substantial, urgent, serious, far-reaching, momentous, seminal ≠ unimportant **2** = powerful, prominent, commanding, dominant, influential, eminent, high-ranking, authoritative

impose

● PHRASES **impose something on or upon someone 1** = levy, introduce, charge, establish, fix, institute, decree, ordain **2** = inflict, force, enforce, visit, press, apply, thrust, saddle (someone) with

imposing = impressive, striking, grand, powerful, commanding, awesome, majestic, dignified ≠ unimposing

imposition 1 = application, introduction, levying **2** = intrusion, liberty, presumption

impossible 1 = not possible, out of the question, impracticable, unfeasible **2** = unachievable, out of the question, vain, unthinkable, inconceivable, far-fetched, unworkable, implausible ≠ possible **3** = absurd, crazy (*informal*), ridiculous, outrageous, ludicrous, unreasonable, preposterous, farcical

impotence = powerlessness, inability, helplessness, weakness, incompetence, paralysis, frailty, incapacity ≠ powerfulness

impoverish 1 = bankrupt, ruin, beggar, break **2** = deplete, drain, exhaust, diminish, use up, sap, wear out, reduce

impoverished = poor, needy, destitute, bankrupt, poverty-stricken, impecunious, penurious ≠ rich

impress VERB = excite, move, strike, touch, affect, inspire, amaze, overcome

● PHRASES **impress something on or upon someone** = stress, bring home to, instil in, drum into, knock into, emphasize to, fix in, inculcate in

impression 1 = idea, feeling, thought, sense, view, assessment, judgment, reaction **2** = effect, influence, impact **3** = imitation, parody, impersonation, send-up (*Brit. informal*), takeoff (*informal*) **4** = mark, imprint, stamp, outline, hollow, dent, indentation

impressive = grand, striking, splendid, good, great (*informal*), fine, powerful, exciting ≠ unimpressive

imprint NOUN = mark, impression, stamp, indentation
- VERB = engrave, print, stamp, impress, etch, emboss

imprison = jail, confine, detain, lock up, put away, intern, incarcerate, send down (*informal*) ≠ free

imprisoned = jailed, confined, locked up, inside (*slang*), in jail, captive, behind bars, incarcerated

imprisonment = confinement, custody, detention, captivity, incarceration

improbable 1 = doubtful, unlikely, dubious, questionable, fanciful, far-fetched, implausible ≠ probable
2 = unconvincing, weak, unbelievable, preposterous ≠ convincing

improper 1 = inappropriate, unfit, unsuitable, out of place, unwarranted, uncalled-for ≠ appropriate 2 = indecent, vulgar, suggestive, unseemly, untoward, risqué, smutty, unbecoming ≠ decent

improve 1 = enhance, better, add to, upgrade, touch up, ameliorate ≠ worsen
2 = get better, pick up, develop, advance

improvement 1 = enhancement, advancement, betterment 2 = advance, development, progress, recovery, upswing

improvise 1 = devise, contrive, concoct, throw together 2 = ad-lib, invent, busk, wing it (*informal*), play it by ear (*informal*), extemporize, speak off the cuff (*informal*)

impulse = urge, longing, wish, notion, yearning, inclination, itch, whim

inaccurate = incorrect, wrong, mistaken, faulty, unreliable, defective, erroneous, unsound ≠ accurate

inadequacy 1 = shortage, poverty, dearth, paucity, insufficiency, meagreness, scantiness 2 = incompetence, inability, deficiency, incapacity, ineffectiveness
3 = shortcoming, failing, weakness, defect, imperfection

inadequate 1 = insufficient, meagre, poor, lacking, scant, sparse, sketchy ≠ adequate 2 = incapable, incompetent, faulty, deficient, unqualified, not up to scratch (*informal*) ≠ capable

inadvertently = unintentionally, accidentally, by accident, mistakenly, unwittingly, by mistake, involuntarily

≠ deliberately

inaugural = first, opening, initial, maiden, introductory

incarnation = embodiment, manifestation, epitome, type, personification

incense = anger, infuriate, enrage, irritate, madden, inflame, rile (*informal*), make your blood boil (*informal*)

incensed = angry, furious, fuming, infuriated, enraged, maddened, indignant, irate, tooshie (*Austral. slang*), off the air (*Austral. slang*)

incentive = inducement, encouragement, spur, lure, bait, motivation, carrot (*informal*), stimulus ≠ disincentive

incident 1 = disturbance, scene, clash, disorder, confrontation, brawl, fracas, commotion 2 = adventure, drama, excitement, crisis, spectacle
3 = happening, event, affair, business, fact, matter, occasion, episode

incidentally = by the way, in passing, en passant, parenthetically, by the bye

inclination 1 = desire, longing, aspiration, craving, hankering 2 = tendency, liking, disposition, penchant, propensity, predisposition, predilection, proclivity ≠ aversion

incline VERB = predispose, influence, persuade, prejudice, sway, dispose
- NOUN = slope, rise, dip, grade, descent, ascent, gradient

inclined 1 = disposed, given, prone, likely, liable, apt, predisposed 2 = willing, minded, disposed

include 1 = contain, involve, incorporate, cover, consist of, take in, embrace, comprise ≠ exclude 2 = count 3 = add, enter, put in, insert

inclusion = addition, incorporation, introduction, insertion ≠ exclusion

inclusive = comprehensive, general, global, sweeping, blanket, umbrella, across-the-board, all-embracing ≠ limited

income = revenue, earnings, pay, returns, profits, wages, yield, proceeds

incoming 1 = arriving, landing, approaching, entering, returning, homeward ≠ departing 2 = new

incompatible = inconsistent, conflicting, contradictory, incongruous, unsuited, mismatched ≠ compatible

incompetence = ineptitude, inability,

inadequacy, incapacity, ineffectiveness, uselessness, unfitness, incapability

incompetent = <u>inept</u>, useless, incapable, floundering, bungling, unfit, ineffectual, inexpert ≠ competent

incomplete = <u>unfinished</u>, partial, wanting, deficient, imperfect, fragmentary, half-pie (*N.Z. informal*) ≠ complete

inconsistency 1 = <u>unreliability</u>, instability, unpredictability, fickleness, unsteadiness 2 = <u>incompatibility</u>, discrepancy, disparity, disagreement, variance, divergence, incongruity

inconsistent 1 = <u>changeable</u>, variable, unpredictable, unstable, erratic, fickle, capricious, unsteady ≠ consistent 2 = <u>incompatible</u>, conflicting, at odds, contradictory, incongruous, discordant, out of step, irreconcilable ≠ compatible

inconvenience NOUN = <u>trouble</u>, difficulty, bother, fuss, disadvantage, disturbance, disruption, nuisance, uphill (*S. African*)
● VERB = <u>trouble</u>, bother, disturb, upset, disrupt, put out, discommode

incorporate 1 = <u>include</u>, contain, take in, embrace, integrate, encompass, assimilate, comprise of 2 = <u>integrate</u>, include, absorb, merge, fuse, assimilate, subsume 3 = <u>blend</u>, combine, compound, mingle

incorrect = <u>false</u>, wrong, mistaken, flawed, faulty, inaccurate, untrue, erroneous ≠ correct

increase VERB 1 = <u>raise</u>, extend, boost, expand, develop, advance, strengthen, widen ≠ decrease 2 = <u>grow</u>, develop, spread, expand, swell, enlarge, escalate, multiply ≠ shrink
● NOUN = <u>growth</u>, rise, development, gain, expansion, extension, proliferation, enlargement

increasingly = <u>progressively</u>, more and more

incredible 1 (*Informal*) = <u>amazing</u>, wonderful, stunning, extraordinary, overwhelming, astonishing, staggering, sensational (*informal*) 2 = <u>unbelievable</u>, unthinkable, improbable, inconceivable, preposterous, unconvincing, unimaginable, far-fetched

incumbent NOUN = <u>holder</u>, keeper, bearer
● ADJECTIVE (*Formal*) = <u>obligatory</u>, required, necessary, essential, binding, compulsory, mandatory, imperative

incur = <u>sustain</u>, experience, suffer, gain,

earn, collect, meet with, provoke

indecent 1 = <u>obscene</u>, lewd, dirty, inappropriate, rude, crude, filthy, improper ≠ decent 2 = <u>unbecoming</u>, unsuitable, vulgar, unseemly, undignified, indecorous ≠ proper

indeed 1 = <u>certainly</u>, yes, definitely, surely, truly, undoubtedly, without doubt, indisputably 2 = <u>really</u>, actually, in fact, certainly, genuinely, in truth, in actuality

indefinitely = <u>endlessly</u>, continually, for ever, ad infinitum

independence = <u>freedom</u>, liberty, autonomy, sovereignty, self-rule, self-sufficiency, self-reliance, rangatiratanga (*N.Z.*) ≠ subjugation

independent 1 = <u>separate</u>, unattached, uncontrolled, unconstrained ≠ controlled 2 = <u>self-sufficient</u>, free, liberated, self-contained, self-reliant, self-supporting 3 = <u>self-governing</u>, free, autonomous, liberated, sovereign, self-determining, nonaligned ≠ subject

independently = <u>separately</u>, alone, solo, on your own, by yourself, unaided, individually, autonomously

indicate 1 = <u>show</u>, suggest, reveal, display, demonstrate, point to, imply, manifest 2 = <u>imply</u>, suggest, hint, intimate, signify, insinuate 3 = <u>point to</u>, point out, specify, gesture towards, designate 4 = <u>register</u>, show, record, read, express, display, demonstrate

indication = <u>sign</u>, mark, evidence, suggestion, symptom, hint, clue, manifestation

indicator = <u>sign</u>, mark, measure, guide, signal, symbol, meter, gauge

indict = <u>charge</u>, accuse, prosecute, summon, impeach, arraign

indictment = <u>charge</u>, allegation, prosecution, accusation, impeachment, summons, arraignment

indifference = <u>disregard</u>, apathy, negligence, detachment, coolness, coldness, nonchalance, aloofness ≠ concern

indifferent 1 = <u>unconcerned</u>, detached, cold, cool, callous, aloof, unmoved, unsympathetic ≠ concerned 2 = <u>mediocre</u>, ordinary, moderate, so-so (*informal*), passable, undistinguished, no great shakes (*informal*), half-pie (*N.Z. informal*) ≠ excellent

indignation = <u>resentment</u>, anger, rage, exasperation, pique, umbrage

indirect 1 = <u>related</u>, secondary, subsidiary, incidental, unintended 2 = <u>circuitous</u>, roundabout, curving, wandering, rambling, deviant, meandering, tortuous ≠ direct

indispensable = <u>essential</u>, necessary, needed, key, vital, crucial, imperative, requisite ≠ dispensable

individual ADJECTIVE 1 = <u>separate</u>, independent, isolated, lone, solitary ≠ collective 2 = <u>unique</u>, special, fresh, novel, exclusive, singular, idiosyncratic, unorthodox ≠ conventional
● NOUN = <u>person</u>, being, human, unit, character, soul, creature

individually = <u>separately</u>, independently, singly, one by one, one at a time

induce 1 = <u>cause</u>, produce, create, effect, lead to, occasion, generate, bring about ≠ prevent 2 = <u>persuade</u>, encourage, influence, convince, urge, prompt, sway, entice ≠ dissuade

indulge VERB 1 = <u>gratify</u>, satisfy, feed, give way to, yield to, pander to, gladden 2 = <u>spoil</u>, pamper, cosset, humour, give in to, coddle, mollycoddle, overindulge
● PHRASES **indulge yourself** = <u>treat</u> yourself, splash out, spoil yourself, luxuriate in something, overindulge yourself

indulgence 1 = <u>luxury</u>, treat, extravagance, favour, privilege 2 = <u>gratification</u>, satisfaction, fulfilment, appeasement, satiation

industrialist = <u>capitalist</u>, tycoon, magnate, manufacturer, captain of industry, big businessman

industry 1 = <u>business</u>, production, manufacturing, trade, commerce 2 = <u>trade</u>, world, business, service, line, field, profession, occupation 3 = <u>diligence</u>, effort, labour, hard work, trouble, activity, application, endeavour

ineffective 1 = <u>unproductive</u>, useless, futile, vain, unsuccessful, pointless, fruitless, ineffectual ≠ effective 2 = <u>inefficient</u>, useless, poor, powerless, unfit, worthless, inept, impotent

inefficient 1 = <u>wasteful</u>, uneconomical, profligate 2 = <u>incompetent</u>, inept, weak, bungling, ineffectual, disorganized ≠ efficient

inequality = <u>disparity</u>, prejudice, difference, bias, diversity, irregularity, unevenness, disproportion

inevitable = <u>unavoidable</u>, inescapable, inexorable, sure, certain, fixed, assured, fated ≠ avoidable

inevitably = <u>unavoidably</u>, naturally, necessarily, surely, certainly, as a result, automatically, consequently

inexpensive = <u>cheap</u>, reasonable, budget, bargain, modest, economical ≠ expensive

inexperienced = <u>new</u>, green, raw, callow, immature, untried, unpractised, unversed ≠ experienced

infamous = <u>notorious</u>, ignominious, disreputable, ill-famed ≠ esteemed

infancy = <u>beginnings</u>, start, birth, roots, seeds, origins, dawn, outset ≠ end

infant = <u>baby</u>, child, babe, toddler, tot, bairn (*Scot.*), littlie (*Austral. informal*), ankle-biter (*Austral. slang*), tacker (*Austral. slang*)

infect 1 = <u>contaminate</u> 2 = <u>pollute</u>, poison, corrupt, contaminate, taint, defile 3 = <u>affect</u>, move, upset, overcome, stir, disturb

infection = <u>disease</u>, condition, complaint, illness, virus, disorder, corruption, poison

infectious = <u>catching</u>, spreading, contagious, communicable, virulent, transmittable

inferior ADJECTIVE = <u>lower</u>, minor, secondary, subsidiary, lesser, humble, subordinate, lowly ≠ superior
● NOUN = <u>underling</u>, junior, subordinate, lesser, menial, minion

infertility = <u>sterility</u>, barrenness, unproductiveness, infecundity

infiltrate = <u>penetrate</u>, pervade, permeate, percolate, filter through to, make inroads into, sneak into (*informal*), insinuate yourself

infinite 1 = <u>vast</u>, enormous, immense, countless, measureless 2 = <u>limitless</u>, endless, unlimited, eternal, never-ending, boundless, everlasting, inexhaustible ≠ finite

inflame = <u>enrage</u>, stimulate, provoke, excite, anger, arouse, rouse, infuriate ≠ calm

inflamed = <u>swollen</u>, sore, red, hot, infected, fevered

inflate 1 = <u>blow up</u>, pump up, swell, dilate,

distend, bloat, puff up *or* out ≠ deflate
2 = <u>increase</u>, expand, enlarge ≠ diminish
3 = <u>exaggerate</u>, embroider, embellish, enlarge, amplify, overstate, overestimate, overemphasize

inflated = <u>exaggerated</u>, swollen, overblown

inflation = <u>increase</u>, expansion, extension, swelling, escalation, enlargement

inflict = <u>impose</u>, administer, visit, apply, deliver, levy, wreak, mete *or* deal out

influence NOUN **1** = <u>control</u>, power, authority, direction, command, domination, supremacy, mastery, mana (*N.Z.*) **2** = <u>power</u>, authority, pull (*informal*), importance, prestige, clout (*informal*), leverage **3** = <u>spell</u>, hold, power, weight, magic, sway, allure, magnetism
● VERB **1** = <u>affect</u>, have an effect on, have an impact on, control, concern, direct, guide, bear upon **2** = <u>persuade</u>, prompt, urge, induce, entice, coax, incite, instigate

influential 1 = <u>important</u>, powerful, telling, leading, inspiring, potent, authoritative, weighty ≠ unimportant
2 = <u>instrumental</u>, important, significant, crucial

influx = <u>arrival</u>, rush, invasion, incursion, inundation, inrush

inform VERB = <u>tell</u>, advise, notify, instruct, enlighten, communicate to, tip someone off
● PHRASES **inform on someone** = <u>betray</u>, denounce, shop (*slang, chiefly Brit.*), give someone away, incriminate, blow the whistle on (*informal*), grass on (*Brit. slang*), double-cross (*informal*), dob someone in (*Austral. & N.Z. slang*)

informal 1 = <u>natural</u>, relaxed, casual, familiar, unofficial, laid-back, easy-going, colloquial **2** = <u>relaxed</u>, easy, comfortable, simple, natural, casual, cosy, laid-back (*informal*) ≠ formal **3** = <u>casual</u>, comfortable, leisure, everyday, simple **4** = <u>unofficial</u>, irregular ≠ official

information = <u>facts</u>, news, report, message, notice, knowledge, data, intelligence, drum (*Austral. informal*)

informative = <u>instructive</u>, revealing, educational, forthcoming, illuminating, enlightening, chatty, communicative

informed = <u>knowledgeable</u>, up to date, enlightened, learned, expert, familiar, versed, in the picture

infuriate = <u>enrage</u>, anger, provoke, irritate, incense, madden, exasperate, rile ≠ soothe

infuriating = <u>annoying</u>, irritating, provoking, galling, maddening, exasperating, vexatious

ingenious = <u>creative</u>, original, brilliant, clever, bright, shrewd, inventive, crafty ≠ unimaginative

ingredient = <u>component</u>, part, element, feature, piece, unit, item, aspect

inhabit = <u>live in</u>, occupy, populate, reside in, dwell in, abide in

inhabitant = <u>occupant</u>, resident, citizen, local, native, tenant, inmate, dweller

inhabited = <u>populated</u>, peopled, occupied, developed, settled, tenanted, colonized

inhale = <u>breathe in</u>, gasp, draw in, suck in, respire ≠ exhale

inherent = <u>intrinsic</u>, natural, essential, native, fundamental, hereditary, instinctive, innate ≠ extraneous

inherit = <u>be left</u>, come into, be willed, succeed to, fall heir to

inheritance = <u>legacy</u>, heritage, bequest, birthright, patrimony

inhibit 1 = <u>hinder</u>, check, frustrate, curb, restrain, constrain, obstruct, impede ≠ further **2** = <u>prevent</u>, stop, frustrate ≠ allow

inhibited = <u>shy</u>, reserved, guarded, subdued, repressed, constrained, self-conscious, reticent ≠ uninhibited

initial = <u>opening</u>, first, earliest, beginning, primary, maiden, introductory, embryonic ≠ final

initially = <u>at first</u>, first, firstly, originally, primarily, in the beginning, at *or* in the beginning

initiate VERB **1** = <u>begin</u>, start, open, launch, kick off (*informal*), embark on, originate, set about **2** = <u>introduce</u>, admit, enlist, enrol, launch, establish, invest, recruit
● NOUN = <u>novice</u>, member, pupil, convert, amateur, newcomer, beginner, trainee
● PHRASES **initiate someone into something** = <u>instruct in</u>, train in, coach in, acquaint with, drill in, make aware of, teach about, tutor in

initiative 1 = <u>advantage</u>, start, lead, upper hand **2** = <u>enterprise</u>, drive, energy, leadership, ambition, daring, enthusiasm, dynamism

inject 1 = <u>vaccinate</u>, administer, inoculate 2 = <u>introduce</u>, bring in, insert, instil, infuse, breathe

injection 1 = <u>vaccination</u>, shot (*informal*), jab (*informal*), dose, booster, immunization, inoculation 2 = <u>introduction</u>, investment, insertion, advancement, dose, infusion

injunction = <u>order</u>, ruling, command, instruction, mandate, precept, exhortation

injure 1 = <u>hurt</u>, wound, harm, damage, smash, crush, mar, shatter, mangulate (*Austral. slang*) 2 = <u>damage</u>, harm, ruin, wreck, spoil, impair, crool *or* cruel (*Austral. slang*) 3 = <u>undermine</u>, damage

injured 1 = <u>hurt</u>, damaged, wounded, broken, cut, crushed, disabled, weakened, crook (*Austral. & N.Z. slang*)

injury 1 = <u>wound</u>, cut, damage, trauma (*Pathology*), gash, lesion, laceration 2 = <u>harm</u>, suffering, damage, ill, hurt, disability, misfortune, affliction 3 = <u>wrong</u>, offence, insult, detriment, disservice

injustice 1 = <u>unfairness</u>, discrimination, prejudice, bias, inequality, oppression, intolerance, bigotry ≠ justice 2 = <u>wrong</u>, injury, crime, error, offence, sin, misdeed, transgression

inland = <u>interior</u>, internal, upcountry

inner 1 = <u>inside</u>, internal, interior, inward ≠ outer 2 = <u>central</u>, middle, internal, interior 3 = <u>hidden</u>, deep, secret, underlying, obscure, repressed, unrevealed ≠ obvious

innocence 1 = <u>naiveté</u>, simplicity, inexperience, credulity, gullibility, ingenuousness, artlessness, unworldliness ≠ worldliness 2 = <u>blamelessness</u>, clean hands, uprightness, irreproachability, guiltlessness ≠ guilt 3 = <u>chastity</u>, virtue, purity, modesty, celibacy, continence, maidenhood

innocent 1 = <u>not guilty</u>, in the clear, blameless, clean, honest, uninvolved, irreproachable, guiltless ≠ guilty 2 = <u>naive</u>, open, trusting, simple, childlike, gullible, unsophisticated, unworldly ≠ worldly 3 = <u>harmless</u>, innocuous, inoffensive, well-meant, unobjectionable, well-intentioned

innovation 1 = <u>change</u>, revolution, departure, introduction, variation, transformation, upheaval, alteration 2 = <u>newness</u>, novelty, originality, freshness, modernization, uniqueness

inquest = <u>inquiry</u>, investigation, probe, inquisition

inquire *or* **enquire** VERB = <u>ask</u>, question, query, quiz

● PHRASES **inquire into something** = <u>investigate</u>, study, examine, research, explore, look into, probe into, make inquiries into

inquiry *or* **enquiry** 1 = <u>question</u>, query, investigation 2 = <u>investigation</u>, study, review, survey, examination, probe, inspection, exploration 3 = <u>research</u>, investigation, analysis, inspection, exploration, interrogation

insane 1 = <u>mad</u>, crazy, mentally ill, crazed, demented, deranged, out of your mind, off the air (*Austral. slang*), porangi (*N.Z.*) ≠ sane 2 = <u>stupid</u>, foolish, daft (*informal*), irresponsible, irrational, senseless, preposterous, impractical ≠ reasonable

insect = <u>bug</u>, creepy-crawly (*Brit. informal*), gogga (*S. African informal*)

insecure 1 = <u>unconfident</u>, worried, anxious, afraid, shy, uncertain, unsure, timid ≠ confident 2 = <u>unsafe</u>, exposed, vulnerable, wide-open, unprotected, defenceless, unguarded ≠ safe

insecurity = <u>anxiety</u>, fear, worry, uncertainty ≠ confidence

insert = <u>put</u>, place, position, slip, slide, slot, thrust, stick in

inside NOUN = <u>interior</u>, contents, core, nucleus

● PLURAL NOUN (*Informal*) = <u>stomach</u>, guts, belly, bowels, innards (*informal*), entrails, viscera, vitals

● ADJECTIVE 1 = <u>inner</u>, internal, interior, inward ≠ outside 2 = <u>confidential</u>, private, secret, internal, exclusive, restricted, privileged, classified

● ADVERB = <u>indoors</u>, in, within, under cover

insight 1 = <u>understanding</u>, perception, sense, knowledge, vision, judgment, awareness, grasp 2 *with into* = <u>understanding of</u>, perception of, awareness of, experience of, description of, introduction to, observation of, judgment of

insignificant = <u>unimportant</u>, minor, irrelevant, petty, trivial, meaningless, trifling, paltry ≠ important

insist 1 lay down the law, put your foot down (*informal*) 2 = <u>demand</u>, order, require, command, dictate, entreat

3 = assert, state, maintain, claim, declare, repeat, vow, swear

insistence 1 = demand, command, dictate, entreaty, importunity **2** = assertion, claim, statement, declaration, persistence, pronouncement

inspect 1 = examine, check, look at, view, survey, look over, scrutinize, go over *or* through **2** = check, examine, investigate, look at, survey, vet, look over, go over *or* through

inspection 1 = examination, investigation, scrutiny, once-over (*informal*) **2** = check, search, investigation, review, survey, examination, scrutiny, once-over (*informal*)

inspector = examiner, investigator, supervisor, monitor, superintendent, auditor, censor, surveyor

inspiration 1 = imagination, creativity, ingenuity, insight, originality, inventiveness, cleverness **2** = motivation, example, model, boost, spur, incentive, revelation, stimulus ≠ deterrent **3** = influence, spur, stimulus, muse

inspire 1 = motivate, stimulate, encourage, influence, spur, animate, enliven, galvanize ≠ discourage **2** = give rise to, produce, result in, engender

inspired 1 = brilliant, wonderful, impressive, outstanding, thrilling, memorable, dazzling, superlative **2** = stimulated, uplifted, exhilarated, enthused, elated

inspiring = uplifting, exciting, moving, stirring, stimulating, rousing, exhilarating, heartening ≠ uninspiring

instability 1 = uncertainty, insecurity, vulnerability, volatility, unpredictability, fluctuation, impermanence, unsteadiness ≠ stability **2** = imbalance, variability, unpredictability, unsteadiness, changeableness

install 1 = set up, put in, place, position, station, establish, lay, fix **2** = institute, establish, introduce, invest, ordain, inaugurate, induct **3** = settle, position, plant, establish, lodge, ensconce

installation 1 = setting up, fitting, instalment, placing, positioning, establishment **2** = appointment, ordination, inauguration, induction, investiture

instalment 1 = payment, repayment,

part payment **2** = part, section, chapter, episode, portion, division

instance NOUN = example, case, occurrence, occasion, sample, illustration
● VERB = name, mention, identify, point out, advance, quote, refer to, point to

instant NOUN **1** = moment, second, flash, split second, jiffy (*informal*), trice, twinkling of an eye (*informal*) **2** = time, point, hour, moment, stage, occasion, phase, juncture
● ADJECTIVE **1** = immediate, prompt, instantaneous, direct, quick, on-the-spot, split-second **2** = ready-made, fast, convenience, ready-mixed, ready-cooked, precooked

instantly = immediately, at once, straight away, now, directly, right away, instantaneously, this minute

instead ADVERB = rather, alternatively, preferably, in preference, in lieu, on second thoughts
● PHRASES **instead of** = in place of, rather than, in preference to, in lieu of, in contrast with

instinct 1 = natural inclination, talent, tendency, faculty, inclination, knack, predisposition, proclivity **2** = talent, skill, gift, capacity, bent, genius, faculty, knack **3** = intuition, impulse

instinctive = natural, inborn, automatic, unconscious, inherent, spontaneous, reflex, innate ≠ acquired

instinctively = intuitively, naturally, automatically, without thinking, involuntarily, by instinct

institute NOUN = establishment, body, centre, school, university, society, association, college
● VERB = establish, start, found, launch, set up, introduce, fix, organize ≠ end

institution 1 = establishment, body, centre, school, university, society, association, college **2** = custom, practice, tradition, law, rule, procedure, convention, ritual

institutional = conventional, accepted, established, formal, routine, orthodox, procedural

instruct 1 = order, tell, direct, charge, bid, command, mandate, enjoin **2** = teach, school, train, coach, educate, drill, tutor

instruction NOUN **1** = order, ruling, command, rule, demand, regulation, dictate, decree **2** = <u>teaching</u>, schooling, training, grounding, education, coaching, lesson(s), guidance

● PLURAL NOUN = <u>information</u>, rules, advice, directions, recommendations, guidance, specifications

instructor = <u>teacher</u>, coach, guide, adviser, trainer, demonstrator, tutor, mentor

instrument 1 = <u>tool</u>, device, implement, mechanism, appliance, apparatus, gadget, contraption (*informal*) **2** = <u>agent</u>, means, medium, agency, vehicle, mechanism, organ

instrumental = <u>active</u>, involved, influential, useful, helpful, contributory

insufficient = <u>inadequate</u>, scant, meagre, short, sparse, deficient, lacking ≠ ample

insulate = <u>isolate</u>, protect, screen, defend, shelter, shield, cut off, cushion

insult VERB = <u>offend</u>, abuse, wound, slight, put down, snub, malign, affront ≠ praise

● NOUN **1** = <u>jibe</u>, slight, put-down, abuse, snub, barb, affront, abusive remark **2** = <u>offence</u>, slight, snub, slur, affront, slap in the face (*informal*), kick in the teeth (*informal*), insolence

insulting = <u>offensive</u>, rude, abusive, degrading, contemptuous, disparaging, scurrilous, insolent ≠ complimentary

insurance 1 = <u>assurance</u>, cover, security, protection, safeguard, indemnity **2** = <u>protection</u>, security, guarantee, shelter, safeguard, warranty

insure 1 = <u>assure</u>, cover, protect, guarantee, warrant, underwrite, indemnify **2** = <u>protect</u>, cover, safeguard

intact = <u>undamaged</u>, whole, complete, sound, perfect, entire, unscathed, unbroken ≠ damaged

integral = <u>essential</u>, basic, fundamental, necessary, component, constituent, indispensable, intrinsic ≠ inessential

integrate = <u>join</u>, unite, combine, blend, incorporate, merge, fuse, assimilate ≠ separate

integrity 1 = <u>honesty</u>, principle, honour, virtue, goodness, morality, purity, probity ≠ dishonesty **2** = <u>unity</u>, unification, cohesion, coherence, wholeness, soundness, completeness

intellect = <u>intelligence</u>, mind, reason, understanding, sense, brains (*informal*), judgment

intellectual ADJECTIVE = <u>scholarly</u>, learned, academic, lettered, intelligent, cerebral, erudite, scholastic ≠ stupid

● NOUN = <u>academic</u>, expert, genius, thinker, master, mastermind, maestro, highbrow, fundi (*S. African*), acca (*Austral. slang*) ≠ idiot

intelligence 1 = <u>intellect</u>, understanding, brains (*informal*), sense, knowledge, judgment, wit, perception ≠ stupidity **2** = <u>information</u>, news, facts, report, findings, knowledge, data, notification ≠ misinformation

intelligent = <u>clever</u>, bright, smart, sharp, enlightened, knowledgeable, well-informed, brainy (*informal*) ≠ stupid

intend = <u>plan</u>, mean, aim, propose, purpose, have in mind *or* view

intense 1 = <u>extreme</u>, great, severe, fierce, deep, powerful, supreme, acute ≠ mild **2** = <u>fierce</u>, tough **3** = <u>passionate</u>, emotional, fierce, heightened, ardent, fanatical, fervent, heartfelt ≠ indifferent

intensify 1 = <u>increase</u>, raise, add to, strengthen, reinforce, widen, heighten, sharpen ≠ decrease **2** = <u>escalate</u>, increase, widen, deepen

intensity 1 = <u>force</u>, strength, fierceness **2** = <u>passion</u>, emotion, fervour, force, strength, fanaticism, ardour, vehemence

intensive = <u>concentrated</u>, thorough, exhaustive, full, demanding, detailed, complete, serious

intent ADJECTIVE = <u>absorbed</u>, intense, fascinated, preoccupied, enthralled, attentive, watchful, engrossed ≠ indifferent

● NOUN = <u>intention</u>, aim, purpose, meaning, end, plan, goal, design ≠ chance

intention = <u>aim</u>, plan, idea, goal, end, design, target, wish

inter = <u>bury</u>, lay to rest, entomb, consign to the grave

intercept = <u>catch</u>, stop, block, seize, cut off, interrupt, head off, obstruct

intercourse 1 = <u>sexual intercourse</u>, sex (*informal*), copulation, coitus, carnal knowledge **2** = <u>contact</u>, communication, commerce, dealings

interest NOUN **1** *often plural* = <u>hobby</u>, activity, pursuit, entertainment, recreation, amusement, preoccupation, diversion **2** *often plural* = <u>advantage</u>, good, benefit, profit **3** = <u>stake</u>, investment

● **VERB** = <u>arouse your curiosity</u>, fascinate, attract, grip, entertain, intrigue, divert, captivate ≠ bore

interested 1 = <u>curious</u>, attracted, excited, drawn, keen, gripped, fascinated, captivated ≠ uninterested 2 = <u>involved</u>, concerned, affected, implicated

interesting = <u>intriguing</u>, absorbing, appealing, attractive, engaging, gripping, entrancing, stimulating ≠ uninteresting

interface = <u>connection</u>, link, boundary, border, frontier

interfere **VERB** = <u>meddle</u>, intervene, intrude, butt in, tamper, pry, encroach, stick your oar in (*informal*)

● **PHRASES interfere with something** **or someone** = <u>conflict with</u>, check, clash, handicap, hamper, disrupt, inhibit, thwart

interference = <u>intrusion</u>, intervention, meddling, opposition, conflict, obstruction, prying

interim = <u>temporary</u>, provisional, makeshift, acting, caretaker, improvised, stopgap

interior **NOUN** = <u>inside</u>, centre, heart, middle, depths, core, nucleus

● **ADJECTIVE** 1 = <u>inside</u>, internal, inner ≠ exterior 2 = <u>mental</u>, emotional, psychological, private, personal, secret, hidden, spiritual

intermediary = <u>mediator</u>, agent, middleman, broker, go-between

intermediate = <u>middle</u>, mid, halfway, in-between (*informal*), midway, intervening, transitional, median

internal 1 = <u>domestic</u>, home, national, local, civic, in-house, intramural 2 = <u>inner</u>, inside, interior ≠ external

international = <u>global</u>, world, worldwide, universal, cosmopolitan, intercontinental

Internet

● **PHRASES the Internet** = <u>the information superhighway</u>, the net (*informal*), the web (*informal*), the World Wide Web, cyberspace

interpret 1 = <u>take</u>, understand, explain, construe 2 = <u>translate</u>, transliterate 3 = <u>explain</u>, make sense of, decode, decipher, elucidate 4 = <u>understand</u>, read, crack, solve, figure out (*informal*), comprehend, decode, deduce 5 = <u>portray</u>, present, perform, render, depict, enact, act out

interpretation 1 = <u>explanation</u>, analysis, exposition, elucidation 2 = <u>performance</u>, portrayal, presentation, reading, rendition 3 = <u>reading</u>, study, review, version, analysis, explanation, examination, evaluation

interpreter = <u>translator</u>

interrogation = <u>questioning</u>, inquiry, examination, grilling (*informal*), cross-examination, inquisition, third degree (*informal*)

interrupt 1 = <u>intrude</u>, disturb, intervene, interfere (with), break in, heckle, butt in, barge in (*informal*) 2 = <u>suspend</u>, stop, end, delay, cease, postpone, shelve, put off

interruption 1 = <u>disruption</u>, break, disturbance, hitch, intrusion 2 = <u>stoppage</u>, pause, suspension

interval 1 = <u>period</u>, spell, space, stretch, pause, span 2 = <u>break</u>, interlude, intermission, rest, gap, pause, respite, lull 3 = <u>delay</u>, gap, hold-up, stoppage 4 = <u>stretch</u>, space

intervene 1 = <u>step in</u> (*informal*), interfere, mediate, intrude, intercede, arbitrate, take a hand (*informal*) 2 = <u>interrupt</u>, involve yourself 3 = <u>happen</u>, occur, take place, follow, arise, ensue, befall, materialize

intervention = <u>mediation</u>, interference, intrusion, arbitration, conciliation, agency

interview **NOUN** 1 = <u>meeting</u> 2 = <u>audience</u>, talk, conference, exchange, dialogue, consultation, press conference

● **VERB** 1 = <u>examine</u>, talk to 2 = <u>question</u>, interrogate, examine, investigate, pump, grill (*informal*), quiz, cross-examine

interviewer = <u>questioner</u>, reporter, investigator, examiner, interrogator

intimacy = <u>familiarity</u>, closeness, confidentiality ≠ aloofness

intimate¹ **ADJECTIVE** 1 = <u>close</u>, dear, loving, near, familiar, thick (*informal*), devoted, confidential ≠ distant 2 = <u>private</u>, personal, confidential, special, individual, secret, exclusive ≠ public 3 = <u>detailed</u>, minute, full, deep, particular, immediate, comprehensive, profound 4 = <u>cosy</u>, relaxed, friendly, informal, harmonious, snug, comfy (*informal*), warm

● **NOUN** = <u>friend</u>, close friend, crony, cobber (*Austral. & N.Z. old-fashioned informal*), confidant *or* confidante, (constant) companion (*N.Z.*) ≠ stranger

intimate² 1 = <u>suggest</u>, indicate, hint, imply, insinuate 2 = <u>announce</u>, state, declare, communicate, make known

intimately 1 = <u>closely</u>, personally, warmly, familiarly, tenderly, affectionately, confidentially, confidingly **2** = <u>fully</u>, very well, thoroughly, in detail, inside out

intimidate = <u>frighten</u>, pressure, threaten, scare, bully, plague, hound, daunt

intimidation = <u>bullying</u>, pressure, threat(s), menaces, coercion, arm-twisting (*informal*), browbeating, terrorization

intricate = <u>complicated</u>, involved, complex, fancy, elaborate, tangled, tortuous, convoluted ≠ simple

intrigue NOUN **1** = <u>plot</u>, scheme, conspiracy, manoeuvre, collusion, stratagem, chicanery, wile **2** = <u>affair</u>, romance, intimacy, liaison, amour
● VERB **1** = <u>interest</u>, fascinate, attract, rivet, titillate **2** = <u>plot</u>, scheme, manoeuvre, conspire, connive, machinate

intriguing = <u>interesting</u>, fascinating, absorbing, exciting, engaging, gripping, stimulating, compelling

introduce 1 = <u>bring in</u>, establish, set up, start, found, launch, institute, pioneer **2** = <u>present</u>, acquaint, make known, familiarize **3** = <u>suggest</u>, air, advance, submit, bring up, put forward, broach, moot **4** = <u>add</u>, insert, inject, throw in (*informal*), infuse

introduction 1 = <u>launch</u>, institution, pioneering, inauguration ≠ elimination **2** = <u>opening</u>, prelude, preface, lead-in, preamble, foreword, prologue, intro (*informal*) ≠ conclusion

introductory 1 = <u>preliminary</u>, first, initial, inaugural, preparatory ≠ concluding **2** = <u>starting</u>, opening, initial

intruder = <u>trespasser</u>, invader, prowler, interloper, infiltrator, gate-crasher (*informal*)

intrusion 1 = <u>interruption</u>, interference, infringement, trespass, encroachment **2** = <u>invasion</u>, breach, infringement, encroachment, infraction, usurpation

intuition 1 = <u>instinct</u>, perception, insight, sixth sense **2** = <u>feeling</u>, idea, impression, suspicion, premonition, inkling, presentiment

invade 1 = <u>attack</u>, storm, assault, capture, occupy, seize, raid, overwhelm **2** = <u>infest</u>, swarm, overrun, ravage, beset, pervade, permeate

invader = <u>attacker</u>, raider, plunderer, aggressor, trespasser

invalid¹ NOUN = <u>patient</u>, sufferer, convalescent, valetudinarian
● ADJECTIVE = <u>disabled</u>, ill, sick, ailing, frail, infirm, bedridden

invalid² 1 = <u>null and void</u>, void, worthless, inoperative ≠ valid **2** = <u>unfounded</u>, false, illogical, irrational, unsound, fallacious ≠ sound

invaluable = <u>precious</u>, valuable, priceless, inestimable, worth your *or* its weight in gold ≠ worthless

invariably = <u>always</u>, regularly, constantly, repeatedly, consistently, continually, eternally, habitually

invasion 1 = <u>attack</u>, assault, capture, takeover, raid, offensive, occupation, conquering **2** = <u>intrusion</u>, breach, violation, disturbance, disruption, infringement, encroachment, infraction

invent 1 = <u>create</u>, make, produce, design, discover, manufacture, devise, conceive **2** = <u>make up</u>, devise, concoct, forge, fake, fabricate, feign, falsify

invention 1 = <u>creation</u>, machine, device, design, instrument, discovery, innovation, gadget **2** = <u>development</u>, design, production, setting up, foundation, construction, creation, discovery **3** = <u>fiction</u>, fantasy, lie, yarn, fabrication, falsehood, untruth **4** = <u>creativity</u>, imagination, initiative, enterprise, genius, ingenuity, originality, inventiveness

inventive = <u>creative</u>, original, innovative, imaginative, inspired, fertile, ingenious, resourceful ≠ uninspired

inventor = <u>creator</u>, maker, author, designer, architect, coiner, originator

inventory = <u>list</u>, record, catalogue, listing, account, roll, file, register

invest VERB **1** = <u>spend</u>, expend, advance, venture, put in, devote, lay out, sink in **2** = <u>empower</u>, provide, charge, sanction, license, authorize, vest
● PHRASES **invest in something** = <u>buy</u>, get, purchase, pay for, obtain, acquire, procure

investigate = <u>examine</u>, study, research, go into, explore, look into, inspect, probe into

investigation = <u>examination</u>, study, inquiry, review, search, survey, probe, inspection

investigator = <u>examiner</u>, researcher,

monitor, detective, analyser, explorer, scrutinizer, inquirer

investment 1 = <u>investing</u>, backing, funding, financing, contribution, speculation, transaction, expenditure **2** = <u>stake</u>, interest, share, concern, portion, ante (*informal*) **3** = <u>buy</u>, asset, acquisition, venture, risk, gamble

invisible = <u>unseen</u>, imperceptible, indiscernible, unseeable ≠ visible

invitation = <u>request</u>, call, invite (*informal*), summons

invite 1 = <u>ask</u> **2** = <u>request</u>, look for, bid for, appeal for **3** = <u>encourage</u>, attract, cause, court, ask for (*informal*), generate, foster, tempt

inviting = <u>tempting</u>, appealing, attractive, welcoming, enticing, seductive, alluring, mouthwatering ≠ uninviting

invoke 1 = <u>apply</u>, use, implement, initiate, resort to, put into effect **2** = <u>call upon</u>, appeal to, pray to, petition, beseech, entreat, supplicate

involve 1 = <u>entail</u>, mean, require, occasion, imply, give rise to, necessitate **2** = <u>concern</u>, draw in, bear on

involved = <u>complicated</u>, complex, intricate, hard, confused, confusing, elaborate, tangled ≠ straightforward

involvement = <u>connection</u>, interest, association, commitment, attachment

inward 1 = <u>incoming</u>, entering, inbound, ingoing **2** = <u>internal</u>, inner, private, personal, inside, secret, hidden, interior ≠ outward

Ireland = <u>Hibernia</u> (*Latin*)

iron ADJECTIVE **1** = <u>ferrous</u>, ferric **2** = <u>inflexible</u>, hard, strong, tough, rigid, adamant, unconditional, steely ≠ weak ● PHRASES **iron something out** = <u>settle</u>, resolve, sort out, get rid of, reconcile, clear up, put right, straighten out

RELATED WORDS
adjectives: ferric, ferrous

ironic *or* **ironical 1** = <u>sarcastic</u>, dry, acid, bitter, mocking, wry, satirical, tongue-in-cheek **2** = <u>paradoxical</u>, contradictory, puzzling, baffling, confounding, enigmatic, incongruous

irony 1 = <u>sarcasm</u>, mockery, ridicule, satire, cynicism, derision **2** = <u>paradox</u>, incongruity

irrational = <u>illogical</u>, crazy, absurd, unreasonable, preposterous, nonsensical

≠ rational

irregular 1 = <u>variable</u>, erratic, occasional, random, casual, shaky, sporadic, haphazard ≠ steady **2** = <u>uneven</u>, rough, ragged, crooked, jagged, bumpy, contorted, lopsided ≠ even **3** = <u>inappropriate</u>, unconventional, unethical, unusual, extraordinary, exceptional, peculiar, unofficial **4** = <u>unofficial</u>, underground, guerrilla, resistance, partisan, rogue, paramilitary, mercenary

irrelevant = <u>unconnected</u>, unrelated, unimportant, inappropriate, peripheral, immaterial, extraneous, beside the point ≠ relevant

irresistible = <u>overwhelming</u>, compelling, overpowering, urgent, compulsive

irresponsible = <u>thoughtless</u>, reckless, careless, unreliable, untrustworthy, shiftless, scatterbrained ≠ responsible

irritate 1 = <u>annoy</u>, anger, bother, needle (*informal*), infuriate, exasperate, nettle, irk ≠ placate **2** = <u>inflame</u>, pain, rub, scratch, scrape, chafe

irritated = <u>annoyed</u>, cross, angry, bothered, put out, exasperated, nettled, vexed, tooshie (*Austral. slang*), hoha (*N.Z.*)

irritating = <u>annoying</u>, trying, infuriating, disturbing, nagging, troublesome, maddening, irksome ≠ pleasing

irritation 1 = <u>annoyance</u>, anger, fury, resentment, gall, indignation, displeasure, exasperation ≠ pleasure **2** = <u>nuisance</u>, irritant, drag (*informal*), pain in the neck (*informal*), thorn in your flesh

island = <u>isle</u>, atoll, islet, ait *or* eyot (*dialect*), cay *or* key

RELATED WORD
adjective: insular

isolate 1 = <u>separate</u>, break up, cut off, detach, split up, insulate, segregate, disconnect **2** = <u>quarantine</u>

isolated = <u>remote</u>, far, distant, lonely, out-of-the-way, hidden, secluded, inaccessible

isolation = <u>separation</u>, segregation, detachment, solitude, seclusion, remoteness

issue NOUN **1** = <u>topic</u>, point, matter, problem, question, subject, theme **2** = <u>point</u>, question, bone of contention **3** = <u>edition</u>, printing, copy, publication, number, version **4** = <u>children</u>, offspring, babies, kids (*informal*), heirs, descendants,

progeny ≠ parent

● VERB = <u>give out</u>, release, publish, announce, deliver, spread, broadcast, distribute

● PHRASES **take issue with something** or **someone** = <u>disagree with</u>, question, challenge, oppose, dispute, object to, argue with, take exception to

itch VERB 1 = <u>prickle</u>, tickle, tingle 2 = <u>long</u>, ache, crave, pine, hunger, lust, yearn, hanker

● NOUN 1 = <u>irritation</u>, tingling, prickling, itchiness 2 = <u>desire</u>, longing, craving, passion, yen (*informal*), hunger, lust, yearning

item 1 = <u>article</u>, thing, object, piece, unit, component 2 = <u>matter</u>, point, issue, case, question, concern, detail, subject 3 = <u>report</u>, story, piece, account, note, feature, notice, article

itinerary = <u>schedule</u>, programme, route, timetable

j

jab VERB = <u>poke</u>, dig, punch, thrust, tap, stab, nudge, prod

● NOUN = <u>poke</u>, dig, punch, thrust, tap, stab, nudge, prod

jacket = <u>covering</u>, casing, case, cover, skin, shell, coat, wrapping

jackpot = <u>prize</u>, winnings, award, reward, bonanza

jail NOUN = <u>prison</u>, penitentiary (*U.S.*), confinement, dungeon, nick (*Brit. slang*), slammer (*slang*), reformatory, boob (*Austral. slang*)

● VERB = <u>imprison</u>, confine, detain, lock up, put away, intern, incarcerate, send down

jam NOUN 1 = <u>predicament</u>, tight spot, situation, trouble, hole (*slang*), fix (*informal*), mess, pinch

● VERB 1 = <u>pack</u>, force, press, stuff, squeeze, ram, wedge, cram 2 = <u>crowd</u>, throng, crush, mass, surge, flock, swarm,

congregate 3 = <u>congest</u>, block, clog, stick, stall, obstruct

jar¹ = <u>pot</u>, container, drum, vase, jug, pitcher, urn, crock

jar² 1 *usually with on* = <u>irritate</u>, annoy, offend, nettle, irk, grate on, get on your nerves (*informal*) 2 = <u>jolt</u>, rock, shake, bump, rattle, vibrate, convulse

jargon = <u>parlance</u>, idiom, usage, argot

jaw PLURAL NOUN = <u>opening</u>, entrance, mouth

● VERB (*Informal*) = <u>talk</u>, chat, gossip, chatter, spout, natter

jealous 1 = <u>suspicious</u>, protective, wary, doubtful, sceptical, vigilant, watchful, possessive 2 = <u>envious</u>, grudging, resentful, green, green with envy, desirous, covetous ≠ satisfied

jealousy = <u>suspicion</u>, mistrust, possessiveness, doubt, spite, resentment, wariness, dubiety

jeer VERB = <u>mock</u>, deride, heckle, barrack, ridicule, taunt, scoff, gibe ≠ cheer

● NOUN = <u>mockery</u>, abuse, ridicule, taunt, boo, derision, gibe, catcall ≠ applause

jeopardy = <u>danger</u>, risk, peril, vulnerability, insecurity

jerk VERB = <u>jolt</u>, bang, bump, lurch

● NOUN = <u>lurch</u>, movement, thrust, twitch, jolt

jet NOUN = <u>stream</u>, current, spring, flow, rush, flood, burst, spray

● VERB = <u>fly</u>, wing, cruise, soar, zoom

jewel 1 = <u>gemstone</u>, gem, ornament, sparkler (*informal*), rock (*slang*) 2 = <u>treasure</u>, wonder, darling, pearl, gem, paragon, pride and joy, taonga (*N.Z.*)

jewellery = <u>jewels</u>, treasure, gems, trinkets, ornaments, finery, regalia

job 1 = <u>position</u>, work, calling, business, field, career, employment, profession 2 = <u>task</u>, duty, work, venture, enterprise, undertaking, assignment, chore

jobless = <u>unemployed</u>, redundant, out of work, inactive, unoccupied, idle

jog 1 = <u>run</u>, trot, canter, lope 2 = <u>nudge</u>, push, shake, prod 3 = <u>stimulate</u>, stir, prod

join 1 = <u>enrol in</u>, enter, sign up for, enlist in 2 = <u>connect</u>, unite, couple, link, combine, attach, fasten, add ≠ detach

joint ADJECTIVE = <u>shared</u>, mutual, collective, communal, united, joined, allied, combined

● NOUN = <u>junction</u>, connection, brace,

bracket, hinge, intersection, node, nexus

jointly = <u>collectively</u>, together, in conjunction, as one, in common, mutually, in partnership, in league ≠ separately

joke NOUN 1 = <u>jest</u>, gag (informal), wisecrack (informal), witticism, crack (informal), quip, pun, one-liner (informal) 2 = <u>laugh</u>, jest, jape 3 = <u>prank</u>, trick, practical joke, lark (informal), escapade, jape 4 = <u>laughing stock</u>, clown, buffoon
● VERB = <u>jest</u>, kid (informal), mock, tease, taunt, quip, banter, play the fool

joker = <u>comedian</u>, comic, wit, clown, wag, jester, prankster, buffoon

jolly = <u>happy</u>, cheerful, merry, upbeat (informal), playful, cheery, genial, chirpy (informal) ≠ miserable

jolt VERB 1 = <u>jerk</u>, push, shake, knock, jar, shove, jog, jostle 2 = <u>surprise</u>, stun, disturb, stagger, startle, perturb, discompose
● NOUN 1 = <u>jerk</u>, start, jump, shake, bump, jar, jog, lurch 2 = <u>surprise</u>, blow, shock, setback, bombshell, bolt from the blue

journal 1 = <u>magazine</u>, publication, gazette, periodical 2 = <u>newspaper</u>, paper, daily, weekly, monthly 3 = <u>diary</u>, record, history, log, notebook, chronicle, annals, yearbook

journalist = <u>reporter</u>, writer, correspondent, newsman or newswoman, commentator, broadcaster, hack (derogatory), columnist

journey NOUN 1 = <u>trip</u>, drive, tour, flight, excursion, trek, expedition, voyage 2 = <u>progress</u>, voyage, pilgrimage, odyssey
● VERB = <u>travel</u>, go, move, tour, progress, proceed, wander, trek, go walkabout (Austral.)

joy = <u>delight</u>, pleasure, satisfaction, ecstasy, enjoyment, bliss, glee, rapture ≠ sorrow

jubilee = <u>celebration</u>, holiday, festival, festivity

judge NOUN 1 = <u>magistrate</u>, justice, beak (Brit. slang), His, Her or Your Honour 2 = <u>referee</u>, expert, specialist, umpire, mediator, examiner, connoisseur, assessor 3 = <u>critic</u>, assessor, arbiter
● VERB 1 = <u>adjudicate</u>, referee, umpire, mediate, officiate, arbitrate 2 = <u>evaluate</u>, rate, consider, view, value, esteem 3 = <u>estimate</u>, guess, assess, calculate, evaluate, gauge

■ **RELATED WORD**
adjective: judicial

judgment 1 = <u>opinion</u>, view, estimate, belief, assessment, diagnosis, valuation, appraisal 2 = <u>verdict</u>, finding, ruling, decision, sentence, decree, arbitration, adjudication 3 = <u>sense</u>, good sense, understanding, discrimination, perception, wisdom, wit, prudence

judicial = <u>legal</u>, official

jug = <u>container</u>, pitcher, urn, carafe, creamer (U.S. & Canad.), vessel, jar, crock

juggle = <u>manipulate</u>, change, alter, modify, manoeuvre

juice 1 = <u>liquid</u>, extract, fluid, liquor, sap, nectar 2 = <u>secretion</u>

juicy 1 = <u>moist</u>, lush, succulent 2 (Informal) = <u>interesting</u>, colourful, sensational, vivid, provocative, spicy (informal), suggestive, racy

jumble NOUN = <u>muddle</u>, mixture, mess, disorder, confusion, clutter, disarray, mishmash
● VERB = <u>mix</u>, mistake, confuse, disorder, shuffle, muddle, disorganize

jumbo = <u>giant</u>, large, huge, immense, gigantic, oversized ≠ tiny

jump VERB 1 = <u>leap</u>, spring, bound, bounce, hop, skip 2 = <u>vault</u>, hurdle, go over, sail over, hop over 3 = <u>spring</u>, bound, bounce 4 = <u>recoil</u>, start, jolt, flinch, shake, jerk, quake, shudder 5 = <u>increase</u>, rise, climb, escalate, advance, soar, surge, spiral 6 = <u>miss</u>, avoid, skip, omit, evade
● NOUN 1 = <u>leap</u>, spring, skip, bound, hop, vault 2 = <u>rise</u>, increase, upswing, advance, upsurge, upturn, increment

jumped-up = <u>conceited</u>, arrogant, pompous, overbearing, presumptuous, insolent

jumper = <u>sweater</u>, top, jersey, cardigan, woolly, pullover

junior 1 = <u>minor</u>, lower, secondary, lesser, subordinate, inferior 2 = <u>younger</u> ≠ senior

junk = <u>rubbish</u>, refuse, waste, scrap, litter, debris, garbage (chiefly U.S.), trash

jurisdiction 1 = <u>authority</u>, power, control, rule, influence, command, mana (N.Z.) 2 = <u>range</u>, area, field, bounds, province, scope, sphere, compass

just ADVERB 1 = <u>recently</u>, lately, only now 2 = <u>merely</u>, only, simply, solely 3 = <u>barely</u>, hardly, by a whisker, by the skin of your teeth **4** = <u>exactly</u>, really, quite, completely, totally, perfectly, entirely, truly

● ADJECTIVE **1** = <u>fair</u>, good, legitimate, upright, honest, equitable, conscientious, virtuous ≠ unfair **2** = <u>fitting</u>, due, correct, deserved, appropriate, justified, decent, merited ≠ inappropriate

justice 1 = <u>fairness</u>, equity, integrity, honesty, decency, rightfulness, right ≠ injustice **2** = <u>justness</u>, fairness, legitimacy, right, integrity, honesty, legality, rightfulness **3** = <u>judge</u>, magistrate, beak (*Brit. slang*), His, Her or Your Honour

justification = <u>reason</u>, grounds, defence, basis, excuse, warrant, rationale, vindication

justify = <u>explain</u>, support, warrant, defend, excuse, uphold, vindicate, exonerate

juvenile NOUN = <u>child</u>, youth, minor, girl, boy, teenager, infant, adolescent ≠ adult

● ADJECTIVE **1** = <u>young</u>, junior, adolescent, youthful, immature ≠ adult **2** = <u>immature</u>, childish, infantile, puerile, young, youthful, inexperienced, callow

k

kai (*N.Z. informal*) = <u>food</u>, grub (*slang*), provisions, fare, tucker (*Austral. & N.Z. informal*), refreshment, foodstuffs

kak (*S. African taboo*) **1** = <u>faeces</u>, excrement, manure, dung, droppings, waste matter **2** = <u>rubbish</u>, nonsense, garbage (*informal*), rot, drivel, tripe (*informal*), bizzo (*Austral. slang*), bull's wool (*Austral. & N.Z. slang*)

keen 1 = <u>eager</u>, intense, enthusiastic, passionate, ardent, avid, fervent, impassioned ≠ unenthusiastic **2** = <u>earnest</u>, fierce, intense, vehement, passionate, heightened, ardent, fanatical **3** = <u>sharp</u>, incisive, cutting, edged, razor-like ≠ dull **4** = <u>perceptive</u>, quick, sharp, acute, smart, wise, clever, shrewd ≠ obtuse **5** = <u>intense</u>,

strong, fierce, relentless, cut-throat

keep[1] VERB **1** *usually with from* = <u>prevent</u>, restrain, hinder, keep back **2** = <u>hold on to</u>, maintain, retain, save, preserve, nurture, cherish, conserve ≠ lose **3** = <u>store</u>, put, place, house, hold, deposit, stack, stow **4** = <u>carry</u>, stock, sell, supply, handle **5** = <u>support</u>, maintain, sustain, provide for, mind, fund, finance, feed **6** = <u>raise</u>, own, maintain, tend, farm, breed, look after, rear **7** = <u>manage</u>, run, administer, be in charge (of), direct, handle, supervise **8** = <u>delay</u>, detain, hinder, impede, obstruct, set back ≠ release

● NOUN = <u>board</u>, food, maintenance, living, kai (*N.Z. informal*)

● PHRASES **keep something up 1** = <u>continue</u>, make, maintain, carry on, persist in, persevere with **2** = <u>maintain</u>, sustain, perpetuate, retain, preserve, prolong ◆ **keep up** = <u>keep pace</u>

keep[2] = <u>tower</u>, castle

keeper = <u>curator</u>, guardian, steward, attendant, caretaker, preserver

keeping NOUN = <u>care</u>, charge, protection, possession, custody, guardianship, safekeeping

● PHRASES **in keeping with** = <u>in agreement with</u>, in harmony with, in accord with, in compliance with, in conformity with, in balance with, in correspondence with, in proportion with

key NOUN **1** = <u>opener</u>, door key, latchkey **2** = <u>answer</u>

● ADJECTIVE = <u>essential</u>, leading, major, main, important, necessary, vital, crucial ≠ minor

kia ora (*N.Z.*) = <u>hello</u>, hi (*informal*), greetings, gidday or g'day (*Austral. & N.Z.*), how do you do?, good morning, good evening, good afternoon

kick VERB **1** = <u>boot</u>, knock, punt **2** (*Informal*) = <u>give up</u>, break, stop, abandon, quit, cease, eschew, leave off

● NOUN (*Informal*) = <u>thrill</u>, buzz (*slang*), tingle, high (*slang*)

● PHRASES **kick off** (*Informal*) = <u>begin</u>, start, open, commence, initiate, get on the road ◆ **kick someone out** (*Informal*) = <u>dismiss</u>, remove, get rid of, expel, eject, evict, sack (*informal*)

kid[1] (*Informal*) = <u>child</u>, baby, teenager, youngster, infant, adolescent, juvenile, toddler, littlie (*Austral. informal*), ankle-biter (*Austral. slang*), tacker (*Austral. slang*)

kid² = tease, joke, trick, fool, pretend, wind up (*Brit. slang*), hoax, delude

kidnap = abduct, capture, seize, snatch (*slang*), hijack, hold to ransom

kill 1 = slay, murder, execute, slaughter, destroy, massacre, butcher, cut down **2** (*Informal*) = destroy, crush, scotch, stop, halt, wreck, shatter, suppress

killer = murderer, slayer, hit man (*slang*), butcher, gunman, assassin, terminator, executioner

killing NOUN = murder, massacre, slaughter, dispatch, manslaughter, elimination, slaying, homicide
● ADJECTIVE (*Informal*) = tiring, taxing, exhausting, punishing, fatiguing, gruelling, sapping, debilitating
● PHRASES **make a killing** (*Informal*) = profit, gain, clean up (*informal*), be lucky, be successful, make a fortune, strike it rich (*informal*), make a bomb (*slang*)

kind¹ 1 = class, sort, type, variety, brand, category, genre **2** = sort, set, type, family, species, breed

kind² = considerate, kindly, concerned, friendly, generous, obliging, charitable, benign ≠ unkind

kindly ADJECTIVE = benevolent, kind, caring, warm, helpful, pleasant, sympathetic, benign ≠ cruel
● ADVERB = benevolently, politely, generously, thoughtfully, tenderly, lovingly, cordially, affectionately ≠ unkindly

kindness = goodwill, understanding, charity, humanity, compassion, generosity, philanthropy, benevolence ≠ malice

king = ruler, monarch, sovereign, leader, lord, Crown, emperor, head of state

kingdom = country, state, nation, territory, realm

kiss VERB **1** = peck (*informal*), osculate, neck (*informal*) **2** = brush, touch, shave, scrape, graze, glance off, stroke
● NOUN = peck (*informal*), snog (*Brit. slang*), smacker (*slang*), French kiss, osculation

kit NOUN **1** = equipment, materials, tackle, tools, apparatus, paraphernalia **2** = gear, things, stuff, equipment, uniform
● PHRASES **kit something** or **someone out** or **up** = equip, fit, supply, provide with, arm, stock, costume, furnish

knack = skill, art, ability, facility, talent, gift, capacity, trick ≠ ineptitude

kneel = genuflect, stoop

knickers = underwear, smalls, briefs, drawers, panties, bloomers

knife NOUN = blade, carver, cutter
● VERB = cut, wound, stab, slash, thrust, pierce, spear, jab

knit 1 = join, unite, link, tie, bond, combine, bind, weave **2** = heal, unite, join, link, bind, fasten, intertwine **3** = furrow, tighten, knot, wrinkle, crease, screw up, pucker, scrunch up

knob = ball, stud, knot, lump, bump, projection, hump, protrusion

knock VERB **1** = bang, strike, tap, rap, thump, pummel **2** = hit, strike, punch, belt (*informal*), smack, thump, cuff **3** (*Informal*) = criticize, condemn, put down, run down, abuse, slate (*informal*), censure, denigrate
● NOUN **1** = knocking, pounding, beating, tap, bang, banging, rap, thump **2** = bang, blow, impact, jar, collision, jolt, smash **3** = blow, hit, punch, crack, clip, slap, bash, smack **4** (*Informal*) = setback, check, defeat, blow, reverse, disappointment, hold-up, hitch
● PHRASES **knock about** or **around** = wander, travel, roam, rove, range, drift, stray, ramble, go walkabout (*Austral.*)
◆ **knock about** or **around with someone** = mix with, associate with, mingle with, consort with, hobnob with, socialize with, accompany ◆ **knock off** (*Informal*) = stop work, get out, call it a day (*informal*), finish work, clock off, clock out ◆ **knock someone about** or **around** = hit, attack, beat, strike, abuse, injure, assault, batter ◆ **knock someone down** = run over, hit, run down, knock over, mow down ◆ **knock something down** = demolish, destroy, flatten, tear down, level, fell, dismantle, bulldoze
◆ **knock something off** (*Slang*) = steal, take, nick (*slang, chiefly Brit.*), thieve, rob, pinch

knockout 1 = killer blow, coup de grâce (*French*), KO or K.O. (*slang*) **2** (*Informal*) = success, hit, winner, triumph, smash, sensation, smash hit ≠ failure

knot NOUN = connection, tie, bond, joint, loop, ligature
● VERB = tie, secure, bind, loop, tether

know 1 = have knowledge of, see,

understand, recognize, perceive, be aware of, be conscious of **2** = be acquainted with, recognize, be familiar with, be friends with, be friendly with, have knowledge of, have dealings with, socialize with ≠ be unfamiliar with **3** *sometimes with* **about** *or of* = be familiar with, understand, comprehend, have knowledge of, be acquainted with, feel certain of, have dealings in, be versed in ≠ be ignorant of

know-how (*Informal*) = expertise, ability, skill, knowledge, facility, talent, command, capability

knowing = meaningful, significant, expressive, enigmatic, suggestive

knowledge 1 = understanding, sense, judgment, perception, awareness, insight, grasp, appreciation **2** = learning, education, intelligence, instruction, wisdom, scholarship, enlightenment, erudition ≠ ignorance **3** = acquaintance, intimacy, familiarity ≠ unfamiliarity

knowledgeable 1 = well-informed, conversant, au fait (*French*), experienced, aware, familiar, in the know (*informal*), cognizant **2** = intelligent, learned, educated, scholarly, erudite

known = famous, well-known, celebrated, noted, acknowledged, recognized, avowed ≠ unknown

kopje *or* **koppie** (*S. African*) = hill, down (*archaic*), fell, mount, hilltop, knoll, hillock, brae (*Scot.*)

label NOUN = tag, ticket, tab, marker, sticker
● VERB = tag, mark, stamp, ticket, tab
labour NOUN **1** = workers, employees, workforce, labourers, hands **2** = work, effort, employment, toil, industry **3** = childbirth, birth, delivery, parturition

● VERB **1** = work, toil, strive, work hard, sweat (*informal*), slave, endeavour, slog away (*informal*) ≠ rest **2** = struggle, work, strain, work hard, strive, grapple, toil, make an effort **3** = overemphasize, stress, elaborate, exaggerate, strain, dwell on, overdo, go on about **4** *usually with* **under** = be disadvantaged by, suffer from, be a victim of, be burdened by

Labour = left-wing, Democrat (*U.S.*)
laboured = difficult, forced, strained, heavy, awkward
labourer = worker, manual worker, hand, blue-collar worker, drudge, navvy (*Brit. informal*)

lace NOUN **1** = netting, net, filigree, meshwork, openwork **2** = cord, tie, string, lacing, shoelace, bootlace
● VERB **1** = fasten, tie, tie up, do up, secure, bind, thread **2** = mix, drug, doctor, add to, spike, contaminate, fortify, adulterate **3** = intertwine, interweave, entwine, twine, interlink

lack NOUN = shortage, want, absence, deficiency, need, inadequacy, scarcity, dearth ≠ abundance
● VERB = miss, want, need, require, not have, be without, be short of, be in need of ≠ have

lad = boy, kid (*informal*), guy (*informal*), youth, fellow, youngster, juvenile, nipper (*informal*)

laden = loaded, burdened, full, charged, weighed down, encumbered

lady 1 = gentlewoman, duchess, noble, dame, baroness, countess, aristocrat, viscountess **2** = woman, female, girl, damsel, charlie (*Austral. slang*), chook (*Austral. slang*), wahine (*N.Z.*)

lag = hang back, delay, trail, linger, loiter, straggle, dawdle, tarry

laid-back = relaxed, calm, casual, easy-going, unflappable (*informal*), unhurried, free and easy ≠ tense

lake = pond, pool, reservoir, loch (*Scot.*), lagoon, mere, lough (*Irish*), tarn

lame 1 = disabled, handicapped, crippled, limping, hobbling, game **2** = unconvincing, poor, pathetic, inadequate, thin, weak, feeble, unsatisfactory

lament VERB = bemoan, grieve, mourn, weep over, complain about, regret, wail

about, deplore
● NOUN 1 = <u>complaint</u>, moan, wailing, lamentation 2 = <u>dirge</u>, requiem, elegy, threnody

land NOUN 1 = <u>ground</u>, earth, dry land, terra firma 2 = <u>soil</u>, ground, earth, clay, dirt, sod, loam 3 = <u>countryside</u>, farmland 4 (*Law*) = <u>property</u>, grounds, estate, real estate, realty, acreage 5 = <u>country</u>, nation, region, state, district, territory, province, kingdom
● VERB 1 = <u>arrive</u>, dock, put down, moor, alight, touch down, disembark, come to rest 2 (*Informal*) = <u>gain</u>, get, win, secure, acquire
● PHRASES **land up** = <u>end up</u>, turn up, wind up, finish up, fetch up (*informal*)
▓▓▓ RELATED WORD
adjective: terrestrial

landlord 1 = <u>owner</u>, landowner, proprietor, freeholder, lessor, landholder 2 = <u>innkeeper</u>, host, hotelier

landmark 1 = <u>feature</u>, spectacle, monument 2 = <u>milestone</u>, turning point, watershed, critical point

landscape = <u>scenery</u>, country, view, land, scene, prospect, countryside, outlook

landslide = <u>landslip</u>, avalanche, rockfall

lane = <u>road</u>, street, track, path, way, passage, trail, pathway

language 1 = <u>tongue</u>, dialect, vernacular, patois 2 = <u>speech</u>, communication, expression, speaking, talk, talking, discourse, parlance

languish 1 = <u>decline</u>, fade away, wither away, flag, weaken, wilt ≠ flourish 2 (*Literary*) = <u>waste away</u>, suffer, rot, be abandoned, be neglected ≠ thrive 3 *often with for* = <u>pine</u>, long, desire, hunger, yearn, hanker

lap¹ = <u>circuit</u>, tour, leg, stretch, circle, orbit, loop

lap² VERB 1 = <u>ripple</u>, wash, splash, swish, gurgle, slosh, purl, plash 2 = <u>drink</u>, sip, lick, swallow, gulp, sup
● PHRASES **lap something up** = <u>relish</u>, like, enjoy, delight in, savour, revel in, wallow in, accept eagerly

lapse NOUN 1 = <u>decline</u>, fall, drop, deterioration 2 = <u>mistake</u>, failing, fault, failure, error, slip, negligence, omission 3 = <u>interval</u>, break, gap, pause, interruption, lull, breathing space, intermission

● VERB 1 = <u>slip</u>, fall, decline, sink, drop, slide, deteriorate, degenerate 2 = <u>end</u>, stop, run out, expire, terminate

lapsed = <u>expired</u>, ended, finished, run out, invalid, out of date, discontinued

large ADJECTIVE 1 = <u>big</u>, great, huge, heavy, massive, vast, enormous, tall ≠ small 2 = <u>massive</u>, great, big, huge, vast, enormous, considerable, substantial ≠ small
● PHRASES **at large** 1 = <u>in general</u>, generally, chiefly, mainly, as a whole, in the main 2 = <u>free</u>, on the run, fugitive, at liberty, on the loose, unchained, unconfined ◆ **by and large** = <u>on the whole</u>, generally, mostly, in general, all things considered, predominantly, in the main, all in all

largely = <u>mainly</u>, generally, chiefly, mostly, principally, primarily, predominantly, by and large

large-scale = <u>wide-ranging</u>, global, sweeping, broad, wide, vast, extensive, wholesale

lash¹ VERB 1 = <u>pound</u>, beat, strike, hammer, drum, smack (*dialect*) 2 = <u>censure</u>, attack, blast, put down, criticize, slate (*informal, chiefly Brit.*), scold, tear into (*informal*) 3 = <u>whip</u>, beat, thrash, birch, flog, scourge
● NOUN = <u>blow</u>, hit, strike, stroke, stripe, swipe (*informal*)

lash² = <u>fasten</u>, tie, secure, bind, strap, make fast

last¹ ADJECTIVE 1 = <u>most recent</u>, latest, previous 2 = <u>hindmost</u>, final, at the end, remotest, furthest behind, most distant, rearmost ≠ foremost 3 = <u>final</u>, closing, concluding, ultimate ≠ first
● ADVERB = <u>in *or* at the end</u>, after, behind, in the rear, bringing up the rear
● PHRASES **the last word** 1 = <u>final decision</u>, final say, final statement, conclusive comment 2 = <u>leading</u>, finest, cream, supreme, elite, foremost, pre-eminent, unsurpassed

last² = <u>continue</u>, remain, survive, carry on, endure, persist, keep on, abide ≠ end

lasting = <u>continuing</u>, long-term, permanent, enduring, remaining, abiding, long-standing, perennial ≠ passing

latch NOUN = <u>fastening</u>, catch, bar, lock, hook, bolt, hasp
● VERB = <u>fasten</u>, bar, secure, bolt, make fast
late ADJECTIVE 1 = <u>overdue</u>, delayed, last-minute, belated, tardy, behind time, behindhand ≠ early 2 = <u>dead</u>, deceased, departed, passed on, former, defunct ≠ alive 3 = <u>recent</u>, new, advanced, fresh ≠ old
● ADVERB = <u>behind time</u>, belatedly, tardily, behindhand, dilatorily ≠ early
lately = <u>recently</u>, of late, just now, in recent times, not long ago, latterly
later ADVERB = <u>afterwards</u>, after, eventually, in time, subsequently, later on, thereafter, in a while
● ADJECTIVE = <u>subsequent</u>, next, following, ensuing
latest = <u>up-to-date</u>, current, fresh, newest, modern, most recent, up-to-the-minute
latitude = <u>scope</u>, liberty, freedom, play, space, licence, leeway, laxity
latter PRONOUN = <u>second</u>, last, last-mentioned, second-mentioned
● ADJECTIVE = <u>last</u>, ending, closing, final, concluding ≠ earlier
laugh VERB = <u>chuckle</u>, giggle, snigger, cackle, chortle, guffaw, titter, be in stitches
● NOUN 1 = <u>chortle</u>, giggle, chuckle, snigger, guffaw, titter 2 (Informal) = <u>joke</u>, scream (informal), hoot (informal), lark, prank 3 (Informal) = <u>clown</u>, character (informal), scream (informal), entertainer, card (informal), joker, hoot (informal)
● PHRASES **laugh something off** = <u>disregard</u>, ignore, dismiss, overlook, shrug off, minimize, brush aside, make light of
laughter = <u>amusement</u>, entertainment, humour, glee, fun, mirth, hilarity, merriment
launch VERB 1 = <u>propel</u>, fire, dispatch, discharge, project, send off, set in motion, send into orbit 2 = <u>begin</u>, start, open, initiate, introduce, found, set up, originate
● PHRASES **launch into something** = <u>start enthusiastically</u>, begin, initiate, embark on, instigate, inaugurate, embark upon
laurel
● PHRASES **rest on your laurels** = <u>sit back</u>, relax, take it easy, relax your efforts
lavatory = <u>toilet</u>, bathroom, loo (Brit. informal), privy, cloakroom (Brit.), urinal, latrine, washroom, dunny (Austral. & N.Z. old-fashioned informal), bogger (Austral. slang), brasco (Austral. slang)
lavish ADJECTIVE 1 = <u>grand</u>, magnificent, splendid, abundant, copious, profuse ≠ stingy 2 = <u>extravagant</u>, wild, excessive, exaggerated, wasteful, prodigal, unrestrained, immoderate ≠ thrifty 3 = <u>generous</u>, free, liberal, bountiful, open-handed, unstinting, munificent ≠ stingy
● VERB = <u>shower</u>, pour, heap, deluge, dissipate ≠ stint
law 1 = <u>constitution</u>, code, legislation, charter 2 = <u>statute</u>, act, bill, rule, order, command, regulation, resolution 3 = <u>principle</u>, code, canon, precept, axiom, kaupapa (N.Z.) 4 = <u>the legal profession</u>, the bar, barristers
▦ RELATED WORDS
adjectives: legal, judicial
lawsuit = <u>case</u>, action, trial, suit, proceedings, dispute, prosecution, legal action
lawyer = <u>legal adviser</u>, attorney, solicitor, counsel, advocate, barrister, counsellor, legal representative
lay¹ VERB 1 = <u>place</u>, put, set, spread, plant, leave, deposit, put down 2 = <u>devise</u>, plan, design, prepare, work out, plot, hatch, contrive 3 = <u>produce</u>, bear, deposit 4 = <u>arrange</u>, prepare, make, organize, position, set out, devise, put together 5 = <u>attribute</u>, assign, allocate, allot, ascribe, impute 6 = <u>put forward</u>, offer, present, advance, lodge, submit, bring forward 7 = <u>bet</u>, stake, venture, gamble, chance, risk, hazard, wager
● PHRASES **lay someone off** = <u>dismiss</u>, fire (informal), release, sack (informal), pay off, discharge, let go, make redundant
◆ **lay someone out** (Informal) = <u>knock out</u>, fell, floor, knock unconscious, knock for six ◆ **lay something out** 1 = <u>arrange</u>, order, design, display, exhibit, put out, spread out 2 (Informal) = <u>spend</u>, pay, invest, fork out (slang), expend, shell out (informal), disburse
lay² 1 = <u>nonclerical</u>, secular, non-ordained 2 = <u>nonspecialist</u>, amateur, unqualified, untrained, inexpert, nonprofessional
layer = <u>tier</u>, level, seam, stratum
layout = <u>arrangement</u>, design, outline, format, plan, formation

lazy 1 = idle, inactive, indolent, slack, negligent, inert, workshy, slothful ≠ industrious **2** = lethargic, languorous, slow-moving, languid, sleepy, sluggish, drowsy, somnolent ≠ quick

leach = extract, strain, drain, filter, seep, percolate

lead VERB **1** = go in front (of), head, be in front, be at the head (of), walk in front (of) **2** = guide, conduct, steer, escort, precede, usher, pilot, show the way **3** = connect to, link, open onto **4** = be ahead (of), be first, exceed, be winning, excel, surpass, come first, transcend **5** = command, rule, govern, preside over, head, control, manage, direct **6** = live, have, spend, experience, pass, undergo **7** = result in, cause, produce, contribute, generate, bring about, bring on, give rise to **8** = cause, prompt, persuade, move, draw, influence, motivate, prevail

• NOUN **1** = first place, winning position, primary position, vanguard **2** = advantage, start, edge, margin, winning margin **3** = example, direction, leadership, guidance, model, pattern **4** = clue, suggestion, hint, indication, pointer, tip-off **5** = leading role, principal, protagonist, title role, principal part **6** = leash, line, cord, rein, tether

• ADJECTIVE = main, prime, top, leading, first, head, chief, premier

• PHRASES **lead someone on** = entice, tempt, lure, mislead, draw on, seduce, deceive, beguile ♦ **lead up to something** = introduce, prepare for, pave the way for

leader = principal, president, head, chief, boss (*informal*), director, manager, chairman, baas (*S. African*) ≠ follower

leadership 1 = authority, control, influence, command, premiership, captaincy, governance, headship **2** = guidance, government, authority, management, direction, supervision, domination, superintendency

leading = principal, top, major, main, first, highest, greatest, chief ≠ minor

leaf NOUN **1** = frond, blade, cotyledon **2** = page, sheet, folio

• PHRASES **leaf through something** (with *book, magazine* etc. as object) = skim, glance, scan, browse, look through, dip into, flick through, flip through

leaflet = booklet, notice, brochure, circular, flyer, tract, pamphlet, handout

leafy = green, shaded, shady, verdant

league 1 = association, union, alliance, coalition, group, corporation, partnership, federation **2** (*Informal*) = class, group, level, category

leak VERB **1** = escape, pass, spill, release, drip, trickle, ooze, seep **2** = disclose, tell, reveal, pass on, give away, make public, divulge, let slip

• NOUN **1** = leakage, discharge, drip, seepage, percolation **2** = hole, opening, crack, puncture, aperture, chink, crevice, fissure **3** = disclosure, exposé, exposure, admission, revelation, uncovering, betrayal, unearthing

lean¹ VERB **1** = bend, tip, slope, incline, tilt, heel, slant **2** = rest, prop, be supported, recline, repose **3** = tend, prefer, favour, incline, be prone to, be disposed to

• PHRASES **lean on someone** = depend on, trust, rely on, cling to, count on, have faith in

lean² = thin, slim, slender, skinny, angular, trim, spare, gaunt ≠ fat

leaning = tendency, bias, inclination, bent, disposition, penchant, propensity, predilection

leap VERB = jump, spring, bound, bounce, hop, skip

• NOUN **1** = jump, spring, bound, vault **2** = rise, change, increase, soaring, surge, escalation, upsurge, upswing

• PHRASES **leap at something** = accept eagerly, seize on, jump at

learn 1 = master, grasp, pick up, take in, familiarize yourself with **2** = discover, hear, understand, find out about, become aware, discern, ascertain, come to know **3** = memorize, commit to memory, learn by heart, learn by rote, learn parrot-fashion, get off pat

learned = scholarly, academic, intellectual, versed, well-informed, erudite, highbrow, well-read ≠ uneducated

learner = student, novice, beginner, apprentice, neophyte, tyro ≠ expert

learning = knowledge, study, education, scholarship, enlightenment

lease = hire, rent, let, loan, charter, rent out, hire out

least = smallest, meanest, fewest, lowest,

tiniest, minimum, slightest, minimal

leave VERB **1** = <u>depart from</u>, withdraw
from, go from, escape from, quit, flee,
exit, pull out of ≠ arrive **2** = <u>quit</u>, give
up, get out of, resign from, drop out of
3 = <u>give up</u>, abandon, dump (*informal*),
drop, surrender, ditch (*informal*), chuck
(*informal*), discard ≠ stay with **4** = <u>entrust</u>,
commit, delegate, refer, hand over, assign,
consign, allot **5** = <u>bequeath</u>, will, transfer,
endow, confer, hand down **6** = <u>forget</u>,
leave behind, mislay **7** = <u>cause</u>, produce,
result in, generate, deposit
● NOUN **1** = <u>holiday</u>, break, vacation, time
off, sabbatical, leave of absence, furlough
2 = <u>permission</u>, freedom, sanction,
liberty, concession, consent, allowance,
warrant ≠ refusal **3** = <u>departure</u>, parting,
withdrawal, goodbye, farewell, retirement,
leave-taking, adieu ≠ arrival
● PHRASES **leave something** *or*
someone out = <u>omit</u>, exclude, miss out,
forget, reject, ignore, overlook, neglect

lecture NOUN **1** = <u>talk</u>, address, speech,
lesson, instruction, presentation,
discourse, sermon **2** = <u>telling-off</u>
(*informal*), rebuke, reprimand, talking-
to (*informal*), scolding, dressing-down
(*informal*), reproof
● VERB **1** = <u>talk</u>, speak, teach, address,
discourse, spout, expound, hold forth
2 = <u>tell off</u> (*informal*), berate, scold,
reprimand, censure, castigate, admonish,
reprove

lees = <u>sediment</u>, grounds, deposit, dregs

left 1 = <u>left-hand</u>, port, larboard (*Nautical*)
2 (*of politics*) = <u>socialist</u>, radical, left-wing,
leftist

left-wing = <u>socialist</u>, communist, red
(*informal*), radical, revolutionary, militant,
Bolshevik, Leninist

leg NOUN **1** = <u>limb</u>, member, shank, lower
limb, pin (*informal*), stump (*informal*)
2 = <u>support</u>, prop, brace, upright **3** = <u>stage</u>,
part, section, stretch, lap, segment, portion
● PHRASES **pull someone's leg**
(*Informal*) = <u>tease</u>, trick, fool, kid
(*informal*), wind up (*Brit. slang*), hoax,
make fun of, lead up the garden path

legacy = <u>bequest</u>, inheritance, gift, estate,
heirloom

legal 1 = <u>judicial</u>, judiciary, forensic,
juridical, jurisdictive **2** = <u>lawful</u>, allowed,
sanctioned, constitutional, valid,

legitimate, authorized, permissible

legend 1 = <u>myth</u>, story, tale, fiction, saga,
fable, folk tale, folk story **2** = <u>celebrity</u>, star,
phenomenon, genius, prodigy, luminary,
megastar (*informal*) **3** = <u>inscription</u>, title,
caption, device, motto, rubric

legendary 1 = <u>famous</u>, celebrated,
well-known, acclaimed, renowned,
famed, immortal, illustrious ≠ unknown
2 = <u>mythical</u>, fabled, traditional, romantic,
fabulous, fictitious, storybook, apocryphal
≠ factual

legion 1 = <u>army</u>, company, force, division,
troop, brigade **2** = <u>multitude</u>, host, mass,
drove, number, horde, myriad, throng

legislation 1 = <u>law</u>, act, ruling, rule,
bill, measure, regulation, charter
2 = <u>lawmaking</u>, regulation, prescription,
enactment

legislative = <u>law-making</u>, judicial, law-
giving

legislator = <u>lawmaker</u>, lawgiver

legislature = <u>parliament</u>, congress,
senate, assembly, chamber

legitimate ADJECTIVE **1** = <u>lawful</u>, legal,
genuine, authentic, authorized, rightful,
kosher (*informal*), dinkum (*Austral. & N.Z.
informal*), licit ≠ unlawful **2** = <u>reasonable</u>,
correct, sensible, valid, warranted, logical,
justifiable, well-founded ≠ unreasonable
● VERB = <u>legitimize</u>, allow, permit, sanction,
authorize, legalize, pronounce lawful

leisure = <u>spare</u>, free, rest, ease, relaxation,
recreation ≠ work

lekker (*S. African slang*) = <u>delicious</u>,
tasty, luscious, palatable, delectable,
mouthwatering, scrumptious (*informal*),
appetizing, yummo (*Austral. slang*)

lemon

RELATED WORDS
adjectives: citric, citrous

lend VERB **1** = <u>loan</u>, advance, sub (*Brit.
informal*) **2** = <u>give</u>, provide, add, supply,
grant, confer, bestow, impart
● PHRASES **lend itself to something**
= <u>be appropriate for</u>, suit, be suitable for,
be appropriate to, be serviceable for

length NOUN **1** = <u>distance</u>, reach, measure,
extent, span, longitude **2** = <u>duration</u>,
term, period, space, stretch, span, expanse
3 = <u>piece</u>, measure, section, segment,
portion
● PHRASES **at length 1** = <u>at last</u>, finally,
eventually, in time, in the end, at long

last **2** = <u>for a long time</u>, completely, fully, thoroughly, for hours, in detail, for ages, in depth

lengthen 1 = <u>extend</u>, continue, increase, stretch, expand, elongate ≠ shorten **2** = <u>protract</u>, extend, prolong, draw out, spin out, make longer ≠ cut down

lengthy 1 = <u>protracted</u>, long, prolonged, tedious, drawn-out, interminable, long-winded, long-drawn-out **2** = <u>very long</u>, rambling, interminable, long-winded, wordy, discursive, extended ≠ brief

lesbian = <u>homosexual</u>, gay, les (*slang*), sapphic, lesbo (*slang*)

less DETERMINER = <u>smaller</u>, shorter, not so much
● PREPOSITION = <u>minus</u>, without, lacking, excepting, subtracting

lessen 1 = <u>reduce</u>, lower, diminish, decrease, ease, narrow, minimize ≠ increase **2** = <u>grow less</u>, diminish, decrease, contract, ease, shrink

lesser = <u>lower</u>, secondary, subsidiary, inferior, less important ≠ greater

lesson 1 = <u>class</u>, schooling, period, teaching, coaching, session, instruction, lecture **2** = <u>example</u>, warning, message, moral, deterrent **3** = <u>Bible reading</u>, reading, text, Bible passage, Scripture passage

let VERB **1** = <u>allow</u>, permit, authorize, give the go-ahead, give permission **2** = <u>lease</u>, hire, rent, rent out, hire out, sublease
● PHRASES **let on** (*Informal*) **1** = <u>reveal</u>, disclose, say, tell, admit, give away, divulge, let slip ◆ **let someone down** = <u>disappoint</u>, fail, abandon, desert, disillusion, fall short, leave stranded, leave in the lurch ◆ **let someone off** = <u>excuse</u>, release, discharge, pardon, spare, forgive, exempt, exonerate ◆ **let something** or **someone in** = <u>admit</u>, include, receive, welcome, greet, take in, incorporate, give access to ◆ **let something down** = <u>deflate</u>, empty, exhaust, flatten, puncture ◆ **let something off 1** = <u>fire</u>, explode, set off, discharge, detonate **2** = <u>emit</u>, release, leak, exude, give off ◆ **let something out 1** = <u>release</u>, discharge **2** = <u>emit</u>, make, produce, give vent to ◆ **let up** = <u>stop</u>, diminish, decrease, subside, relax, ease (up), moderate, lessen

lethal = <u>deadly</u>, terminal, fatal, dangerous,

devastating, destructive, mortal, murderous ≠ harmless

letter 1 = <u>message</u>, line, note, communication, dispatch, missive, epistle **2** = <u>character</u>, mark, sign, symbol

level NOUN = <u>position</u>, standard, degree, grade, standing, stage, rank, status
● ADJECTIVE **1** = <u>equal</u>, balanced, at the same height **2** = <u>horizontal</u>, even, flat, smooth, uniform ≠ slanted **3** = <u>even</u>, tied, equal, drawn, neck and neck, all square, level pegging
● VERB **1** = <u>equalize</u>, balance, even up **2** = <u>destroy</u>, devastate, demolish, flatten, knock down, pull down, tear down, bulldoze ≠ build **3** = <u>direct</u>, point, turn, train, aim, focus **4** = <u>flatten</u>, plane, smooth, even off *or* out
● PHRASES **on the level** (*Informal*) = <u>honest</u>, genuine, straight, fair, square, dinkum (*Austral. & N.Z. informal*), above board

lever NOUN = <u>handle</u>, bar
● VERB = <u>prise</u>, force

leverage 1 = <u>influence</u>, authority, pull (*informal*), weight, clout (*informal*) **2** = <u>force</u>, hold, pull, strength, grip, grasp

levy NOUN = <u>tax</u>, fee, toll, tariff, duty, excise, exaction
● VERB = <u>impose</u>, charge, collect, demand, exact

liability 1 = <u>disadvantage</u>, burden, drawback, inconvenience, handicap, nuisance, hindrance, millstone **2** = <u>responsibility</u>, accountability, culpability, answerability

liable 1 = <u>likely</u>, tending, inclined, disposed, prone, apt **2** = <u>vulnerable</u>, subject, exposed, prone, susceptible, open, at risk of **3** = <u>responsible</u>, accountable, answerable, obligated

liaison 1 = <u>contact</u>, communication, connection, interchange **2** = <u>intermediary</u>, contact, hook-up **3** = <u>affair</u>, romance, intrigue, fling, love affair, amour, entanglement

liar = <u>falsifier</u>, perjurer, fibber, fabricator

libel NOUN = <u>defamation</u>, misrepresentation, denigration, smear, calumny, aspersion
● VERB = <u>defame</u>, smear, slur, blacken, malign, denigrate, revile, vilify

liberal 1 = <u>tolerant</u>, open-minded, permissive, indulgent, easy-going, broad-minded ≠ intolerant 2 = progressive, radical, reformist, libertarian, forward-looking, free-thinking ≠ conservative 3 = abundant, generous, handsome, lavish, ample, rich, plentiful, copious ≠ limited 4 = generous, kind, charitable, extravagant, open-hearted, bountiful, magnanimous, open-handed ≠ stingy

liberate = free, release, rescue, save, deliver, let out, set free, let loose ≠ imprison

liberty NOUN = independence, sovereignty, liberation, autonomy, immunity, self-determination, emancipation, self-government ≠ restraint

● PHRASES **at liberty 1** = free, escaped, unlimited, at large, not confined, untied, on the loose, unchained 2 = able, free, allowed, permitted, entitled, authorized

◆ **take liberties** or **a liberty** = not show enough respect, show disrespect, act presumptuously, behave too familiarly, behave impertinently

licence NOUN 1 = certificate, document, permit, charter, warrant 2 = permission, the right, authority, leave, sanction, liberty, immunity, entitlement ≠ denial 3 = freedom, creativity, latitude, independence, liberty, deviation, leeway, free rein ≠ restraint 4 = laxity, excess, indulgence, irresponsibility, licentiousness, immoderation ≠ moderation

● PHRASES **under licence** = with permission, under a charter, under warrant, under a permit, with authorization, under a patent

license = permit, sanction, allow, warrant, authorize, empower, certify, accredit ≠ forbid

lick VERB 1 = taste, lap, tongue 2 (*Informal*) = beat, defeat, overcome, rout, outstrip, outdo, trounce, vanquish 3 (*of flames*) = flicker, touch, flick, dart, ripple, play over

● NOUN 1 = dab, bit, touch, stroke 2 (*Informal*) = pace, rate, speed, clip (*informal*)

lie¹ NOUN = falsehood, deceit, fabrication, fib, fiction, invention, deception, untruth

● VERB = fib, fabricate, falsify, prevaricate, not tell the truth, equivocate, dissimulate, tell untruths

● PHRASES **give the lie to something** = disprove, expose, discredit, contradict, refute, negate, invalidate, rebut

lie² 1 = recline, rest, lounge, sprawl, stretch out, loll, repose 2 = be placed, be, rest, exist, be situated 3 = be situated, sit, be located, be positioned 4 = be buried, remain, rest, be, be entombed

life 1 = being, existence, vitality, sentience 2 = existence, being, lifetime, time, days, span 3 = way of life, situation, conduct, behaviour, life style 4 = liveliness, energy, spirit, vitality, animation, vigour, verve, zest 5 = biography, story, history, profile, confessions, autobiography, memoirs, life story

▩ RELATED WORDS
adjectives: animate, vital

lifelong = long-lasting, enduring, lasting, persistent, long-standing, perennial

lifetime = existence, time, day(s), span

lift VERB 1 = raise, pick up, hoist, draw up, elevate, uplift, heave up, upraise ≠ lower 2 = revoke, end, remove, withdraw, stop, cancel, terminate, rescind ≠ impose 3 = disappear, clear, vanish, disperse, dissipate, rise, be dispelled

● NOUN 1 = boost, encouragement, stimulus, pick-me-up, fillip, shot in the arm (*informal*), gee-up ≠ blow 2 = elevator (*chiefly U.S.*), hoist, paternoster 3 = ride, run, drive, hitch (*informal*)

● PHRASES **lift off** = take off, be launched, blast off, take to the air

light¹ NOUN 1 = brightness, illumination, luminosity, shining, glow, glare, gleam, brilliance ≠ dark 2 = lamp, torch, candle, flare, beacon, lantern, taper 3 = match, spark, flame, lighter 4 = aspect, context, angle, point of view, interpretation, viewpoint, slant, standpoint

● ADJECTIVE 1 = bright, brilliant, shining, illuminated, luminous, well-lit, lustrous, well-illuminated ≠ dark 2 = pale, fair, faded, blonde, blond, bleached, pastel, light-coloured ≠ dark

● VERB 1 = illuminate, light up, brighten ≠ darken 2 = ignite, inflame, kindle, touch off, set alight ≠ put out

● PHRASES **light up 1** = cheer, shine, blaze, sparkle, animate, brighten, lighten, irradiate 2 = shine, flash, beam, blaze, sparkle, flare, glare, gleam

light² ADJECTIVE 1 = insubstantial, thin, slight, portable, buoyant, airy, flimsy, underweight ≠ heavy 2 = weak, soft, gentle, moderate, slight, mild, faint, indistinct ≠ strong **3** = <u>digestible</u>, modest, frugal ≠ substantial **4** = <u>insignificant</u>, small, slight, petty, trivial, trifling, inconsequential, inconsiderable ≠ serious **5** = <u>light-hearted</u>, funny, entertaining, amusing, witty, humorous, frivolous, unserious ≠ serious **6** = <u>nimble</u>, graceful, deft, agile, sprightly, lithe, limber, lissom ≠ clumsy

● PHRASES **light on** *or* **upon something**
1 = <u>settle</u>, land, perch, alight **2** = <u>come across</u>, find, discover, encounter, stumble on, hit upon, happen upon

lighten¹ 1 = <u>brighten</u>, illuminate, light up, irradiate, become light

lighten² 1 = <u>ease</u>, relieve, alleviate, allay, reduce, lessen, mitigate, assuage ≠ intensify **2** = <u>cheer</u>, lift, revive, brighten, perk up, buoy up ≠ depress

lightly 1 = <u>moderately</u>, thinly, slightly, sparsely, sparingly ≠ heavily **2** = <u>gently</u>, softly, slightly, faintly, delicately ≠ forcefully **3** = <u>carelessly</u>, breezily, thoughtlessly, flippantly, frivolously, heedlessly ≠ seriously **4** = <u>easily</u>, simply, readily, effortlessly, unthinkingly, without thought, flippantly, heedlessly ≠ with difficulty

lightweight 1 = <u>thin</u>, fine, delicate, sheer, flimsy, gossamer, diaphanous, filmy **2** = <u>unimportant</u>, shallow, trivial, insignificant, slight, petty, worthless, trifling ≠ significant

like¹ = <u>similar to</u>, same as, equivalent to, parallel to, identical to, alike, corresponding to, comparable to ≠ different

like² 1 = <u>enjoy</u>, love, delight in, go for, relish, savour, revel in, be fond of ≠ dislike **2** = <u>admire</u>, approve of, appreciate, prize, take to, esteem, cherish, hold dear ≠ dislike **3** = <u>wish</u>, want, choose, prefer, desire, fancy, care, feel inclined

likelihood = <u>probability</u>, chance, possibility, prospect

likely 1 = <u>inclined</u>, disposed, prone, liable, tending, apt **2** = <u>probable</u>, expected, anticipated, odds-on, on the cards, to be expected **3** = <u>plausible</u>, possible, reasonable, credible, feasible, believable

liken = <u>compare</u>, match, relate, parallel, equate, set beside

likewise = <u>similarly</u>, the same, in the same way, in similar fashion, in like manner

liking = <u>fondness</u>, love, taste, weakness, preference, affection, inclination, penchant ≠ dislike

limb 1 = <u>part</u>, member, arm, leg, wing, extremity, appendage **2** = <u>branch</u>, spur, projection, offshoot, bough

limelight = <u>publicity</u>, recognition, fame, the spotlight, attention, prominence, stardom, public eye

limit NOUN **1** = <u>end</u>, ultimate, deadline, breaking point, extremity **2** = <u>boundary</u>, edge, border, frontier, perimeter
● VERB = <u>restrict</u>, control, check, bound, confine, curb, restrain, ration

limitation 1 = <u>restriction</u>, control, check, curb, restraint, constraint **2** = <u>weakness</u>, failing, qualification, reservation, defect, flaw, shortcoming, imperfection

limited = <u>restricted</u>, controlled, checked, bounded, confined, curbed, constrained, finite ≠ unlimited

limp¹ VERB = <u>hobble</u>, stagger, stumble, shuffle, hop, falter, shamble, totter
● NOUN = <u>lameness</u>, hobble

limp² = <u>floppy</u>, soft, slack, drooping, flabby, pliable, flaccid ≠ stiff

line NOUN **1** = <u>stroke</u>, mark, score, band, scratch, slash, streak, stripe **2** = <u>wrinkle</u>, mark, crease, furrow, crow's foot **3** = <u>row</u>, queue, rank, file, column, convoy, procession **4** = <u>string</u>, cable, wire, rope, thread, cord **5** = <u>trajectory</u>, way, course, track, channel, direction, route, path **6** = <u>boundary</u>, limit, edge, border, frontier, partition, borderline **7** = <u>occupation</u>, work, calling, business, job, area, trade, field
● VERB **1** = <u>border</u>, edge, bound, fringe **2** = <u>mark</u>, crease, furrow, rule, score
● PHRASES **in line for** = <u>due for</u>, shortlisted for, in the running for

lined 1 = <u>wrinkled</u>, worn, furrowed, wizened **2** = <u>ruled</u>, feint

line-up = <u>arrangement</u>, team, row, selection, array

linger = <u>stay</u>, remain, stop, wait, delay, hang around, idle, dally

link NOUN **1** = <u>connection</u>, relationship, association, tie-up, affinity **2** = <u>relationship</u>, association, bond, connection, attachment, affinity **3** = <u>component</u>, part, piece, element, constituent
● VERB **1** = <u>associate</u>, relate, identify, connect, bracket **2** = <u>connect</u>, join, unite,

couple, tie, bind, attach, fasten ≠ separate

lip 1 = <u>edge</u>, rim, brim, margin, brink
2 = <u>impudence</u>, insolence,
impertinence, cheek (*informal*), effrontery,
backchat (*informal*), brass neck (*informal*)

liquid NOUN = <u>fluid</u>, solution, juice, sap
● ADJECTIVE **1** = <u>fluid</u>, running, flowing,
melted, watery, molten, runny, aqueous
2 (*of assets*) = <u>convertible</u>, disposable,
negotiable, realizable

liquor 1 = <u>alcohol</u>, drink, spirits, booze
(*informal*), hard stuff (*informal*), strong
drink **2** = <u>juice</u>, stock, liquid, extract, broth

list¹ NOUN = <u>inventory</u>, record, series, roll,
index, register, catalogue, directory
● VERB = <u>itemize</u>, record, enter, register,
catalogue, enumerate, note down,
tabulate

list² VERB = <u>lean</u>, tip, incline, tilt, heel over,
careen
● NOUN = <u>tilt</u>, leaning, slant, cant

listen 1 = <u>hear</u>, attend, pay attention,
lend an ear, prick up your ears **2** = <u>pay
attention</u>, observe, obey, mind, heed, take
notice, take note of, take heed of

literacy = <u>education</u>, learning, knowledge

literal 1 = <u>exact</u>, close, strict, accurate,
faithful, verbatim, word for word
2 = <u>actual</u>, real, true, simple, plain, genuine,
bona fide, unvarnished

literally = <u>exactly</u>, really, closely, actually,
truly, precisely, strictly, faithfully

literary = <u>well-read</u>, learned, formal,
intellectual, scholarly, erudite, bookish

literate = <u>educated</u>, informed,
knowledgeable

literature = <u>writings</u>, letters,
compositions, lore, creative writing

litigation = <u>lawsuit</u>, case, action,
prosecution

litter NOUN **1** = <u>rubbish</u>, refuse, waste, junk,
debris, garbage (*chiefly U.S.*), trash, muck
2 = <u>brood</u>, young, offspring, progeny
● VERB **1** = <u>clutter</u>, mess up, clutter up, be
scattered about, disorder, disarrange,
derange **2** = <u>scatter</u>, spread, shower, strew

little ADJECTIVE **1** = <u>small</u>, minute, short,
tiny, wee, compact, miniature, diminutive
≠ big **2** = <u>young</u>, small, junior, infant,
immature, undeveloped, babyish
● ADVERB **1** = <u>hardly</u>, barely, scarcely
≠ much **2** = <u>rarely</u>, seldom, scarcely, not
often, infrequently, hardly ever ≠ always
● NOUN = <u>bit</u>, touch, spot, trace, hint,
particle, fragment, speck ≠ lot
● PHRASES **a little** = <u>to a small extent</u>,
slightly, to some extent, to a certain
extent, to a small degree

live¹ 1 = <u>dwell</u>, board, settle, lodge, occupy,
abide, inhabit, reside **2** = <u>exist</u>, last,
prevail, be, have being, breathe, persist,
be alive **3** = <u>survive</u>, get along, make a
living, make ends meet, subsist, eke out a
living, support yourself, maintain yourself
4 = <u>thrive</u>, flourish, prosper, have fun,
enjoy yourself, live life to the full

live² 1 = <u>living</u>, alive, breathing, animate
2 = <u>active</u>, unexploded **3** = <u>topical</u>,
important, pressing, current, hot, burning,
controversial, prevalent

livelihood = <u>occupation</u>, work,
employment, living, job, bread and butter
(*informal*)

lively 1 = <u>animated</u>, spirited, quick,
keen, active, alert, dynamic, vigorous
≠ dull **2** = <u>vivid</u>, strong, striking, bright,
exciting, stimulating, bold, colourful ≠ dull
3 = <u>enthusiastic</u>, strong, keen, stimulating,
eager, formidable, vigorous, animated

living NOUN = <u>lifestyle</u>, ways, situation,
conduct, behaviour, customs, lifestyle, way
of life
● ADJECTIVE **1** = <u>alive</u>, existing, moving,
active, breathing, animate ≠ dead
2 = <u>current</u>, present, active, contemporary,
in use, extant ≠ obsolete

load VERB **1** = <u>fill</u>, stuff, pack, pile, stack,
heap, cram, freight **2** = <u>make ready</u>,
charge, prime
● NOUN **1** = <u>cargo</u>, delivery, haul,
shipment, batch, freight, consignment
2 = <u>oppression</u>, charge, worry, trouble,
weight, responsibility, burden, onus
● PHRASES **load someone down**
= <u>burden</u>, worry, oppress, weigh down,
saddle with, encumber, snow under

loaded 1 = <u>tricky</u>, charged, sensitive,
delicate, manipulative, emotive, insidious,
artful **2** = <u>biased</u>, weighted, rigged,
distorted **3** (*Slang*) = <u>rich</u>, wealthy, affluent,
well off, flush (*informal*), well-heeled
(*informal*), well-to-do, moneyed

loaf¹ 1 = <u>lump</u>, block, cake, cube, slab
2 (*Slang*) = <u>head</u>, mind, sense, common
sense, nous (*Brit. slang*), gumption (*Brit.
informal*)

loaf² = <u>idle</u>, hang around, take it easy, lie
around, loiter, laze, lounge around

loan NOUN = <u>advance</u>, credit, overdraft
● VERB = <u>lend</u>, advance, let out

loathe = <u>hate</u>, dislike, despise, detest, abhor, abominate

loathing = <u>hatred</u>, hate, disgust, aversion, revulsion, antipathy, repulsion, abhorrence

lobby VERB = <u>campaign</u>, press, pressure, push, influence, promote, urge, persuade
● NOUN 1 = <u>pressure group</u>, group, camp, faction, lobbyists, interest group, special-interest group, ginger group 2 = <u>corridor</u>, passage, entrance, porch, hallway, foyer, entrance hall, vestibule

lobola (*S. African*) = <u>dowry</u>, portion, marriage settlement, dot (*archaic*)

local ADJECTIVE 1 = <u>community</u>, regional 2 = <u>confined</u>, limited, restricted
● NOUN = <u>resident</u>, native, inhabitant

locate 1 = <u>find</u>, discover, detect, come across, track down, pinpoint, unearth, pin down 2 = <u>place</u>, put, set, position, seat, site, establish, settle

location = <u>place</u>, point, setting, position, situation, spot, venue, locale

lock¹ VERB 1 = <u>fasten</u>, close, secure, shut, bar, seal, bolt 2 = <u>unite</u>, join, link, engage, clench, entangle, interlock, entwine 3 = <u>embrace</u>, press, grasp, clutch, hug, enclose, clasp, encircle
● NOUN = <u>fastening</u>, catch, bolt, clasp, padlock
● PHRASES **lock someone up** = <u>imprison</u>, jail, confine, cage, detain, shut up, incarcerate, send down (*informal*)

lock² = <u>strand</u>, curl, tuft, tress, ringlet

lodge NOUN 1 = <u>cabin</u>, shelter, cottage, hut, chalet, gatehouse 2 = <u>society</u>, group, club, section, wing, chapter, branch
● VERB 1 = <u>register</u>, enter, file, submit, put on record 2 = <u>stay</u>, room, board, reside 3 = <u>stick</u>, remain, implant, come to rest, imbed

lodging *often plural* = <u>accommodation</u>, rooms, apartments, quarters, digs (*Brit. informal*), shelter, residence, abode

lofty 1 = <u>noble</u>, grand, distinguished, renowned, elevated, dignified, illustrious, exalted ≠ humble 2 = <u>high</u>, raised, towering, soaring, elevated ≠ low 3 = <u>haughty</u>, proud, arrogant, patronizing, condescending, disdainful, supercilious ≠ modest

log NOUN 1 = <u>stump</u>, block, branch, chunk, trunk 2 = <u>record</u>, account, register, journal, diary, logbook
● VERB = <u>record</u>, enter, note, register, chart, put down, set down

logic = <u>reason</u>, reasoning, sense, good sense

logical 1 = <u>rational</u>, clear, reasoned, sound, consistent, valid, coherent, well-organized ≠ illogical 2 = <u>reasonable</u>, sensible, natural, wise, plausible ≠ unlikely

lone = <u>solitary</u>, single, one, only, sole, unaccompanied

loneliness = <u>solitude</u>, isolation, desolation, seclusion

lonely 1 = <u>solitary</u>, alone, isolated, abandoned, lone, withdrawn, single, forsaken ≠ accompanied 2 = <u>desolate</u>, deserted, remote, isolated, out-of-the-way, secluded, uninhabited, godforsaken ≠ crowded

lonesome (*Chiefly U.S. & Canad.*) = <u>lonely</u>, gloomy, dreary, desolate, forlorn, friendless, companionless

long¹ 1 = <u>elongated</u>, extended, stretched, expanded, extensive, lengthy, far-reaching, spread out ≠ short 2 = <u>prolonged</u>, sustained, lengthy, lingering, protracted, interminable, spun out, long-drawn-out ≠ brief

long² = <u>desire</u>, want, wish, burn, pine, lust, crave, yearn

longing = <u>desire</u>, hope, wish, burning, urge, ambition, hunger, yen (*informal*) ≠ indifference

long-standing = <u>established</u>, fixed, enduring, abiding, long-lasting, long-established, time-honoured

look VERB 1 = <u>see</u>, view, consider, watch, eye, study, survey, examine 2 = <u>search</u>, seek, hunt, forage, fossick (*Austral. & N.Z.*) 3 = <u>consider</u>, contemplate 4 = <u>face</u>, overlook 5 = <u>hope</u>, expect, await, anticipate, reckon on 6 = <u>seem</u>, appear, look like, strike you as
● NOUN 1 = <u>glimpse</u>, view, glance, observation, sight, examination, gaze, inspection 2 = <u>appearance</u>, bearing, air, style, aspect, manner, expression, impression
● PHRASES **look after something** or **someone** = <u>take care of</u>, mind, protect, tend, guard, nurse, care for, supervise
◆ **look down on** or **upon someone** = <u>disdain</u>, despise, scorn, sneer at, spurn,

contemn (*formal*) ◆ **look forward to something** = anticipate, expect, look for, wait for, await, hope for, long for ◆ **look out for something** = be careful of, beware, watch out for, pay attention to, be wary of, keep an eye out for ◆ **look someone up** = visit, call on, drop in on (*informal*), look in on ◆ **look something up** = research, find, search for, hunt for, track down, seek out ◆ **look up** = improve, develop, advance, pick up, progress, get better, shape up (*informal*), perk up ◆ **look up to someone** = respect, honour, admire, esteem, revere, defer to, think highly of

lookout 1 = watchman, guard, sentry, sentinel 2 = watch, guard, vigil 3 = watchtower, post, observatory, observation post 4 (*Informal*) = concern, business, worry

loom = appear, emerge, hover, take shape, threaten, bulk, menace, come into view

loop NOUN = curve, ring, circle, twist, curl, spiral, coil, twirl

• VERB = twist, turn, roll, knot, curl, spiral, coil, wind round

loophole = let-out, escape, excuse

loose ADJECTIVE 1 = free, detached, insecure, unfettered, unrestricted, untied, unattached, unfastened 2 = slack, easy, relaxed, sloppy, loose-fitting ≠ tight 3 (*Old-fashioned*) = promiscuous, fast, abandoned, immoral, dissipated, profligate, debauched, dissolute ≠ chaste 4 = vague, random, inaccurate, rambling, imprecise, ill-defined, indistinct, inexact ≠ precise

• VERB = free, release, liberate, detach, unleash, disconnect, set free, untie ≠ fasten

loosen VERB = untie, undo, release, separate, detach, unloose

• PHRASES **loosen up** = relax, chill (*slang*), soften, unwind, go easy (*informal*), hang loose, outspan (*S. African*), ease up *or* off

loot VERB = plunder, rob, raid, sack, rifle, ravage, ransack, pillage

• NOUN = plunder, goods, prize, haul, spoils, booty, swag (*slang*)

lord NOUN 1 = peer, nobleman, count, duke, gentleman, earl, noble, baron 2 = ruler, leader, chief, master, governor, commander, superior, liege

• PHRASES **lord it over someone** = boss around *or* about (*informal*), order around, threaten, bully, menace, intimidate, hector, bluster ◆ **the Lord** *or* **Our Lord** = Jesus Christ, God, Christ, Messiah, Jehovah, the Almighty

lose 1 = be defeated, be beaten, lose out, come to grief 2 = mislay, drop, forget, be deprived of, lose track of, misplace 3 = forfeit, miss, yield, be deprived of, pass up (*informal*)

loser = failure, flop (*informal*), also-ran, no-hoper (*Austral. slang*), dud (*informal*), non-achiever

loss NOUN 1 = losing, waste, squandering, forfeiture ≠ gain 2 *sometimes plural* = deficit, debt, deficiency, debit, depletion ≠ gain 3 = damage, cost, injury, hurt, harm ≠ advantage

• PHRASES **at a loss** = confused, puzzled, baffled, bewildered, helpless, stumped, perplexed, mystified

lost = missing, disappeared, vanished, wayward, misplaced, mislaid

lot NOUN 1 = bunch (*informal*), group, crowd, crew, set, band, quantity, assortment 2 = destiny, situation, circumstances, fortune, chance, accident, fate, doom

• PHRASES **a lot** *or* **lots** 1 = plenty, scores, masses (*informal*), load(s) (*informal*), wealth, piles (*informal*), a great deal, stack(s) 2 = often, regularly, a great deal, frequently, a good deal

lotion = cream, solution, balm, salve, liniment, embrocation

lottery 1 = raffle, draw, lotto (*Brit., N.Z., & S. African*), sweepstake 2 = gamble, chance, risk, hazard, toss-up (*informal*)

loud 1 = noisy, booming, roaring, thundering, forte (*Music*), resounding, deafening, thunderous ≠ quiet 2 = garish, bold, glaring, flamboyant, brash, flashy, lurid, gaudy ≠ sombre

loudly = noisily, vigorously, vehemently, vociferously, uproariously, lustily, shrilly, fortissimo (*Music*)

lounge VERB = relax, loaf, sprawl, lie about, take it easy, loiter, loll, laze, outspan (*S. African*)

• NOUN = sitting room, living room, parlour, drawing room, front room, reception room, television room

love VERB 1 = adore, care for, treasure, cherish, prize, worship, be devoted to, dote on ≠ hate **2** = <u>enjoy</u>, like, appreciate, relish, delight in, savour, take pleasure in, have a soft spot for ≠ dislike

● NOUN **1** = <u>passion</u>, affection, warmth, attachment, intimacy, devotion, tenderness, adoration, aroha (*N.Z.*) ≠ hatred **2** = <u>liking</u>, taste, bent for, weakness, relish for, enjoyment, devotion to, penchant for **3** = <u>beloved</u>, dear, dearest, lover, darling, honey, sweetheart, truelove ≠ enemy **4** = <u>sympathy</u>, understanding, pity, humanity, warmth, mercy, sorrow, kindness, aroha (*N.Z.*)

● PHRASES **make love** = <u>have sexual intercourse</u>, have sex, go to bed, sleep together, do it (*informal*), mate, have sexual relations, have it off (*slang*)

love affair = <u>romance</u>, relationship, affair, intrigue, liaison, amour

lovely 1 = <u>beautiful</u>, appealing, attractive, charming, pretty, handsome, good-looking, exquisite ≠ ugly **2** = <u>wonderful</u>, pleasing, nice, pleasant, engaging, marvellous, delightful, enjoyable ≠ horrible

lover = <u>sweetheart</u>, beloved, loved one, flame (*informal*), mistress, admirer, suitor, woman friend

loving 1 = <u>affectionate</u>, dear, devoted, tender, fond, doting, amorous, warm-hearted ≠ cruel **2** = <u>tender</u>, kind, caring, warm, gentle, sympathetic, considerate

low 1 = <u>small</u>, little, short, stunted, squat ≠ tall **2** = <u>inferior</u>, bad, poor, inadequate, unsatisfactory, deficient, second-rate, shoddy, half-pie (*N.Z. informal*), bodger *or* bodgie (*Austral. slang*) **3** = <u>quiet</u>, soft, gentle, whispered, muted, subdued, hushed, muffled ≠ loud **4** = <u>dejected</u>, depressed, miserable, fed up, moody, gloomy, glum, despondent ≠ happy **5** = <u>coarse</u>, common, rough, crude, rude, vulgar, undignified, disreputable **6** = <u>ill</u>, weak, frail, stricken, debilitated ≠ strong

lower ADJECTIVE **1** = <u>subordinate</u>, under, smaller, junior, minor, secondary, lesser, inferior **2** = <u>reduced</u>, cut, diminished, decreased, lessened, curtailed ≠ increased

● VERB **1** = <u>drop</u>, sink, depress, let down, submerge, take down, let fall ≠ raise **2** = <u>lessen</u>, cut, reduce, diminish, slash, decrease, prune, minimize ≠ increase

low-key = <u>subdued</u>, quiet, restrained, muted, understated, toned down

loyal = <u>faithful</u>, true, devoted, dependable, constant, staunch, trustworthy, trusty ≠ disloyal

loyalty = <u>faithfulness</u>, commitment, devotion, allegiance, fidelity, homage, obedience, constancy

luck NOUN **1** = <u>good fortune</u>, success, advantage, prosperity, blessing, windfall, godsend, serendipity **2** = <u>fortune</u>, lot, stars, chance, accident, fate, destiny, twist of fate

● PHRASES **in luck** = <u>fortunate</u>, successful, favoured, well-off, jammy (*Brit. slang*)

◆ **out of luck** = <u>unfortunate</u>, cursed, unlucky, unsuccessful

luckily = <u>fortunately</u>, happily, opportunely

lucky = <u>fortunate</u>, successful, favoured, charmed, blessed, jammy (*Brit. slang*), serendipitous ≠ unlucky

lucrative = <u>profitable</u>, rewarding, productive, fruitful, well-paid, advantageous, remunerative

ludicrous = <u>ridiculous</u>, crazy, absurd, preposterous, silly, laughable, farcical, outlandish ≠ sensible

luggage = <u>baggage</u>, things, cases, bags, gear, suitcases, paraphernalia, impedimenta

lull NOUN = <u>respite</u>, pause, quiet, silence, calm, hush, let-up (*informal*)

● VERB = <u>calm</u>, soothe, subdue, quell, allay, pacify, tranquillize

lumber¹ VERB (*Brit. informal*) = <u>burden</u>, land, load, saddle, encumber

● NOUN (*Brit.*) = <u>junk</u>, refuse, rubbish, trash, clutter, jumble

lumber² = <u>plod</u>, shuffle, shamble, trudge, stump, waddle, trundle

lumbering = <u>awkward</u>, heavy, hulking, ponderous, ungainly

lump NOUN **1** = <u>piece</u>, ball, block, mass, chunk, hunk, nugget **2** = <u>swelling</u>, growth, bump, tumour, bulge, hump, protrusion

● VERB = <u>group</u>, throw, mass, combine, collect, pool, consolidate, conglomerate

lunatic NOUN = <u>madman</u>, maniac, psychopath, nutcase (*slang*)

● ADJECTIVE = <u>mad</u>, crazy, insane, irrational, daft, deranged, crackpot (*informal*), crackbrained, off the air (*Austral. slang*)

lunge VERB = <u>pounce</u>, charge, dive, leap, plunge, thrust

● NOUN = <u>thrust</u>, charge, pounce, spring, swing, jab

lurch 1 = <u>tilt</u>, roll, pitch, list, rock, lean, heel **2** = <u>stagger</u>, reel, stumble, weave, sway, totter

lure VERB = <u>tempt</u>, draw, attract, invite, trick, seduce, entice, allure
● NOUN = <u>temptation</u>, attraction, incentive, bait, carrot (*informal*), inducement, enticement, allurement

lurk = <u>hide</u>, sneak, prowl, lie in wait, slink, skulk, conceal yourself

lush 1 = <u>abundant</u>, green, flourishing, dense, rank, verdant **2** = <u>luxurious</u>, grand, elaborate, lavish, extravagant, sumptuous, plush (*informal*), ornate

lust NOUN **1** = <u>lechery</u>, sensuality, lewdness, lasciviousness **2** = <u>desire</u>, longing, passion, appetite, craving, greed, thirst
● PHRASES **lust for** *or* **after someone** = <u>desire</u>, want, crave, yearn for, covet, hunger for *or* after ◆ **lust for** *or* **after something** = <u>desire</u>, crave, yearn for, covet

luxurious = <u>sumptuous</u>, expensive, comfortable, magnificent, splendid, lavish, plush (*informal*), opulent

luxury 1 = <u>opulence</u>, splendour, richness, extravagance, affluence, hedonism, a bed of roses, the life of Riley ≠ poverty **2** = <u>extravagance</u>, treat, extra, indulgence, frill ≠ necessity

lying NOUN = <u>dishonesty</u>, perjury, deceit, misrepresentation, mendacity, untruthfulness
● ADJECTIVE = <u>deceitful</u>, false, deceiving, treacherous, dishonest, two-faced, mendacious, perfidious ≠ truthful

lyrical = <u>enthusiastic</u>, inspired, poetic, impassioned, effusive, rhapsodic

machine 1 = <u>appliance</u>, device, apparatus, engine, tool, instrument, mechanism, gadget **2** = <u>system</u>, structure, organization, machinery, setup (*informal*)

machinery = <u>equipment</u>, gear, instruments, apparatus, technology, tackle, tools, gadgetry

macho = <u>manly</u>, masculine, chauvinist, virile

mad 1 = <u>insane</u>, crazy (*informal*), nuts (*slang*), raving, unstable, psychotic, demented, deranged, off the air (*Austral. slang*) ≠ sane **2** = <u>foolish</u>, absurd, wild, stupid, daft (*informal*), irrational, senseless, preposterous ≠ sensible **3** (*Informal*) = <u>angry</u>, furious, incensed, enraged, livid (*informal*), berserk, berko (*Austral. slang*), tooshie (*Austral. slang*), off the air (*Austral. slang*) ≠ calm **4** = <u>enthusiastic</u>, wild, crazy (*informal*), ardent, fanatical, avid, impassioned, infatuated ≠ nonchalant **5** = <u>frenzied</u>, wild, excited, frenetic, uncontrolled, unrestrained

madden = <u>infuriate</u>, irritate, incense, enrage, upset, annoy, inflame, drive you crazy ≠ calm

madly 1 (*Informal*) = <u>passionately</u>, wildly, desperately, intensely, to distraction, devotedly **2** = <u>foolishly</u>, wildly, absurdly, ludicrously, irrationally, senselessly **3** = <u>energetically</u>, wildly, furiously, excitedly, recklessly, speedily, like mad (*informal*) **4** = <u>insanely</u>, frantically, hysterically, crazily, deliriously, distractedly, frenziedly

madness 1 = <u>insanity</u>, mental illness, delusion, mania, dementia, distraction, aberration, psychosis **2** = <u>foolishness</u>, nonsense, folly, absurdity, idiocy, wildness, daftness (*informal*), foolhardiness

magazine = <u>journal</u>, publication, supplement, rag (*informal*), issue, glossy (*informal*), pamphlet, periodical

magic NOUN **1** = <u>sorcery</u>, wizardry, witchcraft, enchantment, black art, necromancy **2** = <u>conjuring</u>, illusion, trickery, sleight of hand, legerdemain, prestidigitation **3** = <u>charm</u>, power, glamour, fascination, magnetism, enchantment, allurement
● ADJECTIVE = <u>miraculous</u>, entrancing, charming, fascinating, marvellous, magical, enchanting, bewitching

magician 1 = <u>conjuror</u>, illusionist, prestidigitator **2** = <u>sorcerer</u>, witch, wizard, illusionist, warlock, necromancer, enchanter *or* enchantress

magistrate = <u>judge</u>, justice, justice of the

peace, J.P.

magnetic = <u>attractive</u>, irresistible, seductive, captivating, charming, fascinating, charismatic, hypnotic ≠ repulsive

magnificent 1 = <u>splendid</u>, impressive, imposing, glorious, gorgeous, majestic, regal, sublime ≠ ordinary 2 = <u>brilliant</u>, fine, excellent, outstanding, superb, splendid

magnify 1 = <u>enlarge</u>, increase, boost, expand, intensify, blow up (*informal*), heighten, amplify ≠ reduce 2 = <u>make worse</u>, exaggerate, intensify, worsen, exacerbate, increase, inflame 3 = <u>exaggerate</u>, overstate, inflate, overplay, overemphasize ≠ understate

magnitude 1 = <u>importance</u>, consequence, significance, moment, note, weight, greatness ≠ unimportance 2 = <u>immensity</u>, size, extent, enormity, volume, vastness ≠ smallness 3 = <u>intensity</u>, amplitude

maid 1 = <u>servant</u>, chambermaid, housemaid, menial, maidservant, female servant, domestic (*archaic*), parlourmaid 2 (*Literary*) = <u>girl</u>, maiden, lass, damsel, lassie (*informal*), wench

maiden NOUN (*Literary*) = <u>girl</u>, maid, lass, damsel, virgin, lassie (*informal*), wench
● ADJECTIVE 1 = <u>first</u>, initial, inaugural, introductory 2 = <u>unmarried</u>, unwed

mail NOUN = <u>letters</u>, post, correspondence
● VERB = <u>post</u>, send, forward, e-mail, dispatch

main ADJECTIVE = <u>chief</u>, leading, head, central, essential, primary, principal, foremost ≠ minor
● PLURAL NOUN 1 = <u>pipeline</u>, channel, pipe, conduit, duct 2 = <u>cable</u>, line, electricity supply, mains supply
● PHRASES **in the main** = <u>on the whole</u>, generally, mainly, mostly, in general, for the most part

mainly = <u>chiefly</u>, mostly, largely, principally, primarily, on the whole, predominantly, in the main

mainstream = <u>conventional</u>, general, established, received, accepted, current, prevailing, orthodox ≠ unconventional

maintain 1 = <u>continue</u>, retain, preserve, sustain, carry on, keep up, prolong, perpetuate ≠ end 2 = <u>assert</u>, state, claim, insist, declare, contend, profess, avow ≠ disavow 3 = <u>look after</u>, care for, take care

of, conserve, keep in good condition

maintenance 1 = <u>upkeep</u>, keeping, care, repairs, conservation, nurture, preservation 2 = <u>allowance</u>, support, keep, alimony 3 = <u>continuation</u>, carrying-on, perpetuation, prolongation

majestic = <u>grand</u>, magnificent, impressive, superb, splendid, regal, stately, monumental ≠ modest

majesty = <u>grandeur</u>, glory, splendour, magnificence, nobility ≠ triviality

major 1 = <u>important</u>, critical, significant, great, serious, crucial, outstanding, notable 2 = <u>main</u>, higher, greater, bigger, leading, chief, senior, supreme ≠ minor

majority 1 = <u>most</u>, mass, bulk, best part, better part, lion's share, preponderance, greater number 2 = <u>adulthood</u>, maturity, age of consent, seniority, manhood *or* womanhood

make VERB 1 = <u>produce</u>, cause, create, effect, lead to, generate, bring about, give rise to 2 = <u>perform</u>, do, effect, carry out, execute 3 = <u>force</u>, cause, compel, drive, require, oblige, induce, constrain 4 = <u>create</u>, build, produce, manufacture, form, fashion, construct, assemble 5 = <u>earn</u>, get, gain, net, win, clear, obtain, bring in 6 = <u>amount to</u>, total, constitute, add up to, count as, tot up to (*informal*)
● NOUN = <u>brand</u>, sort, style, model, kind, type, variety, marque
● PHRASES **make for something** = <u>head for</u>, aim for, head towards, be bound for
◆ **make it** (*Informal*) = <u>succeed</u>, prosper, arrive (*informal*), get on, crack it (*informal*)
◆ **make off** = <u>flee</u>, clear out (*informal*), bolt, take to your heels, run away *or* off
◆ **make something up** = <u>invent</u>, create, construct, compose, frame, coin, devise, originate ◆ **make up** = <u>settle your differences</u>, bury the hatchet, call it quits, declare a truce, be friends again ◆ **make up for something** = <u>compensate for</u>, make amends for, atone for, balance out, offset, make recompense for ◆ **make up something** 1 = <u>form</u>, account for, constitute, compose, comprise 2 = <u>complete</u>, supply, fill, round off

maker = <u>manufacturer</u>, producer, builder, constructor

makeshift = <u>temporary</u>, provisional, substitute, expedient, stopgap

make-up 1 = <u>cosmetics</u>, paint (*informal*),

powder, face (*informal*), greasepaint (*Theatre*) **2** = <u>nature</u>, character, constitution, temperament, disposition **3** = <u>structure</u>, organization, arrangement, construction, assembly, constitution, format, composition

making NOUN = <u>creation</u>, production, manufacture, construction, assembly, composition, fabrication
● PLURAL NOUN = <u>beginnings</u>, potential, capacity, ingredients

male = <u>masculine</u>, manly, macho, virile ≠ female

malicious = <u>spiteful</u>, malevolent, resentful, vengeful, rancorous, ill-disposed, ill-natured ≠ benevolent

mammoth = <u>colossal</u>, huge, giant, massive, enormous, immense, gigantic, monumental ≠ tiny

man NOUN **1** = <u>male</u>, guy (*informal*), fellow (*informal*), gentleman, bloke (*Brit. informal*), chap (*Brit. informal*), dude (*U.S. informal*), geezer (*informal*) **2** = <u>human</u>, human being, person, individual, soul **3** = <u>mankind</u>, humanity, people, human race, humankind, Homo sapiens
● VERB = <u>staff</u>, people, crew, occupy, garrison

mana (*N.Z.*) = <u>authority</u>, influence, power, might, standing, status, importance, eminence

manage **1** = <u>be in charge of</u>, run, handle, direct, conduct, command, administer, supervise **2** = <u>organize</u>, use, handle, regulate **3** = <u>cope</u>, survive, succeed, carry on, make do, get by (*informal*), muddle through **4** = <u>perform</u>, do, achieve, carry out, undertake, cope with, accomplish, contrive **5** = <u>control</u>, handle, manipulate

management **1** = <u>administration</u>, control, running, operation, handling, direction, command, supervision **2** = <u>directors</u>, board, executive(s), administration, employers

manager = <u>supervisor</u>, head, director, executive, boss (*informal*), governor, administrator, organizer, baas (*S. African*)

mandate = <u>command</u>, order, commission, instruction, decree, directive, edict

mandatory = <u>compulsory</u>, required, binding, obligatory, requisite ≠ optional

manhood = <u>manliness</u>, masculinity, virility

manifest ADJECTIVE = <u>obvious</u>, apparent, patent, evident, clear, glaring, noticeable, blatant ≠ concealed
● VERB = <u>display</u>, show, reveal, express, demonstrate, expose, exhibit ≠ conceal

manifestation **1** = <u>sign</u>, symptom, indication, mark, example, evidence, proof, testimony **2** = <u>display</u>, show, exhibition, expression, demonstration

manipulate **1** = <u>influence</u>, control, direct, negotiate, exploit, manoeuvre **2** = <u>work</u>, use, operate, handle

mankind = <u>people</u>, man, humanity, human race, humankind, Homo sapiens

manly = <u>virile</u>, masculine, strong, brave, bold, strapping, vigorous, courageous ≠ effeminate

man-made = <u>artificial</u>, manufactured, mock, synthetic, ersatz

manner NOUN **1** = <u>style</u>, way, fashion, method, custom, mode **2** = <u>behaviour</u>, air, bearing, conduct, aspect, demeanour **3** = <u>type</u>, form, sort, kind, variety, brand, category
● PLURAL NOUN **1** = <u>conduct</u>, behaviour, demeanour **2** = <u>politeness</u>, courtesy, etiquette, refinement, decorum, p's and q's **3** = <u>protocol</u>, customs, social graces

mannered = <u>affected</u>, artificial, pretentious, stilted, arty-farty (*informal*) ≠ natural

manoeuvre VERB **1** = <u>scheme</u>, wangle (*informal*), machinate **2** = <u>manipulate</u>, arrange, organize, set up, engineer, fix, orchestrate, contrive
● NOUN **1** = <u>stratagem</u>, scheme, trick, tactic, intrigue, dodge, ploy, ruse **2** *often plural* = <u>movement</u>, operation, exercise, war game

mansion = <u>residence</u>, manor, hall, villa, seat

mantle **1** = <u>covering</u>, screen, curtain, blanket, veil, shroud, canopy, pall **2** = <u>cloak</u>, wrap, cape, hood, shawl

manual ADJECTIVE **1** = <u>physical</u>, human **2** = <u>hand-operated</u>, hand, non-automatic
● NOUN = <u>handbook</u>, guide, instructions, bible

manufacture VERB **1** = <u>make</u>, build, produce, construct, create, turn out, assemble, put together **2** = <u>concoct</u>, make up, invent, devise, fabricate, think up, cook up (*informal*), trump up
● NOUN = <u>making</u>, production, construction, assembly, creation

manufacturer = <u>maker</u>, producer,

builder, creator, industrialist, constructor

many DETERMINER = <u>numerous</u>, various, countless, abundant, myriad, innumerable, manifold, umpteen (*informal*)

● PRONOUN = <u>a lot</u>, lots (*informal*), plenty, scores, heaps (*informal*)

mar 1 = <u>harm</u>, damage, hurt, spoil, stain, taint, tarnish 2 = <u>ruin</u>, spoil, scar, flaw, impair, detract from, deform, blemish ≠ improve

march VERB 1 = <u>parade</u>, walk, file, pace, stride, swagger 2 = <u>walk</u>, strut, storm, sweep, stride, flounce

● NOUN 1 = <u>walk</u>, trek, slog, yomp (*Brit. informal*), routemarch 2 = <u>progress</u>, development, advance, evolution, progression

margin = <u>edge</u>, side, border, boundary, verge, brink, rim, perimeter

marginal 1 = <u>insignificant</u>, small, minor, slight, minimal, negligible 2 = <u>borderline</u>, bordering, on the edge, peripheral

marijuana = <u>cannabis</u>, pot (*slang*), dope (*slang*), grass (*slang*), hemp, dagga (*S. African*)

marine = <u>nautical</u>, maritime, naval, seafaring, seagoing

mariner = <u>sailor</u>, seaman, sea dog, seafarer, salt

marital = <u>matrimonial</u>, nuptial, conjugal, connubial

maritime 1 = <u>nautical</u>, marine, naval, oceanic, seafaring 2 = <u>coastal</u>, seaside, littoral

mark NOUN 1 = <u>spot</u>, stain, streak, smudge, line, scratch, scar, blot 2 = <u>characteristic</u>, feature, standard, quality, measure, stamp, attribute, criterion 3 = <u>indication</u>, sign, symbol, token 4 = <u>brand</u>, impression, label, device, flag, symbol, token, emblem 5 = <u>target</u>, goal, aim, purpose, object, objective

● VERB 1 = <u>scar</u>, scratch, stain, streak, blot, smudge, blemish 2 = <u>label</u>, identify, brand, flag, stamp, characterize 3 = <u>grade</u>, correct, assess, evaluate, appraise 4 = <u>distinguish</u>, show, illustrate, exemplify, denote 5 = <u>observe</u>, mind, note, notice, attend to, pay attention to, pay heed to

marked = <u>noticeable</u>, clear, decided, striking, obvious, prominent, patent, distinct ≠ imperceptible

markedly = <u>noticeably</u>, clearly, obviously, considerably, distinctly, decidedly, strikingly, conspicuously

market NOUN = <u>fair</u>, mart, bazaar, souk (*Arabic*)

● VERB = <u>sell</u>, promote, retail, peddle, vend

maroon = <u>abandon</u>, leave, desert, strand, leave high and dry (*informal*)

marriage = <u>wedding</u>, match, nuptials, wedlock, matrimony

RELATED WORDS

adjectives: conjugal, marital, nuptial

marry 1 = <u>tie the knot</u> (*informal*), wed, get hitched (*slang*) 2 = <u>unite</u>, join, link, bond, ally, merge, knit, unify

marsh = <u>swamp</u>, bog, slough, fen, quagmire, morass

marshal 1 = <u>conduct</u>, take, lead, guide, steer, escort, shepherd, usher 2 = <u>arrange</u>, group, order, line up, organize, deploy, array, draw up

martial = <u>military</u>, belligerent, warlike, bellicose

marvel VERB = <u>be amazed</u>, wonder, gape, be awed

● NOUN 1 = <u>wonder</u>, phenomenon, miracle, portent 2 = <u>genius</u>, prodigy

marvellous = <u>excellent</u>, great (*informal*), wonderful, brilliant, amazing, extraordinary, superb, spectacular, booshit (*Austral. slang*), exo (*Austral. slang*), sik (*Austral. slang*) ≠ terrible

masculine = <u>male</u>, manly, mannish, manlike, virile

mask NOUN = <u>façade</u>, disguise, front, cover, screen, veil, guise, camouflage

● VERB = <u>disguise</u>, hide, conceal, obscure, cover (up), screen, blanket, veil

mass NOUN 1 = <u>lot</u>, collection, load, pile, quantity, bunch, stack, heap 2 = <u>piece</u>, block, lump, chunk, hunk 3 = <u>matter</u>, weight, extent, bulk, magnitude, greatness

● ADJECTIVE = <u>large-scale</u>, general, widespread, extensive, universal, wholesale, indiscriminate

● VERB = <u>gather</u>, assemble, accumulate, collect, rally, swarm, throng, congregate

massacre NOUN = <u>slaughter</u>, murder, holocaust, carnage, extermination, annihilation, butchery, blood bath

● VERB = <u>slaughter</u>, kill, murder, butcher, wipe out, exterminate, mow down, cut to pieces

massage NOUN = <u>rub-down</u>, manipulation

● VERB 1 = <u>rub down</u>, manipulate, knead 2 = <u>manipulate</u>, alter, distort, doctor, cook (*informal*), fix (*informal*), rig, fiddle (*informal*)

massive = <u>huge</u>, big, enormous, immense, hefty, gigantic, monumental, mammoth ≠ tiny

master NOUN 1 = <u>lord</u>, ruler, commander, chief, director, manager, boss (*informal*), head, baas (*S. African*) ≠ servant 2 = <u>expert</u>, maestro, ace (*informal*), genius, wizard, virtuoso, doyen, past master, fundi (*S. African*) ≠ amateur 3 = <u>teacher</u>, tutor, instructor ≠ student

● ADJECTIVE = <u>main</u>, principal, chief, prime, foremost, predominant ≠ lesser

● VERB 1 = <u>learn</u>, understand, pick up, grasp, get the hang of (*informal*), know inside out, know backwards 2 = <u>overcome</u>, defeat, conquer, tame, triumph over, vanquish ≠ give in to

masterly = <u>skilful</u>, expert, crack (*informal*), supreme, world-class, consummate, first-rate, masterful

mastermind VERB = <u>plan</u>, manage, direct, organize, devise, conceive

● NOUN = <u>organizer</u>, director, manager, engineer, brain(s) (*informal*), architect, planner

masterpiece = <u>classic</u>, tour de force (*French*), pièce de résistance (*French*), magnum opus, jewel

mastery 1 = <u>understanding</u>, skill, know-how, expertise, prowess, finesse, proficiency, virtuosity 2 = <u>control</u>, command, domination, superiority, supremacy, upper hand, ascendancy, mana (*N.Z.*), whip hand

match NOUN 1 = <u>game</u>, test, competition, trial, tie, contest, fixture, bout 2 = <u>marriage</u>, pairing, alliance, partnership 3 = <u>equal</u>, rival, peer, counterpart

● VERB 1 = <u>correspond with</u>, go with, fit with, harmonize with 2 = <u>correspond</u>, agree, accord, square, coincide, tally, conform, match up 3 = <u>rival</u>, equal, compete with, compare with, emulate, measure up to

matching = <u>identical</u>, like, twin, equivalent, corresponding, coordinating ≠ different

mate NOUN 1 (*Informal*) = <u>friend</u>, pal (*informal*), companion, buddy (*informal*), comrade, chum (*informal*), mucker (*Brit. informal*), crony, cobber (*Austral. & N.Z. old-fashioned informal*), E hoa (*N.Z.*)

2 = <u>partner</u>, lover, companion, spouse, consort, helpmeet, husband *or* wife 3 = <u>assistant</u>, subordinate, apprentice, helper, accomplice, sidekick (*informal*) 4 = <u>colleague</u>, associate, companion

● VERB = <u>pair</u>, couple, breed

material NOUN 1 = <u>substance</u>, matter, stuff 2 = <u>cloth</u>, fabric, textile 3 = <u>information</u>, details, facts, notes, evidence, particulars, data, info (*informal*)

● ADJECTIVE 1 = <u>physical</u>, solid, substantial, concrete, bodily, tangible, palpable, corporeal 2 = <u>relevant</u>, important, significant, essential, vital, serious, meaningful, applicable

materially = <u>significantly</u>, much, greatly, essentially, seriously, gravely, substantially ≠ insignificantly

maternal = <u>motherly</u>, protective, nurturing, maternalistic

maternity = <u>motherhood</u>, parenthood, motherliness

matted = <u>tangled</u>, knotted, unkempt, knotty, tousled, ratty, uncombed

matter NOUN 1 = <u>situation</u>, concern, business, question, event, subject, affair, incident 2 = <u>substance</u>, material, body, stuff

● VERB = <u>be important</u>, make a difference, count, be relevant, make any difference, carry weight, cut any ice (*informal*), be of account

matter-of-fact = <u>unsentimental</u>, plain, sober, down-to-earth, mundane, prosaic, deadpan, unimaginative

mature VERB = <u>develop</u>, grow up, bloom, blossom, come of age, age

● ADJECTIVE 1 = <u>matured</u>, seasoned, ripe, mellow 2 = <u>grown-up</u>, adult, of age, fully fledged, full-grown ≠ immature

maturity 1 = <u>adulthood</u>, puberty, coming of age, pubescence, manhood *or* womanhood ≠ immaturity 2 = <u>ripeness</u>

maul 1 = <u>mangle</u>, claw, lacerate, tear, mangulate (*Austral. slang*) 2 = <u>ill-treat</u>, abuse, batter, molest, manhandle

maverick NOUN = <u>rebel</u>, radical, dissenter, individualist, protester, eccentric, heretic, nonconformist ≠ traditionalist

● ADJECTIVE = <u>rebel</u>, radical, dissenting, individualistic, eccentric, heretical, iconoclastic, nonconformist

maximum ADJECTIVE = <u>greatest</u>, highest, supreme, paramount, utmost, most, topmost ≠ minimal

● NOUN = <u>top</u>, peak, ceiling, utmost, upper limit ≠ minimum

maybe = <u>perhaps</u>, possibly, perchance (*archaic*)

mayhem = <u>chaos</u>, trouble, violence, disorder, destruction, confusion, havoc, fracas

maze = <u>web</u>, confusion, tangle, labyrinth, imbroglio, complex network

meadow = <u>field</u>, pasture, grassland, lea (*poetic*)

mean¹ 1 = <u>signify</u>, indicate, represent, express, stand for, convey, spell out, symbolize 2 = <u>imply</u>, suggest, intend, hint at, insinuate 3 = <u>intend</u>, want, plan, expect, design, aim, think

mean² 1 = <u>miserly</u>, stingy, parsimonious, niggardly, mercenary, penny-pinching, ungenerous, tight-fisted, snoep (*S. African informal*) ≠ generous 2 = <u>dishonourable</u>, petty, shameful, shabby, vile, callous, sordid, despicable, scungy (*Austral. & N.Z.*) ≠ honourable

mean³ NOUN = <u>average</u>, middle, balance, norm, midpoint

● ADJECTIVE = <u>average</u>, middle, standard

meaning 1 = <u>significance</u>, message, substance, drift, connotation, gist 2 = <u>definition</u>, sense

meaningful = <u>significant</u>, important, material, useful, relevant, valid, worthwhile, purposeful ≠ trivial

meaningless = <u>nonsensical</u>, senseless, inconsequential, inane ≠ worthwhile

means PLURAL NOUN 1 = <u>method</u>, way, process, medium, agency, instrument, mode 2 = <u>money</u>, funds, capital, income, resources, fortune, wealth, affluence

● PHRASES **by all means** = <u>certainly</u>, surely, of course, definitely, doubtlessly

◆ **by no means** = <u>in no way</u>, definitely not, not in the least, on no account

meantime *or* **meanwhile** = <u>at the same time</u>, simultaneously, concurrently

meanwhile *or* **meantime** = <u>for now</u>, in the interim

measure VERB = <u>quantify</u>, determine, assess, weigh, calculate, evaluate, compute, gauge

● NOUN 1 = <u>quantity</u>, share, amount, allowance, portion, quota, ration, allotment 2 = <u>action</u>, act, step, procedure, means, control, initiative, manoeuvre

3 = <u>gauge</u>, rule, scale, metre, ruler, yardstick 4 = <u>law</u>, act, bill, legislation, resolution, statute

measured 1 = <u>steady</u>, even, slow, regular, dignified, stately, solemn, leisurely 2 = <u>considered</u>, reasoned, studied, calculated, deliberate, sober, well-thought-out

measurement = <u>calculation</u>, assessment, evaluation, valuation, computation, calibration, mensuration

meat = <u>food</u>, flesh, kai (*N.Z. informal*)

mechanical 1 = <u>automatic</u>, automated, mechanized, power-driven, motor-driven ≠ manual 2 = <u>unthinking</u>, routine, automatic, instinctive, involuntary, impersonal, cursory, perfunctory ≠ conscious

mechanism 1 = <u>process</u>, way, means, system, operation, agency, method, technique 2 = <u>machine</u>, device, tool, instrument, appliance, apparatus, contrivance

mediate = <u>intervene</u>, step in (*informal*), intercede, referee, umpire, reconcile, arbitrate, conciliate

mediation = <u>arbitration</u>, intervention, reconciliation, conciliation, intercession

mediator = <u>negotiator</u>, arbitrator, referee, umpire, intermediary, middleman, arbiter, peacemaker

medicine = <u>remedy</u>, drug, cure, prescription, medication, nostrum, medicament

mediocre = <u>second-rate</u>, average, ordinary, indifferent, middling, pedestrian, inferior, so-so (*informal*), half-pie (*N.Z. informal*) ≠ excellent

meditation = <u>reflection</u>, thought, study, musing, pondering, contemplation, rumination, cogitation

medium ADJECTIVE = <u>average</u>, mean, middle, middling, fair, intermediate, midway, mediocre ≠ extraordinary

● NOUN 1 = <u>spiritualist</u>, seer, clairvoyant, fortune teller, channeller 2 = <u>middle</u>, mean, centre, average, compromise, midpoint

meet 1 = <u>encounter</u>, come across, run into, happen on, find, contact, confront, bump into (*informal*) ≠ avoid 2 = <u>gather</u>, collect, assemble, get together, come together, muster, convene, congregate ≠ disperse 3 = <u>fulfil</u>, match (up to), answer, satisfy, discharge, comply with, come up to, conform to ≠ fall short of **4** = <u>experience</u>, face, suffer, bear, go through, encounter, endure, undergo **5** = <u>converge</u>, join, cross, touch, connect, come together, link up, intersect ≠ diverge

meeting 1 = <u>conference</u>, gathering, assembly, congress, session, convention, get-together (*informal*), reunion, hui (*N.Z.*) **2** = <u>encounter</u>, introduction, confrontation, engagement, rendezvous, tryst, assignation

melancholy ADJECTIVE = <u>sad</u>, depressed, miserable, gloomy, glum, mournful, despondent, dispirited ≠ happy
● NOUN = <u>sadness</u>, depression, misery, gloom, sorrow, unhappiness, despondency, dejection ≠ happiness

mellow ADJECTIVE **1** = <u>full-flavoured</u>, rich, sweet, delicate **2** = <u>ripe</u>, mature, ripened ≠ unripe
● VERB **1** = <u>relax</u>, improve, settle, calm, mature, soften, sweeten **2** = <u>season</u>, develop, improve, ripen

melody 1 = <u>tune</u>, song, theme, air, music, strain **2** = <u>tunefulness</u>, harmony, musicality, euphony, melodiousness

melt 1 = <u>dissolve</u>, run, soften, fuse, thaw, defrost, liquefy, unfreeze **2** *often with away* = <u>disappear</u>, fade, vanish, dissolve, disperse, evaporate, evanesce **3** = <u>soften</u>, relax, disarm, mollify

member = <u>representative</u>, associate, supporter, fellow, subscriber, comrade, disciple

membership 1 = <u>participation</u>, belonging, fellowship, enrolment **2** = <u>members</u>, body, associates, fellows

memoir = <u>account</u>, life, record, journal, essay, biography, narrative, monograph

memoirs = <u>autobiography</u>, diary, life story, experiences, memories, journals, recollections, reminiscences

memorable = <u>noteworthy</u>, celebrated, historic, striking, famous, significant, remarkable, notable ≠ forgettable

memorandum = <u>note</u>, minute, message, communication, reminder, memo, jotting

memorial NOUN = <u>monument</u>, shrine, plaque, cenotaph
● ADJECTIVE = <u>commemorative</u>, remembrance, monumental

memory 1 = <u>recall</u>, mind, retention, ability to remember, powers of recall,

powers of retention **2** = <u>recollection</u>, reminder, reminiscence, impression, echo, remembrance **3** = <u>commemoration</u>, respect, honour, recognition, tribute, remembrance, observance

menace NOUN **1** (*Informal*) = <u>nuisance</u>, plague, pest, annoyance, troublemaker **2** = <u>threat</u>, warning, intimidation, ill-omen, ominousness
● VERB = <u>bully</u>, threaten, intimidate, terrorize, frighten, scare

menacing = <u>threatening</u>, frightening, forbidding, looming, intimidating, ominous, louring *or* lowering ≠ encouraging

mend VERB **1** = <u>repair</u>, fix, restore, renew, patch up, renovate, refit, retouch **2** = <u>darn</u>, repair, patch, stitch, sew **3** = <u>heal</u>, improve, recover, get better, be all right, be cured, recuperate, pull through **4** = <u>improve</u>, reform, correct, revise, amend, rectify, ameliorate, emend
● PHRASES **on the mend** = <u>convalescent</u>, improving, recovering, getting better, recuperating

mental 1 = <u>intellectual</u>, rational, theoretical, cognitive, brain, conceptual, cerebral **2** (*Informal*) = <u>insane</u>, mad, disturbed, unstable, mentally ill, psychotic, unbalanced, deranged

mentality = <u>attitude</u>, character, personality, psychology, make-up, outlook, disposition, cast of mind

mentally = <u>psychologically</u>, intellectually, inwardly

mention VERB = <u>refer to</u>, point out, bring up, state, reveal, declare, disclose, intimate
● NOUN **1** *often with of* = <u>reference to</u>, observation, indication, remark on, allusion to **2** = <u>acknowledgment</u>, recognition, tribute, citation, honourable mention

mentor = <u>guide</u>, teacher, coach, adviser, tutor, instructor, counsellor, guru

menu = <u>bill of fare</u>, tariff (*chiefly Brit.*), set menu, table d'hôte, carte du jour (*French*)

merchandise = <u>goods</u>, produce, stock, products, commodities, wares

merchant = <u>tradesman</u>, dealer, trader, broker, retailer, supplier, seller, salesman

mercy 1 = <u>compassion</u>, pity, forgiveness, grace, kindness, clemency, leniency, forbearance ≠ cruelty **2** = <u>blessing</u>, boon, godsend

mere 1 = <u>simple</u>, nothing more than, common, plain, pure 2 = <u>bare</u>, slender, trifling, meagre, just, only, basic, no more than

merge 1 = <u>combine</u>, blend, fuse, amalgamate, unite, join, mix, mingle ≠ separate 2 = <u>join</u>, unite, combine, fuse ≠ separate 3 = <u>melt</u>, blend, mingle

merger = <u>union</u>, fusion, consolidation, amalgamation, combination, coalition, incorporation

merit NOUN = <u>advantage</u>, value, quality, worth, strength, asset, virtue, strong point
● VERB = <u>deserve</u>, warrant, be entitled to, earn, have a right to, be worthy of

merry 1 = <u>cheerful</u>, happy, carefree, jolly, festive, joyous, convivial, blithe ≠ gloomy 2 (*Brit. informal*) = <u>tipsy</u>, happy, mellow, tiddly (*slang, chiefly Brit.*), squiffy (*Brit. informal*)

mesh NOUN = <u>net</u>, netting, network, web, tracery
● VERB = <u>engage</u>, combine, connect, knit, coordinate, interlock, dovetail, harmonize

mess NOUN 1 = <u>untidiness</u>, disorder, confusion, chaos, litter, clutter, disarray, jumble 2 = <u>shambles</u> 3 = <u>difficulty</u>, dilemma, plight, hole (*informal*), fix (*informal*), jam (*informal*), muddle, pickle (*informal*), uphill (*S. African*)
● PHRASES **mess about** or **around** = <u>potter about</u>, dabble, amuse yourself, fool about or around, muck about or around (*informal*), play about or around, trifle ◆ **mess something up** 1 = <u>botch</u>, muck something up (*Brit. slang*), muddle something up 2 = <u>dirty</u>, pollute, clutter, disarrange, dishevel ◆ **mess with something** or **someone** = <u>interfere</u>, play, fiddle (*informal*), tamper, tinker, meddle

message 1 = <u>communication</u>, note, bulletin, word, letter, dispatch, memorandum, communiqué 2 = <u>point</u>, meaning, idea, moral, theme, import, purport

messenger = <u>courier</u>, runner, carrier, herald, envoy, go-between, emissary, delivery boy

messy 1 = <u>disorganized</u>, sloppy (*informal*), untidy 2 = <u>dirty</u> 3 = <u>untidy</u>, disordered, chaotic, muddled, cluttered, shambolic, disorganized ≠ tidy 4 = <u>dishevelled</u>, ruffled, untidy, rumpled, bedraggled, tousled, uncombed 5 = <u>confusing</u>, difficult, complex, confused, tangled, chaotic, tortuous

metaphor = <u>figure of speech</u>, image, symbol, analogy, conceit (*literary*), allegory, trope, figurative expression

method 1 = <u>manner</u>, process, approach, technique, way, system, style, procedure 2 = <u>orderliness</u>, planning, order, system, purpose, pattern, organization, regularity

midday = <u>noon</u>, twelve o'clock, noonday

middle NOUN = <u>centre</u>, heart, midst, halfway point, midpoint, midsection
● ADJECTIVE 1 = <u>central</u>, medium, mid, intervening, halfway, intermediate, median 2 = <u>intermediate</u>, intervening

middle-class = <u>bourgeois</u>, traditional, conventional

middling 1 = <u>mediocre</u>, all right, indifferent, so-so (*informal*), unremarkable, tolerable, run-of-the-mill, passable, half-pie (*N.Z. informal*) 2 = <u>moderate</u>, medium, average, fair, ordinary, modest, adequate

midnight = <u>twelve o'clock</u>, middle of the night, dead of night, the witching hour

midst
PHRASES **in the midst of** = <u>among</u>, during, in the middle of, surrounded by, amidst, in the thick of

midway ADJECTIVE or ADVERB = <u>halfway</u>, in the middle of, part-way, equidistant, at the midpoint, betwixt and between

might NOUN = <u>power</u>, force, energy, strength, vigour
● PHRASES **with all your might** = <u>forcefully</u>, vigorously, mightily, manfully, lustily

mighty = <u>powerful</u>, strong, strapping, robust, vigorous, sturdy, forceful, lusty ≠ weak

migrant NOUN = <u>wanderer</u>, immigrant, traveller, rover, nomad, emigrant, itinerant, drifter
● ADJECTIVE = <u>itinerant</u>, wandering, drifting, roving, travelling, shifting, immigrant, transient

migrate = <u>move</u>, travel, journey, wander, trek, voyage, roam, emigrate

migration = <u>wandering</u>, journey, voyage, travel, movement, trek, emigration, roving

mild 1 = <u>gentle</u>, calm, easy-going, meek, placid, docile, peaceable, equable ≠ harsh 2 = <u>temperate</u>, warm, calm, moderate, tranquil, balmy ≠ cold **3** = bland, thin, smooth, tasteless, insipid, flavourless

militant = aggressive, active, vigorous, assertive, combative ≠ peaceful

military ADJECTIVE = warlike, armed, soldierly, martial
 • NOUN = armed forces, forces, services, army

milk = exploit, pump, take advantage of
 RELATED WORD
 adjective: lactic

mill NOUN **1** = grinder, crusher, quern **2** = factory, works, plant, workshop, foundry
 • VERB = grind, pound, crush, powder, grate
 • PHRASES **mill about** or **around** = swarm, crowd, stream, surge, throng

mimic VERB = imitate, do (*informal*), take off (*informal*), ape, parody, caricature, impersonate
 • NOUN = imitator, impressionist, copycat (*informal*), impersonator, caricaturist

mince **1** = cut, grind, crumble, dice, hash, chop up **2** = tone down, spare, moderate, weaken, soften

mincing = affected, camp (*informal*), precious, pretentious, dainty, sissy, effeminate, foppish

mind NOUN **1** = memory, recollection, remembrance, powers of recollection **2** = intelligence, reason, reasoning, understanding, sense, brain(s) (*informal*), wits, intellect **3** = intention, wish, desire, urge, fancy, leaning, notion, inclination **4** = sanity, reason, senses, judgment, wits, marbles (*informal*), rationality, mental balance
 • VERB **1** = take offence at, dislike, care about, object to, resent, disapprove of, be bothered by, be affronted by **2** = be careful, watch, take care, be wary, be cautious, be on your guard **3** = look after, watch, protect, tend, guard, take care of, attend to, keep an eye on **4** = pay attention to, mark, note, listen to, observe, obey, heed, take heed of
 RELATED WORD
 adjective: mental

mine NOUN **1** = pit, deposit, shaft, colliery, excavation **2** = source, store, fund, stock, supply, reserve, treasury, wealth
 • VERB = dig up, extract, quarry, unearth, excavate, hew, dig for

miner = coalminer, pitman (*Brit.*), collier (*Brit.*)

mingle **1** = mix, combine, blend, merge, unite, join, interweave, intermingle ≠ separate **2** = associate, consort, socialize, rub shoulders (*informal*), hobnob, fraternize, hang about or around ≠ dissociate

miniature = small, little, minute, tiny, toy, scaled-down, diminutive, minuscule ≠ giant

minimal = minimum, smallest, least, slightest, token, nominal, negligible, least possible

minimize **1** = reduce, decrease, shrink, diminish, prune, curtail, miniaturize ≠ increase **2** = play down, discount, belittle, disparage, decry, underrate, deprecate, make light or little of ≠ praise

minimum ADJECTIVE = lowest, smallest, least, slightest, minimal, least possible ≠ maximum
 • NOUN = lowest, least, lowest level, nadir

minister NOUN = clergyman, priest, vicar, parson, preacher, pastor, cleric, rector
 • VERB often with **to** = attend, serve, tend, take care of, cater to, pander to, administer to

ministry **1** = department, office, bureau, government department **2** = administration, council **3** = the priesthood, the church, the cloth, holy orders

minor = small, lesser, slight, petty, trivial, insignificant, unimportant, inconsequential ≠ major

mint = make, produce, strike, cast, stamp, punch, coin

minute[1] NOUN = moment, second, bit, flash, instant, tick (*Brit. informal*), sec (*informal*), short time
 • PLURAL NOUN = record, notes, proceedings, transactions, transcript, memorandum

minute[2] **1** = small, little, tiny, miniature, microscopic, diminutive, minuscule, infinitesimal ≠ huge **2** = precise, close, detailed, critical, exact, meticulous, exhaustive, painstaking ≠ imprecise

miracle = wonder, phenomenon, sensation, marvel, amazing achievement, astonishing feat

miraculous = wonderful, amazing, extraordinary, incredible, astonishing,

unbelievable, phenomenal, astounding
≠ ordinary

mirror NOUN = <u>looking-glass</u>, glass (Brit.),
reflector

● VERB = <u>reflect</u>, follow, copy, echo,
emulate

miscarriage = <u>failure</u>, error, breakdown,
mishap, perversion

misconduct = <u>immorality</u>, wrongdoing,
mismanagement, malpractice,
impropriety

miserable 1 = <u>sad</u>, depressed, gloomy,
forlorn, dejected, despondent, sorrowful,
wretched ≠ happy 2 = <u>pathetic</u>, sorry,
shameful, despicable, deplorable,
lamentable ≠ respectable

misery 1 = <u>unhappiness</u>, distress, despair,
grief, suffering, depression, gloom,
torment ≠ happiness 2 (Brit. informal)
= <u>moaner</u>, pessimist, killjoy, spoilsport,
prophet of doom, wet blanket (informal),
sourpuss (informal), wowser (Austral. &
N.Z. slang)

misfortune 1 often plural = <u>bad luck</u>,
adversity, hard luck, ill luck, infelicity
2 = <u>mishap</u>, trouble, disaster, reverse,
tragedy, setback, calamity, affliction
≠ good luck

misguided = <u>unwise</u>, mistaken,
misplaced, deluded, ill-advised,
imprudent, injudicious

mislead = <u>deceive</u>, fool, delude, take
someone in (informal), misdirect,
misinform, hoodwink, misguide

misleading = <u>confusing</u>, false,
ambiguous, deceptive, evasive,
disingenuous ≠ straightforward

miss VERB 1 = <u>fail to notice</u>, overlook, pass
over 2 = <u>long for</u>, yearn for, pine for, long
to see, ache for, feel the loss of, regret
the absence of 3 = <u>not go to</u>, skip, cut,
omit, be absent from, fail to attend, skive
off (informal), play truant from, bludge
(Austral. & N.Z. informal) 4 = <u>avoid</u>, beat,
escape, skirt, duck, cheat, bypass, dodge

● NOUN = <u>mistake</u>, failure, error, blunder,
omission, oversight

missile = <u>projectile</u>, weapon, shell, rocket

missing = <u>lost</u>, misplaced, not present,
astray, unaccounted for, mislaid

mission = <u>task</u>, job, commission, duty,
undertaking, quest, assignment, vocation

missionary = <u>evangelist</u>, preacher,
apostle

mist = <u>fog</u>, cloud, steam, spray, film, haze,
vapour, smog

mistake NOUN 1 = <u>error</u>, blunder,
oversight, slip, gaffe (informal),
miscalculation, faux pas 2 = <u>oversight</u>,
error, slip, fault, howler (informal), erratum

● VERB 1 = <u>confuse with</u>, take for, mix up
with 2 = <u>misunderstand</u>, misinterpret,
misjudge, misread, misconstrue,
misapprehend

mistaken 1 = <u>wrong</u>, incorrect,
misguided, wide of the mark ≠ correct
2 = <u>inaccurate</u>, false, faulty, erroneous,
unsound ≠ accurate

mistress = <u>lover</u>, girlfriend, concubine,
kept woman, paramour

misunderstand 1 = <u>misinterpret</u>,
misread, mistake, misjudge, misconstrue,
misapprehend, be at cross-purposes with
2 = <u>miss the point</u>, get the wrong end of
the stick

misunderstanding = <u>mistake</u>, error,
mix-up, misconception, misinterpretation,
misjudgment

misuse NOUN 1 = <u>waste</u>, squandering
2 = <u>abuse</u> 3 = <u>misapplication</u>, abuse,
illegal use, wrong use 4 = <u>perversion</u>,
desecration 5 = <u>misapplication</u>

● VERB 1 = <u>abuse</u>, misapply, prostitute
2 = <u>waste</u>, squander, embezzle,
misappropriate

mix VERB 1 = <u>combine</u>, blend, merge, join,
cross, fuse, mingle, jumble 2 = <u>socialize</u>,
associate, hang out (informal), mingle,
circulate, consort, hobnob, fraternize
3 often with up = <u>combine</u>, marry, blend,
integrate, amalgamate, coalesce, meld

● NOUN = <u>mixture</u>, combination, blend,
fusion, compound, assortment, alloy,
medley

● PHRASES **mix something up**
1 = <u>confuse</u>, scramble, muddle, confound
2 = <u>blend</u>, beat, mix, stir, fold

mixed 1 = <u>varied</u>, diverse, different,
differing, cosmopolitan, assorted, jumbled,
disparate ≠ homogeneous 2 = <u>combined</u>,
blended, united, compound, composite,
mingled, amalgamated ≠ pure

mixed-up = <u>confused</u>, disturbed, puzzled,
bewildered, at sea, upset, distraught,
muddled

mixture 1 = <u>blend</u>, mix, variety, fusion,
assortment, brew, jumble, medley
2 = <u>composite</u>, compound 3 = <u>cross</u>,

combination, blend **4** = <u>concoction</u>, compound, blend, brew, amalgam

mix-up = <u>confusion</u>, mistake, misunderstanding, mess, tangle, muddle

moan VERB **1** = <u>groan</u>, sigh, sob, whine, lament **2** (*Informal*) = <u>grumble</u>, complain, groan, whine, carp, grouse, whinge (*informal*), bleat

● NOUN **1** = <u>groan</u>, sigh, sob, lament, wail, grunt, whine **2** (*Informal*) = <u>complaint</u>, protest, grumble, whine, grouse, gripe (*informal*), grouch (*informal*)

mob NOUN **1** = <u>crowd</u>, pack, mass, host, drove, flock, swarm, horde **2** (*Slang*) = <u>gang</u>, group, set, lot, crew (*informal*)

● VERB = <u>surround</u>, besiege, jostle, fall on, set upon, crowd around, swarm around

mobile = <u>movable</u>, moving, travelling, wandering, portable, itinerant, peripatetic

mobilize 1 = <u>rally</u>, organize, stimulate, excite, prompt, marshal, activate, awaken **2** = <u>deploy</u>, prepare, ready, rally, assemble, call up, marshal, muster

mock VERB = <u>laugh at</u>, tease, ridicule, taunt, scorn, sneer, scoff, deride ≠ respect

● ADJECTIVE = <u>imitation</u>, pretended, artificial, fake, false, dummy, sham, feigned ≠ genuine

mocking = <u>scornful</u>, scoffing, satirical, contemptuous, sarcastic, sardonic, disrespectful, disdainful

mode 1 = <u>method</u>, way, system, form, process, style, technique, manner **2** = <u>fashion</u>, style, trend, rage, vogue, look, craze

model NOUN **1** = <u>representation</u>, image, copy, miniature, dummy, replica, imitation, duplicate **2** = <u>pattern</u>, example, standard, original, ideal, prototype, paradigm, archetype **3** = <u>sitter</u>, subject, poser

● VERB **1** = <u>show off</u> (*informal*), wear, display, sport **2** = <u>shape</u>, form, design, fashion, carve, mould, sculpt

moderate ADJECTIVE **1** = <u>mild</u>, reasonable, controlled, limited, steady, modest, restrained, middle-of-the-road ≠ extreme **2** = <u>average</u>, middling, fair, ordinary, indifferent, mediocre, so-so (*informal*), passable, half-pie (*N.Z. informal*)

● VERB **1** = <u>soften</u>, control, temper, regulate, curb, restrain, subdue, lessen **2** = <u>lessen</u>, ease ≠ intensify

modern 1 = <u>current</u>, contemporary, recent, present-day, latter-day **2** = up-to-

date, fresh, new, novel, newfangled ≠ old-fashioned

modest 1 = <u>moderate</u>, small, limited, fair, ordinary, middling, meagre, frugal **2** = <u>unpretentious</u>, reserved, retiring, shy, coy, reticent, self-effacing, demure

modesty = <u>reserve</u>, humility, shyness, reticence, timidity, diffidence, coyness, bashfulness ≠ conceit

modification = <u>change</u>, variation, qualification, adjustment, revision, alteration, refinement

modify 1 = <u>change</u>, reform, convert, alter, adjust, adapt, revise, remodel **2** = <u>tone down</u>, lower, qualify, ease, moderate, temper, soften, restrain

mogul = <u>tycoon</u>, baron, magnate, big shot (*informal*), big noise (*informal*), big hitter (*informal*), heavy hitter (*informal*), V.I.P.

moist = <u>damp</u>, wet, soggy, humid, clammy, dewy

moisture = <u>damp</u>, water, liquid, dew, wetness

molecule = <u>particle</u>, jot, speck

moment 1 = <u>instant</u>, second, flash, twinkling, split second, jiffy (*informal*), trice **2** = <u>time</u>, point, stage, juncture

momentous = <u>significant</u>, important, vital, critical, crucial, historic, pivotal, fateful ≠ unimportant

momentum = <u>impetus</u>, force, power, drive, push, energy, strength, thrust

monarch = <u>ruler</u>, king *or* queen, sovereign, tsar, potentate, emperor *or* empress, prince *or* princess

monarchy 1 = <u>sovereignty</u>, autocracy, kingship, royalism, monocracy **2** = <u>kingdom</u>, empire, realm, principality

monastery = <u>abbey</u>, convent, priory, cloister, nunnery, friary

monetary = <u>financial</u>, money, economic, capital, cash, fiscal, budgetary, pecuniary

money = <u>cash</u>, capital, currency, hard cash, readies (*informal*), riches, silver, coin

monitor VERB = <u>check</u>, follow, watch, survey, observe, keep an eye on, keep track of, keep tabs on

● NOUN **1** = <u>guide</u>, observer, supervisor, invigilator **2** = <u>prefect</u> (*Brit.*), head girl, head boy, senior boy, senior girl

monk (*Loosely*) = <u>friar</u>, brother

RELATED WORD
adjective: monastic

monkey 1 = <u>simian</u>, ape, primate

2 = rascal, horror, devil, rogue, imp, tyke, scallywag, scamp, nointer (*Austral. slang*)

■ RELATED WORD

adjective: simian

monster NOUN **1** = giant, mammoth, titan, colossus, monstrosity **2** = brute, devil, beast, demon, villain, fiend

● ADJECTIVE = huge, massive, enormous, tremendous, immense, gigantic, mammoth, colossal

monstrous 1 = outrageous, shocking, foul, intolerable, disgraceful, scandalous, inhuman, diabolical ≠ decent **2** = huge, massive, enormous, tremendous, immense, mammoth, colossal, prodigious ≠ tiny **3** = unnatural, horrible, hideous, grotesque, gruesome, frightful, freakish, fiendish ≠ normal

monument = memorial, cairn, marker, shrine, tombstone, mausoleum, commemoration, headstone

monumental 1 = important, significant, enormous, historic, memorable, awesome, majestic, unforgettable ≠ unimportant **2** (*Informal*) = immense, great, massive, staggering, colossal ≠ tiny

mood = state of mind, spirit, humour, temper, disposition, frame of mind

moody 1 = changeable, volatile, unpredictable, erratic, fickle, temperamental, impulsive, mercurial ≠ stable **2** = sulky, irritable, temperamental, touchy, ill-tempered, tooshie (*Austral. slang*) ≠ cheerful **3** = gloomy, sad, sullen, glum, morose ≠ cheerful **4** = sad, gloomy, melancholy, sombre

moon NOUN = satellite

● VERB = idle, drift, loaf, languish, waste time, daydream, mope

■ RELATED WORD

adjective: lunar

moor¹ = moorland, fell (*Brit.*), heath

moor² = tie up, secure, anchor, dock, lash, berth, make fast

mop NOUN **1** = squeegee, sponge, swab **2** = mane, shock, mass, tangle, mat, thatch

● VERB = clean, wash, wipe, sponge, swab

moral ADJECTIVE = good, just, right, principled, decent, noble, ethical, honourable ≠ immoral

● NOUN = lesson, meaning, point, message, teaching, import, significance, precept

● PLURAL NOUN = morality, standards, conduct, principles, behaviour, manners, habits, ethics

morale = confidence, heart, spirit, self-esteem, team spirit, esprit de corps

morality 1 = virtue, justice, morals, honour, integrity, goodness, honesty, decency **2** = ethics, conduct, principles, morals, manners, philosophy, mores **3** = rights and wrongs, ethics

moratorium = postponement, freeze, halt, suspension, standstill

more ADJECTIVE = extra, additional, new, other, added, further, new-found, supplementary

● ADVERB **1** = to a greater extent, longer, better, further, some more **2** = moreover, also, in addition, besides, furthermore, what's more, on top of that, to boot

moreover = furthermore, also, further, in addition, too, as well, besides, additionally

morning 1 = before noon, forenoon, morn (*poetic*), a.m. **2** = dawn, sunrise, first light, daybreak, break of day

mortal ADJECTIVE **1** = human, worldly, passing, fleshly, temporal, transient, ephemeral, perishable **2** = fatal, killing, terminal, deadly, destructive, lethal, murderous, death-dealing

● NOUN = human being, being, man, woman, person, human, individual, earthling

mortality 1 = humanity, transience, impermanence, corporeality, impermanency **2** = death, dying, fatality

mostly 1 = mainly, largely, chiefly, principally, primarily, on the whole, predominantly **2** = generally, usually, on the whole, as a rule

mother NOUN = female parent, mum (*Brit. informal*), ma (*informal*), mater, dam, mummy (*Brit. informal*), foster mother, biological mother

● VERB = nurture, raise, protect, tend, nurse, rear, care for, cherish

● ADJECTIVE = native, natural, innate, inborn

■ RELATED WORD

adjective: maternal

motherly = maternal, loving, caring, comforting, sheltering, protective, affectionate

motif 1 = design, shape, decoration, ornament **2** = theme, idea, subject, concept, leitmotif

motion NOUN **1** = movement,

mobility, travel, progress, flow, locomotion **2** = proposal, suggestion, recommendation, proposition, submission
● VERB = gesture, direct, wave, signal, nod, beckon, gesticulate

motivate 1 = inspire, drive, stimulate, move, cause, prompt, stir, induce **2** = stimulate, drive, inspire, stir, arouse, galvanize, incentivize

motivation = incentive, inspiration, motive, stimulus, reason, spur, inducement, incitement

motive = reason, ground(s), purpose, object, incentive, inspiration, stimulus, rationale

motto = saying, slogan, maxim, rule, adage, proverb, dictum, precept

mould¹ NOUN **1** = cast, shape, pattern **2** = design, style, fashion, build, form, kind, shape, pattern **3** = nature, character, sort, kind, quality, type, stamp, calibre
● VERB **1** = shape, make, work, form, create, model, fashion, construct **2** = influence, make, form, control, direct, affect, shape

mould² = fungus, blight, mildew

mound 1 = heap, pile, drift, stack, rick **2** = hill, bank, rise, dune, embankment, knoll, hillock, kopje or koppie (S. African)

mount VERB **1** = increase, build, grow, swell, intensify, escalate, multiply ≠ decrease **2** = accumulate, increase, collect, gather, build up, pile up, amass **3** = ascend, scale, climb (up), go up, clamber up ≠ descend **4** = get (up) on, jump on, straddle, climb onto, hop on to, bestride, get on the back of ≠ get off **5** = display, present, prepare, put on, organize, put on display
● NOUN **1** = horse, steed (literary) **2** = backing, setting, support, stand, base, frame

mountain 1 = peak, mount, horn, ridge, fell (Brit.), berg (S. African), alp, pinnacle **2** = heap, mass, masses, pile, a great deal, ton, stack, abundance

mourn 1 often with **for** = grieve for, lament, weep for, wail for **2** = bemoan, rue, deplore, bewail

mourning 1 = grieving, grief, bereavement, weeping, woe, lamentation **2** = black, sackcloth and ashes, widow's weeds

mouth 1 = lips, jaws, gob (slang, esp. Brit.), maw, cakehole (Brit. slang) **2** = entrance, opening, gateway, door, aperture, orifice

3 = opening **4** = inlet, outlet, estuary, firth, outfall, debouchment
███ RELATED WORD
adjective: oral

move VERB **1** = transfer, change, switch, shift, transpose **2** = go, advance, progress, shift, proceed, stir, budge, make a move **3** = relocate, leave, remove, quit, migrate, emigrate, decamp, up sticks (Brit. informal) **4** = drive, cause, influence, persuade, shift, inspire, prompt, induce ≠ discourage **5** = touch, affect, excite, impress, stir, disquiet **6** = propose, suggest, urge, recommend, request, advocate, submit, put forward
● NOUN **1** = action, step, manoeuvre **2** = ploy, action, measure, step, initiative, stroke, tactic, manoeuvre **3** = transfer, posting, shift, removal, relocation **4** = turn, go, play, chance, shot (informal), opportunity

movement 1 = group, party, organization, grouping, front, faction **2** = campaign, drive, push, crusade **3** = move, action, motion, manoeuvre **4** = activity, moving, stirring, bustle **5** = advance, progress, flow **6** = transfer, transportation, displacement **7** = development, change, variation, fluctuation **8** = progression, progress **9** (Music) = section, part, division, passage

movie = film, picture, feature, flick (slang)

moving 1 = emotional, touching, affecting, inspiring, stirring, poignant ≠ unemotional **2** = mobile, running, active, going, operational, in motion, driving, kinetic ≠ stationary

mow VERB = cut, crop, trim, shear, scythe
● PHRASES **mow something or someone down** = massacre, butcher, slaughter, cut down, shoot down, cut to pieces

much ADVERB **1** = greatly, a lot, considerably, decidedly, exceedingly, appreciably ≠ hardly **2** = often, a lot, routinely, a great deal, many times, habitually, on many occasions, customarily
● DETERMINER = great, a lot of, plenty of, considerable, substantial, piles of (informal), ample, abundant ≠ little
● PRONOUN = a lot, plenty, a great deal, lots (informal), masses (informal), loads (informal), tons (informal), heaps (informal) ≠ little

muck 1 = dirt, mud, filth, ooze, sludge, mire, slime, gunge (*informal*), kak (*S. African informal*) **2** = manure, dung, ordure

mud = dirt, clay, ooze, silt, sludge, mire, slime

muddle NOUN = confusion, mess, disorder, chaos, tangle, mix-up, disarray, predicament
● **VERB 1** = jumble, disorder, scramble, tangle, mix up **2** = confuse, bewilder, daze, confound, perplex, disorient, stupefy, befuddle

muddy 1 = boggy, swampy, marshy, quaggy **2** = dirty, soiled, grimy, mucky, mud-caked, bespattered

mug¹ = cup, pot, beaker, tankard

mug² (*Informal*) **1** = face, features, countenance, visage **2** = fool, sucker (*slang*), chump (*informal*), simpleton, easy *or* soft touch (*slang*), dorba *or* dorb (*Austral. slang*), bogan (*Austral. slang*)

mug³ VERB = attack, assault, beat up, rob, set about *or* upon
● **PHRASES mug up (on) something** = study, cram (*informal*), bone up on (*informal*), swot up on (*Brit. informal*)

multiple = many, several, various, numerous, sundry, manifold, multitudinous

multiply 1 = increase, extend, expand, spread, build up, proliferate ≠ decrease **2** = reproduce, breed, propagate

multitude 1 = great number, host, army, mass, horde, myriad **2** = crowd, host, mass, mob, swarm, horde, throng

mundane 1 = ordinary, routine, commonplace, banal, everyday, day-to-day, prosaic, humdrum ≠ extraordinary **2** = earthly, worldly, secular, mortal, terrestrial, temporal ≠ spiritual

municipal = civic, public, local, council, district, urban, metropolitan

murder NOUN = killing, homicide, massacre, assassination, slaying, bloodshed, carnage, butchery
● **VERB** = kill, massacre, slaughter, assassinate, eliminate (*slang*), butcher, slay, bump off (*slang*)

murderer = killer, assassin, slayer, butcher, slaughterer, cut-throat, hit man (*slang*)

murderous = deadly, savage, brutal, cruel, lethal, ferocious, cut-throat, bloodthirsty

murky 1 = dark, gloomy, grey, dull, dim,

cloudy, misty, overcast ≠ bright **2** = dark, cloudy

murmur VERB = mumble, whisper, mutter
● **NOUN** = whisper, drone, purr

muscle NOUN 1 = tendon, sinew **2** = strength, might, power, weight, stamina, brawn
● **PHRASES muscle in** (*Informal*) = impose yourself, encroach, butt in, force your way in

muscular = strong, powerful, athletic, strapping, robust, vigorous, sturdy, sinewy

muse = ponder, consider, reflect, contemplate, deliberate, brood, meditate, mull over

musical = melodious, lyrical, harmonious, melodic, tuneful, dulcet, sweet-sounding, euphonious ≠ discordant

must = necessity, essential, requirement, fundamental, imperative, requisite, prerequisite, sine qua non (*Latin*)

muster VERB 1 = summon up, marshal **2** = rally, gather, assemble, marshal, mobilize, call together **3** = assemble, convene
● **NOUN** = assembly, meeting, collection, gathering, rally, convention, congregation, roundup, hui (*N.Z.*), runanga (*N.Z.*)

mutation 1 = anomaly, variation, deviant, freak of nature **2** = change, variation, evolution, transformation, modification, alteration, metamorphosis, transfiguration

mute 1 = close-mouthed, silent **2** = silent, dumb, unspoken, tacit, wordless, voiceless, unvoiced **3** = dumb, speechless, voiceless

mutter = grumble, complain, murmur, rumble, whine, mumble, grouse, bleat

mutual = shared, common, joint, returned, reciprocal, interchangeable, requited

myriad NOUN = multitude, host, army, swarm, horde
● **ADJECTIVE** = innumerable, countless, untold, incalculable, immeasurable, multitudinous

mysterious 1 = strange, puzzling, secret, weird, perplexing, uncanny, mystifying, arcane ≠ clear **2** = secretive, enigmatic, evasive, discreet, covert, reticent, furtive, inscrutable

mystery = puzzle, problem, question, secret, riddle, enigma, conundrum, teaser

mystic *or* **mystical** = supernatural, mysterious, transcendental, occult, metaphysical, paranormal, inscrutable, otherworldly

myth 1 = <u>legend</u>, story, fiction, saga, fable, allegory, fairy story, folk tale 2 = <u>illusion</u>, story, fancy, fantasy, imagination, invention, delusion, superstition

mythology = <u>legend</u>, folklore, tradition, lore

n

nab = <u>catch</u>, arrest, apprehend, seize, grab, capture, collar (*informal*), snatch

nag¹ VERB = <u>scold</u>, harass, badger, pester, worry, plague, hassle (*informal*), upbraid
• NOUN = <u>scold</u>, complainer, grumbler, virago, shrew, tartar, moaner, harpy

nag² = <u>horse</u> (*U.S.*), hack

nagging 1 = <u>continuous</u>, persistent, continual, niggling, repeated, constant, endless, perpetual 2 = <u>scolding</u>, shrewish

nail NOUN 1 = <u>tack</u>, spike, rivet, hobnail, brad (*technical*) 2 = <u>fingernail</u>, toenail, talon, thumbnail, claw
• VERB 1 = <u>fasten</u>, fix, secure, attach, pin, hammer, tack 2 (*informal*) = <u>catch</u>, arrest, capture, apprehend, trap, snare, ensnare, entrap

naive *or* **naïve** = <u>gullible</u>, trusting, credulous, unsuspicious, green, simple, innocent, callow ≠ worldly

naked = <u>nude</u>, stripped, exposed, bare, undressed, starkers (*informal*), stark-naked, unclothed ≠ dressed

name NOUN = <u>title</u>, nickname, designation, term, handle (*slang*), epithet, sobriquet, moniker *or* monicker (*slang*)
• VERB 1 = <u>call</u>, christen, baptize, dub, term, style, label, entitle 2 = <u>nominate</u>, choose, select, appoint, specify, designate

namely = <u>specifically</u>, to wit, viz.

nap¹ NOUN = <u>sleep</u>, rest, kip (*Brit. slang*), siesta, catnap, forty winks (*informal*)
• VERB = <u>sleep</u>, rest, drop off (*informal*), doze, kip (*Brit. slang*), snooze (*informal*), nod off (*informal*), catnap

nap² = <u>pile</u>, down, fibre, weave, grain

napkin = <u>serviette</u>, cloth

narcotic NOUN = <u>drug</u>, anaesthetic, painkiller, sedative, opiate, tranquillizer, anodyne, analgesic
• ADJECTIVE = <u>sedative</u>, calming, hypnotic, analgesic, soporific, painkilling

narrative = <u>story</u>, report, history, account, statement, tale, chronicle

narrator = <u>storyteller</u>, writer, author, reporter, commentator, chronicler

narrow ADJECTIVE 1 = <u>thin</u>, fine, slim, slender, tapering, attenuated ≠ broad 2 = <u>limited</u>, restricted, confined, tight, close, meagre, constricted ≠ wide 3 = <u>insular</u>, prejudiced, partial, dogmatic, intolerant, narrow-minded, small-minded, illiberal ≠ broad-minded
• VERB 1 = <u>restrict</u>, limit, reduce, constrict 2 = <u>get narrower</u>, taper, shrink, tighten, constrict

narrowly = <u>just</u>, barely, only just, scarcely, by the skin of your teeth

nasty 1 = <u>unpleasant</u>, ugly, disagreeable ≠ pleasant 2 = <u>spiteful</u>, mean, offensive, vicious, unpleasant, vile, malicious, despicable ≠ pleasant 3 = <u>disgusting</u>, unpleasant, offensive, vile, distasteful, obnoxious, objectionable, disagreeable, festy (*Austral. slang*), yucko (*Austral. slang*) 4 = <u>serious</u>, bad, dangerous, critical, severe, painful

nation 1 = <u>country</u>, state, realm 2 = <u>public</u>, people, society

national ADJECTIVE = <u>nationwide</u>, public, widespread, countrywide
• NOUN = <u>citizen</u>, subject, resident, native, inhabitant

nationalism = <u>patriotism</u>, loyalty to your country, chauvinism, jingoism, allegiance

nationality 1 = <u>citizenship</u>, birth 2 = <u>race</u>, nation

nationwide = <u>national</u>, general, widespread, countrywide

native ADJECTIVE = <u>mother</u>, indigenous, vernacular
• NOUN = <u>inhabitant</u>, national, resident, citizen, countryman, aborigine (*often offensive*), dweller

natural 1 = <u>logical</u>, valid, legitimate 2 = <u>normal</u>, common, regular, usual, ordinary, typical, everyday ≠ abnormal 3 = <u>innate</u>, native, characteristic, inherent, instinctive, intuitive, inborn, essential 4 = <u>unaffected</u>, open, genuine, spontaneous, unpretentious, unsophisticated, dinkum (*Austral. & N.Z. informal*), ingenuous, real ≠ affected 5 = <u>pure</u>, plain, organic, whole, unrefined ≠ processed

naturally 1 = <u>of course</u>, certainly 2 = <u>typically</u>, simply, normally, spontaneously

nature 1 = <u>creation</u>, world, earth, environment, universe, cosmos, natural world 2 = <u>quality</u>, character, make-up, constitution, essence, complexion 3 = <u>temperament</u>, character, personality, disposition, outlook, mood, humour, temper 4 = <u>kind</u>, sort, style, type, variety, species, category, description

naughty 1 = <u>disobedient</u>, bad, mischievous, badly behaved, wayward, wicked, impish, refractory ≠ good 2 = <u>obscene</u>, vulgar, improper, lewd, risqué, smutty, ribald ≠ clean

nausea = <u>sickness</u>, vomiting, retching, squeamishness, queasiness, biliousness

naval = <u>nautical</u>, marine, maritime

navigation = <u>sailing</u>, voyaging, seamanship, helmsmanship

navy = <u>fleet</u>, flotilla, armada

near 1 = <u>close</u>, neighbouring, nearby, adjacent, adjoining ≠ far 2 = <u>imminent</u>, forthcoming, approaching, looming, impending, upcoming, nigh, in the offing ≠ far-off

nearby = <u>neighbouring</u>, adjacent, adjoining

nearly 1 = <u>practically</u>, almost, virtually, just about, as good as, well-nigh 2 = <u>almost</u>, approaching, roughly, just about, approximately

neat 1 = <u>tidy</u>, trim, orderly, spruce, shipshape, spick-and-span ≠ untidy 2 = <u>methodical</u>, tidy, systematic, fastidious ≠ disorganized 3 = <u>smart</u>, trim, tidy, spruce, dapper, natty (*informal*), well-groomed, well-turned out 4 = <u>graceful</u>, elegant, adept, nimble, adroit, efficient ≠ clumsy 5 = <u>clever</u>, efficient, handy, apt, well-judged ≠ inefficient 6 = <u>cool</u>, great (*informal*), excellent, brilliant, superb, fantastic (*informal*), tremendous, fabulous (*informal*), booshit (*Austral. slang*), exo (*Austral. slang*), sik (*Austral. slang*) ≠ terrible 7 (*of alcoholic drinks*) = <u>undiluted</u>, straight, pure, unmixed

neatly 1 = <u>tidily</u>, smartly, systematically, methodically, fastidiously 2 = <u>smartly</u>, elegantly, tidily, nattily 3 = <u>gracefully</u>, expertly, efficiently, adeptly, skilfully, nimbly, adroitly, dexterously 4 = <u>cleverly</u>, efficiently

necessarily 1 = <u>automatically</u>, naturally, definitely, undoubtedly, certainly 2 = <u>inevitably</u>, of necessity, unavoidably, incontrovertibly, nolens volens (*Latin*)

necessary 1 = <u>needed</u>, required, essential, vital, compulsory, mandatory, imperative, indispensable ≠ unnecessary 2 = <u>inevitable</u>, certain, unavoidable, inescapable ≠ avoidable

necessity NOUN 1 = <u>essential</u>, need, requirement, fundamental, requisite, prerequisite, sine qua non (*Latin*), desideratum 2 = <u>inevitability</u>, certainty ● PLURAL NOUN = <u>essentials</u>, needs, requirements, fundamentals

need VERB 1 = <u>want</u>, miss, require, lack, have to have, demand 2 = <u>require</u>, want, demand, call for, entail, necessitate 3 = <u>have to</u>, be obliged to ● NOUN 1 = <u>requirement</u>, demand, essential, necessity, requisite, desideratum 2 = <u>necessity</u>, call, demand, obligation 3 = <u>emergency</u>, want, necessity, urgency, exigency 4 = <u>poverty</u>, deprivation, destitution, penury

needed = <u>necessary</u>, wanted, required, lacked, called for, desired

needle = <u>irritate</u>, provoke, annoy, harass, taunt, nag, goad, rile

needless = <u>unnecessary</u>, pointless, gratuitous, useless, unwanted, redundant, superfluous, groundless ≠ essential

needy = <u>poor</u>, deprived, disadvantaged, impoverished, penniless, destitute, poverty-stricken, underprivileged ≠ wealthy

negative ADJECTIVE 1 = <u>pessimistic</u>, cynical, unwilling, gloomy, jaundiced, uncooperative ≠ optimistic 2 = <u>dissenting</u>, contradictory, refusing, denying, rejecting, opposing, resisting, contrary ≠ assenting ● NOUN = <u>denial</u>, no, refusal, rejection, contradiction

neglect VERB 1 = <u>disregard</u>, ignore, fail to look after ≠ look after 2 = <u>shirk</u>, forget, overlook, omit, evade, pass over, skimp, be remiss in or about 3 = <u>fail</u>, forget, omit ● NOUN 1 = <u>negligence</u>, inattention

≠ care **2** = shirking, failure, oversight, carelessness, dereliction, slackness, laxity

neglected 1 = uncared-for, abandoned, underestimated, disregarded, undervalued, unappreciated **2** = run down, derelict, overgrown, uncared-for

negligence = carelessness, neglect, disregard, dereliction, slackness, inattention, laxity, thoughtlessness

negotiate 1 = bargain, deal, discuss, debate, mediate, hold talks, cut a deal, conciliate **2** = arrange, work out, bring about, transact **3** = get round, clear, pass, cross, get over, get past, surmount

negotiation 1 = bargaining, debate, discussion, transaction, dialogue, mediation, arbitration, wheeling and dealing (*informal*) **2** = arrangement, working out, transaction, bringing about

negotiator = mediator, ambassador, diplomat, delegate, intermediary, moderator, honest broker

neighbourhood 1 = district, community, quarter, region, locality, locale **2** = vicinity, environs

neighbouring = nearby, next, near, bordering, surrounding, connecting, adjacent, adjoining ≠ remote

neighbourly = helpful, kind, friendly, obliging, harmonious, considerate, sociable, hospitable

nerve NOUN **1** = bravery, courage, bottle (*Brit. slang*), resolution, daring, guts (*informal*), pluck, grit **2** (*informal*) = impudence, cheek (*informal*), audacity, boldness, temerity, insolence, impertinence, brazenness

● PLURAL NOUN = tension, stress, strain, anxiety, butterflies (in your stomach) (*informal*), nervousness, cold feet (*informal*), worry

● PHRASES **nerve yourself** = brace yourself, prepare yourself, steel yourself, fortify yourself, gear yourself up, gee yourself up

nervous = apprehensive, anxious, uneasy, edgy, worried, tense, fearful, uptight (*informal*), toey (*Austral. slang*) ≠ calm

nest = refuge, retreat, haunt, den, hideaway

nestle = snuggle, cuddle, huddle, curl up, nuzzle

nestling = chick, fledgling, baby bird

net¹ NOUN = mesh, netting, network, web, lattice, openwork

● VERB = catch, bag, capture, trap, entangle, ensnare, enmesh

net² *or* **nett** ADJECTIVE = after taxes, final, clear, take-home

● VERB = earn, make, clear, gain, realize, bring in, accumulate, reap

network 1 = web, system, arrangement, grid, lattice **2** = maze, warren, labyrinth

neurotic = unstable, nervous, disturbed, abnormal, obsessive, compulsive, manic, unhealthy ≠ rational

neutral 1 = unbiased, impartial, disinterested, even-handed, uninvolved, nonpartisan, unprejudiced, nonaligned ≠ biased **2** = expressionless, dull **3** = uncontroversial *or* noncontroversial, inoffensive **4** = colourless

never 1 = at no time, not once, not ever ≠ always **2** = under no circumstances, not at all, on no account, never

nevertheless = even so, still, however, yet, regardless, nonetheless, notwithstanding, in spite of that

new 1 = modern, recent, contemporary, up-to-date, latest, current, original, fresh ≠ old-fashioned **2** = brand new **3** = extra, more, added, new-found, supplementary **4** = unfamiliar, strange **5** = renewed, changed, improved, restored, altered, revitalized

newcomer 1 = new arrival, stranger **2** = beginner, novice, new arrival, parvenu, Johnny-come-lately (*informal*)

news = information, latest (*informal*), report, story, exposé, intelligence, rumour, revelation

next ADJECTIVE **1** = following, later, succeeding, subsequent **2** = adjacent, closest, nearest, neighbouring, adjoining

● ADVERB = afterwards, then, later, following, subsequently, thereafter

nice 1 = pleasant, delightful, agreeable, good, attractive, charming, pleasurable, enjoyable ≠ unpleasant **2** = kind, helpful, obliging, considerate ≠ unkind **3** = likable *or* likeable, friendly, engaging, charming, pleasant, agreeable **4** = polite, courteous, well-mannered ≠ vulgar **5** = precise, fine, careful, strict, subtle, delicate, meticulous, fastidious ≠ vague

nicely 1 = pleasantly, well, delightfully, attractively, charmingly, agreeably, acceptably, pleasurably ≠ unpleasantly

2 = <u>kindly</u>, politely, thoughtfully, amiably, courteously

niche 1 = <u>recess</u>, opening, corner, hollow, nook, alcove **2** = <u>position</u>, calling, place, slot (*informal*), vocation, pigeonhole (*informal*)

nick VERB **1** (*Slang*) = <u>steal</u>, pinch (*informal*), swipe (*slang*), pilfer **2** = <u>cut</u>, mark, score, chip, scratch, scar, notch, dent
● NOUN = <u>cut</u>, mark, scratch, chip, scar, notch, dent

nickname = <u>pet name</u>, label, diminutive, epithet, sobriquet, moniker *or* monicker (*slang*)

night = <u>darkness</u>, dark, night-time

████ RELATED WORD
adjective: nocturnal

nightly ADJECTIVE = <u>nocturnal</u>, night-time
● ADVERB = <u>every night</u>, nights (*informal*), each night, night after night

nightmare 1 = <u>bad dream</u>, hallucination **2** = <u>ordeal</u>, trial, hell, horror, torture, torment, tribulation, purgatory

nil 1 = <u>nothing</u>, love, zero **2** = <u>zero</u>, nothing, none, naught

nip[1] VERB **1** = <u>pop</u>, go, run, rush, dash **2** = <u>bite</u> **3** = <u>pinch</u>, squeeze, tweak
● PHRASES **nip something in the bud** = <u>thwart</u>, check, frustrate

nip[2] = <u>dram</u>, shot (*informal*), drop, sip, draught, mouthful, snifter (*informal*)

nirvana = <u>paradise</u>, peace, joy, bliss, serenity, tranquillity

no INTERJECTION = <u>not at all</u>, certainly not, of course not, absolutely not, never, no way, nay ≠ yes
● NOUN = <u>refusal</u>, rejection, denial, negation ≠ consent

noble ADJECTIVE **1** = <u>worthy</u>, generous, upright, honourable, virtuous, magnanimous ≠ despicable **2** = <u>dignified</u>, great, imposing, impressive, distinguished, splendid, stately ≠ lowly **3** = <u>aristocratic</u>, lordly, titled, patrician, blue-blooded, highborn ≠ humble
● NOUN = <u>lord</u>, peer, aristocrat, nobleman ≠ commoner

nobody PRONOUN = <u>no-one</u>
● NOUN = <u>nonentity</u>, lightweight (*informal*), zero, cipher ≠ celebrity

nod VERB **1** = <u>incline</u>, bow **2** = <u>signal</u>, indicate, motion, gesture **3** = <u>salute</u>, acknowledge
● NOUN **1** = <u>signal</u>, sign, motion,

gesture, indication **2** = <u>salute</u>, greeting, acknowledgment

noise = <u>sound</u>, row, racket, clamour, din, uproar, commotion, hubbub ≠ silence, calm

noisy 1 = <u>rowdy</u>, strident, boisterous, vociferous, uproarious, clamorous ≠ quiet **2** = <u>loud</u>, piercing, deafening, tumultuous, ear-splitting, cacophonous, clamorous ≠ quiet

nominal 1 = <u>titular</u>, formal, purported, in name only, supposed, so-called, theoretical, professed **2** = <u>token</u>, small, symbolic, minimal, trivial, trifling, insignificant, inconsiderable

nominate 1 = <u>propose</u>, suggest, recommend, put forward **2** = <u>appoint</u>, name, choose, select, elect, assign, designate

nomination 1 = <u>proposal</u>, suggestion, recommendation **2** = <u>appointment</u>, election, selection, designation, choice

nominee = <u>candidate</u>, applicant, entrant, contestant, aspirant, runner

none 1 = <u>not any</u>, nothing, zero, not one, nil **2** = <u>no-one</u>, nobody, not one

nonetheless = <u>nevertheless</u>, however, yet, even so, despite that, in spite of that

non-existent *or* **nonexistent** = <u>imaginary</u>, fictional, mythical, unreal, hypothetical, illusory ≠ real

nonsense 1 = <u>rubbish</u>, hot air (*informal*), twaddle, drivel, tripe (*informal*), gibberish, claptrap (*informal*), double Dutch (*Brit. informal*), bizzo (*Austral. slang*), bull's wool (*Austral. & N.Z. slang*) ≠ sense **2** = <u>idiocy</u>, stupidity

non-stop *or* **nonstop** ADJECTIVE = <u>continuous</u>, constant, relentless, uninterrupted, endless, unbroken, interminable, incessant ≠ occasional
● ADVERB = <u>continuously</u>, constantly, endlessly, relentlessly, perpetually, incessantly, ceaselessly, interminably

noon NOUN = <u>midday</u>, high noon, noonday, twelve noon, noontide
● ADJECTIVE = <u>midday</u>, noonday, noontide

norm = <u>standard</u>, rule, pattern, average, par, criterion, benchmark, yardstick

normal 1 = <u>usual</u>, common, standard, average, natural, regular, ordinary, typical ≠ unusual **2** = <u>sane</u>, reasonable, rational, well-adjusted, compos mentis (*Latin*), in your right mind, mentally sound

normally 1 = usually, generally, commonly, regularly, typically, ordinarily, as a rule, habitually 2 = as usual, naturally, properly, conventionally, in the usual way

north ADJECTIVE = northern, polar, arctic, boreal, northerly

● ADVERB = northward(s), in a northerly direction

nose NOUN = snout, bill, beak, hooter (slang), proboscis

● VERB = ease forward, push, edge, shove, nudge

▪ RELATED WORD
adjective: nasal

nostalgia = reminiscence, longing, pining, yearning, remembrance, homesickness, wistfulness

nostalgic = sentimental, longing, emotional, homesick, wistful, maudlin, regretful

notable ADJECTIVE 1 = remarkable, striking, unusual, extraordinary, outstanding, memorable, uncommon, conspicuous ≠ imperceptible 2 = prominent, famous ≠ unknown

● NOUN = celebrity, big name, dignitary, luminary, personage, V.I.P.

notably = remarkably, unusually, extraordinarily, noticeably, strikingly, singularly, outstandingly, uncommonly

notch NOUN 1 = level (Informal), step, degree, grade 2 = cut, nick, incision, indentation, mark, score, cleft

● VERB = cut, mark, score, nick, scratch, indent

note NOUN 1 = message, letter, communication, memo, memorandum, epistle 2 = record, reminder, memo, memorandum, jotting, minute 3 = annotation, comment, remark 4 = document, form, record, certificate 5 = symbol, mark, sign, indication, token 6 = tone, touch, trace, hint, sound

● VERB 1 = notice, see, observe, perceive 2 = bear in mind, be aware, take into account 3 = mention, record, mark, indicate, register, remark 4 = write down, record, scribble, set down, jot down

notebook = notepad, exercise book, journal, diary

noted = famous, celebrated, distinguished, well-known, prominent, acclaimed, notable, renowned ≠ unknown

nothing 1 = nought, zero, nil, not a thing, zilch (slang) 2 = a trifle 3 = nobody, cipher, nonentity 4 = void, emptiness, nothingness, nullity

notice VERB = observe, see, note, spot, distinguish, perceive, detect, discern ≠ overlook

● NOUN 1 = notification, warning, advice, intimation, news, communication, announcement, instruction 2 = attention, interest, note, regard, consideration, observation, scrutiny, heed ≠ oversight 3 = the sack (informal), dismissal, the boot (slang), the push (slang), marching orders (informal)

noticeable = obvious, clear, striking, plain, evident, manifest, conspicuous, perceptible

notify = inform, tell, advise, alert to, announce, warn, make known to

notion 1 = idea, view, opinion, belief, concept, impression, sentiment, inkling 2 = whim, wish, desire, fancy, impulse, inclination, caprice

notorious = infamous, disreputable, opprobrious

notoriously = infamously, disreputably

notwithstanding = despite, in spite of, regardless of

nought or (Archaic or literary) **naught** = zero, nothing, nil

nourish 1 = feed, supply, sustain, nurture 2 = encourage, support, maintain, promote, sustain, foster

nourishing = nutritious, beneficial, wholesome, nutritive

novel[1] = story, tale, fiction, romance, narrative

novel[2] = new, different, original, fresh, unusual, innovative, uncommon ≠ ordinary

novelty 1 = newness, originality, freshness, innovation, surprise, uniqueness, strangeness, unfamiliarity 2 = curiosity, rarity, oddity, wonder 3 = trinket, souvenir, memento, bauble, trifle, knick-knack

novice = beginner, pupil, amateur, newcomer, trainee, apprentice, learner, probationer ≠ expert

now ADVERB 1 = nowadays, at the moment 2 = immediately, promptly, instantly, at once, straightaway

● PHRASES **now and then** or **again** = occasionally, sometimes, from time to time, on and off, intermittently, infrequently, sporadically

nowadays = now, today, at the moment, in this day and age

nucleus = centre, heart, focus, basis, core, pivot, kernel, nub

nude = naked, stripped, bare, undressed, stark-naked, disrobed, unclothed, unclad ≠ dressed

nudge VERB 1 = push, touch, dig, jog, prod, elbow, shove, poke 2 = prompt, influence, persuade, spur, prod, coax
● NOUN 1 = push, touch, dig, elbow, bump, shove, poke, jog 2 = prompting, push, encouragement, prod

nuisance = trouble, problem, trial, drag (*informal*), bother, pest, irritation, hassle (*informal*) ≠ benefit

numb ADJECTIVE 1 = unfeeling, dead, frozen, paralysed, insensitive, deadened, immobilized, torpid ≠ sensitive
2 = stupefied, deadened, unfeeling
● VERB 1 = stun, knock out, paralyse, daze 2 = deaden, freeze, dull, paralyse, immobilize, benumb

number NOUN 1 = numeral, figure, character, digit, integer 2 = amount, quantity, collection, aggregate ≠ shortage
3 = crowd, horde, multitude, throng
4 = group, set, band, crowd, gang
5 = issue, copy, edition, imprint, printing
● VERB 1 = amount to, come to, total, add up to 2 = calculate, account, reckon, compute, enumerate ≠ guess 3 = include, count

numerous = many, several, countless, lots, abundant, plentiful, innumerable, copious ≠ few

nurse 1 = look after, treat, tend, care for, take care of, minister to 2 = harbour, have, maintain, preserve, entertain, cherish
3 = breast-feed, feed, nurture, nourish, suckle, wet-nurse

nursery = crèche, kindergarten, playgroup

nurture VERB = bring up, raise, look after, rear, care for, develop ≠ neglect
● NOUN = upbringing, training, education, instruction, rearing, development

nut 1 (*Slang*) = madman, psycho (*slang*), crank (*informal*), lunatic, maniac, nutcase (*slang*) 2 (*Slang*) = head, skull

nutrition = food, nourishment, sustenance, nutriment

O

oath 1 = promise, bond, pledge, vow, word, affirmation, avowal 2 = swear word, curse, obscenity, blasphemy, expletive, four-letter word, profanity

obedience = compliance, respect, reverence, observance, subservience, submissiveness, docility ≠ disobedience

obey 1 = submit to, surrender (to), give way to, bow to, give in to, yield to, do what you are told by ≠ disobey 2 = carry out, follow, implement, act upon, carry through ≠ disregard 3 = abide by, keep, follow, comply with, observe, heed, conform to, keep to

object[1] 1 = thing, article, body, item, entity 2 = purpose, aim, end, point, plan, idea, goal, design 3 = target, victim, focus, recipient

object[2] 1 *with to* = protest against, oppose, argue against, draw the line at, take exception to, cry out against, complain against, expostulate against ≠ accept 2 = disagree, demur, remonstrate, express disapproval ≠ agree

objection = protest, opposition, complaint, doubt, dissent, outcry, protestation, scruple ≠ agreement

objective NOUN = purpose, aim, goal, end, plan, hope, idea, target
● ADJECTIVE 1 = factual, real 2 = unbiased, detached, fair, open-minded, impartial, impersonal, disinterested, even-handed ≠ subjective

objectively = impartially, neutrally, fairly, justly, without prejudice, dispassionately, with an open mind, equitably

obligation 1 = duty, compulsion 2 = task, job, duty, work, charge, role, function, mission 3 = responsibility, duty, liability, accountability, answerability

oblige 1 = compel, make, force, require, bind, constrain, necessitate, impel
2 = help, assist, benefit, please, humour, accommodate, indulge, gratify ≠ bother

obliged 1 = forced, required, bound,

compelled, duty-bound **2** = <u>grateful</u>, in (someone's) debt, thankful, indebted, appreciative, beholden

obliging = <u>accommodating</u>, kind, helpful, willing, polite, cooperative, agreeable, considerate ≠ unhelpful

obscene 1 = <u>indecent</u>, dirty, offensive, filthy, improper, immoral, pornographic, lewd ≠ decent **2** = <u>offensive</u>, shocking, evil, disgusting, outrageous, revolting, sickening, vile

obscure ADJECTIVE **1** = <u>unknown</u>, little-known, humble, unfamiliar, out-of-the-way, lowly, unheard-of, undistinguished ≠ famous **2** = <u>abstruse</u>, complex, confusing, mysterious, vague, unclear, ambiguous, enigmatic ≠ straightforward **3** = <u>unclear</u>, uncertain, confused, mysterious, doubtful, indeterminate ≠ well-known **4** = <u>indistinct</u>, vague, blurred, dark, faint, dim, gloomy, murky ≠ clear
● VERB **1** = <u>obstruct</u>, hinder **2** = <u>hide</u>, screen, mask, disguise, conceal, veil, cloak, camouflage ≠ expose

observation 1 = <u>watching</u>, study, survey, review, investigation, monitoring, examination, inspection **2** = <u>comment</u>, thought, note, statement, opinion, remark, explanation, reflection **3** = <u>remark</u>, comment, statement, reflection, utterance **4** = <u>observance of</u>, compliance with, honouring of, fulfilment of, carrying out of

observe 1 = <u>watch</u>, study, view, look at, check, survey, monitor, keep an eye on (*informal*) **2** = <u>notice</u>, see, note, discover, spot, regard, witness, distinguish **3** = <u>remark</u>, say, comment, state, note, reflect, mention, opine **4** = <u>comply with</u>, keep, follow, respect, carry out, honour, discharge, obey ≠ disregard

observer 1 = <u>witness</u>, viewer, spectator, looker-on, watcher, onlooker, eyewitness, bystander **2** = <u>commentator</u>, reporter, special correspondent **3** = <u>monitor</u>, watchdog, supervisor, scrutineer

obsessed = <u>absorbed</u>, dominated, gripped, haunted, distracted, hung up (*slang*), preoccupied ≠ indifferent

obsession = <u>preoccupation</u>, thing (*informal*), complex, hang-up (*informal*), mania, phobia, fetish, fixation

obsessive = <u>compulsive</u>, gripping, consuming, haunting, irresistible, neurotic,

besetting, uncontrollable

obsolete = <u>outdated</u>, old, passé, old-fashioned, discarded, extinct, out of date, archaic ≠ up-to-date

obstacle 1 = <u>obstruction</u>, block, barrier, hurdle, snag, impediment, blockage, hindrance **2** = <u>hindrance</u>, bar, difficulty, barrier, handicap, hurdle, hitch, drawback, uphill (*S. African*) ≠ help

obstruct 1 = <u>block</u>, close, bar, plug, barricade, stop up, bung up (*informal*) **2** = <u>hold up</u>, stop, check, block, restrict, slow down, hamper, hinder **3** = <u>impede</u>, hamper, hold back, thwart, hinder ≠ help **4** = <u>obscure</u>, screen, cover

obtain 1 = <u>get</u>, gain, acquire, land, net, pick up, secure, procure ≠ lose **2** = <u>achieve</u>, get, gain, accomplish, attain **3** (*Formal*) = <u>prevail</u>, hold, exist, be the case, abound, predominate, be in force, be current

obvious = <u>clear</u>, plain, apparent, evident, distinct, manifest, noticeable, conspicuous ≠ unclear

obviously 1 = <u>clearly</u>, of course, without doubt, assuredly **2** = <u>plainly</u>, patently, undoubtedly, evidently, manifestly, markedly, without doubt, unquestionably

occasion NOUN **1** = <u>time</u>, moment, point, stage, instance, juncture **2** = <u>function</u>, event, affair, do (*informal*), happening, experience, gathering, celebration **3** = <u>opportunity</u>, chance, time, opening, window **4** = <u>reason</u>, cause, call, ground(s), excuse, incentive, motive, justification
● VERB (*Formal*) = <u>cause</u>, produce, lead to, inspire, result in, generate, prompt, provoke

occasional = <u>infrequent</u>, odd, rare, irregular, sporadic, intermittent, few and far between, periodic ≠ constant

occasionally = <u>sometimes</u>, at times, from time to time, now and then, irregularly, now and again, periodically, once in a while ≠ constantly

occult NOUN = <u>magic</u>, witchcraft, sorcery, wizardry, enchantment, black art, necromancy
● ADJECTIVE = <u>supernatural</u>, magical, mysterious, psychic, mystical, unearthly, esoteric, uncanny

occupant = <u>occupier</u>, resident, tenant, inmate, inhabitant, incumbent, dweller, lessee

occupation 1 = <u>job</u>, calling, business,

line (of work), trade, career, employment, profession **2** = <u>hobby</u>, pastime, diversion, relaxation, leisure pursuit, (leisure) activity **3** = <u>invasion</u>, seizure, conquest, incursion, subjugation **4** = <u>occupancy</u>, residence, holding, control, possession, tenure, tenancy

occupied 1 = <u>in use</u>, taken, full, engaged, unavailable **2** = <u>inhabited</u>, peopled, lived-in, settled, tenanted ≠ uninhabited **3** = <u>busy</u>, engaged, employed, working, active, hard at work, rushed off your feet

occupy 1 = <u>inhabit</u>, own, live in, dwell in, reside in, abide in ≠ vacate **2** = <u>invade</u>, take over, capture, seize, conquer, overrun, annex, colonize ≠ withdraw **3** = <u>hold</u>, control, dominate, possess **4** = <u>take up</u>, consume, tie up, use up, monopolize **5** often passive = <u>engage</u>, involve, employ, divert, preoccupy, engross **6** = <u>fill</u>, take up, cover, fill up, pervade, permeate, extend over

occur VERB **1** = <u>happen</u>, take place, come about, turn up (informal), crop up (informal), transpire (informal), befall **2** = <u>exist</u>, appear, be found, develop, turn up, be present, manifest itself, present itself

● PHRASES **occur to someone** = <u>come to mind</u>, strike someone, dawn on someone, spring to mind, cross someone's mind, enter someone's head, suggest itself to someone

occurrence 1 = <u>incident</u>, happening, event, fact, matter, affair, circumstance, episode **2** = <u>existence</u>, instance, appearance, manifestation, materialization

odd 1 = <u>peculiar</u>, strange, unusual, extraordinary, bizarre, offbeat, freakish **2** = <u>unusual</u>, strange, rare, extraordinary, remarkable, bizarre, peculiar, irregular ≠ normal **3** = <u>occasional</u>, various, random, casual, irregular, periodic, sundry, incidental ≠ regular **4** = <u>spare</u>, remaining, extra, surplus, solitary, leftover, unmatched, unpaired ≠ matched

odds PLURAL NOUN **1** = <u>probability</u>, chances, likelihood

● PHRASES **at odds 1** = <u>in conflict</u>, arguing, quarrelling, at loggerheads, at daggers drawn **2** = <u>at variance</u>, conflicting, contrary to, at odds, out of line, out of step, at sixes and sevens (informal)

♦ **odds and ends** = <u>scraps</u>, bits, remains, fragments, debris, remnants, bits and pieces, bric-a-brac

odour = <u>smell</u>, scent, perfume, fragrance, stink, bouquet, aroma, stench

odyssey = <u>journey</u>, tour, trip, quest, trek, expedition, voyage, crusade

off ADVERB = <u>away</u>, out, apart, elsewhere, aside, hence, from here

● ADJECTIVE **1** = <u>absent</u>, gone, unavailable **2** = <u>cancelled</u>, abandoned, postponed, shelved **3** = <u>bad</u>, rotten, rancid, mouldy, turned, spoiled, sour, decayed

offence 1 = <u>crime</u>, sin, fault, violation, wrongdoing, trespass, felony, misdemeanour **2** = <u>outrage</u>, shock, anger, trouble, bother, resentment, irritation, hassle (informal) **3** = <u>insult</u>, slight, hurt, outrage, injustice, snub, affront, indignity

offend 1 = <u>distress</u>, upset, outrage, wound, slight, insult, annoy, snub ≠ please **2** = <u>break the law</u>, sin, err, do wrong, fall, go astray

offended = <u>upset</u>, hurt, bothered, disturbed, distressed, outraged, stung, put out (informal), tooshie (Austral. slang)

offender = <u>criminal</u>, convict, crook, villain, culprit, sinner, delinquent, felon

offensive ADJECTIVE **1** = <u>insulting</u>, rude, abusive, degrading, contemptuous, disparaging, objectionable, disrespectful ≠ respectful **2** = <u>disgusting</u>, gross, foul, unpleasant, revolting, vile, repellent, obnoxious, festy (Austral. slang), yucko (Austral. slang) ≠ pleasant **3** = <u>attacking</u>, threatening, aggressive, striking, hostile, invading, combative ≠ defensive

● NOUN = <u>attack</u>, charge, campaign, strike, push (informal), assault, raid, drive

offer VERB **1** = <u>provide</u>, present, furnish, afford ≠ withhold **2** = <u>volunteer</u>, come forward, offer your services **3** = <u>propose</u>, suggest, advance, submit **4** = <u>give</u>, show, bring, provide, render, impart **5** = <u>put up for sale</u>, sell **6** = <u>bid</u>, submit, propose, tender, proffer

● NOUN **1** = <u>proposal</u>, suggestion, proposition, submission **2** = <u>bid</u>, tender, bidding price

offering 1 = <u>contribution</u>, gift, donation, present, subscription, hand-out **2** = <u>sacrifice</u>, tribute, libation, burnt offering

office 1 = <u>place of work</u>, workplace, base,

workroom, place of business **2** = <u>branch</u>, department, division, section, wing, subdivision, subsection **3** = <u>post</u>, place, role, situation, responsibility, function, occupation

officer 1 = <u>official</u>, executive, agent, representative, appointee, functionary, office-holder, office bearer **2** = <u>police officer</u>, detective, PC, police constable, police man, police woman

official ADJECTIVE **1** = <u>authorized</u>, formal, sanctioned, licensed, proper, legitimate, authentic, certified ≠ unofficial **2** = <u>formal</u>, bureaucratic, ceremonial, solemn, ritualistic

● NOUN = <u>officer</u>, executive, agent, representative, bureaucrat, appointee, functionary, office-holder

offset = <u>cancel out</u>, balance, set off, make up for, compensate for, counteract, neutralize, counterbalance

offspring 1 = <u>child</u>, baby, kid (*informal*), youngster, infant, successor, babe, toddler, littlie (*Austral. informal*), ankle-biter (*Austral. slang*), tacker (*Austral. slang*) ≠ parent **2** = <u>children</u>, young, family, issue, stock, heirs, descendants, brood

often = <u>frequently</u>, generally, commonly, repeatedly, time and again, habitually, not infrequently ≠ never

oil VERB = <u>lubricate</u>, grease

● NOUN **1** = <u>lubricant</u>, grease, lubrication, fuel oil **2** = <u>lotion</u>, cream, balm, salve, liniment, embrocation, solution

oily = <u>greasy</u>, slimy, fatty, slippery, oleaginous

OK or **okay** ADJECTIVE (*Informal*) **1** = <u>all right</u>, fine, fitting, in order, permitted, suitable, acceptable, allowable ≠ unacceptable **2** = <u>fine</u>, good, average, fair, all right, acceptable, adequate, satisfactory ≠ unsatisfactory **3** = <u>well</u>, all right, safe, sound, healthy, unharmed, uninjured

● INTERJECTION = <u>all right</u>, right, yes, agreed, very good, roger, very well, ya (*S. African*), righto (*Brit. informal*), yebo (*S. African informal*)

● VERB = <u>approve</u>, allow, agree to, permit, sanction, endorse, authorize, rubber-stamp (*informal*)

● NOUN = <u>authorization</u>, agreement, sanction, approval, go-ahead (*informal*), blessing, permission, consent

old 1 = <u>aged</u>, elderly, ancient, mature, venerable, antiquated, senile, decrepit ≠ young **2** = <u>former</u>, earlier, past, previous, prior, one-time, erstwhile **3** = <u>long-standing</u>, established, fixed, enduring, abiding, long-lasting, long-established, time-honoured **4** = <u>stale</u>, worn-out, banal, threadbare, trite, overused, timeworn

old-fashioned 1 = <u>out of date</u>, dated, outdated, unfashionable, outmoded, passé, old hat, behind the times ≠ up-to-date **2** = <u>oldfangled</u>, square (*informal*), outdated, obsolescent

ominous = <u>threatening</u>, sinister, grim, fateful, foreboding, unpromising, portentous, inauspicious ≠ promising

omission 1 = <u>exclusion</u>, removal, elimination, deletion, excision ≠ inclusion **2** = <u>gap</u>, space, exclusion, lacuna **3** = <u>failure</u>, neglect, negligence, oversight, carelessness, dereliction, slackness, laxity

omit 1 = <u>leave out</u>, drop, exclude, eliminate, skip ≠ include **2** = <u>forget</u>, overlook, neglect, pass over, lose sight of

once ADVERB **1** = <u>on one occasion</u>, one time, one single time **2** = <u>at one time</u>, previously, formerly, long ago, once upon a time

● CONJUNCTION = <u>as soon as</u>, when, after, the moment, immediately, the instant

● PHRASES **at once 1** = <u>immediately</u>, now, straight away, directly, promptly, instantly, right away, forthwith **2** = <u>simultaneously</u>, together, at the same time, concurrently

one-sided 1 = <u>unequal</u>, unfair, uneven, unjust, unbalanced, lopsided, ill-matched ≠ equal **2** = <u>biased</u>, prejudiced, weighted, unfair, partial, distorted, partisan, slanted ≠ unbiased

ongoing = <u>in progress</u>, developing, progressing, evolving, unfolding, unfinished

onlooker = <u>spectator</u>, witness, observer, viewer, looker-on, watcher, eyewitness, bystander

only ADJECTIVE = <u>sole</u>, one, single, individual, exclusive, unique, lone, solitary

● ADVERB **1** = <u>just</u>, simply, purely, merely **2** = <u>hardly</u>, just, barely, only just, scarcely, at a push

onset = <u>beginning</u>, start, birth, outbreak, inception, commencement ≠ end

onslaught = <u>attack</u>, charge, campaign, strike, assault, raid, invasion, offensive

≠ retreat

onward or **onwards** = forward, on, forwards, ahead, beyond, in front, forth

ooze[1] 1 = seep, well, escape, leak, drain, filter, drip, trickle 2 = emit, release, leak, drip, dribble, give off, pour forth 3 = exude, emit

ooze[2] = mud, clay, dirt, silt, sludge, mire, slime, alluvium

open VERB 1 = unfasten, unlock ≠ close 2 = unwrap, uncover, undo, unravel, untie ≠ wrap 3 = uncork 4 = unfold, spread (out), expand, unfurl, unroll ≠ fold 5 = clear, unblock ≠ block 6 = undo, unbutton, unfasten ≠ fasten 7 = begin business 8 = start, begin, launch, trigger, kick off (informal), initiate, commence, get going ≠ end 9 = begin, start, commence ≠ end

• ADJECTIVE 1 = unclosed, unlocked, ajar, unfastened, yawning ≠ closed 2 = unsealed, unstoppered ≠ unopened 3 = extended, unfolded, stretched out, unfurled, straightened out, unrolled ≠ shut 4 = frank, direct, straightforward, sincere, transparent, honest, candid, truthful ≠ sly 5 = receptive, sympathetic, responsive, amenable 6 = unresolved, unsettled, undecided, debatable, moot, arguable 7 = clear, passable, unhindered, unimpeded, navigable, unobstructed ≠ obstructed 8 = available, to hand, accessible, handy, at your disposal 9 = general, public, free, universal, blanket, across-the-board, unrestricted, overarching ≠ restricted 10 = vacant, free, available, empty, unoccupied, unfilled

open-air = outdoor, outside, out-of-door(s), alfresco

opening ADJECTIVE = first, earliest, beginning, premier, primary, initial, maiden, inaugural

• NOUN 1 = beginning, start, launch, dawn, outset, initiation, inception, commencement ≠ ending 2 = hole, space, tear, crack, gap, slot, puncture, aperture ≠ blockage 3 = opportunity, chance, time, moment, occasion, look-in (informal) 4 = job, position, post, situation, opportunity, vacancy

openly = frankly, plainly, honestly, overtly, candidly, unreservedly, unhesitatingly, forthrightly ≠ privately

open-minded = unprejudiced, liberal, balanced, objective, reasonable, tolerant, impartial, receptive ≠ narrow-minded

operate 1 = manage, run, direct, handle, supervise, be in charge of 2 = function, work, act 3 = run, work, use, control, manoeuvre 4 = work, go, run, perform, function ≠ break down

operation = performance, action, movement, motion

operational = working, going, running, ready, functioning, operative, viable, functional ≠ inoperative

operative ADJECTIVE = in force, effective, functioning, active, in effect, operational, in operation ≠ inoperative

• NOUN 1 = worker, employee, labourer, workman, artisan 2 (U.S. & Canad.) = spy, undercover agent, mole, nark (Brit., Austral., & N.Z. slang)

operator = worker, driver, mechanic, operative, conductor, technician, handler

opinion 1 = belief, feeling, view, idea, theory, conviction, point of view, sentiment 2 = estimation, view, impression, assessment, judgment, appraisal, considered opinion

opponent 1 = adversary, rival, enemy, competitor, challenger, foe, contestant, antagonist ≠ ally 2 = opposer, dissident, objector ≠ supporter

opportunity = chance, opening, time, turn, moment, possibility, occasion, slot

oppose = be against, fight (against), block, take on, counter, contest, resist, combat ≠ support

opposed 1 with to = against, hostile, adverse, in opposition, averse, antagonistic, (dead) set against 2 = contrary, conflicting, clashing, counter, adverse, contradictory, dissentient

opposing 1 = conflicting, different, contrasting, opposite, differing, contrary, contradictory, incompatible 2 = rival, conflicting, competing, enemy, opposite, hostile

opposite PREPOSITION = facing, face to face with, across from, eyeball to eyeball (informal)

• ADJECTIVE 1 = facing, other, opposing 2 = different, conflicting, contrasted, contrasting, unlike, contrary, dissimilar, divergent ≠ alike 3 = rival, conflicting, opposing, competing

• NOUN = reverse, contrary, converse,

antithesis, contradiction, inverse, obverse

opposition 1 = <u>hostility</u>, resistance, resentment, disapproval, obstruction, animosity, antagonism, antipathy ≠ support **2** = <u>opponent(s)</u>, competition, rival(s), enemy, competitor(s), other side, challenger(s), foe

oppress 1 = <u>subjugate</u>, abuse, suppress, wrong, master, overcome, subdue, persecute ≠ liberate **2** = <u>depress</u>, burden, discourage, torment, harass, afflict, sadden, vex

oppression = <u>persecution</u>, control, abuse, injury, injustice, cruelty, domination, repression ≠ justice

oppressive 1 = <u>tyrannical</u>, severe, harsh, cruel, brutal, authoritarian, unjust, repressive ≠ merciful **2** = <u>stifling</u>, close, sticky, stuffy, humid, sultry, airless, muggy

opt VERB = <u>choose</u>, decide, prefer, select, elect ≠ reject

● PHRASES **opt for something** or **someone** = <u>choose</u>, pick, select, adopt, go for, designate, decide on, plump for

optimistic 1 = <u>hopeful</u>, positive, confident, encouraged, cheerful, rosy, buoyant, sanguine ≠ pessimistic **2** = <u>encouraging</u>, promising, bright, good, reassuring, rosy, heartening, auspicious ≠ discouraging

optimum or **optimal** = <u>ideal</u>, best, highest, finest, perfect, supreme, peak, outstanding ≠ worst

option = <u>choice</u>, alternative, selection, preference, freedom of choice, power to choose

optional = <u>voluntary</u>, open, discretionary, possible, extra, elective ≠ compulsory

opus = <u>work</u>, piece, production, creation, composition, work of art, brainchild, oeuvre (French)

oral = <u>spoken</u>, vocal, verbal, unwritten

orbit NOUN **1** = <u>path</u>, course, cycle, circle, revolution, rotation, trajectory, sweep **2** = <u>sphere of influence</u>, reach, range, influence, province, scope, domain, compass

● VERB = <u>circle</u>, ring, go round, revolve around, encircle, circumscribe, circumnavigate

orchestrate 1 = <u>organize</u>, plan, run, set up, arrange, put together, marshal, coordinate **2** = <u>score</u>, set, arrange, adapt

ordain 1 = <u>appoint</u>, name, commission, select, invest, nominate, anoint, consecrate **2** (Formal) = <u>order</u>, will, rule, demand, require, direct, command, dictate

ordeal = <u>hardship</u>, trial, difficulty, test, suffering, nightmare, torture, agony ≠ pleasure

order VERB **1** = <u>command</u>, instruct, direct, charge, demand, require, bid, compel ≠ forbid **2** = <u>decree</u>, rule, demand, prescribe, pronounce, ordain ≠ ban **3** = <u>request</u>, ask (for), book, seek, reserve, apply for, solicit, send away for **4** = <u>arrange</u>, group, sort, position, line up, organize, catalogue, sort out ≠ disarrange

● NOUN **1** = <u>instruction</u>, ruling, demand, direction, command, dictate, decree, mandate **2** = <u>request</u>, booking, demand, commission, application, reservation, requisition **3** = <u>sequence</u>, grouping, series, structure, chain, arrangement, line-up, array **4** = <u>organization</u>, system, method, pattern, symmetry, regularity, neatness, tidiness ≠ chaos **5** = <u>peace</u>, control, law, quiet, calm, discipline, law and order, tranquillity **6** = <u>society</u>, company, group, club, community, association, institute, organization **7** = <u>class</u>, set, rank, grade, caste **8** = <u>kind</u>, group, class, family, sort, type, variety, category

orderly 1 = <u>well-behaved</u>, controlled, disciplined, quiet, restrained, law-abiding, peaceable ≠ disorderly **2** = <u>well-organized</u>, regular, in order, organized, precise, neat, tidy, systematic ≠ disorganized

ordinary 1 = <u>usual</u>, standard, normal, common, regular, typical, conventional, routine **2** = <u>commonplace</u>, plain, modest, humble, mundane, banal, unremarkable, run-of-the-mill ≠ extraordinary

organ 1 = <u>body part</u>, part of the body, element, biological structure **2** = <u>newspaper</u>, medium, voice, vehicle, gazette, mouthpiece

organic 1 = <u>natural</u>, biological, living, live, animate **2** = <u>systematic</u>, ordered, structured, organized, integrated, orderly, methodical

organism = <u>creature</u>, being, thing, body, animal, structure, beast, entity

organization 1 = <u>group</u>, company, party, body, association, band, institution, corporation **2** = <u>management</u>, running, planning, control, operation, handling, structuring, administration **3** = <u>structure</u>, form, pattern, make-up, arrangement, construction, format, formation

organize 1 = <u>arrange</u>, run, plan, prepare, set up, devise, put together, take care of, jack up (*N.Z. informal*) ≠ disrupt 2 = <u>put in order</u>, arrange, group, list, file, index, classify, inventory ≠ muddle

orient *or* **orientate** 1 = <u>adjust</u>, adapt, alter, accustom, align, familiarize, acclimatize 2 = <u>get your bearings</u>, establish your location

orientation 1 = <u>inclination</u>, tendency, disposition, predisposition, predilection, proclivity, partiality 2 = <u>induction</u>, introduction, adjustment, settling in, adaptation, assimilation, familiarization, acclimatization 3 = <u>position</u>, situation, location, bearings, direction, arrangement, whereabouts

origin 1 = <u>beginning</u>, start, birth, launch, foundation, creation, emergence, onset ≠ end 2 = <u>root</u>, source, basis, base, seed, foundation, nucleus, derivation

original ADJECTIVE 1 = <u>first</u>, earliest, initial 2 = <u>initial</u>, first, starting, opening, primary, introductory ≠ final 3 = <u>new</u>, fresh, novel, unusual, unprecedented, innovative, unfamiliar, seminal ≠ unoriginal 4 = <u>creative</u>, inspired, imaginative, artistic, fertile, ingenious, visionary, inventive
● NOUN = <u>prototype</u>, master, pattern ≠ copy

originally = <u>initially</u>, first, firstly, at first, primarily, to begin with, in the beginning

originate 1 = <u>begin</u>, start, emerge, come, happen, rise, appear, spring ≠ end 2 = <u>invent</u>, create, design, launch, introduce, institute, generate, pioneer

ornament NOUN 1 = <u>decoration</u>, trimming, accessory, festoon, trinket, bauble, knick-knack 2 = <u>embellishment</u>, decoration, embroidery, elaboration, adornment, ornamentation
● VERB = <u>decorate</u>, adorn, array, do up (*informal*), embellish, festoon, beautify, prettify

orthodox 1 = <u>established</u>, official, accepted, received, common, traditional, normal, usual ≠ unorthodox 2 = <u>conformist</u>, conservative, traditional, strict, devout, observant ≠ nonconformist

orthodoxy 1 = <u>doctrine</u>, teaching, opinion, principle, belief, convention, creed, dogma 2 = <u>conformity</u>, received

wisdom, traditionalism, conventionality ≠ nonconformity

other 1 = <u>additional</u>, more, further, new, added, extra, fresh, spare 2 = <u>different</u>, alternative, contrasting, distinct, diverse, dissimilar, separate, alternative

otherwise 1 = <u>or else</u>, or, if not, or then 2 = <u>apart from that</u>, in other ways, in (all) other respects 3 = <u>differently</u>, any other way, contrarily

ounce = <u>shred</u>, bit, drop, trace, scrap, grain, fragment, atom

oust = <u>expel</u>, turn out, dismiss, exclude, exile, throw out, displace, topple

out ADJECTIVE 1 = <u>not in</u>, away, elsewhere, outside, gone, abroad, from home, absent 2 = <u>extinguished</u>, ended, finished, dead, exhausted, expired, used up, at an end ≠ alight 3 = <u>in bloom</u>, opening, open, flowering, blooming, in flower, in full bloom 4 = <u>available</u>, on sale, in the shops, to be had, purchasable 5 = <u>revealed</u>, exposed, common knowledge, public knowledge, (out) in the open ≠ kept secret
● VERB = <u>expose</u>

outbreak 1 = <u>eruption</u>, burst, explosion, epidemic, rash, outburst, flare-up, upsurge 2 = <u>onset</u>, beginning, outset, opening, dawn, commencement

outburst = <u>explosion</u>, fit, surge, outbreak, flare-up, eruption, spasm, outpouring

outcome = <u>result</u>, end, consequence, conclusion, payoff (*informal*), upshot

outcry = <u>protest</u>, complaint, objection, dissent, outburst, clamour, uproar, commotion

outdated = <u>old-fashioned</u>, dated, obsolete, out of date, passé, archaic, unfashionable, antiquated ≠ modern

outdoor = <u>open-air</u>, outside, out-of-door(s), alfresco ≠ indoor

outer 1 = <u>external</u>, outside, outward, exterior, exposed, outermost ≠ inner 2 = <u>surface</u> 3 = <u>outlying</u>, distant, provincial, out-of-the-way, peripheral, far-flung ≠ central

outfit 1 = <u>costume</u>, dress, clothes, clothing, suit, get-up (*informal*), kit, ensemble 2 (*Informal*) = <u>group</u>, company, team, party, unit, crowd, squad, organization

outgoing 1 = <u>leaving</u>, former, previous, retiring, withdrawing, prior, departing, erstwhile ≠ incoming 2 = <u>sociable</u>, open, social, warm, friendly, expansive, affable, extrovert ≠ reserved

outgoings = expenses, costs, payments, expenditure, overheads, outlay

outing = journey, run, trip, tour, expedition, excursion, spin (*informal*), jaunt

outlaw VERB 1 = ban, bar, veto, forbid, exclude, prohibit, disallow, proscribe ≠ legalise 2 = banish, put a price on (someone's) head
● NOUN (*History*) = bandit, criminal, thief, robber, fugitive, outcast, felon, highwayman

outlet 1 = shop, store, supermarket, market, boutique, emporium, hypermarket 2 = channel, release, medium, avenue, vent, conduit 3 = pipe, opening, channel, exit, duct

outline VERB 1 = summarize, draft, plan, trace, sketch (in), sum up, encapsulate, delineate 2 = silhouette, etch
● NOUN 1 = summary, review, résumé, rundown, synopsis, précis, thumbnail sketch, recapitulation 2 = shape, lines, form, figure, profile, silhouette, configuration, contour(s)

outlook 1 = attitude, opinion, position, approach, mood, perspective, point of view, stance 2 = prospect(s), future, expectations, forecast, prediction, probability, prognosis

out of date 1 = old-fashioned, dated, outdated, obsolete, démodé (*French*), antiquated, outmoded, passé ≠ modern 2 = invalid, expired, lapsed, void, null and void

output = production, manufacture, manufacturing, yield, productivity

outrage VERB = offend, shock, upset, wound, insult, infuriate, incense, madden
● NOUN = indignation, shock, anger, rage, fury, hurt, resentment, scorn

outrageous 1 = atrocious, shocking, terrible, offensive, appalling, cruel, savage, horrifying ≠ mild 2 = unreasonable, unfair, steep (*informal*), shocking, extravagant, scandalous, preposterous, unwarranted ≠ reasonable

outright ADJECTIVE 1 = absolute, complete, total, perfect, sheer, thorough, unconditional, unqualified 2 = definite, clear, certain, flat, absolute, black-and-white, straightforward, unequivocal
● ADVERB 1 = openly, frankly, plainly,

overtly, candidly, unreservedly, unhesitatingly, forthrightly 2 = absolutely, completely, totally, fully, entirely, thoroughly, wholly, utterly

outset = beginning, start, opening, onset, inauguration, inception, commencement, kickoff (*informal*) ≠ finish

outside NOUN = exterior, face, front, covering, skin, surface, shell, coating
● ADJECTIVE 1 = external, outer, exterior, outward, extraneous ≠ inner 2 = remote, small, unlikely, slight, slim, distant, faint, marginal
● ADVERB = outdoors, out of the house, out-of-doors

outsider = stranger, incomer, visitor, newcomer, intruder, interloper, odd one out

outskirts = edge, boundary, suburbs, fringe, perimeter, periphery, suburbia, environs

outspan (*S. African*) = relax, chill out (*slang, chiefly U.S.*), take it easy, loosen up, put your feet up

outspoken = forthright, open, frank, straightforward, blunt, explicit, upfront (*informal*), unequivocal ≠ reserved

outstanding 1 = excellent, good, great, important, special, fine, brilliant, impressive, booshit (*Austral. slang*), exo (*Austral. slang*), sik (*Austral. slang*) ≠ mediocre 2 = unpaid, remaining, due, pending, payable, unsettled, uncollected 3 = undone, left, omitted, unfinished, unfulfilled, unperformed

outward = apparent, seeming, surface, ostensible ≠ inward

outwardly = apparently, externally, seemingly, it seems that, on the surface, it appears that, ostensibly, on the face of it

outweigh = override, cancel (out), eclipse, offset, compensate for, supersede, neutralize, counterbalance

oval = elliptical, egg-shaped, ovoid

ovation = applause, hand, cheers, praise, tribute, acclaim, clapping, accolade ≠ derision

over PREPOSITION 1 = above, on top of 2 = on top of, on, across, upon 3 = across, (looking) onto 4 = more than, above, exceeding, in excess of, upwards of 5 = about, regarding, relating to, concerning, apropos of
● ADVERB 1 = above, overhead, in the sky, on high, aloft, up above 2 = extra, more,

further, beyond, additional, in addition, surplus, in excess

● ADJECTIVE = <u>finished</u>, done (with), through, ended, closed, past, completed, complete

▓▓▓▓ RELATED WORDS
prefixes: hyper-, super-

overall ADJECTIVE = <u>total</u>, full, whole, general, complete, entire, global, comprehensive

● ADVERB = <u>in general</u>, generally, mostly, all things considered, on average, on the whole, predominantly, in the main

overcome VERB 1 = <u>defeat</u>, beat, conquer, master, overwhelm, subdue, rout, overpower 2 = <u>conquer</u>, beat, master, subdue, triumph over, vanquish

● ADJECTIVE = <u>overwhelmed</u>, moved, affected, emotional, choked, speechless, bowled over (*informal*), at a loss for words

overdue 1 = <u>delayed</u>, belated, late, behind schedule, tardy, unpunctual, behindhand ≠ early 2 = <u>unpaid</u>, owing

overflow VERB = <u>spill over</u>, well over, run over, pour over, bubble over, brim over

● NOUN 1 = <u>flood</u>, spilling over 2 = <u>surplus</u>, extra, excess, overspill, overabundance, additional people *or* things

overhaul VERB 1 = <u>check</u>, service, maintain, examine, restore, tune (up), repair, go over 2 = <u>overtake</u>, pass, leave behind, catch up with, get past, outstrip, get ahead of, outdistance

● NOUN = <u>check</u>, service, examination, going-over (*informal*), inspection, once-over (*informal*), checkup, reconditioning

overhead ADJECTIVE = <u>raised</u>, suspended, elevated, aerial, overhanging

● ADVERB = <u>above</u>, in the sky, on high, aloft, up above ≠ underneath

overheads = <u>running costs</u>, expenses, outgoings, operating costs

overlook 1 = <u>look over</u> *or* out on, have a view of 2 = <u>miss</u>, forget, neglect, omit, disregard, pass over ≠ notice 3 = <u>ignore</u>, excuse, forgive, pardon, disregard, condone, turn a blind eye to, wink at

overpower 1 = <u>overcome</u>, master, overwhelm, overthrow, subdue, quell, subjugate, prevail over 2 = <u>defeat</u>, crush, triumph over, vanquish 3 = <u>overwhelm</u>, overcome, bowl over (*informal*), stagger

override 1 = <u>outweigh</u>, eclipse, supersede, take precedence over, prevail over 2 = <u>overrule</u>, cancel, overturn, repeal, rescind, annul, nullify, countermand 3 = <u>ignore</u>, reject, discount, overlook, disregard, pass over, take no notice of

overrun 1 = <u>overwhelm</u>, attack, assault, occupy, raid, invade, penetrate, rout 2 = <u>spread over</u>, overwhelm, choke, swamp, infest, inundate, permeate, swarm over 3 = <u>exceed</u>, go beyond, surpass, overshoot, run over *or* on

overshadow 1 = <u>spoil</u>, ruin, mar, wreck, blight, crool *or* cruel (*Austral. slang*), mess up, put a damper on 2 = <u>outshine</u>, eclipse, surpass, dwarf, tower above, leave *or* put in the shade

overt = <u>open</u>, obvious, plain, public, manifest, blatant, observable, undisguised ≠ hidden

overtake 1 = <u>pass</u>, leave behind, overhaul, catch up with, get past, outdistance, go by *or* past 2 = <u>outdo</u>, top, exceed, eclipse, surpass, outstrip, get the better of, outclass 3 = <u>befall</u>, hit, happen to, catch off guard, catch unawares 4 = <u>engulf</u>, overwhelm, hit, strike, swamp, envelop, swallow up

overthrow VERB = <u>defeat</u>, overcome, conquer, bring down, oust, topple, rout, overpower ≠ uphold

● NOUN = <u>downfall</u>, fall, defeat, collapse, destruction, ousting, undoing, unseating ≠ preservation

overturn 1 = <u>tip over</u>, topple, upturn, capsize, upend, keel over, overbalance 2 = <u>knock over</u> *or* down, upturn, tip over, upend 3 = <u>reverse</u>, change, cancel, abolish, overthrow, set aside, repeal, quash 4 = <u>overthrow</u>, defeat, destroy, overcome, bring down, oust, topple, depose

overweight = <u>fat</u>, heavy, stout, hefty, plump, bulky, chunky, chubby ≠ underweight

overwhelm 1 = <u>overcome</u>, devastate, stagger, bowl over (*informal*), knock (someone) for six (*informal*), sweep (someone) off his *or* her feet, take (someone's) breath away 2 = <u>destroy</u>, defeat, overcome, crush, massacre, conquer, wipe out, overthrow

overwhelming 1 = <u>overpowering</u>, strong, powerful, towering, stunning, crushing, devastating, shattering ≠ negligible 2 = <u>vast</u>, huge, massive, enormous, tremendous, immense, very large

≠ insignificant

owe = be in debt (to), be in arrears (to), be overdrawn (by), be obligated *or* indebted (to)

owing to = because of, thanks to, as a result of, on account of, by reason of

own ADJECTIVE = personal, special, private, individual, particular, exclusive

● VERB = possess, have, keep, hold, enjoy, retain, be in possession of, have to your name

owner = possessor, holder, proprietor, titleholder, landlord *or* landlady

ownership = possession, occupation, tenure, dominion

p

pace NOUN 1 = speed, rate, tempo, velocity 2 = step, walk, stride, tread, gait 3 = footstep, step, stride

● VERB = stride, walk, pound, patrol, march up and down

pack VERB 1 = package, load, store, bundle, stow 2 = cram, crowd, press, fill, stuff, jam, ram, compress

● NOUN 1 = packet, box, package, carton 2 = bundle, parcel, load, burden, rucksack, knapsack, back pack, kitbag 3 = group, crowd, company, band, troop, gang, bunch, mob

● PHRASES **pack someone off** = send away, dismiss, send packing (*informal*)

◆ **pack something in** 1 (*Brit. informal*) = resign from, leave, give up, quit (*informal*), chuck (*informal*), jack in (*informal*) 2 = stop, give up, kick in (*informal*), cease, chuck (*informal*)

package NOUN 1 = parcel, box, container, packet, carton 2 = collection, lot, unit, combination, compilation

● VERB = pack, box, parcel (up)

packet 1 = container, box, package, carton 2 = package, parcel 3 (*Slang*) = a fortune, a bomb (*Brit. slang*), a pile (*informal*), a small fortune, a tidy sum (*informal*), a king's ransom (*informal*)

pact = agreement, alliance, treaty, deal, understanding, bargain, covenant

pad¹ NOUN 1 = wad, dressing, pack, padding, compress, wadding 2 = cushion, filling, stuffing, pillow, bolster, upholstery 3 = notepad, block, notebook, jotter, writing pad 4 (*Slang*) = home, flat, apartment, place 5 = paw, foot, sole

● VERB = pack, fill, protect, stuff, cushion

pad² = sneak, creep, steal, go barefoot

padding 1 = filling, stuffing, packing, wadding 2 = waffle (*informal, chiefly Brit.*), hot air (*informal*), verbiage, wordiness, verbosity

paddle¹ NOUN = oar, scull

● VERB = row, pull, scull

paddle² = wade, splash (about), slop

pagan ADJECTIVE = heathen, infidel, polytheistic, idolatrous

● NOUN = heathen, infidel, polytheist, idolater

page¹ = folio, side, leaf, sheet

page² VERB = call, summon, send for

● NOUN 1 = attendant, pageboy 2 = servant, attendant, squire, pageboy

pain NOUN 1 = suffering, discomfort, hurt, irritation, tenderness, soreness 2 = ache, stinging, aching, cramp, throb, throbbing, pang, twinge 3 = sorrow, suffering, torture, distress, despair, misery, agony, sadness

● PLURAL NOUN = trouble, effort, care, bother, diligence

● VERB 1 = distress, hurt, torture, grieve, torment, sadden, agonize, cut to the quick 2 = hurt

painful 1 = sore, smarting, aching, tender ≠ painless 2 = distressing, unpleasant, grievous, distasteful, agonizing, disagreeable ≠ pleasant 3 = difficult, arduous, trying, hard, troublesome, laborious ≠ easy

painfully = distressingly, clearly, sadly, unfortunately, dreadfully

paint NOUN = colouring, colour, stain, dye, tint, pigment, emulsion

● VERB 1 = colour, cover, coat, stain, whitewash, daub, distemper, apply paint to 2 = depict, draw, portray, picture, represent, sketch

pair NOUN 1 = set 2 = couple, brace, duo

● VERB = team, match (up), join, couple, twin, bracket

pal (*Informal*) = friend, companion, mate (*informal*), buddy (*informal*), comrade, chum (*informal*), crony, cobber (*Austral. & N.Z. old-fashioned informal*), E hoa (*N.Z.*)

pale ADJECTIVE 1 = <u>light</u>, soft, faded, subtle, muted, bleached, pastel, light-coloured 2 = <u>dim</u>, weak, faint, feeble, thin, wan, watery 3 = <u>white</u>, pasty, bleached, wan, colourless, pallid, ashen ≠ rosy-cheeked
● VERB = <u>become pale</u>, blanch, whiten, go white, lose colour

pamper = <u>spoil</u>, indulge, pet, cosset, coddle, mollycoddle

pamphlet = <u>booklet</u>, leaflet, brochure, circular, tract

pan¹ NOUN = <u>pot</u>, container, saucepan
● VERB 1 (*Informal*) = <u>criticize</u>, knock, slam (*slang*), censure, tear into (*informal*) 2 = <u>sift out</u>, look for, search for

pan² = <u>move along</u> or <u>across</u>, follow, track, sweep

panic NOUN = <u>fear</u>, alarm, terror, anxiety, hysteria, fright, trepidation, a flap (*informal*)
● VERB 1 = <u>go to pieces</u>, become hysterical, lose your nerve 2 = <u>alarm</u>, scare, unnerve

panorama 1 = <u>view</u>, prospect, vista 2 = <u>survey</u>, perspective, overview, overall picture

pant = <u>puff</u>, blow, breathe, gasp, wheeze, heave

pants 1 (*Brit.*) = <u>underpants</u>, briefs, drawers, knickers, panties, boxer shorts, broekies (*S. African*), underdaks (*Austral. slang*) 2 (*U.S.*) = <u>trousers</u>, slacks

paper NOUN 1 = <u>newspaper</u>, daily, journal, gazette 2 = <u>essay</u>, article, treatise, dissertation 3 = <u>examination</u>, test, exam 4 = <u>report</u>
● PLURAL NOUN 1 = <u>letters</u>, records, documents, file, diaries, archive, paperwork, dossier 2 = <u>documents</u>, records, certificates, identification, deeds, identity papers, I.D. (*informal*)
● VERB = <u>wallpaper</u>, hang

parade NOUN 1 = <u>procession</u>, march, pageant, cavalcade 2 = <u>show</u>, display, spectacle
● VERB 1 = <u>march</u>, process, promenade 2 = <u>flaunt</u>, display, exhibit, show off (*informal*) 3 = <u>strut</u>, show off (*informal*), swagger, swank

paradigm = <u>model</u>, example, pattern, ideal

paradise 1 = <u>heaven</u>, Promised Land, Happy Valley (*Islam*), Elysian fields

2 = <u>bliss</u>, delight, heaven, felicity, utopia

paradox = <u>contradiction</u>, puzzle, anomaly, enigma, oddity

paragraph = <u>section</u>, part, item, passage, clause, subdivision

parallel NOUN 1 = <u>equivalent</u>, counterpart, match, equal, twin, analogue ≠ opposite 2 = <u>similarity</u>, comparison, analogy, resemblance, likeness ≠ difference
● ADJECTIVE 1 = <u>matching</u>, corresponding, like, similar, resembling, analogous ≠ different 2 = <u>equidistant</u>, alongside, side by side ≠ divergent

paralyse 1 = <u>disable</u>, cripple, lame, incapacitate 2 = <u>freeze</u>, stun, numb, petrify, halt, immobilize 3 = <u>immobilize</u>, freeze, halt, disable, cripple, incapacitate, bring to a standstill

paralysis 1 = <u>immobility</u>, palsy 2 = <u>standstill</u>, breakdown, stoppage, halt

parameter (*Informal*) *usually plural* = <u>limit</u>, restriction, framework, limitation, specification

paramount = <u>principal</u>, prime, first, chief, main, primary, supreme, cardinal ≠ secondary

paranoid 1 (*Informal*) = <u>suspicious</u>, worried, nervous, fearful, antsy (*informal*) 2 = <u>obsessive</u>, disturbed, manic, neurotic, mentally ill, psychotic, deluded, paranoiac

parasite = <u>sponger</u> (*informal*), leech, hanger-on, scrounger (*informal*), bloodsucker (*informal*), quandong (*Austral. slang*)

parcel NOUN = <u>package</u>, case, box, pack, bundle
● VERB *often with **up*** = <u>wrap</u>, pack, package, tie up, do up, gift-wrap, box up, fasten together

pardon VERB 1 = <u>forgive</u>, excuse ≠ condemn 2 = <u>acquit</u>, let off (*informal*), exonerate, absolve ≠ punish
● NOUN 1 = <u>forgiveness</u>, absolution ≠ condemnation 2 = <u>acquittal</u>, amnesty, exoneration ≠ punishment

parent = <u>father</u> or <u>mother</u>, sire, progenitor, procreator, old (*Austral. & N.Z. informal*), patriarch

parish 1 = <u>district</u>, community 2 = <u>community</u>, flock, church, congregation

park 1 = <u>recreation ground</u>, garden, playground, pleasure garden, playpark, domain (*N.Z.*), forest park (*N.Z.*)

2 = parkland, grounds, estate, lawns, woodland, grassland **3** = field, pitch, playing field

parliament 1 = assembly, council, congress, senate, convention, legislature **2** = sitting

parliamentary = governmental, legislative, law-making

parlour or (U.S.) **parlor 1** (Old-fashioned) = sitting room, lounge, living room, drawing room, front room **2** = establishment, shop, store, salon

parody NOUN = takeoff (informal), satire, caricature, send-up (Brit. informal), spoof (informal), skit, burlesque
● **VERB** = take off (informal), caricature, send up (Brit. informal), burlesque, satirize, do a takeoff of (informal)

parrot = repeat, echo, imitate, copy, mimic

parry 1 = evade, avoid, dodge, sidestep **2** = ward off, block, deflect, repel, rebuff, repulse

parson = clergyman, minister, priest, vicar, preacher, pastor, cleric, churchman

part NOUN 1 = piece, share, proportion, percentage, bit, section, scrap, portion ≠ entirety **2** often plural = region, area, district, neighbourhood, quarter, vicinity **3** = component, bit, unit, constituent **4** = branch, division, office, section, wing, subdivision, subsection **5** = organ, member, limb **6** (Theatre) = role, representation, persona, portrayal, depiction, character part **7** (Theatre) = lines, words, script, dialogue **8** = side, behalf
● **VERB 1** = divide, separate, break, tear, split, rend, detach, sever ≠ join **2** = part company, separate, split up ≠ meet
● **PHRASES in good part** = good-naturedly, well, cheerfully, without offence

partial 1 = incomplete, unfinished, imperfect, uncompleted ≠ complete **2** = biased, prejudiced, discriminatory, partisan, unfair, one-sided, unjust ≠ unbiased

partially = partly, somewhat, in part, not wholly, fractionally, incompletely

participant = participator, member, player, contributor, stakeholder

participate = take part, be involved, perform, join, partake ≠ refrain from

participation = taking part, contribution, involvement, sharing in, joining in, partaking

particle = bit, piece, scrap, grain, shred, mite, jot, speck

particular ADJECTIVE 1 = specific, special, exact, precise, distinct, peculiar ≠ general **2** = special, exceptional, notable, uncommon, marked, unusual, remarkable, singular **3** = fussy, demanding, fastidious, choosy (informal), picky (informal), finicky, pernickety (informal) ≠ indiscriminate
● **NOUN** usually plural = detail, fact, feature, item, circumstance, specification

particularly 1 = specifically, expressly, explicitly, especially, in particular, distinctly **2** = especially, notably, unusually, exceptionally, singularly, uncommonly

parting 1 = farewell, goodbye **2** = division, breaking, split, separation, rift, rupture

partisan ADJECTIVE = prejudiced, one-sided, biased, partial, sectarian ≠ unbiased
● **NOUN 1** = supporter, devotee, adherent, upholder ≠ opponent **2** = underground fighter, guerrilla, freedom fighter, resistance fighter

partition NOUN 1 = screen, wall, barrier **2** = division, separation, segregation
● **VERB** = separate, screen, divide

partly = partially, somewhat, slightly ≠ completely

partner 1 = spouse, consort, significant other (U.S. informal), mate, husband or wife **2** = companion, ally, colleague, associate, mate, comrade **3** = associate, colleague, collaborator

partnership 1 = cooperation, alliance, sharing, union, connection, participation, copartnership **2** = company, firm, house, interest, society, cooperative

party 1 = faction, set, side, league, camp, clique, coterie **2** = get-together (informal), celebration, do (informal), gathering, function, reception, festivity, social gathering **3** = group, team, band, company, unit, squad, crew, gang

pass VERB 1 = go by or past, overtake, drive past, lap, leave behind, pull ahead of ≠ stop **2** = move, travel, progress, flow, proceed **3** = run, move, stroke **4** = give, hand, send, transfer, deliver, convey **5** = be left, come, be bequeathed, be inherited by **6** = kick, hit, loft, head, lob **7** = elapse, progress, go by, lapse, wear on, go past, tick by **8** = end, go, cease, blow over **9** = spend, fill, occupy, while away

10 = <u>exceed</u>, beat, overtake, go beyond, surpass, outstrip, outdo **11** = <u>be successful in</u>, qualify (in), succeed (in), graduate (in), get through, do, gain a pass in ≠ fail **12** = <u>approve</u>, accept, decree, enact, ratify, ordain, legislate (for) ≠ ban

● NOUN **1** = <u>licence</u>, ticket, permit, passport, warrant, authorization **2** = <u>gap</u>, route, canyon, gorge, ravine

● PHRASES **pass away** or **on** (*Euphemistic*) = <u>die</u>, pass on, expire, pass over, snuff it (*informal*), kick the bucket (*slang*), shuffle off this mortal coil, cark it (*Austral. & N.Z. informal*)

◆ **pass out** (*Informal*) = <u>faint</u>, black out (*informal*), lose consciousness, become unconscious ◆ **pass something over** = <u>disregard</u>, ignore, not dwell on ◆ **pass something up** (*Informal*) = <u>miss</u>, let slip, decline, neglect, forgo, abstain from, give (something) a miss (*informal*)

passage 1 = <u>corridor</u>, hall, lobby, vestibule **2** = <u>alley</u>, way, close (*Brit.*), course, road, channel, route, path **3** = <u>extract</u>, reading, piece, section, text, excerpt, quotation **4** = <u>journey</u>, crossing, trip, trek, voyage **5** = <u>safe-conduct</u>, right to travel, freedom to travel, permission to travel

passenger = <u>traveller</u>, rider, fare, commuter, fare payer

passer-by = <u>bystander</u>, witness, observer, viewer, spectator, looker-on, watcher, onlooker

passing 1 = <u>momentary</u>, fleeting, short-lived, transient, ephemeral, brief, temporary, transitory **2** = <u>superficial</u>, short, quick, glancing, casual, summary, cursory, perfunctory

passion 1 = <u>love</u>, desire, lust, infatuation, ardour **2** = <u>emotion</u>, feeling, fire, heat, excitement, intensity, warmth, zeal ≠ indifference **3** = <u>mania</u>, enthusiasm, obsession, bug (*informal*), craving, fascination, craze **4** = <u>rage</u>, fit, storm, anger, fury, outburst, frenzy, paroxysm

passionate 1 = <u>emotional</u>, eager, strong, intense, fierce, ardent, fervent, heartfelt ≠ unemotional **2** = <u>loving</u>, erotic, hot, ardent, amorous, lustful ≠ cold

passive 1 = <u>submissive</u>, compliant, receptive, docile, quiescent ≠ spirited **2** = <u>inactive</u>, uninvolved ≠ active

past NOUN **1** = <u>former times</u>, long ago, days gone by, the olden days ≠ future

2 = <u>background</u>, life, history, past life, life story, career to date

● ADJECTIVE **1** = <u>former</u>, early, previous, ancient, bygone, olden ≠ future **2** = <u>previous</u>, former, one-time, ex- **3** = <u>last</u>, previous **4** = <u>over</u>, done, ended, finished, gone

● PREPOSITION **1** = <u>after</u>, beyond, later than **2** = <u>by</u>, across, in front of

● ADVERB = <u>on</u>, by, along

paste NOUN **1** = <u>adhesive</u>, glue, cement, gum **2** = <u>purée</u>, pâté, spread

● VERB = <u>stick</u>, glue, cement, gum

pastel = <u>pale</u>, light, soft, delicate, muted ≠ bright

pastime = <u>activity</u>, game, entertainment, hobby, recreation, amusement, diversion

pastor = <u>clergyman</u>, minister, priest, vicar, parson, rector, curate, churchman

pastoral 1 = <u>ecclesiastical</u>, priestly, ministerial, clerical **2** = <u>rustic</u>, country, rural, bucolic

pasture = <u>grassland</u>, grass, meadow, grazing

pat VERB = <u>stroke</u>, touch, tap, pet, caress, fondle

● NOUN = <u>tap</u>, stroke, clap

patch NOUN **1** = <u>spot</u>, bit, scrap, shred, small piece **2** = <u>plot</u>, area, ground, land, tract **3** = <u>reinforcement</u>, piece of fabric, piece of cloth, piece of material, piece sewn on

● VERB *often with* ***up*** = <u>mend</u>, cover, repair, reinforce, stitch (up), sew (up)

patent NOUN = <u>copyright</u>, licence, franchise, registered trademark

● ADJECTIVE = <u>obvious</u>, apparent, evident, clear, glaring, manifest

path 1 = <u>way</u>, road, walk, track, trail, avenue, footpath, berm (*N.Z.*) **2** = <u>route</u>, way, course, direction **3** = <u>course</u>, way, road, route

pathetic = <u>sad</u>, moving, touching, affecting, distressing, tender, poignant, plaintive ≠ funny

patience 1 = <u>forbearance</u>, tolerance, serenity, restraint, calmness, sufferance ≠ impatience **2** = <u>endurance</u>, resignation, submission, fortitude, long-suffering, perseverance, stoicism, constancy

patient NOUN = <u>sick person</u>, case, sufferer, invalid

● ADJECTIVE **1** = <u>forbearing</u>, understanding, forgiving, mild, tolerant, indulgent, lenient, even-tempered ≠ impatient **2** = long-suffering, resigned, calm, enduring, philosophical, persevering, stoical, submissive

patriot = nationalist, loyalist, chauvinist

patriotic = nationalistic, loyal, chauvinistic, jingoistic

patriotism = nationalism, jingoism

patrol VERB = police, guard, keep watch (on), inspect, safeguard, keep guard (on)
● NOUN = guard, watch, watchman, sentinel, patrolman

patron 1 = supporter, friend, champion, sponsor, backer, helper, benefactor, philanthropist **2** = customer, client, buyer, frequenter, shopper, habitué

patronage = support, promotion, sponsorship, backing, help, aid, assistance

pattern 1 = order, plan, system, method, sequence **2** = design, arrangement, motif, figure, device, decoration **3** = plan, design, original, guide, diagram, stencil, template

pause VERB = stop briefly, delay, break, wait, rest, halt, cease, interrupt ≠ continue
● NOUN = stop, break, interval, rest, gap, halt, respite, lull ≠ continuance

pave = cover, floor, surface, concrete, tile

paw (*Informal*) = manhandle, grab, maul, molest, handle roughly

pay VERB **1** = reward, compensate, reimburse, recompense, requite, remunerate **2** = spend, give, fork out (*informal*), remit, shell out (*informal*) **3** = settle **4** = bring in, earn, return, net, yield **5** = be profitable, make money, make a return **6** = benefit, repay, be worthwhile **7** = give, extend, present with, grant, hand out, bestow
● NOUN = wages, income, payment, earnings, fee, reward, salary, allowance
● PHRASES **pay off** = succeed, work, be effective ◆ **pay something off** = settle, clear, square, discharge, pay in full

payable = due, outstanding, owed, owing

payment 1 = remittance, advance, deposit, premium, instalment **2** = settlement, paying, discharge, remittance **3** = wages, fee, reward, hire, remuneration

peace 1 = truce, ceasefire, treaty, armistice ≠ war **2** = stillness, rest, quiet, silence, calm, hush, tranquillity, seclusion **3** = serenity, calm, composure, contentment, repose, equanimity, peacefulness, harmoniousness **4** = harmony, accord, agreement, concord

peaceful 1 = at peace, friendly, harmonious, amicable, nonviolent ≠ hostile **2** = peace-loving, conciliatory, peaceable, unwarlike ≠ belligerent **3** = calm, still, quiet, tranquil, restful ≠ agitated **4** = serene, placid, undisturbed

peak NOUN **1** = high point, crown, climax, culmination, zenith, acme **2** = point, top, tip, summit, brow, crest, pinnacle, apex
● VERB = culminate, climax, come to a head

peasant = rustic, countryman

peck VERB **1** = pick, hit, strike, tap, poke, jab, prick **2** = kiss, plant a kiss, give someone a smacker, give someone a peck *or* kiss
● NOUN = kiss, smacker, osculation (*rare*)

peculiar 1 = odd, strange, unusual, bizarre, funny, extraordinary, curious, weird ≠ ordinary **2** = special, particular, unique, characteristic ≠ common

peddle = sell, trade, push (*informal*), market, hawk, flog (*slang*)

pedestrian NOUN = walker, foot-traveller ≠ driver
● ADJECTIVE = dull, ordinary, boring, commonplace, mundane, mediocre, banal, prosaic, half-pie (*N.Z. informal*) ≠ exciting

pedigree ADJECTIVE = purebred, thoroughbred, full-blooded
● NOUN = lineage, family, line, race, stock, blood, breed, descent

peel NOUN = rind, skin, peeling
● VERB = skin, scale, strip, pare, shuck, flake off, take the skin *or* rind off

peep VERB = peek, look, eyeball (*slang*), sneak a look, steal a look
● NOUN = look, glimpse, peek, look-see (*slang*)

peer¹ = squint, look, spy, gaze, scan, inspect, peep, peek

peer² **1** = noble, lord, aristocrat, nobleman **2** = equal, like, fellow, contemporary, compeer

peg NOUN = pin, spike, rivet, skewer, dowel, spigot
● VERB = fasten, join, fix, secure, attach

pen¹ = write (down), draft, compose, pencil, draw up, scribble, take down, inscribe

pen² NOUN = enclosure, pound, fold, cage, coop, hutch, sty
● VERB = enclose, confine, cage, fence in,

coop up, hedge in, shut up *or* in

penalty = <u>punishment</u>, price, fine, handicap, forfeit

pending ADJECTIVE 1 = <u>undecided</u>, unsettled, in the balance, undetermined 2 = <u>forthcoming</u>, imminent, prospective, impending, in the wind
● PREPOSITION = <u>awaiting</u>, until, waiting for, till

penetrate 1 = <u>pierce</u>, enter, go through, bore, stab, prick 2 = <u>grasp</u>, work out, figure out (*informal*), comprehend, fathom, decipher, suss (out) (*slang*), get to the bottom of

penetrating 1 = <u>sharp</u>, harsh, piercing, carrying, piping, loud, strident, shrill ≠ sweet 2 = <u>pungent</u> 3 = <u>piercing</u> 4 = <u>intelligent</u>, quick, sharp, keen, acute, shrewd, astute, perceptive ≠ dull 5 = <u>perceptive</u>, sharp, keen ≠ unperceptive

penetration 1 = <u>piercing</u>, entry, entrance, puncturing, incision 2 = <u>entry</u>, entrance

pension = <u>allowance</u>, benefit, welfare, annuity, superannuation

pensioner = <u>senior citizen</u>, retired person, retiree (*U.S.*), old-age pensioner, O.A.P.

people PLURAL NOUN 1 = <u>persons</u>, individuals, folk (*informal*), men and women, humanity, mankind, mortals, the human race 2 = <u>nation</u>, public, community, subjects, population, residents, citizens, folk 3 = <u>race</u>, tribe 4 = <u>family</u>, parents, relations, relatives, folk, folks (*informal*), clan, kin
● VERB = <u>inhabit</u>, occupy, settle, populate, colonize

pepper NOUN = <u>seasoning</u>, flavour, spice
● VERB 1 = <u>pelt</u>, hit, shower, blitz, rake, bombard, assail, strafe 2 = <u>sprinkle</u>, spot, scatter, dot, fleck, intersperse, speck, spatter

perceive 1 = <u>see</u>, notice, note, identify, discover, spot, observe, recognize 2 = <u>understand</u>, gather, see, learn, realize, grasp, comprehend, suss (out) (*slang*) 3 = <u>consider</u>, believe, judge, suppose, rate, deem, adjudge

perception 1 = <u>awareness</u>, understanding, sense, impression, feeling, idea, notion, consciousness 2 = <u>understanding</u>, intelligence,

observation, discrimination, insight, sharpness, cleverness, keenness

perch VERB 1 = <u>sit</u>, rest, balance, settle 2 = <u>place</u>, put, rest, balance 3 = <u>land</u>, alight, roost
● NOUN = <u>resting place</u>, post, branch, pole

perennial = <u>continual</u>, lasting, constant, enduring, persistent, abiding, recurrent, incessant

perfect ADJECTIVE 1 = <u>faultless</u>, correct, pure, impeccable, exemplary, flawless, foolproof ≠ deficient 2 = <u>excellent</u>, ideal, supreme, superb, splendid, sublime, superlative 3 = <u>immaculate</u>, impeccable, flawless, spotless, unblemished ≠ flawed 4 = <u>complete</u>, absolute, sheer, utter, consummate, unmitigated ≠ partial 5 = <u>exact</u>, true, accurate, precise, correct, faithful, unerring
● VERB = <u>improve</u>, develop, polish, refine ≠ mar

perfection = <u>excellence</u>, integrity, superiority, purity, wholeness, sublimity, exquisiteness, faultlessness

perfectly 1 = <u>completely</u>, totally, absolutely, quite, fully, altogether, thoroughly, wholly ≠ partially 2 = <u>flawlessly</u>, ideally, wonderfully, superbly, supremely, impeccably, faultlessly ≠ badly

perform 1 = <u>do</u>, achieve, carry out, complete, fulfil, accomplish, execute, pull off 2 = <u>fulfil</u>, carry out, execute, discharge 3 = <u>present</u>, act (out), stage, play, produce, represent, put on, enact 4 = <u>appear on stage</u>, act 5 = <u>function</u>, go, work, run, operate, handle, respond, behave

performance 1 = <u>presentation</u>, playing, acting (out), staging, production, exhibition, rendering, portrayal 2 = <u>show</u>, appearance, concert, gig (*informal*), recital 3 = <u>work</u>, acts, conduct, exploits, feats 4 = <u>carrying out</u>, practice, achievement, execution, completion, accomplishment, fulfilment

performer = <u>artiste</u>, player, Thespian, trouper, actor *or* actress

perfume 1 = <u>fragrance</u>, scent 2 = <u>scent</u>, smell, fragrance, bouquet, aroma, odour

perhaps = <u>maybe</u>, possibly, it may be, it is possible (that), conceivably, perchance (*archaic*), feasibly, happen (*Northern English dialect*)

peril 1 = <u>danger</u>, risk, threat, hazard,

menace, jeopardy, perilousness **2** *often plural* = <u>pitfall</u>, problem, risk, hazard ≠ safety

perimeter = <u>boundary</u>, edge, border, bounds, limit, margin, confines, periphery ≠ centre

period 1 = <u>time</u>, term, season, space, run, stretch, spell, phase

periodic = <u>recurrent</u>, regular, repeated, occasional, cyclical, sporadic, intermittent

peripheral 1 = <u>secondary</u>, minor, marginal, irrelevant, unimportant, incidental, inessential **2** = <u>outermost</u>, outside, external, outer, exterior

perish 1 = <u>die</u>, be killed, expire, pass away, lose your life, cark it (*Austral. & N.Z. slang*) **2** = <u>be destroyed</u>, fall, decline, collapse, disappear, vanish **3** = <u>rot</u>, waste away, decay, disintegrate, decompose, moulder

perk (*Brit. informal*) = <u>bonus</u>, benefit, extra, plus, fringe benefit, perquisite

permanent 1 = <u>lasting</u>, constant, enduring, persistent, eternal, abiding, perpetual, everlasting ≠ temporary **2** = <u>long-term</u>, established, secure, stable, steady ≠ temporary

permission = <u>authorization</u>, sanction, licence, approval, leave, go-ahead (*informal*), liberty, consent ≠ prohibition

permit VERB **1** = <u>allow</u>, grant, sanction, let, entitle, license, authorize, consent to ≠ forbid **2** = <u>enable</u>, let, allow, cause ● NOUN = <u>licence</u>, pass, document, certificate, passport, visa, warrant, authorization ≠ prohibition

perpetual 1 = <u>everlasting</u>, permanent, endless, eternal, lasting, perennial, infinite, never-ending ≠ temporary **2** = <u>continual</u>, repeated, constant, endless, continuous, persistent, recurrent, never-ending ≠ brief

perpetuate = <u>maintain</u>, preserve, keep going, immortalize ≠ end

persecute 1 = <u>victimize</u>, torture, torment, oppress, pick on, ill-treat, maltreat ≠ mollycoddle **2** = <u>harass</u>, bother, annoy, tease, hassle (*informal*), badger, pester ≠ leave alone

persist 1 = <u>continue</u>, last, remain, carry on, keep up, linger **2** = <u>persevere</u>, continue, go on, carry on, keep on, keep going, press on, not give up

persistence = <u>determination</u>, resolution, grit, endurance, tenacity, perseverance, doggedness, pertinacity

persistent 1 = <u>continuous</u>, constant, repeated, endless, perpetual, continual, never-ending, incessant **2** = <u>determined</u>, dogged, steady, stubborn, persevering, tireless, tenacious, steadfast ≠ irresolute

person NOUN = <u>individual</u>, being, body, human, soul, creature, mortal, man *or* woman ● PHRASES **in person 1** = <u>personally</u>, yourself **2** = <u>in the flesh</u>, actually, physically, bodily

personal 1 = <u>own</u>, special, private, individual, particular, peculiar **2** = <u>individual</u>, special, particular, exclusive **3** = <u>private</u> **4** = <u>offensive</u>, nasty, insulting, disparaging, derogatory

personality 1 = <u>nature</u>, character, make-up, identity, temperament, disposition, individuality **2** = <u>character</u>, charm, attraction, charisma, magnetism **3** = <u>celebrity</u>, star, notable, household name, famous name, personage, megastar (*informal*)

personally 1 = <u>in your opinion</u>, in your book, for your part, from your own viewpoint, in your own view **2** = <u>by yourself</u>, alone, independently, solely, on your own **3** = <u>individually</u>, specially, subjectively, individualistically **4** = <u>privately</u>, in private, off the record

personnel = <u>employees</u>, people, staff, workers, workforce, human resources, helpers

perspective 1 = <u>outlook</u>, attitude, context, angle, frame of reference **2** = <u>objectivity</u>, proportion, relation, relativity, relative importance

persuade 1 = <u>talk (someone) into</u>, urge, influence, win (someone) over, induce, sway, entice, coax ≠ dissuade **2** = <u>cause</u>, lead, move, influence, motivate, induce, incline, dispose **3** = <u>convince</u>, satisfy, assure, cause to believe

persuasion 1 = <u>urging</u>, inducement, wheedling, enticement, cajolery **2** = <u>belief</u>, views, opinion, party, school, side, camp, faith

persuasive = <u>convincing</u>, telling, effective, sound, compelling, influential, valid, credible ≠ unconvincing

pervasive = <u>widespread</u>, general, common, extensive, universal, prevalent, ubiquitous, rife

perverse 1 = <u>stubborn</u>, contrary, dogged, troublesome, rebellious, wayward, intractable, wilful ≠ cooperative 2 = <u>ill-natured</u>, cross, surly, fractious, churlish, ill-tempered, stroppy (*Brit. slang*), peevish ≠ good-natured 3 = <u>abnormal</u>, unhealthy, improper, deviant

pervert VERB 1 = <u>distort</u>, abuse, twist, misuse, warp, misrepresent, falsify
2 = <u>corrupt</u>, degrade, deprave, debase, debauch, lead astray
● NOUN = <u>deviant</u>, degenerate, sicko (*informal*), weirdo or weirdie (*informal*)

pessimistic = <u>gloomy</u>, dark, despairing, bleak, depressed, cynical, hopeless, glum ≠ optimistic

pest 1 = <u>infection</u>, bug, insect, plague, epidemic, blight, scourge, pestilence, gogga (*S. African informal*) 2 = <u>nuisance</u>, trial, pain (*informal*), drag (*informal*), bother, irritation, annoyance, bane

pet ADJECTIVE = <u>favourite</u>, favoured, dearest, cherished, fave (*informal*), dear to your heart
● NOUN = <u>favourite</u>, treasure, darling, jewel, idol
● VERB 1 = <u>fondle</u>, pat, stroke, caress
2 = <u>pamper</u>, spoil, indulge, cosset, baby, dote on, coddle, mollycoddle 3 = <u>cuddle</u>, kiss, snog (*Brit. slang*), smooch (*informal*), neck (*informal*), canoodle (*slang*)

petition NOUN 1 = <u>appeal</u>, round robin, list of signatures 2 = <u>entreaty</u>, appeal, suit, application, request, prayer, plea, solicitation
● VERB = <u>appeal</u>, plead, ask, pray, beg, solicit, beseech, entreat

petty 1 = <u>trivial</u>, insignificant, little, small, slight, trifling, negligible, unimportant ≠ important 2 = <u>small-minded</u>, mean, shabby, spiteful, ungenerous, mean-minded ≠ broad-minded

phantom = <u>spectre</u>, ghost, spirit, shade (*literary*), spook (*informal*), apparition, wraith, phantasm

phase NOUN = <u>stage</u>, time, point, position, step, development, period, chapter
● PHRASES **phase something in** = <u>introduce</u>, incorporate, ease in, start
◆ **phase something out** = <u>eliminate</u>, close, remove, withdraw, pull out, wind up, run down, terminate

phenomenal = <u>extraordinary</u>, outstanding, remarkable, fantastic, unusual, marvellous, exceptional, miraculous ≠ unremarkable

phenomenon 1 = <u>occurrence</u>, happening, fact, event, incident, circumstance, episode 2 = <u>wonder</u>, sensation, exception, miracle, marvel, prodigy, rarity

philosopher = <u>thinker</u>, theorist, sage, wise man, logician, metaphysician

philosophical or **philosophic**
1 = <u>theoretical</u>, abstract, wise, rational, logical, thoughtful, sagacious ≠ practical
2 = <u>stoical</u>, calm, composed, cool, collected, serene, tranquil, unruffled ≠ emotional

philosophy 1 = <u>thought</u>, knowledge, thinking, reasoning, wisdom, logic, metaphysics 2 = <u>outlook</u>, values, principles, convictions, thinking, beliefs, doctrine, ideology

phone NOUN 1 = <u>telephone</u>, blower (*informal*) 2 = <u>call</u>, ring (*informal*, *chiefly Brit.*), tinkle (*Brit. informal*)
● VERB = <u>call</u>, telephone, ring (up) (*informal*, *chiefly Brit.*), give someone a call, give someone a ring (*informal*, *chiefly Brit.*), make a call, give someone a tinkle (*Brit. informal*), get on the blower (*informal*)

photograph NOUN = <u>picture</u>, photo (*informal*), shot, print, snap (*informal*), snapshot, transparency
● VERB = <u>take a picture of</u>, record, film, shoot, snap (*informal*), take (someone's) picture

photographic 1 = <u>pictorial</u>, visual, graphic, cinematic, filmic 2 = <u>accurate</u>, exact, precise, faithful, retentive

phrase NOUN = <u>expression</u>, saying, remark, construction, quotation, maxim, idiom, adage
● VERB = <u>express</u>, say, word, put, voice, communicate, convey, put into words

physical 1 = <u>corporal</u>, fleshly, bodily, corporeal 2 = <u>earthly</u>, fleshly, mortal, incarnate 3 = <u>material</u>, real, substantial, natural, solid, tangible, palpable

physician = <u>doctor</u>, doc (*informal*), medic (*informal*), general practitioner, medical practitioner, doctor of medicine, G.P., M.D.

pick VERB 1 = <u>select</u>, choose, identify, elect, nominate, specify, opt for, single out ≠ reject 2 = <u>gather</u>, pull, collect, take in, harvest, pluck, garner **3** = <u>provoke</u>, start, cause, stir up, incite, instigate **4** = <u>open</u>, force, crack (*informal*), break into, break open

● NOUN **1** = <u>choice</u>, decision, option, selection, preference **2** = <u>best</u>, prime, finest, elect, elite, cream, jewel in the crown, crème de la crème (*French*)

● PHRASES **pick on someone 1** = <u>torment</u>, bully, bait, tease, get at (*informal*), badger, persecute, hector **2** = <u>choose</u>, select, prefer, elect, single out, fix on, settle upon ◆ **pick something or someone out** = <u>identify</u>, recognize, distinguish, perceive, discriminate, make someone *or* something out, tell someone *or* something apart ◆ **pick something or someone up 1** = <u>lift</u>, raise, gather, take up, grasp, uplift **2** = <u>collect</u>, get, call for ◆ **pick something up 1** = <u>learn</u>, master, acquire, get the hang of (*informal*), become proficient in **2** = <u>obtain</u>, get, find, buy, discover, purchase, acquire, locate ◆ **pick up 1** = <u>improve</u>, recover, rally, get better, bounce back, make progress, perk up, turn the corner **2** = <u>recover</u>, improve, rally, get better, mend, turn the corner, be on the mend, take a turn for the better

picket VERB = <u>blockade</u>, boycott, demonstrate outside

● NOUN **1** = <u>demonstration</u>, strike, blockade **2** = <u>protester</u>, demonstrator, picketer **3** = <u>lookout</u>, watch, guard, patrol, sentry, sentinel **4** = <u>stake</u>, post, pale, paling, upright, stanchion

pickle VERB = <u>preserve</u>, marinade, steep

● NOUN **1** = <u>chutney</u>, relish, piccalilli **2** (*Informal*) = <u>predicament</u>, fix (*informal*), difficulty, bind (*informal*), jam (*informal*), dilemma, scrape (*informal*), hot water (*informal*), uphill (*S. African*)

pick-up = <u>improvement</u>, recovery, rise, rally, strengthening, revival, upturn, change for the better

picnic = <u>excursion</u>, barbecue, barbie (*informal*), cookout (*U.S. & Canad.*), alfresco meal, clambake (*U.S. & Canad.*), outdoor meal, outing

picture NOUN **1** = <u>representation</u>, drawing, painting, portrait, image, print, illustration, sketch **2** = <u>photograph</u>, photo, still, shot, image, print, frame, slide **3** = <u>film</u>, movie (*U.S. informal*), flick (*slang*), feature film, motion picture **4** = <u>idea</u>, vision, concept,

impression, notion, visualization, mental picture, mental image **5** = <u>description</u>, impression, explanation, report, account, image, sketch, depiction **6** = <u>personification</u>, embodiment, essence, epitome

● VERB **1** = <u>imagine</u>, see, envision, visualize, conceive of, fantasize about, conjure up an image of **2** = <u>represent</u>, show, draw, paint, illustrate, sketch, depict **3** = <u>show</u>, photograph, capture on film

picturesque 1 = <u>interesting</u>, pretty, beautiful, attractive, charming, scenic, quaint ≠ unattractive **2** = <u>vivid</u>, striking, graphic, colourful, memorable ≠ dull

piece 1 = <u>bit</u>, slice, part, block, quantity, segment, portion, fragment **2** = <u>component</u>, part, section, bit, unit, segment, constituent, module **3** = <u>item</u>, report, story, study, review, article **4** = <u>composition</u>, work, production, opus **5** = <u>work of art</u>, work, creation **6** = <u>share</u>, cut (*informal*), slice, percentage, quantity, portion, quota, fraction

pier 1 = <u>jetty</u>, wharf, quay, promenade, landing place **2** = <u>pillar</u>, support, post, column, pile, upright, buttress

pierce = <u>penetrate</u>, stab, spike, enter, bore, drill, puncture, prick

piercing 1 (*of sound*) = <u>penetrating</u>, sharp, loud, shrill, high-pitched, ear-splitting ≠ low **2** = <u>perceptive</u>, sharp, keen, alert, penetrating, shrewd, perspicacious, quick-witted ≠ unperceptive **3** = <u>sharp</u>, acute, severe, intense, painful, stabbing, excruciating, agonizing **4** (*of weather*) = <u>cold</u>, biting, freezing, bitter, arctic, wintry, nippy

pig 1 = <u>hog</u>, sow, boar, swine, porker **2** (*Informal*) = <u>slob</u>, glutton **3** (*Informal*) = <u>brute</u>, monster, scoundrel, rogue, swine, rotter, boor

pigment = <u>colour</u>, colouring, paint, stain, dye, tint, tincture

pile¹ NOUN **1** = <u>heap</u>, collection, mountain, mass, stack, mound, accumulation, hoard **2** (*Informal*) *often plural* = <u>lot(s)</u>, mountain(s), load(s) (*informal*), oceans, wealth, great deal, stack(s), abundance **3** = <u>mansion</u>, building, residence, manor, country house, seat, big house, stately home

● VERB **1** = <u>load</u>, stuff, pack, stack, charge, heap, cram, lade **2** = <u>crowd</u>, pack, rush,

climb, flood, stream, crush, squeeze
● PHRASES **pile up** = <u>accumulate</u>, collect, gather (up), build up, amass

pile² = <u>foundation</u>, support, post, column, beam, upright, pillar

pile³ = <u>nap</u>, fibre, down, hair, fur, plush

pile-up (*Informal*) = <u>collision</u>, crash, accident, smash, smash-up (*informal*), multiple collision

pilgrim = <u>traveller</u>, wanderer, devotee, wayfarer

pilgrimage = <u>journey</u>, tour, trip, mission, expedition, excursion

pill = <u>tablet</u>, capsule, pellet

pillar 1 = <u>support</u>, post, column, prop, shaft, upright, pier, stanchion 2 = <u>supporter</u>, leader, mainstay, leading light (*informal*), upholder

pilot NOUN 1 = <u>airman</u>, flyer, aviator, aeronaut 2 = <u>helmsman</u>, navigator, steersman
● VERB 1 = <u>fly</u>, operate, be at the controls of 2 = <u>navigate</u>, drive, direct, guide, handle, conduct, steer 3 = <u>direct</u>, conduct, steer
● ADJECTIVE = <u>trial</u>, test, model, sample, experimental

pin NOUN 1 = <u>tack</u>, nail, needle, safety pin 2 = <u>peg</u>, rod, brace, bolt
● VERB 1 = <u>fasten</u>, stick, attach, join, fix, secure, nail, clip 2 = <u>hold fast</u>, hold down, constrain, immobilize, pinion
● PHRASES **pin someone down** = <u>force</u>, pressure, compel, put pressure on, pressurize, nail someone down, make someone commit themselves ◆ **pin something down** = <u>determine</u>, identify, locate, name, specify, pinpoint

pinch VERB 1 = <u>nip</u>, press, squeeze, grasp, compress 2 = <u>hurt</u>, crush, squeeze, pain, cramp 3 (*Brit. informal*) = <u>steal</u>, lift (*informal*), nick (*slang, chiefly Brit.*), swipe (*slang*), knock off (*slang*), pilfer, purloin, filch
● NOUN 1 = <u>nip</u>, squeeze 2 = <u>dash</u>, bit, mite, jot, speck, soupçon (*French*) 3 = <u>emergency</u>, crisis, difficulty, plight, scrape (*informal*), strait, uphill (*S. African*), predicament

pine VERB = <u>waste</u>, decline, sicken, fade, languish
● PHRASES **pine for something** or **someone** 1 = <u>long</u>, ache, crave, yearn, eat your heart out over 2 = <u>hanker after</u>, crave, wish for, yearn for, thirst for, hunger for

pink NOUN or ADJECTIVE = <u>rosy</u>, rose, salmon, flushed, reddish, roseate

pinnacle 1 = <u>summit</u>, top, height, peak 2 = <u>height</u>, top, crown, crest, zenith, apex, vertex

pinpoint 1 = <u>identify</u>, discover, define, distinguish, put your finger on 2 = <u>locate</u>, find, identify, zero in on

pioneer NOUN 1 = <u>founder</u>, leader, developer, innovator, trailblazer 2 = <u>settler</u>, explorer, colonist
● VERB = <u>develop</u>, create, establish, start, discover, institute, invent, initiate

pipe NOUN = <u>tube</u>, drain, canal, pipeline, line, main, passage, cylinder
● VERB = <u>convey</u>, channel, conduct
● PHRASES **pipe down** (*Informal*) = <u>be quiet</u>, shut up (*informal*), hush, stop talking, quieten down, shush, shut your mouth, hold your tongue

pipeline = <u>tube</u>, passage, pipe, conduit, duct

pirate NOUN = <u>buccaneer</u>, raider, marauder, corsair, freebooter
● VERB = <u>copy</u>, steal, reproduce, bootleg, appropriate, poach, crib (*informal*), plagiarize

pit NOUN 1 = <u>coal mine</u>, mine, shaft, colliery, mine shaft 2 = <u>hole</u>, depression, hollow, crater, trough, cavity, abyss, chasm
● VERB = <u>scar</u>, mark, dent, indent, pockmark

pitch NOUN 1 = <u>sports field</u>, ground, stadium, arena, park, field of play 2 = <u>tone</u>, sound, key, frequency, timbre, modulation 3 = <u>level</u>, point, degree, summit, extent, height, intensity, high point 4 = <u>talk</u>, patter, spiel (*informal*)
● VERB 1 = <u>throw</u>, cast, toss, hurl, fling, chuck (*informal*), sling, lob (*informal*) 2 = <u>fall</u>, drop, plunge, dive, tumble, topple, plummet, fall headlong 3 = <u>set up</u>, raise, settle, put up, erect 4 = <u>toss (about)</u>, roll, plunge, lurch
● PHRASES **pitch in** = <u>help</u>, contribute, participate, join in, cooperate, chip in (*informal*), get stuck in (*Brit. informal*), lend a hand

pitfall *usually plural* = <u>danger</u>, difficulty, peril, catch, trap, hazard, drawback, snag, uphill (*S. African*)

pity NOUN 1 = <u>compassion</u>, charity, sympathy, kindness, fellow feeling ≠ mercilessness 2 = <u>shame</u>, sin (*informal*), misfortune, bummer (*slang*), crying shame 3 = <u>mercy</u>, kindness, clemency, forbearance

● VERB = <u>feel sorry for</u>, feel for, sympathize with, grieve for, weep for, bleed for, have compassion for

pivotal = <u>crucial</u>, central, vital, critical, decisive

place NOUN 1 = <u>spot</u>, point, position, site, area, location, venue, whereabouts 2 = <u>region</u>, quarter, district, neighbourhood, vicinity, locality, locale, dorp (*S. African*) 3 = <u>position</u>, point, spot, location 4 = <u>space</u>, position, seat, chair 5 = <u>rank</u>, standing, position, footing, station, status, grade, niche 6 = <u>situation</u>, position, circumstances, shoes (*informal*) 7 = <u>job</u>, position, post, situation, office, employment, appointment 8 = <u>home</u>, house, room, property, accommodation, pad (*slang*), residence, dwelling 9 (In this context, the construction is always negative) = <u>duty</u>, right, job, charge, concern, role, affair, responsibility

● VERB 1 = <u>lay (down)</u>, put (down), set (down), stand, position, rest, station, stick (*informal*) 2 = <u>put</u>, lay, set, invest, pin 3 = <u>classify</u>, class, group, put, order, sort, rank, arrange 4 = <u>entrust to</u>, give to, assign to, appoint to, allocate to, find a home for 5 = <u>identify</u>, remember, recognize, pin someone down, put your finger on, put a name to

● PHRASES **take place** = <u>happen</u>, occur, go on, go down (*U.S. & Canad.*), arise, come about, crop up, transpire (*informal*)

plague NOUN 1 = <u>disease</u>, infection, epidemic, pestilence 2 = <u>infestation</u>, invasion, epidemic, influx, host, swarm, multitude

● VERB 1 = <u>torment</u>, trouble, torture 2 = <u>pester</u>, trouble, bother, annoy, tease, harry, harass, hassle

plain ADJECTIVE 1 = <u>unadorned</u>, simple, basic, severe, bare, stark, austere, spartan ≠ ornate 2 = <u>clear</u>, obvious, patent, evident, visible, distinct, understandable, manifest ≠ hidden 3 = <u>straightforward</u>, open, direct, frank, blunt, outspoken, honest, downright ≠ roundabout 4 = <u>ugly</u>, unattractive, homely (*U.S. & Canad.*), unlovely, unprepossessing, not beautiful, no oil painting (*informal*), ill-favoured ≠ attractive 5 = <u>ordinary</u>, common, simple, everyday, commonplace, unaffected,

unpretentious ≠ sophisticated

● NOUN = <u>flatland</u>, plateau, prairie, grassland, steppe, veld

plan NOUN 1 = <u>scheme</u>, system, design, programme, proposal, strategy, method, suggestion 2 = <u>diagram</u>, map, drawing, chart, representation, sketch, blueprint, layout

● VERB 1 = <u>devise</u>, arrange, scheme, plot, draft, organize, outline, formulate 2 = <u>intend</u>, aim, mean, propose, purpose 3 = <u>design</u>, outline, draw up a plan of

plane NOUN 1 = <u>aeroplane</u>, aircraft, jet, airliner, jumbo jet 2 = <u>flat surface</u>, the flat, horizontal, level surface 3 = <u>level</u>, position, stage, condition, standard, degree, rung, echelon

● ADJECTIVE = <u>level</u>, even, flat, regular, smooth, horizontal

● VERB = <u>skim</u>, sail, skate, glide

plant¹ NOUN = <u>flower</u>, bush, vegetable, herb, weed, shrub

● VERB 1 = <u>sow</u>, scatter, transplant, implant, put in the ground 2 = <u>seed</u>, sow, implant 3 = <u>place</u>, put, set, fix 4 = <u>hide</u>, put, place, conceal 5 = <u>place</u>, put, establish, found, fix, insert

plant² 1 = <u>factory</u>, works, shop, yard, mill, foundry 2 = <u>machinery</u>, equipment, gear, apparatus

plaster NOUN 1 = <u>mortar</u>, stucco, gypsum, plaster of Paris 2 = <u>bandage</u>, dressing, sticking plaster, Elastoplast®, adhesive plaster

● VERB = <u>cover</u>, spread, coat, smear, overlay, daub

plastic = <u>pliant</u>, soft, flexible, supple, pliable, ductile, mouldable ≠ rigid

plate NOUN 1 = <u>platter</u>, dish, dinner plate, salver, trencher (*archaic*) 2 = <u>helping</u>, course, serving, dish, portion, platter, plateful 3 = <u>layer</u>, panel, sheet, slab 4 = <u>illustration</u>, picture, photograph, print, engraving, lithograph

● VERB = <u>coat</u>, gild, laminate, cover, overlay

plateau 1 = <u>upland</u>, table, highland, tableland 2 = <u>levelling off</u>, level, stage, stability

platform 1 = <u>stage</u>, stand, podium, rostrum, dais, soapbox 2 = <u>policy</u>, programme, principle, objective(s), manifesto, party line

plausible 1 = <u>believable</u>, possible, likely, reasonable, credible, probable, persuasive, conceivable ≠ unbelievable **2** = glib, smooth, specious, smooth-talking, smooth-tongued

play VERB **1** = amuse yourself, have fun, sport, fool, romp, revel, trifle, entertain yourself **2** = take part in, be involved in, engage in, participate in, compete in **3** = compete against, challenge, take on, oppose, contend against **4** = perform, carry out **5** = act, portray, represent, perform, act the part of **6** = perform on, strum, make music on
● NOUN **1** = amusement, pleasure, leisure, games, sport, fun, entertainment, relaxation **2** = drama, show, piece, comedy, tragedy, farce, soapie (*Austral. slang*), pantomime
● PHRASES **play on** or **upon something** = take advantage of, abuse, exploit, impose on, trade on, capitalize on ◆ **play something down** = minimize, make light of, gloss over, talk down, underrate, underplay, pooh-pooh (*informal*), soft-pedal (*informal*) ◆ **play something up** = emphasize, highlight, underline, stress, accentuate ◆ **play up 1** (*Brit. informal*) = hurt, be painful, bother you, trouble you, be sore, pain you **2** (*Brit. informal*) = malfunction, not work properly, be on the blink (*slang*) **3** (*Brit. informal*) = be awkward, misbehave, give trouble, be disobedient, be stroppy (*Brit. slang*)

playboy = womanizer, philanderer, rake, lady-killer (*informal*), roué, ladies' man

player 1 = sportsman or sportswoman, competitor, participant, contestant **2** = musician, artist, performer, virtuoso, instrumentalist **3** = performer, entertainer, Thespian, trouper, actor or actress

plea 1 = appeal, request, suit, prayer, petition, entreaty, intercession, supplication **2** = excuse, defence, explanation, justification

plead = appeal, ask, request, beg, petition, implore, beseech, entreat

pleasant 1 = pleasing, nice, fine, lovely, amusing, delightful, enjoyable, agreeable, lekker (*S. African slang*) ≠ horrible **2** = friendly, nice, agreeable, likable or likeable, engaging, charming, amiable, genial ≠ disagreeable

please = delight, entertain, humour, amuse, suit, satisfy, indulge, gratify ≠ annoy

pleased = happy, delighted, contented, satisfied, thrilled, glad, gratified, over the moon (*informal*)

pleasing 1 = enjoyable, satisfying, charming, delightful, gratifying, agreeable, pleasurable ≠ unpleasant **2** = likable or likeable, engaging, charming, delightful, agreeable ≠ disagreeable

pleasure 1 = happiness, delight, satisfaction, enjoyment, bliss, gratification, gladness, delectation ≠ displeasure **2** = amusement, joy ≠ duty

pledge NOUN **1** = promise, vow, assurance, word, undertaking, warrant, oath, covenant **2** = guarantee, security, deposit, bail, collateral, pawn, surety
● VERB = promise, vow, swear, contract, engage, give your word, give your oath

plentiful = abundant, liberal, generous, lavish, ample, overflowing, copious, bountiful ≠ scarce

plenty 1 = abundance, wealth, prosperity, fertility, profusion, affluence, plenitude, fruitfulness **2** *usually with* **of** = lots of (*informal*), enough, a great deal of, masses of, piles of (*informal*), stacks of, heaps of (*informal*), an abundance of

plight = difficulty, condition, state, situation, trouble, predicament

plot¹ NOUN **1** = plan, scheme, intrigue, conspiracy, cabal, stratagem, machination **2** = story, action, subject, theme, outline, scenario, narrative, story line
● VERB **1** = plan, scheme, conspire, intrigue, manoeuvre, contrive, collude, machinate **2** = devise, design, lay, conceive, hatch, contrive, concoct, cook up (*informal*) **3** = chart, mark, map, locate, calculate, outline

plot² = patch, lot, area, ground, parcel, tract, allotment

plough VERB = turn over, dig, till, cultivate
● PHRASES **plough through something** = forge, cut, drive, press, push, plunge, wade

ploy = tactic, move, trick, device, scheme, manoeuvre, dodge, ruse

pluck VERB **1** = pull out or off, pick, draw, collect, gather, harvest **2** = tug, catch, snatch, clutch, jerk, yank, tweak, pull at **3** = strum, pick, finger, twang
● NOUN = courage, nerve, bottle (*Brit. slang*), guts (*informal*), grit, bravery, backbone, boldness

plug NOUN 1 = <u>stopper</u>, cork, bung, spigot 2 (*Informal*) = <u>mention</u>, advertisement, advert (*Brit. informal*), push, publicity, hype

● VERB 1 = <u>seal</u>, close, stop, fill, block, stuff, pack, cork 2 (*Informal*) = <u>mention</u>, push, promote, publicize, advertise, build up, hype

● PHRASES **plug away** (*Informal*) = <u>slog away</u>, labour, toil away, grind away (*informal*), peg away, plod away

plum = <u>choice</u>, prize, first-class

plumb VERB = <u>delve into</u>, explore, probe, go into, penetrate, gauge, unravel, fathom

● ADVERB = <u>exactly</u>, precisely, bang, slap, spot-on (*Brit. informal*)

plummet 1 = <u>drop</u>, fall, crash, nose-dive, descend rapidly 2 = <u>plunge</u>, fall, drop, crash, tumble, nose-dive, descend rapidly

plump = <u>chubby</u>, fat, stout, round, tubby, dumpy, roly-poly, rotund ≠ scrawny

plunder VERB 1 = <u>loot</u>, strip, sack, rob, raid, rifle, ransack, pillage 2 = <u>steal</u>, rob, take, nick (*informal*), pinch (*informal*), embezzle, pilfer, thieve

● NOUN 1 = <u>pillage</u> 2 = <u>loot</u>, spoils, booty, swag (*slang*), ill-gotten gains

plunge VERB 1 = <u>descend</u>, fall, drop, crash, pitch, sink, dive, tumble 2 = <u>hurtle</u>, charge, career, jump, tear, rush, dive, dash 3 = <u>submerge</u>, dip 4 = <u>throw</u>, cast, pitch, propel 5 = <u>fall steeply</u>, drop, crash (*informal*), slump, plummet, take a nosedive (*informal*)

● NOUN 1 = <u>dive</u>, jump, duck, descent 2 = <u>fall</u>, crash (*informal*), slump, drop, tumble

plus PREPOSITION = <u>and</u>, with, added to, coupled with

● NOUN (*Informal*) = <u>advantage</u>, benefit, asset, gain, extra, bonus, good point

● ADJECTIVE = <u>additional</u>, added, extra, supplementary, add-on

plush = <u>luxurious</u>, luxury, lavish, rich, sumptuous, opulent, de luxe

ply = <u>work at</u>, follow, exercise, pursue, carry on, practise

pocket NOUN = <u>pouch</u>, bag, sack, compartment, receptacle

● ADJECTIVE = <u>small</u>, compact, miniature, portable, little

● VERB = <u>steal</u>, take, lift (*informal*), appropriate, pilfer, purloin, filch

pod = <u>shell</u>, case, hull, husk, shuck

podium = <u>platform</u>, stand, stage, rostrum, dais

poem = <u>verse</u>, song, lyric, rhyme, sonnet, ode, verse composition

poet = <u>bard</u>, rhymer, lyricist, lyric poet, versifier, elegist

poetic 1 = <u>figurative</u>, creative, lyric, symbolic, lyrical 2 = <u>lyrical</u>, lyric, elegiac, metrical

poetry = <u>verse</u>, poems, rhyme, rhyming, verse composition

poignant = <u>moving</u>, touching, sad, bitter, intense, painful, distressing, pathetic

point NOUN 1 = <u>essence</u>, meaning, subject, question, heart, import, drift, thrust 2 = <u>purpose</u>, aim, object, end, reason, goal, intention, objective 3 = <u>aspect</u>, detail, feature, quality, particular, respect, item, characteristic 4 = <u>place</u>, area, position, site, spot, location, locality, locale 5 = <u>moment</u>, time, stage, period, phase, instant, juncture, moment in time 6 = <u>stage</u>, level, position, condition, degree, pitch, circumstance, extent 7 = <u>end</u>, tip, sharp end, top, spur, spike, apex, prong 8 = <u>score</u>, tally, mark 9 = <u>pinpoint</u>, mark, spot, dot, fleck

● VERB 1 = <u>aim</u>, level, train, direct 2 = <u>indicate</u>, show, signal, point to, gesture towards 3 = <u>face</u>, look, direct

● PHRASES **point at** *or* **to something** *or* **someone** = <u>indicate</u>, point out, specify, designate, gesture towards

pointed 1 = <u>sharp</u>, edged, acute, barbed 2 = <u>cutting</u>, telling, biting, sharp, keen, acute, penetrating, pertinent

pointer 1 = <u>hint</u>, tip, suggestion, recommendation, caution, piece of information, piece of advice 2 = <u>indicator</u>, hand, guide, needle, arrow

pointless = <u>senseless</u>, meaningless, futile, fruitless, stupid, silly, useless, absurd ≠ worthwhile

poised 1 = <u>ready</u>, waiting, prepared, standing by, all set 2 = <u>composed</u>, calm, together (*informal*), collected, dignified, self-confident, self-possessed ≠ agitated

poison NOUN = <u>toxin</u>, venom, bane (*archaic*)

● VERB 1 = <u>murder</u>, kill, give someone poison, administer poison to 2 = <u>contaminate</u>, foul, infect, spoil, pollute, blight, taint, befoul 3 = <u>corrupt</u>, colour, undermine, bias, sour, pervert, warp, taint

poisonous 1 = <u>toxic</u>, fatal, deadly, lethal,

mortal, virulent, noxious, venomous **2** = <u>evil</u>, malicious, corrupting, pernicious, baleful

poke VERB **1** = <u>jab</u>, push, stick, dig, stab, thrust, shove, nudge **2** = <u>protrude</u>, stick, thrust, jut

● NOUN = <u>jab</u>, dig, thrust, nudge, prod

pole = <u>rod</u>, post, support, staff, bar, stick, stake, paling

police NOUN = <u>the law</u> (*informal*), police force, constabulary, fuzz (*slang*), boys in blue (*informal*), the Old Bill (*slang*), rozzers (*slang*)

● VERB = <u>control</u>, patrol, guard, watch, protect, regulate

policy 1 = <u>procedure</u>, plan, action, practice, scheme, code, custom **2** = <u>line</u>, rules, approach

polish NOUN **1** = <u>varnish</u>, wax, glaze, lacquer, japan **2** = <u>sheen</u>, finish, glaze, gloss, brightness, lustre **3** = <u>style</u>, class (*informal*), finish, breeding, grace, elegance, refinement, finesse

● VERB **1** = <u>shine</u>, wax, smooth, rub, buff, brighten, burnish **2** *often with* **up** = <u>perfect</u>, improve, enhance, refine, finish, brush up, touch up

polished 1 = <u>elegant</u>, sophisticated, refined, polite, cultivated, suave, well-bred ≠ unsophisticated **2** = <u>accomplished</u>, professional, masterly, fine, expert, skilful, adept, superlative ≠ amateurish **3** = <u>shining</u>, bright, smooth, gleaming, glossy, burnished ≠ dull

polite 1 = <u>mannerly</u>, civil, courteous, gracious, respectful, well-behaved, complaisant, well-mannered ≠ rude **2** = <u>refined</u>, cultured, civilized, polished, sophisticated, elegant, genteel, well-bred ≠ uncultured

politic = <u>wise</u>, diplomatic, sensible, prudent, advisable, expedient, judicious

political = <u>governmental</u>, government, state, parliamentary, constitutional, administrative, legislative, ministerial

politician = <u>statesman</u> *or* stateswoman, representative, senator (*U.S.*), congressman (*U.S.*), Member of Parliament, legislator, public servant, congresswoman (*U.S.*)

politics 1 = <u>affairs of state</u>, government, public affairs, civics **2** = <u>political beliefs</u>, party politics, political allegiances, political leanings, political sympathies

3 = <u>political science</u>, statesmanship, civics, statecraft

poll NOUN **1** = <u>survey</u>, figures, count, sampling, returns, ballot, tally, census **2** = <u>election</u>, vote, voting, referendum, ballot, plebiscite

● VERB **1** = <u>question</u>, interview, survey, sample, ballot, canvass **2** = <u>gain</u>, return, record, register, tally

pollute 1 = <u>contaminate</u>, dirty, poison, soil, foul, infect, spoil, stain ≠ decontaminate **2** = <u>defile</u>, corrupt, sully, deprave, debase, profane, desecrate, dishonour ≠ honour

pollution 1 = <u>contamination</u>, dirtying, corruption, taint, foulness, defilement, uncleanness **2** = <u>waste</u>, poisons, dirt, impurities

pond = <u>pool</u>, tarn, small lake, fish pond, duck pond, millpond

ponder = <u>think about</u>, consider, reflect on, contemplate, deliberate about, muse on, brood on, meditate on

pool¹ 1 = <u>swimming pool</u>, lido, swimming bath(s) (*Brit.*), bathing pool (*archaic*) **2** = <u>pond</u>, lake, mere, tarn **3** = <u>puddle</u>, drop, patch

pool² NOUN **1** = <u>supply</u>, reserve, fall-back **2** = <u>kitty</u>, bank, fund, stock, store, pot, jackpot, stockpile

● VERB = <u>combine</u>, share, merge, put together, amalgamate, lump together, join forces on

poor 1 = <u>impoverished</u>, broke (*informal*), hard up (*informal*), short, needy, penniless, destitute, poverty-stricken ≠ rich **2** = <u>unfortunate</u>, unlucky, hapless, pitiful, luckless, wretched, ill-starred, pitiable ≠ fortunate **3** = <u>inferior</u>, unsatisfactory, mediocre, second-rate, rotten (*informal*), low-grade, below par, substandard, half-pie (*N.Z. informal*), bodger *or* bodgie (*Austral. slang*) ≠ excellent **4** = <u>meagre</u>, inadequate, insufficient, lacking, incomplete, scant, deficient, skimpy ≠ ample

poorly ADVERB = <u>badly</u>, incompetently, inadequately, unsuccessfully, insufficiently, unsatisfactorily, inexpertly ≠ well

● ADJECTIVE (*Informal*) = <u>ill</u>, sick, unwell, crook (*Austral. & N.Z. informal*), seedy (*informal*), below par, off colour, under the weather (*informal*), feeling rotten (*informal*) ≠ healthy

pop NOUN = bang, report, crack, noise, burst, explosion

● VERB 1 = burst, crack, snap, bang, explode, go off (with a bang) 2 = put, insert, push, stick, slip, thrust, tuck, shove

pope = Holy Father, pontiff, His Holiness, Bishop of Rome, Vicar of Christ

popular 1 = well-liked, liked, in, accepted, favourite, approved, in favour, fashionable ≠ unpopular 2 = common, general, prevailing, current, conventional, universal, prevalent ≠ rare

popularity 1 = favour, esteem, acclaim, regard, approval, vogue 2 = currency, acceptance, circulation, vogue, prevalence

populate 1 = inhabit, people, live in, occupy, reside in, dwell in (formal) 2 = settle, occupy, pioneer, colonize

population = inhabitants, people, community, society, residents, natives, folk, occupants

pore = opening, hole, outlet, orifice

pornography = obscenity, porn (informal), dirt, filth, indecency, smut

port = harbour, haven, anchorage, seaport

portable = light, compact, convenient, handy, manageable, movable, easily carried

porter¹ (Chiefly Brit.) = doorman, caretaker, janitor, concierge, gatekeeper

porter² = baggage attendant, carrier, bearer, baggage-carrier

portion 1 = part, bit, piece, section, scrap, segment, fragment, chunk 2 = helping, serving, piece, plateful 3 = share, allowance, lot, measure, quantity, quota, ration, allocation

portrait 1 = picture, painting, image, photograph, representation, likeness 2 = description, profile, portrayal, depiction, characterization, thumbnail sketch

portray 1 = play, take the role of, act the part of, represent, personate (rare) 2 = describe, present, depict, evoke, delineate, put in words 3 = represent, draw, paint, illustrate, sketch, figure, picture, depict 4 = characterize, represent, depict

portrayal 1 = performance, interpretation, characterization 2 = depiction, picture, representation, sketch, rendering 3 = description, account,

representation 4 = characterization, representation, depiction

pose VERB 1 = position yourself, sit, model, arrange yourself 2 = put on airs, posture, show off (informal)

● NOUN 1 = posture, position, bearing, attitude, stance 2 = act, façade, air, front, posturing, pretence, mannerism, affectation

● PHRASES **pose as something** or **someone** = impersonate, pretend to be, profess to be, masquerade as, pass yourself off as

posh (Informal, chiefly Brit.) 1 = smart, grand, stylish, luxurious, classy (slang), swish (informal, chiefly Brit.), up-market, swanky (informal) 2 = upper-class, high-class

position NOUN 1 = location, place, point, area, post, situation, station, spot 2 = posture, attitude, arrangement, pose, stance 3 = status, place, standing, footing, station, rank, reputation, importance 4 = job, place, post, opening, office, role, situation, duty 5 = place, standing, rank, status 6 = attitude, view, perspective, point of view, opinion, belief, stance, outlook

● VERB = place, put, set, stand, arrange, locate, lay out

positive 1 = beneficial, useful, practical, helpful, progressive, productive, worthwhile, constructive ≠ harmful 2 = certain, sure, convinced, confident, satisfied, assured, free from doubt ≠ uncertain 3 = definite, real, clear, firm, certain, express, absolute, decisive ≠ inconclusive 4 (Informal) = absolute, complete, perfect, right (Brit. informal), real, total, sheer, utter

positively 1 = definitely, surely, firmly, certainly, absolutely, emphatically, unquestionably, categorically 2 = really, completely, simply, plain (informal), absolutely, thoroughly, utterly, downright

possess 1 = own, have, hold, be in possession of, be the owner of, have in your possession 2 = be endowed with, have, enjoy, benefit from, be possessed of, be gifted with 3 = seize, hold, control, dominate, occupy, take someone over, have power over, have mastery over

possession NOUN = ownership, control, custody, hold, hands, tenure

● PLURAL NOUN = <u>property</u>, things, effects, estate, assets, belongings, chattels

possibility 1 = <u>feasibility</u>, likelihood, potentiality, practicability, workableness 2 = <u>likelihood</u>, chance, risk, odds, prospect, liability, probability 3 *often plural* = <u>potential</u>, promise, prospects, talent, capabilities, potentiality

possible 1 = <u>feasible</u>, viable, workable, achievable, practicable, attainable, doable, realizable ≠ unfeasible 2 = <u>likely</u>, potential, anticipated, probable, odds-on, on the cards ≠ improbable 3 = <u>conceivable</u>, likely, credible, plausible, hypothetical, imaginable, believable, thinkable ≠ inconceivable 4 = <u>aspiring</u>, would-be, promising, hopeful, prospective, wannabe (*informal*)

possibly = <u>perhaps</u>, maybe, perchance (*archaic*)

post¹ NOUN 1 = <u>mail</u>, collection, delivery, postal service, snail mail (*informal*) 2 = <u>correspondence</u>, letters, cards, mail
● VERB = <u>send (off)</u>, forward, mail, get off, transmit, dispatch, consign
● PHRASES **keep someone posted** = <u>notify</u>, brief, advise, inform, report to, keep someone informed, keep someone up to date, apprise

post² NOUN 1 = <u>job</u>, place, office, position, situation, employment, appointment, assignment 2 = <u>position</u>, place, base, beat, station
● VERB = <u>station</u>, assign, put, place, position, situate, put on duty

post³ NOUN = <u>support</u>, stake, pole, column, shaft, upright, pillar, picket
● VERB = <u>put something up</u>, display, affix, pin something up

poster = <u>notice</u>, bill, announcement, advertisement, sticker, placard, public notice

postpone = <u>put off</u>, delay, suspend, adjourn, shelve, defer, put back, put on the back burner (*informal*) ≠ go ahead with

posture NOUN = <u>bearing</u>, set, attitude, stance, carriage, disposition
● VERB = <u>show off</u> (*informal*), pose, affect, put on airs

pot = <u>container</u>, bowl, pan, vessel, basin, cauldron, skillet

potent 1 = <u>powerful</u>, commanding, dynamic, dominant, influential, authoritative 2 = <u>strong</u>, powerful, mighty, vigorous, forceful ≠ weak

potential ADJECTIVE 1 = <u>possible</u>, future, likely, promising, probable 2 = <u>hidden</u>, possible, inherent, dormant, latent
● NOUN = <u>ability</u>, possibilities, capacity, capability, aptitude, wherewithal, potentiality

potter *usually with **around** or **about*** = <u>mess about</u>, tinker, dabble, footle (*informal*)

pottery = <u>ceramics</u>, terracotta, crockery, earthenware, stoneware

pounce = <u>attack</u>, strike, jump, leap, swoop

pound¹ = <u>enclosure</u>, yard, pen, compound, kennels

pound² 1 *sometimes with **on*** = <u>beat</u>, strike, hammer, batter, thrash, thump, clobber (*slang*), pummel 2 = <u>crush</u>, powder, pulverize 3 = <u>pulsate</u>, beat, pulse, throb, palpitate 4 = <u>stomp</u>, tramp, march, thunder (*informal*)

pour 1 = <u>let flow</u>, spill, splash, dribble, drizzle, slop (*informal*), slosh (*informal*), decant 2 = <u>flow</u>, stream, run, course, rush, emit, cascade, gush 3 = <u>rain</u>, pelt (down), teem, bucket down (*informal*) 4 = <u>stream</u>, crowd, flood, swarm, gush, throng, teem

pout VERB = <u>sulk</u>, glower, look petulant, pull a long face
● NOUN = <u>sullen look</u>, glower, long face

poverty 1 = <u>pennilessness</u>, want, need, hardship, insolvency, privation, penury, destitution ≠ wealth 2 = <u>scarcity</u>, lack, absence, want, deficit, shortage, deficiency, inadequacy ≠ abundance

powder NOUN = <u>dust</u>, talc, fine grains, loose particles
● VERB = <u>dust</u>, cover, scatter, sprinkle, strew, dredge

power 1 = <u>control</u>, authority, influence, command, dominance, domination, mastery, dominion, mana (*N.Z.*) 2 = <u>ability</u>, capacity, faculty, property, potential, capability, competence, competency ≠ inability 3 = <u>authority</u>, right, licence, privilege, warrant, prerogative, authorization 4 = <u>strength</u>, might, energy, muscle, vigour, potency, brawn ≠ weakness 5 = <u>forcefulness</u>, force, strength, punch (*informal*), intensity, potency, eloquence, persuasiveness

powerful 1 = <u>influential</u>, dominant,

controlling, commanding, prevailing, authoritative ≠ **powerless 2** = <u>strong</u>, strapping, mighty, vigorous, potent, energetic, sturdy ≠ weak **3** = <u>persuasive</u>, convincing, telling, moving, striking, storming, dramatic, impressive

powerless 1 = <u>defenceless</u>, vulnerable, dependent, subject, tied, ineffective, unarmed **2** = <u>weak</u>, disabled, helpless, incapable, frail, feeble, debilitated, impotent ≠ strong

practical 1 = <u>functional</u>, realistic, pragmatic ≠ impractical **2** = <u>empirical</u>, real, applied, actual, hands-on, in the field, experimental, factual ≠ theoretical **3** = <u>sensible</u>, ordinary, realistic, down-to-earth, matter-of-fact, businesslike, hard-headed ≠ impractical **4** = <u>feasible</u>, possible, viable, workable, practicable, doable ≠ impractical **5** = <u>useful</u>, ordinary, appropriate, sensible, everyday, functional, utilitarian, serviceable **6** = <u>skilled</u>, experienced, efficient, accomplished, proficient ≠ inexperienced

practically 1 = <u>almost</u>, nearly, essentially, virtually, basically, fundamentally, all but, just about **2** = <u>sensibly</u>, reasonably, matter-of-factly, realistically, rationally, pragmatically

practice 1 = <u>custom</u>, way, system, rule, method, tradition, habit, routine, tikanga (*N.Z.*) **2** = <u>training</u>, study, exercise, preparation, drill, rehearsal, repetition **3** = <u>profession</u>, work, business, career, occupation, pursuit, vocation **4** = <u>business</u>, company, office, firm, enterprise, partnership, outfit (*informal*) **5** = <u>use</u>, experience, action, operation, application, enactment

practise 1 = <u>rehearse</u>, study, prepare, perfect, repeat, go through, go over, refine **2** = <u>do</u>, train, exercise, drill **3** = <u>carry out</u>, follow, apply, perform, observe, engage in **4** = <u>work at</u>, pursue, carry on

practised = <u>skilled</u>, trained, experienced, seasoned, able, expert, accomplished, proficient ≠ inexperienced

pragmatic = <u>practical</u>, sensible, realistic, down-to-earth, utilitarian, businesslike, hard-headed ≠ idealistic

praise VERB 1 = <u>acclaim</u>, approve of, honour, cheer, admire, applaud, compliment, congratulate ≠ criticize **2** = <u>give thanks to</u>, bless, worship, adore, glorify, exalt

● **NOUN 1** = <u>approval</u>, acclaim, tribute, compliment, congratulations, eulogy, commendation, approbation ≠ criticism **2** = <u>thanks</u>, glory, worship, homage, adoration

pray 1 = <u>say your prayers</u>, offer a prayer, recite the rosary **2** = <u>beg</u>, ask, plead, petition, request, solicit, implore, beseech

prayer 1 = <u>supplication</u>, devotion **2** = <u>orison</u>, litany, invocation, intercession **3** = <u>plea</u>, appeal, request, petition, entreaty, supplication

preach 1 *often with* **to** = <u>deliver a sermon</u>, address, evangelize, preach a sermon **2** = <u>urge</u>, teach, champion, recommend, advise, counsel, advocate, exhort

preacher = <u>clergyman</u>, minister, parson, missionary, evangelist

precarious 1 = <u>insecure</u>, dangerous, tricky, risky, dodgy (*Brit., Austral., & N.Z. informal*), unsure, hazardous, shaky ≠ secure **2** = <u>dangerous</u>, shaky, insecure, unsafe, unreliable ≠ stable

precaution 1 = <u>safeguard</u>, insurance, protection, provision, safety measure **2** = <u>forethought</u>, care, caution, prudence, providence, wariness

precede 1 = <u>go before</u>, antedate **2** = <u>go ahead of</u>, lead, head, go before **3** = <u>preface</u>, introduce, go before

precedent = <u>instance</u>, example, standard, model, pattern, prototype, paradigm, antecedent

precinct = <u>area</u>, quarter, section, sector, district, zone

precious 1 = <u>valuable</u>, expensive, fine, prized, dear, costly, invaluable, priceless ≠ worthless **2** = <u>loved</u>, prized, dear, treasured, darling, beloved, adored, cherished **3** = <u>affected</u>, artificial, twee (*Brit. informal*), overrefined, overnice

precipitate VERB 1 = <u>quicken</u>, trigger, accelerate, advance, hurry, speed up, bring on, hasten **2** = <u>throw</u>, launch, cast, hurl, fling, let fly

● **ADJECTIVE 1** = <u>hasty</u>, rash, reckless, impulsive, precipitous, impetuous, heedless **2** = <u>sudden</u>, quick, brief, rushing, rapid, unexpected, swift, abrupt

precise 1 = <u>exact</u>, specific, particular, express, correct, absolute, accurate, explicit ≠ vague **2** = <u>strict</u>, particular, exact, formal, careful, stiff, rigid, meticulous ≠ inexact

precisely 1 = <u>exactly</u>, squarely, correctly, absolutely, strictly, accurately, plumb (*informal*), square on 2 = <u>just so</u>, yes, absolutely, exactly, quite so, you bet (*informal*), without a doubt, indubitably 3 = <u>just</u>, entirely, absolutely, altogether, exactly, in all respects 4 = <u>word for word</u>, literally, exactly, to the letter

precision = <u>exactness</u>, care, accuracy, particularity, meticulousness, preciseness

predecessor 1 = <u>previous job holder</u>, precursor, forerunner, antecedent 2 = <u>ancestor</u>, forebear, antecedent, forefather, tupuna *or* tipuna (*N.Z.*)

predicament = <u>fix</u> (*informal*), situation, spot (*informal*), hole (*slang*), mess, jam (*informal*), dilemma, pinch

predict = <u>foretell</u>, forecast, divine, prophesy, augur, portend

predictable = <u>likely</u>, expected, sure, certain, anticipated, reliable, foreseeable ≠ unpredictable

prediction = <u>prophecy</u>, forecast, prognosis, divination, prognostication, augury

predominantly = <u>mainly</u>, largely, chiefly, mostly, generally, principally, primarily, for the most part

prefer 1 = <u>like better</u>, favour, go for, pick, fancy, opt for, incline towards, be partial to 2 = <u>choose</u>, opt for, pick, desire, would rather, would sooner, incline towards

preferable = <u>better</u>, best, chosen, preferred, recommended, favoured, superior, more suitable ≠ undesirable

preferably = <u>ideally</u>, if possible, rather, sooner, by choice, in *or* for preference

preference 1 = <u>liking</u>, wish, taste, desire, leaning, bent, bias, inclination 2 = <u>first choice</u>, choice, favourite, pick, option, selection 3 = <u>priority</u>, first place, precedence, favouritism, favoured treatment

pregnant 1 = <u>expectant</u>, expecting (*informal*), with child, in the club (*Brit. slang*), big *or* heavy with child 2 = <u>meaningful</u>, pointed, charged, significant, telling, loaded, expressive, eloquent

prejudice NOUN 1 = <u>discrimination</u>, injustice, intolerance, bigotry, unfairness, chauvinism, narrow-mindedness 2 = <u>bias</u>, preconception, partiality, preconceived notion, prejudgment

● VERB 1 = <u>bias</u>, influence, colour, poison, distort, slant, predispose 2 = <u>harm</u>, damage, hurt, injure, mar, undermine, spoil, impair, crool *or* cruel (*Austral. slang*)

prejudiced = <u>biased</u>, influenced, unfair, one-sided, bigoted, intolerant, opinionated, narrow-minded ≠ unbiased

preliminary ADJECTIVE 1 = <u>first</u>, opening, trial, initial, test, pilot, prior, introductory 2 = <u>qualifying</u>, eliminating

● NOUN = <u>introduction</u>, opening, beginning, start, prelude, preface, overture, preamble

prelude 1 = <u>introduction</u>, beginning, start 2 = <u>overture</u>, opening, introduction, introductory movement

premature 1 = <u>early</u>, untimely, before time, unseasonable 2 = <u>hasty</u>, rash, too soon, untimely, ill-timed, overhasty

premier NOUN = <u>head of government</u>, prime minister, chancellor, chief minister, P.M.

● ADJECTIVE = <u>chief</u>, leading, first, highest, head, main, prime, primary

premiere = <u>first night</u>, opening, debut

premise = <u>assumption</u>, proposition, argument, hypothesis, assertion, supposition, presupposition, postulation

premises = <u>building(s)</u>, place, office, property, site, establishment

premium NOUN 1 = <u>fee</u>, charge, payment, instalment 2 = <u>surcharge</u>, extra charge, additional fee *or* charge 3 = <u>bonus</u>, reward, prize, perk (*Brit. informal*), bounty, perquisite

● PHRASES **at a premium** = <u>in great demand</u>, rare, scarce, in short supply, hard to come by

preoccupation 1 = <u>obsession</u>, fixation, bee in your bonnet 2 = <u>absorption</u>, abstraction, daydreaming, immersion, reverie, absent-mindedness, engrossment, woolgathering

preoccupied 1 = <u>absorbed</u>, lost, wrapped up, immersed, engrossed, rapt 2 = <u>lost in thought</u>, distracted, oblivious, absent-minded

preparation 1 = <u>groundwork</u>, preparing, getting ready 2 *usually plural* = <u>arrangement</u>, plan, measure, provision 3 = <u>mixture</u>, medicine, compound, concoction

prepare 1 = <u>make *or* get ready</u>, arrange, jack up (*N.Z. informal*) 2 = <u>train</u>, guide, prime, direct, brief, discipline, put someone in the picture 3 = <u>make</u>, cook, put together, get, produce, assemble, muster, concoct 4 = <u>get ready</u> 5 = <u>practise</u>, get ready, train, exercise, warm up, get into shape

prepared 1 = <u>willing</u>, inclined, disposed 2 = <u>ready</u>, set 3 = <u>fit</u>, primed, in order, arranged, in readiness

prescribe 1 = <u>specify</u>, order, direct, stipulate, write a prescription for 2 = <u>ordain</u>, set, order, rule, recommend, dictate, lay down, decree

prescription 1 = <u>instruction</u>, direction, formula, script (*informal*), recipe 2 = <u>medicine</u>, drug, treatment, preparation, cure, mixture, dose, remedy

presence NOUN 1 = <u>being</u>, existence, residence, attendance, showing up, occupancy, inhabitance 2 = <u>personality</u>, bearing, appearance, aspect, air, carriage, aura, poise
● PHRASES **presence of mind** = <u>level-headedness</u>, assurance, composure, poise, cool (*slang*), wits, countenance, coolness

present[1] ADJECTIVE 1 = <u>current</u>, existing, immediate, contemporary, present-day, existent 2 = <u>here</u>, there, near, ready, nearby, at hand ≠ absent 3 = <u>in existence</u>, existing, existent, extant
● PHRASES **the present** = <u>now</u>, today, the time being, here and now, the present moment

present[2] NOUN = <u>gift</u>, offering, grant, donation, hand-out, endowment, boon, gratuity, bonsela (*S. African*), koha (*N.Z.*)
● VERB 1 = <u>give</u>, award, hand over, grant, hand out, confer, bestow 2 = <u>put on</u>, stage, perform, give, show, render 3 = <u>launch</u>, display, parade, exhibit, unveil 4 = <u>introduce</u>, make known, acquaint someone with

presentation 1 = <u>giving</u>, award, offering, donation, bestowal, conferral 2 = <u>appearance</u>, look, display, packaging, arrangement, layout 3 = <u>performance</u>, production, show

presently 1 = <u>at present</u>, currently, now, today, these days, nowadays, at the present time, in this day and age 2 = <u>soon</u>, shortly, directly, before long, momentarily (*U.S. & Canad.*), by and by, in a jiffy

(*informal*)

preservation 1 = <u>upholding</u>, support, maintenance 2 = <u>protection</u>, safety, maintenance, conservation, salvation, safeguarding, safekeeping

preserve VERB 1 = <u>maintain</u>, keep, continue, sustain, keep up, prolong, uphold, conserve ≠ end 2 = <u>protect</u>, keep, save, maintain, defend, shelter, shield, care for ≠ attack
● NOUN = <u>area</u>, department, field, territory, province, arena, sphere

preside = <u>officiate</u>, chair, moderate, be chairperson

press 1 = <u>push (down)</u>, depress, lean on, press down, force down 2 = <u>push</u>, squeeze, jam, thrust, ram, wedge, shove 3 = <u>hug</u>, squeeze, embrace, clasp, crush, hold close, fold in your arms 4 = <u>urge</u>, beg, petition, exhort, implore, pressurize, entreat 5 = <u>plead</u>, present, lodge, submit, tender, advance insistently 6 = <u>steam</u>, iron, smooth, flatten 7 = <u>compress</u>, grind, reduce, mill, crush, pound, squeeze, tread 8 = <u>crowd</u>, push, gather, surge, flock, herd, swarm, seethe

pressing = <u>urgent</u>, serious, vital, crucial, imperative, important, high-priority, importunate ≠ unimportant

pressure 1 = <u>force</u>, crushing, squeezing, compressing, weight, compression 2 = <u>power</u>, influence, force, constraint, sway, compulsion, coercion 3 = <u>stress</u>, demands, strain, heat, load, burden, urgency, hassle (*informal*), uphill (*S. African*)

prestige = <u>status</u>, standing, credit, reputation, honour, importance, fame, distinction, mana (*N.Z.*)

prestigious = <u>celebrated</u>, respected, prominent, great, important, esteemed, notable, renowned ≠ unknown

presumably = <u>it would seem</u>, probably, apparently, seemingly, on the face of it, in all probability, in all likelihood

presume 1 = <u>believe</u>, think, suppose, assume, guess (*informal, chiefly U.S. & Canad.*), take for granted, infer, conjecture 2 = <u>dare</u>, venture, go so far as, take the liberty, make so bold as

pretend 1 = <u>feign</u>, affect, assume, allege, fake, simulate, profess, sham 2 = <u>make believe</u>, suppose, imagine, act, make up

pretty ADJECTIVE = <u>attractive</u>, beautiful,

lovely, charming, fair, good-looking, bonny, comely ≠ plain
● ADVERB (*Informal*) = fairly, rather, quite, kind of (*informal*), somewhat, moderately, reasonably

prevail 1 = win, succeed, triumph, overcome, overrule, be victorious 2 = be widespread, abound, predominate, be current, be prevalent, exist generally

prevailing 1 = widespread, general, established, popular, common, current, usual, ordinary 2 = predominating, ruling, main, existing, principal

prevalent = common, established, popular, general, current, usual, widespread, universal ≠ rare

prevent = stop, avoid, frustrate, hamper, foil, inhibit, avert, thwart ≠ help

prevention = elimination, safeguard, precaution, thwarting, avoidance, deterrence

preview = sample, sneak preview, trailer, taster, foretaste, advance showing

previous 1 = earlier, former, past, prior, preceding, erstwhile ≠ later 2 = preceding, past, prior, foregoing

previously = before, earlier, once, in the past, formerly, hitherto, beforehand

prey 1 = quarry, game, kill 2 = victim, target, mug (*Brit. slang*), dupe, fall guy (*informal*)

price NOUN 1 = cost, value, rate, charge, figure, worth, damage (*informal*), amount 2 = consequences, penalty, cost, result, toll, forfeit
● VERB = evaluate, value, estimate, rate, cost, assess

priceless = valuable, expensive, precious, invaluable, dear, costly ≠ worthless

prick VERB = pierce, stab, puncture, punch, lance, jab, perforate
● NOUN = puncture, hole, wound, perforation, pinhole

prickly 1 = spiny, barbed, thorny, bristly 2 = itchy, sharp, smarting, stinging, crawling, tingling, scratchy

pride 1 = satisfaction, achievement, fulfilment, delight, content, pleasure, joy, gratification 2 = self-respect, honour, ego, dignity, self-esteem, self-image, self-worth 3 = conceit, vanity, arrogance, pretension, hubris, self-importance, egotism, self-love ≠ humility

priest = clergyman, minister, father, divine, vicar, pastor, cleric, curate

primarily 1 = chiefly, largely, generally, mainly, essentially, mostly, principally, fundamentally 2 = at first, originally, initially, in the first place, in the beginning, first and foremost, at *or* from the start

primary = chief, main, first, highest, greatest, prime, principal, cardinal ≠ subordinate

prime ADJECTIVE 1 = main, leading, chief, central, major, key, primary, supreme 2 = best, top, select, highest, quality, choice, excellent, first-class
● NOUN = peak, flower, bloom, height, heyday, zenith
● VERB 1 = inform, tell, train, coach, brief, fill in (*informal*), notify, clue in (*informal*) 2 = prepare, set up, load, equip, get ready, make ready

primitive 1 = early, first, earliest, original, primary, elementary, primordial, primeval ≠ modern 2 = crude, simple, rough, rudimentary, unrefined ≠ elaborate

prince = ruler, lord, monarch, sovereign, crown prince, liege, prince regent, crowned head

princely 1 = substantial, considerable, large, huge, massive, enormous, sizable *or* sizeable 2 = regal, royal, imperial, noble, sovereign, majestic

princess = ruler, lady, monarch, sovereign, liege, crowned head, crowned princess, dynast

principal ADJECTIVE = main, leading, chief, prime, first, key, essential, primary ≠ minor
● NOUN 1 = headmaster *or* headmistress, head (*informal*), dean, head teacher, rector, master *or* mistress 2 = star, lead, leader, prima ballerina, leading man *or* lady, coryphée 3 = capital, money, assets, working capital

principally = mainly, largely, chiefly, especially, mostly, primarily, above all, predominantly

principle NOUN 1 = morals, standards, ideals, honour, virtue, ethics, integrity, conscience, kaupapa (*N.Z.*) 2 = rule, law, truth, precept
● PHRASES **in principle** 1 = in general 2 = in theory, ideally, on paper, theoretically, in an ideal world, en principe (*French*)

print VERB 1 = run off, publish, copy, reproduce, issue, engrave 2 = publish,

release, circulate, issue, disseminate
3 = <u>mark</u>, impress, stamp, imprint
• NOUN 1 = <u>photograph</u>, photo, snap
2 = <u>picture</u>, plate, etching, engraving, lithograph, woodcut, linocut 3 = <u>copy</u>, photo (*informal*), picture, reproduction, replica

prior ADJECTIVE = <u>earlier</u>, previous, former, preceding, foregoing, pre-existing, pre-existent
• PHRASES **prior to** = <u>before</u>, preceding, earlier than, in advance of, previous to

priority 1 = <u>prime concern</u>
2 = <u>precedence</u>, preference, primacy, predominance 3 = <u>supremacy</u>, rank, precedence, seniority, right of way, pre-eminence

prison = <u>jail</u>, confinement, nick (*Brit. slang*), cooler (*slang*), jug (*slang*), dungeon, clink (*slang*), gaol, boob (*Austral. slang*)

prisoner 1 = <u>convict</u>, con (*slang*), lag (*slang*), jailbird 2 = <u>captive</u>, hostage, detainee, internee

privacy = <u>seclusion</u>, isolation, solitude, retirement, retreat

private 1 = <u>exclusive</u>, individual, privately owned, own, special, reserved ≠ public
2 = <u>secret</u>, confidential, covert, unofficial, clandestine, off the record, hush-hush (*informal*) ≠ public 3 = <u>personal</u>, individual, secret, intimate, undisclosed, unspoken, innermost, unvoiced
4 = <u>secluded</u>, secret, separate, isolated, sequestered ≠ busy 5 = <u>solitary</u>, reserved, retiring, withdrawn, discreet, secretive, self-contained, reclusive ≠ sociable

privilege = <u>right</u>, due, advantage, claim, freedom, liberty, concession, entitlement

privileged = <u>special</u>, advantaged, favoured, honoured, entitled, elite

prize[1] NOUN 1 = <u>reward</u>, cup, award, honour, medal, trophy, accolade
2 = <u>winnings</u>, haul, jackpot, stakes, purse
• ADJECTIVE = <u>champion</u>, best, winning, top, outstanding, award-winning, first-rate

prize[2] = <u>value</u>, treasure, esteem, cherish, hold dear

prize[3] *or* **prise** 1 = <u>force</u>, pull, lever
2 = <u>drag</u>, force, draw, wring, extort

probability 1 = <u>likelihood</u>, prospect, chance, odds, expectation, liability, likeliness 2 = <u>chance</u>, odds, possibility, likelihood

probable = <u>likely</u>, possible, apparent,
reasonable to think, credible, plausible, feasible, presumable ≠ unlikely

probably = <u>likely</u>, perhaps, maybe, possibly, presumably, most likely, doubtless, perchance (*archaic*)

probation = <u>trial period</u>, trial, apprenticeship

probe VERB 1 *often with into* = <u>examine</u>, go into, investigate, explore, search, look into, analyze, dissect 2 = <u>explore</u>, examine, poke, prod, feel around
• NOUN = <u>investigation</u>, study, inquiry, analysis, examination, exploration, scrutiny, scrutinization

problem 1 = <u>difficulty</u>, trouble, dispute, plight, obstacle, dilemma, headache (*informal*), complication 2 = <u>puzzle</u>, question, riddle, enigma, conundrum, poser

problematic = <u>tricky</u>, puzzling, doubtful, dubious, debatable, problematical ≠ clear

procedure = <u>method</u>, policy, process, course, system, action, practice, strategy

proceed 1 = <u>begin</u>, go ahead
2 = <u>continue</u>, go on, progress, carry on, go ahead, press on ≠ discontinue 3 = <u>go on</u>, continue, progress, carry on, go ahead, move on, move forward, press on ≠ stop
4 = <u>arise</u>, come, issue, result, spring, flow, stem, derive

proceeding = <u>action</u>, process, procedure, move, act, step, measure, deed

proceeds = <u>income</u>, profit, revenue, returns, products, gain, earnings, yield

process NOUN 1 = <u>procedure</u>, means, course, system, action, performance, operation, measure 2 = <u>development</u>, growth, progress, movement, advance, evolution, progression 3 = <u>method</u>, system, practice, technique, procedure
• VERB = <u>handle</u>, manage, action, deal with, fulfil

procession = <u>parade</u>, train, march, file, cavalcade, cortege

proclaim 1 = <u>announce</u>, declare, advertise, publish, indicate, herald, circulate, profess ≠ keep secret
2 = <u>pronounce</u>, announce, declare

prod VERB 1 = <u>poke</u>, push, dig, shove, nudge, jab 2 = <u>prompt</u>, move, urge, motivate, spur, stimulate, rouse, incite
• NOUN 1 = <u>poke</u>, push, dig, shove, nudge, jab 2 = <u>prompt</u>, signal, cue, reminder, stimulus

prodigy = genius, talent, wizard, mastermind, whizz (*informal*)

produce VERB 1 = cause, effect, generate, bring about, give rise to 2 = make, create, develop, manufacture, construct, invent, fabricate 3 = create, develop, write, turn out, compose, originate, churn out (*informal*) 4 = yield, provide, grow, bear, give, supply, afford, render 5 = bring forth, bear, deliver, breed, give birth to, beget, bring into the world 6 = show, provide, present, advance, demonstrate, offer, come up with, exhibit 7 = display, show, present, proffer 8 = present, stage, direct, put on, do, show, mount, exhibit
● NOUN = fruit and vegetables, goods, food, products, crops, yield, harvest, greengrocery (*Brit.*)

producer 1 = director, promoter, impresario 2 = maker, manufacturer, builder, creator, fabricator 3 = grower, farmer

product 1 = goods, produce, creation, commodity, invention, merchandise, artefact 2 = result, consequence, effect, outcome, upshot

production 1 = producing, making, manufacture, manufacturing, construction, formation, fabrication 2 = creation, development, fashioning, composition, origination 3 = management, administration, direction 4 = presentation, staging, mounting

productive 1 = fertile, rich, prolific, plentiful, fruitful, fecund ≠ barren 2 = creative, inventive 3 = useful, rewarding, valuable, profitable, effective, worthwhile, beneficial, constructive ≠ useless

productivity = output, production, capacity, yield, efficiency, work rate

profess 1 = claim, allege, pretend, fake, make out, purport, feign 2 = state, admit, announce, declare, confess, assert, proclaim, affirm

professed 1 = supposed, would-be, alleged, so-called, pretended, purported, self-styled, ostensible 2 = declared, confirmed, confessed, proclaimed, self-confessed, avowed, self-acknowledged

profession = occupation, calling, business, career, employment, office, position, sphere

professional ADJECTIVE 1 = qualified, trained, skilled, white-collar 2 = expert, experienced, skilled, masterly, efficient, competent, adept, proficient ≠ amateurish
● NOUN = expert, master, pro (*informal*), specialist, guru, adept, maestro, virtuoso, fundi (*S. African*)

professor = don (*Brit.*), fellow (*Brit.*), prof (*informal*)

profile 1 = outline, lines, form, figure, silhouette, contour, side view 2 = biography, sketch, vignette, characterization, thumbnail sketch

profit NOUN 1 often plural = earnings, return, revenue, gain, yield, proceeds, receipts, takings ≠ loss 2 = benefit, good, use, value, gain, advantage, advancement ≠ disadvantage
● VERB 1 = make money, gain, earn 2 = benefit, help, serve, gain, promote, be of advantage to

profitable 1 = money-making, lucrative, paying, commercial, worthwhile, cost-effective, fruitful, remunerative 2 = beneficial, useful, rewarding, valuable, productive, worthwhile, fruitful, advantageous ≠ useless

profound 1 = sincere, acute, intense, great, keen, extreme, heartfelt, deeply felt ≠ insincere 2 = wise, learned, deep, penetrating, philosophical, sage, abstruse, sagacious ≠ uninformed

programme 1 = schedule, plan, agenda, timetable, listing, list, line-up, calendar 2 = course, curriculum, syllabus 3 = show, performance, production, broadcast, episode, presentation, transmission, telecast

progress NOUN 1 = development, growth, advance, gain, improvement, breakthrough, headway ≠ regression 2 = movement forward, passage, advancement, course, advance, headway ≠ movement backward
● VERB 1 = move on, continue, travel, advance, proceed, go forward, make headway ≠ move back 2 = develop, improve, advance, grow, gain ≠ get behind
● PHRASES in progress = going on, happening, continuing, being done, occurring, taking place, proceeding, under way

progression 1 = progress, advance,

advancement, gain, headway, furtherance, movement forward **2** = sequence, course, series, chain, cycle, string, succession

progressive 1 = enlightened, liberal, modern, advanced, radical, revolutionary, avant-garde, reformist **2** = growing, continuing, increasing, developing, advancing, ongoing

prohibit 1 = forbid, ban, veto, outlaw, disallow, proscribe, debar ≠ permit **2** = prevent, restrict, stop, hamper, hinder, impede ≠ allow

prohibition = ban, boycott, embargo, bar, veto, prevention, exclusion, injunction

project NOUN **1** = scheme, plan, job, idea, campaign, operation, activity, venture **2** = assignment, task, homework, piece of research

● VERB **1** = forecast, expect, estimate, predict, reckon, calculate, gauge, extrapolate **2** = stick out, extend, stand out, bulge, protrude, overhang, jut

projection = forecast, estimate, reckoning, calculation, estimation, computation, extrapolation

proliferation = multiplication, increase, spread, expansion

prolific 1 = productive, creative, fertile, inventive, copious **2** = fruitful, fertile, abundant, luxuriant, profuse, fecund ≠ unproductive

prolong = lengthen, continue, perpetuate, draw out, extend, delay, stretch out, spin out ≠ shorten

prominence 1 = fame, name, reputation, importance, celebrity, distinction, prestige, eminence **2** = conspicuousness, markedness

prominent 1 = famous, leading, top, important, main, distinguished, well-known, notable ≠ unknown **2** = noticeable, obvious, outstanding, pronounced, conspicuous, eye-catching, obtrusive ≠ inconspicuous

promise VERB **1** = guarantee, pledge, vow, swear, contract, assure, undertake, warrant **2** = seem likely, look like, show signs of, augur, betoken

● NOUN **1** = guarantee, word, bond, vow, commitment, pledge, undertaking, assurance **2** = potential, ability, talent, capacity, capability, aptitude

promising 1 = encouraging, likely, bright, reassuring, hopeful, favourable, rosy,

auspicious ≠ unpromising **2** = talented, able, gifted, rising

promote 1 = help, back, support, aid, forward, encourage, advance, boost ≠ impede **2** = advertise, sell, hype, publicize, push, plug (*informal*) **3** = raise, upgrade, elevate, exalt ≠ demote

promotion 1 = rise, upgrading, move up, advancement, elevation, exaltation, preferment **2** = publicity, advertising, plugging (*informal*) **3** = encouragement, support, boosting, advancement, furtherance

prompt VERB **1** = cause, occasion, provoke, give rise to, elicit **2** = remind, assist, cue, help out

● ADJECTIVE = immediate, quick, rapid, instant, timely, early, swift, speedy ≠ slow

● ADVERB (*Informal*) = exactly, sharp, promptly, on the dot, punctually

promptly 1 = immediately, swiftly, directly, quickly, at once, speedily **2** = punctually, on time, spot on (*informal*), bang on (*informal*), on the dot, on the button (*U.S.*), on the nail

prone 1 = liable, given, subject, inclined, tending, bent, disposed, susceptible ≠ disinclined **2** = face down, flat, horizontal, prostrate, recumbent ≠ face up

pronounce 1 = say, speak, sound, articulate, enunciate **2** = declare, announce, deliver, proclaim, decree, affirm

pronounced = noticeable, decided, marked, striking, obvious, evident, distinct, definite ≠ imperceptible

proof NOUN = evidence, demonstration, testimony, confirmation, verification, corroboration, authentication, substantiation

● ADJECTIVE = impervious, strong, resistant, impenetrable, repellent

prop VERB **1** = lean, place, set, stand, position, rest, lay, balance **2** *often with* **up** = support, sustain, hold up, brace, uphold, bolster, buttress

● NOUN **1** = support, stay, brace, mainstay, buttress, stanchion **2** = mainstay, support, sustainer, anchor, backbone, cornerstone, upholder

propaganda = information, advertising, promotion, publicity, hype, disinformation

propel 1 = drive, launch, force, send, shoot, push, thrust, shove ≠ stop **2** = impel, drive, push, prompt, spur, motivate ≠ hold back

proper 1 = real, actual, genuine, true, bona fide, dinkum (*Austral. & N.Z. informal*) 2 = correct, accepted, established, appropriate, right, formal, conventional, precise ≠ improper 3 = polite, right, becoming, seemly, fitting, fit, mannerly, suitable ≠ unseemly

properly 1 = correctly, rightly, fittingly, appropriately, accurately, suitably, aptly ≠ incorrectly 2 = politely, decently, respectably ≠ badly

property 1 = possessions, goods, effects, holdings, capital, riches, estate, assets 2 = land, holding, estate, real estate, freehold 3 = quality, feature, characteristic, attribute, trait, hallmark

prophecy 1 = prediction, forecast, prognostication, augury 2 = second sight, divination, augury, telling the future, soothsaying

prophet *or* **prophetess** = soothsayer, forecaster, diviner, oracle, seer, sibyl, prophesier

proportion NOUN 1 = part, share, amount, division, percentage, segment, quota, fraction 2 = relative amount, relationship, ratio 3 = balance, harmony, correspondence, symmetry, concord, congruity
● PLURAL NOUN = dimensions, size, volume, capacity, extent, expanse

proportional *or* **proportionate**
= correspondent, corresponding, even, balanced, consistent, compatible, equitable, in proportion ≠ disproportionate

proposal = suggestion, plan, programme, scheme, offer, project, bid, recommendation

propose 1 = put forward, present, suggest, advance, submit 2 = intend, mean, plan, aim, design, scheme, have in mind 3 = nominate, name, present, recommend 4 = offer marriage, pop the question (*informal*), ask for someone's hand (in marriage)

proposition NOUN 1 = task, problem, activity, job, affair, venture, undertaking 2 = theory, idea, argument, concept, thesis, hypothesis, theorem, premiss 3 = proposal, plan, suggestion, scheme, bid, recommendation 4 = advance, pass (*informal*), proposal, overture, improper suggestion, come-on (*informal*)
● VERB = make a pass at, solicit, accost, make an improper suggestion to

proprietor *or* **proprietress** = owner, titleholder, landlord *or* landlady

prosecute (*Law*) = take someone to court, try, sue, indict, arraign, put someone on trial, litigate, bring someone to trial

prospect NOUN 1 = likelihood, chance, possibility, hope, promise, odds, expectation, probability 2 = idea, outlook 3 = view, landscape, scene, sight, outlook, spectacle, vista
● PLURAL NOUN = possibilities, chances, future, potential, expectations, outlook, scope
● VERB = look, search, seek, dowse

prospective 1 = potential, possible 2 = expected, coming, future, likely, intended, anticipated, forthcoming, imminent

prospectus = catalogue, list, programme, outline, syllabus, synopsis

prosper = succeed, advance, progress, thrive, get on, do well, flourish

prosperity = success, riches, plenty, fortune, wealth, luxury, good fortune, affluence ≠ poverty

prosperous 1 = wealthy, rich, affluent, well-off, well-heeled (*informal*), well-to-do, moneyed ≠ poor 2 = successful, booming, thriving, flourishing, doing well ≠ unsuccessful

prostitute NOUN = whore, hooker (*U.S. slang*), pro (*slang*), tart (*informal*), call girl, harlot, streetwalker, loose woman
● VERB = cheapen, sell out, pervert, degrade, devalue, squander, demean, debase

protagonist 1 = supporter, champion, advocate, exponent 2 = leading character, principal, central character, hero *or* heroine

protect = keep someone safe, defend, support, save, guard, preserve, look after, shelter ≠ endanger

protection 1 = safety, care, defence, protecting, security, custody, safeguard, aegis 2 = safeguard, cover, guard, shelter, screen, barrier, shield, buffer 3 = armour, cover, screen, barrier, shelter, shield

protective 1 = protecting 2 = caring, defensive, motherly, fatherly, maternal, vigilant, watchful, paternal

protector 1 = defender, champion, guard,

guardian, patron, bodyguard **2** = <u>guard</u>, screen, protection, shield, pad, cushion, buffer

protest VERB **1** = <u>object</u>, demonstrate, oppose, complain, disagree, cry out, disapprove, demur **2** = <u>assert</u>, insist, maintain, declare, affirm, profess, attest, avow

● NOUN **1** = <u>demonstration</u>, march, rally, sit-in, demo (*informal*), hikoi (*N.Z.*) **2** = <u>objection</u>, complaint, dissent, outcry, protestation, remonstrance

protocol = <u>code of behaviour</u>, manners, conventions, customs, etiquette, propriety, decorum

prototype = <u>original</u>, model, first, example, standard

protracted = <u>extended</u>, prolonged, drawn-out, spun out, dragged out, long-drawn-out

proud 1 = <u>satisfied</u>, pleased, content, thrilled, glad, gratified, joyful, well-pleased ≠ dissatisfied **2** = <u>conceited</u>, arrogant, lordly, imperious, overbearing, haughty, snobbish, self-satisfied ≠ humble

prove 1 = <u>turn out</u>, come out, end up **2** = <u>verify</u>, establish, determine, show, confirm, demonstrate, justify, substantiate ≠ disprove

proven = <u>established</u>, proved, confirmed, tested, reliable, definite, verified, attested

provide VERB **1** = <u>supply</u>, give, distribute, outfit, equip, donate, furnish, dispense ≠ withhold **2** = <u>give</u>, bring, add, produce, present, serve, afford, yield

● PHRASES **provide for someone** = <u>support</u>, care for, keep, maintain, sustain, take care of, fend for ♦ **provide for something** = <u>take precautions against</u>, plan for, prepare for, anticipate, plan ahead for, forearm for

provided *often with **that*** = <u>if</u>, given, on condition, as long as

provider 1 = <u>supplier</u>, giver, source, donor **2** = <u>breadwinner</u>, supporter, earner, wage earner

providing *often with **that*** = <u>on condition that</u>, given that, as long as

province 1 = <u>region</u>, section, district, zone, patch, colony, domain **2** = <u>area</u>, business, concern, responsibility, line, role, department, field

provincial ADJECTIVE **1** = <u>regional</u>, state, local, county, district, territorial, parochial

2 = <u>rural</u>, country, local, rustic, homespun, hick (*informal*, *chiefly U.S. & Canad.*), backwoods ≠ urban **3** = <u>parochial</u>, insular, narrow-minded, unsophisticated, limited, narrow, small-town (*chiefly U.S.*), inward-looking ≠ cosmopolitan

provision NOUN **1** = <u>supplying</u>, giving, providing, supply, delivery, distribution, catering, presentation **2** = <u>condition</u>, term, requirement, demand, rider, restriction, qualification, clause

● PLURAL NOUN = <u>food</u>, supplies, stores, fare, rations, foodstuff, kai (*N.Z. informal*), victuals, edibles

provisional 1 = <u>temporary</u>, interim ≠ permanent **2** = <u>conditional</u>, limited, qualified, contingent, tentative ≠ definite

provocation 1 = <u>cause</u>, reason, grounds, motivation, stimulus, incitement **2** = <u>offence</u>, challenge, insult, taunt, injury, dare, grievance, annoyance

provocative = <u>offensive</u>, provoking, insulting, stimulating, annoying, galling, goading

provoke 1 = <u>anger</u>, annoy, irritate, infuriate, hassle (*informal*), aggravate (*informal*), incense, enrage ≠ pacify **2** = <u>rouse</u>, cause, produce, promote, occasion, prompt, stir, induce ≠ curb

prowess 1 = <u>skill</u>, ability, talent, expertise, genius, excellence, accomplishment, mastery ≠ inability **2** = <u>bravery</u>, daring, courage, heroism, mettle, valour, fearlessness, valiance ≠ cowardice

proximity = <u>nearness</u>, closeness

proxy = <u>representative</u>, agent, deputy, substitute, factor, delegate

prudent 1 = <u>cautious</u>, careful, wary, discreet, vigilant ≠ careless **2** = <u>wise</u>, politic, sensible, shrewd, discerning, judicious ≠ unwise **3** = <u>thrifty</u>, economical, sparing, careful, canny, provident, frugal, far-sighted ≠ extravagant

prune 1 = <u>cut</u>, trim, clip, dock, shape, shorten, snip **2** = <u>reduce</u>, cut, cut back, trim, cut down, pare down, make reductions in

psyche = <u>soul</u>, mind, self, spirit, personality, individuality, anima, wairua (*N.Z.*)

psychiatrist = <u>psychotherapist</u>, analyst, therapist, psychologist, shrink (*slang*), psychoanalyst, headshrinker (*slang*)

psychic ADJECTIVE **1** = <u>supernatural</u>,

mystic, occult **2** = mystical, spiritual, magical, other-worldly, paranormal, preternatural **3** = psychological, emotional, mental, spiritual, inner, psychiatric, cognitive
● NOUN **1** = clairvoyant, fortune teller

psychological 1 = mental, emotional, intellectual, inner, cognitive, cerebral **2** = imaginary, psychosomatic, irrational, unreal, all in the mind

psychology 1 = behaviourism, study of personality, science of mind **2** (*Informal*) = way of thinking, attitude, behaviour, temperament, mentality, thought processes, mental processes, what makes you tick

pub *or* **public house** = tavern, bar, inn, saloon

public NOUN **1** = people, society, community, nation, everyone, citizens, electorate, populace
● ADJECTIVE **1** = civic, government, state, national, local, official, community, social **2** = general, popular, national, shared, common, widespread, universal, collective **3** = open, accessible, communal, unrestricted ≠ private **4** = well-known, leading, important, respected, famous, celebrated, recognized, distinguished **5** = known, open, obvious, acknowledged, plain, patent, overt ≠ secret

publication 1 = pamphlet, newspaper, magazine, issue, title, leaflet, brochure, periodical **2** = announcement, publishing, broadcasting, reporting, declaration, disclosure, proclamation, notification

publicity 1 = advertising, press, promotion, hype, boost, plug (*informal*) **2** = attention, exposure, fame, celebrity, fuss, public interest, limelight, notoriety

publish 1 = put out, issue, produce, print **2** = announce, reveal, spread, advertise, broadcast, disclose, proclaim, circulate

pudding = dessert, afters (*Brit. informal*), sweet, pud (*informal*)

puff VERB **1** = smoke, draw, drag (*slang*), suck, inhale, pull at *or* on **2** = breathe heavily, pant, exhale, blow, gasp, gulp, wheeze, fight for breath
● NOUN **1** = drag, pull (*slang*), moke **2** = blast, breath, whiff, draught, gust

pull VERB **1** = draw, haul, drag, trail, tow, tug, jerk, yank ≠ push **2** = extract, pick, remove, gather, take out, pluck, uproot,

draw out ≠ insert **3** (*Informal*) = attract, draw, bring in, tempt, lure, interest, entice, pull in ≠ repel **4** = strain, tear, stretch, rip, wrench, dislocate, sprain
● NOUN **1** = tug, jerk, yank, twitch, heave ≠ shove **2** = puff, drag (*slang*), inhalation **3** (*Informal*) = influence, power, weight, muscle, clout (*informal*), kai (*N.Z. informal*)
● PHRASES **pull out (of) 1** = withdraw, quit **2** = leave, abandon, get out, quit, retreat from, depart, evacuate ◆ **pull someone up** = reprimand, rebuke, admonish, read the riot act to, tell someone off (*informal*), reprove, bawl someone out (*informal*), tear someone off a strip (*Brit. informal*) ◆ **pull something off** (*Informal*) = succeed in, manage, carry out, accomplish ◆ **pull something out** = produce, draw, bring out, draw out
◆ **pull up** = stop, halt, brake

pulp NOUN **1** = paste, mash, mush **2** = flesh, meat, soft part
● ADJECTIVE = cheap, lurid, trashy, rubbishy
● VERB = crush, squash, mash, pulverize

pulse NOUN = beat, rhythm, vibration, beating, throb, throbbing, pulsation
● VERB = beat, throb, vibrate, pulsate

pump 1 = supply, send, pour, inject **2** = interrogate, probe, quiz, cross-examine

punch[1] VERB = hit, strike, box, smash, belt (*informal*), sock (*slang*), swipe (*informal*), bop (*informal*)
● NOUN **1** = blow, hit, sock (*slang*), jab, swipe (*informal*), bop (*informal*), wallop (*informal*) **2** (*Informal*) = effectiveness, bite, impact, drive, vigour, verve, forcefulness

punch[2] = pierce, cut, bore, drill, stamp, puncture, prick, perforate

punctuate = interrupt, break, pepper, sprinkle, intersperse

puncture NOUN **1** = flat tyre, flat, flattie (*N.Z.*) **2** = hole, opening, break, cut, nick, leak, slit
● VERB = pierce, cut, nick, penetrate, prick, rupture, perforate, bore a hole

punish = discipline, correct, castigate, chastise, sentence, chasten, penalize

punishing = hard, taxing, wearing, tiring, exhausting, gruelling, strenuous, arduous ≠ easy

punishment 1 = penalizing, discipline, correction, retribution, chastening, chastisement 2 = <u>penalty</u>, penance

punitive = <u>retaliatory</u>, in reprisal, retaliative

punt VERB = <u>bet</u>, back, stake, gamble, lay, wager

● NOUN = <u>bet</u>, stake, gamble, wager

punter 1 = <u>gambler</u>, better, backer 2 (*Informal*) = <u>person</u>, man in the street

pupil 1 = <u>student</u>, schoolboy *or* schoolgirl, schoolchild ≠ teacher 2 = <u>learner</u>, novice, beginner, disciple ≠ instructor

puppet 1 = <u>marionette</u>, doll, glove puppet, finger puppet 2 = <u>pawn</u>, tool, instrument, mouthpiece, stooge, cat's-paw

purchase VERB = <u>buy</u>, pay for, obtain, get, score (*slang*), gain, pick up, acquire ≠ sell

● NOUN 1 = <u>acquisition</u>, buy, investment, property, gain, asset, possession 2 = <u>grip</u>, hold, support, leverage, foothold

pure 1 = <u>unmixed</u>, real, simple, natural, straight, genuine, neat, authentic ≠ adulterated 2 = <u>clean</u>, wholesome, sanitary, spotless, sterilized, squeaky-clean, untainted, uncontaminated ≠ contaminated 3 = <u>complete</u>, total, perfect, absolute, sheer, patent, utter, outright ≠ qualified 4 = <u>innocent</u>, modest, good, moral, impeccable, righteous, virtuous, squeaky-clean ≠ corrupt

purely = <u>absolutely</u>, just, only, completely, simply, entirely, exclusively, merely

purge VERB 1 = <u>rid</u>, clear, cleanse, strip, empty, void 2 = <u>get rid of</u>, remove, expel, wipe out, eradicate, do away with, exterminate

● NOUN = <u>removal</u>, elimination, expulsion, eradication, ejection

purity 1 = <u>cleanness</u>, cleanliness, wholesomeness, pureness, faultlessness, immaculateness ≠ impurity 2 = <u>innocence</u>, virtue, integrity, honesty, decency, virginity, chastity, chasteness ≠ immorality

purport = <u>claim</u>, allege, assert, profess

purpose NOUN 1 = <u>reason</u>, point, idea, aim, object, intention 2 = <u>aim</u>, end, plan, hope, goal, wish, desire, object 3 = <u>determination</u>, resolve, will, resolution, ambition, persistence, tenacity, firmness

● PHRASES **on purpose** = <u>deliberately</u>, purposely, intentionally, knowingly, designedly

purposely = <u>deliberately</u>, expressly, consciously, intentionally, knowingly, with intent, on purpose ≠ accidentally

purse NOUN 1 = <u>pouch</u>, wallet, money-bag 2 (*U.S.*) = <u>handbag</u>, bag, shoulder bag, pocket book, clutch bag 3 = <u>funds</u>, means, money, resources, treasury, wealth, exchequer

● VERB = <u>pucker</u>, contract, tighten, pout, press together

pursue 1 = <u>engage in</u>, perform, conduct, carry on, practise 2 = <u>try for</u>, seek, desire, search for, aim for, work towards, strive for 3 = <u>continue</u>, maintain, carry on, keep on, persist in, proceed in, persevere in 4 = <u>follow</u>, track, hunt, chase, dog, shadow, tail (*informal*), hound ≠ flee

pursuit 1 = <u>quest</u>, seeking, search, aim of, aspiration for, striving towards 2 = <u>pursuing</u>, seeking, search, hunt, chase, trailing 3 = <u>occupation</u>, activity, interest, line, pleasure, hobby, pastime

push VERB 1 = <u>shove</u>, force, press, thrust, drive, knock, sweep, plunge ≠ pull 2 = <u>press</u>, operate, depress, squeeze, activate, hold down 3 = <u>make or force your way</u>, move, shoulder, inch, squeeze, thrust, elbow, shove 4 = <u>urge</u>, encourage, persuade, spur, press, incite, impel ≠ discourage

● NOUN 1 = <u>shove</u>, thrust, butt, elbow, nudge ≠ pull 2 (*Informal*) = <u>drive</u>, go (*informal*), energy, initiative, enterprise, ambition, vitality, vigour

● PHRASES **the push** (*Informal, chiefly Brit.*) = <u>dismissal</u>, the sack (*informal*), discharge, the boot (*slang*), your cards (*informal*)

put VERB 1 = <u>place</u>, leave, set, position, rest, park (*informal*), plant, lay 2 = <u>express</u>, state, word, phrase, utter

● PHRASES **put someone off** 1 = <u>discourage</u>, intimidate, deter, daunt, dissuade, demoralize, scare off, dishearten 2 = <u>disconcert</u>, confuse, unsettle, throw (*informal*), dismay, perturb, faze, discomfit ◆ **put someone up** 1 = <u>accommodate</u>, house, board, lodge, quarter, take someone in, billet 2 = <u>nominate</u>, put forward, offer, present, propose, recommend, submit ◆ **put something across** *or* **over** = <u>communicate</u>, explain, convey, make clear, get across, make yourself understood ◆ **put something off** = <u>postpone</u>, delay, defer, adjourn, hold over, put on the back burner (*informal*), take a rain check on (*U.S. & Canad. informal*) ◆ **put something up** 1 = build, raise, set up, construct, erect, fabricate 2 = offer, present, mount, put forward

puzzle VERB = perplex, confuse, baffle, stump, bewilder, confound, mystify, faze ● NOUN 1 = problem, riddle, question, conundrum, poser 2 = mystery, problem, paradox, enigma, conundrum

puzzling = perplexing, baffling, bewildering, involved, enigmatic, incomprehensible, mystifying, abstruse ≠ simple

q

quake = shake, tremble, quiver, move, rock, shiver, shudder, vibrate

qualification 1 = eligibility, quality, ability, skill, fitness, attribute, capability, aptitude 2 = condition, proviso, requirement, rider, reservation, limitation, modification, caveat

qualified 1 = capable, trained, experienced, seasoned, able, fit, expert, chartered ≠ untrained 2 = restricted, limited, provisional, conditional, reserved, bounded, adjusted, moderated ≠ unconditional

qualify 1 = certify, equip, empower, train, prepare, fit, ready, permit ≠ disqualify 2 = restrict, limit, reduce, ease, moderate, regulate, diminish, temper

quality 1 = standard, standing, class, condition, rank, grade, merit, classification 2 = excellence, status, merit, position, value, worth, distinction, virtue 3 = characteristic, feature, attribute, point, side, mark, property, aspect 4 = nature, character, make, sort, kind

quantity 1 = amount, lot, total, sum, part, number 2 = size, measure, mass, volume, length, capacity, extent, bulk

quarrel NOUN = disagreement, fight, row, argument, dispute, controversy, breach, contention, biffo (*Austral. slang*) ≠ accord ● VERB = disagree, fight, argue, row, clash, dispute, differ, fall out (*informal*) ≠ get on or along (with)

quarry = prey, victim, game, goal, aim, prize, objective

quarter NOUN 1 = district, region, neighbourhood, place, part, side, area, zone 2 = mercy, pity, compassion, charity, sympathy, tolerance, kindness, forgiveness ● PLURAL NOUN = lodgings, rooms, chambers, residence, dwelling, barracks, abode, habitation ● VERB = accommodate, house, lodge, place, board, post, station, billet

quash 1 = annul, overturn, reverse, cancel, overthrow, revoke, overrule, rescind 2 = suppress, crush, put down, beat, overthrow, squash, subdue, repress

queen 1 = sovereign, ruler, monarch, leader, Crown, princess, majesty, head of state 2 = leading light, star, favourite, celebrity, darling, mistress, big name

queer 1 = strange, odd, funny, unusual, extraordinary, curious, weird, peculiar ≠ normal 2 = faint, dizzy, giddy, queasy, light-headed

query NOUN 1 = question, inquiry, problem 2 = doubt, suspicion, objection ● VERB 1 = question, challenge, doubt, suspect, dispute, object to, distrust, mistrust 2 = ask, inquire or enquire, question

quest 1 = search, hunt, mission, enterprise, crusade 2 = expedition, journey, adventure

question NOUN 1 = inquiry, enquiry, query, investigation, examination, interrogation ≠ answer 2 = difficulty, problem, doubt, argument, dispute, controversy, query, contention 3 = issue, point, matter, subject, problem, debate, proposal, theme ● VERB 1 = interrogate, cross-examine, interview, examine, probe, quiz, ask questions 2 = dispute, challenge, doubt, suspect, oppose, query, mistrust, disbelieve ≠ accept ● PHRASES **out of the question** = impossible, unthinkable, inconceivable, not on (*informal*), hopeless, unimaginable, unworkable, unattainable

questionable = dubious, suspect, doubtful, controversial, suspicious, dodgy (*Brit., Austral., & N.Z. informal*), debatable, moot ≠ indisputable

queue = line, row, file, train, series, chain, string, column

quick 1 = <u>fast</u>, swift, speedy, express, cracking (*Brit. informal*), smart, rapid, fleet ≠ slow **2** = <u>brief</u>, passing, hurried, flying, fleeting, summary, lightning, short-lived ≠ long **3** = <u>immediate</u>, instant, prompt, sudden, abrupt, instantaneous **4** = <u>excitable</u>, passionate, irritable, touchy, irascible, testy ≠ calm **5** = <u>intelligent</u>, bright (*informal*), alert, sharp, acute, smart, clever, shrewd ≠ stupid

quicken 1 = <u>speed up</u>, hurry, accelerate, hasten, gee up (*informal*) **2** = <u>stimulate</u>, inspire, arouse, excite, revive, incite, energize, invigorate

quickly 1 = <u>swiftly</u>, rapidly, hurriedly, fast, hastily, briskly, apace ≠ slowly **2** = <u>soon</u>, speedily, as soon as possible, momentarily (*U.S.*), instantaneously, pronto (*informal*), a.s.a.p. (*informal*) **3** = <u>immediately</u>, at once, directly, promptly, abruptly, without delay

quiet ADJECTIVE 1 = <u>soft</u>, low, muted, lowered, whispered, faint, suppressed, stifled ≠ loud **2** = <u>peaceful</u>, silent, hushed, soundless, noiseless ≠ noisy **3** = <u>calm</u>, peaceful, tranquil, mild, serene, placid, restful ≠ exciting **4** = <u>still</u>, calm, peaceful, tranquil ≠ troubled **5** = <u>undisturbed</u>, isolated, secluded, private, sequestered, unfrequented ≠ crowded **6** = <u>silent</u> **7** = <u>reserved</u>, retiring, shy, gentle, mild, sedate, meek ≠ excitable
● **NOUN** = <u>peace</u>, rest, tranquillity, ease, silence, solitude, serenity, stillness ≠ noise

quietly 1 = <u>noiselessly</u>, silently **2** = <u>softly</u>, inaudibly, in an undertone, under your breath **3** = <u>calmly</u>, serenely, placidly, patiently, mildly **4** = <u>silently</u>, mutely

quilt = <u>bedspread</u>, duvet, coverlet, eiderdown, counterpane, doona (*Austral.*), continental quilt

quip = <u>joke</u>, sally, jest, riposte, wisecrack (*informal*), retort, pleasantry, gibe

quirky = <u>odd</u>, unusual, eccentric, idiosyncratic, peculiar, offbeat

quit 1 = <u>resign (from)</u>, leave, retire (from), pull out (of), step down (from) (*informal*), abdicate **2** = <u>stop</u>, give up, cease, end, drop, abandon, halt, discontinue ≠ continue **3** = <u>leave</u>, depart from, go out of, go away from, pull out from

quite 1 = <u>somewhat</u>, rather, fairly, reasonably, relatively, moderately **2** = <u>absolutely</u>, perfectly, completely, totally, fully, entirely, wholly

quiz NOUN = <u>examination</u>, questioning, interrogation, interview, investigation, grilling (*informal*), cross-examination, cross-questioning
● **VERB** = <u>question</u>, ask, interrogate, examine, investigate

quota = <u>share</u>, allowance, ration, part, limit, slice, quantity, portion

quotation 1 = <u>passage</u>, quote (*informal*), excerpt, reference, extract, citation **2** (*Commerce*) = <u>estimate</u>, price, tender, rate, cost, charge, figure, quote (*informal*)

quote 1 = <u>repeat</u>, recite, recall **2** = <u>refer to</u>, cite, give, name, detail, relate, mention, instance

r

race¹ NOUN 1 = <u>competition</u>, contest, chase, dash, pursuit **2** = <u>contest</u>, competition, rivalry
● **VERB 1** = <u>compete against</u>, run against **2** = <u>compete</u>, run, contend, take part in a race **3** = <u>run</u>, fly, career, speed, tear, dash, hurry, dart

race² 1 = <u>people</u>, nation, blood, stock, type, folk, tribe

racial = <u>ethnic</u>, ethnological, national, folk, genetic, tribal, genealogical

rack NOUN = <u>frame</u>, stand, structure, framework
● **VERB** = <u>torture</u>, torment, afflict, oppress, harrow, crucify, agonize, pain

racket 1 = <u>noise</u>, row, fuss, disturbance, outcry, clamour, din, pandemonium **2** = <u>fraud</u>, scheme

radiate 1 = <u>emit</u>, spread, send out, pour, shed, scatter **2** = <u>shine</u>, be diffused **3** = <u>show</u>, display, demonstrate, exhibit, emanate, give off *or* out **4** = <u>spread out</u>, diverge, branch out

radical ADJECTIVE 1 = <u>extreme</u>, complete, entire, sweeping, severe, thorough, drastic **2** = <u>revolutionary</u>, extremist, fanatical **3** = <u>fundamental</u>, natural, basic, profound, innate, deep-seated ≠ superficial
● **NOUN** = <u>extremist</u>, revolutionary, militant,

fanatic ≠ conservative

rage NOUN 1 = <u>fury</u>, temper, frenzy, rampage, tantrum, foulie (*Austral. slang*) ≠ calmness 2 = <u>anger</u>, passion, madness, wrath, ire 3 = <u>craze</u>, fashion, enthusiasm, vogue, fad (*informal*), latest thing

● VERB = <u>be furious</u>, blow up (*informal*), fume, lose it (*informal*), seethe, lose the plot (*informal*), go ballistic (*slang, chiefly U.S.*), lose your temper ≠ stay calm

ragged 1 = <u>tatty</u>, worn, torn, run-down, shabby, seedy, scruffy, in tatters ≠ smart 2 = <u>rough</u>, rugged, unfinished, uneven, jagged, serrated

raid VERB 1 = <u>steal from</u>, plunder, pillage, sack 2 = <u>attack</u>, invade, assault 3 = <u>make a search of</u>, search, bust (*informal*), make a raid on, make a swoop on

● NOUN 1 = <u>attack</u>, invasion, foray, sortie, incursion, sally, inroad 2 = <u>bust</u> (*informal*), swoop 3 = <u>robbery</u>, sacking

raider = <u>attacker</u>, thief, robber, plunderer, invader, marauder

railing = <u>fence</u>, rails, barrier, paling, balustrade

rain NOUN = <u>rainfall</u>, fall, showers, deluge, drizzle, downpour, raindrops, cloudburst

● VERB 1 = <u>pour</u>, pelt (down), teem, bucket down (*informal*), drizzle, come down in buckets (*informal*) 2 = <u>fall</u>, shower, be dropped, sprinkle, be deposited

rainy = <u>wet</u>, damp, drizzly, showery ≠ dry

raise 1 = <u>lift</u>, elevate, uplift, heave 2 = <u>set upright</u>, lift, elevate 3 = <u>increase</u>, intensify, heighten, advance, boost, strengthen, enhance, enlarge ≠ reduce 4 = <u>make louder</u>, heighten, amplify, louden 5 = <u>collect</u>, gather, obtain 6 = <u>cause</u>, start, produce, create, occasion, provoke, originate, engender 7 = <u>put forward</u>, suggest, introduce, advance, broach, moot 8 = <u>bring up</u>, develop, rear, nurture 9 = <u>build</u>, construct, put up, erect ≠ demolish

rake[1] 1 = <u>gather</u>, collect, remove 2 = <u>search</u>, comb, scour, scrutinize, fossick (*Austral. & N.Z.*)

rake[2] = <u>libertine</u>, playboy, swinger (*slang*), lecher, roué, debauchee ≠ puritan

rally NOUN 1 = <u>gathering</u>, convention, meeting, congress, assembly, hui (*N.Z.*) 2 = <u>recovery</u>, improvement, revival, recuperation ≠ relapse

● VERB 1 = <u>gather together</u>, unite, regroup, reorganize, reassemble 2 = <u>recover</u>, improve, revive, get better, recuperate ≠ get worse

ram 1 = <u>hit</u>, force, drive into, crash, impact, smash, dash, butt 2 = <u>cram</u>, force, stuff, jam, thrust

ramble NOUN = <u>walk</u>, tour, stroll, hike, roaming, roving, saunter

● VERB 1 = <u>walk</u>, range, wander, stroll, stray, roam, rove, saunter, go walkabout (*Austral.*) 2 often with **on** = <u>babble</u>, rabbit (on) (*Brit. informal*), waffle (*informal, chiefly Brit.*), witter on (*informal*)

ramp = <u>slope</u>, incline, gradient, rise

rampage VERB = <u>go berserk</u>, storm, rage, run riot, run amok

● PHRASES on the rampage = <u>berserk</u>, wild, violent, raging, out of control, amok, riotous, berko (*Austral. slang*)

rampant 1 = <u>widespread</u>, prevalent, rife, uncontrolled, unchecked, unrestrained, profuse, spreading like wildfire 2 (*Heraldry*) = <u>upright</u>, standing, rearing, erect

random ADJECTIVE 1 = <u>chance</u>, casual, accidental, incidental, haphazard, fortuitous, hit or miss, adventitious ≠ planned 2 = <u>casual</u>

● PHRASES at random = <u>haphazardly</u>, randomly, arbitrarily, by chance, willy-nilly, unsystematically

randy (*Informal*) = <u>lustful</u>, hot, turned-on (*slang*), aroused, horny (*slang*), amorous, lascivious

range NOUN 1 = <u>series</u>, variety, selection, assortment, lot, collection, gamut 2 = <u>limits</u>, reach 3 = <u>scope</u>, area, bounds, province, orbit, radius

● VERB 1 = <u>vary</u>, run, reach, extend, stretch 2 = <u>roam</u>, wander, rove, ramble, traverse

rank[1] NOUN 1 = <u>status</u>, level, position, grade, order, sort, type, division 2 = <u>class</u>, caste 3 = <u>row</u>, line, file, column, group, range, series, tier

● VERB 1 = <u>order</u>, dispose 2 = <u>arrange</u>, sort, line up, array, align

rank[2] 1 = <u>absolute</u>, complete, total, gross, sheer, utter, thorough, blatant 2 = <u>foul</u>, bad, offensive, disgusting, revolting, stinking, noxious, rancid, festy (*Austral. slang*) 3 = <u>abundant</u>, lush, luxuriant, dense, profuse

ransom = <u>payment</u>, money, price, payoff

rant = <u>shout</u>, roar, yell, rave, cry, declaim

rap VERB = <u>hit</u>, strike, knock, crack, tap

● NOUN 1 = <u>blow</u>, knock, crack, tap, clout (*informal*) 2 (*Slang*) = <u>rebuke</u>, blame, responsibility, punishment

rape VERB = <u>sexually assault</u>, violate, abuse, ravish, force, outrage

● NOUN = <u>sexual assault</u>, violation, ravishment, outrage

rapid 1 = <u>sudden</u>, prompt, speedy, express, swift ≠ gradual 2 = <u>quick</u>, fast, hurried, swift, brisk, hasty ≠ slow

rapidly = <u>quickly</u>, fast, swiftly, briskly, promptly, hastily, hurriedly, speedily

rare 1 = <u>uncommon</u>, unusual, few, strange, scarce, singular, sparse, infrequent ≠ common 2 = <u>superb</u>, great, fine, excellent, superlative, choice, peerless

rarely = <u>seldom</u>, hardly, hardly ever, infrequently ≠ often

raring (in construction *raring to do something*) = <u>eager</u>, impatient, longing, ready, keen, desperate, enthusiastic

rarity 1 = <u>curio</u>, find, treasure, gem, collector's item 2 = <u>uncommonness</u>, scarcity, infrequency, unusualness, shortage, strangeness, sparseness

rash[1] 1 = <u>reckless</u>, hasty, impulsive, imprudent, careless, ill-advised, foolhardy, impetuous ≠ cautious

rash[2] 1 = <u>outbreak of spots</u>, (skin) eruption 2 = <u>spate</u>, series, wave, flood, plague, outbreak

rate NOUN 1 = <u>speed</u>, pace, tempo, velocity, frequency 2 = <u>degree</u>, standard, scale, proportion, ratio 3 = <u>charge</u>, price, cost, fee, figure

● VERB 1 = <u>evaluate</u>, consider, rank, reckon, value, measure, estimate, count 2 = <u>deserve</u>, merit, be entitled to, be worthy of

● PHRASES **at any rate** = <u>in any case</u>, anyway, anyhow, at all events

rather 1 = <u>preferably</u>, sooner, more readily, more willingly 2 = <u>to some extent</u>, quite, a little, fairly, relatively, somewhat, moderately, to some degree

ratify = <u>approve</u>, establish, confirm, sanction, endorse, uphold, authorize, affirm ≠ annul

rating = <u>position</u>, placing, rate, order, class, degree, rank, status

ratio = <u>proportion</u>, rate, relation, percentage, fraction

ration NOUN = <u>allowance</u>, quota, allotment, helping, part, share, measure, portion

● VERB = <u>limit</u>, control, restrict, budget

rational = <u>sensible</u>, sound, wise, reasonable, intelligent, realistic, logical, sane ≠ insane

rationale = <u>reason</u>, grounds, theory, principle, philosophy, logic, motivation, raison d'être (*French*)

rattle 1 = <u>clatter</u>, bang, jangle 2 = <u>shake</u>, jolt, vibrate, bounce, jar 3 (*Informal*) = <u>fluster</u>, shake, upset, disturb, disconcert, perturb, faze

ravage VERB = <u>destroy</u>, ruin, devastate, spoil, demolish, ransack, lay waste, despoil

● PLURAL NOUN = <u>damage</u>, destruction, devastation, ruin, havoc, ruination, spoliation

rave 1 = <u>rant</u>, rage, roar, go mad (*informal*), babble, be delirious 2 (*Informal*) = <u>enthuse</u>, praise, gush, be mad about (*informal*), be wild about (*informal*)

raving = <u>mad</u>, wild, crazy, hysterical, insane, irrational, crazed, delirious, berko (*Austral. slang*), off the air (*Austral. slang*)

raw 1 = <u>unrefined</u>, natural, crude, unprocessed, basic, rough, coarse, unfinished ≠ refined 2 = <u>uncooked</u>, natural, fresh ≠ cooked 3 = <u>inexperienced</u>, new, green, immature, callow ≠ experienced 4 = <u>chilly</u>, biting, cold, freezing, bitter, piercing, parky (*Brit. informal*)

ray = <u>beam</u>, bar, flash, shaft, gleam

re = <u>concerning</u>, about, regarding, with regard to, with reference to, apropos

reach VERB 1 = <u>arrive at</u>, get to, make, attain 2 = <u>attain</u>, get to 3 = <u>touch</u>, grasp, extend to, stretch to, contact 4 = <u>contact</u>, get in touch with, get through to, communicate with, get hold of

● NOUN 1 = <u>grasp</u>, range, distance, stretch, capacity, extent, extension, scope 2 = <u>jurisdiction</u>, power, influence

react = <u>respond</u>, act, proceed, behave

reaction 1 = <u>response</u>, answer, reply 2 = <u>counteraction</u>, backlash, recoil 3 = <u>conservatism</u>, the right

reactionary ADJECTIVE = <u>conservative</u>,

right-wing
● NOUN = <u>conservative</u>, die-hard, right-winger ≠ radical

read 1 = <u>scan</u>, study, look at, pore over, peruse 2 = <u>understand</u>, interpret, comprehend, construe, decipher, see, discover 3 = <u>register</u>, show, record, display, indicate

readily 1 = <u>willingly</u>, freely, quickly, gladly, eagerly ≠ reluctantly 2 = <u>promptly</u>, quickly, easily, smoothly, effortlessly, speedily, unhesitatingly ≠ with difficulty

readiness 1 = <u>willingness</u>, eagerness, keenness 2 = <u>promptness</u>, facility, ease, dexterity, adroitness

reading 1 = <u>perusal</u>, study, examination, inspection, scrutiny 2 = <u>learning</u>, education, knowledge, scholarship, erudition 3 = <u>recital</u>, performance, lesson, sermon 4 = <u>interpretation</u>, version, impression, grasp

ready 1 = <u>prepared</u>, set, primed, organized ≠ unprepared 2 = <u>completed</u>, arranged 3 = <u>mature</u>, ripe, mellow, ripened, seasoned 4 = <u>willing</u>, happy, glad, disposed, keen, eager, inclined, prone ≠ reluctant 5 = <u>prompt</u>, smart, quick, bright, sharp, keen, alert, clever ≠ slow 6 = <u>available</u>, handy, present, near, accessible, convenient ≠ unavailable

real 1 = <u>true</u>, genuine, sincere, factual, dinkum (*Austral. & N.Z. informal*), unfeigned 2 = <u>genuine</u>, authentic, dinkum (*Austral. & N.Z. informal*) ≠ fake 3 = <u>proper</u>, true, valid 4 = <u>true</u>, actual 5 = <u>typical</u>, true, genuine, sincere, dinkum (*Austral. & N.Z. informal*), unfeigned 6 = <u>complete</u>, total, perfect, utter, thorough

realistic 1 = <u>practical</u>, real, sensible, common-sense, down-to-earth, matter-of-fact, level-headed ≠ impractical 2 = <u>attainable</u>, sensible 3 = <u>lifelike</u>, true to life, authentic, true, natural, genuine, faithful

reality 1 = <u>fact</u>, truth, realism, validity, verity, actuality 2 = <u>truth</u>, fact, actuality

realization 1 = <u>awareness</u>, understanding, recognition, perception, grasp, conception, comprehension, cognizance 2 = <u>achievement</u>, accomplishment, fulfilment

realize 1 = <u>become aware of</u>, understand, take in, grasp, comprehend, get the message 2 = <u>fulfil</u>, achieve, accomplish,

make real 3 = <u>achieve</u>, do, effect, complete, perform, fulfil, accomplish, carry out *or* through

really 1 = <u>certainly</u>, genuinely, positively, surely 2 = <u>truly</u>, actually, in fact, indeed, in actuality

realm 1 = <u>field</u>, world, area, province, sphere, department, branch, territory 2 = <u>kingdom</u>, country, empire, land, domain, dominion

reap 1 = <u>get</u>, gain, obtain, acquire, derive 2 = <u>collect</u>, gather, bring in, harvest, garner, cut

rear[1] NOUN 1 = <u>back part</u>, back ≠ front 2 = <u>back</u>, end, tail, rearguard, tail end
● ADJECTIVE = <u>back</u>, hind, last, following ≠ front

rear[2] 1 = <u>bring up</u>, raise, educate, train, foster, nurture 2 = <u>breed</u>, keep 3 = <u>rise</u>, tower, soar, loom

reason NOUN 1 = <u>cause</u>, grounds, purpose, motive, goal, aim, object, intention 2 = <u>sense</u>, mind, understanding, judgment, logic, intellect, sanity, rationality ≠ emotion
● VERB = <u>deduce</u>, conclude, work out, make out, infer, think
● PHRASES **reason with someone** = <u>persuade</u>, bring round, urge, win over, prevail upon (*informal*), talk into *or* out of

reasonable 1 = <u>sensible</u>, sound, practical, wise, logical, sober, plausible, sane ≠ irrational 2 = <u>fair</u>, just, right, moderate, equitable, tenable ≠ unfair 3 = <u>within reason</u>, fit, proper ≠ impossible 4 = <u>low</u>, cheap, competitive, moderate, modest, inexpensive 5 = <u>average</u>, fair, moderate, modest, O.K. *or* okay (*informal*)

reassure = <u>encourage</u>, comfort, hearten, gee up, restore confidence to, put *or* set your mind at rest

rebate = <u>refund</u>, discount, reduction, bonus, allowance, deduction

rebel NOUN 1 = <u>revolutionary</u>, insurgent, secessionist, revolutionist 2 = <u>nonconformist</u>, dissenter, heretic, apostate, schismatic
● VERB 1 = <u>revolt</u>, resist, rise up, mutiny 2 = <u>defy</u>, dissent, disobey
● ADJECTIVE = <u>rebellious</u>, revolutionary, insurgent, insurrectionary

rebellion 1 = <u>resistance</u>, rising, revolution, revolt, uprising, mutiny 2 = <u>nonconformity</u>, defiance, heresy, schism

rebellious 1 = <u>defiant</u>, difficult, resistant, unmanageable, refractory ≠ obedient
2 = <u>revolutionary</u>, rebel, disorderly, unruly, insurgent, disloyal, seditious, mutinous ≠ obedient

rebound 1 = <u>bounce</u>, ricochet, recoil
2 = <u>misfire</u>, backfire, recoil, boomerang

rebuff VERB = <u>reject</u>, refuse, turn down, cut, slight, snub, spurn, knock back (*slang*) ≠ encourage
● NOUN = <u>rejection</u>, snub, knock-back, slight, refusal, repulse, cold shoulder, slap in the face (*informal*) ≠ encouragement

rebuke VERB = <u>scold</u>, censure, reprimand, castigate, chide, dress down (*informal*), admonish, tell off (*informal*) ≠ praise
● NOUN = <u>scolding</u>, censure, reprimand, row, dressing down (*informal*), telling-off (*informal*), admonition ≠ praise

recall VERB 1 = <u>recollect</u>, remember, evoke, call to mind 2 = <u>call back</u> 3 = annul, withdraw, cancel, repeal, revoke, retract, countermand
● NOUN 1 = <u>recollection</u>, memory, remembrance 2 = <u>annulment</u>, withdrawal, repeal, cancellation, retraction, rescindment

recede = <u>fall back</u>, withdraw, retreat, return, retire, regress

receipt 1 = <u>sales slip</u>, proof of purchase, counterfoil 2 = <u>receiving</u>, delivery, reception, acceptance

receive 1 = <u>get</u>, accept, be given, pick up, collect, obtain, acquire, take
2 = <u>experience</u>, suffer, bear, encounter, sustain, undergo 3 = <u>greet</u>, meet, admit, welcome, entertain, accommodate

recent = <u>new</u>, modern, up-to-date, late, current, fresh, novel, present-day ≠ old

recently = <u>not long ago</u>, newly, lately, currently, freshly, of late, latterly

reception 1 = <u>party</u>, gathering, get-together, social gathering, function, celebration, festivity, soirée 2 = <u>response</u>, reaction, acknowledgment, treatment, welcome, greeting

recess 1 = <u>break</u>, rest, holiday, interval, vacation, respite, intermission 2 = <u>alcove</u>, corner, bay, hollow, niche, nook

recession = <u>depression</u>, drop, decline, slump ≠ boom

recipe = <u>directions</u>, instructions, ingredients

recital 1 = <u>performance</u>, rendering, rehearsal, reading 2 = <u>account</u>, telling, statement, relation, narrative
3 = <u>recitation</u>

recite = <u>perform</u>, deliver, repeat, declaim

reckless = <u>careless</u>, wild, rash, precipitate, hasty, mindless, headlong, thoughtless ≠ cautious

reckon 1 (*Informal*) = <u>think</u>, believe, suppose, imagine, assume, guess (*informal, chiefly U.S. & Canad.*)
2 = <u>consider</u>, rate, account, judge, regard, count, esteem, deem 3 = <u>count</u>, figure, total, calculate, compute, add up, tally, number

reckoning = <u>count</u>, estimate, calculation, addition

reclaim 1 = <u>retrieve</u>, regain 2 = <u>regain</u>, salvage, recapture

recognition 1 = <u>identification</u>, recollection, discovery, remembrance
2 = <u>acceptance</u>, admission, allowance, confession

recognize 1 = <u>identify</u>, know, place, remember, spot, notice, recall, recollect
2 = <u>acknowledge</u>, allow, accept, admit, grant, concede ≠ ignore 3 = <u>appreciate</u>, respect, notice

recollection = <u>memory</u>, recall, impression, remembrance, reminiscence

recommend 1 = <u>advocate</u>, suggest, propose, approve, endorse, commend ≠ disapprove of 2 = <u>put forward</u>, approve, endorse, commend, praise 3 = <u>advise</u>, suggest, advance, propose, counsel, advocate, prescribe, put forward

recommendation 1 = <u>advice</u>, proposal, suggestion, counsel 2 = <u>commendation</u>, reference, praise, sanction, approval, endorsement, advocacy, testimonial

reconcile 1 = <u>resolve</u>, settle, square, adjust, compose, rectify, put to rights
2 = <u>reunite</u>, bring back together, conciliate
3 = <u>make peace between</u>, reunite, propitiate

reconciliation = <u>reunion</u>, conciliation, pacification, reconcilement ≠ separation

reconsider = <u>rethink</u>, review, revise, think again, reassess

reconstruct 1 = <u>rebuild</u>, restore, recreate, remake, renovate, remodel, regenerate
2 = <u>build up a picture of</u>, build up, piece together, deduce

record NOUN 1 = <u>document</u>, file, register, log, report, account, entry, journal

2 = evidence, trace, documentation, testimony, witness **3** = disc, single, album, LP, vinyl **4** = background, history, performance, career

● **VERB 1** = set down, minute, note, enter, document, register, log, chronicle **2** = make a recording of, video, tape, video-tape, tape-record **3** = register, show, indicate, give evidence of

recorder = chronicler, archivist, historian, clerk, scribe, diarist

recording = record, video, tape, disc

recount = tell, report, describe, relate, repeat, depict, recite, narrate

recover 1 = get better, improve, get well, recuperate, heal, revive, mend, convalesce ≠ relapse **2** = rally **3** = save, rescue, retrieve, salvage, reclaim ≠ abandon **4** = recoup, restore, get back, regain, retrieve, reclaim, redeem, recapture ≠ lose

recovery 1 = improvement, healing, revival, mending, recuperation, convalescence **2** = retrieval, repossession, reclamation, restoration

recreation = leisure, play, sport, fun, entertainment, relaxation, enjoyment, amusement

recruit VERB 1 = gather, obtain, engage, procure **2** = assemble, raise, levy, muster, mobilize **3** = enlist, draft, enrol ≠ dismiss

● **NOUN** = beginner, trainee, apprentice, novice, convert, initiate, helper, learner

recur = happen again, return, repeat, persist, revert, reappear, come again

recycle = reprocess, reuse, salvage, reclaim, save

red NOUN or **ADJECTIVE 1** = crimson, scarlet, ruby, vermilion, cherry, coral, carmine **2** = flushed, embarrassed, blushing, florid, shamefaced **3** (of hair) = chestnut, reddish, flame-coloured, sandy, Titian, carroty

● **PHRASES** in the red (Informal) = in debt, insolvent, in arrears, overdrawn ◆ see red (Informal) = lose your temper, lose it (informal), go mad (informal), crack up (informal), lose the plot (informal), go ballistic (slang, chiefly U.S.), fly off the handle (informal), blow your top

redeem 1 = reinstate, absolve, restore to favour **2** = make up for, compensate for, atone for, make amends for **3** = buy back, recover, regain, retrieve, reclaim, repurchase **4** = save, free, deliver, liberate, ransom, emancipate

redemption 1 = compensation, amends, reparation, atonement **2** = salvation, release, rescue, liberation, emancipation, deliverance

redress VERB 1 = make amends for, make up for, compensate for **2** = put right, balance, correct, adjust, regulate, rectify, even up

● **NOUN** = amends, payment, compensation, reparation, atonement, recompense

reduce 1 = lessen, cut, lower, moderate, weaken, diminish, decrease, cut down ≠ increase **2** = degrade, downgrade, break, humble, bring low ≠ promote

redundancy 1 = layoff, sacking, dismissal **2** = unemployment, the sack (informal), the axe (informal), joblessness

redundant = superfluous, extra, surplus, unnecessary, unwanted, inessential, supernumerary ≠ essential

reel 1 = stagger, rock, roll, pitch, sway, lurch **2** = whirl, spin, revolve, swirl

refer VERB = direct, point, send, guide

● **PHRASES** refer to something or someone **1** = allude to, mention, cite, speak of, bring up **2** = relate to, concern, apply to, pertain to, be relevant to **3** = consult, go, apply, turn to, look up

referee NOUN = umpire, judge, ref (informal), arbiter, arbitrator, adjudicator

● **VERB** = umpire, judge, mediate, adjudicate, arbitrate

reference 1 = allusion, note, mention, quotation **2** = citation **3** = testimonial, recommendation, credentials, endorsement, character reference

referendum = public vote, popular vote, plebiscite

refine 1 = purify, process, filter, cleanse, clarify, distil **2** = improve, perfect, polish, hone

refined 1 = purified, processed, pure, filtered, clean, clarified, distilled ≠ unrefined **2** = cultured, polished, elegant, polite, cultivated, civilized, well-bred ≠ coarse **3** = discerning, fine, sensitive, delicate, precise, discriminating, fastidious

reflect 1 = show, reveal, display, indicate, demonstrate, manifest **2** = throw back, return, mirror, echo, reproduce **3** = consider, think, muse, ponder, meditate, ruminate, cogitate, wonder

reflection 1 = <u>image</u>, echo, mirror image
2 = <u>consideration</u>, thinking, thought, idea, opinion, observation, musing, meditation

reflective = <u>thoughtful</u>, contemplative, meditative, pensive

reform NOUN = <u>improvement</u>, amendment, rehabilitation, betterment
● VERB 1 = <u>improve</u>, correct, restore, amend, mend, rectify 2 = <u>mend your ways</u>, go straight (*informal*), shape up (*informal*), turn over a new leaf, clean up your act (*informal*), pull your socks up (*Brit. informal*)

refrain[1] = <u>stop</u>, avoid, cease, renounce, abstain, leave off, desist, forbear

refrain[2] = <u>chorus</u>, tune, melody

refresh 1 = <u>revive</u>, freshen, revitalize, stimulate, brace, enliven, invigorate
2 = <u>stimulate</u>, prompt, renew, jog

refreshing 1 = <u>new</u>, original, novel
2 = <u>stimulating</u>, fresh, bracing, invigorating ≠ tiring

refreshment = <u>food and drink</u>, drinks, snacks, titbits, kai (*N.Z. informal*)

refuge 1 = <u>protection</u>, shelter, asylum
2 = <u>haven</u>, retreat, sanctuary, hide-out

refugee = <u>exile</u>, émigré, displaced person, escapee

refund NOUN = <u>repayment</u>, reimbursement, return
● VERB = <u>repay</u>, return, restore, pay back, reimburse

refurbish = <u>renovate</u>, restore, repair, clean up, overhaul, revamp, mend, do up (*informal*)

refusal = <u>rejection</u>, denial, rebuff, knock-back (*slang*)

refuse[1] 1 = <u>decline</u>, reject, turn down, say no to 2 = <u>deny</u>, decline, withhold ≠ allow

refuse[2] = <u>rubbish</u>, waste, junk (*informal*), litter, garbage, trash

regain 1 = <u>recover</u>, get back, retrieve, recapture, win back, take back, recoup
2 = <u>get back to</u>, return to, reach again

regal = <u>royal</u>, majestic, kingly or queenly, noble, princely, magnificent

regard VERB 1 = <u>consider</u>, see, rate, view, judge, think of, esteem, deem 2 = <u>look at</u>, view, eye, watch, observe, clock (*Brit. slang*), check out (*informal*), gaze at
● NOUN 1 = <u>respect</u>, esteem, thought, concern, care, consideration 2 = <u>look</u>, gaze, scrutiny, stare, glance

● PLURAL NOUN = <u>good wishes</u>, respects, greetings, compliments, best wishes
● PHRASES as regards = <u>concerning</u>, regarding, relating to, pertaining to

regarding = <u>concerning</u>, about, on the subject of, re, respecting, as regards, with reference to, in or with regard to

regardless 1 = <u>in spite of everything</u>, anyway, nevertheless, in any case 2 *with of* = <u>irrespective of</u>, heedless of, unmindful of

regime 1 = <u>government</u>, rule, management, leadership, reign 2 = <u>plan</u>, course, system, policy, programme, scheme, regimen

region = <u>area</u>, place, part, quarter, section, sector, district, territory

regional = <u>local</u>, district, provincial, parochial, zonal

register NOUN = <u>list</u>, record, roll, file, diary, catalogue, log, archives
● VERB 1 = <u>enrol</u>, enlist, list, note, enter 2 = <u>record</u>, catalogue, chronicle
3 = <u>indicate</u>, show 4 = <u>show</u>, mark, indicate, manifest 5 = <u>express</u>, show, reveal, display, exhibit

regret VERB 1 = <u>be or feel sorry about</u>, rue, deplore, bemoan, repent (of), bewail ≠ be satisfied with 2 = <u>mourn</u>, miss, grieve for or over
● NOUN 1 = <u>remorse</u>, compunction, bitterness, repentance, contrition, penitence 2 = <u>sorrow</u> ≠ satisfaction

regular 1 = <u>frequent</u> ≠ normal, common, usual, ordinary, typical, routine, customary, habitual ≠ infrequent
3 = <u>steady</u>, consistent 4 = <u>even</u>, level, balanced, straight, flat, fixed, smooth, uniform ≠ uneven

regulate 1 = <u>control</u>, run, rule, manage, direct, guide, handle, govern
2 = <u>moderate</u>, control, modulate, fit, tune, adjust

regulation 1 = <u>rule</u>, order, law, dictate, decree, statute, edict, precept 2 = <u>control</u>, government, management, direction, supervision

rehearsal = <u>practice</u>, rehearsing, run-through, preparation, drill

rehearse = <u>practise</u>, prepare, run through, go over, train, repeat, drill, recite

reign VERB 1 = <u>be supreme</u>, prevail, predominate, hold sway 2 = <u>rule</u>, govern, be in power, influence, command

● NOUN = rule, power, control, command, monarchy, dominion

rein = control, harness, bridle, hold, check, brake, curb, restraint

reincarnation = rebirth, transmigration of souls

reinforce 1 = support, strengthen, fortify, toughen, stress, prop, supplement, emphasize 2 = increase, extend, add to, strengthen, supplement

reinforcement NOUN 1 = strengthening, increase, fortification, augmentation 2 = support, stay, prop, brace, buttress
● PLURAL NOUN = reserves, support, auxiliaries, additional or fresh troops

reinstate = restore, recall, re-establish, return

reiterate (Formal) = repeat, restate, say again, do again

reject VERB 1 = rebuff, jilt, turn down, spurn, refuse, say no to, repulse ≠ accept 2 = deny, exclude, veto, relinquish, renounce, disallow, forsake, disown ≠ approve 3 = discard, decline, eliminate, scrap, jettison, throw away or out ≠ accept
● NOUN 1 = castoff, second, discard ≠ treasure 2 = failure, loser, flop

rejection 1 = denial, veto, dismissal, exclusion, disowning, thumbs down, renunciation, repudiation ≠ approval 2 = rebuff, refusal, knock-back (slang), kick in the teeth (slang), brushoff (slang) ≠ acceptance

rejoice = be glad, celebrate, be happy, glory, be overjoyed, exult ≠ lament

rejoin = reply, answer, respond, retort, riposte

relate VERB = tell, recount, report, detail, describe, recite, narrate
● PHRASES **relate to something or someone** 1 = concern, refer to, apply to, have to do with, pertain to, be relevant to 2 = connect with, associate with, link with, couple with, join with, correlate to

related 1 = associated, linked, joint, connected, affiliated, akin, interconnected ≠ unconnected 2 = akin, kindred ≠ unrelated

relation NOUN 1 = similarity, link, bearing, bond, comparison, correlation, connection 2 = relative, kin, kinsman or kinswoman
● PLURAL NOUN 1 = dealings, relationship, affairs, contact, connections, interaction, intercourse 2 = family, relatives, tribe, clan, kin, kindred, kinsmen, kinsfolk, ainga (N.Z.)

relationship 1 = association, bond, connection, affinity, rapport, kinship 2 = affair, romance, liaison, amour, intrigue 3 = connection, link, parallel, similarity, tie-up, correlation

relative NOUN = relation, kinsman or kinswoman, member of your or the family
● ADJECTIVE 1 = comparative 2 = corresponding 3 with **to** = in proportion to, proportionate to

relatively = comparatively, rather, somewhat

relax 1 = be or feel at ease, chill out (slang, chiefly U.S.), take it easy, lighten up (slang), outspan (S. African) ≠ be alarmed 2 = calm down, calm, unwind 3 = make less tense, rest 4 = lessen, reduce, ease, relieve, weaken, loosen, let up, slacken ≠ tighten 5 = moderate, ease, relieve, weaken, slacken ≠ tighten up

relaxation = leisure, rest, fun, pleasure, recreation, enjoyment

relay = broadcast, carry, spread, communicate, transmit, send out

release VERB 1 = set free, free, discharge, liberate, drop, loose, undo, extricate ≠ imprison 2 = acquit, let go, let off, exonerate, absolve 3 = issue, publish, make public, make known, launch, distribute, put out, circulate ≠ withhold
● NOUN 1 = liberation, freedom, liberty, discharge, emancipation, deliverance ≠ imprisonment 2 = acquittal, exemption, absolution, exoneration 3 = issue, publication, proclamation

relegate = demote, degrade, downgrade

relentless 1 = merciless, fierce, cruel, ruthless, unrelenting, implacable, remorseless, pitiless ≠ merciful 2 = unremitting, persistent, unrelenting, incessant, nonstop, unrelieved

relevant = significant, appropriate, related, fitting, to the point, apt, pertinent, apposite ≠ irrelevant

reliable 1 = dependable, trustworthy, sure, sound, true, faithful, staunch ≠ unreliable 2 = safe, dependable 3 = definitive, sound, dependable, trustworthy

reliance 1 = dependency, dependence 2 = trust, confidence, belief, faith

relic = remnant, vestige, memento, trace, fragment, souvenir, keepsake

relief 1 = ease, release, comfort, cure, remedy, solace, deliverance, mitigation 2 = rest, respite, relaxation, break, breather (*informal*) 3 = aid, help, support, assistance, succour

relieve 1 = ease, soothe, alleviate, relax, comfort, calm, cure, soften ≠ intensify 2 = help, support, aid, sustain, assist, succour

religion = belief, faith, theology, creed

religious 1 = spiritual, holy, sacred, devotional 2 = conscientious, faithful, rigid, meticulous, scrupulous, punctilious

relinquish (*Formal*) = give up, leave, drop, abandon, surrender, let go, renounce, forsake

relish VERB 1 = enjoy, like, savour, revel in ≠ dislike 2 = look forward to, fancy, delight in
● NOUN 1 = enjoyment, liking, love, taste, fancy, penchant, fondness, gusto ≠ distaste 2 = condiment, seasoning, sauce

reluctance = unwillingness, dislike, loathing, distaste, aversion, disinclination, repugnance

reluctant = unwilling, hesitant, loath, disinclined, unenthusiastic ≠ willing

rely on 1 = depend on, lean on 2 = be confident of, bank on, trust, count on, bet on

remain 1 = stay, continue, go on, stand, dwell 2 = stay behind, wait, delay ≠ go 3 = continue, be left, linger

remainder = rest, remains, balance, excess, surplus, remnant, residue, leavings

remains 1 = remnants, leftovers, rest, debris, residue, dregs, leavings 2 = corpse, body, carcass, cadaver 3 = relics

remark VERB 1 = comment, say, state, reflect, mention, declare, observe, pass comment 2 = notice, note, observe, perceive, see, mark, make out, espy
● NOUN = comment, observation, reflection, statement, utterance

remarkable = extraordinary, striking, outstanding, wonderful, rare, unusual, surprising, notable ≠ ordinary

remedy NOUN = cure, treatment, medicine, nostrum
● VERB = put right, rectify, fix, correct, set to rights

remember 1 = recall, think back to, recollect, reminisce about, call to mind ≠ forget 2 = bear in mind, keep in mind 3 = look back (on), commemorate

remembrance 1 = commemoration, memorial 2 = souvenir, token, reminder, monument, memento, keepsake 3 = memory, recollection, thought, recall, reminiscence

remind = jog your memory, prompt, make you remember

reminiscent = suggestive, evocative, similar

remnant = remainder, remains, trace, fragment, end, rest, residue, leftovers

remorse = regret, shame, guilt, grief, sorrow, anguish, repentance, contrition

remote 1 = distant, far, isolated, out-of-the-way, secluded, inaccessible, in the middle of nowhere ≠ nearby 2 = far, distant 3 = slight, small, outside, unlikely, slim, faint, doubtful, dubious ≠ strong 4 = aloof, cold, reserved, withdrawn, distant, abstracted, detached, uncommunicative ≠ outgoing

removal 1 = extraction, withdrawal, uprooting, eradication, dislodgment, taking away or off or out 2 = dismissal, expulsion, elimination, ejection 3 = move, transfer, departure, relocation, flitting (*Scot. & Northern English dialect*)

remove 1 = take out, withdraw, extract ≠ insert 2 = take off ≠ put on 3 = erase, eliminate, take out 4 = dismiss, eliminate, get rid of, discharge, abolish, expel, throw out, oust ≠ appoint 5 = get rid of, erase, eradicate, expunge 6 = take away, detach, displace ≠ put back 7 = delete, get rid of, erase, excise 8 = move, depart, relocate, flit (*Scot. & Northern English dialect*)

renaissance or **renascence** = rebirth, revival, restoration, renewal, resurgence, reappearance, reawakening

rend (*Literary*) = tear, rip, separate, wrench, rupture

render 1 = make, cause to become, leave 2 = provide, give, pay, present, supply, submit, tender, hand out 3 = represent, portray, depict, do, give, play, act, perform

renew 1 = recommence, continue, extend, repeat, resume, reopen, recreate, reaffirm 2 = reaffirm, resume, recommence 3 = replace, refresh, replenish, restock 4 = restore, repair, overhaul, mend, refurbish, renovate, refit, modernize

renounce 1 = disown, quit, forsake,

recant, forswear, abjure 2 = <u>disclaim</u>, deny, give up, relinquish, waive, abjure ≠ assert

renovate = <u>restore</u>, repair, refurbish, do up (*informal*), renew, overhaul, refit, modernize

renowned = <u>famous</u>, noted, celebrated, well-known, distinguished, esteemed, notable, eminent ≠ unknown

rent[1] VERB 1 = <u>hire</u>, lease 2 = <u>let</u>, lease
● NOUN = <u>hire</u>, rental, lease, fee, payment

rent[2] 1 = <u>tear</u>, split, rip, slash, slit, gash, hole 2 = <u>opening</u>, hole

repair VERB 1 = <u>mend</u>, fix, restore, heal, patch, renovate, patch up ≠ damage 2 = <u>put right</u>, make up for, compensate for, rectify, redress
● NOUN 1 = <u>mend</u>, restoration, overhaul 2 = <u>darn</u>, mend, patch 3 = <u>condition</u>, state, form, shape (*informal*)

repay = <u>pay back</u>, refund, settle up, return, square, compensate, reimburse, recompense

repeal VERB = <u>abolish</u>, reverse, revoke, annul, recall, cancel, invalidate, nullify ≠ pass
● NOUN = <u>abolition</u>, cancellation, annulment, invalidation, rescindment ≠ passing

repeat VERB 1 = <u>reiterate</u>, restate 2 = <u>retell</u>, echo, replay, reproduce, rerun, reshow
● NOUN 1 = <u>repetition</u>, echo, reiteration 2 = <u>rerun</u>, replay, reshowing

repeatedly = <u>over and over</u>, often, frequently, many times

repel 1 = <u>drive off</u>, fight, resist, parry, hold off, rebuff, ward off, repulse ≠ submit to 2 = <u>disgust</u>, offend, revolt, sicken, nauseate, gross out (*U.S. slang*) ≠ delight

repertoire = <u>range</u>, list, stock, supply, store, collection, repertory

repetition 1 = <u>recurrence</u>, repeating, echo 2 = <u>repeating</u>, replication, restatement, reiteration, tautology

replace 1 = <u>take the place of</u>, follow, succeed, oust, take over from, supersede, supplant 2 = <u>substitute</u>, change, exchange, switch, swap 3 = <u>put back</u>, restore

replacement 1 = <u>replacing</u> 2 = <u>successor</u>, double, substitute, stand-in, proxy, surrogate, understudy

replica 1 = <u>reproduction</u>, model, copy, imitation, facsimile, carbon copy ≠ original 2 = <u>duplicate</u>, copy, carbon copy

replicate = <u>copy</u>, reproduce, recreate, mimic, duplicate, reduplicate

reply VERB = <u>answer</u>, respond, retort, counter, rejoin, retaliate, reciprocate
● NOUN = <u>answer</u>, response, reaction, counter, retort, retaliation, counterattack, rejoinder

report VERB 1 = <u>inform of</u>, communicate, recount 2 *often with* **on** = <u>communicate</u>, tell, state, detail, describe, relate, broadcast, pass on 3 = <u>present yourself</u>, come, appear, arrive, turn up
● NOUN 1 = <u>article</u>, story, piece, write-up 2 = <u>account</u>, record, statement, communication, description, narrative 3 *often plural* = <u>news</u>, word 4 = <u>bang</u>, sound, crack, noise, blast, boom, explosion, discharge 5 = <u>rumour</u>, talk, buzz, gossip, hearsay

reporter = <u>journalist</u>, writer, correspondent, hack (*derogatory*), pressman, journo (*slang*)

represent 1 = <u>act for</u>, speak for 2 = <u>stand for</u>, serve as 3 = <u>express</u>, correspond to, symbolize, mean 4 = <u>exemplify</u>, embody, symbolize, typify, personify, epitomize 5 = <u>depict</u>, show, describe, picture, illustrate, outline, portray, denote

representation 1 = <u>picture</u>, model, image, portrait, illustration, likeness 2 = <u>portrayal</u>, depiction, account, description

representative NOUN 1 = <u>delegate</u>, member, agent, deputy, proxy, spokesman *or* spokeswoman 2 = <u>agent</u>, salesman, rep, commercial traveller
● ADJECTIVE 1 = <u>typical</u>, characteristic, archetypal, exemplary ≠ uncharacteristic 2 = <u>symbolic</u>

repress 1 = <u>control</u>, suppress, hold back, bottle up, check, curb, restrain, inhibit ≠ release 2 = <u>hold back</u>, suppress, stifle 3 = <u>subdue</u>, abuse, wrong, persecute, quell, subjugate, maltreat ≠ liberate

repression 1 = <u>subjugation</u>, control, constraint, domination, tyranny, despotism 2 = <u>suppression</u>, crushing, quashing 3 = <u>inhibition</u>, control, restraint, bottling up

reprieve VERB = <u>grant a stay of execution to</u>, pardon, let off the hook (*slang*)
● NOUN = <u>stay of execution</u>, amnesty, pardon, remission, deferment, postponement of punishment

reproduce 1 = copy, recreate, replicate, duplicate, match, mirror, echo, imitate 2 = print, copy 3 (*Biology*) = breed, procreate, multiply, spawn, propagate

reproduction 1 = copy, picture, print, replica, imitation, duplicate, facsimile ≠ original 2 (*Biology*) = breeding, increase, generation, multiplication

Republican ADJECTIVE = right-wing, Conservative

● NOUN = right-winger, Conservative

reputation = name, standing, character, esteem, stature, renown, repute

request VERB 1 = ask for, appeal for, put in for, demand, desire 2 = invite, entreat 3 = seek, ask (for), solicit

● NOUN 1 = appeal, call, demand, plea, desire, entreaty, suit 2 = asking, plea

require 1 = need, crave, want, miss, lack, wish, desire 2 = order, demand, command, compel, exact, oblige, call upon, insist upon 3 = ask

requirement = necessity, demand, stipulation, want, need, must, essential, prerequisite

rescue VERB 1 = save, get out, release, deliver, recover, liberate ≠ desert 2 = salvage, deliver, redeem

● NOUN = saving, salvage, deliverance, release, recovery, liberation, salvation, redemption

research NOUN = investigation, study, analysis, examination, probe, exploration

● VERB = investigate, study, examine, explore, probe, analyse

resemblance = similarity, correspondence, parallel, likeness, kinship, sameness, similitude ≠ dissimilarity

resemble = be like, look like, mirror, parallel, be similar to, bear a resemblance to

resent = be bitter about, object to, grudge, begrudge, take exception to, take offence at ≠ be content with

resentment = bitterness, indignation, ill feeling, ill will, grudge, animosity, pique, rancour

reservation 1 *often plural* = doubt, scruples, hesitancy 2 = reserve, territory, preserve, sanctuary

reserve VERB 1 = book, prearrange, engage 2 = put by, secure 3 = keep, hold, save, store, retain, set aside, stockpile, hoard

● NOUN 1 = store, fund, savings, stock, supply, reservoir, hoard, cache 2 = park, reservation, preserve, sanctuary, tract, forest park (*N.Z.*) 3 = shyness, silence, restraint, constraint, reticence, secretiveness, taciturnity 4 = reservation, doubt, delay, uncertainty, indecision, hesitancy, vacillation, irresolution

● ADJECTIVE = substitute, extra, spare, secondary, fall-back, auxiliary

reserved 1 = uncommunicative, retiring, silent, shy, restrained, secretive, reticent, taciturn ≠ uninhibited 2 = set aside, taken, kept, held, booked, retained, engaged, restricted

reservoir 1 = lake, pond, basin 2 = store, stock, source, supply, reserves, pool

reside (*Formal*) = live, lodge, dwell, stay, abide ≠ visit

residence = home, house, dwelling, place, flat, lodging, abode, habitation

resident 1 = inhabitant, citizen, local ≠ nonresident 2 = tenant, occupant, lodger 3 = guest, lodger

residue = remainder, remains, remnant, leftovers, rest, extra, excess, surplus

resign VERB 1 = quit, leave, step down (*informal*), vacate, abdicate, give *or* hand in your notice 2 = give up, abandon, yield, surrender, relinquish, renounce, forsake, forgo

● PHRASES **resign yourself to something** = accept, succumb to, submit to, give in to, yield to, acquiesce to

resignation 1 = leaving, departure, abandonment, abdication 2 = acceptance, patience, submission, compliance, endurance, passivity, acquiescence, sufferance ≠ resistance

resigned = stoical, patient, subdued, long-suffering, compliant, unresisting

resist 1 = oppose, battle against, combat, defy, stand up to, hinder ≠ accept 2 = refrain from, avoid, keep from, forgo, abstain from, forbear ≠ indulge in 3 = withstand, be proof against

resistance 1 = opposition, hostility, aversion 2 = fighting, fight, battle, struggle, defiance, obstruction, impediment, hindrance

resistant 1 = opposed, hostile, unwilling, intractable, antagonistic, intransigent 2 = impervious, hard, strong, tough, unaffected

resolution 1 = <u>declaration</u> 2 = <u>decision</u>, resolve, intention, aim, purpose, determination, intent 3 = <u>determination</u>, purpose, resolve, tenacity, perseverance, willpower, firmness, steadfastness

resolve VERB 1 = <u>work out</u>, answer, clear up, crack, fathom 2 = <u>decide</u>, determine, agree, purpose, intend, fix, conclude
● NOUN 1 = <u>determination</u>, resolution, willpower, firmness, steadfastness, resoluteness ≠ indecision 2 = <u>decision</u>, resolution, objective, purpose, intention

resort 1 = <u>holiday centre</u>, spot, retreat, haunt, tourist centre 2 = <u>recourse to</u>, reference to

resound 1 = <u>echo</u>, resonate, reverberate, re-echo 2 = <u>ring</u>

resounding = <u>echoing</u>, full, ringing, powerful, booming, reverberating, resonant, sonorous

resource NOUN 1 = <u>facility</u> 2 = <u>means</u>, course, resort, device, expedient
● PLURAL NOUN 1 = <u>funds</u>, holdings, money, capital, riches, assets, wealth 2 = <u>reserves</u>, supplies, stocks

respect VERB 1 = <u>think highly of</u>, value, honour, admire, esteem, look up to, defer to, have a good or high opinion of 2 = <u>show consideration for</u>, honour, observe, heed 3 = <u>abide by</u>, follow, observe, comply with, obey, heed, keep to, adhere to ≠ disregard
● NOUN 1 = <u>regard</u>, honour, recognition, esteem, admiration, estimation ≠ contempt 2 = <u>consideration</u>, kindness, deference, tact, thoughtfulness, considerateness 3 = <u>particular</u>, way, point, matter, sense, detail, feature, aspect

respectable 1 = <u>honourable</u>, good, decent, worthy, upright, honest, reputable, estimable ≠ disreputable 2 = <u>decent</u>, neat, spruce 3 = <u>reasonable</u>, considerable, substantial, fair, ample, appreciable, sizable or sizeable ≠ small

respective = <u>specific</u>, own, individual, particular, relevant

respite = <u>pause</u>, break, rest, relief, halt, interval, recess, lull

respond 1 = <u>answer</u>, return, reply, counter, retort, rejoin ≠ remain silent 2 often with **to** = <u>reply to</u>, answer 3 = <u>react</u>, retaliate, reciprocate

response = <u>answer</u>, return, reply, reaction, feedback, retort, counterattack, rejoinder

responsibility 1 = <u>duty</u>, business, job, role, task, accountability, answerability 2 = <u>fault</u>, blame, liability, guilt, culpability 3 = <u>obligation</u>, duty, liability, charge, care 4 = <u>authority</u>, power, importance, mana (N.Z.) 5 = <u>job</u>, task, function, role 6 = <u>level-headedness</u>, rationality, dependability, trustworthiness, conscientiousness, sensibleness

responsible 1 = <u>to blame</u>, guilty, at fault, culpable 2 = <u>in charge</u>, in control, in authority 3 = <u>accountable</u>, liable, answerable ≠ unaccountable 4 = <u>sensible</u>, reliable, rational, dependable, trustworthy, level-headed ≠ unreliable

responsive = <u>sensitive</u>, open, alive, susceptible, receptive, reactive, impressionable ≠ unresponsive

rest¹ VERB 1 = <u>relax</u>, take it easy, sit down, be at ease, put your feet up, outspan (S. African) ≠ work 2 = <u>stop</u>, have a break, break off, take a breather (informal), halt, cease ≠ keep going 3 = <u>place</u>, repose, sit, lean, prop 4 = <u>be placed</u>, sit, lie, be supported, recline
● NOUN 1 = <u>relaxation</u>, repose, leisure ≠ work 2 = <u>pause</u>, break, stop, halt, interval, respite, lull, interlude 3 = <u>refreshment</u>, release, relief, ease, comfort, cure, remedy, solace 4 = <u>inactivity</u> 5 = <u>support</u>, stand, base, holder, prop 6 = <u>calm</u>, tranquillity, stillness

rest² = <u>remainder</u>, remains, excess, remnants, others, balance, surplus, residue

restaurant = <u>café</u>, diner (chiefly U.S. & Canad.), bistro, cafeteria, tearoom, eatery or eaterie

restless 1 = <u>unsettled</u>, nervous, edgy, fidgeting, on edge, restive, jumpy, fidgety ≠ relaxed 2 = <u>moving</u>, wandering, unsettled, unstable, roving, transient, nomadic ≠ settled

restoration 1 = <u>reinstatement</u>, return, revival, restitution, re-establishment, replacement ≠ abolition 2 = <u>repair</u>, reconstruction, renewal, renovation, revitalization ≠ demolition

restore 1 = <u>reinstate</u>, re-establish, reintroduce ≠ abolish 2 = <u>revive</u>, build up, strengthen, refresh, revitalize ≠ make worse 3 = <u>re-establish</u>, replace, reinstate, give back 4 = <u>repair</u>, refurbish, renovate, reconstruct, fix (up), renew, rebuild, mend ≠ demolish 5 = <u>return</u>, replace, recover, bring back, send back, hand back

restrain 1 = <u>hold back</u>, control, check, contain, restrict, curb, hamper, hinder ≠ encourage **2** = <u>control</u>, inhibit

restrained 1 = <u>controlled</u>, moderate, self-controlled, calm, mild, undemonstrative ≠ hot-headed **2** = <u>unobtrusive</u>, discreet, subdued, tasteful, quiet ≠ garish

restraint 1 = <u>limitation</u>, limit, check, ban, embargo, curb, rein, interdict ≠ freedom **2** = <u>self-control</u>, self-discipline, self-restraint, self-possession ≠ self-indulgence **3** = <u>constraint</u>, limitation, inhibition, control, restriction

restrict 1 = <u>limit</u>, regulate, curb, ration ≠ widen **2** = <u>hamper</u>, handicap, restrain, inhibit

restriction 1 = <u>control</u>, rule, regulation, curb, restraint, confinement **2** = <u>limitation</u>, handicap, inhibition

result NOUN **1** = <u>consequence</u>, effect, outcome, end result, product, sequel, upshot ≠ cause **2** = <u>outcome</u>, end
● VERB = <u>arise</u>, follow, issue, happen, appear, develop, spring, derive

resume = <u>begin again</u>, continue, go on with, proceed with, carry on, reopen, restart ≠ discontinue

résumé = <u>summary</u>, synopsis, précis, rundown, recapitulation

resumption = <u>continuation</u>, carrying on, reopening, renewal, restart, resurgence, re-establishment

resurgence = <u>revival</u>, return, renaissance, resurrection, resumption, rebirth, re-emergence

resurrect 1 = <u>revive</u>, renew, bring back, reintroduce **2** = <u>restore to life</u>, raise from the dead

resurrection 1 = <u>revival</u>, restoration, renewal, resurgence, return, renaissance, rebirth, reappearance ≠ killing off **2** usually caps = <u>raising or rising from the dead</u>, return from the dead ≠ demise

retain 1 = <u>maintain</u>, reserve, preserve, keep up, continue to have **2** = <u>keep</u>, save ≠ let go

retaliate = <u>pay someone back</u>, hit back, strike back, reciprocate, take revenge, get even with (informal), get your own back (informal) ≠ turn the other cheek

retaliation = <u>revenge</u>, repayment, vengeance, reprisal, an eye for an eye, reciprocation, requital, counterblow

retard = <u>slow down</u>, check, arrest, delay, handicap, hinder, impede, set back ≠ speed up

retire 1 = <u>stop working</u>, give up work **2** = <u>withdraw</u>, leave, exit, go away, depart **3** = <u>go to bed</u>, turn in (informal), hit the sack (slang), hit the hay (slang)

retirement = <u>withdrawal</u>, retreat, privacy, solitude, seclusion

retiring = <u>shy</u>, reserved, quiet, timid, unassuming, self-effacing, bashful, unassertive ≠ outgoing

retort VERB = <u>reply</u>, return, answer, respond, counter, come back with, riposte
● NOUN = <u>reply</u>, answer, response, comeback, riposte, rejoinder

retreat VERB = <u>withdraw</u>, back off, draw back, leave, go back, depart, fall back, pull back ≠ advance
● NOUN **1** = <u>flight</u>, retirement, departure, withdrawal, evacuation ≠ advance **2** = <u>refuge</u>, haven, shelter, sanctuary, hideaway, seclusion

retrieve 1 = <u>get back</u>, regain, recover, restore, recapture **2** = <u>redeem</u>, save, win back, recoup

retrospect = <u>hindsight</u>, review, re-examination ≠ foresight

return VERB **1** = <u>come back</u>, go back, retreat, turn back, revert, reappear ≠ depart **2** = <u>put back</u>, replace, restore, reinstate ≠ keep **3** = <u>give back</u>, repay, refund, pay back, reimburse, recompense ≠ keep **4** = <u>recur</u>, repeat, persist, revert, happen again, reappear, come again **5** = <u>elect</u>, choose, vote in
● NOUN **1** = <u>reappearance</u> ≠ departure **2** = <u>restoration</u>, reinstatement, re-establishment ≠ removal **3** = <u>recurrence</u>, repetition, reappearance, reversion, persistence **4** = <u>profit</u>, interest, gain, income, revenue, yield, proceeds, takings **5** = <u>statement</u>, report, form, list, account, summary

revamp = <u>renovate</u>, restore, overhaul, refurbish, do up (informal), recondition

reveal 1 = <u>make known</u>, disclose, give away, make public, tell, announce, proclaim, let out ≠ keep secret **2** = <u>show</u>, display, exhibit, unveil, uncover, manifest, unearth, unmask ≠ hide

revel VERB = <u>celebrate</u>, carouse, live it up (informal), make merry
● NOUN often plural = <u>merrymaking</u>, party,

celebration, spree, festivity, carousal

revelation 1 = <u>disclosure</u>, news, announcement, publication, leak, confession, divulgence 2 = <u>exhibition</u>, publication, exposure, unveiling, uncovering, unearthing, proclamation

revenge NOUN = <u>retaliation</u>, vengeance, reprisal, retribution, an eye for an eye
● VERB = <u>avenge</u>, repay, take revenge for, get your own back for (*informal*)

revenue = <u>income</u>, returns, profits, gain, yield, proceeds, receipts, takings ≠ expenditure

revere = <u>be in awe of</u>, respect, honour, worship, reverence, exalt, look up to, venerate ≠ despise

reverse VERB 1 (*Law*) = <u>change</u>, cancel, overturn, overthrow, undo, repeal, quash, revoke ≠ implement 2 = <u>turn round</u>, turn over, turn upside down, upend 3 = <u>transpose</u>, change, move, exchange, transfer, switch, shift, alter 4 = <u>go backwards</u>, retreat, back up, turn back, move backwards, back ≠ go forward
● NOUN 1 = <u>opposite</u>, contrary, converse, inverse 2 = <u>misfortune</u>, blow, failure, disappointment, setback, hardship, reversal, adversity 3 = <u>back</u>, rear, other side, wrong side, underside ≠ front
● ADJECTIVE = <u>opposite</u>, contrary, converse

revert 1 = <u>go back</u>, return, come back, resume 2 = <u>return</u>

review NOUN 1 = <u>survey</u>, study, analysis, examination, scrutiny 2 = <u>critique</u>, commentary, evaluation, notice, criticism, judgment 3 = <u>inspection</u>, parade, march past 4 = <u>magazine</u>, journal, periodical, zine (*informal*)
● VERB 1 = <u>reconsider</u>, revise, rethink, reassess, re-examine, re-evaluate, think over 2 = <u>assess</u>, study, judge, evaluate, criticize 3 = <u>inspect</u>, check, survey, examine, vet 4 = <u>look back on</u>, remember, recall, reflect on, recollect

reviewer = <u>critic</u>, judge, commentator

revise 1 = <u>change</u>, review 2 = <u>edit</u>, correct, alter, update, amend, rework, redo, emend 3 = <u>study</u>, go over, run through, cram (*informal*), swot up on (*Brit. informal*)

revision 1 = <u>emendation</u>, updating, correction 2 = <u>change</u>, amendment 3 = <u>studying</u>, cramming (*informal*), swotting (*Brit. informal*), homework

revival 1 = <u>resurgence</u> ≠ decline

2 = <u>reawakening</u>, renaissance, renewal, resurrection, rebirth, revitalization

revive 1 = <u>revitalize</u>, restore, renew, rekindle, invigorate, reanimate 2 = <u>bring round</u>, awaken 3 = <u>come round</u>, recover 4 = <u>refresh</u> ≠ exhaust

revolt NOUN = <u>uprising</u>, rising, revolution, rebellion, mutiny, insurrection, insurgency
● VERB 1 = <u>rebel</u>, rise up, resist, mutiny 2 = <u>disgust</u>, sicken, repel, repulse, nauseate, gross out (*U.S. slang*), turn your stomach, make your flesh creep

revolting = <u>disgusting</u>, foul, horrible, sickening, horrid, repellent, repulsive, nauseating, yucko (*Austral. slang*) ≠ delightful

revolution 1 = <u>revolt</u>, rising, coup, rebellion, uprising, mutiny, insurgency 2 = <u>transformation</u>, shift, innovation, upheaval, reformation, sea change 3 = <u>rotation</u>, turn, cycle, circle, spin, lap, circuit, orbit

revolutionary ADJECTIVE 1 = <u>rebel</u>, radical, extremist, subversive, insurgent ≠ reactionary 2 = <u>innovative</u>, new, different, novel, radical, progressive, drastic, ground-breaking ≠ conventional
● NOUN = <u>rebel</u>, insurgent, revolutionist ≠ reactionary

revolve 1 = <u>go round</u>, circle, orbit 2 = <u>rotate</u>, turn, wheel, spin, twist, whirl

reward NOUN 1 = <u>punishment</u>, retribution, comeuppance (*slang*), just deserts 2 = <u>payment</u>, return, prize, wages, compensation, bonus, premium, repayment ≠ penalty
● VERB = <u>compensate</u>, pay, repay, recompense, remunerate ≠ penalize

rewarding = <u>satisfying</u>, fulfilling, valuable, profitable, productive, worthwhile, beneficial, enriching ≠ unrewarding

rhetoric 1 = <u>hyperbole</u>, bombast, wordiness, verbosity, grandiloquence, magniloquence 2 = <u>oratory</u>, eloquence, public speaking, speech-making, elocution, declamation, grandiloquence, whaikorero (*N.Z.*)

rhetorical = <u>high-flown</u>, bombastic, verbose, oratorical, grandiloquent, declamatory, arty-farty (*informal*), magniloquent

rhyme = <u>poem</u>, song, verse, ode

rhythm 1 = <u>beat</u>, swing, accent, pulse, tempo, cadence, lilt 2 = <u>metre</u>, time

rich 1 = <u>wealthy</u>, affluent, well-off, loaded (*slang*), prosperous, well-heeled (*informal*), well-to-do, moneyed ≠ poor 2 = <u>well-stocked</u>, full, productive, ample, abundant, plentiful, copious, well-supplied ≠ scarce 3 = <u>full-bodied</u>, sweet, fatty, tasty, creamy, luscious, succulent ≠ bland 4 = <u>fruitful</u>, productive, fertile, prolific ≠ barren 5 = <u>abounding</u>, luxurious, lush, abundant

riches 1 = <u>wealth</u>, assets, plenty, fortune, substance, treasure, affluence ≠ poverty 2 = <u>resources</u>, treasures

richly 1 = <u>elaborately</u>, lavishly, elegantly, splendidly, exquisitely, expensively, luxuriously, gorgeously 2 = <u>fully</u>, well, thoroughly, amply, appropriately, properly, suitably

rid VERB = <u>free</u>, clear, deliver, relieve, purge, unburden, make free, disencumber
● PHRASES **get rid of something** *or* **someone** = <u>dispose of</u>, throw away *or* out, dump, remove, eliminate, expel, eject

riddle[1] 1 = <u>puzzle</u>, problem, conundrum, poser 2 = <u>enigma</u>, question, secret, mystery, puzzle, conundrum, teaser, problem

riddle[2] 1 = <u>pierce</u>, pepper, puncture, perforate, honeycomb 2 = <u>pervade</u>, fill, spread through

riddled = <u>filled</u>, spoilt, pervaded, infested, permeated

ride VERB 1 = <u>control</u>, handle, manage 2 = <u>travel</u>, be carried, go, move
● NOUN = <u>journey</u>, drive, trip, lift, outing, jaunt

ridicule VERB = <u>laugh at</u>, mock, make fun of, sneer at, jeer at, deride, poke fun at, chaff
● NOUN = <u>mockery</u>, scorn, derision, laughter, jeer, chaff, gibe, raillery

ridiculous = <u>laughable</u>, stupid, silly, absurd, ludicrous, farcical, comical, risible ≠ sensible

rife = <u>widespread</u>, rampant, general, common, universal, frequent, prevalent, ubiquitous

rifle = <u>ransack</u>, rob, burgle, loot, strip, sack, plunder, pillage

rift 1 = <u>breach</u>, division, split, separation, falling out (*informal*), disagreement, quarrel 2 = <u>split</u>, opening, crack, gap, break, fault, flaw, cleft

rig VERB 1 = <u>fix</u>, engineer (*informal*), arrange, manipulate, tamper with, gerrymander 2 (*Nautical*) = <u>equip</u>, fit out, kit out, outfit, supply, furnish
● PHRASES **rig something up** = <u>set up</u>, build, construct, put up, arrange, assemble, put together, erect

right ADJECTIVE 1 = <u>correct</u>, true, genuine, accurate, exact, precise, valid, factual, dinkum (*Austral. & N.Z. informal*) ≠ wrong 2 = <u>proper</u>, done, becoming, seemly, fitting, fit, appropriate, suitable ≠ inappropriate 3 = <u>just</u>, good, fair, moral, proper, ethical, honest, equitable ≠ unfair
● ADVERB 1 = <u>correctly</u>, truly, precisely, exactly, genuinely, accurately ≠ wrongly 2 = <u>suitably</u>, fittingly, appropriately, properly, aptly ≠ improperly 3 = <u>exactly</u>, squarely, precisely 4 = <u>directly</u>, straight, precisely, exactly, unswervingly, without deviation, by the shortest route, in a beeline 5 = <u>straight</u>, directly, quickly, promptly, straightaway ≠ indirectly
● NOUN 1 = <u>prerogative</u>, business, power, claim, authority, due, freedom, licence 2 = <u>justice</u>, truth, fairness, legality, righteousness, lawfulness ≠ injustice
● VERB = <u>rectify</u>, settle, fix, correct, sort out, straighten, redress, put right

right away = <u>immediately</u>, now, directly, instantly, at once, straightaway, forthwith, pronto (*informal*)

righteous = <u>virtuous</u>, good, just, fair, moral, pure, ethical, upright ≠ wicked

rigid 1 = <u>strict</u>, set, fixed, exact, rigorous, stringent ≠ flexible 2 = <u>inflexible</u>, uncompromising, unbending 3 = <u>stiff</u>, inflexible, inelastic ≠ pliable

rigorous = <u>strict</u>, hard, demanding, tough, severe, exacting, harsh, stern ≠ soft

rim 1 = <u>edge</u>, lip, brim 2 = <u>border</u>, edge, trim 3 = <u>margin</u>, border, verge, brink

ring[1] VERB 1 = <u>phone</u>, call, telephone, buzz (*informal, chiefly Brit.*) 2 = <u>chime</u>, sound, toll, reverberate, clang, peal 3 = <u>reverberate</u>
● NOUN 1 = <u>call</u>, phone call, buzz (*informal, chiefly Brit.*) 2 = <u>chime</u>, knell, peal

ring[2] NOUN 1 = <u>circle</u>, round, band, circuit, loop, hoop, halo 2 = <u>arena</u>, enclosure, circus, rink 3 = <u>gang</u>, group, association, band, circle, mob, syndicate, cartel
● VERB = <u>encircle</u>, surround, enclose, girdle, gird

rinse VERB = <u>wash</u>, clean, dip, splash, cleanse, bathe

● NOUN = <u>wash</u>, dip, splash, bath

riot NOUN 1 = <u>disturbance</u>, disorder, confusion, turmoil, upheaval, strife, turbulence, lawlessness 2 = <u>display</u>, show, splash, extravaganza, profusion 3 = <u>laugh</u>, joke, scream (*informal*), hoot (*informal*), lark

● VERB = <u>rampage</u>, run riot, go on the rampage

● PHRASES **run riot** 1 = <u>rampage</u>, go wild, be out of control 2 = <u>grow profusely</u>, spread like wildfire

rip VERB 1 = <u>tear</u>, cut, split, burst, rend, slash, claw, slit 2 = <u>be torn</u>, tear, split, burst

● NOUN = <u>tear</u>, cut, hole, split, rent, slash, slit, gash

● PHRASES **rip someone off** (*Slang*) = <u>cheat</u>, rob, con (*informal*), skin (*slang*), fleece, defraud, swindle

ripe 1 = <u>ripened</u>, seasoned, ready, mature, mellow ≠ unripe 2 = <u>right</u>, suitable 3 = <u>mature</u> 4 = <u>suitable</u>, timely, ideal, favourable, auspicious, opportune ≠ unsuitable

rip-off *or* **ripoff** (*Slang*) = <u>cheat</u>, con (*informal*), scam (*slang*), con trick (*informal*), fraud, theft, swindle

rise VERB 1 = <u>get up</u>, stand up, get to your feet 2 = <u>arise</u> 3 = <u>go up</u>, climb, ascend ≠ descend 4 = <u>loom</u>, tower 5 = <u>get steeper</u>, ascend, go uphill, slope upwards ≠ drop 6 = <u>increase</u>, mount ≠ decrease 7 = <u>grow</u>, go up, intensify 8 = <u>rebel</u>, revolt, mutiny 9 = <u>advance</u>, progress, get on, prosper

● NOUN 1 = <u>upward slope</u>, incline, elevation, ascent, kopje *or* koppie (*S. African*) 2 = <u>increase</u>, upturn, upswing, upsurge ≠ decrease 3 = <u>pay increase</u>, raise (*U.S.*), increment 4 = <u>advancement</u>, progress, climb, promotion

● PHRASES **give rise to something** = <u>cause</u>, produce, effect, result in, bring about

risk NOUN 1 = <u>danger</u>, chance, possibility, hazard 2 = <u>gamble</u>, chance, speculation, leap in the dark 3 = <u>peril</u>, jeopardy

● VERB 1 = <u>stand a chance of</u> 2 = <u>dare</u>, endanger, jeopardize, imperil, venture, gamble, hazard

risky = <u>dangerous</u>, hazardous, unsafe, perilous, uncertain, dodgy (*Brit., Austral., & N.Z. informal*), dicey (*informal, chiefly Brit.*), chancy (*informal*) ≠ safe

rite = <u>ceremony</u>, custom, ritual, practice, procedure, observance

ritual NOUN 1 = <u>ceremony</u>, rite, observance 2 = <u>custom</u>, tradition, routine, convention, practice, procedure, habit, protocol, tikanga (*N.Z.*)

● ADJECTIVE = <u>ceremonial</u>, conventional, routine, customary, habitual

rival NOUN = <u>opponent</u>, competitor, contender, contestant, adversary ≠ supporter

● VERB = <u>compete with</u>, match, equal, compare with, come up to, be a match for

● ADJECTIVE = <u>competing</u>, conflicting, opposing

rivalry = <u>competition</u>, opposition, conflict, contest, contention

river 1 = <u>stream</u>, brook, creek, waterway, tributary, burn (*Scot.*) 2 = <u>flow</u>, rush, flood, spate, torrent

riveting = <u>enthralling</u>, gripping, fascinating, absorbing, captivating, hypnotic, engrossing, spellbinding

road 1 = <u>roadway</u>, highway, motorway, track, route, path, lane, pathway 2 = <u>way</u>, path

roam = <u>wander</u>, walk, range, travel, stray, ramble, prowl, rove

roar VERB 1 = <u>thunder</u> 2 = <u>guffaw</u>, laugh heartily, hoot, split your sides (*informal*) 3 = <u>cry</u>, shout, yell, howl, bellow, bawl, bay

● NOUN 1 = <u>guffaw</u>, hoot 2 = <u>cry</u>, shout, yell, howl, outcry, bellow

rob 1 = <u>steal from</u>, hold up, mug (*informal*) 2 = <u>raid</u>, hold up, loot, plunder, burgle, pillage 3 = <u>dispossess</u>, con (*informal*), cheat, defraud 4 = <u>deprive</u>, do out of (*informal*)

robber = <u>thief</u>, raider, burglar, looter, fraud, cheat, bandit, plunderer

robbery 1 = <u>burglary</u>, raid, hold-up, rip-off (*slang*), stick-up (*slang, chiefly U.S.*) 2 = <u>theft</u>, stealing, mugging (*informal*), plunder, swindle, pillage, larceny

robe = <u>gown</u>, costume, habit

robot = <u>machine</u>, automaton, android, mechanical man

robust = <u>strong</u>, tough, powerful, fit, healthy, strapping, hardy, vigorous ≠ weak

rock[1] = <u>stone</u>, boulder

rock[2] 1 = <u>sway</u>, pitch, swing, reel, toss, lurch, roll 2 = <u>shock</u>, surprise, shake, stun, astonish, stagger, astound

rocky[1] = <u>rough</u>, rugged, stony, craggy

rocky² = <u>unstable</u>, shaky, wobbly, rickety, unsteady

rod 1 = <u>stick</u>, bar, pole, shaft, cane 2 = <u>staff</u>, baton, wand

rogue 1 = <u>scoundrel</u>, crook (*informal*), villain, fraud, blackguard, skelm (*S. African*), rorter (*Austral. slang*) 2 = <u>scamp</u>, rascal, scally (*Northwest English dialect*), nointer (*Austral. slang*)

role 1 = <u>job</u>, part, position, post, task, duty, function, capacity 2 = <u>part</u>, character, representation, portrayal

roll VERB 1 = <u>turn</u>, wheel, spin, go round, revolve, rotate, whirl, swivel 2 = <u>trundle</u>, go, move 3 = <u>flow</u>, run, course 4 *often with* **up** = <u>wind</u>, bind, wrap, swathe, envelop, furl, enfold 5 = <u>level</u>, even, press, smooth, flatten 6 = <u>toss</u>, rock, lurch, reel, tumble, sway

● NOUN 1 = <u>rumble</u>, boom, roar, thunder, reverberation 2 = <u>register</u>, record, list, index, census 3 = <u>turn</u>, spin, rotation, cycle, wheel, revolution, reel, whirl

romance 1 = <u>love affair</u>, relationship, affair, attachment, liaison, amour 2 = <u>excitement</u>, colour, charm, mystery, glamour, fascination 3 = <u>story</u>, tale, fantasy, legend, fairy tale, love story, melodrama

romantic ADJECTIVE 1 = <u>loving</u>, tender, passionate, fond, sentimental, amorous, icky (*informal*) ≠ unromantic 2 = <u>idealistic</u>, unrealistic, impractical, dreamy, starry-eyed ≠ realistic 3 = <u>exciting</u>, fascinating, mysterious, colourful, glamorous ≠ unexciting

● NOUN = <u>idealist</u>, dreamer, sentimentalist

romp VERB 1 = <u>frolic</u>, sport, have fun, caper, cavort, frisk, gambol

● NOUN = <u>frolic</u>, lark (*informal*), caper

room 1 = <u>chamber</u>, office, apartment 2 = <u>space</u>, area, capacity, extent, expanse 3 = <u>opportunity</u>, scope, leeway, chance, range, occasion, margin

root¹ NOUN 1 = <u>stem</u>, tuber, rhizome 2 = <u>source</u>, cause, heart, bottom, base, seat, seed, foundation

● PLURAL NOUN = <u>sense of belonging</u>, origins, heritage, birthplace, home, family, cradle

● PHRASES **root something** *or* **someone out** = <u>get rid of</u>, remove, eliminate, abolish, eradicate, do away with, weed out, exterminate

root² = <u>dig</u>, burrow, ferret

rope NOUN = <u>cord</u>, line, cable, strand, hawser

● PHRASES **know the ropes** = <u>be experienced</u>, be knowledgeable, be an old hand ◆ **rope someone in** *or* **into something** (*Brit.*) = <u>persuade</u>, involve, engage, enlist, link into, inveigle

rosy ADJECTIVE 1 = <u>glowing</u>, blooming, radiant, ruddy, healthy-looking ≠ pale 2 = <u>promising</u>, encouraging, bright, optimistic, hopeful, cheerful, favourable, auspicious ≠ gloomy

● NOUN = <u>pink</u>, red

rot VERB 1 = <u>decay</u>, spoil, deteriorate, perish, decompose, moulder, go bad, putrefy 2 = <u>crumble</u> 3 = <u>deteriorate</u>, decline, waste away

● NOUN 1 = <u>decay</u>, decomposition, corruption, mould, blight, canker, putrefaction 2 (*Informal*) = <u>nonsense</u>, rubbish, drivel, twaddle, garbage (*chiefly U.S.*), trash, tripe (*informal*), claptrap (*informal*), bizzo (*Austral. slang*), bull's wool (*Austral. & N.Z. slang*)

▇▇ RELATED WORD
adjective: putrid

rotate 1 = <u>revolve</u>, turn, wheel, spin, reel, go round, swivel, pivot 2 = <u>follow in sequence</u>, switch, alternate, take turns

rotation 1 = <u>revolution</u>, turning, turn, wheel, spin, spinning, reel, orbit 2 = <u>sequence</u>, switching, cycle, succession, alternation

rotten 1 = <u>decaying</u>, bad, rank, corrupt, sour, stinking, perished, festering, festy (*Austral. slang*) ≠ fresh 2 = <u>crumbling</u>, perished 3 (*Informal*) = <u>despicable</u>, mean, base, dirty, nasty, contemptible 4 (*Informal*) = <u>inferior</u>, poor, inadequate, duff (*Brit. informal*), unsatisfactory, lousy (*slang*), substandard, crummy (*slang*), bodger *or* bodgie (*Austral. slang*) 5 = <u>corrupt</u>, immoral, crooked (*informal*), dishonest, dishonourable, perfidious ≠ honourable

rough ADJECTIVE 1 = <u>uneven</u>, broken, rocky, irregular, jagged, bumpy, stony, craggy ≠ even 2 = <u>boisterous</u>, hard, tough, arduous 3 = <u>ungracious</u>, blunt, rude, coarse, brusque, uncouth, impolite, uncivil ≠ refined 4 = <u>unpleasant</u>, hard, difficult, tough, uncomfortable ≠ easy 5 = <u>approximate</u>, estimated ≠ exact 6 = <u>vague</u>, general, sketchy, imprecise,

inexact 7 = <u>basic</u>, crude, unfinished, incomplete, imperfect, rudimentary, sketchy, unrefined ≠ complete 8 = <u>stormy</u>, wild, turbulent, choppy, squally ≠ calm 9 = <u>harsh</u>, tough, nasty, cruel, unfeeling ≠ gentle
● NOUN = <u>outline</u>, draft, mock-up, preliminary sketch
● PHRASES **rough and ready**
1 = <u>makeshift</u>, crude, provisional, improvised, sketchy, stopgap
2 = <u>unrefined</u>, shabby, untidy, unkempt, unpolished, ill-groomed ◆ **rough something out** = <u>outline</u>, plan, draft, sketch

round NOUN 1 = <u>series</u>, session, cycle, sequence, succession 2 = <u>stage</u>, turn, level, period, division, session, lap 3 = <u>sphere</u>, ball, band, ring, circle, disc, globe, orb 4 = <u>course</u>, tour, circuit, beat, series, schedule, routine
● ADJECTIVE 1 = <u>spherical</u>, rounded, curved, circular, cylindrical, rotund, globular
2 = <u>plump</u>, full, ample, fleshy, rotund, full-fleshed
● VERB = <u>go round</u>, circle, skirt, flank, bypass, encircle, turn
● PHRASES **round something or someone up** = <u>gather</u>, muster, group, drive, collect, rally, herd, marshal

roundabout 1 = <u>indirect</u>, devious, tortuous, circuitous, evasive, discursive ≠ direct 2 = <u>oblique</u>, implied, indirect, circuitous

roundup = <u>muster</u>, collection, rally, assembly, herding

rouse 1 = <u>wake up</u>, call, wake, awaken 2 = <u>excite</u>, move, stir, provoke, anger, animate, agitate, inflame 3 = <u>stimulate</u>, provoke, incite

rousing = <u>lively</u>, moving, spirited, exciting, inspiring, stirring, stimulating ≠ dull

rout VERB = <u>defeat</u>, beat, overthrow, thrash, destroy, crush, conquer, wipe the floor with (*informal*)
● NOUN = <u>defeat</u>, beating, overthrow, thrashing, pasting (*slang*), debacle, drubbing

route 1 = <u>way</u>, course, road, direction, path, journey, itinerary 2 = <u>beat</u>, circuit

routine NOUN = <u>procedure</u>, programme, order, practice, method, pattern, custom
● ADJECTIVE 1 = <u>usual</u>, standard, normal, customary, ordinary, typical, everyday,

habitual ≠ unusual 2 = <u>boring</u>, dull, predictable, tedious, tiresome, humdrum

row[1] NOUN = <u>line</u>, bank, range, series, file, string, column
● PHRASES **in a row** = <u>consecutively</u>, running, in turn, one after the other, successively, in sequence

row[2] NOUN (*Informal*) 1 = <u>quarrel</u>, dispute, argument, squabble, tiff, trouble, brawl
2 = <u>disturbance</u>, noise, racket, uproar, commotion, rumpus, tumult
● VERB = <u>quarrel</u>, fight, argue, dispute, squabble, wrangle

royal 1 = <u>regal</u>, kingly, queenly, princely, imperial, sovereign 2 = <u>splendid</u>, grand, impressive, magnificent, majestic, stately

rub VERB 1 = <u>stroke</u>, massage, caress
2 = <u>polish</u>, clean, shine, wipe, scour
3 = <u>chafe</u>, scrape, grate, abrade
● NOUN 1 = <u>massage</u>, caress, kneading
2 = <u>polish</u>, stroke, shine, wipe
● PHRASES **rub something out** = <u>erase</u>, remove, cancel, wipe out, delete, obliterate, efface

rubbish 1 = <u>waste</u>, refuse, scrap, junk (*informal*), litter, garbage (*chiefly U.S.*), trash, lumber 2 = <u>nonsense</u>, garbage (*chiefly U.S.*), twaddle, rot, trash, hot air (*informal*), tripe (*informal*), claptrap (*informal*), bizzo (*Austral. slang*), bull's wool (*Austral. & N.Z. slang*)

rude 1 = <u>impolite</u>, insulting, cheeky, abusive, disrespectful, impertinent, insolent, impudent ≠ polite
2 = <u>uncivilized</u>, rough, coarse, brutish, boorish, uncouth, loutish, graceless
3 = <u>vulgar</u> ≠ refined 4 = <u>unpleasant</u>, sharp, sudden, harsh, startling, abrupt
5 = <u>roughly-made</u>, simple, rough, raw, crude, primitive, makeshift, artless ≠ well-made

rue (*Literary*) = <u>regret</u>, mourn, lament, repent, be sorry for, kick yourself for

ruffle 1 = <u>disarrange</u>, disorder, mess up, rumple, tousle, dishevel 2 = <u>annoy</u>, upset, irritate, agitate, nettle, fluster, peeve (*informal*) ≠ calm

rugged 1 = <u>rocky</u>, broken, rough, craggy, difficult, ragged, irregular, uneven ≠ even 2 = <u>strong-featured</u>, rough-hewn, weather-beaten ≠ delicate 3 = <u>well-built</u>, strong, tough, robust, sturdy 4 = <u>tough</u>, strong, robust, muscular, sturdy, burly, husky (*informal*), brawny ≠ delicate

ruin VERB 1 = <u>destroy</u>, devastate, wreck, defeat, smash, crush, demolish, lay waste ≠ create 2 = <u>bankrupt</u>, break, impoverish, beggar, pauperize 3 = <u>spoil</u>, damage, mess up, blow (*slang*), screw up (*informal*), botch, make a mess of, crool *or* cruel (*Austral. slang*) ≠ improve
● NOUN 1 = <u>bankruptcy</u>, insolvency, destitution 2 = <u>disrepair</u>, decay, disintegration, ruination, wreckage 3 = <u>destruction</u>, fall, breakdown, defeat, collapse, wreck, undoing, downfall ≠ preservation

rule NOUN 1 = <u>regulation</u>, law, direction, guideline, decree 2 = <u>precept</u>, principle, canon, maxim, tenet, axiom 3 = <u>custom</u>, procedure, practice, routine, tradition, habit, convention 4 = <u>government</u>, power, control, authority, command, regime, reign, jurisdiction, mana (*N.Z.*)
● VERB 1 = <u>govern</u>, control, direct, have power over, command over, have charge of 2 = <u>reign</u>, govern, be in power, be in authority 3 = <u>decree</u>, decide, judge, settle, pronounce 4 = <u>be prevalent</u>, prevail, predominate, be customary, preponderate
● PHRASES **as a rule** = <u>usually</u>, generally, mainly, normally, on the whole, ordinarily ◆ **rule someone out** = <u>exclude</u>, eliminate, disqualify, ban, reject, dismiss, prohibit, leave out ◆ **rule something out** = <u>reject</u>, exclude, eliminate

ruler 1 = <u>governor</u>, leader, lord, commander, controller, monarch, sovereign, head of state 2 = <u>measure</u>, rule, yardstick

ruling ADJECTIVE 1 = <u>governing</u>, reigning, controlling, commanding 2 = <u>predominant</u>, dominant, prevailing, preponderant, chief, main, principal, pre-eminent ≠ minor
● NOUN = <u>decision</u>, verdict, judgment, decree, adjudication, pronouncement

rumour = <u>story</u>, news, report, talk, word, whisper, buzz, gossip

run VERB 1 = <u>race</u>, rush, dash, hurry, bolt, gallop, hare (*Brit. informal*) ≠ dawdle 2 = <u>flee</u>, escape, take off (*informal*), bolt, beat it (*slang*), leg it (*informal*), take flight, do a runner (*slang*) ≠ stay 3 = <u>take part</u>, compete 4 = <u>continue</u>, go, stretch, reach, extend, proceed ≠ stop 5 (*Chiefly U.S. & Canad.*) = <u>compete</u>, stand, contend, be a candidate, put yourself up for,

take part 6 = <u>manage</u>, lead, direct, be in charge of, head, control, operate, handle 7 = <u>go</u>, work, operate, perform, function 8 = <u>perform</u>, carry out 9 = <u>work</u>, go, operate, function 10 = <u>pass</u>, go, move, roll, glide, skim 11 = <u>flow</u>, pour, stream, go, leak, spill, discharge, gush 12 = <u>publish</u>, feature, display, print 13 = <u>melt</u>, dissolve, liquefy, go soft 14 = <u>smuggle</u>, traffic in, bootleg
● NOUN 1 = <u>race</u>, rush, dash, sprint, gallop, jog, spurt 2 = <u>ride</u>, drive, trip, spin (*informal*), outing, excursion, jaunt 3 = <u>sequence</u>, period, stretch, spell, course, season, series, string 4 = <u>enclosure</u>, pen, coop
● PHRASES **run away** = <u>flee</u>, escape, bolt, abscond, do a runner (*slang*), make a run for it, scram (*informal*), fly the coop (*U.S. & Canad. informal*) ◆ **run into someone** = <u>meet</u>, encounter, bump into, run across, come across *or* upon ◆ **run into something** 1 = <u>be beset by</u>, encounter, come across *or* upon, face, experience 2 = <u>collide with</u>, hit, strike ◆ **run out** 1 = <u>be used up</u>, dry up, give out, fail, finish, be exhausted 2 = <u>expire</u>, end, terminate ◆ **run over something** 1 = <u>exceed</u>, overstep, go over the top of, go over the limit of 2 = <u>review</u>, check, go through, go over, run through, rehearse ◆ **run over something** *or* **someone** = <u>knock down</u>, hit, run down, knock over ◆ **run something** *or* **someone down** 1 = <u>criticize</u>, denigrate, belittle, knock (*informal*), rubbish (*informal*), slag (off) (*slang*), disparage, decry 2 = <u>downsize</u>, cut, reduce, trim, decrease, cut back, curtail 3 = <u>knock down</u>, hit, run into, run over, knock over

run-down *or* **rundown** 1 = <u>exhausted</u>, weak, drained, weary, unhealthy, worn-out, debilitated, below par ≠ fit 2 = <u>dilapidated</u>, broken-down, shabby, worn-out, seedy, ramshackle, decrepit

runner 1 = <u>athlete</u>, sprinter, jogger 2 = <u>messenger</u>, courier, errand boy, dispatch bearer

running NOUN 1 = <u>management</u>, control, administration, direction, leadership, organization, supervision 2 = <u>working</u>, performance, operation, functioning, maintenance
● ADJECTIVE 1 = <u>continuous</u>, constant, perpetual, uninterrupted, incessant 2 = <u>in succession</u>, unbroken 3 = <u>flowing</u>, moving,

streaming, coursing

rupture NOUN = break, tear, split, crack, rent, burst, breach, fissure

● VERB = break, separate, tear, split, crack, burst, sever

rural 1 = agricultural, country 2 = rustic, country, pastoral, sylvan ≠ urban

rush VERB 1 = hurry, run, race, shoot, fly, career, speed, tear ≠ dawdle 2 = push, hurry, press, hustle 3 = attack, storm, charge at

● NOUN 1 = dash, charge, race, scramble, stampede 2 = hurry, haste, hustle 3 = surge, flow, gush 4 = attack, charge, assault, onslaught

● ADJECTIVE = hasty, fast, quick, hurried, rapid, urgent, swift ≠ leisurely

rust NOUN 1 = corrosion, oxidation 2 = mildew, must, mould, rot, blight

● VERB = corrode, oxidize

rusty 1 = corroded, rusted, oxidized, rust-covered 2 = out of practice, weak, stale, unpractised 3 = reddish-brown, chestnut, reddish, russet, coppery, rust-coloured

ruthless = merciless, harsh, cruel, brutal, relentless, callous, heartless, remorseless ≠ merciful

S

sabotage VERB = damage, destroy, wreck, disable, disrupt, subvert, incapacitate, vandalize

● NOUN = damage, destruction, wrecking

sack¹ NOUN 1 = bag, pocket, sac, pouch, receptacle 2 = dismissal, discharge, the boot (*slang*), the axe (*informal*), the push (*slang*)

● VERB (*Informal*) = dismiss, fire (*informal*), axe (*informal*), discharge, kiss off (*slang, chiefly U.S. & Canad.*), give (someone) the push (*informal*)

sack² VERB = plunder, loot, pillage, strip, rob, raid, ruin

● NOUN = plundering, looting, pillage

sacred 1 = holy, hallowed, blessed,

divine, revered, sanctified ≠ secular 2 = religious, holy, ecclesiastical, hallowed ≠ unconsecrated 3 = inviolable, protected, sacrosanct, hallowed, inalienable, unalterable

sacrifice VERB 1 = offer, offer up, immolate 2 = give up, abandon, relinquish, lose, surrender, let go, do without, renounce

● NOUN 1 = offering, oblation 2 = surrender, loss, giving up, rejection, abdication, renunciation, repudiation, forswearing

sad 1 = unhappy, down, low, blue, depressed, melancholy, mournful, dejected ≠ happy 2 = tragic, moving, upsetting, depressing, dismal, pathetic, poignant, harrowing 3 = deplorable, bad, sorry, terrible, unfortunate, regrettable, lamentable, wretched ≠ good

sadden = upset, depress, distress, grieve, make sad, deject

saddle = burden, load, lumber (*Brit. informal*), encumber

sadness = unhappiness, sorrow, grief, depression, the blues, misery, melancholy, poignancy ≠ happiness

safe ADJECTIVE 1 = protected, secure, impregnable, out of danger, safe and sound, in safe hands, out of harm's way ≠ endangered 2 = all right, intact, unscathed, unhurt, unharmed, undamaged, O.K. *or* okay (*informal*) 3 = risk-free, sound, secure, certain, impregnable

● NOUN = strongbox, vault, coffer, repository, deposit box, safe-deposit box

safeguard VERB = protect, guard, defend, save, preserve, look after, keep safe

● NOUN = protection, security, defence, guard

safely = in safety, with impunity, without risk, safe and sound

safety 1 = security, protection, safeguards, precautions, safety measures, impregnability ≠ risk 2 = shelter, haven, protection, cover, retreat, asylum, refuge, sanctuary

sag 1 = sink, bag, droop, fall, slump, dip, give way, hang loosely 2 = drop, sink, slump, flop, droop, loll 3 = decline, tire, flag, weaken, wilt, wane, droop

saga 1 = carry-on (*informal, chiefly Brit.*), performance (*informal*), pantomime (*informal*) 2 = epic, story, tale, narrative, yarn

sage NOUN = wise man, philosopher, guru, master, elder, tohunga (*N.Z.*)
● ADJECTIVE = wise, sensible, judicious, sagacious, sapient

sail NOUN = sheet, canvas
● VERB 1 = go by water, cruise, voyage, ride the waves, go by sea 2 = set sail, embark, get under way, put to sea, put off, leave port, hoist sail, cast *or* weigh anchor 3 = pilot, steer 4 = glide, sweep, float, fly, wing, soar, drift, skim

sailor = mariner, marine, seaman, sea dog, seafarer

sake NOUN = purpose, interest, reason, end, aim, objective, motive
● PHRASES **for someone's sake** = in someone's interests, to someone's advantage, on someone's account, for the benefit of, for the good of, for the welfare of, out of respect for, out of consideration for

salary = pay, income, wage, fee, payment, wages, earnings, allowance

sale 1 = selling, marketing, dealing, transaction, disposal 2 = auction, fair, mart, bazaar

salt NOUN = seasoning
● ADJECTIVE = salty, saline, brackish, briny

salute VERB 1 = greet, welcome, acknowledge, address, hail, mihi (*N.Z.*) 2 = honour, acknowledge, recognize, pay tribute *or* homage to
● NOUN = greeting, recognition, salutation, address

salvage = save, recover, rescue, get back, retrieve, redeem

salvation = saving, rescue, recovery, salvage, redemption, deliverance ≠ ruin

same 1 = identical, similar, alike, equal, twin, corresponding, duplicate ≠ different 2 = the very same, one and the same, selfsame 3 = aforementioned, aforesaid 4 = unchanged, consistent, constant, unaltered, invariable, unvarying, changeless ≠ altered

sample NOUN 1 = specimen, example, model, pattern, instance 2 = cross section
● VERB = test, try, experience, taste, inspect
● ADJECTIVE = test, trial, specimen, representative

sanction VERB = permit, allow, approve, endorse, authorize ≠ forbid
● NOUN 1 *often plural* = ban, boycott, embargo, exclusion, penalty, coercive measures ≠ permission 2 = permission, backing, authority, approval, authorization, O.K. *or* okay (*informal*), stamp *or* seal of approval ≠ ban

sanctuary 1 = protection, shelter, refuge, haven, retreat, asylum 2 = reserve, park, preserve, reservation, national park, tract, nature reserve, conservation area

sane 1 = rational, all there (*informal*), of sound mind, compos mentis (*Latin*), in your right mind, mentally sound ≠ insane 2 = sensible, sound, reasonable, balanced, judicious, level-headed ≠ foolish

sap[1] 1 = juice, essence, vital fluid, lifeblood 2 (*Slang*) = fool, jerk (*slang, chiefly U.S. & Canad.*), idiot, wally (*slang*), twit (*informal*), simpleton, ninny, dorba *or* dorb (*Austral. slang*), bogan (*Austral. slang*)

sap[2] = weaken, drain, undermine, exhaust, deplete

satanic = evil, demonic, hellish, black, wicked, devilish, infernal, fiendish ≠ godly

satire 1 = mockery, irony, ridicule 2 = parody, mockery, caricature, lampoon, burlesque

satisfaction 1 = fulfilment, pleasure, achievement, relish, gratification, pride ≠ dissatisfaction 2 = contentment, content, comfort, pleasure, happiness, enjoyment, satiety, repletion ≠ discontent

satisfactory = adequate, acceptable, good enough, average, fair, all right, sufficient, passable ≠ unsatisfactory

satisfy 1 = content, please, indulge, gratify, pander to, assuage, pacify, quench ≠ dissatisfy 2 = convince, persuade, assure, reassure ≠ dissuade 3 = comply with, meet, fulfil, answer, serve, fill, observe, obey ≠ fail to meet

saturate 1 = flood, overwhelm, swamp, overrun 2 = soak, steep, drench, imbue, suffuse, wet through, waterlog, souse

saturated = soaked, soaking (wet), drenched, sodden, dripping, waterlogged, sopping (wet), wet through

sauce = dressing, dip, relish, condiment

savage ADJECTIVE 1 = cruel, brutal, vicious, fierce, harsh, ruthless, ferocious, sadistic ≠ gentle 2 = wild, fierce, ferocious, unbroken, feral, untamed, undomesticated ≠ tame 3 = primitive, undeveloped, uncultivated, uncivilized 4 = uncultivated, rugged, unspoilt, uninhabited, rough, uncivilized

≠ cultivated

● NOUN = lout, yob (*Brit. slang*), barbarian, yahoo, boor, hoon (*Austral. & N.Z.*), boor, cougan (*Austral. slang*), scozza (*Austral. slang*), bogan (*Austral. slang*)

● VERB = maul, tear, claw, attack, mangle, lacerate, mangulate (*Austral. slang*)

save 1 = rescue, free, release, deliver, recover, get out, liberate, salvage ≠ endanger 2 = keep, reserve, set aside, store, collect, gather, hold, hoard ≠ spend 3 = protect, keep, guard, preserve, look after, safeguard, salvage, conserve 4 = put aside, keep, reserve, collect, retain, set aside, put by

saving NOUN = economy, discount, reduction, bargain

● PLURAL NOUN = nest egg, fund, store, reserves, resources

saviour = rescuer, deliverer, defender, protector, liberator, redeemer, preserver

Saviour = Christ, Jesus, the Messiah, the Redeemer

savour VERB 1 = relish, delight in, revel in, luxuriate in 2 = enjoy, appreciate, relish, delight in, revel in, luxuriate in

● NOUN = flavour, taste, smell, relish, smack, tang, piquancy

say VERB 1 = state, declare, remark, announce, maintain, mention, assert, affirm 2 = speak, utter, voice, express, pronounce 3 = suggest, express, imply, communicate, disclose, give away, convey, divulge 4 = suppose, supposing, imagine, assume, presume 5 = estimate, suppose, guess, conjecture, surmise

● NOUN 1 = influence, power, control, authority, weight, clout (*informal*), mana (*N.Z.*) 2 = chance to speak, vote, voice

saying = proverb, maxim, adage, dictum, axiom, aphorism

scale¹ = flake, plate, layer, lamina

scale² NOUN 1 = degree, size, range, extent, dimensions, scope, magnitude, breadth 2 = system of measurement, measuring system 3 = ranking, ladder, hierarchy, series, sequence, progression 4 = ratio, proportion

● VERB = climb up, mount, ascend, surmount, clamber up, escalade

scan 1 = glance over, skim, look over, eye, check, examine, check out (*informal*), run over 2 = survey, search, investigate, sweep, scour, scrutinize

scandal 1 = disgrace, crime, offence, sin, embarrassment, wrongdoing, dishonourable behaviour, discreditable behaviour 2 = gossip, talk, rumours, dirt, slander, tattle, aspersion 3 = shame, disgrace, stigma, infamy, opprobrium 4 = outrage, shame, insult, disgrace, injustice, crying shame

scant = inadequate, meagre, sparse, little, minimal, barely sufficient ≠ adequate

scapegoat = fall guy, whipping boy

scar NOUN 1 = mark, injury, wound, blemish 2 = trauma, suffering, pain, torture, anguish

● VERB = mark, disfigure, damage, mar, mutilate, blemish, deface

scarce 1 = in short supply, insufficient ≠ plentiful 2 = rare, few, uncommon, few and far between, infrequent ≠ common

scarcely 1 = hardly, barely 2 (*Often used ironically*) = by no means, hardly, definitely not

scare VERB = frighten, alarm, terrify, panic, shock, startle, intimidate, dismay

● NOUN 1 = fright, shock, start 2 = panic, hysteria 3 = alert, warning, alarm

scared = afraid, alarmed, frightened, terrified, shaken, startled, fearful, petrified

scary (*Informal*) = frightening, alarming, terrifying, chilling, horrifying, spooky (*informal*), creepy (*informal*), spine-chilling

scatter 1 = throw about, spread, sprinkle, strew, shower, fling, diffuse, disseminate ≠ gather 2 = disperse, dispel, disband, dissipate ≠ assemble

scenario 1 = situation 2 = story line, résumé, outline, summary, synopsis

scene 1 = act, part, division, episode 2 = setting, set, background, location, backdrop 3 = site, place, setting, area, position, spot, locality 4 (*Informal*) = world, business, environment, arena 5 = view, prospect, panorama, vista, landscape, outlook 6 = fuss, to-do, row, performance, exhibition, carry-on (*informal, chiefly Brit.*), tantrum, commotion

scenery 1 = landscape, view, surroundings, terrain, vista 2 (*Theatre*) = set, setting, backdrop, flats, stage set

scenic = picturesque, beautiful, spectacular, striking, panoramic

scent NOUN 1 = fragrance, smell, perfume, bouquet, aroma, odour 2 = trail, track, spoor
● VERB = smell, sense, detect, sniff, discern, nose out

scented = fragrant, perfumed, aromatic, sweet-smelling, odoriferous

sceptic 1 = doubter, cynic, disbeliever 2 = agnostic, doubter, unbeliever, doubting Thomas

sceptical = doubtful, cynical, dubious, unconvinced, disbelieving, incredulous, mistrustful ≠ convinced

scepticism = doubt, suspicion, disbelief, cynicism, incredulity

schedule NOUN = plan, programme, agenda, calendar, timetable
● VERB = plan, set up, book, programme, arrange, organize

scheme NOUN 1 = plan, programme, strategy, system, project, proposal, tactics 2 = plot, ploy, ruse, intrigue, conspiracy, manoeuvre, subterfuge, stratagem
● VERB = plot, plan, intrigue, manoeuvre, conspire, contrive, collude, machinate

scheming = calculating, cunning, sly, tricky, wily, artful, conniving, underhand ≠ straightforward

scholar 1 = intellectual, academic, savant, acca (Austral. slang) 2 = student, pupil, learner, schoolboy or schoolgirl

scholarly = learned, academic, intellectual, lettered, erudite, scholastic, bookish ≠ uneducated

scholarship 1 = grant, award, payment, endowment, fellowship, bursary 2 = learning, education, knowledge, erudition, book-learning

school NOUN 1 = academy, college, institution, institute, seminary 2 = group, set, circle, faction, followers, disciples, devotees, denomination
● VERB = train, coach, discipline, educate, drill, tutor, instruct

science = discipline, body of knowledge, branch of knowledge

scientific = systematic, accurate, exact, precise, controlled, mathematical

scientist = researcher, inventor, boffin (informal), technophile

scoff[1] = scorn, mock, laugh at, ridicule, knock (informal), despise, sneer, jeer

scoff[2] = gobble (up), wolf, devour, bolt, guzzle, gulp down, gorge yourself on

scoop VERB = win, get, land, gain, achieve, earn, secure, obtain
● NOUN 1 = ladle, spoon, dipper 2 = exclusive, exposé, revelation, sensation
● PHRASES **scoop someone up** = gather up, lift, pick up, take up, sweep up or away ◆ **scoop something out** 1 = take out, empty, spoon out, bail or bale out 2 = dig, shovel, excavate, gouge, hollow out

scope 1 = opportunity, room, freedom, space, liberty, latitude 2 = range, capacity, reach, area, outlook, orbit, span, sphere

scorch = burn, sear, roast, wither, shrivel, parch, singe

scorching = burning, boiling, baking, flaming, roasting, searing, fiery, red-hot

score VERB 1 = gain, win, achieve, make, get, attain, notch up (informal), chalk up (informal) 2 (Music) = arrange, set, orchestrate, adapt 3 = cut, scratch, mark, slash, scrape, graze, gouge, deface
● NOUN 1 = rating, mark, grade, percentage 2 = points, result, total, outcome 3 = composition, soundtrack, arrangement, orchestration 4 = grievance, wrong, injury, injustice, grudge
● PLURAL NOUN = lots, loads, many, millions, hundreds, masses, swarms, multitudes
● PHRASES **score something out** or **through** = cross out, delete, strike out, cancel, obliterate

scorn NOUN = contempt, disdain, mockery, derision, sarcasm, disparagement ≠ respect
● VERB = despise, reject, disdain, slight, be above, spurn, deride, flout ≠ respect

scour[1] = scrub, clean, polish, rub, buff, abrade

scour[2] = search, hunt, comb, ransack

scout NOUN = vanguard, lookout, precursor, outrider, reconnoitrer, advance guard
● VERB = reconnoitre, investigate, watch, survey, observe, spy, probe, recce (slang)

scramble VERB 1 = struggle, climb, crawl, swarm, scrabble 2 = strive, rush, contend, vie, run, push, jostle 3 = jumble, mix up, muddle, shuffle
● NOUN 1 = clamber, ascent 2 = race, competition, struggle, rush, confusion, commotion, melee or mêlée

scrap[1] NOUN 1 = piece, fragment, bit, grain, particle, portion, part, crumb 2 = waste, junk, off cuts

● PLURAL NOUN = leftovers, remains, bits, leavings

● VERB = get rid of, drop, abandon, ditch (slang), discard, write off, jettison, throw away or out ≠ bring back

scrap[2] (Informal) NOUN = fight, battle, row, argument, dispute, disagreement, quarrel, squabble, biffo (Austral. slang)

● VERB = fight, argue, row, squabble, wrangle

scrape VERB 1 = rake, sweep, drag, brush 2 = grate, grind, scratch, squeak, rasp 3 = graze, skin, scratch, bark, scuff, rub 4 = clean, remove, scour

● NOUN (Informal) = predicament, difficulty, fix (informal), mess, dilemma, plight, tight spot, awkward situation

scratch VERB 1 = rub, scrape, claw at 2 = mark, cut, score, damage, grate, graze, etch, lacerate

● NOUN = mark, scrape, graze, blemish, gash, laceration, claw mark

● PHRASES up to scratch (Informal) = adequate, acceptable, satisfactory, sufficient, up to standard

scream VERB = cry, yell, shriek, screech, bawl, howl

● NOUN = cry, yell, howl, shriek, screech, yelp

screen NOUN = cover, guard, shade, shelter, shield, partition, cloak, canopy

● VERB 1 = broadcast, show, put on, present, air, cable, beam, transmit 2 = cover, hide, conceal, shade, mask, veil, cloak 3 = investigate, test, check, examine, scan 4 = process, sort, examine, filter, scan, evaluate, gauge, sift 5 = protect, guard, shield, defend, shelter

screw NOUN = nail, pin, tack, rivet, fastener, spike

● VERB 1 = fasten, fix, attach, bolt, clamp, rivet 2 = turn, twist, tighten 3 (Informal) = cheat, do (slang), rip (someone) off (slang), skin (slang), trick, con, sting (informal), fleece 4 (Informal) often with out of = squeeze, wring, extract, wrest

● PHRASES screw something up 1 = contort, wrinkle, distort, pucker 2 (Informal) = bungle, botch, mess up, spoil, mishandle, make a mess of (slang), make a hash of (informal), crool or cruel (Austral. slang)

scribble = scrawl, write, jot, dash off

script NOUN 1 = text, lines, words, book, copy, dialogue, libretto 2 = handwriting, writing, calligraphy, penmanship

● VERB = write, draft

scripture = The Bible, The Gospels, The Scriptures, The Good Book, Holy Scripture, Holy Writ, Holy Bible

scrub 1 = scour, clean, polish, rub, wash, cleanse, buff 2 (Informal) = cancel, drop, give up, abolish, forget about, call off, delete

scrutiny = examination, study, investigation, search, analysis, inspection, exploration, perusal

sculpture NOUN = statue, figure, model, bust, effigy, figurine, statuette

● VERB = carve, form, model, fashion, shape, mould, sculpt, chisel

sea NOUN 1 = ocean, the deep, the waves, main 2 = mass, army, host, crowd, mob, abundance, swarm, horde

● PHRASES at sea = bewildered, lost, confused, puzzled, baffled, perplexed, mystified, flummoxed

RELATED WORDS
adjectives: marine, maritime

seal VERB = settle, clinch, conclude, consummate, finalize

● NOUN 1 = sealant, sealer, adhesive 2 = authentication, stamp, confirmation, ratification, insignia, imprimatur

seam 1 = joint, closure 2 = layer, vein, stratum, lode

sear = wither, burn, scorch, sizzle

search VERB = examine, investigate, explore, inspect, comb, scour, ransack, scrutinize, fossick (Austral. & N.Z.)

● NOUN = hunt, look, investigation, examination, pursuit, quest, inspection, exploration

● PHRASES search for something or someone = look for, hunt for, pursue

searching = keen, sharp, probing, close, intent, piercing, penetrating, quizzical ≠ superficial

searing 1 = acute, intense, shooting, severe, painful, stabbing, piercing, gut-wrenching 2 = cutting, biting, bitter, harsh, barbed, hurtful, caustic

season NOUN = period, time, term, spell

● VERB = flavour, salt, spice, enliven, pep up

seasoned = experienced, veteran, practised, hardened, time-served ≠ inexperienced

seasoning = flavouring, spice, salt and pepper, condiment

seat NOUN 1 = chair, bench, stall, stool, pew, settle 2 = membership, place, constituency, chair, incumbency 3 = centre, place, site, heart, capital, situation, source, hub 4 = mansion, house, residence, abode, ancestral hall
● VERB 1 = sit, place, settle, set, fix, locate, install 2 = hold, take, accommodate, sit, contain, cater for

second¹ ADJECTIVE 1 = next, following, succeeding, subsequent 2 = additional, other, further, extra, alternative 3 = inferior, secondary, subordinate, lower, lesser
● NOUN = supporter, assistant, aide, colleague, backer, helper, right-hand man
● VERB = support, back, endorse, approve, go along with

second² = moment, minute, instant, flash, sec (informal), jiffy (informal), trice

secondary 1 = subordinate, minor, lesser, lower, inferior, unimportant ≠ main 2 = resultant, contingent, derived, indirect ≠ original

second-hand = used, old, hand-me-down (informal), nearly new

secondly = next, second, moreover, furthermore, also, in the second place

secrecy 1 = mystery, stealth, concealment, furtiveness, secretiveness, clandestineness, covertness 2 = confidentiality, privacy 3 = privacy, silence, seclusion

secret ADJECTIVE 1 = undisclosed, unknown, confidential, underground, undercover, unrevealed 2 = concealed, hidden, disguised ≠ unconcealed 3 = undercover, furtive ≠ open 4 = secretive, reserved, close ≠ frank 5 = mysterious, cryptic, abstruse, occult, clandestine, arcane ≠ straightforward
● NOUN = private affair
● PHRASES **in secret** = secretly, surreptitiously, slyly

secretive = reticent, reserved, close, deep, uncommunicative, tight-lipped ≠ open

secretly = in secret, privately, surreptitiously, quietly, covertly, furtively, stealthily, clandestinely

sect = group, division, faction, party,

camp, denomination, schism

section 1 = part, piece, portion, division, slice, passage, segment, fraction 2 = district, area, region, sector, zone

sector 1 = part, division 2 = area, part, region, district, zone, quarter

secular = worldly, lay, earthly, civil, temporal, nonspiritual ≠ religious

secure VERB 1 = obtain, get, acquire, score (slang), gain, procure ≠ lose 2 = attach, stick, fix, bind, fasten ≠ detach
● ADJECTIVE 1 = safe, protected, immune, unassailable ≠ unprotected 2 = fast, firm, fixed, stable, steady, fastened, immovable ≠ insecure 3 = confident, sure, easy, certain, assured, reassured ≠ uneasy

security 1 = precautions, defence, safeguards, protection, safety measures 2 = assurance, confidence, conviction, certainty, reliance, sureness, positiveness ≠ insecurity 3 = pledge, insurance, guarantee, hostage, collateral, pawn, gage, surety 4 = protection, safety, custody, refuge, sanctuary, safekeeping ≠ vulnerability

sediment = dregs, grounds, residue, lees, deposit

seduce 1 = tempt, lure, entice, mislead, deceive, beguile, lead astray, inveigle 2 = corrupt, deprave, dishonour, debauch, deflower

seductive = tempting, inviting, attractive, enticing, provocative, alluring, bewitching

see VERB 1 = perceive, spot, notice, sight, witness, observe, distinguish, glimpse 2 = understand, get, follow, realize, appreciate, grasp, comprehend, fathom 3 = find out, learn, discover, determine, verify, ascertain 4 = consider, decide, reflect, deliberate, think over 5 = make sure, ensure, guarantee, make certain, see to it 6 = accompany, show, escort, lead, walk, usher 7 = speak to, receive, interview, consult, confer with 8 = meet, come across, happen on, bump into, run across, chance on 9 = go out with, court, date (informal, chiefly U.S.), go steady with (informal)
● PHRASES **seeing as** = since, as, in view of the fact that, inasmuch as

seed NOUN 1 = grain, pip, germ, kernel, egg, embryo, spore, ovum 2 = beginning, start, germ 3 = origin, source, nucleus 4 (Chiefly Bible) = offspring, children, descendants, issue, progeny

● PHRASES **go** or **run to seed** = decline, deteriorate, degenerate, decay, go downhill (*informal*), let yourself go, go to pot

seek 1 = look for, pursue, search for, be after, hunt 2 = try, attempt, aim, strive, endeavour, essay, aspire to

seem = appear, give the impression of being, look

seep = ooze, well, leak, soak, trickle, exude, permeate

seethe 1 = be furious, rage, fume, simmer, see red (*informal*), be livid, go ballistic (*slang, chiefly U.S.*) 2 = boil, bubble, foam, fizz, froth

segment = section, part, piece, division, slice, portion, wedge

segregate = set apart, divide, separate, isolate, discriminate against, dissociate ≠ unite

segregation = separation, discrimination, apartheid, isolation

seize 1 = grab, grip, grasp, take, snatch, clutch, snap up, pluck ≠ let go 2 = take by storm, take over, acquire, occupy, conquer 3 = capture, catch, arrest, apprehend, take captive ≠ release

seizure 1 = attack, fit, spasm, convulsion, paroxysm 2 = taking, grabbing, annexation, confiscation, commandeering 3 = capture, arrest, apprehension

seldom = rarely, not often, infrequently, hardly ever ≠ often

select VERB 1 = choose, take, pick, opt for, decide on, single out, adopt, settle upon ≠ reject

● ADJECTIVE 1 = choice, special, excellent, superior, first-class, hand-picked, top-notch (*informal*) ≠ ordinary 2 = exclusive, elite, privileged, cliquish ≠ indiscriminate

selection 1 = choice, choosing, pick, option, preference 2 = anthology, collection, medley, choice

selective = particular, discriminating, careful, discerning, tasteful, fastidious ≠ indiscriminate

selfish = self-centred, self-interested, greedy, ungenerous, egoistic or egoistical, egotistic or egotistical ≠ unselfish

sell VERB 1 = trade, exchange, barter ≠ buy 2 = deal in, market, trade in, stock, handle, retail, peddle, traffic in ≠ buy

● PHRASES **sell out of something** = run

out of, be out of stock of

seller = dealer, merchant, vendor, agent, retailer, supplier, purveyor, salesman or saleswoman

send VERB 1 = dispatch, forward, direct, convey, remit 2 = propel, hurl, fling, shoot, fire, cast, let fly

● PHRASES **send something** or **someone up** (*Brit. informal*) = mock, mimic, parody, spoof (*informal*), imitate, take off (*informal*), make fun of, lampoon

send-off = farewell, departure, leave-taking, valediction

senior 1 = higher ranking, superior ≠ subordinate 2 = the elder, major (*Brit.*) ≠ junior

sensation 1 = feeling, sense, impression, perception, awareness, consciousness 2 = excitement, thrill, stir, furore, commotion

sensational 1 = amazing, dramatic, thrilling, astounding ≠ dull 2 = shocking, exciting, melodramatic, shock-horror (*facetious*) ≠ unexciting 3 (*Informal*) = excellent, superb, mean (*slang*), impressive, smashing (*informal*), fabulous (*informal*), marvellous, out of this world (*informal*), booshit (*Austral. slang*), exo (*Austral. slang*), sik (*Austral. slang*) ≠ ordinary

sense NOUN 1 = faculty 2 = feeling, impression, perception, awareness, consciousness, atmosphere, aura 3 = understanding, awareness 4 *sometimes plural* = intelligence, reason, understanding, brains (*informal*), judgment, wisdom, wit(s), common sense ≠ foolishness 5 = meaning, significance, import, implication, drift, gist

● VERB = perceive, feel, understand, pick up, realize, be aware of, discern, get the impression ≠ be unaware of

sensibility *often plural* = feelings, emotions, sentiments, susceptibilities, moral sense

sensible 1 = wise, practical, prudent, shrewd, judicious ≠ foolish 2 = intelligent, practical, rational, sound, realistic, sage, shrewd, down-to-earth ≠ senseless

sensitive 1 = thoughtful, kindly, concerned, patient, attentive, tactful, unselfish 2 = delicate, tender 3 = susceptible to, responsive to, easily affected by 4 = touchy, oversensitive, easily upset, easily offended, easily hurt ≠ insensitive **5** = <u>precise</u>, fine, acute, keen, responsive ≠ imprecise

sensitivity 1 = <u>susceptibility</u>, responsiveness, receptiveness, sensitiveness **2** = <u>consideration</u>, patience, thoughtfulness **3** = <u>touchiness</u>, oversensitivity **4** = <u>responsiveness</u>, precision, keenness, acuteness

sensual 1 = <u>sexual</u>, erotic, raunchy (*slang*), lewd, lascivious, lustful, lecherous **2** = <u>physical</u>, bodily, voluptuous, animal, luxurious, fleshly, carnal

sentence NOUN **1** = <u>punishment</u>, condemnation **2** = <u>verdict</u>, order, ruling, decision, judgment, decree

● VERB **1** = <u>condemn</u>, doom **2** = <u>convict</u>, condemn, penalize

sentiment 1 = <u>feeling</u>, idea, view, opinion, attitude, belief, judgment **2** = <u>sentimentality</u>, emotion, tenderness, romanticism, sensibility, emotionalism, mawkishness

sentimental = <u>romantic</u>, touching, emotional, nostalgic, maudlin, weepy (*informal*), slushy (*informal*), schmaltzy (*slang*) ≠ unsentimental

separate ADJECTIVE **1** = <u>unconnected</u>, individual, particular, divided, divorced, isolated, detached, disconnected ≠ connected **2** = <u>individual</u>, independent, apart, distinct ≠ joined

● VERB **1** = <u>divide</u>, detach, disconnect, disjoin ≠ combine **2** = <u>come apart</u>, split, come away ≠ connect **3** = <u>sever</u>, break apart, split in two, divide in two ≠ join **4** = <u>split up</u>, part, divorce, break up, part company, get divorced, be estranged **5** = <u>distinguish</u>, mark, single out, set apart ≠ link

separated 1 = <u>estranged</u>, parted, separate, apart, disunited **2** = <u>disconnected</u>, parted, divided, separate, disassociated, disunited, sundered

separately 1 = <u>alone</u>, apart, not together, severally ≠ together **2** = <u>individually</u>, singly

separation 1 = <u>division</u>, break, dissociation, disconnection, disunion **2** = <u>split-up</u>, parting, split, divorce, break-up, rift

sequel 1 = <u>follow-up</u>, continuation, development **2** = <u>consequence</u>, result,

outcome, conclusion, end, upshot

sequence = <u>succession</u>, course, series, order, chain, cycle, arrangement, progression

series 1 = <u>sequence</u>, course, chain, succession, run, set, order, train **2** = <u>drama</u>, serial, soap (*informal*), sitcom (*informal*), soap opera, soapie (*Austral. slang*), situation comedy

serious 1 = <u>grave</u>, bad, critical, dangerous, acute, severe **2** = <u>important</u>, crucial, urgent, pressing, worrying, significant, grim, momentous ≠ unimportant **3** = <u>thoughtful</u>, detailed, careful, deep, profound, in-depth **4** = <u>deep</u>, sophisticated **5** = <u>solemn</u>, earnest, grave, sober, staid, humourless, unsmiling ≠ light-hearted **6** = <u>sincere</u>, earnest, genuine, honest, in earnest ≠ insincere

seriously 1 = <u>truly</u>, in earnest, all joking aside **2** = <u>badly</u>, severely, gravely, critically, acutely, dangerously

seriousness 1 = <u>importance</u>, gravity, urgency, significance **2** = <u>solemnity</u>, gravity, earnestness, gravitas

sermon = <u>homily</u>, address

servant = <u>attendant</u>, domestic, slave, maid, help, retainer, skivvy (*chiefly Brit.*)

serve 1 = <u>work for</u>, help, aid, assist, be in the service of **2** = <u>perform</u>, do, complete, fulfil, discharge **3** = <u>be adequate</u>, do, suffice, suit, satisfy, be acceptable, answer the purpose **4** = <u>present</u>, provide, supply, deliver, set out, dish up

service NOUN **1** = <u>facility</u>, system, resource, utility, amenity **2** = <u>ceremony</u>, worship, rite, observance **3** = <u>work</u>, labour, employment, business, office, duty **4** = <u>check</u>, maintenance check

● VERB = <u>overhaul</u>, check, maintain, tune (up), go over, fine tune

session = <u>meeting</u>, hearing, sitting, period, conference, congress, discussion, assembly

set¹ VERB **1** = <u>put</u>, place, lay, position, rest, plant, station, stick **2** = <u>arrange</u>, decide (upon), settle, establish, determine, fix, schedule, appoint **3** = <u>assign</u>, give, allot, prescribe **4** = <u>harden</u>, stiffen, solidify, cake, thicken, crystallize, congeal **5** = <u>go down</u>, sink, dip, decline, disappear, vanish, subside **6** = <u>prepare</u>, lay, spread, arrange, make ready

● ADJECTIVE **1** = <u>established</u>, planned,

decided, agreed, arranged, rigid, definite, inflexible 2 = <u>strict</u>, rigid, stubborn, inflexible ≠ flexible 3 = <u>conventional</u>, traditional, stereotyped, unspontaneous
● NOUN 1 = <u>scenery</u>, setting, scene, stage set 2 = <u>position</u>, bearing, attitude, carriage, posture
● PHRASES **be set on** or **upon something** = <u>be determined to</u>, be intent on, be bent on, be resolute about ◆ **set something up** 1 = <u>arrange</u>, organize, prepare, prearrange 2 = <u>establish</u>, begin, found, institute, initiate 3 = <u>build</u>, raise, construct, put up, assemble, put together, erect 4 = <u>assemble</u>, put up
set² 1 = <u>series</u>, collection, assortment, batch, compendium, ensemble 2 = <u>group</u>, company, crowd, circle, band, gang, faction, clique
setback = <u>hold-up</u>, check, defeat, blow, reverse, disappointment, hitch, misfortune
setting = <u>surroundings</u>, site, location, set, scene, background, context, backdrop
settle 1 = <u>resolve</u>, work out, put an end to, straighten out 2 = <u>pay</u>, clear, square (up), discharge 3 = <u>move to</u>, take up residence in, live in, dwell in, inhabit, reside in, set up home in, put down roots in 4 = <u>colonize</u>, populate, people, pioneer 5 = <u>land</u>, alight, descend, light, come to rest 6 = <u>calm</u>, quiet, relax, relieve, reassure, soothe, lull, quell ≠ disturb
settlement 1 = <u>agreement</u>, arrangement, working out, conclusion, establishment, confirmation 2 = <u>payment</u>, clearing, discharge 3 = <u>colony</u>, community, outpost, encampment, kainga or kaika (N.Z.)
settler = <u>colonist</u>, immigrant, pioneer, frontiersman
set-up (Informal) = <u>arrangement</u>, system, structure, organization, conditions, regime
sever 1 = <u>cut</u>, separate, split, part, divide, detach, disconnect, cut in two ≠ join 2 = <u>discontinue</u>, terminate, break off, put an end to, dissociate ≠ continue
several ADJECTIVE = <u>some</u>, a few, a number of, a handful of
● PRONOUN = <u>various</u>, different, diverse, sundry
severe 1 = <u>serious</u>, critical, terrible, desperate, extreme, awful, drastic, catastrophic 2 = <u>acute</u>, intense, violent, piercing, harrowing, unbearable, agonizing, insufferable 3 = <u>strict</u>, hard,

harsh, cruel, rigid, drastic, oppressive, austere ≠ lenient 4 = <u>grim</u>, serious, grave, forbidding, stern, unsmiling, tight-lipped ≠ genial 5 = <u>plain</u>, simple, austere, classic, restrained, Spartan, unadorned, unfussy ≠ fancy
severely 1 = <u>seriously</u>, badly, extremely, gravely, acutely 2 = <u>strictly</u>, harshly, sternly, sharply
severity = <u>strictness</u>, harshness, toughness, hardness, sternness, severeness
sew = <u>stitch</u>, tack, seam, hem
sex 1 = <u>gender</u> 2 (Informal) = <u>lovemaking</u>, sexual relations, copulation, fornication, coitus, coition
sexual 1 = <u>carnal</u>, erotic, intimate 2 = <u>sexy</u>, erotic, sensual, arousing, naughty, provocative, seductive, sensuous
sexuality = <u>desire</u>, lust, eroticism, sensuality, sexiness (informal), carnality
sexy = <u>erotic</u>, sensual, seductive, arousing, naughty, provocative, sensuous, suggestive
shabby 1 = <u>tatty</u>, worn, ragged, scruffy, tattered, threadbare ≠ smart 2 = <u>run-down</u>, seedy, mean, dilapidated 3 = <u>mean</u>, low, rotten (informal), cheap, dirty, despicable, contemptible, scurvy ≠ fair
shack = <u>hut</u>, cabin, shanty, whare (N.Z.)
shade NOUN 1 = <u>hue</u>, tone, colour, tint 2 = <u>shadow</u> 3 = <u>dash</u>, trace, hint, suggestion 4 = <u>nuance</u>, difference, degree 5 = <u>screen</u>, covering, cover, blind, curtain, shield, veil, canopy 6 (Literary) = <u>ghost</u>, spirit, phantom, spectre, apparition, kehua (N.Z.)
● VERB 1 = <u>darken</u>, shadow, cloud, dim 2 = <u>cover</u>, protect, screen, hide, shield, conceal, obscure, veil
shadow NOUN 1 = <u>silhouette</u>, shape, outline, profile 2 = <u>shade</u>, dimness, darkness, gloom, cover, dusk
● VERB 1 = <u>shade</u>, screen, shield, darken, overhang 2 = <u>follow</u>, tail (informal), trail, stalk
shady 1 = <u>shaded</u>, cool, dim ≠ sunny 2 (Informal) = <u>crooked</u>, dodgy (Brit., Austral., & N.Z. informal), unethical, suspect, suspicious, dubious, questionable, shifty ≠ honest
shaft 1 = <u>tunnel</u>, hole, passage, burrow, passageway, channel 2 = <u>handle</u>, staff, pole, rod, stem, baton, shank 3 = <u>ray</u>,

beam, gleam

shake VERB 1 = jiggle, agitate 2 = tremble, shiver, quake, quiver 3 = rock, totter 4 = wave, wield, flourish, brandish 5 = upset, shock, frighten, disturb, distress, rattle (*informal*), unnerve, traumatize
● NOUN = vibration, trembling, quaking, jerk, shiver, shudder, jolt, tremor

shaky 1 = unstable, weak, precarious, rickety ≠ stable 2 = unsteady, faint, trembling, faltering, quivery 3 = uncertain, suspect, dubious, questionable, iffy (*informal*) ≠ reliable

shallow = superficial, surface, empty, slight, foolish, trivial, meaningless, frivolous ≠ deep

sham NOUN = fraud, imitation, hoax, pretence, forgery, counterfeit, humbug, impostor ≠ the real thing
● ADJECTIVE = false, artificial, bogus, pretended, mock, imitation, simulated, counterfeit ≠ real

shambles 1 = chaos, mess, disorder, confusion, muddle, havoc, disarray, madhouse 2 = mess, jumble, untidiness

shame NOUN 1 = embarrassment, humiliation, ignominy, mortification, abashment ≠ shamelessness 2 = disgrace, scandal, discredit, smear, disrepute, reproach, dishonour, infamy ≠ honour
● VERB 1 = embarrass, disgrace, humiliate, humble, mortify, abash ≠ make proud 2 = dishonour, degrade, stain, smear, blot, debase, defile ≠ honour

shameful = disgraceful, outrageous, scandalous, mean, low, base, wicked, dishonourable ≠ admirable

shape NOUN 1 = appearance, form, aspect, guise, likeness, semblance 2 = form, profile, outline, lines, build, figure, silhouette, configuration 3 = pattern, model, frame, mould 4 = condition, state, health, trim, fettle
● VERB 1 = form, make, produce, create, model, fashion, mould 2 = mould, form, make, fashion, model, frame

share NOUN = part, portion, quota, ration, lot, due, contribution, allowance
● VERB 1 = divide, split, distribute, assign 2 = go halves on, go fifty-fifty on (*informal*)

sharp ADJECTIVE 1 = keen, jagged, serrated ≠ blunt 2 = quick-witted, clever, astute, knowing, quick, bright, alert,

penetrating ≠ dim 3 = cutting, biting, bitter, harsh, barbed, hurtful, caustic ≠ gentle 4 = sudden, marked, abrupt, extreme, distinct ≠ gradual 5 = clear, distinct, well-defined, crisp ≠ indistinct 6 = sour, tart, pungent, hot, acid, acrid, piquant ≠ bland 7 = acute, severe, intense, painful, shooting, stabbing, piercing, gut-wrenching
● ADVERB = promptly, precisely, exactly, on time, on the dot, punctually ≠ approximately

sharpen = make sharp, hone, whet, grind, edge

shatter 1 = smash, break, burst, crack, crush, pulverize 2 = destroy, ruin, wreck, demolish, torpedo

shattered 1 = devastated, crushed, gutted (*slang*) 2 (*Informal*) = exhausted, drained, worn out, done in (*informal*), all in (*slang*), knackered (*slang*), tired out, ready to drop

shave 1 = trim, crop 2 = scrape, trim, shear, pare

shed[1] 1 = hut, shack, outhouse, whare (*N.Z.*)

shed[2] 1 = drop, spill, scatter 2 = cast off, discard, moult, slough off 3 = give out, cast, emit, give, radiate

sheen = shine, gleam, gloss, polish, brightness, lustre

sheer 1 = total, complete, absolute, utter, pure, downright, out-and-out, unmitigated ≠ moderate 2 = steep, abrupt, precipitous ≠ gradual 3 = fine, thin, transparent, see-through, gossamer, diaphanous, gauzy ≠ thick

sheet 1 = page, leaf, folio, piece of paper 2 = plate, piece, panel, slab 3 = coat, film, layer, surface, stratum, veneer, overlay, lamina 4 = expanse, area, stretch, sweep, covering, blanket

shell NOUN 1 = husk, case, pod 2 = carapace 3 = frame, structure, hull, framework, chassis
● VERB = bomb, bombard, attack, blitz, strafe
● PHRASES **shell something out** (with money or a specified sum of money as object) = pay out, fork out (*slang*), give, hand over

shelter NOUN 1 = cover, screen 2 = protection, safety, refuge, cover 3 = refuge, haven, sanctuary, retreat, asylum

• VERB 1 = take shelter, hide, seek refuge, take cover 2 = protect, shield, harbour, safeguard, cover, hide, guard, defend ≠ endanger

sheltered 1 = screened, covered, protected, shielded, secluded ≠ exposed 2 = protected, screened, shielded, quiet, isolated, secluded, cloistered

shelve = postpone, defer, freeze, suspend, put aside, put on ice, put on the back burner (informal), take a rain check on (U.S. & Canad. informal)

shepherd NOUN = drover, stockman, herdsman, grazier
• VERB = guide, conduct, steer, herd, usher
▬ RELATED WORD
adjective: pastoral

shield NOUN = protection, cover, defence, screen, guard, shelter, safeguard
• VERB = protect, cover, screen, guard, defend, shelter, safeguard

shift VERB 1 = move, move around, budge 2 = remove, move, displace, relocate, rearrange, reposition
• NOUN 1 = change, shifting, displacement 2 = move, rearrangement

shimmer VERB = gleam, twinkle, glisten, scintillate
• NOUN = gleam, iridescence

shine VERB 1 = gleam, flash, beam, glow, sparkle, glitter, glare, radiate 2 = polish, buff, burnish, brush 3 = be outstanding, stand out, excel, be conspicuous
• NOUN 1 = polish, gloss, sheen, lustre 2 = brightness, light, sparkle, radiance

shining = bright, brilliant, gleaming, beaming, sparkling, shimmering, radiant, luminous

shiny = bright, gleaming, glossy, glistening, polished, lustrous

ship = vessel, boat, craft

shiver VERB = shudder, shake, tremble, quake, quiver
• NOUN = tremble, shudder, quiver, trembling, flutter, tremor

shock NOUN 1 = upset, blow, trauma, bombshell, turn (informal), distress, disturbance 2 = impact, blow, clash, collision 3 = start, scare, fright, turn, jolt
• VERB 1 = shake, stun, stagger, jolt, stupefy 2 = horrify, appal, disgust, revolt, sicken, nauseate, scandalize

shocking 1 (Informal) = terrible, appalling, dreadful, bad, horrendous,

ghastly, deplorable, abysmal 2 = appalling, outrageous, disgraceful, disgusting, dreadful, horrifying, revolting, sickening ≠ wonderful

shoot VERB 1 = open fire on, blast (slang), hit, kill, plug (slang), bring down 2 = fire, launch, discharge, project, hurl, fling, propel, emit 3 = speed, race, rush, charge, fly, tear, dash, barrel (along) (informal, chiefly U.S. & Canad.)
• NOUN = sprout, branch, bud, sprig, offshoot

shop = store, supermarket, boutique, emporium, hypermarket, dairy (N.Z.)

shore = beach, coast, sands, strand (poetic), seashore

short ADJECTIVE 1 = brief, fleeting, momentary ≠ long 2 = concise, brief, succinct, summary, compressed, terse, laconic, pithy ≠ lengthy 3 = small, little, squat, diminutive, petite, dumpy ≠ tall 4 = abrupt, sharp, terse, curt, brusque, impolite, discourteous, uncivil ≠ polite 5 = scarce, wanting, low, limited, lacking, scant, deficient ≠ plentiful
• ADVERB = abruptly, suddenly, without warning ≠ gradually

shortage = deficiency, want, lack, scarcity, dearth, paucity, insufficiency ≠ abundance

shortcoming = failing, fault, weakness, defect, flaw, imperfection

shorten 1 = cut, reduce, decrease, diminish, lessen, curtail, abbreviate, abridge ≠ increase 2 = turn up

shortly = soon, presently, before long, in a little while

shot 1 = discharge, gunfire, crack, blast, explosion, bang 2 = ammunition, bullet, slug, pellet, projectile, lead, ball 3 = marksman, shooter, markswoman 4 (Informal) = strike, throw, lob 5 = attempt, go (informal), try, turn, effort, stab (informal), endeavour

shoulder 1 = bear, carry, take on, accept, assume, be responsible for 2 = push, elbow, shove, jostle, press

shout VERB = cry (out), call (out), yell, scream, roar, bellow, bawl, holler (informal)
• NOUN = cry, call, yell, scream, roar, bellow
• PHRASES **shout someone down** = drown out, overwhelm, drown, silence

shove VERB = push, thrust, elbow, drive, press, propel, jostle, impel

● NOUN = <u>push</u>, knock, thrust, elbow, bump, nudge, jostle

● PHRASES **shove off** (*Informal*) = <u>go away</u>, leave, clear off (*informal*), depart, push off (*informal*), scram (*informal*)

shovel 1 = <u>move</u>, scoop, dredge, load, heap **2** = <u>stuff</u>, ladle

show VERB 1 = <u>indicate</u>, demonstrate, prove, reveal, display, point out, manifest, testify to ≠ disprove **2** = <u>display</u>, exhibit **3** = <u>guide</u>, lead, conduct, accompany, direct, escort **4** = <u>demonstrate</u>, describe, explain, teach, illustrate, instruct **5** = <u>be visible</u> ≠ be invisible **6** = <u>express</u>, display, reveal, indicate, register, demonstrate, manifest ≠ hide **7** = <u>turn up</u>, appear, attend **8** = <u>broadcast</u>, transmit, air, beam, relay, televise, put on the air

● NOUN **1** = <u>display</u>, sight, spectacle, array **2** = <u>exhibition</u>, fair, display, parade, pageant **3** = <u>appearance</u>, display, pose, parade **4** = <u>pretence</u>, appearance, illusion, affectation **5** = <u>programme</u>, broadcast, presentation, production **6** = <u>entertainment</u>, production, presentation

● PHRASES **show off** (*Informal*) = <u>boast</u>, brag, blow your own trumpet, swagger
♦ **show someone up** (*Informal*) = <u>embarrass</u>, let down, mortify, put to shame ♦ **show something off** = <u>exhibit</u>, display, parade, demonstrate, flaunt ♦ **show something up** = <u>reveal</u>, expose, highlight, lay bare

showdown (*Informal*) = <u>confrontation</u>, clash, face-off (*slang*)

shower NOUN = <u>deluge</u>
● VERB **1** = <u>cover</u>, dust, spray, sprinkle **2** = <u>inundate</u>, heap, lavish, pour, deluge

show-off (*Informal*) = <u>exhibitionist</u>, boaster, poseur, braggart

shred 1 = <u>strip</u>, bit, piece, scrap, fragment, sliver, tatter **2** = <u>particle</u>, trace, scrap, grain, atom, jot, iota

shrewd = <u>astute</u>, clever, sharp, keen, smart, calculating, intelligent, cunning ≠ naive

shriek VERB = <u>scream</u>, cry, yell, screech, squeal
● NOUN = <u>scream</u>, cry, yell, screech, squeal

shrink = <u>decrease</u>, dwindle, lessen, grow *or* get smaller, contract, narrow, diminish, shorten ≠ grow

shroud NOUN 1 = <u>winding sheet</u>, grave

clothes **2** = <u>covering</u>, veil, mantle, screen, pall
● VERB = <u>conceal</u>, cover, screen, hide, blanket, veil, cloak, envelop

shudder VERB = <u>shiver</u>, shake, tremble, quake, quiver, convulse
● NOUN = <u>shiver</u>, tremor, quiver, spasm

shuffle 1 = <u>shamble</u>, stagger, stumble, dodder **2** = <u>scuffle</u>, drag, scrape **3** = <u>rearrange</u>, jumble, mix, disorder, disarrange

shun = <u>avoid</u>, steer clear of, keep away from

shut VERB = <u>close</u>, secure, fasten, seal, slam ≠ open
● ADJECTIVE = <u>closed</u>, fastened, sealed, locked ≠ open
● PHRASES **shut down** = <u>stop work</u>, halt work, close down

shuttle = <u>go back and forth</u>, commute, go to and fro, alternate

shy ADJECTIVE 1 = <u>timid</u>, self-conscious, bashful, retiring, shrinking, coy, self-effacing, diffident ≠ confident **2** = <u>cautious</u>, wary, hesitant, suspicious, distrustful, chary ≠ reckless
● VERB *sometimes with* **off** *or* **away** = <u>recoil</u>, flinch, draw back, start, balk

sick 1 = <u>unwell</u>, ill, poorly (*informal*), diseased, crook (*Austral. & N.Z. informal*), ailing, under the weather, indisposed ≠ well **2** = <u>nauseous</u>, ill, queasy, nauseated **3** = <u>tired</u>, bored, fed up, weary, jaded **4** (*Informal*) = <u>morbid</u>, sadistic, black, macabre, ghoulish

sicken 1 = <u>disgust</u>, revolt, nauseate, repel, gross out (*U.S. slang*), turn your stomach **2** = <u>fall ill</u>, take sick, ail

sickening = <u>disgusting</u>, revolting, offensive, foul, distasteful, repulsive, nauseating, loathsome, yucko (*Austral. slang*) ≠ delightful

sickness 1 = <u>illness</u>, disorder, ailment, disease, complaint, bug (*informal*), affliction, malady **2** = <u>nausea</u>, queasiness **3** = <u>vomiting</u>

side NOUN 1 = <u>border</u>, margin, boundary, verge, flank, rim, perimeter, edge ≠ middle **2** = <u>face</u>, surface, facet **3** = <u>party</u>, camp, faction, cause **4** = <u>point of view</u>, viewpoint, position, opinion, angle, slant, standpoint **5** = <u>team</u>, squad, line-up **6** = <u>aspect</u>, feature, angle, facet
● ADJECTIVE = <u>subordinate</u>, minor,

secondary, subsidiary, lesser, marginal, incidental, ancillary ≠ main

● PHRASES **side with someone** = support, agree with, stand up for, favour, go along with, take the part of, ally yourself with

sidewalk (*U.S. & Canad.*) = pavement, footpath (*Austral. & N.Z.*)

sideways ADVERB 1 = indirectly, obliquely 2 = to the side, laterally

● ADJECTIVE = sidelong, oblique

sift 1 = part, filter, strain, separate, sieve 2 = examine, investigate, go through, research, analyse, work over, scrutinize

sight NOUN 1 = vision, eyes, eyesight, seeing, eye 2 = spectacle, show, scene, display, exhibition, vista, pageant 3 = view, range of vision, visibility 4 (*Informal*) = eyesore, mess, monstrosity

● VERB = spot, see, observe, distinguish, perceive, make out, discern, behold

▬ RELATED WORDS
adjectives: optical, visual

sign NOUN 1 = symbol, mark, device, logo, badge, emblem 2 = figure 3 = notice, board, warning, placard 4 = indication, evidence, mark, signal, symptom, hint, proof, gesture 5 = omen, warning, portent, foreboding, augury, auspice

● VERB 1 = gesture, indicate, signal, beckon, gesticulate 2 = autograph, initial, inscribe

signal NOUN 1 = flare, beam, beacon 2 = cue, sign, prompting, reminder 3 = sign, gesture, indication, mark, note, expression, token

● VERB = gesture, sign, wave, indicate, motion, beckon, gesticulate

significance = importance, consequence, moment, weight

significant 1 = important, serious, material, vital, critical, momentous, weighty, noteworthy ≠ insignificant 2 = meaningful, expressive, eloquent, indicative, suggestive ≠ meaningless

signify = indicate, mean, suggest, imply, intimate, be a sign of, denote, connote

silence NOUN 1 = quiet, peace, calm, hush, lull, stillness ≠ noise 2 = reticence, dumbness, taciturnity, muteness ≠ speech

● VERB = quieten, still, quiet, cut off, stifle, cut short, muffle, deaden ≠ make louder

silent 1 = mute, dumb, speechless, wordless, voiceless ≠ noisy 2 = uncommunicative, quiet, taciturn

3 = quiet, still, hushed, soundless, noiseless, muted ≠ loud

silently 1 = quietly, in silence, soundlessly, noiselessly, inaudibly, without a sound 2 = mutely, in silence, wordlessly

silhouette NOUN = outline, form, shape, profile

● VERB = outline, etch

silly 1 = stupid, ridiculous, absurd, daft, inane, senseless, idiotic, fatuous ≠ clever 2 = foolish, stupid, unwise, rash, irresponsible, thoughtless, imprudent ≠ sensible

similar 1 = alike, resembling, comparable ≠ different 2 *with* **to** = like, comparable to, analogous to, close to

similarity = resemblance, likeness, sameness, agreement, correspondence, analogy, affinity, closeness ≠ difference

simmer VERB 1 = bubble, boil gently, seethe 2 = fume, seethe, smoulder, rage, be angry

● PHRASES **simmer down** (*Informal*) = calm down, control yourself, cool off *or* down

simple 1 = uncomplicated, clear, plain, understandable, lucid, recognizable, comprehensible, intelligible ≠ complicated 2 = easy, straightforward, not difficult, effortless, painless, uncomplicated, undemanding 3 = plain, natural, classic, unfussy, unembellished ≠ elaborate 4 = pure, mere, sheer, unalloyed 5 = artless, innocent, naive, natural, sincere, unaffected, childlike, unsophisticated ≠ sophisticated 6 = unpretentious, modest, humble, homely, unfussy, unembellished ≠ fancy

simplicity 1 = straightforwardness, ease, clarity, clearness ≠ complexity 2 = plainness, restraint, purity, lack of adornment ≠ elaborateness

simplify = make simpler, streamline, disentangle, dumb down, reduce to essentials

simply 1 = just, only, merely, purely, solely 2 = totally, really, completely, absolutely, wholly, utterly 3 = clearly, straightforwardly, directly, plainly, intelligibly 4 = plainly, naturally, modestly, unpretentiously 5 = without doubt, surely, certainly, definitely, beyond question

simulate = pretend, act, feign, affect, put

on, sham

simultaneous = coinciding, concurrent, contemporaneous, coincident, synchronous, happening at the same time

simultaneously = at the same time, together, concurrently

sin NOUN 1 = wickedness, evil, crime, error, transgression, iniquity 2 = crime, offence, error, wrongdoing, misdeed, transgression, act of evil, guilt

• VERB = transgress, offend, lapse, err, go astray, do wrong

sincere = honest, genuine, real, true, serious, earnest, frank, candid, dinkum (Austral. & N.Z. informal) ≠ false

sincerely = honestly, truly, genuinely, seriously, earnestly, wholeheartedly, in earnest

sincerity = honesty, truth, candour, frankness, seriousness, genuineness

sing 1 = croon, carol, chant, warble, yodel, pipe 2 = trill, chirp, warble

singer = vocalist, crooner, minstrel, soloist, chorister, balladeer

single ADJECTIVE 1 = one, sole, lone, solitary, only, only one 2 = individual, separate, distinct 3 = unmarried, free, unattached, unwed 4 = separate, individual, exclusive, undivided, unshared 5 = simple, unmixed, unblended

• PHRASES **single something** or **someone out** = pick, choose, select, separate, distinguish, fix on, set apart, pick on or out

singly = one by one, individually, one at a time, separately

singular 1 = single, individual 2 = remarkable, outstanding, exceptional, notable, eminent, noteworthy ≠ ordinary 3 = unusual, odd, strange, extraordinary, curious, peculiar, eccentric, queer ≠ conventional

sinister = threatening, evil, menacing, dire, ominous, malign, disquieting ≠ reassuring

sink 1 = go down, founder, go under, submerge, capsize 2 = slump, drop 3 = fall, drop, slip, plunge, subside, abate 4 = drop, fall 5 = stoop, be reduced to, lower yourself 6 = decline, fade, fail, flag, weaken, diminish, decrease, deteriorate ≠ improve 7 = dig, bore, drill, drive, excavate

sip VERB = drink, taste, sample, sup

• NOUN = swallow, drop, taste, thimbleful

sit 1 = take a seat, perch, settle down 2 = place, set, put, position, rest, lay, settle, deposit 3 = be a member of, serve on, have a seat on, preside on 4 = convene, meet, assemble, officiate

site NOUN 1 = area, plot 2 = location, place, setting, point, position, situation, spot

• VERB = locate, put, place, set, position, establish, install, situate

situation 1 = position, state, case, condition, circumstances, equation, plight, state of affairs 2 = scenario, state of affairs 3 = location, place, setting, position, site, spot

size NOUN = dimensions, extent, range, amount, mass, volume, proportions, bulk

• PHRASES **size something** or **someone up** (Informal) = assess, evaluate, appraise, take stock of

sizeable or **sizable** = large, considerable, substantial, goodly, decent, respectable, largish

sizzle = hiss, spit, crackle, fry, frizzle

skeleton = bones, bare bones

sketch NOUN = drawing, design, draft, delineation

• VERB = draw, outline, represent, draft, depict, delineate, rough out

skilful = expert, skilled, masterly, able, professional, clever, practised, competent ≠ clumsy

skill = expertise, ability, proficiency, art, technique, facility, talent, craft ≠ clumsiness

skilled = expert, professional, able, masterly, skilful, proficient ≠ unskilled

skim 1 = remove, separate, cream 2 = glide, fly, coast, sail, float 3 usually with **over** or **through** = scan, glance, run your eye over

skin NOUN 1 = hide, pelt, fell 2 = peel, rind, husk, casing, outside, crust 3 = film, coating

• VERB 1 = peel 2 = scrape, flay

skinny = thin, lean, scrawny, emaciated, undernourished ≠ fat

skip 1 = hop, dance, bob, trip, bounce, caper, prance, frisk 2 = miss out, omit, leave out, overlook, pass over, eschew, give (something) a miss

skirt 1 = border, edge, flank 2 often with **around** or **round** = go round, circumvent

3 *often with* **around** *or* **round** = <u>avoid</u>, evade, steer clear of, circumvent

sky = <u>heavens</u>, firmament, rangi (*N.Z.*)

▓▓ RELATED WORD

adjective: celestial

slab = <u>piece</u>, slice, lump, chunk, wedge, portion

slack ADJECTIVE **1** = <u>limp</u>, relaxed, loose, lax **2** = <u>loose</u>, baggy ≠ taut **3** = <u>slow</u>, quiet, inactive, dull, sluggish, slow-moving ≠ busy **4** = <u>negligent</u>, lazy, lax, idle, inactive, slapdash, neglectful, slipshod ≠ strict

● VERB = <u>shirk</u>, idle, dodge, skive (*Brit. slang*), bludge (*Austral. & N.Z. informal*)

● NOUN **1** = <u>surplus</u>, excess, glut, surfeit, superabundance, superfluity **2** = <u>room</u>, excess, leeway, give (*informal*)

slam 1 = <u>bang</u>, crash, smash **2** = <u>throw</u>, dash, hurl, fling

slant VERB **1** = <u>slope</u>, incline, tilt, list, bend, lean, heel, cant **2** = <u>bias</u>, colour, twist, angle, distort

● NOUN **1** = <u>slope</u>, incline, tilt, gradient, camber **2** = <u>bias</u>, emphasis, prejudice, angle, point of view, one-sidedness

slanting = <u>sloping</u>, angled, inclined, tilted, tilting, bent, diagonal, oblique

slap VERB = <u>smack</u>, beat, clap, cuff, swipe, spank, clobber (*slang*), wallop (*informal*)

● NOUN = <u>smack</u>, blow, cuff, swipe, spank

slash VERB **1** = <u>cut</u>, slit, gash, lacerate, score, rend, rip, hack **2** = <u>reduce</u>, cut, decrease, drop, lower, moderate, diminish, cut down

● NOUN = <u>cut</u>, slit, gash, rent, rip, incision, laceration

slate (*Informal, chiefly Brit.*) = <u>criticize</u>, censure, rebuke, scold, tear into (*informal*)

slaughter VERB **1** = <u>kill</u>, murder, massacre, destroy, execute, assassinate **2** = <u>butcher</u>, kill, slay, massacre

● NOUN = <u>slaying</u>, killing, murder, massacre, bloodshed, carnage, butchery

slave NOUN **1** = <u>servant</u>, serf, vassal **2** = <u>drudge</u>, skivvy (*chiefly Brit.*)

● VERB = <u>toil</u>, drudge, slog

slavery = <u>enslavement</u>, servitude, subjugation, captivity, bondage ≠ freedom

slay 1 (*Archaic or literary*) = <u>kill</u>, slaughter, massacre, butcher **2** = <u>murder</u>, kill, massacre, slaughter, mow down

sleaze (*Informal*) = <u>corruption</u>, fraud,

dishonesty, bribery, extortion, venality, unscrupulousness

sleek = <u>glossy</u>, shiny, lustrous, smooth ≠ shaggy

sleep NOUN = <u>slumber(s)</u>, nap, doze, snooze (*informal*), hibernation, siesta, forty winks (*informal*), zizz (*Brit. informal*)

● VERB = <u>slumber</u>, doze, snooze (*informal*), hibernate, take a nap, catnap, drowse

sleepy = <u>drowsy</u>, sluggish, lethargic, heavy, dull, inactive ≠ wide-awake

slender 1 = <u>slim</u>, narrow, slight, lean, willowy ≠ chubby **2** = <u>faint</u>, slight, remote, slim, thin, tenuous ≠ strong **3** = <u>meagre</u>, little, small, scant, scanty ≠ large

slice NOUN = <u>piece</u>, segment, portion, wedge, sliver, helping, share, cut

● VERB = <u>cut</u>, divide, carve, sever, dissect, bisect

slick ADJECTIVE **1** = <u>skilful</u>, deft, adroit, dexterous, professional, polished ≠ clumsy **2** = <u>glib</u>, smooth, plausible, polished, specious

● VERB = <u>smooth</u>, sleek, plaster down

slide = <u>slip</u>, slither, glide, skim, coast

slight ADJECTIVE **1** = <u>small</u>, minor, insignificant, trivial, feeble, trifling, meagre, unimportant ≠ large **2** = <u>slim</u>, small, delicate, spare, fragile, lightly-built ≠ sturdy

● VERB = <u>snub</u>, insult, ignore, affront, scorn, disdain ≠ compliment

● NOUN = <u>insult</u>, snub, affront, rebuff, slap in the face (*informal*), (the) cold shoulder ≠ compliment

slightly = <u>a little</u>, a bit, somewhat

slim ADJECTIVE **1** = <u>slender</u>, slight, trim, thin, narrow, lean, svelte, willowy ≠ chubby **2** = <u>slight</u>, remote, faint, slender ≠ strong

● VERB = <u>lose weight</u>, diet ≠ put on weight

sling 1 (*Informal*) = <u>throw</u>, cast, toss, hurl, fling, chuck (*informal*), lob (*informal*), heave **2** = <u>hang</u>, suspend

slip VERB **1** = <u>fall</u>, skid **2** = <u>slide</u>, slither **3** = <u>sneak</u>, creep, steal

● NOUN = <u>mistake</u>, failure, error, blunder, lapse, omission, oversight

● PHRASES **give someone the slip** = <u>escape from</u>, get away from, evade, elude, lose (someone), flee, dodge

◆ **slip up** = <u>make a mistake</u>, blunder, err, miscalculate

slippery 1 = <u>smooth</u>, icy, greasy, glassy, slippy (*informal, dialect*), unsafe

2 = <u>untrustworthy</u>, tricky, cunning, dishonest, devious, crafty, evasive, shifty

slit VERB = <u>cut (open)</u>, rip, slash, knife, pierce, lance, gash

● NOUN **1** = <u>cut</u>, gash, incision, tear, rent **2** = <u>opening</u>, split

slogan = <u>catch phrase</u>, motto, tag-line, catchword

slope NOUN = <u>inclination</u>, rise, incline, tilt, slant, ramp, gradient

● VERB = <u>slant</u>, incline, drop away, fall, rise, lean, tilt

● PHRASES **slope off** (*Informal*) = <u>slink away</u>, slip away, creep away

sloping = <u>slanting</u>, leaning, inclined, oblique

sloppy 1 (*Informal*) = <u>careless</u>, slovenly, slipshod, messy, untidy **2** (*Informal*) = <u>sentimental</u>, soppy (*Brit. informal*), slushy (*informal*), gushing, mawkish, icky (*informal*)

slot NOUN **1** = <u>opening</u>, hole, groove, vent, slit, aperture **2** (*Informal*) = <u>place</u>, time, space, opening, position, vacancy

● VERB = <u>fit</u>, insert

slow ADJECTIVE **1** = <u>unhurried</u>, sluggish, leisurely, lazy, ponderous, dawdling, laggard, lackadaisical ≠ quick **2** = <u>prolonged</u>, protracted, long-drawn-out, lingering, gradual **3** = <u>late</u>, behind, tardy **4** = <u>stupid</u>, dim, dense, thick, retarded, dozy (*Brit. informal*), obtuse, braindead (*informal*) ≠ bright

● VERB **1** often with **down** = <u>decelerate</u>, brake **2** often with **down** = <u>delay</u>, hold up, handicap, retard ≠ speed up

slowly = <u>gradually</u>, unhurriedly ≠ quickly

sluggish = <u>inactive</u>, slow, lethargic, heavy, dull, inert, indolent, torpid ≠ energetic

slum = <u>hovel</u>, ghetto, shanty

slump VERB **1** = <u>fall</u>, sink, plunge, crash, collapse, slip ≠ increase **2** = <u>sag</u>, hunch, droop, slouch, loll

● NOUN **1** = <u>fall</u>, drop, decline, crash, collapse, reverse, downturn, trough ≠ increase **2** = <u>recession</u>, depression, stagnation, inactivity, hard *or* bad times

slur = <u>insult</u>, stain, smear, affront, innuendo, calumny, insinuation, aspersion

sly ADJECTIVE **1** = <u>roguish</u>, knowing, arch, mischievous, impish **2** = <u>cunning</u>, scheming, devious, secret, clever, subtle, wily, crafty ≠ open

● PHRASES **on the sly** = <u>secretly</u>, privately, covertly, surreptitiously, on the quiet

smack VERB **1** = <u>slap</u>, hit, strike, clap, cuff, swipe, spank **2** = <u>drive</u>, hit, strike

● NOUN = <u>slap</u>, blow, cuff, swipe, spank

● ADVERB (*Informal*) = <u>directly</u>, right, straight, squarely, precisely, exactly, slap (*informal*)

small 1 = <u>little</u>, minute, tiny, mini, miniature, minuscule, diminutive, petite ≠ big **2** = <u>young</u>, little, junior, wee, juvenile, youthful, immature **3** = <u>unimportant</u>, minor, trivial, insignificant, little, petty, trifling, negligible ≠ important **4** = <u>modest</u>, humble, unpretentious ≠ grand

smart ADJECTIVE **1** = <u>chic</u>, trim, neat, stylish, elegant, spruce, snappy, natty (*informal*) ≠ scruffy **2** = <u>clever</u>, bright, intelligent, quick, sharp, keen, acute, shrewd ≠ stupid **3** = <u>brisk</u>, quick, lively, vigorous

● VERB = <u>sting</u>, burn, hurt

smash VERB **1** = <u>break</u>, crush, shatter, crack, demolish, pulverize **2** = <u>shatter</u>, break, disintegrate, crack, splinter **3** = <u>collide</u>, crash, meet head-on, clash, come into collision **4** = <u>destroy</u>, ruin, wreck, trash (*slang*), lay waste

● NOUN = <u>collision</u>, crash, accident

smashing (*Informal, chiefly Brit.*) = <u>excellent</u>, mean (*slang*), great (*informal*), wonderful, brilliant (*informal*), cracking (*Brit. informal*), superb, fantastic (*informal*), booshit (*Austral. slang*), exo (*Austral. slang*), sik (*Austral. slang*) ≠ awful

smear VERB **1** = <u>spread over</u>, daub, rub on, cover, coat, bedaub **2** = <u>slander</u>, malign, blacken, besmirch **3** = <u>smudge</u>, soil, dirty, stain, sully

● NOUN **1** = <u>smudge</u>, daub, streak, blot, blotch, splotch **2** = <u>slander</u>, libel, defamation, calumny

smell NOUN **1** = <u>odour</u>, scent, fragrance, perfume, bouquet, aroma **2** = <u>stink</u>, stench, pong (*Brit. informal*), fetor

● VERB **1** = <u>stink</u>, reek, pong (*Brit. informal*) **2** = <u>sniff</u>, scent

smile VERB = <u>grin</u>, beam, smirk, twinkle, grin from ear to ear

● NOUN = <u>grin</u>, beam, smirk

smooth ADJECTIVE **1** = <u>even</u>, level, flat, plane, flush, horizontal ≠ uneven **2** = <u>sleek</u>, polished, shiny, glossy, silky, velvety ≠ rough **3** = <u>mellow</u>, pleasant, mild, agreeable **4** = <u>flowing</u>, steady, regular, uniform, rhythmic 5 = easy, effortless, well-ordered 6 = suave, slick, persuasive, urbane, glib, facile, unctuous, smarmy (*Brit. informal*)

● VERB 1 = flatten, level, press, plane, iron 2 = ease, facilitate ≠ hinder

smother 1 = extinguish, put out, stifle, snuff 2 = suffocate, choke, strangle, stifle 3 = suppress, stifle, repress, hide, conceal, muffle

smug = self-satisfied, superior, complacent, conceited

snack = light meal, bite, refreshment(s)

snag NOUN = difficulty, hitch, problem, obstacle, catch, disadvantage, complication, drawback

● VERB = catch, tear, rip

snake = serpent

RELATED WORD

adjective: serpentine

snap VERB 1 = break, crack, separate 2 = pop, click, crackle 3 = speak sharply, bark, lash out at, jump down (someone's) throat (*informal*) 4 = bite at, bite, nip

● ADJECTIVE = instant, immediate, sudden, spur-of-the-moment

● PHRASES **snap something up** = grab, seize, take advantage of, pounce upon

snare NOUN = trap, net, wire, gin, noose

● VERB = trap, catch, net, wire, seize, entrap

snatch VERB 1 = grab, grip, grasp, clutch 2 = steal, take, nick (*slang, chiefly Brit.*), pinch (*informal*), lift (*informal*), pilfer, filch, thieve 3 = win 4 = save, recover, get out, salvage

● NOUN = bit, part, fragment, piece, snippet

sneak VERB 1 = slink, slip, steal, pad, skulk 2 = slip, smuggle, spirit

● NOUN = informer, betrayer, telltale, Judas, accuser, stool pigeon, nark (*Brit., Austral., & N.Z. slang*), fizgig (*Austral. slang*)

sneaking 1 = nagging, worrying, persistent, uncomfortable 2 = secret, private, hidden, unexpressed, unvoiced, undivulged

sneer VERB 1 = scorn, mock, ridicule, laugh, jeer, disdain, deride 2 = say contemptuously, snigger

● NOUN = scorn, ridicule, mockery, derision, jeer, gibe

sniff 1 = breathe in, inhale 2 = smell, scent 3 = inhale, breathe in, suck in, draw in

snub VERB 1 = insult, slight, put down, humiliate, cut (*informal*), rebuff, cold-shoulder

● NOUN = insult, put-down, affront, slap in the face

so = therefore, thus, hence, consequently, then, as a result, accordingly, thence

soak VERB 1 = steep 2 = wet, damp, saturate, drench, moisten, suffuse, wet through, waterlog 3 = penetrate, permeate, seep

● PHRASES **soak something up** = absorb, suck up, assimilate

soaking = soaked, dripping, saturated, drenched, sodden, streaming, sopping, wet through

soar 1 = rise, increase, grow, mount, climb, go up, rocket, escalate 2 = fly, wing, climb, ascend ≠ plunge 3 = tower, climb, go up

sob VERB = cry, weep, howl, shed tears

● NOUN = cry, whimper, howl

sober 1 = abstinent, temperate, abstemious, moderate ≠ drunk 2 = serious, cool, grave, reasonable, steady, composed, rational, solemn ≠ frivolous 3 = plain, dark, sombre, quiet, subdued, drab ≠ bright

so-called = alleged, supposed, professed, pretended, self-styled

social ADJECTIVE 1 = communal, community, collective, group, public, general, common 2 = organized, gregarious

● NOUN = get-together (*informal*), party, gathering, function, reception, social gathering

society 1 = the community, people, the public, humanity, civilization, mankind 2 = culture, community, population 3 = organization, group, club, union, league, association, institute, circle 4 = upper classes, gentry, elite, high society, beau monde 5 (*Old-fashioned*) = companionship, company, fellowship, friendship

sofa = couch, settee, divan, chaise longue

soft 1 = velvety, smooth, silky, feathery, downy, fleecy ≠ rough 2 = yielding, elastic ≠ hard 3 = soggy, swampy, marshy, boggy 4 = squashy, sloppy, mushy, spongy, gelatinous, pulpy 5 = pliable, flexible, supple, malleable, plastic, elastic, bendable, mouldable 6 = quiet, gentle, murmured, muted, dulcet, soft-toned ≠ loud 7 = lenient, easy-going, lax, indulgent, permissive, spineless, overindulgent ≠ harsh **8** = <u>kind</u>, tender, sentimental, compassionate, sensitive, gentle, tenderhearted, touchy-feely (*informal*) **9** (*Informal*) = <u>easy</u>, comfortable, undemanding, cushy (*informal*) **10** = <u>pale</u>, light, subdued, pastel, bland, mellow ≠ bright **11** = <u>dim</u>, faint, dimmed ≠ bright **12** = <u>mild</u>, temperate, balmy

soften 1 = <u>melt</u>, tenderize **2** = <u>lessen</u>, moderate, temper, ease, cushion, subdue, allay, mitigate

soil[1] = <u>earth</u>, ground, clay, dust, dirt **2** = <u>territory</u>, country, land

soil[2] = <u>dirty</u>, foul, stain, pollute, tarnish, sully, defile, besmirch ≠ clean

soldier = <u>fighter</u>, serviceman, trooper, warrior, man-at-arms, squaddie *or* squaddy (*Brit. slang*)

sole = <u>only</u>, one, single, individual, alone, exclusive, solitary

solely = <u>only</u>, completely, entirely, exclusively, alone, merely

solemn 1 = <u>serious</u>, earnest, grave, sober, sedate, staid ≠ cheerful **2** = <u>formal</u>, grand, grave, dignified, ceremonial, stately, momentous ≠ informal

solid 1 = <u>firm</u>, hard, compact, dense, concrete ≠ unsubstantial **2** = <u>strong</u>, stable, sturdy, substantial, unshakable ≠ unstable **3** = <u>reliable</u>, dependable, upstanding, worthy, upright, trusty ≠ unreliable **4** = <u>sound</u>, real, reliable, good, genuine, dinkum (*Austral. & N.Z. informal*) ≠ unsound

solidarity = <u>unity</u>, unification, accord, cohesion, team spirit, unanimity, concordance, like-mindedness, kotahitanga (*N.Z.*)

solitary 1 = <u>unsociable</u>, reclusive, unsocial, isolated, lonely, cloistered, lonesome, friendless ≠ sociable **2** = <u>lone</u>, alone **3** = <u>isolated</u>, remote, out-of-the-way, hidden, unfrequented ≠ busy

solution 1 = <u>answer</u>, key, result, explanation **2** (*Chemistry*) = <u>mixture</u>, mix, compound, blend, solvent

solve = <u>answer</u>, work out, resolve, crack, clear up, unravel, decipher, suss (out) (*slang*)

sombre 1 = <u>gloomy</u>, sad, sober, grave, dismal, mournful, lugubrious, joyless ≠ cheerful **2** = <u>dark</u>, dull, gloomy, sober, drab ≠ bright

somebody = <u>celebrity</u>, name, star, notable, household name, dignitary, luminary, personage ≠ nobody

somehow = <u>one way or another</u>, come what may, come hell or high water (*informal*), by fair means or foul, by hook or (by) crook, by some means or other

sometimes = <u>occasionally</u>, at times, now and then ≠ always

song = <u>ballad</u>, air, tune, carol, chant, chorus, anthem, number, waiata (*N.Z.*)

soon = <u>before long</u>, shortly, in the near future

soothe 1 = <u>calm</u>, still, quiet, hush, appease, lull, pacify, mollify ≠ upset **2** = <u>relieve</u>, ease, alleviate, assuage ≠ irritate

soothing 1 = <u>calming</u>, relaxing, peaceful, quiet, calm, restful **2** = <u>emollient</u>, palliative

sophisticated 1 = <u>complex</u>, advanced, complicated, subtle, delicate, elaborate, refined, intricate ≠ simple **2** = <u>cultured</u>, refined, cultivated, worldly, cosmopolitan, urbane ≠ unsophisticated

sophistication = <u>poise</u>, worldliness, savoir-faire, urbanity, finesse, worldly wisdom

sore 1 = <u>painful</u>, smarting, raw, tender, burning, angry, sensitive, irritated **2** = <u>annoyed</u>, cross, angry, pained, hurt, upset, stung, irritated, tooshie (*Austral. slang*), hoha (*N.Z.*) **3** = <u>annoying</u>, troublesome **4** (*Literary*) = <u>urgent</u>, desperate, extreme, dire, pressing, critical, acute

sorrow NOUN **1** = <u>grief</u>, sadness, woe, regret, distress, misery, mourning, anguish ≠ joy **2** = <u>hardship</u>, trial, tribulation, affliction, trouble, woe, misfortune ≠ good fortune

● VERB = <u>grieve</u>, mourn, lament, be sad, bemoan, agonize, bewail ≠ rejoice

sorry 1 = <u>regretful</u>, apologetic, contrite, repentant, remorseful, penitent, shamefaced, conscience-stricken ≠ unapologetic **2** = <u>sympathetic</u>, moved, full of pity, compassionate, commiserative ≠ unsympathetic **3** = <u>wretched</u>, miserable, pathetic, mean, poor, sad, pitiful, deplorable

sort NOUN = <u>kind</u>, type, class, make, order, style, quality, nature

● VERB = <u>arrange</u>, group, order, rank, divide, grade, classify, categorize

soul 1 = <u>spirit</u>, essence, life, vital force,

wairua (*N.Z.*) 2 = <u>embodiment</u>, essence, epitome, personification, quintessence, type 3 = <u>person</u>, being, individual, body, creature, man or woman

sound¹ NOUN 1 = <u>noise</u>, din, report, tone, reverberation 2 = <u>idea</u>, impression, drift 3 = <u>cry</u>, noise, peep, squeak 4 = <u>tone</u>, music, note

● VERB 1 = <u>toll</u>, set off 2 = <u>resound</u>, echo, go off, toll, set off, chime, reverberate, clang 3 = <u>seem</u>, seem to be, appear to be

<img> RELATED WORDS

adjectives: sonic, acoustic

sound² 1 = <u>fit</u>, healthy, perfect, intact, unhurt, uninjured, unimpaired ≠ frail 2 = <u>sturdy</u>, strong, solid, stable 3 = <u>sensible</u>, wise, reasonable, right, correct, proper, valid, rational ≠ irresponsible 4 = <u>deep</u>, unbroken, undisturbed, untroubled ≠ troubled

sour 1 = <u>sharp</u>, acid, tart, bitter, pungent, acetic ≠ sweet 2 = <u>rancid</u>, turned, gone off, curdled, gone bad, off ≠ fresh 3 = <u>bitter</u>, tart, acrimonious, embittered, disagreeable, ill-tempered, waspish, ungenerous ≠ good-natured

source 1 = <u>cause</u>, origin, derivation, beginning, author 2 = <u>informant</u>, authority 3 = <u>origin</u>, fount

souvenir = <u>keepsake</u>, reminder, memento

sovereign ADJECTIVE 1 = <u>supreme</u>, ruling, absolute, royal, principal, imperial, kingly or queenly 2 = <u>excellent</u>, efficient, effectual

● NOUN = <u>monarch</u>, ruler, king or queen, chief, potentate, emperor or empress, prince or princess

sovereignty = <u>supreme power</u>, domination, supremacy, primacy, kingship, rangatiratanga (*N.Z.*)

sow = <u>scatter</u>, plant, seed, implant

space 1 = <u>room</u>, capacity, extent, margin, scope, play, expanse, leeway 2 = <u>period</u>, interval, time, while, span, duration 3 = <u>outer space</u>, the universe, the galaxy, the solar system, the cosmos 4 = <u>blank</u>, gap, interval

spacious = <u>roomy</u>, large, huge, broad, extensive, ample, expansive, capacious ≠ limited

span NOUN 1 = <u>period</u>, term, duration, spell 2 = <u>extent</u>, reach, spread, length, distance, stretch

● VERB = <u>extend across</u>, cross, bridge, cover, link, traverse

spar = <u>argue</u>, row, squabble, scrap (*informal*), wrangle, bicker

spare ADJECTIVE 1 = <u>back-up</u>, reserve, second, extra, additional, auxiliary 2 = <u>extra</u>, surplus, leftover, over, free, odd, unwanted, unused ≠ necessary 3 = <u>free</u>, leisure, unoccupied 4 = <u>thin</u>, lean, meagre, gaunt, wiry ≠ plump

● VERB 1 = <u>afford</u>, give, grant, do without, part with, manage without, let someone have 2 = <u>have mercy on</u>, pardon, leave, let off (*informal*), go easy on (*informal*), save (from harm) ≠ show no mercy to

sparing = <u>economical</u>, frugal, thrifty, saving, careful, prudent ≠ lavish

spark NOUN 1 = <u>flicker</u>, flash, gleam, glint, flare 2 = <u>trace</u>, hint, scrap, atom, jot, vestige

● VERB *often with* **off** = <u>start</u>, stimulate, provoke, inspire, trigger (off), set off, precipitate

sparkle VERB = <u>glitter</u>, flash, shine, gleam, shimmer, twinkle, dance, glint

● NOUN 1 = <u>glitter</u>, flash, gleam, flicker, brilliance, twinkle, glint 2 = <u>vivacity</u>, life, spirit, dash, vitality, élan, liveliness

spate = <u>flood</u>, flow, torrent, rush, deluge, outpouring

speak 1 = <u>talk</u>, say something 2 = <u>articulate</u>, say, pronounce, utter, tell, state, talk, express 3 = <u>converse</u>, talk, chat, discourse, confer, commune, exchange views, korero (*N.Z.*) 4 = <u>lecture</u>, address an audience

speaker = <u>orator</u>, public speaker, lecturer, spokesperson, spokesman or spokeswoman

spearhead = <u>lead</u>, head, pioneer, launch, set off, initiate, set in motion

special 1 = <u>exceptional</u>, important, significant, particular, unique, unusual, extraordinary, memorable ≠ ordinary 2 = <u>specific</u>, particular, distinctive, individual, appropriate, precise ≠ general

specialist = <u>expert</u>, authority, professional, master, consultant, guru, buff (*informal*), connoisseur, fundi (*S. African*)

speciality = <u>forte</u>, métier, specialty, bag (*slang*), pièce de résistance (*French*)

species = <u>kind</u>, sort, type, group, class, variety, breed, category

specific 1 = <u>particular</u>, special, characteristic, distinguishing ≠ general

2 = <u>precise</u>, exact, explicit, definite, express, clear-cut, unequivocal ≠ vague
3 = <u>peculiar</u>, appropriate, individual, particular, unique

specification = <u>requirement</u>, detail, particular, stipulation, condition, qualification

specify = <u>state</u>, designate, stipulate, name, detail, mention, indicate, define

specimen 1 = <u>sample</u>, example, model, type, pattern, instance, representative, exemplification **2** = <u>example</u>, model, type

spectacle 1 = <u>show</u>, display, exhibition, event, performance, extravaganza, pageant **2** = <u>sight</u>, wonder, scene, phenomenon, curiosity, marvel

spectacular ADJECTIVE = <u>impressive</u>, striking, dramatic, stunning (*informal*), grand, magnificent, splendid, dazzling ≠ unimpressive
● NOUN = <u>show</u>, display, spectacle

spectator = <u>onlooker</u>, observer, viewer, looker-on, watcher, bystander ≠ participant

█ **RELATED WORD**
fear of: arachnophobia

spectre = <u>ghost</u>, spirit, phantom, vision, apparition, wraith, kehua (*N.Z.*)

speculate 1 = <u>conjecture</u>, consider, wonder, guess, surmise, theorize, hypothesize **2** = <u>gamble</u>, risk, venture, hazard

speculation 1 = <u>theory</u>, opinion, hypothesis, conjecture, guess, surmise, guesswork, supposition **2** = <u>gamble</u>, risk, hazard

speculative = <u>hypothetical</u>, academic, theoretical, notional, conjectural, suppositional

speech 1 = <u>communication</u>, talk, conversation, discussion, dialogue **2** = <u>diction</u>, pronunciation, articulation, delivery, fluency, inflection, intonation, elocution **3** = <u>language</u>, tongue, jargon, dialect, idiom, parlance, articulation, diction **4** = <u>talk</u>, address, lecture, discourse, homily, oration, spiel (*informal*), whaikorero (*N.Z.*)

speed NOUN **1** = <u>rate</u>, pace **2** = <u>swiftness</u>, rush, hurry, haste, rapidity, quickness ≠ slowness
● VERB **1** = <u>race</u>, rush, hurry, zoom, career, tear, barrel (along) (*informal*, *chiefly U.S. & Canad.*), gallop ≠ crawl **2** = <u>help</u>, advance, aid, boost, assist, facilitate, expedite ≠ hinder

speedy = <u>quick</u>, fast, rapid, swift, express, immediate, prompt, hurried ≠ slow

spell¹ = <u>indicate</u>, mean, signify, point to, imply, augur, portend

spell² 1 = <u>incantation</u>, charm, makutu (*N.Z.*) **2** = <u>enchantment</u>, magic, fascination, glamour, allure, bewitchment

spell³ = <u>period</u>, time, term, stretch, course, season, interval, bout

spend 1 = <u>pay out</u>, fork out (*slang*), expend, disburse ≠ save **2** = <u>pass</u>, fill, occupy, while away **3** = <u>use up</u>, waste, squander, empty, drain, exhaust, consume, run through ≠ save

sphere 1 = <u>ball</u>, globe, orb, globule, circle **2** = <u>field</u>, department, function, territory, capacity, province, patch, scope

spice 1 = <u>seasoning</u> **2** = <u>excitement</u>, zest, colour, pep, zing (*informal*), piquancy

spicy 1 = <u>hot</u>, seasoned, aromatic, savoury, piquant **2** (*Informal*) = <u>risqué</u>, racy, ribald, hot (*informal*), suggestive, titillating, indelicate

spike NOUN = <u>point</u>, stake, spine, barb, prong
● VERB = <u>impale</u>, spit, spear, stick

spill 1 = <u>tip over</u>, overturn, capsize, knock over **2** = <u>shed</u>, discharge, disgorge **3** = <u>slop</u>, flow, pour, run, overflow

spin VERB **1** = <u>revolve</u>, turn, rotate, reel, whirl, twirl, gyrate, pirouette **2** = <u>reel</u>, swim, whirl
● NOUN **1** (*Informal*) = <u>drive</u>, ride, joy ride (*informal*) **2** = <u>revolution</u>, roll, whirl, gyration
● PHRASES **spin something out** = <u>prolong</u>, extend, lengthen, draw out, drag out, delay, amplify

spine 1 = <u>backbone</u>, vertebrae, spinal column, vertebral column **2** = <u>barb</u>, spur, needle, spike, ray, quill

spiral ADJECTIVE = <u>coiled</u>, winding, whorled, helical
● NOUN = <u>coil</u>, helix, corkscrew, whorl

spirit NOUN **1** = <u>soul</u>, life **2** = <u>life force</u>, vital spark, mauri (*N.Z.*) **3** = <u>ghost</u>, phantom, spectre, apparition, atua (*N.Z.*), kehua (*N.Z.*) **4** = <u>courage</u>, guts (*informal*), grit, backbone, spunk (*informal*), gameness **5** = <u>liveliness</u>, energy, vigour, life, force, fire, enthusiasm, animation **6** = <u>attitude</u>, character, temper, outlook, temperament, disposition 7 = <u>heart</u>, sense, nature, soul, core, substance, essence, quintessence 8 = <u>intention</u>, meaning, purpose, purport, gist 9 = <u>feeling</u>, atmosphere, character, tone, mood, tenor, ambience

● NOUN = <u>mood</u>, feelings, morale, temper, disposition, state of mind, frame of mind

spirited = <u>lively</u>, energetic, animated, active, feisty (*informal*, *chiefly U.S. & Canad.*), vivacious, mettlesome ≠ lifeless

spiritual 1 = <u>nonmaterial</u>, immaterial, incorporeal ≠ material 2 = <u>sacred</u>, religious, holy, divine, devotional

spit VERB 1 = <u>expectorate</u> 2 = <u>eject</u>, throw out

● NOUN = <u>saliva</u>, dribble, spittle, drool, slaver

spite NOUN = <u>malice</u>, malevolence, ill will, hatred, animosity, venom, spleen, spitefulness ≠ kindness

● VERB = <u>annoy</u>, hurt, injure, harm, vex ≠ benefit

● PHRASES **in spite of** = <u>despite</u>, regardless of, notwithstanding, (even) though

splash VERB 1 = <u>paddle</u>, plunge, bathe, dabble, wade, wallow 2 = <u>scatter</u>, shower, spray, sprinkle, wet, spatter, slop 3 = <u>spatter</u>, mark, stain, speck, speckle

● NOUN 1 = <u>dash</u>, touch, spattering 2 = <u>spot</u>, burst, patch, spurt 3 = <u>blob</u>, spot, smudge, stain, smear, fleck, speck

splendid 1 = <u>excellent</u>, wonderful, marvellous, great (*informal*), cracking (*Brit. informal*), fantastic (*informal*), first-class, glorious, booshit (*Austral. slang*), exo (*Austral. slang*), sik (*Austral. slang*) ≠ poor 2 = <u>magnificent</u>, grand, impressive, rich, superb, costly, gorgeous, lavish ≠ squalid

splendour = <u>magnificence</u>, grandeur, show, display, spectacle, richness, nobility, pomp ≠ squalor

splinter NOUN = <u>sliver</u>, fragment, chip, flake

● VERB = <u>shatter</u>, split, fracture, disintegrate

split VERB 1 = <u>break</u>, crack, burst, open, give way, come apart, come undone 2 = <u>cut</u>, break, crack, snap, chop 3 = <u>divide</u>, separate, disunite, disband, cleave 4 = <u>diverge</u>, separate, branch, fork, part 5 = <u>tear</u>, rend, rip 6 = <u>share out</u>, divide, distribute, halve, allocate, partition, allot, apportion

● NOUN 1 = <u>division</u>, breach, rift, rupture, discord, schism, estrangement, dissension 2 = <u>separation</u>, break-up, split-up 3 = <u>crack</u>, tear, rip, gap, rent, breach, slit, fissure

● ADJECTIVE 1 = <u>divided</u> 2 = <u>broken</u>, cracked, fractured, ruptured, cleft

spoil VERB 1 = <u>ruin</u>, destroy, wreck, damage, injure, harm, mar, trash (*slang*), crool or cruel (*Austral. slang*) ≠ improve 2 = <u>overindulge</u>, indulge, pamper, cosset, coddle, mollycoddle ≠ deprive 3 = <u>indulge</u>, pamper, satisfy, gratify, pander to 4 = <u>go bad</u>, turn, go off (*Brit. informal*), rot, decay, decompose, curdle, addle

● PLURAL NOUN = <u>booty</u>, loot, plunder, prey, swag (*slang*)

spoken = <u>verbal</u>, voiced, expressed, uttered, oral, said, told, unwritten

spokesperson = <u>speaker</u>, official, spokesman or spokeswoman, voice, spin doctor (*informal*), mouthpiece

sponsor VERB = <u>back</u>, fund, finance, promote, subsidize, patronize

● NOUN = <u>backer</u>, patron, promoter

spontaneous = <u>unplanned</u>, impromptu, unprompted, willing, natural, voluntary, instinctive, impulsive ≠ planned

sport NOUN 1 = <u>game</u>, exercise, recreation, play, amusement, diversion, pastime 2 = <u>fun</u>, joking, teasing, banter, jest, badinage

● VERB (*Informal*) = <u>wear</u>, display, flaunt, exhibit, flourish, show off, vaunt

sporting = <u>fair</u>, sportsmanlike, game (*informal*) ≠ unfair

sporty = <u>athletic</u>, outdoor, energetic

spot NOUN 1 = <u>mark</u>, stain, speck, scar, blot, smudge, blemish, speckle 2 = <u>pimple</u>, pustule, zit (*slang*) 3 = <u>place</u>, site, point, position, scene, location 4 (*Informal*) = <u>predicament</u>, trouble, difficulty, mess, plight, hot water (*informal*), quandary, tight spot

● VERB 1 = <u>see</u>, observe, catch sight of, sight, recognize, detect, make out, discern 2 = <u>mark</u>, stain, soil, dirty, fleck, spatter, speckle, splodge

spotlight NOUN = <u>attention</u>, limelight, public eye, fame

● VERB = <u>highlight</u>, draw attention to, accentuate

spotted = <u>speckled</u>, dotted, flecked,

mottled, dappled

spouse = partner, mate, husband *or* wife, consort, significant other (*U.S. informal*)

sprawl = loll, slump, lounge, flop, slouch

spray¹ NOUN 1 = droplets, fine mist, drizzle 2 = aerosol, sprinkler, atomizer

● VERB = scatter, shower, sprinkle, diffuse

spray² = sprig, floral arrangement, branch, corsage

spread VERB 1 = open (out), extend, stretch, unfold, sprawl, unroll 2 = extend, open, stretch 3 = grow, increase, expand, widen, escalate, proliferate, multiply, broaden 4 = circulate, broadcast, propagate, disseminate, make known ≠ suppress 5 = diffuse, cast, shed, radiate

● NOUN 1 = increase, development, advance, expansion, proliferation, dissemination, dispersal 2 = extent, span, stretch, sweep

spree = fling, binge (*informal*), orgy

spring NOUN = flexibility, bounce, resilience, elasticity, buoyancy

● VERB 1 = jump, bound, leap, bounce, vault 2 *often with* from = originate, come, derive, start, issue, proceed, arise, stem

RELATED WORD

adjective: vernal

sprinkle = scatter, dust, strew, pepper, shower, spray, powder, dredge

sprinkling = scattering, dusting, few, dash, handful, sprinkle

sprint = run, race, shoot, tear, dash, dart, hare (*Brit. informal*)

sprout 1 = germinate, bud, shoot, spring 2 = grow, develop, ripen

spur VERB = incite, drive, prompt, urge, stimulate, animate, prod, prick

● NOUN = stimulus, incentive, impetus, motive, impulse, inducement, incitement

● PHRASES **on the spur of the moment** = on impulse, impulsively, on the spot, impromptu, without planning

spurn = reject, slight, scorn, rebuff, snub, despise, disdain, repulse ≠ accept

spy NOUN = undercover agent, mole, nark (*Brit., Austral., & N.Z. slang*)

● VERB = catch sight of, spot, notice, observe, glimpse, espy

squabble VERB = quarrel, fight, argue, row, dispute, wrangle, bicker

● NOUN = quarrel, fight, row, argument, dispute, disagreement, tiff

squad = team, group, band, company, force, troop, crew, gang

squander = waste, spend, fritter away, blow (*slang*), misuse, expend, misspend ≠ save

square ADJECTIVE = fair, straight, genuine, ethical, honest, on the level (*informal*), kosher (*informal*), dinkum (*Austral. & N.Z. informal*), above board

● VERB *often with* **with** = agree, match, fit, correspond, tally, reconcile

squash 1 = crush, press, flatten, mash, smash, distort, pulp, compress 2 = suppress, quell, silence, crush, annihilate 3 = embarrass, put down, shame, degrade, mortify

squeeze VERB 1 = press, crush, squash, pinch 2 = clutch, press, grip, crush, pinch, squash, compress, wring 3 = cram, press, crowd, force, stuff, pack, jam, ram 4 = hug, embrace, cuddle, clasp, enfold

● NOUN 1 = press, grip, clasp, crush, pinch, squash, wring 2 = crush, jam, squash, press, crowd, congestion 3 = hug, embrace, clasp

stab VERB = pierce, stick, wound, knife, thrust, spear, jab, transfix

● NOUN 1 (*Informal*) = attempt, go, try, endeavour 2 = twinge, prick, pang, ache

stability = firmness, strength, soundness, solidity, steadiness ≠ instability

stable 1 = secure, lasting, strong, sound, fast, sure, established, permanent ≠ insecure 2 = well-balanced, balanced, sensible, reasonable, rational 3 = solid, firm, fixed, substantial, durable, well-made, well-built, immovable ≠ unstable

stack NOUN 1 = pile, heap, mountain, mass, load, mound 2 = lot, mass, load (*informal*), ton (*informal*), heap (*informal*), great amount

● VERB = pile, heap up, load, assemble, accumulate, amass

staff 1 = workers, employees, personnel, workforce, team 2 = stick, pole, rod, crook, cane, stave, wand, sceptre

stage = step, leg, phase, point, level, period, division, lap

stagger 1 = totter, reel, sway, lurch, wobble 2 = astound, amaze, stun, shock, shake, overwhelm, astonish, confound

stain NOUN 1 = mark, spot, blot, blemish, discoloration, smirch 2 = stigma, shame, disgrace, slur, dishonour 3 = dye, colour, tint

● **VERB 1** = <u>mark</u>, soil, discolour, dirty, tinge, spot, blot, blemish **2** = <u>dye</u>, colour, tint

stake¹ = <u>pole</u>, post, stick, pale, paling, picket, palisade

stake² NOUN = <u>bet</u>, ante, wager

● **VERB 1** = <u>bet</u>, gamble, wager, chance, risk, venture, hazard **2** = <u>interest</u>, share, involvement, concern, investment

stale 1 = <u>old</u>, hard, dry, decayed ≠ fresh **2** = <u>musty</u>, fusty **3** = <u>tasteless</u>, flat, sour **4** = <u>unoriginal</u>, banal, trite, stereotyped, worn-out, threadbare, hackneyed, overused ≠ original

stalk = <u>pursue</u>, follow, track, hunt, shadow, haunt

stall VERB **1** = <u>play for time</u>, delay, hedge, temporize **2** = <u>stop dead</u>, jam, seize up, catch, stick, stop short

● NOUN = <u>stand</u>, table, counter, booth, kiosk

stalwart 1 = <u>loyal</u>, faithful, firm, true, dependable, steadfast **2** = <u>strong</u>, strapping, sturdy, stout ≠ puny

stamina = <u>staying power</u>, endurance, resilience, force, power, energy, strength

stammer = <u>stutter</u>, falter, pause, hesitate, stumble over your words

stamp NOUN = <u>imprint</u>, mark, brand, signature, earmark, hallmark

● **VERB 1** = <u>print</u>, mark, impress **2** = <u>trample</u>, step, tread, crush **3** = <u>identify</u>, mark, brand, label, reveal, show to be, categorize

● PHRASES **stamp something out** = <u>eliminate</u>, destroy, eradicate, crush, suppress, put down, scotch, quell

stance 1 = <u>attitude</u>, stand, position, viewpoint, standpoint **2** = <u>posture</u>, carriage, bearing, deportment

stand VERB **1** = <u>be upright</u>, be erect, be vertical **2** = <u>get to your feet</u>, rise, stand up, straighten up **3** = <u>be located</u>, be, sit, be positioned, be situated or located **4** = <u>be valid</u>, continue, exist, prevail, remain valid **5** = <u>put</u>, place, position, set, mount **6** = <u>sit</u>, mellow **7** = <u>resist</u>, endure, tolerate, stand up to **8** = <u>tolerate</u>, bear, abide, stomach, endure, brook **9** = <u>take</u>, bear, handle, endure, put up with (*informal*), countenance

● NOUN **1** = <u>position</u>, attitude, stance, opinion, determination **2** = <u>stall</u>, booth, kiosk, table

● PHRASES **stand by** = <u>be prepared</u>, wait ◆ **stand for something 1** = <u>represent</u>,

mean, signify, denote, indicate, symbolize, betoken **2** (*Informal*) = <u>tolerate</u>, bear, endure, put up with, brook ◆ **stand in for someone** = <u>be a substitute for</u>, represent, cover for, take the place of, deputize for ◆ **stand up for something** or **someone** = <u>support</u>, champion, defend, uphold, stick up for (*informal*)

standard NOUN **1** = <u>level</u>, grade **2** = <u>criterion</u>, measure, guideline, example, model, average, norm, gauge **3** *often plural* = <u>principles</u>, ideals, morals, ethics **4** = <u>flag</u>, banner, ensign

● ADJECTIVE **1** = <u>usual</u>, normal, customary, average, basic, regular, typical, orthodox ≠ unusual **2** = <u>accepted</u>, official, established, approved, recognized, definitive, authoritative ≠ unofficial

stand-in = <u>substitute</u>, deputy, replacement, reserve, surrogate, understudy, locum, stopgap

standing NOUN **1** = <u>status</u>, position, footing, rank, reputation, eminence, repute **2** = <u>duration</u>, existence, continuance

● ADJECTIVE **1** = <u>permanent</u>, lasting, fixed, regular **2** = <u>upright</u>, erect, vertical

staple = <u>principal</u>, chief, main, key, basic, fundamental, predominant

star NOUN **1** = <u>heavenly body</u>, celestial body **2** = <u>celebrity</u>, big name, megastar (*informal*), name, luminary **3** = <u>leading man</u> or <u>lady</u>, hero or heroine, principal, main attraction

● VERB = <u>play the lead</u>, appear, feature, perform

● ADJECTIVE = <u>leading</u>, major, celebrated, brilliant, well-known, prominent

▬ RELATED WORDS
adjectives: astral, stellar

stare = <u>gaze</u>, look, goggle, watch, gape, eyeball (*slang*), gawp (*Brit. slang*), gawk

stark ADJECTIVE **1** = <u>plain</u>, harsh, basic, grim, straightforward, blunt **2** = <u>sharp</u>, clear, striking, distinct, clear-cut **3** = <u>austere</u>, severe, plain, bare, hard **4** = <u>bleak</u>, grim, barren, hard **5** = <u>absolute</u>, pure, sheer, utter, downright, out-and-out, unmitigated

● ADVERB = <u>absolutely</u>, quite, completely, entirely, altogether, wholly, utterly

start VERB **1** = <u>set about</u>, begin, proceed, embark upon, take the first step, make a beginning ≠ stop **2** = <u>begin</u>, arise, originate, issue, appear, commence ≠ end **3** = <u>set in motion</u>, initiate, instigate, open, trigger, originate, get going, kick-start ≠ stop **4** = <u>establish</u>, begin, found, create, launch, set up, institute, pioneer ≠ terminate **5** = <u>start up</u>, activate, get something going ≠ turn off **6** = <u>jump</u>, shy, jerk, flinch, recoil

● NOUN **1** = <u>beginning</u>, outset, opening, birth, foundation, dawn, onset, initiation ≠ end **2** = <u>jump</u>, spasm, convulsion

startle = <u>surprise</u>, shock, frighten, scare, make (someone) jump

starving = <u>hungry</u>, starved, ravenous, famished

state NOUN **1** = <u>country</u>, nation, land, republic, territory, federation, commonwealth, kingdom

2 = <u>government</u>, ministry, administration, executive, regime, powers-that-be **3** = <u>condition</u>, shape **4** = <u>frame of mind</u>, condition, spirits, attitude, mood, humour **5** = <u>ceremony</u>, glory, grandeur, splendour, majesty, pomp **6** = <u>circumstances</u>, situation, position, predicament

● VERB = <u>say</u>, declare, specify, present, voice, express, assert, utter

stately = <u>grand</u>, majestic, dignified, royal, august, noble, regal, lofty ≠ lowly

statement **1** = <u>announcement</u>, declaration, communication, communiqué, proclamation **2** = <u>account</u>, report

station NOUN **1** = <u>railway station</u>, stop, stage, halt, terminal, train station, terminus **2** = <u>headquarters</u>, base, depot **3** = <u>position</u>, rank, status, standing, post, situation **4** = <u>post</u>, place, location, position, situation

● VERB = <u>assign</u>, post, locate, set, establish, install

stature **1** = <u>height</u>, build, size **2** = <u>importance</u>, standing, prestige, rank, prominence, eminence

status **1** = <u>position</u>, rank, grade **2** = <u>prestige</u>, standing, authority, influence, weight, honour, importance, fame, mana (*N.Z.*) **3** = <u>state of play</u>, development, progress, condition, evolution

staunch = <u>loyal</u>, faithful, stalwart, firm, sound, true, trusty, steadfast

stay VERB **1** = <u>remain</u>, continue to be, linger, stop, wait, halt, pause, abide ≠ go

2 *often with at* = <u>lodge</u>, visit, sojourn, put up at, be accommodated at **3** = <u>continue</u>, remain, go on, survive, endure

● NOUN **1** = <u>visit</u>, stop, holiday, stopover, sojourn **2** = <u>postponement</u>, delay, suspension, stopping, halt, deferment

steady **1** = <u>continuous</u>, regular, constant, consistent, persistent, unbroken, uninterrupted, incessant ≠ irregular **2** = <u>stable</u>, fixed, secure, firm, safe ≠ unstable **3** = <u>regular</u>, established **4** = <u>dependable</u>, sensible, reliable, secure, calm, supportive, sober, level-headed ≠ undependable

steal **1** = <u>take</u>, nick (*slang, chiefly Brit.*), pinch (*informal*), lift (*informal*), embezzle, pilfer, misappropriate, purloin **2** = <u>copy</u>, take, appropriate, pinch (*informal*) **3** = <u>sneak</u>, slip, creep, tiptoe, slink

stealth = <u>secrecy</u>, furtiveness, slyness, sneakiness, unobtrusiveness, stealthiness, surreptitiousness

steep¹ **1** = <u>sheer</u>, precipitous, abrupt, vertical ≠ gradual **2** = <u>sharp</u>, sudden, abrupt, marked, extreme, distinct **3** (*Informal*) = <u>high</u>, exorbitant, extreme, unreasonable, overpriced, extortionate ≠ reasonable

steep² = <u>soak</u>, immerse, marinate (*Cookery*), submerge, drench, moisten, souse

steeped = <u>saturated</u>, pervaded, permeated, filled, infused, imbued, suffused

steer **1** = <u>drive</u>, control, direct, handle, pilot **2** = <u>direct</u>, lead, guide, conduct, escort

stem¹ NOUN = <u>stalk</u>, branch, trunk, shoot, axis

● PHRASES **stem from something** = <u>originate from</u>, be caused by, derive from, arise from

stem² = <u>stop</u>, hold back, staunch, check, dam, curb

step NOUN **1** = <u>pace</u>, stride, footstep **2** = <u>footfall</u> **3** = <u>move</u>, measure, action, means, act, deed, expedient **4** = <u>stage</u>, point, phase **5** = <u>level</u>, rank, degree

● VERB = <u>walk</u>, pace, tread, move

● PHRASES **step in** (*Informal*) = <u>intervene</u>, take action, become involved ♦ **step something up** = <u>increase</u>, intensify, raise

stereotype NOUN = <u>formula</u>, pattern

● VERB = <u>categorize</u>, typecast, pigeonhole,

standardize

sterile 1 = germ-free, sterilized, disinfected, aseptic ≠ unhygienic
2 = barren, infertile, unproductive, childless ≠ fertile

sterling = excellent, sound, fine, superlative

stern 1 = strict, harsh, hard, grim, rigid, austere, inflexible ≠ lenient 2 = severe, serious, forbidding ≠ friendly

stick¹ 1 = twig, branch 2 = cane, staff, pole, rod, crook, baton 3 (Slang) = abuse, criticism, flak (informal), fault-finding

stick² VERB 1 (Informal) = put, place, set, lay, deposit 2 = poke, dig, stab, thrust, pierce, penetrate, spear, prod 3 = fasten, fix, bind, hold, bond, attach, glue, paste
4 = adhere, cling, become joined, become welded 5 = stay, remain, linger, persist
6 (Slang) = tolerate, take, stand, stomach, abide

● PHRASES **stick out** = protrude, stand out, jut out, show, project, bulge, obtrude

◆ **stick up for someone** (Informal) = defend, support, champion, stand up for

sticky 1 = adhesive, gummed, adherent
2 = gooey, tacky (informal), viscous, glutinous, gummy, icky (informal), gluey, clinging 3 (Informal) = difficult, awkward, tricky, embarrassing, nasty, delicate, unpleasant, barro (Austral. slang) 4 = humid, close, sultry, oppressive, sweltering, clammy, muggy

stiff 1 = inflexible, rigid, unyielding, hard, firm, tight, solid, tense ≠ flexible
2 = formal, constrained, forced, unnatural, stilted, unrelaxed ≠ informal 3 = vigorous, great, strong 4 = severe, strict, harsh, hard, heavy, extreme, drastic 5 = difficult, hard, tough, exacting, arduous

stifle 1 = suppress, repress, stop, check, silence, restrain, hush, smother
2 = restrain, suppress, repress, smother

stigma = disgrace, shame, dishonour, stain, slur, smirch

still ADJECTIVE 1 = motionless, stationary, calm, peaceful, serene, tranquil, undisturbed, restful ≠ moving 2 = silent, quiet, hushed ≠ noisy

● VERB = quieten, calm, settle, quiet, silence, soothe, hush, lull ≠ get louder

● ADVERB = however, but, yet, nevertheless, notwithstanding

stimulate = encourage, inspire, prompt, fire, spur, provoke, arouse, rouse

stimulating = exciting, inspiring, stirring, rousing, provocative, exhilarating ≠ boring

stimulus = incentive, spur, encouragement, impetus, inducement, goad, incitement, fillip

sting 1 = hurt, burn, wound 2 = smart, burn, pain, hurt, tingle

stink VERB = reek, pong (Brit. informal)

● NOUN = stench, pong (Brit. informal), foul smell, fetor

stint NOUN = term, time, turn, period, share, shift, stretch, spell

● VERB = be mean, hold back, be sparing, skimp on, be frugal

stipulate = specify, agree, require, contract, settle, covenant, insist upon

stir VERB 1 = mix, beat, agitate
2 = stimulate, move, excite, spur, provoke, arouse, awaken, rouse ≠ inhibit 3 = spur, drive, prompt, stimulate, prod, urge, animate, prick

● NOUN = commotion, excitement, activity, disorder, fuss, disturbance, bustle, flurry

stock NOUN 1 = shares, holdings, securities, investments, bonds, equities 2 = property, capital, assets, funds 3 = goods, merchandise, wares, range, choice, variety, selection, commodities 4 = supply, store, reserve, fund, stockpile, hoard
5 = livestock, cattle, beasts, domestic animals

● VERB 1 = sell, supply, handle, keep, trade in, deal in 2 = fill, supply, provide with, equip, furnish, fit out

● ADJECTIVE 1 = hackneyed, routine, banal, trite, overused 2 = regular, usual, ordinary, conventional, customary

stomach NOUN 1 = belly, gut (informal), abdomen, tummy (informal), puku (N.Z.)
2 = tummy, pot 3 = inclination, taste, desire, appetite, relish

● VERB = bear, take, tolerate, endure, swallow, abide

▨ RELATED WORD
adjective: gastric

stone 1 = masonry, rock 2 = rock, pebble
3 = pip, seed, pit, kernel

stoop VERB 1 = hunch 2 = bend, lean, bow, duck, crouch

● NOUN = slouch, bad posture, round-shoulderedness

stop VERB 1 = quit, cease, refrain, put an end to, discontinue, desist ≠ start

2 = prevent, cut short, arrest, restrain, hold
back, hinder, repress, impede ≠ facilitate
3 = end, conclude, finish, terminate
≠ continue **4** = cease, shut down,
discontinue, desist ≠ continue **5** = halt,
pause ≠ keep going **6** = pause, wait, rest,
take a breather (*informal*), have a breather (*informal*),
stop briefly **7** = stay, rest, lodge
● NOUN **1** = halt, standstill **2** = station,
stage, depot, terminus **3** = stay, break, rest

store NOUN **1** = shop, outlet, market,
mart **2** = supply, stock, reserve, fund,
quantity, accumulation, stockpile, hoard
3 = repository, warehouse, depository,
storeroom
● VERB **1** *often with **away** or **up*** = put by,
save, hoard, keep, reserve, deposit, garner,
stockpile **2** = put away, put in storage, put
in store **3** = keep, hold, preserve, maintain,
retain, conserve

storm NOUN **1** = tempest, hurricane, gale,
blizzard, squall **2** = outburst, row, outcry,
furore, outbreak, turmoil, disturbance,
strife
● VERB **1** = rush, stamp, flounce, fly **2** = rage,
rant, thunder, rave, bluster **3** = attack,
charge, rush, assault, assail

stormy 1 = wild, rough, raging, turbulent,
windy, blustery, inclement, squally
2 = rough, wild, turbulent, raging
3 = angry, heated, fierce, passionate, fiery,
impassioned

story 1 = tale, romance, narrative, history,
legend, yarn **2** = anecdote, account, tale,
report **3** = report, news, article, feature,
scoop, news item

stout 1 = fat, big, heavy, overweight,
plump, bulky, burly, fleshy ≠ slim
2 = strong, strapping, muscular, robust,
sturdy, stalwart, brawny, able-bodied
≠ puny **3** = brave, bold, courageous,
fearless, resolute, gallant, intrepid, valiant
≠ timid

straight ADJECTIVE **1** = direct ≠ indirect
2 = level, even, right, square, true, smooth,
aligned, horizontal ≠ crooked **3** = frank,
plain, straightforward, blunt, outright,
honest, candid, forthright ≠ evasive
4 = successive, consecutive, continuous,
running, solid, nonstop ≠ discontinuous
5 (*Slang*) = conventional, conservative,
bourgeois ≠ fashionable **6** = honest,
just, fair, reliable, respectable, upright,
honourable, law-abiding ≠ dishonest

7 = undiluted, pure, neat, unadulterated,
unmixed **8** = in order, organized, arranged,
neat, tidy, orderly, shipshape ≠ untidy
● ADVERB **1** = directly, precisely, exactly,
unswervingly, by the shortest route,
in a beeline **2** = immediately, directly,
promptly, instantly, at once, straight away,
without delay, forthwith

straight away = immediately, now, at
once, directly, instantly, right away

straighten = neaten, arrange, tidy (up),
order, put in order

straightforward 1 (*Chiefly Brit.*) = simple,
easy, uncomplicated, routine, elementary,
easy-peasy (*slang*) ≠ complicated
2 = honest, open, direct, genuine, sincere,
candid, truthful, forthright, dinkum
(*Austral. & N.Z. informal*) ≠ devious

strain¹ NOUN **1** = pressure, stress, demands,
burden **2** = stress, anxiety **3** = worry,
effort, struggle ≠ ease **4** = burden, tension
5 = injury, wrench, sprain, pull
● VERB **1** = stretch, tax, overtax **2** = strive,
struggle, endeavour, labour, go for
it (*informal*), bend over backwards
(*informal*), give it your best shot
(*informal*), knock yourself out (*informal*)
≠ relax **3** = sieve, filter, sift, purify

strain² **1** = trace, suggestion, tendency,
streak **2** = breed, family, race, blood,
descent, extraction, ancestry, lineage

strained 1 = tense, difficult, awkward,
embarrassed, stiff, uneasy ≠ relaxed
2 = forced, put on, false, artificial,
unnatural ≠ natural

strait NOUN *often plural* = channel, sound,
narrows
● PLURAL NOUN = difficulty, dilemma, plight,
hardship, uphill (*S. African*), predicament,
extremity

strand = filament, fibre, thread, string

stranded 1 = beached, grounded,
marooned, ashore, shipwrecked, aground
2 = helpless, abandoned, high and dry

strange 1 = odd, curious, weird,
wonderful, extraordinary, bizarre, peculiar,
abnormal ≠ ordinary **2** = unfamiliar, new,
unknown, foreign, novel, alien, exotic,
untried ≠ familiar

stranger 1 = unknown person
2 = newcomer, incomer, foreigner, guest,
visitor, alien, outlander

strangle 1 = throttle, choke, asphyxiate,
strangulate **2** = suppress, inhibit, subdue,

stifle, repress, overpower, quash, quell

strap NOUN = tie, thong, belt
● VERB = fasten, tie, secure, bind, lash, buckle

strapping = well-built, big, powerful, robust, sturdy, husky (*informal*), brawny

strategic 1 = tactical, calculated, deliberate, planned, politic, diplomatic 2 = crucial, important, key, vital, critical, decisive, cardinal

strategy 1 = policy, procedure, approach, scheme 2 = plan, approach, scheme

stray VERB 1 = wander, go astray, drift 2 = drift, wander, roam, meander, rove 3 = digress, diverge, deviate, get off the point
● ADJECTIVE 1 = lost, abandoned, homeless, roaming, vagrant 2 = random, chance, accidental

streak NOUN 1 = band, line, strip, stroke, layer, slash, vein, stripe 2 = trace, touch, element, strain, dash, vein
● VERB = speed, fly, tear, flash, sprint, dart, zoom, whizz (*informal*)

stream NOUN 1 = river, brook, burn (*Scot.*), beck, tributary, bayou, rivulet 2 = flow, current, rush, run, course, drift, surge, tide
● VERB 1 = flow, run, pour, issue, flood, spill, cascade, gush 2 = rush, fly, speed, tear, flood, pour

streamlined = efficient, organized, rationalized, slick, smooth-running

street = road, lane, avenue, terrace, row, roadway

strength 1 = might, muscle, brawn ≠ weakness 2 = will, resolution, courage, character, nerve, determination, pluck, stamina 3 = health, fitness, vigour 4 = mainstay 5 = toughness, soundness, robustness, sturdiness 6 = force, power, intensity ≠ weakness 7 = potency, effectiveness, efficacy 8 = strong point, skill, asset, advantage, talent, forte, speciality ≠ failing

strengthen 1 = fortify, harden, toughen, consolidate, stiffen, gee up, brace up ≠ weaken 2 = reinforce, support, intensify, bolster, buttress 3 = bolster, harden, reinforce 4 = heighten, intensify 5 = make stronger, build up, invigorate, restore, give strength to 6 = support, brace, reinforce, consolidate, harden, bolster, augment, buttress 7 = become stronger, intensify, gain strength

stress VERB 1 = emphasize, underline, dwell on 2 = place the emphasis on, emphasize, give emphasis to, lay emphasis upon
● NOUN 1 = emphasis, significance, force, weight 2 = strain, pressure, worry, tension, burden, anxiety, trauma 3 = accent, beat, emphasis, accentuation

stretch VERB 1 = extend, cover, spread, reach, put forth, unroll 2 = last, continue, go on, carry on, reach 3 = expand 4 = pull, distend, strain, tighten, draw out, elongate
● NOUN 1 = expanse, area, tract, spread, distance, extent 2 = period, time, spell, stint, term, space

strict 1 = severe, harsh, stern, firm, stringent ≠ easy-going 2 = stern, firm, severe, harsh, authoritarian 3 = exact, accurate, precise, close, true, faithful, meticulous, scrupulous 4 = absolute, total, utter

strife = conflict, battle, clash, quarrel, friction, discord, dissension

strike NOUN = walkout, industrial action, mutiny, revolt
● VERB 1 = walk out, down tools, revolt, mutiny 2 = hit, smack, thump, beat, knock, punch, hammer, slap 3 = drive, hit, smack, wallop (*informal*) 4 = collide with, hit, run into, bump into 5 = knock, smack, thump, beat 6 = affect, touch, devastate, overwhelm, leave a mark on 7 = attack, assault someone, set upon someone, lay into someone (*informal*) 8 = occur to, hit, come to, register (*informal*), dawn on or upon 9 = seem to, appear to, look to, give the impression to 10 = move, touch, hit, affect, overcome, stir, disturb, perturb

striking = impressive, dramatic, outstanding, noticeable, conspicuous, jaw-dropping ≠ unimpressive

string 1 = cord, twine, fibre 2 = series, line, row, file, sequence, succession, procession 3 = sequence, run, series, chain, succession

stringent = strict, tough, rigorous, tight, severe, rigid, inflexible ≠ lax

strip^1 1 = undress, disrobe, unclothe 2 = plunder, rob, loot, empty, sack, ransack, pillage, divest

strip^2 1 = piece, shred, band, belt 2 = stretch, area, tract, expanse, extent

strive = try, labour, struggle, attempt, toil, go all out (*informal*), bend over backwards (*informal*), do your best

stroke VERB = <u>caress</u>, rub, fondle, pet
● NOUN 1 = <u>apoplexy</u>, fit, seizure, attack, collapse 2 = <u>blow</u>, hit, knock, pat, rap, thump, swipe

stroll VERB = <u>walk</u>, ramble, amble, promenade, saunter
● NOUN = <u>walk</u>, promenade, constitutional, ramble, breath of air

strong 1 = <u>powerful</u>, muscular, tough, athletic, strapping, hardy, sturdy, burly ≠ weak 2 = <u>fit</u>, robust, lusty 3 = <u>durable</u>, substantial, sturdy, heavy-duty, well-built, hard-wearing ≠ flimsy 4 = <u>extreme</u>, radical, drastic, strict, harsh, rigid, forceful, uncompromising 5 = <u>decisive</u>, firm, forceful, decided, determined, resolute, incisive 6 = <u>persuasive</u>, convincing, compelling, telling, sound, effective, potent, weighty 7 = <u>keen</u>, deep, acute, fervent, zealous, vehement 8 = <u>intense</u>, deep, passionate, ardent, fierce, fervent, vehement, fervid 9 = <u>staunch</u>, firm, fierce, ardent, enthusiastic, passionate, fervent 10 = <u>distinct</u>, marked, clear, unmistakable ≠ slight 11 = <u>bright</u>, brilliant, dazzling, bold ≠ dull

stronghold 1 = <u>bastion</u>, fortress, bulwark 2 = <u>refuge</u>, haven, retreat, sanctuary, hide-out

structure NOUN 1 = <u>arrangement</u>, form, make-up, design, organization, construction, formation, configuration 2 = <u>building</u>, construction, erection, edifice
● VERB = <u>arrange</u>, organize, design, shape, build up, assemble

struggle VERB 1 = <u>strive</u>, labour, toil, work, strain, go all out (*informal*), give it your best shot (*informal*), exert yourself 2 = <u>fight</u>, battle, wrestle, grapple, compete, contend
● NOUN 1 = <u>effort</u>, labour, toil, work, pains, scramble, exertion 2 = <u>fight</u>, battle, conflict, clash, contest, brush, combat, tussle, biffo (*Austral. slang*)

strut = <u>swagger</u>, parade, peacock, prance

stubborn = <u>obstinate</u>, dogged, inflexible, persistent, intractable, tenacious, recalcitrant, unyielding ≠ compliant

stuck 1 = <u>fastened</u>, fast, fixed, joined, glued, cemented 2 (*Informal*) = <u>baffled</u>, stumped, beaten

student 1 = <u>undergraduate</u>, scholar 2 = <u>pupil</u>, scholar, schoolchild, schoolboy *or* schoolgirl 3 = <u>learner</u>, trainee, apprentice, disciple

studied = <u>planned</u>, deliberate, conscious, intentional, premeditated ≠ unplanned

studio = <u>workshop</u>, workroom, atelier

study VERB 1 = <u>learn</u>, cram (*informal*), swot (up) (*Brit. informal*), read up, mug up (*Brit. slang*) 2 = <u>examine</u>, survey, look at, scrutinize 3 = <u>contemplate</u>, read, examine, consider, go into, pore over
● NOUN 1 = <u>examination</u>, investigation, analysis, consideration, inspection, scrutiny, contemplation 2 = <u>piece of research</u>, survey, report, review, inquiry, investigation 3 = <u>learning</u>, lessons, school work, reading, research, swotting (*Brit. informal*)

stuff NOUN 1 = <u>things</u>, gear, possessions, effects, equipment, objects, tackle, kit 2 = <u>substance</u>, material, essence, matter
● VERB 1 = <u>shove</u>, force, push, squeeze, jam, ram 2 = <u>cram</u>, fill, pack, crowd

stuffing = <u>wadding</u>, filling, packing

stumble VERB 1 = <u>trip</u>, fall, slip, reel, stagger, falter, lurch 2 = <u>totter</u>, reel, lurch, wobble
● PHRASES **stumble across** *or* **on** *or* **upon something** *or* **someone** = <u>discover</u>, find, come across, chance upon

stump NOUN = <u>tail end</u>, end, remnant, remainder
● VERB = <u>baffle</u>, confuse, puzzle, bewilder, perplex, mystify, flummox, nonplus

stun 1 = <u>overcome</u>, shock, confuse, astonish, stagger, bewilder, astound, overpower 2 = <u>daze</u>, knock out, stupefy, numb, benumb

stunning (*Informal*) = <u>wonderful</u>, beautiful, impressive, striking, lovely, spectacular, marvellous, splendid ≠ unimpressive

stunt = <u>feat</u>, act, trick, exploit, deed

stunted = <u>undersized</u>, little, small, tiny, diminutive

stupid 1 = <u>unintelligent</u>, thick, simple, slow, dim, dense, simple-minded, moronic ≠ intelligent 2 = <u>silly</u>, foolish, daft (*informal*), rash, pointless, senseless, idiotic, fatuous ≠ sensible 3 = <u>senseless</u>, dazed, groggy, insensate, semiconscious

sturdy 1 = <u>robust</u>, hardy, powerful, athletic, muscular, lusty, brawny ≠ puny 2 = <u>substantial</u>, solid, durable, well-made, well-built ≠ flimsy

style NOUN 1 = <u>manner</u>, way, method, approach, technique, mode 2 = <u>elegance</u>, taste, chic, flair, polish, sophistication, panache, élan 3 = <u>design</u>, form, cut 4 = <u>type</u>, sort, kind, variety, category, genre 5 = <u>fashion</u>, trend, mode, vogue, rage 6 = <u>luxury</u>, ease, comfort, elegance, grandeur, affluence
● VERB 1 = <u>design</u>, cut, tailor, fashion, shape, arrange, adapt 2 = <u>call</u>, name, term, label, entitle, dub, designate

stylish = <u>smart</u>, chic, fashionable, trendy (*Brit. informal*), modish, dressy (*informal*), voguish ≠ scruffy

subdue 1 = <u>overcome</u>, defeat, master, break, control, crush, conquer, tame 2 = <u>moderate</u>, suppress, soften, mellow, tone down, quieten down ≠ arouse

subdued 1 = <u>quiet</u>, serious, sad, chastened, dejected, downcast, crestfallen, down in the mouth ≠ lively 2 = <u>hushed</u>, soft, quiet, muted ≠ loud

subject NOUN 1 = <u>topic</u>, question, issue, matter, point, business, affair, object 2 = <u>citizen</u>, resident, native, inhabitant, national 3 = <u>dependant</u>, subordinate
● ADJECTIVE = <u>subordinate</u>, dependent, satellite, inferior, obedient
● VERB = <u>put through</u>, expose, submit, lay open
● PHRASES **subject to** 1 = <u>liable to</u>, open to, exposed to, vulnerable to, prone to, susceptible to 2 = <u>bound by</u> 3 = <u>dependent on</u>, contingent on, controlled by, conditional on

subjective = <u>personal</u>, prejudiced, biased, nonobjective ≠ objective

sublime = <u>noble</u>, glorious, high, great, grand, elevated, lofty, exalted ≠ lowly

submerge 1 = <u>flood</u>, swamp, engulf, overflow, inundate, deluge 2 = <u>immerse</u>, plunge, duck 3 = <u>sink</u>, plunge, go under water 4 = <u>overwhelm</u>, swamp, engulf, deluge

submission 1 = <u>surrender</u>, yielding, giving in, cave-in (*informal*), capitulation 2 = <u>presentation</u>, handing in, entry, tendering 3 = <u>compliance</u>, obedience, meekness, resignation, deference, passivity, docility

submit 1 = <u>surrender</u>, yield, give in, agree, endure, tolerate, comply, succumb 2 = <u>present</u>, hand in, tender, put forward, table, proffer

subordinate NOUN = <u>inferior</u>, junior, assistant, aide, second, attendant ≠ superior
● ADJECTIVE = <u>inferior</u>, lesser, lower, junior, subject, minor, secondary, dependent ≠ superior

subscribe 1 = <u>support</u>, advocate, endorse 2 = <u>contribute</u>, give, donate

subscription (*Chiefly Brit.*) = <u>membership fee</u>, dues, annual payment

subsequent = <u>following</u>, later, succeeding, after, successive, ensuing ≠ previous

subsequently = <u>later</u>, afterwards

subside 1 = <u>decrease</u>, diminish, lessen, ease, wane, ebb, abate, slacken ≠ increase 2 = <u>collapse</u>, sink, cave in, drop, lower, settle

subsidiary NOUN = <u>branch</u>, division, section, office, department, wing, subdivision, subsection
● ADJECTIVE = <u>secondary</u>, lesser, subordinate, minor, supplementary, auxiliary, ancillary ≠ main

subsidy = <u>aid</u>, help, support, grant, assistance, allowance

substance 1 = <u>material</u>, body, stuff, fabric 2 = <u>importance</u>, significance, concreteness 3 = <u>meaning</u>, main point, gist, import, significance, essence 4 = <u>wealth</u>, means, property, assets, resources, estate

substantial = <u>big</u>, significant, considerable, large, important, ample, sizable *or* sizeable ≠ small

substitute VERB = <u>replace</u>, exchange, swap, change, switch, interchange
● NOUN = <u>replacement</u>, reserve, surrogate, deputy, sub, proxy, locum
● ADJECTIVE = <u>replacement</u>, reserve, surrogate, second, alternative, fall-back, proxy

subtle 1 = <u>faint</u>, slight, implied, delicate, understated ≠ obvious 2 = <u>crafty</u>, cunning, sly, shrewd, ingenious, devious, wily, artful ≠ straightforward 3 = <u>muted</u>, soft, subdued, low-key, toned down 4 = <u>fine</u>, minute, narrow, tenuous, hair-splitting

subtlety 1 = <u>fine point</u>, refinement, sophistication, delicacy 2 = <u>skill</u>, ingenuity, cleverness, deviousness, craftiness, artfulness, slyness, wiliness

subversive ADJECTIVE = <u>seditious</u>, riotous, treasonous
● NOUN = <u>dissident</u>, terrorist, saboteur, fifth

columnist

succeed 1 = triumph, win, prevail
2 = work out, work, be successful
3 = make it (*informal*), do well, be
successful, triumph, thrive, flourish, make
good, prosper ≠ fail 4 = take over from,
assume the office of 5 *with* **to** = take over,
assume, attain, come into, inherit, accede
to, come into possession of 6 = follow,
come after, follow after ≠ precede

success 1 = victory, triumph ≠ failure
2 = prosperity, fortune, luck, fame 3 = hit
(*informal*), winner, smash (*informal*),
triumph, sensation ≠ flop (*informal*)
4 = big name, star, hit (*informal*), celebrity,
sensation, megastar (*informal*) ≠ nobody

successful 1 = triumphant, victorious,
lucky, fortunate 2 = thriving, profitable,
rewarding, booming, flourishing, fruitful
≠ unprofitable 3 = top, prosperous,
wealthy

successfully = well, favourably, with
flying colours, victoriously

succession 1 = series, run, sequence,
course, order, train, chain, cycle 2 = taking
over, assumption, inheritance, accession

successive = consecutive, following, in
succession

succumb 1 *often with* **to** = surrender,
yield, submit, give in, cave in (*informal*),
capitulate ≠ beat 2 *with* **to** (with an illness
as object) = catch, fall ill with

suck 1 = drink, sip, draw 2 = take, draw,
pull, extract

sudden = quick, rapid, unexpected, swift,
hurried, abrupt, hasty ≠ gradual

suddenly = abruptly, all of a sudden,
unexpectedly

sue (*Law*) = take (someone) to court,
prosecute, charge, summon, indict

suffer 1 = be in pain, hurt, ache 2 = be
affected, have trouble with, be afflicted,
be troubled with 3 = undergo, experience,
sustain, bear, go through, endure
4 = tolerate, stand, put up with (*informal*),
bear, endure

suffering = pain, distress, agony, misery,
ordeal, discomfort, torment, hardship

suffice = be enough, do, be sufficient, be
adequate, serve, meet requirements

sufficient = adequate, enough, ample,
satisfactory ≠ insufficient

suggest 1 = recommend, propose, advise,
advocate, prescribe 2 = indicate 3 = hint

at, imply, intimate 4 = bring to mind,
evoke

suggestion 1 = recommendation,
proposal, proposition, plan, motion
2 = hint, insinuation, intimation 3 = trace,
touch, hint, breath, indication, whisper,
intimation

suit NOUN 1 = outfit, costume, ensemble,
dress, clothing, habit 2 = lawsuit, case, trial,
proceeding, cause, action, prosecution
● VERB 1 = be acceptable to, please, satisfy,
do, gratify 2 = agree with, become, match,
go with, harmonize with

suitable 1 = appropriate, right, fitting,
fit, becoming, satisfactory, apt, befitting
≠ inappropriate 2 = seemly, fitting,
becoming, proper, correct ≠ unseemly
3 = suited, appropriate, in keeping with
≠ out of keeping 4 = pertinent, relevant,
applicable, fitting, appropriate, to the
point, apt ≠ irrelevant 5 = convenient,
timely, appropriate, well-timed, opportune
≠ inopportune

suite = rooms, apartment

sum 1 = amount, quantity, volume
2 = calculation, figures, arithmetic,
mathematics, maths (*Brit. informal*), tally,
math (*U.S. informal*), arithmetical problem
3 = total, aggregate 4 = totality, whole

summarize = sum up, condense,
encapsulate, epitomize, abridge, précis

summary = synopsis, résumé, précis,
review, outline, rundown, abridgment

summit 1 = peak, top, tip, pinnacle, apex,
head ≠ base 2 = height, pinnacle, peak,
zenith, acme ≠ depths

summon 1 = send for, call, bid, invite
2 *often with* **up** = gather, muster, draw on

sumptuous = luxurious, grand, superb,
splendid, gorgeous, lavish, opulent ≠ plain

sunny 1 = bright, clear, fine, radiant, sunlit,
summery, unclouded ≠ dull 2 = cheerful,
happy, cheery, buoyant, joyful, light-
hearted ≠ gloomy

sunset = nightfall, dusk, eventide, close
of (the) day

superb 1 = splendid, excellent,
magnificent, fine, grand, superior,
marvellous, world-class, booshit (*Austral.
slang*), exo (*Austral. slang*), sik (*Austral.
slang*) ≠ inferior 2 = magnificent, superior,
marvellous, exquisite, superlative
≠ terrible

superficial 1 = shallow, frivolous, empty-headed, silly, trivial ≠ serious **2** = <u>hasty</u>, cursory, perfunctory, hurried, casual, sketchy, desultory, slapdash ≠ thorough **3** = <u>slight</u>, surface, external, on the surface, exterior ≠ profound

superintendent = <u>supervisor</u>, director, manager, chief, governor, inspector, controller, overseer

superior ADJECTIVE **1** = <u>better</u>, higher, greater, grander, surpassing, unrivalled ≠ inferior **2** = <u>first-class</u>, excellent, first-rate, choice, exclusive, exceptional, de luxe, booshit (*Austral. slang*), exo (*Austral. slang*), sik (*Austral. slang*) ≠ average **3** = <u>supercilious</u>, patronizing, condescending, haughty, disdainful, lordly, lofty, pretentious

● NOUN = <u>boss</u>, senior, director, manager, chief (*informal*), principal, supervisor, baas (*S. African*) ≠ subordinate

superiority = <u>supremacy</u>, lead, advantage, excellence, ascendancy, predominance

supernatural = <u>paranormal</u>, unearthly, uncanny, ghostly, psychic, mystic, miraculous, occult

supervise 1 = <u>observe</u>, guide, monitor, oversee, keep an eye on **2** = <u>oversee</u>, run, manage, control, direct, handle, look after, superintend

supervision = <u>superintendence</u>, direction, control, charge, care, management, guidance

supervisor = <u>boss</u> (*informal*), manager, chief, inspector, administrator, foreman, overseer, baas (*S. African*)

supplement VERB = <u>add to</u>, reinforce, augment, extend

● NOUN **1** = <u>pull-out</u>, insert **2** = <u>appendix</u>, add-on, postscript **3** = <u>addition</u>, extra

supply VERB **1** = <u>provide</u>, give, furnish, produce, stock, grant, contribute, yield **2** = <u>furnish</u>, provide, equip, endow

● NOUN = <u>store</u>, fund, stock, source, reserve, quantity, hoard, cache

● PLURAL NOUN = <u>provisions</u>, necessities, stores, food, materials, equipment, rations

support VERB **1** = <u>help</u>, back, champion, second, aid, defend, assist, side with ≠ oppose **2** = <u>provide for</u>, maintain, look after, keep, fund, finance, sustain ≠ live off **3** = <u>bear out</u>, confirm, verify, substantiate, corroborate ≠ refute **4** = <u>bear</u>, carry, sustain, prop (up), reinforce, hold, brace, buttress

● NOUN **1** = <u>furtherance</u>, backing, promotion, assistance, encouragement **2** = <u>help</u>, loyalty ≠ opposition **3** = <u>aid</u>, help, benefits, relief, assistance **4** = <u>prop</u>, post, foundation, brace, pillar **5** = <u>supporter</u>, prop, mainstay, tower of strength, second, backer ≠ antagonist **6** = <u>upkeep</u>, maintenance, keep, subsistence, sustenance

supporter = <u>follower</u>, fan, advocate, friend, champion, sponsor, patron, helper ≠ opponent

supportive = <u>helpful</u>, encouraging, understanding, sympathetic

suppose 1 = <u>imagine</u>, consider, conjecture, postulate, hypothesize **2** = <u>think</u>, imagine, expect, assume, guess (*informal, chiefly U.S. & Canad.*), presume, conjecture

supposed 1 *usually with* **to** = <u>meant</u>, expected, required, obliged **2** = <u>presumed</u>, alleged, professed, accepted, assumed

supposedly = <u>presumably</u>, allegedly, ostensibly, theoretically, hypothetically ≠ actually

suppress 1 = <u>stamp out</u>, stop, check, crush, conquer, subdue, put an end to, overpower ≠ encourage **2** = <u>check</u>, inhibit, subdue, stop, quell **3** = <u>restrain</u>, stifle, contain, silence, conceal, curb, repress, smother

suppression 1 = <u>elimination</u>, crushing, check, quashing **2** = <u>inhibition</u>, blocking, restraint, smothering

supremacy = <u>domination</u>, sovereignty, sway, mastery, primacy, predominance, supreme power

supreme 1 = <u>paramount</u> ≠ least **2** = <u>chief</u>, leading, principal, highest, head, top, prime, foremost ≠ lowest **3** = <u>ultimate</u>, highest, greatest

supremo (*Brit. informal*) = <u>head</u>, leader, boss (*informal*), director, master, governor, commander, principal, baas (*S. African*)

sure 1 = <u>certain</u>, positive, decided, convinced, confident, assured, definite ≠ uncertain **2** = <u>inevitable</u>, guaranteed, bound, assured, inescapable ≠ unsure **3** = <u>reliable</u>, accurate, dependable, undoubted, undeniable, foolproof, infallible, unerring ≠ unreliable

surely 1 = <u>it must be the case that</u> **2** = <u>undoubtedly</u>, certainly, definitely, without doubt, unquestionably, indubitably, doubtlessly

surface NOUN 1 = <u>covering</u>, face, exterior, side, top, veneer 2 = <u>façade</u>

● VERB 1 = <u>emerge</u>, come up, come to the surface 2 = <u>appear</u>, emerge, arise, come to light, crop up (*informal*), transpire, materialize

surge NOUN 1 = <u>rush</u>, flood 2 = <u>flow</u>, wave, rush, roller, gush, outpouring 3 = <u>tide</u>, swell, billowing 4 = <u>rush</u>, wave, storm, torrent, eruption

● VERB 1 = <u>rush</u>, pour, rise, gush 2 = <u>roll</u>, rush, heave 3 = <u>sweep</u>, rush, storm

surpass = <u>outdo</u>, beat, exceed, eclipse, excel, transcend, outstrip, outshine

surpassing = <u>supreme</u>, extraordinary, outstanding, exceptional, unrivalled, incomparable, matchless

surplus NOUN = <u>excess</u>, surfeit ≠ shortage

● ADJECTIVE = <u>extra</u>, spare, excess, remaining, odd, superfluous ≠ insufficient

surprise NOUN 1 = <u>shock</u>, revelation, jolt, bombshell, eye-opener (*informal*) 2 = <u>amazement</u>, astonishment, wonder, incredulity

● VERB 1 = <u>amaze</u>, astonish, stun, startle, stagger, take aback 2 = <u>catch unawares</u> or <u>off-guard</u>, spring upon

surprised = <u>amazed</u>, astonished, speechless, thunderstruck

surprising = <u>amazing</u>, remarkable, incredible, astonishing, unusual, extraordinary, unexpected, staggering

surrender VERB 1 = <u>give in</u>, yield, submit, give way, succumb, cave in (*informal*), capitulate ≠ resist 2 = <u>give up</u>, abandon, relinquish, yield, concede, part with, renounce, waive

● NOUN = <u>submission</u>, cave-in (*informal*), capitulation, resignation, renunciation, relinquishment

surround = <u>enclose</u>, ring, encircle, encompass, envelop, hem in

surrounding ADJECTIVE = <u>nearby</u>, neighbouring

● PLURAL NOUN = <u>environment</u>, setting, background, location, milieu

surveillance = <u>observation</u>, watch, scrutiny, supervision, inspection

survey NOUN 1 = <u>poll</u>, study, research, review, inquiry, investigation 2 = <u>examination</u>, inspection, scrutiny 3 = <u>valuation</u>, estimate, assessment, appraisal

● VERB 1 = <u>interview</u>, question, poll, research, investigate 2 = <u>look over</u>, view, examine, observe, contemplate, inspect, eyeball (*slang*), scrutinize 3 = <u>measure</u>, estimate, assess, appraise

survive 1 = <u>remain alive</u>, last, live on, endure 2 = <u>continue</u>, last, live on 3 = <u>live longer than</u>, outlive, outlast

susceptible 1 = <u>responsive</u>, sensitive, receptive, impressionable, suggestible ≠ unresponsive 2 *usually with* **to** = <u>liable</u>, inclined, prone, given, subject, vulnerable, disposed ≠ resistant

suspect VERB 1 = <u>believe</u>, feel, guess, consider, suppose, speculate ≠ know 2 = <u>distrust</u>, doubt, mistrust ≠ trust

● ADJECTIVE = <u>dubious</u>, doubtful, questionable, iffy (*informal*) ≠ innocent

suspend 1 = <u>postpone</u>, put off, cease, interrupt, shelve, defer, cut short, discontinue ≠ continue 2 = <u>hang</u>, attach, dangle

suspension = <u>postponement</u>, break, breaking off, interruption, abeyance, deferment, discontinuation

suspicion 1 = <u>distrust</u>, scepticism, mistrust, doubt, misgiving, qualm, wariness, dubiety 2 = <u>idea</u>, notion, hunch, guess, impression 3 = <u>trace</u>, touch, hint, suggestion, shade, streak, tinge, soupçon (*French*)

suspicious 1 = <u>distrustful</u>, sceptical, doubtful, unbelieving, wary ≠ trusting 2 = <u>suspect</u>, dubious, questionable, doubtful, dodgy (*Brit., Austral., & N.Z. informal*), fishy (*informal*) ≠ beyond suspicion

sustain 1 = <u>maintain</u>, continue, keep up, prolong, protract 2 = <u>suffer</u>, experience, undergo, feel, bear, endure, withstand 3 = <u>help</u>, aid, assist 4 = <u>keep alive</u>, nourish, provide for 5 = <u>support</u>, bear, uphold

sustained = <u>continuous</u>, constant, steady, prolonged, perpetual, unremitting, nonstop ≠ periodic

swallow 1 = <u>eat</u>, consume, devour, swig (*informal*) 2 = <u>gulp</u>, drink

swamp NOUN = <u>bog</u>, marsh, quagmire, slough, fen, mire, morass, pakihi (*N.Z.*)

● VERB 1 = <u>flood</u>, engulf, submerge, inundate 2 = <u>overload</u>, overwhelm, inundate

swap *or* **swop** = <u>exchange</u>, trade, switch,

interchange, barter

swarm NOUN = <u>multitude</u>, crowd, mass, army, host, flock, herd, horde
● VERB 1 = <u>crowd</u>, flock, throng, mass, stream 2 = <u>teem</u>, crawl, abound, bristle

swathe NOUN = <u>area</u>, section, tract
● VERB = <u>wrap</u>, drape, envelop, cloak, shroud, bundle up

sway VERB 1 = <u>move from side to side</u>, rock, roll, swing, bend, lean 2 = <u>influence</u>, affect, guide, persuade, induce
● NOUN = <u>power</u>, control, influence, authority, clout (*informal*)

swear 1 = <u>curse</u>, blaspheme, be foul-mouthed 2 = <u>vow</u>, promise, testify, attest 3 = <u>declare</u>, assert, affirm

swearing = <u>bad language</u>, cursing, profanity, blasphemy, foul language

sweat NOUN 1 = <u>perspiration</u> 2 (*Informal*) = <u>panic</u>, anxiety, worry, distress, agitation
● VERB 1 = <u>perspire</u>, glow 2 (*Informal*) = <u>worry</u>, fret, agonize, torture yourself

sweep VERB 1 = <u>brush</u>, clean 2 = <u>clear</u>, remove, brush, clean 3 = <u>sail</u>, pass, fly, tear, zoom, glide, skim
● NOUN 1 = <u>movement</u>, move, swing, stroke 2 = <u>extent</u>, range, stretch, scope

sweeping 1 = <u>indiscriminate</u>, blanket, wholesale, exaggerated, overstated, unqualified 2 = <u>wide-ranging</u>, global, comprehensive, wide, broad, extensive, all-inclusive, all-embracing ≠ limited

sweet ADJECTIVE 1 = <u>sugary</u>, cloying, saccharine, icky (*informal*) ≠ sour 2 = <u>fragrant</u>, aromatic ≠ stinking 3 = <u>fresh</u>, clean, pure 4 = <u>melodious</u>, musical, harmonious, mellow, dulcet ≠ harsh 5 = <u>charming</u>, kind, agreeable ≠ nasty 6 = <u>delightful</u>, appealing, cute, winning, engaging, lovable, likable *or* likeable ≠ unpleasant
● NOUN 1 *usually plural* = <u>confectionery</u>, candy (*U.S.*), lolly (*Austral. & N.Z.*), bonbon 2 (*Brit.*) = <u>dessert</u>, pudding

sweetheart 1 = <u>dearest</u>, beloved, sweet, angel, treasure, honey, dear, sweetie (*informal*) 2 = <u>love</u>, boyfriend *or* girlfriend, beloved, lover, darling

swell VERB 1 = <u>increase</u>, rise, grow, mount, expand, accelerate, escalate, multiply ≠ decrease 2 = <u>expand</u>, increase, grow, rise, balloon, enlarge, bulge, dilate ≠ shrink
● NOUN = <u>wave</u>, surge, billow

swelling = <u>enlargement</u>, lump, bump, bulge, inflammation, protuberance, distension

swift 1 = <u>quick</u>, prompt, rapid 2 = <u>fast</u>, quick, rapid, hurried, speedy ≠ slow

swiftly 1 = <u>quickly</u>, rapidly, speedily 2 = <u>fast</u>, promptly, hurriedly

swing VERB 1 = <u>brandish</u>, wave, shake, flourish, wield, dangle 2 = <u>sway</u>, rock, wave, veer, oscillate 3 *usually with* ***round*** = <u>turn</u>, swivel, curve, rotate, pivot 4 = <u>hit out</u>, strike, swipe, lash out at, slap 5 = <u>hang</u>, dangle, suspend
● NOUN 1 = <u>swaying</u>, sway 2 = <u>fluctuation</u>, change, shift, switch, variation

swirl = <u>whirl</u>, churn, spin, twist, eddy

switch NOUN 1 = <u>control</u>, button, lever, on/off device 2 = <u>change</u>, shift, reversal
● VERB 1 = <u>change</u>, shift, divert, deviate 2 = <u>exchange</u>, swap, substitute

swollen = <u>enlarged</u>, bloated, inflamed, puffed up, distended

swoop 1 = <u>pounce</u>, attack, charge, rush, descend 2 = <u>drop</u>, plunge, dive, sweep, descend, pounce, stoop

symbol 1 = <u>metaphor</u>, image, sign, representation, token 2 = <u>representation</u>, sign, figure, mark, image, token, logo, badge

symbolic 1 = <u>representative</u>, emblematic, allegorical 2 = <u>representative</u>, figurative

sympathetic 1 = <u>caring</u>, kind, understanding, concerned, interested, warm, pitying, supportive ≠ uncaring 2 = <u>like-minded</u>, compatible, agreeable, friendly, congenial, companionable ≠ uncongenial

sympathy 1 = <u>compassion</u>, understanding, pity, commiseration, aroha (*N.Z.*) ≠ indifference 2 = <u>affinity</u>, agreement, rapport, fellow feeling ≠ opposition

symptom 1 = <u>sign</u>, mark, indication, warning 2 = <u>manifestation</u>, sign, indication, mark, evidence, expression, proof, token

synthetic = <u>artificial</u>, fake, man-made ≠ real

system 1 = <u>arrangement</u>, structure, organization, scheme, classification 2 = <u>method</u>, practice, technique, procedure, routine

systematic = <u>methodical</u>, organized, efficient, orderly ≠ unmethodical

t

table NOUN 1 = <u>counter</u>, bench, stand, board, surface, work surface 2 = <u>list</u>, chart, tabulation, record, roll, register, diagram, itemization

● VERB (*Brit.*) = <u>submit</u>, propose, put forward, move, suggest, enter, file, lodge

taboo NOUN = <u>prohibition</u>, ban, restriction, anathema, interdict, proscription, tapu (*N.Z.*)

● ADJECTIVE = <u>forbidden</u>, banned, prohibited, unacceptable, outlawed, anathema, proscribed, unmentionable ≠ permitted

tack NOUN = <u>nail</u>, pin, drawing pin

● VERB 1 = <u>fasten</u>, fix, attach, pin, nail, affix 2 (*Brit.*) = <u>stitch</u>, sew, hem, bind, baste

● PHRASES **tack something on to something** = <u>append</u>, add, attach, tag

tackle VERB 1 = <u>deal with</u>, set about, get stuck into (*informal*), come *or* get to grips with 2 = <u>undertake</u>, attempt, embark upon, get stuck into (*informal*), have a go *or* stab at (*informal*) 3 = <u>intercept</u>, stop, challenge

● NOUN 1 = <u>block</u>, challenge 2 = <u>rig</u>, apparatus

tactic NOUN = <u>policy</u>, approach, move, scheme, plans, method, manoeuvre, ploy

● PLURAL NOUN = <u>strategy</u>, campaigning, manoeuvres, generalship

tactical = <u>strategic</u>, shrewd, smart, diplomatic, cunning ≠ impolitic

tag NOUN = <u>label</u>, tab, note, ticket, slip, identification, marker, flap

● VERB = <u>label</u>, mark

tail NOUN 1 = <u>extremity</u>, appendage, brush, rear end, hindquarters, hind part 2 = <u>train</u>, end, trail, tailpiece

● VERB (*Informal*) = <u>follow</u>, track, shadow, trail, stalk

● PHRASES **turn tail** = <u>run away</u>, flee, run off, retreat, cut and run, take to your heels

tailor NOUN = <u>outfitter</u>, couturier, dressmaker, seamstress, clothier, costumier

● VERB = <u>adapt</u>, adjust, modify, style, fashion, shape, alter, mould

taint = <u>spoil</u>, ruin, contaminate, damage, stain, corrupt, pollute, tarnish ≠ purify

take VERB 1 = <u>grip</u>, grab, seize, catch, grasp, clasp, take hold of 2 = <u>carry</u>, bring, bear, transport, ferry, haul, convey, fetch ≠ send 3 = <u>accompany</u>, lead, bring, guide, conduct, escort, convoy, usher 4 = <u>remove</u>, draw, pull, fish, withdraw, extract 5 = <u>steal</u>, appropriate, pocket, pinch (*informal*), misappropriate, purloin ≠ return 6 = <u>capture</u>, seize, take into custody, lay hold of ≠ release 7 = <u>tolerate</u>, stand, bear, stomach, endure, abide, put up with (*informal*), withstand ≠ avoid 8 = <u>require</u>, need, involve, demand, call for, entail, necessitate 9 = <u>understand</u>, follow, comprehend, get, see, grasp, apprehend 10 = <u>regard as</u>, believe to be, consider to be, perceive to be, presume to be 11 = <u>have room for</u>, hold, contain, accommodate, accept

● PHRASES **take off** 1 = <u>lift off</u>, take to the air 2 (*Informal*) = <u>depart</u>, go, leave, disappear, abscond, decamp, slope off ◆ **take someone in** = <u>deceive</u>, fool, con (*informal*), trick, cheat, mislead, dupe, swindle ◆ **take someone off** (*Informal*) = <u>parody</u>, imitate, mimic, mock, caricature, send up (*Brit. informal*), lampoon, satirize ◆ **take something in** = <u>understand</u>, absorb, grasp, digest, comprehend, assimilate, get the hang of (*informal*) ◆ **take something up** 1 = <u>start</u>, begin, engage in, adopt, become involved in 2 = <u>occupy</u>, absorb, consume, use up, cover, fill, waste, squander

takeover = <u>merger</u>, coup, incorporation

tale = <u>story</u>, narrative, anecdote, account, legend, saga, yarn (*informal*), fable

talent = <u>ability</u>, gift, aptitude, capacity, genius, flair, knack

talented = <u>gifted</u>, able, expert, master, masterly, brilliant, ace (*informal*), consummate

talk VERB 1 = <u>speak</u>, chat, chatter, converse, communicate, natter 2 = <u>discuss</u>, confer, negotiate, parley, confabulate, korero (*N.Z.*) 3 = <u>inform</u>, grass (*Brit. slang*), tell all, give the game away, blab, let the cat out of the bag

● NOUN = <u>speech</u>, lecture, presentation, report, address, discourse, sermon, symposium, whaikorero (*N.Z.*)

talking-to (*Informal*) = reprimand, lecture, rebuke, scolding, criticism, reproach, ticking-off (*informal*), dressing-down (*informal*) ≠ praise

tall 1 = lofty, big, giant, long-legged, lanky, leggy **2** = high, towering, soaring, steep, elevated, lofty ≠ short **3** (*Informal*) = implausible, incredible, far-fetched, exaggerated, absurd, unbelievable, preposterous, cock-and-bull (*informal*) ≠ plausible **4** = difficult, hard, demanding, unreasonable, well-nigh impossible

tally NOUN = record, score, total, count, reckoning, running total

● VERB = agree, match, accord, fit, square, coincide, correspond, conform ≠ disagree

tame ADJECTIVE **1** = domesticated, docile, broken, gentle, obedient, amenable, tractable ≠ wild **2** = submissive, meek, compliant, subdued, manageable, obedient, docile, unresisting ≠ stubborn **3** = unexciting, boring, dull, bland, uninspiring, humdrum, uninteresting, insipid ≠ exciting

● VERB **1** = domesticate, train, break in, house-train ≠ make fiercer **2** = subdue, suppress, master, discipline, humble, conquer, subjugate ≠ arouse

tangible = definite, real, positive, material, actual, concrete, palpable, perceptible ≠ intangible

tangle NOUN **1** = knot, twist, web, jungle, coil, entanglement **2** = mess, jam, fix (*informal*), confusion, complication, mix-up, shambles, entanglement

● VERB = twist, knot, mat, coil, mesh, entangle, interweave, ravel ≠ disentangle

● PHRASES **tangle with someone** = come into conflict with, come up against, cross swords with, dispute with, contend with, contest with, lock horns with

tantrum = outburst, temper, hysterics, fit, flare-up, foulie (*Austral. slang*)

tap¹ VERB = knock, strike, pat, rap, beat, touch, drum

● NOUN = knock, pat, rap, touch, drumming

tap² NOUN = valve, stopcock

● VERB = listen in on, monitor, bug (*informal*), spy on, eavesdrop on, wiretap

● PHRASES **on tap 1** (*Informal*) = available, ready, standing by, to hand, on hand, at hand, in reserve **2** = on draught, cask-conditioned, from barrels, not bottled *or* canned

tape NOUN = binding, strip, band, string, ribbon

● VERB **1** = record, video, tape-record, make a recording of **2** *sometimes with* **up** = bind, secure, stick, seal, wrap

target 1 = mark, goal **2** = goal, aim, objective, end, mark, object, intention, ambition **3** = victim, butt, prey, scapegoat

tariff 1 = tax, duty, toll, levy, excise **2** = price list, schedule

tarnish VERB **1** = damage, taint, blacken, sully, smirch ≠ enhance **2** = stain, discolour, darken, blot, blemish ≠ brighten

● NOUN = stain, taint, discoloration, spot, blot, blemish

tart¹ = pie, pastry, pasty, tartlet, patty

tart² = sharp, acid, sour, bitter, pungent, tangy, piquant, vinegary ≠ sweet

tart³ (*Informal*) = slut, prostitute, whore, call girl, trollop, floozy (*slang*)

task NOUN = job, duty, assignment, exercise, mission, enterprise, undertaking, chore

● PHRASES **take someone to task** = criticize, blame, censure, rebuke, reprimand, reproach, scold, tell off (*informal*)

taste NOUN **1** = flavour, savour, relish, smack, tang ≠ blandness **2** = bit, bite, mouthful, sample, dash, spoonful, morsel, titbit **3** = liking, preference, penchant, fondness, partiality, fancy, appetite, inclination ≠ dislike **4** = refinement, style, judgment, discrimination, appreciation, elegance, sophistication, discernment ≠ lack of judgment

● VERB **1** = have a flavour of, smack of, savour of **2** = sample, try, test, sip, savour **3** = distinguish, perceive, discern, differentiate **4** = experience, know, undergo, partake of, encounter, meet with ≠ miss

tasty = delicious, luscious, palatable, delectable, savoury, full-flavoured, scrumptious (*informal*), appetizing, lekker (*S. African slang*), yummo (*Austral. slang*) ≠ bland

taunt VERB = jeer, mock, tease, ridicule, provoke, insult, torment, deride

● NOUN = jeer, dig, insult, ridicule, teasing, provocation, derision, sarcasm

tavern = inn, bar, pub (*informal, chiefly*

Brit.), public house, hostelry, alehouse (*archaic*)

tax NOUN = charge, duty, toll, levy, tariff, excise, tithe

● VERB 1 = charge, rate, assess 2 = strain, stretch, try, test, load, burden, exhaust, weaken

teach VERB = instruct, train, coach, inform, educate, drill, tutor, enlighten

● VERB = show, train

teacher = instructor, coach, tutor, guide, trainer, lecturer, mentor, educator

team NOUN 1 = side, squad 2 = group, company, set, body, band, gang, line-up, bunch

● PHRASES **team up** = join, unite, work together, cooperate, couple, link up, get together, band together

tear VERB 1 = rip, split, rend, shred, rupture 2 = run 3 = scratch, cut (open), gash, lacerate, injure, mangle, cut to pieces, cut to ribbons, mangulate (*Austral. slang*) 4 = pull apart, claw, lacerate, mutilate, mangle, mangulate (*Austral. slang*) 5 = rush, run, charge, race, fly, speed, dash, hurry

● NOUN = hole, split, rip, rent, snag, rupture

tears PLURAL NOUN = crying, weeping, sobbing, wailing, blubbering

● PHRASES **in tears** = weeping, crying, sobbing, blubbering

tease 1 = mock, provoke, torment, taunt, goad, pull someone's leg (*informal*), make fun of 2 = tantalize, lead on, flirt with, titillate

technical = scientific, technological, skilled, specialist, specialized, hi-tech or high-tech

technique 1 = method, way, system, approach, means, style, manner, procedure 2 = skill, performance, craft, touch, execution, artistry, craftsmanship, proficiency

tedious = boring, dull, dreary, monotonous, drab, tiresome, laborious, humdrum ≠ exciting

teenager = youth, minor, adolescent, juvenile, girl, boy

telephone NOUN = phone, mobile (phone), handset, dog and bone (*slang*)

● VERB = call, phone, ring (*chiefly Brit.*), dial

telescope NOUN = glass, scope (*informal*), spyglass

● VERB = shorten, contract, compress,

shrink, condense, abbreviate, abridge ≠ lengthen

television = TV, telly (*Brit. informal*), small screen (*informal*), the box (*Brit. informal*), the tube (*slang*)

tell VERB 1 = inform, notify, state to, reveal to, express to, disclose to, proclaim to, divulge 2 = describe, relate, recount, report, portray, depict, chronicle, narrate 3 = instruct, order, command, direct, bid 4 = distinguish, discriminate, discern, differentiate, identify 5 = have or take effect, register, weigh, count, take its toll, carry weight, make its presence felt

● PHRASES **tell someone off** = reprimand, rebuke, scold, lecture, censure, reproach, berate, chide

telling = effective, significant, considerable, marked, striking, powerful, impressive, influential ≠ unimportant

temper NOUN 1 = irritability, irascibility, passion, resentment, petulance, surliness, hot-headedness ≠ good humour 2 = frame of mind, nature, mind, mood, constitution, humour, temperament, disposition 3 = rage, fury, bad mood, passion, tantrum, foulie (*Austral. slang*) 4 = self-control, composure, cool (*slang*), calmness, equanimity ≠ anger

● VERB 1 = moderate, restrain, tone down, soften, soothe, lessen, mitigate, assuage ≠ intensify 2 = strengthen, harden, toughen, anneal ≠ soften

temperament 1 = nature, character, personality, make-up, constitution, bent, humour, temper 2 = moods, anger, volatility, petulance, excitability, moodiness, hot-headedness

temple = shrine, church, sanctuary, house of God

temporarily = briefly, for the time being, momentarily, fleetingly, pro tem

temporary 1 = impermanent, transitory, brief, fleeting, interim, short-lived, momentary, ephemeral ≠ permanent 2 = short-term, acting, interim, supply, stand-in, fill-in, caretaker, provisional

tempt 1 = attract, allure 2 = entice, lure, lead on, invite, seduce, coax ≠ discourage

temptation 1 = enticement, lure, inducement, pull, seduction, allurement, tantalization ≠ appeal, attraction

tempting = inviting, enticing, seductive, alluring, attractive, mouthwatering, appetizing ≠ uninviting

tenant = leaseholder, resident, renter, occupant, inhabitant, occupier, lodger, boarder

tend¹ = be inclined, be liable, have a tendency, be apt, be prone, lean, incline, gravitate

tend² 1 = take care of, look after, keep, attend, nurture, watch over ≠ neglect 2 = maintain, take care of, nurture, cultivate, manage ≠ neglect

tendency = inclination, leaning, liability, disposition, propensity, susceptibility, proclivity, proneness

tender¹ 1 = gentle, loving, kind, caring, sympathetic, affectionate, compassionate, considerate ≠ harsh 2 = vulnerable, young, sensitive, raw, youthful, inexperienced, immature, impressionable ≠ experienced 3 = sensitive, painful, sore, raw, bruised, inflamed

tender² NOUN = offer, bid, estimate, proposal, submission
● VERB = offer, present, submit, give, propose, volunteer, hand in, put forward

tense ADJECTIVE 1 = strained, uneasy, stressful, fraught, charged, difficult, worrying, exciting 2 = nervous, edgy, strained, anxious, apprehensive, uptight (*informal*), on edge, jumpy ≠ calm 3 = rigid, strained, taut, stretched, tight ≠ relaxed
● VERB = tighten, strain, brace, stretch, flex, stiffen ≠ relax

tension 1 = strain, stress, nervousness, pressure, anxiety, unease, apprehension, suspense ≠ calmness 2 = friction, hostility, unease, antagonism, antipathy, enmity 3 = rigidity, tightness, stiffness, pressure, stress, stretching, tautness

tentative 1 = unconfirmed, provisional, indefinite, test, trial, pilot, preliminary, experimental ≠ confirmed 2 = hesitant, cautious, uncertain, doubtful, faltering, unsure, timid, undecided ≠ confident

term NOUN 1 = word, name, expression, title, label, phrase 2 = period, time, spell, while, season, interval, span, duration
● PLURAL NOUN 1 = conditions, particulars, provisions, provisos, stipulations, qualifications, specifications 2 = relationship, standing, footing, relations, status
● VERB = call, name, label, style, entitle, tag,

dub, designate

terminal ADJECTIVE 1 = fatal, deadly, lethal, killing, mortal, incurable, inoperable, untreatable 2 = final, last, closing, finishing, concluding, ultimate, terminating ≠ initial
● NOUN = terminus, station, depot, end of the line

terminate 1 = end, stop, conclude, finish, complete, discontinue ≠ begin 2 = cease, end, close, finish 3 = abort, end

terrain = ground, country, land, landscape, topography, going

terrestrial = earthly, worldly, global

terrible 1 = awful, shocking, terrifying, horrible, dreadful, horrifying, fearful, horrendous 2 (*Informal*) = bad, awful, dreadful, dire, abysmal, poor, rotten (*informal*) ≠ wonderful 3 = serious, desperate, severe, extreme, dangerous, insufferable ≠ mild

terribly 1 = very much, very, dreadfully, seriously, extremely, desperately, thoroughly, decidedly 2 = extremely, very, dreadfully, seriously, desperately, thoroughly, decidedly, awfully (*informal*)

terrific 1 (*Informal*) = excellent, wonderful, brilliant, amazing, outstanding, superb, fantastic (*informal*), magnificent, booshit (*Austral. slang*), exo (*Austral. slang*), sik (*Austral. slang*), ka pai (*N.Z.*) ≠ awful 2 = intense, great, huge, enormous, tremendous, fearful, gigantic

terrified = frightened, scared, petrified, alarmed, panic-stricken, horror-struck

terrify = frighten, scare, alarm, terrorize

territory = district, area, land, region, country, zone, province, patch

terror 1 = fear, alarm, dread, fright, panic, anxiety 2 = nightmare, monster, bogeyman, devil, fiend, bugbear

test VERB 1 = check, investigate, assess, research, analyse, experiment with, try out, put something to the test 2 = examine, put someone to the test
● NOUN 1 = trial, research, check, investigation, analysis, assessment, examination, evaluation 2 = examination, paper, assessment, evaluation

testament 1 = proof, evidence, testimony, witness, demonstration, tribute 2 = will, last wishes

testify = bear witness, state, swear, certify, assert, affirm, attest, corroborate

≠ disprove

testimony 1 = <u>evidence</u>, statement, submission, affidavit, deposition 2 = <u>proof</u>, evidence, demonstration, indication, support, manifestation, verification, corroboration

testing = <u>difficult</u>, demanding, taxing, challenging, searching, tough, exacting, rigorous ≠ undemanding

text 1 = <u>contents</u>, words, content, wording, body, subject matter 2 = <u>words</u>, wording 3 = <u>transcript</u>, script

texture = <u>feel</u>, consistency, structure, surface, tissue, grain

thank = <u>say thank you to</u>, show your appreciation to

thanks PLURAL NOUN = <u>gratitude</u>, appreciation, credit, recognition, acknowledgment, gratefulness

● PHRASES **thanks to** = <u>because of</u>, through, due to, as a result of, owing to

thaw = <u>melt</u>, dissolve, soften, defrost, warm, liquefy, unfreeze ≠ freeze

theatrical 1 = <u>dramatic</u>, stage, Thespian 2 = <u>exaggerated</u>, dramatic, melodramatic, histrionic, affected, mannered, showy, ostentatious ≠ natural

theft = <u>stealing</u>, robbery, thieving, fraud, embezzlement, pilfering, larceny, purloining

theme 1 = <u>motif</u>, leitmotif 2 = <u>subject</u>, idea, topic, essence, subject matter, keynote, gist

theological = <u>religious</u>, ecclesiastical, doctrinal

theoretical 1 = <u>abstract</u>, speculative ≠ practical 2 = <u>hypothetical</u>, academic, notional, unproven, conjectural, postulatory

theory = <u>belief</u>, feeling, speculation, assumption, hunch, presumption, conjecture, surmise

therapeutic = <u>beneficial</u>, healing, restorative, good, corrective, remedial, salutary, curative ≠ harmful

therapist = <u>psychologist</u>, analyst, psychiatrist, shrink (*informal*), counsellor, healer, psychotherapist, psychoanalyst

therapy = <u>remedy</u>, treatment, cure, healing, method of healing

therefore = <u>consequently</u>, so, thus, as a result, hence, accordingly, thence, ergo

thesis 1 = <u>proposition</u>, theory, hypothesis, idea, view, opinion, proposal, contention

2 = <u>dissertation</u>, paper, treatise, essay, monograph

thick 1 = <u>bulky</u>, broad, big, large, fat, solid, substantial, hefty ≠ thin 2 = <u>wide</u>, across, deep, broad, in extent *or* diameter 3 = <u>dense</u>, close, heavy, compact, impenetrable, lush 4 = <u>heavy</u>, heavyweight, dense, chunky, bulky, woolly 5 = <u>opaque</u>, heavy, dense, impenetrable 6 = <u>viscous</u>, concentrated, stiff, condensed, gelatinous, semi-solid, viscid ≠ runny 7 = <u>crowded</u>, full, covered, bursting, bristling, brimming ≠ empty 8 (*Informal*) = <u>stupid</u>, slow, dense, dopey (*informal*), moronic, obtuse, brainless, dumb-ass (*informal*) ≠ clever 9 (*Informal*) = <u>friendly</u>, close, intimate, familiar, pally (*informal*), devoted, inseparable ≠ unfriendly

thicken = <u>set</u>, condense, congeal, clot, jell, coagulate ≠ thin

thief = <u>robber</u>, burglar, stealer, plunderer, shoplifter, embezzler, pickpocket, pilferer

thin 1 = <u>narrow</u>, fine, attenuated ≠ thick 2 = <u>slim</u>, spare, lean, slight, slender, skinny, skeletal, bony ≠ fat 3 = <u>meagre</u>, sparse, scanty, poor, scattered, inadequate, insufficient, deficient ≠ plentiful 4 = <u>fine</u>, delicate, flimsy, sheer, skimpy, gossamer, diaphanous, filmy ≠ thick 5 = <u>unconvincing</u>, inadequate, feeble, poor, weak, superficial, lame, flimsy ≠ convincing 6 = <u>wispy</u>, thinning, sparse, scarce, scanty

thing NOUN 1 = <u>substance</u>, stuff, being, body, material, fabric, entity 2 (*Informal*) = <u>phobia</u>, fear, complex, horror, terror, hang-up (*informal*), aversion, neurosis 3 (*Informal*) = <u>obsession</u>, liking, preoccupation, mania, fetish, fixation, soft spot, predilection

● PLURAL NOUN 1 = <u>possessions</u>, stuff, gear, belongings, effects, luggage, clobber (*Brit. slang*), chattels 2 = <u>equipment</u>, gear, tools, stuff, tackle, implements, kit, apparatus 3 = <u>circumstances</u>, the situation, the state of affairs, matters, life, affairs

think VERB 1 = <u>believe</u>, be of the opinion, be of the view 2 = <u>judge</u>, consider, estimate, reckon, deem, regard as 3 = <u>ponder</u>, reflect, contemplate, deliberate, meditate, ruminate, cogitate, be lost in thought

● PHRASES **think something up** = <u>devise</u>, create, come up with, invent, contrive, visualize, concoct, dream something up

thinker 1 = <u>philosopher</u>, intellect (*informal*), wise man, sage, brain (*informal*), theorist, mastermind

thinking NOUN = <u>reasoning</u>, idea, view, position, theory, opinion, judgment, conjecture
● ADJECTIVE = <u>thoughtful</u>, intelligent, reasoning, rational, philosophical, reflective, contemplative, meditative

thirst 1 = <u>dryness</u>, thirstiness, drought 2 = <u>craving</u>, appetite, longing, desire, passion, yearning, hankering, keenness ≠ aversion

thorn = <u>prickle</u>, spike, spine, barb

thorough 1 = <u>comprehensive</u>, full, complete, sweeping, intensive, in-depth, exhaustive ≠ cursory 2 = <u>careful</u>, conscientious, painstaking, efficient, meticulous, exhaustive, assiduous ≠ careless 3 = <u>complete</u>, total, absolute, utter, perfect, outright, unqualified, out-and-out ≠ partial

thoroughly 1 = <u>carefully</u>, fully, efficiently, meticulously, painstakingly, scrupulously, assiduously, intensively ≠ carelessly 2 = <u>fully</u> 3 = <u>completely</u>, quite, totally, perfectly, absolutely, utterly, downright, to the hilt ≠ partly

though CONJUNCTION = <u>although</u>, while, even if, even though, notwithstanding
● ADVERB = <u>nevertheless</u>, still, however, yet, nonetheless, for all that, notwithstanding

thought 1 = <u>thinking</u>, consideration, reflection, deliberation, musing, meditation, rumination, cogitation 2 = <u>opinion</u>, view, idea, concept, notion, judgment 3 = <u>consideration</u>, study, attention, care, regard, scrutiny, heed 4 = <u>intention</u>, plan, idea, design, aim, purpose, object, notion 5 = <u>hope</u>, expectation, prospect, aspiration, anticipation

thoughtful 1 = <u>reflective</u>, pensive, contemplative, meditative, serious, studious, deliberative, ruminative ≠ shallow 2 = <u>considerate</u>, kind, caring, kindly, helpful, attentive, unselfish, solicitous ≠ inconsiderate

thrash VERB 1 = <u>defeat</u>, beat, crush, slaughter (*informal*), rout, trounce, run rings around (*informal*), wipe the floor with (*informal*) 2 = <u>beat</u>, wallop, whip, belt (*informal*), cane, flog, scourge, spank

3 = <u>thresh</u>, flail, jerk, writhe, toss and turn
● PHRASES **thrash something out** = <u>settle</u>, resolve, discuss, debate, solve, argue out, have something out, talk something over

thrashing 1 = <u>defeat</u>, beating, hammering (*informal*), hiding (*informal*), rout, trouncing, drubbing 2 = <u>beating</u>, hiding (*informal*), belting (*informal*), whipping, flogging

thread NOUN 1 = <u>strand</u>, fibre, yarn, filament, line, string, twine 2 = <u>theme</u>, train of thought, direction, plot, drift, story line
● VERB = <u>move</u>, pass, ease, thrust, squeeze through, pick your way

threat 1 = <u>danger</u>, risk, hazard, menace, peril 2 = <u>threatening remark</u>, menace 3 = <u>warning</u>, foreshadowing, foreboding

threaten 1 = <u>intimidate</u>, bully, menace, terrorize, lean on (*slang*), pressurize, browbeat ≠ defend 2 = <u>endanger</u>, jeopardize, put at risk, imperil, put in jeopardy, put on the line ≠ protect 3 = <u>be imminent</u>, impend

threshold 1 = <u>entrance</u>, doorway, door, doorstep 2 = <u>start</u>, beginning, opening, dawn, verge, brink, outset, inception ≠ end 3 = <u>limit</u>, margin, starting point, minimum

thrift = <u>economy</u>, prudence, frugality, saving, parsimony, carefulness, thriftiness ≠ extravagance

thrill NOUN = <u>pleasure</u>, kick (*informal*), buzz (*slang*), high, stimulation, tingle, titillation ≠ tedium
● VERB = <u>excite</u>, stimulate, arouse, move, stir, electrify, titillate, give someone a kick

thrilling = <u>exciting</u>, gripping, stimulating, stirring, sensational, rousing, riveting, electrifying ≠ boring

thrive = <u>prosper</u>, do well, flourish, increase, grow, develop, succeed, get on ≠ decline

thriving = <u>successful</u>, flourishing, healthy, booming, blooming, prosperous, burgeoning ≠ unsuccessful

throb VERB 1 = <u>pulsate</u>, pound, beat, pulse, thump, palpitate 2 = <u>vibrate</u>, pulsate, reverberate, shake, judder (*informal*)
● NOUN 1 = <u>pulse</u>, pounding, beat, thump, thumping, pulsating, palpitation 2 = <u>vibration</u>, throbbing, reverberation, judder (*informal*), pulsation

throng NOUN = <u>crowd</u>, mob, horde, host, pack, mass, crush, swarm
- VERB 1 = <u>crowd</u>, flock, congregate, converge, mill around, swarm around ≠ disperse 2 = <u>pack</u>, crowd

throttle = <u>strangle</u>, choke, garrotte, strangulate

through PREPOSITION 1 = <u>via</u>, by way of, by, between, past, from one side to the other of 2 = <u>because of</u>, by way of, by means of 3 = <u>using</u>, via, by way of, by means of, by virtue of, with the assistance of 4 = <u>during</u>, throughout, for the duration of, in
- ADJECTIVE = <u>completed</u>, done, finished, ended
- PHRASES **through and through** = <u>completely</u>, totally, fully, thoroughly, entirely, altogether, wholly, utterly

throughout PREPOSITION 1 = <u>right through</u>, everywhere in, during the whole of, through the whole of 2 = <u>all over</u>, everywhere in, through the whole of
- ADVERB 1 = <u>from start to finish</u>, right through 2 = <u>all through</u>, right through

throw VERB 1 = <u>hurl</u>, toss, fling, send, launch, cast, pitch, chuck (*informal*) 2 = <u>toss</u>, fling, chuck (*informal*), cast, hurl, sling 3 (*Informal*) = <u>confuse</u>, baffle, faze, astonish, confound, disconcert, dumbfound
- NOUN = <u>toss</u>, pitch, fling, sling, lob (*informal*), heave

thrust VERB = <u>push</u>, force, shove, drive, plunge, jam, ram, propel
- NOUN 1 = <u>stab</u>, pierce, lunge 2 = <u>push</u>, shove, poke, prod 3 = <u>momentum</u>, impetus, drive

thug = <u>ruffian</u>, hooligan, tough, heavy (*slang*), gangster, bully boy, bruiser (*informal*), tsotsi (*S. African*)

thump VERB = <u>strike</u>, hit, punch, pound, beat, knock, smack, clout (*informal*)
- NOUN 1 = <u>blow</u>, knock, punch, rap, smack, clout (*informal*), whack, swipe 2 = <u>thud</u>, crash, bang, clunk, thwack

thunder NOUN = <u>rumble</u>, crash, boom, explosion
- VERB 1 = <u>rumble</u>, crash, boom, roar, resound, reverberate, peal 2 = <u>shout</u>, roar, yell, bark, bellow

thus 1 = <u>therefore</u>, so, hence, consequently, accordingly, for this reason, ergo, on that account 2 = <u>in this way</u>, so, like this, as follows

thwart = <u>frustrate</u>, foil, prevent, snooker, hinder, obstruct, outwit, stymie ≠ assist

tick NOUN 1 = <u>check mark</u>, mark, line, stroke, dash 2 = <u>click</u>, tapping, clicking, ticktock 3 (*Brit. informal*) = <u>moment</u>, second, minute, flash, instant, twinkling, split second, trice
- VERB 1 = <u>mark</u>, indicate, check off 2 = <u>click</u>, tap, ticktock

ticket 1 = <u>voucher</u>, pass, coupon, card, slip, certificate, token, chit 2 = <u>label</u>, tag, marker, sticker, card, slip, tab, docket

tide 1 = <u>current</u>, flow, stream, ebb, undertow, tideway 2 = <u>course</u>, direction, trend, movement, tendency, drift

tidy ADJECTIVE 1 = <u>neat</u>, orderly, clean, spruce, well-kept, well-ordered, shipshape ≠ untidy 2 = <u>organized</u>, neat, methodical 3 (*Informal*) = <u>considerable</u>, large, substantial, goodly, healthy, generous, handsome, ample ≠ small
- VERB = <u>neaten</u>, straighten, order, clean, groom, spruce up ≠ disorder

tie VERB 1 = <u>fasten</u>, bind, join, link, connect, attach, knot ≠ unfasten 2 = <u>tether</u>, secure 3 = <u>restrict</u>, limit, confine, bind, restrain, hamper, hinder ≠ free 4 = <u>draw</u>, be level, match, equal
- NOUN 1 = <u>fastening</u>, binding, link, bond, knot, cord, fetter, ligature 2 = <u>bond</u>, relationship, connection, commitment, liaison, allegiance, affiliation 3 = <u>draw</u>, dead heat, deadlock, stalemate

tier = <u>row</u>, bank, layer, line, level, rank, storey, stratum

tight 1 = <u>close-fitting</u>, narrow, cramped, snug, constricted, close ≠ loose 2 = <u>secure</u>, firm, fast, fixed 3 = <u>taut</u>, stretched, rigid ≠ slack 4 = <u>close</u>, even, well-matched, hard-fought, evenly-balanced ≠ uneven 5 (*Informal*) = <u>miserly</u>, mean, stingy, grasping, parsimonious, niggardly, tightfisted ≠ generous 6 (*Informal*) = <u>drunk</u>, intoxicated, plastered (*slang*), under the influence (*informal*), tipsy, paralytic (*informal*), inebriated, out to it (*Austral. & N.Z. slang*) ≠ sober

tighten = <u>close</u>, narrow, strengthen, squeeze, harden, constrict ≠ slacken

till[1] = <u>cultivate</u>, dig, plough, work

till[2] = <u>cash register</u>, cash box

tilt VERB = <u>slant</u>, tip, slope, list, lean, heel, incline
- NOUN 1 = <u>slope</u>, angle, inclination, list,

pitch, incline, slant, camber 2 (*Medieval history*) = <u>joust</u>, fight, tournament, lists, combat, duel

timber 1 = <u>beams</u>, boards, planks 2 = <u>wood</u>, logs

time NOUN 1 = <u>period</u>, term, space, stretch, spell, span 2 = <u>occasion</u>, point, moment, stage, instance, point in time, juncture 3 = <u>age</u>, duration 4 = <u>tempo</u>, beat, rhythm, measure

● VERB = <u>schedule</u>, set, plan, book, programme, set up, fix, arrange

timeless = <u>eternal</u>, lasting, permanent, enduring, immortal, everlasting, ageless, changeless ≠ temporary

timely = <u>opportune</u>, appropriate, well-timed, suitable, convenient, judicious, propitious, seasonable ≠ untimely

timetable 1 = <u>schedule</u>, programme, agenda, list, diary, calendar 2 = <u>syllabus</u>, course, curriculum, programme, teaching programme

tinge NOUN 1 = <u>tint</u>, colour, shade 2 = <u>trace</u>, bit, drop, touch, suggestion, dash, sprinkling, smattering

● VERB = <u>tint</u>, colour

tinker = <u>meddle</u>, play, potter, fiddle (*informal*), dabble, mess about

tint NOUN 1 = <u>shade</u>, colour, tone, hue 2 = <u>dye</u>, wash, rinse, tinge, tincture

● VERB = <u>dye</u>, colour

tiny = <u>small</u>, little, minute, slight, miniature, negligible, microscopic, diminutive ≠ huge

tip¹ NOUN 1 = <u>end</u>, point, head, extremity, sharp end, nib, prong 2 = <u>peak</u>, top, summit, pinnacle, zenith, spire, acme, vertex

● VERB = <u>cap</u>, top, crown, surmount, finish

tip² VERB 1 = <u>reward</u>, remunerate, give a tip to, sweeten (*informal*) 2 = <u>predict</u>, back, recommend, think of

● NOUN 1 = <u>gratuity</u>, gift, reward, present, sweetener (*informal*) 2 = <u>hint</u>, suggestion, piece of advice, pointer

tip³ VERB 1 = <u>pour</u>, drop, empty, dump, drain, discharge, unload, jettison 2 (*Brit.*) = <u>dump</u>, empty, unload, pour out

● NOUN (*Brit.*) = <u>dump</u>, midden, rubbish heap, refuse heap

tire 1 = <u>exhaust</u>, drain, fatigue, weary, wear out ≠ refresh 2 = <u>flag</u>, become tired, fail 3 = <u>bore</u>, weary, exasperate, irritate, irk

tired 1 = <u>exhausted</u>, fatigued, weary,

flagging, drained, sleepy, worn out, drowsy, tuckered out (*Austral. & N.Z. informal*) ≠ energetic 2 = <u>bored</u>, fed up, weary, sick, hoha (*N.Z.*) ≠ enthusiastic about 3 = <u>hackneyed</u>, stale, well-worn, old, corny (*slang*), threadbare, trite, clichéd ≠ original

tiring = <u>exhausting</u>, demanding, wearing, tough, exacting, strenuous, arduous, laborious

title 1 = <u>name</u>, designation, term, handle (*slang*), moniker *or* monicker (*slang*) 2 (*Sport*) = <u>championship</u>, trophy, bays, crown, honour 3 (*Law*) = <u>ownership</u>, right, claim, privilege, entitlement, tenure, prerogative, freehold

toast¹ 1 = <u>brown</u>, grill, crisp, roast 2 = <u>warm (up)</u>, heat (up), thaw, bring back to life

toast² NOUN 1 = <u>tribute</u>, compliment, salute, health, pledge, salutation 2 = <u>favourite</u>, celebrity, darling, talk, pet, focus of attention, hero *or* heroine, blue-eyed boy *or* girl (*Brit. informal*)

● VERB = <u>drink to</u>, honour, salute, drink (to) the health of

together ADVERB 1 = <u>collectively</u>, jointly, as one, with each other, in conjunction, side by side, mutually, in partnership ≠ separately 2 = <u>at the same time</u>, simultaneously, concurrently, contemporaneously, at one fell swoop

● ADJECTIVE (*Informal*) = <u>self-possessed</u>, composed, well-balanced, well-adjusted

toil VERB 1 = <u>labour</u>, work, struggle, strive, sweat (*informal*), slave, graft (*informal*), slog 2 = <u>struggle</u>, trek, slog, trudge, fight your way, footslog

● NOUN = <u>hard work</u>, effort, application, sweat, graft (*informal*), slog, exertion, drudgery ≠ idleness

toilet 1 = <u>lavatory</u>, bathroom, loo (*Brit. informal*), privy, cloakroom (*Brit.*), urinal, latrine, washroom, dunny (*Austral. & N.Z. old-fashioned informal*), bogger (*Austral. slang*), brasco (*Austral. slang*) 2 = <u>bathroom</u>, gents *or* ladies (*Brit. informal*), privy, latrine, water closet, ladies' room, W.C.

token NOUN = <u>symbol</u>, mark, sign, note, expression, indication, representation, badge

● ADJECTIVE = <u>nominal</u>, symbolic, minimal, hollow, superficial, perfunctory

tolerance 1 = broad-mindedness, indulgence, forbearance, permissiveness, open-mindedness ≠ intolerance **2** = endurance, resistance, stamina, fortitude, resilience, toughness, staying power, hardiness **3** = resistance, immunity, resilience, non-susceptibility

tolerant = broad-minded, understanding, open-minded, catholic, long-suffering, permissive, forbearing, unprejudiced ≠ intolerant

tolerate 1 = endure, stand, take, stomach, put up with (*informal*) **2** = allow, accept, permit, take, brook, put up with (*informal*), condone ≠ forbid

toll¹ VERB = ring, sound, strike, chime, knell, clang, peal

● NOUN = ringing, chime, knell, clang, peal

toll² **1** = charge, tax, fee, duty, payment, levy, tariff **2** = damage, cost, loss, roll, penalty, sum, number, roster **3** = adverse effects, price, cost, suffering, damage, penalty, harm

tomb = grave, vault, crypt, mausoleum, sarcophagus, catacomb, sepulchre

tone NOUN **1** = pitch, inflection, intonation, timbre, modulation **2** = volume, timbre **3** = character, style, feel, air, spirit, attitude, manner, mood **4** = colour, shade, tint, tinge, hue

● VERB = harmonize, match, blend, suit, go well with

● PHRASES **tone something down** = moderate, temper, soften, restrain, subdue, play down = reduce, moderate

tongue = language, speech, dialect, parlance

tonic = stimulant, boost, pick-me-up (*informal*), fillip, shot in the arm (*informal*), restorative

too 1 = also, as well, further, in addition, moreover, besides, likewise, to boot **2** = excessively, very, extremely, overly, unduly, unreasonably, inordinately, immoderately

tool 1 = implement, device, appliance, machine, instrument, gadget, utensil, contraption **2** = puppet, creature, pawn, stooge (*slang*), minion, lackey, flunkey, hireling

top NOUN **1** = peak, summit, head, crown, height, ridge, brow, crest ≠ bottom **2** = lid, cover, cap, plug, stopper, bung **3** = first place, head, peak, lead, high point

● ADJECTIVE **1** = highest, loftiest, furthest up, uppermost **2** = leading, best, first, highest, head, finest, elite, foremost ≠ lowest **3** = chief, most important, principal, most powerful, highest, head, leading, main **4** = prime, best, select, first-class, quality, choice, excellent, premier

● VERB **1** = lead, head, be at the top of, be first in **2** = cover, garnish, finish, crown, cap **3** = surpass, better, beat, improve on, cap, exceed, eclipse, excel ≠ not be as good as

topic = subject, point, question, issue, matter, theme, subject matter

topical = current, popular, contemporary, up-to-date, up-to-the-minute, newsworthy

topple 1 = fall over, fall, collapse, tumble, overturn, totter, keel over, overbalance **2** = knock over **3** = overthrow, overturn, bring down, oust, unseat, bring low

torment NOUN = suffering, distress, misery, pain, hell, torture, agony, anguish ≠ bliss

● VERB **1** = torture, distress, rack, crucify ≠ comfort **2** = tease, annoy, bother, irritate, harass, hassle (*informal*), pester, vex

torn 1 = cut, split, rent, ripped, ragged, slit, lacerated **2** = undecided, uncertain, unsure, wavering, vacillating, in two minds (*informal*), irresolute

tornado = whirlwind, storm, hurricane, gale, cyclone, typhoon, tempest, squall

torture VERB **1** = torment, abuse, persecute, afflict, scourge, molest, crucify, mistreat ≠ comfort **2** = distress, torment, worry, trouble, rack, afflict, harrow, inflict anguish on

● NOUN **1** = ill-treatment, abuse, torment, persecution, maltreatment, harsh treatment **2** = agony, suffering, anguish, distress, torment, heartbreak ≠ bliss

toss VERB **1** = throw, pitch, hurl, fling, launch, cast, flip, sling **2** = shake **3** = thrash (about), twitch, wriggle, squirm, writhe

● NOUN = throw, pitch, lob (*informal*)

tot NOUN **1** = infant, child, baby, toddler, mite, littlie (*Austral. informal*), ankle-biter (*Austral. slang*), tacker (*Austral. slang*) **2** = measure, shot (*informal*), finger, nip, slug, dram, snifter (*informal*)

● PHRASES **tot something up** = add up, calculate, total, reckon, compute, tally, enumerate, count up

total NOUN = sum, entirety, grand total, whole, aggregate, totality, full amount, sum total ≠ part

● ADJECTIVE **1** = <u>complete</u>, absolute, utter, whole, entire, undivided, overarching, thoroughgoing ≠ partial

● VERB **1** = <u>amount to</u>, make, come to, reach, equal, run to, number, add up to **2** = <u>add up</u>, work out, compute, reckon, tot up ≠ subtract

totally = <u>completely</u>, entirely, absolutely, fully, comprehensively, thoroughly, wholly, utterly ≠ partly

touch VERB **1** = <u>feel</u>, handle, finger, stroke, brush, make contact with, caress, fondle **2** = <u>come into contact</u>, meet, contact, border, graze, adjoin, be in contact, abut **3** = <u>tap</u> **4** = <u>affect</u>, influence, inspire, impress **5** = <u>consume</u>, take, drink, eat, partake of **6** = <u>move</u>, stir, disturb **7** = <u>match</u>, rival, equal, compare with, parallel, hold a candle to (*informal*)

● NOUN **1** = <u>contact</u>, push, stroke, brush, press, tap, poke, nudge **2** = <u>feeling</u>, handling, physical contact **3** = <u>bit</u>, spot, trace, drop, dash, small amount, jot, smattering **4** = <u>style</u>, method, technique, way, manner, trademark

● PHRASES **touch and go** = <u>risky</u>, close, near, critical, precarious, nerve-racking

◆ **touch on** *or* **upon something** = <u>refer to</u>, cover, raise, deal with, mention, bring in, speak of, hint at

touching = <u>moving</u>, affecting, sad, stirring, pathetic, poignant, emotive, pitiable

tough ADJECTIVE **1** = <u>strong</u> ≠ weak **2** = <u>hardy</u>, strong, seasoned, strapping, vigorous, sturdy, stout **3** = <u>violent</u>, rough, ruthless, pugnacious, hard-bitten **4** = <u>strict</u>, severe, stern, hard, firm, resolute, merciless, unbending ≠ lenient **5** = <u>hard</u>, difficult, troublesome, uphill, strenuous, arduous, laborious **6** = <u>resilient</u>, hard, resistant, durable, strong, solid, rugged, sturdy ≠ fragile

● NOUN = <u>ruffian</u>, bully, thug, hooligan, bruiser (*informal*), roughneck (*slang*), tsotsi (*S. African*)

tour NOUN **1** = <u>journey</u>, expedition, excursion, trip, outing, jaunt, junket

● VERB **1** = <u>travel round</u>, travel through, journey round, trek round, go on a trip through **2** = <u>visit</u>, explore, go round, inspect, walk round, drive round, sightsee

tourist = <u>traveller</u>, voyager, tripper, globetrotter, holiday-maker, sightseer,

excursionist

tournament = <u>competition</u>, meeting, event, series, contest

tow = <u>drag</u>, draw, pull, haul, tug, yank, lug

towards 1 = <u>in the direction of</u>, to, for, on the way to, en route for **2** = <u>regarding</u>, about, concerning, respecting, in relation to, with regard to, with respect to, apropos

tower = <u>column</u>, pillar, turret, belfry, steeple, obelisk

toxic = <u>poisonous</u>, deadly, lethal, harmful, pernicious, noxious, septic, pestilential ≠ harmless

toy NOUN = <u>plaything</u>, game, doll

● PHRASES **toy with something** = <u>play with</u>, consider, trifle with, dally with, entertain the possibility of, amuse yourself with, think idly of

trace VERB **1** = <u>search for</u>, track, unearth, hunt down **2** = <u>find</u>, track (down), discover, detect, unearth, hunt down, ferret out, locate **3** = <u>outline</u>, sketch, draw **4** = <u>copy</u>, map, draft, outline, sketch, reproduce, draw over

● NOUN **1** = <u>bit</u>, drop, touch, shadow, suggestion, hint, suspicion, tinge **2** = <u>remnant</u>, sign, record, mark, evidence, indication, vestige **3** = <u>track</u>, trail, footstep, path, footprint, spoor, footmark

track NOUN **1** = <u>path</u>, way, road, route, trail, pathway, footpath **2** = <u>course</u>, line, path, orbit, trajectory **3** = <u>line</u>, tramline

● VERB = <u>follow</u>, pursue, chase, trace, tail (*informal*), shadow, trail, stalk

● PHRASES **track something** *or* **someone down** = <u>find</u>, discover, trace, unearth, dig up, hunt down, sniff out, run to earth *or* ground

tract[1] = <u>area</u>, region, district, stretch, territory, extent, plot, expanse

tract[2] = <u>treatise</u>, essay, booklet, pamphlet, dissertation, monograph, homily

trade NOUN **1** = <u>commerce</u>, business, transactions, dealing, exchange, traffic, truck, barter **2** = <u>job</u>, employment, business, craft, profession, occupation, line of work, métier

● VERB **1** = <u>deal</u>, do business, traffic, truck, bargain, peddle, transact, cut a deal **2** = <u>exchange</u>, switch, swap, barter **3** = <u>operate</u>, run, deal, do business

trader = <u>dealer</u>, supplier, merchant, seller, purveyor

tradition 1 = <u>customs</u>, institution, ritual,

folklore, lore, tikanga (*N.Z.*) **2** = <u>established practice</u>, custom, convention, habit, ritual

traditional 1 = <u>old-fashioned</u>, old, established, conventional, usual, accustomed, customary, time-honoured ≠ revolutionary **2** = <u>folk</u>, old

traffic NOUN **1** = <u>transport</u>, vehicles, transportation, freight **2** = <u>trade</u>, commerce, business, exchange, truck, dealings, peddling
● VERB = <u>trade</u>, deal, exchange, bargain, do business, peddle, cut a deal, have dealings

tragedy = <u>disaster</u>, catastrophe, misfortune, adversity, calamity ≠ fortune

tragic 1 = <u>distressing</u>, sad, appalling, deadly, unfortunate, disastrous, dreadful, dire ≠ fortunate **2** = <u>sad</u>, miserable, pathetic, mournful ≠ happy

trail NOUN **1** = <u>path</u>, track, route, way, course, road, pathway, footpath **2** = <u>tracks</u>, path, marks, wake, trace, scent, footprints, spoor **3** = <u>wake</u>, stream, tail
● VERB **1** = <u>follow</u>, track, chase, pursue, dog, hunt, shadow, trace **2** = <u>drag</u>, draw, pull, sweep, haul, tow, dangle, droop **3** = <u>lag</u>, follow, drift, wander, linger, trudge, plod, meander

train VERB **1** = <u>instruct</u>, school, prepare, coach, teach, guide, educate, drill **2** = <u>exercise</u>, prepare, work out, practise, do exercise, get into shape **3** = <u>aim</u>, point, level, position, direct, focus, sight, zero in
● NOUN = <u>sequence</u>, series, chain, string, set, cycle, trail, succession

trainer = <u>coach</u>, manager, guide, adviser, tutor, instructor, counsellor, guru

trait = <u>characteristic</u>, feature, quality, attribute, quirk, peculiarity, mannerism, idiosyncrasy

traitor = <u>betrayer</u>, deserter, turncoat, renegade, defector, Judas, quisling, apostate, fizgig (*Austral. slang*) ≠ loyalist

tramp VERB **1** = <u>trudge</u>, stump, toil, plod, traipse (*informal*) **2** = <u>hike</u>, walk, trek, roam, march, ramble, slog, rove
● NOUN **1** = <u>vagrant</u>, derelict, drifter, down-and-out, derro (*Austral. slang*) **2** = <u>tread</u>, stamp, footstep, footfall **3** = <u>hike</u>, march, trek, ramble, slog

trample *often with* **on** = <u>stamp</u>, crush, squash, tread, flatten, run over, walk over

trance = <u>daze</u>, dream, abstraction, rapture, reverie, stupor, unconsciousness

transaction = <u>deal</u>, negotiation, business, enterprise, bargain, undertaking

transcend = <u>surpass</u>, exceed, go beyond, rise above, eclipse, excel, outstrip, outdo

transcript = <u>copy</u>, record, manuscript, reproduction, duplicate, transcription

transfer VERB = <u>move</u>, transport, shift, relocate, transpose, change
● NOUN = <u>transference</u>, move, handover, change, shift, transmission, translation, relocation

transform 1 = <u>change</u>, convert, alter, transmute **2** = <u>make over</u>, remodel, revolutionize

transformation 1 = <u>change</u>, conversion, alteration, metamorphosis, transmutation **2** = <u>revolution</u>, sea change

transit = <u>movement</u>, transfer, transport, passage, crossing, transportation, carriage, conveyance

transition = <u>change</u>, passing, development, shift, conversion, alteration, progression, metamorphosis

transitional 1 = <u>changing</u>, passing, fluid, intermediate, unsettled, developmental **2** = <u>temporary</u>, working, acting, short-term, interim, fill-in, caretaker, provisional

translate = <u>render</u>, put, change, convert, interpret, decode, construe, paraphrase

translation = <u>interpretation</u>, version, rendering, rendition, decoding, paraphrase

transmission 1 = <u>transfer</u>, spread, spreading, passing on, circulation, dispatch, relaying, mediation **2** = <u>broadcasting</u>, showing, putting out, relaying, sending **3** = <u>programme</u>, broadcast, show, production, telecast

transmit 1 = <u>broadcast</u>, televise, relay, air, radio, send out, disseminate, beam out **2** = <u>pass on</u>, carry, spread, send, bear, transfer, hand on, convey

transparent 1 = <u>clear</u>, sheer, see-through, lucid, translucent, crystalline, limpid, diaphanous ≠ opaque **2** = <u>obvious</u>, plain, patent, evident, explicit, manifest, recognizable, unambiguous ≠ uncertain

transplant 1 = <u>implant</u>, transfer, graft **2** = <u>transfer</u>, take, bring, carry, remove, transport, shift, convey

transport NOUN **1** = <u>vehicle</u>, transportation, conveyance **2** = <u>transference</u>, carrying, delivery, distribution, transportation, shipment, freight, haulage **3** *often plural* = <u>ecstasy</u>, delight, heaven, bliss, euphoria, rapture, enchantment, ravishment ≠ despondency

● VERB 1 = <u>convey</u>, take, move, bring, send, carry, bear, transfer 2 = <u>enrapture</u>, move, delight, entrance, enchant, captivate, ravish 3 (*History*) = <u>exile</u>, banish, deport

trap NOUN 1 = <u>snare</u>, net, gin, pitfall, noose 2 = <u>ambush</u>, set-up (*informal*) 3 = <u>trick</u>, set-up (*informal*), deception, ploy, ruse, trickery, subterfuge, stratagem

● VERB 1 = <u>catch</u>, snare, ensnare, entrap, take, corner, bag, lay hold of 2 = <u>trick</u>, fool, cheat, lure, seduce, deceive, dupe, beguile 3 = <u>capture</u>, catch, arrest, seize, take, secure, collar (*informal*), apprehend

trash 1 = <u>nonsense</u>, rubbish, rot, drivel, twaddle, tripe (*informal*), moonshine, hogwash, kak (*S. African taboo slang*), bizzo (*Austral. slang*), bull's wool (*Austral. & N.Z. slang*) ≠ sense 2 (*Chiefly U.S. & Canad.*) = <u>litter</u>, refuse, waste, rubbish, junk (*informal*), garbage, dross

trauma 1 = <u>shock</u>, suffering, pain, torture, ordeal, anguish 2 = <u>injury</u>, damage, hurt, wound, agony

traumatic = <u>shocking</u>, upsetting, alarming, awful, disturbing, devastating, painful, distressing ≠ calming

travel VERB = <u>go</u>, journey, move, tour, progress, wander, trek, voyage

● NOUN *usually plural* = <u>journey</u>, wandering, expedition, globetrotting, tour, trip, voyage, excursion

traveller or (*U.S.*) **traveler** = <u>voyager</u>, tourist, explorer, globetrotter, holiday-maker, wayfarer

tread VERB = <u>step</u>, walk, march, pace, stamp, stride, hike

● NOUN = <u>step</u>, walk, pace, stride, footstep, gait, footfall

treason = <u>disloyalty</u>, mutiny, treachery, duplicity, sedition, perfidy, lese-majesty, traitorousness ≠ loyalty

treasure NOUN 1 = <u>riches</u>, money, gold, fortune, wealth, valuables, jewels, cash 2 (*Informal*) = <u>angel</u>, darling, jewel, gem, paragon, nonpareil

● VERB = <u>prize</u>, value, esteem, adore, cherish, revere, hold dear, love

treasury = <u>storehouse</u>, bank, store, vault, hoard, cache, repository

treat VERB 1 = <u>behave towards</u>, deal with, handle, act towards, use, consider, serve, manage 2 = <u>take care of</u>, minister to, attend to, give medical treatment to, doctor (*informal*), nurse, care for, prescribe medicine for 3 = <u>provide</u>, stand (*informal*), entertain, lay on, regale

● NOUN 1 = <u>entertainment</u>, party, surprise, gift, celebration, feast, outing, excursion 2 = <u>pleasure</u>, delight, joy, thrill, satisfaction, enjoyment, source of pleasure, fun

treatment 1 = <u>care</u>, medical care, nursing, medicine, surgery, therapy, healing, medication 2 = <u>cure</u>, remedy, medication, medicine 3 *often with of* = <u>handling</u>, dealings with, behaviour towards, conduct towards, management, manipulation, action towards

treaty = <u>agreement</u>, pact, contract, alliance, convention, compact, covenant, entente

trek VERB 1 = <u>journey</u>, march, hike, tramp, rove, go walkabout (*Austral.*) 2 = <u>trudge</u>, traipse (*informal*), footslog, slog

● NOUN 1 = <u>slog</u>, tramp 2 = <u>journey</u>, hike, expedition, safari, march, odyssey

tremble VERB 1 = <u>shake</u>, shiver, quake, shudder, quiver, totter 2 = <u>vibrate</u>, shake, quake, wobble

● NOUN = <u>shake</u>, shiver, quake, shudder, wobble, tremor, quiver, vibration

tremendous 1 = <u>huge</u>, great, enormous, terrific, formidable, immense, gigantic, colossal ≠ tiny 2 = <u>excellent</u>, great, wonderful, brilliant, amazing, extraordinary, fantastic (*informal*), marvellous, booshit (*Austral. slang*), exo (*Austral. slang*), sik (*Austral. slang*) ≠ terrible

trench = <u>ditch</u>, channel, drain, gutter, trough, furrow, excavation

trend 1 = <u>tendency</u>, swing, drift, inclination, current, direction, flow, leaning 2 = <u>fashion</u>, craze, fad (*informal*), mode, thing, style, rage, vogue

trendy (*Brit. informal*) = <u>fashionable</u>, with it (*informal*), stylish, in fashion, in vogue, modish, voguish

trial 1 (*Law*) = <u>hearing</u>, case, court case, inquiry, tribunal, lawsuit, appeal, litigation 2 = <u>test</u>, experiment, evaluation, audition, dry run (*informal*), assessment, probation, appraisal 3 = <u>hardship</u>, suffering, trouble, distress, ordeal, adversity, affliction, tribulation

tribe = <u>race</u>, people, family, clan, hapu (*N.Z.*), iwi (*N.Z.*)

tribunal = <u>hearing</u>, court, trial

tribute = <u>accolade</u>, testimonial, eulogy, recognition, compliment, commendation, panegyric ≠ criticism

trick NOUN 1 = <u>joke</u>, stunt, spoof (*informal*), prank, practical joke, antic, jape, leg-pull (*Brit. informal*) 2 = <u>deception</u>, trap, fraud, manoeuvre, ploy, hoax, swindle, ruse 3 = <u>sleight of hand</u>, stunt, legerdemain 4 = <u>secret</u>, skill, knack, hang (*informal*), technique, know-how (*informal*) 5 = <u>mannerism</u>, habit, characteristic, trait, quirk, peculiarity, foible, idiosyncrasy
● VERB = <u>deceive</u>, trap, take someone in (*informal*), fool, cheat, con (*informal*), kid (*informal*), mislead

trickle VERB = <u>dribble</u>, run, drop, stream, drip, ooze, seep, exude
● NOUN = <u>dribble</u>, drip, seepage, thin stream

tricky 1 = <u>difficult</u>, sensitive, complicated, delicate, risky, hairy (*informal*), problematic, thorny ≠ simple 2 = <u>crafty</u>, scheming, cunning, slippery, sly, devious, wily, artful ≠ open

trifle = <u>knick-knack</u>, toy, plaything, bauble, bagatelle

trifling = <u>insignificant</u>, trivial, worthless, negligible, unimportant, paltry, measly ≠ significant

trigger = <u>bring about</u>, start, cause, produce, generate, prompt, provoke, set off ≠ prevent

trim ADJECTIVE 1 = <u>neat</u>, smart, tidy, spruce, dapper, natty (*informal*), well-groomed, shipshape ≠ untidy 2 = <u>slender</u>, fit, slim, sleek, streamlined, shapely, svelte, willowy
● VERB 1 = <u>cut</u>, crop, clip, shave, tidy, prune, pare, even up 2 = <u>decorate</u>, dress, array, adorn, ornament, embellish, deck out, beautify
● NOUN 1 = <u>decoration</u>, edging, border, piping, trimming, frill, embellishment, adornment 2 = <u>condition</u>, health, shape (*informal*), fitness, wellness, fettle 3 = <u>cut</u>, crop, clipping, shave, pruning, shearing, tidying up

trimming NOUN = <u>decoration</u>, edging, border, piping, frill, embellishment, adornment, ornamentation
● PLURAL NOUN = <u>extras</u>, accessories, ornaments, accompaniments, frills, trappings, paraphernalia

trinity = <u>threesome</u>, trio, triad, triumvirate

trio = <u>threesome</u>, trinity, trilogy, triad, triumvirate

trip NOUN 1 = <u>journey</u>, outing, excursion, day out, run, drive, tour, spin (*informal*) 2 = <u>stumble</u>, fall, slip, misstep
● VERB 1 = <u>stumble</u>, fall, fall over, slip, tumble, topple, stagger, misstep 2 = <u>skip</u>, dance, hop, gambol
● PHRASES **trip someone up** = <u>catch out</u>, trap, wrongfoot

triple ADJECTIVE 1 = <u>treble</u>, three times 2 = <u>three-way</u>, threefold, tripartite
● VERB = <u>treble</u>, increase threefold

triumph NOUN 1 = <u>success</u>, victory, accomplishment, achievement, coup, feat, conquest, attainment ≠ failure 2 = <u>joy</u>, pride, happiness, rejoicing, elation, jubilation, exultation
● VERB 1 *often with over* = <u>succeed</u>, win, overcome, prevail, prosper, vanquish ≠ fail 2 = <u>rejoice</u>, celebrate, glory, revel, gloat, exult, crow

triumphant 1 = <u>victorious</u>, winning, successful, conquering ≠ defeated 2 = <u>celebratory</u>, jubilant, proud, elated, exultant, cock-a-hoop

trivial = <u>unimportant</u>, small, minor, petty, meaningless, worthless, trifling, insignificant ≠ important

troop NOUN = <u>group</u>, company, team, body, unit, band, crowd, squad
● PLURAL NOUN = <u>soldiers</u>, men, armed forces, servicemen, army, soldiery
● VERB = <u>flock</u>, march, stream, swarm, throng, traipse (*informal*)

trophy 1 = <u>prize</u>, cup, award, laurels 2 = <u>souvenir</u>, spoils, relic, memento, booty, keepsake

tropical = <u>hot</u>, stifling, steamy, torrid, sultry, sweltering ≠ cold

trot VERB = <u>run</u>, jog, scamper, lope, canter
● NOUN = <u>run</u>, jog, lope, canter

trouble NOUN 1 = <u>bother</u>, problems, concern, worry, stress, difficulty (*informal*), anxiety, distress 2 *usually plural* = <u>distress</u>, problem, worry, pain, anxiety, grief, torment, sorrow ≠ pleasure 3 = <u>ailment</u>, disease, failure, complaint, illness, disorder, defect, malfunction 4 = <u>disorder</u>, fighting, conflict, bother, unrest, disturbance, to-do (*informal*), furore, biffo (*Austral. slang*) ≠ peace 5 = <u>effort</u>, work, thought, care, labour, pains, hassle (*informal*), inconvenience ≠ convenience

● **VERB 1** = <u>bother</u>, worry, upset, disturb, distress, plague, pain, sadden ≠ please **2** = <u>afflict</u>, hurt, bother, cause discomfort to, pain, grieve **3** = <u>inconvenience</u>, disturb, burden, put out, impose upon, incommode ≠ relieve **4** = <u>take pains</u>, take the time, make an effort, exert yourself ≠ avoid

troublesome 1 = <u>bothersome</u>, trying, taxing, demanding, difficult, worrying, annoying, tricky ≠ simple **2** = <u>disorderly</u>, violent, turbulent, rebellious, unruly, rowdy, undisciplined, uncooperative ≠ well-behaved

trough = <u>manger</u>, water trough

truce = <u>ceasefire</u>, peace, moratorium, respite, lull, cessation, let-up (*informal*), armistice

true 1 = <u>correct</u>, right, accurate, precise, factual, truthful, veracious ≠ false **2** = <u>actual</u>, real, genuine, proper, authentic, dinkum (*Austral. & N.Z. informal*) **3** = <u>faithful</u>, loyal, devoted, dedicated, steady, reliable, staunch, trustworthy ≠ unfaithful **4** = <u>exact</u>, perfect, accurate, precise, spot-on (*Brit. informal*), on target, unerring ≠ inaccurate

truly 1 = <u>genuinely</u>, correctly, truthfully, rightly, precisely, exactly, legitimately, authentically ≠ falsely **2** = <u>really</u>, very, greatly, indeed, extremely **3** = <u>faithfully</u>, steadily, sincerely, staunchly, dutifully, loyally, devotedly

trumpet NOUN = <u>horn</u>, clarion, bugle
● **VERB** = <u>proclaim</u>, advertise, tout (*informal*), announce, broadcast, shout from the rooftops ≠ keep secret

trunk 1 = <u>stem</u>, stalk, bole **2** = <u>chest</u>, case, box, crate, coffer, casket **3** = <u>body</u>, torso **4** = <u>snout</u>, nose, proboscis

trust VERB **1** = <u>believe in</u>, have faith in, depend on, count on, bank on, rely upon ≠ distrust **2** = <u>entrust</u>, commit, assign, confide, consign, put into the hands of, allow to look after, hand over **3** = <u>expect</u>, hope, suppose, assume, presume, surmise
● NOUN = <u>confidence</u>, credit, belief, faith, expectation, conviction, assurance, certainty ≠ distrust

trusting *or* **trustful** = <u>unsuspecting</u>, naive, gullible, unwary, credulous, unsuspicious ≠ suspicious

truth 1 = <u>reality</u>, fact(s), real life **2** = <u>truthfulness</u>, fact, accuracy, precision, validity, legitimacy, veracity, genuineness ≠ inaccuracy

try VERB **1** = <u>attempt</u>, seek, aim, strive, struggle, endeavour, have a go, make an effort **2** = <u>experiment with</u>, try out, put to the test, test, taste, examine, investigate, sample
● NOUN = <u>attempt</u>, go (*informal*), shot (*informal*), effort, crack (*informal*), stab (*informal*), bash (*informal*), whack (*informal*)

trying = <u>annoying</u>, hard, taxing, difficult, tough, stressful, exasperating, tiresome ≠ straightforward

tuck VERB = <u>push</u>, stick, stuff, slip, ease, insert, pop (*informal*)
● NOUN **1** (*Brit. informal*) = <u>food</u>, grub (*slang*), kai (*N.Z. informal*), nosh (*slang*) **2** = <u>fold</u>, gather, pleat, pinch

tug VERB **1** = <u>pull</u>, pluck, jerk, yank, wrench **2** = <u>drag</u>, pull, haul, tow, lug, heave, draw
● NOUN = <u>pull</u>, jerk, yank

tuition = <u>training</u>, schooling, education, teaching, lessons, instruction, tutoring, tutelage

tumble VERB = <u>fall</u>, drop, topple, plummet, stumble, flop
● NOUN = <u>fall</u>, drop, trip, plunge, spill, stumble

tumour = <u>growth</u>, cancer, swelling, lump, carcinoma (*Pathology*), sarcoma (*Medical*)

tune NOUN **1** = <u>melody</u>, air, song, theme, strain(s), jingle, ditty **2** = <u>harmony</u>, pitch, euphony
● **VERB 1** = <u>tune up</u>, adjust **2** = <u>regulate</u>, adapt, modulate, harmonize, attune, pitch

tunnel NOUN = <u>passage</u>, underpass, passageway, subway, channel, hole, shaft
● **VERB** = <u>dig</u>, burrow, mine, bore, drill, excavate

turbulent = <u>stormy</u>, rough, raging, tempestuous, furious, foaming, agitated, tumultuous ≠ calm

turf NOUN **1** = <u>grass</u>, sward **2** = <u>sod</u>
● **PHRASES the turf** = <u>horse-racing</u>, the flat, racing

turmoil = <u>confusion</u>, disorder, chaos, upheaval, disarray, uproar, agitation, commotion ≠ peace

turn VERB **1** = <u>change course</u>, swing round, wheel round, veer, move, switch, shift, swerve **2** = <u>rotate</u>, spin, go round (and round), revolve, roll, circle, twist, spiral **3** = <u>change</u>, transform, shape, convert,

alter, mould, remodel, mutate **4** = <u>shape</u>, form, fashion, cast, frame, mould, make **5** = <u>go bad</u>, go off (*Brit. informal*), curdle **6** = <u>make rancid</u>, spoil, sour, taint
● NOUN **1** = <u>rotation</u>, cycle, circle, revolution, spin, twist, whirl, swivel **2** = <u>change of direction</u>, shift, departure, deviation **3** = <u>direction</u>, course, tack, tendency, drift **4** = <u>opportunity</u>, go, time, try, chance, crack (*informal*), stint **5** = <u>deed</u>, service, act, action, favour, gesture
● PHRASES **turn on someone** = <u>attack</u>, assault, fall on, round on, lash out at, assail, lay into (*informal*), let fly at ◆ **turn someone on** (*Informal*) = <u>arouse</u>, attract, excite, thrill, stimulate, please, titillate ◆ **turn something down 1** = <u>refuse</u>, decline, reject, spurn, rebuff, repudiate **2** = <u>lower</u>, soften, mute, lessen, muffle, quieten ◆ **turn something in** = <u>hand in</u>, return, deliver, give up, hand over, submit, surrender, tender ◆ **turn something off** = <u>switch off</u>, turn out, put out, stop, cut out, shut down, unplug, flick off
◆ **turn something on** = <u>switch on</u>, activate, start, start up, ignite, kick-start ◆ **turn something up 1** = <u>find</u>, reveal, discover, expose, disclose, unearth, dig up **2** = <u>increase</u>, raise, boost, enhance, intensify, amplify ◆ **turn up 1** = <u>arrive</u>, come, appear, show up (*informal*), attend, put in an appearance, show your face **2** = <u>come to light</u>, show up, pop up, materialize
turning = <u>turn-off</u>, turn, bend, curve, junction, crossroads, side road, exit
turning point = <u>crossroads</u>, change, crisis, crux, moment of truth
turnout = <u>attendance</u>, crowd, audience, gate, assembly, congregation, number, throng
turnover 1 = <u>output</u>, business, productivity **2** = <u>movement</u>, coming and going, change
tutor NOUN = <u>teacher</u>, coach, instructor, educator, guide, guardian, lecturer, guru
● VERB = <u>teach</u>, educate, school, train, coach, guide, drill, instruct
twig = <u>branch</u>, stick, sprig, shoot, spray
twilight 1 = <u>dusk</u>, evening, sunset, early evening, nightfall, sundown, gloaming (*Scot. poetic*), close of day, evo (*Austral. slang*) ≠ dawn **2** = <u>half-light</u>, gloom, dimness, semi-darkness

twin NOUN = <u>double</u>, counterpart, mate, match, fellow, clone, duplicate, lookalike
● VERB = <u>pair</u>, match, join, couple, link, yoke
twinkle VERB = <u>sparkle</u>, flash, shine, glitter, gleam, blink, flicker, shimmer
● NOUN = <u>sparkle</u>, flash, spark, gleam, flicker, shimmer, glimmer
twist VERB **1** = <u>coil</u>, curl, wind, wrap, screw, twirl **2** = <u>intertwine</u> **3** = <u>distort</u>, screw up, contort, mangle, mangulate (*Austral. slang*) ≠ straighten
● NOUN **1** = <u>surprise</u>, change, turn, development, revelation **2** = <u>development</u>, emphasis, variation, slant **3** = <u>wind</u>, turn, spin, swivel, twirl **4** = <u>curve</u>, turn, bend, loop, arc, kink, zigzag, dog-leg
twitch VERB **1** = <u>jerk</u>, flutter, jump, squirm **2** = <u>pull (at)</u>, tug (at), pluck (at), yank (at)
● NOUN = <u>jerk</u>, tic, spasm, jump, flutter
tycoon = <u>magnate</u>, capitalist, baron, industrialist, financier, fat cat (*slang, chiefly U.S.*), mogul, plutocrat
type = <u>kind</u>, sort, class, variety, group, order, style, species
typical 1 = <u>archetypal</u>, standard, model, normal, stock, representative, usual, regular ≠ unusual **2** = <u>characteristic</u> **3** = <u>average</u>, normal, usual, routine, regular, orthodox, predictable, run-of-the-mill
tyranny = <u>oppression</u>, cruelty, dictatorship, authoritarianism, despotism, autocracy, absolutism, high-handedness ≠ liberality

ubiquitous = <u>ever-present</u>, pervasive, omnipresent, everywhere, universal
ugly 1 = <u>unattractive</u>, homely (*chiefly U.S.*), plain, unsightly, unlovely, unprepossessing, ill-favoured ≠ beautiful **2** = <u>unpleasant</u>, shocking, terrible, nasty, distasteful, horrid, objectionable, disagreeable ≠ pleasant **3** = <u>bad-</u>

tempered, dangerous, menacing, sinister, baleful

ulcer = sore, abscess, peptic ulcer, gumboil

ultimate 1 = final, last, end **2** = supreme, highest, greatest, paramount, superlative **3** = worst, greatest, utmost, extreme **4** = best, greatest, supreme, optimum, quintessential

ultimately 1 = finally, eventually, in the end, after all, at last, sooner or later, in due time **2** = fundamentally, essentially, basically, primarily, at heart, deep down

umpire NOUN = referee, judge, arbiter, arbitrator

● VERB = referee, judge, adjudicate, arbitrate

unable = incapable, powerless, unfit, impotent, unqualified, ineffectual ≠ able

unanimous 1 = agreed, united, in agreement, harmonious, like-minded, of the same mind ≠ divided **2** = united, common, concerted, solid, consistent, harmonious, undivided, congruent ≠ split

unarmed = defenceless, helpless, unprotected ≠ armed

unaware = ignorant, unconscious, oblivious, uninformed, unknowing, not in the loop (*informal*) ≠ aware

unbearable = intolerable, insufferable, too much (*informal*), unacceptable ≠ tolerable

unborn = expected, awaited, embryonic

uncertain = unsure, undecided, vague, unclear, dubious, hazy, irresolute ≠ sure

uncertainty 1 = unpredictability, precariousness, ambiguity, unreliability, fickleness, chanciness, changeableness ≠ predictability **2** = doubt, confusion ≠ confidence **3** = hesitancy, indecision

uncomfortable 1 = uneasy, troubled, disturbed, embarrassed, awkward, discomfited ≠ comfortable **2** = painful, awkward, rough

uncommon 1 = rare, unusual, odd, novel, strange, peculiar, scarce, queer ≠ common **2** = extraordinary, remarkable, special, outstanding, distinctive, exceptional, notable ≠ ordinary

uncompromising = inflexible, strict, rigid, firm, tough, inexorable, intransigent, unbending

unconditional = absolute, full, complete, total, positive, entire, outright, unlimited

≠ qualified

unconscious 1 = senseless, knocked out, out cold (*informal*), out, stunned, dazed, in a coma, stupefied ≠ awake **2** = unaware, ignorant, oblivious, unknowing ≠ aware **3** = unintentional, unwitting, inadvertent, accidental ≠ intentional

uncover 1 = reveal, expose, disclose, divulge, make known ≠ conceal **2** = open, unveil, unwrap, show, strip, expose, bare, lay bare

under PREPOSITION **1** = below, beneath, underneath ≠ over **2** = subordinate to, subject to, governed by, secondary to

● ADVERB = below, down, beneath ≠ up

undercover = secret, covert, private, hidden, concealed ≠ open

underdog = weaker party, little fellow (*informal*), outsider

underestimate 1 = undervalue, understate, diminish, play down, minimize, downgrade, miscalculate, trivialize ≠ overestimate **2** = underrate, undervalue, belittle ≠ overrate

undergo = experience, go through, stand, suffer, bear, sustain, endure

underground ADJECTIVE **1** = subterranean, basement, lower-level, sunken, covered, buried, subterrestrial **2** = secret, covert, hidden, guerrilla, revolutionary, confidential, dissident, closet

● PHRASES **the underground 1** = the tube (*Brit.*), the subway, the metro **2** = the Resistance, partisans, freedom fighters

underline 1 = emphasize, stress, highlight, accentuate ≠ minimize **2** = underscore, mark

underlying = fundamental, basic, prime, primary, elementary, intrinsic

undermine = weaken, sabotage, subvert, compromise, disable ≠ reinforce

understand 1 = comprehend, get, take in, perceive, grasp, see, follow, realize **2** = believe, gather, think, see, suppose, notice, assume, fancy

understandable = reasonable, natural, justified, expected, inevitable, legitimate, predictable, accountable

understanding NOUN **1** = perception, knowledge, grasp, sense, know-how (*informal*), judgment, awareness, appreciation ≠ ignorance **2** = agreement, deal, promise, arrangement, accord, contract, bond, pledge ≠ disagreement

3 = <u>belief</u>, view, opinion, impression, interpretation, feeling, idea, notion
● ADJECTIVE = <u>sympathetic</u>, kind, compassionate, considerate, patient, sensitive, tolerant ≠ unsympathetic

undertake = <u>agree</u>, promise, contract, guarantee, engage, pledge

undertaking 1 = <u>task</u>, business, operation, project, attempt, effort, affair, venture **2** = <u>promise</u>, commitment, pledge, word, vow, assurance

underwear = <u>underclothes</u>, lingerie, undies (*informal*), undergarments, underthings, broekies (*S. African informal*), underdaks (*Austral. slang*)

underworld 1 = <u>criminals</u>, gangsters, organized crime, gangland (*informal*) **2** = <u>nether world</u>, Hades, nether regions

underwrite = <u>finance</u>, back, fund, guarantee, sponsor, insure, ratify, subsidize

undesirable = <u>unwanted</u>, unwelcome, disagreeable, objectionable, unacceptable, unsuitable, unattractive, distasteful ≠ desirable

undo 1 = <u>open</u>, unfasten, loose, untie, unbutton, disentangle **2** = <u>reverse</u>, cancel, offset, neutralize, invalidate, annul **3** = <u>ruin</u>, defeat, destroy, wreck, shatter, upset, undermine, overturn

undone = <u>unfinished</u>, left, neglected, omitted, unfulfilled, unperformed ≠ finished

undoubtedly = <u>certainly</u>, definitely, surely, doubtless, without doubt, assuredly

unearth 1 = <u>discover</u>, find, reveal, expose, uncover **2** = <u>dig up</u>, excavate, exhume, dredge up

unearthly = <u>eerie</u>, strange, supernatural, ghostly, weird, phantom, uncanny, spooky (*informal*)

uneasy 1 = <u>anxious</u>, worried, troubled, nervous, disturbed, uncomfortable, edgy, perturbed ≠ relaxed **2** = <u>precarious</u>, strained, uncomfortable, tense, awkward, shaky, insecure

unemployed = <u>out of work</u>, redundant, laid off, jobless, idle ≠ working

unfair 1 = <u>biased</u>, prejudiced, unjust, one-sided, partial, partisan, bigoted **2** = <u>unscrupulous</u>, dishonest, unethical, wrongful, unsporting ≠ ethical

unfit 1 = <u>out of shape</u>, feeble, unhealthy, flabby, in poor condition ≠ healthy

2 = <u>incapable</u>, inadequate, incompetent, no good, useless, unqualified ≠ capable **3** = <u>unsuitable</u>, inadequate, useless, unsuited ≠ suitable

unfold 1 = <u>reveal</u>, tell, present, show, disclose, uncover, divulge, make known **2** = <u>open</u>, spread out, undo, expand, unfurl, unwrap, unroll

unfortunate 1 = <u>disastrous</u>, calamitous, adverse, ill-fated ≠ opportune **2** = <u>regrettable</u>, deplorable, lamentable, unsuitable, unbecoming ≠ becoming **3** = <u>unlucky</u>, unhappy, doomed, cursed, unsuccessful, hapless, wretched ≠ fortunate

unhappy 1 = <u>sad</u>, depressed, miserable, blue, melancholy, mournful, dejected, despondent ≠ happy **2** = <u>unlucky</u>, unfortunate, hapless, cursed, wretched, ill-fated ≠ fortunate

unhealthy 1 = <u>harmful</u>, detrimental, unwholesome, insanitary, insalubrious ≠ beneficial **2** = <u>sick</u>, sickly, unwell, delicate, crook (*Austral. & N.Z. informal*), ailing, frail, feeble, invalid ≠ well **3** = <u>weak</u>, ailing ≠ strong

unification = <u>union</u>, uniting, alliance, coalition, federation, confederation, amalgamation, coalescence

uniform NOUN **1** = <u>regalia</u>, suit, livery, colours, habit **2** = <u>outfit</u>, dress, costume, attire, gear (*informal*), get-up (*informal*), ensemble, garb
● ADJECTIVE **1** = <u>consistent</u>, unvarying, similar, even, same, matching, regular, constant ≠ varying **2** = <u>alike</u>, similar, like, same, equal

unify = <u>unite</u>, join, combine, merge, consolidate, confederate, amalgamate ≠ divide

union 1 = <u>joining</u>, uniting, unification, combination, coalition, merger, mixture, blend **2** = <u>alliance</u>, league, association, coalition, federation, confederacy

unique 1 = <u>distinct</u>, special, exclusive, peculiar, only, single, lone, solitary **2** = <u>unparalleled</u>, unmatched, unequalled, matchless, without equal

unit 1 = <u>entity</u>, whole, item, feature **2** = <u>section</u>, company, group, force, detail, division, cell, squad **3** = <u>measure</u>, quantity, measurement **4** = <u>part</u>, section, segment, class, element, component, constituent, tutorial

unite 1 = join, link, combine, couple, blend, merge, unify, fuse ≠ separate **2** = cooperate, ally, join forces, band, pool, collaborate ≠ split

unity 1 = union, unification, coalition, federation, integration, confederation, amalgamation **2** = wholeness, integrity, oneness, union, entity, singleness ≠ disunity **3** = agreement, accord, consensus, harmony, solidarity, unison, assent, concord ≠ disagreement

universal 1 = widespread, general, common, whole, total, unlimited, overarching **2** = global, worldwide, international, pandemic

universally = without exception, everywhere, always, invariably

universe = cosmos, space, creation, nature, heavens, macrocosm, all existence

unknown 1 = strange, new, undiscovered, uncharted, unexplored, virgin, remote, alien **2** = unidentified, mysterious, anonymous, unnamed, nameless, incognito **3** = obscure, humble, unfamiliar ≠ famous

unlike 1 = different from, dissimilar to, distinct from, unequal to ≠ similar to **2** = contrasted with, not like, in contradiction to, in contrast with or to, as opposed to, differently from, opposite to

unlikely 1 = improbable, doubtful, remote, slight, faint ≠ probable **2** = unbelievable, incredible, implausible, questionable ≠ believable

unload 1 = empty, clear, unpack, dump, discharge **2** = unburden

unnatural 1 = abnormal, odd, strange, unusual, extraordinary, perverted, queer, irregular ≠ normal **2** = false, forced, artificial, affected, stiff, feigned, stilted, insincere ≠ genuine

unpleasant 1 = nasty, bad, horrid, distasteful, displeasing, objectionable, disagreeable ≠ nice **2** = obnoxious, rude ≠ likable or likeable

unravel 1 = solve, explain, work out, resolve, figure out (informal) **2** = undo, separate, disentangle, free, unwind, untangle

unrest = discontent, rebellion, protest, strife, agitation, discord, sedition, dissension ≠ peace

unsettled 1 = unstable, shaky, insecure, disorderly, unsteady **2** = restless, tense, shaken, confused, disturbed, anxious, agitated, flustered **3** = inconstant, changing, variable, uncertain

unstable 1 = changeable, volatile, unpredictable, variable, fluctuating, fitful, inconstant ≠ constant **2** = insecure, shaky, precarious, unsettled, wobbly, tottering, unsteady **3** = unpredictable, irrational, erratic, inconsistent, temperamental, capricious, changeable ≠ level-headed

unthinkable 1 = impossible, out of the question, inconceivable, absurd, unreasonable **2** = inconceivable, incredible, unimaginable

untold 1 = indescribable, unthinkable, unimaginable, undreamed of, unutterable, inexpressible **2** = countless, incalculable, innumerable, myriad, numberless, uncountable

untrue 1 = false, lying, wrong, mistaken, incorrect, inaccurate, dishonest, deceptive ≠ true **2** = unfaithful, disloyal, deceitful, treacherous, faithless, false, untrustworthy, inconstant ≠ faithful

unusual 1 = rare, odd, strange, extraordinary, different, curious, queer, uncommon ≠ common **2** = extraordinary, unique, remarkable, exceptional, uncommon, singular, unconventional ≠ average

upbeat (Informal) = cheerful, positive, optimistic, encouraging, hopeful, cheery

upbringing = education, training, breeding, rearing, raising

update = bring up to date, improve, correct, renew, revise, upgrade, amend, overhaul

upgrade 1 = improve, better, update, reform, add to, enhance, refurbish, renovate **2** = promote, raise, advance, boost, move up, elevate, kick upstairs (informal), give promotion to ≠ demote

upheaval = disturbance, revolution, disorder, turmoil, disruption

uphill 1 = ascending, rising, upward, mounting, climbing ≠ descending **2** = arduous, hard, taxing, difficult, tough, exhausting, gruelling, strenuous

uphold 1 = support, back, defend, aid, champion, maintain, promote, sustain **2** = confirm, endorse

uplift VERB = improve, better, raise, advance, inspire, refine, edify
● **NOUN** = improvement, enlightenment,

advancement, refinement, enhancement, enrichment, edification

upper 1 = topmost, top ≠ bottom 2 = higher, high ≠ lower 3 = superior, senior, higher-level, greater, top, important, chief, most important ≠ inferior

upper class = aristocratic, upper-class, noble, high-class, patrician, blue-blooded, highborn

upright 1 = vertical, straight, standing up, erect, perpendicular, bolt upright ≠ horizontal 2 = honest, good, principled, just, ethical, honourable, righteous, conscientious ≠ dishonourable

uprising = rebellion, rising, revolution, revolt, disturbance, mutiny, insurrection, insurgence

uproar 1 = commotion, noise, racket, riot, turmoil, mayhem, din, pandemonium 2 = protest, outrage, complaint, objection, fuss, stink (informal), outcry, furore

upset ADJECTIVE 1 = distressed, shaken, disturbed, worried, troubled, hurt, bothered, unhappy 2 = sick, queasy, bad, ill 3 = overturned, upside down, capsized, spilled

● VERB 1 = distress, trouble, disturb, worry, alarm, bother, grieve, agitate 2 = tip over, overturn, capsize, knock over, spill 3 = mess up, spoil, disturb, change, confuse, disorder, unsettle, disorganize

● NOUN 1 = distress, worry, trouble, shock, bother, disturbance, agitation 2 = reversal, shake-up (informal), defeat 3 = illness, complaint, disorder, bug (informal), sickness, malady

upside down or **upside-down** ADVERB = wrong side up

● ADJECTIVE 1 = inverted, overturned, upturned 2 (Informal) = confused, disordered, chaotic, muddled, topsy-turvy, higgledy-piggledy (informal)

up-to-date = modern, fashionable, trendy (Brit. informal), current, stylish, in vogue, up-to-the-minute ≠ out of date

urban = civic, city, town, metropolitan, municipal, dorp (S. African)

urge VERB 1 = beg, exhort, plead, implore, beseech, entreat 2 = advocate, recommend, advise, support, counsel ≠ discourage

● NOUN = impulse, longing, wish, desire, drive, yearning, itch (informal), thirst ≠ reluctance

urgency = importance, need, necessity, gravity, pressure, hurry, seriousness, extremity

urgent = crucial, desperate, pressing, great, important, crying, critical, immediate ≠ unimportant

usage 1 = use, operation, employment, running, control, management, handling 2 = practice, method, procedure, habit, regime, custom, routine, convention

use VERB 1 = employ, utilize, work, apply, operate, exercise, practise, resort to 2 sometimes with **up** = consume, exhaust, spend, run through, expend 3 = take advantage of, exploit, manipulate

● NOUN 1 = usage, employment, operation, application 2 = purpose, end, reason, object 3 = good, point, help, service, value, benefit, profit, advantage

used = second-hand, cast-off, nearly new, shopsoiled ≠ new

used to = accustomed to, familiar with

useful = helpful, effective, valuable, practical, profitable, worthwhile, beneficial, fruitful ≠ useless

useless 1 = worthless, valueless, impractical, fruitless, unproductive, ineffectual, unsuitable ≠ useful 2 = pointless, futile, vain ≠ worthwhile 3 (Informal) = inept, no good, hopeless, incompetent, ineffectual

usher VERB = escort, lead, direct, guide, conduct

● NOUN = attendant, guide, doorman, escort, doorkeeper

usual = normal, customary, regular, general, common, standard, ordinary, typical ≠ unusual

usually = normally, generally, mainly, commonly, mostly, on the whole, as a rule, habitually

utility = usefulness, benefit, convenience, practicality, efficacy, serviceableness

utilize = use, employ, deploy, take advantage of, make use of, put to use, bring into play, avail yourself of

utmost ADJECTIVE 1 = greatest, highest, maximum, supreme, paramount, pre-eminent 2 = farthest, extreme, last, final

● NOUN = best, greatest, maximum, highest, hardest

utter¹ = say, state, speak, voice, express, deliver, declare, mouth

utter² = absolute, complete, total,

sheer, outright, thorough, downright, unmitigated

utterly = totally, completely, absolutely, perfectly, fully, entirely, extremely, thoroughly

V

vacancy 1 = opening, job, post, place, position, role, situation, opportunity 2 = room, space, available accommodation, unoccupied room

vacant 1 = empty, free, available, abandoned, deserted, for sale, on the market, void ≠ occupied 2 = unfilled, unoccupied ≠ taken 3 = blank, vague, dreamy, empty, abstracted, idle, vacuous, inane ≠ thoughtful

vacuum 1 = gap, lack, absence, space, deficiency, void 2 = emptiness, space, void, gap, nothingness, vacuity

vague 1 = unclear, indefinite, hazy, confused, loose, uncertain, unsure, superficial ≠ clear 2 = imprecise, unspecified, generalized, rough, loose, ambiguous, hazy, equivocal 3 = absent-minded, distracted, vacant, preoccupied, oblivious, inattentive 4 = indistinct, unclear, faint, hazy, indeterminate, nebulous, ill-defined ≠ distinct

vain ADJECTIVE 1 = futile, useless, pointless, unsuccessful, idle, worthless, senseless, fruitless ≠ successful 2 = conceited, narcissistic, proud, arrogant, swaggering, egotistical, self-important ≠ modest
● PHRASES **in vain** 1 = useless, to no avail, unsuccessful, fruitless, vain 2 = uselessly, to no avail, unsuccessfully, fruitlessly, vainly, ineffectually

valid 1 = sound, good, reasonable, telling, convincing, rational, logical, viable ≠ unfounded 2 = legal, official, legitimate, genuine, authentic, lawful, bona fide ≠ invalid

validity 1 = soundness, force, power, weight, strength, cogency 2 = legality, authority, legitimacy, right, lawfulness

valley = hollow, dale, glen, vale, depression, dell

valuable ADJECTIVE 1 = useful, important, profitable, worthwhile, beneficial, helpful ≠ useless 2 = treasured, prized, precious 3 = precious, expensive, costly, dear, high-priced, priceless, irreplaceable ≠ worthless
● PLURAL NOUN = treasures, prized possessions, precious items, heirlooms, personal effects, costly article

value NOUN 1 = importance, benefit, worth, merit, point, service, sense, profit ≠ worthlessness 2 = cost, price, worth, rate, market price, face value, asking price, selling price
● PLURAL NOUN = principles, morals, ethics, mores, standards of behaviour, (moral) standards
● VERB 1 = appreciate, rate, prize, regard highly, respect, admire, treasure, esteem ≠ undervalue 2 = evaluate, price, estimate, rate, cost, assess, set at, appraise

vanish 1 = disappear, dissolve, evaporate, fade away, melt away, evanesce ≠ appear 2 = die out, disappear, pass away, end, fade, dwindle, cease to exist, become extinct

vanity = pride, arrogance, conceit, narcissism, egotism, conceitedness ≠ modesty

variable = changeable, unstable, fluctuating, shifting, flexible, uneven, temperamental, unsteady ≠ constant

variant NOUN = variation, form, version, development, alternative, adaptation, revision, modification
● ADJECTIVE = different, alternative, modified, divergent

variation 1 = alternative, variety, modification, departure, innovation, variant 2 = variety, change, deviation, difference, diversity, diversion, novelty ≠ uniformity

varied = different, mixed, various, diverse, assorted, miscellaneous, sundry, motley ≠ unvarying

variety 1 = diversity, change, variation, difference, diversification, heterogeneity, multifariousness ≠ uniformity 2 = range, selection, assortment, mix, collection, line-up, mixture, array 3 = type, sort, kind, class, brand, species, breed, strain

various 1 = different, assorted, miscellaneous, varied, distinct, diverse, disparate, sundry ≠ similar 2 = many, numerous, countless, several, abundant, innumerable, sundry, profuse

varnish NOUN = lacquer, polish, glaze, gloss

● VERB = lacquer, polish, glaze, gloss

vary 1 = differ, be different, be dissimilar, disagree, diverge 2 = change, shift, swing, alter, fluctuate, oscillate, see-saw 3 = alternate

vast = huge, massive, enormous, great, wide, immense, gigantic, monumental ≠ tiny

vault¹ 1 = strongroom, repository, depository 2 = crypt, tomb, catacomb, cellar, mausoleum, charnel house, undercroft

vault² = jump, spring, leap, clear, bound, hurdle

veer = change direction, turn, swerve, shift, sheer, change course

vehicle 1 = conveyance, machine, motor vehicle 2 = medium, means, channel, mechanism, organ, apparatus

veil NOUN 1 = mask, cover, shroud, film, curtain, cloak 2 = screen, mask, disguise, blind 3 = film, cover, curtain, cloak, shroud

● VERB = cover, screen, hide, mask, shield, disguise, conceal, obscure ≠ reveal

veiled = disguised, implied, hinted at, covert, masked, concealed, suppressed

vein 1 = blood vessel 2 = mood, style, note, tone, mode, temper, tenor 3 = seam, layer, stratum, course, current, bed, deposit, streak

velocity = speed, pace, rapidity, quickness, swiftness

vengeance = revenge, retaliation, reprisal, retribution, requital ≠ forgiveness

vent NOUN = outlet, opening, aperture, duct, orifice

● VERB = express, release, voice, air, discharge, utter, emit, pour out ≠ hold back

venture NOUN = undertaking, project, enterprise, campaign, risk, operation, activity, scheme

● VERB 1 = go, travel, journey, set out, wander, stray, plunge into, rove 2 = dare, presume, have the courage to, be brave enough, hazard, go out on a limb (*informal*), take the liberty, go so far as

3 = put forward, volunteer

verbal = spoken, oral, word-of-mouth, unwritten

verdict = decision, finding, judgment, opinion, sentence, conclusion, conviction, adjudication

verge NOUN 1 = brink, point, edge, threshold 2 = border, edge, margin, limit, boundary, threshold, brim

● PHRASES **verge on something** = come near to, approach, border on, resemble, incline to, be similar to, touch on, be more or less

verify 1 = check, make sure, examine, monitor, inspect 2 = confirm, prove, substantiate, support, validate, bear out, corroborate, authenticate ≠ disprove

versatile 1 = adaptable, flexible, all-round, resourceful, multifaceted ≠ unadaptable 2 = all-purpose, variable, adjustable ≠ limited

versed = knowledgeable, experienced, seasoned, familiar, practised, acquainted, well-informed, proficient ≠ ignorant

version 1 = form, variety, variant, sort, class, design, style, model 2 = adaptation, edition, interpretation, form, copy, rendering, reproduction, portrayal 3 = account, report, description, record, reading, story, view, understanding

vertical = upright, sheer, perpendicular, straight (up and down), erect, plumb, on end, precipitous, vertiginous ≠ horizontal

very ADVERB = extremely, highly, greatly, really, deeply, unusually, profoundly, decidedly

● ADJECTIVE 1 = exact, precise, selfsame 2 = ideal

vessel 1 = ship, boat, craft 2 = container, receptacle, can, bowl, tank, pot, drum, barrel

vest VERB

● PHRASES **vest in something** or **someone** *usually passive* = place, invest, entrust, settle, confer, endow, bestow, consign ◆ **vest with something** *usually passive* = endow with, entrust with

vet = check, examine, investigate, review, appraise, scrutinize

veteran NOUN = old hand, past master, warhorse (*informal*), old stager ≠ novice

● ADJECTIVE = long-serving, seasoned, experienced, old, established, qualified, mature, practised

veto VERB = <u>ban</u>, block, reject, rule out, turn down, forbid, boycott, prohibit ≠ pass
● NOUN = <u>ban</u>, dismissal, rejection, vetoing, boycott, embargo, prohibiting, prohibition ≠ ratification

viable = <u>workable</u>, practical, feasible, suitable, realistic, operational, applicable, usable ≠ unworkable

vibrant 1 = <u>energetic</u>, dynamic, sparkling, vivid, spirited, storming, alive, vigorous 2 = <u>vivid</u>, bright, brilliant, intense, clear, rich, glowing

vice 1 = <u>fault</u>, failing, weakness, limitation, defect, deficiency, flaw, shortcoming ≠ good point 2 = <u>wickedness</u>, evil, corruption, sin, depravity, immorality, iniquity, turpitude ≠ virtue

vice versa = <u>the other way round</u>, conversely, in reverse, contrariwise

vicious 1 = <u>savage</u>, brutal, violent, cruel, ferocious, barbarous ≠ gentle 2 = <u>malicious</u>, vindictive, spiteful, mean, cruel, venomous

victim 1 = <u>casualty</u>, sufferer, fatality ≠ survivor 2 = <u>scapegoat</u>, sacrifice, martyr

victor = <u>winner</u>, champion, conqueror, vanquisher, prizewinner ≠ loser

victorious = <u>winning</u>, successful, triumphant, first, champion, conquering, vanquishing, prizewinning ≠ losing

victory = <u>win</u>, success, triumph, conquest, walkover (*informal*) ≠ defeat

vie = <u>compete</u>, struggle, contend, strive

view NOUN 1 *sometimes plural* = <u>opinion</u>, belief, feeling, attitude, impression, conviction, point of view, sentiment 2 = <u>scene</u>, picture, sight, prospect, perspective, landscape, outlook, spectacle 3 = <u>vision</u>, sight, visibility, perspective, eyeshot
● VERB = <u>regard</u>, see, consider, perceive, treat, estimate, reckon, deem

viewer = <u>watcher</u>, observer, spectator, onlooker

vigorous 1 = <u>strenuous</u>, energetic, arduous, hard, taxing, active, rigorous 2 = <u>spirited</u>, lively, energetic, active, dynamic, animated, forceful, feisty (*informal*) ≠ lethargic 3 = <u>strong</u>, powerful, lively, lusty ≠ weak

vigorously 1 = <u>energetically</u>, hard, forcefully, strongly, strenuously, lustily 2 = <u>forcefully</u>, strongly, vehemently, strenuously

vigour *or* (*U.S.*) **vigor** = <u>energy</u>, vitality, power, spirit, strength, animation, verve, gusto ≠ weakness

vile 1 = <u>wicked</u>, evil, corrupt, perverted, degenerate, depraved, nefarious ≠ honourable 2 = <u>disgusting</u>, foul, revolting, offensive, nasty, sickening, horrid, repulsive, yucko (*Austral. slang*) ≠ pleasant

villain 1 = <u>evildoer</u>, criminal, rogue, scoundrel, wretch, reprobate, miscreant, blackguard 2 = <u>baddy</u> (*informal*), antihero ≠ hero

vindicate 1 = <u>clear</u>, acquit, exonerate, absolve, let off the hook, exculpate ≠ condemn 2 = <u>support</u>, defend, excuse, justify

vintage NOUN (always used of wines) = <u>harvest</u>
● ADJECTIVE 1 (always used of wines) = <u>high-quality</u>, best, prime, quality, choice, select, superior 2 = <u>classic</u>, old, veteran, historic, heritage, enduring, antique, timeless

violate 1 = <u>break</u>, infringe, disobey, transgress, ignore, defy, disregard, flout ≠ obey 2 = <u>invade</u>, infringe on, disturb, upset, shatter, disrupt, impinge on, encroach on 3 = <u>desecrate</u>, profane, defile, abuse, pollute, deface, dishonour, vandalize ≠ honour 4 = <u>rape</u>, molest, sexually assault, ravish, abuse, assault, interfere with, sexually abuse

violation 1 = <u>breach</u>, abuse, infringement, contravention, abuse, trespass, transgression, infraction 2 = <u>invasion</u>, intrusion, trespass, breach, disturbance, disruption, interruption, encroachment 3 = <u>desecration</u>, sacrilege, defilement, profanation, spoliation 4 = <u>rape</u>, sexual assault, molesting, ravishing (*old-fashioned*), abuse, sexual abuse, indecent assault, molestation

violence 1 = <u>brutality</u>, bloodshed, savagery, fighting, terrorism 2 = <u>force</u>, power, strength, might, ferocity, forcefulness, powerfulness 3 = <u>intensity</u>, force, cruelty, severity, fervour, vehemence

violent 1 = <u>brutal</u>, aggressive, savage, wild, fierce, bullying, cruel, vicious ≠ gentle 2 = <u>sharp</u> 3 = <u>passionate</u>, uncontrollable, unrestrained 4 = <u>fiery</u>, fierce, passionate

VIP = <u>celebrity</u>, big name, star, somebody, luminary, big hitter (*informal*), heavy hitter (*informal*)

virgin NOUN = maiden, girl (*archaic*)
● ADJECTIVE = pure, chaste, immaculate, virginal, vestal, uncorrupted, undefiled ≠ corrupted

virtual = practical, essential, in all but name

virtually = practically, almost, nearly, in effect, in essence, as good as, in all but name

virtue 1 = goodness, integrity, worth, morality, righteousness, probity, rectitude, incorruptibility ≠ vice 2 = merit, strength, asset, plus (*informal*), attribute, good point, strong point ≠ failing 3 = advantage, benefit, merit, credit, usefulness, efficacy

visible = perceptible, observable, clear, apparent, evident, manifest, in view, discernible ≠ invisible

vision 1 = image, idea, dream, plans, hopes, prospect, ideal, concept 2 = hallucination, illusion, apparition, revelation, delusion, mirage, chimera 3 = sight, seeing, eyesight, view, perception 4 = foresight, imagination, perception, insight, awareness, inspiration, innovation, creativity

visionary NOUN 1 = idealist, romantic, dreamer, daydreamer ≠ realist 2 = prophet, diviner, mystic, seer, soothsayer, sibyl, scryer, spaewife (*Scot.*)
● ADJECTIVE 1 = idealistic, romantic, unrealistic, utopian, speculative, impractical, unworkable, quixotic ≠ realistic 2 = prophetic, mystical, predictive, oracular, sibylline

visit VERB 1 = call on, drop in on (*informal*), stay at, stay with, stop by, spend time with, look someone up, go see (*U.S.*) 2 = stay in, stop by
● NOUN 1 = call, social call 2 = trip, stop, stay, break, tour, holiday, vacation (*informal*), stopover

visitor = guest, caller, company, manu(w)hiri (*N.Z.*)

vista = view, scene, prospect, landscape, panorama, perspective

visual 1 = optical, optic, ocular 2 = observable, visible, perceptible, discernible ≠ imperceptible

vital 1 = essential, important, necessary, key, basic, significant, critical, crucial ≠ unnecessary 2 = lively, vigorous,

energetic, spirited, dynamic, animated, vibrant, vivacious ≠ lethargic

vitality = energy, vivacity, life, strength, animation, vigour, exuberance, liveliness ≠ lethargy

vivid 1 = clear, detailed, realistic, telling, moving, affecting, arresting, powerful ≠ vague 2 = bright, brilliant, intense, clear, rich, glowing, colourful ≠ dull

vocabulary 1 = language, words, lexicon 2 = wordbook, dictionary, glossary, lexicon

vocal 1 = outspoken, frank, forthright, strident, vociferous, articulate, expressive, eloquent ≠ quiet 2 = spoken, voiced, uttered, oral, said

vocation = profession, calling, job, trade, career, mission, pursuit

vogue = fashion, trend, craze, style, mode, passing fancy, dernier cri (*French*)

voice NOUN 1 = tone, sound, articulation 2 = utterance 3 = opinion, will, feeling, wish, desire 4 = say, view, vote, comment, input
● VERB = express, declare, air, raise, reveal, mention, mouth, pronounce
▬ RELATED WORD
adjective: vocal

void NOUN 1 = gap, space, lack, hole, emptiness 2 = emptiness, space, vacuum, oblivion, blankness, nullity, vacuity
● ADJECTIVE = invalid, null and void, inoperative, useless, ineffective, worthless
● VERB = invalidate, nullify, cancel, withdraw, reverse, undo, repeal, quash

volatile 1 = changeable, shifting, variable, unsettled, unstable, explosive, unreliable, unsteady ≠ stable 2 = temperamental, erratic, mercurial, up and down (*informal*), fickle, over-emotional ≠ calm

volley = barrage, blast, burst, shower, hail, bombardment, salvo, fusillade

volume 1 = amount, quantity, level, body, total, measure, degree, mass 2 = capacity, size, mass, extent, proportions, dimensions, bulk, measurements 3 = book, work, title, opus, publication, manual, tome, treatise 4 = loudness, sound, amplification

voluntarily = willingly, freely, by choice, off your own bat, of your own accord, of your own volition

voluntary 1 = intentional, deliberate, planned, calculated, wilful ≠ unintentional 2 = optional, discretionary, up to the individual, open, unforced, at your discretion, open to choice ≠ obligatory **3** = unpaid, free, willing, pro bono (*Law*)

volunteer = offer, step forward ≠ refuse

vomit 1 = be sick, throw up (*informal*), spew, chuck (*Austral. & N.Z. informal*), heave (*slang*), retch **2** *often with* **up** = bring up, throw up, regurgitate, emit (*informal*), disgorge, spew out *or* up

vote NOUN = poll, election, ballot, referendum, popular vote, plebiscite, straw poll, show of hands
● VERB = cast your vote

voucher = ticket, token, coupon, pass, slip, chit, chitty (*Brit. informal*), docket

vow VERB = promise, pledge, swear, commit, engage, affirm, avow, bind yourself
● NOUN = promise, commitment, pledge, oath, profession, avowal

voyage NOUN = journey, trip, passage, expedition, crossing, sail, cruise, excursion
● VERB = travel, journey, tour, cruise, steam, take a trip, go on an expedition

vulgar 1 = tasteless, common ≠ tasteful **2** = crude, rude, coarse, indecent, tasteless, risqué, ribald **3** = uncouth, unrefined, impolite, ill-bred ≠ refined

vulnerable 1 = susceptible, helpless, unprotected, defenceless, exposed, weak, sensitive, tender ≠ immune **2** = exposed, open, unprotected, defenceless, accessible, wide open, assailable ≠ well-protected

W

waddle = shuffle, totter, toddle, sway, wobble

wade 1 = paddle, splash, splash about, slop **2** = walk through, cross, ford, travel across

wag VERB **1** = wave, shake, waggle, stir, quiver, vibrate, wiggle **2** = waggle, wave, shake, flourish, brandish, wobble, wiggle
3 = shake, bob, nod
● NOUN **1** = wave, shake, quiver, vibration, wiggle, waggle **2** = nod, bob, shake

wage NOUN *often plural* = payment, pay, remuneration, fee, reward, income, allowance, recompense
● VERB = engage in, conduct, pursue, carry on, undertake, practise, prosecute, proceed with

wail VERB = cry, weep, grieve, lament, howl, bawl, yowl
● NOUN = cry, moan, howl, lament, yowl

wait VERB **1** = stay, remain, stop, pause, rest, linger, loiter, tarry ≠ go **2** = stand by, hold back, hang fire **3** = be postponed, be suspended, be delayed, be put off, be put back, be deferred, be put on hold (*informal*), be shelved
● NOUN = delay, gap, pause, interval, stay, rest, halt, hold-up

waiter *or* **waitress** = attendant, server, flunkey, steward *or* stewardess, servant

waive 1 = give up, relinquish, renounce, forsake, drop, abandon, set aside, dispense with ≠ claim **2** = disregard, ignore, discount, overlook, set aside, pass over, dispense with, brush aside

wake¹ VERB **1** = awake, stir, awaken, come to, arise, get up, rouse, get out of bed ≠ fall asleep **2** = awaken, arouse, rouse, waken **3** = evoke, recall, renew, stimulate, revive, induce, arouse, call up
● NOUN = vigil, watch, funeral, deathwatch, tangi (*N.Z.*)

wake² NOUN = slipstream, wash, trail, backwash, train, track, waves, path
● PHRASES **in the wake of** = in the aftermath of, following, because of, as a result of, on account of, as a consequence of

walk VERB **1** = stride, stroll, go, move, step, march, pace, hike **2** = travel on foot **3** = escort, take, see, show, partner, guide, conduct, accompany
● NOUN **1** = stroll, hike, ramble, march, trek, trudge, promenade, saunter **2** = gait, step, bearing, carriage, tread **3** = path, footpath, track, way, road, lane, trail, avenue, berm (*N.Z.*)
● PHRASES **walk of life** = area, calling, business, line, trade, class, field, career

walker = hiker, rambler, wayfarer, pedestrian

wall 1 = partition, screen, barrier,

enclosure 2 = <u>barrier</u>, obstacle, barricade, obstruction, check, bar, fence, impediment

wallet = <u>purse</u>, pocketbook, pouch, case, holder, money-bag

wander VERB = <u>roam</u>, walk, drift, stroll, range, stray, ramble, prowl

● NOUN = <u>excursion</u>, walk, stroll, cruise, ramble, meander, promenade, mosey (*informal*)

wanderer = <u>traveller</u>, rover, nomad, drifter, gypsy, explorer, rambler, voyager

wane 1 = <u>decline</u>, weaken, diminish, fail, fade, decrease, dwindle, lessen ≠ grow **2** = <u>diminish</u>, decrease, dwindle ≠ wax

want VERB **1** = <u>wish for</u>, desire, long for, crave, covet, hope for, yearn for, thirst for ≠ have **2** = <u>need</u>, demand, require, call for **3** = <u>should</u>, need, must, ought **4** = <u>desire</u>, long for, crave, wish for, yearn for, thirst for, hanker after, burn for **5** = <u>lack</u>, need, require, miss

● NOUN **1** = <u>lack</u>, need, absence, shortage, deficiency, famine, scarcity, dearth ≠ abundance **2** = <u>poverty</u>, hardship, privation, penury, destitution, neediness, pennilessness ≠ wealth **3** = <u>wish</u>, will, need, desire, requirement, longing, appetite, craving

wanting 1 = <u>deficient</u>, poor, inadequate, insufficient, faulty, defective, imperfect, unsound, bodger *or* bodgie (*Austral. slang*) ≠ adequate **2** = <u>lacking</u>, missing, absent, incomplete, short, shy ≠ complete

war NOUN **1** = <u>conflict</u>, drive, attack, fighting, fight, operation, battle, movement ≠ peace **2** = <u>campaign</u>, drive, attack, operation, movement, push, mission, offensive

● VERB = <u>fight</u>, battle, clash, wage war, campaign, combat, do battle, take up arms ≠ make peace

ward NOUN **1** = <u>room</u>, department, unit, quarter, division, section, apartment, cubicle **2** = <u>district</u>, constituency, area, division, zone, parish, precinct **3** = <u>dependant</u>, charge, pupil, minor, protégé

● PHRASES **ward someone off** = <u>drive off</u>, resist, fight off, hold off, repel, fend off ◆ **ward something off 1** = <u>avert</u>, fend off, stave off, avoid, frustrate, deflect, repel **2** = <u>parry</u>, avert, deflect, avoid, repel, turn aside

warden 1 = <u>steward</u>, guardian, administrator, superintendent, caretaker, curator, custodian **2** = <u>jailer</u>, prison officer, guard, screw (*slang*) **3** = <u>governor</u>, head, leader, director, manager, chief, executive, commander, baas (*S. African*) **4** = <u>ranger</u>, keeper, guardian, protector, custodian, official

wardrobe 1 = <u>clothes cupboard</u>, cupboard, closet (*U.S.*), cabinet **2** = <u>clothes</u>, apparel, attire

warehouse = <u>store</u>, depot, storehouse, repository, depository, stockroom

wares = <u>goods</u>, produce, stock, products, stuff, commodities, merchandise

warfare = <u>war</u>, fighting, battle, conflict, combat, hostilities, enmity ≠ peace

warm ADJECTIVE **1** = <u>balmy</u>, mild, temperate, pleasant, fine, bright, sunny, agreeable ≠ cool **2** = <u>cosy</u>, snug, toasty (*informal*), comfortable, homely, comfy (*informal*) **3** = <u>moderately hot</u>, heated ≠ cool **4** = <u>thermal</u>, winter, thick, chunky, woolly ≠ cool **5** = <u>mellow</u>, relaxing, pleasant, agreeable, restful **6** = <u>affable</u>, kindly, friendly, affectionate, loving, tender, amicable, cordial ≠ unfriendly **7** = <u>near</u>, close, hot, near to the truth

● VERB = <u>warm up</u>, heat, thaw (out), heat up ≠ cool down

● PHRASES **warm something** *or* **someone up** = <u>heat</u>, thaw, heat up

warmth 1 = <u>heat</u>, snugness, warmness, comfort, homeliness, hotness ≠ coolness **2** = <u>affection</u>, feeling, love, goodwill, kindness, tenderness, cordiality, kindliness ≠ hostility

warn 1 = <u>notify</u>, tell, remind, inform, alert, tip off, give notice, make someone aware **2** = <u>advise</u>, urge, recommend, counsel, caution, commend, exhort, admonish

warning 1 = <u>caution</u>, information, advice, injunction, notification **2** = <u>notice</u>, notification, sign, alarm, announcement, alert, tip-off (*informal*) **3** = <u>omen</u>, sign, forecast, indication, prediction, prophecy, foreboding, portent, rahui (*N.Z.*) **4** = <u>reprimand</u>, admonition

warp VERB **1** = <u>distort</u>, bend, twist, buckle, deform, disfigure, contort, malform **2** = <u>become distorted</u>, bend, twist, contort, become deformed, become misshapen **3** = <u>pervert</u>, twist, corrupt, degrade, deprave, debase, debauch, lead astray

● NOUN = <u>twist</u>, bend, defect, flaw,

distortion, imperfection, kink, contortion

warrant VERB 1 = <u>call for</u>, demand, require, merit, rate, earn, deserve, permit 2 = <u>guarantee</u>, declare, pledge, promise, ensure, affirm, certify, attest

● NOUN 1 = <u>authorization</u>, permit, licence, permission, authority, sanction 2 = <u>justification</u>, reason, grounds, basis, licence, rationale, vindication, authority

warranty = <u>guarantee</u>, promise, contract, bond, pledge, certificate, assurance, covenant

warrior = <u>soldier</u>, combatant, fighter, gladiator, trooper, man-at-arms

wary 1 = <u>suspicious</u>, sceptical, guarded, distrustful, chary 2 = <u>watchful</u>, careful, alert, cautious, vigilant, circumspect, heedful ≠ careless

wash VERB 1 = <u>clean</u>, scrub, sponge, rinse, scour, cleanse 2 = <u>launder</u>, clean, rinse, dry-clean 3 = <u>rinse</u>, clean, scrub, lather 4 = <u>bathe</u>, bath, clean yourself, soak, douse, scrub yourself down 5 = <u>move</u>, overcome, touch, upset, stir, disturb, perturb, surge through 6 (*Informal*) = <u>be plausible</u>, stand up, hold up, pass muster, hold water, stick, carry weight, be convincing

● NOUN 1 = <u>laundering</u>, cleaning, clean, cleansing 2 = <u>bathe</u>, dip, soak, scrub, rinse 3 = <u>backwash</u>, slipstream, path, trail, train, track, waves, aftermath 4 = <u>splash</u>, surge, swell, rise and fall, undulation 5 = <u>coat</u>, film, covering, layer, coating, overlay

● PHRASES **wash something** or **someone away** = <u>sweep away</u>, carry off, bear away ◆ **wash something away** = <u>erode</u>, wear away, wash away

waste VERB 1 = <u>squander</u>, throw away, blow (*slang*), lavish, misuse, dissipate, fritter away ≠ save 2 = <u>wear out</u>, wither

● NOUN 1 = <u>squandering</u>, misuse, extravagance, frittering away, dissipation, wastefulness, prodigality ≠ saving 2 = <u>rubbish</u>, refuse, debris, scrap, litter, garbage, trash, leftovers

● PLURAL NOUN = <u>desert</u>, wilderness, wasteland

● ADJECTIVE 1 = <u>unwanted</u>, useless, worthless, unused, leftover, superfluous, unusable, supernumerary ≠ necessary 2 = <u>uncultivated</u>, wild, bare, barren, empty, desolate, unproductive, uninhabited

≠ cultivated

● PHRASES **waste away** = <u>decline</u>, dwindle, wither, fade, crumble, decay, wane, wear out

watch VERB 1 = <u>look at</u>, observe, regard, eye, see, view, contemplate, eyeball (*slang*) 2 = <u>spy on</u>, follow, track, monitor, keep an eye on, stake out, keep tabs on (*informal*), keep watch on 3 = <u>guard</u>, keep, mind, protect, tend, look after, shelter, take care of

● NOUN 1 = <u>wristwatch</u>, timepiece, chronometer 2 = <u>guard</u>, surveillance, observation, vigil, lookout

watchdog 1 = <u>guardian</u>, monitor, protector, custodian, scrutineer 2 = <u>guard dog</u>

water NOUN = <u>liquid</u>, H_2O, wai (*N.Z.*)

● PLURAL NOUN = <u>sea</u>, main, waves, ocean, depths, briny

● VERB 1 = <u>sprinkle</u>, spray, soak, irrigate, hose, dampen, drench, douse 2 = <u>get wet</u>, cry, weep, become wet, exude water

● PHRASES **water something down** = <u>dilute</u>, weaken, water, doctor, thin

▓ RELATED WORD
adjective: aquatic

waterfall = <u>cascade</u>, fall, cataract

wave VERB 1 = <u>signal</u>, sign, gesture, gesticulate 2 = <u>guide</u>, point, direct, indicate, signal, motion, gesture, nod 3 = <u>brandish</u>, swing, flourish, wag, shake 4 = <u>flutter</u>, flap, stir, shake, swing, wag, oscillate

● NOUN 1 = <u>gesture</u>, sign, signal, indication, gesticulation 2 = <u>ripple</u>, breaker, swell, ridge, roller, billow 3 = <u>outbreak</u>, rash, upsurge, flood, surge, ground swell 4 = <u>stream</u>, flood, surge, spate, current, flow, rush, tide

waver 1 = <u>hesitate</u>, dither (*chiefly Brit.*), vacillate, falter, fluctuate, seesaw, hum and haw ≠ be decisive 2 = <u>flicker</u>, shake, tremble, wobble, quiver, totter

wax 1 = <u>increase</u>, grow, develop, expand, swell, enlarge, magnify ≠ wane 2 = <u>become fuller</u>, enlarge

way 1 = <u>method</u>, means, system, process, technique, manner, procedure, mode 2 = <u>manner</u>, style, fashion, mode 3 *often plural* = <u>custom</u>, manner, habit, style, practice, nature, personality, wont, tikanga (*N.Z.*) 4 = <u>route</u>, direction, course, road, path 5 = <u>access</u>, road, track, channel, route, path, trail, pathway **6** = <u>journey</u>, approach, passage **7** = <u>distance</u>, length, stretch

wayward = <u>erratic</u>, unruly, unmanageable, unpredictable, capricious, ungovernable, inconstant ≠ obedient

weak 1 = <u>feeble</u>, frail, debilitated, fragile, sickly, puny, unsteady, infirm ≠ strong **2** = <u>slight</u>, faint, feeble, pathetic, hollow **3** = <u>fragile</u>, brittle, flimsy, fine, delicate, frail, dainty, breakable **4** = <u>unsafe</u>, exposed, vulnerable, helpless, unprotected, defenceless, unguarded ≠ secure **5** = <u>unconvincing</u>, unsatisfactory, lame, flimsy, pathetic ≠ convincing **6** = <u>tasteless</u>, thin, diluted, watery, runny, insipid ≠ strong

weaken 1 = <u>reduce</u>, undermine, moderate, diminish, lessen, sap ≠ boost **2** = <u>wane</u>, diminish, dwindle, lower, flag, fade, lessen ≠ grow **3** = <u>sap the strength of</u> ≠ strengthen

weakness 1 = <u>frailty</u>, fatigue, exhaustion, fragility, infirmity, feebleness, decrepitude ≠ strength **2** = <u>liking</u>, appetite, penchant, soft spot, passion, inclination, fondness, partiality ≠ aversion **3** = <u>powerlessness</u>, vulnerability, meekness, spinelessness, timorousness, cravenness, cowardliness **4** = <u>inadequacy</u>, deficiency, transparency, lameness, hollowness, implausibility, flimsiness, unsoundness **5** = <u>failing</u>, fault, defect, deficiency, flaw, shortcoming, blemish, imperfection ≠ strong point

wealth 1 = <u>riches</u>, fortune, prosperity, affluence, money, opulence ≠ poverty **2** = <u>property</u>, capital, fortune **3** = <u>abundance</u>, plenty, richness, profusion, fullness, cornucopia, copiousness ≠ lack

wealthy = <u>rich</u>, prosperous, affluent, well-off, flush (*informal*), opulent, well-heeled (*informal*), well-to-do ≠ poor

wear VERB 1 = <u>be dressed in</u>, have on, sport (*informal*), put on **2** = <u>show</u>, present, bear, display, assume, put on, exhibit **3** = <u>deteriorate</u>, fray, wear thin
● **NOUN 1** = <u>clothes</u>, things, dress, gear (*informal*), attire, costume, garments, apparel **2** = <u>damage</u>, wear and tear, erosion, deterioration, attrition, corrosion, abrasion ≠ repair
● **PHRASES wear off** = <u>subside</u>, disappear, fade, diminish, decrease, dwindle, wane, peter out

wearing = <u>tiresome</u>, trying, fatiguing,

oppressive, exasperating, irksome, wearisome ≠ refreshing

weary ADJECTIVE 1 = <u>tired</u>, exhausted, drained, worn out, done in (*informal*), flagging, fatigued, sleepy, clapped out (*Austral. & N.Z. informal*) ≠ energetic **2** = <u>tiring</u>, arduous, tiresome, laborious, wearisome ≠ refreshing
● **VERB** = <u>grow tired</u>, tire, become bored ≠ invigorate

weather NOUN = <u>climate</u>, conditions, temperature, forecast, outlook, meteorological conditions, elements
● **VERB** = <u>withstand</u>, stand, survive, overcome, resist, brave, endure, come through ≠ surrender to

weave 1 = <u>knit</u>, intertwine, plait, braid, entwine, interlace **2** = <u>zigzag</u>, wind, crisscross **3** = <u>create</u>, tell, recount, narrate, build, relate, make up, spin

web 1 = <u>cobweb</u>, spider's web **2** = <u>mesh</u>, lattice **3** = <u>tangle</u>, network

wed 1 = <u>get married to</u>, be united to ≠ divorce **2** = <u>get married</u>, marry, be united, tie the knot (*informal*), take the plunge (*informal*) ≠ divorce **3** = <u>unite</u>, combine, join, link, ally, blend, merge, interweave ≠ divide

wedding = <u>marriage</u>, nuptials, wedding ceremony, marriage service, wedding service

wedge VERB = <u>squeeze</u>, force, lodge, jam, crowd, stuff, pack, thrust
● **NOUN** = <u>block</u>, lump, chunk

weep = <u>cry</u>, shed tears, sob, whimper, mourn, lament, blubber, snivel ≠ rejoice

weigh 1 = <u>have a weight of</u>, tip the scales at (*informal*) **2** *often with* **up** = <u>consider</u>, examine, contemplate, evaluate, ponder, think over, reflect upon, meditate upon **3** = <u>compare</u>, balance, contrast, juxtapose, place side by side **4** = <u>matter</u>, carry weight, count

weight NOUN 1 = <u>heaviness</u>, mass, poundage, load, tonnage **2** = <u>importance</u>, force, power, value, authority, influence, impact, import, mana (*N.Z.*)
● **VERB 1** *often with* **down** = <u>load</u> **2** = <u>bias</u>, load, slant, unbalance

weird 1 = <u>strange</u>, odd, unusual, bizarre, mysterious, queer, eerie, unnatural ≠ normal **2** = <u>bizarre</u>, odd, strange, unusual, queer, unnatural, creepy (*informal*), freakish ≠ ordinary

welcome VERB 1 = <u>greet</u>, meet, receive, embrace, hail, karanga (*N.Z.*), mihi (*N.Z.*) ≠ reject 2 = <u>accept gladly</u>, appreciate, embrace, approve of, be pleased by, give the thumbs up to (*informal*), be glad about, express pleasure *or* satisfaction at
● NOUN = <u>greeting</u>, welcoming, reception, acceptance, hail, hospitality, salutation ≠ rejection

● ADJECTIVE 1 = <u>pleasing</u>, appreciated, acceptable, pleasant, desirable, refreshing, delightful, gratifying ≠ unpleasant 2 = <u>wanted</u> ≠ unwanted 3 = <u>free</u>

weld 1 = <u>join</u>, link, bond, bind, connect, fuse, solder 2 = <u>unite</u>, combine, blend, unify, fuse

welfare 1 = <u>wellbeing</u>, good, interest, health, security, benefit, safety, protection 2 = <u>state benefit</u>, support, benefits, pensions, dole (*slang*), social security, unemployment benefit, state benefits

well¹ ADVERB 1 = <u>skilfully</u>, expertly, adeptly, professionally, correctly, properly, efficiently, adequately ≠ badly 2 = <u>satisfactorily</u>, nicely, smoothly, successfully, pleasantly, splendidly, agreeably ≠ badly 3 = <u>thoroughly</u>, completely, fully, carefully, effectively, efficiently, rigorously 4 = <u>intimately</u>, deeply, fully, profoundly ≠ slightly 5 = <u>favourably</u>, highly, kindly, warmly, enthusiastically, approvingly, admiringly, with admiration ≠ unfavourably 6 = <u>considerably</u>, easily, very much, significantly, substantially, markedly 7 = <u>fully</u>, highly, greatly, amply, very much, thoroughly, considerably, substantially 8 = <u>possibly</u>, probably, certainly, reasonably, conceivably, justifiably 9 = <u>decently</u>, right, kindly, fittingly, fairly, properly, politely, suitably ≠ unfairly 10 = <u>prosperously</u>, comfortably, splendidly, in comfort, in (the lap of) luxury, without hardship

● ADJECTIVE 1 = <u>healthy</u>, sound, fit, blooming, in fine fettle, in good condition ≠ ill 2 = <u>satisfactory</u>, right, fine, pleasing, proper, thriving ≠ unsatisfactory 3 = <u>advisable</u>, proper, agreeable ≠ inadvisable

well² NOUN = <u>hole</u>, bore, pit, shaft
● VERB 1 = <u>flow</u>, spring, pour, jet, surge, gush, spurt, spout 2 = <u>rise</u>, increase, grow, mount, surge, intensify

wet ADJECTIVE 1 = <u>damp</u>, soaking, saturated, moist, watery, soggy, sodden, waterlogged ≠ dry 2 = <u>rainy</u>, damp, drizzly, showery, raining, pouring, drizzling, teeming ≠ sunny 3 (*Informal*) = <u>feeble</u>, soft, weak, ineffectual, weedy (*informal*), spineless, effete, timorous
● VERB = <u>moisten</u>, spray, dampen, water, soak, saturate, douse, irrigate ≠ dry
● NOUN 1 = <u>rain</u>, drizzle ≠ fine weather 2 = <u>moisture</u>, water, liquid, damp, humidity, condensation, dampness, wetness ≠ dryness

whack (*Informal*) VERB = <u>strike</u>, hit, belt (*informal*), bang, smack, thrash, thump, swipe
● NOUN 1 = <u>blow</u>, hit, stroke, belt (*informal*), bang, smack, thump, swipe 2 (*Informal*) = <u>share</u>, part, cut (*informal*), bit, portion, quota 3 (*Informal*) = <u>attempt</u>, go (*informal*), try, turn, shot (*informal*), crack (*informal*), stab (*informal*), bash (*informal*)

wharf = <u>dock</u>, pier, berth, quay, jetty, landing stage

wheel NOUN = <u>disc</u>, ring, hoop
● VERB 1 = <u>push</u>, trundle, roll 2 = <u>turn</u>, swing, spin, revolve, rotate, whirl, swivel 3 = <u>circle</u>, go round, twirl, gyrate

whereabouts = <u>position</u>, situation, site, location

whiff = <u>smell</u>, hint, scent, sniff, aroma, odour

whim = <u>impulse</u>, caprice, fancy, urge, notion

whine VERB 1 = <u>cry</u>, sob, wail, whimper, sniffle, snivel, moan 2 = <u>complain</u>, grumble, gripe (*informal*), whinge (*informal*), moan, grouse, grizzle (*informal*, *chiefly Brit.*), grouch (*informal*)
● NOUN 1 = <u>cry</u>, moan, sob, wail, whimper 2 = <u>drone</u>, note, hum 3 = <u>complaint</u>, moan, grumble, grouse, gripe (*informal*), whinge (*informal*), grouch (*informal*)

whip NOUN = <u>lash</u>, cane, birch, crop, scourge, cat-o'-nine-tails
● VERB 1 = <u>lash</u>, cane, flog, beat, strap, thrash, birch, scourge 2 (*Informal*) = <u>dash</u>, shoot, fly, tear, rush, dive, dart, whisk 3 = <u>whisk</u>, beat, mix vigorously, stir vigorously 4 = <u>incite</u>, drive, stir, spur, work up, get going, agitate, inflame

whirl VERB 1 = <u>spin</u>, turn, twist, rotate, twirl 2 = <u>rotate</u>, roll, twist, revolve, swirl, twirl, pirouette 3 = <u>feel dizzy</u>, swim, spin, reel, go round

● NOUN 1 = <u>revolution</u>, turn, roll, spin, twist, swirl, rotation, twirl 2 = <u>bustle</u>, round, series, succession, flurry, merry-go-round 3 = <u>confusion</u>, daze, dither (*chiefly Brit.*), giddiness 4 = <u>tumult</u>, spin

whisk VERB 1 = <u>flick</u>, whip, sweep, brush 2 = <u>beat</u>, mix vigorously, stir vigorously, whip, fluff up

● NOUN 1 = <u>flick</u>, sweep, brush, whip 2 = <u>beater</u>, mixer, blender

whisper VERB 1 = <u>murmur</u>, breathe ≠ shout 2 = <u>rustle</u>, sigh, hiss, swish

● NOUN 1 = <u>murmur</u>, mutter, mumble, undertone 2 (*Informal*) = <u>rumour</u>, report, gossip, innuendo, insinuation 3 = <u>rustle</u>, sigh, hiss, swish

white = <u>pale</u>, wan, pasty, pallid, ashen

white-collar = <u>clerical</u>, professional, salaried, nonmanual

whittle VERB = <u>carve</u>, cut, hew, shape, trim, shave, pare

● PHRASES **whittle something** or **someone down** = <u>reduce</u>, cut down, cut, decrease, prune, scale down ◆ **whittle something away** = <u>undermine</u>, reduce, consume, erode, eat away, wear away

whole NOUN = <u>unit</u>, ensemble, entirety, totality ≠ part

● ADJECTIVE 1 = <u>complete</u>, full, total, entire, uncut, undivided, unabridged ≠ partial 2 = <u>undamaged</u>, intact, unscathed, unbroken, untouched, unharmed, in one piece ≠ damaged

● PHRASES **on the whole** 1 = <u>all in all</u>, altogether, all things considered, by and large 2 = <u>generally</u>, in general, as a rule, chiefly, mainly, mostly, principally, on average

wholesale ADJECTIVE = <u>extensive</u>, total, mass, sweeping, broad, comprehensive, wide-ranging, blanket ≠ limited

● ADVERB = <u>extensively</u>, comprehensively, across the board, indiscriminately

wholly = <u>completely</u>, totally, perfectly, fully, entirely, altogether, thoroughly, utterly ≠ partly

whore = <u>prostitute</u>, tart (*informal*), streetwalker, call girl

wide ADJECTIVE 1 = <u>spacious</u>, broad, extensive, roomy, commodious ≠ confined 2 = <u>baggy</u>, full, loose, ample, billowing, roomy, voluminous, capacious 3 = <u>expanded</u>, dilated, distended ≠ shut

4 = <u>broad</u>, extensive, wide-ranging, large, sweeping, vast, immense, expansive ≠ restricted 5 = <u>extensive</u>, general, far-reaching, overarching 6 = <u>large</u>, broad, vast, immense 7 = <u>distant</u>, remote, off course, off target

● ADVERB 1 = <u>fully</u>, completely ≠ partly 2 = <u>off target</u>, astray, off course, off the mark

widen 1 = <u>broaden</u>, expand, enlarge, dilate, spread, extend, stretch ≠ narrow 2 = <u>get wider</u>, spread, extend, expand, broaden ≠ narrow

widespread = <u>common</u>, general, popular, broad, extensive, universal, far-reaching, pervasive ≠ limited

width = <u>breadth</u>, extent, span, scope, diameter, compass, thickness, girth

wield 1 = <u>brandish</u>, flourish, manipulate, swing, use, manage, handle, employ 2 = <u>exert</u>, maintain, exercise, have, possess

wife = <u>spouse</u>, partner, mate, bride, better half (*humorous*), vrou (*S. African*), wahine (*N.Z.*)

wild ADJECTIVE 1 = <u>untamed</u>, fierce, savage, ferocious, unbroken, feral, undomesticated, free, warrigal (*Austral. literary*) ≠ tame 2 = <u>uncultivated</u>, natural ≠ cultivated 3 = <u>stormy</u>, violent, rough, raging, choppy, tempestuous, blustery 4 = <u>excited</u>, crazy (*informal*), enthusiastic, raving, hysterical ≠ unenthusiastic 5 = <u>uncontrolled</u>, disorderly, turbulent, wayward, unruly, rowdy, unfettered, riotous ≠ calm 6 = <u>mad</u> (*informal*), furious, fuming, infuriated, incensed, enraged, very angry, irate, tooshie (*Austral. slang*), off the air (*Austral. slang*) 7 = <u>uncivilized</u>, fierce, savage, primitive, ferocious, barbaric, brutish, barbarous ≠ civilized

● PLURAL NOUN = <u>wilderness</u>, desert, wasteland, middle of nowhere (*informal*), backwoods, back of beyond (*informal*)

wilderness = <u>wilds</u>, desert, wasteland, uncultivated region

will NOUN 1 = <u>determination</u>, drive, purpose, commitment, resolution, resolve, spine, backbone 2 = <u>wish</u>, mind, desire, intention, fancy, preference, inclination 3 = <u>choice</u>, prerogative, volition 4 = <u>decree</u>, wish, desire, command, dictate, ordinance 5 = <u>testament</u>, bequest(s), last wishes, last will and testament

● VERB 1 = <u>wish</u>, want, prefer, desire, see

fit 2 = bequeath, give, leave, transfer, gift, hand on, pass on, confer

willing 1 = inclined, prepared, consenting, agreeable, compliant, amenable ≠ unwilling 2 = ready, game (*informal*) ≠ reluctant

willingly = readily, freely, gladly, happily, eagerly, voluntarily, cheerfully, by choice ≠ unwillingly

willingness = inclination, will, agreement, wish, consent, volition ≠ reluctance

wilt 1 = droop, wither, sag, shrivel 2 = weaken, languish, droop 3 = wane, flag, fade

win VERB 1 = be victorious in, succeed in, prevail in, come first in, be the victor in ≠ lose 2 = be victorious, succeed, triumph, overcome, prevail, conquer, come first, sweep the board ≠ lose 3 = gain, get, land, achieve, earn, secure, obtain, acquire ≠ forfeit
● NOUN = victory, success, triumph, conquest ≠ defeat
● PHRASES **win someone over** or **round** = convince, influence, persuade, convert, sway, prevail upon, bring or talk round

wince VERB = flinch, start, shrink, cringe, quail, recoil, cower, draw back
● NOUN = flinch, start, cringe

wind[1] NOUN 1 = air, blast, hurricane, breeze, draught, gust, zephyr 2 = flatulence, gas 3 = breath, puff, respiration 4 = nonsense, talk, boasting, hot air, babble, bluster, humbug, twaddle (*informal*), bizzo (*Austral. slang*), bull's wool (*Austral. & N.Z. slang*)
● PHRASES **get wind of something** = hear about, learn of, find out about, become aware of, be told about, be informed of, be made aware of, hear tell of

wind[2] VERB 1 = meander, turn, bend, twist, curve, snake, ramble, twist and turn 2 = wrap, twist, reel, curl, loop, coil 3 = coil, curl, spiral, encircle
● PHRASES **wind someone up** (*Informal*) 1 = irritate, provoke, excite, anger, annoy, exasperate, nettle, work someone up, pique 2 = tease, kid (*informal*), have someone on (*informal*), annoy, rag (*informal*), rib (*informal*), josh (*informal*), vex ◆ **wind something up** 1 = end, finish, settle, conclude, tie up, wrap up, finalize 2 = close down, close, dissolve,

terminate, put something into liquidation
◆ **wind up** = end up, be left, finish up, fetch up (*informal*), land up

windfall = godsend, find, jackpot, bonanza, manna from heaven ≠ misfortune

windy = breezy, wild, stormy, windswept, blustery, gusty, squally, blowy ≠ calm

wing NOUN = faction, group, arm, section, branch
● VERB 1 = fly, soar, glide, take wing 2 = wound, hit, clip

wink VERB 1 = blink, bat, flutter 2 = twinkle, flash, shine, sparkle, gleam, shimmer, glimmer
● NOUN = blink, flutter

winner = victor, champion, master, champ (*informal*), conqueror, prizewinner ≠ loser

winning ADJECTIVE 1 = victorious, first, top, successful, unbeaten, conquering, triumphant, undefeated 2 = charming, pleasing, attractive, engaging, cute, disarming, enchanting, endearing ≠ unpleasant
● PLURAL NOUN = spoils, profits, gains, prize, proceeds, takings

wipe VERB 1 = clean, polish, brush, rub, sponge, mop, swab 2 = erase, remove
● NOUN = rub, brush
● PHRASES **wipe something** or **someone out** = destroy, massacre, erase, eradicate, obliterate, annihilate, exterminate, expunge

wisdom = understanding, learning, knowledge, intelligence, judgment, insight, enlightenment, erudition ≠ foolishness

wise 1 = sage, clever, intelligent, sensible, enlightened, discerning, perceptive, erudite ≠ foolish 2 = sensible, clever, intelligent, prudent, judicious ≠ unwise

wish NOUN = desire, want, hope, urge, intention, fancy (*informal*), ambition, yen (*informal*) ≠ aversion
● VERB = want, feel, choose, please, desire, think fit
● PHRASES **wish for something** = desire, want, hope for, long for, crave, aspire to, yearn for, hanker for

wit 1 = humour, quips, banter, puns, repartee, wordplay, witticisms, badinage ≠ seriousness 2 = humorist, card (*informal*), comedian, wag, joker, dag (*N.Z. informal*) 3 *often plural* = cleverness, sense, brains, wisdom, common sense, intellect, ingenuity, acumen ≠ stupidity

witch = enchantress, magician, hag, crone, sorceress, Wiccan

witchcraft = magic, voodoo, wizardry, black magic, enchantment, occultism, sorcery, Wicca, makutu (N.Z.)

withdraw 1 = remove, take off, pull out, extract, take away, pull back, draw out, draw back 2 = take out, extract, draw out

withdrawal = removal, ending, stopping, taking away, abolition, elimination, cancellation, termination

withdrawn = uncommunicative, reserved, retiring, distant, shy, taciturn, introverted, unforthcoming ≠ outgoing

wither 1 = wilt, decline, decay, disintegrate, perish, shrivel ≠ flourish 2 = waste, decline, shrivel 3 = fade, decline, perish ≠ increase

withering = scornful, devastating, humiliating, snubbing, hurtful, mortifying

withhold 1 = keep secret, refuse, hide, reserve, retain, conceal, suppress, hold back ≠ reveal 2 = hold back, suppress, keep back ≠ release

withstand = resist, suffer, bear, oppose, cope with, endure, tolerate, stand up to ≠ give in to

witness NOUN 1 = observer, viewer, spectator, looker-on, watcher, onlooker, eyewitness, bystander 2 = testifier ● VERB 1 = see, view, watch, note, notice, observe, perceive 2 = countersign, sign, endorse, validate

witty = humorous, funny, clever, amusing, sparkling, whimsical, droll, piquant ≠ dull

wizard = magician, witch, shaman, sorcerer, occultist, magus, conjuror, warlock, tohunga (N.Z.)

wobble VERB 1 = shake, rock, sway, tremble, teeter, totter 2 = tremble, shake ● NOUN 1 = unsteadiness, shake, tremble 2 = unsteadiness, shake, tremor

woe 1 = misery, distress, grief, agony, gloom, sadness, sorrow, anguish ≠ happiness 2 = problem, grief, misery, sorrow

woman = lady, girl, female, sheila (Austral. & N.Z. informal), vrou (S. African), adult female, charlie (Austral. slang), chook (Austral. slang), wahine (N.Z.) ≠ man

womanly 1 = feminine, motherly, female, warm, tender, matronly, ladylike

2 = curvaceous, ample, voluptuous, shapely, curvy (informal), busty (informal), buxom, full-figured

wonder VERB 1 = think, question, puzzle, speculate, query, ponder, meditate, conjecture 2 = be amazed, stare, marvel, be astonished, gape ● NOUN 1 = amazement, surprise, admiration, awe, fascination, astonishment, bewilderment, wonderment 2 = phenomenon, sight, miracle, spectacle, curiosity, marvel, prodigy, rarity

wonderful 1 = excellent, great (informal), brilliant, outstanding, superb, fantastic (informal), tremendous, magnificent, booshit (Austral. slang), exo (Austral. slang), sik (Austral. slang) ≠ terrible 2 = remarkable, amazing, extraordinary, incredible, astonishing, staggering, startling, phenomenal ≠ ordinary

woo 1 = seek, cultivate 2 = court, pursue

wood 1 = timber, planks, planking, lumber (U.S.) 2 or **woods** = woodland, forest, grove, thicket, copse, coppice 3 = firewood, fuel, logs, kindling

wooded = tree-covered, forested, timbered, sylvan (poetic), tree-clad

wooden 1 = made of wood, timber, woody, ligneous 2 = expressionless, lifeless, deadpan, unresponsive

wool 1 = fleece, hair, coat 2 = yarn

word NOUN 1 = term, name, expression 2 = chat, tête-à-tête, talk, discussion, consultation, confab (informal), heart-to-heart, powwow (informal) 3 = comment, remark, utterance 4 = message, news, report, information, notice, intelligence, dispatch, communiqué 5 = promise, guarantee, pledge, vow, assurance, oath 6 = command, order, decree, bidding, mandate ● VERB = express, say, state, put, phrase, utter, couch, formulate

■ RELATED WORDS
adjectives: lexical, verbal

wording = phraseology, words, language, phrasing, terminology

work VERB 1 = be employed, be in work 2 = labour, sweat, slave, toil, slog (away), drudge, peg away, exert yourself ≠ relax 3 = function, go, run, operate, be in working order ≠ be out of order 4 = succeed, work out, pay off (informal), be successful, be effective, do the trick (*informal*), do the business (*informal*), get results **5** = <u>cultivate</u>, farm, dig, till, plough **6** = <u>operate</u>, use, move, control, drive, manage, handle, manipulate **7** = <u>manipulate</u>, form, fashion, shape, mould, knead

● NOUN **1** = <u>employment</u>, business, job, trade, duty, profession, occupation, livelihood ≠ play **2** = <u>effort</u>, industry, labour, sweat, toil, exertion, drudgery, elbow grease (*facetious*) ≠ leisure **3** = <u>task</u>, jobs, projects, commissions, duties, assignments, chores, yakka (*Austral. & N.Z. informal*) **4** = <u>handiwork</u>, doing, act, feat, deed **5** = <u>creation</u>, piece, production, opus, achievement, composition, handiwork

● PLURAL NOUN **1** = <u>factory</u>, plant, mill, workshop **2** = <u>writings</u>, output, canon, oeuvre (*French*) **3** = <u>mechanism</u>, workings, parts, action, movement, machinery

● PHRASES **work something out** = <u>solve</u>, find out, calculate, figure out

worker = <u>employee</u>, hand, labourer, workman, craftsman, artisan, tradesman

workman = <u>labourer</u>, hand, worker, employee, mechanic, operative, craftsman, artisan

workshop 1 = <u>factory</u>, plant, mill **2** = <u>workroom</u>, studio

world 1 = <u>earth</u>, planet, globe **2** = <u>mankind</u>, man, everyone, the public, everybody, humanity, humankind **3** = <u>sphere</u>, area, field, environment, realm, domain **4** (usually used in phrase *a world of difference*) = <u>huge amount</u>, mountain, wealth, great deal, good deal, abundance, enormous amount, vast amount

worldly 1 = <u>earthly</u>, physical, secular, terrestrial, temporal, profane ≠ spiritual **2** = <u>materialistic</u>, grasping, selfish, greedy ≠ nonmaterialistic **3** = <u>worldly-wise</u>, knowing, experienced, sophisticated, cosmopolitan, urbane, blasé ≠ naive

worn = <u>ragged</u>, frayed, shabby, tattered, tatty, threadbare, the worse for wear

worried = <u>anxious</u>, concerned, troubled, afraid, frightened, nervous, tense, uneasy ≠ unworried

worry VERB **1** = <u>be anxious</u>, be concerned, be worried, obsess, brood, fret, agonize, get in a lather (*informal*) ≠ be unconcerned **2** = <u>trouble</u>, upset, bother, disturb, annoy, unsettle, pester, vex ≠ soothe

● NOUN **1** = <u>anxiety</u>, concern, fear, trouble, unease, apprehension, misgiving, trepidation ≠ peace of mind **2** = <u>problem</u>, care, trouble, bother, hassle (*informal*)

worsen 1 = <u>deteriorate</u>, decline, sink, decay, get worse, degenerate, go downhill (*informal*) ≠ improve **2** = <u>aggravate</u>, damage, exacerbate, make worse ≠ improve

worship VERB **1** = <u>revere</u>, praise, honour, adore, glorify, exalt, pray to, venerate ≠ dishonour **2** = <u>love</u>, adore, idolize, put on a pedestal ≠ despise

● NOUN = <u>reverence</u>, praise, regard, respect, honour, glory, devotion, adulation

worth 1 = <u>value</u>, price, rate, cost, estimate, valuation ≠ worthlessness **2** = <u>merit</u>, value, quality, importance, excellence, goodness, worthiness ≠ unworthiness **3** = <u>usefulness</u>, value, quality, importance, excellence, goodness ≠ uselessness

worthless 1 = <u>valueless</u>, rubbishy, negligible ≠ valuable **2** = <u>useless</u>, unimportant, ineffectual, negligible ≠ useful **3** = <u>good-for-nothing</u>, vile, despicable, contemptible ≠ honourable

worthwhile = <u>useful</u>, valuable, helpful, profitable, productive, beneficial, meaningful, constructive ≠ useless

worthy = <u>praiseworthy</u>, deserving, valuable, worthwhile, admirable, virtuous, creditable, laudable ≠ disreputable

would-be = <u>budding</u>, self-styled, wannabe (*informal*), unfulfilled, self-appointed

wound NOUN **1** = <u>injury</u>, cut, hurt, trauma (*Pathology*), gash, lesion, laceration **2** *often plural* = <u>trauma</u>, offence, slight, insult

● VERB **1** = <u>injure</u>, cut, wing, hurt, pierce, gash, lacerate **2** = <u>offend</u>, hurt, annoy, sting, mortify, cut to the quick

wrangle VERB = <u>argue</u>, fight, row, dispute, disagree, contend, quarrel, squabble

● NOUN = <u>argument</u>, row, dispute, quarrel, squabble, bickering, tiff, altercation

wrap VERB **1** = <u>cover</u>, enclose, shroud, swathe, encase, enfold, bundle up **2** = <u>pack</u>, package, parcel (up), tie up, gift-wrap ≠ unpack **3** = <u>bind</u>, swathe ≠ unwind

● NOUN = <u>cloak</u>, cape, stole, mantle, shawl

● PHRASES **wrap something up** **1** = <u>giftwrap</u>, pack, package, bundle up **2** (*Informal*) = <u>end</u>, conclude, wind up, terminate, finish off, round off, polish off

wrath = anger, rage, temper, fury, resentment, indignation, ire, displeasure ≠ satisfaction

wreck VERB 1 = destroy, break, smash, ruin, devastate, shatter, spoil, demolish ≠ build 2 = spoil, ruin, devastate, shatter, crool or cruel (*Austral. slang*) ≠ save
● NOUN = shipwreck, hulk

wreckage = remains, pieces, ruin, fragments, debris, rubble

wrench VERB 1 = twist, force, pull, tear, rip, tug, jerk, yank 2 = sprain, strain, rick
● NOUN 1 = twist, pull, rip, tug, jerk, yank 2 = sprain, strain, twist 3 = blow, shock, upheaval, pang 4 = spanner, adjustable spanner

wrestle = fight, battle, struggle, combat, grapple, tussle, scuffle

wrinkle NOUN 1 = line, fold, crease, furrow, crow's-foot, corrugation 2 = crease, fold, crumple, furrow, crinkle, corrugation
● VERB = crease, gather, fold, crumple, furrow, rumple, pucker, corrugate ≠ smooth

writ = summons, document, decree, indictment, court order, subpoena, arraignment

write 1 = record, scribble, inscribe, set down, jot down 2 = compose, draft, pen, draw up 3 = correspond, get in touch, keep in touch, write a letter, drop a line, drop a note

writer = author, novelist, hack, scribbler, scribe, wordsmith, penpusher

writing = script, hand, printing, fist (*informal*), scribble, handwriting, scrawl, calligraphy

wrong ADJECTIVE 1 = amiss, faulty, unsatisfactory, not right, defective, awry 2 = incorrect, mistaken, false, inaccurate, untrue, erroneous, wide of the mark, fallacious 3 = inappropriate, incorrect, unsuitable, unacceptable, undesirable, incongruous, unseemly, unbecoming ≠ correct 4 = bad, criminal, illegal, evil, unlawful, immoral, unjust, dishonest ≠ moral 5 = defective, faulty, awry, askew
● ADVERB 1 = incorrectly, badly, wrongly, mistakenly, erroneously, inaccurately ≠ correctly 2 = amiss, astray, awry, askew
● NOUN = offence, injury, crime, error, sin, injustice, misdeed, transgression ≠ good deed
● VERB = mistreat, abuse, hurt, harm, cheat, take advantage of, oppress, malign ≠ treat well

X-ray = radiograph, x-ray image

yank VERB = pull, tug, jerk, seize, snatch, pluck, hitch, wrench
● NOUN = pull, tug, jerk, snatch, hitch, wrench, tweak

yarn 1 = thread, fibre, cotton, wool 2 (*Informal*) = story, tale, anecdote, account, narrative, fable, reminiscence, urban myth

yawning = gaping, wide, huge, vast, cavernous

yearly ADJECTIVE = annual, each year, every year, once a year
● ADVERB = annually, every year, by the year, once a year, per annum

yearn *often with for* = long, desire, hunger, ache, crave, covet, itch, hanker after

yell VERB = scream, shout, cry out, howl, call out, wail, shriek, screech ≠ whisper
● NOUN = scream, cry, shout, roar, howl, shriek, whoop, screech ≠ whisper

yen = longing, desire, craving, yearning, passion, hunger, ache, itch

yet ADVERB 1 = so far, until now, up to now, still, as yet, even now, thus far, up till now 2 = now, right now, just now, so soon 3 = still, in addition, besides, to boot, into the bargain
● CONJUNCTION = nevertheless, still, however, for all that, notwithstanding, just the same, be that as it may

yield VERB 1 = bow, submit, give in, surrender, succumb, cave in (*informal*), capitulate 2 = relinquish, resign, hand

over, surrender, turn over, make over, give over, bequeath ≠ retain ≠ resist
3 = <u>produce</u>, give, provide, return, supply, bear, net, earn ≠ use up
● NOUN 1 = <u>produce</u>, crop, harvest, output
2 = <u>profit</u>, return, income, revenue, earnings, takings ≠ loss

yielding 1 = <u>soft</u>, pliable, springy, elastic, supple, spongy, unresisting
2 = <u>submissive</u>, obedient, compliant, docile, flexible, accommodating, pliant, acquiescent ≠ obstinate

yob or **yobbo** = <u>thug</u>, hooligan, lout, hoon (*Austral. & N.Z. slang*), ruffian, roughneck (*slang*), tsotsi (*S. African*), cougan (*Austral. slang*), scozza (*Austral. slang*), bogan (*Austral. slang*)

young ADJECTIVE 1 = <u>immature</u>, juvenile, youthful, little, green, junior, infant, adolescent ≠ old 2 = <u>early</u>, new, undeveloped, fledgling ≠ advanced
● PLURAL NOUN = <u>offspring</u>, babies, litter, family, issue, brood, progeny ≠ parents

youngster = <u>youth</u>, girl, boy, kid (*informal*), lad, teenager, juvenile, lass

youth 1 = <u>immaturity</u>, adolescence, boyhood or girlhood, salad days ≠ old age 2 = <u>boy</u>, lad, youngster, kid (*informal*), teenager, young man, adolescent, teen (*informal*) ≠ adult

youthful = <u>young</u>, juvenile, childish, immature, boyish, girlish ≠ elderly

district, territory, belt, sphere
zoom = <u>speed</u>, shoot, fly, rush, flash, dash, whizz (*informal*), hurtle

Z

zeal = <u>enthusiasm</u>, passion, zest, spirit, verve, fervour, eagerness, gusto ≠ apathy

zero 1 = <u>nought</u>, nothing, nil 2 = <u>rock bottom</u>, the bottom, an all-time low, a nadir, as low as you can get

zip VERB = <u>speed</u>, shoot, fly, flash, zoom, whizz (*informal*)
● NOUN (*Informal*) = <u>energy</u>, drive, vigour, verve, zest, gusto, liveliness ≠ lethargy

zone = <u>area</u>, region, section, sector,

THEMED
LISTS

THEMED
LISTS

ACIDS

SPECIFIC ACIDS

abietic acid
acetic acid
alginic acid
aminobenzoic acid
aspartic acid
barbituric acid
benzoic acid
boric acid
butyric acid
carbonic acid
chloric acid
chloroacetic acid
chlorous acid
cholic acid
chromic acid
cinnamic acid
citric acid
crotonic acid
cyanic acid
decanedioic acid
decanoic acid
dichromic acid
dithionous acid
deoxyribonucleic acid
dodecanoic acid
erucic acid
formic acid
fulminic acid
fumaric acid
gallic acid
glacial acetic acid

glyceric acid
heptadecanoic acid
hexanoic acid
hydnocarpic acid
hydrochloric acid
hydrofluoric acid
hypochlorous acid
hypophosphoric acid
hypophosphorous
isocyanic acid
itaconic acid
lactic acid
linoleic acid
linolenic acid
lysergic acid
manganic acid
mucic acid
nitric acid
nitrous acid
nonanoic acid
octanedioic acid
oleic acid
orthophosphoric acid
oxalic acid
pantothenic acid
para-aminobenzoic acid
pectic acid
pentanoic acid
permanganic acid
phosphoric acid
phthalic acid

picric acid
platinocyanic acid
polyphosphoric acid
propanoic acid
prussic acid
pyroboric acid
pyrophosphoric acid
pyrosulphuric acid
racemic acid
ricinoleic acid
saccharic acid
selenic acid
selenious acid
silicic acid
sorbic acid
spiraeic acid (modern
  salicylic acid)
stearic acid
suberic acid
succinic acid
sulphonic acid
sulphurous acid
tantalic acid
tartaric acid
telluric acid
terebic acid
terephthalic acid
thiocyanic acid
thiosulphuric acid
trichloroacetic acid
uric acid

TYPES OF ACID

amino acid	dicarboxylic acid	mineral acid	polycarboxylic acid
carboxylic acid	fatty acid	nucleic acid	
dibasic acid	iodic acid	periodic acid	

AMINO ACIDS

alanine	glutamine	leucine	proline
arginine	glycine	lysine	serine
citrulline	histidine	ethionine	threonine
cystine	isoleucine	ornithine	triiodothyronine

AIRCRAFT

TYPES OF AIRCRAFT

aerodyne	bomber	dive bomber	gyrodyne
aerostat	canard	drone	hang-glider
airliner	coleopter	fighter	helicopter
airship	convertiplane,	fighter-bomber	helicopter gunship
amphibian	convertaplane, or	flying boat	hot-air balloon
autogiro or autogyro	convertoplane	flying wing	interceptor or
balloon	cyclogiro	freighter	intercepter
biplane	delta-wing	gas-filled balloon	jet or jet plane
blimp	dirigible	glider	jetliner

jumbo jet
jump jet
lifting body
light aircraft
microlight or microlite
monoplane
multiplane
night fighter
ornithopter or orthopter
rotaplane
sailplane
seaplane
skiplane
Stealth bomber or
Stealth plane
STOL
swept-wing
swing-wing
tanker
triplane
troop carrier
turbofan
turbojet
turboprop or propjet
VTOL
warplane
wing
zeppelin

AIRCRAFT PARTS

aerofoil
aerometeorograph
aerostructure
afterburner
aileron
airframe
air-intake
airlock
air scoop
airscrew
all-flying tail
altimeter
anti-icer
arrester
artificial horizon
astrodome or astrohatch
athodyd
autopilot
auxiliary power unit
basket
black box
blister
body
bomb bay
bombsight
bulkhead
cabin
canopy
cantilever
capsule
chassis
clamshell
cockpit
control column or control stick
cowling or cowl
dashboard
drop tank
ejection seat
elevator
elevon
empennage
engine
engine pod
fairing
fin
flap
flight deck
flight recorder
fuel tank
fuselage
galley
gondola
heat sink
hold
horn or horn balance
hydroplane
inclinometer
instrument panel
jet engine
jet pipe
joystick
keel
landing gear
landing light
launching shoe or launch shoe
longeron
main plane
nacelle
nose
nose wheel
Pitot tube
pod
propeller
pulsejet
pusher
pylon
ramjet or ramjet engine
rotor
rudder
slat
slinger ring
spinner
spoiler
stabilizer
tab
tail
tailplane
tailskid
tail wheel
trailing edge
trim tab
turret
undercarriage
waist
wing
winglet
wing tip

ALCOHOLIC DRINKS

apéritif
busera
Campari (trademark)
chaser
cider, cyder, or (U.S. & Canad.) hard cider
caudle
Cinzano (trademark)
cocktail
cordial
dram
Dubonnet (trademark)
elderberry wine
frappé
French vermouth
ginger wine
glogg
gluhwein
grog
hippocras
Irish coffee or Gaelic coffee
Italian vermouth
kvass, kvas, or quass
liqueur
malt liquor
Martini (trademark)
mead
mulled wine
negus
nor'wester
palm wine
posset
pousse-café
pulque
sake, saké, saki, or rice wine
samshu
shooter
skokiaan
slammer
snakebite
soma
spruce beer
toddy
vermouth
waragi

ALGAE

blackfish weed (Austral.)
bladderwrack
brown algae
carrageen, carragheen, or
carageen
diatom

		phytoplankton *or*	sea lettuce
dinoflagellate	Irish moss	plankton	sea tangle
dulse	kelp	red algae	seaweed
euglena	laver	reindeer moss	sea wrack
fucoid *or* fucus	lichen	rockweed	spirogyra
green algae	Neptune's necklace	sargasso *or*	stonewort
gulfweed	(*Austral.*)	sargassum	wrack
Iceland moss	oarweed		

ALLOYS

Alnico (*trademark*)	constantan	Manganin (*trademark*)	pinchbeck
amalgam	cupronickel	misch metal	platina
austenitic stainless	Duralumin (*trademark*)	Monel *or* Monell	platiniridium
steel	electrum	metal	soft solder
Babbit metal	ferrochromium	Nichrome (*trademark*)	speculum metal
bell bronze	ferromanganese	nickel silver	steel
bell metal	ferromolybdenum	nimonic alloy	Stellite (*trademark*)
billon	ferronickel	ormolu	sterling silver
brass	ferrosilicon	oroide	terne
brazing solder	Invar (*trademark*)	osmiridium	tombac *or* tambac
Britannia metal	kamacite	permalloy	type metal
bronze	magnolia metal	pewter	white gold
chromel	magnox	phosphor bronze	zircalloy

ALPHABETS

RELATED VOCABULARY

Cyrillic	kanji	Latin	Linear B	Nagari
hiragana	katakana	lexigraphy	logogram *or*	Roman
kana	Kufic *or* Cufic	Linear A	logograph	

ARABIC LETTERS

alif	ḥā	zā	ṭā	qāf	hā
bā	khā	sīn	ẓā	kāf	wāw
tā	dāl	shīn	`ain	lām	yā
thā	dhāl	ṣād	ghain	mīm	
jīm	rā	ḍād	fā	nūn	

GREEK LETTERS

alpha	epsilon	kappa	omega	psi	theta
beta	eta	lambda	omicron	rho	upsilon
chi	gamma	mu	phi	sigma	xi
delta	iota	nu	pi	tau	zeta

HEBREW LETTERS

aleph	he	mem	tsade	teth
ayin *or* ain	heth *or* cheth	nun	samekh	vav *or* waw
beth	kaph	pe	shin	yod *or* yodh
daleth *or* daled	koph *or* qoph	resh	sin	zayin
gimel	lamed *or* lamedh	sadhe, sade, *or*	tav *or* taw	

COMMUNICATIONS CODE WORDS FOR THE ALPHABET

Alpha	Golf	Mike	Sierra	Yankee
Bravo	Hotel	November	Tango	Zulu
Charlie	India	Oscar	Uniform	
Delta	Juliet	Papa	Victor	
Echo	Kilo	Quebec	Whiskey	
Foxtrot	Lima	Romeo	X-Ray	

ENGLISH AND AMERICAN EQUIVALENCES

English	American	English	American
aeroplane	airplane	foyer	lobby
American football	football	fringe	bangs
antenatal	prenatal	garden	yard
aubergine	eggplant	gear lever	stick shift
autumn	fall	goose pimples	goose bumps
bad-tempered	mean	ground floor	first floor
banknote	bill	hair grip	bobby pin
bat	paddle	hairpin bend	switchback
benefit	welfare	handbag	purse
bin or dustbin	trashcan	hessian	burlap
biscuit	cookie	high street	main street
black pudding	blood sausage	holiday	vacation
blinds	shades	indicator	blinker
bonnet (car)	hood	invigilator	proctor
boot (car)	trunk	ironmonger	hardware store
braces (teeth)	retainer	jam	jelly
braces (lingerie)	suspenders	janitor	caretaker
breve	double whole note	lawyer	attorney
broad bean	fava bean	lift	elevator
building society	savings and loan	mangetout	snowpea
burgle	burglarize	mate	friend
candy floss	cotton candy	merry-go-round	carousel
car	automobile	methylated spirits	denatured alcohol
car park	parking lot	mince	ground beef
chemist	drug store	minim	half note
chips	French fries	nappy	diaper
clothes peg	clothes pin	neat (of drinks)	straight
coffin	casket	noughts and crosses	tick-tack-toe
condom	rubber	nursery	kindergarten
cornflour	corn starch	off-licence	liquor store
courgette	zucchini	paraffin	kerosene
crisps	chips or potato chips	pavement	sidewalk
crossroads	intersection	pepper	bell pepper
crotchet	quarter note	petrol	gas or gasoline
current account	checking account	pissed	drunk
curtains	drapes	plait	braid
cutlery	flatware or silverware	plasterboard	dry lining
CV	résumé	plot	lot
dialling code	area code	porridge	oatmeal
dinner jacket	tuxedo	postcode	zip code
double cream	heavy cream	postman	mail man
drapery	dry goods	pub or public house	bar
draughts	checkers	public school	private school
drawing pin	thumb tack	purse	pocketbook
dressing gown	robe	pushchair	stroller
dummy	pacifier or soother	quaver	eighth note
engaged tone	busy signal	quilt or eiderdown	comforter
estate agent	realtor	railway	railroad
estate car	station wagon	receptionist	desk clerk
fire lighter	fire starter	reverse charge	collect
first floor	second floor	ring road	beltway
flat	apartment	roll or bap	bun
flick knife	switch blade	rubber	eraser
football	soccer	rubbish	trash or garbage

English	American	English	American
semibreve	whole note	tap	faucet
semi-detached	duplex	tarmac	asphalt
semiquaver	sixteenth note	telegram	wire
shop	store	thread	cotton
silencer	muffler	tights	pantihose
skip	dumpster	timber	lumber
skirting board	baseboard	torch	flashlight
sleeper (railway)	tie	town centre	downtown
slowcoach	slowpoke	trainers	sneakers
soft drink	soda	tram	streetcar
spanner	wrench	trousers	pants
spring onion *or* salad	scallion	turn up	cuff
onion		VAT	sales tax
state school	public school	vest	undershirt
stream	creek	waistcoast	vest
surgical spirit	rubbing alcohol	windscreen	windshield
sweet	candy		

AMPHIBIANS

axolotl	eft	midwife toad	Queensland cane
brown-striped frog	frog *or (Caribbean)*	mud puppy	toad
(*Austral.*)	crapaud	natterjack	salamander
bullfrog	Goliath frog	newt *or (dialect or*	siren
caecilian	hairy frog	*archaic)* eft	toad *or (Caribbean)*
cane toad (*Austral.*)	hellbender	olm	crapaud
congo eel *or* snake	hyla	pipa *or* Surinam toad	tree frog

ANGELS

ANGELS

Azrael	Gabriel	Michael	Raphael	Uriel

ANGELIC ORDERS

angels	dominations *or*	principalities *or*	thrones
archangels	dominions	princedoms	virtues
cherubim	powers	seraphim	

ANIMALS

RELATED WORDS

ant	formic	fish	piscine *or* icthyoid	ox	bovine
ass	asinine	fowl	gallinaceous	parrot	psittacine
bear	ursine	fox	vulpine	peacock	pavonine
bee	apian	goat	caprine *or* hircine	pig	porcine
bird	avian *or* ornithic	goose	anserine *or*	puffin	alcidine
bull	taurine		anserous	seal	phocine
cat	feline	gull	larine	sheep	ovine
crab	cancroid	hare	leporine	snake	serpentine,
crow	corvine	hawk	accipitrine		anguine,
deer	cervine	horse	equine		ophidian, *or*
dog	canine	lion	leonine		colubrine
dove	columbine	lynx	lyncean	swallow	hirundine
eagle	aquiline	mite *or*	acaroid	wasp	vespine
elephant	elephantine	tick		wolf	lupine
falcon	falconine	monkey	simian		

COLLECTIVE ANIMALS

Animal	Collective term
antelopes	herd
apes	shrewdness
asses	pace or herd
badgers	cete
bears	sloth
bees	swarm or grist
birds	flock, congregation, flight, or volery
bitterns	sedge or siege
boars	sounder
bucks	brace or lease
buffaloes	herd
capercailzies	tok
cats	clowder
cattle	drove or herd
choughs	chattering
colts	rag
coots	covert
cranes	herd, sedge, or siege
crows	murder
cubs	litter
curlews	herd
curs	cowardice
deer	herd
dolphins	school
doves	flight or dule
ducks	paddling or team
dunlins	flight
elk	gang
fish	shoal, draught, haul, run, or catch
flies	swarm or grist
foxes	skulk
geese	gaggle or skein
giraffes	herd
gnats	swarm or cloud
goats	herd or tribe
goldfinches	charm
grouse	brood, covey, or pack
gulls	colony
hares	down or husk
hawks	cast
hens	brood
herons	sedge or siege
herrings	shoal or glean
hounds	pack, mute, or cry
insects	swarm
kangaroos	troop
kittens	kindle
lapwings	desert
larks	exaltation
leopards	leap
lions	pride or troop
mallards	sord or sute
mares	stud
martens	richesse
moles	labour
monkeys	troop
mules	barren
nightingales	watch
owls	parliament
oxen	yoke, drove, team, or herd
partridges	covey
peacocks	muster
pheasants	nye or nide
pigeons	flock or flight
pigs	litter
plovers	stand or wing
pochards	flight, rush, bunch, or knob
ponies	herd
porpoises	school or gam
poultry	run
pups	litter
quails	bevy
rabbits	nest
racehorses	field or string
ravens	unkindness
roes	bevy
rooks	building or clamour
ruffs	hill
seals	herd or pod
sheep	flock
sheldrakes	dopping
snipe	walk or wisp
sparrows	host
starlings	murmuration
swallows	flight
swans	herd or bevy
swifts	flock
swine	herd, sounder, or dryft
teal	bunch, knob, or spring
whales	school, gam, or run
whelps	litter
whiting	pod
wigeon	bunch, company, knob, or flight
wildfowl	plump, sord, or sute
wolves	pack, rout, or herd
woodcocks	fall

HABITATIONS

Animal	Habitation
ant	ant hill or formicary
badger	set or sett
beaver	lodge
bee	hive or apiary
bird	nest
eagle	aerie or eyrie
fish	redd
fox	earth
otter	holt
pig	sty
puffin	puffinry
rabbit	warren
rook	rookery
seal	sealery
squirrel	drey or dray
termite	termitarium
wasp	vespiary or bike

MALE

Animal	Male
ass	jack
bird	cock
cat	tom
deer	hart or stag
donkey	jack
duck	drake
elephant	bull
falcon	tercel or tiercel
ferret	hob
fowl	cock
fox	dog
goat	billy or buck
goose	gander
hare	buck
horse	stallion
kangaroo	buck or old man
lobster	cock
ox	bull
peafowl	peacock
pig	boar
rabbit	buck
reindeer	buck
ruff	ruff
sheep	ram or tup
swan	cob
weasel	whittret
whale	bull

FEMALE

Animal	Female	Animal	Female	Animal	Female	Animal	Female
ass	jenny			lobster	hen	swan	pen
bird	hen	fowl	hen	mink	sow	tiger	tigress
cat	tabby	fox	vixen	ox	cow	whale	cow
deer	doe or hind	goat	nanny	peafowl	peahen	wolf	bitch
dog	bitch	hare	doe	pig	sow	wren	jenny
donkey	jenny	horse	mare	rabbit	doe		
elephant	cow	leopard	leopardess	ruff	reeve		
ferret	gill or jill (dialect)	lion	lioness	sheep	ewe		

YOUNG

Animal	Young	Animal	Young	Animal	Young
bear	cub	falcon	eyas	owl	owlet
bird	chick, fledg(e)ling, or nestling	ferret	kit	ox	calf
butterfly	caterpillar, chrysalis, or chrysalid	fish	fry or fingerling	pig	piglet
		frog	tadpole	pigeon	squab
cat	kitten	fox	kit or cub	salmon	alevin, grilse, parr, or smolt
cod	codling	goat	kid or yeanling		
deer	fawn	goose	gosling	seal	pup
dog	pup or puppy	hare	leveret	sheep	lamb or yeanling
duck	duckling	herring	alevin, brit, or sparling	sprat	brit
eagle	eaglet			swan	cygnet
eel	elver or grig	horse	foal, colt, or filly	tiger	cub
elephant	calf	kangaroo	joey	toad	tadpole
		lion	cub	whale	calf
		moth	caterpillar	wolf	cub or whelp

ANNIVERSARIES

Year	Traditional	Modern	Year	Traditional	Modern
1st	Paper	Clocks	13th	Lace	Textile, furs
2nd	Cotton	China	14th	Ivory	Gold jewellery
3rd	Leather	Crystal, glass	15th	Crystal	Watches
4th	Linen (silk)	Electrical appliances	20th	China	Platinum
5th	Wood	Silverware	25th	Silver	Sterling silver
6th	Iron	Wood	30th	Pearl	Diamond
7th	Wool (copper)	Desk sets	35th	Coral (jade)	Jade
8th	Bronze	Linen, lace	40th	Ruby	
9th	Pottery (china)	Leather	45th	Sapphire	
10th	Tin (aluminium)	Diamond jewellery	50th	Gold	
11th	Steel	Fashion jewellery, accessories	55th	Emerald	
12th	Silk	Pearls or coloured gems	60th	Diamond	

ANTS, BEES, AND WASPS

Amazon ant
ant or (archaic or dialect) emmet
army ant or legionary ant
bee
blue ant (Austral.)
bulldog ant, bull ant, or (Austral.) bull Joe
bumblebee or humblebee
carpenter bee
cicada hunter (Austral.)
cuckoo bee
digger wasp
driver ant
flower wasp (Austral.)
gall wasp
honeypot ant or honey ant (Austral.)
honeybee or hive bee
horntail or wood wasp
ichneumon fly or ichneumon wasp
killer bee
kootchar (Austral.)
leafcutter ant
leafcutter bee
mason bee
mason wasp
minga (Austral.)
mining bee
mud dauber
native bee or sugarbag fly (Austral.)
Pharaoh ant
policeman fly (Austral.)
ruby-tail wasp
sand wasp
Sirex wasp (Austral.)
slave ant
spider-hunting wasp
termite or white ant
velvet ant
wasp
wood ant
yellow jacket

FOUR HORSEMEN OF THE APOCALYPSE

white - Christ	red - War	black - Famine	pale - Death

APPLES

biffin (Brit.)	Egremont Russet	Jonathon	Rosemary Russet
Blenheim Orange	Elstar	Jonagold	Royal Gala
Braeburn	Empire	Laxton Superb	russet
bramley	Fuji	Lobo	Spartan
Charles Ross	Golden Delicious	Lord Lambourne	sturmer
codlin or codling	Granny Smith	Pink Lady	sunset
costard	Greensleeves	pippin	sweeting
Cox's orange pippin	Grenadier	Prince Albert	Worcester Pearmain
crab apple	Idared	Red Delicious	
Discovery	James Grieve	Red Ellison	

TYPES OF ARCH

acute, gothic, lancet, pointed arch, or ogive	horseshoe arch	arch	Roman arch
	keel arch	gee arch	skew arch
	Norman or Roman	proscenium arch	triumphal arch

ARCHAEOLOGY

ARCHAEOLOGICAL PERIODS

Acheulean or Acheulian	Châtelperronian	Levalloisian or Levallois	Neo-Babylonian
Asturian	Eneolithic	Magdalenian	Neolithic or New Stone Age
Aurignacian	Gravettian	Mesolithic	Old Babylonian
Azilian	Helladic	Minoan	Palaeolithic or Old Stone Age
Bronze Age	Ice age	Mousterian	Solutrean
chalcolithic	Iron Age	Mycenaean	
	La Tène		

ARCHAEOLOGICAL TERMS

acropolis	cartouch or cartouche	graffito	patella
alignment	caveman	henge	pylon
arcade	celt	hillfort	radiocarbon dating
archaeomagnetism or archeomagnetism	cirque	hogback	retouch
	cist or kist	hut circle	robber trench
barrow	clovis point	larnax	sondage
baulk	core	ley line	souterrain
bifacial	cromlech	microlith	stela or stele
blade	cross-dating	megalith	stone circle
bogman	dolmen	mound	stratigraphy
bracteate	earthwork	neolith	tribrach
burin	eolith	obelisk	tumulus
cairn	flake	palmette	vallum
callais	flint	palstave	

ARCHITECTURE

ARCHITECTURAL STYLES

Art Deco	churrigueresque or churrigueresco	Decorated	Empire
Art Nouveau		Doric	Federation (Austral.)
Baroque	classical	Early Christian	functionalism
Bauhaus	colonial	Early English	Georgian
brutalist	Composite	Edwardian	Gothic
Byzantine	Corinthian	Elizabethan	Gothic Revival

Greek Revival
International Style or Modernist
Ionic
Jacobean
Louis Quatorze
Louis Quinze
Louis Seize

Louis Treize
Mannerist
moderne
Moorish or Morisco
Mudéjar
neoclassicist
new brutalist
Norman

Palladian
perpendicular
postmodernist
Queen-Anne
Regency
Renaissance
Rococo
Roman

Romanesque
Saracen
Saxon
transition or transitional
Tudor
Tuscan
Victorian

ARCHITECTURAL TERMS

abutment or abuttal
architectonic
architectonics
architectural
astylar
bolster
bracket
castellated or castled
cinquecento
cloistered
colossal or giant
composite
cradling
crenellate or (U.S.) crenelate
denticulate
diastyle
diminish
dipteral
discharge
drum
elevation
engaged
eurhythmy

fenestrated
filler
flamboyant
floor plan
floriated or floreated
florid
fluted
foliated
foliation
galilee
galleria
ground plan
hexastyle
high-pitched
hip
hipped
hypostyle
imbricate or imbricated
intercolumniation
invert
joggle post or king post
lanceted

lierne
lintel or summer
listed
loggia
member
module
Moresque
naos
order
orientation
polychromy
postiche
profile
prostyle
pulvinate or pulvinated
queen post
rampant
rendering
respond
return
rhythm
ribbon development
rise

rusticate
sexpartite
shaft
shafting
shell
soffit
springing, spring, springing line, or springing point
stilted
storey
stria
stringer, string, or string course
stylobate
subbase
summer or summer tree
supercolumnar
surbase
tailpiece or tail beam
trabeate or trabeated
tympanic
underpitch vault

ARCHITECTURAL FEATURES

abacus
acanthus
accolade
acroter
aisle
ambulatory
amphiprostyle
amphistylar
ancon or ancone
annulet
anta
antefix
anthemion
apophyge or hypophyge
apse or apsis
apteral
arcade
arcature
arch
architrave
archivolt

arcuation
arris
articulation
astragal
atlas (plural atlantes) or telamon
atrium
attic
baguette or baguet
balcony
baldachin
balk
ballflower
baluster
band
banderole, banderol, or bannerol
barge couple
barge course
barrel vault, tunnel vault, or wagon vault

base
basement
bay window
bead
beak
bed moulding
belfry
bezant, bezzant, or byzant
billet
binder
bolection or bilection
bottom house
bow
bow window
bracket
brattishing
breast
broach
buttress
caisson, coffer, or lacuna

calotte
canopy
cantilever
capital, chapiter, or cap
cartouche
caryatid
case or casing
casement
Catherine wheel
cavetto
ceiling
cella or naos
cellar
channel
chaplet
cheek
chevron or dancette
choir
choir loft
cinquefoil
clerestory

cloister
colonnade
columbarium
column
columniation
compass window
concha or conch
congé
corbeil or corbeille
corbel or truss
corbie gable
corbie-step, corbel step, or crow step
cordon, string course, belt course, or table
cornice
corona
cove or coving
crenel or crenelle
cresting
crocket or crochet
crossing
crown
cullis
cupola
curb roof
curtail step
curtain wall
cushion
cusp
cuspidation
cyma
cymatium
dado
decastyle
dentil
die
dogtooth
drip
dripstone, label, or hood mould
echinus
ectype
egg and dart, egg and tongue, or egg and anchor
ell
embrasure
entablature
entasis
exedra
extrados
facade
facet
fan
fanlight
fantail

fan tracery
fan or palm vaulting
fascia or facia
fascial or facial
fenestella
fenestra
festoon
fillet or listel
finial
flèche
fluting
flying buttress or arc-boutant
foil
footing
footstall
French windows or doors
frieze
frontispiece
frustum
gable
gable end
gable window
gadroon or godroon
gallery
gambrel
gargoyle
garret
garth
gatehouse
gazebo
glyph
gradin
griffe
groin
grotto
gutta
half landing
haunch or hance
headstone
headwork
helicline
hipped or hip roof
imperial
impost
intrados
jube
keystone, quoin, or headstone
lancet arch, Gothic arch, or ogive
lancet window
landing
lantern
leaded
loggia

long-and-short work
louvre
lucarne
machicolation
mansard
meander
medallion
metope
minaret
modillion
moulding
mullion
mutule
narthex
neck
necking or gorgerin
newel
niche
Norman arch or Roman arch
obelisk
oeil-de-boeuf
offset
ogee, ogee arch, or talon
ogive
onion dome
oriel or oriel window
ovolo, quarter round, or thumb
pace
parapet
patio
pedestal
pediment
pendant
penthouse
peristyle
perpend
perron
piazza
pier
pillar
pinnacle
platform
plinth
podium
predella
pylon
quad
poppyhead
porch or portico
portal
porte-cochere
postern
propylaeum
quadrangle

quatrefoil
quirk
quoin, coign, or coigne
reed
reeding
reglet
relief
respond
return
reveal
rib
ridge
rose window, rosace, or rosette
rotunda
roundel
saddle roof or saddleback
sash window
scotia
screen
scrollwork
semidome
shaft
shafting
sill
skew arch
skylight
soffit
spandrel or spandril
spire
splay
springer
squinch
squint or hagioscope
steeple
stele or stela
stoa
straining piece
strap work
stria
strigil
stylobate or stereobate
summer
taenia or (U.S.) tenia
tambour
tellamon
term, terminal, or terminus
torus or tore
tracery
transept
traverse
trefoil
tribune

triforium	turret	veranda *or* verandah	water table
triglyph	tympanum *or* tympan	verge	web
trophy	underpitch vault	vignette	whispering gallery
trumeau	vault	volute *or* helix	xyst

ARMOUR

armet	crinet	jack	roundel
basinet *or* bascinet	cuirass	jambeau, jambart, *or*	sabaton
breastplate	cuisse *or* cuish	jamber	sword belt
camail	culet	jupon	tasset, tasse, *or* tace
chamfrain, chamfron,	gauntlet	lance rest	umbo
or chanfron	gorget	mail	vambrace
coat-of-mail	greave	nosepiece	ventail
corselet *or* corslet	gusset	pavloron	visor *or* vizor
couter	helmet	poleyn	

ART

ART STYLES AND MOVEMENTS

abstract	constructivism	minimal art	postmodernism
expressionism	cubism	modernism	Pre-Raphaelite
abstractionism	Dada *or* Dadaism	Nabis	realism
Art Deco	De Stijl	naturalism	rococo
Arte Povera	divisionism	Nazarene	Romanesque
Art Nouveau	expressionism	neoclassicism	romanticism
Barbizon School	Fauvism	neoimpressionism	Suprematism
baroque	futurism	neoplasticism	surrealism
Der Blaue Reiter	Gothic	op art	symbolism
Brücke	Impressionism	pointillism	synthetism
classicism	Jugendstil	pop art	ukiyo-e
conceptual art	mannerism	postimpressionism	vorticism

ART EQUIPMENT

acrylic	crayon	ink	paintbrush	spatula
airbrush	drawing paper	lay figure	palette	spray gun
brush	easel	linseed oil	palette knife	varnish
canvas	fixative	oil paint	pastel	watercolour
chalk	glaze	paint	pencil	
charcoal	ground	paintbox	sketchbook	

ARTHURIAN LEGEND

CHARACTERS IN ARTHURIAN LEGEND

Arthur	Gareth (of	Lancelot *or*	Morgan Le Fay	Uther Pendragon
Bedivere	Orkney)	Launcelot du	Nimue	Viviane *or* the
Bors	Gawain *or*	Lac	Parsifal *or*	Lady of the
Caradoc	Gawayne	Launfal	Perceval	Lake
Elaine	Guinevere	Merlin	Tristan *or*	
Galahad	Igraine	Modred	Tristram	

PLACES IN ARTHURIAN LEGEND

| Astolat | Avalon | Camelot | Glastonbury | Lyonnesse | Tintagel |

ASTEROIDS

| Ceres | Eros | Hermes | Hesperia | Juno | Pallas | Phaethon |

ASTROLOGY TERMS

air
Ascendant or Ascendent
aspect
birthchart
cardinal
conjunction
cusp
Descendant or Descendent
earth
element
fire
fixed
horoscope
house
Midheaven or MC
mutable
opposition
quintile
ruling planet
satellitium
square
stars
star sign
sun sign
trine
water
zodiac

ASTRONOMY TERMS

achondrite
aerolite
aerospace
aerosphere
albedo
almucantar or almacantar
altitude
analemma
annular eclipse
anthelion
aphelion
apocynthion
apolune
appulse
apapsis
apsis or apse
asteroid
asteroid belt
astrobleme
atmosphere
aureola or aureole
aurora
aurora australis
aurora borealis
azimuth
barycentre
basin
binary star
black drop
black hole
blue straggler
bolide
brown dwarf
burst
cataclysmic variable
Cepheid variable
Chandrasekhar limit
chemosphere
chondrite
chromosphere
circumlunar
circumpolar
circumsolar
circumstellar
cislunar
cluster
collapsar
colour index
colure
coma
comet
companion
conjunction
constellation
cooordinate system
Copernican system
corona
cosmic
cosmogony
cosmology
crater
crescent
crust
culmination
cusp
dwarf
dynamics
eccentric
ecosphere
effective temperature
ejecta
ellipse
elongation
emersion
ephemeris
epoch
equator
escape velocity
equinox
evection
evolved star
exosphere
extinction
facula
farside
filament
fireball
flare
flocculus
galactic centre
galactic equator
galactic rotation
galaxy
giant
gravitation
heliocentric system
heliosphere
immersion or ingress
inclination
inequality
inertia
inferior planet
inner planet
insolation
interplanetary
interstellar
ionosphere
jet
light year
limb
lodestar or loadstar
luminosity
lunar
lunar eclipse
magnetosphere
magnitude
major planet
maria
mass
mass loss
mass transfer
merger
meridian
meridian passage
mesosphere
metallicity
metal ratio
meteor
meteorite
meteoroid
meteoroid stream
meteor shower
meteor storm
missing mass
molecular cloud
moonquake
moving cluster
multiple star
nadir
naked singularity
nearside
nebula
neutron star
new moon
node
north celestial pole
northern hemisphere
northern lights
northing
north polar distance
nova
nucleosynthesis
nucleus
nutation
oblateness
obliquity
observatory
occultation
octant
open cluster
opposition
orbit
orbital elements
orbital velocity
oscillating
universe
outer planet
parallax
partial eclipse
penumbral eclipse
periapsis
periastron
percentre
perigee
perihelion
photosphere
physical libration
plages
planetary
planetary alignment
planetary system
planetesimal
planetoid
plasmasphere
plerion
polar axis
pole
precession
precession of the equinoxes
primary
prominence
proper motion
protogalaxy
protoplanet
protostar
Ptolemaic system
pulsating universe
pulsating variable
quadrature
quarter
quasar
quasi-stellar object
quiet

radiant
radio source
ray
reciprocal mass
red giant
red supergiant
regolith
retardation
revolution
ring
ring plain
rising
rotation
rupes
saros
satellite
Schwarzschild
  radius
scintillation
secondary

sextile
Seyfert galaxy
shell star
shepherd
  satellite
sidereal time
singularity
solar
solar constant
solar eclipse
solar spectrum
solar system
solstice
south celestial
  pole
southern
  hemisphere
southern lights
southing
south polar

distance
space
spacetime
spectral type or
  spectral class
spherule
spicule
spinar
spray
star
star cloud
stellar
stellar evolution
stellar structure
stellar wind
Strömgren
  sphere
sublunar point
subsolar point
substellar point

sunspot
sunspot cycle
supercluster
supergiant
superior planet
supernova
symbiotic star
synodic period
syzygy
telluric line
terminator
terrestrial planet
tidal capture
tidal force
tidal friction
tide
total eclipse
total magnitude
thermosphere
train

transient lunar
  phenomena
triple star
tropical year
troposphere
universal time
universe
variable star
variation
velocity
  dispersion
vertical circle
visual magnitude
white dwarf
white hole
zenith
zenith distance

ATHLETIC EVENTS

100 metres
110 metres
  hurdles
200 metres
400 metres
400 metres
  hurdles

800 metres
1500 metres
3000 metres
5000 metres
10 000 metres
cross-country
  running

decathlon
discus
half marathon
hammer
heptathlon
high jump
javelin

long jump
marathon
orienteering
pentathlon
pole vault
relay
shot put

steeplechase
triathlon
triple jump
walking

REGIONS OF THE ATMOSPHERE

ionosphere
mesosphere

ozone layer or
  ozonosphere

stratosphere
thermosphere

troposphere

AVIATION TERMS

aerobatics
air corridor
air miss
airside
airspeed
air traffic control
anhedral
approach or
  approach path
attitude
automatic pilot
  or autopilot
autorotation
bank
barrel roll
batsman
belly landing
bird strike
boarding pass
bunt

ceiling
chandelle
charter flight
clearway
contact flight
copilot
crab
crash-dive
crash-land
cruise
dihedral
ditch
dive
drogue
feather
flameout
flight
  management
  systems
flight path

fly-by-wire
gate
glide
groundspeed
head-up display
holding pattern
hunt
Immelmann turn
  or Immelmann
in-flight
landing
landside
loading
loop
Mach
navigator
nose dive
overfly
overshoot
pancake landing

pilot
pitch
pitch axis
power dive
rake
redeye or redeye
  flight
reheat
roll
roll axis
runway
SBA or standard
  beam approach
scheduled flight
shockstall
sideslip
snap roll
sonic boom
sound barrier
spin

stack
stall
subsonic
supersonic
tailspin
takeoff
taxi
taxiway
trim
undershoot
vapour trail
victory roll
wide-body
wingover
yaw
yaw axis

BALL GAMES

American football
Australian Rules
badminton
bagatelle
bar billiards
baseball
billiards
boules
bowling
bumble-puppy
Canadian football
crazy golf
croquet
fives
football or (U.S.) soccer
goalball
golf
handball
hockey
hurling
korfball
lacrosse
netball
paintball
piggy in the middle
pinball
pocket billiards
punchball
pushball
pyramid
rounders
snooker
squash
Subbuteo (trademark)
tennis
volleyball

BATS

barbastelle
false vampire
flying fox
fruit bat
hammerhead
horseshoe bat
insectivorous bat
kalong
noctule
pipistrelle
serotine
vampire bat

FAMOUS BATTLES

Aboukir Bay or Abukir Bay	1798	Hastings	1066	Prestonpans	1745
Actium	31 B.C.	Hohenlinden	1800	Pydna	168 B.C.
Agincourt	1415	Imphal	1944	Quatre Bras	1815
Alamo	1836	Inkerman	1854	Ramillies	1706
Arnhem	1944	Issus	333 B.C.	Roncesvalles	778
Atlantic	1939-45	Jemappes	1792	Sadowa or Sadová	1866
Austerlitz	1805	Jena	1806	Saint-Mihiel	1918
Balaklava or Balaclava	1854	Killiecrankie	1689	Salamis	480 B.C.
Bannockburn	1314	Kursk	1943	Sedgemoor	1685
Barnet	1471	Ladysmith	1899-1900	Sempach	1386
Bautzen	1813	Le Cateau	1914	Shiloh	1862
Belleau Wood	1918	Leipzig	1813	Shipka Pass	1877-78
Blenheim	1704	Lepanto	1571	Somme	1916; 1918
Borodino	1812	Leyte Gulf	1944	Stalingrad	1941-42
Bosworth Field	1485	Little Bighorn	1876	Stamford Bridge	1066
Boyne	1690	Lützen	1632	Stirling Bridge	1297
Britain	1940	Manassas	1861; 1862	Tannenberg	1410; 1914
Bulge	1944-45	Mantinea or Mantineia	418 B.C.; 362 B.C.	Tewkesbury	1471
Bull Run	1861;1862	Marathon	490 B.C.	Thermopylae	480 B.C.
Bunker Hill	1775	Marengo	1800	Tobruk	1941; 1942
Cannae	216 B.C.	Marston Moor	1644	Trafalgar	1805
Crécy	1346	Missionary Ridge	1863	Trenton	1776
Culloden	1746	Naseby	1645	Verdun	1916
Dien Bien Phu	1954	Navarino	425 B.C.	Vitoria	1813
Edgehill	1642	Omdurman	1898	Wagram	1809
El Alamein	1942	Passchendaele	1917	Waterloo	1815
Falkirk	1298; 1746	Philippi	42 B.C.	Ypres	1914; 1915; 1917; 1918
Flodden	1513	Plains of Abraham	1759		
Gettysburg	1863	Plassey	1757	Zama	202 B.C.
Guadalcanal	1942-3	Plataea	479 B.C.		
		Poltava	1709		

BEERS

ale
barley wine
Bière de Garde
black and tan
bock beer or bock
boilermaker
bottle-conditioned beer or ale
brown ale
cask-conditioned beer or ale
Christmas beer or ale
draught beer
eighty shilling or eighty
export

fruit beer
guest beer
gueuze
half-and-half
heavy *(Scot.)*
home-brew
ice beer
India Pale Ale *or* IPA
Kaffir beer
keg beer

Kölsch
lager
lambic
light *(Scot.)*
light ale
mild
milk stout
nog *or* nogg *(dialect)*
pale ale
Pils

Pilsner *or* Pilsener
plain *(Irish)*
porter
Rauchbier
real ale
seventy shilling *or*
  seventy
shandy
shebeen *or* shebean
  (Irish) (U.S.)

sixty shilling *or* sixty
special
stingo
stout
sweet stout
Trappist beer
Weissbier
Weizenbier
wheat beer

BEETLES

ambrosia beetle
Asiatic beetle
bacon beetle
bark beetle
bee beetle
black beetle *or (N.Z.)*
  kekerengu *or* Māori
  bug
blister beetle
bloody-nosed beetle
boll weevil
bombardier beetle
burying beetle *or*
  sexton
cabinet beetle
cardinal beetle
carpet beetle *or (U.S.)*
  carpet bug
carrion beetle
chafer
Christmas beetle *or*

king beetle
churchyard beetle
click beetle, snapping
  beetle, *or* skipjack
cockchafer, May
  beetle, *or* May bug
Colorado beetle *or*
  potato beetle
curculio
deathwatch beetle
devil's coach-horse
diving beetle
dor
dung beetle *or* chafer
elater
firefly
flea beetle
furniture beetle
glow-worm
gold beetle *or* goldbug
goldsmith beetle

goliath beetle
ground beetle
Hercules beetle
huhu
Japanese beetle
June bug, June beetle,
  May bug, *or* May
  beetle
ladybird *or (U.S. &*
  Canad.) ladybug
larder beetle
leaf beetle
leather beetle
longicorn (beetle) *or*
  long-horned beetle
May beetle,
  cockchafer, *or* June
  bug
museum beetle
oil beetle
pill beetle

rhinoceros beetle
rose chafer *or* rose
  beetle
rove beetle
scarab
scavenger beetle
snapping beetle
snout beetle
soldier beetle
Spanish fly
stag beetle
tiger beetle
timberman beetle
tortoise beetle
vedalia
water beetle
weevil *or* snout beetle
weevil, pea weevil, *or*
  bean weevil
whirligig beetle

BIBLE

BOOKS OF THE BIBLE (OLD TESTAMENT)

Genesis	1 Samuel	Esther	Lamentations	Micah
Exodus	2 Samuel	Job	Ezekiel	Nahum
Leviticus	1 Kings	Psalms	Daniel	Habakkuk
Numbers	2 Kings	Proverbs	Hosea	Zephaniah
Deuteronomy	1 Chronicles	Ecclesiastes	Joel	Haggai
Joshua	2 Chronicles	Song of Solomon	Amos	Zechariah
Judges	Ezra	Isaiah	Obadiah	Malachi
Ruth	Nehemiah	Jeremiah	Jonah	

BOOKS OF THE BIBLE (NEW TESTAMENT)

Matthew	1 Corinthians	1 Thessalonians	Hebrews	3 John
Mark	2 Corinthians	2 Thessalonians	James	Jude
Luke	Galatians	1 Timothy	1 Peter	Revelation
John	Ephesians	2 Timothy	2 Peter	
Acts	Philippians	Titus	1 John	
Romans	Colossians	Philemon	2 John	

BOOKS OF THE BIBLE (APOCRYPHA)

Tobit	2 Maccabees	Baruch	Daniel, Bel and	Esdras
Judith	Wisdom	Daniel and	the Snake	Manasseh
1 Maccabees	Ecclesiasticus	Susanna	Song of the Three	

CHARACTERS IN THE BIBLE

Aaron	Dinah	James	Mark	Rachel
Abednego	Dives	Japheth	Martha	Rebecca
Abel	Dorcas	Jehoshaphat	Mary	Reuben
Abigail	Elias	Jehu	Mary Magdalene	Ruth
Abraham	Elijah	Jephthah or	Matthew	Salome
Absalom	Elisha	Jephte	Matthias	Samson
Achitophel or	Enoch	Jeremiah	Melchior	Samuel
Ahithophel	Enos	Jeroboam	Melchizedek or	Sarah
Adam	Ephraim	Jesse	Melchisedech	Saul
Ahab	Esau	Jesus Christ	Meshach	Seth
Ahasuerus	Esther	Jethro	Methuselah	Shadrach
Ammon	Eve	Jezebel	Micah	Shem
Amos	Ezekiel	Joab	Midian	Simeon
Ananias	Ezra	Job	Miriam	Simon
Andrew	Gabriel	Joel	Mordecai	Solomon
Asher	Gad	John	Moses	Susanna
Balaam	Gideon	John the Baptist	Nabonidus	Tetragrammaton
Balthazar	Gilead	Jonah or Jonas	Naboth	Thaddeus or
Barabbas	Gog and Magog	Jonathan	Nahum	Thadeus
Bartholomew	Goliath	Joseph	Naomi	Thomas
Baruch	Good Samaritan	Joshua	Naphtali	Tobit
Bathsheba	Habakkuk	Josiah	Nathan	Tubal-cain
Beelzebub	Hagar	Jubal	Nathanael	Uriah
Belial	Haggai	Judah	Nebuchadnezzar	Virgin Mary
Belshazzar	Ham	Judas Iscariot	or	Zacharias,
Benjamin	Hannah	Jude	Nebuchadrezzar	Zachariah, or
Boanerges	Herod	Judith	Nehemiah	Zachary
Boaz	Hezekiah	Laban	Nicodemus	Zebedee
Caiaphas	Hiram	Lazarus	Nimrod	Zebulun
Cain	Holofernes	Leah	Noah	Zechariah
Caspar	Hosea	Levi	Obadiah	Zedekiah
Cush or Kush	Isaac	Lot	Paul	Zephaniah
Dan	Isaiah	Lot's wife	Peter	Zilpah
Daniel	Ishmael	Luke	Philip	
David	Issachar	Magus	Potiphar	
Deborah	Jacob	Malachi	Prodigal Son	
Delilah	Jael	Manasseh	Queen of Sheba	

PLACE NAMES IN THE BIBLE

Aceldama	Calvary	Gethsemane	land of milk and	Shinar
Antioch	Cana	Golgotha	honey	Shittim
Aram	Canaan	Gomorrah or	land of Nod	Sodom
Ararat	Capernaum	Gomorrha	Moab	Tadmor
Arimathaea or	Eden	Goshen	Nazareth	Tophet or
Arimathea	Galilee	Horeb	On	Topheth
Babel	Garden of Eden	Jericho	Ophir	wilderness
Bashan	Gath	Jerusalem	Rabbath Ammon	
Bethesda	Gaza	Judaea or Judea	Samaria	
Bethlehem	Gehenna	Judah	Shiloh	

BICYCLES

BICYCLE PARTS

bell	crossbar	mileometer	pedal	saddlebag
bicycle chain	handlebars	mudguard	rat-trap	stabilizer
bicycle pump	kickstand	pannier	saddle	wheel

TYPES OF BICYCLE

autocycle	boneshaker	fairy cycle	roadster
bicycle	chopper	mountain bike	tandem
BMX	exercise bike	penny-farthing	velocipede

BIOLOGY

BRANCHES OF BIOLOGY

actinobiology	biogeography	cytogenetics	oceanography	radiobiology
aerobiology	biometry	cytology	organography	sociobiology
agrobiology	biophysics	ecology	organology	somatology
astrobiology	biostatics	genetics	palaeontology	stoichiology
bacteriology	biostatics	histology	parasitology	taxonomy
biochemistry	botany	microbiology	photobiology	teratology
biodynamics	chronobiology	morphology	photodynamics	zoology
	cryobiology			

BIOLOGY TERMS

aerobic	dorsal	kingdom	protoplasm
agglutination	ecosystem	Krebs cycle	puberty
albino	egg	life cycle	recessive
allele or allelomorph	embryo	meiosis	reproduction
anaerobic	environment	menstruation	respiration
anterior	enzyme	metabolism	RNA or ribose nucleic
asexual reproduction	epidermis	metamorphosis	acid
assimilation	evolution	mitosis	ribosome
bacteria	excretion	muscle	root
binary fission	family	mutation	seed
biomass	fermentation	natural selection	sexual reproduction
blood	fertilization	nitrogen cycle	skeleton
blood vessel	flower	nucleus	skin
bone	foetus	order	soil
cell	food chain	organ	species
chromosome	fossil	osmosis	spermatozoon or
circulation	fruit	ovulation	sperm
circulatory system	fungus	ovum	spore
class	gamete	parasite	symbiosis
clone	gene	pathogen	translocation
codominance	genus	pectoral	transpiration
cold-blooded	germination	photosynthesis	ventral
conception	gestation	phylum	vertebrate
copulation	gland	poikilothermic	virus
cytoplasm	gonad	pollen	vitamin
diffusion	growth	pollination	viviparous
digestion	haploid	pollution	warm-blooded
diploid	heredity	posterior	X-chromosome
division	hermaphrodite	predator	Y-chromosome
DNA or	hormone	pregnancy	zygote
deoxyribonucleic	hybrid	progeny	
acid	inheritance	propagation	
dominant	invertebrate	protein	

BIRDS

accentor	family bird (Austral.)	Baltimore oriole	bee-eater
amazon	avadavat or amadavat	banded dotterel (N.Z.)	bellbird or (N.Z.)
amokura (N.Z.)	avocet	banded rail (N.Z.)	koromako or
ani	axebird (Austral.)	barbet	makomako
apostle bird or happy	babbler	beccafico	bird of paradise

bishopbird
bittern
blackbird
blackcap
blackcock
black-fronted tern or tara (N.Z.)
black grouse
blackpoll
black robin (N.Z.)
bluebird
blue duck, mountain duck, whio or whistling duck (N.Z.)
blue grouse
blue jay
bluethroat
bluetit
boatbill or boat-billed heron
bobolink
bobwhite
bokmakierie
boobook (Austral.)
bowerbird
brain-fever bird or (Austral.) pallid cuckoo
brambling
broadbill
brolga, Australian crane, or (Austral.) native companion
brown creeper or pipipi (N.Z.)
brown duck (N.Z.)
brown kiwi (N.Z.)
budgerigar or (Austral.) zebra parrot
bulbul
bullfinch
bunting
bush shrike
bushtit
bush wren (N.Z.)
bustard or (Austral.) plain turkey, plains turkey, or wild turkey
button quail or (Austral.) bustard quail
cacique
Californian quail (N.Z.)
canary
Cape Barren goose

Cape pigeon
capercaillie or capercailzie
Cape sparrow
capuchin
cardinal or cardinal grosbeak
carrion crow
cassowary
catbird
chaffinch
chat
chickadee
chicken or (Austral. informal) chook
chiffchaff
chimney swallow or chimney swift
chipping sparrow
chough
chuck-will's-widow
chukar
cliff swallow
coal tit or coletit
cockatiel, cockateel, or cockatoo-parrot
cockatoo
cock-of-the-rock
collared dove
coly or mousebird
conure
coppersmith
coquette
corella
corn bunting
corncrake
cotinga or chatterer
coucal, pheasant coucal, or swamp pheasant
cowbird
crake
crane
crested tit
crocodile bird
crombec
crossbill
crow or (Scot.) corbie
cuckoo
cuckoo-shrike
cumulet
curassow
curlew
currawong or bell magpie
dabchick
darter, anhinga, or snakebird

demoiselle (crane) or Numidian crane
diamond bird or pardalote
dipper or water ouzel
diver
dollarbird
dotterel or dottrel
dove or (archaic or poetic) culver
dowitcher
drongo
dunlin or red-backed sandpiper
egret
emperor penguin
emu
emu-wren
fantail or (N.Z.) piwakawaka
fernbird (N.Z.)
fieldfare
fig-bird
finch
finfoot
firebird
firecrest
flamingo
flower-pecker
flycatcher
francolin
friarbird
frogmouth
galah or (Austral.) galar or gillar
gang-gang
gnatcatcher
go-away bird
godwit
goldcrest
golden oriole
goldfinch
Gouldian finch, painted finch, or purple-breasted finch
grackle or crow blackbird
grassfinch
grassquit
great crested grebe or loon
great northern diver
great tit
grebe
greenfinch
green leek
greenlet

greenshank
green woodpecker
grey-crowned babbler, happy family bird, Happy Jack, or parson bird (Austral.)
grey warbler or rirориro (N.Z.)
grosbeak
grouse
guan
guinea fowl
hadedah
hawfinch
hazelhen
hedge sparrow or dunnock
helldiver, pie-billed grebe, or dabchick
hen harrier or (U.S. & Canad.) marsh harrier
heron
hill myna
hoatzin or hoactzin
homing pigeon
honey creeper
honeyeater
honey guide
honeysucker
hooded crow
hoopoe
hornbill
house martin
house sparrow
hummingbird or trochilus
ibis
jabiru or (Austral.) policeman bird
jacamar
jaçana or lily-trotter
jackdaw
jacksnipe
Jacobin
jaeger (U.S.) (Canad.)
Java sparrow
jay
junco
jungle fowl
kagu
kaka (N.Z.)
kakapo (N.Z.)
kakariki (N.Z.)
karoro or blackbacked gull (N.Z.)
kea (N.Z.)

killdeer
kingbird
kingfisher or (N.Z.) kotare
king penguin
kiwi or apteryx
knot
koel or (Austral.) black cuckoo or cooee bird
kokako or blue-wattled crow (N.Z.)
kookaburra, laughing jackass, or (Austral.) bushman's clock, settler's clock, goburra, or great brown kingfisher
kotuku or white heron (N.Z.)
Lahore
lapwing or green plover
lark
limpkin or courlan
linnet
locust bird
loggerhead shrike
longspur
long-tailed tit
lorikeet
lory
lourie
lovebird
lyrebird or (Austral.) buln-buln
macaw
magpie or (Austral.) piping shrike or piping crow-shrike
magpie lark or (Austral.) mudlark, Murray magpie, mulga, or peewit
Major Mitchell or Leadbeater's cockatoo
makomako (Austral.)
marabou
marsh tit
martin
meadowlark
meadow pipit
metallic starling or shining starling (Austral.)
minivet
miromiro (N.Z.)

mistle thrush or missel thrush
mistletoe bird (Austral.)
mockingbird
mohua or bush canary (N.Z.)
monal or monaul
motmot or sawbill
mourning dove
myna, mynah, or mina
New Zealand pigeon or kereru (N.Z.)
nighthawk, bullbat, or mosquito hawk
night heron
nightingale
nightjar, (U.S. & Canad.) goatsucker, or (Austral.) nighthawk
noddy
noisy friarbird or leatherhead
noisy miner or (Austral.) micky or soldier bird
notornis
nun
nutcracker
nuthatch
oil bird or guacharo
oriole
ortolan or ortolan bunting
ostrich
ouzel or ousel
ovenbird
oxpecker or tick-bird
paradise duck or putangitangi (N.Z.)
parakeet or parrakeet
pardalote (Austral.)
parrot
partridge
peacock
peafowl
peewit
pelican
penguin
phalarope
pheasant
pied goose or magpie goose
pied wagtail
pigeon
pipit or (N.Z.) pihoihoi
pipiwharauroa or

bronze-winged cuckoo (N.Z.)
pitta (Austral.)
plover
pratincole
ptarmigan
puffbird
puffin
pukeko
purple gallinule
pyrrhuloxia
quail
quarrian or quarrion
quetzal
racket-tail
rail
rainbow bird
rainbow lorikeet
raven
red-backed shrike
redbreast
red grouse
red-legged partridge
redpoll
redshank
redstart
redwing
reedbird
reed bunting
reedling or bearded tit
reed warbler
regent-bird or regent bowerbird
regent honeyeater
rhea or American ostrich
ricebird
riflebird
rifleman or (N.Z.) titipounamu
ringed plover
ring-necked pheasant
ringneck parrot, Port Lincoln parrot, or buln-buln (Austral.)
ring ouzel
roadrunner or chaparral cock
robin or robin redbreast
rock dove or rock pigeon
rockhopper
roller
rook
rosella
rosy finch
ruff

ruffed grouse
runt
saddleback
saddlebill or jabiru
sage grouse
sanderling
sandgrouse
sand martin
sandpiper
sapsucker
satin bowerbird
Scandaroon
scarlet tanager
scrub bird
sedge warbler
seriema
serin
sheathbill
shoebill
shore bird or (Brit.) wader
shrike or butcherbird
sicklebill
silver-eye (Austral.)
siskin or (formerly) aberdevine
sitella or tree-runner
skimmer
skylark
snipe
snow bunting
snowy egret
solitaire
song sparrow
song thrush or mavis
sora
sparrow
spoonbill
spotted crake or (Austral.) water crake
spotted flycatcher
spotted sandpiper or (U.S.) peetweet
squacco
starling
stilt
stint
stock dove
stonechat
stone curlew or thick-knee
stork
sugar bird
sulphur-crested cockatoo or white cockatoo
sunbird

sun bittern
superb blue wren (Austral.)
superb lyrebird (Austral.)
surfbird
swallow
swift
swiftlet
swordbill
tailorbird
takahe
tanager
tattler
tawny pippit
tern
thornbill
thrasher
thrush or (poetic) throstle
tit
titmouse
tody
topknot pigeon
(Austral.)
toucan
touraco, turaco, or plantain-eater
towhee
tragopan
tree creeper
tree sparrow
trochilus
trogon
tropicbird
troupial
trumpeter
tui or parson bird (N.Z.)
turtledove
twite
umbrella bird
veery
verdin
wader or wading bird
wagtail
wall creeper
warbler
water rail
water thrush
wattlebird
waxbill
waxwing
weaverbird or weaver
weka, weka rail, Māori hen, or wood hen (N.Z.)
wheatear
whimbrel
whinchat
whip bird
whippoorwill
white-eye or (N.Z.) blighty, silvereye, tauhou or waxeye
white-fronted tern or kahawai bird (N.Z.)
whitethroat
whooping crane
willet
willow grouse
willow tit
willow warbler
wonga-wonga or wonga pigeon
woodchat or woodchat shrike
woodcock
wood ibis
woodlark
woodpecker
wood pigeon, ringdove, cushat, (Scot.) cushie-doo, or (English dialect) quist
woodswallow
wood warbler
wren
wrybill
wryneck
yellowhammer
yellowtail or yellowtail kingfisher (Austral.)
zebra finch

EXTINCT BIRDS

archaeopteryx
archaeornis
dodo
great auk
huia (N.Z.)
ichthyornis
moa
notornis
passenger pigeon
piopio (N.Z.)
solitaire

BISCUITS

abernethy
amaretti
bannock (Scot.)
Bath Oliver
bourbon
brandy snap
captain's biscuit
caramel wafer
chocolate digestive
cookie (chiefly U.S.) (Canad.)
cracker
cracknel
cream cracker
crispbread
digestive
Empire biscuit
fairing
farl
flapjack
Florentine
garibaldi
gingerbread man
ginger nut or ginger snap
graham cracker (U.S.)
hardtack, ship's biscuit, pilot biscuit, or sea biscuit
Jaffa cake (trademark)
langue de chat
lebkuchen
love letter
macaroon
matzo
oatcake
petit four
pretzel
ratafia
rich tea
rusk
shortbread
shortcake
soda biscuit
sweetmeal biscuit or digestive
Tararua biscuit (N.Z.)
tea biscuit
wafer
water biscuit

BLOOD CELLS

phagocytic white blood cell
erythrocyte
haemocyte
leucocyte
lymphocyte
macrocyte
microcyte
poikilocyte
polymorph
reticulocyte

BOARD GAMES

acey-deucy
backgammon
bagatelle
chequers
chess
Chinese chequers
Cluedo (trademark)
draughts
fox and geese
go or I-go
halma
kriegspiel
lightning chess
ludo
Monopoly (trademark)
nine men's morris
Parcheesi (trademark)
reversi
shove-halfpenny
snakes and ladders
solitaire
speed chess

BOATS AND SHIPS

airboat
aircraft carrier
auxiliary
banker
barge
barque
barquentine *or* barquintine
bateau
bathyscaph, bathyscaphe, *or* bathyscape
battlecruiser
battleship
Bermuda rig
boatel
brigantine
bulk carrier
bumboat
cabin cruiser
canal boat
canoe
caravel *or* carvel
carrack
catamaran
catboat
caïque
clipper
coble
cockboat *or* cockleboat
cockleshell
coracle
corvette
crabber
cruiser
cutter
destroyer

destroyer escort
dhow
dinghy
dogger
dory
dreadnought *or* dreadnaught
dredger
drifter
dromond *or* dromon
E-boat
factory ship
faltboat
felucca
ferry
fireboat
fishing boat
flatboat
flotel *or* floatel
flyboat
fore-and-after
foyboat
freighter
frigate
galleas
galleon
galley
gig
gondola
gunboat
hooker
houseboat
hoy
hydrofoil
hydroplane
icebreaker
ice yacht *or*

scooter
Indiaman
ironclad
jet-boat
jolly boat
junk
kayak
keelboat
ketch
laker
landing craft
lapstrake *or* lapstreak
launch
lifeboat
lightship
liner
longboat
longship
lugger
man-of-war *or* man o' war
maxi
merchantman
minehunter
minelayer
minesweeper
monitor
monohull
motorboat
MTB (motor torpedo boat)
multihull
MY *or* motor yacht
narrow boat
nuggar
outboard

outrigger
oysterman
packet boat
paddle steamer
pink
pocket battleship
polacre *or* polacca
powerboat
proa *or* prau
PT boat
púcán
punt
quinquereme
raft
randan
revenue cutter
rowboat
rowing boat
sailing boat *or* (U.S. & Canad.) sailboat
scow
schooner
scull
sealer
shallop
shell
ship of the line
sidewheeler
skiff
skipjack
sloop
speedboat
steamboat
steamer
steamship

stern-wheeler
submarine
supertanker
surfboat
swamp boat
tall ship
tanker
tartan
tender
threedecker
torpedo boat
torpedo-boat destroyer
towboat
trawler
trimaran
trireme
troopship
tub
tug *or* tugboat
U-boat
umiak *or* oomiak
vaporetto
vedette
VJ (vaucluse junior)
warship
weathership
whaler
wherry
windjammer
xebec, zebec, *or* zebeck
yacht
yawl

PARTS OF THE BODY

Part of the body	Technical name	Related adjective	Part of the body	Technical name	Related adjective
abdomen	-	abdominal	belly	venter	ventral
adenoids	pharyngeal tonsil	adenoid *or* adenoidal	bladder	urinary bladder	vesical
alimentary canal	-		blood	-	haemal, haemic, *or* haematic
ankle	talus	-	bone	os	osseous, osteal, *or* osteoid
anus	-	anal			
appendix	vermiform appendix	appendicular	brain	encephalon	cerebral
			breast	-	-
arm	brachium	brachial	buttocks	nates	natal *or* gluteal
armpit	axilla	axillary	caecum	-	caecal
artery	-	arterial	calf	-	-
back	-	dorsal	capillary	-	capillary

Part of the body	Technical name	Related adjective	Part of the body	Technical name	Related adjective
cervix	-	cervical	knee	genu	genicular
cheek	gena	genal	knuckle	-	-
chest	-	pectoral	labia majora	-	labial
chin	-	genial or mental	labia minora	-	labial
clitoris	-	clitoral	large intestine	-	-
colon	-	colonic	leg	crus	crural
duodenum	-	duodenal	lip	-	labial
ear	-	aural	liver	-	hepatic
elbow	-	-	loin	lumbus	lumbar
epiglottis	-	epiglottal	lung	-	pulmonary
external ear	auricle or pinna	-	lymph cell	lymphocyte	-
eye	-	ocular or ophthalmic	lymph node	-	-
eyebrow	-	superciliary	midriff	diaphragm	-
eyelash	cilium	ciliary	mons pubis	-	-
eyelid	-	palpebral	mons veneris		
Fallopian tube	oviduct	oviducal or oviductal	mouth	-	stomatic
finger	-	digital	nape	nucha	nuchal
fingernail	-	ungual or ungular	navel or omphalos	umbilicus	umbilical
fist	-	-	neck	cervix	cervical
follicle	-	follicular	nerve	-	neural
fontanelle or (chiefly U.S.) fontanel	-	-	nerve cell	neuron or neurone	neuronic|
foot	pes	pedal	nipple or teat	mamilla or papilla	mamillary
forearm	-	cubital	nose	-	nasal
forehead	-	frontal	nostril	naris	narial or narine
foreskin	prepuce	preputial	occiput	-	occipital
gall bladder	-	-	ovary	-	ovarian
gland	-	adenoid	pancreas	-	pancreatic
glottis	-	glottic	penis	-	penile
groin	-	inguinal	pharynx	-	pharyngeal
gullet	oesophagus	oesophageal	pubes	-	pubic
gum	gingiva	gingival	rectum	-	rectal
hamstring	-	popliteal	red blood cell	erythrocyte	erythrocytic
hard palate	-	-	ribcage	-	-
hair	-	-	scalp	-	-
half-moon	lunula or lunule	-	scrotum	-	scrotal
hand	manus	manual	shin	-	-
head	caput	capital	shoulder	-	-
heart	-	cardiac	side	-	-
heel	-	-	skin	cutis	cutaneous
hip	-	-	small intestine		
ileum	-	ileac or ileal	soft palate	-	-
inner ear or internal ear	labyrinth	-	sole	-	plantar
instep	-	-	spleen	-	lienal or splenetic
intestine	-	alvine	stomach	-	gastric
jaw	-	gnathic or gnathal	tear duct	lacrimal duct	-
jejunum	-	jejunal			
jugular vein	-	-			
kidney	-	renal or nephritic			

Part of the body	Technical name	Related adjective	Part of the body	Technical name	Related adjective
temple	-	temporal	umbilical cord	umbilicus	-
tendon	-	-	ureter	-	ureteral or ureteric
testicle	-	testicular	urethra	-	urethral
thigh	-	femoral or crural	vagina	-	vaginal
thorax	-	thoracic	vein	vena	venous
throat	-	guttural, gular, or jugular	vocal cords	glottis	glottal
			voice box	larynx	laryngeal
thumb	pollex	pollical	vulva	-	vulval, vulvar, or vulvate
toe	-	-			
toenail	-	ungual or ungular	waist	-	-
tongue	lingua	lingual or glottic	white blood cell	leucocyte	leucocytic
tonsil	-	tonsillar or tonsillary			
torso	-	-	windpipe	trachea	tracheal or tracheate
transverse colon	-	-	womb	uterus	uterine
trunk	-	-	wrist	carpus	-

BOMBS

atom bomb or A-bomb	fusion bomb	incendiary bomb	pipe bomb
bangalore torpedo	grenade	Mills bomb	plastic bomb
blockbuster	hand grenade	Molotov cocktail	stun grenade
bouncing bomb	hydrogen bomb	nail bomb	time bomb
cluster bomb	improvised explosive device or IED	neutron bomb	
depth charge	incendiary or	nuclear bomb	
		petrol bomb	

BONES

Bone	Nontechnical names	Bone	Nontechnical names
astragalus	anklebone	occipital bone	-
calcaneus	heel bone	parietal bone	-
carpal	wrist	patella	kneecap
carpus	wrist	pelvis	-
clavicle	collarbone	phalanx	-
coccyx	-	pubis	-
costa	rib	radius	-
cranium	brainpan	rib	-
cuboid	-	sacrum	-
ethmoid	-	scapula	shoulder blade
femur	thighbone	skull	-
fibula	-	sphenoid	-
frontal bone	-	spinal column or spine	backbone
hallux	-	stapes	stirrup
humerus	-	sternum	breastbone
hyoid	-	talus	anklebone
ilium	-	tarsal	-
incus	anvil	tarsus	-
innominate bone	hipbone	temporal bone	-
ischium	-	tibia	shinbone
malleus	hammer	ulna	-
mandible	lower jawbone	vertebra	-
maxilla	upper jawbone	vertebral column	backbone
metacarpal	-	zygomatic bone	cheekbone
metatarsal	-		
metatarsus	-		

BOOKS

TYPES OF BOOK

album
almanac
anatomy
annual
anthology
armorial
A to Z
atlas
autobiography
Baedeker
bestiary
bibelot
Bible
biography
breviary
brochure
casebook
catalogue
catechism
coffee-table
    book
comic book
commonplace
    book
companion
compendium
concordance
confessional
cookery book
copybook
diary
dictionary
directory
dispensatory
encyclopedia or
    encyclopaedia
exercise book
formulary
gazetteer
gradus
grammar
graphic novel
grimoire
guidebook
handbook
hymn book
jotter
journal
lectionary
ledger
lexicon
log or logbook
manual
miscellany
missal
monograph
notebook
novel
novelette
novella
ordinal
peerage
pharmacopoeia
phrase book
prayer book
primer
prospectus
psalter
reader
reference book
register
road book
score
scrapbook
service book
sketchbook
song book
speller
statute book
storybook
telephone
    directory
textbook
thesaurus
vade mecum
who's who
wordbook
workbook
yearbook

PARTS OF A BOOK

acknowledgments
addendum
afterword
appendix
back
back matter
bibliography
binding
blurb
chapter
contents
corrigenda
cover
dedication
dust jacket or cover
endpaper
epigraph
epilogue
errata
flyleaf
folio
fore-edge
foreword
frontispiece
front matter
glossary
gutter
half-title
illustration
index
interleaf
introduction
leaf
margin
page
plate
postscript
preface
prelims
proem
prolegomenon
prologue
recto
rubric
running head
slipcase
spine
tail
title page
verso
wrapper

BOTANY

BRANCHES OF BOTANY

agrostology
algology
archaeobotany or
    archeobotany
astrobotany
bryology
carpology
dendrology
ethnobotany
floristics
mycology
palaeobotany
palaeoethnobotany
phytogenesis
phytogeography
phytography
phytopathology
pteridology

BOTANY TERMS

abscission
androecium
androgynous
anther
archegonium
auxin
axil
axis
berry
bulb
calyx
cambium
carpel
chlorophyll
chloroplast
corm
corolla
corona
cortex
cotyledon
cross-pollination
cuticle
dicotyledon
epidermis
filament
flower
foliation
fruit
geotropism
germination
guard cell
gynaecium
hilum
hydrotropism
inflorescence
insect pollination
integument
key
lamina
leaf

legume
lenticel
meristem
mesophyll
micropyle
monocotyledon
nastic movement
nut
operculum
ovary
ovule
palisade mesophyll
phloem
photosynthesis
phototropism
pistil
pith
plumule
pollen
pollination
raceme
radicle
receptacle
rhizome
root
root cap
root hair
root nodule
rosette
runner
sap
seed
seed capsule or
  seedcase
seed pod
seed vessel
self-pollination
sepal
shoot
spadix
spongy mesophyll
sporangium
spore
stamen
stem
stigma
stolon
stoma
style
testa
translocation
transpiration
tropism
tuber
vascular bundle
vegetative
  reproduction
wind pollination
xylem

BOXING WEIGHTS

Weight	Amateur	Professional	Weight	Amateur	Professional
Light flyweight	48 kg	49 kg	Welterweight	67 kg	66.6 kg
Flyweight	51 kg		Light middleweight	71 kg	70 kg
Bantamweight	54 kg	53.5 kg	Middleweight	75 kg	72.5 kg
Featherweight	57 kg		Light heavyweight	81 kg	79 kg
Junior lightweight	-	59 kg	Cruiserweight	-	88.5 kg
Lightweight	60 kg	61 kg	Heavyweight	91 kg	+88.5 kg
Light welterweight	63.5 kg		Superheavyweight	+91 kg	-

PARTS OF THE BRAIN

amygdala
brainstem
Broca's area
central sulcus
cerebellum
cerebral aqueduct
cerebral cortex or
  (nontechnical) grey
  matter
cerebrospinal fluid
cerebrum
choroid plexus
corpus callosum
diencephalon
fourth ventricle
frontal lobe
hippocampus
hypothalamus
infundibulum
limbic system
mamillary body
medulla oblongata
meninges
midbrain
myelencephalon
  or (nontechnical)
  afterbrain
occipital lobe
optic chiasma
parietal lobe
pineal body
pituitary gland
pons Varolli
substantia alba or
  (nontechnical) white
  matter
temporal lobe
thalamus
third ventricle
vermis
Wernicke's area

BREADS

bagel or beigel
baguette
bap
barm cake
  (dialect)
barmbrack (Irish)
barm cake
  (Lancashire)
batch loaf
billy-bread (N.Z.)
black bread
bloomer
bridge roll
brioche
brown bread,
  loaf, or roll
bun
buttery (Scot.)
challah or hallah
chapati or
  chapatti
ciabatta
cob
coburg
corn bread, corn
  pone, or Indian
  bread (U.S.)
cottage loaf
croissant
damper (Austral.)
farmhouse
focaccia
French bread
French stick
fruit loaf
Granary
  (trademark)
gluten bread
griddlebread
half-quartern
johnny cake
long tin
matzo, matzoh,
  matza, or
  matzah
muffin
naan or nan
pan bread or loaf
(Scot.)
paratha
pitta
plain bread or loaf
  (Scot.)
plait
poppadom or
  poppadum
puri
quartern
roll
roti
rye bread or rye
schnecken
soda bread
sourdough
split tin
square tin
stollen
tortilla
unleavened
  bread
wheaten bread
white bread, loaf,
  or roll
wholemeal
  or (esp U.S. &
  Canad.) whole-
  wheat

TYPES OF BRIDGE

aqueduct
Bailey bridge
balance, bascule, or counterpoise bridge
box-girder bridge
cable-stayed bridge
cantilever bridge
clapper bridge
deck bridge
drawbridge
flyover
footbridge
pivot, swing, or turn bridge
pontoon bridge
snow bridge
suspension bridge
truss bridge
turn bridge
viaduct

SCHOOLS OF BUDDHISM

Foism
Geluk
Hinayana
Jodo
Kagyü
Lamaism
Mahayana
Nichiren
Nyingma
Pure Land Buddhism
Rinjai
Sakya
Soka Gakkai
Soto
Tendai
Theravada
Vajrayana
Zen

BUTTERFLIES AND MOTHS

apollo
argus
bag moth (N.Z.)
bagworm moth
bell moth
bogong or bugong (moth)
brimstone
brown-tail moth
buff-tip moth
cabbage white
cactoblastis
Camberwell beauty or (U.S.) mourning cloak
cardinal
carpenter moth
carpet moth
cleopatra
comma butterfly
copper
cecropia moth
cinnabar
clearwing or clearwing moth
Clifden nonpareil
codlin(g) moth
death's-head moth
drinker moth or drinker
egger or eggar
ermine moth or ermine
festoon
ghost moth
gipsy moth
goldtail moth or yellowtail (moth)
grass moth
grayling
hairstreak
herald moth
hawk moth, sphinx moth, or hummingbird moth
house moth
Io moth
Kentish glory
kitten moth
lackey moth
lappet moth
large white or cabbage white
leopard moth
lobster moth
luna moth
magpie moth
marbled white
monarch
mother-of-pearl moth
Mother Shipton
old lady
orange-tip
painted lady
peacock butterfly
peppered moth
privet hawk
processionary moth
purple emperor
puss moth
red admiral
red underwing
ringlet
silver-Y
skipper
small white
snout
speckled wood
swallowtail
swift
tapestry moth
thorn (moth)
tiger (moth)
tussock moth
two-tailed pasha
umber (moth)
vapourer moth
wave (moth)
wax moth, honeycomb moth, or bee moth
wall brown
white
white admiral
winter moth
yellow
yellow underwing

CAKES AND PASTRIES

almond cake
angel cake or angel food cake
Bakewell tart
baklava
Banbury cake
Battenburg cake
black bun
Black forest gateau
brownie
carrot cake
cherry cake
chocolate cake
Christmas cake
coconut cake
coffee kiss
cream cake
cream puff
cruller or kruller (U.S.) (Canad.)
crumpet
cupcake
Danish pastry
devil's food cake
doughnut or donut
drop scone or pancake (Scot.)
dumpling
Dundee cake
Eccles cake
eclair
fairy cake
flapjack
frangipane
French pastry
fruitcake
fudge cake
gateau
Genoa cake
Genoese sponge
gingerbread
hot cross bun
johnny cake (Austral.)
jumble or jumbal
koeksister (S. African)
kuchen
kuglehopf
ladyfinger or sponge finger
lamington (Austral.) (N.Z.)
lardy cake
layer cake
Linzer torte
Madeira cake
madeleine

marble cake
meringue
millefeuille
mince pie
muffin
pancake
pandowdy
panettone
parkin

petit four
pound cake
profiterole
queencake
rock cake
rum baba
Sally Lunn
sandwich cake
scone

seedcake
Selkirk bannock
simnel cake
singing hinny
sponge cake
stollen
swiss roll
tart
teabread

teacake
tipsy cake
torte
turnover
upside-down cake
Victoria sponge
wedding cake
yumyum

CARS

CAR PARTS

accelerator
air bag
alternator
ammeter
anti-roll bar
ashtray
automatic choke
axle
battery
bearing
big end
body
bonnet
boot
brake
brake light
brake pad
bucket seat
bulb
bumper
camshaft
carburettor
catalytic
  converter
chassis
childproof lock
choke
clutch
coil
connecting rod
convertible top

cowl
crank
crankcase
crankshaft
cylinder
cylinder head
dashboard
demister
dipstick
disc brakes
distributor
distributor cap
door
door handle
driveshaft
engine
exhaust
fan
fan belt
fascia
fender (U.S.)
  (Canad.)
flywheel
fog lamp
fuel gauge
fuse
fuse box
gasket
gear
gearbox
gear lever or

(U.S. & Canad.)
  gearshift
generator
glove
  compartment
grille or radiator
  grille
handbrake
hard top
hazard light
headlight
headrest
heater
hood
horn
hubcap
ignition
indicator
jack
light
little end
lock
luggage rack
manifold
mileometer,
  milometer, or
  (U.S. & Canad.)
  odometer
mud flap
numberplate
oil filter

oil-pressure
  gauge
oil pump
parcel shelf
parking light
pedal
petrol cap
petrol gauge
petrol tank
piston
plug
points
radiator
radius arm
rear light or
  (U.S. & Canad.)
  taillight
rear-view mirror
reversing light
roof
seat
seat belt or safety
  belt
shock absorber
silencer
soft top
spare wheel
speedometer
springs
sprocket
starter

steering column
steering wheel
sump
sunroof or
  sunshine roof
suspension
tailgate
tailpipe
tank
top
torsion bar
towbar
transmission
trim
tyre
universal joint
valve
wheel
wheel brace
wheel nut
wheel trim
window
windscreen
windscreen
  wiper
wing
wing mirror
wing nut

CARDS

CARD GAMES

auction bridge
baccarat
beggar-my-
  neighbour
bezique
blackjack
boston
bridge
canasta

canfield
casino
chemin-de-fer
  or chemmy
cinch
contract
  bridge
cooncan or
  conquian

cribbage
duplicate
  bridge
écarté
euchre
faro
five hundred
gin rummy
happy families

hearts
loo
monte
nap or
  napoleon
old maid
ombre
patience
pinochle,

penuchle,
penuckle or
pinocle
piquet
poker
pontoon
quinze
rouge et noir
rubber bridge

rummy	slapjack	solo whist	strip poker	trente et
seven up	snap	spoilfive	stud poker	quarante
skat	solo	stops	switch	whist

BRIDGE TERMS

contract	grand slam	redouble	south	yarborough
double	little slam or	rubber	trick	
dummy	small slam	ruff	trump	
east	north	singleton	vulnerable	
finesse	no-trump	slam	west	

POKER TERMS

ante	pair	see	stand pat	straight flush
flush	raise	showdown	straddle	
full house	royal flush	shy	straight	

OTHER CARD TERMS

ace	cut	hand	knave	trey
clubs	deal	hearts	queen	wild
court card or (U.S.	deck	jack	revoke	
& Canad.) face	deuce	joker	spades	
card	diamonds	king	suit	

CARNIVORES

aardwolf	ermine	linsang	red fox
arctic fox	fennec	lion	rooikat
badger	ferret	lynx	sable
bear	fox	margay	sea otter
binturong	genet or genette	marten	serval
black bear	giant panda	meerkat	silver fox
bobcat	grey fox (U.S.)	mink	skunk
brown bear	grey wolf or timber	mongoose	sloth bear
cacomistle or	wolf	mountain lion	snow leopard or
cacomixle	grison	ocelot	ounce
caracal or desert lynx	grizzly bear or grizzly	otter	stoat
cat	hog badger	otter shrew	stone marten
see breeds of cat	hognosed skunk	palm civet	strandwolf
catamount,	hyena or hyaena	panda	sun bear
catamountain, or	ichneumon	panther	swift fox or kit fox
cat-o'-mountain	jackal	pine marten or sweet	tayra
cheetah or chetah	jaguar	marten	teledu
cinnamon bear	jaguarondi,	polar bear or (N.	tiger
civet	jaguarundi, or	Canad.) nanook	tiger cat
corsac	(Austral.) eyra	polecat	timber wolf
coyote or prairie wolf	kinkajou, honey bear,	prairie dog	weasel
dhole	or potto	puma or cougar	wolf
dingo or (Austral.)	Kodiak bear	raccoon, racoon, or	wolverine, glutton, or
native dog or	kolinsky	coon	carcajou
warrigal	laughing hyena or	raccoon dog	zibeline
dog	spotted hyena	rasse	zibet
see breeds of dog	leopard or panther	ratel	zorilla or zorille

BREEDS OF CAT

Abyssinian	colourpoint	Maine coon	Rex	tortoiseshell
Angora	or (U.S.)	Manx	Russian blue	Turkish
Bengal leopard	Himalayan	Persian	Siamese	
Burmese	Havana	ragdoll	tabby	

CATTLE

BREEDS OF CATTLE

Aberdeen Angus
Africander
Alderney
Ayrshire
Belted Galloway
Blonde
  d'Aquitaine
Brown Swiss
cattalo or catalo
Charolais or
  Charollais
Devon
dexter
Durham
Friesian
Galloway
Gelbvieh
Guernsey
Hereford
Highland
Holstein
Illawarra
  (shorthorn)
Jersey
Kerry
kyloe
Limousin
longhorn
Meuse-Rhine-
  Ijssel
Normandy
Norwegian Red
Red Poll or Red
  Polled
Santa Gertrudis
shorthorn
Simmental
Sussex
Texas longhorn
Wagyu

CATTLE AND OTHER ARTIODACTYLS

addax
alpaca or alpacca
antelope
aoudad
argali or argal
ariel
axis (plural axises)
  or chital
babirusa
Bactrian camel
bharal
bison
blacktail
blaubok
blesbok
boar
boer goat
bongo
bontebok
brocket
bubal or bubalis
buffalo
bull
  see breeds of
  cattle
bushbuck or
  boschbok
bushpig
camel or (Anglo-
  Indian) oont
Cape buffalo
caribou
chamois or izard
chevrotain or
  mouse deer
Chinese water
  deer
cow
  see breeds of
  cattle
dik-dik
dromedary
duiker or duyker
eland
elk
gaur
gayal
gazelle
gemsbok
gerenuk
giraffe or
  (obsolete)
  cameleopard
gnu
goa
goat
goral
grysbok
guanaco
harnessed
  antelope
hartebeest or
  hartbeest
hippopotamus
ibex
impala
Jacob or Jacob
  sheep
karakul or caracul
Kashmir goat
klipspringer
kob
kongoni
kouprey
kudu or koodoo
llama
markhor or
  markhoor
marshbuck
moose
mouflon or
  moufflon
mountain goat
mule deer
muntjac,
  muntjak, or
  barking deer
musk deer
nilgai, nilghau, or
  nylghau
nyala
okapi
oribi
oryx
ox
  see breeds of
  cattle
peccary
Père David's deer
pig
  see breeds of pig
pronghorn
pudu
razorback
red deer
reedbuck or nagor
reindeer
rhebok or reebok
Rocky Mountain
  goat
roe deer
sable antelope
saiga
sambar or sambur
sassaby
serow
sheep or (Austral.
  slang) jumbuck
  see breeds of
  sheep
sika
springbok
stag
steenbok
tahr or thar
takin
vicuña or vicuna
wapiti
wart hog
waterbuck
water buffalo,
  water ox, or
  carabao
white-tailed deer
wild boar
wildebeest
yak
zebu
zo or zho, or dzo

TYPES OF CHAIR

armchair
banquette
barrel chair
bar stool
basket chair
Bath chair
beanbag
bench
bentwood chair
berbice chair
bergère
bucket seat
campaign chair
camp chair
cane chair
carver
cathedra
corner chair
curule chair
deck chair
dining chair
director's chair
dos-à-dos
easy chair
fauteuil
fiddle-back
folding chair
form
garden chair
gestatorial chair
hassock
highchair
jampan (kneeling
  chair)
ladder-back chair
lounger
milking stool
Morris chair
music stool (office
  chair)
opsitbank (S.
  African)
ottoman
pew
piano stool
platform rocker
pouf or pouffe
reclining chair or
  recliner
rocking chair or
  rocker
sedan chair
settle
shooting stick
stool
straight chair
súgán chair
swing
swivel chair
throne
tub chair
wheelchair
window seat
Windsor chair
Windsor rocker
wing chair

CHAMPAGNE BOTTLES

Bottle	Capacity	Bottle	Capacity
magnum	2 bottles	salmanazar	6 magnums
jeroboam	2 magnums	balthazar	8 magnums
rehoboam	3 magnums	nebuchadnezzar	10 magnums
methuselah	4 magnums		

CHEESES

Bavarian blue
Bel Paese
Bleu d'Auvergne
Bleu de Bresse
blue cheese or
  blue vein
Blue Shropshire
Blue Stilton
Blue Vinney or
  Blue Vinny
Bonchester
Brie
Caboc
caciocavallo
Caerphilly
Cambazolla
Camembert
canestrato

Cantal
Chaumes
Cheddar
Cheshire
chèvre
cottage cheese
cream cheese
crowdie
curd cheese
Danish blue
Derby
Dolcelatte
Double
  Gloucester
Dunlop
Dunsyre Blue
Edam
Emmenthal or

Emmental
Ermite
Esrom
feta
fontina
fromage frais
Gjetost
goats' cheese
Gorgonzola
Gouda
Gruyère
Havarti
Jarlsberg
Lanark Blue
Lancashire
Leicester
Limburger
mascarpone

Monterey jack
mousetrap
mozzarella
muenster
mycella
Neufchâtel
Oka
Parmesan
pecorino
Port-Salut
pot cheese
provolone
quark
Reblochon
Red Leicester
Red Windsor
Ribblesdale
ricotta

Romano
Roquefort
Sage Derby
Saint Agur
Samsø
sapsago
Stilton
Stinking Bishop
Taleggio
Tornegus
Vacherin
vignotte
wensleydale
yarg

CHEMICAL ELEMENTS

	Symbols	Atomic numbers		Symbols	Atomic numbers
hydrogen	H	1	cobalt	Co	27
helium	He	2	nickel	Ni	28
lithium	Li	3	copper	Cu	29
beryllium	Be	4	zinc	Zn	30
boron	B	5	gallium	Ga	31
carbon	C	6	germanium	Ge	32
nitrogen	N	7	arsenic	As	33
oxygen	O	8	selenium	Se	34
fluorine	F	9	bromine	Br	35
neon	Ne	10	krypton	Kr	36
sodium	Na	11	rubidium	Rb	37
magnesium	Mg	12	strontium	Sr	38
aluminium or (U.S.)			yttrium	Y	39
aluminum	Al	13	zirconium	Zr	40
silicon	Si	14	niobium	Nb	41
phosphorus	P	15	molybdenum	Mo	42
sulphur or (U.S.) sulfur	S	16	technetium	Tc	43
chlorine	Cl	17	ruthenium	Ru	44
argon	Ar	18	rhodium	Rh	45
potassium	K	19	palladium	Pd	46
calcium	Ca	20	silver	Ag	47
scandium	Sc	21	cadmium	Cd	48
titanium	Ti	22	indium	In	49
vanadium	V	23	tin	Sn	50
chromium	Cr	24	antimony	Sb	51
manganese	Mn	25	tellurium	Te	52
iron	Fe	26	iodine	I	53

	Symbols	Atomic numbers		Symbols	Atomic numbers
xenon	Xe	54	bismuth	Bi	83
caesium or (U.S.)			polonium	Po	84
cesium	Cs	55	astatine	At	85
barium	Ba	56	radon	Rn	86
lanthanum	La	57	francium	Fr	87
cerium	Ce	58	radium	Ra	88
praseodymium	Pr	59	actinium	Ac	89
neodymium	Nd	60	thorium	Th	90
promethium	Pm	61	protactinium	Pa	91
samarium	Sm	62	uranium	U	92
europium	Eu	63	neptunium	Np	93
gadolinium	Gd	64	plutonium	Pu	94
terbium	Tb	65	americium	Am	95
dysprosium	Dy	66	curium	Cm	96
holmium	Ho	67	berkelium	Bk	97
erbium	Er	68	californium	Cf	98
thulium	Tm	69	einsteinium	Es	99
ytterbium	Yb	70	fermium	Fm	100
lutetium or lutecium	Lu	71	mendelevium	Md	101
hafnium	Hf	72	nobelium	No	102
tantalum	Ta	73	lawrencium	Lr	103
tungsten or wolfram	W	74	rutherfordium	Rf	104
rhenium	Re	75	dubnium	Db	105
osmium	Os	76	seaborgium	Sg	106
iridium	Ir	77	bohrium	Bh	107
platinum	Pt	78	hassium	Hs	108
gold	Au	79	meitnerium	Mt	109
mercury	Hg	80	darmstadtium	Ds	110
thallium	Tl	81	roentgenium	Rg	111
lead	Pb	82			

CHEMISTRY

BRANCHES OF CHEMISTRY

analytical chemistry	histochemistry	organic chemistry	stereochemistry
astrochemistry	immunochemistry	petrochemistry	stoichiometry
biochemistry	inorganic chemistry	phonochemistry	thermochemistry
chemurgy	kinetics	photochemistry	zoochemistry
cytochemistry	magnetochemistry	physical chemistry	zymurgy
electrochemistry	neurochemistry	phytochemistry	
geochemistry	nuclear chemistry	radiochemistry	

CHEMISTRY TERMS

acid	atom	chain reaction	electrode	fission
alcohol	atomic mass	chromatography	electrolysis	foam
alkali	atomic number	combustion	electron	formula
alkali metal	base	compound	electrovalency	fuel
alkaline earth	boiling point	concentrated	element	fusion
metal	bond	condensation	emulsion	gas
alkane	Brownian	corrosion	equation	halogen
allotrope	motion	covalent bond	ester	hydrocarbon
alloy	carbohydrate	crystal	ether	hydrolysis
amino acid	catalyst	crystallization	evaporation	inert
analysis	cathode	diffusion	fat	inorganic
anion	cation	dilute	fatty acid	insoluble
anode	chain	distillation	fermentation	ion

ionic bond
ionization
isomer
isotope
lanthanide *or*
  rare-earth
  element
liquid
litmus test
melting point
metal
metalloid
mineral
mixture
molality
molarity
mole
molecule
monomer
neutral
neutron
noble gas *or* inert
  gas
nonmetal
nucleus
oil
ore
organic
oxidation
periodic table
pH
plastic
polymer
precipitate
proton
radioactivity
reaction
reagent
redox reaction
reduction
salt
saponification
saturated
soap
solid
soluble
solution
solvent
sublimation
substitution
  reaction
sugar
suspension
synthesis
transition metal
unsaturated
valency
van der Waals
  forces

CHESS PIECES

Piece	Abbreviation	Piece	Abbreviation	Piece	Abbreviation
Bishop	B	King's rook	KR	Queen's bishop	QB
King	K	Knight	N	Queen's knight	QN
King's bishop	KB	Pawn	P	Queen's rook	
King's knight	KN	Queen	Q	QR	

CHRISTIAN DENOMINATIONS AND SECTS

Adventism
Amish
Anabaptism
Anglicanism
Baptist Church
Byzantine Church
Calvinism
Catholicism
Christadelphianism
Christian Science
Congregationalism
Coptic Church
Dutch Reformed
  Church
Eastern Orthodox
  Church
Episcopal Church
evangelicalism
Greek Orthodox
  Church
Jehovah's Witnesses
Lutheranism
Maronite Church
Methodism
Moravian Church
Mormons *or* Latter-
  day Saints
New Jerusalem
  Church
Orthodox Church
Pentecostalism
Plymouth Brethren
Presbyterianism
Protestantism
Quakerism
Roman Catholicism
Russian Orthodox
  Church
Salvation Army
Seventh-Day
  Adventism
Shakerism
Society of Friends
Unification Church
Unitarianism

CLOTHING

ARTICLES OF CLOTHING

apron
baldric
basque
bathing suit
bathrobe
bib and brace
bikini
blouse
body
body stocking
bodysuit
boubou
braces *or* (U.S.)
  suspenders
bustier
cardigan *or*
  (informal) cardie
  or cardy
chapeau
chaps,
  chaparajos, *or*
  chaparejos
chausses
chuddah,
  chuddar,
  chudder, *or*
  chador
cilice
coat
coatee
codpiece
cummerbund *or*
  kummerbund
dolman
dress
dressing gown
dungarees
frock
galluses *(dialect)*
gambeson
garter
gilet
glove
gown
haik
halter
hauberk
hose
housecoat
jacket
jerkin
jersey
jubbah
jumper
jump suit
jupon
kaftan *or* caftan
kameez
kanzu
kaross
kimono
kilt
kittel
leotard
loincloth *or*
  breechcloth
maillot
manteau
mantle *(archaic)*
mitten
muff
negligee *or*
  negligée
nightdress,
  nightgown, *or*
  (Brit. informal)
nightie
nightshirt
overall
overcoat
overskirt
oversleeve
paletot
pallium
partlet
pashmina
peignoir
plaid
pullover
pyjamas *or* (U.S.)
  pajamas
robe
rompers
sash
sanbenito

sari or saree	skivvy (slang)	costume,	tallit	tunic
sarong	(chiefly U.S.)	bathing	tanga	undergarment
serape	slop	costume,	tank top	waistcoat or (U.S.
shalwar	smock	costume,	thong	& Canad.) vest
shawl	sock	or (Austral.	tie or (U.S.)	wrap
shift	sporran	informal) cossie	necktie	wrapper
shirt	surcoat	swimming	tights or hose	yashmak or
shoe	sweater	trunks or trunks	toga	yashmac
shorts	swimming	swimsuit	T-shirt or tee shirt	

PARTS OF CLOTHING

arm	cuff	hemline	neckline	sleeve
armhole	dicky	hood	patch pocket	tail
armlet	epaulette	jabot	pocket	train
bodice	flounce	lapel	seam	waist
buttonhole	gusset	leg	shawl collar	waistline
collar	hem	lining	shoulder	yoke

TYPES OF CLOTHING

academic dress	evening dress	long-coats or	sackcloth	undergarments
armour	fancy dress	(archaic) long	samfoo	underthings
baby clothes	fatigues	clothes	separates	underwear
beachwear	froufrou	millinery	skivvies (slang)	uniform
black tie	Highland dress	morning dress	(chiefly U.S.)	weepers
canonicals	hose	mufti	slops	white tie
civvies or civies	hosiery	neckwear	sportswear	widow's weeds
clericals	knitwear	nightclothes	swaddling	
coordinates	lingerie	nightwear	clothes	
coveralls	livery	overgarments	swimwear	

TYPES OF CLOUD

altocumulus	cirrostratus	cumulus	fractostratus	stratocumulus
altostratus	cirrus	false cirrus	nimbostratus	stratus
cirrocumulus	cumulonimbus	fractocumulus	nimbus	

TYPES OF CLUB

blackjack	knobstick	nightstick	shillelagh or shillala
bludgeon	lathi	nulla-nulla	truncheon
cudgel	life preserver	patu (N.Z.)	waddy
knobkerrie or	mere (N.Z.)	quarterstaff	

COATS AND CLOAKS

afghan	coat dress	duster coat	joseph	overcoat
balmacaan	coatee	fearnought or	loden coat	paletot
bathrobe	cope	fearnaught	mac or mack	pea jacket or
box coat	covert coat	frock coat	Mackinaw coat	peacoat
Burberry	Crombie	fun fur coat	mackintosh or	parka
(trademark)	(trademark)	fur coat	macintosh	peignoir
burnous,	cutaway	gabardine	manta	pelisse
burnouse, or	dolman	greatcoat	mantelet	peplum
burnoose	domino	hacking coat	mantilla	poncho
cape	dreadnought or	himation	mantle	Prince Albert
capote	dreadnaught	housecoat	morning coat	raglan
capuchin	dress coat	Inverness	newmarket	raincoat
cardinal	dressing gown	jellaba or jellabah	opera cloak or	redingote
chesterfield	duffel coat	Jodhpuri coat	opera hood	roquelaure

sheepskin coat	snorkel	surtout	tailcoat or tails	ulster
sherwani	sou'wester	swallow-	tippet	undercoat
slicker (U.S.)	spencer	tailed coat or	topcoat	waterproof
(Canad.)	surcoat	swallowtail	trench coat	

COCKTAILS

Americano	Cuba libre	Long Island Tea	pink gin	Wall
Bellini	cup	manhattan	planter's punch	snowball
Black Russian	daiquiri	margarita	punch	spritzer
black velvet	dry martini	martini	rickey	stinger or
Bloody Mary	eggnog or egg flip	milk punch	Rusty Nail	stengah
Brandy Alexander	Gibson	mint julep	sangaree	swizzle
buck's fizz	gimlet	mojito	sangria	syllabub or
bullshot	gin sling	Moscow Mule	sazerac	sillabub
caudle	glogg	negroni	screwdriver	Tom Collins
claret cup	Harvey	nog or nogg	sidecar	whiskey sour
cobbler	Wallbanger	oenomel	Singapore sling	whisky mac
cold duck	highball	old-fashioned	sling	white lady
collins	julep	orgasm	Slow Screw	zombie
cooler	kir	piña colada	Against the	

COFFEES

americano	café au lait	decaffeinated or	Irish or Gaelic	mocha
arabica	café noir	decaf	coffee	mochaccino
black coffee	cappuccino	espresso	Java	robusta
Blue mountain	Colombian	frappuccino	Kenyan	skinny latte
Brazilian	Continental	French roast	latte	Turkish coffee
brown coffee	Costa Rican	instant coffee	macchiato	white coffee

COLLECTORS AND ENTHUSIASTS

ailurophile	cats	herbalist	herbs
arctophile	teddy bears	lepidopterist	moths and butterflies
audiophile	high-fidelity sound	medallist	medals
reproduction		numismatist	coins
automobilist	cars	oenophile	wine
bibliophile	books	paranumismatist	coin-like objects
brolliologist	umbrellas	philatelist	stamps
campanologist	bell-ringing	phillumenist	matchbox labels
cartophilist	cigarette cards	phraseologist	phrases
cruciverbalist	crosswords	scripophile	share certificates
deltiologist	picture postcards	vexillologist	flags
discophile	gramophone records	zoophile	animals
fusilatelist	phonecards		

COMPASS POINTS

Compass Point	Abbreviation	Compass Point	Abbreviation
North	N	East by South	E by S
North by East	N by E	East South East	ESE
North North East	NNE	South East by East	SE by E
North East by North	NE by N	South East	SE
North East	NE	South East by South	SE by S
North East by East	NE by E	South South East	SSE
East North East	ENE	South by East	S by E
East by North	E by N	South	S
East	E	South by West	S by W

Compass Point	Abbreviation	Compass Point	Abbreviation
South South West	SSW	North West	NW
South West by South	SW by S	North West by North	NW by N
South West	SW	North North West	NNW
South West by West	SW by W	North by West	N by W
West South West	WSW	**Cardinal point**	**Related adjective**
West by South	W by S	north	arctic or boreal
West	W	east	oriental
West by North	W by N	south	meridional or austral
West North West	WNW	west	occidental or
North West by West	NW by W		hesperidan

COMPUTERS

COMPUTER PARTS

analogue-digital converter	digital camera	keyboard	port
arithmetic logic unit or ALU	digitizer	laser printer	printed circuit board
	DIMM	LCD panel	printer
cartridge	disk	line printer	processor
case	disk drive	magnetic tape unit or MTU	scanner
CD-rewriter	disk unit		screen
CD-Rom drive	DRAM	memory	SDRAM
central processing unit or CPU	DVD reader	microprocessor	SIMM
	DVD writer	modem	sound card
chip	emulator	monitor	speaker
coaxial cable	encoder	motherboard	trackball
console	flatbed scanner	mouse	transistor
control key	floppy disk	MP3 player	USB port
counter	graphics card	multiplexor	visual display unit or VDU
daisywheel	hard drive	optical character reader	
DDR-RAM	integrated circuit		webcam
digital audio player	interface	optical disk	
	joystick	optical scanner	

COMPUTER TYPES

desktop or desktop computer	Macintosh, MacBook, or iMac	computer
laptop or laptop computer		PC or personal computer
notebook or notebook computer	trademark	tablet or tablet computer
	palmtop or palmtop	

COMPUTER TERMS

absolute address	area	beta-test	bulletin board
access	array	binary notation	bundle
access time	artificial intelligence or AI	bit or binary digit	bus or busbar
address		BitTorrent (trademark)	bus master
address bus	ASCII	black box	byte
ADSL	assemble	Bluetooth	cache memory
adware	assembler	boilerplate	capture
algorithm	assembly language	bomb	CD-Rom
alpha-test	audio response	boot or bootstrap	character
analogue computer	automatic repeat	bottom-up processing	chipset
AND gate	backbone	bpi (bits per inch)	clip art
antivirus	backing store	branch instruction	clock
applet	backup	broadband	code
application program	bandwidth	buffer	COM
architecture	base address	bug	command
archival storage	batch processing	buggy	command language

communications
compatible
compiler
complex instruction
  set computer or CISC
computer-aided
  design or CAD
computer-aided
  design and
  manufacture or
  CADCAM
computer-aided
  engineering or CAE
computer-aided
  instruction or CAI
computer-aided (or
  -assisted) learning
  or CAL
computer-aided
  management or CAM
computer-based
  manufacture or CAM
computer-aided
  teaching or CAT
computer aided
  trading or CAT
computerate
computer-based
  training or CBT
computer
  conferencing
computer graphics
computer input on
  microfilm or CIM
computer integrated
  manufacture or CIM
computerize
computer science
computer typesetting
concordance
concurrent
  processing
condition codes
configuration
connectivity
constant
control commands
cookie
core memory
co-routine
corrupt
crash
cross assembler
cursor
cut and paste
cybercafé
cyberpunk
cyberspace

cycle
DAC
data
data bank
database
database
  management
databus
data capture
dataflow architecture
data processing
data protection
data structure
Datel (trademark)
debugging
decision support
  system
decision table
default
desktop
desktop publishing
  or DTP
development system
device
digit
digital computer
digital fount
digital imaging
digital mapping
digital watermark
digitize
digitized
direct-access or
  random-access
  storage
direct memory access
  or DMA
directory
disassembler
distributed array
  processor
distributed logic
dithering
document
document reader
DOS or disk operating
  system (trademark)
dot matrix
download
downsize
down time
dumb terminal
dump
dpi or dots per inch
driver
dump
duplex
EBCDIC or extended

binary-coded
  decimal-
  interchange code
echo
ecommerce
edit
editor
EEPROM
electronic flight
  information
  systems
electronic mail or
  E-mail
electronic office
electronic publishing
emulator
encryption
error message
escape routine
exclusive OR circuit
exit
expansion slot
expert system
extranet
fail-safe
field
fifth-generation
file
file manager
filename
file sharing
firewall
FireWire
firmware
flag
flops or floating-point
  operations per
  second
flowchart
freeware
front-end processor
FTP or file transfer
  protocol
function
function key
fuzzy
gate
gateway
gif
giga-
gigabyte
global search
graphical user
  interface
graphics
greyed out
hacker
hand-held computer

handshake
hard card
hard copy
hardware
hard-wired
help screens
hexadecimal notation
high-level language
host
hot key
hotspot
housekeeping
HTML
hybrid computer
hypermedia
hypertext
icon
idle time
IM or instant
  messaging
image enhancement
incremental plotter
incremental recorder
infect
information
  technology
initialize
input
input device
input/output or I/O
install
instruction
intelligent
  knowledge-based
  system or IKBS
intelligent terminal
interactive
interactive video
Internet
interpreter
interrupt
intranet
ISDN
iTunes (trademark)
job
jpeg
key in
keyword
kilo-
kilobyte
LAN
language
lapheld
laptop
legacy
linked list
liveware
load

local area network
location
logic bomb
logic circuit
logic programming
login
log in
log out
loop
low-level language
machine code
machine learning
machine readable
machine translation
macro
magnetic bubble
mail bombing
mailbox
mainframe
main memory
malware
manager
mega-
megabyte
memory mapping
menu
menu-driven
microcomputer
microprocessor
midi
minicomputer
mobile device
module
morphing
mpeg
MP3
multiaccess
multiprogramming
multi-threaded
multi-user
NAND circuit or gate
network
neurocomputer or neural computer
node
NOR gate
notebook computer
NOT gate
object program
OEM or original equipment manufacturer
offline
online
open
open-source
operating system
optimize

OR gate
output
overflow
package
packet
packet-switching
palette
palmtop computer
parallel processing
parameter
parity check
parser
password
patch
patch board
PC or personal computer
PDA
PDF
personal computer or PC
piggyback
pixel
platform
plug compatible
podcast
pointer
polymorphic function
pop-up
portable
power down
power up
printout
procedure
process
program
program generator
programmable read only memory or PROM
programmer
programming language
program statement
prompt
protocol
query language
queue
queuing theory
random access memory or RAM
Random Instruction Set Computer or RISC
raster
read in
read out
read only memory or ROM

real-time processing
reboot
record
remote access
rerun
reserved word
reset
restricted users group
retrieval
RISC or reduced instruction set computer
robustness
routine
run
run time
screensaver
scroll
SCSI or Small Computer Systems Interface
search engine
sense
sequential access
serial access memory or SAM
serial processing
server
SGML
shareware
shell program
skinning
slide-show
smart card
software
software engineering
sort
source document
source program
spam
speech recognition
spreadsheet
sprite
spyware
stack
statement
storage capacity
storage device
store
store and forward
string
subroutine
supercomputer
SWITCH
syntax
system
systems analysis
systems disk

taskbar
teleprocessing
telesoftware
terabyte
terminal
tetrabyte
text processing
3D graphics
throughput
time out
time sharing
toggle
toolbar
top-down processing
topology
transcribe
translator
transputer
tristate
turnkey system
underflow
UNIX (trademark)
uptime
USB
user-defined key
user group
utility
vaccine
variable
virtual address
virtual memory
virtual reality
virtual storage
virus
visual programming
voice input
voice recognition
voice response
volatile memory
WAN
WAP
warez
webcasting
web development
Wi-Fi
wild card
window
windows icons menus pointers or WIMP
wireless
wizard
word
word processor
work station
World Wide Web
worm
WYSIWIG
XML

CONTAINERS FOR LIQUID

amphora
ampulla
Balthazar
barrel
bottle
can
carafe
carton
cask
coldie (Austral.) (slang)
decanter
firkin
flagon
flask
gourd
half-bottle
hogshead
jar
jeroboam
jug
keg
magnum
Methuselah
miniature
Nebuchadnezzar
pitcher
polypin
rehoboam
Salmanazar
screw-top (informal)
stubby (Austral.)
  (informal)
tantalus
tin
tinny (Austral.) (slang)
tube

COOKERY

GENERAL COOKERY TERMS

à la king
à la mode
antipasto
au gratin
au jus
au lait
au naturel
bake
barbecue or
  (Austral. slang)
  barbie
bard or barde
baste
batter
blackened
blanch
boil
boil-in-the-bag
braise
broth
browning
caramelize
carbonado
casserole
caterer
chafing dish
char-grill
chasseur
chef
cobbler
coddle
colander
commis
confectioner
consommé
cook
cookbook or
  cookery book
cook-chill
corned
creole
cuisine
cuisine minceur
cured
curried
custard
dice
dough
dressing
en brochette
en croute
entrée
entremets
fajita
farci
fillet
flambé
flour
fondue
fricassee
fry
fumet
garnish
gelatine
ghee
giblets
glacé
glaze
goujon
goulash
grate
gravy
grill
hors d'oeuvre
ice
icing
jardinière
jerk
julienne
knead
ladle
lard
lardon or lardoon
leaven
liaison
luau
lyonnaise
macedoine
marengo
marinade
marinate
marmite
mask
mash
médaillons or
  medallions
meunière
meze
mirepoix
mornay
Newburg
nouvelle cuisine
offal
oven-ready
panada
parboil
Parmentier
paste
poach
potage
Provençale
purée
ragout
rijsttafel
rise
rissole
roast
roulade
roux
royal icing
salpicon
sauce
sauté
scramble
season
silver service
sippet
smoked
soup
steam
stew
stock
stroganoff
supreme
sweat
sweet-and-sour
tandoori
tenderize
teriyaki
tikka
timbale
topping
undressed
unleavened
unsmoked
whip
wholemeal or
  (chiefly U.S.
  and Canad.)
  wholewheat
wholemeal flour
  or (chiefly U.S.
  and Canad.)
  Graham flour
yeast

CUISINES AND COOKING STYLES

balti
Cantonese
Caribbean
Californian
Chinese
cordon bleu
cuisine minceur
fast food
French
Greek
gutbürgerlich
halal
haute cuisine
home cooking
Indian
Indonesian
international
ital
Italian
Japanese
kosher
Malaysian
Mediterranean
Mexican
nouvelle cuisine
Provençal
seafood
Sichuan or Szechuan
tapas
Tex-Mex
Thai
Turkish
vegan
vegetarian

CRAFTS

basketry or basket-making
batik
calligraphy
ceramics
cloisonnage
crewelwork
crochet
decoupage
dressmaking
embroidery
flower arranging
knitting
knotwork
macramé
needlepoint
patchwork
pottery
quilling
quilting
raffia work
sewing
spinning
sugarcraft
tapestry
weaving
wickerwork

CRICKET TERMS

appeal
Ashes
bail
ball
bat
batsman
bouncer or bumper
boundary
bowl
bowled
bowler
bye
catch
caught
century
chinaman
cover point
covers
crease
cut
declare
doosra
drive
duck
edge
extra
extra cover
fast bowler
fielder or fieldsman
fine leg
follow on
four
full toss
glance or glide
googly
gully
hit wicket
hook
in
innings
leg before wicket
leg break
leg bye
leg slip
long leg
long off
long on
maiden (over)
mid off
mid on
mid wicket
nightwatchman
no ball
off break
off side
off spin
off-spinner
on side or leg side
opener or opening batsman
out
over
pad
pitch
pull
run
run out
seam
short leg
silly mid on
silly mid off
single
six
slip
spin
square leg
stump
stumped
sweep
swing
test match
third man
twelfth man
Twenty20
umpire or (Austral. slang) umpie
wicket
wicketkeeper
wide
yorker

CRUSTACEANS

barnacle
crab
crayfish, crawfish, (U.S.) or (Austral. & N.Z. informal) craw
Dublin Bay prawn
freshwater shrimp
goose barnacle
gribble
hermit crab
horseshoe crab or king crab
king prawn
koura (N.Z.)
krill
land crab
langoustine
lobster
Norway lobster
opossum shrimp
oyster crab
prawn
robber crab
sand hopper, beach flea, or sand flea
sand shrimp
scorpion
sea spider
shrimp
soft-shell crab
spider crab
spiny lobster, rock lobster, crawfish, or langouste
water flea

CUPS AND OTHER DRINKING VESSELS

canteen
champagne flute
chalice
copita
cup
demitasse
glass
goblet
mug
porrón
quaich
schooner
tankard
tassie
tumbler
water bottle

CUPBOARDS AND CABINETS

ambry
armoire
bookcase
buffet
bureau
cabinet
canterbury
cellaret
chest
chest of drawers
chest-on-chest
chiffonier or chiffonnier
closet
clothes-press
commode
console
Coolgardie safe
court cupboard
credence table or credenza
dooket (Scot.)
drawer
dresser
filing cabinet
étagère
garderobe
(archaic) highboy (U.S.)
larder
locker
lowboy (U.S.)
medicine chest
pantry
press
safe
shelf
sideboard
stand
tallboy
vitrine
wardrobe
Welsh dresser
whatnot

TYPES OF CURRY

achari	chasni	jalfrezi	madras	pathia	tikka
balti	dhal	jaipuri	masala	phal	vindaloo
biryani	dhansak	karahi	mussalman	red thai	
bhoona *or* bhuna	dopiaza	kofta	nentara	rogan josh	
	green thai	korma	pasanda	tandoori	

DANCE

DANCES

allemande	country dance	lambada	round
apache dance	courante	Lambeth walk	round dance
ballroom dance	czardas	lancers	roundelay *or* roundel
barn dance	Dashing White Sergeant	ländler	rumba
beguine	ecossaise	limbo	salsa
belly dance	eightsome reel	line dance	saltarello
black bottom	excuse-me	macarena	samba
body popping	fan dance	malagueña	saraband
bogle	fandango	mambo	saunter
bolero	farandole	maxixe	schottische
boogaloo	flamenco	mazurka	seguidilla
boogie	folk dance	merengue	shake
bossa nova	formation dance	minuet	shimmy
boston	foxtrot	Morisco *or* Moresco	shuffle
bourrée	galliard	morris dance	siciliano
branle	galop	mosh	Sir Roger de Coverley
brawl	gavotte	musette	skank
break dance	Gay Gordons	nautch	snake dance
breakdown	german	old-time dance	snowball
buck and wing	ghost dance	one-step	square dance
bump	gigue	palais glide	step dance
bunny hug	gopak	paso doble	stomp
butterfly	habanera	passacaglia	strathspey
cachucha	haka *(N.Z.)*	Paul Jones	strip the willow
cakewalk	hay *or* hey	pavane	sword dance
calypso	Highland fling	pogo	tambourin
cancan	hoedown	poi dance	tango
carioca	hokey cokey	polka	tap dance
carmagnole	hora	pole dance	tarantella
carol	hornpipe	polonaise	toe dance
cha-cha-cha *or* cha-cha	hula *or* hula-hula	pyrrhic	twist
chaconne	hustle	quadrille	two-step
charleston	jig	quickstep	Tyrolienne
clog dance	jitterbug	redowa	Virginia reel
conga	jive	reel	vogueing
contredanse *or* contradance	jota	rigadoon *or* rigaudon	volta
Cossack dance	juba	ring-shout	waltz
cotillion	kazachok	robot dancing *or* robotics	war dance
	kolo	ronggeng	Zapata

GENERAL DANCE STEPS AND TERMS

chassé	grand chain	pas	pigeonwing	routine	shuffle
choreography	keep step	pas de basque	progressive	score	slip step
dosido	in step	pas seul	promenade	sequence	steps
glide	out of step	phrase	rhythm	set	time

ACADEMIC DEGREES

DEGREE

	Abbreviation		Abbreviation
Bachelor of Agriculture	BAgr	Doctor of Laws	LLD
Bachelor of Arts	BA	Doctor of Letters or Literature	DLitt or
Bachelor of Commerce	BCom		LittD
Bachelor of Dental Surgery	BDS		
Bachelor of Divinity	BD	Doctor of Medicine	MD
Bachelor of Education	BEd	Doctor of Music	DMus,
Bachelor of Engineering	BEng		MusD, or
Bachelor of Law	BL		MusDoc
Bachelor of Laws	LLB	Doctor of Philosophy	PhD
Bachelor of Letters	BLitt	Higher National Certificate	HNC
Bachelor of Medicine	BM or MB	Higher National Diploma	HND
Bachelor of Music	BMus,	Master of Arts	MA
MusB, or		Master of Education	MEd
		Master of Laws	LLM
	MusBac	Master of Letters	MLitt
Bachelor of Pharmacy	BPharm	Master of Music	MMus
Bachelor of Philosophy	BPhil	Master of Philosophy	MPhil
Bachelor of Science	BSc	Master of Science	MSc
Bachelor of Surgery	BS	Master of Surgery	MCh
Diploma in Education	DipEd	Master of Technology	MTech
Doctor of Dental Surgery	DDS or	Ordinary National Certificate	ONC
or Science	DDSc	Ordinary National Diploma	OND
Doctor of Divinity	DD		

DESSERTS AND SWEET DISHES

Atholl Brose or
Athole Brose
baked Alaska
banana split
bavarois or
Bavarian cream
Black Forest
gateau
blancmange
blintz
bombe
bread and butter
pudding
cabinet pudding
cassata
charlotte
charlotte russe
cheesecake
Christmas
pudding
cobbler

college pudding
compote
coupe
cranachan
crème brûlée
crème caramel
crêpe
crêpe suzette
crumble
custard
death by
chocolate
duff
dumpling
Easter-ledge
pudding
Eve's pudding
flummery
fondant
fool
fruit cup

fruit salad or
cocktail
gâteau
hasty pudding
ice cream
Île Flottante
jelly or (U.S.) jello
junket
kissel
knickerbocker
glory
kulfi
marrons glacés
milk pudding
Mississippi mud
pie
mousse
Neapolitan ice
cream
nesselrode
panocha (U.S.)

parfait
pashka
pavlova or
(Austral. & N.Z.
informal) pav
peach Melba
plum duff
plum pudding
queen of
puddings
rice pudding
roly-poly
sabayon
sago
semolina
shoofly pie (U.S.)
shortcake
slump (U.S.)
sorbet
soufflé
sponge pudding

spotted dick
spumone or
spumoni
steamed pudding
strudel
suet pudding
summer pudding
sundae
syllabub or
sillabub
tapioca
tartlet
tiramisu
torte
trifle
tutti-frutti
vacherin
water ice
whip
yogurt
zabaglione

DIETS

Atkins diet
breatharian diet or
inedia
cabbage soup diet

Cambridge diet
CRON-diet
dairy-free diet
detox diet

Diet Smart Plan
DASH diet
fat resistance diet
Feingold diet

Fit for Life diet
flexitarian diet
food combining diet
F-Plan diet

fruitarian diet
gluten-free, casein-free diet
GI diet
Graham diet
grapefruit diet or Hollywood diet
hacker's diet
halal diet
hallelujah diet
high protein diet
kosher diet
lacto-vegetarian diet
low-protein diet
macrobiotic diet
Master Cleanse diet
Mediterranean diet
Montignac diet
natural food diet
negative calorie diet
no-grain diet
Okinawa diet
Optimal diet
organic food diet
Ornish diet
ovo-lacto-vegetarian diet
Palaeolithic diet
Perricone Weight-Loss diet
pescetarian diet or pesco-vegetarianism
pollotarian diet or pollo-vegetarianism
Pritikin diet
raw food diet
rice diet
Rosemary Conley diet
Scarsdale Medical
diet
sex diet
Shangri-La diet
Slimming World diet
South Beach diet
Stillman diet
Subway diet
veganism
vegetarianism
very low calorie diet or VLCD
weigh down diet
Weight Watchers
zone diet

DINOSAURS

allosaur(us)
ankylosaur(us)
apatosaur(us)
atlantosaur(us)
brachiosaur(us)
brontosaur(us)
ceratosaur(us)
compsognathus
dimetrodon
diplodocus
dolichosaur(us)
dromiosaur(us)
elasmosaur(us)
hadrosaur(us)
ichthyosaur(us)
iguanodon or iguanodont
megalosaur(us)
mosasaur(us)
oviraptor
plesiosaur(us)
pteranodon
pterodactyl or pterosaur
protoceratops
stegodon or stegodont
stegosaur(us)
theropod
titanosaur(us)
trachodon
triceratops
tyrannosaur(us)
velociraptor

THE DISCIPLES OF JESUS

Andrew	James	John	Jude	Peter	Simon
Bartholomew	James	Judas	Matthew	Philip	Thomas

DISEASES

HUMAN DISEASES

absinthism
acariasis
acne
acromegaly
actinodermatitis
actinomycosis
Addison's disease
adrenoleukody-strophy or ALD
aeroneurosis
agranulocytosis
ague
Aids or AIDS
alcoholism
Alzheimer's disease
amoebiasis
ancylostomiasis, anchylostomiasis, or ankylostomiasis
angina
anorexia or anorexia nervosa
anthracosis
anthrax
aortitis
appendicitis
apraxia
arteriosclerosis
arthritis
asbestosis
ascariasis
asthma
atherosclerosis
athlete's foot
avian flu
avitaminosis
Bell's palsy
beriberi
bilharzia
bilharziasis or bilharziosis
bird flu
Black Death
black measles
blackwater fever
Bornholm disease
Bright's disease
bronchiolitis
bronchitis
bronchopneumonia
brucellosis
bubonic plague
bulimia or bulimia nervosa
Burkitt lymphoma or Burkitt's lymphoma
bursitis
byssinosis
calenture
cancer
cardiomyopathy
carditis
caries
carpal tunnel syndrome
cellulitis
cerebellar syndrome
Chagas' disease
chickenpox
chin cough
chloracne
chlorosis
cholera
chorea
Christmas disease
chronic fatigue syndrome or CFS
cirrhosis
coal miner's lung
coccidioidomycosis
coeliac disease
cold
colitis
common cold
conjunctivitis
constipation
consumption
cor pulmonale

coxalgia
Creutzfeldt-Jakob
  disease
Crohn's disease
Cushing's disease
cystic fibrosis
cystitis
dead fingers
decompression
  sickness
dengue
dermatitis
dhobi itch
diabetes
diarrhoea
diphtheria
diverticulitis
double pneumonia
dropsy
dysentery
earache
ebola virus disease
Economo's disease
eczema
elephantiasis
emphysema
encephalitis
encephalomyelitis
encephalopathy
endocarditis
enteritis
enterobiasis
enterocolitis
epilepsy
ergotism
erysipelas
erythroblastosis
exophthalmic goitre
farmer's lung
favus
fibrositis
filariasis
fishskin disease
flu
framboesia
furunculosis
gastritis
gastroenteritis
genital herpes
German measles
gingivitis
glandular fever
glaucoma
glomerulonephritis
glossitis
glue ear
goitre
gonorrhoea

gout
grand mal
green monkey disease
greensickness
haemoglobinopathy
haemophilia
Hansen's disease
hebephrenia
hepatitis
hepatitis A
hepatitis B
herpes
herpes simplex
herpes zoster
hidrosis
histoplasmosis
Hodgkin's disease
Huntington's chorea
hypothermia
hypothyroidism
ichthyosis
icterus
impetigo
infectious hepatitis
infectious
  mononucleosis
influenza
iritis
jaundice
jungle fever
kala-azar
Kaposi's sarcoma
Kawasaki's disease
Korsakoff's psychosis
kuru
labyrinthitis
laryngitis
Lassa fever
lathyrism
legionnaire's disease
leishmaniasis or
  leishmaniosis
leprosy
leptospirosis
leukaemia
listeriosis
lockjaw
lumbago
lupus
lupus erythematosus
lupus vulgaris
Lyme disease
lymphoma
malaria
Marburg disease
mastitis
measles
Ménière's syndrome

meningitis
metabolic syndrome
milk sickness
motor neurone
  disease
multiple sclerosis
mumps
muscular dystrophy
myalgic
  encephalomyelitis
  or ME
myasthenia gravis
myiasis
myopathy
myxoedema
narcolepsy
necrotising fasciitis
nephritis
nephrosis
neuropathy
non-A, non-B
  hepatitis
non-Hodgkin's
  lymphoma
onchocerciasis
ornithosis
osteitis
osteitis deformans
osteoarthritis
osteomalacia
osteomyelitis
osteoporosis
otitis
Paget's disease
paratyphoid fever
Parkinson's disease
pellagra
pelvic inflammatory
  disease
pemphigus
pericarditis
petit mal
pharyngitis
phlebitis
phthisis
pinta
pityriasis
pleurisy
pleuropneumonia
pneumoconiosis
pneumonia
poliomyelitis or polio
polycythaemia
porphyria
Pott's disease
pox
presenile dementia
prurigo

psittacosis
psoriasis
purpura
pyorrhoea
Q fever
quinsy
rabies
radiation sickness
ratbite fever or ratbite
  disease
Raynaud's disease
relapsing fever
retinitis
retinopathy
Reye's syndrome
rheumatic fever
rheumatoid arthritis
rhinitis
rickets
rickettsial disease
ringworm
Rocky Mountain
  spotted fever
rubella
Saint Vitus's dance
salmonella or
  salmonellosis
salpingitis
sapraemia
sarcomatosis
scabies
scarlet fever or
  scarlatina
schistosomiasis
schizophrenia
schizothymia
sciatica
scleroderma,
  sclerodermia, or
  scleriasis
scrofula
scrub typhus
scurvy
seasonal affective
  disorder
seborrhoea
senile dementia
septicaemia
serpigo
serum sickness
shell shock
shingles
sickle-cell anaemia
siderosis
silicosis
sinusitis
sleeping sickness
smallpox

spina bifida
spirochaetosis
splenitis
splenomegaly
spondylitis
spotted fever
sprue
stomatitis
strongyloidiasis or
  strongyloidosis
sunstroke
sweating sickness
swinepox
sycosis
Sydenham's chorea

synovitis
syphilis
syringomyelia
tarantism
Tay-Sachs disease
tetanus
thalassaemia
thrush
tick fever
tinea
tonsillitis
Tourette syndrome
toxic shock syndrome
trachoma
trench fever

trench mouth
trichinosis
trypanosomiasis
tsutsugamushi
  disease
tuberculosis
typhoid fever
typhus
uncinariasis
uraemia
urethritis
urticaria
utriculitis
uveitis
vaginitis

vagotonia
valvulitis
varicosis
variola
varioloid
venereal disease
Vincent's angina or
  Vincent's disease
vulvitis
vulvovaginitis
Weil's disease
whooping cough
yaws
yellow fever

ANIMAL DISEASES

actinomycosis or
  (nontechnical) lumpy jaw
anbury
anthrax
blackleg
bots
braxy
brucellosis or undulant fever
BSE (bovine spongiform
  encephalopathy) or
  (informal) mad cow disease
bull nose
bush sickness (N.Z.)
canker
cowpox
distemper
dourine
foot-and-mouth disease or
  hoof-and-mouth disease
fowl pest
furunculosis
gallsickness or anaplasmosis
gapes
gid
glanders
grapes
hard pad
heaves or broken wind
laminitis or founder
lampas or lampers

loco disease
Lyme disease
malanders, mallanders, or
  mallenders
Marburg disease or green
  monkey disease
milk fever
moon blindness or mooneye
murrain
myxomatosis
nagana
Newcastle disease or fowl
  pest
ornithosis
pinkeye
pip
pityriasis
psittacosis
pullorum disease or bacillary
  white diarrhoea
quarter crack
quittor
red water
rinderpest
ringbone
roaring
rot
roup
sand crack
scab

scrapie
scratches
seedy toe
sheep measles
sitfast
spavin
staggers, blind staggers, or
  megrims
strangles or equine distemper
stringhalt or springhalt
surra
swamp fever or equine
  infectious anaemia
sweating sickness
sweeny
swine fever or (U.S.) hog
  cholera
swinepox or variola porcina
swine vesicular disease
Texas fever
thoroughpin
thrush
toe crack
trembles or milk sickness
warble
whistling
windgall

DIVINATION

METHODS OF DIVINATION

astrology
clairvoyance
crystal gazing
dice

dowsing
I Ching
numerology
palmistry

runes
scrying
sortilege
tarot

tea leaves

MEANS OF DIVINATION

ailuromancy	cats	hydromancy	water
alphitomancy	wheat or barley cakes	lampadomancy	oil lamps
arachnomancy	spiders	lithomancy	precious stones
astragalomancy	dice	lychnomancy	flames of wax candles
bibliomancy	passages from books	molybdomancy	molten lead
cartomancy	cards	necromancy	the dead
catoptromancy	mirror	oneiromancy	dreams
ceromancy	melted wax	ornithomancy	birds
chiromancy	hands	pegomancy	sacred pool
cleidomancy	suspended key	pyromancy	fire or flames
crithomancy	freshly baked bread	radiesthesia	pendulum
cromniomancy	onions	rhabdomancy	rod or wand
crystallomancy	crystal ball	sciomancy	ghosts
dactylomancy	suspended ring	tasseography	tea leaves
geomancy	earth, sand, or dust	theomancy	god
hippomancy	horses	tyromancy	cheese

BREEDS OF DOG

affenpinscher
Afghan hound
Airedale terrier
Akita
Alaskan malamute
Alpine spaniel
Alsatian or German
   shepherd
Australian cattle
   dog, blue
   cattle dog, or
   (Queensland) blue
   heeler (Austral.)
Australian terrier
Australian silky
   terrier or Sydney
   silky
barb (Austral.)
basenji
basset hound
beagle
bearded collie
Bedlington terrier
Belvoir hound
Bichon Frise
Blenheim spaniel
bloodhound,
   sleuthhound, or
   sleuth
blue Gascon hound
Border collie
Border terrier
borzoi or Russian
   wolfhound
Boston terrier or bull
   terrier
bouvier

boxer
briard
Bruxellois
bulldog
bull mastiff
bull terrier
cairn terrier or cairn
chihuahua
chow-chow or chow
clumber spaniel
cocker spaniel
collie
corgi or Welsh corgi
Cuban bloodhound
dachshund
Dalmatian or
   (formerly) carriage
   dog or coach dog
Dandie Dinmont
   (terrier)
deerhound
Doberman pinscher
   or Doberman
Egyptian basset
elkhound or
   Norwegian
   elkhound
English setter
Eskimo dog
field spaniel
foxhound
fox terrier
French bulldog
golden retriever
Gordon setter
Great Dane
greyhound

griffon
harrier
Highland terrier
husky
Irish setter or red
   setter
Irish terrier
Irish water spaniel
Irish wolfhound
Italian greyhound
Jack Russell (terrier)
Japanese spaniel
Japanese tosa
keeshond
kelpie
Kerry blue terrier
King Charles spaniel
komondor
Labrador retriever,
   Labrador, or lab
Lakeland terrier
Lhasa apso
malamute or
   malemute
Maltese
Manchester terrier
   or black-and-tan
   terrier
mastiff
Mexican hairless
Newfoundland
Norfolk springer
   spaniel
Norfolk terrier
Norwich terrier
Old English
   sheepdog

otterhound
papillon
Pekingese
pit bull terrier or
   American pit bull
   terrier
pointer
Pomeranian
poodle
pug
puli
Pyrenean mountain
   dog
raccoon dog or
   coonhound
retriever
Rhodesian
   ridgeback
Rottweiler
rough collie
Saint Bernard or St.
   Bernard
Saluki or Persian
   greyhound
Samoyed
schipperke
schnauzer
Scottish, Scotch, or
   (formerly) Aberdeen
   terrier or Scottie
Sealyham terrier
setter
Shetland sheepdog
   or sheltie
shih-tzu
Skye terrier
spaniel

spitz
springer spaniel
Staffordshire bull
  terrier
staghound
Sussex spaniel
talbot
terrier
vizsla
water spaniel
Weimaraner
Welsh terrier
West Highland white
  terrier
whippet
wire-haired terrier
wolfhound
Yorkshire terrier

DRESSES

ballgown
burka
busuuti
button-through dress
chemise
cheongsam
chiton
coat dress
cocktail dress
dirndl
gymslip
kaftan or caftan
kimono
mantua
maxidress
microdress
midi
minidress
Mother Hubbard
muu-muu
negligee or negligée
nightdress or (U.S. &
  Canad.) nightrobe
nightgown or
(informal) nightie or
  nighty
nightshirt
overdress
peignoir
pinafore dress,
  pinafore, pinny
  (informal), or (U.S. &
  Canad.) jumper
riding habit
sack
sari or saree
sheath
shift
shirtdress
shirtwaister or
  (U.S. and Canad.)
  shirtwaist
sundress
sweater dress
tea gown
tunic
wedding dress

SOFT DRINKS

alcohol-free or non-
  alcoholic beer
apple juice
barley water
bitter lemon
Bovril (trademark)
buttermilk
cassis
Coca-Cola or Coke
  (trademark)
cocoa
coffee
cola
cordial
cream soda
crush
dandelion and
  burdock
fruit juice
fruit tea
ginger ale
ginger beer
grapefruit juice
herb tea or herbal
  infusion
hot chocolate
ice-cream soda
iron brew
juice
kumiss, koumiss,
  koumis, or koumyss
lassi
lemonade
lemon squash
lemon tea or Russian
  tea
limeade
lime cordial
lolly water (Austral.)
  (N.Z.)
Lucozade (trademark)
maté or mate
milk
milk shake
mineral water
nectar
orangeade
orange juice
orgeat
peppermint cordial
Perrier or Perrier
  water (trademark)
prairie oyster
Ribena (trademark)
root beer
sarsaparilla
Seltzer or Seltzer
water
sherbet
smoothie
soapolallie
soda
soda water
spremuta
squash
sweet cider (U.S.)
  (Canad.)
tea
tisane
Tizer (trademark)
tomato juice
tonic
vichy water
Vimto (trademark)
water

DRUGS

DRUGS

acetanilide or
  acetanilid
acriflavine
allopurinol
aloin
alum or potash alum
amitriptyline
amphetamine,
  Benzedrine
  (trademark), or (slang)
  speed
ampicillin
amyl nitrite or (slang)
  popper
Amytal (trademark)
Antabuse (trademark)
antipyrine
apomorphine
araroba or Goa
  powder
Argyrol (trademark)
arsphenamine
aspirin or
  acetylsalicylic acid
atropine or atropin
azathioprine
azedarach
bacitracin
barbitone or (U.S.)
  barbital
barbiturate
belladonna
Benadryl (trademark)
benzocaine
benzodiazepine
berberine
bhang or bang
bitter aloes
bromal
bupivacaine
caffeine
calomel
cannabis
cantharides
carbamazepine
carbimazole
cascara sagrada
chlorambucil

chloramphenicol
chlordiazepoxide
chloroquine
chlorothiazide
chlorpromazine
chlorpropamide
chlortetracycline
chlorthalidone
chrysarobin
cinchona
cinchonine
cocaine, cocain, or (slang) coke or Charlie
codeine
contrayerva
cortisone
co-trimoxazole
crystal methamphetamine or (informal) crystal meth
curare or curari
cyclopropane
cyclosporin-A
dapsone
DET or diethyltryptamine
dextroamphetamine
digitalis
dimenhydrinate or Dramamine (trademark)
disulfiram
ecstasy
DMT or dimethyltryptamine
ephedrin or ephedrine
fentanyl
ganja
gemfibrozil
hashish or charas
hemlock
hemp
heroin or diamorphine
hydrocortisone or cortisol
hyoscyamine

ibuprofen
imipramine
indomethacin
ipecac or ipecacuanha
ivermectin
kaolin or kaoline
ketamine
laudanum
Librium (trademark)
LSD, lysergic acid diethylamide, or (slang) acid
marijuana or marihuana
MDMA
mecamylamine
mepacrine, quinacrine (U.S.), Atebrin (trademark), or Atabrine U.S. trademark
meperidine or meperidene hydrochloride
merbromin
mercaptopurine
mescaline or mescalin
methadone or methadon
methamphetamine
methicillin
methotrexate
methyldopa
Mogadon (trademark)
morphine or morphia
neomycin
nepenthe
nicotine
nitrazepam
nitrous oxide, dinitrogen oxide, or laughing gas
Novocaine (trademark) or procaine hydrochloride
nux vomica
opium
Paludrine (trademark)

paracetamol
paraldehyde
paregoric
PCP (trademark), phencyclidine, or (informal) angel dust
penicillin
pentamidine
pentaquine
pentazocine
pentobarbitone sodium, sodium pentabarbital (U.S.), or Nembutal (trademark)
pentylenetetrazol
phenacaine
phenacetin or acetophenetidin
phenformin
phenobarbitone
phenolphthalein
phenothiazine
phenylbutazone
phenytoin
poppy
prednisolene
prednisone
primaquine
promethazine
propranolol
Prozac (trademark)
psilocybin
quercetin or quercitin
quinidine
quinine
reserpine
rhatany or krameria
rifampicin or (U.S.) rifampin
safflower or false saffron
salicin or salicine
saloop
salts
sanguinaria
santonin
scammony

scopolamine or hyoscine
scopoline
Seidlitz powder, Seidlitz powders, or Rochelle powder
senna leaf
senna pods
squill
STP
stramonium
streptomycin
sulphadiazine
sulphadimidine or (U.S.) sulfamethazine
sulpha drug
sulphanilamide
sulphathiozole
sulphisoxazole
temazepam
terebene
Terramycin (trademark)
tetracycline
thalidomide
thiopentone sodium, thiopental sodium, or Sodium Pentothal (trademark)
thiouracil
tricyclic
turpeth
valerian
Valium (trademark) or diazepam
verapamil
Viagra (trademark)
vinblastine
vinca alkaloid
vincristine
witch hazel or wych hazel
wormseed
yohimbine
zidovudine or Retrovir (trademark)

TYPES OF DRUG

abirritant
abortifacient
ACE inhibitor
adjuvant
agrypnotic
alexipharmic
alkylating agent

alterative
anaesthetic or (U.S.) anesthetic
analeptic
analgesic
anaphrodisiac
anodyne

antagonist
antibiotic
anticholinergic
anticonvulsant
antidepressant
antidote
antiemetic

antifebrile
antihistamine
anti-inflammatory
antimalarial
antimetabolite
antimycotic
antiperiodic

antiphlogistic
antipyretic
antispasmodic
antitussive
anxiolytic
aphrodisiac
astringent
ataractic or ataraxic
attenuant
beta-blocker
bronchodilator
calcium antagonist or
  blocker
calmative
cardiac
carminative
cathartic
cholagogue
cimetidine
cisplatin
clomiphene
colestipol
contraceptive
convulsant
cytotoxin
decongestant
demulcent
depressant
depressomotor
diaphoretic
diuretic

ecbolic
emetic
emmenagogue
errhine
euphoriant
excitant
expectorant
expellant or expellent
febrifuge
general anaesthetic
  or (U.S.) general
  anesthetic
haemagogue or (U.S.)
  hemagogue or
  hemagog
haemostatic or (U.S.)
  hemostatic
hallucinogen
hepatic
hypnotic
immunosuppressive
inotropic
laxative
lenitive
local anaesthetic
  or (U.S.) local
  anesthetic
masticatory
miticide
narcotic
nervine

neuroleptic
NSAID or nonsteroidal
  anti-inflammatory
  drug
opiate
oxytocic
painkiller
palliative
pectoral
preventive
prophylactic
psychedelic or
  psychodelic
psychoactive
psychotomimetic
pulmonic (rare)
purgative
radio mimetic
recreational
relaxant
resolvent
restorative
revulsive
roborant
sedative
sialagogue or
  sialogogue
soporific
sorbefacient
spermicide or
  (less commonly)

spermatocide
steroid
stimulant
stupefacient
styptic
suppurative
sympatholytic
sympathomimetic
synergist
taeniacide or (U.S.)
  teniacide
taeniafuge or (U.S.)
  teniafuge
tetanic
tonic
tranquillizer,
  tranquilliser, or (U.S.)
  tranquilizer
tumefacient
vasoconstrictor
vasodilator
vasoinhibitor
vermifuge,
  anthelminthic,
  anthelmintic, or
  helminthic
vesicant or vesicatory
vomit
vulnerary

GENERAL DRUG TERMS

absorption
addiction
addictive
adiaphorous
ana
antimonial
aromatic
arsenical
autacoid
bacterin
bioassay
bioavailability
biological
blockade
botanical
chalybeate
chemoprophylaxis
cohobate
confection
contraindicate
control group
decoction
dependency
designer drug

dosage
dose
electuary
elixir
embrocation
emulsion
endermic
ethical
excipient
exhaust
external
extract
fluidextract
galenical
glycoside
hard
hypersensitive
hypodermic
hypodermic needle
hypodermic syringe
idiosyncrasy
incompatible
inhalant
intermediate-acting

intoxicating
lethal dose or LD
linctus
liquor
local
long-acting
magistral
mass
median lethal dose or
  mean lethal dose
medication
menstruum
mercurial
mind-expanding
minimum lethal dose
  or MLD
mixture
normal
officinal (obsolete)
oleoresin
oral
overdose
over-the-counter
parenteral

pessary
placebo
positive
potentiate
prescription
proprietary
reaction
reactor
remedy
route
sensitivity
sensitize or sensitise
short-acting
side effect
signature (U.S.)
soft
spansule
specific
spirit
suppository
tincture
succedaneum
synergism or synergy
tachyphylaxis

tolerant	unit	venipuncture *or*	wafer
topical	unofficial	venepuncture	wine
trituration	vehicle	vinegar	withdrawal

DRUG ABUSE TERMS

acid	fix	lit up	smoke
acidhead	freebase	loaded (*chiefly U.S.*)	snort
angel dust	gear	(*Canad.*)	snowball
blow	get off	magic mushroom	solvent abuse
blow someone's mind	get through (*U.S.*)	mainline	space cadet
bombed	glue-sniffing	make it	spaced out *or* spaced
bong	gone	Man (*U.S.*)	speed
bring down	goof	Mickey Finn	speedball
bummer	goofball (*U.S.*)	mind-expanding	speedfreak
burned	grass	monkey (*U.S.*) (*Canad.*)	spliff
bust	habit	nail	stash
buzz	hash	narc (*U.S.*)	step on
Charlie	head	nod out	stoned
chillum	high	number	strung out
coke	hit	OD *or* overdose	stuff
cold turkey	hooked	opium den	swacked
comedown	hop (*obsolete*)	pep pill	switch on
connection	hophead (*chiefly U.S.*)	pop	tab
cook up	hop up (*dated*)	popper	toke
cop	hype	pot	toot
crack	hyped up	pothead	trip
crackhead	jack up	pusher	turn on
crank up	jag	reefer	upper
dadah (*Austral.*)	jellies	roach	user
(*slang*)	joint	score	wasted
dealer	joypop	shooting gallery	weight
do	junk	shoot up	withdrawal
dope	junkie	skin-pop	withdrawal
downer	kick	skin up	symptoms
drop	kif	smack	wrap
dry out	knockout drops	smackhead	wrecked
ecstasy *or* E	line	smashed	zonked

SNOW WHITE'S SEVEN DWARFS

Bashful	Doc	Dopey	Grumpy	Happy	Sleepy	Sneezy

PARTS OF THE EAR

ancus	external auditory canal	round window
auditory nerve	incus	saccule
cochlea	malleus	semicircular canals
eardrum, tympanic	meatus *or* auditory canal	stapes
membrane, *or* tympanum	organ of Corti	tragus
ear lobe	oval window	utricle
Eustachian tube	pinna	

LAYERS OF THE EARTH'S CRUST

asthenosphere	lithosphere	discontinuity	sial
basement	lower mantle	oceanic crust	transition zone
continental crust	Mohorovicíc	sima	upper mantle

SPECIFIC EATING HABITS

HABIT

Food

anthropophagic *or* anthropophagous	fellow humans
apivorous	bees
cannibalistic	other members of the same species
carnivorous	meat
carpophagous, frugivorous, *or* fruitarian	fruit
carrion	dead and rotting flesh
coprophagous	dung
geophagous	earth
herbivorous	plants
hylophagous	wood
insectivorous	insects
limivorous	mud

Food

macrophagous	relatively large pieces of food
monophagous	only one food
mycetophagous	fungi
myrmecophagous	ants
nectarivorous	nectar
nucivorous	nuts
omnivorous	meat and plants
omophagic *or* omophagous	raw food
piscivorous	fish
theophagous	gods
vegan	no animal products
vegetarian	no flesh
zoophagous	animals

ECONOMICS

BRANCHES OF ECONOMICS

agronomics	econometrics	industrial economics	microeconomics
cliometrics	economic history	macroeconomics	welfare economics

ECONOMICS TERMS

arbitration	capital good	cost effectiveness	disposable income
asset	capitalism	cost of living	diversification
autarky	cartel	cost-push inflation	divestment
automation	cash	credit	dividend
balanced budget	central bank	credit controls	division of labour
balance of payments	Chamber of Commerce	credit squeeze	dumping
balance of trade	closed shop	currency	duopoly
balance sheet	collective bargaining	current account	durable good
bank	command economy *or* planned economy	customs union	Dutch disease
bankruptcy		debt	duty
barriers to entry	commercial bank *or* clearing bank	deflation	earned income
barriers to exit		deindustrialization	earnings
barter	commission	demand	economic growth
base rate	commodity	demand management *or* stabilization policy	economic policy
bear market	common market		economic sanctions
bid	comparative advantage	demand-pull inflation	economies of scale
black economy		deposit account	embargo
boom	competition	depreciation	employee
boycott	conspicuous consumption	depression	employer
bridging loan		deregulation	employment
budget	consumer	devaluation	entrepreneur
budget deficit	consumer good	diminishing returns	environmental audit
building society	consumption	discount	exchange
bull market	cooperative	discount house (*Brit.*)	exchange rate
business cycle	corporation	discount rate	expenditure
buyer's market	corporation tax	disequilibrium	export
capacity	cost-benefit analysis	disinflation	finance
capital			financial year

fiscal drag
fiscal policy
fiscal year
Five-Year Plan
fixed assets
fixed costs
fixed exchange-rate
 system
fixed investment
floating exchange-
 rate system
foreclosure
foreign exchange
 controls
foreign exchange
 market
forfaiting
franchise
free-market economy
free rider
free trade
free trade area
free trade zone or
 freeport
freight
friendly society
fringe benefits
full employment
funding
futures market or
 forward exchange
 market
gains from trade
game theory
gilt-edged security or
 government bond
gold standard
greenfield investment
gross domestic
 product or GDP
gross national
 product or GNP
gross profit
hard currency
hedging
hire
hire purchase or HP
hoarding
holding
horizontal integration
hot money
human capital
hyperinflation
imperfect
 competition
import
import restrictions
income

income support
income tax
index-linked
indirect tax
industrial dispute
industrial estate
industrial policy
industrial relations
industrial sector
inflationary spiral
information
 agreement
infrastructure
inheritance tax
insolvency
instalment credit
institutional investors
insurance
intangible assets
intangibles
intellectual property
 right
interest
interest rate
international
 competitiveness
international debt
international reserves
investment
invisible balance
invisible hand
invoice
joint-stock company
joint venture
junk bond
labour
labour market
labour theory of value
laissez faire or laisser
 faire
lease
legal tender
lender
liability
liquidation
liquid asset
liquidity
listed company
loan
lockout
macroeconomic
 policy
management buy-out
marginal revenue
marginal utility
market
market failure
mass production

means test
mediation
medium of exchange
medium-term
 financial strategy
mercantilism
merchant bank
merger
microeconomic policy
middleman
mint
mixed economy
monetarism
monetary
 compensatory
 amounts, MCAs, or
 green money
monetary policy
money
money supply
monopoly
moonlighting
mortgage
multinational
national debt
national income
national insurance
 contributions
nationalization
national product
natural rate of
 unemployment
net profit
nondurable good
offshore
oligopoly
overheads
overheating
overmanning
overtime
patent
pawnbroker
pay
pay-as-you-earn or
 PAYE
payroll
pension
pension fund
per capita income
perfect competition
personal equity plan
 or PEP
picket
piecework
polluter pays principle
portfolio
poverty trap
premium

premium bond
price
prices and incomes
 policy
primary sector
private enterprise
private property
privatization
producer
production
productivity
profit
profitability
profit-and-loss
 account
profit margin
profit sharing
progressive taxation
protectionism
public expenditure
public finance
public interest
public-sector
 borrowing
 requirement or PSBR
public-sector debt
 repayment
public utility
public works
pump priming
purchasing power
quality control
ratchet effect
rational expectations
rationalization
rationing
recession
recommended retail
 price
recovery
recycling
redundancy
reflation
regional policy
rent
rent controls
research and
 development or
 R & D
residual
 unemployment
restrictive labour
 practice
retail
retail price index
revaluation
revenue
risk analysis

salary
sales
saving
savings bank
seasonal
  unemployment
self-employment
self service
self-sufficiency
seller's market
sequestration
service sector
share
shareholder
share issue
share price index
shop
shop steward
simple interest
slump
social costs
socio-economic

group
soft currency
specialization
speculation
stagflation
standard of living
stock
stockbroker
stock control
stock exchange, stock
  market, or (N.Z.)
  share market
stop-go cycle
structural
  unemployment
subsidiary company
subsidy
supplier
supply
supply-side
  economics
surplus

synergy
takeover
tangible assets
tariff
tax
taxation
tax avoidance
tax evasion
tax haven
terms of trade
trade
trade barrier
trademark
trade union
trade-weighted index
training
transaction
trust
trustee
underwriter
unearned income
unemployment

unemployment
  benefit
uniform business rate
  or UBR
unit of account
unit trust
utility
value-added tax or
  VAT
variable costs
venture capital
vertical integration
voluntary
  unemployment
wage
wage restraint
wealth
welfare state
wholesaler
worker participation
working capital
yield

ECONOMICS SCHOOLS AND THEORIES

Austrian school
Chicago school
Classical school
Keynesianism

Marxism
mercantilism
monetarism
neoclassical school

neoKeynesians
Physiocrats
Reaganomics
Rogernomics (N.Z.)

Thatcherism

EDUCATION TERMS

A bursary (N.Z.)
academic
accredit (N.Z.)
accumulation
Advanced level or A level (Brit.)
adviser or advisor (Brit.)
advisory teacher (Brit.)
aegrotat (Brit.)
alumnus or alumna (chiefly
  U.S.) (Canad.)
assignment
assistant (U.S.) (Canad.)
associate (U.S.) (Canad.)
baccalaureate
banding (Brit.)
battels (Brit.)
B bursary (N.Z.)
bedder (Brit.)
binary
boarder (Brit.)
boarding house (Austral.)
bubs grade (Austral.) (N.Z.
  (slang))
bursar
bursarial
bursary or bursarship (Scot.)
  (N.Z.)

campus
campus university
catalogue (U.S.) (Canad.)
catchment (Brit.)
Certificate of Pre-vocational
  Education or CPVE (Brit.)
Certificate of Proficiency or
  COP (N.Z.)
chancellor (Brit.) (U.S.
  (Canad.))
chapterhouse (U.S.)
class
classmate
classroom
co-ed (U.S.)
coeducation
collegial
collegian
collegiate
comedown (Brit.)
commencement (U.S.)
  (Canad.)
commoner (Brit.)
Common Entrance (Brit.)
conductive education
congregation (chiefly Brit.)
continuous assessment

convocation
core subjects (Brit.)
coursework
crammer
credit
crib (Brit.)
cross-curricular (Brit.)
Cuisenaire rod (trademark)
curricular
curriculum
dean
deanery
degree
delegacy
department
detention
dissertation
docent (U.S.)
dominie (Scot.)
don (Brit.)
donnish
dropout
dunce
dunce cap
dux
Easter term
educate

education
educational
eleven-plus (obsolete)
emeritus
entry
essay
examination or exam
exercise
exhibition (Brit.) (Austral.)
exhibitioner (Brit.)
expel
extension
external
extracurricular
extramural
faculty
fail
family grouping or vertical
  grouping
federal
fellow
fellowship
ferule
flunk (chiefly U.S.) (Canad.
  (N.Z.)) (informal)
fresher or freshman
full professor (U.S.) (Canad.)
further education (Brit.)
gaudy (Brit.)
General Certificate of
  Education or GCE (Brit.)
General Certificate of
  Secondary Education or
  GCSE (Brit.)
gown
grade (U.S.) (Canad.)
graded post (Brit.)
graduand (chiefly Brit.)
graduate (Brit.) (U.S. (Canad.))
graduation
grant
grant-in-aid
grant-maintained
Great Public Schools or GPS
  (Austral.)
Greats (Brit.)
gymnasium
hall
hall of residence
headmaster or headmistress
headmastership or
  headmistress-ship
headship (Brit.)
higher (Scot.)
high school
Hilary term
homework
honours or (U.S.) honors

hood
hooky or hookey (chiefly U.S.)
  (Canad. (N.Z.)) (informal)
house
housefather
housemaster
housemother
imposition (Brit.)
incept (Brit.)
infant (Brit.)
in residence
instructor (U.S.) (Canad.)
internal
interscholastic
intramural (chiefly U.S.)
  (Canad.)
invigilate (Brit.)
invigilator (Brit.)
janitor (Scot.)
jig (Austral.) (slang)
junior
junior common room
key stage (Brit.)
lecture
lecturer
level of attainment (Brit.)
liaison officer (N.Z.)
lines
literae humaniores (Brit.)
LMS or local management of
  schools (Brit.)
local examinations
lowerclassman (U.S.)
lower school
lycée (French)
manciple
marking
master
matriculate
matriculation or matric
mature student
Michaelmas term
middle common room
midterm
mistress
mitch or mich (dialect)
mocks (informal)
moderator (Brit.) (N.Z.)
muck-up day (Austral.) (slang)
National Curriculum (Brit.)
Nuffield teaching project
  (Brit.)
open learning
Ordinary grade or O grade
  (Scot.)
Ordinary level or O level (Brit.)
Ordinary National Certificate
  or ONC (Brit.)

pandy (chiefly Scot.) (Irish)
parent teacher association
  or PTA
parietal (U.S.)
pass
pedant (archaic)
pipe (U.S.) (slang)
porter
postgraduate
prefect (Brit.)
prelims (Scot.)
prepositor (Brit.) (rare)
primers (N.Z.) (informal)
principal
Privatdocent
proctor (U.S.)
professor
professoriate
prospectus
provost
punishment exercise
reader (chiefly Brit.)
readership (chiefly Brit.)
reception (Brit.)
recess (U.S.) (Canad.)
record of achievement (Brit.)
recreation
rector (chiefly Brit.)
redbrick (Brit.)
refresher course
regent
registrar
Regius professor (Brit.)
remedial
remove (Brit.)
report (Brit.)
resit
rusticate (Brit.)
sabbatical
sandwich course
SCE or Scottish Certificate of
  Education
scholastic
School Certificate (Brit.) (N.Z.
  (old-fashioned))
schoolleaver
schoolman
schoolmarm
schoolmaster
schoolmistress
schoolteacher
second (Brit.)
self-educated
semester (chiefly U.S.) (Canad.)
seminar
senate
send down
senior

senior common room
session
set
shell (Brit.)
sixth form (Brit.)
sixth-form college (Brit.)
sizar (Brit.)
sophomore (chiefly U.S.)
 (Canad.)
sorority (chiefly U.S.)
speech day (Brit.)
sports day (Brit.)
stage
Standard Grade (Scot.)
standard assessment tasks
 or SATS (Brit.)
statement (Brit.)
stream (Brit.)

student teacher
subject
subprincipal
summa cum laude
summative assessment
 (Brit.)
supervisor
teach-in
term
tertiary bursary (Brit.)
test
thesis
transcript (chiefly U.S.)
 (Canad.)
transfer
trimester (chiefly U.S.)
 (Canad.)
Trinity term

truant
tuition
tutee
tutor
tutorial
tutorial system
union
university entrance
 (examination) or UE (N.Z.)
undergraduate
unstreamed (Brit.)
upper school
vice chancellor (Brit.)
visiting professor
wag (slang)
warden (Brit.)
wrangler (Brit.)
year

EMBROIDERY STITCHES

Arrowhead stitch
Back stitch
Barb stitch
Basque stitch
Beaded stitch
Berlin stitch
Berwick stitch
Blanket stitch
Briar stitch
Bullion stitch
Buttonhole Bar
Buttonhole Wheel
Buttonhole
Casalguidi
Cast on stitch
Catch stitch
Caterpillar stitch
Chain stitch
Chevron stitch
Chinese stitch
Closed Buttonhole
Closed Feather

stitch
Coil stitch
Convent stitch
Coral stitch
Cretan stitch
Crewel stitch
Cross stitch
Crossed Buttonhole
Crossed corners
Crow's-foot
Daisy stitch
Damask stitch
Double Cross
Eyelet stitch
Feather stitch
Feathered Chain
Fern stitch
Fly stitch
French Knot
German Knot stitch
Ghiordes Knot
Greek stitch

Herringbone
Kloster stitch
Ladder stitch
Lazy Daisy stitch
Montenegrin
Open Chain stitch
Outline stitch
Pekinese
Plaited stitch
Porto Rico rose
Portuguese stitch
Post stitch
Quilt Knot stitch
Renaissance
Ribbed Wheel
Rice stitch
Roman Chain stitch
Running stitch
Russian Cross stitch
Russian stitch
Sampler stitch
Satin stitch

Scottish stitch
Scroll stitch
Sham Hem stitch
Split stitch
Stem stitch
Threaded
 Arrowhead
Threaded Fly stitch
Threaded Running
Twisted Chain
Twisted Lattice
 Band
Wheatear
Whipped Back
Whipped Chain
Whipped Fly
Whipped Running
Whipped Stem
Woven Spider's
 Wheel
Zigzag Chain

BRANCHES OF ENGINEERING

aerodynamics
aeronautical engineering
aerospace engineering
agricultural engineering
astronautics
automotive engineering
bioengineering
chemical engineering
civil engineering
computer-aided engineering
cosmonautics

electrical engineering
electronics engineering
environmental engineering
ergonomics
fluid dynamics
genetic engineering
geotechnics
hydraulics
mechanical engineering
mechatronics
military engineering

mining engineering
naval engineering
nuclear engineering
process engineering
production engineering
sanitary engineering
structural engineering
traffic engineering

ENTERTAINMENT

TYPES OF ENTERTAINMENT

acrobatics
aerobatics
agon
airshow
all-dayer
all-nighter
antimasque
après-ski
aquashow
ball
ballet
B and S *(Austral.)*
  (informal)
banquet
bear-baiting
bullfighting
burlesque show
busking
cabaret
carnival
ceilidh
charade
circus
cockfighting
comedy
command
  performance
concert
conjuring
cotillion *or* cotillon
  (U.S.) (Canad.)
dance
escapology
exhibition
fair
farce
fashion show
feast
fête *or* fete
film
fireworks *or*
  pyrotechnics
floor show
funambulism *or*
  tightrope-walking
gala
galanty show
garden party
gaudy
gig *(informal)*
ice show
juggling
karaoke
kermis *or* kirmess
  (U.S.) (Canad.)
levee
light show
magic
masked ball
masque
melodrama
minstrel show
musical
music hall
opera
operetta
pantomime
party
play
puppet show
raree show
rave
reading
reception
recital
recitation
revue *or* review
ridotto
road show
rodeo
shadow play
show
sideshow
singsong
slide show
slot machine
soiree
son et lumière
street theatre
striptease
tragedy
variety
vaudeville
ventriloquism
video game
wall of death
waltzer
warehouse party
whist drive
zarzuela

TYPES OF ENTERTAINER

acrobat
actor *or (fem.)* actress
artist
artiste
auguste
bareback rider
busker
chorus girl
circus artist
clown
comedian *or (fem.)*
  comedienne
conjurer
contortionist
dancer
diva
equilibrist
escapologist
exotic dancer
fire eater
fool
funambulist *or*
  tightrope walker
funnyman
go-go dancer
gracioso
guiser
harlequin
illusionist
impersonator
impressionist
jester
jongleur
juggler
lion tamer
magician
merry-andrew
mimic
minstrel
mummer
musician
organ-grinder
performer
prima ballerina
prima donna
puppeteer
quick-change artist
raconteur
ringmaster
show girl
singer
snake charmer
stripteaser *or* stripper
strolling player
strongman
sword swallower
tightrope walker
tragedian *or (fem.)*
  tragedienne
trapeze artist
trouper
tumbler
unicyclist
vaudevillian
ventriloquist

PLACES OF ENTERTAINMENT

amphitheatre
amusement arcade
  (Brit.)
arena
auditorium
ballroom
bandstand
big top
bingo hall
carnival
cinema
circus
coliseum *or*
  colosseum
concert hall
dance hall
disco
fairground
funfair
gallery
hall
leisure centre
lido
marquee
museum
music hall
nightclub
nightspot
niterie *(slang)*
opera house
social club
stadium
theatre
vaudeville
waxworks
zoo

EQUESTRIANISM

EQUESTRIAN EVENTS AND SPORTS

Ascot
Badminton
buckjumping
  (Austral.)
cavalcade
claiming race (U.S.)
  (Canad.)
classic
Derby
dressage
eventing
Grand National
gymkhana
harness racing
horse racing
hunt
joust
jump-off
Kentucky Derby
meeting
nursery stakes
Oaks
One Thousand
  Guineas
picnic race (Austral.)
plate
point-to-point
polo
puissance
race meeting
races, the
Saint Leger
showjumping
steeplechase
sweepstake or (esp
  U.S.) sweepstakes
three-day eventing
Two Thousand
  Guineas

CLASSIC ENGLISH HORSE RACES

Race	Course	Distance
One Thousand Guineas (fillies)	Newmarket	one mile
Two Thousand Guineas (colts)	Newmarket	one mile
Derby (colts)	Epsom	one and a half miles
the Oaks (fillies)	Epsom	one and a half miles
St. Leger (colts and fillies)	Doncaster	one and three quarter miles

HORSE RACING TERMS

accumulator
allowance
also-ran
ante post betting
apprentice
auction plate
away
blanket finish
boring
break
break away
card or race card
chaser
claiming race (U.S.)
  (Canad.)
classic
clerk of the course
clerk of the scales
colt
come in
course
daily double
dead heat
distance
dope sheet (slang)
draw
each way or (U.S.)
  across-the-board
faller
fence
filly
finish
flat
flat jockey
flat racing
flight
furlong
gate
going
green horse
handicap
handicapper
handy
harness race or (N.Z.)
  trotting race
head
home straight or
  (U.S.) home stretch
hurdle
hurdling
impost
jockey
Jockey Club
jump jockey
length
maiden
meeting
milepost
nap
National Hunt
neck
novice
objection
pacemaker or
  pacesetter
pacer
paddock
photo finish
place
plater
point-to-point (Brit.)
pole (chiefly U.S.)
  (Canad.)
post
roughie
scratch
scurry
selling race or plate
short head
silver ring
stakes
starter
starting post
starting price
starting stalls or
  (U.S.) starting gate
stayer
steeplechase or
  chase
steward
stewards' inquiry
straight or (U.S.)
  straightaway
stretch
sweat (chiefly U.S.)
sweat up
ticktack
track
trainer
turf
under starter's
  orders
unplaced
unseated rider
walkover
weigh in
winning post
wire (U.S.) (Canad.)
yearling

TYPES OF JUMP

brush and rails
double oxer
gate
hog's back
narrow stile
parallel poles
planks
post and rails
triple bars
wall
water jump

PARTS OF THE EYE

aqueous humour
blind spot
choroid or chorioid
ciliary body
cone
conjunctiva
cornea
eyeball
fovea
iris
lens
ocular muscle
optic nerve
pupil
retina
retinal vessels
rod
sclera
suspensory ligament
vitreous body
vitreous humour

FABRICS

Acrilan (trademark)
alpaca
armure
baize
balbriggan
barathea
barège
batik or battik
batiste
bayadere
beige
bengaline
bird's-eye
bobbinet
bombazine or bombasine
bouclé
brilliantine
broadcloth
brocade
buckskin
bunting
burlap
calamanco
calico
cambric
camlet
cavalry twill
challis or challie
chambray
Charmeuse (trademark)
cheesecloth
chenille
cheviot
chiffon
chintz
cilice
ciré
cloqué
cord
corduroy
cotton
cottonade
cotton flannel
covert cloth
crepe or crape

cretonne
Crimplene (trademark)
crinoline
cypress or cyprus
Dacron (trademark)
damask
delaine
denim
diamanté
dimity
Donegal tweed
drab
drabbet
Dralon (trademark)
drugget
duck
dungaree
duvetyn, duvetine, or duvetyne
etamine or etamin
façonné or faconne
faille
fearnought or fearnaught
felt
fishnet
flannel
fleece
folk weave
foulard
frieze
frisé
fur
fustian
gaberdine
galatea
georgette
gingham
gloria
Gore-Tex (trademark)
gossamer
grogram
gros de Londres
grosgrain
gunny (chiefly U.S.)
Harris Tweed (trademark)

hessian
honan
hopsack
huckaback or huck
India print
jaconet
Jacquard or Jacquard weave
jean
jersey
khaki
kincob
knit
lace
lambskin
lamé
lawn
leather
linen
linsey-woolsey
lisle
Lurex (trademark)
Lycra (trademark)
madras
marabou
marocain
marquisette
marseille or marseilles
melton
messaline
mohair
moire or moiré
moleskin
monk's cloth
moquette
moreen
mousseline
mull
muslin
nainsook
nankeen or nankin
needlecord
net
ninon
nun's cloth or veiling
oilskin
organdie

organza
organzine
Orlon (trademark)
ottoman
Oxford
paduasoy
paisley pattern
panne
paramatta or parramatta
peau de soie
percale
percaline
petersham
piña cloth
piqué
plush
pongee
poplin
poult or poult-de-soie
prunella, prunelle, or prunello
rayon
russet
sailcloth
samite
sarcenet or sarsenet
sateen
satin
satinet or satinette
saxony
say (archaic)
schappe
scrim
seersucker
sendal
serge
shag
shalloon
shantung
sharkskin
sheeting
shirting
shoddy
silesia
silk
silkaline

slipper satin
spandex
spun silk
stockinet
stroud
stuff
suiting
surah
surat
swan's-down
swanskin
swiss muslin

tabaret
tabby
taffeta
tammy
tarlatan
tarpaulin
tartan
tattersall
terry
Terylene (trademark)
tick
ticking

tiffany
toile
towelling
tricot
tricotine
tulle
tussore, tusser, or
(chiefly U.S.) tussah
tweed
twill
velours
velure

velvet
velveteen
Viyella (trademark)
voile
wadmal
webbing
whipcord
wild silk
winceyette
wool
worsted

THE FATES

Atropos

Clotho

Lachesis

FENCING TERMS

backsword
bracer
carte
feint
guard
mask

octave
parade
parry
piste
prime
quarte or carte

quinte
reach
repechage
sabre
seconde
septime

singlestick
sixte
terce or tierce
touch
touché
volt

FIGURES OF SPEECH

alliteration
allusion
anacoluthia
anadiplosis
analogy
anaphora
anastrophe
antiphrasis
antithesis
antonomasia
apophasis
aporia
aposiopesis
apostrophe
catachresis

chiasmus
circumlocution
climax
emphasis
epanaphora
epanorthosis
exclamation
gemination
hendiadys
hypallage
hyperbaton
hyperbole
hysteron proteron
inversion
irony

kenning
litotes
malapropism
meiosis
metaphor
metonymy
onomatopoeia
oxymoron
paralipsis or
    paraleipsis
parenthesis
periphrasis
personification
pleonasm
polysyndeton

prolepsis
prosopopoeia or
    prosopopeia
repetition
rhetorical question
sarcasm
simile
spoonerism
syllepsis
synechdoche
tmesis
zeugma

FISH

TYPES OF FISH

ahi
ahuru (N.Z.)
alewife
albacore
alfonsino
amberjack
anabantid
anabas
anableps
anchoveta
anchovy

angelfish
arapaima
archerfish
argentine
aua (N.Z.)
Australian salmon,
    native salmon,
    salmon trout, bay
    trout or kahawai
    (N.Z.) (Austral.)
barbel

barracouta or
    (Austral.) hake
barracuda
barramunda
barramundi or
    (Austral.) barra or
    giant perch
bass
batfish
beluga
bib, pout, or whiting

pout
bigeye
billfish
bitterling
black bass
black bream
black cod or Māori
    chief (N.Z.)
blackfish or (Austral.)
    nigger
bleak

blenny
blindfish
bloodfin
blowfish or (Austral.) toado
blue cod, rock cod, or (N.Z.) rawaru, pakirikiri, or patutuki
bluefin tuna
bluefish or snapper
bluegill
blue nose (N.Z.)
boarfish
bonefish
bonito or (Austral.) horse mackerel
bony bream (Austral.)
bowfin or dogfish
bream or (Austral.) brim
brill
brook trout or speckled trout
brown trout
buffalo fish
bullhead
bull trout
bully or (N.Z.) pakoko, titarakura, or toitoi
burbot, eelpout, or ling
butterfish
butterfish, greenbone, or (N.Z.) koaea or marari
butterfly fish
cabezon or cabezone
cabrilla
callop
candlefish or eulachon
capelin or caplin
carp
catfish
cavalla or cavally
cavefish
cero
characin or characid
chimaera
Chinook salmon, quinnat salmon, or king salmon
chub
chum
cichlid
cisco or lake herring
climbing fish or climbing perch

clingfish
coalfish or (Brit.) saithe or coley
cobia, black kingfish, or sergeant fish
cockabully
cod or codfish
coelacanth
coho or silver salmon
coley
conger
coral trout
crappie
croaker
crucian
dab
dace
damselfish
danio
dart (Austral.)
darter
dealfish
dentex
dollarfish
dorado
dory
dragonet
eel or (N.Z.) tuna
eelpout
electric eel
fallfish
father lasher or short-spined sea scorpion
fighting fish or betta
filefish
flatfish or (N.Z.) flattie
flathead
flounder or (N.Z.) patiki
flying fish
flying gurnard
four-eyed fish
frogfish
garpike, garfish, gar, or (Austral.) ballahoo
geelbek
gemfish or (Austral.) hake
gilthead
goby
golden perch, freshwater bream, Murray perch, or yellow-belly (Austral.)
goldeye
goldfish
goldsinny or goldfinny

gourami
grayling or (Austral.) yarra herring
greenling
grenadier or rat-tail
groper or grouper
grunion
grunt
gudgeon
guitarfish
gunnel
guppy
gurnard or gurnet
gwyniad
haddock
hagfish, hag or blind eel
hairtail or (U.S.) cutlass fish
hake
halfbeak
halibut
hapuku (Austral.) (N.Z.)
herring
hogfish
hoki (N.Z.)
horned pout or brown bullhead
horse mackerel
houndfish
houting
ice fish
jacksmelt
javelin fish or Queensland trumpeter
jewelfish
jewfish or (Austral. informal) jewie
John Dory
jurel
kelpfish or (Austral. informal) kelpie
killifish
kingfish
kingklip (S. African)
kokanee
kokopu (N.Z.)
labyrinth fish
lampern or river lamprey
lamprey or lamper eel
lancet fish
lantern fish
largemouth bass
latimeria
leatherjacket

lemon sole
lepidosiren
ling or (Austral.) beardie
lingcod
lionfish
loach
louvar
luderick or (N.Z.) parore
lumpfish or lumpsucker
lungfish
mackerel or (colloquial) shiner
mangrove Jack (Austral.)
manta, manta ray, devilfish, or devil ray
maomao (N.Z.)
marlin or spearfish
megrim
menhaden
milkfish
miller's thumb
minnow or (Scot.) baggie minnow
mirror carp
moki or blue moki (N.Z.)
molly
monkfish or (U.S.) goosefish
mooneye
moonfish
Moorish idol
moray
morwong, black perch, or (N.Z.) porae
mudcat
mudfish
mudskipper
opah, moonfish, or kingfish
orange chromide
orange roughy (Austral.)
orfe
ouananiche
ox-eye herring (Austral.)
paddlefish
panchax
pandora
paradise fish
parore, blackfish, black rockfish or mangrove fish (N.Z.)

parrotfish
pearl perch (Austral.)
perch or (Austral.) redfin
pickerel
pigfish or hogfish
pike, luce, or jackfish
pikeperch
pilchard or (Austral. informal) pillie
pilot fish
pinfish or sailor's choice
pipefish or needlefish
piranha or piraña
plaice
platy
pogge or armed bullhead
pollack or pollock
pollan
pomfret
pompano
porae (N.Z.)
porcupine fish or globefish
porgy or pogy
pout
powan or lake herring
puffer or globefish
pumpkinseed
Queensland halibut
Queensland lungfish
rabbitfish
rainbow trout
ray
red cod
red emperor
redfin
redfish
red mullet or (U.S.) goatfish
red salmon
red snapper
remora
ribbonfish
roach
robalo

rock bass
rock cod
rockfish or (formerly) rock salmon
rockling
rosefish
rudd
ruffe, ruff, or pope
runner
salmon
salmon trout
sand dab
sand eel, sand lance, or launce
sardine
sauger
saury or skipper
sawfish
scabbard fish
scad
scaldfish
scat
scorpion fish
sculpin (U.S.) (Canad.)
scup or northern porgy
sea bass
sea bream
sea horse
sea lamprey
sea perch
sea raven
sea robin
sea scorpion
sea snail or snailfish
sea trout
Sergeant Baker
sergeant major
shad
shanny
sheepshead
shiner
shovelnose
Siamese fighting fish
sild
silver belly (N.Z.)
silverfish
silverside or silversides

skate
skelly
skipjack or skipjack tuna
sleeper or sleeper goby
smallmouth bass
smelt
smooth hound
snapper, red bream, or (Austral.) wollomai or wollamai
snipefish or bellows fish
snoek
snook
sockeye or red salmon
sole
solenette
spadefish
Spanish mackerel or Queensland kingfish
spotted mackerel or school mackerel
sprat
squeteague
squirrelfish
steelhead
sterlet
stickleback
stingray
stone bass or wreckfish
stonefish
stone roller
sturgeon
sucker
sunfish
surfperch or sea perch
surgeonfish
swordfish
swordtail
tailor
tarakihi or terakihi (N.Z.)
tarpon
tarwhine
tautog or blackfish

tench
teraglin
tetra
thornback
threadfin
tilapia
tilefish
toadfish
tommy rough or tommy ruff (Austral.)
topminnow
torsk or (U.S. & Canadian) cusk
trevalla (Austral.)
trevally, araara or samson fish (Austral.) (N.Z.)
triggerfish
tripletail
trout
trunkfish, boxfish, or cowfish
tuna or tunny
turbot
vendace
wahoo
walleye, walleyed pike, or dory
warehou (N.Z.)
weakfish
weever
whitebait
whitefish
whiting
wirrah
witch
wobbegong, wobbygong, or wobegong
wolffish or catfish
wrasse
yellowfin (N.Z.)
yellowfin tuna
yellow jack
yellowtail
zander

EXTINCT FISH

ceratodus

ostracoderm

placoderm

FLOWERS

acacia
acanthus
African violet

aloe
alyssum
amaranth

amaryllis
anemone
arbutus

asphodel
aspidistra
aster

aubrietia, aubrieta, or aubretia
azalea
babe-in-a-cradle (Austral.)
begonia
betony
bignonia
black-eyed Susan
bluebell
bog asphodel
bougainvillea
burdock
Busy Lizzie
buttercup
cactus
calendula
camellia
camomile or chamomile
cardinal flower
carnation
celandine
Christmas cactus
chrysanthemum
clematis
clianthus
columbine
Cooktown orchid (Austral.)
cornflower
cotoneaster
cowslip
crocus
cyclamen
daffodil
dahlia
daisy
dandelion
deadly nightshade
delphinium
digitalis
dog rose
edelweiss
eglantine
forget-me-not
foxglove
freesia
geranium
gilliflower or gillyflower
gladiolus
godetia
grape hyacinth
groundsel
guelder-rose
gypsophila
harebell
heartsease or heart's-ease
heliotrope
hellebore
hemlock
hibiscus
hollyhock
hyacinth
hydrangea
iris
jasmine
jonquil
larkspur
lavender
lily
lily of the valley
lobelia
London pride
lotus
love-in-idleness
love-lies-bleeding
lupin
magnolia
mallow
mandrake
marguerite
marigold
marjoram
meadowsweet
monkshood
Michaelmas daisy
morning-glory
narcissus
nasturtium
old man's beard
orchid
oxeye daisy
oxlip
oxtongue
pansy
passionflower
peony or paeony
petunia
phlox
pimpernel
pink
poppy
primrose
primula
ragged robin
ragweed
rose
saffron
samphire
saxifrage
scarlet pimpernel
snapdragon
snowdrop
speedwell
stock
(Sturt's) desert pea (Austral.)
sunflower
sweetbrier
sweet pea
sweet william
tiger lily
tulip
valerian
verbena
violet
wallflower
water lily
willowherb
wintergreen
wisteria
wood anemone
woodbine
yarrow
zinnia

FLIES

antlion or antlion fly
aphid or plant louse
aphis
apple blight or American blight
bee fly
beetfly or mangold fly
blackfly or bean aphid
blowfly, bluebottle, or (Austral. informal) blowie
botfly
buffalo gnat or black fly
bulb fly
bushfly
carrot fly
chalcid or chalcid fly
cluster fly
crane fly or (Brit.) daddy-longlegs
damselfly
dobsonfly
dragonfly or (colloquial) devil's darning-needle
drosophila, fruit fly, or vinegar fly
fly
frit fly
fruit fly
gadfly
gallfly
gnat
grannom
green blowfly or (Austral. informal) blue-arsed fly
greenbottle
greenfly
horsefly or cleg
housefly
hoverfly
lacewing
lantern fly
mayfly or dayfly
Mediterranean fruit fly or Medfly
needle fly
onion fly
robber fly, bee killer, or assassin fly
sandfly
scorpion fly
screwworm fly
silverhorn
snake fly
stable fly
stonefly
tachina fly
tsetse fly or tzetze fly
vinegar fly
warble fly
whitefly
willow fly

FOOTBALL

TERMS USED IN (ASSOCIATION) FOOTBALL

aggregate (score)
back
ballplayer
ballwinner
booking or caution
breakaway
cap
catenaccio
centre circle
centre forward
centre half
clearance
cross
crossbar or bar
corner (kick)
cut out
defender
derby
direct free kick
dribble
dummy
extra time
FA
FIFA
finishing
forward
foul
free kick
fullback

full time
goal
goal area or six-yard
  box
goalkeeper or goalie
goal kick or bye kick
goal net or net
goalpost or post
golden goal
half
halfback
half time
half way line
handball
indirect free kick
inside left
inside right
inswinger
international
kick off
lay off
left back
linesman
long ball
mark
midfield
midfielder
nil
non-league

nutmeg
offside
offside trap
onside
one-two
outside left
outside right
own goal
pass
pass-back
penalty (kick) or spot
  kick
penalty area or
  penalty box
penalty shoot-out
penalty spot
playoff
professional foul
promotion
red card
referee
relegation
reserves
right back
Route One
save
score draw
sending-off or
  ordering-off

SFA
shot
silver goal
six-pointer
six-yard line
sliding tackle
stoppage time or
  injury time
striker
square
substitute
sweeper
tackle
target man
technical area
throw in
total football
touchline
transfer
trap
UEFA
wall
wall pass
wing
winger
yellow card

TERMS USED IN AUSTRALIAN RULES FOOTBALL

Australian Football
  League or AFL
back pocket
behind or point
behind line
behind post
boundary
eighteen, the
field umpire
flank

footy, Aussie Rules,
  or (jocular) aerial
  ping-pong
follower
forward pocket
free kick
goal
goal umpire
guernsey
half-back

half-forward
handball
interchange
mark
nineteenth man
quarter
rove
rover
rub out
ruck

ruckrover
scrimmage
shepherd
shirt front
stab kick
stanza
throw in
twentieth man

TERMS USED IN AMERICAN FOOTBALL

backfield
blitz
block
center
complete
cornerback
defense
defensive back
defensive end
down
end zone
field goal

football or pigskin
fullback
gridiron
guard
halfback
incomplete
interception
kicker
line or line of
  scrimmage
line backer
lineman

offense
overtime
pass
play
point after
punt
punter
quarterback
run or rush
running back
sack
safety

scrimmage
secondary
shotgun
snap
special team
Super Bowl
tackle
tight end
touchback
touchdown
turnover
wide receiver

FRUITS

ananas
anchovy pear
apple
apricot
avocado, avocado pear, or (U.S.) alligator pear
babaco
banana
Bartlett pear
beach plum
bergamot pear
berry
Beurre Hardy pear
bigarreau cherry
bilberry, blaeberry, huckleberry, whortleberry, or (Irish) fraughan
blackberry or (Scot.) bramble
black cherry
blackcurrant
blackheart cherry
blood orange
blueberry
Bon Chretien pear
boxberry
boysenberry
breadfruit
calamondin
cantaloup or cantaloupe melon
carambola or star fruit
casaba or cassaba melon
Charentais melon
chayote
chempaduk
cherry
chokecherry

choko
citron
clementine
cloudberry or (Canad.) bakeapple
Concord grape
Conference pear
cranberry
custard apple
damson
date
dewberry
durian or durion
elderberry
fig
Galia melon
gooseberry or (informal) goosegog
grape
grapefruit
greengage
guava
hackberry
heart cherry
honeydew melon
jackfruit or jack
Jaffa orange
kiwano (trademark)
Kiwi fruit or Chinese gooseberry
kumquat or cumquat
lemon
lime
lychee, litchi, lichee, or lichi
loganberry
longan
loquat or Japan plum

mandarin
mango
mangosteen
May apple
medlar
melon
minneola
morello cherry
mulberry
muskmelon
nashi or Asian pear
navel orange
nectarine
Ogen melon
olive
orange
ortanique
papaw or pawpaw
papaya
passion fruit or granadilla
peach
pear
pepper
physalis, Cape gooseberry, or strawberry tomato
pineapple
plantain
plum
pomegranate
pomelo or shaddock
prickly pear
prune
pumpkin
Queensland blue
quince
raisin
rambutan
raspberry
redcurrant

rockmelon
salmonberry
sapota
sapodilla, sapodilla plum, or naseberry
saskatoon
satsuma
Seville orange
serviceberry
sharon fruit or persimmon
sloe
snowberry
sour cherry
sour gourd
soursop
star-apple
strawberry
sultana
sweet cherry
sweetie
sweetsop
tamarillo or tree tomato
tamarind
tangelo
tangerine or (S. African) naartje
tayberry
tomato or (archaic) love apple
UGLI (trademark)
victoria or victoria plum
watermelon
white currant
Williams pear
winter melon
youngberry

FUNGI

agaric
bird's-nest fungus
boletus
bracket fungus
cramp ball
death cap
dry rot
earthstar
elf-cup

ergot
funnel cap
ink-cap
jelly fungus
horn of plenty
liberty cap
mildew
milk cap
miller

mould
mushroom
puffball
rust or rust fungus
shaggy cap
sickener
smut
stinkhorn
sulphur tuft

toadstool
truffle
velvet shank
wax cap
wet rot
wood hedgehog
wood woollyfoot
yeast

FURNITURE

TYPES OF FURNITURE

bedpost
bedstead
canopy
cheval glass
coatstand
dumbwaiter
epergne
footstool
girandole or girandola
grandfather clock
grandmother clock
hallstand
hatstand
headboard
lectern
litter
longcase clock
screen
tester
trolley
umbrella stand
vanitory or vanity unit
washstand

FURNITURE STYLES

Art Deco
Bauhaus
Cape Dutch
Edwardian
Elizabethan
Empire
Georgian
Gothic
Greek Revival
Jacobean
Louis Quatorze
Louis Quinze
Louis Seize
Louis Treize
Medieval
New Georgian
Norman
Puritan
Queen Anne
Regency
Restoration
Saxon
Second Empire
Shaker
Tudor
Victorian
William and Mary

GAMES

PARTY GAMES

blind man's buff
charades
Chinese whispers
consequences
follow-my-leader
hide-and-seek
I-spy
musical chairs
postman's knock
Simon says
statues

WORD GAMES

acrostic
anagram
crambo
crossword or crossword
puzzle
hangman
logogriph
The Minister's Cat (Scot.)
rebus
Scrabble (trademark)
twenty questions or animal, vegetable, or mineral

OTHER GAMES

bar billiards
battleships
beetle
bingo or housey-housey
British bulldog
caber tossing
conkers
craps
crown and anchor
deck tennis
dominoes
foosball or table football
French cricket
hoopla
hopscotch
horseshoes
jacks
jigsaw puzzle
keno, keeno, kino, or quino
king of the castle
knur and spell
lansquenet
leapfrog
lotto
mahjong or mah-
jongg
marbles
nim
noughts and crosses
paintball
pall-mall
pegboard
pinball
pitch-and-toss
quoits
ring taw
roque
roulette
Russian roulette
sack race
scavenger hunt
shuffleboard
skipping
spillikins or jackstraws
tag or tig
tangram
thimblerig
tiddlywinks
tipcat
trictrac or tricktrack
trugo
wall game
war game

GASES

TYPES OF GAS

acetylene
afterdamp
ammonia
argon
arsine
biogas
butadiene
butane
butene
Calor gas (trademark)
carbon dioxide or carbonic-acid gas
carbon monoxide
chlorine
coal gas

compressed natural gas (CNG)
cyanogen
diazomethane
diborane
dichlorodifluoromethane
electrolytic gas
ethane
ethylene
flue gas
fluorine
formaldehyde
helium
hydrogen
hydrogen bromide
hydrogen chloride
hydrogen fluoride
hydrogen iodide
hydrogen sulphide
ketene
krypton
laughing gas or nitrous oxide (LNG)
liquefied petroleum gas (LPG)
marsh gas
methane
methylamine
methyl bromide
methyl chloride
natural gas
neon
nitric oxide
nitrogen
nitrogen dioxide
nitrous oxide
oil gas
oxygen
ozone
phosgene
phosphine
producer gas or air gas
propane
radon
sewage gas
stibine
synthetic natural gas (SNG)
sulphur dioxide
synthesis gas
tail gas
tetrafluoroethene
tetrafluoroethylene
town gas
vinyl chloride
water gas
xenon

CHEMICAL WARFARE GASES

blister gas	mustard gas	sarin	tear gas
CS gas	nerve gas	soman	VX
lewisite	nitrogen mustard	tabun	

GEMSTONES

adularia
agate
alexandrite
almandine
amazonite
amethyst
andalusite
andradite
aquamarine
aventurine, aventurin, or avanturine
balas
beryl
black opal
bloodstone
bone turquoise
cairngorm
carnelian
cat's-eye
chalcedony
chrysoberyl
chrysolite
chrysoprase
citrine
Colorado ruby
Colorado topaz
corundum
cymophane
demantoid
diamond
diopside
emerald
fire opal
garnet
girasol, girosol, or girasole
grossularite
hawk's-eye
helidor
heliotrope
hessonite
hiddenite
hyacinth
indicolite or indigolite
jacinth
jadeite or jade
jasper
jet
kunzite
lapis lazuli
liver opal
Madagascar aquamarine
melanite
moonstone
morganite
morion
moss agate
New Zealand greenstone
odontolite
onyx
opal
Oriental almandine
Oriental emerald
peridot
plasma
pyrope
quartz
rhodolite
rose quartz
rubellite
ruby
sapphire
sard or sardine
sardonyx
smoky quartz
Spanish topaz
spessartite
sphene
spinel
spodumene
staurolite
sunstone
titanite
topaz
topazolite
tourmaline
turquoise
uvarovite
vesuvianite
water sapphire
white sapphire
zircon

GEOGRAPHY

BRANCHES OF GEOGRAPHY

biogeography
cartography
chorography
chorology
climatology
demography
geology
geomorphology
glaciology
hydrology
human geography
meteorology
oceanography
oceanology
orography or orology
pedology
physical geography
political geography
or geopolitics
seismology
topography
vulcanology

GEOGRAPHY TERMS AND FEATURES

afforestation	deforestation	ice cap	ocean	South Pole
antipodes	delta	infrastructure	Ordnance Survey	spit
arête	desert	International	oriental	spring
atlas	desertification	Date Line	ozone layer	spur
atmosphere	dormitory	irrigation	permafrost	stack
atoll	dyke	isobar	plate tectonics	steppe
basin	earthquake	isobath	pollution	subsoil
bay	eastings	isohyet	precipitation	suburb
beach	environment	isotherm	rainforest	tarn
canyon	epicentre	isthmus	rain shadow	temperate
cliff	equator	jungle	reef	Third World
climate	erosion	lagoon	relief map	topsoil
col	escarpment	latitude	ridge	tor
conservation	estuary	levée	rift valley	tropics
continent	fault	loch	rill	tsunami
continental drift	fell	longitude	river basin	tundra
continental shelf	fjord	longshore drift	rivulet	urbanization
contour	flood plain	mantle	salt flat	veld or veldt
conurbation	glaciation	map	salt lake	volcano
coombe	glacier	meander	sandbank	wadi
coral reef	glade	Mercator	sand bar	watercourse
core	glen	projection	sand dune	water cycle
corrie, cirque, or	global warming	moraine	savanna or	waterfall
cwm	green belt	new town	savannah	watershed
crag	greenhouse	northern	scree	water table
crater	effect	hemisphere	sierra	weathering
crevasse	grid reference	northings	snow line	wetland
crust	hanging valley	North Pole	southern	whirlpool
culvert	headland	occidental	hemisphere	

GEOLOGY

GEOLOGICAL ERAS

Cenozoic	Mesozoic	Palaeozoic	Precambrian

GEOLOGICAL PERIODS

Quaternary	Jurassic	Carboniferous	Ordovician
Tertiary	Triassic	Devonian	Cambrian
Cretaceous	Permian	Silurian	

EPOCHS OF THE CENOZOIC ERA

Holocene	Pliocene	Oligocene	Palaeocene
Pleistocene	Miocene	Eocene	

GOLF TERMS

ace (U.S.)	ball	trap	cut	fade
air shot or fresh	bandit	caddie	divot	fairway
air shot	better-ball	caddie car	dormie	fluff
albatross	birdie	carry	downswing	foozle
approach	blade	casual water	draw	fore
apron	bogey	chip	drive	four-ball
back nine (chiefly	borrow	club	driver	foursome
U.S.)	bunker, trap,	clubhouse	driving range	front nine (chiefly
backswing	or (esp U.S. &	course	duff	U.S.)
bag	Canad.) sand	cup	eagle	gimme

green
green fee
green keeper
greensome
grip
half
half shot
handicap
hazard
heel
hole
hole in one
honour
hook
hosel
iron
ladies' tee

lag
lie
links
local rules
loft
long iron
marker
match play
medal play
medal tee
midiron
nine-hole course
nineteenth hole
par
pin
pitch and run
pitching wedge

pitch shot
play through
plus fours
plus twos
practice swing
pull
putt
putter
putting green
rabbit
recovery
rough
round
rub of the green
run
Royal and
    Ancient or R & A

sand wedge
sclaff
score
score card
scratch
shaft
shank
short iron
single
slice
slow play
spoon
Stableford
    system
stance
stroke
stroke play

stymie
sweetspot
swing
take-away
tee
thin
tiger
threesome
top
trolley
waggle
wedge
wood
yips

TYPES OF GOVERNMENT

absolutism	by an absolute ruler	isocracy	by equals
anarchy	absence of government	meritocracy	by rulers chosen according to ability
aristocracy	by nobility	mobocracy	by the mob
autarchy or autocracy	by an unrestricted individual	monarchy	by monarch
		monocracy	by one ruler
bureaucracy	by officials	nomocracy	by rule of law
communalism	by self-governing communities	ochlocracy	by mob
		octarchy	by eight rulers
constitutionalism	according to a constitution	oligarchy	by the few
		pantisocracy	by all equally
corporatism	by corporate groups	pentarchy	by five rulers
democracy	by the people	plutocracy	by the rich
despotism	by a despot or absolute ruler	pornocracy	by whores
		ptochocracy	by the poor
diarchy or dyarchy	by two rulers	quangocracy	by quangos
dictatorship	by dictator	slavocracy	by slaveholders
ergatocracy	by the workers	squirearchy or	
gerontocracy	by old people	squirarchy	by squires
gynaecocracy or		stratocracy	by the army
gynarchy	by women	technocracy	by experts
hagiocracy or hagiarchy	by holy men	tetrarchy	by four rulers
heptarchy	by seven rulers	theocracy or thearchy	by a deity
hexarchy	by six rulers	triarchy	by three rulers
hierocracy or hierarchy	by priests	tyranny	by a tyrant
imperialism	by an emperor or empire		

THE GRACES

Aglaia	Euphrosyne	Thalia

GRAMMATICAL CASES

ablative	elative	instrumental	oblique
accusative	ergative	locative	possessive
agentive	genitive	nominative	subjective
dative	illative	objective	vocative

GRAPES USED IN MAKING WINE

WHITE WINE

aligoté
chardonnay
chenin blanc or steen
colombard
furmint
gewürztraminer
grüner veltliner
hárslevelü
malvasia
marsanne
müller-thurgau
muscadelle
muscat or moscatel
pinot blanc
pinot gris, pinot grigio, ruländer, or Tokay-Pinot Gris
riesling or rhine riesling
sauvignon blanc
scheurebe
semillon or sémillon
seyval blanc
silvaner or sylvaner
trebbiano or ugni blanc
verdelho
verdicchio
viognier
viura
welschriesling, olasz rizling, or laški rizling

RED WINE

barbera
cabernet franc
cabernet sauvignon
cinsault
dolcetto
gamay
grenache or garnacha
kékfrankos
malbec
merlot
montepulciano
mourvèdre
nebbiolo or
spanna
negroamoro
pinotage
pinot noir or spätburgunder
sangiovese
shiraz or syrah
tempranillo
zinfandel

GRASSES

barley
Bermuda grass
blady grass, bladey grass, or kunai (Austral.)
bluegrass
buffalo grass
buffel grass
cane grass
citronella
corkscrew grass (Austral.)
cotton grass
couch grass or (Austral.) quack grass, quick grass or quitch grass
crab grass
danthonia or
wallaby grass (Austral.)
darnel
elephant grass
esparto
fescue
kangaroo grass (Austral.)
maize
marram grass
millet
oat
pampas grass
paspalum
reed
rice
rye
rye-grass
snowgrass (N.Z.)
sorghum
spear grass (Austral.)
spinifex
sugar cane
wheat
wild oat
wild rye

GUNS

AK-47 or Kalashnikov
anti-aircraft gun or ack-ack gun
Armalite (trademark)
arquebus
BAR
Big Bertha
blunderbuss
Bofors gun
breech-loader
Bren gun
Browning
burp gun
carbine
carronade
chassepot
chokebore
Colt
culverin
derringer or deringer
Enfield rifle
firelock
flintlock
forty-five
fusil
Garand rifle
Gatling
howitzer
Lewis gun
Luger (trademark)
M-1 rifle
M-14
M-16
machine gun
Magnum (trademark)
matchlock
Mauser
Maxim gun
mitrailleuse
musket
muzzle-loader
Owen gun
petronel
pistol
pom-pom
pump gun
Quaker gun
repeater
revolver
rifle
scatter-gun
shotgun
six-shooter
Springfield rifle
Sten gun
stern-chaser
sub-machine-gun
Thompson sub-machine gun (trademark)
trench mortar
Uzi (trademark)
Winchester rifle
zip gun

HAIRSTYLES

Afro
beehive
bob
bouffant
bun
bunches
buzz cut
chignon
corn row
crew cut
crop
dreadlocks
duck's arse or DA
Eton crop
feather-cut
flat top
French pleat or roll
marcel or marcel wave
mohican
mullet
pageboy
perm or permanent wave
pigtail
plait
pompadour
ponytail
pouf
razor-cut
shingle
skinhead
wedge

HATS

Akubra (Austral.) (trademark)	busby	flat cap	nightcap	stocking cap
anadem (poetic)	calash or caleche	fool's cap	opera hat or gibus	stovepipe
babushka	calotte	forage cap	Panama hat	straw hat
Balaclava helmet or Balaclava	calpac, calpack, or kalpak	frontlet or frontal	paper hat	sunbonnet
Balmoral or bluebonnet	capuche or capouch	Gandhi cap	peaked cap	sunhat
bandanna or bandana	castor	glengarry	petasus	taj
bandeau	chaplet	hard hat	Phrygian cap	tam-o'-shanter or tammy (Scot.)
barret	cheese cutter	havelock	picture hat	tarboosh, tarbouche or tarbush
baseball cap	circlet	headband	pillbox	tarpaulin, ten-gallon hat
basinet or bascinet	cloche	headdress	pinner	tiara
beanie or beany	cloth cap	heaume	pith helmet, topee, or topi	tin hat (informal)
bearskin	cocked hat	helmet	poke or poke bonnet	tricorn or tricorne
beaver	coif	homburg	porkpie hat	toorie or tourie (Scot.)
beret	commode	hood	sailor hat	top hat
billycock (rare) (chiefly Brit.)	coonskin	Juliet cap	sallet, salet, or salade	topper (informal)
biretta or berretta	cornet	keffiyeh, kaffiyeh, or kufiyah	shako or shacko	toque
blackcap	coronet	kepi	shovel hat	tricorn
bluebonnet or bluecap	cossack hat	laurels	shower cap	trilby
boater	crash helmet	leghorn	silk hat	tuque
bonnet	crown	liberty cap	skullcap	turban
bowler or (U.S. & Canad.) derby	curch or curchef	lum-hat (Scot.)	slouch hat	veil
broadbrim	deerstalker	mitre	snood	visor or vizor
	diadem	mobcap or mob	sombrero	watch cap
	Dolly Varden	montero	songkok	wimple
	dunce cap	morion	sou'wester or nor'wester	yarmulke
	earmuff	mortarboard, trencher, or trencher cap	stetson	
	fascinator (rare)	mutch		
	fedora			
	fez			

PARTS OF THE HEART

aorta	pulmonary artery	septum	ventricle
atrium or auricle	pulmonary vein	tricuspid valve	
bicuspid valve	semilunar valve	vena cava	

HERALDRY TERMS

achievement	blazonry	cognisance	embattled	gironny or gyronny
annulet	bordure	college of arms	emblazon	griffon
argent	cadency	compony or compone	ermine	guardant or gardant
armes parlantes	canting arms	coronet	escutcheon	gules
armiger	canton	couchant	falcon	hatchment
armory	chaplet	crescent	fesse or fess	herald
bandeau	charge	crest	field	heraldic or fetial
bar	checky	cross	fillet	impale or empale
base	chevron	crosslet	fleur-de-lis or fleur-de-lys	inescutcheon
baton	chief	crown	flory or fleury	issuant
bearing	cinquefoil	dexter	fret	king-of-arms
bend	Clarenceux	difference	fur	label
bend sinister	coat armour	dimidiate	fusil	leopard
bezzant, bezant, or byzant	coat of arms	dormant	garland	lion
blazon	cockatrice	eagle	giron or gyron	
	cognizance or			

lozenge	officer of arms	potent	sable	torse
lozengy	or	proper	saltire	tressure
Lyon King of Arms	ordinary	purpure	sejant *or* sejant	urdé *or* urdée
mantling *or*	orle	pursuivant	scutcheon	urinant
lambrequin	pale	quarter	semé (of) *or*	vair
mascle *or* voided	pall	quartered	semée (of)	vert
lozenge	paly	quartering	shield	voided
matriculation	parted	quarterly	sinister	volant
moline	party	rampant	spread eagle	wreath
naissant	passant	rebus	statant	wyvern
nombril	pean	regardant	sun in splendour	yale
octofoil	pile	roundel	supporter	

HERBS, SPICES AND SEASONINGS

alligator pepper	cayenne pepper	five spice powder	nutmeg	sauce, shoyu, *or*
allspice	chervil	galangal *or*	oregano	tamari
aniseed	chilli	galingale	paprika	star anise
asafoetida *or*	chive	garam masala	parsley	sunflower seed
asafetida	cinnamon	garlic	peppercorn	Szechuan,
basil	clove	ginger	poppy seed	Szechwan,
bayleaf	coconut	Kaffir lime leaf	red pepper	*or* Sichuan
black pepper	coconut milk	lemon grass	rocambole	peppercorns
borage	coriander	mace	rosemary	tansy
calendula	cress	marjoram	saffron	tarragon
canella	cumin	mint	sage	thyme
capers	curry powder	miso	salt	turmeric
caraway seed	dill	mustard	savory	wasabi
cardamom	fennel	nam pla *or* fish	sesame seed	white pepper
cassia bark	fines herbes	sauce	soy sauce, soya	

LABOURS OF HERCULES

the slaying of the Nemean lion	the capture of the horses of Diomedes
the slaying of the Lernaean hydra	the taking of the girdle of Hippolyte
the capture of the hind of Ceryneia	the capture of the cattle of Geryon
the capture of the wild boar of Erymanthus	the recovery of the golden apples of
the cleansing of the Augean stables	Hesperides
the shooting of the Stymphalian birds	the taking of Cerberus
the capture of the Cretan bull	

HINDU DENOMINATIONS AND SECTS

Hare Krishna	Saivaism	Saktas	Vaishnavism

TYPES OF HOME

adobe	shingle	Cape Cod	cottage	embassy
apartment	(*Caribbean*)	cottage	cottage flat	farmhouse
bachelor	boarding house	caravan	crannog	flat
apartment	booth	castle	croft	flatlet
(*Canadian*)	bungalow	chalet	dacha (*Russian*)	flophouse
back-to-back	bunker	chateau or	deanery	flotel
barrack	but and ben	château	digs	garret
bedsitter	(*Scot.*)	chattel house	doss house	grange
black house	cabin	consulate	duplex *or* duplex	guest house
(*Scot.*)	caboose (*Canad.*)	cot *or* cote	apartment	hacienda
board-and-	camboose	(*dialect*)	(*U.S.*) (*Canad.*)	hall

hogan
hostel
hotel
house
houseboat
hovel
hut
igloo *or* iglu
inn
lake dwelling
lodge
log cabin
long house
maisonette
manor
manse
mansion
mattamore
mews *(informal)*
mobile home
motel
motor caravan
mud hut
palace
parsonage
penthouse
pied-à-terre
prefab
priory
ranch
rath *(Irish)*
rectory
rest-home
roadhouse
semi
shack
shanty
shooting box
show house
single-end *(Scot.)*
  (dialect)
slum
starter home
stately home
studio flat
tavern
tenement
tent
tepee
town house
trailer *(U.S.)*
  (Canad.)
tree house
tupik *or* tupek
  (Canad.)
vicarage
villa
whare *(N.Z.)*
wigwam

HORMONES

adrenaline *or* epinephrine
adrenocorticotrophic
  hormone
androsterone
antidiuretic hormone
bursicon
calcitonin
cholecystokinin *or*
  pancreozymin
chorionic gonadotrophin
corpus luteum hormone *or*
  progesterone
corticosteroid
corticosterone *or*
  adrenocorticotrophic
  hormone
cortisone
deoxycorticosterone
ecdysone
enterogastrone
erythropoietin
florigen
follicle-stimulating hormone
glucagon
gibberellic acid
gastrin
gonadotrophin
growth hormone *or*
  somatotrophin
insulin
interstitial-cell-stimulating
  hormone *or* luteinizing
  hormone
juvenile hormone
lactogenic hormone
luteinizing hormone-
  releasing hormone
luteotrophin *or* prolactin
noradrenaline
oestradiol
oestriol
oestrone
oxytocin
progesterone
parathyroid hormone
relaxin
secretin
sex hormone
somatomedin
somatostatin
stilboestrol
testosterone
thyroid-stimulating hormone
  or thyrotropin
thyroxine
trichlorophenoxyacetic acid
triiodothyronine
vasopressin

BODILY HUMOURS

black bile	yellow bile	blood	phlegm

HYDROCARBONS

alkane	cubane	decane	pentane	xylene
alkene	cycloalkane	indene	pyrene	
alkyne	cyclopentadiene	isooctane	retene	
arene	cyclopropane	naphthalene	stilbene	
cetane	diene	octane	triptane	

INSECTS

TYPES OF INSECT

apple maggot
body louse,
  cootie *(U.S. &
  N.Z.)*, *or (N.Z.
  slang)* kutu
bollworm
booklouse
bookworm
bristletail
cabbageworm
caddis worm *or*
  casewórm
cankerworm
cochineal *or*
cochineal
  insect
cockroach
cotton stainer
crab (louse)
cricket
dust mite
earwig, *or*
  (Scot. dialect)
  clipshears, *or*
  clipshear
flea
German
  cockroach *or*
(U.S.) Croton
  bug
grasshopper
katydid
lac insect
locust
louse *or (N.Z.)*

kutu
mantis or praying mantis
measuring worm, looper, or inchworm
midge
mole cricket
mosquito
nit
phylloxera
scale insect
seventeen-year locust
or periodical cicada
sheep ked or sheep tick
silkworm
silverfish
stick insect or
(U.S. & Canad.) walking stick
sucking louse
tent caterpillar
thrips
treehopper
wax insect
web spinner
weta (N.Z.)
wheel bug
wireworm
woodworm

PARTS OF INSECTS

acetabulum
air sac
antenna
arista
cercus
cirrus
clasper
clypeus
compound eye
corium
coxa
elytron
endocuticle
epicuticle
exocuticle
femur
flagellum
forewing
glossa
gonopod
hamulus
haustellum
hemelytron
ileum
jaw
labium
labrum
ligula
Malpighian tubule
mandible
maxilla
mesothorax
metathorax
notum
ocellus
ovipositor
pedicel
proboscis
proleg
pronotum
prosternum
prothorax
proventriculus
pulvillus
scape
scutellum
scutum
snout
spinneret
spiracle
stigma
tarsus
tegmen
thigh
thorax
tibia
trachea
trochanter
underwing
ventriculus

MUSICAL INSTRUMENTS

accordion
aeolian harp
alphorn or alpenhorn
althorn
Autoharp (trademark)
baby grand
Bach trumpet
bagpipes
balalaika
bandore
banjo
barrel organ
baryton
bass drum
basset horn
bass guitar
bassoon
bass viol
bell
bodhrán
Böhm flute
bombardon
bongo
boudoir grand
bouzouki
bugle
calliope
carillon
castanets
celesta or
celeste
cello or violoncello
cembalo
chamber organ
Chapman stick (trademark)
chime
Chinese block
chitarrone
chitarra
cimbalon or cymbalon
cithara or kithara
cittern, cither or cithern
clarinet
clarion
clarsach
clave
clavicembalo
clavichord
clavier
concert grand
concertina
conga
contrabass
contrabassoon
cor anglais
cornet
cornett
cottage piano
cowbell
crumhorn or krummhorn
crwth
cymbal
cymbalo
didgeridoo
Dobro (trademark)
double bass
double bassoon
drum
drum machine
dulcimer
electric guitar
electronic organ
English horn
euphonium
fiddle
fife
flageolet
flugelhorn
flute
French horn
gittarone
gittern
glass harmonica
glockenspiel
gong
gran cassa
grand piano
guitar
Hammond organ (trademark)
handbell
harmonica
harmonium
harp
harpsichord
Hawaiian guitar
helicon
horn
hornpipe
hunting horn
hurdy-gurdy
idiophone
jew's-harp
kazoo
kettledrum
keyboard
kit
kora
koto
lur or lure
lute
lyra viol
lyre
mandola
mandolin or mandoline
maraca
marimba
mbira
mellophone
melodeon or melodion
metallophone
Moog (trademark)
mouth organ
musette
naker
ngoma
nickelodeon
nose flute
oboe
oboe da caccia
oboe d'amore
ocarina
octachord
ondes Martenot
ophicleide
orchestrina or orchestrion
organ
orpharion
oud
panpipes
pedal steel guitar
penny whistle
piano
Pianola (trademark)
piccolo

pipe	saxhorn	syrinx	trigon	viola d'amore
player piano	saxophone	tabla	trombone	violin
portative organ	shawm	tabor or tabour	trumpet	violone
racket	side drum	tambour	tuba	virginal
rebec or rebeck	sistrum	tamboura	tubular bells	vocoder
recorder	sitar	tambourine	uillean pipes	washboard
reco-reco	slide guitar	tam-tam	ukulele or	Welsh harp
reed organ	snare drum	theorbo	ukelele	whip
reed pipe	sousaphone	Theremin	upright piano	whistle
regal	Spanish guitar	(trademark)	vibraphone	wood block
rote	spinet	timbal or	vihuela	Wurlitzer
sackbut	square piano	tymbal	vina	(trademark)
samisen	steam organ	timpani or	viol	xylophone
sarangi	steel guitar	tympani	viola	xylorimba
sarod	stylophone	tom-tom	viola da braccio	zither
sarrusophone	synthesizer	triangle	viola da gamba	

INSULTS AND TERMS OF ABUSE

airhead	dipstick	imbecile	plonker
article	divvy	jerk	prat
berk	donkey	lamebrain	rascal
bird-brain	doofus	loon	rogue
bitch	dope	mincer	scab
blockhead	dork	minger	scoundrel
bonehead	doughnut	mong	scrubber
bozo	drip	moron	scutter
bushpig	dumb-ass	mug	simpleton
cabbage	dumbo	muppet	slag
charlie	dummy	nerd	slapper
cheeky monkey	dunce	nincompoop	tart
chicken	dweeb	ninny	thickhead
chuckie	eejit	nit	thicko
chump	fathead	nitwit	twerp
clod	fool	numbskull or	twit
clot	galah	numskull	wally
clown	geek	numpty	whore or 'ho
coot	git	oaf	wimp
cow	goose	ogre	wretch
cretin	halfwit	pea-brain	wuss
devil	heifer	pillock	
dimwit	idiot	plank	

INTERNET TERMS

blog, blogger, or	hit	or podcasting	VPN
blogging	home page	portal	Web 2.0
bookmark	hotspot	RSS	web address
broadband	ISP or Internet service	search engine	WebBoard
browse or browser	provider	search engine	webcam
chatroom	leetspeak or	optimization or SEO	webcast
cookie	1337speak	Skype (trademark)	web directory
domain name	lurk, lurker, or lurking	spam	weblog
download	message board	spoofing	webmail
eBay (trademark)	netiquette	surf, surfer, or surfing	webmaster
e-book	newsgroup	upload	webpage
FTP or ftp	offline	URL or universe	website
Generation C	online	resource locator	Wi-Fi
Google (trademark)	podcast, podcaster,	voip	Yahoo (trademark)

INVERTEBRATES

TYPES OF INVERTEBRATE

amoeba or (U.S.) ameba
animalcule or animalculum
arrowworm
arthropod
Balmain bug
bardy, bardie, or bardi (Austral.)
bivalve
bladder worm
blue-ringed octopus (Austral.)
Bluff oyster (N.Z.)
box jellyfish or (Austral.) sea wasp
brachiopod or lamp shell
brandling
bryozoan or (colloquial) sea mat
catworm, white worm, or white cat
centipede
chicken louse
chiton or coat-of-

mail shell
clam
clappy-doo or clabby-doo (Scot.)
cockle
cone (shell)
coral
crown-of-thorns (starfish)
ctenophore or comb jelly
cunjevoi or cunje (Austral.)
cuttlefish or cuttle
daphnia
earthworm
eelworm
gaper
gapeworm
gastropodart
Guinea worm
horseleech
jellyfish or (Austral. slang) blubber
kina (N.Z.)
lancelet or amphioxus

leech
liver fluke
lugworm, lug, or lobworm
lungworm
millipede, millepede, or milleped
mollusc
mussel
octopus or devilfish
oyster
paddle worm
paper nautilus, nautilus, or argonaut
pearly nautilus, nautilus, or chambered nautilus
piddock
pipi or ugari (Austral.)
Portuguese man-of-war or (Austral.) bluebottle
quahog, hard-

shell clam, hard-shell, or round clam
ragworm or (U.S.) clamworm
razor-shell or (U.S.) razor clam
red coral or precious coral
roundworm
sandworm or (Austral.) pumpworm
scallop
sea anemone
sea cucumber
sea lily
sea mouse
sea pen
sea slater
sea squirt
sea urchin
seed oyster
soft-shell (clam)
sponge
squid
starfish
stomach worm
stony coral

sunstar
tapeworm
tardigrade or water bear
tellin
teredo or shipworm
trepang or bêche-de-mer
tube worm
tubifex
tusk shell or tooth shell
Venus's flower basket
Venus's-girdle
Venus shell
vinegar eel, vinegar worm, or eelworm
water louse or water slater
water measurer
water stick insect
wheatworm
whipworm
woodborer
worm

EXTINCT INVERTEBRATES

ammonite | belemnite | eurypterid | graptolite | trilobite

JACKETS

acton
anorak
báinín
banyan
Barbour jacket (trademark)
bed jacket
biker jacket
blazer
blouson
body warmer
bolero
bomber jacket

boxy jacket
bush jacket
cagoule or cag
cardigan
combat jacket
cymar
denim jacket
dinner jacket or (U.S. & Canad.) tuxedo or tux
dolman
donkey jacket
doublet

duvet or duvet jacket
Eton jacket or bumfreezer
flak jacket
fustian jacket
gambeson
gilet
hacking jacket
hug-me-tight
jerkin
leather jacket
life jacket

lumberjacket
Mackinaw coat or mackinaw (chiefly U.S.) (Canad.)
matinée jacket
mess jacket
monkey jacket
Norfolk jacket
pourpoint
reefing jacket
sack or sacque
safari jacket

shell jacket
shrug
smoking jacket
spencer
sports jacket or coat
tabard
windcheater or windjammer

JEWISH DENOMINATIONS AND SECTS

Chassidism, Chasidism, Hassidism, or Hasidism

Conservative Judaism
Liberal Judaism

Orthodox Judaism
Reform Judaism
Zionism

KITCHEN EQUIPMENT

Aga (trademark)
bain-marie
baking tray
barbecue or
    (Austral. slang)
    barbie
batterie de
    cuisine
blender
bottle opener
bread knife
cafetiere
cake tin
carving knife
casserole
chip pan
chopping board
chopsticks
coffee grinder
coffeepot
colander
cooker
cooling rack
corkscrew
deep fat fryer
dessertspoon
double saucepan
    or (U.S. &
    Canad.) double
    boiler
egg beater or egg
    whisk
fan-assisted oven
fish slice
flan tin
food processor
fork
frying pan
grater
gravy boat or
    sauce boat
griddle or (Scot.)
girdle
grill
ice-cream maker
icing bag
jelly bag
juicer or juice
    extractor
kettle
knife
ladle
lemon squeezer
liquidizer
loaf tin
mandoline
measuring jug
mezzaluna
microwave or
    microwave
    oven
mixing bowl
mortar and
    pestle
nutcracker
olla
oven
pastry cutter
peeler
pepper mill
percolator
poacher
pot
pot-au-feu
ramekin
ricer (U.S.)
    (Canad.)
rolling pin
rotisserie
saucepan
scales
sieve
skillet
spatula
spoon
spurtle
steamer
strainer
tablespoon
tagine
tandoor
teapot
teaspoon
tenderizer
timbale
tin-opener
toaster
toasting fork
whisk
wok
wooden spoon

KNITTING STITCHES

box stitch
cable stitch
diagonal rib
double seed or
double moss
    stitch
fisherman's rib
garter rib
garter stitch
layette
mistake rib
moss panels
moss stitch
pavilion
rib
roman stripe
seed stitch
slip stitch
stocking stitch

KNOTS

barrell knot
bend
Blackwall hitch
bow or bowknot
bowline
bowstring knot
carrick bend
cat's paw
clinch knot
clove hitch
diamond knot
Englishman's tie
figure of eight
fisherman's bend
fisherman's or
    truelover's knot
girth hitch
granny knot
half hitch
hangman's knot
harness hitch
hawser bend
half-hitch
hitch
loop knot
love knot
magnus hitch
Matthew Walker
monkey fist
overhand knot or
    thumb knot
prusik knot
reef knot, flat
    knot, or square
    knot
rolling hitch
running bowline
running knot
sailor's knot
sheepshank
sheet bend,
    becket bend,
    weaver's hitch,
    or mesh knot
shroud knot
slipknot
slippery hitch
stevedore's knot
surgeon's knot
swab hitch
timber hitch
truelove knot
Turk's-head
wale knot
wall knot
water knot
Windsor knot

LAW

LAW TERMS

abandonee
abate
abator
abet
abeyance
able
absente reo
absolute
acceptance
(Contract law)
accessory or
    accessary
accretion
accrue
accusation
accusatorial
accuse
accused, the
acquit
action
actionable
act of God
adjective
ad litem
adminicle
administration
    order
admissible
adopt
adult
advocate
advocation
affiant
affidavit
affiliate or filiate
affiliation or
filiation
affiliation order
affiliation
    proceedings or
    (U.S.) paternity
    suit
affirm
affirmation
affray

agist
alibi
alienable
alienate
alienation
alienee
alienor
alimony
allege
alluvion
ambulatory
a mensa et thoro
amerce (obsolete)
amicus curiae
amnesty
ancient
annulment
answer
Anton Piller order
appeal
appearance
appellant
appellate
appellee
appendant
approve
arbitrary
arbitration
arraign
array
arrest judgment
arrest of
  judgement
articled clerk
assault
assessor
assets
assign
assignee
assignment
assignor
assumpsit
attach
attachment
attainder
attaint (archaic)
attorn
attorney
attorney-at-law
attorney general
authentic
authority
automatism
aver
avoid
avoidance
avow (rare)
avulsion

award
bail
bailable
bailee (Contract
  law)
bailiff
bailiwick
bailment
  (Contract law)
bailor (Contract
  law)
bailsman (rare)
ban
bankrupt
bar
baron (English
  law)
barratry or
  barretry
barrister or
  barrister-at-law
bench, the
bencher
beneficial
beneficiary
bequeath
bequest
bigamy
bill of attainder
bill of indictment
bill of sale
blasphemy or
  blasphemous
  libel
body corporate
bona fides
bona vacantia
bond
bondsman
breach of
  promise
breach of the
  peace
breach of trust
brief
briefless
bring
burden of proof
capias
capital
caption
carnal
  knowledge
cartulary or
  chartulary
case
case law
case stated or

stated case
cassation
cause
caution
CAV, Cur. adv.
  vult, or Curia
  advisari vult
caveat
caveator
certificate of
  incorporation
  (Company law)
chamber counsel
  or counsellor
chambers
certification
certiorari
cessor
cessionary
challenge
challenge to the
  array
challenge to the
  polls
champerty
chance-medley
chancery
change of venue
charge
chargeable
cheat
chief justice
chose
circuit (English
  law)
citation
cite
civil death
civil marriage
clerk to the
  justices
close
codicil
codification
coexecutor
cognizable or
  cognisable
cognizance or
  cognisance
collusion
come on
commitment,
  committal,
  or (especially
  formerly)
  mittimus
common
commonage

common law
commutable
commutation
commute
competence
competency
competent
complainant
complaint
  (English law)
complete (Land
  law)
compound
compliance
  officer
composition
compurgation
conclusion
condemn
condition
condone
confiscate
connivance
connive
conscience
  clause
consensual
consideration
consolidation
consortium
constituent
constitute
constructive
contempt
contentious
continuance
  (U.S.)
contraband
contract
contractor
contributory
  (Company law)
contributory
  negligence
contumacy
convene
conventional
conversion
convert
conveyance
convincing
coparcenary or
  coparceny
coparcener or
  parcener
copyhold
copyholder
co-respondent

coroner
coroner's inquest
coroner's jury
corpus delicti
corpus juris
Corpus Juris
  Civilis
costs
counsel
counselor or
  counselor-at-
  law (U.S.)
count
countercharge
counterclaim
counterpart
countersign
county court
court
court of first
  instance
covenant
coverture
covin
criminal
  conversation
criminate (rare)
cross-examine
crown attorney
  (Canad)
crown court
  (English law)
cruelty
culpa (Civil law)
culprit
cumulative
  evidence
custodian
custody
custom
customary
cy pres
damages
damnify
dead letter
debatable
decedent (chiefly
  U.S.)
declarant
declaration
declaratory
decree
decree absolute
decree nisi
deed
deed poll
defalcate
defamation

default
defeasible
defeat
defence
defendant
deferred
  sentence
de jure
delict (Roman
  law)
demand
demandant
demisit sine prole
demur
demurrer
denunciation
  (obsolete)
deodand (English
  law)
deponent
depose
deposition
deraign or
  darraign
  (obsolete)
dereliction
descendible or
  descendable
desertion
detainer
determinable
determination
determine
detinue
devil
devisable
devise
devolve
dies non or dies
  non juridicus
digest
diligence
diminished
  responsibility
direct evidence
disaffirm
disafforest
  or disforest
  (English law)
disannul
disbar
discharge
disclaim
discommon
discontinue
discovert
discovery
disinherit

dismiss
disorderly
disorderly
  conduct
disorderly house
dissent
distrain or
  distress
distrainee
distraint
distributee
  (chiefly U.S.)
distribution
distringas
disturbance
dividend
divorce from
  bed and board
  (U.S.)
docket
documentation
Doe
domain
donee
donor
dot (Civil law)
dotation
dowable
dower
droit
due process of
  law
duress
earnest or
  earnest money
  (Contract law)
effectual
emblements
eminent domain
empanel or
  impanel
encumbrance
encumbrancer
enfranchise
  (English law)
engross
engrossment
enjoin
enter
equitable
equity
escheat
escrow
estop
estoppel
estovers
estray
estreat

evict
evidence
evocation (French
  law)
examination
examine
examine-in-chief
exception
execute
execution
executor or (fem.)
  executrix
executory
exemplary
  damages
exemplify
exhibit
ex parte
expectancy
expropriate
extend
extent (U.S.)
extinguish
extraditable
extradite
extrajudicial
eyre (English legal
  history)
fact
factor
  (Commercial
  law)
false
  imprisonment
Family Division
felo de se
feme
feme covert
feme sole
fiction
fideicommissary
  (Civil law)
fideicommissum
  (Civil law)
fiduciary or
  fiducial
fieri facias
file
filiate
filiation
find
finding
first offender
fiscal
flaw
folio
forbearance
force majeure

foreclose
foreign
foreman
forensic
forensic
  medicine,
  legal medicine,
  or medical
  jurisprudence
forest
forfeit
forjudge or
  forejudge
fornication
free
fungible
garnish
garnishee
garnishment
gavelkind (English
  law)
gist
goods and
  chattels
grand jury (chiefly
  U.S.)
grand larceny
grantee
grant
grantor
gratuitous
gravamen
grith (English legal
  history)
ground rent
guarantee
guardian
guilty
habeas corpus
hand down (U.S.)
  (Canad.)
handling
hear
hearing
hearsay
heir or (fem.)
  heiress (Civil
  law)
heirship
hereditary
heres or haeres
  (Civil law)
heritable
heritage
heritor
holder
homologate
hung jury

hypothec (Roman
  law)
hypothecate
immovable
impartible
impediment
imperfect
implead (rare)
imprescriptable
in articles
in banc
in camera
incapacitate
incapacity
in chancery
incompetent
incorporeal
incriminate
indefeasible
indemnity
indenture
indeterminate
  sentence
inducement
in escrow
infant
in fee
inferior court
infirm
in flagrante
  delicto or
  flagrante
  delicto
ingoing
inheritance
injunction
injury
innuendo
in personam
in posse
inquest
inquisition
inquisitorial
in rem
insanity
in specie
instanter
institutes
instruct
instructions
instrument
insurable interest
intendment
intent
intention
interdict (Civil
  law)
interlocutory

interplead
interpleader
interrogatories
intervene
inter vivos
intestate
invalidate
in venter
ipso jure
irrepleviable *or*
  irreplevisable
issuable
issue
jail delivery
  (English law)
jeopardy
joinder
joint
jointress
jointure
judge
judge-made
judges' rules
judgment *or*
  judgement
judgment by
  default
judicable
judicative
judicatory
judicature
judicial
judicial
  separation
  (Family law)
judiciary
junior
jural
jurat
juratory
juridical
jurisconsult
jurisprudence
jurisprudent
jurist
juristic
juror
jury
juryman *or (fem.)*
  jurywoman
jury process
jus
jus gentium
  (Roman law)
jus naturale
  (Roman law)
jus sanguinis
jus soli

justice
justice court
justice of the
  peace
justiciable
justices in eyre
  *(English legal
  history)*
justify
juvenile court
laches
land
lapse
larceny
Law French
Law Lords
law merchant
  (Mercantile law)
lawsuit
law term
lawyer
leasehold
leaseholder
legist
letters of
  administration
lex loci
lex non scripta
lex scripta
lex talionis
libel
lien
limit
limitation
lis pendens
litigable
litigant
litigation
locus standi
magistrate
magistrates'
  court *or* petty
  sessions
maintenance
malfeasance
malice
manager
mandamus
mandate *(Roman
  law) (Contract
  law)*
manslaughter
manus
mare clausum
mare liberum
material
matter
mayhem *or*

maihem
memorandum
mens rea
mental disorder
mental
  impairment
merger
merits
mesne
ministerial
misadventure
mise
misfeasance
misjoinder
mispleading
mistrial
misuser
mittimus
monopoly
moral
moratorium
morganatic *or*
  left-handed
mortgagee
mortmain *or (less
  commonly)* dead
  hand
motion
moveable *or*
  movable
muniments
mute
naked
Napoleonic Code
necessaries
negligence
next friend
nisi
nisi prius *(History)*
  (U.S.)
nolle prosequi,
  nol. pros., *or*
  nolle pros.
nolo contendere
  (chiefly U.S.)
nonage
non compos
  mentis
nonfeasance
nonjoinder
non liquet
non prosequitur
  or non pros.
nonsuit
notary public
not guilty
novation
novel *(Roman law)*

nude
nudum pactum
nuisance
oath
obiter dictum
obligation
oblivion
obreption
obscene
obtaining by
  deception
occupancy
occupant
offer *(Contract
  law)*
Official Referee
onerous
onomastic
on, upon *or* under
  oath
onus probandi
open
opening
ordinary
overt
owelty
oyer *(English legal
  history)*
oyer and
  terminer
panel
paraphernalia
pardon
parol
Particulars of
  Claim
party
paterfamilias
  (Roman law)
peculium *(Roman
  law)*
pecuniary
pecuniary
  advantage
pendente lite
perception
peremptory
persistent cruelty
personal
personal
  property *or*
  personalty
petit
petition
petitioner
petit jury *or* petty
  jury
petit larceny *or*

petty larceny
petty
place of safety
  order
plaint
plaintiff
plea
plea bargaining
plead
pleading
pleadings
portion
port of entry
posse
posse comitatus
possessory
post-obit
prayer
precedent
precept
predispose
pre-emption
prefer
preference
premeditation
premises
prescribe
prescription
presentment
  (chiefly U.S.)
presents
presume
presumption
preterition
  (Roman law)
prima facie
primogeniture
principal
private law
private nuisance
privilege
privileged
privity
privy
prize court
probable cause
probate
proceed
proceeding
process
process-server
procuration
procuratory
prohibition
promisee
  (Contract law)
promisor
  (Contract law)

CRIMINAL LAW TERMS

PROPERTY LAW TERMS

SCOTS LAW TERMS

LITERATURE

LITERATURE TERMS

Beat Generation or Beats
belles-lettres
belletrist
bibliography
Bildungsroman
black comedy
Bloomsbury group
bodice-ripper
bombast
bowdlerization
Brechtian
bricolage
Byronic
carnivalesque
campus novel
causerie
Celtic Revival
cento
chiller
Ciceronian
classicism
coda
colloquialism
comedy
comedy of manners
commedia dell'arte
conceit
courtly love
cultural materialism
cut-up technique
cyberpunk
death of the author

decadence
deconstruction
denouement
Derridian
dialectic
dialogue
Dickensian
discourse
double entendre
drama
epic
epilogue
epistle
epistolary novel
epitaph
erasure
essay
exegesis
expressionism
fable
fabulist
faction
fantastique
fantasy
feminist theory
festschrift
figure of speech
fin de siècle
foreword
Foucauldian
Futurism
gloss
Gongorism
Gothic
hagiography
Hellenism
hermeneutics
historical novel

historicism
Homeric
Horatian
hudibrastic verse
imagery
interior monologue
intertextuality
invective
Jacobean
Janeite
Johnsonian
journalese
Joycean
Juvenalian
Kafkaesque
kailyard
kenning
kiddy lit
lampoon
Laurentian or Lawrentian
legend
literary criticism
littérateur
locus classicus
Lost Generation
magic realism or magical realism
marxist theory
maxim
melodrama
metafiction
metalanguage
metaphor
mock-heroic
modernism
motif

myth
mythopoeia
narrative
narratology
narrator
naturalism
new criticism
new historicism
nom de plume
nouveau roman
novel
novelette
novella
onomatopoeia
oxymoron
palindrome
paraphrase
parody
pastiche
pastoral
pathos
picaresque
plagiarism
plot
polemic
pornography
post-colonialism
postmodernism
post-structuralism
post-theory
pot-boiler
queer theory
realism
Restoration comedy
roman
roman à clef

Romanticism
saga
samizdat
satire
science fiction or SF
sentimental novel
shopping-and-fucking or S & F novel
short story
signifier and signified
simile
sketch
socialist realism
splatterpunk
Spoonerism
story
stream of consciousness
structuralism
Sturm und Drang
subplot
subtext
Surrealism
Swiftian
theme
theory
thesis
tragedy
tragicomedy
trope
verse
vignette

EXTINCT MAMMALS

apeman
aurochs
australopithecine
baluchitherium
chalicothere
creodont

dinoceras or uintathere
dinothere
dryopithecine
eohippus
glyptodont

Irish elk
labyrinthodont
mammoth
mastodon
megathere
nototherium

quagga
sabre-toothed tiger or cat
tarpan
titanothere

TYPES OF MANIA

ablutomania	washing	arithmomania	counting
agoramania	open spaces	automania	solitude
		autophonomania	suicide
ailuromania	cats	balletomania	ballet
andromania	men	ballistomania	bullets
Anglomania	England	bibliomania	books
anthomania	flowers	chionomania	snow
apimania	bees	choreomania	dancing

chrematomania	money
cremnomania	cliffs
cynomania	dogs
dipsomania	alcohol
doramania	fur
dromomania	travelling
egomania	yourself
eleuthromania	freedom

entheomania	religion	macromania	becoming larger
entomomania	insects		
ergasiomania	work	megalomania	your own importance
eroticomania	erotica		
erotomania	sex	melomania	music
florimania	plants	mentulomania	penises
gamomania	marriage	micromania	becoming smaller
graphomania	writing		
gymnomania	nakedness	monomania	one thing
gynomania	women	musicomania	music
hamartiomania	sin	musomania	mice
hedonomania	pleasure	mythomania	lies
heliomania	sun	necromania	death
hippomania	horses	noctimania	night
homicidomania	murder	nudomania	nudity
hydromania	water	nymphomania	sex
hylomania	woods	ochlomania	crowds
hypnomania	sleep	oikomania	home
ichthyomania	fish	oinomania	wine
iconomania	icons	ophidiomania	reptiles
kinesomania	movement	orchidomania	testicles
kleptomania	stealing	ornithomania	birds
logomania	talking	phagomania	eating

pharmacomania	medicines
phonomania	noise
photomania	light
plutomania	great wealth
potomania	drinking
pyromania	fire
scribomania	writing
siderodromo-mania	railway travel
sitomania	food
sophomania	your own wisdom
thalassomania	the sea
thanatomania	death
theatromania	theatre
timbromania	stamps
trichomania	hair
verbomania	words
xenomania	foreigners
zoomania	animals

MARSUPIALS

agile wallaby, river wallaby, sandy wallaby, or jungle kangaroo

antechinus

antelope kangaroo or antilopine wallaby

bandicoot

barred bandicoot or marl

Bennett's tree kangaroo or tcharibeena

bettong

bilby, rabbit(-eared) bandicoot, long-eared bandicoot, dalgyte, or dalgite

bobuck or mountain (brushtail) possum

boodie (rat), burrowing rat-kangaroo, Lesueur's rat-kangaroo, tungoo, or tungo

boongary or Lumholtz's tree kangaroo

bridled nail-tail wallaby or merrin

brindled bandicoot or northern brown

bandicoot

brush-tail(ed) possum

burramys or (mountain) pygmy possum

crest-tailed marsupial mouse, Cannings' little dog, or mulgara

crescent nail-tail wallaby or wurrung

cuscus

dasyurid, dasyure, native cat, marsupial cat, or wild cat

desert bandicoot

desert-rat kangaroo

dibbler

diprotodon

dunnart

eastern grey kangaroo, great grey kangaroo, forest kangaroo, or (grey) forester

fluffy glider or yellow-bellied glider

flying phalanger, flying squirrel, glider, or pongo

green ringtail possum or toolah

hairy-nosed wombat

hare-wallaby

honey mouse, honey possum, noolbenger, or tait

jerboa, jerboa pouched mouse, jerboa kangaroo, or kultarr

kangaroo or (Austral. informal) roo

koala (bear) or (Austral.) native bear

kowari

larapinta or Darling Downs dunnart

Leadbeater's possum or fairy possum

lemuroid ringtail possum

long-nosed bandicoot

mardo or yellow-footed antechinus

marlu

marsupial mole

marsupial mouse

mongan or Herbert River ringtail possum

munning

musky rat-kangaroo

naked-nose wombat

ningaui

northern nail-tail wallaby or karrabul

northern native cat or satanellus

numbat or banded anteater

opossum or possum

pademelon or paddymelon

parma wallaby

phalanger

pig-footed bandicoot

pitchi-pitchi or wuhl-wuhl

platypus, duck-billed platypus, or duckbill

potoroo

pretty-face wallaby or whiptail wallaby

pygmy glider, feather glider, or flying mouse

quenda or (southern) brown bandicoot

quokka

quoll

rat kangaroo

red kangaroo or plains kangaroo

red(-necked) wallaby, Bennett's wallaby,

eastern brush wallaby, rufous wallaby, or brush kangaroo
ringtail or ringtail(ed) possum
rock wallaby or brush-tailed wallaby
rufous rat-kangaroo
scrub wallaby
short-eared bandicoot
short-nosed bandicoot
short-nosed rat kangaroo or

squeaker
squirrel glider
striped possum
sugar glider
swamp wallaby, black wallaby, or black-tailed wallaby
tammar, damar, or dama
Tasmanian barred bandicoot or Gunn's bandicoot
Tasmanian devil or ursine dasyure
thylacine, Tasmanian wolf, or Tasmanian

tiger
tiger cat or spotted native cat
toolache or Grey's brush wallaby
tree kangaroo
tuan, phascogale, or wambenger
wallaby
wallaroo, uroo, or biggada
warabi
western grey kangaroo, black-faced kangaroo, sooty kangaroo, or

mallee kangaroo
wintarro or golden bandicoot
wogoit or rock possum
wombat or (Austral.) badger
woylie or brush-tailed bettong
yapok
yallara
yellow-footed rock wallaby or ring-tailed rock wallaby

MARTIAL ARTS AND TERMS

MARTIAL ARTS

aikido
capoeira
Crane style kung fu
Goju Kai karate
Goju Ryu karate
hapkido
Hung Gar or Tiger style kung fu
iai-do
iai-jutsu
Ishin Ryu karate
Jeet Kune Do

judo
ju jitsu, jiu jitsu or ju-jitsu
karate or karate-do
kendo
kick boxing
kung fu
Kyokushinkai karate
kyudo
naginata-do
ninjitsu or ninjutsu
Praying Mantis style

kung fu
Sankukai karate
Shito Ryu karate
Shotokai karate
Shotokan karate
Shukokai karate
sumo or sumo wrestling
tae kwon-do
tai chi chuan
tai chi qi gong
Ta Sheng Men or

Monkey style kung fu
Thai boxing or Muay Thai
Tomiki aikido
Tukido (trademark)
Wado Ryu karate
Wing Chun or Wing Tsun kung fu
yari-jutsu

MARTIAL ARTS TERMS

Term	Meaning	Term	Meaning
basho	sumo turnament	katsu	resuscitation techniques
bo	staff	keikogi	kendo jacket
bogu	kendo armour	kesho-mawashi	embroidered sumo apron
bokuto	kendo wooden sword	ki, chi or qi	inner power
budo or bushido	warrior's way	kiai	yell accompanying movement
dan	black belt grade		
do	kendo breastplate	kihon	repetition of techniques
-do	the way	kote	kendo gauntlets
dohyo	sumo ring	kyu	student grade
dojo	practice room or mat	makiwara	practice block
gi	suit	mawashi	sumo fighting belt
hachimaki or tenugui	kendo headcloth	men	kendo mask
		nage-waza or tachi-waza	ju jitsu competition
hakama	divided skirt		
ippon	one competition point	naginata	curved-blade spear
jiu-kumite	freestyle karate competition	ne-waza	ju jitsu competition
		ninin-dori	aikido competition
-jutsu	fighting art	ninja	Japanese trained assassin
-ka	student	nunchaku	hinged flails
kama	hand sickle	obi	coloured belt
kata	sequence of techniques	ozeki	sumo champion
katana	kendo sword	qi gong	breath control

Term	Meaning	Term	Meaning
randori kyoghi	aikido competition	tanto randori	aikido competition
rikishi	sumo wrestler	tare	kendo apron
rokushakubo	six-foot staff	te	hand fighting
ryu	martial arts school	ton-fa *or* tui-fa	hardwood weapon
sai	short trident	tsuna	sumo grand champion's belt
samurai	Japanese warrior caste		
sensei	teacher	waza-ari	half competition point
shinai	kendo bamboo sword	yari	spear
sifu	teacher	yokozuna	sumo grand champion
suneate	naginata shin guards	zanshin	total awareness

MATHEMATICS

BRANCHES OF MATHEMATICS

algebra
analysis
analytical geometry *or* coordinate geometry
applied mathematics
arithmetic
Boolean algebra
calculus
chaos geometry
conics
differential calculus
Euclidean geometry
game theory
geometry
group theory
integral calculus
nomography
non-Euclidean geometry
number theory
numerical analysis
probability
theory
pure mathematics
set theory
statistics
topology
trigonometry

MATHEMATICAL TERMS

acute angle
addition
algorithm *or* algorism
angle
arc
area
average
axis
base
binary
binomial
cardinal number
Cartesian coordinates
chord
circle
circumference
closed set
coefficient
common denominator
common factor
complex number
concentric
cone
constant
coordinate *or* co-ordinate
cosecant
cosine
cotangent
cube

cube root
cuboid
curve
cusp
cylinder
decagon
decimal
denary
denominator
diagonal
diameter
digit
division
dodecahedron
ellipse
equals
equation
equilateral
even
exponential
factor
factorial
formula
fraction
frequency
function
graph
helix
hemisphere
heptagon
hexagon
hyperbola
hypotenuse

icosahedron
imaginary number
improper fraction
index
infinity
integer
integral
intersection
irrational number
isosceles
locus
logarithm *or* log
lowest common denominator
lowest common multiple
Mandelbrot set
matrix
mean
median
minus
mode
multiplication
natural logarithm
natural number
node
nonagon
number
numerator

oblong
obtuse angle
octagon
octahedron
odd
open set
operation
operator
ordinal number
origin
parabola
parallel
parallelogram
pentagon
percentage
perfect number
pi
plus
polygon
polyhedron
polynomial
power
prime number
prism
probability
product
proof
proper fraction
Pythagoras' theorem
quadrant
quadratic equation

quadrilateral
quotient
radian
radius
ratio
rational number
real number
reciprocal
rectangle
recurring decimal
reflex angle
remainder
rhombus
right angle
right-angled triangle
root
scalar
scalene
secant
sector
semicircle
set
significant figures
simultaneous equations
sine
slide rule
solid
sphere
square
square root

strange attractor	tangent	union	Venn diagram	z-axis
subset	tetrahedron	universal set	volume	zero
subtraction	torus	value	vulgar fraction	
sum	trapezium	variable	x-axis	
surd	triangle	vector	y-axis	

TYPES OF MEAL

afternoon tea	breakfast	elevenses	luncheon	tapas
banquet	brunch	feast	picnic	tiffin
barbecue or	buffet	fish fry (U.S.)	smorgasbord	
(Austral.) barbie	cream tea	high tea or tea	snack	
beanfeast	dinner	lunch or	supper	

TYPES AND CUTS OF MEAT

bacon	collar	knockwurst	(archaic)	sausage
baron of beef	colonial goose	Kobe beef or	offal	saveloy
Bath chap	corned beef	Wagyu	oxtail	scrag
beef	crown roast	lamb	oxtongue	shank
beef-ham	Cumberland	lamb's fry	Parma ham	shoulder
black pudding	sausage	leg	parson's nose	silverside
bockwurst	cutlet	lights	pastrami	sirloin
boerewors	devon	liver	pemmican	skirt
bratwurst	duck	liver sausage	pepperoni	Spam
breast	entrecôte	or (esp U.S.)	pheasant	(trademark)
brisket	escalope	liverwurst	pigeon	sparerib
cervelat	fillet	loin	polony	steak
charqui	forehock	Lorne sausage,	pope's eye	stewing steak
Chateaubriand	foreshank	square	pork	sweetbread
chicken	game	sausage, or	porterhouse	T-bone
chipolata	gammon	square slice	steak	tenderloin
chitterlings,	gigot	(Scot.)	prosciutto	tongue
chitlings, or	goose	luncheon meat	rack	topside
chitlins	gristle	médaillons	rib	tournedos
chop	ham	mince	rolled lamb	tripe
chorizo	haslet	minute steak	round	turkey
chuck or chuck	hogg or hogget	mortadella	rump	undercut
steak	hough or hock	mutton	saddle	veal
chump	kidney	noisette	salami	venison
cold cuts	knackwurst or	numbles	salt pork	

MEDALS

Bronze Star (U.S.)	Distinguished Service Order	Militaire Willemsorde
Congressional Medal of	(Britain)	(Netherlands)
Honor (U.S.)	George Cross (Britain)	Purple Heart (U.S.)
Croix de Guerre (France)	Iron Cross (Germany)	Royal Red Cross (Britain)
Distinguished Service Cross	Légion d'Honneur (France)	Silver Star (U.S.)
(U.S.)	Legion of Merit (U.S.)	Victoria Cross

MEDICINE

BRANCHES OF MEDICINE

aetiology or etiology	andrology	bacteriology	cardiology
anaesthetics	angiology	balneology	chiropody
anaplasty	audiology	bioastronautics	dental hygiene or oral
anatomy	aviation medicine	biomedicine	hygiene

dental surgery
dentistry
dermatology
diagnostics
eccrinology
electrophysiology
electrotherapeutics
embryology
encephalography
endocrinology
endodontics
epidemiology
exodontics
forensic or legal
  medicine
gastroenterology
genitourinary
  medicine
geratology
geriatrics
gerontology
gynaecology or (U.S.)
  gynecology
haematology or (U.S.)
  hematology

hydrotherapeutics
immunochemistry
immunology
industrial medicine
internal medicine
laryngology
materia medica
midwifery
morbid anatomy
myology
neonatology
nephrology
neuroanatomy
neuroendocrinology
neurology
neuropathology
neurophysiology
neuropsychiatry
neurosurgery
nosology
nostology
nuclear medicine
nutrition
obstetrics
odontology

oncology
ophthalmology
optometry
orthodontics or
  orthodontia
orthopaedics or (U.S.)
  orthopedics
orthoptics
orthotics
osteology
osteoplasty
otolaryngology
otology
paediatrics or (U.S.)
  pediatrics
pathology
periodontics
pharyngology
physical medicine
physiotherapy or
  (U.S.) physiatrics
plastic surgery
posology
preventive medicine
proctology

psychiatry
psychoanalysis
psychology
radiology
rheumatology
rhinology
serology
space medicine
spare-part surgery
speech therapy
sports medicine
stomatology
surgery
symptomatology
syphilology
therapeutics
tocology or tokology
toxicology
trichology
urology
venereology
veterinary science or
  medicine
virology

MEDICAL PRACTITIONERS AND SPECIALISTS

aetiologist or
  etiologist
anaesthetist
anatomist
andrologist
audiologist
bacteriologist
balneologist
barefoot doctor
cardiologist
chiropodist
consultant
dental hygienist or
  oral hygienist
dentist or dental
  surgeon
dermatologist
diagnostician
dietitian
district nurse
doctor
electrophysiologist
embryologist
endocrinologist
endodontist
epidemiologist
exodontist
extern or externe
  (U.S.) (Canad.)
forensic scientist

gastroenterologist
general practitioner
  or GP
geriatrician or
  geriatrist
gerontologist
gynaecologist or
  (U.S.) gynecologist
haematologist
  or (U.S.)
  hematologist
health visitor
house physician
houseman
hydrotherapist
immunologist
intern or interne
  (U.S.) (Canad.)
internist
junior doctor
laboratory
  technician
laryngologist
matron
midwife
myologist
neonatologist
nephrologist
neuroanatomist
neurologist

neuropathologist
neurophysiologist
neuropsychiatrist
neurosurgeon
nosologist
nurse
nursing officer
nutritionist
obstetrician
occupational
  therapist
odontologist
oncologist
ophthalmologist
optician
optometrist
orderly
orthodontist
orthopaedist or
  (U.S.) orthopedist
orthoptist
orthotist
osteologist
otolaryngologist
otologist
paediatrician or
  (U.S.) pediatrician
paramedic
pathologist
pharyngologist

physiotherapist or
  physio
plastic surgeon
proctologist
psychiatrist
psychoanalyst
psychologist
radiographer
radiologist
registrar
resident (U.S.)
  (Canad.)
rheumatologist
rhinologist
serologist
speech therapist
surgeon
syphilologist
therapist
toxicologist
trichologist
urologist
venereologist
veterinary surgeon,
  vet or (U.S.)
  veterinarian
virologist

MEDICAL AND SURGICAL INSTRUMENTS AND EQUIPMENT

arthroscope
artificial heart
artificial kidney
aspirator
bandage
bedpan
bistoury
bronchoscope
cannula or canula
cardiograph
catheter
catling
clamp
clinical thermometer
colonoscope
colposcope
compressor
CT scanner or CAT
   scanner
curet or curette
cystoscope
defibrillator
depressor
dialysis machine
drain
electrocardiograph
electroencephalo-
   graph
electromyograph
encephalogram

endoscope
fetoscope
fibrescope or (U.S.)
   fiberscope
fluoroscope
forceps
gamma camera
gastroscope
gonioscope
haemostat or (U.S.)
   hemostat
heart-lung machine
heat lamp
hypodermic or
   hypodermic needle
hypodermic or
   hypodermic syringe
inhalator
inspirator
iron lung
kidney machine
kymograph or
   cymograph
lancet or lance
laparoscope
laryngoscope
life-support machine
microscope
nebulizer
needle

nephroscope
oesophagoscope
   or (U.S.)
   esophagoscope
ophthalmoscope
orthoscope
otoscope
oxygen mask
oxygen tent
pacemaker
packing
perimeter
pharyngoscope
plaster cast
pneumatometer
pneumograph
probe
proctoscope
Pulmotor (trademark)
raspatory
respirator
resuscitator
retinoscope
retractor
rheometer
rhinoscope
roentgenoscope or
   röntgenoscope
scalpel
scanner

skiascope
sling
sound
specimen bottle
speculum
sphygmograph
sphygmomanometer
spirograph
spirometer
splint
stethoscope
stomach pump
stretcher
stupe
stylet
styptic pencil
suture
swab
syringe
thoracoscope
tourniquet
trepan
trephine
trocar
ultrasound scanner
urethroscope
urinometer
ventilator
wet pack
X-ray machine

BRANCHES OF ALTERNATIVE MEDICINE

acupressure
acupuncture
Alexander technique
aromatherapy
autogenic training
Bach flower remedy

biofeedback
chiropractic
herbalism
homeopathy or
   homoeopathy
hydrotherapy

hypnosis
hypnotherapy
iridology
kinesiology
massage
moxibustion

naturopathy
osteopathy
radionics
reflexology
shiatsu

METALS

Metal	Symbol	Metal	Symbol	Metal	Symbol
actinium	Ac	chromium	Cr	hafnium	Hf
aluminium	Al	cobalt	Co	holmium	Ho
americium	Am	copper	Cu	indium	In
antimony	Sb	curium	Cm	iridium	Ir
barium	Ba	dysprosium	Dy	iron	Fe
berkelium	Bk	einsteinium	Es	lanthanum	La
beryllium	Be	erbium	Er	lawrencium	Lr
bismuth	Bi	europium	Eu	lead	Pb
cadmium	Cd	fermium	Fm	lithium	Li
caesium or		francium	Fr	lutetium	Lu
(U.S.) cesium	Cs	gadolinium	Gd	magnesium	Mg
calcium	Ca	gallium	Ga	manganese	Mn
californium	Cf	germanium	Ge	mendelevium	Md
cerium	Ce	gold	Au	mercury	Hg

Metal	Symbol	Metal	Symbol	Metal	Symbol
molybdenum	Mo	protactinium	Pa	thallium	Tl
neodymium	Nd	radium	Ra	thorium	Th
neptunium	Np	rhenium	Re	thulium	Tm
nickel	Ni	rhodium	Rh	tin	Sn
niobium	Nb	rubidium	Rb	titanium	Ti
nobelium	No	ruthenium	Ru	tungsten or wolfram	W
osmium	Os	samarium	Sm	uranium	U
palladium	Pd	scandium	Sc	vanadium	V
platinum	Pt	silver	Ag	ytterbium	Yb
plutonium	Pu	sodium	Na	yttrium	Y
polonium	Po	strontium	Sr	zinc	Zn
potassium	K	tantalum	Ta	zirconium	Zr
praseodymium	Pr	technetium	Tc		
promethium	Pm	terbium	Tb		

MILITARY RANKS

able rating
able seaman or able-bodied
    seaman (AB)
acting sublieutenant
admiral (Adm)
admiral of the fleet
air chief marshal (ACM)
air commodore (AC)
aircraftmen (AC)
air marshal (AM)
air officer
air vice-marshal (AVM)
branch officer (BO)
brigadier (Brig)
captain (Capt)
chief of staff (COS)
chief petty officer (CPO)
chief technician
colonel (Col)
colour sergeant (Col Sgt)
commander (Cdr)
commander in chief (C-in-C)
commanding officer (CO)
commissioned officer
commodore (Cdre)
company sergeant major
    (CSM)

corporal (Corp, Cpl)
drum major
field marshal (FM)
field officer (FO)
fleet admiral
fleet chief petty officer
flight engineer
flight lieutenant (Flt Lt)
flight mechanic (FM)
flight sergeant (Flt Sgt)
flying officer (FO)
general (Gen, Genl)
group captain (G Capt)
junior technician
lance corporal (L-Cpl)
leading aircraftman (LAC)
leading rating
lieutenant (Lt)
lieutenant colonel (Lt-Col)
lieutenant commander
    (Lt-Comm)
lieutenant general (Lt-Gen)
major (Maj)
major general (Maj-Gen)
marine
marshal
marshal of the Royal Air

Force (MRAF)
master aircrew
medical officer (MO)
midshipman
noncommissioned officer
    (NCO)
ordinary rating
ordinary seaman (OS)
petty officer (PO)
pilot officer (PO)
private (Pte)
quartermaster (QM)
rear admiral (RA)
regimental sergeant major
    (RSM)
second lieutenant
senior aircraftman
senior medical officer (SMO)
sergeant (Sgt, Sergt)
sergeant major (SM)
squadron leader (Sqn-Ldr)
staff sergeant
subaltern
sublieutenant (Sub L)
vice admiral (VA)
warrant officer (WO)
wing commander

MINERALS

actinolite
agate
albite
allanite
allophane
alunite
amalgam
amblygonite
analcite or
    analcime

anatase
andalusite
andesine
anglesite
anhydrite
ankerite
annabergite
anorthite
apatite
apophyllite

aragonite
argentite
arsenopyrite
augite
autunite
axinite
azurite
baddeleyite
barytes
bastnaesite or

bastnasite
bauxite
beryl
biotite
bismuthinite
    or bismuth
    glance
Boehmite
boracite
borax

bornite
braunite
brookite
calaverite
calcite
carnallite
carnotite
cassiterite
celestite or
    celestine

cerargyrite
chabazite
chalcanthite
chalcocite
chalcopyrite
chlorite
chromite
chrysoberyl
chrysotile
cinnabar
clay mineral
cleveite
clinopyroxene
cobaltite or
  cobaltine
colemanite
columbite
cordierite
corundum
cristobalite
crocidolite
crocoite or
  crocoisite
cryolite
cuprite
cyanite
datolite
diallage
diamond
diaspore
diopside
dioptase
dolomite
dumortierite
emery
enstatite
epidote
erythrite
euxenite
fayalite
feldspar or
  felspar
feldspathoid
fluorapatite
fluorspar,
  fluor or (U.S.

& Canad.)
fluorite
forsterite
franklinite
gahnite
galena or
  galenite
garnet
garnierite
gehlenite
germanite
geyserite
gibbsite
glauconite
goethite or
  göthite
graphite
greenockite
gummite
gypsum
halite
harmotome
hematite or
  haematite
hemimorphite
hessite
heulandite
hiddenite
hornblende
hyacinth
hypersthene
illite
ilmenite
jadeite
jarosite
jasper
kainite
kaolinite
kernite
kieserite
kunzite
labradorite
lapis lazuli
lazulite
lazurite
leucite

limonite
magnesite
magnetite
malachite
manganite
marcasite
margarite
massicot
meerschaum
metamict
mica
microcline
millerite
mimetite
molybdenite
monazite
montmorillon-
  ite
monzonite
mullite
muscovite
natrolite
nepheline or
  nephelite
nephrite
niccolite
norite
oligoclase
olivenite
olivine
opal
orpiment
orthoclase
ozocerite or
  ozokerite
pentlandite
periclase
perovskite
petuntse or
  petuntze
phenacite or
  phenakite
phosgenite
phosphorite
piedmontite
pinite

pitchblende
pollucite
polybasite
proustite
psilomelane
pyrargyrite
pyrite
pyrolusite
pyromorphite
pyrophyllite
pyroxene
pyroxenite
pyrrhotite or
  pyrrhotine
quartz
realgar
rhodochrosite
rhodonite
rutile
samarskite
saponite
sapphirine
scapolite
scheelite
scolecite
senarmontite
serpentine
siderite
sillimanite
smaltite
smaragdite
smectite
smithsonite
sodalite
sperrylite
sphalerite
sphene
spinel
spodumene
stannite
staurolite
stibnite
stilbite
strontianite
sylvanite
sylvite or sylvine

talc
tantalite
tenorite
tetradymite
tetrahedrite
thenardite
thorianite
thorite
tiemannite
topaz
torbernite
tourmaline
tremolite
triphylite
trona
troostite
tungstite
turgite
turquoise
uralite
uraninite
uranite
vanadinite
variscite
vermiculite
vesuvianite
wavellite
willemite
witherite
wolframite
wollastonite
wulfenite
zaratite
zeolite
zincite
zinkenite or
  zinckenite
zircon
zoisite

MISSILES

cruise missile
Exocet
guided missile
ICBM or
  intercontinental
  ballistic missile
Minuteman
MIRV or multiple

independently
  targeted re-entry
  vehicle
Patriot
Pershing
Polaris
rocket
Scud

SLBM or submarine-
  launched ballistic
  missile
SLCM or sea-
  launched cruise
  missile
SS-18
SS-20

standoff missile
Trident
V-1, doodlebug, buzz
  bomb, or flying
  bomb
V-2

MONKEYS, APES AND OTHER PRIMATES

aye-aye
baboon
Barbary ape
bonnet monkey
bushbaby or
  galago
capuchin
chacma
chimpanzee or
  chimp
colobus

douc
douroucouli
drill
flying lemur or
  colugo
gelada
gibbon
gorilla
green monkey
grivet
guenon

guereza
howler monkey
indris or indri
langur
lemur
loris
macaco
macaque
mandrill
mangabey
marmoset

mona
monkey or
  (archaic)
  jackanapes
orang-outang,
  orang-utan, or
  orang
proboscis
  monkey
rhesus monkey
saki

siamang
sifaka
spider monkey
squirrel monkey
talapoin
tamarin
tana
tarsier
titi
vervet
wanderoo

MOTOR SPORTS

autocross
drag racing
karting

motocross
motor-cycle racing
motor racing

motor rallying or
  rallying
rallycross

scrambling
speedway
stock car racing

MUSCLES

accelerator
accessorius
adductor
agonist
antagonist
arytenoid
biceps
buccinator
compressor
constrictor

contractor
corrugator
deltoid
depressor
digrastic
dilator
elevator
erector
evertor
extensor

flexor
gastrocnemius
gluteus or
  gluteaus
levator
lumbricalis
masseter
opponent
pectoral
peroneal muscle

pronator
psoas
quadriceps
rectus
retractor
rhomboideus
rotator
sartorius
scalenus
soleus

sphincter
supinator
suspensory or
  suspensor
tensor
trapezius
triceps

MUSES

Calliope	epic poetry	Polyhymnia	singing, mime, and sacred dance
Clio	history		
Erato	love poetry	Terpsichore	dance and choral song
Euterpe	lyric poetry and music	Thalia	comedy and pastoral poetry
Melpomene	tragedy	Urania	astronomy

MUSHROOMS AND OTHER EDIBLE FUNGI

black truffle
blewit
button mushroom
cep or porcini
champignon

chanterelle
horn of plenty
meadow mushroom
morel
oyster mushroom

puffball
shaggy ink cap or
  lawyer's wig
shiitake mushroom
straw mushroom

white truffle
wood ear mushroom

MUSIC

CLASSICAL MUSIC GENRES

ars antiqua
ars nova
baroque
classical
early music
expressionist

galant
Gothic
impressionist
minimalist
music concrète
nationalist

neoclassical
post-romantic
Renaissance
rococo
romantic
salon music

serial music
twelve-tone or
  dodecaphonic

TYPES OF COMPOSITION

air	concerto	humoresque	passacaglia	schottische
albumblatt	concerto grosso	impromptu	passepied	septet
allemande	concertstück	interlude	Passion	serenade
anthem	contredanse or	lament	pastiche	sextet
aria	contradance	ländler	pastorale	sinfonia
bagatelle	czardas	lied	pavane	concertante
ballade	dirge	madrigal	phantasy	sinfonietta
ballet	divertimento	march	pibroch	Singspiel
barcarole	divertissement	mass	polka	sonata
barceuse	duet	mazurka	polonaise	sonatina
bolero	dumka	medley	prelude	song
bourrée	duo	minuet	psalm	song cycle
canon	ecossaise	motet	quadrille	strathspey
cantata	elegy	nocturne	quartet	suite
canticle	étude	nonet	quintet	symphonic
canzona	fantasy or	notturno	raga	poem
canzone	fantasia	octet	reel	symphony
canzonetta	farandole	opera	Requiem	toccata
capriccio	fugue	opera buffa	rhapsody	tone poem
cavatina	galliard	opera seria	ricercar or	trio
chaconne	galop	operetta	ricercare	trio sonata
chorale	gavotte	oratorio	rigadoon or	waltz
chorus	gigue	overture	rigadoun	
concertante	grand opera	partita	romance	
concertino	hornpipe	part song	scherzo	

POPULAR MUSIC TYPES

acid house	country blues	grunge	(trademark)	rhythm and blues
acid jazz	country rock	hardbop	Muzak	rock
acid rock	Cu-bop	hardcore	(trademark)	rockabilly
ambient	death metal	harmolodics	New Age	rock and roll
bebop	disco	heavy metal	New Country	rock and roll
bhangra	Dixieland	hip-hop	New Orleans jazz	salsa
bluebeat	doo-wop	House	new romantic	ska
bluegrass	dub	Indie	New Wave	skiffle
blues	folk music	industrial	P-funk	soul
boogie-woogie	folk rock	jazz	pop	surf music
bop	free jazz	jazz-funk	progressive rock	swing
bubblegum	funk	jazz-rock	psychobilly	swingbeat
Cajun	fusion	jungle	punk	techno
calypso	gangsta rap	mainstream jazz	ragga	thrash metal
cool jazz	glam rock	Merseybeat	rap	trad jazz
country and	gospel	modern jazz	rave	world music
western	Goth	Motown	reggae	zydeco

MUSICAL EXPRESSIONS AND TEMPO INSTRUCTIONS

Instruction	Meaning	Instruction	Meaning
accelerando	with increasing speed	animato	in a lively manner
adagio	slowly	appassionato	impassioned
agitato	in an agitated manner	assai	(in combination) very
allegretto	fairly quickly or briskly	calando	with gradually decreasing
allegro	quickly, in a brisk, lively		tone and speed
	manner	cantabile	in a singing style
amoroso	lovingly	con	(in combination) with
andante	at a moderately slow tempo	con affeto	with tender emotion
andantino	slightly faster than andante	con amore	lovingly

Instruction	Meaning	Instruction	Meaning
con anima	with spirit	piano	softly
con brio	vigorously	più	(in combination) more
con fuoco	with fire	pizzicato	(in music for stringed
con moto	quickly		instruments) to be
crescendo	gradual increase in loudness		plucked with the finger
diminuendo	gradual decrease in loudness	poco or un	(in combination) a little
dolce	gently and sweetly	poco	
doloroso	in a sorrowful manner	pomposo	in a pompous manner
energico	energetically	presto	very fast
espressivo	expressively	prestissimo	faster than presto
forte	loud or loudly	quasi	(in combination) almost, as if
fortissimo	very loud	rallentando	becoming slower
furioso	in a frantically rushing manner	rubato	with a flexible tempo
		scherzando	in jocular style
giocoso	merry	sciolto	free and easy
grave	solemn and slow	semplice	simple and unforced
grazioso	graceful	sforzando	with strong initial attack
lacrimoso	sad and mournful	smorzando	dying away
largo	slowly and broadly	sospirando	'sighing', plaintive
larghetto	slowly and broadly, but less so than largo	sostenuto	in a smooth and sustained manner
legato	smoothly and connectedly	sotto voce	extremely quiet
leggiero	light	staccato	(of notes) short, clipped, and separate
lento	slowly		
maestoso	majestically	strascinando	stretched out
marziale	martial	strepitoso	noisy
mezzo	(in combination) moderately	stringendo	with increasing speed
moderato	at a moderate tempo	tanto	(in combination) too much
molto	(in combination) very	tardo	slow
non troppo or non tanto	(in combination) not too much	troppo	(in combination) too much
		vivace	in a brisk lively manner
pianissimo	very quietly	volante	'flying', fast and light

RANKS OF NOBILITY

RANKS OF BRITISH NOBILITY (IN ORDER OF PRECEDENCE)

royal duke or (fem.) royal duchess
duke or (fem.) duchess
marquess or marquis or (fem.) marchioness
earl or (fem.) countess

viscount or (fem.) viscountess
baron or (fem.) baroness
baronet

RANKS OF FOREIGN NOBILITY

archduke or (fem.) archduchess
boyar
burgrave
count or (fem.) countess

grand duke or (fem.) grand duchess
grandee
landgrave or (fem.) landgravine

marchese or (fem.) marchesa
margrave or (fem.) margravine
marquis or (fem.) marquise
prince or (fem.) princess
vicomte or (fem.) vicomtesse

MUSICAL NOTES AND RESTS

British name	American name	British name	American name
breve	double-whole note	quaver	eighth note
semibreve	whole note	semiquaver	sixteenth note
minim	half note	demisemiquaver	thirty-second note
crotchet	quarter note	hemidemisemiquaver	sixty-fourth note

MUSLIM DENOMINATIONS AND SECTS

Alaouites *or* Alawites	Ismaili *or* Isma'ili	Sufism	Wahabism
Druse *or* Druze	Nizari	Sunni	Zaidi
Imami	Shiah, Shia *or* Shiite	Wahhabism *or*	

NUTS

almond	chinquapin,	pignut	nut, *or* bauple	pecan
beech nut	chincapin, *or*	hazelnut, filbert,	nut	pine nut *or* pine
brazil nut	chinkapin	cobnut, *or* cob	marron	kernel
butternut	coco de mer	macadamia	peanut, monkey	pistachio
cashew	dwarf chestnut	(nut),	nut, *or*	quandong
chestnut	earthnut *or*	Queensland	groundnut	walnut

OILS

EDIBLE OILS

benne, gingili, *or*	cottonseed	oleo	peppermint
sesame	fixed	olive	soya
butyrin	maize	palm	sunflower seed
corn	nut	peanut	vegetable

INDUSTRIAL OILS

benzaldehyde	colza	heavy	rosin
banana *or* pentyl	diesel	linseed	shale
acetate	drying	mineral	sperm
bone	fuel	neat's foot	stand
crude	fusel	paraffin	train
Chinese wood *or* tung	glutaraldehyde	parathion	turpentine
coal	gas	rapeseed	whale oil

OILS USED IN PERFUME AND MEDICINE

attar	citronella	evening primrose	neroli	sassafras
bergamot	clove	jojoba	palm	savin
cajuput	coconut	lavender	patchouli	tea tree
camphorated	cod-liver	Macassar	peanut	wintergreen
castor	croton	musk	rapeseed	ylang-ylang
chaulmoogra	eucalyptus	mustard	sandalwood	

INSTRUMENTS IN A FULL ORCHESTRA

cello *or*	piano	cor anglais	trumpet	bass-drum
violoncello	harp	contra-bassoon	tuba	xylophone
violin	piccolo	bassoon	trombone	celesta
viola	flute	clarinet	timpani	snare drum
double bass	oboe	french horn	gong	tubular bells

TYPES OF PASTA

agnolotti	cappelletti	fettuccine, fettucine,	lasagne
bavette	cellentani	*or* fettucini	lasagnette
bombolotti	conchiglie	fusilli	linguine
bucatini	ditali	gnocchetti	lumache
cannelloni	farfalle	gnocchi	macaroni

maultaschen	penne	spaghetti	tortelloni
noodles	pipe	spätzle *or* spaetzle	tortiglioni
orecchiette	ravioli	tagliatelle	vermicelli
paglia e fieno	rigatoni	taglioni	zita *or* ziti
pappardelle	ruote	tortellini	

PEOPLES

AFRICAN PEOPLES

Bantu	Ghanaian *or*	Maninke	Ovambo	Tsonga
Barotse	Ghanian	Masai	Pondo	Tswana
Basotho	Griqua *or*	Matabele	Pygmy *or* Pigmy	Tuareg
Berber	Grikwa	Moor	Rif, Riff, *or* Rifi	Tunisian
Bushman	Hausa	Mosotho	Shangaan	Tutsi
Chewa	Herero	Mossi	Shluh	Venda
Damara	Hottentot	Nama *or*	Shona	Watusi *or*
Dinka	Hutu	Namaqua	Somali	Watutsi
Duala	Ibibio	Ndebele	Songhai	Wolof
Edo	Ibo *or* Igbo	Negrillo	Sotho	Xhosa
Eritrean	Kabyle	Negro	Strandloper	Yoruba
Ethiopian	Kikuyu	Nguni	Susu	Zulu
Ewe	Kongo	Nuba	Swahili	
Gabonese	Luba	Nupe	Swazi	
Galla	Luo	Nyanja	Temne	
Gambian	Malinke *or*	Nyoro	Tiv	

ASIAN PEOPLES

Adivasi	Chuvash	Kabardian	Moro	Sumerian
Ainu	Cossack	Kalmuck *or*	Motu	Tadzhik, Tadjik,
Akkadian *or*	Cumans	Kalmyk	Munda	*or* Tajik
Accadian	Dani	Kanarese *or*	Naga	Tagalog
Amalekite	Dard	Canarese	Negrito	Talaing
Amorite	Dyak *or* Dayak	Kara-Kalpak	Nogay	Tamil
Andamanese	Elamite	Karen	Nuri *or* Kafir	Tatar *or* Tartar
Arab	Ephesian	Kashmiri	Palestinian	Thai
Babylonian	Ephraimite	Kassite	Pathan, Pashto,	Tocharian *or*
Bakhtyari	Essene	Kazakh *or* Kazak	Pushto, *or*	Tokharian
Baluchi *or* Balochi	Evenki	Khmer	Pushtu	Tongan
Bashkir	Fulani	Kurd	Phoenician	Tungus
Bedouin *or*	Gond	Lao	Punjabi *or*	Turanian
Beduin	Gujarati *or*	Lepcha	Panjabi	Turk
Bengali	Gujerati	Lycian	Sabaean *or*	Turkmen
Bihari	Gurkha	Lydian	Sabean	Uigur *or* Uighur
Burmese	Hittite	Malay	Samoyed	Uzbek
Buryat	Hui	Maratha *or*	Saracen	Vedda *or* Veddah
Chaldean *or*	Hun	Mahratta	Semite	Visayan *or*
Chaldaean	Hurrian	Mede	Shan	Bisayan
Cham	Igorot *or* Igorrote	Mishmi	Sherpa	Yakut
Chinese	Israeli	Mon	Sindhi	
Chukchee *or*	Jat	Mongol	Sinhalese	
Chukchi	Jewish	Montagnard	Sogdian	

AUSTRALASIAN PEOPLES

Aborigine	Dayak	Māori	Polynesian
Aranda	Gurindji	Melanesian	Tagalog

CENTRAL AND SOUTH AMERICAN INDIAN PEOPLES

Araucanian	Cashinahua	Inca	Quechua,	Zapotec
Arawakan	Chibca	Makuna	Kechua, or	
Aymara	Chimú	Maya	Quichua	
Aztec	Ge	Mixtec	Toltec	
Carib	Guarani	Nahuatl	Tupi	

ESKIMO PEOPLES

Aleut or Aleutian	Caribou Eskimo	Inuit or Innuit	Yupik

EUROPEAN PEOPLES

Achaean or	Castilian	Galician	Luxembourger	Serbian
Achaian	Catalan	Gascon	Macedonian	Sicilian
Aeolian or Eolian	Celt	Gaul	Magyar	Silures
Albanian	Celtiberi	Georgian	Maltese	Slav
Alemanni	Chechen	German	Manx	Slovak
Andalusian	Cheremis or	Goidel	Montenegrin	Slovene
Angle	Cheremiss	Goth	Mordvin	Sorb
Anglo-Norman	Cimbri	Greek	Norman	Swabian
Anglo-Saxon	Cornish	Gypsy or Gipsy	Norse	Swede
Aragonese	Corsican	Hellenic	Norwegian	Swiss
Armenian	Croatian or Croat	Iberian or	Ostrogoth	Teuton
Aryan	Cymry or Kymry	Celtiberian	Ostyak	Thracian
Ashkenazi	Czech	Icelandic	Pict	Turk
Austrian	Dane	Iceni	Pole	Tyrolese
Azerbaijani or	Dorian	Illyrian	Portuguese	Ugrian
Azeri	Dutch	Indo-European	Provençal	Ukrainian
Azorean	English	Ingush	Prussian	Vandal
Basque	Faeroese	Ionian	Romanian	Viking
Bavarian	Finn	Irish	Russian	Visigoth
Belgae	Ephesian	Jute	Sabellian	Vlach or Walach
Belorussian	Estonian or	Karelian	Sabine	Volsci
Bosnian Muslim	Esthonian	Komi	Salain	Votyak
Breton	Etruscan or	Lapp	Samnite	Walloon
Briton	Etrurian	Latin	Samoyed	Welsh
Brython	Fleming	Latvian	Sardinian	Wend
Bulgar	Frank	Lithuanian	Saxon	
Bulgarian	French	Lombard or	Scot	
Burgundian	Frisian	Langobard	Scythian	
Carinthian	Gaelic	Lusatian	Sephardi	

NATIVE AMERICAN TRIBES

Abnaki	Aymara	Chilcal	Flathead	Kickapoo
Aguaruna	Aztec	Chinook	Fox	Kiowa
Algonquian or	Bella Coola	Chippewa or	Haida	Kootenay
Algonkian	Biloxi	Chippeway	Hidatsa	Kwakiutl
Algonquin or	Blackfoot	Choctaw	Hopi	Leni-Lenapé
Algonkin	Blood	Cocopa	Hupa	Lipan
Apache	Caddo	Comanche	Huron	Mandan
Apalachee	Campa	Cree	Illinois	Mapuche
Arapaho	Carib	Creek	Inca	Maya
Araucan	Catawba	Crow	Iowa	Menomini or
Arikara	Cayuga	Dakota	Iroquois	Menominee
Ashochimi	Cherokee	Delaware	Kansa	Miami
Assiniboine	Cheyenne	Dene	Karankawa	Micmac
Athabascan	Chickasaw	Dogrib	Kichai	Minnetaree

Mixtec
Mohave or
  Mojave
Mohawk
Mohegan
Mohican or
  Mahican
Moki or Moqui
Montagnard
Muskogean or
  Muskhogean
Nahuatl
Narraganset
Natchez

Navaho or Navajo
Nez Percé
Nootka
Ojibwa or
  Ojibway
Omaha
Oneida
Onondaga
Orejone
Osage
Ostiak
Ottawa
Paiute
Pasamaquoddy

Pawnee
Penobscot
Pequot
Pericu
Piegan
Pima
Powhatan
Pueblo
Quakaw
Quechua,
  Quichua, or
  Kechua
Root-digger
Salish

Santee
Sarcee
Sauk
Seminole
Seneca
Shawnee
Shoshoni
Shushwap
Sioux
Stonies
Susquehanna
Teton
Tlingit
Toltec

Tonkawa
Tuscarora
Ute
Wappo
Warrau
Wichita
Winnebago
Wyandot
Yaqui
Yuchi
Yuma
Yunca
Zuni

PHILOSOPHY

PHILOSOPHICAL SCHOOLS AND DOCTRINES

animism
Aristotelianism
atomism
behaviourism
Cartesianism
conceptualism
Confucianism
consequentialism
conventionalism
critical realism
cynicism
deism
determinism
dualism

Eleaticism
empiricism
epicureanism
essentialism
existentialism
fatalism
fideism
hedonism
Hegelianism
humanism
idealism
immaterialism
Kantianism
logical atomism

logical positivism
Marxism
materialism
monism
neo-Platonism
nihilism
nominalism
phenomenalism
Platonism
pluralism
positivism
pragmatism
Pyrrhonism
Pythagoreanism

rationalism
realism
scepticism
scholasticism
sensationalism
Stoicism
structuralism
Taoism
theism
Thomism
utilitarianism
utopianism

PHOBIAS

Phobia	Meaning	Phobia	Meaning
acerophobia	sourness	atephobia	ruin
achluophobia	darkness	aulophobia	flute
acrophobia	heights	bacilliphobia	microbes
aerophobia	air	barophobia	gravity
agoraphobia	open spaces	basophobia	walking
aichurophobia	points	batrachophobia	reptiles
ailurophobia	cats	belonephobia	needles
akousticophobia	sound	bibliophobia	books
algophobia	pain	brontophobia	thunder
amakaphobia	carriages	cancerophobia	cancer
amathophobia	dust	cheimaphobia	cold
androphobia	men	chionophobia	snow
anemophobia	wind	chrematophobia	money
anginophobia	narrowness	chronophobia	duration
anthropophobia	man	chrystallophobia	crystals
antlophobia	flood	claustrophobia	closed spaces
apeirophobia	infinity	cnidophobia	stings
aquaphobia	water	cometophobia	comets
arachnophobia	spiders	cromophobia	colour
asthenophobia	weakness	cyberphobia	computers
astraphobia	lightning	cynophobia	dogs

Phobia	Meaning	Phobia	Meaning
demonophobia	demons	nephophobia	clouds
demophobia	crowds	nosophobia	disease
dermatophobia	skin	nyctophobia	night
dikephobia	justice	ochlophobia	crowds
doraphobia	fur	ochophobia	vehicles
eisoptrophobia	mirrors	odontophobia	teeth
electrophobia	electricity	oikophobia	home
enetephobia	pins	olfactophobia	smell
entomophobia	insects	ommatophobia	eyes
eosophobia	dawn	oneirophobia	dreams
eremophobia	solitude	ophidiophobia	snakes
ereuthophobia	blushing	ornithophobia	birds
ergasiophobia	work	ouranophobia	heaven
genophobia	sex	panphobia	everything
geumaphobia	taste	pantophobia	everything
graphophobia	writing	parthenophobia	girls
gymnophobia	nudity	pathophobia	disease
gynophobia	women	peniaphobia	poverty
hadephobia	hell	phasmophobia	ghosts
haematophobia	blood	phobophobia	fears
hamartiophobia	sin	photophobia	light
haptophobia	touch	pnigerophobia	smothering
harpaxophobia	robbers	poinephobia	punishment
hedonophobia	pleasure	polyphobia	many things
helminthophobia	worms	potophobia	drink
hodophobia	travel	pteronophobia	feathers
homichlophobia	fog	pyrophobia	fire
homophobia	homosexuals	Russophobia	Russia
hormephobia	shock	rypophobia	soiling
hydrophobia	water	Satanophobia	Satan
hypegiaphobia	responsibility	selaphobia	flesh
hypnophobia	sleep	siderophobia	stars
ideophobia	ideas	sitophobia	food
kakorraphiaphobia	failure	spermaphobia	germs
katagelophobia	ridicule	spermatophobia	germs
kenophobia	void	stasiphobia	standing
kinesophobia	motion	stygiophobia	hell
kleptophobia	stealing	taphephobia	being buried alive
kopophobia	fatigue	technophobia	technology
kristallophobia	ice	teratophobia	giving birth to a monster
laliophobia	stuttering		
linonophobia	string	thaasophobia	sitting
logophobia	words	thalassophobia	sea
lyssophobia	insanity	thanatophobia	death
maniaphobia	insanity	theophobia	God
mastigophobia	flogging	thermophobia	heat
mechanophobia	machinery	tonitrophobia	thunder
metallophobia	metals	toxiphobia	poison
meteorophobia	meteors	tremophobia	trembling
misophobia	contamination	triskaidekaphobia	thirteen
monophobia	one thing	xenophobia	strangers or foreigners
musicophobia	music	zelophobia	jealousy
musophobia	mice	zoophobia	animals
necrophobia	corpses		
nelophobia	glass		
neophobia	newness		

PHYSICS

BRANCHES OF PHYSICS

acoustics
aerodynamics
aerostatics
applied physics
astrophysics
atomic physics
biophysics
condensed-matter physics *or* solid-state physics
cosmology
cryogenics *or* low-temperature physics
dynamics
electromagnetism
electronics
electrostatics
geophysics
harmonics
high-energy physics *or* particle physics
kinetics
macrophysics
magnetics *or* magnetism
magnetostatics
mechanics
mesoscopics
microphysics
nuclear physics
nucleonics
optics
photometry
pneumatics
quantum mechanics
quantum physics
rheology
solar physics
sonics
spectroscopy
statistical mechanics
statics
superaerodynamics
theoretical physics
thermodynamics
thermometry
thermostatics
ultrasonics

PHYSICS TERMS

acceleration
alternating current
ampere
amplifier
angstrom
anion
antimatter
atom
baryon
becquerel
Boyle's law
Brownian motion
cacion
calorie
capacitance
cathode ray
centre of gravity
centrifugal force
centripetal force
charge
Charles' law
conductor
convection
cosmic ray
coulomb
current
cyclotron
decibel
density
diffraction
diffusion
diode
direct current
Doppler effect
earth
electricity
electromotive force
electron
energy
farad
field
fission
fluorescence
force
frequency
friction
fuse
fusion
gamma ray
generator
gravity
half-life
hertz
hyperon
impetus
inductance
inertia
infrared
joule
kelvin
kinetic energy
laser
lens
lepton
luminescence
mass
matter
meson
microwave
moment
momentum
muon
neutrino
neutron
newton
nucleon
nucleus
ohm
Ohm's law
particle
pascal
Planck constant *or* Planck's constant
potential difference
potential energy
proton
quantum
radiation
radioactivity
radio wave
red shift
reflection
refraction
relativity
resistance
rutherford
semiconductor
simple harmonic motion
spectrum
static electricity
subatomic particle
super-conductivity
superfluidity
surface tension
tau particle
tension
terminal velocity
thermostat
transformer
transistor
ultraviolet
vacuum
velocity
viscosity
volt
watt
wave
wavelength
x-ray

BREEDS OF PIG

Berkshire
Cheshire
Chester White
Duroc
Gloucester Old Spot
Hampshire
Landrace
Large Black
Large White
Middle White
Pietrain
Saddleback
Small White
Tamworth
Vietnamese pot-bellied
Welsh

PLANETS

Earth
Jupiter
Mars
Mercury
Neptune
Saturn
Uranus
Venus

PARTS OF PLANTS

androecium
anther
anthophore
blossom
bract
bud
bulbil
calyx
capitulum
carpel
carpophore
catkin
caulis
clinandrium
commissure
corolla
corymb
costa
cyathium
cyme
dichasium
epidermis
filament

floral envelope
floret
foliage
fruit
gametophore
guard cell
glume
gynoecium
head
hibernaculum
hypanthium
inflorescence
internode
involucel
involucre
joint
leaf
lemma
lip
micropyle
monochasium
nectary
nucellus

offshoot
ovary
ovule
palea
panicle
pedicel
peduncle
perianth
petal
phloem
pistil
placenta
pod
pollen
pollen grain
pollinium
raceme
rachis
receptacle, thalamus,
    or torus
root
root cap
root hair

secundine
seed
seed pod
sepal
sheath
spadix
spathe
spike
spikelet
spur
stamen
stem
stigma
stoma
style
taproot
tassel
tepal
umbel
vascular bundle
xylem

POETRY

POETRY AND PROSODY TERMS

accentual metre
accentual-syllabic
    metre or stress-
    syllabic metre
Adonic
Alcaic
Alexandrine
alliteration
amoebaean or
    amoebean
amphibrach
amphimacer
anacrusis
anapaest or anapest
anapaestic or
    anapestic
antistrophe
arsis
assonance
bacchius
ballad stanza
blank verse
bob
cadence or cadency
caesura or cesura
canto
catalectic
choriamb or
    choriambus
closed couplet

common measure
common metre
consonance or
    consonancy
couplet
cretic or amphimacer
dactyl
dactylic
diaeresis or dieresis
dipody
distich
elision
end-stopped
enjambement
envoy or envoi
epode
eye rhyme
feminine ending
feminine rhyme
foot
free verse or vers libre
half-rhyme
hemistich
heptameter
heptastich
heroic couplet
hexameter
hypermeter
iamb or iambus
iambic

ictus
internal rhyme
ionic
jabberwocky
leonine rhyme
long metre
macaronic
masculine ending
masculine rhyme
metre
octameter
octave or octet
onomatopoeia
ottava rima
paeon
paeonic
pararhyme
pentameter
pentastich
perfect rhyme or full
    rhyme
Pindaric
pyhrric
quantitative metre
quatrain
quintain or quintet
refrain
rhyme
rhyme royal
rhyme scheme

rhythm
rime riche
Sapphic
scansion
septet
sestet
sestina or sextain
short metre
Spenserian stanza
spondee
spondaic
sprung rhythm
stanza
stichic
strophe
syllabic metre
tercet
terza rima
tetrabrach
tetrameter
tetrapody
tetrastich
triplet
trochaic
trochee
unstopped
verse paragraph
wheel

POETRY MOVEMENTS AND GROUPINGS

Alexandrians
Decadents
Georgian Poets
imagists
Lake Poets
Liverpool Poets
Metaphysical Poets
the Movement
Petrarchans
Romantics
Scottish Chaucerians
symbolists

POISONS

POISONOUS SUBSTANCES AND GASES

aconite
acrolein
adamsite
afterdamp
Agent Orange
aldrin
allyl alcohol
aniline
antimony potassium
   tartrate
arsenic *or* arsenic
   trioxide
arsine
atropine *or* atropin
barium hydroxide
benzene
benzidine
brucine
cacodyl
carbon disulphide
carbon monoxide
coniine, conin, *or*
   conine
curare
cyanic acid
cyanide
cyanogen
digitalin
emetine
formaldehyde
hemlock
hydrastine
hydrogen cyanide
hydrogen fluoride
hydrogen iodide
hydrogen sulphide
hyoscyamine
lead monoxide
lewisite
lindane
mercuric chloride
mercuric oxide
methanol
methyl bromide
muscarine
mustard gas
nerve gas
nitrogen dioxide
osmium tetroxide
ouabain
oxalic acid
Paraquat
Paris green
phenol
phosgene
picrotoxin
poison gas
potassium cyanide
potassium
   permanganate
prussic acid
ratsbane
red lead
sarin
silver nitrate
sodium cyanide
sodium fluoroacetate
stibine
strychnine
tetramethyldiarsine
thallium
thebaine
tropine
urushiol
veratrine
whitedamp
zinc chloride

TYPES OF POISONING

botulism
bromism
digitalism
ergotism
fluorosis
hydrargyria
iodism
lead poisoning
listeriosis
mercurialism
phosphorism
plumbism
ptomaine poisoning
salmonella
saturnism
strychninism

POISONOUS PLANTS

aconite
amanita
baneberry
belladonna
black bryony
black nightshade
castor-oil plant
cowbane
coyotillo
deadly nightshade
death camass
death cap *or* angel
destroying angel
dieffenbachia
dog's mercury
ergot
fly agaric
foxglove
hemlock
henbane
Indian liquorice
laburnum
liberty cap
locoweed
manchineel
monkshood
mountain laurel
Noogoora burr
nux vomica
oleander
poison dogwood *or*
   elder
poison ivy
poison oak
poison sumach
pokeweed, pokeberry,
   or pokeroot
sassy, sasswood, *or*
   sassy wood
staggerbush
stavesacre
thorn apple
tutu
upas
water hemlock
wolfsbane *or* wolf's-
   bane
woody nightshade

BIRDS OF PREY

accipiter
Australian goshawk
   or chicken hawk
bald eagle
barn owl
bateleur eagle
boobook
brown owl
buzzard
caracara
condor
Cooper's hawk
duck hawk
eagle
eagle-hawk *or* wedge-
tailed eagle
falcon *or* (N.Z.) bush-
   hawk *or* karearea
falconet
golden eagle

goshawk
gyrfalcon or gerfalcon
harrier
hawk
hawk owl
hobby
honey buzzard
hoot owl
horned owl
kestrel

kite
lammergeier,
  lammergeyer,
  bearded vulture, or
  (archaic) ossifrage
lanner
little owl
long-eared owl
merlin
Montagu's harrier

mopoke or (N.Z.) ruru
osprey, fish eagle, or
  (archaic) ossifrage
owl
peregrine falcon
red kite or (archaic)
  gled(e)
rough-legged buzzard
saker
screech owl

sea eagle, erne, or ern
secretary bird
snowy owl
sparrowhawk
tawny owl
turkey buzzard or
  vulture
vulture

PROGRAMMING LANGUAGES

Ada	C#	Haskell	Perl	RPG
Algol	COBOL or Cobol	Java	PL/1	Simula
BASIC or Basic	FORTH or Forth	LISP	Postscript	Smalltalk
C	FORTRAN or	LOGO	PROLOG or	SNOBOL
C++	Fortran	Pascal	Prolog	SQL

PROTEINS

actin	dystrophin	hordein	ossein
actomyosin	factor VIII	keratin	prion
aleurone	ferritin	lactalbumin	properdin
alpha-fetoprotein	fibrin	lactoprotein	ricin
amyloid	fibrinogen	lectin	sclerotin
apoprotein	fibroin	legumin	sericin
avidin	flagellin	leptin	spongin
calmodulin	gliadin	lymphokine	thrombogen
caseinogen	globin	myosin	vitellin
conchiolin	gluten	opsin	zein

PSYCHOLOGY

BRANCHES OF PSYCHOLOGY

analytic psychology	experimental psychology	psychiatry
child psychology	hedonics	psycholinguistics
clinical psychology	industrial psychology	psychometrics
comparative psychology	neuropsychology	psychophysics
developmental psychology	organizational psychology	psychophysiology
educational psychology	parapsychology	social psychology

PSYCHOLOGY TERMS

alter ego	extrovert	Oedipus complex	repression
anal	fixation	paranoia	Rorschach test or
analysis	Freudian slip	persecution complex	inkblot test
angst	Gestalt therapy	persona	schizophrenia
anxiety	group therapy	personality	self
complex	hypnosis	personality disorder	stress
compulsion	hypochondria	phobia	subconscious
conditioning	hysteria	primal therapy or	sublimation
consciousness	id	primal scream	superego
death wish	inferiority complex	therapy	syndrome
delusion	introvert	psyche	trauma
dementia	mania	psychoanalysis	unconscious
depression	mind	psychosis	
ego	neurosis	psychosomatic	
Electra complex	obsession	regression	

RELIGION

RELIGIONS

animism
Babi or Babism
Baha'ism
Buddhism
Christianity
Confucianism
druidism
heliolatry

Hinduism or
  Hindooism
Islam
Jainism
Judaism
Macumba
Manichaeism or
  Manicheism

Mithraism or
  Mithraicism
Orphism
paganism
Rastafarianism
Ryobu Shinto
Santeria
Satanism

Scientology
  (trademark)
shamanism
Shango
Shembe
Shinto
Sikhism
Taoism

voodoo or
  voodooism
Yezidis
Zoroastrianism or
  Zoroastrism

RELIGIOUS BOOKS

Adi Granth
Apocrypha
Atharveda
Ayurveda
Bhagavad-Gita
Bible
Book of Mormon

Granth or Guru
  Granth Sahib
I Ching
Koran or Quran
Li Chi
Lu
Mahabharata

New Testament
Old Testament
Ramayana
Rigveda
Samaveda
Shi Ching
Siddhanta

Su Ching
Talmud
Tipitaka
Torah
Tripitaka
Veda
Yajurveda

RELIGIOUS BUILDINGS

abbey
bethel
cathedral

chapel
church
convent

gurdwara
Kaaba
marae

monastery
mosque
synagogue

tabernacle
temple

RELIGIOUS CLOTHING

alb
almuce
amice
biretta or berretta
calotte
canonicals
capuche or capouche
cassock
chasuble
chimere, chimer, or
  chimar

clerical collar
clericals
coif
cope
cornet
cotta
cowl
dalmatic
dog collar (informal)
gremial
guimpe

habit
infulae
maniple
mantelletta
mitre
mozzetta or mozetta
pallium
peplos or peplus
pontificals
rochet
scapular

shovel hat
soutane
superhumeral
surcingle
surplice
tippet
wimple
zucchetto

RELIGIOUS FESTIVALS

Advent
Al Hijrah
Ascension Day
Ash Wednesday
Baisakhi
Bodhi Day
Candlemas
Chanukah or
  Hanukkah
Ching Ming
Christmas
Corpus Christi
Day of Atonement
Dhammacakka
Diwali
Dragon Boat Festival

Dussehra
Easter
Eid ul-Adha or Id-ul-
  Adha
Eid ul-Fitr or Id-ul-Fitr
Epiphany
Feast of Tabernacles
Good Friday
Guru Nanak's
  Birthday
Hirja
Hola Mohalla
Holi
Janamashtami
Lailat ul-Barah
Lailat ul-Isra Wal

Mi'raj
Lailat ul-Qadr
Lent
Mahashivaratri
Maundy Thursday
Michaelmas
Moon Festival
Palm Sunday
Passion Sunday
Passover
Pentecost
Pesach
Purim
Quadragesima
Quinquagesima
Raksha Bandhan

Ramadan
Rama Naumi
Rogation
Rosh Hashanah
Septuagesima
Sexagesima
Shavuot
Shrove Tuesday
Sukkoth or Succoth
Trinity
Wesak
Whitsun
Winter Festival
Yom Kippur
Yuan Tan

REPTILES

adder
agama
agamid
alligator
amphisbaena
anaconda or (Caribbean) camoodi
anole
asp
bandy-bandy
black snake or red-bellied black snake
blind snake
blue racer
blue tongue
boa
boa constrictor
boomslang
box turtle
brown snake or (Austral.) mallee snake
bull snake or gopher snake
bushmaster
carpet snake or python
cayman or caiman
cerastes
chameleon
chuckwalla
cobra
cobra de capello
constrictor
copperhead
coral snake
crocodile
death adder or deaf adder
diamondback,

diamondback terrapin, or diamondback turtle
diamond snake or diamond python
dugite or dukite
elapid
fer-de-lance
flying lizard or flying dragon
freshwater crocodile or (Austral. informal) freshy
frill-necked lizard, frilled lizard, bicycle lizard, cycling lizard, or (Austral. informal) frillie
gaboon viper
galliwasp
garter snake
gavial, gharial, or garial
gecko
giant tortoise
Gila monster
glass snake
goanna, bungarra (Austral.), or go (Austral. informal)
grass snake
green turtle
habu
harlequin snake
hawksbill or hawksbill turtle
hognose snake or puff adder
hoop snake
horned toad or lizard

horned viper
iguana
indigo snake
jew lizard, bearded lizard, or bearded dragon
kabaragoya or Malayan monitor
king cobra or hamadryad
king snake
Komodo dragon or Komodo lizard
krait
leatherback or (Brit.) leathery turtle
leguan
lizard
loggerhead or loggerhead turtle
mamba
massasauga
milk snake
moloch, thorny devil, thorn lizard, or mountain devil
monitor
mud turtle
ngarara (N.Z.)
perentie or perenty
pit viper
puff adder
python
racer
rat snake
rattlesnake or (U.S. & Canad. informal) rattler
ringhals
rock snake,

rock python, amethystine python, or Schneider python
saltwater crocodile or (Austral. informal) saltie
sand lizard
sand viper
sea snake
sidewinder
skink
slowworm or blindworm
smooth snake
snake
snapping turtle
soft-shelled turtle
swift
taipan
terrapin
tiger snake
tokay
tortoise
tree snake
tuatara or (technical) sphenodon (N.Z.)
turtle
viper
wall lizard
water moccasin, moccasin, or cottonmouth
water snake
whip snake
worm lizard

RICE AND OTHER CEREALS

arborio rice
basmati rice
bran
brown rice
bulgur wheat

corn
couscous
Indian rice or wild rice
long grain rice
maize

millet
oatmeal
oats
Patna rice
ragi

sago
short grain rice
tapioca
wheat
wild rice

TYPES OF ROCK

andesite
anorthosite
anthracite
arkose
basalt

breccia
chalk
chert
clay
coal

conglomerate
diorite
dolerite
dolomite
dunite

eclogite
felsite or felstone
flint
gabbro
gneiss

granite	lava	peridotite	schist
granodiorite	lignite	perknite	shale
gravel	limestone	phyllite	skarn
greywacke or (U.S.)	loess	pitchstone	slate
graywacke	marble	pumice	soapstone
grit	monzonite	pyroxenite	syenite
hornblendite	mudstone	quartzite	trachyte
hornfels	obsidian	rhyolite	
lamprophyre	pegmatite	sandstone	

RODENTS

acouchi or acouchy	gerbil, gerbille, or	jerboa	red squirrel or
agouti	jerbil	jumping mouse	chickaree
beaver	gopher or pocket	kangaroo rat	spinifex hopping
black rat	gopher	kiore (N.Z.)	mouse or (Austral.)
brown rat or Norway	gopher or ground	lemming	dargawarra
rat	squirrel	Māori rat or (N.Z.)	springhaas
cane rat	grey squirrel	kiore	squirrel
capybara	groundhog or	mara	suslik or souslik
cavy	woodchuck	marmot	taguan
chinchilla	ground squirrel or	mole rat	tucotuco
chipmunk	gopher	mouse	viscacha or vizcacha
coypu or nutria	guinea pig or cavy	muskrat or	vole
deer mouse	hamster	musquash	water rat
desert rat	harvest mouse	paca	water vole or water
dormouse	hedgehog	pack rat	rat
fieldmouse	hopping mouse or	pocket mouse	white-footed mouse
flying squirrel	jerboa rat	porcupine	white rat
fox squirrel	house mouse	rat	

RUGBY TERMS

back	full back	pass
back row	garryowen (Rugby union)	penalty
ball	goalpost	prop forward
centre	half back	punt
conversion	hooker	referee
crossbar	knock on	ruck (Rugby union)
drop goal	line-out (Rugby union)	scrum half
lock forward	mark (Rugby union)	second row
loose forward	maul (Rugby union)	tackle
loose head	number eight forward (Rugby	three-quarter
five-eighth (Austral.) (N.Z.)	union)	tight head
flanker or wing forward	scrum or scrummage	touch judge
(Rugby union)	stand-off half, fly half, or	try
forward	outside half	up and under (Rugby league)
front row	pack	winger

RULERS

TITLES OF RULERS

amir or ameer	chief	emir	hospodar
archduke	Chogyal	emperor or (fem.)	imam or imaum
Caesar	Dalai Lama	empress	Inca
caliph, calif, kalif, or	doge	Gaekwar or Gaikwar	kabaka
khalif	duke	Great Mogul	Kaiser

khan
khedive
king
maharajah or maharaja
maharani or maharanee
mikado

nawab or nabob
Negus
Nizam
oba
pasha or pacha
Pharaoh
podesta
pope

queen
rajah or raja
rani or ranee
satrap
shah
sheik or sheikh
sherif, shereef, or sharif

shogun
stadholder or stadtholder
sultan
tenno
tsar or czar
viceroy or (fem.) vicereine

FAMOUS RULERS

Alexander the Great
Alfred the Great
Idi Amin
Augustus
Bismarck
Boudicca
Caligula
Castro
Catherine the Great
Charlemagne

Churchill
Cleopatra
Cromwell
de Gaulle
Edward the Confessor
Elizabeth I
Elizabeth II
Franco
Genghis Khan
Haile Selassie

Herod
Hirohito
Hitler
Ivan the Terrible
Julius Caesar
Kublai Khan
Lenin
Louis XIV
Mao Ze Dong or Mao Tse-tung

Montezuma
Mussolini
Napoleon Bonaparte
Nasser
Nero
Nicholas II
Pericles

SAUCES

apple
à la king
barbecue
Béarnaise
béchamel
black bean
bolognese or bolognaise
Bordelaise
brandy butter or hard sauce
bread
brown
chasseur
chaudfroid
cheese
chilli

chocolate
chow-chow
coulis
cranberry
cream
creole
cumberland
curry
custard
French dressing
fudge
gravy
hoisin
hollandaise
horseradish
ketchup
mayonnaise

Melba sauce
mint
mornay
mousseline
nam pla or fish sauce
orange
oyster
pesto
piccalilli
red pesto
rémoulade
Russian dressing
sabayon
salad cream
salad dressing
salsa
salsa verde

soubise
soy sauce, shoyu, or tamari
suprême
sweet-and-sour
Tabasco (trademark)
tartare
tomato
velouté
verjuice sauce
vinaigrette
white
wine
Worcester or Worcestershire

SEA BIRDS

albatross or (informal) gooney bird
auk
auklet
black-backed gull
black guillemot
black shag or kawau (N.Z.)
blue penguin, korora or little blue penguin (N.Z.)
blue shag (N.Z.)
booby (Austral.)
caspian tern or taranui (N.Z.)
coot
cormorant

fairy penguin, little penguin, or (N.Z.) korora
fish hawk
fulmar
gannet
glaucous gull
guillemot
gull or (archaic or dialect) cob(b)
herring gull
ivory gull
kittiwake
man-of-war bird or frigate bird
murrelet

old squaw or oldwife
oystercatcher
petrel
prion
razorbill or razor-billed auk
scoter
sea duck
sea eagle, erne, or ern
seagull
shearwater
short-tailed shearwater, (Tasmanian) mutton bird, or (N.Z.) titi
skua

storm petrel, stormy petrel,
    or Mother Carey's chicken
surf scoter or surf duck
takapu (N.Z.)

velvet scoter
wandering albatross
white-fronted tern, black
    cap, kahawai bird, sea

swallow or tara (N.Z.)
Wilson's petrel

SEAFOOD

abalone
anchovy
Balmain bug (Austral.)
banana prawn (Austral.)
barramundi
bass
blackfish
bloater
blue cod
blue swimmer, blue manna, or
    sand crab (Austral.)
bonito
bream
brill
butterfish
callop
carp
catfish
clam
clappy-doo or clabby-doo
    (Scot.)
cockle
coalfish or saithe
cockle
cod
codling
crab
crayfish, crawfish, or (N.Z.)
    koura
crayfish, craybob, craydab,
    crawbob, clawchie, lobster,
    marron, or yabby (Austral.)
dab
dogfish
dorado
Dover sole
Dublin Bay prawn
eel
flounder
gemfish
grayling
Greenland halibut
haddock

hake
halibut
herring
huss
jewfish
John Dory
kahawai or Australian salmon
kingfish
king prawn
kipper
langoustine
lemon sole
ling
lobster
lumpfish
mackerel
marron
megrim
monkfish
Moreton Bay bug or shovel-
    nosed lobster (Austral.)
morwong
mud crab
mullet
mulloway
mussel
nannygai
Norway lobster
octopus
oyster
parrotfish
perch
pike
pilchard or (Austral. informal)
    pillie
pipi
plaice
pollack
pomfret
pout
prawn
queenie or queen scallop
rainbow trout

redfish
red snapper
roach
rockfish
salmon
sardine
scallop or scollop
school prawn (Austral.)
sea cucumber
shad
shark
shrimp
sild
skate
skipjack tuna
snapper
snoek
snook
sockeye or red salmon
sole
sprat
squid
swordfish
tarakihi or terakihi
teraglin
tiger prawn
tilefish
trevally (Austral.) (N.Z.)
trout
tuna or tunny
turbot
wahoo
whelk
whitebait
whiting
winkle
witch
wolffish
yabby or yabbie (Austral.)
yellow belly (Austral.)
zander

SEA MAMMALS

dugong
eared seal
earless seal
elephant seal

harp seal
hooded seal
manatee
sea cow

seal
sea lion
walrus or (archaic) sea horse

SEASONS

Season	Related adjective	Season	Related adjective
spring	vernal	autumn	autumnal
summer	aestival or estival	winter	hibernal or hiemal

SEXUAL PRACTICES AND TERMS

adultery
afterplay
algolagnia
anal intercourse, sodomy, or buggery
anilingus
autoeroticism
bagpiping
bestiality
bisexuality
bondage
coprophilia
cottaging
cunnilingus

felching
fellatio
fetishism
fisting or fist-fucking
flagellation
foreplay
fornication
frottage
heterosexuality
homosexuality
impotence
incest
lesbianism
masochism

masturbation
narcissism
necrophilia
nymphomania
oral sex
paedophilia
paraphilia
pederasty
premature ejaculation
rimming
rough trade
sadism
sadomasochism or

S&M
safe sex
satyriasis
scopophilia
shrimping
soixante-neuf or sixty-nine
tribadism
troilism
voyeurism
water sports, urolagnia, or golden shower
zoophilia

SHAKESPEARE

PLAYS OF SHAKESPEARE

All's Well that Ends Well
Antony and Cleopatra
As You Like It
The Comedy of Errors
Coriolanus
Cymbeline
Hamlet
Henry IV Part I
Henry IV Part II
Henry V
Henry VI Part I
Henry VI Part II
Henry VI Part III

Henry VIII
Julius Caesar
King John
King Lear
Love's Labour's Lost
Macbeth
Measure for Measure
The Merchant of Venice
The Merry Wives of Windsor
A Midsummer Night's Dream
Much Ado About Nothing
Othello
Pericles, Prince of Tyre

Richard II
Richard III
Romeo and Juliet
The Taming of the Shrew
The Tempest
Timon of Athens
Titus Andronicus
Troilus and Cressida
Twelfth Night
The Two Gentlemen of Verona
The Winter's Tale

POEMS OF SHAKESPEARE

The Passionate Pilgrim
The Phoenix and the Turtle

The Rape of Lucrece
Sonnets

Venus and Adonis

SHARKS

angel shark, angelfish, or monkfish
basking shark, sailfish or (N.Z.) reremai
blue pointer or (N.Z.) blue shark or blue whaler
bronze whaler (Austral.)
carpet shark or (Austral.) wobbegong
cow shark or six-gilled shark

dogfish or (Austral.) dog shark
grey nurse shark
gummy (shark)
hammerhead
mako
nursehound
nurse shark
porbeagle or mackerel shark
requiem shark
school shark (Austral.)

seven-gill shark (Austral.)
shovelhead
soupfin or soupfin shark
thrasher or thresher shark
tiger shark
tope
whale shark
whaler shark

BREEDS OF SHEEP

Beulah Speckled-face
bighorn or mountain sheep
Blackface
Black Welsh Mountain
Blue-faced or Hexham
  Leicester
Border Leicester
Boreray
Brecknock Hill Cheviot
British Bleu du Maine
British Charollais
British Friesland
British Milksheep
British Oldenburg
British Texel
British Vendéen
Cambridge
Cheviot
Clun Forest
Colbred
Corriedale
Cotswold
Dalesbred
Dartmoor
Derbyshire Gritstone
Devon and Cornwall
  Longwool
Devon Closewool
Dorset Down
Dorset Horn
East Friesland
English Halfbred
Exmoor Horn
Hampshire Down
Hebridian or St. Kilda
Herdwick
Hill Radnor
Île de France
Jacob
karakul, caracul, or broadtail
Kerry Hill
Leicester Longwool
Lincoln Longwool
Llanwenog
Lleyn
Lonk
Manx Loghtan
Masham
Merino
Mule
Norfolk Horn
North Country Cheviot
Orkney or North Ronaldsay
Oxford or Oxfordshire Down
Polwarth
Portland
Rambouillet
Romney Marsh
Rouge de l'Ouest
Rough Fell
Ryeland
Scottish Blackface
Scottish Halfbred
Shetland
Shropshire
Soay
Southdown
South Wales Mountain
Suffolk
Swaledale
Teeswater
Texel
Welsh Halfbred
Welsh Hill Speckled
Welsh Mountain
Welsh Mountain Badger
  Faced
Welsh Mule
Wensleydale Longwool
White Face Dartmoor
Whitefaced Woodland
Wiltshire Horn

SHELLFISH

banana prawn (Austral.)
blue swimmer, blue manna, or
  sand crab (Austral.)
clam
clappy-doo or clabby-doo
  (Scot.)
cockle
crab
crayfish, crawfish, or (N.Z.)
  koura
crayfish, craybob, craydab,
  crawbob, clawchie, lobster,
  marron, or yabby (Austral.)
Dublin Bay prawn
freshwater shrimp
king prawn
langoustine
lobster
Moreton Bay bug or shovel-
  nosed lobster (Austral.)
mud crab
mussel
Norway lobster
oyster
prawn
scallop or scollop
school prawn (Austral.)
soldier crab

SHOES AND BOOTS

ankle boot
arctic (U.S.)
Balmoral
biker boot
blucher (obsolete)
bootee
bottine
bovver boot (Brit.)
  (slang)
brogan
brogue
brothel creeper
  (informal)
buskin
chopine or chopin
chukka boot
clog
co-respondent
cothurnus or
  cothurn
court shoe
cowboy boot
creeper (informal)
crowboot
deck shoe
Doc Marten
  (trademark)
espadrille
field boot
flat or flatty
flip-flop
football boot
gaiter or spat
galosh
ghillie (Scot.)
golf shoe
gumboot
gumshoe
gym shoe
half boot
Hessian boot
high heel
hobnail boot
jackboot

Jandal (N.Z.) (trademark)
kitten heel
lace-up
larrigan
loafer
moccasin
moonboot
mukluk
mule
overshoe
Oxford
pantofle, pantoffle, or pantoufle (archaic)
platform
plimsoll or plimsole
pump
racket or racquet
running shoe
rock boot
sabot
sandal
sandshoe
scuff
slingback
slip-on
slipper
sneaker
snowshoe
spike
stiletto
surgical boot
tennis shoe
thigh boot
top boot
track shoe
training shoe or trainer
veldskoen
wader
wedge or wedge heel
welly
Wellington boot
winkle-picker

SHREWS AND OTHER INSECTIVORES

desman
elephant shrew
mole
moon rat
shrew or shrewmouse
shrew mole
solenodon
star-nosed mole
tenrec
tree shrew
water shrew

SHRUBS

acacia
acanthus
arbutus
banksia
bauera
bilberry
black boy, yacca (bush), or yacka (Austral.)
blackcurrant
blackthorn
blueberry
bluebush
boronia
bottlebrush (Austral.)
box
bramble
briar or brier
broom
buckthorn
buddleia
camellia
caper
Christmas bush (Austral.)
clematis
coca
correa
cotton
cottonbush (Austral.)
cottonwood, blanket bush, tawine, tarwine, or
tauhinu (Austral.)
cranberry
crowea
crown-of-thorns
daphne
dogwood
emu bush (Austral.)
eriostemon
forsythia
frangipani
fuchsia
gardenia
geebung, geebong, or jibbong (Austral.)
Geraldton waxflower (Austral.)
gooseberry
gorse
grevillea
hakea (Austral.)
hawthorn
heath
heather
honeysuckle
hydrangea
jasmine
juniper
kerrawang (Austral.)
laburnum
laurel
lilac
liquorice
magnolia
mistletoe
mock orange
myrtle
oleander
olearia or daisy bush (Austral.)
pittosporum
pituri (Austral.)
poinsettia
poison ivy
poison oak
potentilla
privet
pyracantha
raspberry
redcurrant
rhododendron
rose
rosemary
rue
saltbush (Austral.)
strawberry
tea
thyme
waratah (Austral.)
wax(flower)

SEVEN DEADLY SINS

anger
covetousness or avarice
envy
gluttony
lust
pride
sloth

SKIRTS

A-line
button-through
crinoline
dirndl
divided skirt
drop-waisted
filibeg, fillibeg, or philibeg
full skirt
fustanella or fustanelle
gaberdine or gabardine

grass skirt
half-slip or waist-slip
hobble skirt
hoop skirt
kilt
lava-lava
maxiskirt
microskirt
midiskirt
miniskirt

overskirt
pencil skirt
petticoat
puffball skirt
ra-ra skirt
riding skirt
sarong
tutu
underskirt
wrapover or wrapround

SNAILS, SLUGS AND OTHER GASTROPODS

abalone or ear shell
conch
cowrie or cowry
limpet
murex
nudibranch or sea slug

ormer or sea-ear
periwinkle or winkle
ramshorn snail
Roman snail
sea hare
slug

snail
top-shell
triton
wentletrap
whelk

SNOOKER AND BILLIARDS TERMS

baize
ball
baulk
baulkline
black
blue
bouclée
break
bricole
brown
cannon
carom (chiefly U.S.) (Canad.)
chalk
clearance
cue ball

cue extension
cue tip
cushion
D or d
double
draw
drop cannon
fluke
foul
frame
free ball
green
half-butt
hazard
headrail
in-off
jenny

kick
kiss
lag
long jenny
massé
maximum break or 147
miscue
nurse
nursery cannon
object ball
pink
plain ball
plant
pocket
pot
red
rest

safety
scratch
screw
short jenny
side or (U.S. & Canad.) English
snooker
spider
spot
spot ball
stun
top
triangle or (U.S. & Canad.) rack
white
Whitechapel
yellow

SOCKS AND TIGHTS

ankle sock or (U.S.) anklet
argyle
bed sock
bobby sock
half-hose

hose (History)
knee-high sock
legwarmer
lisle stocking
maillot
nylons

pop sock
puttee or putty
tights or (esp U.S. & Austral.) pantihose or pantyhose
sock

slouch sock
stay-up
stock (archaic)
stocking

TYPES OF SOFA

bergère
canapé
chaise longue or chaise
chesterfield

couch
davenport (U.S.)
day bed
divan
futon

lounge
love seat
settee
settle
sofa bed

squab
studio couch
tête-à-tête
vis-à-vis

SPIDERS AND OTHER ARACHNIDS

bird spider
black widow
book scorpion
cardinal spider
cheese mite
chigger, chigoe, or (U.S. & Canad.) redbug
chigoe, chigger, jigger, or sand flea
false scorpion
funnel-web
harvestman or (U.S. & Canad.) daddy-longlegs
house spider
itch mite
jockey spider
jumping spider
katipo (N.Z.)
mite
money spider
red-back (spider) (Austral.) spider
spider mite
tarantula
tick
trap-door spider
vinegarroon
water spider
whip scorpion
wolf spider or hunting spider

SPIRITS

absinth or absinthe
aguardiente
applejack, applejack brandy, or apple brandy
aquavit or akvavit
aqua vitae (archaic)
Armagnac
arrack or arak
Bacardi (trademark)
brandy
bitters
Calvados
Cognac
dark rum
eau de vie
firewater
framboise
gin
grappa
Hollands
hooch
Kirsch or Kirschwasser
korn
marc
mescal
ouzo
palinka
poteen or poitín
raki or rakee
rum
schnapps or schnaps
slivovitz
sloe gin
taffia
tequila
triple sec
vodka
whisky
white rum

SPORTS

TEAM SPORTS

American football
association football or soccer
Australian Rules or Australian Rules football
baseball
bandy
basketball
camogie
Canadian football
cricket
curling
five-a-side football
football
Gaelic football
goalball
handball
hockey
hurling or hurley
ice hockey
kabbadi
korfball
lacrosse
netball
polo
roller hockey
rounders
rugby or rugby football
rugby league
rugby union
shinty
softball
stool ball
tug-of-war
volleyball
water polo

COMBAT SPORTS

boxing
fencing
sambo or sambo wrestling
savate
wrestling

OTHER SPORTS

angling or fishing
archery
badminton
ballooning
billiards
boules
bowls
bullfighting
candlepins
canyoning
clay pigeon shooting
cockfighting
coursing
croquet
cycling
cyclo-cross
darts
decathlon
falconry
fives
fly-fishing
fox-hunting
gliding
golf
greyhound racing
gymnastics
hang gliding
jai alai
lawn tennis
modern pentathlon
mountaineering
paddleball
parachuting
paragliding
parascending
paraskiing
pelota
pétanque
pigeon racing
pool

potholing	roller skating	squash *or* squash rackets	trapshooting
quoits	shooting		triathlon
rackets	skeet	table tennis	weightlifting
real tennis	skittles	tennis	
rhythmic gymnastics	skydiving	tenpin bowling	
rock climbing	snooker	trampolining	

STARS AND CONSTELLATIONS

STARS

Aldebaran	Sirius, the Dog Star, Canicula, *or* Sothis
Betelgeuse *or* Betelgeux	the Sun
Polaris, the Pole Star, *or* the North Star	

CONSTELLATIONS

Latin name	English name	Latin name	English name
Andromeda	Andromeda	Hydra	Sea Serpent
Antila	Air Pump	Hydrus	Water Snake
Apus	Bird of Paradise	Indus	Indian
Aquarius	Water Bearer	Lacerta	Lizard
Aquila	Eagle	*Latin name*	*English name*
Ara	Altar	Leo	Lion
Aries	Ram	Leo Minor	Little Lion
Auriga	Charioteer	Lepus	Hare
Boötes	Herdsman	Libra	Scales
Caelum	Chisel	Lupus	Wolf
Camelopardalis	Giraffe	Lynx	Lynx
Cancer	Crab	Lyra	Harp
Canes Venatici	Hunting Dogs	Mensa	Table
Canis Major	Great Dog	Microscopium	Microscope
Canis Minor	Little Dog	Monoceros	Unicorn
Capricornus	Sea Goat	Musca	Fly
Carina	Keel	Norma	Level
Cassiopeia	Cassiopeia	Octans	Octant
Centaurus	Centaur	Ophiuchus	Serpent Bearer
Cepheus	Cepheus	Orion	Orion
Cetus	Whale	Pavo	Peacock
Chamaeleon	Chameleon	Pegasus	Winged Horse
Circinus	Compasses	Perseus	Perseus
Columba	Dove	Phoenix	Phoenix
Coma Bernices	Bernice's Hair	Pictor	Easel
Corona Australis	Southern Crown	Pisces	Fishes
Corona Borealis	Northern Crown	Piscis Austrinus	Southern Fish
Corvus	Crow	Puppis	Ship's Stern
Crater	Cup	Pyxis	Mariner's Compass
Crux	Southern Cross	Reticulum	Net
Cygnus	Swan	Sagitta	Arrow
Delphinus	Dolphin	Sagittarius	Archer
Dorado	Swordfish	Scorpius	Scorpion
Draco	Dragon	Sculptor	Sculptor
Equuleus	Little Horse	Scutum	Shield
Eridanus	River Eridanus	Serpens	Serpent
Fornax	Furnace	Sextans	Sextant
Gemini	Twins	Taurus	Bull
Grus	Crane	Telescopium	Telescope
Hercules	Hercules	Triangulum	Triangle
Horologium	Clock	Triangulum Australe	Southern Triangle
		Tucana	Toucan

Ursa Major	Great Bear (contains the Plough or (U.S.) Big Dipper)	Vela	Sails
		Virgo	Virgin
		Volans	Flying Fish
Ursa Minor	Little Bear or (U.S.) Little Dipper	Vulpecula	Fox

SUGARS

EDIBLE SUGARS

beet sugar	crystallized sugar	jaggery	powdered sugar
brown sugar	demerara sugar	maple sugar	panocha
cane sugar	granulated sugar	muscovado sugar	refined sugar
caster sugar	icing sugar	palm sugar	white sugar

BIOCHEMICAL SUGARS

aldose	fructose or laevulose	maltose	sorbose
arabinose	galactose	mannose	trehalose
deoxyribose	glucose	raffinose	triose
dextrose or grape sugar	invert sugar	rhamnose	xylose or wood sugar
	lactose or milk sugar	ribose	

SUITS

boiler suit	lounge suit	sailor suit	swimsuit
buckskins	Mao suit	scrubs	three-piece suit
catsuit	morning dress	shell suit	tracksuit
double-breasted suit	penguin suit	single-breasted suit	trouser suit or (U.S. & Canad.) pant suit
dress suit	playsuit	ski suit	
evening dress	pyjamas or (U.S.) pajamas	slack suit	wet suit
G-suit or anti-G suit		spacesuit	zoot suit
judogi	romper suit	sunsuit	
jump suit	safari suit	sweat suit or sweats	

THE SUPERNATURAL

PEOPLE WITH SUPERNATURAL POWERS

archimage	enchanter	magician	siren	water diviner
channeller	enchantress	magus	sorcerer	water witch
clairaudient	exorcist	medium	sorceress	white witch
clairvoyant	fortune-teller	necromancer	spaewife (Scot.)	witch
conjurer	hag	rainmaker	superhero	witch doctor
diviner	hex	seer	thaumaturge	witch master
dowser	mage	shaman	warlock	wizard

SUPERNATURAL CREATURES

angel	fay	hobgoblin	monster	succubus
banshee	genie	imp	ogre	sylph
brownie	ghost	incubus	peri	troll
demon	ghoul	jinni, jinnee, djinni, or djinny	phantom	vampire
devil	giant		pixie	werewolf or lycanthrope
dwarf	gnome	kachina	poltergeist	
dybbuk	goblin	kelpie	sandman	wraith
elf	god or goddess	lamia	selkie or silkie (Scot.)	zombie or zombi
fairy	golem	leprechaun	spectre	
fairy godmother	gremlin	little people or folk	sprite	
familiar	guardian angel			

SUPERNATURAL TERMS

abracadabra
amulet
apport
aura
black magic or the
  Black Art
charm
clairaudience
clairvoyance
cryptaesthesia
curse
divination
ectoplasm
evil eye
exorcism
extrasensory
perception or ESP
fate
fetish
grigri, gris-gris, or
  greegree
grimoire
hex
hoodoo
incantation
invultuation
Indian sign
jinx
juju
kismet
levitation
magic circle
magic spell
magic wand
mojo
necromancy
obi or obeah
Ouija (trademark)
parapsychology
pentagram
philtre
portent
possession
premonition
reincarnation
rune
seance or séance
second sight
sigil
sixth sense
spell
talisman
talking in tongues,
  xenoglossia, or
  xenoglossy
telaesthesia
telegnosis
telekinesis or
  psychokinesis
telepathy
voodoo
wand
white magic
witching hour

SWEATERS

Aran sweater
cardigan
Cowichan sweater, Indian
  sweater, siwash, or siwash
  sweater (Canad.)
cowl-necked sweater
crew-neck or crew-necked
  sweater
Fairisle
Guernsey (Austral.)
hoodie (informal)
Icelandic
jersey
jumper
polo or polo neck
pullover
rollneck
skivvy (Austral.) (N.Z.)
slipover
sloppy joe
sweatshirt
turtleneck
V-neck or V-necked sweater

SWORDS AND OTHER WEAPONS WITH BLADES

assegai or assagai
backsword
battle-axe
bayonet
bill
bowie knife
broadsword
claymore
cutlass
dagger
dirk
épée
falchion
foil
halberd
hatchet
jackknife
jerid, jereed, or jerreed
knife or (slang) chiv
kris
kukri
machete
parang
partisan
pike
poleaxe
poniard
rapier
sabre or saber
scimitar
sgian-dhu
sheath knife
skean
smallsword
snickersnee
spear

TABLES AND DESKS

bar
bedside table
billiard table
breakfast bar
breakfast table
buffet
bureau
card table
carrel
coffee table
console table
counter
davenport (Brit.)
desk
dining table
dressing table
drop-leaf table
drum table
escritoire
folding table
gate-leg or gate-
  legged table
kitchen table
lapboard
lowboy (U.S.) (Canada)
nest of tables
occasional table
pedestal desk
Pembroke table
piecrust table
reading desk
refectory table
roll-top desk
secretaire
side table
snooker table
teapoy
tea table
tea trolley
traymobile (Austral.)
trestle table
wool table
workbench
worktable
writing desk
writing table

TEAS

Assam	Darjeeling	jasmine tea	post-and-rail tea
bohea	Earl Grey	Lapsang Souchong	*(archaic)*
camomile tea	green tea	lemon tea	Russian tea
Ceylon	gunpowder tea	mint tea	
Chinese tea	herb *or* herbal tea	oolong	
congou *or* congo	Indian tea	orange pekoe	

TELECOMMUNICATION TERMS

Blackberry	instant messaging	mobile phone	Skype
Bluetooth	*or* IM	MSN	SMS *or* text
e-mail	MMS	pager	messaging

TENNIS TERMS

ace	deuce	line call	server
advantage	double fault	linesman	service
approach shot	doubles	lob	service line
backhand	drop shot	love	set
ball	fault	love game	set point
baseline	foot fault	match	sideline
baseliner	forecourt	mixed doubles	singles
break of serve	forehand	net	slice
break point	game	net cord	smash
cannonball	grass court	passing shot	tie-break *or* tiebreaker
centre line	ground stroke	racket *or* racquet	topspin
centre mark	half-volley	rally	tramline
chip	hard court	receiver	umpire
clay court	lawn tennis	return	undercut
court	let	serve and volleyer	volley

TEXT MESSAGING ABBREVIATIONS AND SYMBOLS

Abbreviation or symbol	Meaning	Abbreviation or symbol	Meaning
A3	anytime, anywhere, anyplace	BWD	backward
AAM	as a matter of fact	BY	busy
AFAIK	as far as I know	C	see
AFK	away from keyboard	CIAO	goodbye
al2gethr	altogether	CMIIW	correct me if I'm wrong
ALrlt	all right	CU	see you
ATB	all the best	CUL8R	see you later
ATK	at the keyboard	CYA	see you
ATM	at the moment	EVR	ever
ATTN	attention	EZ	easy
B	be	FC	fingers crossed
B4	before	FONE	phone
BAK	back at keyboard	4	for *or* four
BBL	be back later	4EVA	for ever
BCNU	be seeing you	F2T	free to talk
BFN *or* B4N	bye for now	FWD	forward
BK *or* COZ	because	FWIW	for what it's worth
BF	boyfriend	FYI	for your information
BR	bathroom	GAL	get a life
BRB	be right back	G9	genius
BRT	be right there	GF	girlfriend
BS	bullshit	GG	good game

Abbreviation or symbol	Meaning	Abbreviation or symbol	Meaning
GGG or GGL	giggle	PRW	parents are watching
GMTA	great minds think alike	Q	queue
GR8	great	QL	cool
HAND	have a nice day	QT	quiet
H8	hate	R	are
HD	hold	RGDS	regards
IC	I see	ROFL	rolling on floor laughing
IDD	indeed	ROFLOL	rolling on floor laughing out loud
ILU	I love you		
IMHO	in my humble or honest opinion	ROTFL	rolling on the floor laughing
IMNSHO	in my not so humble opinion	ROTFLOL	rolling on the floor laughing out loud
IMO	in my opinion		
IOW	in other words	RUOK	are you OK?
IRL	in real life	SIT	stay in touch
IRW	in the real world	SK8	skate
IFYWIMAITYD	if you know what I mean and I think you do	SOHF	sense of humour failure
		SOM1	someone
K	okay	THX or TX	thanks
KISS	keep it simple, stupid	Ti2GO	time to go
KIT	keep in touch	2	to, too, or two
L8	late	2DAY	today
L8R	later	2MORO	tomorrow
LDR	long-distance relationship	2NITE	tonight
LO	hello	TTYL	talk to you later
LOL	laughing out loud	TXT	text
LTNS	long time no see	U	you
LUV	love	U2	you too
LZ	loser	U4E	yours for ever
M8	mate	UR	you are or your
MSG	message	W8	wait
MT	empty	WADYA	what do you
MTG	meeting	WAN2	want to
NE	any	WAN2TLK	want to talk?
NE1	anyone	WB	welcome back
Njoy	enjoy	WK	week
NO1	no-one	WKND	weekend
NRN	no reply necessary	WIV	with
OFN	often	W/O	without
OIC	oh I see	WOT	what
PCM	please call me	WTG	way to go!
PLS	please	X	kiss
PLU	people like us	XLNT	excellent
PPL	people	XOXO	hugs and kisses
PRT	party		

EMOTICONS

Emoticon	Meaning	Emoticon	Meaning
:-)	happy	:-*	kissing
:-))	cheerful	:-(	sad
:-)))	really happy	:'-(	crying
:-()	smiling with mouth open	:-C	very sad
8-)	smiling with glasses	:-@	screaming
D:-)	smiling with baseball cap	:-O	shocked or surprised
;-)	winking		

SIGNS OF THE ZODIAC

Aquarius (the Water Carrier)
Aries (the Ram)
Cancer (the Crab)

Capricorn (the Goat)
Gemini (the Twins)
Leo (the Lion)
Libra (the Scales)

Pisces (the Fishes)
Sagittarius (the Archer)
Scorpio (the Scorpion)

Taurus (the Bull)
Virgo (the Virgin)

CHINESE ANIMAL YEARS

Chinese	English			Years		
Shu	Rat	1960	1972	1984	1996	2008
Niu	Ox	1961	1973	1985	1997	2009
Hu	Tiger	1962	1974	1986	1998	2010
Tu	Hare	1963	1975	1987	1999	2011
Long	Dragon	1964	1976	1988	2000	2012
She	Serpent	1965	1977	1989	2001	2013
Ma	Horse	1966	1978	1990	2002	2014
Yang	Sheep	1967	1979	1991	2003	2015
Hou	Monkey	1968	1980	1992	2004	2016
Ji	Cock	1969	1981	1993	2005	2017
Gou	Dog	1970	1982	1994	2006	2018
Zhu	Boar	1971	1983	1995	2007	2019

ZOOLOGY

BRANCHES OF ZOOLOGY

arachnology
archaeozoology
cetology
entomology
ethology

herpetology
ichthyology
malacology
mammalogy
myrmecology

ophiology
ornithology
palaeozoology
primatology
protozoology

zoogeography
zoography
zoometry
zootomy

ZOOLOGY TERMS

abdomen
aestivation
amphibian
antenna
anterior
appendage
arachnid
arthropod
biped
bivalve
carnivore
caudal
chordate
chrysalis
cocoon
coelenterate

coelom
colony
crustacean
decapod
dipteran
dorsal
echinoderm
edentate
fin
gastropod or gasteropod
gill
herbivore
hibernation
imago
insectivore

invertebrate
larva
lepidopteran
marsupial
metamorphosis
migration
omnivore
parenchyma
passerine
pectoral
placenta
posterior
predator
prey
primate
protozoan

pupa
quadruped
raptor
reptile
rodent
ruminant
segment
skeleton
spawn
spine
sucker
thorax
ventral
vertebrate

QbA, Qualitätswein bestimmter Anbaugebiet, *or* Qualitätswein
QmP *or* Qualitätswein mit Prädikat
recioto
récolte
reserva
rosé
riserva
Ruby Port
sec
secco
second wine
Sekt
sin crianza
Sigle Quinta Port
solera
sparkling wine
Spätlese
spumante
sur lie
sweet
table wine
Tafelwein
tannin
Tawny Port
terroir
tinto
trocken
Trockenbeeren- auslese *or* TBA
varietal
VDQS *or* Vin Délimité de Qualité Supérieure
vendage tardive
vieilles vignes
vigneron
vignoble
vin de pays
vin de table
vin doux naturel
vin gris
vino da tavola
vintage
Weingut
Weissherbst
Winzergenossen- schaft

WINTER SPORTS

Alpine skiing
biathlon
bobsleigh
curling
downhill racing
ice dancing
ice hockey
ice skating *or* figure skating
luge
Nordic skiing
Nordic walking
skating
skibobbing
skiing
skijoring
ski jumping
slalom
snowboarding
speed skating
super-G
tobogganing

SEVEN WONDERS OF THE ANCIENT WORLD

Colossus of Rhodes
Hanging Gardens of Babylon
Mausoleum of Halicarnassus
Pharos of Alexandria
Phidias' statue of Zeus at Olympia
Pyramids of Egypt
Temple of Artemis at Ephesus

TYPES OF WOOD

African mahogany
afrormosia
alerce
amboyna *or* amboina
apple
ash
assegai *or* assagai
balsa
basswood
baywood
beech
beefwood
birch
black walnut
bog oak
boxwood
brazil, brasil, *or* brazil wood
bulletwood
butternut
cade
calamander
camwood
candlewood
cedar
cherry
chestnut
citron wood
coachwood
corkwood
crabwood
cypress
durmast *or* durmast oak
eaglewood
ebony
elm
fiddlewood
fir
gaboon
gopher wood
greenheart
guaiacum *or* guaiocum
gumtree *or* gumwood
hackbèrry
hardwood
hazel
hemlock
hickory
hornbeam
iroko
ironwood
jacaranda
jelutong
kauri
kiaat
kingwood
koa
lancewood
larch
locust
mahogany
maple
marblewood
nutwood
oak
olive
orangewood
padauk *or* padouk
Paraná pine
partridge-wood
pear
persimmon
pine
pitch pine
poon
poplar
pulpwood
quassia
quebracho
red cedar
red fir
red gum
red oak
ribbonwood
rosewood
sandalwood
sandarac
sappanwood
sassy, sasswood, *or* sassy wood
satinwood
Scots pine
shagbark *or* shellbark
sneezewood
softwood
spotted gum
spruce
stinkwood
sumach *or* sumac (U.S.)
sycamore
tamarack
tamarind
teak
thorn
toon
torchwood
tulipwood
tupelo
walnut
western red cedar
white cedar
white pine
whitewood
willow
yellowwood
yew
zebrawood

Pommard	riesling	Saint-Émilion	sherry	Verdicchio
port	Rioja	Saint-Estèphe	straw wine	Vinho Verde
Pouilly-Fuissé	Roero	Saint-Julien	Tavel	vin ordinaire
Pouilly-Fumé	Rosé d'Anjou	Saint-Véran	Teroldego	Vino Nobile di
Quarts de	Rosso Cònero	Salice Salentino	Rotaliano	Montepulciano
Chaume	Rüdesheimer	Sancerre	Tokaji	Vosne-Romanée
Quincy	Rueda	Saumur	Tokay-Pinot Gris	Vouvray
retsina	Rully	Sauternes	Valdepeñas	
Rhine wine	sack	scuppernong	Valpolicella	

WINE-PRODUCING AREAS

	Country		Country		Country
Ahr	Germany	Hawkes Bay	New	Oregon	U.S.A.
Alsace	France		Zealand	Padthaway	Australia
Alto Adige or		Hessiches		Penedès	Spain
Südtirol	Italy	Bergstrasse	Germany	Piedmont	Italy
Anjou	France	Greece	–	Portugal	–
Argentina	–	Hungary	–	Provence	France
Austria	–	Hunter Valley	Australia	Rheingau	Germany
Barossa Valley	Australia	Languedoc	France	Rheinhessen	Germany
Baden	Germany	Loire	France	Rheinpfalz	Germany
Bordeaux	France	Marlborough	New	Rhône	France
Bulgaria	–		Zealand	Ribera del Duro	Spain
Burgundy	France	Margaret River	Australia	Rioja	Spain
California	U.S.A.	Martinborough	New	Romania	–
Chablis	France		Zealand	Sicily	Italy
Champagne	France	McLaren Vale	Australia	Sonoma	U.S.A.
Chianti	Italy	Mendocino	U.S.A.	South Africa	–
Chile	–	Mittelrhein	Germany	Switzerland	–
Clare Valley	Australia	Moldavia	–	Touraine	France
Coonawarra	Australia	Mornington		Tuscany	Italy
Côte d'Or	France	Peninsula	Australia	Umbria	Italy
Finger Lakes	U.S.A.	Mosel-Saar-		Valdepeñas	Spain
Franken	Germany	Ruwer	Germany	Veneto	Italy
Friuli	Italy	Nahe	Germany	Washington State	U.S.A.
Gisborne	New	Napa Valley	U.S.A.	Württemberg	Germany
	Zealand	Navarra	Spain	Yarra Valley	Australia
Goulburn Valley	Australia	New York State	U.S.A.		

WINE TERMS

abbocatto	cru bourgeois	flor	medium-sweet
AC or appellation	cru classé	fino	méthode
contrôlée	cuvée	fortified wine	champenoise
amabile	demi-sec	garrafeira	moelleux
amontillado	dessert wine	grand cru	mousseux
AOC or appellation	DOC or	gran reserva	noble rot
d'origine contrôlée	denominazione di	Grosslage	NV or non-vintage
aszú	origine controllata	halbtrocken	Oechsle
Ausbruch	DOCG or	Kabinett	oloroso
Auslese	denominazione di	late harvest	organic
Baumé	origine controllata e	LBV or Late-Bottled	pale cream
Beerenauslese	garantita	Vintage (Port)	passito
botrytis	dolce	malmsey	pétillant
botrytized	dry	malolactic	plonk
Brix	Einzellage	fermentation	pourriture noble
brut	Eiswein	manzanilla	prädikat
cream	erzeugerabfüllung	medium	premier cru
crianza	estate bottled	medium-dry	puttonyos

WHALES AND DOLPHINS

beluga	bowhead	grampus, or	porpoise	cachalot
baleen whale	dorado	orca	right whale or	toothed whale
blue whale	Greenland whale	minke whale	(Austral.) bay	whalebone
or sulphur-	greyback or grey	narwhal	whale	whale
bottom	whale	pilot whale,	rorqual	white whale
bottlenose	humpback whale	black whale, or	sei whale	
dolphin	killer whale,	blackfish	sperm whale or	

WHISKIES

blend	grain whisky	whisky	rye	single malt
blended whisky	hokonui (N.Z.)	poteen or poitín	Scotch	sour mash
bourbon	Irish whiskey	redeye (U.S.)	shebeen or	vatted malt
corn whisky	malt or malt	(slang)	shebean (Irish)	

WINDS

Wind	Location	Wind	Location
berg wind	South Africa	meltemi or	NE Mediterranean
bise	Switzerland	etesian wind	
bora	Adriatic Sea	mistral	S France to
buran or bura	central Asia		Mediterranean
Cape doctor	Cape Town, South Africa	monsoon	S Asia
chinook	Washington & Oregon	nor'wester	Southern Alps, New
	coasts		Zealand
föhn or foehn	N slopes of the Alps	pampero	S America
harmattan	W African coast	simoom or simoon	Arabia & N Africa
khamsin, kamseen	Egypt	sirocco	N Africa to S Europe
or kamsin		tramontane or	W coast of Italy
levanter	W Mediterranean	tramontana	
libeccio or libecchio	Corsica		

WINES

WINES

Amarone	Brouilly	Tricastin	Gigondas	Minervois
Asti Spumante	Brunello di	Côte de Beaune-	Grange	Monbazillac
Bairrada	Montalcino	Villages	Hermitage	Montepulciano
Bandol	Bucelas	Côte Rôtie	Graves	d'Abruzzo
Banyuls	Bull's Blood or	Côtes du Rhône	Hermitage	montilla
Barbaresco	Egri Bikaver	Crémant d'Alsace	hock	Moscato d'Asti
Barbera d'Albi	Burgundy	Crémant de Loire	jerepigo	Moselle
Barbera d'Asti	Cahors	Crozes-	Jurançon	muscadet
Barolo	canary	Hermitage	lachryma Christi	Muscat de
Barsac	Carema	crusted port	Lambrusco	Beaumes-de-
beaujolais	Cava	Dão	Liebfraumilch	Venise
beaujolais	Chablis	Entre-Deux-Mers	Lirac	muscatel
nouveau	Chambertin	Faugères	Liqueur Muscat	Niersteiner
Bereich	Champagne	Fitou	Liqueur Tokay	Nuits-Saint-
Bernkastel	chardonnay	Fleurie	Mâcon	Georges
Bergerac	chianti	Frascati	Mâcon-Villages	Orvieto
blanc de blancs	Colheita Port	Fumé Blanc	Madeira	Parrina
Blanquette de	claret	Gaillac	Málaga	Pauillac
Limoux	Condrieu	Gattinara	Margaux	Pessac-Léognan
Bordeaux	Constantia	Gavi	Marsala	Pinot Grigio
Bourgogne	Corbières	Gevrey-	Médoc	Piesporter
Bourgueil	Coteaux du	Chambertin	Meursault	Pomerol

heatwave	precipitation	smirr *(Scot.)*	thunder	wind
hurricane	pressure	snow	tidal wave	willy-willy
ice	rain	squall	tornado	*(Austral.)*
lightning	sandstorm	storm	tsunami	zephyr
mist	sheet lightning	sunshine	typhoon	
peasouper *(chiefly*	shower	tempest *(literary)*	waterspout	
Brit.)*	sleet	thaw	whirlwind	

METEOROLOGICAL TERMS

anticyclone	front	lee wave	synoptic chart	warm front
cold front	heat-island	occluded front	thermal	
cyclone	isallobar	ridge	trough	
depression	isobar	scud	virga	

GATHERERS OF WEATHER DATA

dropsonde	*or* Met. Office	weather ship	weatherwoman
meteorograph	pilot balloon	weather station	
Meteorological Office	radiosonde	weatherman	

MEASURING INSTRUMENTS

Phenomenon measured		*Phenomenon measured*	
anemometer	wind velocity	rain gauge	rainfall and snowfall
anemoscope	wind direction	rawinsonde	atmospheric wind velocity
atmometer	rate of water evaporation into atmosphere	Stevenson's screen	temperature
barograph	atmospheric pressure	sunshine recorder	hours of sunshine
barometer	atmospheric pressure		
baroscope	atmospheric pressure	thermometer	temperature
hygrometer	humidity	weathercock	wind direction
maximum-minimum thermometer	temperature variation	weather vane	wind direction
		wet-and-dry-bulb thermometer	humidity
nephoscope	cloud velocity, altitude, and direction of movement		
		wind gauge	wind velocity
psychrometer	humidity	wind tee	wind direction

WEIGHTS AND MEASURES

IMPERIAL SYSTEM

Linear	*Square*	*Weight*	*Land*	*Volume*	*Liquid volume*
mile	square mile	ton	square mile	cubic yard	gallon
furlong	acre	hundredweight	acre	cubic foot	quart
rod	square rod	stone	square rod	cubic inch	pint
yard	square yard	pound	square yard	-	fluid ounce
foot	square foot	ounce			
inch	square inch	-			
mil	-	-			

METRIC SYSTEM

Linear	*Square*	*Weight*	*Land*	*Volume*	*Liquid Volume*
kilometre	square kilometre	tonne			
metre	square metre	kilogram	square kilometre	cubic metre	litre
centimetre	square centimetre	gram	hectare	cubic decimetre	millilitre
millimetre	square millimetre	-	are	cubic centimetre	-
			-	cubic millimetre	-

roadroller
road train (Austral.)
rocket
scooter
scout car
shandrydan
ship
single-decker (Brit.)
skibob
sledge or (especially
    U.S. & Canad.) sled
sleigh
Sno-Cat (trademark)
snowmobile
snow plough
space capsule

spacecraft
space probe
spaceship
space shuttle
sports car
stagecoach
steamroller
sulky
SUV or sports utility
    vehicle
tandem
tank
tank engine or
    locomotive
tanker
tarantass

taxi
telega
three-wheeler
tipper truck or lorry
toboggan
tonga
tourer or (especially
    U.S.) touring car
traction engine
tractor
trail bike
trailer
train
tram, tramcar, or (U.S.
    & Canad.) streetcar or
    trolley car

travois
tricycle
troika
trolley
trolleybus
troop carrier
truck
tuk-tuk
tumbrel or tumbril
unicycle
van
wagon or waggon
wagonette or
    waggonette
wheelbarrow

WATER SPORTS

aquabobbing
canoeing
canoe polo
diving

parasailing
powerboating
    or powerboat
    racing

rowing
sailing
skin diving
surfing

swimming
synchronized
    swimming
water polo

water-skiing
windsurfing
yachting

WEAPONS

PROJECTILE WEAPONS

ballista
bazooka
blowpipe

catapult
crossbow
fléchette

grapeshot
gun
longbow

onager
quarrel
rifle grenade

torpedo
trebuchet or
    trebucket

MISCELLANEOUS WEAPONS

biological warfare
bomb
chemical warfare
club

death ray
flame-thrower
germ warfare or
    bacteriological

warfare
Greek fire
knuckle-duster
Mace (trademark)

mustard gas
napalm
pepper spray
poison gas

WEATHER

WEATHER DESCRIPTIONS

arctic
baking
balmy
bland
blistering
blustery
breezy
clammy
clear
clement
close

cloudy
cold
dirty
dreich (Scot.)
drizzly
dry
dull
filthy
fine
foggy
foul

freezing
    (informal)
fresh
hazy
hot
humid
icy
inclement
mild
misty
muggy

nippy
overcast
parky (informal)
perishing
    (informal)
rainy
raw
scorching
    (informal)
showery
snowy

sticky
stormy
sultry
sunny
thundery
tropical
wet
windy
wintry

WEATHER PHENOMENA

acid rain
ball lightning
breeze

cloud
cold snap
cyclone

drizzle
dust devil
dust storm

fog
freeze
gale

gust
haar (Scot.)
hail

VEGETABLES

ackee
adjigo or warran (Austral.)
asparagus
aubergine or (esp U.S., Canad., and Austral.) eggplant
baby corn
bean sprout
beef tomato
beetroot or beet
bok choy, Chinese leaf, Chinese cabbage, or pak-choi
broad bean
broccoli
Brussels sprout or sprout
butternut pumpkin
cabbage
calabrese
calalu or calaloo
cardoon
carrot
cauliflower
celeriac
celery
chard
chayote
cherry tomato
chicory
chive
choko
collard
corn on the cob
cos, cos lettuce, or (U.S. & Canad.) romaine
courgette or (U.S., Canad. & Austral.) zucchini
cress
cucumber
endive
fennel
finocchio
frisee
gherkin
globe artichoke
greens
horseradish
iceberg lettuce
Jerusalem artichoke
kale or kail
kohlrabi
lamb's lettuce or corn salad
leek
lettuce
marrow squash
okra, lady's finger, or bhindi
onion
orache
pak-choi
parsnip
pea
pepper, capsicum, or (U.S.) bell pepper
pe-tsai cabbage
pimiento or pimento
potato
puha, puwha, or rauriki (N.Z.)
radicchio
radish
salsify or oyster plant
savoy cabbage
shallot
silver beet
sorrel
Spanish onion
spinach
spring greens
spring onion, salad onion, scallion (chiefly U.S.), or syboe (Scot.)
squash
swede
sweet corn or (chiefly U.S.) corn
sweet potato, batata, or (N.Z.) kumera or kumara
turnip or (dialect) neep
vegetable marrow or marrow
yam

TYPES OF VEHICLE

aircraft
ambulance
articulated lorry or (informal) artic
autocycle
autorickshaw
barrow
bicycle or (informal) bike
Black Maria
boat
breakdown van or truck, tow truck, or (Austral. slang) towie
bulldozer
bus
cab
cabriolet
camion
camper (U.S.) (Canad.)
camper van
car
caravan
carriage
Caterpillar (trademark)
chaise
charabanc (Brit.)
chariot
coach
combine harvester
Conestoga wagon (U.S.) (Canad.)
coupé
cycle
delivery van or (U.S. & Canad.) panel truck
Dormobile (trademark)
double-decker (chiefly Brit.)
dray
dump truck or dumper-truck
dustcart or (U.S. & Canad.) garbage truck
estate car
fire engine
fork-lift truck
four-wheel drive
gritter (Brit.)
hansom or hansom cab
hatchback or hatch
hog (informal)
Humvee or (informal) Hummer
hybrid car or hybrid
jaunting car or jaunty car
JCB (trademark)
Jeep (trademark)
jet ski
jinricksha, jinricksha, jinrikisha or jinriksha
jitney (U.S.) (rare)
kart, go-cart, or go-kart
kibitka
komatik
koneke (N.Z.)
landaulet or landaulette
light engine or (U.S.) wildcat
limousine
litter
locomotive
lorry
low-loader
luge
milk float
minibus
moped
motorbicycle
motorbike
motorbus
motorcar
motor caravan
motorcycle
motor scooter
motor vehicle
off-road vehicle
omnibus
paddock-basher (Austral.) (slang)
panda car (Brit.)
pantechnicon (Brit.)
people carrier, people mover, or (U.S.) minivan
pick-up (Austral. & N.Z.), utility truck, or (informal) ute
police car
postbus
post chaise
pram
racing car
railcar
ratha
rickshaw

cajuput or cajeput (Austral.)
camphor laurel (Austral.)
carbeen, carbean, karbeen, or Moreton Bay ash (Austral.)
carob
cashew
cassia
casuarina or native oak (Austral.)
cedar
cedar of Lebanon
celery pine or celery-top pine (Austral.)
cherry
chestnut
cinnamon
citrus
coachwood (Austral.)
coco
coconut
coolabah or coolibah
coral tree (Austral.)
cork oak
corkwood or cork tree
cypress
date palm
deal
dogwood
Douglas fir
ebony
elder
elm
eucalyptus or eucalypt
eumung or eumong (Austral.)
fig
fir
firewheel tree (Austral.)
flame tree or Illawarra flame tree (Austral.)
flooded gum (Austral.)
ghost gum (Austral.)
gidgee or stinking wattle (Austral.)
golden wattle (Austral.)
grapefruit
grasstree or black boy (Austral.)
grey gum (Austral.)
ground ash
ground oak
guava
gum (tree)
gympie
hawthorn
hazel
hemlock
hickory

holly
hoop pine (Austral.)
hornbeam
horse chestnut
huon pine (Austral.)
ilex
ironbark
iron gum
ironwood
jacaranda
jarrah (Austral.)
Judas tree
juniper
karri
kauri
kentia palm (Austral.)
kurrajong or currajong (Austral.)
laburnum
larch
laurel
lemon
lilac
lilly pilly or lilli pilli (Austral.)
lime
lind
linden
lotus
macadamia, bauple nut, or Queensland nut (Austral.)
macrocarpa
magnolia
mahogany
mallee (Austral.)
mango
mangrove
manuka, kahikatoa, or kanuka (N.Z.)
maple
marri (Austral.)
melaleuca
mimosa
monkey puzzle or Chile pine
Moreton Bay fig (Austral.)
mountain ash
mugga (Austral.)
mulberry
myall (Austral.)
Norfolk Island pine (Austral.)
nutmeg
oak
olive
orange
osier
palm
papaya
paperbark
pawpaw or papaw

peach
pear
peppermint gum (Austral.)
persimmon
pine
plane
plum
pomegranate
poplar
pussy willow
quandong or quondong (Austral.)
quince
radiata pine, insignis pine, or Monterey pine (Austral.)
raffia
redwood
rivergum or river red gum (Austral.)
rosewood
rowan
sandalwood
sassafras
Scots fir
Scots pine
scribbly gum (Austral.)
sequoia
silky oak (Austral.)
silver birch
snow gum (Austral.)
spotted gum (Austral.)
spruce
stinging tree or gympie nettle (Austral.)
stringy-bark
sycamore
tamarind
Tasmanian blue gum (Austral.)
teak
tea-tree
umbrella tree
walnut
wandoo (Austral.)
wattle
weeping willow
white ash
whitebeam
wilga (Austral.)
willow
wirilda (Austral.)
witch
witch elm
yellow box (Austral.)
yew
ylang-ylang
yucca

gouger
graver
gympie (*Austral.*)
hack
hack hammer
half-round chisel
hammer
hammer drill
hob
hoe
hone
icebreaker
ice pick
jackhammer
jointer
jumper
kevel
knapping hammer
mallet
mattock
maul
mitre square
monkey wrench
nibbler
nippers
padsaw
percussion tool
pestle
pick
piledriver
pitching tool
plane
pliers
ploughstaff
pneumatic
  hammer
power drill
pruning hook
punch
rabble *or* rabbler
rake
rawhide hammer
ripple
rocker
rounder
router
sander
saw
sax
scorper *or* scauper
screwdriver
screw tap
scriber
scutch *or* scutcher
scythe
shave
shears
sickle
slasher (*Austral.*)
  (*N.Z.*)
sledgehammer
snake
slick
soldering iron
spade
spanner
spider
spitsticker
spud *or* spudder
stiletto
stylus
swage
tack hammer
tilt hammer
triphammer
trepan
trowel
wimble
wrench

TEETH

canine
incisor *or* foretooth
molar
premolar
wisdom tooth

TORTURE

INSTRUMENTS OF TORTURE

boot
brake
cat-o'-nine-tails
iron maiden
pilliwinks
Procrustean bed
rack
scourge
thumbscrew
wheel

TYPES OF TORTURE

bastinado
Chinese water torture
gauntlet
strappado
water cure
water torture

TREES

acacia
akee
alder
almond
aloe
angophora (*Austral.*)
Antarctic beech
apple
apricot
ash
aspen
balsa
banana
bangalay *or* bastard
  mahogany (*Austral.*)
bangalow (palm) *or*
  piccabean (*Austral.*)
banyalla *or* tallowwood
  (*Austral.*)
banyan
baobab *or* boab
bat's wing coral-tree
  (*Austral.*)
bay
beech
beefwood (*Austral.*)
belah, belar, billar, *or* black
  oak (*Austral.*)
berrigan *or* bitterbush
  (*Austral.*)
bimble box (*Austral.*)
birch
bitterbark (*Austral.*)
black bean *or* Moreton Bay
  chestnut
blackbutt (*Austral.*)
black pine *or* matai (*Austral.*)
black wattle (*Austral.*)
blackwood *or* mudgerabah
  (*Austral.*)
blanket-leaf (*Austral.*)
bloodwood (*Austral.*)
bonsai
boree (*Austral.*)
bottle tree (*Austral.*)
box
brazil
brigalow (*Austral.*)
bulwaddy, bullwaddy,
  bullwaddie, *or* bulwaddee
  (*Austral.*)
bunya *or* bunya-bunya (pine)
burrawang *or* zamia (*Austral.*)
butternut
cabbage tree (palm) (*Austral.*)
cacao
cadagi *or* cadaga (*Austral.*)

TIME

RELATED VOCABULARY

calends or kalends	ides	lunar year	week
civil day	intercalary	month	year
civil year	Julian calendar	nones	
day	leap year	Roman calendar	
Gregorian calendar	lunar month	synodic month	

GREGORIAN CALENDAR

January	April	July	October
February	May	August	November
March	June	September	December

JEWISH CALENDAR

Tishri	Tevet	Nisan	Tammuz
Cheshvan or Heshvan	Shevat or Shebat	Iyar or Iyyar	Av or Ab
Kislev	Adar	Sivan	Elul

MUSLIM CALENDAR

Muharram or Moharram	Rabia II	Shaban or Shaaban	Shawwal
Safar or Saphar	Jumada I	Ramadan, Rhamadhan, or Ramazan	Dhu'l-Qa'dah
Rabia I	Jumada II		Dhu'l-Hijjah
	Rajab		

FRENCH REVOLUTIONARY CALENDAR

Vendémiaire	Nivôse	Germinal	Messidor
Brumaire	Pluviôse	Floréal	Thermidor or Fervidor
Frimaire	Ventôse	Prairial	Fructidor

TIME ZONES

Atlantic Daylight Time	Eastern Standard Time	Pacific Daylight Time
Atlantic Standard Time	Greenwich Mean Time	Pacific Standard Time
British Summer Time	Mountain Daylight Time	Yukon Daylight Time
Central Daylight Time	Mountain Standard Time	Yukon Standard Time
Central European Time	Newfoundland Daylight Time	
Central Standard Time	Newfoundland Standard Time	
Eastern Daylight Time		

TOOLS

Allen key	broach	croze	fillet
alligator	broad	diamond point	firmer chisel
auger	burin	dibble	flange
awl	bushhammer	drawknife or drawshave	flatter
axe	centre punch	dresser	float
ball-peen hammer	chaser	drift or driftpin	floatcut file
beetle	chisel	drill	fork
billhook	claw hammer	drill press	former
bit	clink	drove or drove chisel	fraise
bitstock	clippers	edge tool	froe or frow
bodkin	cold chisel	eyeleteer	fuller
bolster	comb	facer	gab
borer	comber	file	gad
bosh	countersink		gavel
brace and bit	cradle		gimlet